# LASKIN'S
# CANADIAN
# CONSTITUTIONAL
# LAW

*Fifth Edition*

### NEIL FINKELSTEIN

VOLUME 2

# LASKIN'S CANADIAN CONSTITUTIONAL LAW

## Fifth Edition

### NEIL FINKELSTEIN

B.A., C.A., LL.B. (McGill), LL.M. (Harvard)
*Member of the Ontario Bar*

## VOLUME 2

CARSWELL

Toronto • Calgary • Vancouver

1986

**Canadian Cataloguing in Publication Data**

Laskin, Bora.
  Laskin's Canadian constitutional law

ISBN 0-459-38450-3 (set). — ISBN 0-459-38430-9 (v. 1). —
ISBN 0-459-38440-6 (v. 2)

1. Canada — Constitutional law.   2. Canada.
Canadian Charter of Rights and Freedoms.
I. Finkelstein, Neil, 1951-     II. Canada.
Constitution.   III. Title.   IV. Title: Canadian
constitutional law.

JL141.L37  1986        342.71        C86-093682-1

First Edition (1951) . . .Bora Laskin
Second Edition (1960) . . . Bora Laskin
Third Edition (1965) . . . Bora Laskin
Revised Third Edition (1969) . . . Bora Laskin
Fourth Edition (1973) . . . Albert S. Abel
Revised Fourth Edition (1975) . . . Albert S. Abel
Fifth Edition (1986) . . . Neil Finkelstein

© The Carswell Company Limited
1986

# Contents

## VOLUME 1

### PART I
### LEGISLATIVE POWER

# VOLUME 2

# PART II

# CANADIAN CHARTER OF RIGHTS AND FREEDOMS

# 11

# Incorporation and Regulation of Companies and Securities

## 1. The "Dominion" Company in the Provinces

### GREAT WEST SADDLERY CO. v. THE KING

In the Privy Council. [1921] 2 A.C. 91.

Viscount Haldane, Viscount Cave, Lord Sumner and Lord Parmoor.
Feb. 25, 1921.

Consolidated appeals by special leave from two judgments of the Supreme Court of Canada, 59 S.C.R. 19 and 35, and a judgment of the Ontario Appellate Division, 41 O.L.R. 475, on the validity of Saskatchewan, Manitoba and Ontario legislation in so far as it purported to apply to Dominion companies.

VISCOUNT HALDANE: In this case their Lordships are called on to interpret and apply the implications of a judgment, delivered by the Judicial Committee on November 2, 1914, in *John Deere Plow Co. v. Wharton*, [1915] A.C. 330. It was there laid down that the *British North America Act of 1867* had so enabled the Parliament of the Dominion to prescribe the extent of the powers of companies incorporated under Dominion law with objects which extended to the Dominion generally, that the status and powers so far as there in question of one of the three appellant companies could not as matter of principle be validly interfered with by the Provincial Legislature of British Columbia. It was held that laws which had been passed by the Legislature of that Province, and which sought to compel a Dominion company to obtain a certain kind of Provincial licence or to be registered in the way brought before the Judicial Committee, as a condition of exercising its powers in the Province or of suing in the Courts, were *ultra vires*. The reason given was that their Lordships interpreted what had been done by the Province in that case as interfering in a manner not consistent with the principles laid down with the status and corporate capacity of a company with Dominion objects to which the Parliament of Canada had given powers to carry on its business in every part of the Dominion.

In the consolidated appeals now before their Lordships analogous questions are raised by legislation in varying forms enacted in three other Provinces, Saskatchewan, Manitoba, and Ontario.

Since the decision in 1914 the Province of Saskatchewan has passed an Act, in 1915, which supersedes its earlier Companies Acts, and apparently seeks to avoid the features in these which might conflict with the decision of this Committee in

*John Deere Plow Co. v. Wharton* as to the British Columbia legislation. The question raised as regards Manitoba arises out of older legislation of 1913 (subsequently amended and re-enacted in 1916), and as regards Ontario under an older Ontario Companies Act and the Extra-Provincial Corporations Act of 1914. No question is raised from British Columbia, or from any Provinces other than Saskatchewan, Manitoba and Ontario, on this occasion.

The proceedings out of which the present appeals arise concern several Dominion companies, and are, as to Saskatchewan, two cases before a magistrate for infraction of the provisions of the Provincial Companies Act, and an action by a shareholder in one of the Dominion companies concerned, to restrain it from attempting to carry on its business without complying with the requirements of the Companies Act of the Province. The main issue in all these proceedings is substantially the same. In Manitoba an analogous question was raised in a shareholders' action, and also in an action by the Attorney-General of the Province. The main issue in Ontario was similar to that in Saskatchewan, but there was also raised a question as to whether a Dominion company could hold land in the Province without being authorized to do so by its Government, in accordance with Ontario statute law. In the proceedings referred to judgments were delivered in the Courts of first instance and by the appellate Courts in Saskatchewan and Manitoba and by the Courts of first instance and the appellate Court in Ontario. In the cases in the two former Provinces there was an appeal to the Supreme Court of Canada, but in the Ontario litigation the appeal has been brought directly to the King in Council from the judgment of the appellate Court of the Province. On August 18, 1919, special leave to appeal to the Privy Council was granted, and it was ordered that the appeals, six in number, from judgments which had been adverse to the Dominion companies concerned, should be consolidated and heard together. The Attorneys-General for Canada and for the Provinces have intervened throughout.

It will be convenient, having regard to the course taken in the argument, to consider in the first place the appeal from the Court of Appeal in Ontario.

In order to ascertain the real points now in controversy, it is important to refer in some detail to what was actually decided in 1914 in *John Deere Plow Co. v. Wharton*. The British Columbia Companies Act had provided that, in the case of an incorporated company which was not one incorporated under the laws of the Province, and was called in the Act an extra-provincial company, certain conditions must be complied with. If such a company had gain for its object it must be licensed or registered under the law of the Province, and no agent was to carry on its business until this had been done. If this condition were complied with, such an extra-provincial company might sue in the Courts of the Province and hold land there. Such a company might also, if it were only duly incorporated under the laws of, among other authorities, the Dominion, and if authorized by its charter to carry out purposes to which the legislative authority of the Province extended, obtain from the Registrar, under the general Companies Act of the Province, a licence to carry on business within the Province on complying with the provisions of the Act and paying a proper licence fee. It was then to have the same powers and privileges in the Province as though incorporated under the Provincial Act. If such a company carried on business without a licence it was made liable to penalties, and its agents were similarly made liable. So long as unlicensed, the company could not sue in the

Courts of the Province in respect of contracts in connection with its business made within the Province. The Registrar might refuse a licence where the name of the company was identical with or resembled that by which a company, society or firm in existence was carrying on business or had been incorporated, licensed or registered, or where the Registrar was of opinion that the name was calculated to deceive, or disapprove of it for any other reason.

Their Lordships pointed out that, under the Dominion Companies Act, which they held to have been validly passed, the charter of the John Deere Plow Company incorporated it with the powers to which the legislative authority of the Parliament of Canada extended. The Dominion Interpretation Act provided that the meaning of such an incorporation included this, that the corporate body created should have power to sue, to contract in its corporate name, and to acquire and hold personal property for its purposes. There was in the Dominion Companies Act a provision that such a company should not be incorporated with a name likely to be confounded with the name of any other known company, incorporated or unincorporated, and it gave the Secretary of State the discretion in this connection. On incorporation the company was to be vested with all the powers, privileges, and immunities, requisite or incidental to the carrying on of its undertaking. It was to have an office in the city or town in which its chief place of business in Canada was situated, which should be its legal domicile in Canada, and could establish other offices and agencies elsewhere. No person acting as its agent was to be subjected, if acting within his authority, to individual penalty.

Their Lordships made reference to the circumstance that the concluding words of s. 91 of the British North America Act, "Any matter coming within any of the classes of subjects enumerated in this section shall not be deemed to come within the class of matters of a local or private nature comprised in the enumeration of the classes of subjects by this Act assigned exclusively to the Legislatures of the Provinces," render it necessary to do more than ascertain whether the subject-matter in question apparently falls within any of the heads of s. 92; for if it also falls within any of the enumerated heads of s. 91, then it cannot be treated as covered by any of those in s. 92. As is now well settled the words quoted apply, not only to the merely local or private matters in the Province referred to in head 16 of s. 92, but to the whole of the sixteen heads in that section: *A.-G. for Ontario v. A.-G. for Canada*, [1896] A.C. 348. The effect, as was pointed out in the decision just cited, is to effect a derogation from what might otherwise have been literally the authority of the Provincial Legislatures, to the extent of enabling the Parliament of Canada to deal with matters local and private where, though only where, such legislation is necessarily incidental to the exercise of the enumerated powers conferred on it by s. 91.

If therefore in legislating for the incorporation of companies under Dominion law and in validly endowing them with powers, the Dominion Parliament has by necessary implication given these companies a status which enables them to exercise these powers in the Provinces, they cannot be interfered with by any Provincial law in such a fashion as to derogate from their status and their consequent capacities, or, as the result of this restriction, to prevent them from exercising the powers conferred on them by Dominion law. Their Lordships, however, observed that when a company has been incorporated by the Dominion Government with powers to trade in any Province it may not the less, consistently with the general scheme, be subject to Provincial laws of general application, such as laws imposing taxes, or relating to mortmain, or even requiring licences for certain purposes, or as to the forms of contracts; but they were careful not to say that the sanctions by which such Provincial laws might be enforced could validly be so directed by the Provincial Legislatures as indirectly to sterilize or even to effect, if the local laws were not obeyed, the destruction of the capacities and powers which the Dominion had validly conferred. To have said so would have been to misread the scheme of the *British North America Act*, which is one that establishes interlacing and independent legislative authorities. Within the spheres allotted to them by the Act the Dominion and the Provinces are rendered on general principle coordinate Governments. As a consequence, where one has legislative power the other has not, speaking broadly, the capacity to pass laws which will interfere with its exercise. What cannot be done directly cannot be done indirectly. This is a principle which has to be kept closely in view in testing the validity of the Provincial legislation under consideration as affecting Dominion companies. . . .

The general Companies Act of Ontario was passed before that decision of the *John Deere Plow* case, and has no special bearing on the question in this appeal. The important statute is the *Extra-Provincial Corporations Act*, which was also passed before that decision. The purpose of the latter statute is to provide that certain classes of extra-Provincial corporations (which mean corporations created otherwise than by or under the authority of an Act of the Ontario Legislature), including those created under any Act of the Dominion and authorized to carry on business in Ontario, must take out a licence (s. 4) under the Ontario statute. On complying with its provisions a corporation coming within these classes is entitled to receive a licence (s. 5) to carry on its business and exercise its powers within Ontario. In the absence of such a licence it is forbidden to do so (s. 7), and its agents are subjected to a like prohibition. A penalty of $20 a day is imposed for any contravention of this provision. An extra-Provincial corporation coming within the classes referred to may apply to the Lieutenant-Governor in Council for a licence to carry on its business and exercise its powers in Ontario, and no limitations or conditions are to be included in any such licence which would interfere with the rights of such a corporation — for example, a Dominion company — carry on in Ontario all such part of its powers as by its Act or charter of incorporation it may be authorized to carry on and exercise there (s. 9, sub-ss. 1 and 2). A corporation receiving a licence may, subject to the limitations and conditions of the licence, and the provisions of its own constitution, hold and dispose of real estate in Ontario, just as an Ontario company might (s. 12). A corporation receiving a licence may be called on to make returns comprising such information as is required from an Ontario company (s. 14). The Lieutenant-Governor in Council may make regulations for, among other things, the appointment and continuance by the extra-Provincial company of a representative in Ontario on whom service of process and notices may be made (s. 10, sub-s. 1(b)). If such a company, having received a licence, makes default in complying with the limitations and conditions of the licence or of the provision as to returns, or the regulations respecting the appointment of a representative, its licence may be revoked (s. 15). If such a corporation carries on in Ontario without a licence any part of its business, it is to incur a penalty of $50 a day, and is rendered incapable of suing in the Ontario Courts in respect of any contract made in whole or in part within Ontario in relation to business for which it ought to have been licensed (s. 16). The Lieutenant-Governor in Council may prescribe fees on the transmission of the statement or return required under s. 14. Such fees are to vary with the capital stock of the company (s. 20).

It is obvious that the Act thus summarised assumes that the Legislature of the Province can impose on a Dominion company conditions which, if not complied with, will restrict the exercise of its powers within the Province. These conditions do not appear to their Lordships to be merely a means for the attainment of some exclusively Provincial object, such as direct taxation for Provincial purposes. They apparently assume a general right to limit the exercise of the powers of extra-Provincial companies if they seek to exercise these powers within Ontario. A question of principle is thus raised broadly. . . .

Their Lordships turn next to the case which has been brought forward as regards the legislation on the subject in Manitoba. In the Courts of that Province analogous questions were raised in a shareholder's action. The Attorney-General of the Province intervened in the course of the subsequent appeal.

In Manitoba there was passed in 1913 a general *Companies Act*, of which Part IV deals with extra-Provincial companies and includes Dominion corporations. Under s. 108 every such corporation is required to take out a licence under this part of the Act, and by s. 109 (*inter alia*) such a corporation, on complying with the provisions of that part and with the regulations made under the Act, is entitled to receive a licence to carry on its business and exercise its powers in Manitoba. By s. 111 (*inter alia*) such a corporation may apply to the Lieutenant-Governor in Council "for a licence to carry on its business or part thereof, and exercise its powers or part thereof, in Manitoba, and upon the granting of such licence such corporation may thereafter, while such licence is in force, carry on in Manitoba the whole or such parts of its business and exercise in Manitoba the whole or such parts of its powers as may be embraced in the licence; subject, however, to the provisions of this part and to such limitations and conditions as may be specified in the licence." On such an application the corporation is to file certain evidence and a power of attorney to someone in the Province appointing him to accept service. This is not to apply if the head office is within the Province (s. 114, sub-s. 3). By s. 118 no such corporation is to carry on within Manitoba any of its business, and no agent is to act for it, until a licence has been granted to it, and then only so long as this is in force. Sect. 120 requires annual returns of information to be made. By s. 121 the Lieutenant-Governor in Council may suspend or revoke the licence for default in observing the provisions of the Act. Sect. 122 provides, as in the case of the Ontario statute, for penalties for the carrying on of business in the absence of the licence, and incapacitates the corporation from suing without it in the Courts of the Province. Sect. 126 enables the Lieutenant-Governor to fix the fees to be paid. These are for the exchequer of the Province, and are to vary in part according to the nature and importance of the business to be carried on in the Province, and in part according to the amount of the entire capital stock of the corporation. In addition to these provisions, s. 112 enables a duly licensed corporation to hold real estate in the Province, but limited, in its licence, by s. 113 to such annual value as may have been deemed proper, as fully as if it had been a Manitoba company under the general Act. There is no Mortmain Act in the Province, but the registration of titles to land requires a licence and the registration of title to real estate in the case of extra-Provincial companies.

Thus there does not appear to be anything in the form or substance of the *Manitoba Act* which differentiates it materially from the corresponding Ontario Act. . . .

The four *Saskatchewan Companies Acts*, now operative, differ from those of Ontario and Manitoba in the circumstance that they were passed in 1915, 1916 and 1917, after the decision in *John Deere Plow Co. v. Wharton* by this Committee. It is the first of these four Acts that alone is important for the purposes of the present question. This is a general Companies Act, the provisions in which have nothing unusual in them, but which extends to (*inter alia*) Dominion companies having gain for their object, and carrying on business in the Province. The effect of s. 23 is that a Dominion company of this nature must be registered under the Act, and that if it does not register, the Dominion company and its representatives are liable to penalties for carrying on business in the Province. The effect of s. 24 is that registration cannot be refused to a Dominion company. By s. 25 the company may, on complying with the provisions of the Act, receive an annual licence, for which it is to pay fees to the Government of the Province, and then may carry on its business, subject to the provisions of the instrument creating it, as if it had been incorporated under the Act; but a company carrying on business without a licence is liable to penalties. By s. 27 the Lieutenant-Governor in Council may prescribe such regulations as he may deem expedient for the registration of all companies, and for fixing the fees payable. By s. 29 if the registrar thinks that a company registered has ceased to carry on business he may, after finding on inquiry that this is so, strike the company off the register, whereupon it is dissolved; but by an amending Act passed since the commencement of these proceedings the provision as to dissolution is to take effect only as to Saskatchewan companies. By s. 30 if the prescribed fee is not paid the company may be struck off the register.

Proceedings were taken in Saskatchewan before a Justice of the Peace against a Dominion company for not being licensed or registered, and an action was brought by a shareholder, as in the cases of the other Provinces already referred to. The substantial question was again the validity of the Provincial statute. . . .

. . . . Can the relevant provisions of all or any of the three sets of Provincial statutes be justified as directed exclusively to the attainment of an object of legislation assigned by s. 92 to the Legislatures, such as is the collection of direct taxes for Provincial purposes; or do these provisions interfere with such powers as are conferred on a Dominion company by the Parliament of Canada to carry on its business anywhere in the Dominion, and so affect its status? The question is one primarily of the interpretation of the *British North America Act* and in the second place of the meaning of the principle already laid down by this Committee in the *John Deere Plow* case. The constitution of Canada is so framed by the *British North America Act* that the difficulty was almost certain to arise. For the power of a Province to legislate for the incorporation of companies is limited to companies with Provincial objects, and there is no express power conferred to incorporate companies with powers to carry on business throughout the Dominion and in every Province. But such a power is covered by the general enabling words of s. 91, which, because of the gap, confer it exclusively on the Dominion. It must now be taken as established that s. 91 enables the Parliament of Canada to incorporate companies with such status and powers as to restrict the Provinces from interfering with the general right of such companies to carry on their business where they choose, and that the effect of the concluding words of s. 91 is to make the exercise of this capacity of the Dominion Parliament prevail in case of conflict over the exercise by the Provincial legislatures of their capacities under the enumerated heads of s. 92. It is clear that the mere power of direct taxation is saved to the Province, for that power is specifically given and is to be taken, so far as necessary, on a proper construction to be an exception from the general language of s. 91, as was explained by Sir Montague Smith in delivering the judgment of the Judicial Committee in *Citizens Insurance Co. v. Parsons*, 7 App. Cas. 96. Nevertheless, the methods by which the direct taxation is to be enforced may be restricted to the bringing of an action, with the usual consequences, which was all that was decided to be legal in *Bank of Toronto v. Lambe*, 12 App. Cas. 575. It does not follow that because the Government of the Province can tax it can put an end to the existence or even the powers of the company it taxes for non-compliance with the demands of the tax-gatherer. Their Lordships find themselves unable to agree with an observation made by Meredith C.J. toward the conclusion of his judgment [in 41 O.L.R. 475]. "It is," he says, "I think to be regretted that at the outset it was not determined that the authority of the Parliament of Canada to incorporate companies was limited to creating them and endowing them with capacity to exercise such powers as it might be deemed proper that they should possess, but leaving to each Province the power of determining how far, if at all, those powers should be exercised within its limits." Such a construction would have left an hiatus in the *British North America Act*, for there would have been in the Act so read no power to create a company with effective powers directed to other than merely Provincial objects. It was decided as long ago as 1883, in *Colonial Building Investment Association v. A.-G. for Quebec*, 9 App. Cas. 157, that there was no such hiatus. Nor does it appear, if reference may be made as matter of historical curiosity to the resolutions on which the *British North America Act* was founded, and which were passed at Quebec on October 10, 1864, for the guidance of the Imperial Parliament in enacting the Constitution of 1867, that these resolutions gave countenance to the idea that a different construction on the point in question was desired. The learned Chief Justice refers to them without quoting their language. But, in connection with the topic in controversy, all that was desired by the words of these resolutions to be assigned to the Provincial Legislatures was "the incorporation of Private or Local Companies, except such as relate to matters assigned to the General Parliament." . . .

The principle of interpretation to be followed in applying the test laid down in the *John Deere Plow Co.* case, that Provincial legislation cannot validly destroy the status and powers conferred on a Dominion company by Act of the Parliament of Canada, does not appear to be obscure when read in this light. Turning to its application, the first thing to be observed is the nature of the question to be answered. Their Lordships will dispose in the first place of a subsidiary matter, which is whether a Dominion company can be precluded from acquiring and holding land in a province by a Provincial law of the nature of a general Mortmain Act. It is clear, both on principle and from previous decisions, that it is within the competence of a Provincial Legislature to enact such legislation, and the question is therefore answered in the affirmative. If there be a provision to this effect, occurring even in a statute which in other respects is *ultra vires*, and that provision be severable, it is valid. In the Ontario case there is therefore no doubt that the broad result of the contention of the Province under this head is well founded; for there the Legislature has passed a Mortmain Act of General application, and in regard to this Act a Dominion company is in no better position than any other corporation which desires to hold land.

In Manitoba there is no general Mortmain Act, but s. 112 of the *Manitoba Companies Act* enables a corporation receiving a licence under Part IV of the Act, relating to extra-Provincial companies, to acquire and hold land as freely as could any company under Part I of the Act. Even if the provision as to the licensing of extra-Provincial companies is held to be *ultra vires*, so as to prevent such a provision from being operative, as being inseverable, it is plain that the substance of a provision which is of the character of a mortmain law is within the power of the Province.

In Saskatchewan there is no general Mortmain Act, but the *Companies Act* of 1915, by s. 19, enables a company incorporated under the law of the Province to hold land. By s. 25 a company not so incorporated (and this includes a Dominion company) may, if it has been licensed, carry on its business as if it had been incorporated under the law of the Province. This enables it to hold land unless the provisions as to the grant to it of a licence are inoperative. Their Lordships do not think that s. 29 of the Companies Act of Canada, which purports to enable a Dominion company to acquire and hold real estate requisite for the carrying on of its undertaking, can prevail against any severable provision by a Provincial Legislature restricting the power of corporations generally to acquire or hold real estate in the Province.

Their Lordships now pass to the question of a more general order, which is the main one in these appeals. Had the Provinces of Ontario, Manitoba and Saskatchewan power to impose on Dominion companies the obligation to obtain a licence from the Provincial Government as a condition of the exercise in those Provinces respectively of the powers conferred on them by the Dominion?

If the condition of taking out a licence had been introduced, not so as to affect the status of the Dominion company, but simply for the purpose of obtaining payment of a direct tax for Provincial purposes, or of securing the observance of some restriction as to contracts to be observed by the public generally in the province, or of causing the doing, by that public generally, of some act of a purely local character only under licence, their Lordships would, for reasons already given, have been prepared to regard the condition as one which it was within the power of the Province to impose. Even then it would have been requisite to see, as was pointed out by Lord Herschell, in delivering the judgment of the Judicial Committee in the *Brewers and Maltsters* case, that the Provincial Legislature was not, under the guise of imposing such direct taxation in the form of which he was speaking as being within their power, really doing something else, such as imposing indirect taxation. As to any inquiry in the future whether this or anything analogous has been in substance attempted, their Lordships hold themselves unfettered. If, for example, such a question were to arise hereafter, involving consideration of whether the real effect of the licence required by a Provincial law has been to abrogate capacity which it was within the power of the Parliament of Canada to bestow, or whether for a breach of conditions a Provincial Legislature could impose, not an ordinary penalty but one extending to the destruction of the status of the company and its capacity in the Province, nothing that has been here said is intended to prejudice the decision of such a question, should it occur. It is sufficient to observe once more that in such matters what cannot be done directly can no more be effected by indirect methods.

What remains is to apply the principle of the decision in the *John Deere Plow* case as so interpreted to the actual Provincial legislation challenged.

As to Ontario, the statute impugned is the Extra-Provincial Corporations Act in its application to Dominion companies. Their Lordships have come to the conclusion that the real effect of this Act, as expressed or implied by its provisions, is to preclude companies of this character from exercising the powers of carrying on business in Ontario, to the same extent as in other parts of Canada, unless they comply with a condition sought to be imposed, that of obtaining a licence to do so from the Government of the Province. By s. 7 such companies are expressly prohibited from doing so, and the provision in s. 9, sub-s. 2, that no limitations or conditions are to be included in such a licence as would limit a Dominion company, for example, from carrying on in the Province all such parts of its business, or from exercising there all such parts of its powers, as its Act or charter of incorporation authorizes, does not in their Lordships' opinion sufficiently mend matters. For the assertion remains of the right to impose the obtaining of a licence as a condition of doing anything at all in the Province. By s. 11 the grant of the licence is made dependent on compliance with such regulations as may happen to have been made by the Lieutenant-Governor in Council under ss. 2 and 10 of the Act. By s. 16, and also under s. 7 itself an extra-Provincial corporation required to take out a licence is to be fined for not doing so, and, under s. 16, is to be incapable of suing in the Courts of the Province. Their Lordships are of opinion that these provisions cannot be regarded as confined only to such limited purposes as would be legitimate, and that they are therefore *ultra vires*.

Taking next the *Companies Act of Manitoba*, Part IV of this Act deals with extra-Provincial corporations, including Dominion companies. The effect of the scheme of this part does not appear to their Lordships to differ in any feature that is material from that of the Ontario Act. *Inter alia*, a Dominion company must take out a licence, which it is entitled to receive if it complies with the provisions of the Act and with regulations to be made by the Lieutenant-Governor in Council. There may, under s. 111, be limitations and conditions specified in the licence, and if the company makes default in complying with these or certain other provisions, the licence may be revoked under s. 121. Unless the company obtains a licence it cannot, nor can any of its agents carry on business in Manitoba. Penalties are imposed for carrying on business without a licence, and so long as unlicensed the company cannot invoke the jurisdiction of the Courts of the Province. It does not alter the scope of these provisions that by s. 126 fees are payable for the licence, to be applied to the benefit of the revenue of the Province.

Their Lordships are unable to take the view that these sections regarded together are directed solely to the purposes specified in s. 92. They interpret them, like those of the Ontario statute, as designed to subject generally to conditions the activity within the Province of companies incorporated under the Act of the Parliament of Canada. The restrictions in this statute as to the holding of land cannot be severed from the general provisions as to licensing so as to make those restrictions enforceable as being in the nature of the Mortmain legislation.

The statute remaining to be considered is that passed by the Legislature of Saskatchewan in 1915, a general Companies Act which, however, contains provisions applicable to Dominion companies. By s. 23, if such companies carry on business in Saskatchewan, they must be registered under this Act, and if they carry on business without registering, the companies, and also the agents acting for them, are made liable on summary conviction to penalties. By s. 24 such companies are entitled to be registered on complying with the provisions of the Act and on paying the prescribed fees. There are also payable annual fees. By s. 25 such companies may upon certain conditions receive a licence to carry on business in Saskatchewan, and if they carry on business without a licence are guilty of an offence and liable to penalties. By s. 29, where the Registrar satisfies himself in the prescribed manner that a company registered under the Act has ceased to carry on business, he may strike the company off the register, and it is then to be dissolved. By s. 30, if the registration fees prescribed by the regulations made by the Lieutenant-Governor in Council be not paid, the Registrar is to strike the company off the register.

Here again their Lordships think that the Provincial Legislature has failed to confine its legislation to the objects prescribed in s. 92, and has trenched on what is exclusively given by the *British North America Act* to the Parliament of Canada. If the Act had merely required a Dominion company, within a reasonable time after commencing to carry on business in Saskatchewan, to register its name and other particulars in the Provincial register and to pay fees not exceeding those payable by Provincial companies, and had imposed upon it a daily penalty for not complying with this obligation, it could (their Lordships think) be supported as legitimate machinery for obtaining information and levying a tax. But the effect of imposing upon such a company a penalty for carrying on business while unregistered is to make it impossible for the company to enter into or to enforce its ordinary business engagements and contracts until registration is effected, and so to destroy for the time being the status and powers conferred upon it by the Dominion. Further, if it is the intention and effect of the Act that a Dominion company when registered in the Province shall be subject (by virtue of the definition section or otherwise) to the general provisions of the *Saskatchewan Companies Act* or shall become liable to dissolution under s. 29, the Act would be open to question on that ground; but it is right to say that such a construction was disclaimed by counsel for the Attorney-General of Saskatchewan and (as regards the liability to dissolution) has been excluded by an amending Act passed while these proceedings were pending. Sect. 25 of the *Saskatchewan Act*, which requires a Dominion company to obtain a licence, stands on the same footing as the enactments in Ontario and Manitoba which have been held void as *ultra vires*; and in this case also the restrictions on the holding of land are not severable from the licensing provisions and are invalid on that ground.

The result is that their Lordships take the view which commended itself to a minority of the judges in the Courts below, and find themselves unable to agree on the main question argued, either with the preponderating opinion expressed in the Supreme Court of Canada on the Saskatchewan and Manitoba legislation, or with that of the majority of the Appellate Division in Ontario on the validity of the statute of that Province, but that on the subsidiary question as to the Mortmain Act of Ontario they agree with the Ontario Courts.

*Appeals allowed.*

# CANADIAN INDEMNITY CO. v. ATTORNEY-GENERAL OF BRITISH COLUMBIA

In the Supreme Court of Canada. [1977] 2 S.C.R. 504.

Laskin, C.J.C., Martland, Judson, Ritchie, Spence, Pigeon, Dickson and Beetz, JJ. October 5, 1976.

Appeal from a judgment of the British Columbia Court of Appeal, [1976] 2 W.W.R. 499, dismissing an appeal from a judgment of Aikins, J., [1975] 1 W.W.R. 481, dismissing an action for a declaration of invalidity of the *Automobile Insurance Act* (B.C.) and the *Insurance Corporation of British Columbia Act* (B.C.).

The judgment of the Court was delivered by

MARTLAND J.: — The appellants, who are the plaintiffs in these proceedings, are 37 insurance companies, all of which carry on the business, in Canada, *inter alia*, of automobile insurance. Seventeen of the appellants are Canadian corporations. The respondent is the Attorney-General of British Columbia. The appellants, in their suit against him, sought to obtain a judgment declaring that the *Automobile Insurance Act*, S.B.C. 1973, c. 6, and the *Insurance Corporation of British Columbia Act*, S.B.C. 1973, c. 44, are both *ultra vires* of the Legislature of British Columbia to enact and are, therefore, invalid and of no force or effect.

The learned trial Judge, Aikins, J., made a careful study of the relevant portions of these statutes, the evidence submitted to him and the authorities cited in argument. His reasons are reported in [1975] 1 W.W.R. 481, and they make it unnecessary to review the statutory provisions and the evidence in detail. The two statutes under attack introduced in British Columbia a universal compulsory automobile insurance plan, known as "Autoplan", to be administered by the Insurance Corporation of British Columbia, hereinafter referred to as "the Corporation", which was created by the second of the above-mentioned statutes, and which is an agent of the Crown. The learned trial Judge describes the plan in the following passages from his judgment [at pp. 493 and 510 W.W.R.]:

> The two statutes under attack do not themselves reveal the whole plan because there are related statutes which were amended in order to implement the overall plan. The related statutes are the *Motor-vehicle Act*, R.S.B.C. 1960, c. 253; the *Motor Carrier Act*, R.S.B.C. 1960, c. 252, and the *Insurance Act*, R.S.B.C. 1960, c. 197. I will describe generally the legislative scheme enacted by the impugned statutes and by amendments to related Acts. Motor vehicle insurance is compulsory. Every driver licensed to drive in British Columbia must have driver's insurance evidenced by a driver's certificate. Driver's insurance is valid from and expires on the same date as does the driver's licence: it is conterminous with the driver's licence. A driver cannot get a driver's licence without driver's insurance; put shortly, no driver's insurance, no driver's licence. Every owner of a motor-vehicle registered and licensed in British Columbia must have insurance on his vehicle and

that insurance must be evidenced by an owner's certificate. Owner's insurance runs for the licence year of the motor vehicle and, therefore, is conterminous with the vehicle licence. Again, put shortly, no owner's insurance, no motor vehicle licence.

The legislative plan provides that the driver's certificate and owner's certificate must be issued by the Corporation. I should note that the Corporation does not issue actual policies of insurance. The Corporation simply issues driver's and owner's certificates. The contract of insurance, and the terms and conditions thereof, are not found in an issued policy of insurance but are to be found in the Regulations made pursuant to the *Automobile Insurance Act*. These Regulations provide, *inter alia*, that owners and drivers must insure to minimum prescribed limits and that extension insurance is available for those who wish to protect themselves to higher limits than the limits of the compulsory minimum coverage.

. . . . .

This complicated network of statutory and regulatory provisions comes down to this. An owner of a motor vehicle or trailer licensed and registered in British Columbia must have motor vehicle insurance and an owner's certificate evidencing such insurance. The only source of the required motor vehicle insurance and the required owner's certificate is the Corporation.

He concluded that the matter of the legislation is the establishment of a universal compulsory scheme of motor vehicle insurance in the Province of British Columbia with a monopoly in that class of insurance for the Corporation.

The *Automobile Insurance Act* provides for its provisions coming into effect on dates fixed by proclamation and for different dates being fixed for the coming into force of the several provisions. Some of the provisions of the Act had not come into effect at the date of the trial and were not in effect when the appeal to this Court was heard. Of these, the most important, in relation to this appeal, are ss. 8 [am. 1973 (2nd Sess.), c. 152, s. 2] 77, 78, 79 and 80.

Section 8 provides:

8. Notwithstanding any other Act or regulation, where the corporation is authorized under section 2 to engage in and carry on the activity of automobile insurance,
  (a) every person who applies in the Province for a policy of automobile or trailer insurance or a motor-vehicle liability policy in respect of a motor-vehicle or trailer registered or licensed in the Province shall apply to the corporation and, upon compliance with this Act and the regulations and paying the appropriate premium, he shall be provided with a motor-vehicle liability policy sufficient for the purposes of the *Motor-vehicle Act*, and such extension insurance as he applies for and pays for on the terms and conditions set out in the plan; and
  (b) every contract of automobile insurance in the Province and every motor-vehicle liability policy made or issued in the Province, after the coming into force of this section, in respect of a motor-vehicle or trailer registered or licensed in the Province by an insurer other than the corporation is void and of no effect.

The other four sections provide for amendments to the *Insurance Act*, R.S.B.C. 1960, c. 197, and their effect is indicated by the following extracts from those sections:

77(2) . . . a contract of automobile insurance made by any insurer in respect of an automobile or trailer licensed in the Province, on or after the date to be fixed by Order of the Lieutenant-Governor in Council, is void and of no effect; and the insurer shall forthwith upon demand refund to the insured any unearned premium paid in respect of the contract.

78(2) . . . on or after a date to be fixed by Order of the Lieutenant-Governor in Council, no insurer shall be licensed to carry on, in the Province, any class of automobile insurance.

79(2) ... every licence authorizing an insurer to carry on in the Province any class of automobile insurance is revoked and cancelled, in respect of that class of insurance, on a date to be fixed by Order of the Lieutenant-Governor in Council.

. . . . .

80(3) On or after a date to be fixed by Order of the Lieutenant-Governor in Council, no insurer, other than the Insurance Corporation of British Columbia, shall make a contract in respect of an automobile or trailer licensed in the Province.

(4) A contract made by an insurer in contravention of subsection (3) is void and of no effect.

The appellants had all been licensed under the *Insurance Act* to carry on the business of automobile insurance in British Columbia. Their last licences were for the period from March 1, 1973, to February 28, 1974. Renewals of these licences were refused.

The attack made by the appellants upon the constitutional validity of the two statutes was based upon two main submissions:

1. That the legislation related to a matter exclusively within the jurisdiction of the federal Parliament by virtue of s. 91(2) of the *British North America Act, 1867, i.e.*, "the regulation of trade and commerce".
2. That the effect of the legislation was in relation to and directed at the status and capacities of federally-incorporated companies, and was, therefore, *ultra vires* of the Legislature of British Columbia.

[His Lordship's discussion of section 91(2) is omitted.]


## STERILIZATION OF FEDERALLY-INCORPORATED COMPANIES

The appellants, relying upon the authority of such cases as *John Deere Plow Co. v. Wharton*, [1915] A.C. 330 (P.C.); *Great West Saddlery Co. v. The King*, [1921] 2 A.C. 91 (P.C.); *Lukey v. Ruthenian Farmers' Elevator Co.*, [1924] S.C.R. 56, and *A.-G. Man. v. A.-G. Can.*, [1929] A.C. 260 (P.C.), contend that the legislation in question here impairs, in a substantial degree, the status and capacities of each of the appellants incorporated under Canadian law and, in consequence, is *ultra vires* of the Legislature of British Columbia. This submission was accepted by Robertson, J.A., in the Court of Appeal.

The effect of this line of case law was the subject of comment recently in this Court by Chief Justice Laskin, when delivering the judgment of the Court, in *Morgan v. A.-G. P.E.I.*, [1976] 2 S.C.R. 349 at 364:

The issue here is not unlike that which has governed the determination of the validity of provincial legislation embracing federally-incorporated companies. The case law, dependent so largely on the judicial appraisal of the thrust of the particular legislation, has established, in my view, that federally-incorporated companies are not constitutionally entitled, by virtue of their federal incorporation, to any advantage, as against provincial regulatory legislation, over provincial corporations or over extra-provincial or foreign corporations, so long as their capacity to establish themselves as viable corporate entities (beyond the mere fact of their incorporation), as by raising capital through issue of shares and debentures, is not precluded by the provincial legislation. Beyond this, they are subject to competent provincial regulations in respect of businesses or activities which fall within provincial legislative power.

The particular legislation which was in issue in the *John Deere* case was a British Columbia statute which required every extra-provincial company (which included a federally-incorporated company) to be licensed or registered under that Act, failing which it would not be capable of carrying on business in the Province or able to maintain legal proceedings in the provincial Courts in respect of a contract made in the Province.

Viscount Haldane, at 341 A.C., said:

> It is enough for present purposes to say that the province cannot legislate so as to deprive a Dominion company of its status and powers.

However, he went on to say, on the same page:

> This does not mean that these powers can be exercised in contravention of the laws of the province restricting the rights of the public in the province generally. What it does mean is that the status and powers of a Dominion company as such cannot be destroyed by provincial legislation.

In the *Great West Saddlery* case, a consolidation of three cases, the issue involved the validity of provincial legislation in Ontario, Manitoba and Saskatchewan. Again the legislation in question purported to preclude federally-incorporated companies from carrying on business in the Province unless registered or licensed by the Province. Penalties were imposed for non-compliance. The Acts were held to be *ultra vires* of the provincial Legislatures.

There was also in issue, in one of these cases, the validity of the Ontario *Mortmain and Charitable Uses Act* in its application to federally-incorporated companies. Dealing with this matter, Viscount Haldane said, at 119 A.C.:

> Their Lordships will dispose in the first place of a subsidiary matter, which is whether a Dominion company can be precluded from acquiring and holding land in a province by a provincial law of the nature of a general Mortmain Act. It is clear, both on principle and from previous decisions, that it is within the competence of a Provincial Legislature to enact such legislation, and the question is therefore answered in the affirmative. If there be a provision to this effect, occurring even in a statute which in other respects is *ultra vires*, and that provision be severable, it is valid. In the Ontario case there is therefore no doubt that the broad result of the contention of the Province under this head is well founded; for there the Legislature has passed a Mortmain Act of general application, and in regard to this Act a Dominion company is in no better position than any other corporation which desires to hold land.

In the *Lukey* case this Court considered the validity of the Saskatchewan *Sale of Shares Act* in relation to its application to the sale of its own shares in the Province by a federally-incorporated company. The statute provided that no person should sell shares of a company, or offer such shares for sale, without first obtaining a certificate from the Local Government Board. Duff, J., as he then was, said at 73 S.C.R.:

> The enactments of the impugned statute necessarily have as already mentioned the immediate effect of preventing Dominion companies with head offices in Saskatchewan exercising in the normal way the power to obtain capital through subscription for their shares. Not only is that the effect of the legislation, it is of the essence of its design. For by its provisions the exercise of the powers of such a company is made conditional upon submission by the company to a provincial control which would deprive it of the free right of exercising its capacities according to the constitution validly imposed upon it by the Dominion, the constitution, the arrangements between the company and its members, between different classes of members, between the members and the management as touching the control of its affairs, and the distribution of profits are all subjected to the supervision of the Provincial Local Board.

He went on to say, at 74 S.C.R.:

> This is not to say that such companies are withdrawn from the operation of provincial laws dealing generally with matters that may be embraced in whole or in part within the objects of the company. Dominion companies empowered to deal in intoxicating liquors for example are subject to provincial laws regulating or suppressing the sale of liquor; but such laws are not laws aimed at Dominion companies as such or at joint stock companies as such and do not in effect or in purpose prohibit or impose conditions upon the exercise of powers of Dominion companies which are essential in the sense that they are necessary to enable them in a practical way to function as corporations according to the constitutions imposed upon them by the Dominion.

The case of *A.-G. Man. v. A.-G. Can.*, decided by the Privy Council, dealt with two Manitoba statutes, the *Sale of Shares Act* and the *Municipal and Public Utility Board Act*, which had provisions similar to the legislation considered by this Court in the *Lukey* case and which were held, for similar reasons, to be invalid.

The four cases above-mentioned all dealt with provincial company law or securities legislation and their effect in frustrating the effect of federal incorporation. In each case the legislation was held to be *ultra vires* of the provincial Legislature. They were followed by the important Privy Council decision in the case of *Lymburn v. Mayland*, [1932] A.C. 318. In this case it was argued that the *Security Frauds Prevention Act*, 1930, of Alberta, was *ultra vires* the provincial Legislature in so far as it applied to federally-incorporated companies. The Act provided that no person could trade in securities unless he was registered with the approval of the Attorney-General. A corporation could be registered which would obviate the necessity for its officials registering. A public company was not permitted to sell its shares unless it did so through a registered person or was itself registered. Section 9 of the Act provided that the Attorney-General, or his delegate, could examine any person or company to ascertain whether any "fraudulent act" had been, was being, or was about to be committed. The case arose when the Attorney-General of Alberta appointed an examiner to examine into the affairs of three federal companies. The Alberta Courts granted an interim injunction to prevent the Attorney-General's nominee from examining the federal company and held that s. 9 of the Act was *ultra vires* in relation to such companies. On appeal, Lord Atkin, speaking for the Privy Council, said, at pp. 322-3 A.C.:

> Before the Board the attack was made on a broader ground. The whole Act was invalid so far as it related to Dominion companies because it destroyed their status by making it impossible for them to issue their share capital. In this respect it was said the case was covered by the decision of this Board in *A.-G. Man v. A.-G. Can.*, [1929] A.C. 260. . . . Their Lordships cannot accept any of these contentions.

The Court considered the argument that the provisions of this statute, so far as they affected federal companies, were *ultra vires* according to the principles of *John Deere Plow, Great West Saddlery* and *A.-G. Man. v. A.-G. Can.* The Board's answer to that submission is contained in the following language, found on pp. 324-5 A.C.:

> It appears to their Lordships impossible to bring this legislation within such a principle. A Dominion company constituted with powers to carry on a particular business is subject to the competent legislation of the Province as to that business and may find its special activities completely paralysed as by legislation against drink traffic or by the laws as to holding land. If it is formed to trade in securities there appears no reason why it should not be subject to the competent laws of the Province as to the business of all persons who trade in securities. As to the issue of capital there is no complete prohibition, as in *A.-G. Man. v. A.-G. Can.* in 1929; and no reason to

suppose that any honest company would have any difficulty in finding registered persons in the Province through whom it could lawfully issue its capital. There is no material upon which their Lordships could find that the functions and activities of a company were sterilized or its status and essential capacities impaired in a substantial degree.

The learned trial Judge dealt with the issues now being considered in the following passage in his judgment [at pp. 587-9 W.W.R.]:

> The principle which I think can properly be drawn from these cases and the principle which I apply in holding that the impugned legislation is not *ultra vires* the Province, in so far as it affects Dominion companies, is that which was stated by the Appellate Division of the Alberta Supreme Court in *R. v. Arcadia Coal Co.*, [1932] 1 W.W.R. 771 (Alta. C.A.). In that case the constitutional validity of the Alberta *Coal Miner's Security Act* was challenged. The statute had purported to prohibit the operation of any mine within the Province where a bond or security satisfactory to the Minister had not been furnished to him. McGillivray, J.A., for the Court, declared the Act to be *ultra vires* the Province, and in coming to that conclusion stated, at pp. 784-5 W.W.R., what he took to be the effect of the authorities:
>
>> A provincial Legislature may enact laws, province wide, of general application (*i.e.*, including the public generally) in respect of any of the subjects enumerated in s. 92 and in so doing may completely paralyze all activities of a Dominion trading company provided that in the enactment of such laws it does not enter the field of company law and in that field encroach upon the status and powers of a Dominion company as such.
>>
>> In my view an enactment of a provincial Legislature limited in direct effect by provincial boundaries which relates to a particular trade or business carried on within its boundaries, quite regardless of whether or not that trade or business is carried on by natural persons or companies, is valid, but the moment that a provincial Legislature legislates concerning companies as such, then, if such legislation constitutes regulation or impairment or sterilization of the powers and capacities which the Dominion has conferred, the legislation will be invalid.
>>
>> I may add, as pointed out by Viscount Sumner in *A.-G. Man. v. A.-G. Can.*, such last-mentioned legislation is not saved by the fact that all kinds of companies provincial as well as Dominion are aimed at without special discrimination against Dominion companies.
>>
>> The distinction between enactments affecting Dominion companies that are of general application and those that may be termed company law, is simply this: in the former case there is no attempt to interfere with powers validly granted to the company by the Dominion nor with the status of the company as such. The circumstance that the company consistently with the general laws of the Province may not exercise those powers, does not destroy or impair the powers. In the latter case the enactment prohibits or imposes conditions upon the exercise of the powers of Dominion companies as such. In short it is aimed at and affects Dominion company powers as distinguished from being aimed at and affecting a trade or business in the Province which Dominion companies may happen to be engaged in common with provincial companies and natural persons.
>>
>> In the one case the legislation has to do with a provincial matter, Dominion companies being only incidentally affected; in the other case the legislation is aimed either at Dominion companies or at all companies which includes Dominion companies, and so the Province with power to legislate only as to Provincial companies must be said to have entered the Dominion field.

The *Arcadia Coal* case was decided shortly after the decision of the Privy Council in *Lymburn v. Mayland*, which judgment is referred to in it.

I am in agreement with this statement which accords with that of Chief Justice Laskin in the *Morgan* case, previously quoted. Parliament can create and maintain the legal existence of a corporate entity, with which a Province cannot interfere. But a provincial Legislature within its own field of legislative power can regulate, in the Province, a particular business or activity. The fact that a federally-incorporated company has, by federal legislation, derived existence as a legal person, with designated powers, does not mean that it is thereby exempted from the operation of such provincial regulation. It is subject to such regulation in the same way as a natural person or a provincially-incorporated company.

In my opinion the second submission of the appellants also fails. I would dismiss the appeal, with costs to the respondent. There should be no costs payable by or to any of the intervenants.

*Appeal dismissed.*

# CHURCHILL FALLS (LABRADOR) CORP. LTD. v. A.G. NFLD.

In the Supreme Court of Canada. [1984] 1 S.C.R. 297.

Laskin C.J.C.*, Ritchie, Dickson, Beetz, Estey, McIntyre, Chouinard, Lamer and Wilson JJ. May 3, 1984.

*The Chief Justice took no part in the judgment.

[The facts of this case are set out in Chapter 8, *supra.*]

The judgment of the Court was delivered by McINTYRE J.: — ...

## VII

It was contended by the appellants that the *Reversion Act* was *ultra vires* of the Legislature of Newfoundland, because it impaired the status and essential powers of a federally-incorporated company. This argument was rejected in the Court of Appeal. It concluded that, while the *Reversion Act* deprived CFLCo of most of its assets, it did not affect the essential corporate capacity of the company. It was still at liberty to raise capital by the issue of shares and securities and could thus effectively further its corporate objects and purposes. It went on to conclude that the fact that the Act was not a law of general application in Newfoundland — it affected only CFLCo — was not a factor in deciding whether the Act was *intra vires*. The court held that it could be supported under the general power of the Province to expropriate property and civil rights within the Province, saying:

> If, as was held in the *Great-West Saddlery Co.* [2 A.C. 91], a federal company dealing only in land is subject to provincial mortmain legislation it would, in our view, be equally subject to provincial expropriation legislation which is the subject matter of the Reversion Act.

It then went on to conclude that any inadequacy in compensation did not restrict CFLCo in its corporate capacity and that, while s. 12 of the *Reversion Act* deprives the company of any right to sue in the courts of Newfoundland for compensation, it does not affect the company's general right to sue, to contract, and to carry on its business within Newfoundland.

The appellants argued that the Act effectively sterilizes the Company by expropriating all its operating assets. By limiting compensation to direct payment to creditors and shareholders, and excluding CFLCo, it deprives the Company of any means by which it could function and perform its covenants under the Power Contract, in respect of which it remained liable. In addition, it was argued that, since the objects and powers of the company are limited to hydro-electric power generation and distribution, and in practical terms to the fulfilment of the project on the Upper Churchill River, the Act strips CFLCo of its essential powers and capacity to function as a company. Reference was made to *B.C. Power Corporation v. Attorney General of British Columbia* (1963), 44 W.W.R. 65 (B.C.S.C.).

The respondent Attorney General of Newfoundland supported the Court of Appeal's judgment on this point and asserted that the Province had, because of its general competence to legislate with respect to property and civil rights within the Province, full power to pass the *Reversion Act* and to expropriate the assets of CFLCo. Such an expropriation, despite the fact that it deprives CFLCo of virtually all its assets, does not impair the status or essential powers of the corporation.

Generally speaking, a federally-incorporated company carrying on business in a province is bound to obey any of the provincial laws which ordinarily apply to it and the trade or business with which it is concerned. In this respect it does not, by virtue of its corporate status, obtain any advantage over a provincially-incorporated company or a natural person. Such a company will be liable to pay taxes competently imposed under provincial legislation. It will be subject to ordinary licensing requirements and regulations under valid provincial legislation, as would be natural persons. In short, it will be subject to all competently enacted laws of general application in the Province. The one exception to this general application of provincial laws is described by Professor Hogg in his *Constitutional Law of Canada* (1977), at p. 355, in this manner:

> There is one important exception to the general principle that a company is obliged to obey any valid law which is apt to apply to it. A province may not impair the "status and essential powers" of a federally-incorporated company (hereinafter referred to as a federal company). What this means is that if a province enacts a law which is within its legislative competence, but which would have the effect of impairing the status or essential powers of a federal company, then the law will be held inapplicable to any federal company.

The following question therefore arises: Does the *Reversion Act* impair the status and essential powers of CFLCo?

There are many cases dealing with the subject. The starting point for consideration is generally taken to be *John Deere Plow Co. v. Wharton*, [1915] A.C. 330; and *Great West Saddlery Co. v. The King*, [1921] 2 A.C. 91. It is not necessary here to go into detail regarding the cases, but in *John Deere Plow Co.* a provincial enactment (the *Companies Act* of British Columbia) which provided for the licensing of federal companies under the Act as a condition of carrying on business in the Province or of maintaining proceedings in the courts was held *ultra vires*. In the *Great West Saddlery Co.* case the *Mortmain and Charitable Uses Act* of Ontario, which required the federally-incorporated company — and all other companies — to have a provincial licence as a condition of their right to hold land, was held to be *intra vires* as being a law of general application. The Privy Council noted that a Dominion company acquired no more favourable position than any other corporation when it sought to own land within a province.

In *Attorney-General for Manitoba v. Attorney-General for Canada* (the *Manitoba Securities* case), [1929] A.C. 260, it was held by the Judicial Committee of the Privy Council that a provincial enactment prohibiting the sale of shares by any company, provincial or federal, except on terms provided in the Act and with the consent of a provincial commissioner was *ultra vires* in that it struck at the basic capacity of the federal company to create its corporate being by raising capital. In *Lymburn v. Mayland*, [1932] A.C. 318, the *Security Frauds Prevention Act, 1930* of Alberta required registration of anyone, including a company, trading in securities. The Judicial Committee held the Act *intra vires* and distinguished the *Manitoba Securities* case, saying at pp. 324-25, after deciding that the principle enunciated in *John Deere Plow* and the *Great West Saddlery* cases was not applicable to the *Security Frauds Prevention Act*:

> A Dominion company constituted with powers to carry on a particular business is subject to the competent legislation of the Province as to that business and may find its special activities completely paralysed, as by legislation against drink traffic or by the laws as to holding land. If it is formed to trade in securities there appears no reason why it should not be subject to the competent laws of the Province as to the business of all persons who trade in securities. As to the issue of capital there is no complete prohibition, as in the *Manitoba* case in 1929; and no reason to suppose that any honest company would have any difficulty in finding registered persons in the Province through whom it could lawfully issue its capital. There is no material upon which their Lordships could find that the functions and activities of a company were sterilized or its status and essential capacities impaired in a substantial degree.

In *Morgan v. Attorney-General of Prince Edward Island*, [1976] 2 S.C.R. 349, a case which did not involve a question of sterilization of a federal company by provincial legislation, Laskin C.J. made the following observation, at pp. 364-65, which is relevant to the issue before us:

> The issue here is not unlike that which has governed the determination of the validity of provincial legislation embracing federally-incorporated companies. The case law, dependent so largely on the judicial appraisal of the thrust of the particular legislation, has established, in my view, that federally-incorporated companies are not constitutionally entitled, by virtue of their federal incorporation, to any advantage, as against provincial regulatory legislation, over provincial corporations or over extra-provincial or foreign corporations, so long as their capacity to establish themselves as viable corporate entities (beyond the mere fact of their incorporation), as by raising capital through issue of shares and debentures, is not precluded by the provincial legislation. Beyond this, they are subject to competent provincial regulations in respect of businesses or activities which fall within provincial legislative power.

In *Canadian Indemnity Co. v. Attorney-General of British Columbia*, [1977] 2 S.C.R. 504, this Court dealt with a case where the appellant, a company engaged in the business of writing automobile insurance, was refused a licence for the conduct of its business in the year 1974, because the provincial government had introduced a statutory scheme of compulsory government insurance which excluded private insurers. It was argued *inter alia* that the legislation creating the plan was *ultra vires* of the Province as legislation in relation to and directed at the status and capacity of a federal company. The legislation was held to be *intra vires* of the provincial legislature. Martland J., writing for this Court, reviewed the relevant authorities and quoted a lengthy passage from the judgment of Aikens J. at trial in the Supreme Court of British Columbia. The passage quoted includes, at p. 518 ([1977] 2 S.C.R.), the words of McGillivray J.A., speaking for the Appellate Division of the Alberta Supreme Court in *R. v. Arcadia Coal Co.*, [1932] 1 W.W.R. 771 at pp. 784-85, where he said:

The distinction between enactments affecting Dominion companies that are of general application and those that may be termed company law is simply this: In the former case there is no attempt to interfere with powers validly granted to the company by the Dominion nor with the status of the company as such. The circumstance that the company consistently with the general laws of the province may not exercise those powers does not destroy or impair the powers. In the latter case the enactment prohibits or imposes conditions upon the exercise of the powers of Dominion companies as such. In short it is aimed at and affects Dominion company powers as distinguished from being aimed at and affecting a trade or business in the province which Dominion companies may happen to be engaged in in common with provincial companies and natural persons.

Martland J. then went on to say that he approved of the passage quoted from the trial judgment and he observed that it accorded with the words of Laskin C.J. in the *Morgan* case which have already been reproduced above.

There are, of course, many other authorities which have dealt with this question. Many are referred to and discussed in the cases cited above. I do not consider that more extensive reference to them is necessary here, because the governing principle in this matter emerges from the cases already cited. The authorities make it clear that it is not competent for a provincial legislature to legislate to impair or destroy the essential status and capacities of a federal company. However, a federal company carrying on business within a province is subject to all laws of general application in the province and as well is subject to all laws of particular application to the business, trade or function with which the federal company is concerned, and the federal company does not acquire any favoured position in relation to other companies or to natural persons or obtain any peculiar advantages by reason only of its federal incorporation. Provincial legislation may license and regulate the activities of federal companies within the field of provincial competence and may impose sanctions for the enforcement of its regulations, but such sanctions may not be such as to strike at the essential capacities and status of a federal company. In exercising its legislative powers, however, the provincial legislature may not venture into the field of company law in respect of the federal company. It may not legislate so as to affect the corporate structure of the federal entity or so as to render the federal company incapable of creating its corporate being and exercising its essential corporate powers as a company. I now turn to a consideration of the facts in the present case.

The *Reversion Act* on it face does nothing more than expropriate for all practical purposes all of the assets of CFLCo and make certain provisions regarding compensation to shareholders and creditors but no compensation to the Company. While the result of the Act would be to deprive CFLCo of the business it formerly conducted, in my view it cannot be said that the corporate being of CFLCo would be affected. It would still be a corporation in being and its essential structure would remain unchanged. It seems perfectly clear that if the *Reversion Act* applied to a provincially-incorporated company no challenge could be maintained as to its constitutionality on this branch of the argument. Can it be said then that the mere fact of federal incorporation clothes CFLCo with any immunity from expropriation under valid provincial law not possessed by a provincial company or for that matter a natural person? In addressing this question the Court of Appeal quoted from *Abitibi Power and Paper Co. v. Montreal Trust Co.*, [1943] A.C. 536 at p. 548:

There appears to be no authority, and no reason for the opinion, that legislation in respect of property and civil rights must be general in character and not aimed at a particular right. Such a restriction would appear to eliminate the possibility of special legislation aimed at transferring a particular right or property from private hands to a public authority for public purposes. The legislature is supreme in these matters, and its actions must be assumed to be taken with due regard for justice and good conscience. They are not, in any case, subject to control by the courts.

A federal company is entitled to establish itself as a corporation in a province and for this purpose it is entitled to raise capital and to create its corporate being without interference from provincial legislation. Having done so, however, it is in no better position with respect to the conduct or continuation of its business than a provincial company or natural person. As has been pointed out in a "Note on the Favoured Position of the Dominion Company Under the B.C. Power Case", in *Laskin's Canadian Constitutional Law*, 4th ed., 1975, p. 559 at 561:

If, as has been held, a federal company dealing only in land is subject to provincial mortmain legislation, it would be equally subject to provincial expropriation legislation. And why would a federal company dealing in shares of provincial companies or in the shares of only one provincial company be in any different position?

It is difficult to conceive how ownership of all the shares of a provincial company as a federal company's choice of business can go to the matter of its incorporation. The argument of "impairment of the status and capacities of a federal company in a substantial degree" cannot go beyond protection of the federal company's right to become launched as a corporation by raising capital. Does a federal company by limiting itself to one line of business within provincial competence obtain a constitutional right to be left alone in its ownership, thus enjoying an advantage not open to a natural person?

On the authorities already discussed, the question posed in the Note requires a negative answer. It will be evident from what I have said that I do not regard *B.C. Power Corporation v. The Attorney General of British Columbia* as authoritative on this point. It is not, in my view, in accordance with the governing authorities.

In the case at bar the Legislature of Newfoundland in passing the *Reversion Act* effectively transferred the assets of CFLCo from privat ownership to ownership by the Government. CFLCo is left with its corporate structure intact and with the capability to raise new capital and issue shares. It is my opinion that, whatever attacks may be made on the validity of the *Reversion Act* under other heads of argument raised in this case, the Legislature in passing the *Reversion Act* did not contravene the constitutional strictures against interference with the essential status and powers of a federally-incorporated company.

*Appeal allowed with costs.*

## Note

The cases on legislative authority in relation to companies are discussed in Wegenast, *Canadian Companies*, chap. 3. For a general survey, see Ziegel, *Constitutional Aspects of Canadian Companies*, chap. 5 of Ziegel (ed.), "Studies in Canadian Company Law" (1968). See also Lederman, "The Creation of Corporate Bodies and the Functional Regulation of Legal Persons in the Canadian Federal System" in *Continuing Canadian Constitutional Dilemmas* (1981).

A foreign incorporated company does not enjoy the same constitutional protection against certain kinds of provincial legislation as does a federally incorporated company: see *Van Buren Bridge Co. v. Madawaska and A.-G. N.B.* (1958), 15 D.L.R. (2d) 763 (N.B.C.A.).

Assuming the immunity of "Dominion" companies from provincial general licensing legislation, it does not cover particular licences required for engaging in a controlled activity in the Province. Thus, a federally incorporated company authorized to engage in or practise engineering could not by reason only of such incorporation claim to take engineering work without complying with provincial licensing legislation; and this would be equally true as to other controlled professions or activities, even if there were a licensing requirement for any type of business: see *Motor Car Supply Co. v. A.G. Alta.*, [1939] 3 W.W.R. 65 (Alta. S.C.). If this is so, does it mean that a province may competently exclude a corporation, whether federally incorporated or not, from engaging in particular kinds of business for which a licence is required? See *Giffels & Vallet of Canada Ltd. v. The King*, [1952] O.W.N. 196 (C.A.), aff'g [1951] O.R. 652 (H.C.).

In *Public Accountants Council for Ontario v. Premier Trust Co.*, [1964] 1 O.R. 386 (H.C.), the question arose whether a federally incorporated trust company empowered by its charter to execute the offices of accountant and auditor in connection with its primary business of trustee and fiduciary, was caught by the *Public Accountancy Act*, R.S.O. 1960, c. 317 which forbade a corporation to practise public accountancy. Schatz J. said that "the restriction upon the defendant operating as a public accountant does not 'impair the status and essential capacities of the company in a substantial degree' and that the defendant is not sterilized in all its functions and activities", because the business of acting as public accountant was not contemplated as a basic or substantial part of the company's activities. Hence the Act was properly applicable.

Accepting that a Dominion company no less than a foreign company operating in a Province is subject to provincial taxing legislation, is there any tenable constitutional objection in either case against discriminatory taxation? See *Van Buren Bridge Co. v. Madawaska and A.-G. N.B., supra; Charlottetown v. Foundation Maritime Ltd.*, [1932] 1 D.L.R. 453 (P.E.I.S.C.), aff'd [1932] S.C.R. 589. Does it make any difference if the Dominion company is an ordinary trading company or is a bank? See *A.-G. Alta. v. A.-G. Can.*, [1939] A.C. 117 (P.C.).

Flowing from the foregoing is the question whether there is any limitation on the objects or powers with which a company may be incorporated by the Dominion. Presumably, it could not incorporate a municipality within a Province, but are there any other limitations on its power to incorporate? It is the Provinces that are limited in their powers of incorporation under section 92(11) of the *Constitution Act, 1867*: for a detailed judicial treatment of the provincial incorporation power, see Laskin J.'s (as he then was) judgment in *Kootenay and Elk Railway Co. v. C.P.R.*, [1974] S.C.R. 955. Is it open to the Parliament of Canada to authorize the incorporation of a college or a university? See *The Frontier College Act*, S.C. 1922, c. 77, which empowered the incorporated college to grant degrees in arts. But *cf. In re the Brothers of the Christian Schools in Canada* (1876), Cout. S.C. 1.

How far if at all may the Dominion in incorporating a company regulate its domestic administration? May it circumscribe the kind or range of investments? Or the liability of the company or its directors to creditors? See *Reference re Section 110 of the Dominion Companies Act*, [1934] S.C.R. 653; *Montel v. Groupe de Consultants P.G.L. Inc.; A.G. Can. v. Groupe de Consultants P.G.L. Inc.*, [1982] C.A. 336. In *Montel*, the Quebec Court of Appeal upheld the federal remedy against oppression in section 234 of the *Canada Business Corporations Act*, S.C. 1974-75-76, c. 33 which empowered the court, upon application of a complainant, to make orders, *inter alia*, appointing receivers, regulating corporate affairs by amending its articles, and varying or setting aside contracts to which the corporation is a party and awarding compensation to an aggrieved person. Dubé J.A. speaking for the Court, said at pp. 667-9 D.L.R.:

> Moreover, from the fact that the Canadian Parliament has the power to incorporate companies having other than provincial objects, the evidence indicates that this power is not limited simply to the creation of such companies: clearly this power must include the power to legislate with respect to the internal constitution of such a company, the power to determine the procedure to become a member of that company, the power to define relationships between the members and many other related powers; if some of these powers belong to the provincial authorities which s. 92 of the *Constitution Act, 1867* calls exclusive powers, for example powers with respect to property and civil rights in the province, I do not think that we must therefore conclude that the federal legislation is unconstitutional; in fact, although this legislation has the appearance of legislation affecting property and civil rights, it is actually corporate legislation.
>
> In support of this claim, I cite the Supreme Court decision in the case of *Lukey v. Ruthenian Farmers Elevator Co.*, [1924] S.C.R. 56 at 72-3:
>
>> The authority to incorporate companies and endow them with status and powers, maintainable and exercisable independently of provincial sanction, would appear at least to involve the authority to dictate the constitution of the company including the procedure by which membership in the corporation is acquired, as well as to prescribe the character of relations which shall obtain between the corporation and its members. And legislation defining this procedure and creating powers expressly or impliedly to enable it to be carried out, is strictly not within the scope of legislation on the subject of "civil rights" as contemplated by 92(13) but belongs to the class of legislation on the subject of "incorporation of companies" and therefore is not within the scope of section 92 when governing companies with objects other than "provincial rights" within the meaning of 92(1).
>
> According to the prevailing jurisprudence of the Supreme Court, it is appropriate to conclude that the competence devolving upon the Parliament of Canada with respect to the incorporation of companies is broad enough to serve as a constitutional basis for any legislation whose object is to regulate the internal life of companies constituted under the regime of a federal statute and accordingly, to deal with the repression of what the Legislature might regard as abusive behaviour on the part of such a company with respect to its shareholders, directors or even creditors. In 1934, the Supreme Court was called upon to deal with the constitutional validity of s. 110 of the Dominion *Companies Act*, R.S.C. 1927, c. 27, with respect to the personal responsibility of directors of a company to that company, as well as to its shareholders and its creditors, for the debts of the company in the event of the payment of a dividend when the company is insolvent; Chief Justice Duff said as follows with respect to this matter in the case *Reference re Section 110 Dominion Companies Act*, [1934] S.C.R. 653 at 659:
>
>> It appears to me that you are strictly within what might properly be called the defining of the construction of the company when you are making provision for limiting the liability of shareholders in respect of the debts of the company; when you are making co-ordinate provisions for the protection of the assets of the company in the interests of the creditors of the company; when you are providing safeguards against the malfeasance of the managers and, particularly, when, in the interests of persons dealing with the company, you are providing safeguards against the improper or colourable employment by the managers or the shareholders of their powers in wasting the assets of the company.

I would hasten to point out the appropriateness of Chief Justice Duff's remarks with respect to the case before us.

May the Dominion in its company legislation validly restrict the transfer of shares by or to certain persons or companies or generally? May it compel minority shareholders to sell if a prescribed majority approves of a proposed sale of the company's shares or any class thereof? See *Rathie v. Montreal Trust Co.* (1952), 5 W.W.R. (N.S.) 675 (B.C.S.C.), affd (1952), 6 W.W.R. (N.S.) 652 (B.C.C.A.), rev'd on other grounds [1953] 2 S.C.R. 204; *Esso Standard (Inter-America) Inc. v. J.W. Enterprises Inc. and Morrisroe*, [1963] S.C.R. 144.

Federal legislation which provides that letters patent are "conclusive proof" of the facts set out therein cannot preclude a party in a provincial court from adducing evidence that in fact the letters patent bear a date which is earlier than that on which they were actually signed: see *Letain v. Conwest Explor. Co. Ltd.*, [1961] S.C.R. 98.

The fact that a federally incorporated company confines its activities to one province does not affect the validity of its constitution: see *Colonial Building & Investment Assoc. v. A.-G. Que.* (1883), 9 App. Cas. 157 (P.C.). Is there any constitutional objection then to a federal incorporation which limits territorially the operations of the company?

In a number of cases it has been held that a provincial Attorney-General may (apart from any authority in federal legislation) take proceedings by way of *scire facias* to revoke the charter of a federally incorporated company: see *Guimond v. National Real Estate & Investment Co.* (1915), 16 Que. P.R. 328. Some reliance has been placed for this result on section 130 of the *Constitution Act, 1867*, but it is difficult to see how this helps in the case of a post-confederation federally incorporated company: see *Loranger v. Montreal Telegraph Co.* (1882), 5 L.N. 429. If provincial legislation is incompetent to destroy the status and capacity of a Dominion company, what justification is there for permitting this through exercise of a provincial executive or prerogative authority? The issue was canvassed in *People's Holding Co. v. A.-G. Que.*, [1931] S.C.R. 452 and the right of the provincial Attorney-General to seek forfeiture of the charter of a federally incorporated company was upheld, subject to any contrary federal legislation. However, the Supreme Court refrained from passing on the question whether the courts could order the dissolution or winding-up of a Dominion company at the instance of the provincial Attorney-General. The fact that the Dominion company has been a constant violator of provincial law is surely no basis for supporting the result reached by the Supreme Court. In view of decisions precluding dismemberment of interprovincial (federal) undertakings through resort to provincial legislation, it is submitted that the *People's Holding Co.* case cannot stand as an untarnished authority.

## Note on the Downfall of the B.C. Power Case

Prior to the Supreme Court of Canada decisions in *Canadian Indemnity, supra*, and *Churchill Falls, supra*, the judgment of the late Chief Justice Lett of the British Columbia Supreme Court in *British Columbia Power Corp. v. A.-G. B.C.* (1963), 44 W.W.R. 65 (B.C.S.C.), had made the federally incorporated company a pampered darling of Canadian constitutional law; it was accorded an advantage not enjoyed by a human. The settlement of the hard-fought dispute in the matter avoided an appeal, and the trial judgment stood as a monument to detailed diligence perhaps unsurpassed in Canadian constitutional litigation. It also amounts to a considerable extension of the line of cases which had theretofore defined the scope of the undoubted federal power to incorporate companies. Stripped of a number of entangling elements which were relevant to a total assessment of the constitutional issues raised in the case, the decision stood for this proposition: a federally-incorporated company which exercises its powers by limiting itself to ownership of all the common shares of a provincially-incorporated company engaged in public utility operations in electricity, gas and transportation, and which has no other business but the management of its wholly-owned subsidiary, may not constitutionally be divested of ownership of the common shares of the provincial company by the Legislature of the province of incorporation. Although the adequacy of the compensation may be said to have been an element in the decision, it was not the determinant in a conclusion that was difficult to reconcile with a long line of decision on the federal incorporation power. The conclusion was arrived at by a considerable sentence parsing by Lett C.J.S.C. of earlier judgments, and by analogical application of abstract propositions.

From the *Parsons* case on, a distinction has been drawn between the federal powers to incorporate a company and federal power to regulate its activities; the one did not necessarily carry the other, unless, as in the case of banking, interprovincial railways and aviation (to take a few examples), the activity was otherwise within federal regulatory competence. The evolution of doctrine in respect of the federal company cases from *John Deere Plow v. Wharton* through to the *Great West Saddlery* case and down to *Lymburn v. Mayland* showed a recognition that federal companies *qua corporate* entities were entitled to become established as such, and without limitation or discrimination against them in achieving corporate life through the raising of capital by the issue of shares and debentures. But they had no constitutional guarantee of being entitled to carry on any particular business within provincial regulatory power in the teeth of provincial requirements. If such businesses were open to private entry or competition, the federal company could ask no more than to be treated in the same way as a provincial company or private individual. If the business was one in which a limited number of franchises for it were available, the federal company had no preferential claim to a grant. Moreover, if the business was one which was withdrawn from competition and was a government or public monopoly, as in the *Canadian Indemnity* case, *supra*, federal incorporation would be of no avail to shatter the provincial policy.

Some of the language of some of the cases no doubt went beyond these propositions; an example is found in the judgment of Duff C.J.C. in *Reference re Alberta Debt Adjustment Act*, [1942] S.C.R. 31. On the other hand, standards formulated to help assess the validity of provincial legislation in relation to Dominion companies have been erected into rigid canons and given a different context than that in which they originated. This is true of the phrase "laws of general application" as pointing to subjection of Dominion companies to regulatory legislation equally applicable to other persons or corporations in the regulated field. It could not rationally be applied to preclude a Province from expropriating shares of a company which it incorporated merely because such shares constituted the only assets of a federal company. To say, as did the Judge in the *B.C. Power* case, that the expropriating provincial legislation was not a law of general application but was in truth selective legislation directed against a Dominion company, was simply to play a game of numbers without regard to the pervasiveness of the provincial company's business and the provincial government's policy in relation thereto. The object of the expropriation of the shares was to gain operating control for the government of a power business in furtherance of a policy to make the generation and distribution of power a government enterprise. This was an object within provincial competence over and above competence to deal with the shares of a creature of the Province.

Ownership of the shares of a provincial company and regulation of the business or activities of the company are different things. If it be the case that a provincial company engages in business which as such is within federal jurisdiction, federal regulatory power is not excluded by reason of compulsory change of ownership of the shares; not even if they became vested in the Crown in right of the Province. The fact that the business was managed by a federal company by reason of its ownership of the provincial company's shares has in truth very little to do with the issue of provincial competence to take the shares. It would be no different if the federal company was concerned only in the management of land which it owned in a Province and asserted a right of immunity from that Province's expropriation legislation. The tenability of the assertion would depend not on the fact of federal company ownership but on whether the land was connected with, if it was not an integral part of, a business or undertaking which as such was within federal competence. If, as has been held, a federal company dealing only in land is subject to provincial mortmain legislation, it would be equally subject to provincial expropriation legislation. And why would a federal company dealing in shares of provincial companies or in the shares of only one provincial company be in any different position?

It is difficult to conceive how ownership of all the shares of a provincial company as a federal company's choice of business can go to the matter of its incorporation.

The Supreme Court of Canada recently expressed its disapproval of *B.C. Power* in *Churchill Falls (Labrador) Corporation v. A.G. Newfoundland*, [1984] 1 S.C.R. 297. In dismissing the argument that a Newfoundland statute, which expropriated all assets of the federally incorporated Churchill Falls (Labrador) Corporation, contravened the constitutional strictures against interference with the essential status and powers of a federally incorporated company, McIntyre J. said:

> A federal company is entitled to establish itself as a corporation in a province and for this purpose it is entitled to raise capital and to create its corporate being without interference from provincial legislation. Having done so, however, it is in no better position with respect to the conduct or continuation of its business than a provincial company or a natural person.

*B.C. Power* was viewed as not in accordance with the governing authorities and the approach of Lett C.J.S.C. can now be treated as an historical anomaly.

[*Quaere*, as to the correctness of *R. v. New Westminster; Ex parte Canadian Wirevision Ltd.* (1965), 54 W.W.R. 238 (B.C.C.A.), holding that a federally-incorporated company was subject to a general municipal by-law requiring trades licences to be obtained, where the company's business was cable television, a matter within exclusive federal competence! Does the application of the licensing by-law depend on the authority given to the company in its federal incorporation or on the reach of provincial (or municipal) legislation to businesses within exclusive federal regulatory power?]

## 2. Securities Regulation and Corporate Affairs

# LYMBURN v. MAYLAND

In the Privy Council. [1932] A.C. 318.

Viscount Dunedin, Lord Blanesburgh, Lord Atkin, Lord Russell of Killowen and Sir George Lowndes. Feb. 4, 1932.

Appeal from a judgment of the Alberta Appellate Division, [1931] 1 W.W.R. 735, holding, *inter alia*, that s. 9 of the Security Frauds Prevention Act (Alta.), c. 8, could not apply to a Dominion company.

LORD ATKIN: This is an appeal from the Supreme Court of Alberta in proceedings taken by the plaintiffs to challenge powers sought to be exercised by the Attorney-General of Alberta under the provisions of the Security Frauds Prevention Act, 1930 (Alberta), Statutes of Alberta, 20 Geo. V, c. 8. Under the terms of s. 9 of that Act the Attorney-General or any delegate appointed by him has power to examine any person or company at any time in order to ascertain whether any fraudulent act as defined by the statute or any offence against the Act or the regulations has been, is being, or is about to be, committed. The Attorney-General, Mr. Lymburn, had appointed the defendant, Mr. Frawley, to hold the examination in question, and Mr. Frawley had summoned the plaintiff, Mr. Mayland, to attend him for examination on an inquiry amongst other things into items appearing in the balance sheet of the other plaintiff, Mercury Oils, Ltd., as at December 31, 1930. Mr. Frawley also gave notice that he intended to inquire into a transaction between Solloway Mills & Co., Ltd., and the plaintiff Mayland respecting the exchange of certain shares and the assumption by Mayland of an underwriting agreement entered into between Solloway Mills & Co., Ltd., and Mill City Petroleums Ltd. All the companies mentioned are incorporated under the provisions of the *Dominion Companies Act.* . . .

[It was alleged before the Board that] the whole Act was invalid so far as it related to Dominion companies, because it destroyed their status by making it impossible for them to issue their share capital. In this respect it was said the case was covered by the decision of this Board in *Attorney-General for Manitoba v. Attorney-General for Canada*, [1929] A.C. 260. It was further contended that apart altogether from Dominion companies the Act was invalid because under the colour of dealing with the prevention of fraud in share transactions it was assuming to legislate as to criminal law, a class of subject reserved to the Dominion. Apart from invalidity, it was further said that if the terms of the Act were examined the three Dominion companies in question, as well as the plaintiff Mayland, did not carry on any business as brokers in shares; and it was only to transactions by brokers that the provisions of s. 9 applied. Their Lordships cannot accept any of these contentions.

When the framework of the Act is examined it will be found that after an elaborate definition clause it is divided into five parts. The material definitions are those of broker, which includes every person, other than a "salesman" as defined, who is engaged in the business of "trading" in securities, and "trading" includes the solicitation or obtaining a subscription to any security. "Salesman" includes every person employed by a company to trade in securities. Part I is entitled "Registration of brokers and salesmen," and provides in substance that no person may trade in securities unless he is registered as a broker or salesman. The prohibition is confined to "persons" which by the definition clause does not include corporations. A corporation may however be registered, in which event its officials do not need separate registration. Registration is made subject to the approval of the Attorney-General, who may direct that registration be refused for any reason which he may deem sufficient. Registered persons must enter into a personal bond, and may be required to enter into a surety bond each in the sum of $500, conditioned for payment if the registered person, amongst other events, is (in the former bond) "charged with," (in the latter bond) "convicted of," a criminal offence, or found to have committed an offence against the Act or the regulations made thereunder. It was contended on behalf of the Attorney-General for the Dominion that to impose a condition making the bond fall due upon conviction for a criminal offence was to encroach upon the sole right of the Dominion to legislate in respect of the criminal law. It indirectly imposed an additional punishment for a criminal offence. Their Lordships do not consider this objection well founded. If the legislation be otherwise *intra vires*, the imposition of such an ordinary condition in a bond taken to secure good conduct does not appear to invade in any degree the field of criminal law.

There is no reason to doubt that the main object sought to be secured in this part of the Act is to secure that persons who carry on the business of dealing in securities shall be honest and of good repute, and in this way to protect the public from being defrauded. Incidentally the net has been drawn so wide as to cover the issue of shares by a public company, with the result that a company cannot issue its shares to the public unless for that purpose it employs a registered broker or salesman, or unless the company itself is registered. It is said that these provisions so far as they affect Dominion companies are *ultra vires* according to the principles adopted by this Board in *John Deere Plow Co. v. Wharton; Great West Saddlery Co. v. The King;* and *Attorney-General for Manitoba v. Attorney-General for Canada.* In those cases there was a general prohibition to companies either to trade at all or to issue their capital unless the company was registered. The legislation was held *ultra vires* because the legislative powers of the Province are restricted so that "the status and powers of the Dominion company as such cannot be destroyed" (*John Deere Plow Co.* case) and legislation will be invalid if a Dominion company is "sterilized in all its functions and activities" or "its status and essential capacities are impaired in a substantial degree" (*Great West Saddlery Co.* case). It appears to their Lordships impossible to bring this legislation within such a principle. A Dominion company constituted with powers to carry on a particular business is subject to the competent legislation of the Province as to that business and may find its special activities completely paralysed, as by legislation against drink traffic or by the laws as to holding land. If it is formed to trade in securities there appears no reason why it should not be subject to the competent laws of the Province as to the business of all persons who trade in securities. As to the issue of capital there is no complete prohibition, as in the Manitoba case in 1929; and no reason to suppose that any honest company would have any difficulty in finding registered persons in the Province through whom it could lawfully issue its capital. There is no material upon which their Lordships could find that the functions and activities of a company were sterilized or its status and essential capacities impaired in a substantial degree.

Their Lordships have discussed this part of the Act because the attack of the respondents was mainly directed to it, partly because it was said that the pith and substance of the Act was contained in it and that by sterilizing Dominion companies it was inseverably invalid; and partly because it was said that, even if severable so far as registration of Dominion companies was concerned, inasmuch as inquiry could be made under Part II, as to an offence against the Act, an inquiry under Part II might be directed to an alleged offence invalidly created, and therefore the inquiry provisions of Part II themselves were invalid. This brings their Lordships to the consideration of Part II, and it will be found that once the main attack on registration has failed there is little to be said against this part of the Act.

Section 9, under which the examination in dispute in these proceedings was ordered, empowers the Attorney-General or any delegate appointed by him to examine any person or company in order to ascertain whether any fraudulent act or any offence against the Act or regulations has been, is being, or is about to be, committed. The definition of "fraudulent act" appears to be very wide, in some cases having no relation to securities or dealing in securities; and it is possible that if the question becomes relevant a limited construction would be put upon the very general terms used. But this has no bearing upon the question of validity. The examination is not confined to questions of registration, nor are the persons or companies to be examined limited to persons or companies who themselves trade in securities. It seems obvious that the object of the section would be defeated unless the powers of examination extended to persons who might have relevant knowledge, including companies and the officials of companies whose securities might be or be about to be the subject of dealings with the public. The provisions of this part of the Act may appear to be far-reaching; but if they fall, as their Lordships conceive them to fall, within the scope of legislation dealing with property and civil rights the legislature of the Province, sovereign in this respect, has the sole power and responsibility of determining what degree of protection it will afford to the public. There appears to be no reason for excluding Dominion companies from the inquiries of the Attorney-General under this section; and no inconsistency between this legislation and the powers of inquiry under the Dominion Companies Act made on application of members of a company and for a limited purpose — namely, the investigation of the affairs of the company. Their Lordships are unable to agree with the view which was adopted by the Appellate Division that in respect of the subject-matter under discussion the legislature of the Province has only a limited right to require information.

Part III of the Act provides for the appointment of auditors to audit the accounts of brokers and to advise the executive committees of stock exchanges in the Province. There appears to be no ground for disputing the validity of these provisions.

Part IV by s. 14 contains a provision making it an offence for a broker in certain transactions for customers to place beyond his control securities he may be carrying for customers, and ss. 15 and 16 provide for the necessary records of such transactions. The penal provisions of s. 14 have been subsequently incorporated into the Criminal Code of the Dominion by 20 & 21 Geo. V, c. 11 (Canada), s. 5, which now presumably occupies the field so far as the criminal law is concerned. The substantive provisions of the section avoiding the impugned transaction at the option of the customer and the provisions of the other sections of this part cannot be attacked. Part V has general provisions which need not be noticed except as to the argument of the respondents founded on the words of s. 20, which provide (*inter alia*) that any person who does any fraudulent act not punishable under the provisions of the Criminal Code of Canada shall be liable to fine and imprisonment. It is said that this encroaches on the exclusive legislative power of the Dominion as to criminal law. Having regard to the wide definition of "fraudulent act" above referred to, it may well be that this argument is well founded. But so far as the section is invalid it appears to be clearly severable. In any case it appears to their Lordships, after reviewing the whole Act, that there is no ground for holding that the Act is a colourable attempt to encroach upon the exclusive legislative power of the Dominion as to criminal law. They have already given their reasons for holding that the Act cannot be considered invalid as destroying the status of Dominion companies. The provisions therefore of Part II of the Act appear to be competent Provincial enactments dealing with property and civil rights and have to be obeyed by persons subject to them.

In the result the order of the Appellate Division should be set aside. . . .

*Appeal allowed.*

### Note

In *A.-G. Man. v. A.-G. Can.*, [1929] A.C. 260, where provincial legislation was held *ultra vires* in so far as it prohibited a Dominion company from selling its shares without obtaining a licence, Lord Sumner, said, *inter alia*:

> The capacity of a Dominion company to obtain capital by the subscription or so-called sale, of its shares, is essential in a sense in which holding particular kinds of property in a province or selling particular commodities, subject to provincial conditions or regulations, is not. Neither is the legislation which is in question saved by the fact that all kinds of companies are aimed at and that there is no special discrimination against Dominion companies. The matter depends upon the effect of the legislation and its purpose.

See also *Lukey v. Ruthenian Farmers' Elevator Co. Ltd.*, [1924] S.C.R. 56. On the applicability of provincial legislation to Dominion companies: see *R. v. Arcadia Coal Co. Ltd.*, [1932] 1 W.W.R. 771 (Alta. C.A.); *Re Hretchka and Chromex Invts. Ltd.*, [1971] 1 W.W.R. 163; appeal quashed [1972] S.C.R. 119 (*sub nom. Hretchka v. A.-G. B.C.*).

To what extent can a province require regulatory approval of transfers of shares of federally incorporated companies? See Kay, "Constitutional Aspects of Share Transactions" (1981), 19 Osgoode Hall L.J. 100 in which the author argues such requirements are *ultra vires* a province.

Despite the holding in *Lymburn v. Mayland, supra*, would it be open to the Dominion to enact federal securities legislation applicable at least to the marketing of the shares and bonds of federally incorporated companies? Do *MacDonald v. Vapor Canada Ltd.*, [1977] 2 S.C.R. 134 and *Multiple Access Corp. v. McCutcheon* (1982), 138 D.L.R. (3d) 1 (S.C.C.) bear on the issue of federal power to enact valid securities legislation? See Anisman, *Proposals for a Securities Market Law for Canada* (1979) and, in particular Anisman and Hogg, "Constitutional Aspects of Federal Securities Legislation," Vol. 3, p. 136 For comment on the *Proposals*, see Anisman, "The Proposals for a Securities Market Law for Canada: Purpose and Process" (1981), 19 Osgoode Hall L.J. 329.

May a province condition the right of a Dominion lending company to enforce its claims in the provincial courts by requiring the prior consent of (a) an administrative board; or (b) the Lieutenant-Governor in Council; or (c) a Judge? See *Reference re Debt Adjustment Act, 1937 (Alta.)*, [1942] S.C.R. 31, aff'd on other grounds [1943] A.C. 356 (P.C.).

The position of the province as owner of property (*e.g.* timber, minerals) may be different from its position when exercising legislative authority: see *Brooks-Bidlake and Whittall Ltd. v. A.-G. B.C.*, [1923] A.C. 450 (P.C.).

The limitations on provincial power to interfere with the operations of Dominion companies apply to pre-confederation companies which were given a corporate existence throughout the former province of Canada: *Dobie v. Temporalities Board* (1881), 7 App. Cas. 136. Only the Dominion can deal with the constitution of such companies. Can the province add to the powers of such companies where there is no inconsistency with their "federal" charter? See *Sun Life Assurance Co. v. Sisters Adorers of the Precious Blood*, [1942] O.R. 708 (C.A.).

# MULTIPLE ACCESS LTD. v. McCUTCHEON

In the Supreme Court of Canada. [1982] 2 S.C.R. 161.

Laskin, C.J.C., Martland, Ritchie, Dickson, Beetz, Estey, McIntyre, Chouinard and Lamer JJ. August 9, 1982.

Appeal from a judgment of the Ontario Court of Appeal, 19 O.R. (2d) 516*n*, dismissing an appeal from a judgment of the Ontario Divisional Court, 16 O.R. (2d) 593, allowing an appeal from a decision of Henry J., 11 O.R. (2d) 249, holding that the insider trading provisions of the *Securities Act* (Ont.) are not invalidated by similar provisions in the *Canada Corporations Act*.

The judgment of Laskin C.J.C., Martland, Ritchie, Dickson, McIntyre and Lamer JJ. was delivered by

DICKSON J.: — This appeal raises the issue of "insider trading" in securities. Insider trading is the purchase or sale of the securities of a company by a person who, by reason of his position in the company, has access to confidential information not known to other shareholders or the general public. He learns, for example, that the company is going to be the object of a take-over bid at a price per share well above the market. He buys shares. Or, to take a more common occurrence of late, he learns that the company is in dire straits. He sells shares. He thus places personal benefit or advantage in conflict with, and superior to, his relationship with, and duty to, other shareholders and to the company.

The social and economic evil thus exemplified was controlled in part by common law remedies but it has been recognized, since the Second World War that something more was needed. Under the rules of common law and equity, the outsider was almost totally unprotected largely as a result of the decision in *Percival v. Wright*, [1902] 2 Ch. 421, which declared that ordinarily a director is not a fiduciary relationship with individual shareholders. Parliament responded by enacting "insider trading" legislation. So did a number of the provinces, of which Ontario has been, without doubt, the coryphaeus.

This appeal raises the issue of the constitutionality of provincially, and federally, enacted "insider trading" legislation, and, more specifically, very similar sections in provincial and federal statutes which deal with the use of confidential information by insiders. At trial and on appeal it was common ground that both the federal and provincial statutes were *intra vires*, the only issue being the application of the doctrine of paramountcy.

. . . .

## I

The facts are of little importance. Multiple Access Limited (the Company) is a public company incorporated under the laws of Canada having its head office in Metropolitan Toronto and capital stock listed for trading by the public on the Toronto Stock Exchange. The defendant McCutcheon was president and director, Lowrie a director and the other defendants senior managing officers of the Company. By an order of Addy J., on a motion made by two shareholders of the Company pursuant to s. 114(1) of the *Securities Act*, it was ordered that the Ontario Securities Commission commence action, in the name of and on behalf of the Company, to enforce the liability created by the alleged "insider trading" of the defendants. . . .

## II

I should like to turn now to the first constitutional question, namely, are ss. 100.4 and 100.5 of the *Canada Corporations Act* [the federal insider trading provisions] *ultra vires* the Parliament of Canada in whole or in part? As I have indicated, in the courts below the case was argued on the assumption that the relevant sections of the *Canada Corporations Act* are *intra vires*. The parties at trial did not contest the validity of either enactment. "It is common ground that . . . it was competent to Parliament and the Legislature to enact respectively these provisions so that each is *intra vires*", *per* Henry J. [65 D.L.R. (3d) at p. 580]. The question is now raised for the first time. It is to be regretted that we do not have the advantage of judgments on the point from the three courts of Ontario before whom these proceedings have already come. Counsel for Canada urges that, for that reason, the first question be left unanswered: *Montcalm Construction Inc. v. Minimum Wage Com'n*, [1979] 1 S.C.R. 754, and *Solicitor-General of Canada v. Royal Commission of Inquiry into the Confidentiality of Health Records in Ontario* [(1981), 23 C.R. (3d) 338], *per* Laskin C.J.C. I do not incline to this view. I think we must answer, as best we can, the question which has been stated.

Before directly addressing the question posed, two prefatory observations. First, in the legislative scheme of things we find ss. 100.4 and 100.5 in a corporations act dealing with company law matters. Part I of the Act, entitled "Companies with Share Capital", comprises some 150 sections and 120 pages of text. Part II is entitled "Corporations without Share Capital"; Part III, "Special Act Corporations"; Part IV, "Company Clauses"; Part V, "Incidental Powers of Corporate Bodies Created otherwise than by Letters Patent"; Part VI, "Provisions of General Application".

The sections with which we are here concerned, ss. 100.4 and 100.5 are found in Part I of the Act. Among the headings one finds in Part I are "Formation of New

Companies", "General Powers and Duties of Companies", "Transfer of Shares", "Calls", "Liability of Shareholders", "Prospectuses and Offers to the Public" and "Directors". Under this last heading are detailed provisions respecting the directors of a company, their number, qualifications, election, responsibilities, action to be taken where serious impairment of capital is discovered, duty of a director who is in any way interested in a contract or proposed contract with the company. Section 98(5) relieves a director who has made a declaration of his interest in such a contract and has not voted in respect of the contract, from being accountable to the company or any of its shareholders or creditors by reason only of such director holding that office or of the fiduciary relationship thereby established, for any profit realized by such contract. Section 100(1) provides that where a director or officer or controlling shareholder purchases or sells any of the shares of the company, such director, officer or shareholder must furnish to the secretary of the company a statement setting forth the details of such purchase or sale. Such statement is immediately available for inspection by shareholders and is disclosed to the annual meeting following. Then come the impugned ss. 100.4 and 100.5.

Parliament has not yet enacted any comprehensive scheme of securities legislation. To date the Canadian experience has been that the provinces have taken control of the marketing of securities, differing in this respect from the United States where the Securities and Exchange Commission has regulated trading and primary distribution of securities. I should not wish by anything said in this case to affect prejudicially the contitutional right of Parliament to enact a general scheme of securities legislation pursuant to its power to make laws in relation to interprovincial and export trade and commerce. This is of particular significance considering the interprovincial and indeed international character of the securities industry. The federal government, it may be noted, has already produced "Proposals for a Securities Market Law for Canada" (1979). Professor Anisman, writing in 1981 in respect of those proposals expressed the view that:

> [T]he factors that indicated a need for federal regulatory involvement in the securities market in 1979 are still present and, if anything, have been reinforced by events during the past two years. The *Proposals* are premised ultimately on the national and international character of the Canadian securities market and its importance to the economic welfare of the country. The fact that the market is national in scope has long been acknowledged and is demonstrated by the cooperative efforts of the provincial commissions with respect to the adoption of national policies and by the statutory authorization for and increasing frequency of joint hearings held by a number of provincial commissions to decide issues that transcend provincial boundaries.

("The Proposals for a Securities Market Law for Canada: Purpose and Process" (1981), 19 Osgoode Hall L.J. 329 at 352, footnotes omitted.)

Until recent statutory changes, which need not here concern us, insider trading provisions were found in the *Business Corporations Act* of Ontario, R.S.O. 1970, c. 53 [now R.S.O. 1980, c. 54], as affecting Ontario companies, and a like set of provisions were found in the *Securities Act*, as affecting, broadly speaking, non-Ontario companies, including those incorporated federally, that (i) have issued equity shares that are distributed in the course of a primary distribution to the public, in respect of which a prospectus is filed with the Ontario Securities Commission or (ii) any of whose shares are listed and posted for trading on any stock exchange in Ontario recognized by the Commission.

It is not without significance that Ontario thought it appropriate to place insider trading provisions, affecting Ontario companies, in the *Business Corporations Act* of that province. It would seem axiomatic that if the province can validly enact insider trading legislation under s. 92(11) of the *Constitution Act, 1867* (the incorporation of companies with provincial objects), then the federal Parliament can validly enact insider trading legislation under the residual clause authorizing the incorporation of companies with *other* than provincial objects (*Citizens Ins. Co. of Canada v. Parsons* (1881), 7 App. Cas. 96 at 117: "it follows that the incorporation of companies for objects other than provincial falls within the general powers of the parliament of Canada", *per* Sir Montague Smith). In one of its aspects, insider trading legislation, dealing as it does with fundamental corporate relationships, may certainly be characterized as company law. Some commentators such as Williamson go so far as to say that:

> The insider reporting requirements seem, in the light of the history of Canadian corporation and securities law, more properly part of a companies act than of a securities act.

("Supplement to Securities Regulation in Canada", at p. 358.) And Professor Ziegel has written (*Studies in Canadian Company Law* (1967), at p. 170):

> Prima facie the regulation of proxies and insider trading belong exclusively to the domain of company law because they affect the relationship between the directors and its shareholders and the solicitation of voting powers at meetings of the company.

The second introductory observation. There may be a temptation to regard the insider trading provisions of the *Canada Corporations Act* as redundant having regard to the almost identical provisions found in the Ontario legislation applicable to federal companies as well as Ontario companies. Any such temptation should be resisted. The validity of the federal legislation must be determined without heed to the Ontario legislation. Further, a number of the provinces have not yet enacted insider trading legislation. Striking down the federal legislation would leave federal companies, having head offices in those provinces, and their shareholders, without the double protection, which Ontario shareholders now enjoy. A declaration of invalidity of the federal Act would create a potential gap in the present regulatory schemes that might be exploited by the unprincipled.

I turn now to the main question. Does the "matter" (or pith and substance) of the insider trading provisions of the federal Act fall within a "class of subject" (or head of power) allocated to Parliament? Counsel for the Company and for the Attorney-General of Ontario contends that s. 100.4 applies to a very large class of individuals or companies and the apparent purpose of the section is to impose possible civil liability on members of a large class of persons who are involved in transactions relating to the securities of the company. These provisions, it is said, do not relate to the status of a federal company or to domestic or internal constitution of the company but rather create civil rights or obligations which can only be the subject-matter of provincial legislation in relation to property and civil rights in a province.

With respect, I do not agree. Sections 100.4 and 100.5 put teeth into s. 100 of the Act. Viewed in isolation it can no doubt be argued that their matter is the trading in securities. Viewed in context, however, they are, in my opinion, company law. They fit properly and comfortably into Part I of the *Canada Corporations Act*. The provisions deal with obligations attached to the ownership of shares in a federal company, which extend to shareholders, officers and employees of such companies, a subject-matter that is not within the exclusive jurisdiction of provincial legislatures. The provisions are also directed to the relationship between management and shareholders of federal companies. Their enactment by Parliament is in the discharge of its company law power.

It has been well established ever since *John Deere Plow Co. v. Wharton*, [1915] A.C. 330 (P.C.), that the power of legislating with reference to the incorporation of companies with other than provincial objects belonged exclusively to the Dominion Parliament as a matter covered by the expression "the peace, order and good government of Canada". Additionally, the power to regulate trade and commerce, at all events, enabled the Parliament of Canada to prescribe to what extent the powers of companies the objects of which extend to the entire Dominion should be exercisable and what limitations should be placed on such powers. Viscount Haldane L.C., delivering the judgment of their Lordships, stated further that ". . . if it can be established that the Dominion Parliament can create such companies, then it becomes a question of general interest throughout the Dominion in what fashion they should be permitted to trade" (at p. 340 A.C.). The power of Parliament in relation to the incorporation of companies with other than provincial objects has not been narrowly defined. The authorities are clear that it goes well beyond mere incorporation. It extends to such matters as the maintenance of the company, the protection of creditors of the company and the safeguarding of the interests of the shareholders. It is all part of the internal ordering as distinguished from the commercial activities. Section 124 of the *Companies Act*, S.C. 1934, c. 33, providing for the acquisition of shares of dissenting shareholders, against their will, was held to be properly part of company legislation: *Rathie v. Montreal Trust Co.* (1952), 6 W.W.R. (N.S.) 652 [rev'd [1953] 2 S.C.R. 204]. As Professor Hogg has said in his book at p. 351: "The federal power to incorporate companies . . . is simply the residue of the entire possible power to incorporate companies after subtracting the provincial power" and ". . . it also authorizes all laws of a company law character, for example, the laws pertaining to corporate powers, organization, internal management and financing" (at p. 353). Insider malfeasance affects, directly and adversely, corporate powers, organization, internal management. It affects also financing because shareholders and potential shareholders must be assured the company's affairs will be scrupulously and fairly conducted; otherwise the raising of capital, clearly an element of company law, will be inhibited: *Lukey v. Ruthenian Farmers' Elevator Co.*, [1924] S.C.R. 56 at 72; *A.-G. Man. v. A.-G. Can.*, [1929] A.C. 260 at 266-7.

Duff C.J.C. in *Reference re Section 110 Dominion Companies Act*, [1934] S.C.R. 653 at 658, recognized the right of the federal Parliament to provide for the constitution of the companies it created and for the conditions under which membership could be acquired; for the management by directors or other managers; the terms and conditions upon which profits should be divided or dividends declared; the conditions under which the capital of the company could be increased or diminished; the responsibility of the members of the company in respect to the debts of the corporation; the responsibility of the directors in respect of such debts. The Reference was concerned with the constitutional competence of Parliament to enact legislation making the directors of the company liable for the payment of any dividend when the company was insolvent or which impaired the capital of the company. The liability imposed was joint and several, to the company and to the individual share-holders and creditors, for all the debts of the company then existing and for all debts thereafter contracted during their continuance in office. The court held the enactment to be of a character that brought it within the class of topics that the legislature must be supposed to have contemplated as falling within the subject of "Incorporation of Companies" as used in the *Constitution Act, 1867* (formerly the *British North America Act, 1867*).

Duff C.J.C., speaking for the court, made it abundantly clear that any definition of the constitution of the company would call for answers to such questions as: what provision is being made for the protection of the assets of the company?; what safeguards are provided against the malfeasance of the managers?; what are the safeguards against the improper or colourable employment by the managers of their powers, in wasting the assets of the company?

In *Esso Standard (Inter-America) Inc. v. J.W. Enterprises Inc.*, [1963] S.C.R. 144, this court considered the provisions of the *Companies Act*, R.S.C. 1952, c. 53, respecting the compulsory acquisition of minority shares in take-over bids. Judson J., speaking for the court, said (at p. 153 S.C.R.):

> It is truly legislation in relation to the incorporation of companies with other than provincial objects and it is not legislation in relation to property and civil rights in the Province or in relation to any matter coming within the classes of subject assigned exclusively to the Legislature of the Province. It deals with certain conditions under which a person may become a shareholder or lose his position as a shareholder in such a company and, in my opinion, this case is completely covered by the reasons of this Court in *Reference re Section 110 Dominion Companies Act. . .*

Earlier in his judgment Judson J. said (at p. 152 S.C.R.):

> There has been complete unanimity throughout that Parliament has the power to enact s. 128. The matter was summarized by Laidlaw, J.A., as follows, [[1962] O.R. 705 (Ont. C.A.)]:
>
>> It is my opinion that the Parliament of Canada having legislative power to create companies whose objects extend to more than one Province possesses also the legislative power to prescribe the manner in which shares of the capital of such companies can be transferred and acquired. That matter is one of general interest throughout the Dominion.

Providing safeguards against the malfeasance of the managers is strictly within what might properly be called the constitution of the company. The proper relationship between a company and its insiders is central to the law of companies and, from the inception of companies, that relationship has been regulated by the legislation sanctioning the company's incorporation. I agree with the submission of counsel for the Attorney-General of Canada that the impugned provisions of the *Canada Corporations Act* are directed at preserving the integrity of federal companies and protecting the shareholders of such companies; they aim at practices, injurious to a company or to shareholders at large of a company, by persons who, because they hold positions of trust or otherwise, are privy to information not available to all shareholders.

Insiders should not benefit, either at the expense of the company or at the expense of other shareholders, from their access to confidential information intended to be available only for a corporate purpose and not for the personal benefit of anyone. Information so acquired is at the expense of the enterprise. Confidential company information is a corporate asset the benefit of which is intended to benefit the company, its shareholders and creditors. See Brudney, "Insiders, Outsiders and Informational Advantages under the Federal Securities Laws", 93 Harv. L.R. 322 (1979), at p. 344.

It is true that the net cast by s. 100.4 of the *Canada Corporations Act* is a broad one but it must be broad if it is to be effective. Section 100.4 speaks of insiders, employees, associates, and affiliates. It may catch more than just directors or managers. There is no reason in principle why this should be fatal to constitutional integrity. Practical considerations no doubt dictate that the net be broad if confidential information, vital to the financial integrity of the company, were to be adequately protected from those unprincipled insiders who were in a position to be privy to such information.

. . . .

Because "[t]he language of [ss. 91 and 92] and of the various heads which they contain obviously cannot be construed as having been intended to embody the exact disjunctions of a perfect logical scheme" (*John Deere Plow Co. v. Wharton, supra*, at p. 338 A.C., *per* Viscount Haldane L.C.), a statute may fall under several heads of either s. 91 or s. 92. For example, a provincial statute will often fall under both s. 92(13), property and civil rights, and s. 92(16), a purely local matter, given the broad generality of the language. There is of course no constitutional difficulty in this. The constitutional difficulty arises, however, when a statute may be characterized, as often happens, as coming within a federal as well as a provincial head of power. "To put the same point in another way, our community life — social, economic, political and cultural — is very complex and will not fit neatly into any scheme of categories or classes without considerable overlap and ambiguity occurring. There are inevitable difficulties arising from this that we must live with so long as we have a federal constitution" (Lederman, "The Concurrent Operation of Federal and Provincial Laws in Canada" (1962-63), 9 McGill L.J. 185. As Professor Ziegel has stated "[s]ecurities legislation clearly has a double character" ("Constitutional Aspects of Canadian Companies" in *Studies in Canadian Company Law* (1967), 149 at p. 167) and, "there is no simple dichotomy between legislation of a company law character and legislation affecting property and civil rights in the province. Viewed in its proper social and economic context the legislation may well have a double character" (at pp. 192-3).

I incline to the view that the impugned insider trading provisions have both a securities law and a companies law aspect. . . .

One reservation with respect to the impugned sections of the federal Act may be in the imposition of civil liability in s. 100.4(1). Does this imposition of civil liability in a federal statute so invade the provincial domain as to render the sections imposing liability *ultra vires*? This, in essence, was the argument of the appellants. But as Professors Anisman and Hogg point out: "Judicial decisions concerning a number of disparate matters such as federal elections, railways, federal corporations and even divorce have upheld Parliament's jurisdiction to provide civil relief in order to effectuate its legislative policies" ("Constitutional Aspects of Federal Securities Legislation" in *Proposals for a Securities Market Law for Canada* (1979), Vol. 3, 137, at p. 192). In my opinion, ss. 100.4 and 100.5 have a general corporate purpose and a "rational, functional connection" with company law. The sections in my view are *intra vires* the Parliament of Canada.

### III

The argument against the validity of ss. 113 and 114 of the Ontario *Securities Act* [the impugned provincial insider trading provisions] is that they are beyond the legislative power of the province in that they purport to apply to companies incorporated under the laws of Canada; these sections are not in pith and substance enactments regulating the securities business; in actuality they define critical corporate relationships; it is beyond the power of a province to enact laws that regulate the corporate relationships of a federally-incorporated company.

I do not think this argument is tenable. It is well established that the provinces have the power, as a matter of property and civil rights, to regulate the trade in corporate securities in the province, provided the statute does not single out federal companies for special treatment or discriminate against them in any way. There must be no impairment of status or of the essential power to raise capital for corporate purpose. But federal incorporation does not render a company immune from securities regulation of general application in a province. Since the decision of the Privy Council in *Lymburn v. Mayland*, [1932] A.C. 318, the provisions of provincial Securities Acts have been given a wide constitutional recognition. Anisman and Hogg in *Proposals for a Securities Market Law of Canada*, at p. 144, speak of "[j]udicial sympathy for provincial securities legislation" adding, at p. 145:

> The reluctance of the courts to strike down provincial securities legislation likely stems in part from the fact that there is no federal securities law so that a declaration of the invalidity of a provincial act or any of its provisions would create a potential gap in the existing regulatory scheme that might be exploited by the unscrupulous.

Federally-incorporated companies are subject, with one important exception, to provincial regulations with respect to trading in securities. The legislative powers of the province are restricted so that "the status and powers of a Dominion company as such cannot be destroyed" (*John Deere Plow Co. v. Wharton, supra*) and legislation will be invalid if a Dominion company is "sterilized in all its functions and activities" or "its status and essential capacities are impaired in a substantial degree" (*Great West Saddlery Co. Ltd. v. The King*, [1921] 2 A.C. 91). Subject to that exception, a federal company empowered to carry on a particular business in a province is subject to the competent legislation of the province as to that business. If it wishes to raise capital through the sale of securities there is no reason why it should not be subject to the laws of the province applicable to all those in the province who wish to raise capital through security sales, and subject thereafter to rules requiring honest dealings in securities, so that the public be not defrauded. Sections 113 and 114 further the provincial object of assuring that persons who carry on the business of dealing in securities shall be honest and of good repute. As Mr. Justice Fauteux, as he then was, stated in *Gregory & Co. v. Quebec Securities Comm.*, [1961] S.C.R. 584 at 588:

> The paramount object of the Act is to ensure that persons who, in the Province, carry on the business of trading in securities or acting as investment counsel, shall be honest and of good repute and, in this way, to protect the public, in the Province or elsewhere, from being defrauded as a result of certain activities initiated in the Province by persons therein carrying on such a business.

In *Smith v. The Queen*, [1960] S.C.R. 776, Mr. Justice Martland stated (at p. 797 S.C.R.):

> The *Securities Act* exists to regulate the securities business. This is achieved through two main forms of control, the first of which is directed towards the persons or companies selling the securities and the second of which is directed to the securities being sold.

And later (at p. 798 S.C.R.):

> Thus control is exercised through the registration of persons and companies before they are permitted to trade in securities coupled with what is essentially the registration of the securities themselves before the securities may be traded in the course of a primary distribution to the public.

In my opinion ss. 113 and 114 of the *Securities Act* of Ontario constitute valid legislative provisions in relation to the subject-matter of property and civil rights in the province, with respect to trading of the capital securities of a company. These sections do not sterilize the functions and activities of a federal company nor do they impair its status or essential powers: see *Canadian Indemnity Co. v. A.-G. B.C.*, [1977] 2 S.C.R. 504.

. . . .

*Appeal allowed.*

[His Lordship's discussion of the paramountcy doctrine is reproduced at Chapter 4, *supra*. The judgment of Estey J., Beetz and Chouinard JJ. concurring, dissenting in part, is omitted. Estey J. would have held the federal insider trading provisions to be *ultra vires*, and those of the provincial legislation *intra vires*.]

## Note on Securities Regulation

In line with the reasoning in the insurance cases, it has been held that regulation of trading in securities falls within provincial legislative authority and that, moreover, such regulation may operate through a commission empowered to license brokers and other security dealers and to require full disclosure to the public in the enforcement of honest trading. Federal authority to punish fraudulent dealings in securities under the criminal law power has long been conceded, but not federal authority to regulate security transactions through a licensing or similar control system: see *Smith v. The Queen*, [1960] S.C.R. 776. Provincial authority is, of course, limited to regulation of business carried on or transactions taking place in the Province, and there is also a special limitation, which can be avoided by drafting (as was indicated in *Lymburn v. Mayland*, [1932] A.C. 318), in respect of the issue of securities of a federally incorporated company.

The relevant constitutional issue in this field today is not the scope or limit of provincial power, but the rationale behind a continued preclusion of supervening federal power. Thus, it is of small constitutional consequence that provincial securities legislation may competently encompass promissory notes within its trading provisions when they are used in a defined way in business ventures, (so long as their character and holders' rights under federal legislation are not impaired): see *Duplain v. Cameron*, [1961] S.C.R. 693. Nor is it surprising that provincial authority should be exercisable against a depository bank by way of a stop order where an investigation into or suspected fraud as to security trading in the Province is involved, even though this goes close to the line where federal power over banks has been exhibited in legislation: see *Gregory & Co. Inc. v. Imperial Bank of Canada and*

*A.-G. Que.*, [1960] C.S. 204. However, in *Gregory & Co. Inc. v. Quebec Securities Commission*, [1961] S.C.R. 584, the question was raised whether provincial competence could reach a securities dealer (having offices in the Province) by an order to cease publication of bulletins which, although produced in the Province, were mailed only to clients outside the Province. The bulletins in fact promoted the sale of shares transferable only in the Province where orders were completed and payment was made. Since all submissions on constitutionality were withdrawn before the Supreme Court the affirmation of the order turned merely on the application of the provincial legislation. However, Cartwright J. stated, speaking for himself alone, that he had difficulty in satisfying himself that the provincial Act, properly construed, authorized the provincial Securities Commission to regulate a business of the sort carried on by the dealer in this case. There is a clear connection here with the question of constitutional power. Today the field is ripe for a judicial inquiry into whether the national and international character of the securities business deserves constitutional recognition as falling within the trade and commerce power in section 91(2) and other federal heads of power. The courts are undoubtedly moving in that direction: see *Multiple Access Ltd. v. McCutcheon, supra*, (which seems to invite properly drafted federal securities legislation); Anisman, *Proposals for a Securities Market Law for Canada* (1979), and in particular Anisman and Hogg, "Constitutional Aspects of Federal Securities Legislation" Vol. 3, p. 136. For comment on the *Proposals*, see Anisman, "The Proposals for a Securities Market Law for Canada: Purpose and Process" (1981), 19 Osgoode Hall L.J. 329.

Pending any legislative attempt by Parliament to enter this regulatory field, it is reasonable to give the broadest construction to provincial legislation and to apply its policing provisions where acts take place in the Province notwithstanding that they are part of an operation which, overall, is extraprovincial. Thus, in *R. v. W. McKenzie Securities Ltd.* (1966), 55 W.W.R. 157, the Manitoba Court of Appeal held that the registration provisions of the Manitoba securities statute validly applied to an Ontario broker-dealer who solicited Manitoba residents by mail and telegraph from Toronto. Hence, that security dealer, having in this way sold shares to a Manitoba resident, could properly be convicted of unlawfully trading in securities, not being registered under the Manitoba legislation.

For a summary of the constitutional limits of provincial competence in securities regulation, see Report of the Attorney General's Committee on Securities Legislation in Ontario (1965), Part IX.

It is competent to the Province to provide for administrative investigations into security trading in enforcement of its regulatory legislation: *Re Williams and Williams*, [1961] O.R. 657 (C.A.); *International Claim Brokers Ltd. v. Kinsey and A.-G. B.C.* (1966), 55 W.W.R. 672 (B.C.C.A.).

Would it be open to Parliament to invoke its exclusive authority in relation to the "postal service" (section 91(5) of the *Constitution Act, 1867*) and to deny (as Congress has) the use of the mails to security dealers who refuse to register under federal regulatory legislation?

Is there any constitutional objection to provincial legislation excluding use of trading stamps as a merchandising device? Would it make any difference if the exclusion was made a condition of a required retail licence which could be cancelled if the licensee engaged in detrimental practices, e.g. used trading stamps? See *R. v. Fleming* (1962), 38 W.W.R. 513 (Alta. Dist. Ct.).

## 3. The "Provincial" Company Outside its Home Province

### BONANZA CREEK GOLD MINING CO. v. THE KING

In the Privy Council. [1916] 1 A.C. 566.

Lord Buckmaster L.C., Viscount Haldane, Lord Parker of Waddington and Lord Sumner. Feb. 24, 1916.

Appeal by special leave from a judgment of the Supreme Court of Canada, 50 S.C.R. 534, affirming the judgment of the Exchequer Court, 6 W.W.R. 1056, dismissing a petition of right for damages for breach by the Crown (Dominion) of the terms of mining leases held by appellants, an Ontario company.

VISCOUNT HALDANE: This is an appeal from a judgment of the Supreme Court of Canada in a petition of right which gave rise to questions of constitutional importance as to the position of joint stock companies, incorporated within the provinces, but seeking to carry on their business beyond the provincial boundaries.

The appellants were incorporated in Ontario by letters patent dated December 23, 1904, and issued under the authority of the *Ontario Companies Act*, and by virtue of any other authority or power then existing, in the name of the Sovereign and under the Great Seal of the province, by its Lieutenant-Governor. The letters patent recite that this Act authorizes the Lieutenant-Governor in Council by letters patent under the Great Seal to create and constitute bodies corporate and politic for any of the purposes or objects to which the legislative authority of the province extends. They go on to incorporate the company to carry on the business of mining and exploration in all their branches, and to acquire real and personal property, including mining claims, with incidental powers. There are no words which limit the area of operation or prohibit the company from carrying out its objects beyond the provincial boundaries.

In the years 1899 and 1900 the Crown, through the Minister of the Interior of the Dominion, had granted to predecessors in title of the appellants leases of certain tracts of land, in what is now the Yukon district, for the purpose of hydraulic mining. Two of these leases contained exclusions of so much of the tracts as had been taken up and entered for placer mining claims. In the year 1900 the Crown entered into agreements with these predecessors in title to the effect that, if any of the placer mining claims within the tracts should be forfeited or surrendered, the Crown would include them in the tracts by supplementary leases. The original leases having subsequently been assigned to the appellants, and certain of the placer mining claims having reverted, the Crown purported in 1907 to demise to the appellants these claims, and to agree to demise to them such other of the claims as might thereafter revert for the same terms of years as those for which the original leases were granted.

In 1906 the Minister of the Interior of the Dominion had purported to issue to the appellants a free miner's certificate. This certificate was issued in conformity with certain regulations under an Order in Council made under the provisions of the Dominion Lands Act, which gives the right to a free miner's certificate to persons of over eighteen and to joint stock companies, the latter being defined to include any company incorporated "for mining purposes under a Canadian charter or licensed by the Government of Canada."

When the Yukon district was, by the statute passed by the Dominion Parliament in 1899, made a separate territory, power to make ordinances was conferred on the Commissioner of the territory. Under this power the Foreign Companies Ordinance was passed, under which any company, incorporated otherwise than by or under the authority of an ordinance of the territory or an Act of the Parliament of Canada, was required to obtain a licence under the ordinance to carry on its business in the Yukon territory. Such a licence when issued was made sufficient evidence in the Courts of the territory of the due licensing of the company. In September, 1905, the appellants obtained such a licence.

In 1908 the appellants presented a petition of right in the Exchequer Court of Canada, alleging that, in breach of the agreement entered into by the Crown, placer mining claims which had reverted to the Crown and should have been leased to the appellants had been wrongly withheld from the appellants, and that by reason of this and other breaches of the agreement the appellants had suffered heavy damage, for which they as suppliants prayed compensation. The respondent delivered an answer to the petition of right, the first two paragraphs of such answer being as follows: "1. The respondent denies that the suppliant has now or ever had the power, either under letters patent, licence, free miner's certificate, or otherwise, to carry on the business of mining in the district of the Yukon, or to acquire any mines, mining claims, or mining locations therein, or any estate or interest by way of lease or otherwise in any such mines, mining claims, or locations. 2. Should a free miner's certificate have been issued to the suppliant, the respondent claims that the same is and always has been invalid and of no force or effect, that there was no power to issue a free miner's certificate to the suppliant, a company incorporated under provincial letters patent, and that there was no power vested in the suppliant to accept such a certificate."

[His Lordship then discussed the views of the Courts below and concluded that the question raised by the second paragraph, *supra*, should be answered in favour of appellants because "if they possessed legal capacity to receive such a Dominion certificate, [they] had it validly bestowed on them and that, if so, they subsequently obtained a good title to the mining locations and also to the Yukon licence to carry on business which was granted to them."]

Their Lordships accordingly turn to the larger question raised by the first of the two paragraphs, a question which is of far-reaching importance. It is whether a company incorporated by provincial letters patent, issued in conformity with legislation under s. 92 of the *British North America Act* can have capacity to acquire and exercise powers and rights outside the territorial boundaries of the province. In the absence of such capacity the certificates, licences, and leases already referred to were wholly inoperative, for if the company had no legal existence or capacity for purposes outside the boundaries of the province conferred on it by the Government of Ontario, by whose grant exclusively it came into being, it is not apparent how any other Government could bestow on it rights and powers which enlarged that existence and capacity. The answer to this question must depend on the construction to be placed on s. 92 of the *British North America Act* and on the *Ontario Companies Act*.

Section 92 confers exclusive power upon the provincial Legislature to make laws in relation to the incorporation of companies with provincial objects. The interpretation of this provision which has been adopted by the majority of the judges in the Supreme Court is that the introduction of the words "with provincial objects" imposes a territorial limit on legislation conferring the power of incorporation so completely that by or under provincial legislation no company can be incorporated with an existence in law that extends beyond the boundaries of the province. Neither directly by the language of a special Act, nor indirectly by bestowal through executive power, do they think that capacity can be given to operate outside the province, or to accept from an outside authority the power of so operating. For the company, it is said, is a pure creature of statute, existing only for objects prescribed by the Legislature within the area of its authority, and is therefore restricted, so far as legal capacity is concerned, on the principle laid down in *Ashbury Railway Carriage and Iron Co. v. Riche*, L.R. 7 H.L. 653.

Their Lordships, however, take the view that this principle amounts to no more than that the words employed to which a corporation owes its legal existence must have their natural meaning whatever that may be. The words of the *British Companies Act* were construed as importing that a company incorporated by the statutory memorandum of association which the Act prescribes could have no legal existence beyond such as was required for the particular objects of incorporation to which that memorandum limited it. A similar rule has been laid down as regards companies created by special Act. The doctrine means simply that it is wrong, in answering the question what powers the corporation possesses when incorporated exclusively by statute, to start by assuming that the Legislature meant to create a company with a capacity resembling that of a natural person, such as a corporation created by charter would have at common law, and then to ask whether there are words in the statute which take away the incidents of such a corporation. This was held by the House of Lords to be the error to which Blackburn, J., and the judges who agreed with him had fallen when they decided in *Riche v. Ashbury Railway Carriage and Iron Co.*, L.R. 9 Ex. 224, in the Court below that the analogy of the status and powers of a corporation created by charter, as expounded in the *Sutton's Hospital Case*, (1663) 10 Rep. 1a. should in the first instance be looked to. For to look to that analogy is to assume that the Legislature has had a common law corporation in view, whereas the wording may not warrant the inference that it has done more than concern itself with its own creature. Such a creature, where its entire existence is derived from the statute, will have the incidents which the common law would attach if, but only if, the statute has by its language gone to attach them. In the absence of such language they are excluded, and if the corporation attempts to act as though they were not, it is doing what is *ultra vires* and so prohibited as lying outside its existence in contemplation of law. The question is simply one of interpretation of the words used. For the statute may be so framed that executive power to incorporate by charter, independently of the statute itself, which some authority, such as a Lieutenant-Governor, possessed before it came into operation, has been left intact. Or the statute may be in such a form that a new power to incorporate by charter has been created, directed to be exercised with a view to the attainment of, for example, merely territorial objects, but not directed in terms which confine the legal personality which the charter creates to existence for the purpose of these objects, and within territorial limits. The language may be such as to show an intention to confer on the corporation the general capacity which the common law ordinarily attaches to corporations created by charter. In such a case a construction like that adopted by Blackburn, J., will be the true one.

Applying the principle so understood to the interpretation of s. 92 and of the *Ontario Companies Act* passed by virtue of it, the conclusion which results is different from that reached by the Court below. For the words of s. 92 are, in their Lordships' opinion, wide enough to enable the Legislature of the province to keep the power alive, if there existed in the Executive at the time of confederation a power to incorporate companies with provincial objects, but with an ambit of vitality wider than that of the geographical limits of the province. Such provincial objects would be of course the only objects in respect of which the province could confer actual rights. Rights outside the province would have to be derived from authorities outside the province. It is therefore important to ascertain what were the powers in this regard of a Lieutenant-Governor before the *British North America Act* passed, and in the second place what the *Ontario Companies Act* has really done.

The Act which was passed by the Imperial Parliament in 1840, 3 & 4 Vict. c. 35, in consequence of the report on the state of affairs in Canada made by Lord Durham, united the Provinces of Upper and Lower Canada under a Governor-General, who had power to appoint deputies to whom he could delegate his authority. This Act established a single Legislature for the new United Province of Canada, and shortly after it had passed responsible government was there set up. In 1867 the *British North America Act* modified the Constitution so established. . . . It is to be observed that the *British North America Act* has made a distribution between the Dominion and the provinces which extends not only to legislative but to executive authority. The executive government and authority over Canada are primarily vested in the Sovereign. But the statute proceeds to enact, by s. 12, that all powers, authorities, and functions which by any Imperial statute or by any statute of the provinces of Upper Canada, Lower Canada, Canada, Nova Scotia, or New Brunswick are at the Union vested in or exercisable by the respective Governors or Lieutenant-Governors of these provinces shall, "as far as the same continue in existence and capable of being exercised after the Union in relation to the government of Canada," be vested in and exercisable by the Governor-General. Section 65, on the other hand, provides that all such powers, authorities, and functions shall, "as far as the same are capable of being exercised after the Union in relation to the government of Ontario and Quebec respectively, be vested in and exercisable by the Lieutenant-Governors of Ontario and Quebec respectively." By s. 64 the constitution of the executive authority in Nova Scotia and New Brunswick was to continue as it existed at the Union until altered under the authority of the Act.

The effect of these sections of the *British North America Act* is that, subject to certain express provisions in that Act and to the supreme authority of the Sovereign, who delegates to the Governor-General and through his instrumentality to the Lieutenant-Governors the exercise of the prerogative on terms defined in their commissions, the distribution under the new grant of executive authority in substance follows the distribution under the new grant of legislative powers: In relation, for example, to the incorporation of companies in Ontario with provincial objects the powers of incorporation which the Governor-General or Lieutenant-Governor possessed before the Union must be taken to have passed to the Lieutenant-Governor of Ontario so far as concerns companies with this class of objects. Under both s. 12 and s. 65 the continuance of the powers thus delegated is made by the implication to depend on the appropriate Legislature not interfering.

There can be no doubt that prior to 1867 the Governor-General was for many purposes entrusted with the exercise of the prerogative power of the Sovereign to incorporate companies throughout Canada, and such prerogative power to that extent became after confederation, and so far as provincial objects required its exercise, vested in the Lieutenant-Governors, to whom provincial Great Seals were assigned as evidences of their authority. Whatever obscurity may at one time have prevailed as to the position of a Lieutenant-Governor appointed on behalf of the Crown by the Governor-General has been dispelled by the decision of this Board in *Liquidators of the Maritime Bank of Canada v. Receiver-General of New Brunswick*, [1892] A.C. 437 (P.C.). It was there laid down that "the act of the Governor-General and his Council in making the appointment is, within the meaning of the statute, the act of the Crown; and a Lieutenant-Governor, when appointed, is as much the representative of Her Majesty for all purposes of provincial government as the Governor-General himself is for all purposes of Dominion government." . . .

Their Lordships have now to consider the question whether legislation before or after confederation has been of such a character that any power of incorporation by charter from the Crown which formerly existed has been abrogated or interfered with to such an extent that companies so created no longer possess that capacity which the charter would otherwise have attached to them.

Prior to confederation the granting of letters patent under the Great Seal of the province of Canada for the incorporation of companies for manufacturing, mining, and certain other purposes was sanctioned and regulated by the Canadian statute of 1864, 27 & 28 Vict. c. 23 (Province of Canada). This statute authorized the Governor in Council to grant a charter of incorporation to persons who should petition for incorporation for the purposes of the enumerated kinds of business. Applicants for such a charter were to give notice in the *Canadian Gazette* of, among other things, the object or purpose for which incorporation was sought. By s. 4 every company so incorporated under that Great Seal for any of the purposes mentioned in this Act was to be a body corporate capable of exercising all the functions of an incorporated company as if incorporated by a special Act of Parliament. Their Lordships construe this provision as an enabling one, and not as intended to restrict the existence of the company to what can be found in the words of the Act as distinguished from the letters patent granted in accordance with its provisions. It appears to them that the doctrine of *Ashbury Railway Carriage and Iron Co. v. Riche*, L.R. 7 H.L. 653, does not apply where, as here, the company purports to derive its existence from the act of the Sovereign and not merely from the words of the regulating statute. No doubt the grant of a charter could not have been validly made in contravention of the provisions of the Act. But, if validly granted, it appears to their Lordships that the charter conferred on the company a status resembling that of a corporation at common law, subject to the restrictions which are imposed on its proceedings. There is nothing in the language used which, for instance, would preclude such a company from having an office or branch in England or elsewhere outside Canada.

The *Dominion Companies Act* (c. 79 of the Revised Statutes of 1906), is, so far as Part I is concerned, framed on the same principle, although the machinery set up is somewhat different. Part II stands on another footing. This part deals only with companies directly incorporated by special Act of Parliament of Canada, and to these it is obvious that other considerations may apply. But the companies to which Part I applies are, like those under the old statute, to be incorporated by letters patent, the only material difference being that the Act enables these to be granted by the Secretary of State under his own seal of office. When granted by s. 5 they constitute the shareholders a body corporate and politic for any of the purposes and objects, with certain exceptions, to which the legislative authority of the Parliament of Canada extends. The Sovereign, through the medium of the Governor-General, in this way delegates the power of incorporation, subject to restrictions on its exercise, to the Secretary of State, and it is by the exercise of the executive power of the Sovereign that the company is brought into existence.

The *Ontario Companies Act*, which governs the present case, is c. 191 of the Revised Statutes of the province, 1897. The principle is similar, save that the letters patent are to be granted directly by the Lieutenant-Governor of the province under the Great Seal of Ontario. Excepting in this respect, the provisions of s. 9, which corresponds to s. 5 of the Dominion Act, are substantially the same as those of the latter section so that, subject to the express restrictions in the statute, it is by the grant under the Great Seal and not by the words of the statute, which merely restrict the cases in which such a grant can be made, that the vitality of the corporation is to be measured. It will be observed that s. 107 enables an extra-provincial company desiring to carry on business within the province of Ontario to do so if authorized by licence from the Lieutenant-Governor, a provision which bears out the view indicated.

It was obviously beyond the powers of the Ontario Legislature to repeal the provisions of the Act of 1864, excepting in so far as the *British North America Act* enabled it to do this in matters relating to the province. If the Legislature of Ontario had not interfered the general character of an Ontario company constituted by grant would remain similar to that of a Canadian company before confederation.

The whole matter may be put thus: The limitations of the legislative powers of a province expressed in s. 92, and in particular the limitation of the power of legislation to such as relates to the incorporation of companies with provincial objects, confine the character of the actual powers and rights which the provincial Government can bestow, either by legislation or through the Executive, to powers and rights exercisable within the province. But actual powers and rights are one thing and capacity to accept extra-provincial powers and rights is quite another. In the case of a company created by charter the doctrine of *ultra vires* has no real application in the absence of statutory restrictions added to what is written in the charter. Such a company has the capacity of a natural person to acquire powers and rights. If by the terms of the charter it is prohibited from doing so, a violation of this prohibition is an act not beyond its capacity, and is therefore not *ultra vires*, although such a violation may well give ground for proceedings by way of *scire facias* for the forfeiture of the charter. In the case of a company the legal existence of which is wholly derived from the words of a statute, the company does not possess the general capacity of a natural person and the doctrine of *ultra vires* applies. Where, under legislation resembling that of the *British Companies Act* by a province of Canada in the exercise of powers which s. 92 confers, a provincial company has been incorporated by means of a memorandum of association analogous to that prescribed by the *British Companies Act*, the principle laid down by the House of Lords in *Ashbury Railway Carriage and Iron Co. v. Riche*, of course, applies. The capacity of such a company may be limited to capacity within the province, either because the memorandum of association has not allowed the company to exist for the purpose of carrying on any business outside the provincial boundaries, or because the statute under which incorporation took place did not authorize, and therefore excluded, incorporation for such a purpose. Assuming, however, that provincial legislation has purported to authorize a memorandum of association permitting operations outside the province if power for the purpose is obtained *ab extra*, and that such a memorandum has been registered, the only question is whether the legislation was competent to the province under s. 92. If the words of this section are to receive the interpretation placed on them by the majority in the Supreme Court the question will be answered in the negative. But their Lordships are of opinion that this interpretation was too narrow. The words "legislation in relation to the incorporation of companies with provincial objects" do not preclude the province from keeping alive the power of the Executive to incorporate by charter in a fashion which confers a general capacity analogous to that of a natural person. Nor do they appear to preclude the province from legislating so as to create, by or by virtue of statute, a corporation with this general capacity. What the words really do is to preclude the grant of such a corporation, whether by legislation or by executive act according with the distribution of legislative authority, of powers and rights in respect of objects outside the province, while leaving untouched the ability of the corporation, if otherwise adequately called into existence, to accept such powers and rights if granted *ab extra*. It is, in their Lordships' opinion, in this narrower sense alone that the restriction to provincial objects is to be interpreted. It follows, as the Ontario Legislature has not thought to restrict the exercise of the Lieutenant-Governor of the prerogative power to incorporate by letters patent with the result of conferring a capacity analogous to that of a natural person, that the appellant company could accept powers and rights conferred on it by outside authorities.

The conclusions at which their Lordships have thus arrived are sufficient to enable them to dispose of this appeal; for, according to these conclusions, the appellant company has a status which enabled it to accept from the Dominion authorities the right of free mining, and to hold the leases in question and take the benefit of the agreements relating to the locations in the Yukon district, as well as of the licence from the Yukon authorities. . . .

*Appeal allowed.*

## Note

It may be noted that in the concluding part of his judgment, not reproduced here, Viscount Haldane considered the question whether the Governor-General or Lieutenant-Governors were in the position of viceroys rather than mere representatives of His Majesty. He concluded that this was not so. Is the conclusion valid today in respect of the Governor-General? See Kennedy, "Office of Governor-General of Canada" (1953), 31 Can. Bar Rev. 994.

While there is an obvious territorial limitation on provincial incorporating power, is the province also limited (as to objects or activities with which it can endow its creatures) by the scheme of distribution of legislative power in sections 91 and 92 of the *Constitution Act, 1867*? Cf. Cudney, "Incorporation of Companies" (1948), 26 Can. Bar Rev. 1182. In *In re International and Interprovincial Ferries* (1905), 36 S.C.R. 206, Taschereau J. said (at p. 209): "No provincial legislature could incorporate a company to run a ferry between . . . two provinces and no provincial government could itself be granted by its legislature the power to run an exclusive ferry between . . . two provinces".

Was it really necessary in the *Bonanza Creek* case to make a constitutional distinction between companies incorporated by letters patent and so-called statutory or memorandum of association companies, so far as concerns capacity to accept powers which a foreign jurisdiction wishes to confer? Why should there be any difference when the exercise of powers in a foreign jurisdiction depends on the laws thereof? Issues may arise, as between an incorporating jurisdiction and a foreign jurisdiction relative to the status of a company, its continuing existence and operation, but these are matters which are independent of any question of capacity arising from the form of incorporation: see *National Trust Co. v. Ebro Irrigation & Power Co. Ltd.; Nat. Trust Co. v. Catalonian Land Co.*, [1954] O.R. 463 (H.C.).

Under the *Bonanza Creek*, and other cases it is clear that "capacity" may be conferred on a statutory company to accept powers *ab extra* without any violation of the constitutional limits of section 92(11), and moreover this "capacity" may be conferred by implication as well as expressly: see *Honsberger v. Weyburn Townsite Co.* (1919), 59 S.C.R. 281. Must the powers so conferred be limited to those set out in the incorporating instrument? See *C.P.R. v. Ottawa Fire Ins. Co.* (1907), 39 S.C.R. 405; *In re Incorporation of Companies in Canada* (1913), 48 S.C.R. 331, varied [1916] 1 A.C. 598.

Following the judgment in *Bonanza Creek*, the Ontario Legislature enacted by 1916, c. 35, section 6 what is now section 274 of the *Corporations Act*, R.S.O. 1980, c. 95 which states:

> A corporation unless otherwise expressly provided in the Act or instrument creating it, has and shall be deemed to have had from its creation the capacity of a natural person and may exercise its powers beyond the boundaries of Ontario to the extent to which the laws in force where the powers are sought to be exercised permit, and may accept extra-provincial powers and rights.

In *Walton v. Bank of Nova Scotia*, [1964] 1 O.R. 673 (C.A.), aff'd on other grounds, [1965] S.C.R. 681, Schroeder J.A. commented on the *Bonanza Creek* case as follows:

> Whether the correct deduction from the opinion of Viscount Haldane is that a provincial company being a common law company, could carry on any business that a natural person could, or that the

judgment must be read as deciding no more than that a provincial company could carry on business and had the capacity to carry on business outside of the incorporating jurisdiction and that anything beyond this concept is pure dictum is of very little importance for immediately following the decision of the Privy Council there were enactments in nearly all the Provinces which settled the point.

After referring to the 1916 legislation above mentioned, he continued:

> In *Edwards v. Blackmore* (1918), 42 O.L.R. 105 [(C.A.)], it was held that by virtue of the provisions of that section a company thus incorporated was endowed with all the capacity which a corporation created by charter had at common law — that is, almost unlimited capacity to contract; the statements in the letters patent defining the objects of incorporation did not take away that capacity; and even express restrictions in the charter did not take it away, but should be treated as a declaration of the Crown's pleasure in reference to the purposes beyond which the capacity of the corporation was not to be exercised, a breach whereof gave the Crown a right to annul the charter. That judgment has been followed consistently in Ontario ever since. . . . In my opinion, the word 'expressly' is used in s. 287 in this sense — meaning that a provision of the Act or instrument creating the corporation does not have the effect sought to be attributed to it unless it is stated in express and positive terms, directly, and not merely by implication from the language used.

Does the right of a company incorporated in one province or jurisdiction to sue in another depend on whether it is a letters patent company where there is no prohibitory legislation of the forum? See *Aetna Factors Corp. v. Breau* (1958), 15 D.L.R. (2d) 326 (N.B.C.A.); *Aetna Factors Corp. v. Hachey* (1957), 8 D.L.R. (2d) 105 (N.B. Co. Ct.).

In *Hague v. Cancer Relief and Research Institute*, [1939] 3 W.W.R. 1 (Man. K.B.), Dysart J. declared, *inter alia*, that "there can be no corporation . . . unless and until there is first a group or series of natural persons to compose or constitute the corporation, because although later corporations may be formed of existing corporations, these component corporations in the first instance must consist exclusively of natural persons". Hence, where a corporation was created by provincial statute without named corporators and without members, and a separate board of trustees was established to manage the affairs of the corporation, Dysart J. held that the corporation "was nothing". Is this a limitation on constitutional power under section 92(11), and if so what is its basis? And if it is such a limitation, does it or could it equally apply to the federal power of incorporation?

A common law municipal corporation is also unaffected by the doctrine of *ultra vires*: see *A.-G. N.B. v. St. John*, [1948] 3 D.L.R. 693 (N.B.C.A.). To what extent, having regard to section 92(8) of the *Constitution Act, 1867*, may a municipal corporation exercise powers conferred by federal legislation? Must it obtain "capacity" from the province? See *G.T.R. v. Toronto* (1900), 32 O.R. 120.

## 4. Foreign Companies in Canada

### Note

In so far as any foreign company purports to engage in activities falling within federal or provincial authority it would be subject to regulation by Dominion or Province as the case may be. Is there any federal authority over foreign companies which are in a business that falls within provincial authority? It has already been pointed out that a foreign company does not enjoy protection against provincial legislation (within the *Great West Saddlery* doctrine) that is accorded to federally incorporated companies. In *A.-G. Can. v. A.-G. Alta.*, [1916] 1 A.C. 588 (P.C.) in answer to the question whether the Dominion has power to require a foreign company to take out a licence as a condition of doing business, even if the company wishes to confine its business to a single province, Viscount Haldane said that "in such a case it would be within the power of the Parliament of Canada, by properly framed legislation, to impose such restriction. It appears . . . that such a power is given by the heads in s. 91 which refer to the regulation of trade and commerce and to aliens." This observation was referred to by the Privy Council in *A.-G. Ont. v. Reciprocal Insurers*, [1924] A.C. 328. It was qualified, however, in *In re Insurance Act of Canada*, [1932] A.C. 41, where the Privy Council said that the Dominion cannot under the guise of legislation in relation to aliens inter-meddle with the conduct of a business which is exclusively subject to provincial laws, e.g., insurance. Is the Dominion then limited to conditioning merely the entry of foreign companies into Canada without attempting to license them to carry on a "provincial" business? May it require guarantees of solvency? May it control their range of investments?

### Note on Inter-Jurisdictional Reincorporation and Amalgamation

A provincial Legislature may competently provide for the amalgamation of corporations originally created under its laws, and Parliament may similarly provide for amalgamation of Dominion companies. This proposition must, however, be qualified to exclude provincial power in this connection to destroy or limit extra-provincial rights of creditors, and also to exclude federal power in this connection to interfere with rights of creditors save where this may be done when the businesses or undertakings are as such within federal legislative jurisdiction.

Inter-jurisdictional reincorporation and amalgamation raise different and more difficult problems, both where the corporations of two different Provinces are involved and where a provincial and a federal corporation are involved. Company legislation in some of the Provinces, e.g. Manitoba and Ontario, provides for the reincorporation in the Province of extra-provincial corporations if authorized by the laws of the incorporating jurisdiction; and, conversely, permits the reincorporation (or continuing incorporation) of a creature of the Province under the laws of another jurisdiction whereupon it ceases to be a creature of the Province of original incorporation or ceases to be subject to its companies legislation: see *Corporations Act*, S.M. 1976, c. 40, sections 181 and 182; *Corporations Act*, R.S.O. 1980, c. 95, section 313. The theory appears to be that reincorporation of an extra-provincial corporation will domesticate it, and amalgamation with a local corporation can then follow without liability to constitutional pitfalls.

The pitfall at the level of reincorporation and amalgamation as between corporations of different Provinces is the prohibition against extra-territorial exercise of legislative power. It is arguable that this prohibition, which affects all provincial legislative power, is not dissolved merely because of permissive legislation of the Province whose creature is to be reincorporated in another Province. No direct comfort can be derived from *A.-G. Ont. v. Scott, supra*, at p. 555 on this question; but the point can be made, independently of that case, that if a provincial corporation may properly exercise powers in and under the laws of another Province, it may be stamped with corporate identity under such laws. The matter is not, however, free from doubt.

Extraterritoriality is not a factor in federal legislative power but there is a problem in the fact that provincial powers of incorporation are limited to the incorporation of companies with provincial objects. Inter-jurisdictional reincorporation and amalgamation of a provincial and a federal company could not, in any event, involve on the part of a Province reincorporation of a federal company whose business or undertaking is within exclusive federal legislative power. Where the federal company carries on a business which is subject to provincial regulatory authority, and provincial reincorporation is permitted under federal legislation, the situation should be as constitutionally manageable as it would be between two corporations of different Provinces. Federal reincorporation of a provincial company, where permitted by provincial legislation, should give rise to even less doubt of its constitutional propriety.

The two-step procedure of, first, reincorporation and then amalgamation (if desired) at least blunts an attack that would be harder to meet if there was an attempt at direct amalgamation between two companies incorporated by different Provinces or between a federal and a provincial company; and there is an additional counter to any argument of invalidity in the permission of the jurisdiction of original incorporation so to deal with its creature. However, the legislation on the matter still remains to be tested in judicial decision.

# 12

# Problems Relating to Credit Systems and Credit Transactions

## 1. Banking and Credit

*Note*

The *Constitution Act, 1867* contains overwhelming internal evidence of the conviction that money, banking and credit (in its public aspect) should be exclusively of federal concern. Among the enumerated classes of subjects in section 91 are (1) currency and coinage (head 14); (2) banking, incorporation of banks and issue of paper money (head 15); (3) savings banks (head 16); (4) bills of exchange and promissory notes (head 18); (5) interest (head 19); and (6) legal tender (head 20); these are in addition to federal power in relation to bankruptcy and insolvency (head 21). From the outset, the courts took a broad view of the federal banking power. In *Tennant v. Union Bank of Canada*, [1894] A.C. 31, the Privy Council declared that "banking" was "wide enough to embrace every transaction coming within the legitimate business of a banker"; and see also *Merchants Bank v. Smith* (1884), 8 S.C.R. 512. Its opinion did not vary over the years as is indicated in *Reference re Alberta Bill of Rights Act; A.-G. Alta. v. A.-G. Can.*, [1947] A.C. 503 (P.C.), where it reaffirmed a consistent course of decision that what is fairly included within the conception of 'banking' is a matter reserved exclusively for Parliament, and this without any limitation to the extent and kind of business that was carried on by banks in Canada in 1867.

## CANADIAN PIONEER MANAGEMENT LTD. v. LABOUR RELATIONS BOARD OF SASKATCHEWAN

In the Supreme Court of Canada. [1980] 1 S.C.R. 433.

Laskin, C.J.C., Martland, Ritchie, Pigeon, Dickson, Beetz, Estey, Pratte and McIntyre, JJ. March 3, 1980.

Appeal from a judgment of the Saskatchewan Court of Appeal, [1979] 1 W.W.R. 271, dismissing an appeal from a judgment of Halvorson, J., [1978] 5 W.W.R. 157, dismissing applications for orders in the nature of *certiorari* and prohibition in respect of certain certification orders.

The judgment of Laskin C.J.C. and Dickson J. was delivered by

LASKIN C.J.C.: — I have had the advantage of seeing the reasons proposed by my brother Beetz and, like him, I have no difficulty in concluding that the employees of Pioneer Life Assurance Company and their employer are subject, in their labour-management relations, to the jurisdiction of the Labour Relations Board of Saskatchewan under the *Trade Union Act*, 1972 (Sask.), c. 137 [now R.S.S. 1978, c. T-17]. The fact that Pioneer Life Assurance Company, originally a Saskatchewan corporation, was, so to speak, reincorporated under the *Canadian and British Insurance Companies Act*, R.S.C. 1970, c. I-15, and is subject to certain controls under that federal Act, as, for example, in respect of solvency and internal corporate matters, does not affect its subjection to provincial regulatory control of its business of life insurance. There is a long line of decisions which affirm provincial legislative authority in relation to the business of insurance carried on within a Province, and they support the application of provincial labour-management relations legislation to Pioneer Life Assurance Company and its employees in Saskatchewan.

The position of Pioneer Trust Company and its employees with respect to the application of provincial labour-management relations legislation is not as simple. The company is incorporated under the *Trust Companies Act*, R.S.C. 1970, c. T-16, but this alone does not bring it within federal legislative authority in respect of its relations with its employees. The argument that it carries on, in the main, what are popularly regarded as banking functions does not *ipso facto* mean that it is subject only to federal legislative authority, authority extending to its relations with its employees. The Parliament of Canada has been careful not to bring federally incorporated trust companies, companies which are fiduciaries, into the banking system of the country, although endowing them with many powers which are exercised by banks.

The central issue in this case affecting Pioneer Trust Company is not whether it is in fact a bank within s. 2(*g*) of the *Canada Labour Code*, R.S.C. 1970, c. L-1, and s. 28 of the *Interpretation Act*, R.S.C. 1970, c. I-23 — it clearly is not — but whether it falls within the opening words of s. 2 of the *Canada Labour Code* and within s. 108 of Part V of that *Code*, as enacted by 1972 (Can.), c. 18, s. 1, as being "a federal work, undertaking or business" that is within the legislative authority of the Parliament of Canada or within s. 2(*i*) of the *Canada Labour Code* as being "a work, undertaking or business outside the exclusive legislative authority of provincial legislatures". Functionally, the issue concerns only the scope of the term "federal business" and the only such business in which Pioneer Trust Company can claim to be engaged is the business of banking. I have already noted that the mere fact of federal incorporation does not provide a base for federal jurisdiction; but rather there must be an activity carried on by the corporation which is itself subject to federal regulatory authority. Of course, there is no accretion to provincial legislative authority by the failure or unwillingness of Parliament to legislate to the full limit of its power under s. 91 of the *British North America Act, 1867*. The Saskatchewan Labour Relations Board and the intervening Provinces which support its claim of jurisdiction do not rely on any such accretion, but rather assert an independent authority to regulate labour-management relations of trust companies, whether provincially or federally incorporated, which carry on business in the particular Province.

Although Pioneer Trust Company is not a "bank" under federal legislation, it is contended that it is none the less engaged in "banking", within s. 91(15) of the

*British North America Act, 1867,* and that this activity, although not institution-alized through incorporation as a "bank", is as fully within exclusive federal legis-lative authority as an actual incorporation would be. The contention is a cogent one in view of the range of activities in which Pioneer Trust Company is engaged.

One of the difficulties in this case stems from outworn conceptions of the busi-ness of banking reflected in a line of cases in the last century, and some in the present century which borrowed from the former, and which were grounded on English practices untouched by federalism and by the rise of new types of credit institutions which exercise powers similar to those long exercised by banks. Although a bank may be a dealer in credit, not every dealer in credit is a bank. So too, it is no longer correct to say, as was said by Lord Porter in *A.-G. Can. v. A.-G. Que.; Bank of Montreal v. A.-G. Que.*, [1947] A.C. 33 at 44, that "the receipt of deposits and the repayment of the sums deposited to the depositors or their successors as defined above is an essential part of the business of banking", if by that he means that any institution which has this relation of debtor and creditor must necessarily be re-garded as engaged in "banking" within s. 91(15) of the *British North America Act,* 1867.

Even if Parliament could have brought trust companies within its regulatory authority in relation to banking, it has chosen not to do so, and I think that this Court should respect that position. The result is to leave provincial labour-manage-ment relations legislation as the operative code to govern Pioneer Trust Company and its employees. It would, I think, be strange for this Court to hold, in the circum-stances of this case, that, although Pioneer Trust Company is not a "bank" within the meaning of express federal legislation relating to such institutions and has not been brought into the federal regulatory regime governing banking, it can enter by a back door as a "federal business" when that can only be the business of banking.

I would dismiss the appeals with costs. There will be no costs to or against any of the intervenors.

The judgment of Martland, Ritchie, Pigeon, Beetz, Estey and McIntyre JJ. was delivered by

BEETZ, J.: — The two points in issue are whether under the *Trade Union Act,* S.S. 1972, c. 137 [now R.S.S. 1978, c. T-17], the Labour Relations Board of Saskat-chewan (the "Board") has jurisdiction to certify the respondent union to represent the employees of (1) Pioneer Life Assurance Company ("Pioneer Life") and (2) Pioneer Trust Company ("Pioneer Trust"), and to hear charges of unfair labour practices against Pioneer Life and Pioneer Trust.

The jurisdiction of the Board was challenged from the start on the ground that the labour relations of Pioneer Life and Pioneer Trust were regulated by the *Canada Labour Code,* R.S.C. 1970, c. L-1, or otherwise came within the exclusive compe-tence of Parliament. The Board held that it had jurisdiction and certified the respon-dent union to represent employees of the appellants in the City of Regina.

The appellants applied to the Court of Queen's Bench of Saskatchewan for an order of *certiorari* to quash the Board's certification order and for an order of pro-hibition to prevent the Board from proceeding to hear nine complaints of unfair labour practices, [[1978] 5 W.W.R. 157]. Halvorson, J., dismissed both applications and his judgment was affirmed by the unanimous judgment of Culliton, C.J.S., Woods and Brownridge, JJ.A., of the Saskatchewan Court of Appeal, [[1979] 1 W.W.R. 271]. Hence the present appeal, by leave of this Court.

In this Court, all the intervenors except the Attorney-General of Canada supported the judgments of the Courts below. The Attorney-General of Canada took the position that the Courts below were right with respect to the jurisdiction of the Board over Pioneer Life but wrong with respect to the jurisdiction of the Board over Pioneer Trust.

## II PIONEER TRUST

### 1. *The facts*

As was noted above, Pioneer Trust is a wholly-owned subsidiary of Canadian Pioneer Management Ltd. It was incorporated pursuant to the *Trust Companies Act*, R.S.C. 1970, c. T-16, and carries on its business and has offices in Alberta, Saskatchewan and Manitoba.

According to the statement of facts contained in appellants' factum, which has been accepted by the Attorney-General for Saskatchewan and which corresponds substantially to the findings of the Board, and according also to a brochure outlining the services provided by Pioneer Trust, which has been produced as an exhibit and the accuracy of which does no appear to have been challenged, the business or operations of Pioneer Trust can be described in terms of the services which it provides to its customers. These include the following: (1) "chequing" accounts (while cheques drawn on Pioneer Trust are not cheques within the meaning of s. 165(1) of the *Bills of Exchange Act*, R.S.C. 1970, c. B-5, since they are not drawn on a bank, they appear to play the same role as true cheques: they do pass through the clearing system of the banks. Pioneer Trust utilizes the clearing facilities of the Bank of Montreal); (2) savings accounts; (3) loans on the security of mortgages; (4) personal loans against the collateral and lending by way of overdraft; (5) loans under federal Government guarantees pursuant to such statutes as the *Canada Students Loans Act*, R.S.C. 1970, c. S-17, the *Farm Improvement Loans Act*, R.S.C. 1970, c. F-3, the *Fisheries Improvement Loans Act*, R.S.C. 1970, F-22, and the *National Housing Act*, R.S.C. 1970, N-10; (6) commercial loans with securities, other than accounts receivable and inventory, and commercial lending without security; (7) exchange services; (8) money orders; (9) travellers' cheques; (10) strong boxes renting; (11) securities safe-keeping; (12) term deposits, guaranteed investment certificates in amounts of $1,000 or more for terms of from one to five years, guaranteed income averaging certificates and guaranteed deposit receipts; (13) registered retirement savings plans, retirement accumulation savings plans, registered home ownership savings plans and deferred profit sharing plans; (14) estate administration services.

Of the services outlined above, two are not carried on by chartered banks: the issuance of income averaging certificates and estate administration services. But it was contended that Pioneer Trust does very little fiduciary work. On the other hand, and according to the testimony of Mr. Price, vice-president and general manager of Pioneer Trust, the only banking function not open to Pioneer Trust is the provision of commercial loans on the security of accounts receivable and inventory, although Pioneer Trust is involved in commercial lending with other securities and on an unsecured basis. Mr. Price testified that 99% of the actual business conducted by the company is identical to the business carried on by chartered banks. The brochure outlining the services offered by Pioneer Trust carries the slogan: "You Can Bank on Pioneer".

Just as banks, and like all federally incorporated trusts, Pioneer Trust is a member of the Canada Deposit Insurance Corporation, pursuant to s. 9(b) of the *Canada Deposit Insurance Corporation Act*, R.S.C. 1970, c. C-3. It is inspected by the Superintendent of Insurance. It must file with the Government of Canada annual statements, quarterly liquidity statements and semi-annual statements of changes in investments and loans. Pioneer Trust is subject to minimal provincial regulation: it submits an annual summary of capital and shares to the Registrar of Companies in Regina and annual statements to the provincial jurisdictions in which it operates but is not subject to inspection by any of the provincial jurisdictions.

## 2. *Submissions made on behalf of appellants and the Attorney-General for Canada*

It was submitted on behalf of Pioneer Trust that while, *prima facie*, the Provinces have jurisdiction to legislate with respect to labour relations, Parliament has exclusive jurisdiction over the labour relations of federal works, undertakings and businesses. It was further submitted that in order to determine whether the business of Pioneer Trust was a federal business, it was necessary to consider its normal operations without regard to exceptional or casual factors: *Letter Carriers' Union of Canada v. Canadian Union of Postal Workers*, [1975] 1 S.C.R. 178. Ninety-nine per cent of the business of Pioneer Trust was identical to that carried by a chartered bank and was therefore in the nature of a banking business although the company was not chartered as a bank under the *Bank Act*, R.S.C. 1970, c. B-1. "Banking" within the meaning of s. 91(15) of the *British North America Act, 1867*, includes not only the business carried on by chartered banks but also banking carried on by other financial institutions. The *Trust Companies Act* went beyond mere incorporation. The day-to-day operations of Pioneer Trust were regulated pursuant to the provisions of this Act, under the power of Parliament to make laws in relation to banking. It was because of such regulation and because of the banking nature of its operation that Pioneer Trust ought to be considered as a federal business for the purposes of the *Canada Labour Code*. Provincially incorporated trusts doing the same type of business were not federally regulated as was Pioneer Trust and the Provinces could continue to incorporate and regulate them as long as federal law permitted. But Pioneer Trust, being in the business of banking and being subject to federal regulations was a federal business within the meaning of s. 2 of the *Canada Labour Code*:

> 2. In this Act
>
> "federal work, undertaking or business" means any work, undertaking or business that is within the legislative authority of the Parliament of Canada, including without restricting the generality of the foregoing:
>
> . . . . .
>
> (g) a bank;
>
> . . . . .

(*i*) a work, undertaking or business outside the exclusive legislative authority of provincial legislatures;

It was conceded that Pioneer Trust is not a "bank": s. 28 of the *Interpretation Act*, R.S.C. 1970, c. I-23, provides:

28. In every enactment

. . . . .

"bank or chartered bank" means a bank to which the *Bank Act* applies;

and s. 4 of the *Bank Act* provides:

4. This Act applies to each bank named in Schedule A and does not apply to any other bank.

Pioneer Trust is not named in Sched. A [am. 1972, c. 24, s. 6; 1974-75-76, c. 114, s. 5; c. 16, s. 5; 1976-77, c. 28, s. 41] of the *Bank Act* and therefore, by virtue of the *Interpretation Act*, is not a bank within the meaning of s. 2(*g*) of the *Canada Labour Code*.

But is was contended that Pioneer Trust is a federal business within the meaning of s. 2(*i*) of the *Canada Labour Code* quoted above.

Counsel for the Attorney-General of Canada agreed with counsel for Pioneer Trust that, although Pioneer Trust is not a bank, banking is its business. The test was not what Pioneer Trust could do under its corporate powers, but what it actually did. At this point, however, the two counsel parted company. Counsel for the Attorney-General of Canada dismissed any suggestion that there was room for shared or concurrent jurisdiction in the field of banking. Banking came under exclusive federal authority. Once it was held, as it should be, that Pioneer Trust was a banking undertaking, the regulation of its labour relations came under the exclusive authority of Parliament, whether or not the *Canada Labour Code* applied to it: *Reference re Validity of Industrial Relations and Disputes Investigation Act*, (the *Stevedoring* case), [1955] S.C.R. 529. It was contended that Pioneer Trust was a federal work, undertaking or business within the meaning of s. 2(*i*) of the *Canada Labour Code*, but even if it was not, the *Trade Union Act* was inapplicable and the Board was without jurisdiction. The entire scope of Parliament's jurisdiction over banking and the incorporation of banks was not encompassed in the *Bank Act*. The fact that the banking undertaking of *Pioneer Trust* was not regulated by federal legislation under all its aspects did not render provincial legislation applicable to this exclusively federal undertaking: *Union Colliery Co. of B.C. v. Bryden*, [1899] A.C. 580 (P.C.); *Commission du Salaire Minimum v. Bell Telephone Co. of Canada*, [1966] S.C.R. 767 at 772, 774.

If those submissions express the law, the consequences are quite far-reaching.

Thus, should the submissions made on behalf of Pioneer Trust be accepted, a trust company with the same type of business as Pioneer Trust would be subject either to provincial or federal legislation with respect to its labour relations, depending on whether it is provincially incorporated or incorporated under the *Trust Companies Act*. This goes against settled authority according to which the origin of incorporation has no bearing on jurisdiction over labour relations: *C.P.R. Co. v. A.-G. B.C.*, [1950] A.C. 122 (the *Empress Hotel* case); *Canada Labour Relations Board v. C.N.R.*, [1975] 1 S.C.R. 786 (the *Jasper Park Lodge* case); *Morgan v. A.-G. P.E.I.*, [1976] 2 S.C.R. 349 at 364, *per* Laskin, C.J.C.; the *Canadian Indemnity* case, *supra*, *per* Martland, J., at p. 519 S.C.R. Furthermore, trust companies incorporated pursuant to the *Trust Companies Act* and, for that matter, provincially incorporated trust companies would come under either federal or provincial jurisdiction with respect to their labour relations, depending on how little they elect to do fiduciary work and how much they render other types of services resembling those rendered by Pioneer Trust.

The contentions advanced on behalf of the Attorney-General for Canada are even more far-reaching: if acceded to and pushed to their logical consequences, they might mean that provincially incorporated trust companies and perhaps even credit unions and "caisses populaires" with the same type of business as Pioneer Trust were unlawfully incorporated and have been operating invalidly.

The issue turns on the elusive concept of banking.

### 3. *Difficulty of defining banking*

In *The Law of Banking and the Canadian Bank Act*, 2nd ed. (1968, Toronto), the author, Ian F.G. Baxter, wrote at p. 5:

> ... it would be a bold man who would undertake to state categorically which business activities legally appertain and which do not appertain to the business of banking.

Chorley, in his book on the *Law of Banking*, 4th ed., p. 23, has even gone as far as to say that "to construct a definition which would embrace the whole of it is manifestly impossible".

The reasons why banking is so difficult to define are manifold. First,

> Banking is not a technical or legal term but a loose popular one, comprehending activities carried on by those who, likewise popularly, are called bankers.

Coyne, J.A., in *Re Bergethaler Waisenamt* (No. 2), [1949] 1 W.W.R. 323 at 334 (Man. C.A.).

"Banking" on the other hand, while not a legal term, evokes economic notions which are notoriously not amenable to the discipline of the law. Furthermore, the meaning of the word has evolved considerably over the centuries. Finally, because of the expansion of credit and the development of competition between banks and other types of institutions sometimes called near banks, such as trust companies, the latter have entered certain fields of activities previously carried on by banks while banks have begun operations which were not traditionally considered to appertain to the business of banking, leading to considerable overlapping of functions.

Still, many attempts have been made in judicial decisions as well as in doctrinal works, to define the notion of banking or at least to reduce the uncertainties. In some of the attempts, the problem was approached from the point of view of the substance of the matter and, in others, from the point of view of form.

### 4. *Nature of the relationship between the institution and its customers*

One approach related to substance has focused on the nature of the relationship between the institution and its customers. The relation between a banker and a customer who pays money to the bank is not a fiduciary one. It is the ordinary relation of debtor and creditor, with a superadded obligation arising out of the custom of bankers to honour the customer's cheques. Possession of or property in the deposit remains with the bank the obligation of which is a debt under a contract of *mutuum*, not *commodatum*: *Foley v. Hill* (1848), 9 E.R. 1002; *Joachimson v. Swiss Bank Corp.*, [1921] 3 K.B. 110 at 127; *A.-G. Can. v. A.-G. Que.; Bank of Montreal v. A.-G. Que.*, [1947] A.C. 33 at 44, (the *Bank Deposits* case). By contrast, s. 63 [am. R.S.C. 1970, c. 47 (1st Supp.), s. 22] of the *Trust Companies Act* which relates to the powers of a trust company emphasizes their fiduciary nature by the use of words "in trust", "entrusted", "trustee" or some other similar expression in practically each of its subsections; and it would appear that a trust company has no power to receive money on deposit in such a way that it is the simple debtor of the depositor: Daniel J. Baum, "The Near-Banks: Trust Companies of Canada", XLV Tulane L. Rev. 546 (1970-71), at pp. 558 and 568. It has been contended that this legal distinction is of little or no practical effect and that in fact the relationship between a trust company and a depositor "is indistinguishable from the debtor-creditor relationship between a bank and its customer": Peter W. Hogg, *Constitutional Law of Canada* (1977), p. 367, note 97. I cannot subscribe to the view that the distinction entails no practical differences. . . .

In short, under the *Trust Companies Act*, all the transactions of Pioneer Trust, or most of them, appear to be fiduciary by operation of law, whether or not they are so by nature. Furthermore, several of them, described by Pioneer Trust as banking operations, are fiduciary by nature as well as by operation of law and are not banking transactions although some of them, not all, may lawfully be carried on by chartered banks. These factors may not by themselves be determinative of the issue. But they are relevant and indicative that the business of Pioneer Trust is not that of banking.

## 5. *The functional test*

Another approach to the problem of defining banking, also related to the substance of the matter, consists in the consideration of the functions of banking, from an economic or legal point of view.

### (a) The economic point of view
According to a view widely held in the nineteenth century, banks were considered as the main channel for the transfer of savings; the function of banking was one of financial intermediation in which the public had an interest with respect to solvency and allocation of financial resources. But under this particular economic view, the list of financial intermediaries would include, as well as chartered banks, some other very different types of institutions such as life insurance companies, finance companies, mortgage companies, trust companies, etc. (See Patrick N. McDonald, "The B.N.A. Act and the Near Banks: A Case Study in Federalism" (1972), 10 Alta. L. Rev. 155 at 158 ff. This article is, to the best of my knowledge, the most exhaustive study published on the question.)

Judges, however, have not always shrunk from the functional economic approach. They had little choice in *Reference re Alberta Legislation*, [1938] S.C.R. 100 (the *Alberta Statutes Reference*), since they had to deal with the legislative implementation of a specific economic doctrine; the Court found *ultra vires* a provincial legislative scheme the essence of which was to set up a new form of credit and currency within Alberta. Three bills had been referred to the Court: Bill No. 1, "An Act Respecting the Taxation of Banks"; Bill No. 8, "An Act to Amend and Consolidate the Credit of Alberta Regulation Act"; and Bill No. 9, "An Act to ensure the Publication of Accurate News and Information". The three bills were found unconstitutional together with a statute which had not been explicitly referred to the Court but which contained, expressed in legislative terms, the core of the social credit system, the *Alberta Social Credit Act*, 1937 (Alta.), c. 10. Bill No. 9 does not concern us here. Bill No. 1 attempted to tax the banks out of existence and was found *ultra vires* as directed to the frustration of the banking system established by the *Bank Act*. (This part of the judgment was upheld by the Judicial Committee in *A.-G. Alta. v. A.-G. Can.*, [1939] A.C. 117, (the *Alberta Bank Taxation* case). The Judicial Committee did not pronounce on the other issues which had become academic.) The main thrust of the *Alberta Social Credit Act* was described as follows by Duff, C.J.C., at p. 113 S.C.R.:

> ... it is clear ... that the substitution generally in internal commerce of Alberta credit for bank credit and legal tender as the circulating medium is of the very essence of the plan.

The Act provided for the distribution of Alberta credit by the Provincial Treasurer by means of treasury credit certificates. It also provided for the creation of a credit house with branches that could accept deposits, convert currency and negotiable instruments on demand into Alberta credit, etc. The practicability of the scheme would have depended upon the general acceptance by the people of Alberta, of Alberta credit as a medium of payment. The Act was found *ultra vires* by five of the six members of the Court, as relating to "Banking and the Incorporation of Banks", and also, by three of those five, as dealing with "Currency" and the "Regulation of Trade and Commerce". By comparison to what he said with respect to Bill No. 8, Duff, C.J.C., did not deal at great length with the functions of banking; the *Alberta Social Credit Act* was in relation to banking because it purported to set up a parallel system of banks for the issuance and circulation of a parallel system of credit. While the reasons of Duff, C.J.C., may not be capable of being interpreted as meaning that the *Alberta Social Credit Act* would not have been found *ultra vires* had it not interfered with chartered banks, Duff, C.J.C., did say, in the passage quoted above, that the *substitution* of one system for the other was the *very essence* of the plan. And if one couples the *Alberta Social Credit Act* with Bill No. 1, the taxing bill, which would have prevented the continued operation of chartered banks, one can entertain no doubt, looking at the scheme as a whole, that the parallel system was intended to prevail over the established one, and to that extent, to interfere with it.

But it is mostly in relation to Bill No. 8, "An Act to Amend and Consolidate the Credit of Alberta Regulation Act", that Duff, C.J.C., and Kerwin, J., as he then was, dealt in detail with the function of banking, and sought to get hold of its quintessence in terms involving economic concepts. At pp. 124-5 S.C.R., after saying, "A banker is a dealer in credit", Duff, C.J.C., focused upon the monetary function of banks and dwelt upon the particular way in which bankers, as opposed to moneylenders, create credit and deal in credit by way of book-keeping entries. He quoted with approval the following passage from M. Walter Leaf's volume on banking:

... when the creation of credit is discussed there is general agreement that by credit is meant banker's credit, that is to say, the right to draw cheques on a bank. The exercise of this right involves either the withdrawal from the bank of legal tender, in the shape of bank notes or silver and bronze coin, or the transfer of such a right to some other person in the books of the same or another bank.

At pp. 155-6 S.C.R., Kerwin, J., quoted a paragraph of the Encyclopaedia Britannica, 14th ed., containing the following passage:

Banks create credit. It is a mistake to suppose that bank credit is created to any important extent by the payment of money into the banks. Money is always being paid in by tradesmen and others who receive it in the course of business, and drawn out again by employers to pay wages and by depositors in general for use as pocket money. But the change of money into credit money and of credit money back into money does not alter the total amount of the means of payment in the hands of the community. When a bank lends, by granting an advance or discounting a bill, the effect is different. Two debts are created, the trader who borrows becomes indebted to the bank at a future date, and the bank becomes immediately indebted to the trader. The bank's debt is a means of payment; it is credit money. It is a clear addition to the amount of the means of payment in the community. The bank does not lend money. The borrower can, if he pleases, take out the whole amount of the loan in money. He is in that respect in the same position as any other depositor. But like other depositors he is likely in practice to use credit for all major payments and only to draw out money as and when needed for minor payments.

Kerwin, J., then continued at p. 156 S.C.R.:

It is not necessary to refer to the various schools of economists with their divergent views as to the extent to which banks create credit or as to the wisdom or otherwise of a state empowering such institutions to do so. It suffices that by current common understanding a business transaction whereby credit is created, issued, lent, provided or dealt in by means of bookkeeping entries is considered to be part of the business of banking as it has been practised and developed. It is well known that in addition to creating credit banks also issue, lend, provide and deal in credit by means of bookkeeping entries.

The type of provincial legislation found *ultra vires* in the *Alberta Statutes Reference* would still be invalidated today, but whether the same reasons would all be relied upon is a matter of doubt, for economic theory has evolved. Be that as it may, there were other reasons of a more classical type from a legal point of view why Bill No. 8, "An Act to Amend and Consolidate the Credit of Alberta Regulation Act", was found *ultra vires*: it was a licensing statute; it depended upon machinery created by the *Alberta Social Credit Act* which was found *ultra vires*, and it was ancillary to the latter. By themselves, these reasons which were also invoked by Duff, C.J.C., at pp. 122-3 S.C.R., sufficed to dispose of Bill No. 8 and I do not think that the other reasons are decisive of the case at bar. (It should be noted, however, that these other reasons commended themselves to Porter, J.A., whose partly dissenting opinion to the effect that the *Treasury Branches Act*, R.S.A. 155, c. 344, was unconstitutional, was adopted by two members of this Court in *Breckenridge Speedway Ltd. v. The Queen*, [1970] S.C.R. 175; the seven other members of the Court refrained from expressing any view on the question, and I do the same.)

(b) The legal point of view

Attempts to define banking in functional terms but from a strictly legal angle have been studied by C.C. Johnston, in "Judicial Comment on the concept of

'Banking Business' ", 2 Osgoode Hall L.J. 347 (1962). Typical of such attempts is the description of banking given by Richards, J.A., for the majority of the Manitoba Court of Appeal in the *Bergethaler Waisenamt* case, *supra*, at pp. 328-9 W.W.R.:

> Expert opinion was not given in evidence in this case as to what is banking business, but it is common knowledge that during the period of the corporation's operations banking did include the following: (1) Receiving money on deposit from its customers. (2) Paying a customer's cheques or drafts on it to the amount on deposit by such customer, and holding Dominion Government and Bank notes and coin for such purpose. (3) Paying interest by agreement on deposits. (4) Discounting commercial paper for its customers. (5) Dealing in exchange and in gold and silver coin and bullion. (6) Collecting notes and drafts deposited. (7) Arranging credits for itself with banks in other towns, cities and countries. (8) Selling its drafts or cheques on other banks and banking correspondents. (9) Issuing letters of credit. (10) Lending money to its customers: (a) on the customers' notes; (b) by way of overdraft; (c) on bonds, shares and other securities.
>
> The business of a Canadian Chartered bank is wider still because of the statutory rights and powers given to a bank under the provisions of the *Bank Act*.

But Richards, J.A., added the following comment at p. 332 W.W.R.:

> The business carried on by most banks includes the totality of the functions I have enumerated, but, of course, a banking business can be carried on without performing all of them and most corporations and individuals engaged in a financial business of any kind are required to carry on or perform some of them, and it does not follow from the fact that banks perform them that every exercise of one or more of the functions is a form of banking.

I agree with this comment.

Take long term borrowing, by way of term deposits or otherwise. It was held by the English Court of Appeal in *United Dominions Trust Ltd. v. Kirkwood*, [1966] 1 All E.R. 968, that the acceptance of money against deposit receipts, usually in sums ranging between £5,000 and £1,000,000 for definite periods of three; six or nine months, was not an aspect of the business of banking. Under this standard, Pioneer Trust's borrowing by way of guaranteed investment certificates is not a banking activity although it is widely practised by chartered banks and other types of institutions. I should think it is an activity that may be appropriate for savings banks but it could not be said that, on that account, they should have a monopoly thereon.

The hard core of banking is usually what lawyers will try to circumscribe. The issuance of banknotes intended for circulation would probably have been considered as part of that core in earlier days when the issuance of banknotes had not become the monopoly of the central bank: it is significant in this regard that in s. 91(15) of the Constitution, legislative jurisdiction over the issue of paper money is linked with jurisdiction over banking and the incorporation of banks. At the present day in England, the features which, according to most, are characteristic of the business of bankers have been described as follows by Lord Denning, M.R., in the *United Dominions Trust* case, at p. 975:

> ... (i) they accept money from, and collect cheques for, their customers and place them to their credit; (ii) they honour cheques or orders drawn on them by their customers when presented for payment and debit their customers accordingly. These two characteristics carry with them also a third, namely, (iii) they keep current accounts, or something of that nature, in their books in which the credits and debits are entered.
>
> Those three characteristics are much the same as those stated in *Paget's Law of Banking* (6th Edn.) (1961), p. 8:

"No-one and nobody, corporate or otherwise, can be a 'banker' who does not (i) take current accounts; (ii) pay cheques drawn on himself; (iii) collect cheques for his customers."

It will be noticed that this statement links up with the banking concept of Duff, C.J.C., and Kerwin, J., in the *Alberta Statutes Reference* stripped from its economic aspect relating to credit. (See also *Re District Savings Bank Ltd.; Ex parte Coe* (1861), 45 E.R. 907 at 909; *Re Bottomgate Industrial Co-op. Society* (1891), 65 L.T. 712; *Bank of Chettinad Ltd. of Colombo v. Income Tax Com'r of Colombo*, [1948] A.C. 378. In *Re Dominion Trust Co.*, [1918] 3 W.W.R. 1023, and *La Caisse Populaire Notre Dame Ltée v. Moyen* (1967), 59 W.W.R. 129 (Sask. Q.B.), single Judges took the view that a provincial trust company and a provincial credit union could validly provide chequing facilities to their depositors.)

Assuming that no corporation can be said to be in the banking business unless it provides its depositors with chequing privileges, it does not follow that these activities are exclusive to the business of banking. I agree, in this respect with what Coyne, J.A., said in the *Bergethaler Waisenamt* case, *supra*, at p. 334 W.W.R., that:

Chequing privileges accorded depositors ... are characteristic of, and perhaps essential to, banking. But even that does not make them exclusive rights of bankers, even in the absence of prohibition by statute against others carrying them on.

On the whole, I do not think that it is possible, at least for the purpose of this case, to define banking in purely functional terms.

## 6. *The formal and institutional tests*

In the United Kingdom, the peculiar status of bankers, their importance at the centre of the financial community, the expectation of the public that it can grant them implicit and utmost confidence have led, given the uncertainty of substantive tests, to various methods to identify or recognize banks and banking by way of formal and institutional means.

Two of these means which are closely connected with each other, have been elaborated in the cases. The first is the holding out of one-self as a banker. The second is one's reputation as a banker. The holding out is evidently aimed at the acquisition of the reputation.

A banker " 'must hold himself out as a banker and the public take him as such', assuming 'openly, avowedly and notoriously the character of a banker' ": *Stafford v. Henry* (1850), 12 Ir. Eq. 400, quoted by Coyne, J.A., in the *Bergethaler Waisenamt* case, at p. 335 W.W.R.

In Canada, Parliament has recognized the importance of the holding out test and, in order to prevent individuals or institutions which are not banks from acquiring the reputation of being in the banking business, has enacted s. 157(1) of the *Bank Act*:

157(1) Every person who, in any language, uses the word "bank", "banker" or "banking", either alone or in combination with other words, or any word or words of import equivalent thereto, to indicate or describe his business in Canada or any part of his business in Canada without being authorized so to do by this or any other Act, is guilty of an offence against this Act.

Pioneer Trust is not authorized by the *Bank Act* nor any other Act to use the forbidden words to describe its business or any part thereof including its chequing account service. If Parliament, which is the competent authority in the matter, wishes to prevent members of the public from mistaking any part of the business of Pioneer Trust and other trust companies for a banking business, it seems to me that it is because Parliament considers that it is *not* a banking business. I am also of the view that the opinion of Parliament should be considered as decisive in this case.

I accept the submission made on behalf of the Attorney-General for New Brunswick that, to resolve the issue, we should adopt an institutional approach. Such an approach, it is true, emphasizes formal tests. But, in the case at bar, these tests are bolstered by the consideration of the substantive factors referred to above. I agree with the contention which I quote from the factum of the Attorney-General for New Brunswick that:

> "Banking" involves a set of interrelated financial activities carried out by an institution that operates under the nomenclature and terms of incorporation which clearly identify it as having the distinctive institutional character of a bank.

There are several reasons for adopting such an approach.

First, it is the approach taken by Parliament, and federal legislation may properly be considered as an aid to constitutional interpretation: *Citizens Ins. Co. of Canada v. Parsons, supra*, at p. 116.

Second, it is an approach which was also taken by the Courts: in most instances where provincial legislation was found *ultra vires* on the ground that it impinged upon exclusive federal authority over banking, there has also been an attempt to regulate or to interfere with the business of established banks: the *Alberta Bank Taxation* case, *supra*; the *Bank Deposits* case, *supra*; *Reference re Alberta Bill of Rights Act, A.-G. Alta. v. A.-G. Can.*, [1947] A.C. 503, (the *Alberta Bill of Rights* case).

Third, it is an approach which is particularly appropriate in a case where what has to be decided is whether a given institution falls within the concept of banking as a business, and not whether a legislative enactment is constitutionally depending on its relationship to banking within the meaning of s. 91(15) of the Constitution. The characterization of legislation and the characterization of a business are not identical processes. Legislation, for instance, may be divisible whereas a business as a going concern is indivisible and must stand or fall as a whole on one side of the constitutional line or the other. The concept of banking as a business and the meaning of the word "banking" in s. 91(15) are not necessarily co-extensive; the meaning of "banking" in the section might very well be wider than the concept of banking as a business. Some of the reasons for such distinction have been explained by Latham, C.J., in *Commonwealth of Australia v. Bank of New South Wales* (1948), 76 C.L.R. 1 (the *Australian Banking* case) at p. 195:

> I agree with the argument of the plaintiffs that the acquisition of a share in a bank by any person (whether a bank or not) is not itself a banking operation, and similarly that the purchase by any person, whether a bank or not, of assets from a bank is not itself a banking operation and that the taking over of the business of another bank probably would not be described as a banking "transaction". But a law which controls such matters is a law dealing with the business of banking, because such matters affect the conduct and control of the business and are things which may be done from time to time in the course of the business of banking, although they are not banking

transactions between a banker and a customer. It is easy to give examples of laws which are laws having a most immediate relation to banking and which are therefore laws with respect to banking, though they do not deal with banker-customer relations as such. Among such laws would be a law requiring a bank to have a certain minimum capital or to maintain a percentage of uncalled capital, or a law prescribing the persons who may be allowed to hold bank shares, e.g. excluding bankrupts, or a law preventing banks in certain circumstances from disposing of their assets, or a law prescribing permissible forms of investment by banks. A law dealing with the management and staffing of banks would be a law relating to essential elements in the business of banking though not dealing with any transactions between any bank and any customer.

Judicial opinions on the constitutional meaning of the word "banking" in Australia should carry some weight in Canada because s. 51(xiii) of the *Commonwealth of Australia Constitution*, 1900 (63 & 64 Vict.), c. 12 (U.K.), is, except for a reference to state banking, identical to s. 91(15) of the Canadian Constitution and, as was noted by some Australian Judges, seems to have been inspired by the latter. It reads:

> (xiii) Banking, other than State banking, also State banking extending beyond the limits of the State concerned, the incorporation of banks, and the issue of paper money;

Latham, C.J., was dissenting in part in the *Australian Banking* case but, more than his views on the nature of banking, one of the main reasons for his partial dissent would appear to have been his interpretation of another provision of the Australian Constitution, s. 92, relating to the freedom of trade, commerce and intercourse among the States, of which there is no exact counterpart in the Canadian Constitution. The majority view on one of the issues raised in the *Australian Banking* case was upheld in an opinion of the Judicial Committee: [1950] A.C. 235.

One of the earliest pronouncements on the meaning of banking in Canadian constitutional law is to be found in *Tennant v. Union Bank of Canada*, [1894] A.C. 31, where Lord Watson wrote, at p. 46, that "banking" is "an expression which is wide enough to embrace every transaction coming within the legitimate business of a banker".

This statement was again referred to in more recent times: the *Bank Deposits* case, *supra*, at p. 42 A.C., and the *Alberta Bill of Rights* case, *supra*, at p. 517 A.C.

Appellants have relied upon that expression of opinion but I do not think it helps them. It cannot be read literally for it would then mean, for instance, that the borrowing of money or the lending of money, with or without security, which come within the legitimate business of a great many other types of institutions as well as of individuals, would, in every respect, fall under the exclusive legislative competence of Parliament. Such a result was never intended. But Lord Watson was then speaking of the federal legislative authority with respect to institutions which had been chartered as banks and his statement makes sense if understood in institutional terms. Take the business of money-lending on the security of mortgages. This operation was not previously open to banks and, because of the problem of liquidity, would have frightened nineteenth century bankers. That it became open to banks did not mean that it was transformed into a banking operation so that all the institutions such as loan companies, trust companies like Pioneer Trust and individuals who were heavily engaged in this type of transactions found themselves suddenly plunged into the banking business. It could not be contended either that the provincial Legislatures had lost their jurisdiction over the law of mortgages, mortgage companies and their employees. It would be more accurate to say that it was the banks which were beginning a non-banking type of activity, but it is a well established principle that federal undertakings may be empowered by Parliament to engage in business under provincial jurisdiction: the *Empress Hotel* case, *supra*; the *Jasper Park Lodge* case, *supra*.

The same comments and qualifications might apply to other loans made by banks.

### 7. *The objection of the exclusiveness rule*

Only one serious objection to the institutional approach can be raised and it has been raised by Counsel for the Attorney-General of Canada. It is based on the exclusiveness of federal legislative powers relating to banking and the incorporation of banks. It was contended that provincial legislative jurisdiction and the extent and applicability of provincial legislation cannot depend on the abstinence of Parliament from legislating to the full limit of its exclusive powers. The *Union Colliery* and *Commission du Salaire Minimum* cases, both *supra*, were relied upon.

I do not think this objection is valid in this case.

Legislative jurisdiction involves certain powers of definition which are not unlimited but which, depending on the particular manner in which they are exercised, may affect other jurisdictional fields.

For instance, Parliament has exclusive legislative jurisdiction over the establishment, maintenance, and management of penitentiaries under s. 91(28) of the Constitution, and each Province has exclusive legislative jurisdiction over the establishment, maintenance and management of public and reformatory prisons in and for the Province, under s. 92(6). At present the line of demarcation between the two appears to depend in part upon federal legislation such as s. 659 [am. 1974-75-76, c. 93, s. 79; 1976-77, c. 53, s. 13] of the *Criminal Code*.

Another example is provided by the legal status of the Eskimo inhabitants of Quebec. They are not Indians under the *Indian Act*, R.S.C. 1970, c. I-6; s 4(1), but they are Indians within the contemplation of s. 91(24) of the Constitution: *Reference as to whether "Indians" in s. 91(24) of the B.N.A. Act includes Eskimo inhabitants of Quebec* [1939] S.C.R. 104. Should Parliament bring them under the *Indian Act*, provincial laws relating to descent of property and to testamentary matters would cease to apply to them and be replaced by the provisions of the *Indian Act* relating thereto.

Parliament having chosen to exercise its jurisdiction over banking and the incorporation of banks from an institutional aspect rather than in functional terms, as was perhaps unavoidable, did not necessarily exhaust its exclusive jurisdiction; but it left institutions which it did not characterize as being in the banking business to the operation of provincial labour laws.

### 8. *Conclusion*

To summarize and conclude:

The relationship of Pioneer Trust with its customers is of a fiduciary nature and several of its operations appertain to the business of a trust company. A great many of its other operations are not characteristic of the banking business although they are also carried on by chartered banks. The one operation carried on by Pioneer

Trust which may be characteristic of the banking business, the chequing account service, is not exclusive to the business of banking. And finally, Parliament, which is the competent constitutional authority in matters of banks and banking, considers that Pioneer Trust is not a bank and that its business is not the banking business. Hence, Pioneer Trust is not in the business of banking.

The appeal should be dismissed with costs. There should be no order as to cost for or against the intervenors.

[Pratte J. retired on June 30, 1979, and was not a party to these reasons.]

*Appeal dismissed.*

## Note

Would the court show equal deference to Parliament by using the institutional instead of functional test if Parliament tried to assume jurisdiction over credit unions and caisses populaires by designating them as "banks"? See MacPherson, "Developments in Constitutional Law: The 1979-80 Term" (1981), 2 Supreme Court L.R. 49 at pp. 91-94.

Under section 92(3) of the *Constitution Act, 1867*, a provincial legislature may pass laws in relation to "the borrowing of money on the sole credit of the province." To what extent, if at all, does this enable a province to establish a banking system? See *In re Dominion Trust Co.*, [1918] 3 W.W.R. 1023 (B.C. S.C.); *Winnipeg Trustee v. Kenny*, [1924] 1 D.L.R. 952 (Man. K.B.). Cf. *Agricultural Development Finance Act*, R.S.O. 1980, c. 10.

Is "gold clause" legislation competent to a Province insofar as it provides for discharge in legal tender of any obligation which gives the obligee a right to require payment in gold or in a particular kind of currency? See *The Gold Clauses Act*, R.S.O. 1980, c. 189. Is it competent to Parliament to legislate to this effect? See the now repealed *Gold Clauses Act*, R.S.C. 1970, c. G-4. See also *Norman v. B. & O. Ry.*, 294 U.S. 240 (1935); *Perry v. U.S.*, 294 U.S. 330 (1935).

Does the federal banking power preclude provincial legislation in respect of money lending? Cf. The *Credit Union and Caisses Populaires Act*, R.S.O. 1980, c. 102, as amended, authorizing the incorporation of credit unions and caisses populaires for the purpose of receiving money on deposit from members and the making of loans to members with or without security; and see, as to validity, *La Caisse Populaire Notre Dame Ltée v. Moyen* (1967), 59 W.W.R. 129 (Sask. Q.B.).

For a non-constitutional discussion of what is "banking": see *United Dominion Trust Ltd. v. Kirkwood*, [1966] 1 All E.R. 968 (C.A.).

In *A.G. Can. v. A.G. Que.*, [1947] A.C. 33 (P.C.), rev'g [1943] Que. K.B. 543 (Bank Deposits), Lord Porter stated that "the receipt of deposits and the repayment of the sums deposited to the depositors or their successors . . . is an essential part of the business of banking." In consequence, it was held that provincial legislation appropriating unclaimed bank deposits (being merely debts of the bank) was invalid, whether the Province purports to hold such choses in action for the owners or not. Should there be any difference in result if the Crown in right of a Province claims such choses as *bona vacantia*? May the Province define what constitutes *bona vacantia* in such a way as to cover unclaimed bank deposits? Cf. *Prov. Treasurer of*

*Manitoba v. Minister of Finance; A.-G. Man. v. Minister of Finance*, [1943] S.C.R. 370. For the position on these problems in the United States where there is no exclusive federal banking power, see *Anderson National Bank v. Luckett*, 321 U.S. 233 (1944), and *Roth v. Delano*, 338 U.S. 226 (1949), upholding state authority in respect of unclaimed bank deposits so long as there is no interference with the federal banking system.

A provincial legislature has no authority to require a bank to have a provincial licence as a condition of doing business. Nor may it seek to regulate or require that deposits be backed by a specified amount or percentage of reserves: see *A.-G. Alta. v. A.-G. Can.* (Reference re Alberta Bill of Rights Act), [1947] A.C. 503 (P.C.); La Brie, Note (1947), 25 Can. Bar Rev. 888.

To what extent, absent federal legislation, are banks subject to provincial legislation of general application, *e.g.*, provincial registry laws respecting land, conditional sale and chattel mortgage legislation, and garnishment legislation? See *Re Victor Varnish Co.* (1909), 16 O.L.R. 338; *Brantford v. Imperial Bank of Canada* (1930), 65 O.L.R. 625 (C.A.).

Section 3 of the *Mechanics' Lien Act*, R.S.O. 1980, c. 261 established a statutory trust of money received on account of the contract price by a builder, contractor or subcontractor and forbade its conversion by them save to the extent to which workmen, suppliers and subcontractors had been paid. How would this provision affect a bank, in which a contractor has a current account to which he has deposited money received on the contract price, where the bank applies the money to an overdraft? Would the statutory trust operate against the bank in view of s. 100(1) of the *Bank Act*, S.C. 1980-81-82-83, c. 40 which provides that "the bank is not bound to see to the execution of any trust, whether express, implied or constructive, to which any deposit made under the authority of this Act is subject"? See *Fonthill Lumber Ltd. v. Bank of Montreal*, [1959] O.R. 451 (C.A.). Does it, or should it make any difference whether the contract money is actually deposited with the bank or is claimed by the bank under, say, a general assignment of book debts given to the bank by a contractor debtor? See *Canadian Bank of Commerce v. T. McAvity & Sons Ltd.*, [1959] S.C.R. 478.

Is it competent for a Province to empower a landlord to distrain on goods of a tenant which are covered by an assignment to a bank by way of security? No doubt Parliament could protect the bank's security by affirmative legislation but in the absence thereof should provincial legislation apply where it operates to deny the effect of security taken before distress is levied? See *Re Newmarket Lumber Co. Ltd.; International Wood Products Ltd. v. Royal Bank of Canada*, [1951] O.R. 642 (H.C.).

## 2. Federal Power in Relation to Interest

### A.-G. SASK. v. A.-G. CAN.

In the Privy Council. [1949] A.C. 110.

Viscount Simon, Lord Macmillan, Lord Simonds, Lord Oaksey,
Lord MacDermott. Nov. 22, 1948.

Appeal by special leave from a judgment of the Supreme Court of Canada, [1947] S.C.R 394 (Taschereau J. dissenting), invalidating on a reference s. 6 of the *Farm Security Act*, 1944 (Sask. 2nd sess.), c. 30, as amended.

The *Farm Security Act*, 1944, of Saskatchewan was entitled "An Act for the protection of certain mortgagors, purchasers and lessees of farm land," and the main object of the Act was to lighten the contractual obligations of a mortgagor or purchaser of farm land in the event of the yield of grain grown on the land falling below a prescribed minimum. The earlier sections of the Act provided for relief of that nature being granted also to lessees, who rented such land on the terms that the lessor was to receive a share of the crop, but s. 6 was concerned only with the modification of the contractual rights of mortgagees or vendors of farm land in respect of the contractual payments due to them in the event of a "crop failure".

Sub-section 1 of s. 6 defined "crop failure" as meaning a "failure of grain crops grown in any year on mortgaged land or on land sold under agreement of sale, due to causes beyond the control of the mortgagor or purchaser, to the extent that the sum realized from the said crops is less than a sum equal to six dollars per acre sown to grain in each year on such land." The sub-section also contained a definition commencing on the first day of August in the year in which the crop failure occurs and ending on the thirty-first day of July in the next succeeding year. Sub-section 2 of s. 6 ran as follows:

> (2) Notwithstanding anything to the contrary, every mortgage and every agreement of sale shall be deemed to contain a condition that, in case of crop failure in any year and by reason only of such crop failure:
> 1. the mortgagor or purchaser shall not be required to make any payment of principal to the mortgagee or vendor during the period of suspension.
> 2. payment of any principal which falls due during the period of suspension and of any principal which theerafter falls due under the mortgage or agreement of sale shall become automatically postponed for one year;
> 3. the principal outstanding on the fifteenth day of September in the period of suspension shall on that date become automatically reduced by four per cent. thereof or by the same percentage thereof as that at which interest will accrue immediately after the said date on the principal then outstanding, whichever percentage is the greater; provided that, notwithstanding such reduction, interest shall continue to be chargeable, payable and recoverable as if the principal had not been so reduced.

VISCOUNT SIMON: In the view which their Lordships take on the constitutional validity of sub-s. 2, and on its relation to the rest of s. 6, it is not necessary to set out the remaining sub-ss. of s. 6, though they have been carefully examined to see if they throw further light on sub-s. 2. The contention of the respondents is that para. 3 of sub-s. 2 is *ultra vires* of the provincial legislature of Saskatchewan because it is an encroachment in relation to "interest" — a matter which, by s. 91, head 19, of the *British North America Act* is within the exclusive legislative power of the Dominion Parliament. . . .

The appellant argues that the "pith and substance" of para. 3 is "property and civil rights," a matter in relation to which the provincial legislature has an exclusive legislative power, and that in so far as para. 3 affects "interest" it does so only incidentally. In support of this view the Attorney-General for Saskatchewan relies on *Ladore v. Bennett*, [1939] A.C. 468 (P.C.), and especially on the concluding passage of Lord Atkin's judgment. A further ground on which the appellant contends that the impeached paragraph is *intra vires* of the Province is that its "pith and substance" is "agriculture in the Province" within the meaning of s. 95 of the *British North America Act*, and that it is not repugnant to any Act of the Parliament of Canada such as is referred to in that section.

It is convenient to deal first with this last contention, which provided a chief ground on which the dissenting judgment of Taschereau J. was based. There was abundant evidence that agriculture is the main industry of Saskatchewan and that it is the principal source of revenue of its inhabitants. It is moreover clear that the result of the impeached legislation, if it is validly enacted, would be to relieve in some degree a certain class of farmers from financial difficulties due to the uncertainties of their farming operations. But, as Rand J. points out, there is a distinction between legislation "in relation to" agriculture and legislation which may produce a favourable effect on the strength and stability of that industry. Consequential effects are not the same thing as legislative subject-matter. It is "the true nature and character of the legislation" — not its ultimate economic results — that matters (*Russell v. The Queen* (1882), 7 App. Cas. 829 at 840 (P.C.)). Here what is sought to be statutorily modified is a contract between two parties one of which is an agriculturist but the other of which is a lender of money. However broadly the phrase "agriculture in the Province" may be construed, and whatever advantages to farmers the re-shaping of their mortgages or agreements for sale might confer, their Lordships are unable to take the view that this legislation can be regarded as valid on the ground that it is enacted in relation to agriculture.

A more difficult question is raised by the alternative contention that the legislation is in relation to civil rights in the Province. Contractual rights are, generally speaking, one kind of civil rights and, were it not that the Dominion has an exclusive power to legislate in relation to "interest," the argument that the provincial legislature has the power, and the exclusive power, to vary provisions for the payment of interest contained in contracts in the province could not be overthrown. But proper allowance must be made for the allocation of the subject-matter of "interest" to the Dominion legislature under head 19 of s. 91 of the *British North America Act*. There is another qualification to the otherwise unrestricted power of the provincial legislature to deal with civil rights in head 18 "Bills of Exchange and Promissory Notes." The Dominion power to legislate in relation to interest cannot be understood to be limited to a power to pass statutes dealing with usury such as were repealed in the United Kingdom in 1854 (17 & 18 Vict., c. 90). So restricted a construction was rejected by the Judicial Committee in *Lethbridge Nor. Irrigation District Trustees v. Independent Order of Foresters and Attorney-General for Canada*, [1940] A.C. 513 at 530-1 (P.C.), for reasons stated by Viscount Caldecote. The validity of the *Interest*

*Act* of the Parliament of Canada (R.S.C. 1927, c. 102) has not been challenged in any particular. Section 2 of this statute provides:

> Except as otherwise provided by this or by any other Act of the Parliament of Canada, any person may stipulate for, allow and exact, on any contract or agreement whatsoever, any rate of interest or discount which is agreed upon.

It is therefore clear that a provincial statute which varies the stipulation in a contract as to the rate of interest to be exacted would not be consonant with the existence and exercise of the exclusive Dominion power to legislate in respect of interest. The Dominion power would likewise be invaded if the provincial enactment was directed to postponing the contractual date for the payment of interest without altering the rate, for this would equally be legislating in respect of interest.

There thus remain two questions to be considered: first, does the provincial statute now under consideration operate to the above effect? And secondly, even if it does, can the consequent invalidity be avoided because this result should be regarded as merely incidental to the achievement of the real and valid statutory purpose, so that, although the topic of interest is trenched upon, the subject of interest is not the pith and substance of the Act? The first of these questions must be answered in the light of an established rule of construction in such cases, namely, that regard must be had to the substance and not to the mere form of the enactment, so that "you cannot do that indirectly which you are prohibited from doing directly" (per Lord Halsbury in *Madden v. Nelson and Fort Sheppard Ry. Co.*, [1899] A.C. 626 at 627). If, under colour of an arrangement which purports to deal only with the principal of a debt, it is really the contractual obligation to pay interest on the principal which is modified, the enactment should be regarded as dealing with interest. With this rule in mind, their Lordships have examined the language and effect of s. 6 of the *Farm Security Act* with much care, and they have been greatly assisted in this task by the arguments of counsel on either side. Sub-section 2 of s. 6 provides in effect that, in the event of crop failure, (a) the mortgagor or purchaser shall not be required to make any payment of principal during the period of suspension, (b) the payment of any principal which is contractually due during that period and any principal which thereafter falls due shall be postponed for one year, (c) the principal outstanding on September 15 in the period of suspension shall on that date become automatically reduced by 4 per cent. thereof "or by the same percentage thereof as that at which interest will accrue immediately after the said date on the principal then outstanding, whichever percentage is the greater," but (d) notwithstanding such reduction, interest shall continue to be chargeable, payable and recoverable as if the principal had not been so reduced.

It is not in dispute that mortgages or agreements to defer payment of purchase money of land in Saskatchewan, practically without exception, provide for interest on outstanding principal at a rate greater than 4 per cent. per annum. The effect, therefore, is to reduce the outstanding principal, in the event of crop failure, by an amount equal to the amount of interest called for under the contract, but to require this same amount of interest to continue to be paid as though the outstanding principal had not been reduced. If the sub-section had said in plain terms that for the period of suspension there should be no interest charged and that the payment of outstanding principal should be postponed, the result (at any rate in the first year of suspension) to the mortgagee or vendor would be the same. Moreover, such agreements normally stipulate for a "rate" of interest on outstanding principal, and a "rate" is the ratio which the sum payable as interest bears to the amount of such outstanding principal. To provide that principal is to be reduced by statute but that the amount to be paid as interest is to remain unaltered is necessarily to increase the rate on the principal outstanding. But provincial legislation which alters a stipulated rate of interest would conflict with s. 2 of the *Interest Act*. These considerations lead their Lordships to confirm the conclusion at which the majority of the Supreme Court has arrived, that para. 3 of sub-s. 2 of s. 6 trenches upon the Dominion field. It is obvious that the language used has been ingeniously chosen in an endeavour to avoid a conflict with Dominion powers and legislation, but in the view of their Lordships the endeavour is not successful. This view of the matter renders it unnecessary to determine what would be the correct application of the words used in the difficult situation of successive years of suspension analysed in the judgment of Kellock J.

Secondly, can the remaining argument be upheld that this interference with the topic of interest none the less remains valid because it is merely incidental to the exercise of a valid power to legislate for a modification of principal debts? On this, it is to be observed that there is not only an exclusive power to legislate in relation to interest vested in the Dominion Parliament, but that such legislation has been enacted in the *Interest Act*. . . . Apart, however from the obstacle created by the existence of the *Dominion Interest Act*, their Lordships are unable to take the view that the dealing with interest is only incidental, for it lies at the heart of the matter. Their Lordships are not called on to discuss, and do not pronounce on, a case where a provincial enactment renders null and void the whole contract to repay money with interest. Here the contracts survive, and once the conclusion is reached that, as Kerwin J. said, "the legislation here in question is definitely in relation to interest," reliance on such a decision as *Ladore v. Bennett* is misplaced. The provincial legislation there considered was legislation in relation to "municipal institutions in the Province," and, as Viscount Caldecote pointed out in the *Lethbridge* case:

> having come to the conclusion that the pith and substance of the legislation in question related to one or more of the classes of subjects under s. 92, the Board had no difficulty in holding that the regulation of the interest payable on the debentures of the new city was not an invasion of Dominion powers under head 19 of s. 91.

Lastly, does the invalidity of paragraph 3 involve the consequence that section 6 is ultra vires as a whole? Their Lordships agree with the Supreme Court that it does . . .

*Appeal dismissed.*

[Having regard to this decision, is there any substance at all in the current "agriculture" power? Is not the conclusion that the legislation is in relation to interest a negation of a basic assumption of the legislation that the farmer must look to his crop yield to pay off the debt on his farm? Moreover, is there not an inconsistency between the approach to constitutional construction in this case and that in the *Alberta Bank Taxation* case, [1939] A.C. 117? Assuming it to be true that, as Viscount Simon said, "consequential effects are not the same thing as legislative subject matter," how does this conclusion support the conclusion reached in this case? For similar statements that one should look to legislative purpose rather than consequential effects, see *Carnation Company Ltd. v. Quebec Agricultural Marketing Board*, [1968] S.C.R. 238 reproduced above at Chapter 8; *Canadian Indemnity Co. v. A.G.-B.C.*, [1977] 2 S.C.R. 504.

Section 36 of the *Judicature Act*, R.S.O. 1980, c. 223 [now sections 137-140 of the *Courts of Justice Act*, S.O. 1984, c. 11] which allowed a party entitled to judgment for the payment of money, subject to specified exceptions and judicial discretion to have included in the judgment interest on the award was upheld as valid provincial legislation concerning the administration of justice which dealt with interest in only an incidental manner: see *Minister of State of the Principality of Monaco v. Project Planning Associates (Int.) Ltd.* (1980), 32 O.R. (2d) 438 (Ont. C.A.). See also *United Grain Growers Ltd. v. Mott Electric Ltd.* (1981), 124 D.L.R. (3d) 434 (B.C.S.C.) for a similar decision concerning section 1 of the *Court of Order Interest Act*, R.S.B.C. 1979, c. 76.

Is provincial legislation providing for interest on unpaid taxes *intra vires*? See *R. v. Harper* (1971), 22 D.L.R. (3d) 230 (C.A.).]

# A.-G. ONT. v. BARFRIED ENTERPRISES LTD.

In the Supreme Court of Canada. [1963] S.C.R. 570.

Taschereau C.J., Cartwright, Fauteux, Martland, Judson, Ritchie and Hall JJ. Dec. 16, 1963.

Appeal from a judgment of the Ontario Court of Appeal, [1962] O.R. 1103, reversing an order of Clark Co. Ct. J. and declaring The Ontario *Unconscionable Transactions Relief Act* to be invalid.

The judgment of Taschereau C.J.C. and Fauteux, Judson and Hall JJ. was delivered by

JUDSON J.:

The Attorney-General for Ontario appeals from a judgment of the Ontario Court of Appeal which declared the *Unconscionable Transactions Relief Act*, R.S.O. 1960, c. 410, to be unconstitutional. The Attorney-General for Quebec has intervened and supports the appeal. No other province is represented. The appeal is opposed by Barfried Enterprises Ltd., the lender under the impugned transaction, and by the Attorney-General of Canada.

One Ralph Douglas Sampson, the borrower, applied in the County Court of the County of Wellington, to have revised a certain mortgage transaction with the respondent Barfried. The mortgage is dated September 3, 1959, and was for a face amount of $2,250 with interest at 7 per cent. per annum. The sum actually advanced was $1,500 less a commission of $67.50. The difference between the $1,500 and the face amount of $2,250 was made up of a bonus and other charges. The County Judge set aside the mortgage in part and revised it to provide for payment of a principal sum of $1,500 with interest at 11 per cent. per annum. No constitutional issue was raised before him.

Barfried raised this issue for the first time in the Court of Appeal. Briefly, the *Unconscionable Transactions Relief Act* empowers the Court to grant specified relief in respect of money lent where it finds that the 'cost of the loan' is excessive and the transaction harsh and unconscionable. 'Cost of the loan' is defined in the Act to mean, among other things, 'the whole cost to the debtor of money lent and includes interest, discount, subscription, premium, dues, bonus, commission, brokerage fees and charges.' This was held by the Court of appeal to be legislation in relation to interest, its essential purpose being to afford a remedy to a borrower to have the contract of loan modified, by having interest, 'in the broad sense of the term as compensation for the loan', reduced. The Court also held that the Act was in direct conflict with s. 2 of the *Interest Act*, R.S.C. 1952, c. 156.

The essence of the judgment appealed from is contained in the following passage from the reasons for judgment of the Court of Appeal:

> The statute is applicable to only one kind of contract — a money-lending contract. Its essential purpose and object is to provide a remedy to a borrower to enable him to have the terms of such a contract modified. The end result of an application to the Court in accordance with its provisions, if the borrower is entitled to succeed, must be that the interest in the broad sense of that term, payable as compensation for the loan will be reduced. It matters not, in my opinion, whether this result is achieved through the intervention of a provision in the Act itself fixing a stated rate or scale of interest. In either case it is unquestionably legislation in relation to interest under the pith and substance rule, and, in my opinion, clearly invalid as an infringement of the exclusive legislative power committed to Parliament. Moreover it is in direct conflict with the provisions of s. 2 of the *Interest Act*, R.S.C. 1952, c. 156. Accordingly, it is beyond the province's legislative competence to enact.

Both provinces submit common grounds of error:

(a) That the Act is legislation in relation to a matter coming within s. 92(13) of the *British North America Act*, Property and Civil Rights in the Province, the subject-matter being rescission and reformation of a contract of loan under the conditions defined by the Act;

(b) That in so far as the Act affects any matter coming within the Classes of Subjects assigned by the *British North America Act* to the exclusive legislative authority of the Parliament of Canada, it does so only incidentally;

(c) That there is no conflict or repugnancy between the provisions of the Act and any validly enacted federal legislation.

The powers of the Court are stated in s. 2 of the Act, which reads:

> 2. Where in respect of money lent, the court finds that, having regard to the risk and to all the circumstances, the cost of the loan is excessive and that the transaction is harsh and unconscionable, the court may,
>
> (a) re-open the transaction and take an account between the creditor and the debtor;
> (b) notwithstanding any statement or settlement of account or any agreement purporting to close previous dealings and create a new obligation, re-open any account already taken and relieve the debtor from payment of any sum in excess of the sum adjudged by the Court to be fairly due in respect of the principal and the cost of the loan;
> (c) order the creditor to repay any such excess if the same has been paid or allowed on account by the debtor;
> (d) set aside either wholly or in part or revise or alter any security given or agreement made in respect of the money lent, and, if the creditor has parted with the security, order him to indemnify the debtor.

The terms 'money lent' and 'cost of the loan' are defined as follows:

> ' "Money lent" includes money advanced on account of any person in any transaction that, whatever its form may be, is substantially one of money-lending or securing the repayment of money so advanced and includes and has always included a mortgage within the meaning of *The Mortgages Act*, R.S.O. 1950, c. 402, s. 1; 1960, c. 127, s. 1.
> ' "Cost of the loan" means the whole cost to the debtor of money lent and includes interest, discount, subscription, premium, dues, bonus, commission, brokerage fees and charges, but not

actual lawful and necessary disbursements made to a registrar of deeds, a master or local master of titles, a clerk of a county or district court, a sheriff or a treasurer of a municipality.'

In my opinion all these submissions are well founded and the Act is within the power of the provincial Legislature. The foundation for the judgment under appeal is to be found in the adoption of a wide definition of the subject-matter of interest used in [*A. G. Sask. v. A. G. Can.*] (*Saskatchewan Farm Security Act* reference), [1947] S.C.R. 394 at 411. The judgment of this Court in that case was affirmed in the Privy Council, [1949] A.C. 110. Interest was defined:

> In general terms, the return or consideration or compensation for the use or retention by one person of a sum of money, belonging to, in a colloquial sense, or owed to, another.

This is substantially the definition running through the three editions of Halsbury. However, in the third edition (27 Hals. 3rd. ed., p. 7) the text continues:

> Interest accrues *de die in diem* even if payable only at intervals, and is, therefore, apportionable in point of time between persons entitled in succession to the principal.

The day-to-day accrual of interest seems to me to be an essential characteristic. All the other items mentioned in *The Unconscionable Transactions Relief Act* except discount lack this characteristic. They are not interest. In most of these unconscionable schemes of lending the vice is in the bonus.

In the cases decided in this Court under s. 6 of the *Interest Act*, it is settled that a bonus is not interest for the purpose of determining whether there has been compliance with the Act. Section 6 reads:

> ... whenever any principal money or interest secured by mortgage of real estate is, by the same, made payable on the sinking fund plan, or on any plan under which the payments of principal money and interest are blended ... no interest whatever shall be ... recoverable ... unless the mortgage contains a statement showing the amount of such principal money and the rate of interest chargeable thereon, calculated yearly or half-yearly, not in advance.

Schroeder J.A. cited *Singer v. Goldhar* (1924), 55 O.L.R. 267 (C.A.), as defining interest in wide terms. In *Singer v. Goldhar* there was no provision for interest in the mortgage but there was a very big bonus. The Court of Appeal held that this infringed s. 6 of the *Interest Act*, the bonus being the same thing as interest. But in *Asconi Building Corporation v. Vocisano*, [1947] S.C.R. 358 at 365, Kerwin J. pointed out that *London Loan & Savings Co. of Canada v. Meagher*, [1930] S.C.R. 378, had overruled *Singer v. Goldhar*. It is now established that in considering s. 6 of the *Interest Act*, a bonus is not interest in the fact that interest may be payable on a total sum which includes a bonus does not involve an infringement of s. 6 of the Act. This was recognized in all the reasons delivered in the *Asconi* case. It was in this context that the wide definition of interest above referred to was used in the *Saskatchewan Reference* case. The Court held that the subject-matter of the legislation was interest and that to call it a reduction of principal did not change its character.

There is, therefore, error in the judgment of Schroeder J.A. in following *Singer v. Goldhar* in holding that interest in the wide sense includes bonus instead of following the subsequent cases which overrule it.

The *Lethbridge Northern Irrigation* case, [1940] A.C. 513, and the *Saskatchewan Farm Security* case, [1947] S.C.R. 394, do not govern the present case. In the first of these cases, provincial legislation reduced the rate of interest on provincial debentures or provincially-guaranteed debentures. This legislation was concerned with interest in its simplest sense and nothing more and was held to be *ultra vires*.

The *Saskatchewan Farm Security* case was treated as being on the same subject or matter. Legislation which provided that in case of crop failure as defined by the Act, the principal obligation of the mortgagor or purchaser of a farm should be reduced by 4 per cent. in that year but that interest should continue to be payable as if the principal had not been reduced, was held to be legislation in relation to interest.

*Day v. Victoria*, [1938] 3 W.W.R. 161 (B.C.C.A.) and *Ladore v. Bennett*, [1939] A.C. 468, come much closer to the present problem. In *Day v. Victoria*, legislation altering the rate of interest of municipal debentures was held to be incidental to a recasting of the city debt structure and was within the competence of the province under s. 92(8) 'Municipal Institutions in the Province', and s. 92(13) 'Property and Civil Rights in the Province.' In *Ladore v. Bennett* a reduction in the rate of interest on municipal debentures was incidental to an amalgamation of four municipalities and a consolidation of their separate indebtedness and the issue by the new municipality of its own debentures in place of the old but at a reduced rate of interest.

The issue in this appeal is to determine the true nature and character of the Act in question and, in particular, of s. 2 above quoted. The Act deals with rights arising from contract and is *prima facie* legislation in relation to civil rights and, as such, within the exclusive jurisdiction of the province under s. 92(13). Is it removed from the exclusive provincial legislative jurisdiction by s. 91(19) of the Act, which assigns jurisdiction over interest to the federal authority? In my opinion, it is not legislation in relation to interest but legislation relating to annulment or reformation of contract on the grounds set out in the Act, namely, (a) that the cost of the loan is excessive, and (b) that the transaction is harsh and unconscionable. The wording of the statute indicates that it is not the rate or amount of interest which is the concern of the legislation but whether the transaction as a whole is one which it would be proper to maintain as having been freely consented to by the debtor. If one looks at it from the point of view of English law it might be classified as an extension of the doctrine of undue influence. As pointed out by the Attorney-General for Quebec, if one looks at it from the point of view of the civil law, it can be classified as an extension of the doctrine of lesion dealt with in articles 1001 to 1012 of the *Civil Code*. The theory of the legislation is that the Court is enabled to relieve a debtor, at least in part, of the obligations of a contract to which in all the circumstances of the case he cannot be said to have given a free and valid consent. The fact that interference with such a contract may involve interference with interest as one of the constituent elements of the contract is incidental. The legislature considered this type of contract as one calling for its interference because of the vulnerability of the contract as having been imposed on one party by extreme economic necessity. The Court in a proper case is enabled to set aside the contract, rewrite it and impose the new terms.

This legislation raises the very case which the Privy Council refrained from deciding in the *Saskatchewan Farm Security* case when it said, at p. 126 A.C.:

> Their Lordships are not called on to discuss, and do not pronounce on, a case where a provincial enactment renders null and void the whole contract to repay money with interest. Here the contracts survive, and once the conclusion is reached that, as Kerwin J. said, 'the legislation here in

question is definitely in relation to interest,' reliance on such a decision as *Ladore v. Bennett* is misplaced.

Under the Ontario statute an exercise of judicial power necessarily involves the nullity or setting aside of the contract and the substitution of a new contractual obligation based upon what the Court deems it reasonable to write within the statutory limitations. Legislation such as this should not be characterized as legislation in relation to interest. I would hold that it was validly enacted, that no question of conflict arises.

I would therefore reverse the order of the Court of Appeal for Ontario and hold that the *Unconscionable Transactions Relief Act* is within the powers of the Legislature of the Province of Ontario. . . ."

CARTWRIGHT J.: . . . The *Unconscionable Transactions Relief Act* appears to me to be legislation in relation to Property and Civil Rights in the Province and the Administration of Justice in the Province, rather than legislation in relation to Interest. Its primary purpose and effect are to enlarge the equitable jurisdiction to give relief against harsh and unconscionable bargains which the Courts have long exercised; it affects, but only incidentally, the subject-matter of Interest specified in head 19 of s. 91 of the *British North America Act*. For this reason and for the reasons given by my brother Judson I agree with his conclusion that the *Unconscionable Transactions Relief Act* is not *ultra vires* of the Legislature of Ontario.

Particular cases may arise in which the provisions of the Provincial Act will come into conflict with those of the Dominion Act. In such cases the Dominion Act will of course prevail. The case at bar does not appear to me to be such a case. It has not been suggested that the applicant could have obtained any relief from a bargain to pay interest at 7 per cent. on the amount actually advanced to him. It is of the items other than interest making up the 'cost of the loan' that complaint is made. . . ."

The judgment of Martland and Ritchie JJ., dissenting, was delivered by

MARTLAND J.: . . . it is the contention of the appellant, the Attorney-General for Ontario, supported by the intervenant, the Attorney-General of Quebec, that this legislation is within the jurisdiction of the Province to enact, under subss. 13 and 16 of s. 92 of the *British North America Act*, as relating to Property and Civil Rights in the Province and to Matters of a merely local or private Nature in the Province.

Whether or not this contention could be maintained successfully, in the absence of legislation by the Parliament of Canada in the same field, it is unnecessary for me to consider, since I have reached the conclusion that the provisions of the Act under consideration come into conflict directly with the provisions of s. 2 of the *Interest Act*, R.S.C. 1952, c. 156, which provides as follows:

> 2. Except as otherwise provided by this or by any other Act of the Parliament of Canada, any person may stipulate for, allow and exact, on any contract or agreement whatsoever, any rate of interest or discount that is agreed upon.

That the validity of the provisions of the *Interest Act*, under s. 91(19) of the *British North America Act*, is unquestionable was stated by Viscount Caldecote,

L.C. in *Board of Trustees of the Lethbridge Northern Irrigation District v. Independent Order of Foresters*, [1940] A.C. 513 at 531. Section 2 of that Act, above quoted, provides that, except as provided by that Act or any other Act of the Parliament of Canada, a person may not only stipulate for any rate of interest or discount that is agreed upon, but may exact the same. Parliament has, therefore, given to a creditor, who has agreed with his debtor upon a rate of interest or discount, the legal right to demand and to enforce payment of the same. . . .

The power of the Court to act under [the Ontario] Act arises only if it has found that the cost of the loan is excessive. It is true that it must also find the transaction to be harsh and unconscionable, but it may happen, as it did in the present case, that the judge who hears the case decides that the transaction is harsh and unconscionable because of the excessive cost of the loan. The result is that the very Court to which a creditor must resort in order to enforce payment of the interest or discount which the Interest Act says he may exact is, by the Provincial legislation, empowered to decide whether that interest or discount is, in all the circumstances, excessive. Furthermore, if that Court decides that it is excessive and that the transaction is harsh and unconscionable, it may relieve the debtor of the obligation of paying that portion of his obligation which it considers to be excessive, and thus is in a position to relieve him from the payment of an obligation which the Parliament of Canada has stated the creditor is entitled to exact from him.

In these circumstances there is a direct conflict between the two statutes, and, that being so, the legislation of the Canadian Parliament, validly enacted, must prevail. . . .

In my opinion, therefore, the legislation in question is *ultra vires* of the Ontario Legislature . . .

*Appeal allowed.*

### Note

The *Saskatchewan Farm Security Act* case and the *Barfried* case represent the dilemmas for provincial legislatures arising from the federal interest power. Can the two cases stand together? The problem raised by these cases was adumbrated in the early decision of *Lynch v. Canada North-West Land Co.* (1891), 19 S.C.R. 204, where the Supreme Court sustained a provincial statute providing, *inter alia*, that if municipal taxes were paid after a stipulated date, 10 per cent of the amount of the tax was to be paid in addition. After stating that the federal power in relation to interest encompassed contractual interest, Ritchie C.J. said, with reference to the 10 per cent penalty provision, that "had it been specifically named as interest I am of opinion that it was an incident to the right of taxation vested in the municipal authority, and though more than the rate allowed by the Dominion statute in matters of contract, in no way in conflict with the authority secured to the Dominion Parliament over interest by the British North America Act, but must be read consistently with that as within the power given to the local legislature under its power to deal with municipal institutions. . . ."

A different kind of case is *Lethbridge Northern Irrigation District Trustees v. I.O.F. and A.-G. Can; R. v. I.O.F. and A.-G. Can.*, [1940] A.C. 513, where provincial legislation which simply halved the interest payable on provincial debentures and provincially guaranteed debentures was held *ultra vires*. The Court rejected an argument that the legislation respecting the provincial debentures was supportable under section 92(3) of the *Constitution Act, 1867* respecting "the borrowing of money on the sole credit of the Province". Would it have made any difference in this case if the legislation had provided for compulsory refunding and a lower rate of interest as part of the refinancing programme?

The *Lethbridge* case reasserted that federal competence in relation to interest covered contractual interest and, rejecting an argument that it was limited to usurious interest, the Court stated that the Dominion "might very well include in an Act dealing generally with the subject of interest provisions to prevent harsh transactions". *Quaere*, in view of the *Barfried* case, *supra*, is there room for the concurrent operation of the *Small Loans Act*, R.S.C. 1970, c. S-11, section 2 (raising the limit of its application to $1,500) which defines "cost of a loan" in terms similar to those in the Ontario *Unconscionable Transactions Relief Act*, and stipulates the maximum that may be charged by a money-lender on pain of a summary conviction penalty? In *R. v. Exchange Realty Co.* (1963), 45 W.W.R. 346 (Man. C.A.), the Act was held to be valid federal legislation in relation to interest and to have paramount effect when it was challenged by an unlicensed money-lender who refused to permit inspection of his books under section 9 which provides for such inspection for assurance of compliance with the Act.

A practice of "buying" tax refunds at a discount has developed. Clearly the rate of the discount taken determines the cost of the money to the taxpayer of receiving his discount immediately rather than in the future. Can a province limit the discount rate that can be demanded from a taxpayer when buying tax refunds? See section 37 of the *Consumer Protection Act*, R.S.B.C. 1979, c. 65 [am. 1980, c. 6, s. 17] and *Re Hanson and Harbour Tax Services Ltd. (No. 2)* (1978), 87 D.L.R. (3d) 96 (B.C.S.C.) upholding the provincial legislation as being regulation of the specific contract between vendor and purchaser. (See also the *Tax Rebate Discounting Act*, S.C. 1977-78, c. 25.)


# TOMELL INVESTMENTS LTD. v. EAST MARSTOCK LANDS LTD.

In the Supreme Court of Canada. [1978] 1 S.C.R. 974.

Laskin, C.J.C., Martland, Judson, Ritchie, Spence, Pigeon, Dickson and Beetz JJ. June 24, 1977.

Appeal from a judgment of the Ontario Court of Appeal affirming without reasons the judgment of Galligan J., 8 O.R. (2d) 396 holding that section 8(1) of the *Interest Act*, R.S.C. 1970, c. I-18 prevents Tomell Investments Ltd. from recovering a bonus of three months' interest stipulated to be payable on default of payment in a mortgage deed.

Section 8 of the *Interest Act* (Can.) reads as follows:

8(1) No fine or penalty or rate of interest shall be stipulated for, taken, reserved or exacted on any arrears of principal or interest secured by mortgage of real estate, that has the effect of increasing the charge on any such arrears beyond the rate of interest payable on principal money not in arrears.

(2) Nothing in this section has the effect of prohibiting a contract for the payment of interest on arrears of interest or principal at any rate not greater than the rate payable on principal money not in arrears.

The judgment of Laskin C.J.C. and Martland J. was delivered by

LASKIN C.J.C.: —

The central question raised by the constitutional attack on s. 8 of the *Interest Act*, R.S.C. 1970, c. I-18, is ascertainment of its pith and substance or, for convenience of expression, its focus. I agree with my brother Pigeon that it focuses on the maximum charge that can be exacted from a debtor on arrears of principal or interest under a land mortgage by limiting it to the rate of interest payable on principal not in arrears. A charge, whether called or found to be a fine or penalty or rate of interest, which exceeds this limit is precluded. In my opinion, s. 8 is valid legislation in relation to interest.

Parliament's undoubted power to fix or limit rates of interest under any types of contracts or transactions extends to interest on arrears as well as to interest on principal payments as they fall due. Parliament is, in my view, entitled to require creditors to abstain from making or exacting a charge on arrears that goes beyond the rate of interest fixed for principal not in arrears and, in that respect, to prevent them from escaping the stricture through a designation of the charge as a fine or a penalty. This is an assertion of the interest power *simpliciter*, and, as in *A.-G. Can. v. Nykorak*, [1962] S.C.R. 331, it is unnecessary to invoke any doctrine of ancillary power.

I would dispose of the appeal as proposed by my brother Pigeon.

The judgment of Judson, Ritchie, Spence, Pigeon, Dickson and Beetz JJ. was delivered by

PIGEON J.: . . .

At the hearing we were informed by counsel for Tomell Investments that Galligan's judgment had been rendered without any mention of the judgment of this court in *Les Immeubles Fournier Inc. v. Construction St. Hilaire Ltée*, [1975] 2 S.C.R. 2, because it was not known to the parties, not being yet reported. However, it was mentioned at the hearing in the Court of Appeal.

It does not appear to me that counsel for Tomell Investments has made a case for reconsidering this recent decision of the Full Court on the construction of the statute. However, the constitutional issue having been left open, because it was not raised, must now be dealt with.

The argument made by the appellant and the intervenors supporting its position rests mainly on the judgment of this Court in *A.-G. Ont. v. Barfried Enterprises Ltd.*, [1963] S.C.R. 570. The question was the validity of the *Unconscionable Transactions Relief Act*, R.S.O. 1960, c. 410. The Ontario Court of Appeal dealing with a mortgage which included a big bonus had set aside, on the basis that the Act was unconstitutional, the judgment at trial granting relief to the borrower, ([1962] O.R. 1103). For the majority in this Court, Judson J., said (at p. 576 S.C.R.):

Schroeder, J.A., cited *Singer v. Goldhar* (1924), 55 O.L.R. 267 [(C.A.)], as defining interest in wide terms. In *Singer v. Goldhar* there was no provision for interest in the mortgage but there was a very big bonus. The Court of Appeal held that this infringed s. 6 of the *Interest Act*, the bonus being the same thing as interest. But in *Asconi Building Corp. and Vermette v. Vocisano*, [1947]S.C.R. 358 at 365, Kerwin, J., pointed out that *London Loan & Savings Co. v. Meagher*, [1930]S.C.R. 378, had overruled *Singer v. Goldhar*. It is now established that in considering s. 6 of the *Interest Act*, a bonus is not interest and the fact that interest may be payable on a total sum which includes a bonus does not involve an infringement of s. 6 of the Act. This was recognized in all the reasons delivered in the *Asconi* case. It was in this context that the wide definition of interest above referred to was used in the *Saskatchewan Reference* case. The Court held that the subject-matter of the legislation was interest and that to call it a reduction of principal did not change its character.

There is therefore, error in the judgment of Schroeder, J.A., in following *Singer v. Goldhar* in holding that interest in the wide sense includes bonus instead of following the subsequent cases which overrule it.

It must be noted that the *Unconscionable Transactions Relief Act* was found not to be in conflict with the *Interest Act* because s. 6 was not construed as including in "interest" a charge such as a bonus: this would have made "interest" synonymous with "cost of the loan". Section 6 of the *Interest Act* then as now read:

6. Whenever any principal money or interest secured by mortgage of real estate is, by the mortgage, made payable on the sinking fund plan, or on any plan under which the payments of principal money and interest are blended, or on any plan that involves an allowance of interest on stipulated repayments, no interest whatever shall be chargeable, payable or recoverable, on any part of the principal money advanced, unless the mortgage contains a statement showing the amount of such principal money and the rate of interest chargeable thereon, calculated yearly or half-yearly, not in advance.

In *Singer v. Goldhar* (1924), 55 O.L.R. 267 at 271, Masten, J.A., had said, rendering the judgment of the Court of Appeal:

For these reasons, I think we must hold that, notwithstanding the form of the mortgage, the amount actually advanced, $3,500, is the "principal"; that the additional amount which the defendant agreed to pay beyond the $3,500 advanced is in truth and in fact interest; and that in the repayment clause the principal and interest are blended.

As to this, Rand J., had said in *Asconi Building Corp. and Vermette v. Vocisano*, [1947] S.C.R. 358 at 368-9:

No doubt under the usury Acts, the form which the loan or the consideration for interest might take played little part in the question of the real nature of the bargain. An agreement providing for interest at the maximum rate in advance was illegal *ab initio* regardless of its form; what the Court was concerned to ascertain was the actual loan and the consideration for its use. In the language of Lord Mansfield in *Floyer v. Edwards* (1774), 1 Cowp. 112 at pp. 114-5, 98 E.R. 995 at p. 996: "And where the real truth is a loan of money, the wit of man cannot find a shift to take it out of the statute. If the substance is a loan of money, nothing will protect the taking more than 5 per cent."

. . . . .

Now section 6 of the *Interest Act* is not designed to protect a borrower against agreeing to pay any particular rate or amount of interest; in fact, under s. 2 of the Act there is complete freedom of action in a contract for interest. The object of s. 6 is something quite different. It is that where repayment under a mortgage involves, in the forms mentioned, an increment of interest, it shall be made clear in the mortgage what the amount of the principal and the rate of interest are. Obviously no device to defeat the purpose could be tolerated; but where the transaction is not either on its face or by the real intention of the parties within the section and the borrower is fully aware both of the actual amount of interest which he is paying, and the rate and principal with reference to which that calculation is made, the purpose of the section suffers no infringement.

From all this it is apparent that the judgment in *Barfried Enterprises* was predicated on the view that s. 6 of the *Interest Act* deals only with "interest" properly so-called, that is a charge for use of money accruing day by day. This obviously implied the same construction of "interest" in s. 2:

> 2. Except as otherwise provided by this or by any other Act of the Parliament of Canada, any person may stipulate for, allow and exact, on any contract or agreement whatever, any rate of interest or discount that is agreed upon.

In *Immeubles Fournier* the respondent in this Court, plaintiff in the original action, had claimed as liquidated damages stipulated in the mortgage contract a penalty of 15% of the principal amount. The Court of Appeal overruling the trial Judge had found the penalty payable under the terms of the contract, by virtue of the debtor's default and the creditor's action in instituting the proceedings. The question in this Court was whether the recovery of the penalty was barred by s. 8 of the *Interest Act* reading:

> 8(1) No fine or penalty or rate of interest shall be stipulated for, taken, reserved or exacted on any arrears of principal or interest secured by mortgage of real estate, that has the effect of increasing the charge on any such arrears beyond the rate of interest payable on principal money not in arrears.
> (2) Nothing in this section has the effect of prohibiting a contract for the payment of interest on arrears of interest or principal at any rate not greater than the rate payable on principal money not in arrears.

As no constitutional question was raised by the respondent, what this Court had to decide in *Immeubles Fournier* was whether this provision could somehow be read so as to apply to a penalty of a fixed percentage which did not accrue day by day and therefore was not interest. In essence, respondents' submission was that the application of s. 8 should be limited to "interest" properly so-called, that is, a charge accruing day by day. It was urged that in *Asconi* it had been held that the stipulation of a fixed bonus did not make the contract a "plan under which the payments of principal money and *interest* are blended" within the meaning of s. 6. Thus, in that section, "interest" was held not to include a bonus, as previously mentioned.

However, s. 8 is differently worded, it refers to a "fine or penalty or rate of interest . . . that has the effect of increasing the *charge*". In the view of the majority this wording was clearly applicable to any kind of penalty and could not be restricted to a charge accruing day by day. This means, of course, that s. 8 was construed as aiming at something that is not strictly "interest". That such construction might put in doubt the constitutional validity of the enactment was not overlooked, but the majority considered that this difficulty was unavoidable. They saw no escape from the literal construction of the enactment that was clearly applicable, in their view, to any *charge* on "arrears beyond the rate of interest payable on principal money not in arrears".

In my opinion, s. 8 as construed in *Immeubles Fournier*, really deals only with interest. The object of the provision is to define what interest may be charged on "arrears of principal or interest secured by mortgage on real estate". Subsection (2) should, I think, be considered as stating the governing principle, that is, that a stipulation of interest on interest is permissible provided it is at a "rate not greater than the rate payable on principal money not in arrears". The object of s-s. (1) is to invalidate any stipulation of a "charge" beyond such interest. In order to hold that Parliament cannot enact such a provision under the *British North America Act, 1867*, s. 91, head 19, "Interest", it seems to me that one has to say that Parliament is not thereby authorized to prescribe a maximum rate. Any legislation fixing a maximum rate of interest is futile if it does not, expressly or impliedly, prohibit any stipulation that would have the effect of increasing the charge beyond the rate of interest allowed. . . . .

With respect for those who have expressed a contrary opinion in *Immeubles Fournier*, it does not appear to me that the conclusion reached in *Barfried Enterprises* implies a view of the extent of federal power over interest which excludes from its scope enactments such as s. 8 of the *Interest Act*. All that was decided was that the federal jurisdiction over interest does not exclude all provincial jurisdiction over contracts involving the payment of interest so as to invalidate provincial laws authorizing the Courts to grant relief from such contracts, when they are adjudged to be harsh and unconscionable. This conclusion was based on the view that the subject of interest assigned to the federal Parliament was not to be equated with the cost of money, in other words with interest in the widest sense.

This view of the limited scope of this federal power is consonant with the view taken in earlier cases that federal jurisdiction over interest does not extend to interest on all kinds of debts or claims, but only on contractual obligations. For instance, it was held in *Lynch v. Canada North-West Land Co.* (1891), 19 S.C.R. 204, that the federal jurisdiction does not apply to interest on taxes levied under provincial legislation. It seems clear the same would have to be said of interest on provincial government bonds. In fact, it was held that provincial jurisdiction over municipal corporations would authorize a reorganization of defaulting municipalities involving reduced interest on their obligations (*Ladore v. Bennett*, [1939] A.C. 468) although it would not allow a mere reduction of the rate of interest payable on municipal bonds (*Lethbridge Northern Irrigation District v. Independent Order of Foresters*, [1940] A.C. 513).

In my view, the present case calls for the application of the doctrine of ancillary power and its corollary that of the unoccupied field (Lord Tomlin's third and fourth propositions in the *Fish Canneries* case, *Re Fisheries Act, 1914; A.-G. Can. v. A.-G. B.C.*, [1930] A.C. 111 at 118). Although in principle the absention by the federal Parliament to exercise its exclusive legislative power does not enable the provincial Legislatures to enact legislation on the subject, this is true only of what may be called the federal primary power. With respect to matters which are not strictly within such primary power but can be dealt with ancillarily, provincial jurisdiction over property and civil rights and over matters of a local nature remains unimpaired until such time as the field is occupied. In the *Voluntary Assignments* case, *A.-G. Ont. v. A.-G. Can.*, [1894] A.C. 189, a very limited scope was given to the federal primary power over bankruptcy and insolvency. However, a very wide ancillary jurisdiction was recognizd in *Royal Bank of Canada v. Larue*, [1926] S.C.R. 218 (*sub nom. A.-G. Que. v. Larue*), [1928] A.C. 187; in *Reference re Companies' Creditors Arrangement Act*, [1934] S.C.R. 659, and in *Reference re Farmers' Creditors Arrangement Act*, [1936] S.C.R. 384; affirmed [1937] A.C. 391. Similarly, in *A.-G. Que. v. A.-G. Can.*, [1945] S.C.R. 600, this Court recognized the validity of federal legislation dealing with costs in criminal prosecutions brought in provincial Courts, though it refused to accept that criminal law or criminal procedure in the strict sense were involved.

We heard submissions concerning s. 10 of the *Interest Act* (the right of a borrower after five years to tender the capital with three months' further interest in lieu of notice) and I did also give consideration to the *Small Loans Act*, S.C. 1939, c. 23, now R.S.C. 1970, c. S-11, and its preamble. In the circumstances, it appears to me preferable to make no observations with respect to those legislative provisions which are not presently at issue.

In my opinion, s. 8 of the *Interest Act* is valid federal legislation in respect of interest because, although it does not deal exclusively with interest in the strict sense of a charge accruing day by day, it is, in so far as it deals with other charges, a valid exercise of ancillary power designed to make effective the intention that the effective rate of interest over arrears of principle or interest should never be greater than the rate payable on principal money not in arrears.

I would dismiss the appeal with costs but there should be no costs to or against the intervenants.

[Note that Pigeon J. does not refer to *A. G. Can. v. Nykorak*, [1962] S.C.R. 331, the case referred to by Laskin C.J.C., in his discussion of the so-called "ancillary jurisdiction". Note also that none of the cases which he refers to in that connection postdate *Nykorak*. What is the status of the "ancillary" or "necessarily incidental" doctrine after *Tomell?* See "Note on the 'Ancillary' and 'Necessarily Incidental' Doctrines" at Chapter 4, *supra*.]

## 3. Bankruptcy, Insolvency and Debt Adjustment

## A.-G. B.C. v. A.-G. CAN.

In the Privy Council. [1937] A.C. 391.

Lord Atkin, Lord Thankerton, Lord Macmillan, Lord Wright M.R., and Sir Sidney Rowlatt, Jan. 28, 1937.

Appeal by special leave from a judgment of the Supreme Court of Canada, [1936] S.C.R. 384, on a reference to determine the validity of the *Farmers' Creditors Arrangement Act*, S.C. 1934, c. 53, amended 1935, c. 20. The Supreme Court, Cannon J. dissenting, held that the Act was valid. Counsel for appellants argued in part as follows: The effect of the Act has been upheld as bankruptcy legislation coming under head 21 of s. 91 of the *British North America Act, 1867* — "Bankruptcy and Insolvency." The submission of all the Provinces is the same, namely, that the Act is not in its pith and substance bankruptcy, but is colourable legislation. If it is bankruptcy legislation, then it involves the right to interfere incidentally with property and civil rights in the Province. If, on the other hand, it is not bankruptcy legislation as such, but is only colourable, then the matter undoubtedly comes within property and civil rights in the Province. The fundamental characteristic of bankruptcy and insolvency legislation is that it is designed in the interests of creditors as a class. It is to provide for the rateable distribution of the assets of the debtor among his creditors whether or not the debtor is willing. The present Act, on the contrary, has none of the characteristics of bankruptcy and insolvency legislation for the following reasons: (a) It is designed for the purpose of keeping the farmer on his farm, and not to distribute his assets. (b) It is not bankruptcy but the prevention of bankruptcy. (c) The proceedings of the Act are not in course of bankruptcy proceedings, but before such proceedings. (d) An act of bankruptcy is not the basis of the proceedings but follows only thereafter in case of a failure to carry out a compromise under the Act. (e) The proposal of "compromise" so-called is not an ancillary of bankruptcy proceedings, but antecedent to and independent thereof. (f) The essential proposal for a compromise is in its features not a voluntary arrangement but a compulsory arrangement imposed by a Board on the creditors. (g) Such a scheme is made with a view not of the creditors' welfare as a class, or to distribution among them. It is made to defeat distribution. It may be without regard to their interests and solely in the interests of the debtor and with a view to protecting the value of the farm. (h) The scheme is not for the protection of the creditors, but at their expense. (i) It deals not with the assets of the debtor for the benefit of the creditors, but with the assets of the creditors for the benefit of the debtor. (j) The references in the Act to the *Dominion Bankruptcy Act* are colourable and establish no substantial connection between the two enactments. (k) The scheme treats a subject-matter which in part in some aspects may be ancillary to bankruptcy and insolvency legislation as itself the principal or primary subject-matter of legislation. (l) It has no general relation to bankruptcy and insolvency but is special legislation relative to farmers, and is or may be restricted to certain Provinces. . . . The Act sets up a new scheme which in its purpose is not to administer the farmer's property as the assets of his creditors, but to administer it in defiance of that.

[Citation of Authorities.] If those authorities, which show that in all schemes of bankruptcy the basis of the scheme is the distribution of the assets of the debtor among the creditors, are sound, the present Act came in as an independent Act with its own recital for the purpose not to distribute the assets among creditors, but to prevent that in order to promote production in Canada by moneys taken from the secured creditors and given for the benefit of the farmer. . . . The Dominion of Canada does not acquire jurisdiction in regard to property and civil rights of the farmers merely because they are unable to pay their obligations as they arise: the Dominion can only deal with the farmer in that connection in the limited field of bankruptcy. It is not claimed that legislation must conform to what was bankruptcy at federation: it is not contended that matters not strictly bankruptcy legislation may not be included as ancillary or necessarily incidental. Legislation which is the antithesis of bankruptcy, however, such as the present, cannot be ancillary, and still remains within the field of the Province. There is no severable clause in the Act and the legislation is bad *in toto*.

Counsel for the Dominion were not called upon.

LORD THANKERTON: . . . The appellant raises no question as to s. 17 of the Act, which relates to interest, and falls under head 19 of s. 91 of the *British North America Act of 1867*, but he maintains that the rest of the Act does not truly form legislation relating to "bankruptcy and insolvency," but is an invasion of the sphere of the Provincial Legislatures in relation to "property and civil rights in the Province" or "matters of a merely local or private nature in the Province," which is secured to them by heads 13 and 16 of s. 92 of the *British North America Act*.

The appellant submitted that the fundamental characteristic of legislation in relation to bankruptcy and insolvency is that it is conceived in the interests of the creditors as a class, and provides for distribution of the debtor's assets among them, and he maintained that the Act here in question is not only lacking in such a characteristic, but is inconsistent therewith, and he gave twelve reasons which may be compendiously stated as follows: The Act is mainly designed to keep the debtor farmer on the land at the expense of his creditors; it deals with a stage prior to bankruptcy and insolvency, and is designed to prevent bankruptcy by means of a composition which is compulsory on creditors for the benefit of the debtor; the references to bankruptcy are merely ancillary to the main design; and the Act has no general relation to bankruptcy and insolvency, as it refers to farmers only, and may refer to certain Provinces only.

The long title of the Act of 1934 is "An Act to facilitate compromises and arrangements between farmers and their creditors." The relevant sections of the Act of 1934, as amended by the Act of 1935, may now be referred to. [His Lordship then set out various provisions of the Act governing compositions and continued:]

In a general sense, insolvency means inability to meet one's debts or obligations; in a technical sense, it means the condition or standard of inability to meet debts or obligations, upon the occurrence of which the statutory law enables a creditor to intervene, with the assistance of a Court, to stop individual action by creditors and to secure administration of the debtor's assets in the general interest of creditors; the law also generally allows the debtor to apply for the same administration. The justification for such proceeding by a creditor generally consists in an act of bankruptcy by the debtor, the conditions of which are defined and prescribed by the statute law. In a normal community it is certain that these conditions will require reconsideration from time to time. Their Lordships are unable to hold that the statutory conditions of insolvency which enabled a creditor or the debtor to invoke the aid of the bankruptcy laws, or the classes to which these laws applied, were intended to be stereotyped under head 21 of s. 91 of the *British North America Act* so as to confine the jurisdiction of the Parliament of Canada to the legislative provisions then existing as regards these matters.

Further, it cannot be maintained that legislative provision as to compositions, by which bankruptcy is avoided, but which assumes insolvency, is not properly within the sphere of bankruptcy legislation. (*In re Companies' Creditors Arrangement Act*, [1934] S.C.R. 659.)

It will be seen from the sections above quoted that the Act here in question relates only to a farmer who is unable to meet his liabilities as they become due, and enables him to make a proposal for a composition, extension of time or scheme of arrangement either before or after an assignment has been made, for which a precedent existed in the *Canadian Bankruptcy Act of 1919*. As defined in s. 2, an assignment means an assignment made under the *Bankruptcy Act* by a farmer. If the creditors fail to approve of the farmer's proposal, the Board of Review, on written request of a creditor or the debtor, is to endeavour to formulate "an acceptable proposal" for submission to the creditors and the debtor; if the creditors or the debtor decline to approve the Board's proposal, the Board may nevertheless confirm their proposal, and it is to bind the creditors and the debtor.

Subject to the contention by the appellants, now to be dealt with, their Lordships are of opinion that these provisions fall within head 21 of s. 91 of the *British North America Act.*

The appellant maintains that the real object of these provisions is to keep the farmers on the land for the benefit of agricultural production, and that this object is to be attained by the operations of the Board of Review, who have power to sacrifice the interests of the creditors for the benefit of the debtor farmer; he further maintains that under s. 7 the secured creditor may be deprived of that which is his property. To deal first with the last contention, their Lordships are clearly of opinion that s. 7 does not enable any creditor to be deprived of his security, but does enable the proposal for composition to provide for the reduction of the debt itself, or the extension of time for its payment, which is a familiar feature of compositions.

The appellant laid stress on the provisions of sub-s. 8 of s. 12, but that does not appear to their Lordships to be an illegitimate or unusual element to be taken into account in the consideration of composition schemes, and, indeed, the retention of the business under the management of the debtor may well be a consideration in the interests of the creditors as well as of the debtor. Its fair application appears to be well secured by the provisions of sub-ss. 3, 4 and 9. A judicial Chief Commissioner is provided for under sub-s. 3; under sub-s. 4 the Board's proposal is to be designed as an acceptable one to both parties, and this element is emphasized by sub-s. 9. Their Lordships are unable to accept the contention that the Act is not genuine legislation relating to bankruptcy and insolvency. . . .

*Appeal dismissed.*

[In *In re Companies' Creditors Arrangement Act*, [1934] S.C.R. 659, Duff C.J., in upholding the validity of the federal statute, declared that "legislation in respect of compositions and arrangements is a natural and ordinary component of a system of bankruptcy and insolvency law"; and further: "Matters normally constituting part of a bankruptcy scheme but not in their essence matters of bankruptcy and insolvency may, of course, from another point of view and in another aspect be dealt with by a provincial legislature; but when treated as matters pertaining to bankruptcy and insolvency, they clearly fall within the legislative authority of the Dominion."

Provincial legislative power in relation to voluntary assignments was recognized in *A.G. Ont. v. A.G. Can.*, [1894] A.C. 189 reproduced above at Chapter 4. Dominion legislation would, of course, prevail in case of conflict. See also *L'Union St. Jacques de Montreal v. Belisle* (1874), L.R. 6 P.C. 31; *Cushing v. Dupuy* (1880), 5 App. Cas. 409 (P.C.).

"The exclusive authority . . . given to the Dominion Parliament to deal with all matters arising within the domain of bankruptcy and insolvency enables that Parliament to determine by legislation the relative priorities of creditors under a bankruptcy or an authorized assignment": *A.-G. Que. and Royal Bank v. Larue and A.-G. Can.*, [1928] A.C. 187. The Dominion may, hence, by its legislation limit or take away the priority or immunity of the Crown in right of a province (see, for example, *Re Clemenshaw; W.C.B. v. Can. Credit Men's Trust Assn.* (1962), 38 W.W.R. 426 (B.C.S.C.)), but unless it does so expressly the Crown in right of a province may assert its common law priority or immunity: *In re Silver Bros. Ltd.; A.-G. Que. v. A.-G. Can.*, [1932] A.C. 514; *Re Navilla Ice Cream Co.*, [1934] O.R. 772 (S.C.). Federal power embraces not only the order of priorities on a bankruptcy but also the extent: see *Re Gingras Automobile Ltée; Produits de Caoutchouc Marquis Inc. v. Trottier*, [1962] S.C.R. 676. C.f. *Malczewski v. Sansai Securities Ltd.* (1974), 49 D.L.R. (3d) 629 (B.C.S.C.) upholding as a condition of obtaining a licence, the requirement of contribution to a trust fund held for the purpose of satisfying certain claims against security broker dealers who might become bankrupt or insolvent.

Where a provincially-incorporated insurance company has become insolvent and a winding-up order has been made against it under a federal statute, may provincial legislation be applied to the distribution of the proceeds of convertible securities deposited by it as a condition of provincial licensing? If the federal Act prescribes a different order of distribution will it prevail? See *Re Wentworth Insurance Co.*, [1968] 2 O.R. 416 (C.A.), affirmed [1969] S.C.R. 779 (*sub nom. A.-G. Ont. v. Wentworth Insurance Co.*).]

# REFERENCE RE ALBERTA DEBT ADJUSTMENT ACT

In the Supreme Court of Canada. [1942] S.C.R. 31.

Duff C.J., Rinfret, Crocket, Davis, Kerwin, Hudson, and Taschereau JJ.
Dec. 2, 1941.

A provincial statute, the *Debt Adjustment Act*, S.A. 1937, c. 9, as amended provided, *inter alia*, that no action could be brought against a "resident debtor" without a permit from the Debt Adjustment Board. As Duff C.J. described it, the Act converted the owner's legal right to enforce his claim into one which was conditional upon the Board's issuing a permit. Other provisions in the statute empowered the Board to negotiate agreements for the adjustment of resident debtors' debts, and all agreements made through the agency of the Board were binding. The Board was to have extensive powers of inquiry, and was to endeavour to ensure that the agreement, if one was reached, reduced the amount owing to one which the resident debtor was capable of paying.

The judgment of Duff C.J.C. and Rinfret, Davis, Kerwin, Hudson and Taschereau JJ. was delivered by

DUFF C.J.C.: . . .
There is another class of cases that I have just alluded to, the consideration of which leaves it, I think, very clear that in attempting to establish an authority of this character a provincial legislature is exceeding its authority. Section 91 of the *British North America Act* gives to the Parliament of Canada exclusive control over certain types of businesses and undertakings. I particularly refer to two classes of business only. The first of these, that of banks, perhaps illustrates the point most strikingly. The lending of money is a principal part of the business of any bank. A debt arising from a loan by a bank to a customer will, speaking generally, fall within section 8(1)(a), and the bank's right to enforce repayment is by the enactment conditioned upon the existence of a permit. It is in the power of the Board to refuse to permit in all such cases, or in the case of any particular debt. This power of selection seems to involve a considerable power of regulation of the business of the banks. It is, I think, incompetent to the legislature to establish any such authority. I think the case of banking is, perhaps, from this point of view, the most striking case, although the application of the authority of the Board to companies engaged in operating Dominion undertakings, such as Dominion railway companies and companies engaged in operating lines of ocean shipping, might well exceed the ambit of provincial authority.

What I have said is sufficient, in my opinion, to show that subsection (1)(a) of section 8 is *ultra vires*. I assume that debts and liquidated demands falling entirely (that is to say, exclusively) under the regulative authority of the province, as being "civil rights within the province," could be dealt with by a province by an enactment having the characteristics of section 8(1)(a), but limited to such debts and demands. It is not necesary to decide it, but I assume that to be so. I do not think that section 8(1)(a) can properly be construed as limited in its application to such debts and demands and is, therefore, I think, entirely destitute of effect.

Subsection 1(b) of section 8 presents a different question, but it is, in my opinion, *ultra vires* by reason of considerations of much the same character. It is no answer to say that the authority extends to all judgments; because the Board can arbitrarily refuse to grant a permit in any particular case. The Board is authorized to refuse a permit for a writ of execution where the debt sued upon is one which it has no power to regulate and to do so for any reason which to it may appear sufficient; and, of course, to discriminate in this respect between debts which it has power to regulate and debts in respect of which it has no such power.

We are not required to consider the authority of a provincial legislature to restrict the jurisdiction of the provincial Courts to giving declaratory judgments and to deprive them of the power to grant any consequential relief. This legislation affects the jurisdiction of the provincial Courts, but the pith and substance of it is to establish a provincial authority which is empowered to exercise the discriminatory control just mentioned. While in form this is legislation in relation to remedy and procedure, in substance this provision which attempts to regulate the remedial incidents of the right in this manner must, when it is read in light of the context in which it stands in this section 8(1), be regarded as a step in a design to regulate the right itself.

There is a class of creditors occupying a special position which must be considered. I refer to companies incorporated by the Dominion. It is settled that in the case of companies with objects other than provincial objects, the exclusive power to legislative in relation to incorporation is vested in Parliament, and that by the joint operation of the residuary power under section 91 of the *Confederation Act* and the power conferred upon Parliament in relation to the enumerated subject, the regulation of trade and commerce, this power extends to the status and powers of the company. True, where the business of the company is subject to provincial legislative regulation, the provincial legislature may legislate in such a manner as to affect the business of the company by laws of general application in relation to the kind of business in which the company engages in the province; but the provisions of this statute giving to the Board the authority to interfere with the affairs of creditors in the manner set forth in section 8 would not appear to be a general law in this sense.

A company, for example, incorporated by the Dominion with authority to carry on the business of lending money upon various kinds of security in the province, may find itself in a position, under the operation of subsections 1(a) and (b) of section 8, in which it and other Dominion companies are precluded from enforcing their securities in the usual way. In my view, such legislation is not competent and, accordingly, paragraphs (c), (d), (e) and (f) would appear to be incompetent, as well as paragraphs (a) and (b).

As regards interest, subsection (1) of section 8 is plainly repugnant to section 2 of the *Interest Act*. In truth, the scope of subsection (1) of section 8 is indicated by paragraph (g) thereof and by section 41 which withdraws from the operation of the

Act debts owing to The Canadian Farm Loan Board or to the Soldiers' Settlement Board and proceedings for enforcing the payment of any such debts. I think we must conclude that subsection (1) must be treated as a whole, that is to say, that it is valid or invalid as a whole, and for the reasons I have given it is, I think, invalid. The provisions of subsection (3) limiting the application of section 8 in the manner there mentioned do not, it appears to me, affect the force of what has been said. The whole of section 8 is *ultra vires*.

As to section 26, the matters dealt with by this enactment, in my opinion, are so related to the subject-matter of *The Farmers' Creditors Arrangement Act* as to be withdrawn from provincial jurisdiction by force of the last paragraph of section 91.

There remains the contention of the Attorney-General of Canada that the statute as a whole constitutes an attempt to legislate in relation to bankruptcy and insolvency. I have very carefully considered this contention and the first thing that strikes one is that the effect of section 8(1) is, as regards debts where the creditor and debtor reside in the province and the contract has been made in the province and the debt is payable in the province, that the creditor is deprived of his right to present a bankruptcy petition. As appears from what has already been said, section 8(1) does not merely suspend the remedy — it takes away the remedy given by law and substitutes therefor a remedy dependent upon the arbitrary consent of the Board, or the arbitrary determination of a jury. As I have already said, this, in my opinion, strikes at the debt itself and I do not think that in any Court governed by this legislation it could be successfully contended that in respect of an obligation to which the statute applies there is a "debt owing" to the creditor, within the meaning of section 4 of the *Bankruptcy Act*. Moreover, I find it impossible to escape the conclusion that Part III contemplates the use of the Board's powers under section 8(1) to enable it to secure compulsorily the consent of the parties to arrangements proposed by it for composition and settlement. Bankruptcy is not mentioned, but normally the powers and duties of the Board under Part III will come into operation when a state of insolvency exists. It is not too much to say that it is for the purpose of dealing with the affairs of debtors who are pressed and unable to pay their debts as they fall due that these powers and duties are created. Indeed the whole statute is conceived as a means of protecting embarrassed debtors who are residents of Alberta. Most people would agree that in this point of view the motives prompting the legislation may be laudable ones. But the legislature, in seeking to attain its object, seems to have entered upon a field not open to it. The statute, if valid, enables the Board (invested with exclusive possession of the key to the Courts) to employ its position and powers coercively in compelling the creditors of an insolvent debtor and the debtor himself to consent to a disposition of the resources of the debtor prescribed by the Board. In this way the statute seeks to empower the Board to impose upon the insolvent debtor and his creditors a settlement of his affairs, which the creditors must accept in satisfaction of their claims. I cannot escape the conclusion that the statute contemplates the use of the Board in this way. I think this is an attempt to invade the field reserved to the Dominion under Bankruptcy and Insolvency.

. . . .

*Act declared invalid.*

[Crocket J.'s dissent is omitted.]

*Note*

The judgment was affirmed by the Privy Council, (*sub nom. A.-G. Alta. v. A.-G. Can.*) [1943] A.C. 356, on the two grounds that "the Act as a whole constitutes a serious and substantial invasion of the exclusive legislative powers of the Parliament of Canada in relation to bankruptcy and insolvency, and, on the other hand, that it obstructs and interferes with the actual legislation of that Parliament on those matters". See Note (1942), 20 Can. Bar Rev. 343; Note (1943), 21 Can. Bar Rev. 310. See also, Bastedo, "Constitutional Limitations of Provincial Debt Adjustment Legislation" (1941), 6 Sask. Bar Rev. 1.

In *Reference re Legal Proceedings Suspension Act*, [1942] 2 W.W.R. 536, the Alberta Appellate Division, by a majority, held *ultra vires* a temporary enactment of the legislature which would have had the effect of keeping alive the then recently invalidated *Debt Adjustment Act, 1937*, pending a final decision on its validity by the Privy Council. In *Roy and A.-G. Alta. v. Plourde*, [1943] S.C.R. 262, where Alberta legislation extended the period of redemption in pending and prospective mortgage foreclosure and specific performance actions but excepted from the statute actions in which a permit was not required under the *Debt Adjustment Act* or in which a permit was obtained, the Supreme Court upheld the legislation by severing the excepting clause as having no effect by reason of the invalidity of the *Debt Adjustment Act*.

In the earlier case, *A.-G. Alta. and Winstanley v. Atlas Lumber Co.*, [1941] S.C.R. 87, the Supreme Court held that section 8(1)(a) of the Act could not validly apply to actions on bills of exchange and promissory notes, particularly because it was repugnant to section 74 of the *Bills of Exchange Act*, R.S.C. 1927, c. 16, in requiring a permit as a condition of suit. See Note (1940), 18 Can. Bar Rev. 725.

If provincial legislation requiring a permit to sue on a bill of exchange or promissory note is invalid, may a province validly enact a statute of limitations applicable to bills and notes? In any event, on what ground does general provincial limitations legislation apply to actions on bills and notes (as is the assumption: see, for example, *Weingarden v. Moss* (1955), 15 W.W.R. 481 (Man. C.A.)) when there is no referential federal enactment making such provincial legislation applicable? See *Dorfer v. Winchell*, [1941] 1 W.W.R. 541 (Alta. Dist. Ct.) and *A.G. Sask. v. Allen*, [1941] 3 W.W.R. 742, rev'd on other grounds [1942] 2 W.W.R. 239 (Sask. C.A.); Note (1942), 20 Can. Bar Rev. 60. Cf. Note (1945), 58 Harv. L. Rev. 738.

Provincial conditional sales legislation limits a conditional seller to his "lien" upon the chattel and to repossession and sale upon the buyer's default. Is this legislation effective against an assignee of the conditional seller so as to preclude such assignee from recovering for any deficiency where he is holder in due course of a promissory note given to the conditional seller? See *Traders Finance Corp. v. Casselman*, [1960] S.C.R. 242, aff'g (1958), 25 W.W.R. 289 (Man. C.A.), which rev'd (1957), 22 W.W.R. 625 (Man. Q.B.).

Provincial legislation, *e.g., The Gaming Act*, R.S.O. 1980, c. 183 declares that a bill or note given in connection with gaming is deemed to be given for an illegal consideration and that where any person who makes or draws or gives such a bill or note pays to any holder, endorsee or assignee money secured thereby the money is deemed to be paid on account of the person to whom the bill or note was originally given and to be a debt owing to the person who paid it and shall be recoverable by action. Is this legislation competent to a province? See *McGillis v. Sullivan*, [1947] O.R. 650 (C.A.), aff'd [1949] S.C.R. 201.

### Note on the Federal Insolvency Power and Provincial Moratorium Legislation

The decision in the *Alberta Debt Adjustment Act* case, *supra*, had significance for Manitoba and Saskatchewan as well as for Alberta because all three provinces had similar legislation. One immediate result was the promulgation by the federal government of Order-in-Council P.C. 3243 of April 20, 1943, applicable to the three Provinces and empowering the Courts, where mortgage actions and actions by vendors of land were brought against farmers, to order a stay, postpone payments and prescribe terms which would, during the war period, retain on the land efficient and industrious farmers of good faith; and the Courts were also charged, so far as possible and consistent with this purpose, to protect the interests of other persons in the land: see Note (1943), 21 Can. Bar Rev. 416. While the Order-in-Council was a war measure (and easily supportable on that ground) it raised the question, which recent cases have brought into sharper focus, whether a Province is precluded (in view of exclusive federal power in relation to insolvency as well as bankruptcy) from enacting not only compulsory debt adjustment legislation but general moratorium legislation.

Apart from the debt adjustment legislation invalidated by the Courts, other Provinces, *e.g.* Ontario and British Columbia, had enacted moratorium legislation in the early 1930's, applicable to mortgages and sales of land: see *Mortgagors' and Purchasers' Relief Act*, S.O. 1932, c. 49; *Mortgagors' and Purchasers' Relief Act*, S.B.C. 1934, c. 49. These statutes were envisaged as temporary and were re-enacted over successive periods until becoming spent in 1946 and 1949 respectively. Administration was confided to the Courts whose leave was required to enforce mortgages and sales of land where there was default of principal or interest (in British Columbia) or of principal only (in Ontario). In British Columbia provision was made for preliminary inquiry and report by the Court registrar in connection with an application for leave, and in Ontario a debtor was entitled to apply for relief by way of postponement of payments of interest, rent or taxes (apart from the protection afforded him where interest was paid up but principal only was in default).

The distinction between such legislation and the invalidated debt adjustment legislation lay in the administrative machinery in the latter for effecting a composition of debts through withholding a permit to sue. That the effect of Court control in the former type of legislation might be to persuade the parties to a voluntary composition was not, apparently, enough to taint it constitutionally, especially when regard was had to its restricted and temporary nature. Indeed, to borrow a phrase from the Privy Council's earliest decision on the federal bankruptcy and insolvency power, the British Columbia and Ontario relief legislation could be sustained because it did not provide for the administration of the estates of persons who were bankrupt or insolvent: see *L'Union St. Jacques v. Belisle* (1874), L.R. 6 C.P. 31. Although the *Voluntary Assignments* case, [1894] A.C. 189, which sustained provincial legislation respecting administration of estates under a voluntary assignment for benefit of creditors, may be regarded as doubtful authority to-day, moratorium legislation which involves postponement only, without accompanying provisions for enforcing a composition, is supportable on a provincial level; and additional support may be found in the analogy of a stay of proceedings under the rules of procedure of provincial courts.

Admittedly, the line is thin between effective provincial moratorium legislation (which would generally be operable where a condition of insolvency exists) and an invasion of the federal bankruptcy and insolvency power; and, no doubt, Parliament could competently enter the field. As Rand J. pointed out in *Canadian Bankers Association v. A.-G. Sask.*, [1956] S.C.R. 31, a Province cannot justify legislation in relation to bankruptcy or insolvency on the ground that the conditions aimed at by the legislation are of a local or private nature. Two other statements in his judgment bare the nature of the issue presented by provincial legislative concern for hard-pressed debtors: (1) "If the Province steps in and actively assumes the general protection of [an insolvent] debtor, by whatever means, it is acting in relation to insolvency, and assuming the function of Parliament; it is so far administering, coercively as to creditors, the affairs of insolvent debtors. In this it is frustrating the laws of the Dominion in relation to the same subject". (2) "That the Province may in certain circumstances and in proper aspects, enact moratorium legislation . . . may be accepted; its validity will depend upon the facts, circumstances and means adopted, determining its true character". In the same case Locke J. rationalized provincial debt legislation against federal power by declaring that "power to declare a moratorium for the relief of residents of a Province generally in some great emergency, such as existed in 1914 and in the days of the lengthy depression in the thirties is one thing, but power to intervene between insolvent debtors and their creditors irrespective of the reasons which have rendered the debtor unable to meet his liabilities, is something entirely different". The recession from earlier case law conceded some scope for provincial administration of estates of self-declared insolvent persons is shown also by *A.-G. Alta. v. Nash* (1964), 50 W.W.R. 115 (Alta. C.A.), aff'g (1964), 48 W.W.R. 420 (Alta. S.C.), holding invalid the *Alberta Fraudulent Preferences Act*, R.S.A. 1955, c. 120. (But see *Allison & Burnham Concrete Ltd. v. Mountain View Construction Ltd.* (1965), 53 W.W.R. 274 (B.C.S.C.).

The *Canadian Bankers Association* case may usefully be contrasted for the problem at hand with the earlier case of *Abitibi Power & Paper Co. v. Montreal Trust Co.*, [1943] A.C. 536 (P.C.). In the *Abitibi* case, an action was begun in Ontario to enforce a bond mortgage on which there had been default by the company. Shortly afterwards the company was declared insolvent at the instance of a creditor and a winding-up order was made. Under section 21 of the *Winding-up Act*, R.S.C. 1927, c. 213, no action could be commenced or continued after the making of a winding-up order except by leave of the proper provincial Court. Leave to continue with the action on the bond mortgage was obtained, but during the course of the action a provincial commission of inquiry into the affairs of the company was appointed, and in consequence of its report a special moratorium Act was passed staying proceedings for a fixed period to enable consideration to be given to a proposed plan for rehabilitating the company. The Act was renewed after one year's force by another temporary Act expiring in the succeeding calendar year. The validity of these temporary moratorium statutes was successfully attacked in the provincial

Courts as an invasion of the federal bankruptcy and insolvency power and as an interference with federal winding-up legislation. The Privy Council reversed and sustained the provincial enactments, holding that the action against the company had begun and continued (once leave had been given) as a provincial action and could be subjected to provincial control. The core of the matter is found in the following passage of the judgment:

> It was pressed on their Lordships that the real substance of the legislation was an attempt to coerce the bondholders into accepting a plan of reconstruction, and that arrangements such as were contemplated by the report of the Royal Commission were within the exclusive field of the Dominion. So they are, but this Board must have cogent grounds before it arising from the nature of the impugned legislation before it can impute to a provincial legislature some object other than what is to be seen on the face of the enactment itself. In the present case their Lordships see no reason to reject the statement of the Ontario legislature, contained in the preamble to the Act, that the power to stay the action is given so that an opportunity may be given to all the parties concerned to consider the plan submitted in the report of the Royal Commission.

The *Canadian Bankers Association* case was markedly different from the *Abitibi* case and, in substance, the Province of Saskatchewan sought to achieve through two statutes what had been struck down when combined in the *Alberta Debt Adjustment Act*. Under the *Moratorium Act*, R.S.S. 1953, c. 98, enacted in 1943, the Lieutenant-Governor in Council was empowered to make general or particular orders postponing payment of debts or suspending process for a period not exceeding two years. Coupled with this Act was the *Provincial Mediation Board Act*, R.S.S. 1953, c. 40, also enacted in 1943, under which, on a debtor's application, the Board was authorized to try to effect a compromise with his creditors. Force could be lent to the Board's efforts by a government order under the moratorium statute. In invalidating this Saskatchewan scheme, the Supreme Court reinforced the *Alberta Debt Adjustment Act* decision. It refused to find any constitutional distinction in the fact that while a permit to sue was necessary under the legislation in the *Alberta* case no such requirement was included in the Saskatchewan legislation. The reason for this refusal was that the possibility of a suspension order hung over a creditor; and he would thus be "coerced" for two years to arrive at some compromise under the aegis of the Mediation Board just as in the Alberta case the Debt Adjustment Board could bring similar pressure by denying a permit to sue; and nothing of substance turned on the fact that in the Alberta case the permit to sue could be denied without limit of time.

[Is there any constitutional objection to provincial legislation which requires a secured creditor to submit to supervision of the realization of his security, where such legislation is applicable whether the debtor be insolvent or not? See *Montreal Trust Co. v. Abitibi Power & Paper Co.*, [1938] O.R. 81 (S.C.), aff'd on other grounds [1938] O.R. 589 (C.A.); *Canada Trust Co. v. Hanson*, [1949] O.W.N. 803 (C.A.), aff'd [1951] S.C.R. 366.

Is it open to a Province to create a statutory trust in favour of certain creditors, as was done by section 3 of the *Mechanics' Lien Act*, R.S.O. 1980, c. 261 and thus colour the term "trust" as used in section 47(a) of the *Bankruptcy Act*, R.S.C. 1970, c. B-3; so as to remove certain assets of a person who subsequently becomes bankrupt from the claims of creditors generally? See *John M.M. Troup Ltd. v. Royal Bank of Canada*, [1962] S.C.R. 487.]

# ROBINSON v. COUNTRYWIDE FACTORS LTD.

In the Supreme Court of Canada. [1978] 1 S.C.R. 753.

Laskin, C.J.C., Martland, Judson, Ritchie, Spence, Pigeon, Dickson, Beetz and de Grandpré, JJ. January 25, 1977.

Appeal from a judgment of the Saskatchewan Court of Appeal, 19 C.B.R. (N.S.) 24, allowing an appeal from a judgment of MacPherson, J., 16 C.B.R. (N.S.) 120, setting aside a transaction as a fraudulent preference.

The judgment of Laskin C.J.C. and Martland, Dickson and de Grandpré JJ. concurring, dissenting was delivered by

LASKIN, C.J.C. (dissenting): — There are two issues in this appeal which is here by leave of this Court. The first is whether a certain transaction and, in particular, a certain debenture, granted on a debtor's stock-in-trade in pursuance of the transaction between the debtor and the respondent creditor, was a fraudulent preference that was impeachable under ss. 3 and 4 of the *Fraudulent Preferences Act*, R.S.S. 1965, c. 397; and the second is whether, if it was so impeachable, those provisions of the provincial Act were *ultra vires* as an invasion of exclusive federal power in relation to bankruptcy and insolvency or, alternatively, were inoperative in the face of the preference provisions of the *Bankruptcy Act*, R.S.C. 1970, c. B-3.

The appellant is trustee in bankruptcy of Kozan Furniture (Yorkton) Ltd. pursuant to a receiving order of November 19, 1968. On November 19, 1966, Kozan entered into a transaction with a pressing creditor, the respondent, whereby it sold certain stock-in-trade to a third person (payment being made to the respondent which reduced Kozan's indebtedness accordingly) and also agreed to give the respondent a debenture on its stock-in-trade for its remaining indebtedness. The debenture was executed on or about March 20, 1967, and duly registered. After the receiving order against Kozan was made, proceedings were taken by the appellant trustee in bankruptcy to set aside the transaction of November 19, 1966, as constituting a fraudulent preference under the provincial *Fraudulent Preferences Act* and to recover the money paid to the respondent and to annul the debenture.

MacPherson, J., found that Kozan was insolvent at the time of the transaction of November 19, 1966, that there was a concurrent intention of Kozan and the respondent to give and receive a preference, and that, consequently, both the payment made to the respondent and the debenture constituted fraudulent preferences under the provincial statute and were hence impeachable. On appeal, this judgment was set aside on the view of the majority of the Saskatchewan Court of Appeal that the appellant had failed to prove that Kozan was insolvent on November 19, 1966. The trial Judge was not called upon to deal with any constitutional issue, and the majority of the Court of Appeal did not have to do so in view of its finding on insolvency. Hall, J.A., who dissented supported the trial Judge's finding of insolvency, and in a one-sentence assertion, in reliance upon *Re Panfab Corp. Ltd.*, [1971] 2 O.R. 202 (H.C.), he rejected the contention that the *Fraudulent Preferences Act* was *ultra vires*.

I would not interfere with the findings of the Judge of first instance that Kozan was insolvent at the material time and that Kozan intended to give and the respondent intended to receive a preference. This is the view of my brother Spence who, in exhaustive reasons, also concluded that the *Fraudulent Preferences Act* as a whole was not *ultra vires* nor was either s. 3 or s. 4 inoperative in the face of the *Bankruptcy Act*. I have a different opinion on the constitutional issue in this case, as appears from what now follows. That issue does not invite this Court to pronounce on the validity of provincial legislation dealing with fraudulent conveyances or with fraudulent transactions in general. Thus, to take as an example the *Fraudulent Conveyances Act*, R.S.O. 1970, c. 182, nothing said in these reasons is to be taken as impugning the validity of that or similar enactments. They do not, *ex facie*, depend on proof of insolvency or on bankruptcy. In so far as any of the case law, some of it canvassed by my brother Spence, relates to such legislation and carries it into a consideration of the validity of provincial preference legislation which depends, as do ss. 3 and 4 of the Saskatchewan *Fraudulent Preferences Act*, on a condition of insolvency, I find it inapt for the determination of the constitutional question in this appeal.

Sections 3 and 4 aforesaid are in the following terms:

> 3. Subject to sections 8, 9, 10 and 11 every gift, conveyance, assignment or transfer, delivery over or payment of goods, chattels or effects or of bills, bonds, notes or securities or of shares, dividends, premiums or bonus in a bank, company or corporation, or of any other property real or personal, made by a person at a time when he is in insolvent circumstances or is unable to pay his debts in full or knows that he is on the eve of insolvency, with intent to defeat, hinder, delay or prejudice his creditors or any one or more of them, is void as against the creditor or creditors injured, delayed or prejudiced.
>
> 4. Subject to sections 8, 9, 10 and 11 every gift, conveyance, assignment or transfer, delivery over or payment of goods, chattels or effects or of bills, bonds, notes or securities or of shares, dividends, premiums or bonus in a bank, company or corporation, or of any other property real or personal, made by a person at a time when he is in insolvent circumstances or is unable to pay his debts in full or knows that he is on the eve of insolvency to or for a creditor, with intent to give that creditor preference over his other creditors or over any one or more of them, is void as against the creditor or creditors injured, delayed, prejudiced or postponed.

Sections 8, 9, 10 and 11, to which each of the foregoing provisions is subject, do not affect the constitutional issue, being concerned with *bona fide* sales or payments to innocent purchasers, to valid sales for consideration and to protection of security given up by a creditor. The present case does not involve ss. 8 to 11.

I approach the question of validity on principle and on authority. So far as principle is concerned, the starting point is in the relevant words of the *British North America Act, 1867*, namely, s. 91(21), "Bankruptcy and Insolvency", as they relate to s. 92(13), "Property and Civil Rights in the Province". The elucidation of the meaning and scope of s. 91(21), as of the meaning and scope of any other heads of legislative power, can hardly ever be a purely abstract exercise, even where an attempt is made at neutral definition; but I see no reason why judicial pronouncements, especially at the appellate level where they are those of the Court, should not be considered as throwing light upon the integrity of the head of power in the scheme of the *British North America Act, 1867* as a whole.

Four things stand out. First, s. 91(21) is an exclusive federal power; second, it is a power confided to the Parliament of Canada notwithstanding anything else in the

Act; third, it is a power, like the criminal law power, whose ambit did not and does not lie frozen under conceptions held of bankruptcy and insolvency in 1867: see the *Farmers' Creditors Arrangement Act* reference, *A.-G. B.C. v. A.-G. Can.*, [1937] A.C. 391 at 402-3; and, fourth, the term "insolvency" in s. 91(2) has as much an independent operation in the reservation of an exclusive area of legislative competence to the Parliament of Canada as the term "bankruptcy": see *Canadian Bankers' Ass'n and Dominion Mortgage & Investments Ass'n v. A.-G. Sask.*, [1956] S.C.R. 31 at 46, *per* Rand, J.

The view taken by the Privy Council and by this Court as to the meaning of "insolvency", as well after as before the abolition of Privy Council appeals, has been a uniform one. Lord Thankerton, speaking for the Privy Council in the *Farmers' Creditors Arrangement Act* reference, at p. 402 A.C., expressed it as follows:

> In a general sense, insolvency means inability to meet one's debts or obligations; in a technical sense, it means the condition or standard of inability to meet debts or obligations, upon the occurrence of which the statutory law enables a creditor to intervene, with the assistance of a Court, to stop individual action by creditors and to secure administration of the debtor's assets in the general interest of creditors; the law also generally allows the debtor to apply for the same administration.

This definition was referred to with approval in the majority judgment of the Supreme Court of Canada delivered by Kerwin, C.J.C., in *Reference re Validity of the Orderly Payment of Debts Act, 1959 (Alta.), c. 61*, [1960] S.C.R. 571 at 576. Earlier, in *Reference re Debt Adjustment Act, 1937 (Alta.)*, [1942] S.C.R. 31 at 40, [affirmed, *infra*], Duff, C.J.C., speaking for all but one of the members of the Court took as an additional ground for invalidating the challenged provincial legislation in that case that the powers of the provincial statutory tribunal set up under that legislation would normally "come into operation when a state of insolvency exists"; and he continued: "It is not too much to say that it is for the purpose of dealing with the affairs of debtors who are pressed and unable to pay their debts as they fall due that these powers and duties are created." If it is for Parliament alone to deal with insolvency, indeed to define it where it chooses to do so and to leave it otherwise to judicial definition, there can be no argument about unlawful invasion of provincial power in relation to property and civil rights. A limitation upon such power necessarily inheres in the federal catalogue of powers in s. 91, and it was recognized as early as 1880 in *Cushing v. Dupuy* (1880), 5 App. Cas. 409 at 415, in respect of the federal bankruptcy and insolvency power.

I refer to two other propositions before turning to what I consider to be the relevant cases. First, there is the well-recognized proposition that federal abstinence from legislation in relation to an exclusive head of legislative power does not leave that legislative area open to provincial action: see *Union Colliery Co. of British Columbia, Ltd. v. Bryden*, [1899] A.C. 580 at 588. The principle of our Constitution as it relates to legislative power is not one of simple concurrency of authority subject only to a variable doctrine of paramountcy. Exclusiveness is central to the scheme of distribution, save as to a specified number of concurrent powers, such as those in s. 95. It is only under the umbrella of the doctrine of exclusiveness that the relative scope of federal and provincial authority is assessed, the assessment being carried forward to determine whether there is preclusion or supersession where both federal and provincial legislation are in competition. This brings me to the second point. I take the same view here that was taken by Duff, C.J.C., in the *Alberta Debt Adjustment Act* reference and I adopt his words, at p. 40 S.C.R., namely, that although the motives of a provincial Legislature may be laudable ones, it is precluded from seeking to realize its object by entering into a field not open to it.

*A.-G. Ont. v. A.-G. Can.*, [1894] A.C. 189, generally known as the *Voluntary Assignments* case, stands as the general support for provincial legislation of the kind or allied to the kind of legislation that is challenged in the present case. It concerned only one section, s. 9, of the *Ontario Act*, "An Act respecting Assignments and Preferences by Insolvent persons", R.S.O. 1887, c. 124, first enacted in 1885 by 1885 (Can.), c. 26. That section was as follows:

> 9. An assignment for the general benefit of creditors under this Act shall take precedence of all judgments and of all executions not completely executed by payment, subject to the lien, if any, of an execution creditor for his costs where there is but one exception in the sheriff's hands, or to the lien, if any, of the creditor for his costs who has the first execution in the sheriff's hands.

This Act replaced earlier pre-Confederation legislation found in C.S.U.C. 1859, c. 26, under the title the *Indigent Debtor's Act*, which was continued in the post-Confederation legislation of Ontario as "An Act respecting the Fraudulent Preference of Creditors by persons in insolvent circumstances", and included in R.S.O. 1877, c. 118. What is significant in this earlier legislation is that (as set out in s. 2 of R.S.O. 1877, c. 118) it dealt with "any person, being at the time in insolvent circumstances or unable to pay his debts in full, or knowing himself to be on the eve of insolvency". The substituted Act of 1885 continued the reference to insolvency in respect of preferences, but it also introduced new provisions respecting assignments for the benefit of creditors and these provisions, as was noted in the *Voluntary Assignments* case, were not predicated on insolvency and, indeed, were to a large degree separated from the preference provisions of the Act, as is reflected in s. 3 of R.S.O. 1887, c. 124.

Certainly, as the Privy Council noted, the challenged provision, s. 9, had to be taken in the context of the entire Act. There is no doubt, as well, that the issue of validity was recognized as arising at a time when there was no federal bankruptcy or insolvency legislation in force, the only such legislation, the *Insolvency Act of 1875*, 1875 (Can.), c. 16, having been repealed in 1880 by 1880 (Can.), c. 1. The majority of the Ontario Court of Appeal, to which the question of the validity of s. 9 had been referred, found that it was *ultra vires* as invading exclusive federal power in relation to bankruptcy and insolvency: see *Re Assignments and Preferences Act, Section 9* (1893), 20 O.A.R. 489. The reversal of this judgment by the Privy Council was accompanied by an acknowledgement of the broad scope of federal power under s. 91(21) when affirmatively exercised but it was held that this power was not invaded by an enactment relating to an assignment that was purely voluntary.

The explanation for this result is found in two passages of the Privy Council's reasons. First, at p. 198:

> ... it is to be observed that an assignment for the general benefit of creditors has long been known to the jurisprudence of this country and also of Canada, and has its force and effect at common law quite independently of any system of bankruptcy or insolvency, or any legislation relating thereto.

Second, at p. 199:

... the operation of an assignment for the benefit of creditors was precisely the same, whether the
assignor was or was not in fact insolvent. ... The validity of the assignment and its effect would in
no way depend on the insolvency of the assignor, and their Lordships think it clear that the 9th
section would equally apply whether the assignor was or was not insolvent.

What is evident, therefore, from that case is that, unlike the situation here, the
operation of the provincial enactment did not depend on insolvency and the Privy
Council was willing to treat s. 9 as having an object that was independent of it. This
may even be a supportable view today, albeit there is a range of existing federal legislation dealing with bankruptcy and insolvency. I should note, however, that in the
majority judgment of this Court in *Reference re Validity of the Orderly Payment of
Debts Act, 1959 (Alta.), c. 61*, [1960] S.C.R. 571 at 576-7, Kerwin, C.J.C., referring to
the *Voluntary Assignments* reference, said "it is doubtful whether in view of later
pronouncements of the Judicial Committee it would at this date be decided in the
same sense, even in the absence of Dominion legislation upon the subject of bankruptcy and insolvency"

The later pronouncements of the Privy Council include its judgment in the
*Alberta Debt Adjustment Act* reference, [1943] A.C. 356, as well as in the *Farmers'
Creditors Arrangement Act* reference, [1937] A.C. 391. Equally important is the
judgment of this Court in *Canadian Bankers' Ass'n and Dominion Mortgage Investments Ass'n v. A.-G. Sask.*, [1956] S.C.R. 31, dealing with the validity of provincial
moratorium legislation. It was in line with the decision in the *Alberta Debt Adjustment Act* reference in finding an invasion of federal power in relation to bankruptcy
and insolvency. I think it enough, for present purposes, to refer to what Locke, J.,
speaking for the majority of the Court, said, at p. 42 S.C.R.:

> Power to declare a moratorium for the relief of the residents of a Province generally in some
> great emergency, such as existed in 1914 and in the days of the lengthy depression in the thirties, is
> one thing, but power to intervene between insolvent debtors and their creditors, irrespective of the
> reasons which have rendered the debtor unable to meet his liabilities, is something entirely
> different.

Although judgments of the Privy Council and of this Court (and I add to those
already cited *Royal Bank of Canada v. Larue*, [1928] A.C. 187) have recognized the
broad power of Parliament to embrace in its legislation in relation to bankruptcy or
insolvency provisions which might otherwise fall within provincial competence, I
know of no case in those Courts, other than *Ladore v. Bennett*, [1939] A.C. 468,
where provincial legislation has been sustained, either in the absence of or in the face
of federal legislation, when such provincial legislation depends for its operation
only upon insolvency. *Ladore v. Bennett* can best be explained as involving
municipal reorganization and hence as being concerned with the amalgamation and
financial restructuring of units of local Government for which the provincial Legislature has a direct responsibility, albeit some of the municipalities involved in the
legislatively-directed reorganization were insolvent. It is, indeed, a special case of a
piece of special legislation enacted in pursuance of the power conferred by s. 92(8) of
the *British North America Act, 1867* and I do not regard it as offering any lead to continuing legislation relating to private debtors and their creditors.

It is plain to me that if provincial legislation avowedly directed to insolvency,
and to transactions between debtor and creditor consummated in a situation of

insolvency, can be sustained as validly enacted, unless overborne by competent federal legislation, there is a serious breach of the principle of exclusiveness which embraces insolvency under s. 91(21). This Court so held in a series of cases where the encroachment on the federal bankruptcy and insolvency power was less obvious than that exhibited here. I refer, of course, to the *Alberta Debt Adjustment Act* reference, *supra*, to the *Canadian Bankers' Ass'n* case, *supra*, and to the *Orderly Payment of Debts Act, 1959 (Alta.)* reference, *supra*. It would be a curious reversal of the proposition, enunciated in *Madden v. Nelson and Fort Sheppard R. Co.*, [1899] A.C. 626, namely, that you cannot do indirectly what you cannot do directly, to hold that the Province can do directly what it cannot do indirectly.

The case put forward by the appellant and by the intervening Provinces which supported him goes even farther. It is contended that notwithstanding the existence of federal bankruptcy legislation dealing with preferences, the challenged provincial legislation can still operate in respect of a particular preference which is given outside of the time-limits within which the federal control operates, so long at least as the provincial provision is not more stringent.

I do not follow this line of reasoning, especially on the submission of greater or lesser stringency. The relevant federal provision is s. 73 of the *Bankruptcy Act* which reads as follows:

> 73(1) Every conveyance or transfer of property or charge thereon made, every payment made, every obligation incurred, and every judicial proceeding taken or suffered by an insolvent person in favour of any creditor or of any person in trust for any creditor with a view to giving such creditor a preference over the other creditors shall, if the person making, incurring, taking, paying or suffering the same becomes bankrupt within three months after the date of making, incurring, taking, paying or suffering the same, be deemed fraudulent and void as against the trustee in the bankruptcy.
>
> (2) Where any such conveyance, transfer, payment, obligation or judicial proceeding has the effect of giving any creditor a preference over other creditors, or over any one or more of them, it shall be presumed *prima facie* to have been made, incurred, taken, paid or suffered with a view to giving such creditor a preference over other creditors, whether or not it was made voluntarily or under pressure and evidence of pressure shall not be receivable or avail to support such transaction.
>
> (3) For the purposes of this section, the expression "creditor" includes a surety or guarantor for the debt due to such creditor.

This provision cannot be taken in isolation. The *Bankruptcy Act* is a code on the subject of bankruptcy and insolvency, defining what is an act of bankruptcy, who is an insolvent person, prescribing what are vulnerable settlements as well as what are vulnerable preferences, declaring what is comprised in a bankrupt's estate, providing for priorities in distribution and for rateable distribution. It provides also, as in the present s. 31(1), for the making of an assignment by an insolvent person for the benefit of creditors as well as providing by s. 24(1)(*a*) that it is an act of bankruptcy to make an assignment for the benefit of creditors whether the assignment is or is not authorized by the *Bankruptcy Act*. In short, apart from the question whether provincial legislation predicated on insolvency is *ipso facto* invalid, I see no room for any assertion that such provincial legislation can continue to have operative effect in the face of the scope of the *Bankruptcy Act* embracing both bankruptcy and insolvency in its provisions.

It is worth a reminder that there is no common law of bankruptcy and insolvency, and hence it cannot be said that there was an existing common law course of decision which was being embraced by provincial legislation. The common law did not distinguish the fraudulent from the insolvent debtor; it was through legislation that such a distinction was made. If a provincial Legislature wishes to proscribe fraudulent transactions, it is compelled by the *British North America Act, 1867* to ensure that its legislation dealing with such transactions does not focus on insolvency.

[His Lordship reviewed a number of cases dealing with the interaction and conflict between the federal *Bankruptcy Act* and provincial legislation and continued:]

I conclude, therefore, as follows. Provincial legislation which purports to provide for impeachment of preferences to creditors given by a person who is then insolvent, where insolvency is the *sine qua non* of impeachability is invalid as a direct invasion of exclusive federal power in relation to bankruptcy and insolvency. Hence, ss. 3 and 4 of the Saskatchewan *Fraudulent Preferences Act* are *ultra vires*. Moreover, in so far as these sections prescribe an impeachment period which enables a creditor to set aside a preference made beyond the period fixed by the *Bankruptcy Act*, and hence not impeachable under that Act, it interferes with the operation of the *Bankruptcy Act* and is, indeed, repugnant to it. It must be remembered that where, as in the present case, there has been a receiving order, the intrusion of provincial legislation relating to transactions entered into by an insolvent, must interfere with the rateable distribution of the bankrupt's property according to the scheme of distribution prescribed by the *Bankruptcy Act*. Whether that scheme is faulty in the view of a Court is immaterial; the correction must come from the responsible Legislature. No more under bankruptcy and insolvency law than under the criminal law can a Province make unlawful what is lawful under valid federal legislation, nor make lawful what is unlawful under valid federal legislation.

In the result, I would answer the two questions in issue here in the affirmative. The judgment of the Saskatchewan Court of Appeal should be varied so as to restore the finding of insolvency by the trial Judge but the appeal should otherwise be dismissed in view of the affirmative answers aforesaid. Leave is also given for a reference to determine the amount due under the debenture if the parties are unable to agree thereon. The respondent should have its costs in this Court but there should be no order as to costs to or against any of the intervenors.

The judgment of Judson, Ritchie, Spence and Pigeon JJ. was delivered by

SPENCE, J.: —

. . . .

Upon the trustee in bankruptcy obtaining leave to appeal to this Court, the respondent Countrywide Factors Ltd., in accordance with the Rules of this Court, and in view of the fact that it wished to argue the *ultra vires* character of the provincial *Fraudulent Preferences Act*, applied to this Court for directions and this Court ordered that notice of two questions be served on the Attorney-General of Canada and the Attorneys-General of the Provinces. The two questions were:

1. Whether The Fraudulent Preferences Act, R.S.S. 1965, Chapter 397, is *ultra vires* of the Legislature of the Province of Saskatchewan.

2. Alternatively, whether sections 3 and 4 of The Fraudulent Preferences Act, R.S.S. 1965, Chapter 397, while being within the legislative competence of the Legislature of the Province of Saskatchewan, are in conflict with valid legislation of the Parliament of the Dominion of Canada relating to bankruptcy and insolvency, namely, the Bankruptcy Act, R.S.C. 1970, Chapter B3.

. . . .

The *Bankruptcy Act* was only enacted in the year 1919 but in *A.-G. Ont. v. A.-G. Can.*, [1894] A.C. 189, the Judicial Committee dealt with the problem of whether s. 9 of an Ontario statute, the then counterpart of the present Ontario *Assignments and Preferences Act*, R.S.O. 1970, c. 34, was *intra vires* of the Province of Ontario. It is to be remembered that s. 91, heading 21, of the *British North America Act, 1867* granted exclusive legislative jurisdiction to the Parliament of Canada on subjects entitled "Bankruptcy and Insolvency". Section 9 of the Ontario statute, R.S.O. 1887, c. 124, read as follows:

9. An assignment for the general benefit of creditors under this Act shall take precedence of all judgments and of all executions not completely executed by payment, subject to the lien, if any, of an execution creditor for his costs where there is but one execution in the sheriff's hands, or to the lien, if any, of the creditor for his costs who has the first execution in the sheriff's hands.

The Judicial Committee held that such a provision was within the constitutional powers of the Province as granted in s. 92, heading 13, of the *British North America Act, 1867, i.e.*, "Property and Civil Rights in the Province". The Lord Chancellor said at pp. 198-9:

But it is argued that inasmuch as this assignment contemplates the insolvency of the debtor, and would only be made if he were insolvent, such a provision purports to deal with insolvency, and therefore is a matter exclusively within the jurisdiction of the Dominion Parliament. Now it is to be observed that an assignment for the general benefit of creditors has long been known to the jurisprudence of this country and also of Canada, and has its force and effect at common law quite independently of any system of bankruptcy or insolvency, or any legislation relating thereto. So far from being regarded as an essential part of the bankruptcy law, such an assignment was made an act of bankruptcy on which an adjudication might be founded, and by the law of the Province of Canada which prevailed at the time when the Dominion Act was passed, it was one of the grounds for an adjudication of insolvency.

It is to be observed that the word "bankruptcy" was apparently not used in Canadian legislation, but the insolvency law of the Province of Canada was precisely analogous to what was known in England as the bankruptcy law.

Moreover, the operation of an assignment for the benefit of creditors was precisely the same, whether the assignor was or was not in fact insolvent. It was open to any debtor who might deem his solvency doubtful, and who desired in that case that his creditors should be equitably dealt with, to make an assignment for their benefit. The validity of the assignment and its effect would in no way depend on the insolvency of the assignor, and their Lordships think it clear that the 9th section would equally apply whether the assignor was or was not insolvent.

and at pp. 200-1 continued:

It is not necessary in their Lordships' opinion, nor would it be expedient to attempt to define, what is covered by the words "bankruptcy" and "insolvency" in sect. 91 of the British North America Act. But it will be seen that it is a feature common to all the systems of bankruptcy and insolvency to which reference has been made, that the enactments are designed to secure that in the case of an insolvent person his assets shall be rateably distributed amongst his creditors whether he is willing that they shall be so distributed or not. Although provision may be made for a voluntary assignment as an alternative, it is only as an alternative. In reply to a question put by their Lordships the learned counsel for the respondent were unable to point to any scheme of bankruptcy or insolvency legislation which did not involve some power of compulsion by process of law to secure to the creditors the distribution amongst them of the insolvent debtor's estate.

In their Lordships' opinion these considerations must be borne in mind when interpreting the words "bankruptcy" and "insolvency" in the British North America Act. It appears to their Lordships that such provisions as are found in the enactment in question, relating as they do to assignments purely voluntary, do not infringe on the exclusive legislative power conferred upon the Dominion Parliament. They would observe that a system of bankruptcy legislation may frequently require various ancillary provisions for the purpose of preventing the scheme of the Act from being defeated. It may be necessary for this purpose to deal with the effect of executions and other matters which would otherwise be within the legislative competence of the provincial legislature. Their Lordships do not doubt that it would be open to the Dominion Parliament to deal with such matters as part of a bankruptcy law, and the provincial legislature would doubtless be then precluded from interfering with this legislation inasmuch as such interference would affect the bankruptcy law of the Dominion Parliament. But it does not follow that such subjects, as might properly be treated as ancillary to such a law and therefore within the powers of the Dominion Parliament, are excluded from the legislative authority of the provincial legislature when there is no bankruptcy or insolvency legislation of the Dominion Parliament in existence.

It will be seen, therefore, that the Judicial Committee in this decision only determined that a system providing for voluntary assignments enacted in a Province prior to the enactment of any federal Bankruptcy Act was *intra vires* but acknowledged that a subsequently enacted Bankruptcy Act by the federal Parliament might well overcome the provisions of the provincial statute. It would seem that the decision is quite silent as to the effect of provisions in a provincial Assignments and Preferences Act other than one permitting a voluntary assignment of debts except that one might well argue that by implication provisions in the provincial statute dealing with fraudulent preferences would be equally within the purview of the Province under "property" and "civil rights" unless and until overcome by federal legislation ancillary to its power in bankruptcy and insolvency.

[His Lordship reviewed a number of cases dealing with the interaction between federal and provincial legislation and continued:]

I have dealt with what, in my view, are the main cases upon the subject in Canada. Upon considering them all, as well as the decision of the Judicial Committee in *A.-G. Ont. v. A.-G. Can.*, [1894] A.C. 189, I have come to the conclusion that the better view is to confine the effect of what is now s. 73 of the *Bankruptcy Act* to providing for the invalidity of transactions within its exact scope. To that extent, the Parliament of Canada, by valid legislation upon "bankruptcy" and "insolvency", has covered the field but has refrained from completely covering the whole field of transactions avoided by provincial legislation. I am of the opinion that the enactment in 1949 of the provisions now found in s. 50(6) of the *Bankruptcy Act* is a plain indication that Parliament recognized that provisions in provincial statutes dealing with preferential transactions were still valid provincial enactments in reference to "property" and "civil rights" and were valuable aids to trustees in bankruptcy in attacking the validity of such transactions and should be available to the said trustees in bankruptcy.

I am assisted in coming to this conclusion by the view which I believe was behind the Lord Chancellor's reasons in *A.-G. Ont. v. A.-G. Can.* that the words "bankruptcy" and "insolvency" in s. 91, para. 21, of the *British North America Act, 1867* were aimed at legislative schemes which had the purpose of governing the distribution of a debtor's property amongst his creditors. There may well be, and there are, provisions in such legislative schemes, *i.e.*, the *Bankruptcy Act*, dealing with "property" and "civil rights". Such provisions are properly ancillary to the bankruptcy and insolvency legislation, and to the extent to which they go overcome existing valid provincial legislation and bar future provincial legislation *contra* thereto but do not purport to extend beyond that point to invalidate other valid provincial legislation upon "property" and "civil rights".

I have, therefore, come to the conclusion that the provisions of ss. 3 and 4 of the *Fraudulent Preferences Act* of Saskatchewan are valid and subsisting provincial legislation available to the trustee in his attack upon the transactions with which this appeal is concerned. . . .

For these reasons, I am of the opinion that the appeal should be allowed, the judgment of the Court of Appeal of Saskatchewan quashed and judgment at trial restored. As I have already said, the questions upon which leave was given to the various intervenors should be answered as follows:

Question 1:   No.

Question 2:   Sections 3 and 4 of the *Fraudulent Preferences Act*, R.S.S. 1965, c. 397, are not in conflict with the provisions of the *Bankruptcy Act*, R.S.C. 1970, c. B-3.

The appellant should have his costs against the respondent in the Court of Appeal and in this Court. There will be no costs to intervenors.

BEETZ, J.: — I have had the advantage of reading the opinions of the Chief Justice and of Mr. Justice Spence. I agree with Mr. Justice Spence. To his reasons for judgment I would, however, like to add some of my own.

The power to repress fraud by avoiding fraudulent conveyances and preferences is an indisputable part of provincial jurisdiction over property and civil rights. The risk of fraud is increased when a debtor finds himself in a situation of impending or actual insolvency and, in my view, provincial laws can, without undergoing a change in nature, focus upon that situation as upon a proper occasion to attain their object. Given their purpose, they do not cease to be laws in relation to property and civil rights simply because they are timely and effective or because Parliament could enact similar laws in relation to bankruptcy and insolvency.

Insolvency has been defined by Lord Thankerton in the *Farmers' Creditors Arrangement Act* reference, *A.-G. B.C. v. A.-G. Can.*, [1937] A.C. 391 at 402:

> In a general sense, insolvency means inability to meet one's debts or obligations; in a technical sense, it means the condition or standard of inability to meet debts or obligations, upon the occurrence of which the statutory law enables a creditor to intervene, with the assistance of a Court, to stop individual action by creditors and to secure administration of the debtor's assets in the general interest of creditors; the law also generally allows the debtor to apply for the same administration.

The primary meaning of "insolvency" in s. 91(21) of the Constitution is insolvency in the technical sense, not in the general sense. This Lord Thankerton made clear just a few lines after the passage quoted above: with respect to the jurisdiction of Parliament under s. 91(21), he referred to "... the statutory conditions of insolvency which enabled a creditor or the debtor to invoke the aid of the bankruptcy laws . . .".

There is no common law of bankruptcy and insolvency in the technical sense, but the disruptions resulting from insolvency in the general sense had of necessity to be taken into account by general legal systems such as the common law and the civil law. Insolvency lies at the core of those parts of the common law and of the civil law which relate to such matters as mortgage, pledge, pawning, suretyship and the securing of debts generally which are implicitly or explicitly predicated on the risk of insolvency and which produce their full effect when the risk has been converted into reality; so it is with the rules which determine the rank of privileges and hypothecs or which ordain that an insolvent or bankrupt debtor shall lose the benefit of the term: art. 1092 of the Quebec *Civil Code*. Some of the most fundamental principles of the civil law are expressed in arts. 1980, 1981 and 1982 of the Quebec *Civil Code*:

> 1980. Whoever incurs a personal obligation, renders liable for its fulfilment all his property, moveable and immoveable, present and future, except such property as is specially declared to be exempt from seizure.

> 1981. The property of a debtor is the common pledge of his creditors, and where they claim together they share its price rateably, unless there are amongst them legal causes of preference.

> 1982. The legal causes of preference are privileges and hypothecs.

Although not expressly referred to, insolvency forms the web of these articles; there would be little need for them, particularly the last two, were it not for insolvency. But I cannot be persuaded that they are not laws relating to property and civil rights.

When the exclusive power to make laws in relation to bankruptcy and insolvency was bestowed upon Parliament, it was not intended to remove from the general legal systems which regulated property and civil rights a cardinal concept essential to the coherence of those systems. The main purpose was to give to Parliament exclusive jurisdiction over the establishment by statute of a particular system regulating the distribution of a debtor's assets. However, given the nature of general legal systems, the primary jurisdiction of Parliament cannot easily be exercised together with its incidental powers without some degree of overlap in which case federal law prevails. On the other hand, provincial jurisdiction over property and civil rights should not be measured by the ultimate reach of federal power over bankruptcy and insolvency any more than provincial competence in relation to the administration of justice can be determined by every conceivable and potential use of the criminal law power. This, I believe, is the general import of the *Voluntary Assignments* case, *A.-G. Ont. v. A.-G. Can.*, [1894] A.C. 189. The Judicial Committee declared that the validity of the provision it had to consider and of the assignments made under the authority of that provision did not depend on the insolvency of the assignor: an assignment was also open "to any debtor who might deem his insolvency doubtful . . .". All that one can say is that legislation of the type considered in the *Voluntary Assignments* case presents little interest for prosperous persons; it is of concern chiefly to debtors in strained circumstances whose solvency is, at best, uncertain. It should be noted that the impugned voluntary assignments enactment did not only deal with assignments: it also provided that an assignment for the general benefit of creditors should take *precedence* of all judgments and of all executions not completely executed by payment.

I am reinforced in those views by a consideration of the *Civil Code of Lower Canada, 1866*, in light of the *Insolvent Act of 1864*, 1864 (Can.), c. 17. Both were enacted at a time when Confederation was being discussed. The French title of the *Insolvent Act of 1864*, was *l'Acte de Faillite de 1864*, the word "faillite" being the one now currently used to translate the word "bankruptcy". In spite of its English title, the Act was in fact a bankruptcy Act. It applied to all persons in Upper Canada and to traders only in Lower Canada and it contained detailed provisions relating to fraudulent conveyances and preferences. Nevertheless, the *Civil Code* comprised a section of nine articles (arts. 1032 to 1040 incl.), entitled "Of the Avoidance of Contracts and Payments made in Fraud of Creditors", applicable to traders and to non-traders alike except where the *Insolvent Act of 1864* was to prevail. The legislative history of those articles was set forth by Mr. Justice Pigeon in *Gingras v. General Motors Products of Canada Ltd.*, [1976] 1 S.C.R. 426. Some have been amended. It will suffice to quote a few of them as they then read:

> 1034. A gratuitous contract is deemed to be made with intent to defraud, if the debtor be insolvent at the time of making it.
> 1035. An onerous contract made by an insolvent debtor with a person who knows him to be insolvent is deemed to be made with intent to defraud.
> 1036. Every payment by an insolvent debtor to a creditor knowing his insolvency, is deemed to be made with intent to defraud, and the creditor may be compelled to restore the amount or thing received or the value thereof, for the benefit of the creditors according to their respective rights.
> 1037. Further provisions concerning the presumption of fraud and the nullity of acts done in contemplation of insolvency are contained in The Insolvent Act of 1864.

Article 17, para. 23 of the Code defines "bankruptcy" ("faillite") as meaning "the condition of a trader who has discontinued his payments"; insolvency was left undefined, the word being clearly used by the Code in the general sense. Even though arts. 1034, 1035 and 1036 are predicated on insolvency, the Commissioners appointed for codifying the laws of Lower Canada in civil matters would have been astonished had they been told that those articles formed no part of the civil law: except perhaps for art. 1036 which appears to be an improvement of relatively modern origin (although it was not considered new law), such provisions were derived from a division of Roman law called Paulian law and, from time immemorial, had constituted a pivot of the civil law system. Other provisions of the Code are of the same nature and also depend on insolvency, such as art. 803 (revocation of a gift made by an insolvent debtor), and art. 2023 (hypothec consented to by an insolvent debtor). Other provisions still, although not expressly predicated on insolvency are related to insolvency and to the protection of creditors, for instance, art. 655 (the creditors of an heir who renounces a succession to their prejudice can have the renunciation rescinded and accept the succession in his stead).

The constitutional validity of such provisions is not in issue: they antedate Confederation and were continued by s. 129 of the Constitution. The only issue which could arise with respect to them is whether they are in conflict with federal law. But the content and integrity of the *Civil Code* are indicative of the extent of provincial jurisdiction over property and civil rights: *Citizens Ins. Co. of Canada v. Parsons* (1881), 7 App. Cas. 96 at 110-1. The fact that there existed a statutory scheme of bankruptcy and insolvency to which the Code explicitly referred as to a distinct and specific body of law, without curtailing for that reason its own normal ambit, illustrates how the respective domains of property and civil rights and of bankruptcy and insolvency were viewed during the very period when the federal union was being discussed; it also reveals how it was intended that the distribution of powers should operate with respect to those domains.

In the *Alberta Debt Adjustment Act* reference, *Reference re Debt Adjustment Act, 1937 (Alta.)*, [1943] A.C. 356, in *Canadian Bankers' Ass'n and Dominion Mortgage & Investments Ass'n v. A.-G. Sask.*, [1956] S.C.R. 31, and in *Reference re Validity of the Orderly Payment of Debts Act, 1959 (Alta.), c. 61.*, [1960] S.C.R. 571, the various provincial laws found *ultra vires* were predicated upon insolvency. But they went further and set up elaborate statutory schemes involving one or more of the following features: the denial of creditors' access to Courts or the restriction of their right to enforce their claims, the establishment of administrative boards, mediation, composition, arrangements, moratoriums, consolidation orders, staying of proceedings and the relief of debtors from liability to pay their debts. No such features are to be found in the presently-impugned Saskatchewan statute where all that is at stake is the avoidance of fraudulent acts for the better enforcement of civil obligations. Some doubt was expressed in the *Orderly Payment of Debts Act, 1959 (Alta.)* reference, at pp. 576-7 S.C.R., as to whether the *Voluntary Assignments* case would have been decided in the same way at a later date even in the absence of federal legislation on the subject of bankruptcy and insolvency. But even if this doubt was not expressed in an *obiter dictum*, I would regard it as questioning not the general principles enunciated in the *Voluntary Assignments* case, but their application in that particular instance. Accordingly, I do not think that those previous decisions of the Judicial Committee and of this Court preclude my abiding by my conclusions: laws provincial in their purpose, object and nature as those under attack cannot be rendered *ultra vires* because of virtual federal paramountcy: they can only become inoperative in case of actual repugnancy with valid federal laws.

On this latter point, I believe the test of repugnancy to be applied in this case should not differ from the one which was admitted in *Provincial Secretary of Prince Edward Island v. Egan.*, [1941] S.C.R. 396; *O'Grady v. Sparling*, [1960] S.C.R. 804, and *Ross v. Registrar of Motor Vehicles*, [1975] 1 S.C.R. 5: provincial law gives way to federal law in case of operational conflict. Even if the test be one of conflict of legislative policies entailing no operational inconsistency and depending solely "upon the intention of the paramount legislature" as was said by Dixon, J., in a passage of *Ex parte McLean* (1930), 43 C.L.R. 472 at 483, quoted by Mr. Justice Pigeon in the *Ross* case, at p. 15 S.C.R., I am of the view that s. 50(6) of the *Bankruptcy Act*, R.S.C. 1970, c. B-3, provides a clear indication that Parliament, far from intending to depart from the rule of operational conflict, did in fact aim at the highest possible degree of legal integration of federal and provincial laws: attacks upon transactions within the three-month period provided by s. 73 of the *Bankruptcy Act* constitute a minimum but the trustee in bankruptcy is entitled to avail himself of all other rights and remedies provided by provincial law "as supplementary to and in addition to the rights and remedies provided by" the *Bankruptcy Act*.

I would dispose of this appeal as is proposed by Mr. Justice Spence.

*Appeal allowed.*

# 13

# Taxing Powers

## 1. The Scope of Dominion and Provincial Taxing Powers: Definition of Taxation: Taxing and Regulation: Spending

### Note on Taxation, Regulation and Spending

It is convenient to list at the outset those provisions of the *Constitution Act, 1867* which confer upon the Dominion and the Provinces authority to raise money and which, conversely, limit that authority. The Dominion's powers are in section 91(3) ("the raising of money by any mode or system of taxation") and section 122 ("the customs and excise laws of each province shall subject to the provisions of this Act continue in force until altered by the Parliament of Canada"). It is a tenable conclusion that section 122 is now spent and that customs and excise laws are, independently of section 122, competent to the Dominion under section 91(2) and section 91(3). *Cf.* MacDonald, "Taxation Powers in Canada" (1941), 19 Can. Bar Rev. 75 at 95; *A.-G. B.C. v. Kingcome Navigation Co. Ltd.*, [1934] A.C. 45 (P.C.); and *cf. R. v. Shearwater Co.*, [1934] S.C.R. 197. In any event, section 122 may be regarded as confirmatory of some of the things covered by section 91(3): see *P.A.T.A. v. A.-G. Can.*, [1931] A.C. 310 (P.C.). The original taxation powers granted to the provinces were in section 92(2) ("direct taxation within the province in order to the raising of a revenue for provincial purposes") and section 92(9) ("shop, saloon, tavern, auctioneer and other licences in order to the raising of a revenue for provincial, local or municipal purposes"). Two limiting provisions may be noted: section 121 ("all articles of the growth, produce or manufacture of any one of the provinces shall from and after the Union be admitted free into each of the other provinces") and section 125 ("no lands or property belonging to Canada or any province shall be liable to taxation"). The effect of these sections has been partly treated in Chapter 8, *supra*. The *Constitution Act, 1982* added section 92A(4) which allows for provincial taxation "by any mode or system" in respect of non-renewable natural resources, forestry resources and electrical energy generation and primary production therefrom whether or not such production is exported from the province so long as the tax does not differentiate between production exported to another part of Canada and that not exported from the province.

While the primary concern here is to consider the legal aspects of federal and provincial revenue powers, the issues raised by the scope of the respective powers, considered in conjunction with the various subsidy arrangements, first under section 118 (repealed by 1950 (U.K.), c. 6) and later under the *Constitution Act*, 1907 (U.K.), c. 11 and also under federal legislation, transcend legalism and go to the heart of a working federalism. *Cf.* Maxwell, "A Flexible Portion of the *B.N.A. Act*"

(1933), 11 Can. Bar Rev. 149, on the changes in the provision for federal subsidies to the provinces; see also the *Provincial Subsidies Act*, R.S.C. 1970, c. P-26; the *Maritime Provinces Additional Subsidies Act*, 1942 (Can.), c. 14; *Constitution Act, 1949*, No. 1, 1949 (U.K.), c. 22, Terms of Union with Newfoundland, and 1949 (Can.), c. 1. It has become a truism of Canadian constitutional law that judicial interpretation of the *Constitution Act, 1867* has given the provinces substantive legislative authority (especially in respect of social services) that far exceeds their financial resources and their money-raising power, while it has left the Dominion with financial resources through an ample taxing power overshadowing its regulatory authority. Having regard to this result of the legal division of powers, and to the disparate economic strength of the various provinces *inter se*, it is understandable why the financial relations of Dominion and provinces have become a central issue in Canadian federalism — an issue in which the strict legal position is of secondary importance: see Report of Royal Commission on Dominion-Provincial Relations, 1940, Book I, Chaps. 8 and 9; Book II, Chap. 1; Proceedings of Constitutional Conference of Federal and Provincial Governments, 1950; Proceedings of Constitutional Conference of Federal and Provincial Governments (Second Session), 1950; Report of the Dominion-Povincial Conference on Fiscal Relations, 1957; Federal-Provincial Relations, 1958 (A Symposium), (1958) 1 Can. Pub. Adm., No. 3, pp. 1-25. The amendments to the *Constitution Act, 1867* respecting unemployment insurance and old age pensions and supplementary benefits are indicative of piecemeal solutions on a political level which, no doubt, may be extended into other areas where social pressure for governmental action becomes insistent. But these special and particular amendments have left the general legal framework of financial and taxing powers otherwise unimpaired. Within this framework, Dominion and provinces have had to meet and satisfy the claims and demands for various forms of public assistance. Hence, the development of grants in aid by Dominion to provinces, and the growth of what may be called a federal "spending" power involving disbursement of money on stipulated conditions but without any right of compulsory direction or regulation of the beneficiaries: see Gouin and Claxton, "Legislative Expedients and Devices Adopted by the Dominion and the Provinces" (*Royal Commission Study, Appendix 8*), chapter III; Gettys, *Administration of Canadian Conditional Grants*; Smiley, *Conditional Grants and Canadian Federalism* (1963); Cheffins, *The Constitutional Process in Canada*, pp. 143-146 (1969); and *cf. The Family Allowances Act*, 1973, S.C. 1973-4, c. 44.

The Dominion's right to spend money which it has raised through a proper exercise of its taxing power is confirmed, if confirmation be necessary, by section 91(1A) of the *Constitution Act, 1867* ("the public debt and property"). "We are satisfied", said Duff C.J. in his dissenting judgment in *Reference re Employment and Social Insurance Act*, [1936] S.C.R. 427 at 432, "that if Parliament out of public monies exclusively were to constitute a fund for the relief of unemployment and to give to unemployed persons a right to claim unemployment benefits, to be paid out of that fund upon such conditions as Parliament might see fit to prescribe, no plausible argument could be urged against the validity of such legislation". An issue of validity does arise, however, where the legislation is not a mere spending enactment (*e.g. The Family Allowances Act*) but purports to be an exercise of the taxing power or combines taxation (*i.e.* compulsory exactions) with a scheme of disbursement (*e.g. The Employment and Social Insurance Act of 1935*). In *In re Insurance Act of Canada*, [1932] A.C. 41 at 52, reproduced, *supra*, at p. 519, the Privy Council stated the problem as follows: "Now as to the power of the Dominion Parliament to impose taxation there is no doubt. But if the tax as imposed is linked up with an object which is illegal, the tax for that purpose must fall". This principle is, of course, as applicable to provincial taxing measures as it is to federal enactments: see *A.-G. Alta. v. A.-G. Can.*, [1939] A.C. 117. As to Dominion statutes, the problem has been whether the Dominion may exercise its plenary taxing power towards achievement of a regulatory purpose which it cannot realize through direct regulation, either by licensing or otherwise. Thus, in the *Employment and Social Insurance Act* case, Rinfret J. took the position ([1936] S.C.R. 427 at 453) that "the contributions (or the taxes if we are to call them so) are mere incidents of the regulation" of employment service and unemployment insurance, forbidden (at that time) to the Dominion. When the case came before the Privy Council ([1937] A.C. 355), that body went a little farther — too far, perhaps — in warning against an overreaching of the federal taxing power. Said Lord Atkin: "But assuming that the Dominion has collected by means of taxation a fund, it by no means follows that any legislation which disposes of it is necessarily within Dominion competence. It may still be legislation affecting [sic] the classes of subjects enumerated in section 92 and, if so, would be *ultra vires*". More recently, Pigeon J., speaking for a majority of the Supreme Court of Canada on the issue, said in *Reference re Agricultural Products Marketing Act and Two Other Acts* (1978), 84 D.L.R. (3d) 257 at 323 that "federal intrusion into local trade is just as unconstitutional when done by buying and selling, as when done through any other method". These statements have not had any noticeable effect upon Dominion spending. See Driedger, "The Spending Power" (1982), 7 Queen's L.J. 124 for a forceful argument that any constraints on non-regulatory use of the federal spending power are political and not constitutional. For a broad view of Parliament's spending power: see *Central Mortgage and Housing Corp. v. Co-operative College Residences Inc.* (1975), 71 D.L.R. (3d) 83 (Ont. C.A.). For a similar wide view of provincial power to spend money: see *Dunbar v. A.G. Sask.* (1984), 11 D.L.R. (4th) 374 (Sask. Q.B.) upholding provincial spending for international aid.

It ought to be said that in contrasting taxation and regulation, the courts have not been influenced so much by a belief in "pure taxation" (*i.e.* taxation which produces revenue but has no economic effects — an imaginary situation in the modern world) as by a legal view of the distribution of legislative power and of the "pith and substance" doctrine.

Whether legislation imposes a tax is a question which is as important for the provinces as it is for the Dominion. Its relevance for the provinces is in respect of their limitation to direct taxation under section 92(2). For example, are employer contributions to a provincial workmen's compensation fund taxes which must meet the test of "direct taxation"? Or, are they in the nature of premiums statutorily exacted to insure employees against employment hazards, and hence a matter of the exercise of provincial regulatory authority under section 92(13)? The Privy Council indicated in *Workmen's Compensation Board v. C.P.R.*, [1920] A.C. 184, that such contributions were taxes. In the course of his judgment for the Board, Lord Haldane remarked: "Nor can it be successfully contended that the Province had not a general power to impose direct taxation in this form on the respondents if for provincial purposes"; see also *Workmen's Compensation Board v. Bathurst Co.*, [1923] 4 D.L.R.

84 (N.B.C.A.); *Royal Bank of Canada v. Workmen's Compensation Board of N.S.*, [1936] S.C.R. 560 (assessments on employers held to be direct taxation). This view, and its consequence, should be compared with the attitude of the Privy Council in the *Employment and Social Insurance Act* case, *supra*, and the consequence for the Dominion of the view that the contributions there were not taxes. Having regard to the limitations on federal regulatory power, reliance on the plenary taxing power was necessary. This proved adequate in *Reader's Digest Assoc. (Canada) Ltd. v. A.-G. Can.* (1962), 37 D.L.R. (2d) 239 (Que. Q.B.), aff'd. (1965), 59 D.L.R. (2d) 54 (Que. C.A.) to sustain a federal excise tax on the value of advertising material in so-called special editions (as defined) of non-Canadian periodicals published in Canada, although it was clear that the tax was designed to aid or had the effect of aiding Canadian periodicals. The matter has come up in several other cases with respect to provincial legislation. In *Ontario Boys' Wear Ltd. v. Advisory Committee and A.-G. Ont.*, [1944] S.C.R. 349, an issue arose whether the compulsory levy to help defray the expenses of administering codes of working conditions under the *Ontario Industrial Standards Act* was a tax, and, if so, whether it was direct. Kerwin J., speaking for the Court stated that "if the assessment be a tax, it is a direct tax . . .; and, in any event, it may be justified as a fee for services rendered by the Province or by its authorized instrumentalities under the powers given provincial legislatures by section 92(13) and 92(16) of the *B.N.A. Act*". See, to the same effect, *Shannon v. Lower Mainland Dairy Products Board*, [1938] A.C. 708 (P.C.). In *A.-G. B.C. v. E. & N. Ry.*, [1950] A.C. 87, the Privy Council had to consider, *inter alia*, whether section 124 of the *Forest Act*, R.S.B.C. 1948, c. 128, providing for the creation of a forest protection fund through an annual levy on owners of timber lands and through annual provincial grants, imposed a tax or merely a service charge for fire protection services. Although imposed on a defined and limited class of persons, and applicable to a special purpose without ever falling into the general mass of proceeds of taxation, the levy was held to be a tax. The decision on tax or service charge had to be made in this case to determine whether the railway company was exempt from the levy because of a statutory exemption from "taxation". In *Children's Aid Society v. Salmon Arm*, [1941] 1 W.W.R. 68 (B.C.C.A.), it was held that a provincial enactment authorizing the making of an order fixing a municipality with responsibility for maintaining a neglected child, did not impose a tax; hence there was no question of "direct" or "indirect" to be determined.

In *Lower Mainland Dairy Products v. Crystal Dairy Ltd.*, [1933] A.C. 168, the Privy Council held that certain equalization levies designed to effectuate provincial price-fixing schemes as a means of orderly marketing were really taxes. The levies were accordingly struck down as indirect taxes. In fact, they represented a provincial attempt to impose adjustment and expense levies on milk producers as part of a regulatory scheme to effect a pooling of proceeds and to equalize producer returns. *Reference re Agricultural Products Marketing Act and Two Other Acts*, [1978] 2 S.C.R. 1198 has finally and properly written "finis" to the so-called *Crystal Dairy* doctrine, but the course of its diminution and ultimate reverse is interesting. A few years after the *Crystal Dairy* case was decided, its principle was somewhat attenuated where a licensing scheme was used as a means of conjoint regulation and revenue-raising: see *Shannon v. Lower Mainland Dairy Products Board*, [1938] A.C. 708 (P.C.). The marketing scheme in the *Shannon* case did not have to meet the test of direct taxation because the legislation did not involve the type of adjustment levy found in the *Crystal Dairy* case; and the Court was able to sustain the scheme without reference to section 92(2). But it did involve licence fees bound up with marketing administration, and thus reflected on the alternative majority position taken by the Supreme Court in respect of the expenses levy associated with the marketing scheme in *Lawson v. Interior Tree Fruit and Vegetable Committee of Direction*, [1931] S.C.R. 357. The holding of Duff J. for the majority that the expenses levy was taxation (and invalid because indirect) was taken up in the *Crystal Dairy* case which, however, involved an adjustment levy as well as an expenses levy. Certainly, so far as an expenses or administration levy is concerned, case law since the *Shannon* case has followed that case rather than the *Lawson* case: see *Ontario Boys' Wear Ltd. v. Advisory Committee*, [1944] S.C.R. 349; *P.E.I. Potato Marketing Board v. H. B. Willis Inc.*, [1952] 2 S.C.R. 392; *Reference re the Ontario Farm Products Marketing Act*, [1957] S.C.R. 198.

It is a striking comment on *stare decisis* — there is no other rational explanation — that not only in the *Turner's Dairy Ltd.* case, [1941] S.C.R. 573, but also in *P.E.I. Potato Marketing Board v. H. B. Willis Inc.*, [1952] 2 S.C.R. 392 (see the judgments of Rand J. and of Estey J.), the Supreme Court was content with an uncritical acceptance of the *Crystal Dairy* doctrine. With appeals to the Privy Council gone, the Court took a closer look at the doctrine in the *Ontario Farm Products Marketing Act* reference, *supra*, but even there the Court at once distinguished it and applied it. It found that the doctrine did not apply to a marketing scheme involving merely the pooling of products and returns by producers engaged in a statutorily-directed scheme of co-operative disposal of their products. In this respect the scheme did not contemplate (to use the language of Fauteux J.) that one producer or one class of producers should contribute part of his or its returns to another producer or class. This was not taxation; and indeed, the Supreme Court re-emphasized the fact that a mere pooling scheme is not taxation when it reviewed the pooling arrangements in the federal *Canadian Wheat Board Act* in *Murphy v. C.P.R.*, [1958] S.C.R. 626. To have characterized the pooling arrangement as a taxing device might have involved a collision with section 121 of the *Constitution Act, 1867*, although, apart from this risk of invalidity, the Dominion might have as safely argued taxation as regulation of interprovincial and export trade. The importance of the *Murphy* case lies precisely in the fact that the Court regarded the federal enactment constitutionally as what it was in fact, *i.e.* a marketing measure. In overruling *Crystal Dairy*, in *Reference Re Agricultural Products Marketing Act*, [1978] 2 S.C.R. 1198, the Supreme Court of Canada has recognized that whether a compulsory marketing scheme provides for a simple pooling of products and returns in proportion to products pooled, or goes further and embraces a formula for adjustment of returns as between classes of regulated products, the gist of the matter is trade regulation. If there is any vice in such provincial regulation it can only be in an overreaching of the legislation to encompass interprovincial or export trade. See *R. v. Ont. Milk Marketing Board; Ex parte Channel Islands Breeds Milk Producers Association*, [1969] 1 O.R. 309 (S.C.); aff'd [1969] 2 O.R. 121 (C.A.); *cf. Brant Dairy Co. v. Ontario Milk Commission*, [1973] S.C.R. 131.

[In *United States v. Butler* (1935), 297 U.S. 1, where the federal Agricultural Adjustment Act was struck down as relating to agricultural production which was beyond Congressional power, the Court rejected an argument founded on the federal taxing power, saying in part (at p. 61): "A tax, in the general understanding of the term, and as used in the Constitution, is an exaction for the support of the Government. The word has never been thought to connote the expropriation of money from one group for the benefit of another. We may concede that the latter sort of imposition is constitutional when imposed to effectuate regulation of a matter in which both groups are interested and in respect of which there is a power of legislative regulation. But manifestly no justification for it can be found unless as an integral part of such regulation. The exaction cannot be wrested out of its setting, denominated an excise for raising revenue and legalized by ignoring its purpose as a mere instrumentality for bringing about a desired end. To do this would be to shut our eyes to what all others than we can see and understand." What was unconstitutional regulation in the *Butler* case was unconstitutional taxation in the *Crystal Dairy* case. The two cases represent an interesting problem in comparative federalism.]

While it would seem to be a necessary consequence of these cases that there is a legally definable thing called a "tax", it is difficult to square the results of the cases with the indicia of taxation which they lay down. Perhaps the pioneer effort at definition was that made by Duff J., as he then was, in *Lawson v. Interior Tree, Fruit & Vegetable Committee*, [1931] S.C.R. 357, which involved the validity of provincial marketing legislation authorizing an administrative agency to impose levies on any products marketed to defray expenses of operation. According to Duff J., the levies were taxes because they were (1) enforceable by law; (2) imposed under the authority of the legislature; (3) imposed by a public body; and (4) made for a public purpose. It followed in this case that they were invalid because indirect in violation of section 92(2). It is a fair question whether they would not today be considered valid under section 92(9) if enacted under a licensing system established by provincial marketing legislation: see *Shannon v. Lower Mainland Dairy Products Board, supra*. In *A.-G. B.C. v. E. & N. Ry., supra*, it appeared to be enough to mark the forest protection fund levy as a tax that (to use the words of the Privy Council) "it [was] imposed compulsorily by the State and [was] recoverable at the suit of the Crown" ([1950] A.C. 87 at 121); the special features of the levy, already noted, did not matter. This much is clear; a tax under the *Constitution Act, 1867* is not confined to an exaction for the support of the government.

The tests of a tax, indicated in the *Lawson* case and in the *E. & N. Ry.* case were applied by Egbert J. in *Re Unearned Increment Tax Act* (1952), 6 W.W.R. (N.S.) 657 (Alta. S.C.), affirmed at 672 (Alta. C.A.). There a statute imposed a tax of ten per cent (payable on the registration under the *Alberta Land Titles Act* of any transfer of land) on the increase in value of the land at the time of such registration over and above the last preceding value, excluding cost of improvements or of development work. Despite the language of the statute which spoke of a "tax" the learned Judge held that the exaction was not a tax because not imposed directly upon anyone, not made compulsory, nor was it enforceable by law when the only penalty for non-payment was refusal to register a transfer; indeed, a purchaser could escape the consequence of non-payment by registering a caveat. Egbert J. held that exaction was a confiscation or capture of a capital gain, but he went on to hold that if he should be wrong in this and the levy was a tax, it was direct. The Alberta Appellate Division affirmed in a few words, holding the exaction to be a tax and to be direct.

[Are water rates taxes in respect of federal Crown property? See *A.-G. Can. v. Toronto* (1893), 23 S.C.R. 514.]

A few other features of federal and provincial taxing powers may be noted here. The Dominion under section 91(3) may impose a licence tax in connection with matters falling within its regulatory authority, *e.g.* "seacoast and inland fisheries":

*A.-G. Can. v. A.-G. Ont.*, [1898] A.C. 700 (P.C.). Since the *Statute of Westminster*, 1931 (Imp.), c. 4, s. 3, the Dominion may give its tax legislation an extraterritorial operation: see *B.C. Electric Ry. Co. v. The King*, [1946] A.C. 527 (P.C.). While provincial taxing power under section 92(2) is limited both in kind and in area, neither of these limitations affects the plenary authority of the Dominion under section 91(3). The necessary reconciliation of these two grants of power (adverted to in *Citizens Insurance Co. v. Parsons* (1881), 7 App. Cas. 96 at 108 (P.C.) and in *Bank of Toronto v. Lambe* (1887), 12 App. Cas. 575 at 585 (P.C.)) has, however, withdrawn from Dominion authority any power of direct taxation within a province to raise revenue for provincial purposes: *Reference re Agricultural Products Marketing Act*, [1978] 2 S.C.R. 1198.

Because the taxing powers of Dominion and Provinces are independent of each other, there is no constitutional objection to double taxation: see *Forbes v. A.-G. Man.*, [1937] A.C. 260 (P.C.), where Lord Macmillan said: "Both [*i.e.* Dominion and provincial] income taxes may co-exist and be enforced without clashing. The Dominion reaps part of the field of the Manitoba citizen's income. The Province reaps another part of it." What the constitutional position would be if Dominion and provincial income taxation aggregated over 100 per cent. has not yet been decided, but the situation would invite the application of the "paramountcy" doctrine to tax collection: *cf. In re Silver Bros.; A.-G. Que. v. A.-G. Can.*, [1932] A.C. 514 (P.C.). Despite the absence of constitutional difficulty, the existence of common tax fields (as in the case of income tax) has induced Dominion-provincial co-operation in income taxation, both in the interests of economy of administration and of relieving the taxpayer from making multiple returns. Thus, by tax agreements with the Dominion the provinces other than Quebec have undertaken, in return for payments to be made to them by the Dominion, to refrain from levying specified taxes. No delegation of power is involved because the Dominion is clearly entitled in any event to levy such taxes. And it is to be doubted that the Dominion-Provincial tax arrangements can be attacked as involving direct taxation by the Dominion within a Province to raise revenue for provincial purposes. The law on the matter is, however, enmeshed in economic and political considerations which go to the very heart of Canadian federalism: see Scott, "The Constitutional Background of Taxation Agreements" (1955), 2 McGill L.J. 1. Indeed, the taxation agreements are not legally enforceable against the Dominion except as they may involve legislative acceptance of jurisdiction for their implementation: see *In re Taxation Agreement between Saskatchewan and Canada*, [1946] 1 W.W.R. 257 (Arb-Trib.). (*Quaere*, however, whether it is not open to the Crown in one aspect to sue the Crown in another on a contract between them!) Moreover, it is open to a Province to pass valid legislation in derogation of the agreements: see *Van Buren Bridge Co. v. Madawaska and A.-G. N.B.* (1958), 15 D.L.R. (2d) 763 (N.B.C.A.); *Re Lofstrom & Murphy* (1971), 22 D.L.R. (3d) 120 (Sask. C.A.). The contrary intimation in *Alworth Jr. v. A.-G. B.C.* (1959), 20 D.L.R. (2d) 544 (B.C.) (affirmed on appeal with express exclusion of any determination on this point (1960), 24 D.L.R. (2d) 71) is incompatible with well-understood constitutional principle. No so-called contract between Dominion and Province can operate as a constitutional limitation on provincial taxing power to the advantage of a person caught by a provincial statute which violates the contract.

[In *Caron v. The King*, [1924] A.C. 999 (P.C.), Lord Phillimore said: "Upon any view there is nothing in section 92 to take away the power to impose any taxation for Dominion purposes which is *prima facie* given by head 3 of section 91. It is not therefore *ultra vires* on the part of the Parliament of Canada to impose a Dominion income tax for Dominion purposes"; see too Duff C.J. (dissenting) in *Reference re Employment and Social Insurance Act*, [1936] S.C.R. 427 at 433: "The authority, it will be noticed, is an authority to legislate in relation to the raising of money. There is no limitation in those words as respect the purpose or purposes to which the money is to be applied." Note the use of the federal "spending" power in connection with the marketing of wheat by the offer of a fixed price to farmers which they are not, however, legally obliged to accept; and see Chapter 8, *supra*. It is similarly open to the Dominion to spend money on education or on any other objects, either by conditional or unconditional grants.

For further discussion of the topics and cases in this chapter, see Magnet, "The Constitutional Distribution of Taxation Powers in Canada" (1978), 10 Ottawa L.R. 473].

# MASSEY-FERGUSON INDUSTRIES LTD. v. GOVERNMENT OF SASKATCHEWAN

In the Supreme Court of Canada. [1981] 2 S.C.R. 413.

Laskin C.J.C., Martland, Dickson, Estey, McIntyre, Chouinard and Lamer JJ.
October 6, 1981.

Appeal by the plaintiffs from a judgment of the Saskatchewan Court of Appeal, [1980] 6 W.W.R. 604, dismissing their appeal from, and allowing the defendants' cross-appeal to vary, a judgment of Hughes J., [1979] 1 W.W.R. 97, dismissing the plaintiffs' action for a declaration that certain amendments to the *Agricultural Implements Act, 1968* (Sask.) are *ultra vires*.

The judgment of the Court was delivered by

LASKIN C.J.C.: — This appeal, which is here by leave, involves the determination of two constitutional issues posed as follows:

1. Is the Saskatchewan *Agricultural Implements Act*, 1968, as amended, which establishes the Agricultural Implements Board and empowers it to determine compensation as provided in the Act, *ultra vires* section 96 of the *British North America Act*?
2. Does the levy on general provincial distributors, to establish and maintain the Agricultural Implements Compensation Fund, based upon a percentage of their gross sales or other rates or specific sums, amount to an indirect tax in violation of section 92(2) of the *British North America Act*?

These issues were the subject of a declaratory action by the appellants who are farm implement manufacturers and whose products are sold in Saskatchewan and elsewhere in Canada. Each is represented by an independent farm equipment dealer in Saskatchewan and some also sell their products through stores of their own in the Province. All are designated as distributors under the *Agricultural Implements Act*, now R.S.S. 1978, c. A-10. The issues herein fall to be decided under the statute as enacted by 1968 (Sask.), c. 1, and as amended by 1973, c. 1, and 1976, c. 2.

It was the amendment of 1973 which established the Agricultural Implements Board and provided for the Agricultural Implements Compensation Fund and for contributions thereto by distributors. A change was made by 1979-80, c. 10, s. 6, in the way contributions to the fund were to be assessed, and the appellants do not challenge the new mode of assessment. So far then as the second question is concerned, the appellants contest the validity of the assessments only for the period 1973 to 1979.

They succeeded on this point before the trial Judge, Hughes J., who held against them, however, on the s. 96 question [[1979] 1 W.W.R. 97]. A unanimous Court of Appeal, in reasons delivered by Culliton C.J.S., held against the appellants on both issues [[1980] 6 W.W.R. 604]. In this Court, the Attorney-General of Canada, as intervenor, supported the appellants on the indirect tax issue but supported the respondents, the Government of Saskatchewan and the Minister of Agriculture, on the s. 96 point. The Attorneys-General of Ontario and of Quebec, also intervenors, supported the respondents on both issues.

## II

The *Agricultural Implements Act, 1968*, as amended, has a history. It began life, in more modest form, as the *Farm Implements Act*, 1915 (Sask.), c. 28. The purpose of this Act was to provide for some control over contracts for the purchase of farm implements, directed to protection of the purchaser. The Act prescribed statutory forms of contract for the sale and purchase of farm implements, which were classified under the Act as large and small implements, separate contract forms being prescribed for each class. Sellers of implements were required to file annually a list of the implements they have for sale, with the prices thereof, both for cash and on credit and, in the latter case, the credit terms. A lien on implements sold to purchasers on credit (title remaining in the seller until full payment was made) depended upon a lien note being taken in compliance with relevant legislation. If there was repossession for default, arbitration was provided to fix the value of the repossessed implement if the seller and buyer were unable to agree on it, and accounts between them were to be settled on the basis of that value.

The *Farm Implement Act*, with amendments which did not change its essential character as indicated above, continued in force until 1958 when it was replaced by the *Agricultural Machinery Act*, 1958 (Sask.), c. 91 [later R.S.S. 1965, c. 232]. This Act established a Government agency called the Agricultural Machinery Administration and also a board called the Agricultural Machinery Board whose duties were, mainly, to govern and direct the work of the Agricultural Machinery Administration. It was also empowered to conduct inquiries into the distribution and marketing of farm implements in Saskatchewan.

The Agricultural Machinery Administration, subject to the direction of the Board, was invested with power to administer the Act, to test and appraise, under actual working conditions, implements sold or offered for sale in the Province, to undertake development work to improve and develop implements for use in Saskatchewan and to publish reports, pamphlets and bulletins. It introduced the "general provincial distributor", being an agent of a manufacturer or person selling or offering to sell implements in Saskatchewan and required that every such manufacturer or person be represented in the Province by one or more general provincial distributors. Those who were not manufacturers and who sold at retail only were excluded from this requirement. However, retail sellers of farm implements had to be licensed to sell implements and such licensees were limited to selling only implements obtainable from or through a general provincial distributor. The limitation did not extend to second-hand implements or second-hand parts.

General provincial distributors were required to file annually statements showing the name and location of every vendor who obtained or would obtain implements from or through general provincial distributors. A list of large and small implements offered for sale by each provincial distributor was to be filed annually along with illustrations and descriptions, the maximum intended retail price, both for cash and on credit and the usual credit terms and the rate of interest. They were also required to maintain a sufficient supply of repairs for their implements on pain of a summary conviction penalty. So too were licensed sellers on similar pain of a penalty. Liability to penalties was also imposed for default in required filings and failure to satisfy the licensing requirements.

The *Agricultural Machinery Act* continued the prescription of statutory forms of contract in the predecessor Act, including trial periods to enable the purchaser to determine whether the machinery works. The lien or conditional sale provisions of the earlier Act were also continued, and so were the repossession provisions and, as well, the provisions for arbitrating the value in the case of large implements if the parties were unable to agree on it.

What is clear is that there was a tightening of the statutory and administrative controls over the sale of farm implements in Saskatchewan and over the distributors and sellers of such implements. The *Agricultural Machinery Act* was amended by 1965, c. 12, the main change being the dropping of the Agricultural Machinery Administration and the Agricultural Machinery Board; otherwise, the Act remained substantially the same.

The *Agricultural Machinery Act* was replaced in 1968 by the *Agricultural Implements Act, 1968*, and it is this Act, as amended in 1973 and 1976, which, as indicated at the beginning of these reasons, is the focus of the two constitutional questions which were before the Courts below and are now before this Court.

The Act as amended in 1973 established an Agricultural Implements Board whose members were to be appointed by the Lieutenant-Governor in Council. Administration of the Act was confided to the Board under the direction of the Minister and in accordance with Regulations which the Lieutenant-Governor in Council was authorized to make under s. 31 [now s. 53], as amended by 1970, c. 2, s. 5; 1973, c. 1, s. 6, and 1976, c. 2, s. 19. The 1976 amendment [by s. 20] also changed the designation of "general provincial distributors" (as introduced in the 1958 Act) to "distributors" and replaced the term "vendor", used in the predecessor Acts by the term "dealer".

It is unnecessary to examine in any detail those provisions of the 1968 Act which required filings by distributors and dealers and which provided for licensing of dealers. They continued a pre-existing policy with some additional provisions for obtaining information from distributors. Inspection provisions found in previous legislation were also continued and so too were the central provisions which prescribed statutory contracts and delienated repossession procedures. For present purposes, the key terms are those respecting the Board's powers, the Regulation-making authority and the provisions respecting assessments for the compensation fund and respcting claims upon the fund....

[His Lordship's recitation of the Board's administration and regulation-making powers is omitted. He continued with the statute compensation provisions as follows:]

Section 6D [am. 1976, c. 2, ss. 3, 20 — now s. 10] referred to in s. 31(f) above is as follows:

6D(1) A farmer who feels himself aggrieved, or who considers he has incurred a loss, due to an unreasonable delay in the availability of a repair or who considers he has incurred a loss due to the vendor or the general provincial distributor not fulfilling the conditions or warranties as set out in this Act or in a conditional sales contract, in respect of an implement purchased by him or by a person who transferred the implement to him, may apply to the board for an award of compensation for the damages or loss he has suffered.

(2) Upon receipt of an application under subsection (1), the board may, subject to the regulations with respect to notice of the hearing to interested parties and the conduct of the hearing, dismiss the application or make compensation to the applicant farmer out of the Agricultural Implements Compensation Fund.

(3) The decisions and findings of the board upon all questions of law and fact are final and conclusive.

(4) Where a farmer has suffered loss, within the meaning of subsection (1), the farmer may claim compensation under this section or alternatively he may commence an action in any court of competent jurisdiction.

(5) Where an application is made to the board under this section it shall act as a bar to any court action with respect to the matters affected thereby.

(6) Compensation shall not be awarded to a farmer under this section in respect of damages or losses unless notice of the damages or losses is given to the general provincial distributor, the vendor and the board within six months after the damages or losses were alleged to have been incurred and the notice shall set out the name and address of the farmer and shall be sufficient if it states in ordinary language the cause of the damages or losses and where they were incurred.

(7) The notice may be given:

(a) to the general provincial distributor and the vendor by delivering it at or sending it by registered mail addressed to their respective places of business;

(b) to the board by delivering it to or sending it by registered mail addressed to the board.

(8) Failure to give the prescribed notice or any defect or inaccuracy in a notice does not bar the right to compensation if the board is of opinion that the claim to compensation is a just one and ought to be allowed.

Section 6E is an important provision respecting the Agricultural Implements Board's power to deal with applications for compensation. As enacted in 1973 and as amended in 1976, c. 2, s. 4 [now s. 11], it reads as follows:

6E(1) A farmer desirous of claiming compensation under section 6D shall within six months after the damages or losses were allegedly incurred, file with the board an application for the compensation and such further or other evidence of his claim as may be required by the board.

(2) No action lies for the recovery of compensation under section 6D from the board but all claims for compensation shall be heard and determined by the board.

(3) An award for compensation to a farmer under section 6D shall not exceed five thousand dollars.

(4) Compensation payable to farmers in amounts determined by the board and the expenses of investigating and hearing claims for compensation shall be paid out of the Agricultural Implements Compensation Fund.

I come now to the statutory provisions respecting the Agricultural Implements Compensation Fund (referred to in ss. 6D(2) and 6E(4)) out of which farmers' claims, made pursuant to ss. 6D and 6E, are payable. Sections 6F [1976, c. 2, ss. 5, 20 — now s. 12] and 6G [am. 1976, c. 2, s. 20 — now s. 13] are in these terms:

6F(1) The Agricultural Implements Compensation Fund is hereby established and contributions to the Fund shall be made by general provincial distributors in accordance with this section.

(2) The Board shall each year assess and levy upon the general provincial distributors such percentage of their gross sales or other rates, or such specific sums, as it considers sufficient to pay during the current year compensation to farmers, to defray the expenses of investigating and hearing claims for compensation under this Act and to maintain a reserve fund to pay compensation that may become payable in the future.

(3) An assessment under subsection (2) may if the board sees fit be levied provisionally upon the estimate of gross receipts of a provincial distributor reported to the board by the general provincial distributor or upon an estimate of those gross receipts as may be fixed by the board, and where an assessment is levied provisionally, the assessment shall be levied on the actual gross receipts of the general provincial distributor as soon as the actual gross receipts of the general provincial distributor have been ascertained by the board; and the amount to be paid by the general provincial distributor as a result of the levy may, if the board considers it reasonable, be paid in instalments in sums to be determined by the board.

(4) The board shall determine and fix the sum or provisional sum, whether calculated as a percentage or other rate for which each general provincial distributor is assessed under this section, and each general provincial distributor shall, within one month, or such other time as the board may fix, after notice of the assessment and of the sum or provisional sum to be paid has been served upon him, pay to the board the sum or provisional sum fixed by the board or, where the sum is to be paid in instalments pay the first instalment within such time as the board may specify and the remaining instalment or instalments within such time as may be so specified and, in the case of a provisional sum pay, according to terms and at times prescribed by the board, any increased amount resulting from the adjustment in the levy on the actual receipts of the general provincial distributor.

(5) The notice may be served upon the general provincial distributor by sending it to him by registered mail, postage prepaid, and shall be deemed to have been served on the general provincial distributor on the day on which the notice was mailed.

(6) Where at any time it appears that a statement or estimate of gross receipts upon which an assessment or provisional amount of assessment is based, is too low, the general provincial distributor shall upon demand pay to the board such sum, to be fixed by the board, that shall in the opinion of the board be sufficient to bring the payment to the proper amount, and payment of such sum may be enforced in the same manner as the payment of any amount levied by the board may be enforced.

(7) The sum whether calculated as a percentage or other rate determined and fixed by the board under subsection (4) shall be published in the *Gazette* forthwith after being fixed.

6G. For the purpose of assessing general provincial distributors, the board may classify general provincial distributors and assess different rates for any class or classes of general provincial distributors.

. . . .

[His Lordship rejected the argument that the Board was acting as a s. 96 court and continued:]

## IV

An attack has also been mounted against the levy on distributors to establish and maintain the compensation fund. It is submitted that the formula for fixing the levy results in the imposition of an indirect tax which, as such, is beyond provincial competence to impose. There are two issues involved in this submission: first, is the levy a tax within s. 92(2) of the *British North America Act, 1867?*; and, second, if it is a tax is it indirect? It is the Board which assesses under s. 6F in order to create a fund which will satisfy existing and anticipated compensation awards and Board expenses for investigating and hearing claims. The assessment upon the distributors is annual and is upon "such percentage of their gross sales or other rates or such specific sums" as the Board considers sufficient for the above-mentioned purposes. Under s. 6F, distributors may be classified and different rates may be assessed for any class or classes of them.

The contention of the appellants that the levies for the compensation fund are taxes and that as such they are indirect is founded upon a conjoint reliance on *Workmen's Compensation Board v. C.P.R. Co.*, [1920] A.C. 184 (P.C.) and *R. v. Caledonian Collieries Ltd.*, [1928] A.C. 358 (P.C.). The former is relied on to support the submission that the levies are taxes (no less than the assessments upon employers for workmen's compensation) and the latter is relied on to show that a tax on gross sales is necessarily indirect. It must be noted, however, that the Board here is given choices in measuring the levies and is not limited to assessments on gross receipts, except where it assesses provisionally. The ultimate annual assessment may be on a different formula, and emphasis is lent to this by the provision for classifying distributors and fixing different rates for the various classes.

In my opinion, if the assessments are taxes they are no less direct than the assessment upon employers for workmen's compensation in *Workmen's Compensation Board v. C.P.R., supra.* Unlike the *Caledonian Collieries* case, the assessments here are not necessarily related to trading transactions. In the *Workmen's Compensation Board* case, the Privy Council was concerned, *inter alia*, with an accident fund created by assessment of employers and administered by the board for the benefit of injured employees. Although there was also an exaction from employees (through a deduction from wages), it was nominal. The Judicial Committee made short shrift of the direct-indirect tax issue by saying (at p. 190 A.C.): "Nor can it be successfully contended that the Province had not a general power to impose direct taxation in this form on the respondents [employers] if for Provincial purposes."

This Court considered the same question in *Royal Bank v. Workmen's Compensation Bd. of N.S.*, [1936] S.C.R. 560. There, according to the majority of the Court, it was admitted by the appellant that employer assessments for workmen's compensation were taxes and it was held that they were without doubt direct taxes upon the employers. No reference was made, however, to the Privy Council's judgment but it appears from the concurring reasons of Davis J. that the Court raised the question whether the workmen's compensation assessments were taxes and, if so, whether they were indirect. On the assumption that they were taxes, Davis J. was satisfied that they were direct and within provincial competence.

I am not persuaded that the assessments to create and maintain a compensation fund should be characterized as taxes within s. 92(2) of the *British North America Act, 1867*. The levies, as monetary exactions, are liquidating premiums to satisfy farmers' claims under s. 6D and the policy of the Act is to relate the assessments to the compensation awards and to administrative expenses. They are designed to support a limited form of insurance for the benefit of farmers who purchase agricultural implements, related to their use of such implements. There is here no collection of money to go into a consolidated revenue fund which is then chargeable with satisfying awards of compensation. Although the scheme is a public one, created under a public statute, its beneficiaries and obligors are circumscribed by the particular activity or enterprise in which they are engaged.

It is true that previous cases which have considered whether a levy is or is not a tax have had a different focus than the present case, as, for example, in facing the question whether a compulsory levy to defray administration expenses is better characterized as a service charge rather than as a tax: see *Ontario Boys Wear Ltd. v. Advisory Committee*, [1944] S.C.R. 349; *Shannon v. Lower Mainland Dairy Products Board*, [1938] A.C. 708. Although the levy here is intended to meet administrative expenses of the Board, its chief purpose is, as I have already said, to create a limited insurance fund. The distributors who are subject to the levy are under an additional cost of doing business in Saskatchewan, but this does not mean that they are being taxed in a constitutional sense.

V

In the result, the two questions in this appeal should be answered "no". The appeal therefore fails and should be dismissed with costs. There will be no costs to or against any of the intervenors.

*Appeal dismissed.*

## 2. Direct Taxation Within the Province

### *Note on Direct versus Indirect Tax*

The test for determining whether a tax is direct or indirect was laid down in *Bank of Toronto v. Lambe* (1887), 12 App. Cas. 575, where the Privy Council accepted John Stuart Mill's definition in *Political Economy*, Book V, c. 3:

> Taxes are either direct or indirect. A direct tax is one which is demanded from the very persons who it is intended or desired should pay it. Indirect taxes are those which are demanded from one person in the expectation and intention that he shall indemnify himself at the expense of another; such are the excise or customs.
> The producer or importer of a commodity is called upon to pay a tax on it, not with the intention to levy a peculiar contribution upon him, but to tax through him the consumers of the commodity, from whom it is supposed that he will recover the amount by means of an advance in price.

Mills' definition has been accepted "almost from the beginning of Canadian federalism", in the words of Laskin C.J.C. in *Minister of Finance of New Brunswick v. Simpson-Sears*, [1982] 1 S.C.R. 144. See also *Canadian Industrial Gas and Oil Ltd. v. Government of Saskatchewan*, [1978] 2 S.C.R. 545. The critical issue is whether the tax has a "tendency to be passed on" or whether the person who must pay the tax is the one that the legislature intends should ultimately pay it. Thus in *Brewers and Maltsters Association of Ontario v. A.G. Ont.*, [1897] A.C. 231 (P.C.), where legislation imposed a flat licence fee of $100.00 on brewers and distillers engaged in wholesale licensing, the tax was upheld as direct pursuant to section 92(2) of the *Constitution Act, 1867.* Since the fee had no relation to the quantity of goods sold and in the ordinary course there was no intention or expectation of recoupment from customers, it satisfied the test of direct taxation. To the same effect: see *Fortier v. Lambe* (1894), 25 S.C.R. 422 (provincial legislation imposing a licence fee on manufacturers and traders upheld); *Colpitts Ranches v. A.G. Alta.*, [1954] 3 D.L.R. 121 (Alta. S.C.) (municipal business tax on fox farming upheld). Similarly, a tax on net income has always been held to be a direct tax as it does not have a tendency to be passed on. Restated, the incidence of an income tax is not clearly traceable through to each contract of sale: see *Re Newfoundland and Labrador Corporation Ltd. and A.G. Newfoundland*, [1982] 2 S.C.R. 260; *Nickel Rim Mines Ltd. v. A.G. Ont.*, [1967] S.C.R. 270n. The essential attribute of these cases is that, while the commercial taxpayer will naturally seek to pass on the effect of the tax as part of the cost of doing business, he will be unable to specifically pass on the tax itself. As stated by Laskin C.J.C. in *Minister of Finance of New Brunswick v. Simpson-Sears, supra*, at p. 162 S.C.R.:

> The "general tendency" argument, found, for example, in the *Caledonian Collieries* case, is not one that establishes a principle outside of the context in which it was used in that case. Where, as in the present case, the tax imposed in respect of the free distribution of catalogues takes no account of what ultimately happens to the catalogues, whether they are used or discarded, and is unrelated to any purchases made from the catalogues, *it is manifest to me that the tax is so diffused in its impact that it cannot be said that there is any clearly traceable way in which the tax can be passed on* (emphasis added).

On the other hand, the courts have struck down taxes as indirect where they can be specifically allocated to a particular contract of sale and accordingly "cling" to the product through successive stages of sale. Thus in *A.G. Man. v. A.G. Can.*, [1925] A.C. 561, the Privy Council invalidated a provincial statute which imposed a tax on the seller or his broker or agent in respect of every contract of sale of grain for future delivery. Lord Haldane said that:

> it is impossible to doubt that the tax was imposed in a form which contemplated that someone else than the person on whom it was imposed should pay it. The amount will, in the end, become a charge against the amount of the price which is to come to the seller in the world market, and be paid by someone else than the persons primarily taxed.

Similarly, in *R. v. Caledonian Collieries Ltd.*, [1928] A.C. 358 the Privy Council struck down provincial legislation which imposed upon mine owners a percentage tax upon the gross revenues of their coal mines because such taxes have a general tendency to be passed on. See also *Charlottetown v. Foundation Maritime Ltd.*, [1932] S.C.R. 589, where a law requiring all non-resident contractors to pay a graduated tax by way of a percentage of the contract price on every contract for work within the municipality was struck down as an indirect tax.

While each case must be examined on its merits, certain categories have been crystallized through the jurisprudence as being direct or indirect. As stated by Dickson J. (as he then was) in *Canadian Industrial Gas and Oil v. Government of Saskatchewan, supra*, at p. 584 in dissent:

> Historically well-understood categories of taxation have a known jurisprudential fate. Thus, a customs levy cannot be made by the Legislature whereas a property tax or income tax falls unquestionably within their competence.

He went on to say:

> Argument was directed to the Court to the effect that the tax here in question is a commodity tax and, as such, the general tendency would be for the tax to be passed on and therefore categorized as indirect. It is true that a tax on any one commodity whether laid on its production, its importation, its carriage from place to place, or its sale will, as a general rule, raise the value and price of the commodity by at least the amount of the tax: Mill, volume II (1893 ed.), at page 435. That is very old doctrine and for that reason a commodity tax is traditionally conceived as an indirect tax. The Courts have taken that as one criterion in characterizing the tax: *A.G. B.C. v. C.P.R. Co.*, [1927] A.C. 934; *R. v. Caledonian Collieries Ltd., supra; A.G. B.C. v. MacDonald Murphy Lumber Co.*, [1930] A.C. 357. But there is a caveat. *Taxes imposed on the consumers of particular commodities are often called, or seem to be, taxes on commodities but they are not. Consumer taxes are normally regarded as direct.* See *A.G. B.C. v. Kingcome Navigation Co. Ltd., supra*, and *Atlantic Smoke Shops Ltd. v. Conlon*, [1943] A.C. 550, as related to consumption of non-durable goods, and *Cairns Construction Ltd. v. Government of Saskatchewan*, [1960] S.C.R. 619, related to durable goods (emphasis added).

While Dickson J. was speaking in dissent in the above case, the majority's disagreement with him was in the result and not on the principles quoted. In any event, Martland J. at page 559 agreed with Dickson J. in his comments about sales taxes:

> A sales tax, imposed upon vendors of goods, has been generally regarded as an indirect tax. On the other hand, where the tax, although collected through the vendor is actually paid by the ultimate consumer, the tax has been held to be direct: *Atlantic Smoke Shops v. Conlon*, [1943] A.C.550; *Cairns Construction Ltd. v. Government of Saskatchewan*, [1960] S.C.R. 619.

The result is that as long as the tax is imposed upon the ultimate consumer, who by definition will not pass on the tax, the tax will be direct notwithstanding that the vendor may be required by legislation to be the government's collection agent: see *Atlantic Smoke Shops v. Conlon*, [1943] A.C. 550 (P.C.).

It should be noted that the form of legislation is of critical importance in the area of direct versus indirect tax. Much in the jurisprudence on the taxing power in section 92(2) of the *Constitution Act, 1867* turns upon questions of statutory construction: see, for example *A.G.-B.C. v. Canada Trust Co.*, [1980] 2 S.C.R. 466 where the sole distinction between that case and *Provincial Treasurer of Alberta v. Kerr*, [1933] A.C. 710 (P.C.) was whether the tax was on "property" or "persons", and involved a highly technical point of statutory interpretation. The latitude currently being given to provincial Legislatures on matters of statutory construction in the section 92(2) context is clearly illustrated by *Alworth v. Minister of Finance*, [1978] 1 S.C.R. 447. In the *Alworth* case, the Supreme Court of Canada upheld a provincial tax on the basis that, notwithstanding that the charging section said that "the taxpayer shall pay a tax", the real subject of the tax was business operations in the province. Laskin C.J.C. said that it was "too mechanical" to hold that it was an *in personam* tax merely because the charging section said the "taxpayer" must pay it.


# CANADIAN INDUSTRIAL GAS & OIL LTD. v. GOVERNMENT OF SASKATCHEWAN

In the Supreme Court of Canada. [1978] 2 S.C.R. 545.

Laskin, C.J.C., Martland, Judson, Ritchie, Spence, Pigeon, Dickson, Beetz and de Grandpré, JJ. November 23, 1977.

[The facts are set out in Chapter 8, *supra*.]

The judgment of Laskin C.J.C. and Martland, Judson, Ritchie, Spence, Pigeon and Beetz JJ. was delivered by

MARTLAND J.: . . .

*Direct or indirect taxation*

My brother Dickson has reviewed the leading authorities dealing with the distinction between direct and indirect taxation. It is not necessary for me to repeat that review here. He has pointed out that it has been settled that:

> The dividing line between a direct and an indirect tax is referable to and ascertainable by the "general tendencies of the tax and the common understanding of men as to those tendencies" . . . The general tendency of a tax is the relevant criterion.

He has also pointed out that certain well understood categories of taxation have been generally established as falling within one or other of these classes. Thus custom levies are recognized as being indirect taxes, whereas income and property taxes have been recognized as being direct taxes. Similarly, a commodity tax has, as a general rule, been regarded as an indirect tax. The appellant submits that the levies here in question are commodity taxes, and refers to the Privy Council decision in *R. v. Caledonian Collieries Ltd.*, [1928] A.C. 358 at 362 (P.C.), in which Lord Warrington of Clyffe made the following statement:

> The respondents are producers of coal, a commodity the subject of commercial transactions. Their Lordships can have no doubt that the general tendency of a tax upon the sums received from the sale of the commodity which they produce and in which they deal is that they would seek to recover it in the price charged to a purchaser. Under particular circumstances the recovery of the tax may, it is true, be economically undesirable or practically impossible, but the general tendency of the tax remains.
>
> It is said on behalf of the appellant that at the time a sale is made the tax has not become payable, and therefore cannot be passed on. Their Lordships cannot accept this contention; the tax will have to be paid, and there would be no more difficulty in adding to the selling price the amount of the tax in anticipation than there would be if it had been actually paid.

In that case the tax was imposed upon the gross revenue of every mine owner, at a rate not to exceed 2%. The Privy Council considered that the general tendency of the tax would be for a mine owner to seek to recover the tax from his purchasers.

A sales tax, imposed upon vendors of goods, has been generally regarded as an indirect tax. On the other hand, where the tax, although collected through the vendor is actually paid by the ultimate consumer, the tax has been held to be direct: *Atlantic Smoke Shops Ltd. v. Conlon*, [1943] A.C. 550 (P.C.); *Cairns Construction Ltd. v. Government of Saskatchewan*, [1960] S.C.R. 619. However, in the present case the tax is imposed upon and payable by the producer in relation to the sale price of the oil which is produced. It is a sales tax, but the contention of the respondents is that it is not an indirect tax because the legislation does not contemplate and seeks to preclude the recovery of the tax from the purchaser.

The respondent contends that the mineral income tax is, as its name implies, an income tax, and so, a direct tax. I agree with the reasons of my brother Dickson for holding that that tax is not an income tax as that term is understood in the authorities which say that an income tax is a direct tax.

The respondent submits, with respect to the royalty surcharge, that it is not a tax, but that it is a genuine royalty payable to the Crown, as the owner of mineral rights, by its lessees who have been authorized to extract minerals from Crown lands. To determine the validity of this contention it is necessary to consider the nature of the legal relationship between the Crown and the persons from whom payment of the royalty surcharge is demanded.

Some of these persons were the holders of petroleum and natural gas leases from the owners of the freehold interest in such minerals. Their obligation to pay royalties depended upon the terms of the lease from the freehold owner. The effect of Part IV of Bill 42 was to expropriate the rights of the freehold owners in the petroleum and natural gas in their lands, save in the case of freehold owners of producing tracts which had an aggregate total area of 1,280 acres or less. Owners coming within this exemption would retain title to their petroleum and natural gas rights and the legal relationship between them and their lessees would continue. However, Bill 42 imposed on such lessees the obligation to pay mineral income tax in respect of their production.

With respect to lands not falling within the exemption, the owners were divested of their title, which was given, by the statute, to the Crown. This was accomplished by s-s. 28(1) of Bill 42, but the transfer to and vesting of title in the Crown was stated to be "subject to any lease affecting the same that may exist immediately preceding the tenth day of December, 1973". The rights of leaseholders in this category were thus preserved. However, s-s. 33(2) subjected such lessees to the same royalty surcharge as was imposed upon lessees leasing directly from the Crown. It provided:

> 33(2) Any person having a lease of the oil and gas rights or any of them shall be subject to section 63 of *The Petroleum and Natural Gas Regulations, 1969*, when enacted pursuant to section 18 and shall be liable to pay the royalty surcharge provided for therein from the first day of January, 1974, as if the lease came within subsection (1) of section 63.

The levy thus imposed cannot, in my opinion, be a royalty. The royalty payable by the lessee was fixed by the terms of his lease, and that lease was preserved by the terms of s-s. 28(1). It was not expropriated by the Crown. The imposition upon the lessee of the royalty surcharge levy was, in my opinion, a tax upon the lessee's share of the production to which he was lawfully entitled. I agree with my brother Dickson that this levy fell within the criteria laid down by Duff, J., as he then was, in *Lawson v. Interior Tree Fruit & Vegetable Committee*, [1931] S.C.R. 357 at 363, for deciding whether a levy constituted a tax.

Another class of lessees upon whom the royalty surcharge is imposed consists of those who were the holders of Crown leases at the time the royalty surcharge was imposed. In respect of these it was argued by counsel for the respondents that the Crown leases themselves, samples of which were filed as exhibits, contemplate the imposition of such a royalty. These leases contained the following provision:

> And also rendering and paying therefor unto the Lessor any royalties at such rates and in such manner and at such times as are from time to time prescribed by the Order of the Lieutenant Governor in Council: such rents and royalties to be free and clear of and from all rates, taxes and assessments and from all manner of deduction whatsoever.

I do not accept this submission. In my opinion the word "royalty" was used in the leases in its customary sense as meaning a share of the production obtained by the lessee. My view is reinforced by the use of the word "rate" which contemplates the determination of the proportions of production allocated to the lessor. The regulation which imposed the royalty surcharge imposed an obligation upon lessees, holding existing leases, to turn over to the Crown 100% of the proceeds of production beyond the basic well-head price, as fixed by the Government. The existing royalties, which were genuine royalties, continued unchanged.

In my opinion the royalty surcharge made applicable to these Crown leases was not a royalty for which provision was made in the lease agreement. It was imposed as a levy upon the share of production to which, under the lease, the lessee was entitled, and was a tax upon production.

I agree with the reasons of my brother Dickson for concluding that the royalty surcharge is a tax imposed upon Crown lessees of the same nature as the mineral income tax imposed upon lessees holding leases from freehold owners. It is significant that the royalty surcharge is computed in the same manner as the mineral income tax, and that the proceeds of both are to be paid into the same fund.

The reasons given by the Court of Appeal for concluding that the mineral income tax was a direct tax are summarized in the following extract from the judgment [[1976] 2 W.W.R. 356]:

> I think it must be concluded that the tax is one which is demanded from the very persons whom it is intended and desired should pay it. It is not one which is demanded from persons in the expectation and intent that they shall indemnify themselves at the expense of others. In my view, the language of the sections under which the tax is imposed, calculated and payment directed, leaves no doubt but the legislators intended the tax to be paid by the persons upon whom it was imposed and from whom payment is demanded.
>
> If there were any doubt as to this view, I think that doubt would be resolved by an appreciation of the situation that would result if the persons taxed attempted to indemnify themselves at the expense of the purchasers of the oil. If the tax paid pursuant to Bill 42 was added to the sale price of the crude *at the well-head*, then to the extent it was so passed on, it would increase the well-head price. The effect, therefore, would simply be to increase the tax by the amount which the well-head price was so increased. In other words, such action by the taxpayers would result in no benefit to themselves, but could, if the selling price were increased by the total amount of the tax, substantially increase the tax collected by the Government. Surely such a result following from an attempt to pass on the tax clearly indicates that the Legislature intended the tax to be paid by those upon whom it was imposed and from whom payment was demanded.

With respect, my consideration of the real substance and intent of the legislation under review leads me to a different conclusion.

Both the mineral income tax and the royalty surcharge are taxes upon the production of oil virtually all of which is produced for export from the Province of Saskatchewan. Section 3 of Bill 42 imposes the mineral income tax upon every person having an interest in the oil produced from a well in a producing tract. Subsection 63(1) of the *Petroleum and Natural Gas Regulations, 1969*, requires payment of the royalty surcharge upon oil produced or deemed to be produced from Crown lands.

Subsection 4(1) of Bill 42 as originally enacted fixed the tax payable as being the amount of the difference between the basic well-head price and the international well-head price determined by the Minister. Bill 128 repealed that subsection and substituted the formula of the well-head price received for each barrel of oil produced and sold in each month less the basic well-head price. The operation of the new subsection was made subject to a new section, 4A.

Section 4A provides that where the Minister is of the opinion that oil, income from which is subject to tax, has been disposed of in any month at less than its fair value, he shall determine the well-head value of the oil sold, being the price which he determines should have been obtained, and it is that price, so determined by him, which governs in the computation of the tax and not the actual price received. The purpose of this important provision was twofold. First, it enabled the Minister to prevent a reduction in the tax payable by reason of a sale at less than what he considered to be the fair value of the oil. Second, it provided a basis for the computation of tax where oil produced from a Saskatchewan well had not been sold at the well-head but had been shipped out by the producer to be refined and sold.

Under this section it is the Minister who has the power to determine what he considers to be the fair value of the oil produced, which figure will be applicable in the computation of the tax payable. His determination of fair value is final and conclusive. Section 11 of Bill 42 so provides and also states that his determination is not subject to review by any Court of law or by any *certiorari, mandamus*, prohibition, injunction or other proceeding whatsoever.

With respect to the computation of royalty surcharge, I have referred earlier to s-s. 63(1) of the *Petroleum and Natural Gas Regulations, 1969*, as finally amended, which imposes a royalty surcharge calculated as follows:

> (oil produced less Crown royalty oil less Road Allowance Crown levy) times (well-head value, as established by the Minister less basic well-head price);

The effect of this provision is that the royalty surcharge is determined by subtracting from one figure (well-head value) established by the Minister, another figure (basic well-head price) established by the Crown in the Regulations.

These taxing provisions, *i.e.*, both mineral income tax and royalty surcharge, have the following impact upon the Saskatchewan oil producer. In the first place he is effectively precluded from recovering in respect of the oil which he produces any return greater than the basic well-head price per barrel. He is subjected to an income freeze at that figure and can obtain no more than that. In the second place, he is compelled to sell his product at a price which will equal what the Minister determines to be the fair value of the oil which he produces. He must do this, because his production of oil is subject to a tax per barrel representing the difference between fair value and basic well-head price. If he is the lessee of mineral rights in lands in respect of which the mineral rights were expropriated by the Crown, he does not even have the option to discontinue production. Discontinuance of production without ministerial consent is subject to a heavy penalty.

The tax under consideration is essentially an export tax imposed upon oil production. In the past a tax of this nature has been considered to be an indirect tax. In *A.-G. B.C. v. Macdonald Murphy Lumber Co.*, [1930] A.C. 357 (P.C.), the Privy Council considered the validity of a timber tax imposed by s. 58 of the *Forest Act*, R.S.B.C. 1924, c. 93, upon all timber cut within the Province, except that upon which a royalty was payable, but which provided for a rebate of nearly all of the tax in the case of timber used or manufactured in the Province. In his reasons in that case Lord Macmillan, at pp. 364-5 A.C., said:

> Mr. Lawrence, however, contended that although the tax might accurately be described as an export duty, this did not necessarily negative its being a direct tax within the meaning of the Act. Without reviewing afresh the niceties of discrimination between direct and indirect taxation it is enough to point out that an export tax is normally collected on merchantable goods in course of transit in pursuance of commercial transactions. Whether the tax is ultimately borne by the exporting seller at home or by the importing buyer abroad depends on the terms of the contract between them. It may be borne by the one or by the other. It was said in the present case that the conditions of the competitive market in the United States compelled the exporter of timber from British Columbia to that country to bear the whole burden of the tax himself. That, however, is a matter of the exigencies of a particular market, and is really irrelevant in determining the inherent character of the tax. While it is no doubt true that a tax levied on personal property, no less than a tax levied on real property, may be a direct tax where the taxpayer's personal property is selected as the criterion of his ability to pay, a tax which, like the tax here in question, is levied on a commercial commodity on the occasion of its exportation in pursuance of trading transactions, cannot be

described as a tax whose incidence is, by its nature, such that normally it is finally borne by the first payer, and is not susceptible of being passed on. On the contrary, the existence of an export tax is invariably an element in the fixing of prices, and the question whether it is to be borne by seller or purchaser in whole or in part is determined by the bargain made. The present tax thus exhibits the leading characteristic of an indirect tax as defined by authoritative decisions.

The mineral income tax and the royalty surcharge are taxes imposed in a somewhat unusual manner. The mineral income tax purports to be a direct tax upon income imposed upon the taxpayer, which he cannot pass on to his purchaser. The royalty surcharge, while carrying a different title, is the same in nature. What differentiates this legislation from other legislation imposing export taxes is that the true effect of the legislation is to impose a freeze upon the actual income which the producer exporter can derive from the sale of his product. All that he is permitted to retain on the sale of each barrel of oil is the basic well-head price. In addition to being subjected to an income freeze, he is compelled to sell his product at a price equivalent to what the Minister considers to be its fair value in order to obtain the funds necessary to meet the tax. This amount per barrel over and above the basic well-head price he must obtain from his purchaser as a part of the purchase price. In essence the producer is a conduit through which the increased value of each barrel of oil above the basic well-head price is channelled into the hands of the Crown by way of tax. The increase in value is itself the tax and it is paid by the purchaser of the oil.

It is contended that the imposition of these taxes will not result in an increase in the price paid by oil purchasers, who would have been required to pay the same market price even if the taxes had not been imposed, and so there could be no passing on of the tax by the Saskatchewan producer to his purchaser. On this premise it is argued that the tax is not indirect. This, however, overlooks the all important fact that the scheme of the legislation under consideration involves the fixing of the maximum return of the Saskatchewan producers at the basic well-head price per barrel, while at the same time compelling him to sell at a higher price. There are two components in the sale price, first the basic well-head price and second the tax imposed. Both are intended by the legislation to be incorporated into the price payable by the purchaser. The purchaser pays the amount of the tax as a part of the purchase price.

For these reasons it is my opinion that the taxation scheme comprising the mineral income tax and the royalty surcharge does not constitute direct taxation within the Province and is therefore outside the scope of the provincial power under s-s. 92(2) of the *British North America Act, 1867*.

. . . .

[For His Lordship's discussion of section 91(2), see Chapter 8, *supra.*]

The dissenting judgment of Dickson and de Grandpré JJ. was delivered by

DICKSON J. (dissenting): . . .

### Direct or indirect taxation

The appellant claims that the mineral income tax and the royalty surcharge are indirect taxes and hence beyond the power of a provincial Legislature. The established guide for determining the validity of this submission is the classical formulation of John Stuart Mill (*Principles of Political Economy*, Book V. c. 3):

> Taxes are either direct or indirect. A direct tax is one which is demanded from the very person who it is intended or desired should pay it. Indirect taxes are those which are demanded from one person in the expectation and intention that he shall indemnify himself at the expense of another; such are the excise or customs.
>
> The producer or importer of a commodity is called upon to pay a tax on it not with the intention to levy a peculiar contribution upon him, but to tax through him the consumers of the commodity, from whom it is supposed that he will recover the amount by means of an advance in price.

Mill's well-known writings appeared not long before the drafting of the *British North America Act, 1867* and were presumed by the Privy Council to be familiar to the Fathers of Confederation. The definition was first applied in *A.-G. Quebec. v. Reed* (1884), 10 App. Cas. 141. In that case it was held that the question whether a tax is a direct or an indirect tax cannot depend upon special events which may vary in particular cases; the best general rule is to look to the time of payment and if at that time the incidence of the tax is uncertain then it cannot be called direct taxation. Mill's test became firmly established in *Bank of Toronto v. Lambe* (1887), 12 App. Cas. 575. In that case Lord Hobhouse said that while it was proper and, indeed, necessary to have regard to the opinion of economists, the question is a legal one, *viz.*, what the words mean as used in the statute. The problem is primarily one of law rather than of refined economic analysis. The dividing line between a direct and an indirect tax is referable to and ascertainable by the "general tendencies of the tax and the common understanding of men as to those tendencies": *Lambe's* case.

The general tendency of a tax is the relevant criterion. This must be distinguished from the ultimate incidence of the tax in the circumstances of the particular case: *City of Halifax v. Fairbanks*, [1928] A.C. 117 (P.C.); *A.-G. B.C. v. Kingcome Navigation Co. Ltd.*, [1934] A.C. 45 (P.C.).

In *City of Charlottetown v. Foundation Maritime Ltd.*, [1932] S.C.R. 589, Rinfret, J., pointed out that Mill's canon is founded on the theory of the ultimate incidence of the tax, not the ultimate incidence depending on the special circumstances of individual cases.

The nature of the tax is a question of substance and does not turn on the language used by the Legislature: *R. v. Caledonian Collieries Ltd.*, [1928] A.C. 358 (P.C.).

There can be no doubt that by the words "direct and indirect taxation" the Fathers of Confederation contemplated certain distinct categories of taxation, as well as a general test of directness. Only certain of such categories, such as income and property taxes, were to be available to the Legislatures. There were two reasons for this. The first was based on arcane political economy. It was thought that a direct tax would be more perceived than an indirect tax. The effect was thought to provide for greater scrutiny and reticence by the electorate with a resulting parsimony in public expenditure. The second reason proved wrong from the start. It was thought that provincial activities would be limited and revenue needs would be slim; the Legislatures, therefore, would have no necessity to resort to most tax pools.

Clearly, direct and indirect taxation are terms of historical reference, and although there is no reason to believe that the *British North America Act, 1867*, is not a document of evolving meaning, not limited to its original inspiration, jurisprudence, in so far as concerns particular forms of taxation like income or property taxes, has captured the historical spirit of "direct" and "indirect" taxation and preserved it. The effect of this was explained by Viscount Cave, L.C., in *City of Halifax v. Fairbanks, supra*, at p. 125 A.C.:

> What then is the effect to be given to Mill's formula above quoted? No doubt it is valuable as providing a logical basis for the distinction already established between direct and indirect taxes, and perhaps also as a guide for determining as to any new or unfamiliar tax which may be imposed in which of the two categories it is to be placed; but it cannot have the effect of disturbing the established classification of the old and well known species of taxation, and making it necessary to apply a new test to every particular member of those species. The imposition of taxes on property and income, of death duties and of municipal and local rates is, according to the common understanding of the term, direct taxation, just as the exaction of a customs or excise duty on commodities or of a percentage duty on services would ordinarily be regarded as indirect taxation; and although new forms of taxation may from time to time be added to one category or the other in accordance with Mill's formula, it would be wrong to use that formula as a ground for transferring a tax universally recognized as belonging to one class to a different class of taxation.

Historically well-understood categories of taxation have a known jurisprudential fate. Thus, a customs levy cannot be made by the Legislature whereas a property tax or income tax falls unquestionably within their competence. Careful constitutional analysis is required in respect of any unusual or hybrid form of taxation. A hybrid form of taxation may well have aspects which are direct and others which are indirect. By nineteenth century political economy, any element of indirectness was as stigma as tending to obfuscate the actions of the Legislature. That consideration is of minor importance today. In assessing the policy of a new form of taxation the jurisprudence offers no certain guide. One begins with the *British North America Act, 1867*, in which there are two additional criteria — (1) that the taxation be within the Province, and (2) that it be in order to the raising of a revenue for provincial purposes. Implicit in this, and more important than a vestige of indirectness, is the prohibition of the imposition by a Province of any tax upon citizens beyond its borders. Additionally, a Province cannot, through the ostensible use of its power to tax, invade prohibited fields. It cannot by way of taxation regulate trade and commerce or prohibit the free admission of produce or manufactured goods from other Provinces. It must confine itself to the raising of a revenue for provincial purposes.

## VI

Argument was directed to the Court to the effect that the tax here in question is a commodity tax and, as such, the general tendency would be for the tax to be passed on and therefore categorized as indirect. It is true that a tax on any one commodity whether laid on its production, its importation, its carriage from place to place, or its sale, will, as a general rule, raise the value and price of the commodity by at least the amount of the tax: Mill, Vol. II (1893 ed.), at p. 435. That is very old doctrine and for that reason a commodity tax is traditionally conceived as an indirect tax. The Courts have taken that as one criterion in characterizing the tax: *A.-G. B.C. v. C.P.R. Co.*, [1927] A.C. 934 (P.C.); *R. v. Caledonian Collieries Ltd., supra; A.-G. B.C. v. Macdonald Murphy Lumber Co.*, [1930] A.C. 357 (P.C.). But there is a caveat. Taxes imposed on the consumers of particular commodities are often called, or seem to be, taxes on commodities but they are not. Consumer taxes are normally regarded as direct. See *A.-G. B.C. v. Kingcome Navigation Co. Ltd., supra*, and

*Atlantic Smoke Shops Ltd. v. Conlon*, [1943] A.C. 550 (P.C.), as related to consumption of non-durable goods, and *Cairns Construction Ltd. v. Government of Saskatchewan*, [1960] S.C.R. 619, related to durable goods.

This appeal cannot be directed simply on the basis that the mineral income tax is levied on a commercial commodity. The Court is obliged to examine the legislation and relevant facts for the purpose of determining, by the application of the test formulated by Mill, as developed in the authorities, whether the tax is direct or indirect. In *Atlantic Smoke Shops Ltd. v. Conlon*, Viscount Simon, L.C., asserted that two distinct categories of taxes should not be understood as relieving the Courts of the obligation of examining each particular tax, or as justifying the classification of a tax as indirect simply because it was associated with the purchase of a commodity. A similar approach was taken in *A.-G. B.C. v. Esquimalt & Nanaimo R. Co.*, [1950] A.C. 87 (P.C.).

It is hard to see that the mineral income tax fits snugly into the commodity tax category. There are several rough edges. First, the tax falls upon a holder of certain rights in respect of part of the amount received. Secondly, unlike a true commodity tax, *i.e.*, a fixed imposition or a percentage of the commodity — s. 6 of the Act contemplates an imposition varying with production costs. If production costs rise, the share of the Province by taxation falls. Thirdly, the tax is not an "add-to-the price" impost but rather a "take-from-the-owner" levy.

Finally, the tax does not fall on the product but only on certain entitled holders. Owners of rights having an aggregate area of less than 1,280 acres in producing tracts are exempted. For these reasons, the tax resists classification as a commodity tax in so far as constitutional jurisprudence knows that term. It must be subject, therefore, to further constitutional scrutiny.

## VII

Counsel for the Province attempted to support the tax as constituting an income tax on the authority of *Forbes v. A.-G. Man.*, [1937] A.C. 260 (P.C.). The so-called "mineral income tax" is not an income tax in any generally recognized sense of the term. A true income tax means, for taxation purposes, a levy on gains and profits: *R. v. Caledonian Collieries Ltd., supra*. The evidence of Professor Barber in the case at bar confirms that view. He defined income tax as being, according to generally accepted accounting principles and business practice, a tax imposed on net income and in determining such net income any expenses incurred in earning that income are inherently deductible.

In *Nickel Rim Mines Ltd. v. A.-G. Ont.*, [1966] 1 O.R. 345 (C.A.), cited by counsel for the Province, the tax was held to be a direct tax but it was levied upon annual profits, determined after taking into account a "long list of deductions". The tax was described by Wells, J., as one on "net profits ascertained or estimated". On appeal [*loc. cit.*], Porter, C.J.O., referred to the tax as a "profit tax".

In my view, the *Nickel Rim* case does not assist the Province. The tax is not levied upon net income. It is more in the nature of a gross revenue tax — as above a certain statutory figure it becomes a 100% levy — that has generally in the past been regarded as an indirect tax. The tax is in essence a flat sum which will vary according to the sale price of the oil but is not necessarily reflective of *actual* expense experience. Expenses are discretionary and not inherently deductible so as to fall within the definition of an income tax. If s. 4*A* should ever come into play the tax would be levied not on the price received but on a ministerial figure. In sum, an income tax is a tax upon gross receipts less expenses. In the instant tax it is possible that these two figures will be subject to ministerial determination.

## VIII

It should be clear from the foregoing that neat constitutional categories are of marginal assistance in the present case. The tax resists such classification; it is a hybrid. It must be assessed in the light of constitutional analysis, keeping in mind the *indicia* to which I have above referred.

Can it be said, then, that the tax is one which is demanded from the very person who it is intended or desired should pay it, or can it be said, rather, that it is demanded from the oil producer in the expectation and intention that he shall indemnify himself at the expense of another? The question is not easily answered. An example might assist. If we assume a basic well-head price of $3 per barrel and a sale at $7 per barrel, the tax would amount to $4 per barrel. If basic well-head price and production costs remain constant but the selling price increases to $11 per barrel, the tax would amount to $8 per barrel. It is quite obvious that the oil producer will not be in a position to bear the tax of $4 or $8 out of the basic well-head price of $3 per barrel which he retains. On this view it is arguable that the tax is passed on to the purchaser as a component of price. I do not think, however, that this can be said to be the true view. An indirect tax is an amount which is added to what would otherwise be the price of the commodity or service. This appears from Mill's formulation. He says that tax is indirect when the producer is called upon to pay a tax not with the intention of levying a contribution upon him, but to tax through him the consumers of the commodity, from whom it is supposed that he will recover the amount "by means of an advance in price", *i.e.*, as an "add-on". In *A.-G. B.C. v. Esquimalt & Nanaimo R. Co., supra*, Lord Greene pointed out that in order to constitute an indirect tax the *tax itself* must have a general tendency to be passed on. If an article selling for $10 is subjected to a 10% customs duty, the general tendency would be simply to add the amount of the tax or more to the price of the commodity. The purchaser would then pay one dollar or more in excess of the amount he would have paid in the absence of the tax. In *Security Export Co. v. Hetherington*, [1923] S.C.R. 539 at 558, Duff, J., adopted the following definition of a direct tax, taken from the Oxford Dictionary:

> one levied immediately upon the persons who are to bear the burden, as opposed to *indirect* taxes levied upon commodities, of which *the price is thereby increased* so that the persons on whom the incidence ultimately falls pay indirectly a proportion of taxation included in the price of the article.

(Emphasis added.) If the price is increased by reason of the tax, the tendency will be to have the consumer bear the increase. If the price is not increased, the tendency will be to have the producer bear the tax.

For myself, I can find nothing in the language of the Act nor in the oral or documentary evidence to suggest that the price of Saskatchewan oil was increased by the addition of the "mineral income tax" levied, or that the purchaser of Saskatchewan crude paid more per barrel than he would have paid in the absence of the tax. Nor can I discover anything which leads me to conclude that the Legislature of Saskatchewan acted on any view other than that of collecting maximum tax from the persons who are by the statute made liable to pay it, namely, Saskatchewan oil producers.

There is a further consideration which should not be overlooked. If it had been intended that those subject to the tax would pass it on to others the inclusion of the "farmers' section", exempting tracts not exceeding 1,280 acres, would have been quite unnecessary.

The "farmers' section" highlights the essential axis on which the present litigation revolves. It is a dispute concerning who, as between the producers and the Government of Saskatchewan, will reap the benefit of a fortuitous rise in the price of oil. In the case of producers holding rights in producing tracts in excess of 1,280 acres, the Legislature has determined the benefit shall accrue to provincial coffers; in the case of a producer in a smaller tract, the Legislature has abstained from imposition leaving the benefit in the producer's pocket. The ultimate position of the final consumer is unaffected. It is also patent that any attempt by an oil producer to pass on an amount additional to the selling price would be self-defeating. Every increase in selling price will be reflected by an equal increase in tax as, according to the formula, tax equals well-head price received minus basic well-head price.

Reference was made in the Saskatchewan Courts, and in argument in this Court, to the international or "world" price of oil and the effect of such upon the pricing of Saskatchewan crude. It has been contended on behalf of the Province that the world price would place a ceiling on the price of Saskatchewan crude and, therefore, the Saskatchewan producer could not pass on the mineral income tax to the purchaser. Again, to take an example, if world price were $11 per barrel and basic well-head price $3 per barrel, the mineral income tax would amount to $8 per barrel. The producer could not recover this amount by increasing the price to $19 per barrel and for good reasons (i) his oil could not command that price in the market, and (ii) he would be deprived of the additional revenue by the mechanics of the Act.

A similar question lurked, but remained unresolved, in the *Grain Futures* case, *A.-G. Man. v. A.-G. Can.*, [1925] A.C. 561 (P.C.). There "An Act to provide for the collection of a tax from persons selling grain for future delivery", 1923 (Man.), c. 17, was considered. The Act provided that on contracts of sale of grain for future delivery made at an exchange or similar institution in the Province, the seller, or his broker or agent, should pay a tax on the amount sold. When the case reached this Court, [1924] S.C.R. 317 at 322, Duff, J., in speaking of sales in an international market had this to say:

> But a tax on production or upon sales may have, and in special circumstances undoubtedly has, no effect upon price. Where, for example, the ultimate price at which a commodity from time to time is sold is determined in an international market, and is known to everybody concerned, through daily quotations, an annually recurring tax will have no effect, even in determining the price so fixed, unless it be of such magnitude and levied in such circumstances as to reach the marginal supply. And obviously the ultimate price, once fixed in such circumstances, will govern the terms of transactions throughout the entire series, from the initial seller to the ultimate buyer. Again, to take another example, a tax levied on sales by western farmers of grain grown by themselves would be in fact, as well as in intention, a tax to be borne by the very person who is called upon to pay it.

This passage would tend to support the submission of the Province. Judgment on the further appeal to the Privy Council was delivered by Viscount Haldane. He referred to an agreed statement of facts, put in by the Attorneys-General, from which it appeared that the ultimate market price for grain in Canada was determined in the "great importing markets in Great Britain and Europe". His Lordship added "this is a 'world price' which is but little controlled by the producers, and which has to be looked at to cover all the items in costs of production and of transportation". The Board did not decide whether the tendency for the seller to add to the price the amount of tax paid in respect of the sale was negatived because the price of grain was determined by the world market over which the seller had no control. The Board held that in so far as the statute sought to impose a tax on brokers, agents, factors and elevator companies, they would be expected to pass it on, and to that extent the tax was indirect. The task of separating out the cases of such persons and corporations from others in which there was a legitimate imposition of direct taxation was considered by the Board to be a matter of such complication as to be impracticable for a Court of law. To the extent the case appears to recognize as direct a tax upon sales by principals of grain for future delivery it is helpful to the Province.

I might repeat a passage from the judgment of Turgeon, J.A., in *Re Grain Marketing Act, 1931*, [1931] 2 W.W.R. 146 at p. 154 (Sask. C.A.), which echoes the opinion of Duff, J., expressed in the *Grain Futures* case quoted above:

> In the *Lawson* case, *supra* [*Lawson v. Interior Tree Fruit & Vegetable Committee*, [1931] S.C.R. 357], the levies were held to be of such a nature as probably to affect the price of the product; they were therefore indirect taxes. In this case, I can see no such result. It is admitted that Saskatchewan grain is sold at prices fixed outside the province and by general conditions, and these deductions are taken out of the selling price after the grain is sold. They are clearly intended to be paid by the grower out of whose money they are retained. Consequently they are direct and not indirect taxes, and their imposition would be legitimate if the Act was otherwise valid.

If Saskatchewan oil is sold in the market at prevailing market prices, as I understand to be the case, then I do not think it can properly be said that the Eastern Canadian oil consumer pays more by reason of imposition of the tax. There is no added "burden" to "cling" to the commodity unit: see Rand, J., in *C.P.R. Co. v. A.-G. Sask.*, [1952] 2 S.C.R. 231.

One of the cornerstones upon which appellant's case rests is the contention that there resides in the Minister a general power to fix the price at which oil is sold, and that the oil producer, if he is to avoid pecuniary loss, must sell at the ministerially pre-determined price. That is simply not the case. The power of the Minister to determine well-head value in respect of mineral income tax is not an unrestrained and unrestricted general power; it is exercisable only when oil is disposed of at less than fair value, and then, only *after* the sale has taken place. The purpose of s. 4*A* of Bill 42 is obviously to prevent such practices as sale of oil between related companies at artificially low prices. Well-head value is not arbitrarily set by the Minister — it is set by world and national forces determining the market price at the well-head. No evidence was adduced that the Minister has ever set a figure above market price, thus forcing producers into a loss position if unable to sell at the artificially high figure set. In the normal course of events the tax is the difference between basic well-head price and the market price received by the producer in the course of trade. If the producer seeks to evade tax by undercutting the price his product would command at fair market value, then the possibility of ministerial determination arises, but only then. The tax does not set the price. Price sets the tax.

When one comes to consider royalty surcharge, it is apparent that the combined operation of O.C. 1238/74 and Ministerial Order WOV-01/75 is to the same effect. It will be recalled that royalty surcharge is the difference between basic well-head price and the higher of the price per barrel received at the well-head and the price per barrel listed in Order WOV-01/75. As with mineral income tax, in the normal course the amount of tax payable will depend upon the price actually received for the oil and not upon any exercise of ministerial authority. The Minister's power in both cases is a protective measure to discourage tax evasion.

The contention that the mineral income tax and royalty surcharge constitute an indirect tax or export tax must proceed, I think, from the inchoate fear that the Minister will use his powers, not for the intended purpose of preventing tax evasion, but for the purpose of imposing arbitrary and punitive well-head values, exceeding the prices which the oil would command in the market place. There is nothing in the language of the provisions, or on the record before us, to justify that fear.

I cannot stress too strongly the point that purchasers would be paying the same price whether the tax existed or not. This fact, to my mind, conclusively prevents the levy from being in the nature of an indirect tax or an export tax. It is not passed on to purchasers to augment the price they would otherwise pay. Instead, they pay exactly the price they would pay in the absence of the tax and the producers are taxed on the profits they would otherwise receive.

I would hold that, in its true nature and effect, the mineral income tax constitutes direct taxation within the Province in order to the raising of a revenue for provincial purposes.

. . . .

[For a comment on the *CIGOL* decision which suggests Dickson J.'s dissent was the preferable approach, see Buglass, "Comment" (1978-9), 43 Sask. L.R. 177.

Could a tax such as that challenged by CIGOL now be imposed by a provincial government under the authority of section 92A? See Ballem, "Oil and Gas Under the New Constitution" (1983), 61 Can. Bar Rev. 547 who gives a positive answer to this question. See also Moull, "Section 92A of the *Constitution Act, 1867*" (1983), 61 Can. Bar Rev. 715 who agrees that such a tax would not now violate the taxation provisions of the *Constitution Act* but questions whether it might not still face an obstacle under section 92(2).]

## Note

In *A.-G. Que. v. Reed* (1884), 10 App. Cas. 141, referred to in *Bank of Toronto v. Lambe* (1887), 12 App. Cas. 575, the Privy Council asserted that "the question whether it is a direct or an indirect tax cannot depend upon those special events which may vary in particular cases; but the best general rule is to look to the time of payment; and if at the time the ultimate incidence is uncertain then, as it appears to their Lordships, it cannot in this view, be called direct taxation . . ." (at p. 144). In *A.-G. B.C. v. Kingcome Navigation Co. Ltd.*, [1934] A.C. 45 at 52 (P.C.), the Privy Council, referring to the foregoing passage in the *Reed* case said: "It is clear that 'ultimate incidence' is not there used in the sense of the political economists, but refers to the ultimate incidence among the parties to the transaction in respect of which the tax is imposed". Mill's definition of direct and indirect taxation as applied in the *Lambe* case was approved in *Brewers and Maltsters' Association of Ontario v. A.-G. Ont.*, [1897] A.C. 231 (P.C.) where legislation imposing a flat licence fee of $100 on brewers and distillers engaged in wholesale selling was upheld under section

92(2) and section 92(9) of the *Constitution Act, 1867*. Since the fee had no relation to the quantity of goods sold and in the ordinary course there was no intention or expectation of recoupment from customers, it satisfied the accepted test of direct taxation. In *Cottom v. The King*, [1914] A.C. 176 (P.C.), "direct taxation" as used in section 92(2) was held to be settled in meaning by Mill's definition.

Although the *Reed* case was the first in which Mill's definition was mentioned, there was an earlier reference in *A.-G. Que. v. Queen Ins. Co.* (1878), 3 App. Cas. 1090 (P.C.) to the fact that at least two encyclopedias had been produced in support of the conclusion that both the popular and technical use of the term "direct tax" excluded a stamp tax.

In *A.-G. Man. v. A.-G. Can.*, [1925] A.C. 561, the Privy Council invalidated the *Manitoba Grain Futures Taxation Act*, 1923, which (although exempting sales where the seller is the grower or either party to the contract is owner or tenant of the land on which the grain is to be grown) imposed a tax on the seller or his broker or agent in respect of every contract of sale of grain for future delivery. Lord Haldane said that "it is impossible to doubt that the tax was imposed in a form which contemplated that some one else than the person on whom it was imposed should pay it. The amount will, in the end, become a charge against the amount of the price which is to come to the seller in the world market, and be paid by some one else than the persons primarily taxed. The class of those taxed obviously includes an indefinite number who would naturally indemnify themselves out of the property of the owners for whom they were acting".

In *Fortier v. Lambe* (1894), 25 S.C.R. 422, the Supreme Court of Canada followed *Bank of Toronto v. Lambe, supra* and upheld provincial legislation imposing a licence fee on manufacturers and traders as a direct tax. *Fortier v. Lambe* was followed in *Colpitts Ranches v. A.-G. Alta.*, [1954] 3 D.L.R. 121 (Alta. S.C.), sustaining the validity of a municipal business tax on fox farming, as authorized by provincial legislation, where the tax was payable whether or not the fox was pelted or sold or kept for breeding or for show purposes. The authorizing legislation provided for the passing of by-laws for assessing the business of fur farming on the basis of the number and kind of fur bearing animals kept for the purpose of the business at any amount per animal, not exceeding that fixed by the Lieutenant-Governor in Council. The municipality in this case exacted the limit of the permitted amount. Cairns J. held that this was clearly a tax on a business, a tax on plaintiff's personal property imposed with the intention that he should bear it even if in the course of business he might pass it on; consequently it was a direct tax.

## R. v. CALEDONIAN COLLIERIES LTD.

In the Privy Council. [1928] A.C. 358.

Lord Hailsham L.C., Viscount Haldane, Lord Buckmaster, Lord Wrenbury
and Lord Warrington of Clyffe. June 12, 1928.

Appeal by special leave from a judgment of the Supreme Court of Canada, [1927] S.C.R. 257, reversing a judgment of the Alberta Appellate Division, [1926] 2 W.W.R. 280, and holding that the *Alberta Mine Owners Tax Act*, 1923, was *ultra vires*.

LORD WARRINGTON OF CLYFFE: The question raised by this appeal is whether the *Mine Owners Tax Act*, 1923, of the Province of Alberta, which imposes upon mine owners as therein defined a percentage tax upon the gross revenues of their coal mines is *ultra vires* the Province as an attempt to impose indirect taxation . . .

The Act in question was passed by the Legislature of Alberta on April 21, 1923. It contained the following material provisions: "Section 3. Every mine owner shall from the last day of May, 1918, be subject to a tax upon the gross revenue received by him from his mine. Section 4. The said tax shall not be more than 2 per cent. of the said revenue and as determined by the Lieut.-Governor in Council under the provisions of this Act. Section 6. On or before the last day of each month each mine owner shall forward to the Minister a sum of money equal to 2 per cent. of the gross revenue received by him from his mine during the next preceding month."

The Act repealed a previous Act of the Province — the *Mine Owners Tax Act*, 1918 — which also imposed a tax upon gross revenue, taking the form in that Act of 5 c. per ton of the coal removed from the mine premises. The validity of this tax had been disputed by the mine owners who had in many cases refused to pay it.

On August 14, 1925, the Lieutenant-Governor by and with the advice of the Executive Council ordered that the tax in question should be 2 per cent. of the gross revenue received by the mine owner from his mine.

The respondent company is a mine owner within the definition of that term contained in the Act in question. They began business in November, 1923. They refused to pay the tax, and on August 21, 1925, the action, in which the order under appeal was made, was commenced for the purpose of recovering the amount of the tax alleged to be due from them . . .

The question whether a tax is direct or indirect has on many occasions been the subject of decision by this Board, but it is unnecessary to refer to any of these decisions except that of *Bank of Toronto v. Lambe*, in which Lord Hobhouse, in delivering the judgment of the Board, made some useful observations as to the mode in which the question should be approached. . . .

What then is the general tendency of the tax now in question?

First it is necessary to ascertain the real nature of the tax. It is not disputed that, though the tax is called a tax on "gross revenue", such gross revenue is in reality the aggregate of sums received from sales of coal, and is indistinguishable from a tax upon every sum received from the sale of coal.

The respondents are producers of coal, a commodity the subject of commercial transactions. Their Lordships can have no doubt that the general tendency of a tax upon the sums received from the sale of the commodity which they produce and in which they deal is that they would seek to recover it in the price charged to a purchaser. Under particular circumstances the recovery of the tax may, it is true, be economically undesirable or practically impossible, but the general tendency of the tax remains.

It is said on behalf of the appellant that at the time a sale is made the tax has not become payable, and therefore cannot be passed on. Their Lordships cannot accept this contention; the tax will have to be paid, and there would be no more difficulty in adding to the selling price the amount of the tax in anticipation than there would be if it had been actually paid.

*Appeal dismissed.*

*Note*

The *Caledonian Collieries* case was explained by Martland J., speaking for the Supreme Court of Canada in *Re Newfoundland & Labrador Corporation Ltd. and A.G. Nfld.* (1982), 138 D.L.R. (3d) 577 at 588, as not standing for the proposition that, as a tax on gross revenue, it must be indirect. Rather it was indirect as a tax on the aggregate of every sum received from the sale of coal and had a general tendency to be passed on. In *Re Newfoundland & Labrador*, the tax was on net revenues from rentals, royalties and like payments, arrived at by deducting from the total sum received certain specified deductions allowed by the Act. The fact that the deductible amounts were at the discretion of the Minister did not convert the tax to a tax as gross revenue or render it indirect. Martland J. characterized the tax as an income tax, and upheld it as direct.

In *Charlottetown v. Foundation Maritime Ltd.*, [1932] S.C.R. 589, a by-law under authorizing legislation was held invalid as imposing an indirect tax where it required all non-resident contractors to pay a graduated tax by way of a percentage of the contract price on every contract for work within the municipality. See also *Reference Re Agricultural Land Relief Act (Alta.)*, [1938] 3 W.W.R. 186 (Alta. C.A.).

A tax on net profits is, of course, distinguishable from a tax on gross revenue, and it was held in *Nickel Rim Mines Ltd. v. A.-G. Ont.*, [1966] 1 O.R. 345, aff'd [1967] S.C.R. 270 that section 3 of the *Mining Tax Act*, R.S.O. 1960, c. 242, imposed valid direct taxation not only in respect of annual profits received from output sold during the year but also in respect of profits, pre-estimated according to a statutory formula, on unsold ore severed from the mine and treated at the mine or elsewhere.

Where a Province has validly imposed a land tax, it is equally valid to make the tax a special or first lien on the crops grown on the assessed land, although there may be a question of priority if there is competing valid federal legislation: See *Reference re Section 31 of the Municipal District Act Amendment Act*, 1941 *(Alta.)*, [1943] S.C.R. 295.

In *A.G.-B.C. v. McDonald Murphy Lumber Co.*, [1930] A.C. 357 (P.C.), striking down a provincial statute imposing a tax on timber cut within the Province, their Lordships considered it clear on the evidence that the tax was in reality an export tax. In rejecting the argument that the tax was nevertheless direct, Lord MacMillan stated:

> Whether the tax is ultimately borne by the exporting seller at home or by the importing buyer abroad depends upon the terms of the contract between them. It may be borne by one or by the other. It was said in the present case that the conditions of the competitive market in the United States compelled the exporter of timber from British Columbia to that country to bear the whole burden of the tax himself. That, however, is a matter of exigencies of a particular market, and is really irrelevant in determining the inherent character of the tax. While it is no doubt true that a tax levied on personal property, no less than a tax levied on real property, may be a direct tax where the taxpayer's personal property is selected as the criterion of his ability to pay, a tax which, like the tax here in question, is levied on a commercial commodity on the occasion of its exportation in pursuance of trading transactions, cannot be described as a tax whose incidence is, by its nature, such that normally it is finally borne by the first payer, and is not susceptible of being passed on. On the contrary, the existence of an export tax is invariably an element in the fixing of prices, and the question whether it is borne by seller or purchaser in whole or in part is determined by the bargain made. The present tax thus exhibits the leading characteristic of an indirect tax ...

See also *Security Export Co. v. Hetherington*, [1923] S.C.R. 539, rev'd on other grounds, [1924] A.C. 988 (P.C.); *Texada Mines Ltd. v. A.-G. B.C.*, [1960] S.C.R. 713. In *Lawson v. Interior Tree Fruit and Vegetable Committee*, [1931] S.C.R. 357, where the Supreme Court of Canada invalidated the British Columbia Produce Marketing Act, 1927, on the principal ground that it invaded federal legislative power in relation to trade and commerce, Cannon J. in a concurring judgment (to the principal one delivered by Duff J.) said, *inter alia*, (at p. 373):

> By the Produce Marketing Act of 1927, the province of British Columbia imposed levies on the fruits or vegetables grown or produced in a large area, including appellant's farm, and obliged all shippers to secure a licence to market and sell products of the province anywhere within the Dominion under a penalty for each contravention. Even leaving aside the licence, and considering only the levy, I believe, as pointed out by my brother Duff, that such imposts on commodities, on trade in commodities, have always been regarded as indirect taxes for a public purpose and come under the head of "taxation" — which is dealt with in Part VIII of the British North America Act, where is found article 121. It may be considered as an excise tax which necessarily has a tendency to affect, and affects, the price of the product to the customer in another province. To use the words of Lord MacMillan in *Attorney-General for British Columbia v. McDonald Murphy Lumber Company*, [1930] A.C. 357 at 363 (P.C.), the levy in question 'is an export tax falling within the category of duties of customs and excise, and as such, as well as by reason of its inherent nature as an indirect tax, could not competently be imposed by the provincial legislature'. I therefore, reach the conclusion that this legislation is an attempt to impose by indirect taxation and regulations an obstacle to one of the main purposes of Confederation, which was, ultimately, to form an economic unit of all the provinces in British North America with absolute freedom of trade between its constituent parts.

Cf., on the question when goods become "exports", the *Ontario Farm Products Marketing Act Reference, supra*, at 296; and see *Richfield Oil Corp. v. State Board of Equalization* (1946), 329 U.S. 69; Note, (1946) 59 Harv. Law Rev. 627.

# A.-G. B.C. v. KINGCOME NAVIGATION CO. LTD.

In the Privy Council. [1934] A.C. 45.

Lords Blanesburgh, Atkin, Thankerton, and Russell of Killowen and Sir George Lowndes. Oct. 12, 1933.

Appeal from a judgment of the British Columbia Court of Appeal, [1933] 3 D.L.R. 364, affirming a judgment of Morrison C.J., [1933] 1 D.L.R. 688, and holding the British Columbia Fuel-oil Tax Act, 1930, as amended, *ultra vires*.

LORD THANKERTON: The material provisions of the Act of 1930, as amended by the Act of 1932, are as follows:

> 2. For the raising of a revenue for Provincial purposes every person who consumes any fuel-oil in the Province shall pay to the Minister of Finance a tax in respect of that fuel-oil at the rate of one-half cent a gallon.
> 3. The tax imposed by this Act shall be paid and collected at such times and in such manner as the regulations may prescribe. . . .
> 4. The amount of any tax imposed by this Act may be recovered by action in any Court as for a debt due to the Crown in right of the Province, and the Court may make an order as to the costs of

the action in favour of or against the Crown. (2) In every action for the recovery of any tax imposed by this Act, the burden of proving the quantity of fuel-oil consumed by the defendant, and of proving that the tax has been paid in respect of the fuel-oil in question, shall be upon the defendant. (1932, c. 51, s. 2).

5. (1) Upon the expiration of thirty days after the commencement of this Act no person shall keep for sale or sell fuel-oil in the Province unless he is the holder of a licence issued pursuant to this section in respect of each place of business at which fuel-oil is so kept for sale or sold by him. (2) The manner of application and the forms of application and of the licence shall be as prescribed in the regulations. A licence fee of one dollar shall be payable in respect of each licence. (3) The Minister of Finance may, without holding any formal or other hearing, cancel any licence issued pursuant to this section if the licensee is convicted of any offence against this Act, and may during the period of twelve months next succeeding the cancellation of that licence refuse to issue any new licence to the person so convicted.

6. (1) Every collector, constable, and every person authorized in writing by the Minister of Finance to exercise the powers of inspection under this section may without warrant enter upon any premises on which he has cause to believe that any fuel-oil is kept or had in possession, and may inspect the premises and all fuel-oil found thereon, and may interrogate any person who is found on the premises or who owns, occupies or has charge of the premises. (2) Every person interrogated under this section who refuses or fails to answer any question put to him respecting the fuel-oil kept or had on the premises, or who refuses or fails to produce for inspection or to permit inspection of any book, record or document, or any barrel, tank, or receptacle in his possession or under his control which he is required to produce for inspection or of which he is required to permit inspection, shall be guilty of an offence against this Act.

7. (1) Every person who consumes or sells fuel-oil in the Province and every person who keeps for sale or sells fuel-oil in the Province shall keep such books and records and shall make and furnish such returns as are prescribed in the regulations. (2) Every person who refuses or fails to keep any book or record or to make and furnish any return prescribed by the regulations or who withholds any entry or information required by the regulations to be made or entered in any book, record, or return, or who makes any false or deceptive entry or statement in any such book, record, or return, shall be guilty of an offence against this Act.

The respondent challenges the validity of the tax on three grounds — namely: (a) that in its nature it is either an import duty or a duty of excise, and therefore falls into the category of indirect taxes; (b) that it is not direct taxation in respect that the burden may be passed on; and (c) that it invades the legislative sphere of the Dominion parliament in regard to regulation of trade and commerce.

The respondent's first contention is that the tax in question is a customs or excise duty, according to the general understanding current in 1867, and that all customs and excise duties are outside the competence of a Provincial legislature, apart from any question whether the tax is "demanded from the very persons who it is intended or desired should pay it." For this construction he prays in aid s. 122 of the Act of 1867, and, in order to establish that the present tax was in the nature of a customs or excise duty, he relied on the definitions of political economists and the course of customs and excise legislation in this country up to 1867. In their Lordships' opinion this contention is inconsistent with the decisions of this Board, which go back to the year 1878, and have settled that the test be applied in determining what is "direct taxation" within the meaning of s. 92, head 2, of the Act of 1867 is to be found in Mill's definition of direct and indirect taxes.

[His Lordship here discussed *A.-G. Que. v. Queen Insurance Co.* (1878), 3 App. Cas. 1090 (P.C.); *A.-G. Que. v. Reed* (1884), 10 App. Cas. 141 (P.C.); *Bank of Toronto v. Lambe* (1887), 12 App. Cas. 575 (P.C.); *Brewers and Maltsters' Association of Ontario v. A.-G. Ont.*, [1897] A.C. 231 (P.C.) and *Cotton v. The King*, [1941] A.C. 176 (P.C.). He quoted from Lord Moulton's judgment in the *Cotton* case the statement that decided cases have established that "the meaning to be attributed to the phrase 'direct taxation' in s.

92 ... is substantially the definition quoted ... from the treatise of John Stuart Mill, and that this question is no longer open to discussion." He then continued as follows:]

These decisions, in their Lordships' opinion, make clear that if the tax is demanded from the very person who it is intended or desired should pay it, the taxation is direct, and that it is none the less direct even if it might be described as an excise tax, for instance, or is collected as an excise tax. Among the numerous subsequent decisions of the Board, the respondent was only able to refer to two, as containing any suggestion to the contrary — namely, *City of Halifax v. Fairbanks' Estate*, [1928] A.C. 117 (P.C.) and *Attorney-General for British Columbia v. McDonald Murphy Lumber Co.*

In *Fairbanks'* case a city charter, enacted by the Provincial legislature, imposed a "business tax" to be paid by every occupier of real property for the purposes of any trade, profession or other calling carried on for the purposes of gain. Where the property was let to the Crown or to any person exempt from taxation, the owner was to be deemed to be the occupier, and was to be assessed for business tax according to the purposes for which it was occupied. The property in question was let to the Crown, and the respondent estate, as owner, had been assessed to the tax. It was held that the tax was direct taxation even though the owner probably would seek to pass it on to the tenant. Lord Cave, who delivered the judgment of the Board, stated in regard to the Act of 1867:

> The framers of that Act evidently regarded taxes as divisible into two separate and distinct categories — namely, those that are direct and those which cannot be so described, and it is to taxation of the former character only that the powers of a Provincial government are made to extend. From this it is to be inferred that the distinction between direct and indirect taxes was well known before the passing of the Act; and it is undoubtedly the fact that before that date the classification was familiar to statesmen as well as to economists, and that certain taxes were then universally recognized as falling within one or the other category. Thus, taxes on property or income were everywhere treated as direct taxes. ... On the other hand, duties of customs and excise were regarded by every one as typical instances of indirect taxation. When therefore the Act of Union allocated the power of direct taxation for Provincial purposes to the Province, it must surely have intended that the taxation, for those purposes, of property and income should belong exclusively to the Provincial legislatures, and that without regard to any theory as to the ultimate incidence of such taxation. To hold otherwise would be to suppose that the framers of the Act intended to impose on a Provincial legislature the task of speculating as to the probable ultimate incidence of each particular tax which it might desire to impose, at the risk of having such tax held invalid if the conclusion reached should afterwards be held to be wrong.
>
> What then is the effect to be given to Mill's formula above quoted? No doubt it is valuable as providing a logical basis for the distinction already established between direct and indirect taxes, and perhaps also as a guide for determining as to any new or unfamiliar tax which may be imposed in which of the two categories it is to be placed; but it cannot have the effect of disturbing the established classification of the old and well-known species of taxation, and making it necessary to apply a new test to every particular member of those species. The imposition of taxes on property and income, of death duties and of municipal and local rates is, according to the common understanding of the terms, direct taxation, just as the exaction of a customs or excise duty or commodities or of a percentage duty on services would ordinarily be regarded as indirect taxation; and although new forms of taxation may from time to time be added to one category or the other in accordance with Mill's formula, it would be wrong to use that formula as a ground for transferring a tax universally recognized as belonging to one class to a different class of taxation. ...

As has already been pointed out the ultimate incidence of the tax, in the sense of the political economist, is to be disregarded, but where the tax is imposed in respect of a transaction, the taxing authority is indifferent as to which of the parties to the transaction ultimately bears the burden, and, as Mill expresses it, it is not intended as a peculiar contribution upon the particular party selected to pay the tax. Similarly, where the tax is imposed in respect of some dealing with commodities, such as their import or sale, or production for sale, the tax is not a peculiar contribution upon the one of the parties to the trading in the particular commodity who is selected as the taxpayer. This is brought out in the second paragraph of Mill's definition, and is true of the typical customs and excise duties referred to by Lord Cave [in *Fairbanks'* case]. Again, taxes on property and income are imposed in respect of the particular taxpayer's interest in property or the taxpayer's own income, and they are a peculiar contribution upon him, and it is intended and desired that he shall pay it, although it is possible for him, by making his own arrangements to that end, to pass the burden on in the sense of the political economists. The decision in *Fairbanks'* case is in accordance with the principles already stated by their Lordships as those to be derived from the earlier decisions of the Board.

In the *McDonald Murphy Lumber Co.'s* case a Provincial tax upon all timber cut in the Province, with a rebate of nearly the whole tax in the case of timber used or manufactured in the Province was held to be in its nature an export tax "levied on a commercial commodity on the occasion of its exportation in pursuance of trading transactions." The tax was held to be *ultra vires*. . . .

It is clear that this decision applied Mill's definition, as adopted by the previous decisions of the Board, as the test, and that the result was in accordance with those decisions. The present respondent relied on the reference to s. 122 of the Act of 1867 as being of assistance to his argument. In their Lordships' opinion the customs or excise duties on commodities ordinarily regarded as indirect taxation, referred to in the judgment in *Fairbanks'* case and the *McDonald Murphy Lumber Co.'s* case, are duties which are imposed in respect of commercial dealings in commodities, and they would necessarily fall within Mill's definition of indirect taxes. They do not extend, for instance, to a dog tax, which is clearly direct taxation, though the machinery of the excise law might be applied to its collection, or to a licence duty, such as was considered in *Lambe's* case. Customs and excise duties are, in their essence, trading taxes, and may be said to be more concerned with the commodity in respect of which the taxation is imposed than with the particular person from whom the tax is exacted. Sect. 122 of the Act merely provided for the temporary continuation of the then existing legislation as regards customs and excise, and the respondent was unable to point to anything in that legislation which would fall outside the above definition of customs and excise duties. It follows that the tax here in question must be tested by Mill's definition, as adopted by the decisions of the Board.

Turning then to the provisions of the *Fuel-Oil Act* here in question, it is clear that the Act purports to exact the tax from a person who has consumed fuel-oil, the amount of the tax being computed broadly according to the amount consumed. The Act does not relate to any commercial transaction in the commodity between the taxpayer and someone else. Their Lordships are unable to find, on examination of the Act, any justification for the suggestion that the tax is truly imposed in respect of the transaction by which the taxpayer acquires the property in the fuel-oil nor in respect of any contract or arrangement under which the oil is consumed, though it is, of course, possible that individual taxpayers may recoup themselves by such a contract or arrangement; but this cannot affect the nature of the tax. Accordingly their Lordships are of opinion that the tax is direct taxation within the meaning of s. 92, head 2, of the *British North America Act*.

*Appeal allowed.*

[His Lordship concluded by rejecting the argument that the Act invaded the federal "trade and commerce" power.]

## Note

The taxing technique used in the *Kingcome* case in respect of consumables like gasoline was tested in the Supreme Court of Canada in its application to non-consumables (or durable goods) in *Cairns Construction Ltd. v. Government of Saskatchewan*, [1960] S.C.R. 619, aff'g 27 W.W.R. 297, rev'g 22 W.W.R. 193. The *Cairns* case involved the validity of a provincial statute imposing a tax on consumers and users of tangible personalty purchased at retail in the province from a licensed vendor who was required to collect the tax at the time of the retail sale. The "agency" transaction covered by the legislation in *Atlantic Smoke Shops Ltd. v. Conlon and A.G. Can.*, [1943] A.C. 550 (P.C.), was similarly embraced by the legislation in the *Cairns* case, as was the case of the provincial resident bringing into the Province or receiving therein tangible personalty for his own consumption or use. The thin line in the "direct taxation" cases between the validity of the statute (construed in terms of its general tendency) and its application to a particular person was forcibly demonstrated in the *Cairns* case where the tax was demanded of a building contractor who purchased tangible personalty (being pre-fabricated building materials) for incorporation into houses built on the contractor's land for general sale or built on lands of others under a fixed contract price or on a cost-plus basis. The statute pinpointed the elusive division between constitutionality and particular application by its definition of "retail sale" as "a sale to a consumer or user for purposes of consumption or use and not for resale as tangible personal property". The building contractor purchased the materials for resale, but not for resale as personalty; and, considered in terms of general tendency there was no more reason to hold the tax indirect in this case than it would be to hold a gasoline tax to be indirect in respect of a trucking company for which the tax was part of its general overhead. However, accepting the constitutional validity of the tax even as applied to the building contractor, it might still be argued that as a matter of statutory construction the contractor was outside the enactment because he was buying for resale, even though he was at the same time a consumer or user of the building materials. This was not something that could be said in respect of consumables like tobacco and gasoline, so far as concerned a consumer or user of such products. It was this dilemma that was sought to be cured by defining "retail sale" in the terms above set out, terms which permit tax exoneration of a particular purchaser only where the resale of the personalty is in its form as such. Clearly, the legislature was entitled to limit tax exemption in this way as a mere matter of statutory coverage; and any constructional evasion of the limitation would be really a return to a constitutional argument. The Court was hence quite justified (on the given basis of the *Kingcome* and *Conlon* cases) in upholding both the validity of the provincial statute and its particular application to the building contractor.

### Note on Out-of-Province Transactions

As to out-of-province purchases, which are tied up with issues of section 121 as well as section 92(2), see *Atlantic Smoke Shops Ltd. v. Conlon and A. G. Can.*, [1943] A.C. 550 (P.C.), and Note (1942), 20 Can. Bar Rev. 157; Note, "Enforcing State Consumption Taxes on Out of State Purchases" (1951), 65 Harv. L. Rev. 301.

Although a Province may, both constitutionally and practically, be able to enforce a consumer sales tax by licensing retailers who carry on business in the Province and oblige them to collect the tax, what is its constitutional and practical position with respect to extra-provincial retailers who solicit in the Province by catalogue or mail or by a representative therein? See *Minister of Finance of New Brunswick v. Simpsons-Sears*, reproduced below. A consumer in the Province who brings taxable goods in from outside may validly be embraced by a tax, as determined in the *Conlon* case, but collection depends on the reporting of the purchase or other means of ascertaining that it was made. If the goods purchased from an outside vendor are shipped or delivered to the provincial purchaser-consumer rather than brought in by him, is there a constitutional means by which the Province may enforce payment of the tax by such consumer through the imposition of duties or requirements on the outside retailer? May such retailer be prohibited by the Province from shipping goods into the Province or from delivering them therein, unless the registers with the Province? Some assistance may be gained on these questions from *R. v. Thomas Equipment Ltd.*, [1979] 2 S.C.R. 529. See remarks following *Interprovincial Cooperatives v. The Queen* at Chapter 8, *supra*, for comment on this case. Is it open to the Province to constitute an outside retailer an agent of the Province for collection of the tax, or to prohibit suit for recovery of the price of goods sold to a provincial consumer unless the retailer complies with prescribed requirements, or to require security from him? Would section 121 of the *Constitution Act, 1867* be violated in any of the foregoing circumstances? See the excellent note by Beck, "Sales Tax on Interprovincial Transactions — Collection from Non-Resident Retailers — Reciprocal Enforcement of Tax Claims" (1964), 42 Can. Bar Rev. 490.

## MINISTER OF FINANCE OF NEW BRUNSWICK v. SIMPSONS-SEARS LTD.

In the Supreme Court of Canada. [1982] 1 S.C.R. 144.

Laskin C.J.C., Martland, Ritchie, Dickson, Beetz, Estey, McIntyre, Chouinard and Lamer JJ. January 26, 1982.

Appeal from a decision of the Court of Appeal of New Brunswick, 30 N.B.R. (2d) 151 affirming a decision of Stratton J., 27 N.B.R. (2d) 652 declaring certain provisions of the *Social Services and Education Tax Act*, R.S.N.B. 1973, c. S-10 as amended S.N.B. 1978, c. 55 *ultra vires* the legislature.

This case was a follow-up to an earlier case involving essentially the same parties, *Simpsons-Sears Ltd. v. Provincial Secretary of New Brunswick*, [1978] 2 S.C.R. 869. In the earlier case, catalogues were sent by Simpsons-Sears Ltd. in the course of its mail order business from outside New Brunswick to destinations in the

Province free of charge to the recipients thereof. The Provincial Secretary sought to tax Simpsons-Sears Ltd. pursuant to section 4 of the *Social Services and Education Tax Act* (N.B.) which provided that "Every consumer of goods consumed in the Province shall pay to the Minister for the raising of a revenue for Provincial purposes, a tax . . ." Section 1 defined "consumer" as a person who utilized goods in the Province for his own consumption or the consumption of any other person at his expense. A majority of the Supreme Court of Canada held that the statute did not as a matter of construction apply to tax the free distribution of mail order catalogues as "consumption" in the Province. On the constitutional issue of whether the tax, if applicable, was direct or indirect, the Court split four to four with Laskin C.J.C. expressing no opinion. The decision therefore rested on constructional rather than constitutional grounds.

The Legislature amended the statute in 1978 following this first case. The Court considered that these 1978 Amendments caught promotional distributions such as those in the case at bar, and was therefore squarely faced with the constitutional question.

The judgment of the Court was delivered by

LASKIN C.J.C.: . . .

The question in this appeal is whether the Legislature of New Brunswick, in amending its *Social Services and Education Tax Act*, R.S.N.B. 1973, c. S-10, by 1978 (N.B.), c. 55, has overcome the frailties in the Act which precluded it from lawfully taxing the respondent company in respect of the free distribution of catalogues to persons in the Province. This Court decided, by a majority judgment in *Simpsons-Sears Ltd. v. Provincial Secretary of New Brunswick*, [1978] 2 S.C.R. 869, that the taxation could not be supported under the Act as it stood before the 1978 amendments. That judgment related to catalogues distributed in 1972. The present appeal relates to catalogues distributed in 1975, 1976 and 1977. The amendments in 1978 covered those years retroactively, but nothing turns on this feature of the case.

As in the former case, the catalogues were either shipped in bulk from Ontario and distributed in New Brunswick by the respondent (which carries on business in that Province as well as elsewhere in Canada) to customers and prospective customers or were mailed from Ontario directly to individual customers in New Brunswick whose names are made known by the company's New Brunswick offices. The issue raised under the applicable legislation is whether the taxation of the company in respect of the free distribution of its catalogues in New Brunswick is "direct taxation within the Province" under s. 92(2) of the *British North America Act, 1867*. Stratton J. [27 N.B.R. (2d) 652] of the New Brunswick Queen's Bench held that the taxation was indirect and this conclusion was affirmed in a majority judgment of the Court of Appeal, [30 N.B.R. (2d) 151], Limerick J.A., dissenting.

Following the judgments in the New Brunswick Courts, and leave to appeal here having been given, the following constitutional question was fixed for determination:

> Are the provisions of The Social Services and Education Tax Act, R.S.N.B., 1973, Chapter S-10 under which a promotional distributor is taxed in respect of the provision of goods by way of promotional distribution, intra vires the legislature of New Brunswick in respect of:
> (a) catalogues brought into the Province by the Respondent and distributed in the Province to the Respondent's customers and prospective customers, without charge?

(b) catalogues mailed from outside the Province directly to the Respondent's customers in the Province, without charge?

. . . .

Before dealing with the question whether the tax imposed is direct, I wish to mention a company submission that the tax, at least in respect of the mailings from Ontario to individuals in New Brunswick, is not a tax within the Province. Having regard to the definition of "promotional distribution" and "promotional distributor", as carried into the definition of "consumption" and, in turn, into the charging s. 4, the submission is untenable. The company carries on business in the Province and, by way of promotional distribution, has caused the catalogues to be provided to persons in the Province. These facts, all prescribed by the Act, are sufficient to establish a valid tax basis within the Province if the tax imposed is direct.

On this score, it was submitted by the appellant that on the facts and in light of the amended statute, the company was the consumer of the catalogues, coming within the definition of "consumer" and, by extension thereunder, within the charging s. 4. The tax, therefore, in respect of the distribution of catalogues in the Province was a direct tax payable by the company as the consumer and, indeed, as the ultimate consumer. The purported fortification of this conclusion by s. 11.2 would not of itself turn a tax otherwise indirect into a direct tax but it does assist as a statutory determination of ultimate consumption when, under s. 11.2, a person who receives a catalogue free of charge is declared to be exempt from tax in respect of the catalogue. The larger, and more critical question, is whether this assists in determining whether the tax is direct or indirect.

I am in agreement with the contention of the appellant that Hughes C.J.N.B. went too far in his assertion that there was a tendency on the part of the Courts to classify all taxes on businesses as indirect, unless the tax falls within some category traditionally considered as direct. Income taxes and land taxes are, of course, the prime examples of taxes traditionally classified as direct but there are other examples of taxes payable in respect of business operations that have been treated as direct. *A.-G. Nfld. v. Avalon Telephone Co.* (1962), 47 M.P.R. 165 (Nfld. C.A.) provides one example and the recent judgment of Cowan C.J.T.D. of the Nova Scotia Supreme Court in *Re Franklin Enterprises Ltd. and Minister of Finance for Nova Scotia* [now reported 45 N.S.R. (2d) 604 (T.D.)], provides another. This last-mentioned case is relevant because there a hotel enterprise was held to be validly taxable in respect of its purchase for use in its hotel of tangible personalty such as beds, bedspreads, linens, towels, soap, matches and tissue paper. Again, as was pointed out by the appellant, if, as in *Brewers & Maltsters' Ass'n of Ontario v. A.-G. Ont.*, [1897] A.C. 231 (P.C.), the Province of New Brunswick had imposed a licence fee in respect of the free distribution of catalogues, it would be difficult indeed to contend that an indirect tax had been imposed, especially when the fee had no relation to the quantity of goods.

It would be a more apt illustration than that used by Chief Justice Hughes to say that taxes in respect of commodities or commercial transactions at the retail or production level have been generally classified as indirect, as, for example, in the *Caledonian Cotlieries* case, *R. v. Caledonian Collieries Ltd.*, [1928] A.C. 358 (P.C.), and in *Charlottetown v. Foundation Maritime Ltd.*, [1932] S.C.R. 589. The respondent company has invoked this line of cases, not as being directly applicable on their facts but as expressing the principle that where the general tendency of a tax is that it will be passed on and hence paid by someone other than the person upon whom it is initially imposed, it will be regarded as an indirect tax.

This assertion was related by the company to a submission to which I referred earlier, namely, that the tax was a consumption tax or at best a hybrid form of tax and that it remained necessary to determine who was the ultimate consumer. This contention has validity in a case such as *Caledonian Collieries* where the Court was concerned with a sale situation. Here there is no question of a sale, and consumption, in its literal meaning, does not come into the picture save in its artificial meaning as reflected in its extended definition. In that respect, it is only the company that can be regarded as the ultimate consumer for tax purposes.

There is no doubt, on the evidence, and on ordinary economic considerations which are obvious enough to justify a Court in taking judicial notice of them, that the company would seek, if it could, to include the cost to it of its catalogues and the tax payable on their free distribution in its expense of doing business, and thus seek to pass this expense on to its customers. However, economic considerations are not invariable touchstones of legal incidence. Although the tests of direct and indirect taxation have, almost from the beginning of Canadian federalism, been based on Mill's Political Economy, Bk. V, c. 5, they have necessarily been placed in a legal setting and have been applied as providing a legal definition and not an economic one. There is a passage in *Bank of Toronto v. Lambe* (1887), 12 App. Cas. 575 at 583 (P.C.), which is an appropriate reference here, although it deals with a different type of tax. The passage is as follows:

> ... the tax now in question is demanded directly of the bank apparently for the reasonable purpose of getting contributions for provincial purposes from those who are making profits by provincial business. It is not a tax on any commodity which the bank deals in and can sell at an enhanced price to its customers. It is not a tax on its profits, nor on its several transactions. It is a direct lump sum, to be assessed by simple reference to its paid-up capital and its places of business. It may possibly happen that in the intricacies of mercantile dealings the bank may find a way to recoup itself out of the pockets of its Quebec customers. But the way must be an obscure and circuitous one, the amount of recoupment cannot bear any direct relation to the amount of tax paid, and if the bank does manage it, the result will not improbably disappoint the intention and desire of the Quebec Government. For these reasons their Lordships hold the tax to be direct taxation within class 2 of sect. 92 of the Federation Act.

The "general tendency" argument, found, for example, in the *Caledonian Collieries* case, is not one that establishes a principle outside of the context in which it was used in that case. Where, as in the present case, the tax imposed in respect of the free distribution of catalogues takes no account of what ultimately happens to the catalogues, whether they are used or discarded, and is unrelated to any purchases made from the catalogues, it is manifest to me that the tax is so diffused in its impact that it cannot be said that there is any clearly traceable way in which the tax can be passed on.

Moreover, to borrow a phrase from the reasons of Rand J. in *C.P.R. v. A.-G. Sask.*, [1952] 2 S.C.R. 231 at 251, the tax in the present case is not "related or relatable" to any unit of a commodity or its price, indeed, no commodity is involved.

The fact that the company may, competitive and other factors permitting, recoup the tax in its overall pricing structure, is no ground for classifying it as an indirect tax. The tax, indeed, is paid in respect of a dead-end dealing, one that is over when the catalogues are distributed and there is no way in which it can be assigned to recipients of the catalogues. Moreover, the fact that the tax is a cost of carrying on business does not mean that it is not exacted from the very person who it is intended and expected would pay it.

This is sufficient to dispose of the appeal which I would allow and, accordingly, declare that the amended Act is, in respect of the matters put in issue here, *intra vires*. The appellant is entitled to costs throughout. There will be no costs to or against the intervenants.

*Appeal allowed.*

## 3. Taxation Within the Province

### Note on Taxation Within the Province

The territorial limitation of provincial taxing power under section 92(2) invites examination of the charging sections of provincial taxing statutes to determine who or what is being taxed. This question assumed added importance when regard is had to the settled proposition, easier to state than it is at times to apply, that the constitutionality of a tax imposed within the province (and being, of course, a direct tax) is not affected if extra-provincial attributes are used to measure its amount: see *Bank of Toronto v. Lambe* (1887), 12 App. Cas. 575 (P.C.); *Minister of Finance (B.C.) v. Royal Trust Co.*, 61 S.C.R. 127, rev'd on other grounds [1922] 1 A.C. 87 (P.C.); Gunn, "Provincial Taxation of Paid-up Capital of Foreign Corporations" (1941), 19 Can. Bar Rev. 31; and see also *A.-G. B.C. v. E. & N. Ry.*, [1950] A.C. 87 at 115 (P.C.), where Lord Greene said:

> It simply is not the case that a tax on land is the same thing as a tax on timber, however minute or even non-existent may be the difference in value of the land and of the timber.... Their Lordships are in agreement with what was said by O'Halloran J.A. on this topic in the following passage: 'Because land bears a tax which is measured by the reflected value of its products is no reason to say that the tax on the land is a colourable tax on its products, and that such a tax is not in truth a tax on the land itself.'

The constitutional problem thus often dissolves into a matter of statutory construction: Is the tax on a person or on a thing or on some transaction or benefit within the province?

In *A.G.-B.C. v. Canada Trust Co.*, [1980] 2 S.C.R. 466, a provincial statute imposed a tax on resident beneficiaries in respect of personal property outside the Province passing on the death of a non-resident. The Supreme Court of Canada upheld the tax as an *in personam* tax on the resident beneficiaries rather than an *in rem* tax on the extra-provincial assets. The value of the assets were merely used to calculate the amount of the tax. Dickson J. stated the principle this way at 484-485 S.C.R.:

> I am satisfied there is no reason in principle or authority why, in the context of succession duties, the Provinces cannot tax on the basis of the residence of the beneficiary without regard for the *situs* of the property or the domicile of the decedent. In other words, it is within provincial competence to tax a resident beneficiary in respect of property situated outside the Province and passing on the death of a person domiciled outside the Province. It does not matter whether the decedent died

domiciled in the Province or outside, so long as the beneficiary or beneficiaries are within the Province. When a Province decides to impose a succession duty, it is not in the position of having to choose to levy a direct tax upon property, or upon the basis of the artificial subcategory, "transmission of property", or upon the beneficiaries. The Province may, constitutionally, tax on any or all of these bases, provided always that the subject-matter of the tax is situated within the Province.

In *Kerr v. Superintendent of Income Tax*, [1942] S.C.R. 435 an Alberta resident was taxed under Alberta legislation in respect of income deposited to her credit outside of Alberta. The central issue, decided adversely to the taxpayer, was whether the taxing statute charged persons in Alberta or income in Alberta. See, to the same effect, *C.P.R. v. Prov. Treas. of Man.*, [1953] 4 D.L.R. 233 (Man. Q.B.).

*Alworth v. Minister of Finance*, [1978] 1 S.C.R. 449 presented the converse situation where the Supreme Court of Canada upheld a tax on income from logging operations in the Province even where the tax was payable by non-residents. Laskin C.J.C., speaking for the Court at 452 S.C.R., said:

> The definition of taxpayer is not limited to persons who reside in the Province but points rather to a class of persons identified with the operations in respect of which tax is imposed, regardless of their place of residence. It is the income derived from those operations, which themselves are limited to the Province, that, in my view, carries the burden of the tax. Whether the tax be characterized as an income tax or a tax respecting certain economic activity in the Province the result is the same, namely, that it is taxation within the Province.

In *International Harvester Co. v. Provincial Tax Commission*, [1949] A.C. 36 (P.C.), rev'g [1941] S.C.R. 325, the Saskatchewan taxing statute in question charged the income of non-residents carrying on business in the province, and defined it as "the net profit or gain arising from the business . . . in Saskatchewan." The Privy Council noted the distinction between taxing profits *received* in a province and profits *arising* from the business therein; and it agreed with the argument, accepted by Duff C.J. in his dissenting judgment below, that the assessed company could properly exclude a "manufacturing" profit on sales in Saskatchewan attributable to its factory operations in another province. See also *Prov. Treas. of Man. v. Wm. Wrigley Jr. Co.*, [1950] A.C. 1 (P.C.). Similarly, a question of construction, both of a statute and of a contract, faced the courts which dealt with *Firestone Tire & Rubber Co. of Canada Ltd. v. Com'r of Income Tax*, [1942] S.C.R. 476 where a British Columbia statute taxed "income earned within the province" by non-residents. An Ontario manufacturing company had entered into a "distributor's warehouse" contract in Ontario with a distributor in British Columbia to whom it granted the exclusive right to handle its products in that province. The Supreme Court of Canada decided that the contract was one of sale rather than of agency, with the result that the company did not earn any profits in British Columbia. While the Court proceeded on the view that the alternatives were to find a sale to the distributor in Ontario or a sale by the company to purchasers in British Columbia through the distributor, the terms of the contract would support the argument that the distributor remained a bailee until he effected a sale in British Columbia, a transaction which would involve both a purchase by him from the company and a resale by him: see Note (1943), 21 Can. Bar Rev. 61.

The phrase "within the province" in section 92(2) presents no particular difficulty of application to persons or firms or corporations or tangible things. The difficult problems in this connection have arisen in determining the situs of intangibles and in defining the conditions in which a province may levy succession duties or gift taxes in respect of estates of deceased persons, especially where the assets are intangibles. The cases and notes which follow illustrate these problems.

# R. v. NATIONAL TRUST CO.

In the Supreme Court of Canada. [1933] S.C.R. 670.

Duff C.J., Rinfret, Lamont, Smith, Cannon and Crocket JJ. Oct. 3, 1933.

Appeal from a judgment of the Quebec Court of King's Bench, Appeal Side (1932), 54 Que. K.B. 351, affirming a judgment of the Superior Court which dismissed appellant's action.

The judgment of the Court was delivered by

DUFF C.J.: The statutory enactments under consideration are sections 3 and 5 of the Quebec Succession Duties Act. So far as pertinent, the provisions of these sections are as follows:

> 3. All property, moveable or immoveable, the ownership, usufruct, or enjoyment whereof is transmitted owing to death, shall be liable to the following taxes calculated upon the value of the property transmitted, after deducting debts and charges existing at the time of death. . . .
>
> 5. The word 'property' within the meaning of this division includes all property, moveable or immoveable, actually situate within the province, and all debts which are owing to the deceased at the time of his death, or are payable by reason of his death, and which are either payable in the province, or are due by a debtor domiciled therein; the whole whether the deceased at the time of his death had his domicile within or without the province, or whether the transmission takes place within or without the province.
>
> The property in respect of which the dispute arises consists of certain bonds or debentures of the Grand Trunk Pacific Railway Company and the Canadian National Railway Company respectively, guaranteed by the Government of the Dominion of Canada. These bonds were the property of Sir Clifford Sifton who, at the time of his death on the 17th of April, 1929, was domiciled in the province of Ontario where the bonds were in his possession.

The enactments of the statute purport to impose a tax upon property transmitted owing to death; and, therefore, they only affect subjects having a situs within the province (*Woodruff v. Attorney-General for Ontario*, [1908] A.C. 508 (P.C.); *R. v. Lovitt*, [1912] A.C. 212 (P.C.); *Toronto General Trusts Corporation v. The King*, [1919] A.C. 679 (P.C.); *Brassard v. Smith*, [1925] A.C. 371 (P.C.); *Provincial Treasurer of Alberta v. Kerr*, [1933] A.C. 710 (P.C.).

The question we have to consider is whether or not these bonds have, in the relevant sense, a local situation within that province.

Some propositions pertinent to that issue may, we think, be collected from the judgments of the Judicial Committee of the Privy Council, if not laid down explicitly, at least, as implicit in them. First, property, whether moveable or immoveable, can, for the purposes of determining situs among the different provinces of Canada in relation to the incidence of a tax imposed by a provincial law upon property transmitted owing to death, have only one local situation. In applying this proposition, of course, it is necessary to distinguish between a tax upon property and a tax upon persons domiciled or resident in the province.

(*Toronto General Trusts Corp. v. The King; Brassard v. Smith; Provincial Treasurer of Alberta v. Kerr*).

Then, it seems to be a corollary of this proposition that situs, in respect of intangible property (which has no physical existence) must be determined by reference to some principle or coherent system of principles; and again, the courts appear to have acted upon the assumption that the British Legislature, in defining, in part, at all events, by reference to the local situation of such property, the authority of the province in relation to taxation, must be supposed to have had in view the principles of, or deducible from, those of the common law. (*The King v. Lovitt; Toronto General Trusts Corp. v. The King; Brassard v. Smith; Royal Trust Co. v. Attorney-General for Alberta*, [1930] A.C. 144 (P.C.)).

We think it follows that a provincial legislature is not competent to prescribe the conditions fixing the situs of intangible property for the purpose of defining the subjects in respect of which its powers of taxation under s. 92(2) may be put into effect.

On this appeal we are concerned with debts, or obligations to pay money. As is well known, rules for the determination of such situs for various purposes have been drawn from those which defined. the jurisdiction of the ecclesiastical tribunals respecting probate. (*Royal Trust Co. v. Attorney-General for Alberta; English, Scottish & Australian Bank v. The Commissioners of Inland Revenue*, [1932] A.C. 238 at 242 (H.L.)). In those rules, a broad distinction was observed between specialties and simple contract debts. The latter were *bona notabilia* in the jurisdiction in which the debtor had his personal residence; the former, where the instrument constituting the specialty was found at the death of the testator. The case of judgment debts which were deemed to be situated where the judgment was recorded, may be regarded as a special one. . . .

[His Lordship went on to hold that the mere fact that the bonds were registered in Quebec and transferable on the company's register in that Province did not in and of itself render the situs of the obligation to be in Quebec and, further, the fact that the primary debtor was resident in Quebec was not controlling on the issue of situs in the circumstances of this case].

*Appeal dismissed.*

### Note

Duff J. went on to say, later in his judgment in the *National Trust* case, *supra*, that "the rule for determining situs, in applying the enactment of s. 92(2) of the *B.N.A. Act*, must rest upon the principles of the common law in England . . ." In commenting upon this rule, Professor Hogg states:

This implausible proposition is now firmly established [citing *R. v. Williams*, [1942] A.C. 541]. The result is that a body of arcane rules has been transplanted from England and then elaborated in Canada for the purpose of determining the situs of property. The constitutional status of the situs rules has been confirmed by the further rule that a province may not alter the rules in order to assume taxing jurisdiction over property [citing *R. v. National Trust, supra; R. v. Williams, supra*; cf. *Minister of Finance (B.C.) v. First National Bank of Nevada*, [1975] 1 S.C.R. 525]. The judge-made rules as to situs are therefore immune from provincial legislative change.

Hogg, *Constitutional Law of Canada*, (2d ed. 1985) at pp. 617-8.

See also Laskin, "Taxation and Situs: Company Shares" (1941), 19 Can. Bar Rev. 617; Note (1942), 20 Can. Bar Rev. 471; Note (1942), 20 Can. Bar Rev. 640.

Does the *Williams* case deny power to a province to include share certificates within a definition of property subject to taxation if found within the province? *Cf. Stern v. The Queen*, [1896] 1 Q.B. 211. In *In re Brookfield Estate, Royal Trust Co. v. The King*, [1949] S.C.R. 329, rev'g [1948] 4 D.L.R. 210, the deceased, domiciled in Nova Scotia, had registered certain shares in United States companies, which had no share transfer registries in Nova Scotia, in the names of Nova Scotia nominees. The certificates, endorsed in blank, with attached declarations of trust by the registered owners, were held by a Nova Scotia trust company subject to the deceased's instructions. The Supreme Court of Canada held that the deceased's beneficial interest in the shares was not property situate in Nova Scotia within ss. 3(1) and 8(a) of the *Succession Duty Act*, 1945 (N.S.), c. 7. Rand J. said, *inter alia*:

> Under a law-making sovereignty the subject-matter of taxation may in fact be anything on which power can be exerted or in respect of which the payment of money can be made the condition of the doing of an act or exercising a right within its territorial boundaries. In the *Stern* case there were street certificates within England which were essential to an entry of transfer on the register outside of England; and the legislative authority of England extended in effect to restrain the use of these certificates until, or to charge other property admittedly in England with, the payment of certain monies related to them. Whether these monies are taken to be probate or estate duties or legacy or succession duties does not, for purposes of jurisdiction in taxes, appear to be material.
>
> But a province of the Dominion is not apparently in that degree of sovereignty. The power of 'direct taxation within the province', interpreted as it has been by the authorities cited, is to be exercised on the footing that there is only one *situs* for every class of property and that that *situs* must be within the province. And for shares, there can be no such division of interest or powers in or annexed to them as would in the result attribute to them a *situs* in two or more places.
>
> It is not suggested that the law of New York has embodied the visible and exclusive evidence of these rights in one tangible and moveable symbol to be looked upon and dealt with as a chattel as in *Attorney-General v. Bouwens* (1838), 4 M. & W. 171, and that being so, we are remitted to the considerations by which the shares are localized in the place where they may be effectually dealt with. But it is conceded that an entry of the purchaser's name on the registry of the shares in New York would be essential to admitting him to membership in the company and the case comes then directly within the principles laid down.

Would it be competent to a Province, which permits companies incorporated therein to establish share transfer registries outside, to provide by legislation that shares of a deceased shareholder are transferable only on the registry in the Province? Both at trial (*sub nom. Re Wolfenden Estate*, [1971] 5 W.W.R. 168) and at the British Columbia Court of Appeal in *Minister of Finance (B.C.) v. First National Bank of Nevada*, [1972] 5 W.W.R. 443, the courts found that such a provision was a colourable attempt under the guise of company law to alter situs of the shares so as to bring them within the province. It was common ground when the case was argued before the Supreme Court of Canada that the situs of the shares was outside the province on the applicable common law rules and apart from the statutory provision in question. The Supreme Court of Canada affirmed the lower courts decisions at [1975] 1 S.C.R. 525 that no succession duty was payable on the constitutional grounds that the legislation in its terms did not reach the property. Five of the nine Justices did not reach the constitutional issue at all (Abbot, Martland, Judson, Dickson and Laskin JJ.). The remaining four concurred on the constitutional point, but in addition took positions on the constitutional point. Ritchie J., speaking for himself, Fauteux C.J.C. and Pigeon held that the legislation was not a colourable device to alter the situs of the shares and Spence J. held that it was. See also Note

(1944), 22 Can. Bar Rev. 838; Note (Correspondence) (1945), 23 Can. Bar Rev. 77; Note (1945), 23 Can. Bar Rev. 167.

On the question of the situs of "street" certificates, which Lord Uthwatt seemed to treat as open in *Treasurer of Ontario v. Blonde*, [1947] A.C. 24 (P.C.): see, Rand J. in *In re Brookfield Estate, Royal Trust Co. v. The King*, [1949] S.C.R. 329 at 339, where after referring to *Brassard v. Smith* and the *Williams* case, he said:

> These pronouncements, re-affirmed in *Treasurer of Ontario v. Blonde*, treat mere transferability or merchantability of the right to become a shareholder, in the initial stages of the inquiry, as having little if any relevance to situs, but they recognize as matters of a determinative nature which the law creating the shares has provided to evidence their characteristics as property. Registration in a book and representation by a certificate are tangible badges which set conditions to complete transferability of the shares as well as facilitate dealings with them. If, as in the case of bearer shares, in analogy to bearer bonds, the issuing jurisdiction has in effect embodied in a certain instrument the exclusive symbol of the total rights created, then, certainly, as a rule, the situs is taken to be the locality in which the instrument may at any time be.

The rules governing the situs of various kinds of intangibles are discussed by Falconbridge, Essays on the Conflict of Laws (1954 2d ed.), chap. 20. The following illustrative cases may be noted:

1. Simple contract debts: *R. v. Lovitt*, [1912] A.C. 212 (P.C.); *In re Muir Estate, Standard Trust Co. v. Treas. of Man.* (1915), 51 S.C.R. 428; *Bitter v. Secretary of State for Canada*, [1944] Ex. C.R. 61 (corporation debtor with several residences).
2. Specialty debts: *Royal Trust Co. v. A.-G. Alta.*, [1930] A.C. 144 (P.C.); *Toronto General Trusts Corp. v. The King*, [1919] A.C. 679 (P.C.).
3. Judgment debts: *A.-G. v. Bouwens* (1838), 4 M. & W. 171, 150 E.R. 1390.
4. Negotiable instruments: *Crosby v. Prescott*, [1923] S.C.R. 446.
5. Bank deposit receipts: *Prov. Treas. of Man. v. Bennett*, [1937] S.C.R. 138.
6. Bonds: *Re Moore*, [1937] 2 D.L.R. 746 (Ont. S.C.); *Re Mathews*, [1938] 2 D.L.R. 763 (Ont. Surr. Ct.); *R. v. Sanner and Bank of Montreal* (1936), 74 Que. S.C. 42.
7. Debts due from the Crown and statutory government obligations: *R. v. National Trust Co.*, [1933] S.C.R. 670.
8. Mortgages: *Toronto General Trusts Corp. v. The King, supra; Royal Trust Co. v. Prov. Sec.-Treas. of N.B.*, [1925] S.C.R. 94; *Treas. of Ont. v. Pattin* (1910), 22 O.L.R. 184 (C.A.).
9. Agreements for sale of land: *Re Muir, Standard Trust Co. v. Prov. Treas. of Man., supra; Vaughn v. A.-G. Alta.*, [1924] 2 W.W.R. 821; *Schmidt v. Prov. Treas. of Alta.*, [1935] 3 W.W.R. 498 (Alta. C.A.).
10. Trusts: *A.-G. N.S. v. Davis*, [1937] 3 D.L.R. 673. *Cf. A.-G. Ont. v. Fasken*, [1935] O.R. 288 (C.A.); *Re Brookfield, Royal Trust Co. v. The King*, [1949] S.C.R. 329.
11. Life insurance policies: *Re Corlet*, [1939] 2 W.W.R. 478 (Alta.); *Re Lawton*, [1944] 2 W.W.R. 265, aff'd [1945] 2 W.W.R. 529 (Man. C.A.).
12. Interests in estates: *In re Steed and Raeburn Estates, Minister of National Revenue v. Fitzgerald*, [1949] S.C.R. 453; *In re Lunn Estate*, [1925] 2 W.W.R. 608 (B.C.C.A.).

Some of the foregoing cases are discussed in Farwell, *Law of Succession Duties in Ontario* (1942), pp. 67-79; Quigg, *Succession Duties in Canada* (2d ed. 1937), chap. IX; Jameson, *Ontario Succession Duties* (1959), chap. 4; and see also Perry, *Taxation in Canada* (1951), chap. 8. It may be noted that the *Estate Tax Act*, R.S.C. 1970, c. E-9, s. 42, fixes the situs of various kinds of property in places differing from those fixed by the common law rules. The Dominion is not, of course, affected by the constitutional and territorial limitations governing the provinces, and certainly not in respect of federally incorporated companies (see *Hunt v. The Queen*, [1968] S.C.R. 323), but the federal rules taken on importance for the provinces in the light of Dominion-Provincial tax agreements.

[Where provincial legislation prohibits the transfer of shares into the name of the beneficiary without a succession duty clearance is the legislation valid with respect to the transfer of shares in a Dominion company where Dominion legislation declares that the right of the shareholder to transfer his shares shall not be restricted? See *Christie v. British American Oil Co. Ltd.*, [1947] O.R. 842.]

# PROVINCIAL TREASURER OF ALTA. v. KERR

In the Privy Council. [1933] A.C. 710.

Lord Blanesburgh, Lord Atkin, Lord Thankerton, Lord Russell of Killowen and Lord Macmillan. July 27, 1933.

Appeal and cross-appeal from a judgment of the Alberta Appellate Division, [1932] 2 W.W.R. 705, relating to the validity of Alberta succession duty legislation in its application to personal property of an Alberta domiciliary.

LORD THANKERTON: The late Isaac Kendall Kerr died on December 3, 1929, domiciled and resident in the Province of Alberta. He left a large estate, and the respondents in the original appeal, both of whom are resident in the city of Calgary, obtained letters probate as executrix and executor of his will. Thereafter duties amounting to $54,754.21 were assessed under the Alberta Succession Duties Act by the Provincial Treasurer in respect of the property of the deceased, and the respondents, along with a surety, entered into the bond afterwards referred to in order to secure payment of these duties.

The respondents challenged the validity of the imposition of these duties by the Province and a special case was agreed to by the parties, which was referred, pursuant to the Alberta Rules of Court, to the Appellate Division of the Supreme Court of Alberta. In this case two questions were referred for determination, and the decision of the Appellate Division, given July 22, 1932, has led to the original appeal by the Provincial Treasurer and the Attorney-General for Alberta (hereinafter called "the Province"), and a cross appeal by the executrix and executor (hereinafter called "the executors").

The property in respect of which the duties were imposed is described in the special case as follows:

(2.) The property owned by the said Isaac Kendall Kerr at the time of his death consisted of — (a) certain personal property of the aggregate value of $265,703.58 composed of shares and other securities of various companies which had no head office in the Province of Alberta, and none of which had any registration or transfer office within the said Province, together with other personal property locally situate outside of the said Province. The share certificates and other documents evidencing such shares and other securities were found in the City of Calgary, in the Province of Alberta. (b) Certain real property and personal property having an aggregate value of $274,697.03.

The real property is situate within the Province of Alberta and the personal property consists of shares and other securities in companies with head office and transfer office situate within the Province of Alberta, and other personal property locally situate within the said Province. (3.) Within the two years prior to his death the said Isaac Kendall Kerr transferred to Clara E. Kerr, one of the plaintiffs, certain real etate situate within the Province of Alberta, together with certain personal estate.

No question is raised as to the duties in respect of the property in para. 3, and the following questions were submitted for the opinion of the Court:

(1.) Whether or not the succession duties levied in respect of the property mentioned in sub-s. (1) in para. 2 of the special case are valid and payable to the defendants or either of them. (2.) Whether or not the succession duties levied in respect of the property mentioned in sub-s. (b) in para. 2 of the special case are valid and payable to the defendants or either of them.

The determination of the validity of the imposition of the duties depends on the application of the limits placed upon the taxing powers of a Province by s. 92 of the *British North America Act*, 1867 — namely, "Direct taxation within the Province in order to the raising of a revenue for Provincial purposes" to the provisions of the Alberta Succession Duties Act. As regards the first question, which relates to personal property locally situate outside the Province, the issue is twofold — namely, whether the taxation is direct and whether it is within the Province. On the second question, which covers real and personal property situate within the Province, the issue is whether the taxation is direct.

Dealing first with the question of taxation "within the Province", the general law as to the power of taxation of a sovereign state has been thus stated; *Blackwood v. The Queen:* ((1882), 8 App. Cas. 82 at 96 (P.C.))

There is nothing in the law of nations which prevents a Government from taxing its own subjects on the basis of their foreign possessions. It may be inconvenient to do so. The reasons against doing so may apply more strongly to real than to personal estate. But the question is one of discretion, and is to be answered by the statutes under which each state levies its taxes, and not by mere reference to the laws which regulate successions to real and personal property.

There can be no doubt that the Alberta Succession Duties Act purports to impose taxation on the basis (*inter alia*) of personal property situate outside the Province, and therefore, if it possessed unlimited sovereign power, it would be entitled to impose such taxation on its subjects. Accordingly, the present question only arises because of the limitations placed on the legislative powers of the Province by s. 92 of the *British North America Act*, 1867, and, for this reason, the cases on legacy and succession duties in England are of little assistance for the present purpose. Generally speaking, taxation is imposed on persons, the nature and amount of the liability being determined either by individual units, as in the case of a poll tax, or in respect of the taxpayers' interest in property or in respect of transactions or actings of the taxpayers. It is at least unusual to find a tax imposed on property and not on persons — in any event, the duties here in question are not of that nature. In considering the limits placed on Provincial taxation, the Courts have invariably had regard to the basis or subject-matter in respect of which the taxation is imposed, and their Lordships agree with the statement of Anglin J. in *R. v. Cotton* (1912), 45 S.C.R. 469 at 536, where he said: "in order that a Provincial tax should be valid under the British North America Act, in my opionion the subject of taxation must be within the province."

The Province maintained in the first place, that under the Alberta Succession Duties Act the subject-matter of taxation was the transmission of the property and not the property itself, and fell within the principle of the decision of this Board in *Alleyn v. Barthe*.

In their Lordships' opinion, the principle to be derived from the decisions of this Board is that the Province, on the death of a person domiciled within the Province, is not entitled to impose taxation in respect of personal property locally situate outside the Province, but that it is entitled to impose taxation on persons domiciled or resident within the Province in respect of the transmission to them under the Provincial law of personal property locally situate outside the Province.

In *Lambe v. Manuel*, [1903] A.C. 68, a claim was made by the Province of Quebec for succession duties on movable property locally situate in that Province, which formed part of the succession of a testator domiciled in Ontario. The claim was rejected on the view that, on its true construction, the Quebec Succession Duty Act only applied, in the case of movables, to transmissions of property resulting from the devolution of a succession in the Province of Quebec. Sect. 1191B of the Quebec Act of 1892, on which the issue turned, provided as follows: "All transmissions, owing to death, of the property in, usufruct, or enjoyment of, moveable and immoveable property in the province shall be liable to the following taxes . . ." Thus the taxes were held to be imposed in respect of transmissions.

The Quebec Act of 1892 and the later Act of 1906, which re-enacted the words above quoted with alterations immaterial to this point, were considered in the case of *Cotton v. Rex*, and were construed as imposing the duties in respect of the transmission of the property. It was held, on construction, that neither of these Acts imposed any duty upon the transmission of moveable property outside the Province, and also that the taxation was not direct, in respect that it was imposed on "someone who was not intended himself to bear the burden but to be recouped by someone else."

In *Woodruff v. Att.-Gen. for Ontario*, [1908] A.C. 508 (P.C.), the deceased having died domiciled in the Province of Ontario, that Province claimed succession duty in respect of movable property locally situate in the United States. It was held to be an attempt to levy a tax on property locally situate outside the Province, which was beyond their competence. The Ontario Act of 1897, s. 4, sub-s. 1, provided "the following property shall be subject to a succession duty", which clearly was not a tax in respect of the transmission of a succession.

The case of *R. v. Lovitt*, [1912] A.C. 212 (P.C.) provides an interesting contrast to *Lambe's* case, [1903] A.C. 68 (P.C.). The testator, who died domiciled in Nova Scotia, was possessed of certain personal property locally situate in the Province of New Brunswick, in respect of which the latter Province claimed succession duty. It was held that, although called a succession duty, the tax in question was laid on the corpus of the property, and its payment was made a term of the grant of ancillary probate, and the claim to duty was upheld. The *New Brunswick Succession Duty Act, 1896*, s. 5, sub-s. 1, enacted: "All property, whether situate in this province or elsewhere, . . . passing either by will or intestacy . . . shall be subject to a succession duty."

In *Alleyn v. Barthe*, [1922] 1 A.C. 215 (P.C.), though an argument to the contrary was submitted, the judgment clearly proceeds on the footing that the taxation was imposed in respect of the transmission, and it may be noted that by the

*Quebec Succession Duty Act, 1909,* as revised in 1914, s. 1387B, "All transmissions within the Province, owing to the death of a person domiciled therein, of movable property locally situate outside the Province at the time of such death", were made liable to the duties; this provision is substantially the same as that under construction in *Lambe's* case. The main question in *Alleyn's* case was whether the taxation was direct, but, in delivering the judgment of this Board, Lord Phillimore, after referring to the statutory provisions, states:

> The conditions therein stated upon which taxation attaches to property outside the Province are two: (1) that the transmission must be within the Province; and (2) that it must be due to the death of a person domiciled within the Province. The first of these conditions can, in their Lordships' opinion, only be satisfied if the person to whom the property is transmitted is, as the universal legatee in this case was, either domiciled or ordinarily resident within the Province; for, in the connection in which the words are found no other meaning can be attached to the words 'within the Province' which modify and limit the word 'transmission.' So regarded, the taxation is clearly within the powers of the Province.

The identification of the subject-matter of the tax is naturally to be found in the charging section of the statute, and it will only be in the case of some ambiguity in the terms of the charging section that recourse to other sections is proper or necessary. In the present case, s. 7, sub-s. 1, is the charging provision, and as amended provided as follows:

> 7.—(1) Save as otherwise provided, all property of the owner thereof situate within the Province, and in the case of an owner domiciled in the Province, all the personal property of the owner situate outside the Province, and passing on his death, shall be subject to succession duties at the rate or rates set forth in the following table, the percentage payable on the share of any beneficiary being fixed by the following, or by some one or more of the following considerations, as the case may be:
>
> (a) the net value of the property of the deceased;
> (b) the place of residence of beneficiary;
> (c) the degree of kinship or absence of kinship of the beneficiary to the deceased.

In their Lordships' opinion, the terms of this section, which is very similar to that considered in *Lovitt's* case, clearly show that the subject matter of the taxation is the property and not the transmission of property; it is in marked contrast to the terms of the Quebec section considered in the cases of *Lambe* and *Alleyn*. It may be added that s. 9 of the Alberta Act, on which the Province sought to rely, does not modify this view, but merely provides a particular liability for payment of the tax.

The Province next contended that, although locally situate outside the Province, the personal property of a person, who dies domiciled within the Province, is to be treated as "within the Province" for the purposes of s. 92 of the *British North America Act*, by reason of the application of the rule embodied in the maxim "*mobilia sequuntur personam.*" This argument appears to proceed on a misunderstanding of the meaning and effect of that rule. If A dies domiciled in the United States of America, leaving movable property locally situate in England, the latter country has complete jurisdiction over the property, but the law of England, in order to decide on whom the property devolves on the death of A, will not apply English law of succession, but will ascertain and apply the American law. In other words, it is the law of England — not the law of America — that applies the principle of *mobilia sequuntur personam* in exercising its jurisdiction over the movable property in England, the locus of the latter remaining unchanged; in no sense could the property be described as "within America".

The Province further maintained that, as the bond given by the executors limited their liability to the duties in respect of property "coming into their hands", and the property here in question had admittedly come into their hands, the taxation was in respect of property within the Province; but, in their Lordships' opinion, the bond merely defines the extent of the security taken from the executors, and its terms cannot affect the validity or invalidity of the duties imposed under s. 7 of the Act. While that is sufficient to dispose of the contention, it may well be doubted whether "coming into their hands" means anything more than that the executors have completed their title to the property in question, the local situation of the property remaining unchanged.

Accordingly, their Lordships are of opinion that the duties under s. 7, so far as imposed on personal property locally situate outside the Province, did not come within the limits placed on Provincial taxation by s. 92 of the British North America Act . . .

[His Lordship's discussion of the second question, namely whether the tax on locally situated real estate was direct or indirect, is omitted].

*Appeal dismissed; cross-appeal allowed*

## Note

The *Kerr* case is another illustration of the role that statutory construction plays in the determination of constitutionality in section 92(2), especially when viewed in contradistinction to *Canada Trust Co. v. A.G. B.C.*, [1980] 2 S.C.R. 466. In *Canada Trust*, the issue was whether a provincial legislature could impose a tax on a resident beneficiary in respect of property situated outside the Province passing on the death of a non-resident deceased. Dickson J., delivering a judgment of the Supreme Court of Canada, upheld the tax. In the course of his reasons, he commented upon the *Kerr* case as follows at p. 481:

> The second case relied upon in the British Columbia Courts is *Provincial Treasurer v. Kerr*, [[1933] A.C. 710 (P.C.)]. The relevant sections there (ss. 9 and 7 of the *Succession Duties Act*, R.S.A., 1922, c. 28, as amended) provided [pp. 711 and 721 A.C.]:
>
> > 9. Every person resident in the Province to whom passes on the death of any person domiciled in the Province any personal property situate outside the Province, shall pay to the Provincial Treasurer for the use of the Province a tax calculated upon the value of the property in accordance with the rates and subject to the considerations set forth in sections 7 and 8 of this Act.
> >
> > . . . . .
> >
> > 7(1) Save as otherwise provided, all property of the owner thereof situate within the Province, and in the case of an owner domiciled in the Province, all the personal property of the owner situate outside the Province, and passing on his death, shall be subject to succession duties at the rate or rates set forth in the following table . . .
>
> One might think that s. 9 clearly imposed a tax on a resident beneficiary and not on property or on "transmissions". Indeed, the Privy Council appeared to say just that [p. 718 A.C.]:
>
> > Generally speaking, taxation is imposed on persons, the nature and amount of the liability being determined either by individual units, as in the case of a poll tax, or in respect of . . .

transactions or actings of the taxpayers. It is at least unusual to find a tax imposed on property and not on persons — in any event, the duties here in question are not of that nature.

This was followed, however, by an examination of the charging section, s. 7(1), which resulted in the conclusion that the subject-matter of the taxation was the property and not the transmission of property [p. 722 A.C.]:

> Accordingly, their Lordships are of opinion that the duties under s. 7, so far as imposed on personal property locally situate outside the Province, did not come within the limits placed on provincial taxation by s. 92 of the B.N.A. Act.

Since it was the finding of the Privy Council that the duties under s. 7 were on "property", then of course it follows that the section sought to reach, in part, a subject-matter outside the Province. The case has no direct application to the question now before us as to whether, when the tax is on the resident beneficiary, residence within the Province alone is sufficient.

The Courts below relied on the following oft-quoted passage as authority for the proposition that, in the case of property situate outside the Province, residence within the Province of both the testator and beneficiary is a precondition to the valid imposition of a tax [p. 718 A.C.]:

> The Province maintained, in the first place, that under the Alberta Succession Duties Act the subject matter of taxation was the transmission of the property and not the property itself, and fell within the principle of the decision of this Board in *Burland v. The King, Alleyn-Sharples v. Barthe* (1921), 62 D.L.R. 515 (P.C.).
> In their Lordships' opinion, the principle to be derived from the decisions of this Board is that the Province, on the death of a person domiciled within the Province, is not entitled to impose taxation in respect of personal property locally situate outside the Province, but that it is entitled to impose taxation on persons domiciled or resident within the Province in respect of the transmission to them under the provincial law of personal property locally situate outside the Province.

I agree that this statement of principle is an accurate statement of the "transmission doctrine", as generally understood, but I point out that it precedes the conclusion, at p. 721 A.C., that "the subject-matter of the taxation is the property and not the transmission of property". The principle was expressed in the context of an enactment which did not attempt to impose a tax upon, or in respect of a transmission, but rather upon personal property situated outside Alberta, and was clearly *obiter dictum*. The above passage, in my view, may be taken as an illustration of what a Province may validly do, but not as an exhaustive formulation of the minimum requirements which must be satisfied as a condition of constitutional validity. Lord Thankerton's discussion does not flow from an appreciation of the constitutional limits of the Province's taxing power, but rather from an appreciation of the cases concerning a "taxing on transmissions", cases which, as I have suggested, were concerned with rules of construction.

The words "in respect of the transmission to them under the Provincial law" should not be taken as limiting the provincial taxing power, but rather as reflecting the facts of the case before the Board. There, the decedent and the beneficiary were both domiciled in the Province.

*Kerr* is clearly good law in point of principle and indeed was approved as such in the above passage from *Canada Trust*. However *quaere* whether it would be decided the same way today on its facts that a succession duty is invalid where the decedent and beneficiary are both resident in the province but the property is situated outside it. The latitude currently being given to the provincial legislatures on matters of statutory construction is clearly illustrated by *Alworth v. Minister of Finance*, [1978] 1 S.C.R. 449. In *Alworth*, the Supreme Court of Canada upheld a tax even as regards non-residents, notwithstanding that the charging section stipulated that "the taxpayer shall pay a tax", by holding that the real subject of the tax was business operations in the Province. Laskin C.J.C. said that it was "too mechanical" to hold that it was an *in personam* tax merely because the charging section said the "taxpayer" must pay it.

# THE QUEEN IN RIGHT OF MANITOBA v. AIR CANADA

In the Supreme Court of Canada. [1980] 2 S.C.R. 303.

Laskin, C.J.C., Martland, Ritchie, Pigeon, Dickson, Beetz, Estey, McIntyre and Chouinard, JJ. July 18, 1980.

Appeal by the Province of Manitoba from a judgment of the Manitoba Court of Appeal, [1978] 2 W.W.R. 694, allowing its appeal in part and varying the judgment of Morse, J., [1977] 3 W.W.R. 129, allowing in part an appeal of Air Canada from a decision of the Minister of Finance of Manitoba confirming an amended assessment made pursuant to the *Retail Sales Tax Act* (Man.).

The judgment of the Court was delivered by

LASKIN, C.J.C.: — This case concerns the construction and application of the *Retail Sales Tax Act*, R.S.M. 1970, c. R150 (originally entitled the *Revenue Tax Act*), as amended by 1972, c. 6, and by 1974, c. 57, s. 1, Part 1, to Air Canada operations and services in throughflights which do not touch down in Manitoba and in flights which land in Manitoba or which take off in that Province. It arose under an amended assessment of tax under the Act, confirmed by the Manitoba Minister of Finance in the amount of $1,375,387, including interest and penalties, and covering in its various aspects the period of July 1, 1971 to June 30, 1974. Air Canada challenged the assessment and was largely successful in the challenge in litigation in the Manitoba Courts.

. . . .

On appeal by leave to this Court, two constitutional questions were fixed by an order of Pigeon, J., of August 18, 1978, as follows:

1. Is airspace over land territory of the Province of Manitoba "within the Province" so as to permit the Province to tax a corporation in respect of its use of aircraft in such airspace under the *Retail Sales Tax Act*, R.S.M. (1970) Ch. R150.
2. Is it otherwise *intra vires* the Province to so tax a business within the Province.

The Attorney-General of Canada intervened as did the Attorneys-General of Quebec, Nova Scotia, New Brunswick, British Columbia, Alberta and Saskatchewan. The appeal was heard in this Court by a Bench of seven Judges on November 7 and 8, 1979, but on December 21, 1979, the Court ordered a rehearing in the following terms:

A rehearing of this appeal is directed before the full Court [of nine] with particular reference to the question as to whether the taxes assessed against the respondent pursuant to the provisions of the *Retail Sales Tax Act*, R.S.M. 1970, c. R150, and in issue in this appeal, constitute indirect taxation and therefore was beyond the power of the Legislature of the Province of Manitoba to impose.

The rehearing took place on January 23, 1980, and the same intervenors participated.

Counsel for the appellant Government of Manitoba dropped any challenge to the award of interest by the Manitoba Court of Appeal and, similarly, abandoned any claim to tax in respect of Air Canada timetables. At the rehearing, no issue was taken by the appellant with respect to the affirmed order of Morse, J., as to the meal service. The appeal in this Court was thus reduced to a consideration of the liability of Air Canada for tax in respect of throughflights over the airspace above Manitoba and in respect of liquor service to first class and economy passengers during such flights, and in respect of flights that land in Manitoba. Those that land in Manitoba from outside points are flights that involve temporary stopovers pending their continuation to destinations outside the Province. There was no suggestion of tax liability in respect of flights which take off from, *i.e.*, originate in Manitoba, for points beyond. Nor are we concerned in this case with Air Canada operations that begin and end in Manitoba; no such operations were put in issue. I would note here that, as stated by the appellant in its factum on the first hearing in this Court, "the tax is imposed only once during the lifetime of an aircraft, or other items of property at the time of purchase", this last word taking its meaning as defined in the Act.

. Counsel for the appellant conceded that the title, "*Retail Sales Tax Act*" was a misnomer because the Act is not limited to the levy of taxes on retail sales but purports to encompass, in defined circumstances, consumption and use of tangible personal property, whether or not there is an actual retail sale. It also embraces the enjoyment or advantage of services. Prior to May 1, 1972, aircraft in interprovincial and foreign flights through the airspace over Manitoba and repair parts for such aircraft were exempted from tax but the exemption was removed by the 1972 amendment and a certain taxing formula was introduced in respect of aircraft engaged in such flights. . . .

Air Canada has offices in Manitoba and also has maintenance and service facilities for its aircraft which land there or take off from there, and it was contended that, if the tax that is imposed is a tax *in personam*, then Air Canada is liable to pay it, in respect of overflights and in respect of aircraft that land in Manitoba, and also in respect of aircraft parts which are found in Air Canada's facilities in Manitoba, unless the tax is indirect.

This submission involves, initially, the construction of Manitoba's taxing statute as it applies to Air Canada and, indeed, to other air carriers, foreign and domestic, which have places of business in Manitoba and which fly through or into and then out of the Province. There is involved, secondly, the constitutional question, posed by the order of Pigeon, J., in the light of Manitoba's assertion that it has, in any event, legislative jurisdiction over the airspace above the Province and may thus tax upon the entry of aircraft into that airspace. The evidence discloses that Air Canada aircraft on overflights fly at an altitude of at least 31,000 ft., that liquor is served on such overflights but not when aircraft land in Manitoba, and not when taking off until cruising altitude is reached.

[His Lordship's discussion of whether the *Retail Sales Tax Act* catches overflight as a matter of statutory construction is omitted.]

### Overflights: the claim of jurisdiction in the airspace

Manitoba's claim to tax under its statute is, as I have already noted, based on the contentions that (1) it has legislative jurisdiction in the airspace above it and (2) upon entry of Air Canada aircraft into that airspace, that tangible personalty is sufficiently within the Province for tax purposes. In the view that I take of this case, I find it unnecessary to explore the extent to which a Province has legislative jurisdiction in the airspace *per se*. Here the claim to jurisdiction is made without limitation, but that it not the reason for not embarking upon an inquiry into the extent and nature of the jurisdiction under s. 92 of the *British North America Act, 1867*. Such an inquiry would lead much beyond the compass of the facts in the present case and would necessarily involve considerations of federal authority if the airspace *ad infinitum* is to be the focus of inquiry. It is enough here to limit an issue arising in such an uncharted field to the facts out of which it arises and to the statute under which it is pursued.

I am prepared, on this view, to assume that the Province has some legislative jurisdiction in the airspace above it so that the pivotal question is whether Air Canada aircraft, engaged in overflights are "within the Province", as this quoted phrase is used in s. 92(2) which empowers a Province to impose "Direct taxation within the Province in order to the raising of a Revenue for Provincial Purposes".

Merely going through the airspace over Manitoba does not give the aircraft a *situs* there to support a tax which constitutionally must be "within the Province". In the case of aircraft operations, there must be a substantial, at least more than a nominal, presence in the Province to provide a basis for imposing a tax in respect of the entry of aircraft into the Province.

There is a pertinent observation by Jackson, J., in a concurring judgment in *Northwest Airlines, Inc. v. Minnesota* (1943), 322 U.S. 292, to which I wish to refer. He said this, at p. 304:

> Certainly today flight over a state either casually or on regular routes and schedules confers no jurisdiction to tax. Earlier ideas of a state's sovereignty over the air above it might argue for such a right to tax, but it is one of those cases where legal philosophy has to take account of the fact that the world does move.
>
> Does the act of landing within a state, even regularly and on schedule, confer jurisdiction to tax? Undoubtedly a plane, like any other article of personal property, could land or remain within a state in such a way as to become part of the property within the state. But when a plane lands to receive and discharge passengers, to undergo servicing or repairs, or to await a convenient departing schedule, it does not in my opinion lose its character as a plane in transit. Long ago this Court held that the landing of a ship within the ports of a state for similar purposes did not confer jurisdiction to tax. *Hays v. Pacific Mail S. S. Co.*, 17 How. 596; *St. Louis v. Ferry Co.*, 11 Wall. 423; *Morgan v. Parham*, 16 Wall. 471; cf. *Ayer & Lord Tie Co. v. Kentucky*, 202 U.S. 409. I cannot consider that to alight out of the skies onto a landing field and take off again into the air confers any greater taxing jurisdiction on a state than for a ship for the same purposes to come alongside a wharf on the water and get under way again.

The appellant relied on this case and also on *Braniff Airways Inc. v. Nebraska State Board of Equalization and Assessment et al.* (1953), 347 U.S. 590, in support of its contentions that it may properly tax aircraft which enter airspace above it. In my opinion, these cases do not assist the appellant's contention. They turn on considerations that are not relevant to the present case and on constitutional provisions that have no application to the position asserted by Manitoba. The *Northwest Airlines* case concerned a Minnesota personal property tax which was held to be leviable against a Minnesota corporation having its principal place of business in that State, in respect of its entire fleet of aeroplanes, all of which were registered with the federal Civil Aeronautics Authority in a city in the State as the home port. Although the fleet operated in interstate commerce, none of the aeroplanes was continuously out of the State during the taxation year, and it was held that, absent restricting federal legislation, it was open to the State of the domicile, the home

State, to impose the tax without violating either the federal commerce clause or the due process clause of the Constitution. No question of legislative jurisdiction over airspace was involved. In the *Braniff* case, an apportioned *ad valorem* tax by the State of Nebraska levied on the flight equipment of an interstate air carrier was sustained where it was shown that the carrier regularly made 18 stops a day in Nebraska, although it was not incorporated there nor was its home port there. This was held to be a sufficient contact with Nebraska to support the apportioned tax. Again, no question arose as to legislative jurisdiction over the airspace and certainly none in respect of overflights.

What remains for consideration on this aspect of the case is a submission based on *Bank of Toronto v. Lambe, supra*. The submission is that, regardless of whether the airspace above Manitoba is within the Province, the appellant was entitled to tax Air Canada in respect of its aeroplanes, parts and services on overflights by regarding these facilities as merely the means of measuring a tax *in personam*. There are two answers to this contention. First, this is not the way in which the tax has been imposed. I have already adverted to the issue of construction and it is clear from the statute that, although I accept the tax as *in personam*, it is exacted upon the bringing of tangible personal property into the Province. That was not done in this case. Second, I do not agree that *Bank of Toronto v. Lambe* supports the contention. Although that case was concerned with an activity which, like the one here, is within exclusive federal regulatory authority and a provincial tax upon the bank as carrying on business in the Province and measured by extraprovincial considerations was sustained, its principal cannot, in my view, be extended to make interprovincial and transnational aircraft operations as measuring standards to determine the amount of a tax imposed upon an air carrier which has a business office in the taxing Province.

### Flights that land in Manitoba

I need not dwell on this aspect of the case which concerns flights that originate outside Manitoba but which land in the Province temporarily and then proceed out of Manitoba. It is governed by my reasons in respect of overflights, being based on the same principles, but there are a few additional observations that I wish to make.

I emphasize again that the momentary transitory presence of agencies of transportation in the Province cannot bring them under the *Retail Sales Tax Act* any more than they could be brought under it if they did not enter the Province or were over-flying the Province, although the operators of such services had places of business in the Province. Apart from constitutional considerations, I do not see how such operators can be said to be "purchasers", as defined in subcl. (iii) of s. 2(1)(*i*), which alone of the four definitions of "purchaser" in s. 2(1)(*i*) has any possible application. This is not a case of anyone in the Province bringing in or receiving delivery in the Province of tangible personal property "acquired by him outside the Province". There is no acquisition involved, however broadly the word is defined. I doubt, as well, whether there is any "consumption" involved in temporary stopovers, although that word is defined in s. 2(1)(*b*) to include "the consumption or use of tangible personal property". Moreover, there is, at best, merely a notional drawing into the taxation net of interprovincial and extraprovincial operations, and constitutional authority, which is limited to direct taxation within the Province, cannot be extended by self-serving definitions.

The present case, in so far as it concerns the attempted imposition of a tax in respect of personal property brought into the Province, finds no support in *Atlantic Smoke Shops Ltd. v. Conlon*, [1943] A.C. 550 (P.C.). That case, dealing with a tax in respect of tobacco, either purchased in the Province or brought in from outside for consumption in the Province, was based on retail sale transactions, unlike the present case. Moreover, there was reality in its consumption aspect which was its essential feature.

### Conclusion

For the reasons given above, I hold that the *Manitoba Retail Sales Tax Act* is *ultra vires* in so far as it purports to tax Air Canada on overflights of its aircraft through the airspace over Manitoba and on flights which land temporarily in Manitoba from outside points before proceeding onward. The Act does not impose a tax that can be said to be "within the Province" under s. 92(2) of the *British North America Act, 1867*. In addition, I do not think that in its own terms it is applicable to Air Canada in respect of such flights.

In view of this conclusion, I find it unnecessary to deal with the question whether the tax (even on the assumption that it is within the Province) is a direct tax. Although the Court ordered a rehearing with particular reference to this question, I think it preferable to avoid dealing with it, in conformity with the general rule in constitutional cases not to engage issues which do not squarely arise for decision.

I am relieved by my holding from examining a number of issues touching the method of assessment under the Act and the propriety of some of the paragraphs of the formal order of Morse, J., such as paras. (b) and (c). Equally, it is unnecessary to consider taxability in respect of the consumption of liquor by both first class and economy passengers since it follows from my main conclusion that any liquor sales to passengers cannot be said to be sales in Manitoba.

The appeal is, accordingly, dismissed with costs. There was no cross-appeal with respect to the assessment of tax against Air Canada in the sum of $1,856 and that liability therefore stands. There will be no costs to or against any of the intervenors.

*Appeal dismissed.*

[The principal case was followed in *Re Lynden Transport Inc. and Minister of Finance (B.C.)* (1981), 119 D.L.R. (3d) 765 (B.C.C.A.), holding that trucks carrying freight in bond through the Province between foreign points are not subject to provincial sales tax. Notwithstanding that a business is carried on in the Province, it is transitory in nature and not sufficiently connected to the Province to engage its taxing power.]

### Note on "for provincial purposes" in Section 92(2)

In *Reference re Employment and Social Insurance Act*, [1936] S.C.R. 427 at 434, Duff C.J.C. put the matter as follows:

If you read head No. 2 of s. 92 with s. 126, and by the light of the observations of Lord Watson in *St. Catharine's Milling & Lumber Co. v. The Queen* (1888), 14 App. Cas. 46 there is . . . solid ground for the conclusion that the words 'for provincial purposes' mean neither more nor less than this: the taxing power of the legislature is given to them for raising money for the exclusive disposition of the legislature.

The Courts have scotched any notion that the taxing authority in section 92(2) extended only to the raising of money for *general* provincial purposes, *i.e.* by province-wide taxation for the general purposes of the whole province. In *Dow v. Black* (1875), L.R. 6 P.C. 272 the Privy Council stated (at p. 282) that section 92(2) "must be taken to enable the provincial legislature . . . to impose direct taxation for a local purpose upon a particular locality within the province".

## 4. The Provincial Licensing Power

### Note

Under section 92(9) of the *Constitution Act, 1867* the provinces may legislate in relation to "shop, saloon, tavern, auctioneer and other licences in order to the raising of a revenue for provincial, local or municipal purposes." The main problems which this head of power raises are these: (1) Is the phrase "other licences" to be read *ejusdem generis* with the preceding enumeration? (2) Must the revenue-raising provisions of licensing legislation conform to the standards of direct taxation? (3) May the province license for regulatory rather than, or for regulatory as well as, for revenue purposes?

It is well established that the *ejusdem generis* rule does not apply to "other licences": *Brewers and Maltsters Assoc. of Ont. v. A.-G. Ont.*, [1897] A.C. 231 (P.C.); *Shannon v. Lower Mainland Dairy Products Board*, [1938] A.C. 708 (P.C.). Moreover, the provinces enjoy an omnibus licensing power within the limits of section 92. This power, in its regulatory character, can be supported under section 92(13) and section 92(16). In so far as a licensing system established for regulatory purposes also exhibits a revenue purpose by reason of the exaction of licence fees, it now appears that resort may be had to section 92(9); and in this connection, it is unnecessary to meet the requirements of direct taxation. In *Lawson v. Interior Tree Fruit and Vegetable Committee*, [1931] S.C.R. 357, involving, *inter alia*, the validity under provincial legislation of marketing licences and fees authorized in connection therewith and also of certain levies authorized to defray the expenses of operating the marketing scheme, Duff J. spoke for the majority of the Court as follows:

> This brings us to the question whether the levies complained of are levies which can be brought under head No. 9 of s. 92 . . . The question has never yet been decided whether or not the revenue contemplated by this head can in any circumstances be raised by a fee which operates in such a manner as to take it out of the scope of 'direct taxation'. *Prima facie*, it would appear, from inspection of the language of the two several heads, that the taxes contemplated by No. 9 are not confined to taxes of the same character as those authorized by No. 2, and that accordingly imposts which would properly be classed under the general description 'indirect taxation' are not for that reason alone excluded from those which may be exacted under head 9. On the other hand, the last mentioned head authorizes licences for the purpose of raising a revenue, and does not, I think contemplate licences which, in their primary function, are instrumentalities for the control of trade — even local or provincial trade. Here, such is the primary purpose of the legislation. The imposition of these levies is merely ancillary, having for its object the creation of a fund to defray the expenses of working the machinery of the substantive scheme for the regulation of trade. Even the licence fee is discretionary with the Committee. This part of the statute would appear to be *ultra vires*. The levy authorized is not within s. 92(2), and the licence is not within s. 92(9).

*Cf. Russell v. The Queen* (1882), 7 App. Cas. 829, where the Privy Council indicated that section 92(9) could not be invoked for regulation. That part only of Duff J.'s statement which viewed the licensing power as essentially a revenue raising power was rejected by the Privy Council in *Shannon v. Lower Mainland Dairy Products Board, supra*; and Lord Atkin said *inter alia*:

> If regulation of trade within the Province has to be held valid, the ordinary method of regulating trade, *i.e.*, by a system of licences, must also be admissible. A licence itself merely involves a permission to trade subject to compliance with specified conditions. A licence fee, though usual, does not appear to be essential. But, if licences are granted, it appears to be no objection that fees should be charged in order either to defray the costs of administering the local regulation or to increase the general funds of the Province, or for both purposes. The object would appear to be in such a case to raise a revenue for either local or Provincial purposes. On this part of the case their Lordships, with great respect, think that the present Chief Justice, then Duff J., took a somewhat narrow view of the Provincial powers under s. 92(9) in *Lawson v. Interior Tree Fruit and Vegetable Committee of Direction.* . . . It cannot, as their Lordships think, be an objection to a licence plus a fee that it is directed both to the regulation of trade and to the provision of revenue. It would be difficult in the case of saloon and tavern licences to say that the regulation of the trade was not at least as important as the provision of revenue. And, if licences for the specified trades are valid, their Lordships see no reason why the words 'other licences' in s. 92(9) should not be sufficient to support the enactment in question.

See also *Motor Car Supply Co. v. A.-G. Alta.*, [1939] 3 W.W.R. 65 (Alta. S.C.). In *Nelson v. City of Dartmouth* (1964), 45 D.L.R. (2d) 183 (N.S.S.C.), the principle thus expounded was applied to sustain a licence tax on owners of mobile home parks, regardless of the fact that it was indirect in its incidence. It would appear that the Privy Council in the *Shannon* case intended, by its criticism, to do no more than give a basis of support to licence taxes where the purpose was as much regulatory as fiscal. It was certainly unnecessary, even if the explicit terms thereof be overlooked, to extend section 92(9) to cover purely regulatory licences because power to this end exists in other heads of section 92; *cf. Cherry v. The King*, [1938] 2 W.W.R. 12 (Sask. C.A.). For a general discussion, see MacDonald, "The Licensing Power of the Provinces" (1939), 17 Can. Bar Rev. 240.

## 5. Express Limitations on the Taxing Powers

### Note

The meaning of section 121 of the *Constitution Act, 1867* was considered in *Gold Seal Ltd. v. Dominion Express Co. and A.-G. Alta.*, (1921), 62 S.C.R. 424, and in *Atlantic Smoke Shops Ltd. v. Conlon*, [1941] S.C.R. 670, varied [1943] A.C. 550. Additional consideration was given to section 121 in the *Murphy* case reproduced in Chapter 8, and Rand J. there suggested a wider view of the provision. See Chapter 8, *supra*, for further material on section 121.

The tax immunity given by section 125 to "lands or property belonging to Canada or any province" is an immunity in favour of lands or property vested in the Crown in right of the Dominion or of a province: see *St. Catharine's Milling & Lumber Co. v. The Queen* (1888), 14 App. Cas. 46 (P.C.). Section 125 does not operate to confer any immunity on private persons who have some interest in Crown land or other property; nor does it operate to give them any immunity where the Crown acquires some interest in land or other property belonging to such persons. Section 125 in terms deals only with taxes charged on lands or property and not with "personal" taxes. But, it probably also covers taxation on the Crown in right of the Dominion or of a province in respect of lands or property in which the Crown has an interest. In other words, it ought reasonably to be construed as giving immunity from a tax charged on Crown property or on the Crown itself in respect of its interest in such property. In *Halifax v. Halifax Harbour Commrs.*, [1935] S.C.R. 215, a case involving municipal assessment of a federal Crown agency in respect of its occupation of Crown property, Duff C.J. said that any attempt to tax the Dominion Government or the property of the Dominion Government must fail as *ultra vires* a provincial legislature. The converse is equally true: see *Alberta Natural Gas Taxation Reference*, [1982] 1 S.C.R. 1004. However, the constitutional protection of section 125 does not extend to shield a provincial Crown from other types of federal taxation, such as customs duties connected with the regulation of trade and commerce. The statement by Clement, *The Canadian Constitution* (3rd ed.), p. 643, that section 125 "would operate no doubt to exempt from customs duties goods purchased abroad by a provincial government" was later proved wrong by the Privy Council in *A.-G. B.C. v. A.-G. Can.*, [1924] A.C. 222 (P.C.), reproduced below.

Most of the cases in which arguments were raised based on section 125 really turned on the construction of the taxing statute in order to ascertain whether the interest of the Crown was being taxed or the interest of a private person, or whether the tax was on the Crown or on a private person in respect of a property interest. It has been held that a tax may be validly levied on an owner of land leased to the Crown (*Halifax v. Fairbanks Estate*, [1928] A.C. 117 (P.C.); *Vancouver v. A.-G. Can.*, [1944] S.C.R. 23; or on a tenant or occupant of Crown land (*Smith v. Vermillion Hills*, [1916] 2 A.C. 569 (P.C.); *Montreal v. A.-G. Can.*, [1923] A.C. 136 (P.C.)); or on an occupant of Crown land residing thereon in virtue of his employment by the federal Crown (*Phillips and Taylor v. Sault Ste. Marie*, [1954] S.C.R. 404); or on a purchaser under an agreement of sale with the Crown (*Southern Alberta Land Co. v. McLean* (1916), 53 S.C.R. 151). Attempts to realize such taxes must, of course, stop short of interfering with the Crown's rights in the property affected: see *Calgary & Edmonton Land Co. v. A.-G. Alta.* (1911), 45 S.C.R. 170. In *Spooner Oils Ltd. and Spooner v. Turner Valley Gas Conservation Board and A.-G. Alta.*, [1933] S.C.R. 629 at 645, Duff C.J. referred to these matters as follows:

> The occupant of Dominion lands under a legal right may be taxed [by a province] in respect of his occupancy. But it is necessary to be cautious in inferring from this that such taxation can in every case be enforced by remedies involving the sale or appropriation of the occupant's rights, without regard to the nature of that right. Where the right is equivalent to an equitable title in fee simple, probably no difficulty would arise . . ., but if the enforcement of a tax imposed by provincial legislation, would involve a nullification in whole or in part of competent Dominion legislation under which the right is constituted, then it is, to say the least, doubtful, whether such provisions could take effect.

In some cases, the question has arisen whether a corporate body or agency claiming tax immunity when occupying Crown land, is the Crown or a servant or agent of the Crown; and here, too, questions of construction may arise in assessing the character of the corporation or agency to determine whether it is a servant or agent of the Crown: see *Halifax v. Halifax Harbour Commrs.*, [1935] S.C.R. 215; *Re Toronto and C.B.C.*, [1938] O.W.N. 507; *Recorder's Court v. C.B.C.*, 70 Que. K.B. 65 (Que. C.A.); *Northern Saskatchewan Flying Training School v. Buckland*, [1943] 3 W.W.R. 609 (Sask. C.A.); *Montreal v. Montreal Locomotive Works*, [1946] 3 W.W.R. 748 (P.C.); *Regina Industries Ltd. v. R.*, [1947] S.C.R. 345. Similarly, it may be necessary to determine whether occupation of private land is an occupation of or for the Crown or in the private interest of the occupant: see *Stinson v. Middleton; Wright v. Middleton*, [1949] O.R. 237 (C.A.). In *Bennett & White (Calgary) Ltd. v. Sugar City*, [1951] A.C. 786 (P.C.), it was held as a matter of interpretation that under a construction contract between appellant and the Crown, certain property was owned by the Crown and, further, that although appellant was in possession for the purposes of the contract, nevertheless only an owner or an owner in possession was taxed, and hence appellant was not subject to tax measured by the value of the Crown property.

It was held that section 125 only prohibits Dominion taxation of provincial property and provincial taxation of Dominion property. It does not prohibit them from taxing their own property; for example, a province may competently authorize municipal taxation of property vested in a corporate servant of the Crown in right of that province: see *Re Taxation of University of Manitoba Lands*, [1940] 1 W.W.R. 145 (Man. C.A.); *B.C. Power Commission v. Victoria* (1951), 1 W.W.R. (N.S.) 700 (B.C.C.A.). Moreover, the unqualified terms of section 125 indicate that the tax immunity extends to property of any province (*i.e.* vested in the Crown in right thereof) as against taxation by another province. While neither the Dominion nor any province can legally destroy the immunity conferred by section 125 (short of an amendment to that effect), either can "waive" it and submit to taxation through a voluntary payment of money in the exercise of a spending power: see *The Municipal Grants Act*, R.S.C. 1970, c. M-15 and the *Municipal Grants Act, 1980*, S.C. 1980-81-82-83, c. 37; and *cf. Ottawa Public School Board v. Ottawa*, [1953] O.R. 122 (C.A.). For further discussion of section 125, see "Note on Interjurisdictional Immunity", *supra*, Chapter 8.

[A municipality's cost of repairing a sidewalk on failure of the fronting owner to repair, when recoverable as a tax, is within the immunity of section 125: see *R. v. Breton*, [1967] S.C.R. 503.]

There is no express constitutional immunity from taxation of the property of a foreign state; the question would appear to turn on the application of recognized principles of international law in the construction of the taxing statute: see *Reference re Powers to Levy Rates on Foreign Legations and High Commissioners' Residences*, [1943] S.C.R. 208; *Yin-Tso Hsiung v. Toronto*, [1950] O.R. 463 (S.C.); and see Note (1943), 21 Can. Bar Rev. 560. Note also the provisions of the *Diplomatic and Consular Privileges Act*, S.C. 1976-77, c. 31. The Crown in right of Great Britain should stand in no different position; see *Jennings v. Whitby Tp.*, [1943] O.W.N. 170 (Co. Ct.)]

# A.-G. B.C. v. A.-G. CAN.

In the Privy Council. [1924] A.C. 222.

Viscount Haldane, Lord Buckmaster, Lord Atkinson, Lord Shaw and Lord Sumner. Oct. 18, 1923.

Appeal from a judgment of the Supreme Court of Canada, 64 S.C.R. 377, affirming a judgment of the Exchequer Court, 21 Ex. C.R. 281, denying that appellants were entitled to import goods into the province for sale therein without liability to pay certain federal taxes.

LORD BUCKMASTER: The question raised upon this appeal is whether there is power conferred upon the Dominion Parliament by the British North America Act of 1867 to impose customs duties or excise or sales tax upon goods when they enter the Dominion although they are the property of one of the Provinces. The case arises in the following way:—

The Province of British Columbia in 1921 established Government control and sale of alcoholic liquors by various statutes, enumeration of which is unnecessary. The Dominion Parliament, on the other hand, imposed customs or sales or excise duty upon, among other things, alcoholic liquors, imported into the Dominion. In July of 1921 the appellant, acting as duly authorized agent under the British Columbia Liquor Act, purchased in Great Britain in the name and on behalf of His Majesty in right of the Province one case of "Johnny Walker Black Label" whisky, which was duly shipped from Glasgow and consigned to His Majesty in the right of the Province. Upon demand for delivery of this whisky the Collector of Customs, on behalf of the Dominion Government, refused delivery until payment of the customs duty and excise or sales tax. The appellant denied his right to claim these duties, and took the proceedings out of which this appeal has arisen to test his claim. The statutes under which it was claimed the right to impose such duties arose were the following: s. 2 and item A of the Customs Tariff Act, 1907; s. 2, sub-s. 3 of the Customs Act, 1917; s. 19BBB, sub-s. 1, of the Special War Revenue Act, 1915; and s. 6, sub-s. 1, of the Special War Revenue Act, 1915.

Nothing depends upon the language of these statutes. They admittedly embrace all consignments without distinction of consignee. The question is whether there was power so to legislate.

. . . The real issue lies in determining the true meaning to be given to s. 125 of the *British North America Act*, which provides that "No lands or property belonging to Canada or any Province shall be liable to taxation." Taken alone and read without consideration of the scheme of the statute, this section undoubtedly creates a formidable argument in support of the appellant's case. It is plain, however, that the section cannot be regarded in this isolated and disjunctive way. It is only a part of the general scheme established by the statute with its different allocations of powers and authorities to the Provincial and Dominion Governments. Section 91, which assigns powers to the Dominion, provides, among other things, that it shall enjoy exclusive legislative authority over all matters enumerated in the section, included among which are the regulation of trade and commerce and raising of money by any mode or system of taxation. The imposition of customs duties upon goods imported into any country may have many objects; it may be designed to raise revenue or to regulate trade and commerce by protecting native industries, or it may have the two-fold purpose of attempting to secure both ends; in either case it is a power reserved to the Dominion. It has not indeed been denied that such a general power does exist, but it is said that a breach is created in the tariff wall, which the Dominion has the power to erect, by s. 125, which enables goods of the Province or the Dominion to pass through, unaffected by the duties. But s. 125 cannot, in their Lordships' opinion, be so regarded. It is to be found in a series of sections which, beginning with s. 102, distribute as between the Dominion and the Province certain distinct classes of property, and confer control upon the Province with regard to the part allocated to them. But this does not exclude the operation of Dominion laws made in exercise of the authority conferred by s. 91. The Dominion have the power to regulate trade and commerce throughout the Dominion, and, to the extent to which this power applies, there is no partiality in its operation. Section 125 must, therefore, be so considered as to prevent the paramount purpose thus declared from being defeated.

*Appeal dismissed.*

### Note

The distinction made by Lord Buckmaster in *A. G.-B.C. v. A.G. Can. (Johnny Walker* case), *supra* between "regulation" and "taxation" is the key to section 125. Where a piece of federal legislation is in pith and substance directed at the former, it is valid notwithstanding that it may have a taxation element or that, as here, the mode of applying the regulation is through taxation. On the other hand, where the legislation is aimed at taxation and has either a non-existent or subsidiary regulatory aspect, it will be struck down: see *Alberta Natural Gas Taxation Reference* (1982), 42 N.R. 361 (S.C.C.). The question comes down to one of characterization of the matter of the legislation. See "Note on Interjurisdictional Immunity", *supra*, Chapter 8 for further discussion of the *Alberta Natural Gas Taxation Reference.*

A matter which has heretofore been unexplored is the extent to which provincial regulatory legislation of general application with a taxation aspect may, in that aspect, apply to federal Crown property. While there is no distinction made textually in the *Constitution Act, 1867* between the federal and provincial Crowns for the purposes of section 125, the courts would likely take a stricter line as regards provincial legislation. There are no decisions directly on point, but this may be implied from the general course of decisions in interjurisdictional immunity cases and, in particular, from Laskin C.J.C.'s comments in *Reference re Anti-Inflation Act*, [1976] 2 S.C.R. 429-30, where he contemplates the possibility of federal regulation reaching provincial government operations in certain circumstances. It is clear that there is no reciprocal power in the provincial Legislatures: see *Reference re Minimum Wage Act of Saskatchewan*, [1948] S.C.R. 248; *Letter Carriers Union of Canada v. Canadian Union of Postal Workers*, [1975] 1 S.C.R. 178.

For a fuller treatment of these and other interjurisdictional immunity issues, see "Note on Interjurisdictional Immunity," *supra* Chapter 8.

### Note on Taxation of Dominion or Provincial "Instrumentalities"

In *Caron v. The King*, [1924] A.C. 999 at 1006 (P.C.), Lord Phillimore adverted to a proposition laid down in *Great West Saddlery Co. v. The King*, [1921] 2 A.C. 91 (P.C.), that "no provincial legislature could use its special powers as an indirect means of destroying powers given by the Parliament of Canada"; and, he added, "by parity of reason the Parliament of Canada could not exercise its powers of taxation so as to destroy the capacity of officials lawfully appointed by the province". Subject to these principles, Canadian constitutional law does not recognize any immunity of federal or provincial functionaries from valid taxation imposed by province or Dominion, as the case may be. The *Constitution Act, 1867* gives power to the Dominion under section 91(8) in relation to "the fixing of and providing for the salaries and allowances of civil and other officers of the government of Canada"; and by section 92(4) gives power to the provinces in relation to "the establishment and tenure of provincial offices and the appointment and payment of provincial officers". These provisions do not carry the implication that the respective salaries may not be diminished by valid taxation. Thus, in the *Caron* case, in upholding the power of the Dominion to exact income taxes from the Quebec Minister of Agriculture in respect of his salary as minister and his sessional indemnity as a member of the provincial legislative assembly, Lord Phillimore asserted that "their Lordships can see no reason in principle why any of the sources of income of a taxable citizen should be removed from the power of taxation given to the Parliament of Canada". Similarly, an officer of the armed forces and a Dominion civil servant are liable to pay provincial income tax: *Worthington v. A.-G. Man.; Forbes v. A.-G. Man.*, [1936] S.C.R. 40. While two Judges of the Supreme Court dissented on the ground that the provincial tax was imposed on funds in the hands of the Dominion — a view which the majority rejected — and that, admittedly, the province cannot tax Dominion funds, this position raises a drafting problem rather than a constitutional issue. However, one of the dissenting Judges, Cannon J., took a specific constitutional ground in elaborating the proposition that a provincial legislature cannot interfere with the salary fixed by the Dominion for an officer of the permanent forces and a full-time civil servant; moreover, the provincial taxing legislation would interfere with the relationship which under law exists between the Government and its servants by compelling a portion of their services to be given gratuitously with a consequent adverse effect on the efficiency of the federal civil service. The difficulty in the way of this proposition was not only the *Caron* case but also an earlier judgment of the Supreme Court of Canada in *Abbott v. City of St. John* (1908), 40 S.C.R. 597, which affirmed the liability of a Dominion employee to pay municipal taxes levied under provincial legislation. In the *Abbott* case the Supreme Court abruptly halted the development of a principle of immunity which had been earlier asserted in *Leprohon v. City of Ottawa* (1878), 2 O.A.R. 522. The general position may now be considered as settled, in the terms of the *Abbott* case, by the Privy Council's judgment on an appeal by Forbes from the Supreme Court's decision: see *Forbes v. A.-G. Man.*, [1937] A.C. 260 (P.C.); and see also *Reference re Alberta Statutes*, [1938] S.C.R. 100, per Duff C.J. at pp. 130-1, and per Cannon J., at pp. 138-141; *Paquin v. Warden King Ltd. and A.-G. Que.* (1941), 71 Que. K.B. 425 (Que. C.A.) (execution against federal civil servant). There remains, however, the qualification stated at the beginning of this Note — and noticed also in the *Abbott* case and in the *Forbes* case — that the respective taxing powers of Dominion and provinces may not be used by either of them to sterilize powers conferred by the other upon its functionaries or substantially to impair their status. A particular application of this principle has already been illustrated in connection with taxation of banks: see *A.-G. Alta. v. A.-G. Can.*, [1939] A.C. 117 (P.C.). The principle has also had a wide application in the "company" cases: see Chapter 11, *supra*; and *cf. Reference re Debt Adjustment Act*, [1942] S.C.R. 31, affirmed [1943] A.C. 356 (P.C.).

Judges, too, are subject to taxation imposed by Dominion or province. It matters not whether they are County or District Court Judges: see *City of Toronto v. Morson* (1917), 40 O.L.R. 227 (C.A.); or Supreme Court Judges: see *The Judges v. A.-G. Sask.* (1937), 53 T.L.R. 464. Nor is it material that they are members of provincial or Dominion courts. Although Judges of the provincial superior courts have, by section 99 of the *Constitution Act, 1867*, a constitutionally protected tenure (subject now to compulsory retirement at age 75), the Privy Council in *Judges v. A.-G. Sask., supra,* did not think that their independence would be affected by requiring them to pay taxes in respect of their salaries which are for the Dominion to fix and provide under section 100 of the *Constitution Act, 1867.* The judgment of the Privy Council proceeded, in part, as follows:

> An argument had apparently been addressed to the Court [below, the Saskatchewan Court of Appeal, [1936] 2 W.W.R. 443] based on the word "fixed" in section 100. The same word is used in section 91(8) of the *British North America Act* in defining the powers of the Parliament of Canada with respect to the salaries of civil servants, and the Court had before it two decisions of the Supreme Court of Canada — namely, *Abbott v. City of St. John* (1908), 40 S.C.R. 597, and *Forbes v. A.-G. Man.,* [1936] S.C.R. 40, affirmed [1937] A.C. 260 (P.C.), in which a provincial income-tax on such salaries was upheld. The latter of these two cases was appealed to His Majesty in Council: [1937] A.C. 260 (P.C.). The decision of the Supreme Court was affirmed, and the argument under discussion is therefore not now open. This, in effect, disposes of the present case also, unless judicial emoluments are in a class apart, protected by some paramount principle making inapplicable to that form of income a tax imposed by a statute in terms wide enough to include it. There is no foundation in the realities of the situation for any such conception. Neither the independence nor any other attribute of the judiciary can be affected by a general income-tax which charges their official incomes on the same footings as incomes of other citizens. The Court below, agreeing with, though not bound by, two decisions in other Dominions — namely, *Cooper v. Com'r of Income Tax for Queensland* (1907), 4 C.L.R. 1, 304, before the High Court of Australia, and *Krause v. Com'r for Inland Revenue,* [1929] S.A.R. (A.D.) 286, in the Supreme Court of South Africa — found no reason for exempting judicial emoluments from income-tax. Their Lordships are of the same opinion.

One question remains. Would it be competent to the Dominion to legislate expressly against any diminution by provincial taxation of the salaries of Judges or of Dominion functionaries? Would this not be valid legislation under sections 91(8) and 100 which would prevail against any provincial taxing measure?

> [*Cf.* Lederman, "The Independence of the Judiciary" (1956), 34 Can. Bar Rev. 1139 at 1165: "The words 'fixed and provided' are specially entrenched in the constitutional sense as part of section 100 of the *B.N.A. Act* and hence confer a guarantee of salary to superior court judges that cannot be impaired by an ordinary federal statute". The reference is to impairment apart from general income tax legislation applicable to all recipients of income. See Holdsworth, "The Constitutional Position of Judges" (1932), 48 Law Q. Rev. 25; Wade, "His Majesty's Judges" (1932), 173 L. T. 246, 267; Holdsworth, "Reply", 173 L.T. 336; and see (1933), 176 L.T. 103. See also *Beauregard v. The Queen* (1983), 148 D.L.R. (3d) 205 (Fed. C.A.), holding that section 100 does not permit federal legislation requiring judges to contribute to their pension plans.]

# 14

# Criminal Law

## 1. The Scope of the Criminal Law Power

*Note on the Scope of the Criminal Law Power*

In *A.-G. Ont. v. Hamilton Street Ry.*, [1903] A.C. 524, the Privy Council stated that "it is . . . the criminal law in its widest sense that is reserved" for the exclusive authority of the Dominion under section 91(27) of the *Constitution Act, 1867*. Earlier, in the *Russell* case (1882), 7 App. Cas. 829 (P.C.) the Judicial Committee had pointed out that provincial authority in relation to property and civil rights in no way prevented the Dominion from enacting that certain uses of property and certain acts in relation to property were criminal. Illustrations were given of laws making it a criminal offence for a man wilfully to set fire to his own house, or to overwork his horse; or laws restricting the sale or exposure of cattle having a contagious disease. "Laws of this nature," said the Privy Council, "designed for the promotion of public order, safety or morals, and which subject those who contravene them to criminal procedure and punishment, belong to the subject of public wrongs rather than to that of civil rights." In the *Board of Commerce* case, [1922] 1 A.C. 191 (P.C.), Lord Haldane introduced a limited view of federal power under section 91(27) by referring to it "as enabling the Dominion Parliament to exercise exclusive legislative power where the subject matter is one which by its very nature belongs to the domain of criminal jurisprudence." In the context in which he spoke it would have been enough to say (as the Privy Council later said in the *Reciprocal Insurers* case, [1924] A.C. 328 (P.C.)) that merely to attach penal sanctions to designated activity does not necessarily foreclose judicial inquiry into whether the legislation is in pith and substance in relation to the criminal law. In *P.A.T.A. v. A.-G. Can.*, [1931] A.C. 310 (P.C.), the Privy Council found it necessary expressly to dissociate itself from Lord Haldane's view of the criminal law power. In that case, the Privy Council upheld federal legislation making it an offence to combine in restraint of trade, and Lord Atkin speaking for the Judicial Committee restated a broad view of the criminal law power as follows at 323-324 (A.C.):

> In their Lordships' opinion s. 498 of the *Criminal Code* and the greater part of the provisions of the *Combines Investigation Act* fall within the power of the Dominion Parliament to legislate as to matters falling within the class of subjects, 'the criminal law including the procedure in criminal matters' (s. 91, head 27). The substance of the Act is by s. 2 to define, and by s. 32 to make criminal, combines which the legislature in the public interest intends to prohibit. The definition is wide, and may cover activities which have not hitherto been considered to be criminal. But only those combines are affected 'which have operated or are likely to operate to the detriment or against the interest of the public, whether consumers, producers or others'; and if Parliament genuinely determines that commercial activities which can be so described are to be suppressed in the public interest, their Lordships see no reason why Parliament should not make them crimes. 'Criminal law' means

'the criminal law in its widest sense': *Attorney-General for Ontario v. Hamilton Street Ry. Co.* It certainly is not confined to what was criminal by the law of England or of any Province in 1867. The power may extend to legislation to make new crimes. Criminal law connotes only the quality of such acts or omissions as are prohibited under appropriate penal provisions by authority of the State. The criminal quality of an act cannot be discerned by intuition; nor can it be discovered by reference to any standard but one: Is the act prohibited with penal consequences? Morality and criminality are far from co-extensive; nor is the sphere of criminality necessarily part of a more extensive field covered by morality — unless the moral code necessarily disapproves all acts prohibited by the State, in which case the argument moves in a circle. It appears to their Lordships to be of little value to seek to confine crimes to a category of acts which by their very nature belong to the domain of 'criminal jurisprudence'; for the domain of criminal jurisprudence can only be ascertained by examining what acts at any particular period are declared by the State to be crimes, and the only common nature they will be found to possess is that they are prohibited by the State and that those who commit them are punished.

A few years later the Privy Council returned to the exposition of the criminal law power with a qualification of the loose formula of the *P.A.T.A.* case. *A.-G. B.C. v. A.-G. Can.*, [1937] A.C. 368 (P.C.), sustained the validity of section 498A of the *Dominion Criminal Code*, penalizing stipulated acts of unfair competition (*e.g.* discriminatory discounts or rebates; unreasonably low selling prices to destroy competition) and Lord Atkin stated at 375-376 (A.C.):

The only limitation on the plenary power of the Dominion to determine what shall or shall not be criminal is the condition that Parliament shall not in the guise of enacting criminal legislation in truth and in substance encroach on any of the classes of subjects enumerated in s. 92. It is no objection that it does in fact affect them. If a genuine attempt to amend the criminal law, it may obviously affect previously existing civil rights. The object of an amendment of the criminal law as a rule is to deprive the citizen of the right to do that which, apart from the amendment, he could lawfully do. No doubt the plenary power given by s. 91(27) does not deprive the Provinces of their right under s. 92(15) of affixing penal sanctions to their own competent legislation. On the other hand, there seems to be nothing to prevent the Dominion, if it thinks fit in the public interest, from applying the criminal law generally to acts and omissions which so far are only covered by provincial enactments. In the present case there seems to be no reason for supposing that the Dominion are using the criminal law as a pretence or pretext, or that the legislature is in pith and substance only interfering with civil rights in the Province.

However, Lord Atkin preceded these comments with the statement that "the basis of [the *P.A.T.A.*] decision is that there is no other criterion of 'wrongness' than the intention of the Legislature in the public interest to prohibit the act or omission made criminal". On this far-reaching view of the criminal law power, there are no limits to the permissible subject matter of a federal law (assuming there is no colourability factor) beyond a prohibition and a penalty. As Professor Hogg states in his work *Constitutional Law of Canada* (2d ed. 1985), p. 400, those two ingredients alone are not sufficient to preserve a balance in the distribution of federal and provincial legislature powers. A third ingredient, being a "typically criminal purpose", is a necessary element. This third ingredient follows from Rand J.'s remarks in *Reference re Validity of s. 5(a) of the Dairy Industry Act*, [1949] 1 D.L.R. 433 at 472-3 (S.C.C.) (Margarine Reference) where he said:

. . . A crime is an act which the law, with appropriate penal sanctions, forbids: but as prohibitions are not enacted in a vacuum, we can properly look for some evil or injurious or undesirable effect upon the public against which the law is directed. That effect may be in relation to social, economic or political interests; and the legislature has had in mind to suppress the evil or to safeguard the interest threatened. . . .

Is the prohibition then enacted with a view to a public purpose which can support it as being in relation to criminal law? Public peace, order, security, health, morality: these are the ordinary though not exclusive ends served by that law . . .

It should be noted that Parliament may also use the criteria listed by Rand J. above as touchstones for excluding criminality, as is done in the therapeutic abortion provisions in section 251(4) and (5) of the *Criminal Code* where health is used. As stated by Laskin C.J.C. in *Morgentaler v. The Queen* (1976), 53 D.L.R. (3d) 161 at 169 (S.C.C.) (dissenting on other grounds):

I need cite no authority for the proposition that Parliament may determine what is not criminal as well as what is, and may hence introduce dispensations or exemptions in its criminal legislation.

The other side of the coin is, of course, represented by Judson J.'s statement in *O'Grady v. Sparling*, [1960] S.C.R. 804 at 810 that "a provincial enactment does not become a matter of criminal law merely because it consists of a prohibition and makes it an offence for failure to observe the prohibition". For a recent discussion of provincial power to punish pursuant to section 92(15) in respect of violations of provincial law, see *DiIorio v. Warden of Montreal Jail*, [1978] 1 S.C.R. 152.

Resort to the criminal law power to proscribe undesirable commercial practices is today as characteristic of its exercise as has been resort thereto to curb violence or immoral conduct. See, for example, *Krassman v. The Queen* (1979), 102 D.L.R. (3d) 262 (Fed. T.D.) upholding a prohibition of certain tax discounting on the basis of section 91(27). Matters like resale price maintenance as such may properly be the subject of a criminal prohibition by Parliament, even without a requirement of proof of harm to the public, when viewed from the standpoint of the public interest in preserving free and equal competition. For a review of the history of federal competition legislation and the criminal law power, see Finkelstein; "Comment — Constitutional Law — S. 91(2) of the *Constitution Act, 1867* — Competition Legislation" (1984), 62 Can. Bar Rev. 182, reproduced at Chapter 8, *supra*. It should be noted that the provincial Legislatures may also regulate or prohibit unfair trade practices and misleading or deceptive representations in their provincial aspects pursuant to section 92(3): *Re Aamco Automatic Transmissions Inc. and Simpson* (1980), 113 D.L.R. (3d) 650 (Ont. Div. Ct.); *R. v. Clarke* (1982), 137 D.L.R. (3d) 464, affirmed 147 D.L.R. (3d) 763 (Nfld. C.A.).

Whatever be the proper standards for attributing federal legislation to an exercise of the criminal law power, or, correlatively, denying validity to provincial legislation as an invasion of that power, certain propositions in this area are well established. Federal authority in relation to criminal law encompasses not only the creation of new crimes but the legalization of conduct or activity which was criminal at Confederation or which was subsequently proscribed as criminal: see *Toronto Ry. v. The King*, [1917] A.C. 630 at 639 (P.C.); *Amalgamated Builders Council v. Herman*, (1930), 65 O.L.R. 296 (S.C.). Thus, the Dominion may make it an offence to publish, distribute, sell or have in possession a "crime comic": see *R. v. Superior Publishers Ltd. and Zimmermann*, [1954] O.R. 981 (C.A.); sell or give cigarettes or tobacco to a person under age 16: see *R. v. Stelzer* (1957), 24 W.W.R. 130 (Man. C.A.); validly provide for indeterminate preventive detention of habitual criminals (as defined by federal legislation): see *Brusch v. The Queen*, [1953] 1 S.C.R. 373 (and this power is not circumscribed by either the *Canadian Bill of Rights: Ex parte*

*Matticks* (1973), 15 C.C.C. (2d) 213n (S.C.C.); or, the Canadian *Charter of Rights and Freedoms: R. v. Gustavson* (1982), 1 C.C.C. (3d) 470 (B.C.S.C.); *Re Moore and The Queen* (1984), 10 C.C.C. (3d) 306, affirmed [1983] 1 S.C.R. 658; *R. v. Langevin* (1984), 45 O.R. (2d) 705 (Ont. C.A.); *R. v. Lewis* (1984), 46 O.R. (2d) 289 (C.A.); *R. v. Vandale* (1984), 13 W.C.B. 173 (B.C. C.A.));and the Dominion may equally provide for indeterminate preventive detention of criminal sexual psychopaths: see *R. v. Neil*, [1957] S.C.R. 685. While generally prohibiting the keeping of a gaming house and book-making, the Dominion may exempt (*i.e.* permit) pari-mutuel betting: *cf. Re Race-Tracks and Betting* (1921), 49 O.L.R. 339 (C.A.). In other words, federal criminal legislation may be absolute or conditional in operation, may be punitive after the event and also preventive. Where the Dominion has enacted prohibitions, whether absolute or qualified, it is incompetent, of course, for a Province to relax them: see *Re Morrison and Kingston*, [1938] O.R. 21 (C.A.); *R. v. Stanley* (1952), 6 W.W.R. 574 (Alta T.D.); *A.-G. Can. v. Prince Albert*, (1951), 3 W.W.R. (N.S.) 646 (Sask. C.A.). It is equally incompetent for a Province to supplement the punishment prescribed by the Dominion, at least where the Province is acting only to strengthen enforcement of the federal prohibition: see *Prov. Sec. of P.E.I. v. Egan*, [1941] S.C.R. 396; *cf. Boyce v. The Queen* (1959), 22 D.L.R. (2d) 555 (Que. S.C.). There are a number of border-line situations which arise in this connection.

Notice was taken in Chapter 3, "Note on Constitutional Aspects of Procedure in Courts", of the authority of Parliament to legislate in relation to preventive criminal law; as, for example, by binding over a person to keep the peace. Parliament's power extends more obviously to the detention of an accused who has been acquitted on the ground of insanity at the time the offence charged was committed: see *R. v. Trapnell* (1910), 22 O.L.R. 219 (C.A.). Equally, it encompasses authority to order and supervise detention of an accused who is unfit, by reason of mental incompetency, to stand trial for a federal offence. In *Green v. Livermore*, [1940] O.R. 381 (S.C.) it was held that the Province could validly provide for the committal to a mental institution of a person charged with an "offence" (which was the term then used in the Ontario legislation and is the term still used). In rejecting the argument that this was an invasion of the criminal law power, the Court declared that "the action of the magistrate in sending the plaintiff to the hospital does not arise from any crime. . . . It is a step in the control of persons who have always been dealt with by the Province in legislation of the nature of the Mental Hospitals Act." In fact, the person so committed had been charged with a provincial offence and the case left open the question how far, if at all, the provincial enactment could be validly used in respect of a person charged under the federal criminal law.

This question was partly answered by the judgment in *Fawcett v. A.-G. Can.*, [1964] S.C.R. 625. The *Fawcett* case allowed a complementary resort to the provincial legislation where the original remand to a mental institution of a person accused of a federal offence was made under the *Criminal Code*. Criticism of this reliance on provincial legislation in the *Fawcett* case can, to some extent at least, be supported by the earlier judgment of the Supreme Court of Canada in *Re Trenholm*, [1940] S.C.R. 301. Although *Re Trenholm* is distinguishable because there was an attempt there to detain an accused after his remand on a federal criminal charge had expired, and because the reliance for his continued detention before expiry of the remand was on a clause of the provincial statute limited to imprisonment for a provincial offence, nonetheless the case indicates a concern not to mix up the provincial and federal powers of detention. This concern is evident as well in *R. v. P.D.P.* (1979), 94 D.L.R. (3d) 564 (B.C.C.A.).

Having regard to its exclusive authority in relation to criminal procedure as well as substantive criminal law, it is for Parliament alone to legislate in respect of the disposition of fines imposed for violations of federal criminal law: *Toronto v. The King*, [1932] A.C. 98 (P.C.); it is for Parliament alone to provide for payment of fees to witnesses and functionaries in connection with criminal proceedings: *A.-G. Que. v. A.-G. Can.*, [1945] S.C.R. 600; it is for Parliament alone to deal with costs in criminal proceedings, whether in respect of prosecutions under the federal criminal law or in respect of resort to prerogative writs directed to enforcement of that law: *Re Bence*, [1954] 2 D.L.R. 460 (B.C.). See, on the claim of a defendant to a trial in the French language, *Re Poulin*, 64 W.W.R. 705, affirmed 67 W.W.R. 514 (B.C. C.A.) (claim grounded on *Constitution Act, 1867*, section 133, rejected as to prosecution before magistrate); and *R. v. Lajoie*, [1971] 1 W.W.R. 157 (B.C.S.C.) (claim grounded on the *Official Languages Act*, R.S.C. 1970, c. O-2, s. 11, rejected on basis of referential exemption, recognizing provincial procedure). For further discussion on the question of language, see Chapter 23, *infra*.

The federal criminal law power does not extend to the mere attaching of penalties to offences defined by valid provincial legislation: *Boggs v. The Queen*, [1981] 1 S.C.R. 49. There is a category of so-called "provincial crimes" (see *R. v. Nat Bell Liquors Ltd.*, [1922] 2 A.C. 128 (P.C.) By section 92(15) of the *Constitution Act, 1867* exclusive authority is vested in the Provincial legislatures to enforce those offences by appropriate sanction.

While it is clearly settled that the imposition of a penalty does not *ipso facto* validate federal legislation, there has been no settled course of decision on the question whether the character of a penalty may result in invalidation of an otherwise valid provincial enactment. For example, would it be open to a Province to prescribe life imprisonment or whipping or, as an ultimate, hanging, for violation of a provincial enactment? Putting the matter another way, what are the limitations if any, that reside in the words "imposition of punishment by fine, penalty or imprisonment" in section 92(15)?

In *R. v. Wason* (1890), 17 O.A.R. 221 (C.A.) it was stated by members of the Court that provincial enforcement power extended to penalty without limit in amount and to imprisonment without limit in duration; or, as Osler J.A. put it (at p. 240) "the competency of the [provincial] enactment cannot be tested by the severity of the sanction so long as the latter is limited to fine, penalty or imprisonment"; see also *R. v. Chief* (1963), 46 W.W.R. 57, affirmed 44 D.L.R. (2d) 108 (Man. C.A.). "Penalty" would presumably include forfeiture of property (see the *Nat Bell* case, *supra*) and hard labour as an adjunct of imprisonment (see *Hodge v. The Queen* (1883), 9 App. Cas. 117 (P.C.)), but would not include capital punishment.

May a Province validly provide for compulsory sterilization of persons who are convicted of certain offences? In view of the *Charter of Rights*, can Parliament? Cf. *Skinner v. Oklahoma*, 316 U.S. 525 (1942).

On the scope of section 91(7) see Symposium, "The Criminal Law Power in Canada" (1957), 15 Univ. of Tor. Faculty of Law Rev. 1 ff.; Arvay, "The Criminal Law Power and the Constitution: and then came McNeil and Dupond" (1979), 11 Ottawa L.R. 1.

### Note on the Criminal Law Power and the Young Offender

A series of cases has taken the position that the Parliament of Canada may competently exercise its criminal law power against juveniles by asserting a paramount authority over their conduct, whether it be violative of federal criminal law or provincial penal law, and thus exclude a Province's enforcement of its own penal legislation where the offender was a juvenile as defined by federal law.

There is no doubt as to the power of the Province to impose obligations on parents and municipalities for the care of neglected or deprived children, to provide for their proper custody in institutions or elsewhere if parents neglect or abuse them, and to prescribe education and training for them. This is clearly so in the absence of federal legislation; and the question to be answered is whether Parliament may pre-empt part or all of this field of jurisdiction. Certainly, it may exercise control over juveniles through custody and required training as by-products of their violation of federal criminal law.

What arises from the cases discussed below is the question whether federal authority extends to the supervision of juveniles on the broader basis of violation of provincial or even of municipal legislation, or of immoral conduct which may not itself be against the law. The federal *Juvenile Delinquents Act*, (repealed April 2, 1984) asserted federal jurisdiction on this broader basis by creating an offence of "delinquency" which covered violations of federal, provincial or municipal law and covered also sexual immorality or any similar form of vice and the commission of any other act rendering a juvenile liable to be committed to any reformative institution or refuge for children under any federal or provincial statute.

The validity of this federal assertion of jurisdiction came before the Supreme Court of Canada in *A. G.-B. C. v. Smith*, [1967] S.C.R. 702. In that case, a juvenile was convicted of driving a motor vehicle over the speed limit imposed by the *Motor Vehicle Act*, R.S.B.C. 1960, c. 253. He applied for *certiorari* on the grounds that the case had not been dealt with pursuant to the federal *Juvenile Delinquents Act*. Counsel for the provincial Crown argued that the federal statute could not reach "delinquencies" arising out of provincial statutes or municipal bylaws or ordinances. Fauteux J., delivering the judgment of the Supreme Court of Canada, held that the *Juvenile Delinquents Act* was valid pursuant to section 91(27) and, further, that it applied to breaches of provincial law. The point is now considered to be "settled": *R. v. P.D.P.* (1979), 94 D.L.R. (3d) 564 (B.C.C.A.). As stated in P.D.P., a provincial *Corrections Act* may not provide for a remission of punishment for a breach of the *Criminal Code* or other federal statute. Insofar as punishment for breaches of provincial laws are concerned, they are clearly valid pursuant to s. 92(15) but inoperative to the extent the field is occupied by federal juvenile legislation.

What was involved under the *Juvenile Delinquents Act* was the assumption of authority over the conduct of persons because of age. *Quaere* the relevance of age as a lynchpin for the determination of constitutionality in these circumstances. And yet, can *Smith* be reconciled with the later case of *Boggs v. The Queen*, [1981] 1 S.C.R. 49, reproduced below, on any other basis than the existence of the age factor? The question is not whether the conduct as such is within the criminal law power, but whether it comes within it by reason of the age of the offender.

Debate over the scope of federal criminal law jurisdiction over young offenders has been rendered academic by the repeal of the *Juvenile Delinquents Act* and its replacement by the *Young Offenders Act*, S.C. 1980-81-82-83, c. 110. In addition to introducing a new philosophy to the treatment of young law breakers which no longer depends on the board concept of "delinquency", the new statute applies only to "young persons" who perform "an offence created by an Act of Parliament or by any regulation, rule, order, by-law or ordinance authority to legislate to this extent under s. 91(27) is beyond dispute made thereunder . . ." Some of the provincial Legislatures have filled in the lacunae left by the repeal of the *Juvenile Delinquents Act*: see, for example, sections 91a-91q of the *Provincial Offences Act*, R.S.O. 1980, c. 400 as amended by *inter alia* S.O. 1983, c. 80. These sections were proclaimed simultaneously with the repeal of the *Juvenile Delinquents Act*.

## 2. "Criminal Law" and "Property and Civil Rights"

### BEDARD v. DAWSON AND A.-G. QUE.

In the Supreme Court of Canada. [1923] S.C.R. 681.

Idington, Duff, Anglin, Brodeur and Mignault JJ. June 15, 1923.

Appeal from a judgment of the Quebec Court of King's Bench, Appeal Side, 33 Que. K.B. 246, affirming a judgment of the Superior Court and upholding the validity of a Quebec statute, 10 Geo. V, c. 81.

IDINGTON J.: This action was taken by the respondent Dawson under and by virtue of 10 Geo. V., c. 81 of the Quebec Legislature, entitled "An Act respecting the owners of houses used as disorderly houses," which provides, by sections 2, 3, 4 and 7 as follows: —

> 2. It shall be illegal for any person who owns or occupies any house or building of any nature whatsoever, to use or to allow any person to use the same as a disorderly house. A certified copy of any judgment convicting any person of an offence under section 228, 228a, 229 or 229a of the Criminal Code shall be *prima facie* proof of such use of the house in respect of which such conviction was had.
>
> 3. Any person knowing or having reason to believe that any building or part of a building is being made use of as a disorderly house, may send to the registered owner, or to the lessor, or to the agent of the registered owner, or to the lessee of such building, a notice, accompanied by a certified copy of any conviction as aforesaid, if any there be, by registered mail to the last known address of the said owner, agent or lessee, as the case may be.
>
> 4. Ten days after the mailing of such notice, if such building or any part thereof still continues to be used as a disorderly house, any person may apply for and obtain an injunction directed to the owner, lessor, lessee or occupant of such building, or to all such persons, restraining them, their heirs, assigns or successors from using or permitting the use of such building or any other building for the purposes above-mentioned.
>
> 7. If the judge finds that the use of such building as a disorderly house continues, he shall by his final judgment, in addition to all other orders he is by law empowered to make, order the closing of the said building against its use for any purpose whatsoever for a period of not more than one year from the date of judgment.

The power of the legislature to so enact having been questioned, by appellant pleading in defence, the Attorney-General for Quebec became in intervenant immediately thereafter. Thereupon the intervenant pleaded, the now appellant answered same, and the intervenant replied.

The case thus constituted was heard by Mr. Justice Maclennan who gave judgment for the respondent and granted the injunction claimed by him as provided in said section 7 of said Act, and for the intervenant with costs maintaining the constitutionality of the Act....

The Court of King's Bench, [on appeal], by a majority, there being a dissenting judge on the question, upheld the constitutionality of the Act and dismissed the appeal as to that issue, with costs to the responding intervenant....

I have long entertained the opinion that the provincial legislatures have such absolute power over property and civil rights, as given them by section 92 of the *B.N.A. Act*, item 13 thereof, that so long as they did not in fact encroach upon the powers assigned by the said Act to the Dominion Parliament it would be almost impossible to question any such exercise of power so given unless by the exercise of the veto power given the Dominion Government. That veto power was originally designed to prevent an improper exercise of legislative power by the provincial legislatures.

I, therefore, do not see that if properly interpreted and construed the said Act now in question herein can be said to be *ultra vires*.

There is, however, one aspect of it which rather disturbs me, and that is this: The Act takes certain sections of the Criminal Code as the basis of its subject-matter and then proceeds to apply convictions thereunder as the basis of its application.

And if, as might well happen, the keeper of the disorderly house so penalized should also be the owner thereof, and this Act applied in such case, it would look very much like adding as a matter of course to the penalties imposed by Parliament for the offence in question, when Parliament alone is endowed with the power and has imposed on it in so doing the sole responsibility of determining what is the proper measure of punishment.

That, however, is not the case presented on the facts in question herein. I point it out as being the possible cause of future embarrassment and would have preferred to see its enactment somewhat differently framed.

As to the argument addressed to us that the local legislatures cannot legislate to prevent crime, I cannot assent thereto for in a very wide sense it is the duty of the legislature to do the utmost it can within its power to anticipate and remove, so far as practicable, whatever is likely to tend to produce crime; and yet not produce worse forms of it, or tending thereto....

There are many instances of other nuisances which can be better rectified by local legislation within the power of the legislatures over property and civil rights than by designating them crimes and leaving them to be dealt with by Parliament as such....

DUFF J.: The legislation impugned seems to be aimed at suppressing conditions calculated to favour the development of crime rather than at the punishment of crime. This is an aspect of the subject in which the provinces seems to be free to legislate. I think the legislation is not invalid.

ANGLIN J.: . . . I am of the opinion that this statute in no wise impinges on the domain of criminal law but is concerned exclusively with the control and enjoyment of property and the safeguarding of the community from the consequences of an illegal and injurious use being made of it — a pure matter of civil right. In my opinion in enacting the statute now under consideration the legislature exercised the power which it undoubtedly possesses to provide for the suppression of a nuisance and the prevention of its recurrence by civil process. . . .

*Appeal dismissed.*

[Brodeur and Mignealt JJ. also gave reasons upholding the validity of the Act.]

*Note*

In *R. v. Lamontagne*, [1945] O.R. 606 (C.A.), a majority of the Ontario Court of Appeal distinguished *Bedard v. Dawson and A.-G. Que., supra*, and held invalid the *Gaming and Betting Act*, S.O. 1942, c. 19 in the following circumstances. The Act provided that a Court may on application order the closing for a period up to a year of premises in respect of which there has been, within the previous three months, a conviction under enumerated disorderly house, betting and bookmaking provisions of the Criminal Code. Where a closing order was made and the premises were used in violation of the order, the registered owner and any person found therein at the time (unless such person could prove he was there for a lawful purpose) were to be deemed to have violated the order. A person violating the Act or any order thereunder was guilty of an offence. Certain premises were made the subject of an order closing them for all purposes except use as a private residence or boarding house, and expressly forbidding a violation of the particular Criminal Code provision in respect of use of the premises. While the order was in force one L. was convicted under the Criminal Code of keeping a common bawdy house on the premises. The owner of the premises was also convicted under the Criminal Code of knowingly permitting the premises to be used as a common bawdy house. Thereafter, the owner was charged under the *Gaming and Betting Act* of violating the closing order because of the conviction of L. In affirming the setting aside of a conviction under the Ontario Act the majority held that the statute operated essentially as criminal law in a field already covered by the federal Criminal Code. On the facts, the Act that violated the closing order and exposed the accused to punishment was already an offence under the Criminal Code. McRuer J.A., dissenting, could see no difference in principle between the Ontario statute and the enactment in the *Bedard case*.

In *Johnson v. A. G. Alta.*, [1954] S.C.R. 127, the Alberta *Slot Machine Act*, R.S.A. 1942, c. 333 provided that "no slot machine shall be capable of ownership, nor shall the same be the subject of property rights with the Province . . ." "Slot machine" was defined as, *inter alia*, any machine deemed by section 986(4) of the *Criminal Code* as a means or continuance for playing a game of chance. Upon information on oath by any peace officer that there were reasonable grounds for believing a slot machine to be in any premises, a justice of the peace could by warrant authorize the officer to search the premises and seize any slot machines found thereon. If the person in possession of the machine or occupant of the premises could not, after notice before a justice of the peace, show cause why the machine was not a slot machine within the meaning of the *Slot Machine Act*, the justice of the peace was required to make an order confiscating the machine to the Crown.

The case came before the Supreme Court of Canada by way of appeal of an order of the Alberta Court of Appeal setting aside the trial judge's order prohibiting proceedings under the Act. The Supreme Court of Canada allowed the appeal. Rand J. said:

> That the object of the statute is to eliminate what is considered to be a local evil is quite apparent but what evil? I can quite imagine an object of concern to be the waste of time and money, particularly of young persons, in the operation of such machines as were dealt with in [*Regent Vending Machines Ltd. v. Alberta Vending Machines Ltd.*, [1954] S.C.R. 98]. Their operation may even be taken to tend to breed a gambling propensity, although that tendency, if it exists at all, must be admitted to be extremely tenuous. But that the legislative purpose is aimed primarily at the evil of gambling is patent from almost the opening words of the statute. There is the incorporation of the instruments falling with s. 986(4) of the *Code* in subcl. (i); subcls. (ii) and (iii) are couched in language which in its technical description of the functional result of the machines is identical with what is contained in that section. The only difference between subcls. (ii) and (iii) are in the opening words of application in subcl. (ii) "any slot machine and any other machine of a similar nature" against in subcl. (iii) "any machine or device"; in line 5 of subcl. (ii), "any number" against, in lines 4-5 of subcl. (iii), "any given number"; and in line 9 of subcl. (ii) "shall be known" against "may be known" in the second last line of subcl. (iii). If significant differences in the interpretation of the two subclauses exist, they have not been suggested to us. It is therefore, in my opinion, reasonably clear that if the scope of the statute in this respect does go beyond that of s. 986(4), it must be in relation to machines or devices that are of or are used for a gambling nature or purpose.
>
> That being so, what is the scope of the provision of the Code dealing with gaming and gambling instruments? It should be remarked at the outset that, generally, gambling devices are aimed at as the apparatus of gaming-houses. In certain forms they may be found in homes and used if at all in purely private activities beyond the reach of the criminal law. I do not interpret the words of s. 4 of the statute "that any slot machine is *kept* in any building or premises" to extend to an instrument of any kind to be found in a home for family and social entertainment. To be "kept" in the text carries the implication both of keeping in use and for other than purely social purposes. What is intended to be struck at is a public or community evil, not what would involve in its enforcement the invasion of domestic privacy.
>
> In addition to s. 986(4) the provisions of ss. 235 and 641 bear directly on the question. The former makes it an indictable offence to keep in any premises, "any gambling, wagering, or betting machine or device". No definition is given of these machines or devices, and we are left in each case to a determination of fact. Then s. 641 [am. 1974, c. 55, s. 19; 1948, c. 39, s. 17; 1950, c. 11, s. 8] authorizes the seizure within any house, room or place which a Peace Officer believes to be a place kept as a gambling-house, of all instruments of gaming found therein, to be brought before a Justice who, by s-s. (3) is empowered in a proper case to make an order of confiscation. Taken with s. 642 it furnishes the means and the occasion for initiating a prosecution under s. 229.
>
> From this it is seen that the Code has dealt comprehensively with the subject-matter of the provincial statute. An additional process of forfeiture by the Province would both duplicate the sanctions of the Code and introduce an interference with the administration of its provisions. Criminality is primarily personal and sanctions are intended not only to serve as deterrents but to mark a personal delinquency. The enforcement of criminal law is vital to the peace and order of the community. The obvious conflict of administrative action in prosecutions under the Code and proceedings under the statute, considering the more direct and less complicated action of the latter, could lend itself to a virtual nullification of enforcement under the Code and in effect displace the Code so far by the statute. But the criminal law has been enacted to be carried into effect against violations, and any local legislation of a supplementary nature that would tend to weaken or confuse that enforcement would be an interference with the exclusive power of Parliament.

The penalty of the Act, in duplicating forefeiture, is supplementing punishment. That is not legislating either "in relation to" property or to a local object. Every valid enactment made under the authority conferred by means of that phrase is for an object or purpose which is within the power of the enacting jurisdiction, and legislation "in relation to"property is as much subject to that canon as any other head of ss. 91 or 92. Legislation from caprice or perverseness or arbitrary will affecting, say, property, cannot be brought within those words; when of such a nature it passes into another category. That law is reason is in such a sense as applicable to statutes as to the unwritten law. I am unable to agree, therefore, that under its authority to legislate in relation to property the Province can in reality supplement punishment; that it may deal with conditions that conduce to the development of crime where what is proposed is in fact legislation of that character and infringes no legislative field beyond its jurisdiction though undoubted is not in question here.

The result is that since the machines or devices struck at by the statute are the same as those dealt with in similar manner by the Code, it is sufficient to say that the statute is inoperative ...

Locke J. took a somewhat different position. Whereas Rand J. viewed the provincial legislation as an attempt to supplement existing federal criminal legislation, for Locke J. the fact that Parliament had already enacted similar law was not controlling. The provincial legislation was an invasion of the federal criminal law power and was for that reason alone *ultra vires* regardless of the existence, or non-existence, of federal law on the subject. He said:

In essence, the Act was directed against gambling and, in my opinion, nothing else, and, in addition to declaring that no slot machines should be capable of ownership, prohibited any person from keeping or operating such a machine and permitted its seizure and confiscation.

... The determination of this matter does not, in my opinion, depend alone upon the fact that if the provincial legislation was lawfully enacted there would be a direct clash with the terms of the Criminal Code: rather is it my opinion that the main reason is that the exclusive jurisdiction to legislate in relation to gaming lies with Parliament under head (27) of s. 91 ...

I would allow this appeal with costs throughout and declare that the *Slot Machine Act* is *ultra vires* of the Legislature of Alberta.

Cartwright J. said:

I am unable to relate the statute in the case at bar to any provincial purpose falling within heads (13) or (16) of s. 92 of the *B.N.A. Act* as the Courts have been able to do in other cases in which the validity of provincial legislation was called in question on the allegation that infringed upon the field of criminal law, as, for example, in the cases of *Provincial Secretary of P.E.I. v. Egan*, [1941] S.C.R. 396, (the civil regulation of the use of highways), *Bedard v. Dawson*, [1923] S.C.R. 681, (the suppression of a nuisance and the prevention of its recurrence by civil process) and *R. v. Wason* (1890), 17 O.R. 58 (C.A.) (the regulation of the dealings of cheese-makers and their patrons). The statute here in question appears to me to be inserverable, to relate only to the prohibition and punishment of keeping contrivances for playing games of chance, that is to criminal law, and to be *ultra vires* of the Legislature *in toto*.

Kerwin J. (as he then was), with Taschereau J. concurring, dissented on the grounds that the *Slot Machine Act* dealt with property in the province rather than criminal law, and that it was similar to the legislation considered in *Bedard v. Dawson, supra*, which provided "for the suppression of a nuisance and not with criminal law by aiming at the punishment of a crime". Is Kerwin J. correct about the similarity of *Bedard* and *Johnson*? Could *Bedard* be decided the same way today?

Estey J. entered a separate dissent, Kellock J. concurred with Cartwright J. In *Deware v. The Queen*, [1954] S.C.R. 182, in a judgment handed down on the same day as that in the *Johnson* case, the Supreme Court, similarly constituted, split evenly on the validity of the *Slot Machine Act*, R.S.N.B. 1952, c. 212, with Rand J.

taking no position on the issue of validity but going off on a question of application of the Act.

Following the *Johnson* case, Alberta enacted a new *Slot Machine Act*, 1954, c. 99, which *inter alia*, defined a slot machine by specification and excluded any machine which under the Criminal Code is deemed to be a means for playing a game of chance. It went on to declare that the maintenance of a slot machine on any premises in the Province is a nuisance. Confiscation was provided for as before, but with jurisdiction in a Supreme Court or District Court Judge. In reliance on the *Johnson* case, the Act was declared *ultra vires* as seeking to suppress gambling not covered by the Criminal Code and thus trespassing on a forbidden field: *Regent Vending Machines Ltd. v. Alberta Vending Machines Ltd. and A.-G. Alta.* (1956), 19 W.W.R. 509, aff'g 16 W.W.R. 141 (Alta. C.A.).

It should be noted that there is a difference between prohibiting an activity altogether and regulating commerce through zoning. In *Re City of Montreal and Arcade Amusements Inc.*, [1985] 1 S.C.R. 368, The Supreme Court of Canada had to consider section 8 of a City of Montreal bylaw which, *inter alia*, prohibits minors from entering amusement halls or using amusement machines. In addition, the bylaw limited the operation of amusement halls to a small geographical area of the City. The Court struck down section 8 of the bylaw on administrative law grounds, but rejected the constitutional argument that the bylaw, and in particular section 8 thereof, was really legislation to prohibit gaming from the point of view of public morals and the criminal law. Beetz J., speaking for the Court, said at pp. 199-201:

> The argument of illegality made against By-law 5156 by respondents and based on the *Constitution Act, 1867* may be summarized as follows. This by-law is said to be similar to the *Slot Machine Act, 1935* of Alberta, struck down in *Johnson v. A.-G. Alta.*, [1954] S.C.R. 127, and the *Slot Machine Act, 1954* of Alberta, struck down in *Regent Vending Machines Ltd. v. Alberta Vending Machines Ltd. and A.-G. Alta.* (1956), 24 C.R. 297 (Alta. C.A.). It allegedly does not differ in essence from By-laws 2223 and 2229 of the City, prohibiting pinball machines and bagatelle games, repealed by s. 13 of By-law 5156 and themselves declared by the Superior Court to be unconstitutional in *Parkway Amusement Co. Ltd. v. Cité de Montréal*, [1958] Que. S.C. 209. The impugned by-law seeks to prohibit, and in reality to make a crime, the use of gaming machines which the Parliament of Canada "decriminalized" when, in s. 10 of the *Criminal Law Amendment Act*, (1974-75-76 (Can.), c. 93, [it] amended s. 180(3) of the *Criminal Code* by excluding from the definition of "slot machine" "an automatic machine or slot machine that dispenses as prizes only one or more free games on that machine". The essential purpose of By-law 5156 is allegedly to prohibit gaming on grounds of public morals and to fill in what are perceived as gaps created in the *Criminal Code*, contrary to the principles recognized in such cases as *Westendorp v. The Queen*, [1983] 1 S.C.R. 43, and, one might add, *Goldwax v. City of Montreal*, [1984] 2 S.C.R. 525.
>
> This argument of illegality should only be considered if one is of the opinion that By-law 5156 is really prohibitory. Even then, the argument is not necessarily conclusive in constitutional terms. If one concludes, as I did above, that By-law 5156 does not prohibit either amusement machines or amusement halls, but regulates their use and location, the constitutional argument loses all its force and one need go no further in refuting it.
>
> However, I feel I should add certain observations.
>
> Even s. 8 of the by-law, which is prohibitory in form and which is *ultra vires* for the reasons mentioned above, is not thereby unconstitutional. This partial prohibition forms an integral though severable part of a comprehensive regulation regarding commerce and zoning, one which is also adopted for policing purposes to protect youth and prevent delinquency. The regulation of local commerce, zoning, the protection of youth and the prevention of crime are all areas within the authority of the province. [citations omitted]

Additionally, the amusement machines covered by By-law 5156 are, under the definition in s. 2, amusement devices authorized by law, and the amusements which they provide are perfectly innocent in themselves, in terms of public morals and other points of view as well. With such a by-law, one is far from an attempt to wipe out prostitution as in *Westendorp, supra*, and *Goldwax, supra*. I feel that this is also far from being an attempt to prohibit, even for young people, gaming regarded as a vice and from the standpoint of the criminal law, as three out of seven judges held in *Johnson, supra*. This case is not very decisive with respect to characterizing the legislation at issue there. However, its authority has continued to be cited by this court in *Nova Scotia Board of Censors, supra*, at 698-9 S.C.R., when a provincial statute reproduced the provisions of the *Criminal Code*.

I would dismiss the argument of illegality based on the *Constitution Act, 1867*.

It is within the power of the Dominion to provide for the forfeiture of vehicles or other things used in the commission of a criminal offence even though the articles are owned by someone other than the convicted person and even though no exculpatory provision is made in respect of the interest of an innocent person: see *Industrial Acceptance Corp. v. The Queen*, [1953] 2 S.C.R. 273. In *R. v. McManus Agenices Ltd.* (1960), 32 C.R. 252 (N.S. S.C.), it was held to be competent to Parliament to provide for the destruction, on the direction of the Court, of articles seized as evidence of gambling or bookmaking.

Assuming that the Dominion does not provide for the impounding or confiscation of articles used in connection with the commission of (federal) criminal offences, is it open to a Province so to legislate? See *McDonald v. Down*, [1939] 2 D.L.R. 177, aff'd 75 Can. C.C. 404 (Ont. C.A.) (provincial legislation held valid in providing for impounding of automobile in certain circumstances if there has been a conviction under specified provisions of the provincial *Highway Traffic Act* or the federal *Criminal Code* involving use of the automobile).

A licensing by-law passed in pursuance of provincial legislation provided for the licensing of dance halls on certain conditions, including a stipulation that the licensee must not permit gambling or gaming of any kind on the premises. On appeal by a licensee from his conviction for breach of the by-law in permitting gambling on the licensed premises (although he himself was not present at the time), it was contended that the by-law was *ultra vires*. Do you agree? Would it make any difference if the only sanction for breach of the by-law was revocation of the licence? See *Millar v. The Queen* (1953), 10 W.W.R. (N.S.) 145 (Man. C.A.).

A theatre licensing by-law authorized the cancellation of a licence when an immoral or indecent or profane performance takes place. *Held*, applying the *Johnson* case, the by-law was unconstitutional because it purported to supplement the *Criminal Code*: *St. Leonard v. Fournier* (1956), 115 C.C.C. 366 (N.B.C.A.) See also *Hurrell v. Montreal*, [1963] Que. P.R. 89, holding invalid (in view of the obscenity provisions of the Criminal Code) a by-law prohibiting display of pictures of nudes or semi-nudes on news stands without the prior approval of the chief of police.

May a person be convicted of stealing things which by provincial law are declared to be ownerless or incapable of being the objects of property rights? See *R. v. MacEwen; R. v. Bell*, [1947] 2 D.L.R. 62 (P.E.I. S.C.).

A municipal by-law, authorized by provincial legislation, providing that no person shall create any disturbance in any public place or on any street by screaming, shouting, swearing or singing, or by being drunk or by fighting, was held invalid in view of the provisions of *Criminal Code*, section 160 prohibiting the causing of a disturbance in or near a public place by conduct similar to that described in the by-law: *Poole v. Tomlinson* (1957), 21 W.W.R. 511 (Sask. Q.B.). Would the by-law be invalid if there were no *Criminal Code*, section 160?

May a Province make it an offence to speculate in the sale of tickets to places of entertainment? See *R v. Fink*, [1967] 2 O.R. 132.

May a provincial legislature make it an offence for a man to register at a hotel with a woman falsely held out to be his wife? Would the validity of the legislation be affected if it provided merely for cancellation of a hotel licence if the proprietor knowingly permitted a man so to register? See *R. v. Hayduk*, [1938] O.R. 653 (C.A.).

May a provincial legislature provide for committal to jail of a judgment debtor if his examination shows that the debt on which the judgment was founded was contracted by false pretences, which is independently punishable under the federal Criminal Code? See *Re Dunn*, [1939] 4 D.L.R. 382 (N.S. C.A.).

# GOODYEAR TIRE & RUBBER CO. OF CANADA LTD. v. THE QUEEN

In the Supreme Court of Canada. [1956] S.C.R. 303.

Kerwin C.J., Taschereau, Rand, Kellock, Estey, Locke, and Fauteux JJ. Feb. 10, 1956.

Appeal from a judgment of the Ontario Court of Appeal, [1954] O.R. 377 affirming with variations an order of prohibition by Treleaven J., [1953] O.R. 856, under s. 31(1) of the *Combines Investigation Act* (Can.).

LOCKE J.: ... The appellants were indicted together on the charge that they "during the period from 1936 to the 31st day of October 1952, both inclusive, within the jurisdiction of this Honourable Court, did unlawfully conspire, combine, agree or arrange together and within one another and with *Barringham Rubber & Plastics Limited; G. L. Griffith & Sons, Ltd.; Viceroy Manufacturing Company Limited; Firestone Tire & Rubber Company of Canada, Limited and Canalco Limited*, to unduly prevent or lessen competition in the production, manufacture, purchase, barter, sale, transportation or supply in the City of Toronto, in the County of York, and other places throughout the Province of Ontario, and in the City of Montreal, in the Province of Quebec, and other places throughout the Province of Quebec and elsewhere in Canada where the articles or commodities hereinafter mentioned are offered for sale, of articles or commodities which may be the subject of trade or commerce, to wit (then followed a description of the commodities), contrary to the provisions of the Criminal Code, Section 498, subsection 1(d)."

Section 31 of the *Combines Investigation Act* reads:

> 31(1) Where a person has been convicted of an offence under section thirty-two or thirty-four of this Act or under section four hundred and ninety-eight or four hundred and ninety-eight A of the *Criminal Code*

(a) the court may, at the time of such conviction, on the application of the Attorney-General of Canada or the attorney-general of the province, or

(b) a superior court of criminal jurisdiction in the province may at any time within three years thereafter, upon proceedings commenced by information of the Attorney-General of Canada or the attorney-general of the province for the purposes of this section,

and in addition to any other penalty imposed on the person convicted, prohibit the continuation or repetition of the offence or the doing of any act or thing by the person convicted or any other person directed towards the continuation or repetition of the offence and where the conviction is with respect to the formation or operation of a merger, trust or monopoly, direct the person convicted or any other person to do such acts or things as may be necessary to dissolve the merger, trust or monopoly in such manner as the court directs.

(2) Where it appears to a superior court of criminal jurisdiction in proceedings commenced by information of the Attorney-General of Canada or the attorney-general of the province for the purposes of this section that a person is about to do or is likely to do any act or thing constituting or directed towards the commission of an offence under section thirty-two or thirty-four of this Act or section four hundred and ninety-eight or four hundred and ninety-eight A of the *Criminal Code*, the court may prohibit the commission of the offence or the doing of any act or thing by that person or any other person constituting or directed towards the commission of such an offence.

(3) A court may punish any person who contravenes or fails to comply with a prohibition or direction made or given by it under this section by a fine in the discretion of the court, or by imprisonment for a term not exceeding two years.

(4) Any proceedings pursuant to an information of the Attorney-General of Canada or the attorney-general of a province under this section shall be tried by the court without a jury, and the procedure applicable in injunction proceedings in the superior courts of the province shall, in so far as possible, apply.

(5) This section applies in respect of all prosecutions under this Act or under section four hundred and ninety-eight or four hundred and ninety-eight A of the *Criminal Code* whether commenced before or after the coming into force of this section and in respect of all acts or things, whether committed or done before or after the coming into force of this section.

(6) In this section 'superior court of criminal jurisdiction' means a superior court of criminal jurisdiction as defined in the *Criminal Code*. [re-enacted 1952, c. 39, s. 3]

All of the appellants pleaded guilty to the charge and Crown counsel, representing the Attorney-General of Canada and the Attorney-General of Ontario, then applied for an order under the provisions of s. 31 and on September 24, 1953, the learned trial Judge imposed a fine of $10,000 upon each of the accused and directed that an order of prohibition issue, as permitted by the section.

On September 25, 1953, an order issued out of the Supreme Court of Ontario which, after reciting the conviction, read:

1. This Court doth prohibit the continuation or repetition of the said offence by the persons convicted.

2. This Court doth further prohibit the doing of any act or thing by the persons convicted or by any other person directed towards the continuation or repetition of the said offence.

The appellants obtained leave to appeal to the Court of Appeal and contended before that Court that s. 31 was *ultra vires* of Parliament. That appeal was dismissed, the Court, however, directing that para. (2) of the order be altered so that it reads:

This Court doth further prohibit the doing of any act or thing by the persons convicted, and/or their directors, officers, servants and agents, directed towards the continuation or repetition of the said offence.

While, pursuant to the direction of this Court, all of the provincial Attorneys-General were notified of the questions to be raised on the appeal, none were represented before us, the argument in support of the validity of the legislation being made on behalf of the Attorney-General of Canada.

Stated shortly, the contention of the appellants is that s. 31 is either wholly or partially *ultra vires* of Parliament, being a colourable attempt, under the guise of enacting legislation in relation to criminal law, to trench upon the field of property and civil rights in the Province assigned exclusively to the Legislature by head (13) of s. 92 of the *B.N.A. Act*. A subsidiary point is that the Court of Appeal erred in interpreting the reference in s.-ss. (1) and (2) of s. 31 to "any other person" as meaning only those who stood in such a relation to the accused that a prohibitory order against them would affect the accused and be a penalty on the accused.

Counsel for the Attorney-General supports the legislation as a valid exercise of the powers of Parliament under head (27) of s. 91 as criminal law, and under head (2) as the regulation of trade and commerce.

Since 1888 there has been legislation in Canada prohibiting the offences referred to in s. 498 of the *Code*. In substantially the same form, that section appeared as s. 520 when the *Code* was first enacted in 1892 (c. 29).

Following the decision of the Judicial Committee finding the *Board of Commerce Act* and the *Combines and Fair Prices Act*, enacted in 1919, to be *ultra vires* (60 S.C.R. 456, aff'd [1922] 1 A.C. 191), the *Combines Investigation Act*, 1923 (Can.), c. 9, which repealed the said statutes, was enacted.

In 1929 the Governor-General in Council referred to this Court the question as to whether that Act, either in whole or in part, and s. 498 of the *Criminal Code* were *ultra vires*. Both the statute and the section were held to be within the power of Parliament, [1929] S.C.R. 409, and that decision was upheld by the Judicial Committee in *Proprietary Articles Trades Ass'n v. A.-G. Can.*, [1931] A.C. 310 (P.C.).

Section 31 was not part of the Act in 1929, having been first enacted by c. 39 of the Statutes of 1952. It is not a valid objection, in my opinion, to that portion of the section which has been invoked in the present matter, that, since the offence is prohibited by s. 498 of the *Code* and penalties are provided both by the *Code* and by the *Combines Investigation Act*, the power to deal with the matter under head (27) is exhausted. It is to be noted that the making of a prohibitory order is authorized "in addition to any other penalty", being thus treated as a penalty. The power to legislate in relation to criminal law is not restricted, in my opinion, to defining offences and providing penalties for their commission. The power of Parliament extends to legislation designed for the prevention of crime as well as to punishing crime. It was, apparently, considered that to prohibit the continuation or repetition of the offence by order, a breach being punishable under s-s. (3) of s. 31, would tend to restrain its repetition. As to the language "or the doing of any act or thing by the person convicted . . . directed toward the continuation or repetition of the offence", this appears to me to be properly construed as forbidding the taking of any step by the person to whom the order is directed, looking to the continuation of the offence dealt with by the conviction or its repetition by forming another combine, and I do not think it is intended to deal only with attempts to commit the offence. The language appears to me to permit the prohibition of any act such as a preliminary proposal to others regarding the formation of a combine which, in itself, might not fall within the definition of an attempt under s. 72. As Parliament apparently considered that such an order might be of use in preventing the formation of such combines, I think the matter to be wholly within its powers.

This view is supported, in my opinion, by a passage from the judgment of Sir Lyman P. Duff C.J.C. in *Provincial Secretary of P.E.I. v. Egan*, [1941] S.C.R. 396. Section 285(7)(*a*) of the *Code* provides that, where a person is convicted of an offence defined by s-s. (1), (2), (4) or (6) of that section, the Court may "in addition to any other punishment provided for such offence, make an order prohibiting such person from driving a motor vehicle or automobile anywhere in Canada during any period not exceeding three years".

Dealing with the argument that the making of such a prohibitory order did not fall under head (27), the Chief Justice said (p. 308 D.L.R.):

> I may say at once I cannot agree with this view. . . . It appears to me to be quite clear that such prohibitions may be imposed as punishment in exercise of the authority vested in the Dominion to legislate in relation to criminal law and procedure.

In *A.-G. Ont. v. Can. Temperance Federation*, [1946] A.C. 193 (P.C.), Viscount Simon L.C. referring to and rejecting an argument that Parliament was without power to re-enact provisions with the object of preventing a recurrence of a state of affairs which had been deemed to necessitate the passage of an earlier statute, said that to legislate for prevention appears to be on the same base as legislation for cure.

Whether or not it can properly be said that the language referred to was intended to define a new offence, or whether it should be construed as merely providing the means of preventing the commission of the offence, it is, in my opinion, equally within the power of Parliament under head (27) of s. 91.

It is further contended that the power to make a prohibitory order directed to the person convicted "or any other person" is not legislation authorized by head (27). While, literally construed and divorced from the context, these words would permit the making of an order against persons quite unconnected with those against whom a conviction has been made, it is impossible that this was the intention of Parliament and I agree with the learned Judges of the Court of Appeal that it should properly be construed as meaning, in cases such as this where the accused are corporations, the directors, officers, servants and agents of the various companies.

The appellants further submitted that that part of s-s. (1) which reads "and where the conviction is with respect to the formation or operation of a merger, trust or monopoly, direct the person convicted or any other person to do such acts or things as may be necessary to dissolve the merger, trust or monopoly in such manner as the court directs", is *ultra vires*.

This power was not exercised by the Court in the present case and as, in my opinion, this portion of the subsection is clearly severable from that portion which has been invoked, the point as to whether this is within the powers of Parliament should not, in my opinion, be determined. This is not a Reference to the Court in which we are asked to determine the validity of s. 31 as a whole, but rather that portion of it purporting to give to the Court the powers which have been exercised in making the order complained of.

In view of my conclusion that the impugned legislation is *intra vires* of Parliament under head (27), it is unnecessary to consider the question as to whether it might not also fall within head (2) . . .

*Appeal dismissed.*

[Kerwin C.J.C., Taschereau, Kellock and Fauteux JJ. concurred with Locke J. A separate concurring judgment was delivered by Rand J. who said, *inter alia*, that "it is accepted that head (27) of s. 91 . . . is to be interpreted in its widest sense, but that breadth of scope contemplates neither a static catalogue of offences nor order of sanctions". Estey J. took no part in the judgment.

May the Dominion confer upon an informer the right to recover by civil action penalties imposed for breach of the criminal law? See *Doyle v. Bell* (1884), 11 O.A.R. 326.]

## Note

In *Gordon v. Imperial Tobacco Sales Co.*, [1939] O.R. 122 (S.C.), McFarland J., relying on *Transport Oil Co. Ltd. v. Imperial Oil Co. Ltd.*, [1935] O.R. 215 (C.A.) stated that "the principle is quite clearly established that Dominion legislation cannot trespass upon or create any civil right in a province". *Quaere* whether any constitutional principle is raised on whether a civil action arises upon a breach of the criminal enactment where the Dominion criminal legislation is silent! See Finkleman, "Note" (1935), 13 Can. Bar Rev. 517 at 521:

> The right of action for injury caused by a conspiracy, arises not by virtue of any federal legislation but by operation of the common law doctrine which gives a right of action to anyone injured by a criminal conspiracy, in this case a conspiracy to violate a Dominion statute.

In *Floyd v. Edmonton City Dairy Ltd.*, [1934] 3 W.W.R. 326 (Alta. S.C.), Ford J. stated (at p. 756) that "a proven violation of s. 498 of the Criminal Code, if it results in damage, is actionable at the suit of the individual damnified"; and see *Wasney v. Jurazsky*, [1933] 1 D.L.R. 616 (Man. C.A.). Cf. Duff C.J. in *Philco Products Ltd. v. Thermionics Ltd.*, [1940] S.C.R. 501 at 504:

> If B commits an indictable offence and the direct consequence of that indictable offence is that A suffers some special harm different from that of the rest of His Majesty's subjects, then, speaking generally, A has a right of action against B. As at present advised, I think it is not obvious that this well settled doctrine does not apply to indictable offences under section 498 of the Criminal Code.

See, too, *Note* (1941), 19 Can. Bar Rev. 51; *Placatka v. Thompson*, [1941] 1 W.W.R. 528 (Alta. C.A.); *Pullan v. McLellan*, [1946] 2 D.L.R. 606 (B.C. S.C.).

In *Direct Lumber Co. Ltd. v. Western Plywood Co. Ltd.*, [1962] S.C.R. 646, which affirmed dismissal of an action for damages based on alleged discriminatory treatment in violation of prohibitions of the federal criminal law respecting monopolies and illegal trade practices, Judson J. for the Supreme Court commented as follows: "I recognize that there may be a difference between a common law action for damages based on conspiracy and one based on price discrimination. The common law itself imposes liability for harm caused by combinations to injure by unlawful means but the common law never gave any cause of action for price discrimination unaccompanied by conspiracy. To this extent some of the *dicta* in the *Transport Oil* case, which was a conspiracy case, may be open to question, and it may well be doubted whether any constitutional principle is raised when Dominion criminal legislation is silent upon the question whether a civil action arises upon breach of its terms. This doubt has been expressed by Wright in *Cases on the law of Torts*, 2nd ed., p. 279; Laskin, *Canadian Constitutional Law*, 2nd ed., p. 863; and Finkelman (1935), 13 Can. Bar Rev. 517, and it is probably the basis for the statement of Duff C.J.C. in *Philco Products Ltd. v. Thermionics Ltd.* . . . To take the point one step farther, assuming that one may validly imply a civil right of action for breach of a federal criminal statute, does it not follow that there should be no constitutional impediment if Parliament expressly provides one? See Hogg, *Constitutional Law of Canada*, (1977) at p. 288 (not repeated in the 2d ed., 1985). Would this alone be enough to validate section 31.1 of the *Combines Investigation Act*? See Finkelstein, "Comment" reproduced at Chapter 8 above.

In *St. Catharines General Hospital v. Sviergula*, [1961] O.R. 164 (H.C.) it was held that *Criminal Code*, section 186 which imposed a legal duty to provide necessaries of life to, *inter alia*, a child under age 16, did not create any civil liability; and the Court added, "if it did so it might well be challenged as unconstitutional because property and civil rights are involved."

See also *Note*, Implying Civil Remedies from Federal Regulatory Statutes (1963), 77 Harv. L. Rev. 285, alluding to one of the theories underlying liability imposed by the cases as being that "a new cause of action implied from a federal statute creates a federal right." Would this be applicable under Canadian federal regulatory statutes as opposed to criminal enactments?

## 3. Criminal Proceedings and Civil Actions

### Note on Criminal Proceedings and Civil Actions

*Transport Oil Co. Ltd. v. Imperial Oil Co. Ltd.*, [1935]O.R. 215 (Ont. C.A.) and the comment thereon in *Direct Lumber Co. Ltd. v. Western Plywood Co. Ltd.*, [1962] S.C.R. 646 reproduced above touch but one of a number of problems with constitutional implications where, whether by common law or by legislation, civil actions are permitted or restricted in reference to acts or conduct which is criminal. Parliament provided by what was formerly *Criminal Code* section 734 that a person acquitted on a charge of common assault or who, if convicted, has paid or suffered the penalty awarded against him, shall be released from all further civil or criminal proceedings for the same cause. The enactment understandably gave rise to a division of opinion as to its validity in so far as it purported to release a person from civil liability for conduct which, as a tort matter, was subject to provincial legislative authority: see *Rice v. Messenger*, [1929] 2 D.L.R. 669 (N.S. C.A.) and *Dawson v. Muttart*, [1941] 2 D.L.R. 341 (P.E.I. S.C.), holding section 734 to be invalid; and see, holding section 734 to be *intra vires*, *Wilson v. Codyre* (1886), 26 N.B.R. 516; *Flick v. Brisbin* (1895), 26 O.R. 423 (C.A.); *Trinea v. Duleba*, [1924] 2 W.W.R. 1177 (Alta. C.A.); *Dowsett v. Edwards*, [1926] 3 W.W.R. 447 (Alta. C.A.); *Nykiforuk v. Kohut*, [1949] 1 W.W.R. 708 (Sask. Dist. Ct.). What was section 734 was taken from English legislation where it had no constitutional implications: see Note (1948), 26 Can. Bar Rev. 1001. The better reasoning would be against the validity of such a provision: see Note (1941), 19 Can. Bar Rev. 379. Mere initial resort to the criminal law cannot alone be a basis for federal control or denial of civil rights of action otherwise open to an injured person under provincial common or statute law. Certainly, it could not be argued that a Province could control criminal proceedings by making initial resort to a civil action a bar to criminal prosecution. For a holding to this effect in an analogous situation, see *A. G. Que. v. Lechasseur*, [1981] 2 S.C.R. 253.

There is, however, a case to be made for the validity of federal legislation in limiting or even excluding the civil liability of police officers or others for acts done in the enforcement of the federal criminal law. In *Re Royal Canadian Legion (Branch 177)* (1964), 48 W.W.R. 481 (B.C. S.C.) the Court assumed the validity of federal legislation authorizing the giving an order of protection from civil liability to a justice of the peace who wrongly issued a search warrant, and in refusing such an order in favour of policemen who executed the warrant in an indiscriminate fashion. Certainly there is no doubt as to federal authority to give them immunity from criminal liability, and it is also a proper conclusion that no civil liability can arise from the exercise of powers, *e.g.*, of arrest and search, expressly conferred by federal legislation in connection with enforcement of the criminal law; see for example, *Woodward v. Begbie*, [1962] O.R. 60 (H.C.), which accepted this conclusion where the conduct of the police fell within the protective terms of *Criminal Code*, section 25(4); see also *Fletcher v. Collins*, [1968] 2 O.R. 618 (H.C.). It follows, of course, that an expansion of their powers would enlarge the area of civil immunity of police and others, even if no express federal legislation were enacted on the question of immunity from civil suit: see *Criminal Code*, sections 25-31; and cf. *Frey v. Fedoruk*, [1949] 2 W.W.R. 604, rev'd. on other grounds [1950] S.C.R. 517; *Priestman v. Colangelo and Smythson*, [1959] S.C.R. 615; *Kennedy v. Tomlinson* (1959), 20 D.L.R. (2d) 272 (Ont. C.A.), leave to appeal to S.C.C. refused 20 D.L.R. (2d) 273n (S.C.C.).

Similarly, Parliament can, as an exercise of the criminal law power, enact legislation providing for the return of stolen goods to their owner or for restitution of property or money realized therefrom by a thief: see *Criminal Code*, sections 653-655; and see *R. v. Zelensky*, [1978] 2 S.C.R. 940, reproduced in part *infra*; *R. v. Groves* (1977), 79 D.L.R. (3d) 561 (Ont. H.C.); *Re Torek and The Queen* (1974), 44 D.L.R. (3d) 416 (Ont. H.C.); MacPherson, "The Constitutionality of the Compensation and Restitution Provisions of the Criminal Code — The Picture After *R. v. Zelensky*" (1979), 11 Ottawa L.R. 713. It is important to note, however, that, as stressed by Laskin C.J.C. in *Zelensky*, restitution or compensation orders must be made only in situations commensurate with their valid character as part of the sentencing process. They should not be used as a substitute for a civil trial. Laskin C.J.C. gave the example in *Zelensky* of section 653 not being the "platform upon which to unravel involved commercial transactions . . ." *R. v. Groves, supra* provides a further example holding, *inter alia*, that section 663(2)(e) Criminal Code is not wide enough to permit an order for compensation for pain and suffering. On the validity of section 31.1 of the *Combines Investigation Act*, which provides a civil cause of action in respect of breaches of Part V of the Act; see Finkelstein "Comment", reproduced at Chapter 8, *supra* and the cases cited therein. See also the remarks following the *Goodyear* case reproduced above.

In *Hurley v. Foreman* (1962), 35 D.L.R. (2d) 596 (N.B. S.C.) where an order to pay the medical expenses of an aggrieved person was made as a condition of a recognizance under the then *Criminal Code*, section 638, on suspension of a sentence for assault, it was held that the order did not preclude a civil action for the same assault since it did not amount to a judgment enforceable by plaintiff against defendant; failure to obey the order would merely expose defendant to liability to sentence for the offence of which he was convicted. Even if it is not a judgment, would it not be open to the aggrieved person to sue on the order, as indicated in *R. v. Scherstabitoff*, [1963] 2 C.C.C. 208 (B.C. C.A.) where the validity of the compensation provision in section 653 was assumed? The compensation provisions of the Criminal Code are illustrations of the Code giving rise directly to civil liabilities enforceable by action.

*Criminal Code* section 10 provides that "no civil remedy for an act or omission is suspended or affected by reason that the act or omission is a criminal offence". This provision does away with the rule of public policy by which a civil action based on facts also constituting a crime was suspended until the plaintiff had prosecuted the defendant. The validity of the section was questioned by Duff J. in *MacKenzie v. Palmer* (1921), 62 S.C.R. 517 at 520. See also *Kozlowski v. Workers' Benevolent Society*, [1933] 3 W.W.R. 566 at 571 (Man. C.A.).

In *Lamb v. Benoit*, [1959] S.C.R. 321, Cartwright J. raised, and left unanswered, the question whether the law governing an action for malicious prosecution was part of the criminal law defining the privilege or condition of immunity of a person who sets the criminal proceedings in motion or whether it was simply part of the law of torts and hence definable under provincial law. What is the answer? Is the situation any different from that which would arise if a Province purported to deny or confer a civil cause of action consequent upon a criminal conviction or acquittal?

In *Priestman v. Colangelo and Smythson*, [1959] S.C.R. 615, Cartwright J. raised the question, initially one of construction, whether the justification accorded to a police officer under *Criminal Code*, section 25(4) (in respect of the use of force where a person whom the officer is proceeding lawfully to arrest takes flight) operates only as between the officer and the alleged offender or also extends to injuries suffered by innocent bystanders by reason of the force that is used. He answered it as follows:

> The words of the subsection appear to me to be susceptible of either interpretation and that being so I think we ought to ascribe to them the more restricted meaning. In my opinion, if Parliament intended to enact that grievous bodily harm or death might be inflicted upon an entirely innocent person and that such person or his dependants should be deprived of all civil remedies to which they would otherwise have been entitled in circumstances such as are present in this case, it would have used words declaring such intention without any possible ambiguity.

Where a question arises in civil proceedings whether a party thereto has committed a crime, is there any constitutional reason to doubt the power of the provincial court to make an affirmative determination? In *Nordstrom v. Baumann*, [1962] S.C.R. 147, where the question was whether a wife who had set fire to premises in which her husband died could claim an intestate share in his estate, and this depended on whether she was insane at the time, a majority of the British Columbia Court of Appeal when the case was before it (34 W.W.R. 556) held that a finding of crime could not properly be made on an originating summons concerning insanity or criminality. O'Halloran J.A. said that "in view of the divisional heads in ss. 91 and 92 of the B.N.A. Act . . . a provincially constituted court is without jurisdiction to determine in civil proceedings whether or not a person has committed a crime." The Supreme Court of Canada reversed; and Locke J., addressing himself to the constitutional point, remarked that "if it were not permissible in civil actions to make findings of fact which if proven in criminal proceedings would be held criminal, the due administration of justice would be gravely impeded."

Section 22 of the *Evidence Act*, R.S.O. 1980 c. 145, provides that "a witness may be asked whether he has been convicted of any crime . . ." *Held*, on an issue to determine whether a witness in a civil action may be questioned as to a provincial offence, "crime" in section 22 means an offence under the federal criminal law: *Street v. Guelph*, [1964] 2 O.R. 421 (H.C.).

# R. v. ZELENSKY

In the Supreme Court of Canada. [1978] 2 S.C.R. 940.

Laskin, C.J.C., Martland, Ritchie, Spence, Pigeon, Dickson, Beetz, Estey, and Pratte, JJ. May 1, 1978.

Appeal by the Crown from a judgment of the Manitoba Court of Appeal, 33 C.C.C. (2d) 147, 73 D.L.R. (3d) 596, allowing an appeal by the accused from an order requiring her to make compensation and restitution following her conviction on a charge of theft.

The judgment of Laskin C.J.C. and Martland, Ritchie, Spence, Dickson and Estey JJ. was delivered by

LASKIN C.J.C.: — This appeal, brought here by leave to this Court, challenges the majority judgment of the Manitoba Court of Appeal (Matas, J.A., Hall and O'Sullivan, JJ.A, concurring; Monnin, J.A., Guy, J.A., concurring, dissenting) which invalidated s. 653 of the *Criminal Code* and held also, and in any event, that Provincial Court Judge Collerman erred in law in making an order for compensation under that provision and in directing restitution of stolen property under s. 655. The order for compensation and for restitution was a composite order made at the time the respondent Anne Zelensky was sentenced to imprisonment and to a term of probation after pleading guilty to theft and was in pursuance of an application or such relief made by T. Eaton Company Limited, the victim of the theft.

The validity of s. 655 was not impeached before the Manitoba Court of Appeal or before this Court, and there was nothing in the reasons of Matas, J.A. [33 C.C.C. (2d) 147], which pertained particularly to the direction for restitution of the stolen goods by way of contesting that part of the trial Judge's composite order. It appears to have been swept out by reason of its association with the order for compensation. Counsel for the respondent Anne Zelensky did not complain here of the order for restitution and, in my view, it must stand as a severable order validly made under s. 655, whatever be the disposition as to the order for compensation under s. 653 and as to the validity of this last-mentioned provision.

Sections 653 and 655 read as follows:

653(1) A court that convicts an accused of an indictable offence may, upon the application of a person aggrieved, at the time sentence is imposed, order the accused to pay to that person an amount by way of satisfaction or compensation for loss or damage to property suffered by the applicant as a result of the commission of the offence of which the accused is convicted.

(2) Where an amount that is ordered to be paid under subsection (1) is not paid forthwith the applicant may, by filing the order, enter as a judgment, in the superior court of the province in

which the trial was held, the amount ordered to be paid, and that judgment is enforceable against the accused in the same manner as if it were a judgment rendered against the accused in that court in civil proceedings.

(3) All or any part of an amount that is ordered to be paid under subsection (1) may, if the court making the order is satisfied that ownership of or right to possession of those moneys is not disputed by claimants other than the accused and the court so directs, be taken out of moneys found in the possession of the accused at the time of his arrest.

. . . . .

655(1) Where an accused is convicted of an indictable offence the court shall order that any property obtained by the commission of the offence shall be restored to the person entitled to it, if at the time of the trial the property is before the court or has been detained, so that it can be immediately restored to that person under the order.

(2) Where an accused is tried for an indictable offence but is not convicted, and the court finds that an indictable offence has been committed, the court may order that any property obtained by the commission of the offence shall be restored to the person entitled to it, if at the time of the trial the property is before the court or has been detained, so that it can be immediately restored to that person under the order.

(3) An order shall not be made under this section in respect of

(a) property to which an innocent purchaser for value has acquired lawful title,

(b) a valuable security that has been paid or discharged in good faith by a person who was liable to pay or discharge it,

(c) a negotiable instrument that has, in good faith, been taken or received by transfer or delivery for valuable consideration by a person who had no notice and no reasonable cause to suspect that an indictable offence had been committed, or

(d) property in respect of which there is a dispute as to ownership or right of possession by claimants other than the accused.

(4) An order made under this section shall be executed by the peace officers by whom the process of the court is ordinarily executed.

(5) This section does not apply to proceedings against a trustee, banker, merchant, attorney, factor, broker or other agent entrusted with the possession of goods or documents of title to goods, for an offence under section 290, 291, 292 or 296.

I think it desirable to set out s. 654 as well because it stands as a reinforcement and adjunct to the policy reflected in s. 653. It is in these words:

654(1) Where an accused is convicted of an indictable offence and any property obtained as a result of the commission of the offence has been sold to an innocent purchaser, the court may, upon the application of the purchaser after restitution of the property to its owner, order the accused to pay to the purchaser an amount not exceeding the amount paid by the purchaser for the property.

(2) Where an amount that is ordered to be paid under subsection (1) is not paid forthwith the applicant may, by filing the order, enter as a judgment, in the superior court of the province in which the trial was held, the amount ordered to be paid, and that judgment is enforceable against the accused in the same manner as if it were a judgment rendered against the accused in that court in civil proceedings.

(3) All or any part of an amount that is ordered to be paid under subsection (1) may, if the court making the order is satisfied that ownership of or right to possession of those moneys is not disputed by claimants other than the accused and the court so directs, be taken out of moneys found in the possession of the accused at the time of his arrest.

Sections 653, 654 and 655 have been in the *Criminal Code* in similar but not exact formulation since the *Code*'s enactment in 1892: see ss. 836, 837, 838. The original of the present s. 653, namely s. 836, provided for compensation not exceeding $1,000 upon the application of the person aggrieved, the amount to be deemed a judgment debt owing by the accused and enforceable in the same way as an order for costs under s. 832, which provided, *inter alia*, for satisfaction in whole or in part out of money belonging to and taken from the accused on his arrest.

The provision for compensation was not then tied expressly to the sentencing process as is now the case under s. 653. Under the original of the present s. 654, namely, s. 837, where property involved in the offence was sold to a *bona fide* purchaser and restored to the true owner, the purchaser could apply for compensation out of money of the accused taken from him on his apprehension. The present s. 654 clearly goes farther in providing for an order for a money payment, subject to the Court being able to direct that all or part of the compensation to the purchaser be paid out of money in the possession of the accused at the time of his arrest and which is indisputably his. Neither in ss. 836 or 837 was there any such express provision as now exists in ss. 653 and 654 for filing the order for compensation, with effect as a judgment enforceable as if it was a judgment in civil proceedings.

The principle of restitution under the present s. 655 is carried forward from the original s. 838, but the present provision is more explicit (if, indeed, the original provision covers the point at all) that an order will not be made if there is a dispute as to ownership of the property involved by claimants other than the accused. No such issue arose in the present case and, as I have already said, the order for restitution must stand.

It appears to me that ss. 653, 654 and 655, historically and currently, reflect a scheme of criminal law administration under which property, taken or destroyed or damaged in the commission of a crime, is brought into account following the disposition of culpability, and may be ordered by the criminal Court to be returned to the victimized owner if it is under the control of the Court and its ownership is not in dispute or that reparation be made by the offender, either in whole or in part out of money found in his possession when arrested if it is indisputably his and otherwise under an order for compensation, where the property has been destroyed or damaged.

I think s. 655(2) gives particular emphasis to the scheme in providing for an order of restitution, even if the accused has been acquitted, where the property involved in the commission of an offence is under the control of the Court. The integrity of the scheme is seen in s. 654, already mentioned, which enables the criminal Court to tidy up a situation where stolen property has been sold to a *bona fide* purchaser and it is available for restoration to the victimized owner, the Court authorized upon such restitution to inflict upon the offender a liability to pay to the innocent purchaser what he gave for the goods.

I regard s. 654 as of a piece with s. 388(2), (3) which deals with wilful damage to property where the damage does not exceed $50. The summary conviction Court is authorized to make an award of compensation, not exceeding that amount, to the aggrieved person in addition to any punishment imposed, payment being enforced by a term of imprisonment not exceeding two months. The pecuniary sanction under both s. 388 and s. 654 may be regarded as the imposition of restitutionary fines, with a direction as to the destination of the money, a direction which it is open to Parliament to give: see *Toronto v. The King*, [1932] A.C. 98 (P.C.). It is true that in that case the challenged legislation of Parliament, a provision of the *Criminal Code*, provided for certain fines to be paid to the municipal or local authority but I see no departure from principle and from lawful constitutional authority if they are directed to a victim of a crime or to someone, *e.g.*, the *bona fide* purchaser under s. 654 who has also been victimized as a result thereof. Of course, the characterization of the compensation provided under ss. 388 and 654 spills over to the provisions of s. 653 and has a relation as well to s. 655.

There is a passage in the reasons in *Toronto v. The King, supra*, at p. 104 A.C., which is relevant here. Lord Macmillan, speaking for the Privy Council, said this:

> Turning now to s. 91 of the B.N.A. Act, their Lordships find that "notwithstanding anything in this Act," and therefore notwithstanding the provisions of s. 109, "the exclusive legislative authority of the Parliament of Canada extends to all matters coming within . . . the Criminal Law." Plainly, and indeed admittedly, this confers on the Dominion Parliament the exclusive right by legislation to create and define crimes and to impose penalties for their commission. In their Lordships' opinion it no less empowers the Dominion Legislature to direct how penalties for infraction of the criminal law shall be applied. It has always been regarded as within the scope of criminal legislation to make provision for the disposal of penalties inflicted, as innumerable instances show, and the power to do so is, if not essential, at least incidental, to the power to legislate on criminal matters for it may well go to the efficacy of such legislation. If the power to direct the manner of application of penalties were to be dissociated from the power to create such penalties and were to be lodged in another authority, it is easy to see how penal legislation might be seriously affected, if not stultified.

Section 653 is at the heart of the compensation provisions of the *Criminal Code*, and the question of its validity is a matter of first instance in this Court. We have long abandoned the notion expressed in the judgment of the Privy Council in *Re Board of Commerce Act, 1919 and Combines and Fair Prices Act, 1919*, [1922] 1 A.C. 191 at 199, that there is some fixed "domain of criminal jurisprudence". The Privy Council itself had a different view in *A.-G. Ont. v. Hamilton Street Railway*, [1903] A.C. 524 at 529, where it noted that it was "the criminal law in its widest sense" that fell within exclusive federal competence. If that was true of the substantive criminal law, it was equally true of "procedure in criminal matters", which is likewise confided exclusively to Parliament. Indeed, Duff, C.J.C., said in *Provincial Secretary of Prince Edward Island v. Egan*, [1941] S.C.R. 396 at 401, that ". . . the subject of criminal law entrusted to the Parliament of Canada is necessarily an expanding field by reason of the authority of the Parliament to create crimes, impose punishment for such crimes, and to deal with criminal procedure". We cannot, therefore, approach the validity of s. 653 as if the fields of criminal law and criminal procedure and the modes of sentencing have been frozen as of some particular time. New appreciations thrown up by new social conditions, or reassessments of old appreciations which new or altered social conditions induce make it appropriate for this Court to re-examine courses of decision on the scope of legislative power when fresh issues are presented to it, always remembering, of course, that it is entrusted with a very delicate role in maintaining the integrity of the constitutional limits imposed by the *British North America Act, 1867*.

We are concerned in this case not with a novel form of relief to persons aggrieved by another's criminal conduct, resulting in the loss or destruction of property, but with one in respect of which the novelty is that no challenge has come to this Court on the matter until now. Certainly, as has been often said, time does not validate a statute which is unconstitutional, but I point out that there is an instance in our law where time has invalidated a statute which was generally regarded as constitutional. That was the result of the Margarine Reference, *Reference re Validity of s. 5(a) of Dairy Industry Act (Margarine Case)*, [1949] S.C.R. 1; affirmed [1951] A.C. 179 (*sub nom. Canadian Federation of Agriculture v. A.-G. Que.*) (P.C.) holding that federal legislation prohibiting the manufacture, possession and sale of margarine (first enacted in 1886 when there was concern about the nutritional quality of the product and its danger to health), could not be sustained as an exercise, *inter alia*, of the federal criminal law power because in the intervening years, changes in methods of manufacture and of ingredients had removed any danger to health. Correlatively, it seems to me, the passage of time has resulted in new approaches to criminal law administration so as to confirm the propriety of the long standing provisions of the *Criminal Code* for compensation and restitution.

I would refer in this connection to Working Paper 5 of the Law Reform Commission of Canada, October, 1974, where in dealing with restitution (which it conceives in wide terms, covering and going beyond what is embraced by ss. 653, 654 and 655), the Commission says (at p. 6) that "not only is restitution a natural and just response to crime, it is also a rational sanction". In proposing that "restitution ... become a central consideration in sentencing and dispositions" that it should merit foremost but not exclusive consideration, the Commission made a number of relevant observations (at pp. 7-8):

> Recognition of the victim's needs underlines at the same time the larger social interest inherent in the individual victim's loss. Thus, social values are reaffirmed through restitution to victim. Society gains from restitution in other ways as well. To the extent that restitution works toward self-correction, and prevents or at least discourages the offender's committal to a life of crime, the community enjoys a measure of protection, security and savings. Depriving offenders of the fruits of their crimes or ensuring that offenders assist in compensating victims for their losses should assist in discouraging criminal activity. Finally, to the extent that restitution encourages society to perceive crime in a more realistic way, as a form of social interaction, it should lead to more productive responses not only by Parliament, the courts, police and correctional officials but also by ordinary citizens and potential victims.

Until the decision of the majority of the Manitoba Court of Appeal in the present case, there has not been any pronouncement by a Court in this country in challenge of the validity of ss. 653, 654 and 655. There are decisions which have either assumed the validity of s. 653, or have been silent on it, as, for example, *R. v. Scherstabitoff* (1962), 40 W.W.R. 575 (B.C. C.A.) but where validity has been faced it has been affirmed and I shall come to those cases shortly. At the same time, other types of sanctions than the traditional ones of imprisonment and of fines payable to the Crown have been enacted and sustained upon a challenge to their constitutionality. To take three examples, in *Industrial Acceptance Corp. Ltd. v. The Queen*, [1952] 2 S.C.R. 273, this Court upheld the validity of a provision for forfeiture of property used in the commission of a criminal offence, whether or not the property was owned by a person other than the one convicted; in *Goodyear Tire & Rubber Co. of Canada Ltd. v. The Queen*, [1956] S.C.R. 303, this Court sustained the validity of a provision for a prohibitory order against the continuation or repetition of certain offences defined in the provision, the order to be in addition to any other penalty imposed on the person convicted and to be one which could be directed to the convicted person or any other person and, as indicated in *Sunbeam Corp. (Canada) Ltd. v. The Queen*, [1969] S.C.R. 221, one which may prohibit the repetition or continuance of the offence in respect of other persons than those who were the victims under the charge or by other means that those condemned under the particular conviction; and in *R. v. Groves* (1977), 37 C.C.C. (2d) 429 (Ont. H.C.), O'Driscoll, J., of the Ontario Supreme Court upheld the validity under the federal criminal law power of s. 663(2)(*e*) of the *Criminal Code* which provides that the Court may include in a probation order a requirement that the convicted person, "make restitution or reparation to any person aggrieved or injured by the commission of the offence for the actual loss or damage sustained by that person as a result thereof".

I wish to dwell for a moment on s. 663(2)(*e*) because, in the course of argument on this appeal when reference was made to it, there seemed to be little challenge to its validity on the view that provision for restitution or reparation was so integrally a part of the sentence as to distinguish it from s. 653; and there was the further point that a wilful breach of a prohibition order was an offence under s. 666(1) and punishable on summary conviction.

Apart from the question of enforcement under s. 666(1) (which may be contrasted with the enforcement open under s. 653 by filing the compensation order in a superior Court with effect as a judgment thereof), I see no difference in principle between a provision for reparation in a probation order, as an additional term of what is in effect a sentence, and a direction for compensation or reparation by an order under s. 653 which, if made at all, must be made at the time sentence is imposed. I find little to choose, except on the the side of formality, in the requirement of s. 653 that the compensation order must be based on an application by the person aggrieved rather than be made by the Court *suo motu* as is apparently, but only apparently, the position under s. 663(2)(*e*).

The reasons of the majority of the Manitoba Court of Appeal against the validity of s. 653 are those of Matas, J.A., concurred in by Hall, J.A., and fortified by additional concurring reasons of O'Sullivan, J.A. I note that O'Sullivan, J.A., agreed that monetary penalties may constitutionally be directed for the benefit of victims of crime because, in imposing a pecuniary penalty which would benefit the victim, the Court would still be imposing a penal sanction, that is to say, punishment, and the compensation would flow from the imposition of the penalty. Why then would the learned Justice hold s. 653 to be invalid?

He stated his reasons as follows [33 C.C.C. (2d) 147 at 171]:

> The vice of s. 653, in my opinion, is that it does not regard the payment of an amount equivalent to damage done by a criminal as part of a punishment which will vary with the circumstances of the offence and the offender. It seeks to confer directly on the victim of a crime a right to claim compensation from the wrongdoer. The section, if valid, would confer on the victim of a crime an additional and alternative civil right to sue in a criminal Court for that for which he already has the right to sue in a civil Court. In my opinion, this constitutes an invasion of the field of property and civil rights and is beyond the powers of Parliament.

Matas, J.A., acknowledged in his reasons that an order for compensation under s. 653 is part of the sentencing process but qualified this observation in two ways; first, by pointing out that, although it is included, along with orders under ss. 654 and 655 and dispositions under s. 663(1), in the definition of "sentence" under s. 601 [definition of "sentence" rep. & sub. 1974-75-76, c. 93, s. 72], this provision occurs in a Part of the *Criminal Code* relating to appeals; and, secondly, this inclusion in a definition does not itself determine validity, nor is validity established by the fact that an order under s. 653 is, even apart from the definition in s. 601, made part of the sentencing process under its very terms, since it becomes necessary, in either case, to decide whether it can validly be made part of the sentencing process under the federal criminal law power.

I find these provisions in turn diluted by the agreement of Matas, J.A., with the view of Haines, J., in *Re Torek and The Queen* (1974), 2 O.R. (2d) 228 (H.C.) that compensating victims of crime is a valid object in sentencing. I am unable to appreciate, therefore, why there should be any doubt about the validity of a compensation provision, tied to the sentencing process as is s. 653, unless refuge is taken in a renewal of a notion that there is a proper domain of criminal law which forecloses an extension of the scheme of sanctions, although, admittedly, there is a rational connection between that part of s. 653 which is challenged and that part which is valid: see *Papp v. Papp*, [1970] 1 O.R. 331 at 336 (C.A.).

*Re Torek v. The Queen* (1974), 2 O.R. (2d) 228, appears to contain the most extensive consideration of the issue under review prior to the conclusions of the Manitoba Court of Appeal in the present case. It is relied on heavily by Monnin, J.A., Guy, J.A., concurring, in the dissenting reasons. The *Torek* case came before Haines, J., on a motion for *certiorari* by a convicted person to quash a compensation order against him in favour of the victim. (I note in the reasons that the order was sought by the Crown Attorney acting on behalf of the victim.) I reproduce certain portions of the reasons in *Torek* that sum up most of the considerations, pro and con, that were urged in the argument in this Court. At p. 229 O.R., Haines, J., said this:

> Counsel for the applicant argued forcefully that s. 653 is really legislation pertaining to property and civil rights and falls within the ambit of s. 92(13) of the *British North America Act, 1867*, rather than criminal law. Counsel pointed out that under s. 653, the accused is deprived of many of the protections which he would have in an ordinary civil action. For instance, the defendant does not really have notice of the claim beforehand and cannot defend it properly. He has no right to discovery by which he could attempt to elicit proper proof of value of the articles which allegedly have been stolen. In the present case, one of the articles allegedly stolen by the applicant was a ring owned by Mrs. Kaminsky. The value of that ring was placed at $1,500, but no proof of purchase or of the value of the ring was led before the Court. In arriving at the sum of $4,377.50, His Honour Judge Reville clearly accepted Mr. Kaminsky's testimony as to exactly what was stolen in cash, the ring and liquor. The applicant argues that had Mr. Kaminsky been forced to undertake a civil action to recover the sum, he would have been forced to prove his loss in a stricter manner. However, under s. 653, all that the complainant need do is merely testify as to value and the accused cannot really disprove it. In other words, the protection afforded to a defendant by the *Judicature Act*, R.S.O. 1970, c. 228, and the Rules of Practice, are removed, but the consequence is really the same in the sense in that the complainant gets what is, in effect, a judgment, which by s. 653(2) can be enforced in the provincial superior Courts in the ordinary manner.
>
> I do not think that there can be any doubt that the right to bring and defend an ordinary civil action is a civil right, which is within the competence of provincial legislation. Nor can there be any doubt that in these circumstances, Mr. Kaminsky could have commenced an action against the applicant. However, it does not follow that the federal Government is entirely without power to order restitution or compensation in some circumstances.
>
> In my view, proceedings under s. 653 can be considered to be part of the sentencing process. It is worth noting that in s. 601, which deals with appeals on indictable offences, the word "sentence" is defined to include an order made under s. 653. It seems to me that it is a valid object in sentencing to prevent a convicted criminal from profiting from his crime by serving a jail term and then

keeping the gains of his illegal venture. Counsel for the applicant admitted that it would be proper for the order complained of to have been made as a term of probation, pursuant to s. 663(2)(*e*) and (*h*) . . .

. . . . .

I fail to see that there is any meaningful distinction between an order requiring an accused to make restitution or reparation as set out in s. 663(2)(*e*) and an order requiring an accused to pay by way of satisfaction or compensation as set out in s. 653(1).

More than 50 years ago, Perdue, C.J.M., in *R. v. Cohen and Miller*, [1922] 3 W.W.R. 1126 came to a similar conclusion in the Manitoba Court of Appeal, saying, with respect to the provisions for restitution and compensation, that the matters dealt with in the relevant provisions "seem to me to be incidental to the exclusive legislative authority of Parliament over criminal law and procedure in criminal cases and therefore within its powers" (at p. 1127 W.W.R.). Matas, J.A., referred briefly to *R. v. Cohen and Miller* but refused to regard it as an authority for holding s. 653 to be valid, probably because Perdue, C.J.M., was the only member of the Court who took the constitutional point and, in any event, his pronouncement on it was *obiter*.

In line with the view taken by Haines, J., in *Re Torek v. The Queen, supra*, is the judgment of Hugessen, A.C.J., in *Turcotte v. Gagnon*, [1974] Que. P.R. 309 (S.C.) which arose by way of an application to enter as a judgment of the Superior Court of Quebec an order for compensation made under s. 653 against a convicted person in favour of his victim. In sustaining the validity of the compensation order and allowing it to be entered and enforced as a judgment of the Superior Court, Hugessen, A.C.J., made two points: first, the fact that Parliament has made the compensation order enforceable as a judgment in a civil action is more a call on the administrative side of the Superior Court than on the judicial side but it is, in any event, a means open to Parliament to provide for the execution of an order validly made; and secondly, the compensation order may be regarded as a fine or penalty. His reasons contain the following observations (at pp. 317-8):

> In my view, an order for restitution to the victim of a crime is not only incidental to criminal law and procedure; it may be an inherent part of the sentencing process. While it may be true that, historically, the Common Law did not recognize compensatory orders as being part of the criminal process, I can see no reason why appropriate legislation within the exercise of the criminal law power should not render them so.
>
> . . . . .
>
> In my opinion, Parliament has attempted to provide for such compensation, albeit in an imperfect and partial manner, by the provisions of section 653. As is made clear by section 601, an order under section 653 is a part of the sentence rendered by the criminal court. Proceedings such as the present ones taken in a civil court in order to effect the execution of such an order do not cause it thereby to lose its criminal law character. In effect, all that Parliament has done is to impose upon the provincial superior courts, which are equipped for such purpose, the duty of providing for the execution of an order already given by a court of competent jurisdiction. As already stated in the present judgment, the function of the civil court in such a case is not so much judicial as administrative and I would have no right, on a petition of the present sort, to vary the order made by the Court of Sessions of the Peace even were I minded to do so.
>
> That Parliament may, by appropriate legislation, vest in a provincial superior court a jurisdiction which it did not possess at common law has been established almost since the time of Confederation.

I regard the point taken by Hugessen, A.C.J., with reference to the enforcement procedure under s. 653 as a central one, having regard to the position of the majority of the Manitoba Court of Appeal in the present case. It is not unusual for Parliament to invoke the aid of the provincial Courts for the effective administration of its legislation. A prime example is in the field of bankruptcy where Parliament has enacted not only a comprehensive statute on the substantive law but also has provided for rules of procedure which are administered in the provincial Courts. A good deal was made by those attacking the validity of s. 653 of the provision therein for filing and entering a compensation order as a judgment of the provincial superior Court. This, to me, as it was to Justice Hugessen, is machinery which cannot control the issue of validity.

The *Criminal Code* exhibits another illustration in ss. 656 and 657 of the resort to provincial Courts for enforcement of criminal Court orders. Those sections deal with the imposition of costs in defamatory libel prosecutions, and authorize the party in whose favour costs are awarded to enter judgment for the costs by filing the order in the superior Court of the Province in which the trial was held, and the judgment is to be enforceable in the same way as if it were a judgment in a civil proceeding.

In his extensive reasons for judgment, Matas, J.A., adverts to various considerations affecting the applicability of s. 653 and draws an adverse constitutional conclusion when comparisons are drawn between the procedures in a civil action for damages and the relative position of the accused as a defendant in such an action and his position as a convicted person against whom an order is sought under s. 653. I do not disagree that in assessing constitutionality there is merit in such an approach, but relative advantages in applicable procedures cannot, in my opinion, be determinative of validity where the primary consideration is a more functional one, with regard being had to the object of the inpugned legislation and its connection with other admittedly valid aspects of the criminal process. It appears to me that in his stress on the comparisons above-noted Matas, J.A., has put answer before question in remarking [at p. 168 C.C.C.] that "a compensation order which is invalid, as an unwarranted invasion of provincial jurisdiction, does not become valid because of the objective in preventing a criminal from profiting from his crime". In my opinion, the issue before us has been met by Monnin, J.A., in his dissenting reasons where he said this [at pp. 152-3 C.C.C.]:

> In pith and substance, s. 653 is part and parcel of the sentencing process set out in the *Criminal Code* of Canada. If it were not, the hands of our Courts would be sadly tied and the victims of crimes would of necessity have to seek recovery of property or moneys illegally taken away from them through civil courts on the basis that one cannot mix that which is criminal with that which is civil and on the further basis that provincially appointed Judges are not fit persons to deal with matters of civil law. Can one think of a more ridiculous proposition and one bound to bring the entire legal process — already badly challenged — in disrepute? Distinctions for the sake of distinctions have no place in Courts of law.

I agree with his conclusion that s. 653 is valid as part of the sentencing process.

The constitutional basis of s. 653 must, in my opinion, be held in constant view by a Judge called upon to apply its terms. It would be wrong, therefore, to relax in any way the requirement that the application for compensation be directly associated with the sentence imposed as the public reprobation of the offence. Monnin,

J.A., mentioned this in bringing compensation, restitution and probation into relation with one another, saying this in this reasons [p. 153 C.C.C.]:

> I see little or no difference between restitution and compensation as they are described in ss. 653 and 663. Compensation must be requested by the aggrieved person at the time sentence is about to be imposed and there is case law to the effect that a request for compensation must be made at the time of sentencing and cannot be made at a later date. Restitution can be ordered by the sentencing Judge as a part of his total sentence if it forms part of the probation order. In ordering restitution, the Judge may act pursuant to a request by Crown counsel or by the aggrieved party or may also do so of his own free will without any request by anyone.
>
> Restitution has often been equated with compensation except that there is a special section, namely, s. 653, which deals with compensation for loss or damage of property suffered by a victim. So much so that even this Court, though differently constituted in *R. v. Butkans*, decided June 18, 1970, [unreported] — a Court composed of Smith, C.J.M., Dickson, J.A., and myself, — confirmed what we called in that particular case an order of restitution under s. 638(2)(*e*) of the *Criminal Code*, which section is identical to the existing s. 663(2)(*e*). In the *Butkans* case the Court was actually dealing with a matter of compensation, though it had been called an order of restitution. Was that Bench acting *per incuriam*? I doubt it.

There is, moreover, another important aspect of s. 653 that must be kept in mind. The Court's power to make a concurrent order for compensation as part of the sentencing process is discretionary. I am of the view that in exercising that discretion the Court should have regard to whether the aggrieved person is invoking s. 653 to emphasize the sanctions against the offender as well as to benefit himself. A relevant consideration would be whether civil proceedings have been taken and, if so, whether they are being pursued. There are other factors that enter into the exercise of the discretion, such as the means of the offender, and whether the criminal Court will be involved in a long process of assessment of the loss, although I do not read s. 653 as requiring exact measurement. A plea of guilty will, obviously, make the Court's task easier where it is asked to make an order of compensation, but there is no reason why an attempt to secure agreement on the amount of loss should not be made where the conviction follows a plea of not guilty. It is probable, of course, that the likelihood of an appeal will militate against agreement but I would add that I do not regard it as a function of the criminal Court to force agreement to enable it to make an order for compensation. What all of this comes to is that I agree with Matas, J.A., that, constitutionality apart, an order for compensation should only be made with restraint and with caution. . . .

The present case is one in which restraint and caution should have been exercised in a refusal to make a compensation order. The aggrieved company instituted civil proceedings, for the recovery of money and merchandise stolen from it by the offenders, a day before criminal charges were brought against them. It continued with the civil proceedings, taking steps in connection therewith while the criminal proceedings were in progress, and even after the offenders had pleaded guilty to theft. The aggrieved company then decided to seek a compensation order under s. 653 and a dispute arose with respect to the amount of the loss, particularly in relation to the money that was allegedly stolen. So far as appears, the civil proceedings were maintained while the application for compensation order was pursued. The civil proceedings were justified because of the desire to get a garnishment order. In all the circumstances, I would not interfere with that part of the judgment of the majority of the Manitoba Court of Appeal holding that the order for compensation should not have been made.

I wish to dwell further on the course of proceedings in this case in order to provide some guidance to trial Judges on the proper application of s. 653 and in order to make clear that s. 653 is not to be used *in terrorem* as a substitute for or a reinforcement for civil proceedings. Its validity is based, as I have already said, on its association with the sentencing process, and its administration in particular cases must be limited by that consideration.

What emerges from the facts here is that the T. Eaton Company sought to use the criminal process as a more expeditious means of recovering the money lost by the fraudulent activities of the accused. Its co-operation with the Crown during the early course of the criminal proceedings is understandable, but at the same time it was pursuing a civil remedy against the accused, and the civil proceedings had reached the stage of discovery when the accused came up for sentencing by the criminal Court. Eaton's then joined in the criminal proceedings as an "aggrieved person", and it became evident immediately that the amount of the loss suffered by it was in dispute. The dispute was not resolved, as it would have been under the procedures available in a civil Court, and the order for compensation made in the criminal proceedings was somewhat arbitrary as to amount.

Section 653 does not spell out any procedure for resolving a dispute as to quantum; its process is, *ex facie*, summary but I do not think that it precludes an inquiry by the trial Judge to establish the amount of compensation, so long as this can be done expeditiously and without turning the sentencing proceedings into the equivalent of a civil trial or into a reference in a civil proceeding. What is important is to contain s. 653 within its valid character as part of the sentencing process and thus avoid the allegation of intrusion into provincial legislative authority in relation to property and civil rights in the Province. Although, as I have already noted, the Courts have recognized the wide scope of the federal power in relation to criminal law and criminal procedure, and although there is now a broad range of powers in a sentencing Court to deal with offenders, it none the less remains true that the criminal law cannot be used to disguise an encroachment upon provincial legislative authority: see *Re Reciprocal Ins. Legislation*, [1924] A.C. 328 (P.C.); *Reference re Validity of s. 5(q) of the Dairy Industry Act (Margarine Case)*, [1949] S.C.R. 1 at 50; affirmed [1951] A.C. 179 (*sub nom. Canadian Federation of Agriculture v. A.-G. Quebec*).

It must be obvious, therefore, that s. 653 is not the platform upon which to unravel involved commercial transactions in order to provide monetary redress to those entitled thereto as against an accused. The latter, too, may have a proper interest in insisting that civil proceedings be taken against him so that he may avail himself of the procedures for discovery and production of documents, as well as of a proper trial of issues which go to the merit of monetary claims against him. Again, the criminal Court cannot be expected to nor should it act under s. 653 if it would be required to interpret written documents in order to arrive at a sum of money sought through an order of compensation. So too, it would be improper to invoke s. 653 if the effect of provincial legislation would have to be considered in order to determine what order should be made. Indeed, any serious contest on legal or factual issues, or on whether the person alleging himself to be aggrieved is so in fact, should signal a denial of recourse to an order under s. 653.

There looms in this case an obvious question of the effect of a discretionary order for compensation under s. 653 upon subsequent civil proceedings by the victim against the accused, if he has not been made whole by the order. Parliament has not purported to interfere with any right of civil recourse which thus remains open despite s. 653. What is involved is whether the obtaining of an order under s. 653 (not the mere application therefor) amounts to an election against civil proceedings or whether the order goes simply to quantum if civil proceedings are later taken. I am inclined to the view of an election as being consistent with the criminal law character of s. 653, but no argument was addressed to the Court on this point, the respondent being content with a submission in her supplementary factum that if s. 653 was valid, the trial Judge's admitted discretion to make a compensation order should not have been exercised. It does not raise a constitutional issue and since the result here does not call for its determination, I prefer to leave it open.

I wish to advert to one further point and that is the question of appeal from an order for compensation. The filing of such an order in the provincial superior Court does not, in my opinion, put in motion any civil proceedings other than those relating to enforcement. A compensation order, being included in the definition of "sentence" under s. 601 of the *Criminal Code*, is appealable as provided by that *Code*, and I would apply the principle of *Pringle v. Fraser*, [1972] S.C.R. 821, to exclude any suggestion that civil appeal proceedings are open.

Section 616 of the *Criminal Code* deals with the powers of a provincial Court of appeal in respect of an order for compensation and provides for suspension of the operation of the order during the time it is appealable and until appeal proceedings, if taken, are concluded. Section 616(2) empowers the provincial Court of Appeal to annul or vary a compensation order, whether or not the conviction is quashed. It does not itself give a right of appeal, a view expressed on the then similar English legislation in *R. v. Elliott*, [1908] 2 K.B. 452. It appears, therefore, that only the accused has a right of appeal against a compensation order, a right given by s. 603(1)(*b*), and not the person in whose favour the compensation order is made. This, in my view, is consistent with the character of such an order as part of sentence.

I would, accordingly, allow the appeal in part, set aside the order of the Manitoba Court of Appeal in so far as it interfered with the order for restitution and restore that part of the composite order made by the trial Judge. In accordance with the terms of the order of this court granting leave, the Attorney-General of Manitoba will pay the costs of the respondent in this Court. There will be no other order as to costs.

*Appeal allowed in part.*

[The dissenting opinion of Pigeon J., Beetz and Pratte JJ. concurring, is omitted.]

## 4. Attaching Criminal Consequences to Provincially Regulated Matters

## BOGGS v. THE QUEEN

In the Supreme Court of Canada. [1981] 1 S.C.R. 49.

Laskin C.J.C., Dickson, Beetz, Estey, McIntyre, Chouinard and Lamer JJ.
February 3, 1981.

Appeal by the accused from a judgment of the Ontario Court of Appeal, dismissing his appeal from conviction for driving while disqualified contrary to s. 238(3) of the *Criminal Code*.

The judgment of the Court was delivered by

ESTEY J.: — In his appeal we are concerned with a challenge to the constitutionality of s. 238(3) of the *Criminal Code* of Canada. The case arises out of convictions of the appellant on August 5, 1977, in a Provincial Court for driving an automobile while impaired, contrary to s. 234 [am. 1974-75-76, c. 93, s. 14] of the *Criminal Code*; and for refusing to take a breath test, contrary to s. 235 [rep. & sub. *idem*, s. 15] of the *Code*. Following these convictions, the appellant's driver's licence was automatically suspended by administrative action pursuant to s. 20(1) [rep. & sub. 1977, c. 54, s. 2; am. 1978, c. 90, s. 2] of the *Highway Traffic Act*, R.S.O. 1970, c. 202. The appellant was thereafter charged with driving an automobile on August 11, 1979, while disqualified by reason of the suspension of his licence to drive a motor vehicle in the Province of Ontario, contrary to s. 238(3) of the *Code*. In the ensuing proceedings in Provincial Court, the appellant was convicted, the court finding that s. 238(3) was *intra vires* the Parliament of Canada.

The same issue arose in the Ontario Courts in parallel proceedings in *R. v. Akey* (unreported), where Judge Clendenning of the Provincial Court found the *Code* section to be *ultra vires*; the High Court of Ontario, on a stated case, reversed this decision in a judgment by Montgomery J. [1 M.V.R. 78]. The Court of Appeal in both proceedings found s. 238(3) to be *intra vires* and accordingly dismissed the appeal by the appellant Boggs from his conviction on the merits [*loc. cit.*, p. 293].

In this Court, leave to appeal was granted in respect of the following question:

> Did the Court of Appeal err in law in holding that the enactment of s.s. 238(3) of the Criminal Code was *intra vires* of the Parliament of Canada?

Section 238(3) of the *Criminal Code* of Canada provides as follows:

> 238(3)  Every one who drives a motor vehicle in Canada while he is disqualified or prohibited from driving a motor vehicle by reason of the legal suspension or cancellation, in any province, of his permit or licence or of his right to secure a permit or licence to drive a motor vehicle in that province is guilty of
>
> (a)  an indictable offence and is liable to imprisonment for two years; or
> (b)  an offence punishable on summary conviction.
>
> . . . . .

A review of the highway legislation of all the Provinces reveals that generally, provision is made in provincial statutes for the suspension of driver's licences upon conviction of offences in the *Criminal Code* related to the operation of motor vehicles; for the failure to pay motor vehicle related civil judgments, or to make like payments to vehicle accident compensation funds established by the Province; and for failure to pay any such civil judgments rendered in other Provinces or States of the United States with like legislation; for violation of the rules of the road as declared by provincial statute or regulation; and for the violation of provincial schemes relating to the taxation and licensing of motor vehicles, fuel oil, etc. The employment of the device of administrative and judicial disqualification of the driver's licence by the Provinces has apparently come a long way since the days of [*R. v. Whynacht* (1941), 77 C.C.C. 1 (N.S. C.A.)] where Graham J. noted (at p. 8 C.C.C.) that the purpose of the reference in s. 238(3) (then 285(8)), was (and I repeat it for emphasis):

> . . .to prevent an unfit driver from driving on the highway. . . . and the inference from revocation of his licence is that he is not a fit person to drive a motor vehicle and that it would be dangerous to allow him to drive because the revocation must be presumed to have been for just cause . . .

It is obvious that a suspension of an owner's licence for the non-payment of a judgment arising out of the driving of an authorized driver, or suspension or revocation by reason of the non-payment of a fuel oil bill relating to domestic heating oil, have no relationship in practice or in theory to the owner's ability to drive and hence to public safety on the highways of the nation.

The effect of s. 238(3) takes on two separate characteristics. Where the suspension of a driver's licence results from provincial administrative action in response to a conviction for an offence under the *Criminal Code*, s. 238(3), it operates to create a new offence under the *Code* in addition to the provincial offence of driving while under disqualification: see the Ontario *Highway Traffic Act*, ss. 13 [rep. & sub. 1973, c. 167, s. 3; am. 1974, c. 123, s. 3; 1978, c. 24, s. 2; c. 90, s. 1] and 30, or similar legislation in British Columbia, the *Motor Vehicle Act*, R.S.B.C. 1979, c. 288, s. 12(1)(*a*). Where, however, the suspension or cancellation results from the provincial administrative action, as for example under the Ontario *Highway Traffic Act*, s. 138, or by judicial action under a provincial statute, as for example the Alberta legislation s. 238(3) creates a new punishment under the *Code* for breach of the provincial law or regulation without any distinction in the punishment so applied as between the first case, that is where the initial breach was itself a *Code* offence, and the second case, where the breach relates to a provincial regulation. In either case, the offence is complete only after the introductory action taken by a provincial authority (or a Court) under a provincial statute, and the breach of the provincially-ordained suspension, which breach, by s. 238(3), constitutes an offence under the *Code*. This Court, in considering this aspect of s. 238(3) in *R. v. Mansour*, [1979] 2 S.C.R. 916 at 924], said:

> Section 234(1) describes the offence without reference to any provincial statute or licence requirement. All that is required is that a person have the care and control of a motor vehicle as defined in the *Code* while his ability to drive is impaired as likewise defined in the *Code*. In ascertaining the width and breadth of the offence, it is unnecessary to look beyond the *Criminal Code. In contrast, s. 238(3) has no application unless a Province has suspended or cancelled the accused's licence or permit to drive.*

(Emphasis added.)

The issue then is reached, can Parliament validly exercise its criminal power under s. 91(27) by attaching penal consequences by means of a *Criminal Code* provision (here s. 238(3)) to a breach of an order made administratively or judicially under a valid provincial statute, without any necessary relationship to the conduct that led to such an order?

Parliament cannot, of course, invade the proper sphere of the provincial Legislature by simply adopting the guise or disguise of criminal legislation under s. 91(27) of the *British North America Act, 1867.* As Lord Atkin stated in *A.-G. B.C. v. A.-G. Can.*, [1937] A.C. 368 at 375-6:

> The only limitation on the plenary power of the Dominion to determine what shall or shall not be criminal is the condition that Parliament shall not in the guise of enacting criminal legislation in truth and in substance encroach on any of the classes of subjects enumerated in s. 92. It is no objection that it does in fact affect them. If a genuine attempt to amend the criminal law, it may obviously affect previously existing civil rights. The object of an amendment of the criminal law as a rule is to deprive the citizen of the right to do that which, apart from the amendment, he could lawfully do.
>
> No doubt the plenary power given by s. 91(27) does not deprive the Provinces of their right under s. 92(15) of affixing penal sanctions to their own competent legislation. On the other hand, there seems to be nothing to prevent the Dominion, if it thinks fit in the public interest, from applying the criminal law generally to acts and omissions which so far are only covered by provincial enactments.

See also *A.-G. Can. v. A.-G. Alta.*, [1922] 1 A.C. 191 at 198-9 (P.C.), *per* Viscount Haldane, and *Toronto Electric Com'rs v. Snider*, [1925] A.C. 396 at 408 (P.C.), *per* Viscount Haldane:

> It is obvious that these provisions dealt with civil rights, and it was not within the power of the Dominion Parliament to make this otherwise by imposing merely ancillary penalties. The penalties for breach of the restrictions did not render the statute the less an interference with civil rights in its pith and substance. The Act is not one which aims at making striking generally a new crime.

It is to be observed at once that here we have a situation wherein the Province does not seek to subject the citizen to a *quasi*-penal punishment in the sense that the fine or imprisonment or other disadvantage is scaled to the nature of the offence, but rather, at least in this case where administrative action is taken in response to the non-payment of a provincial tax or fee under a provincial regulatory scheme, the imposition of the suspension is directed towards compelling payment of the fee rather than punishing an offence. Thus, we have the situation described in the opening sentence of the above excerpt from the judgment of Viscount Haldane. Here, the Dominion is criminalizing an action which may have been prohibited by the Province only as a coercive measure to bring about the operation of a provincial plan, be it taxation or regulation.

. . . .

[His Lordship reviewed a number of cases on the scope of the federal criminal law power and continued:]

Can it be a valid exercise of the criminal law interest of Parliament to add penal consequences to a provincial suspension order directed to the more efficient administration of a provincial taxation scheme? The difficulty is that there may be circumstances ... where the community interest in safety on the road attracts a proper exercise of legislative authority in the field of criminal law. Especially true is the opposite proposition, namely, that there can be no readily discernible community interest in the criminalization of the administration of a wholesale or retail licensing system. Unfortunately, s. 238 is, on this aspect, wholly inarticulate. There is nothing to sever so as to preserve that which may be constitutionally proper. Nor can the principle of "reading down" be applied as this would entail a scrutiny in each trial of the original disqualification procedure, which may not, as in the *Akey* case, *supra*, be before the Court hearing the charge under s. 238(3).

. . . .

I therefore conclude that s. 238(3) is *ultra vires* Parliament and the appeal should be allowed and the conviction of the appellant set aside.

*Appeal allowed.*

### Note

Estey J. did not refer in *Boggs to A.G.-B.C. v. Smith*, [1967] S.C.R. 702, previously discussed in "Note on the Criminal Law Power and the Young Offender," where the Supreme Court of Canada held that Parliament could validly create the offence of "delinquency" for young offenders covering breaches of federal, provincial or municipal laws pursuant to its criminal law power. The *Smith* holding was not restricted to such provincial laws which might, in addition to their provincial aspect, have a federal criminal law aspect as well. How consistent are *Boggs* and *Smith*? Should age alone be a relevant touchstone of federal jurisdiction pursuant to section 91(27)? See the "Note" referred to above for further elaboration of this idea.

## 5. Public Health and Morality
### SCHNEIDER v. THE QUEEN

In the Supreme Court of Canada. [1982] 2 S.C.R. 112.

Laskin C.J.C., Martland, Ritchie, Dickson, Beetz, Estey, McIntyre, Chouinard and Lamer JJ. August 9, 1982.

Appeal by the plaintiff from a judgment of the British Columbia Court of Appeal, [1981] 1 W.W.R. 511, allowing an appeal by the Crown from a judgment of McEachern C.J.S.C., [1980] 2 W.W.R. 27 and 691, 17 B.C.L.R. 37 and 92, allowing her application for a declaration.

LASKIN C.J.C.: — I am in agreement with Dickson J. that in its thrust as public health legislation in the province, providing thereunder for voluntary and compulsory treatment, the *Heroin Treatment Act*, S.B.C. 1978, c. 24 [now R.S.B.C. 1979, c. 166], is *intra vires*. This conclusion must not be taken as excluding the Parliament of Canada from legislating in relation to public health, viewed as directed to protection of the national welfare. In the present case, there is no preclusive or superseding federal legislation. Even Part II of the *Narcotic Control Act*, R.S.B.C. 1970, c. N-1, providing for custodial treatment upon a conviction of a narcotic offence, remains unproclaimed. However, it is unnecessary to come to a determination whether on such a proclamation the provincial Act would become inoperable.

There is one other point I wish to make and it relates to the difficulties in this case raised by the majority judgment of this court in *R. v. Hauser*, [1979] 1 S.C.R. 984. It appears to be that case, in treating the *Narcotic Control Act* as an exercise of the federal residuary power to legislate for the peace, order and good government of Canada, that underpinned the reasons of McEachern C.J.S.C., invalidating the present provincial Act. Dickson J., in his reasons in this case, adequately disposed of the residuary power as a bar to the provincial Act, but I do not myself hesitate to say that, in my view, the majority judgment in the *Hauser* case ought not to have placed the *Narcotic Control Act* under the residuary power. Unless we revert to a long abandoned view of the peace, order and good government power as embracing the entire catalogue of federal legislative powers, I would myself have viewed the *Narcotic Control Act* as an exercise of the federal criminal law power (as did Dickson J. dissenting on another point in *Hauser*); and, had I sat in *Hauser*, I would have supported the reasons of Spence J. who, in *Hauser*, saw the *Narcotic Control Act* as referable to both the criminal law power and to the trade and commerce power (at pp. 1003-4 S.C.R.).

It is of some relevance to note that this court, speaking through Martland J., in *R. v. Aziz*, [1981] 1 S.C.R. 188, was cautious in its endorsement of *Hauser* as basing the *Narcotic Control Act* entirely on the peace, order and good government clause. There is, in my view, good ground to reconsider that basis of decision, resting as it did on a bare majority judgment.

The judgment of MARTLAND, RITCHIE, DICKSON, BEETZ, McINTYRE, CHOUINARD and LAMER JJ. was delivered by

DICKSON J.: — The appellant, Brenda Ruth Schneider, has brought this action on her own behalf, and on behalf of all persons in British Columbia who are, or who may be, psychologically or physically dependent upon a narcotic as defined in the *Heroin Treatment Act*, 1978 (B.C.), c. 24 [now R.S.B.C. 1979, c. 166]. She challenges the constitutional validity of the Act and seeks a declaration that it is *ultra vires* the provincial Legislature, in particular the plan for compulsory treatment and detention of heroin users established by the Act.

The constitutional question as settled by the order of the Chief Justice is brief and to the point: "Is the *Heroin Treatment Act*, S.B.C. 1978, c. 24 *ultra vires* the legislature of the Province of British Columbia?"

I

*Narcotics control legislation*

The federal Parliament has enacted over the years a series of increasingly elaborate statutes for the control of narcotic drugs. The first, comprising two sections, was passed in 1908, "An Act to prohibit the importation, manufacture and sale of Opium for other than medicinal purposes", 1908 (Can.), c. 50. This was followed in 1911 by the *Opium and Drug Act*, 1911 (Can.), c. 17, in 1923 by the *Opium and Narcotic Drug Act*, 1923 (Can.), c. 22, and in 1961 by "An Act to provide for the Control of Narcotic Drugs", 1961 (Can.), c. 35, what is now in effect the present Act entitled *Narcotic Control Act*, R.S.C. 1970, c. N-1.

Part I of the present Act lists four offences: (i) possession of narcotic, the offender being liable upon conviction on indictment to imprisonment for seven years; (ii) trafficking in a narcotic, the offender being liable to imprisonment for life; (iii) importing or exporting a narcotic, the maximum penalty being imprisonment for life, the minimun penalty being seven years; (iv) cultivating opium poppy or marijuana, the penalty being seven years' imprisonment.

Part II of the Act, not yet proclaimed, bears the title "Preventive Detention and Custody for Treatment", and provides among other things, for a sentence of "custody for treatment for an indeterminate period, in lieu of any other sentence that might be imposed" upon conviction for a narcotic offence (s. 17(1)). Section 19(1) of Part II provides:

> 19(1) Where the legislature of a province enacts legislation that is designed to provide custody for treatment for persons who, although not charged with the offence of possession of a narcotic, are narcotic addicts, the Minister may enter into an agreement with the province, subject to the approval of the Governor in Council, for the confinement and treatment of such persons in institutions maintained and operated pursuant to the Penitentiary Act and for the release and supervision of such persons pursuant to the Parole Act.

Part II of the Act, when enacted in 1961, was expressed to come into force upon proclamation. To date, no proclamation has been made.

. . . .

## III

*Further background*

The question whether jurisdiction in respect of the treatment of narcotic addicts lay in the federal or in the provincial domain was considered in 1955 by the special committee of the Senate on the traffic in narcotic drugs. The committee concluded that it fell within provincial competence (at p. xix):

> The Committee points out that it is not within the constitutional authority of the federal government to assume responsibility for treatment of drug addicts nor to enact the kind of legislation necessary in that connection. This legislation would need to include the compulsory treatment of addiction, the legal supervision and control over the individual during treatment and the right of control of an individual following treatment to prevent his return to the use of drugs, former associations or habits. These are considered to be matters beyond the competence of the federal government.

In 1973 the *Final Report of the Commission of Inquiry into the Non-Medical Use of Drugs* (the LeDain Commission) was published. The report also considered the constitutional framework of legislation in Canada dealing with the non-medical use of drugs. The report comes down firmly on the side of provincial competence with respect to compulsory treatment legislation: "it is directed to the elimination of a medical condition rather than the deterrence of crime" (at p. 927). Earlier in the report one reads (at p. 923):

It is clearly established that the provinces have jurisdiction to provide for civil commitment or compulsory treatment. There is legislation for the involuntary confinement of mentally disordered persons in all of the provinces. The statement of the grounds for such confinement varies but generally speaking it is that the patient suffers from mental disorder in such a degree that hospitalization is required "for his own protection or welfare or that of others" or "in the interests of his own safety or the safety of others". There is also legislative provision in some provinces for the compulsory treatment of drug dependent persons, including alcoholics, either under the mental health legislation or some special statute. The constitutional basis for compulsory treatment legislation in the provinces would appear to be section 92(7) of the *B.N.A. Act* respecting the establishment of hospitals and asylums, section 92(13) respecting property and civil rights, including questions of incapacity and the protection of incapables, and section 92(16) which covers the residual provincial jurisdiction with respect to matters of health.

Finally, we come to the 1977 British Columbia report entitled *A Plan for the Treatment and Rehabilitation of Heroin Users in British Columbia*, prepared by the Alcohol and Drug Commission for the provincial Minister of Health, and which preceded the enactment of the *Heroin Treatment Act*. The report introduces the subject with the statement that the Province of British Columbia has had to contend with a drug addiction problem for 68 years and has within this period had not less than 60% or 70% of all known heroin addicts in Canada living within its borders. The voluntary programmes have, in general, it is said, attracted only a very small proportion of the user population, either the highly motivated or the desperate. Among other statements one reads in the course of a very lengthy report are the following. The problem of heroin use in Canada as well as in British Columbia has increased more than 500% since 1956 and British Columbia has consistently had the most serious problem of any province. It is estimated that 60% of crime in the province is drug related and that the heroin trade generates $255 million annually. In the view of the authors of the report it was a problem which had to be attacked through the co-ordination of treatment and enforcement programmes (at p. 105):

> In conclusion, it appears that since 1956 law enforcement efforts have not succeeded in stopping the spread of heroin or reducing its use in British Columbia. It is probable, however, that these efforts have been responsible for limiting the rate of growth of this problem and that more recent strategies have contributed to an overall decrease in availability and purity and an increase in costs, the effects of which are yet to be determined. What is now required is a more concerted effort, co-ordinated between all levels of enforcement, the criminal justice system and treatment. Only by working together and by viewing the problem as one that is of concern to everybody will observable success be attained.

Among the alternative courses of action listed are (at p. 106):

> Continue the present situation, characterized by the present drug laws and enforcement patterns to control supply, and rely on voluntary treatment programmes to reduce demand. Design a system which would change the law and enforcement patterns by allowing some type of legal heroin supply. Design a system which would allow individuals apprehended under the present legislation to be diverted to a long-term programme aimed at reducing their involvement in the heroin scene. Design a system which would reduce the demand for heroin by intervening directly into the drug use patterns of the current users.

Continuance of the current situation was rejected because "it is clear that our current system puts us on an endless treadmill where a large expenditure on enforcement is essential to keep the problem under control, and a constantly high level of crime is an additional price we pay" (at p. 108). Legalized heroin "does not provide the hope of any lasting solution or significant reduction of the overall problem.

Heroin would be readily available and without an ongoing commitment to enforcement there would always be a potential growing addict population" (at p. 109). The option of sending individuals who are addicted, once they are convicted of an offence, to a programme that would deal with their addiction suffered the disadvantage that "it would still be necessary for someone to be convicted of an offence before they could enter the system" (at p. 110). The fourth alternative, "Direction into Treatment" was favoured (at p. 111):

> A programme of direction into treatment would place a new emphasis on controlling the heroin user to discourage him from using narcotics and to encourage him to effect a significant change in his life-style. The twofold objective of removing the current using population from active use of the illicit drug and rehabilitating as many as possible could be anticipated to have some major positive effects.

The judge at trial and counsel for the appellant laid emphasis upon the following passage from the report (at p. 113):

> Contrary to the opinions of some, the heroin user does not suffer from a disease in the traditional sense, but in fact accepts and in some case enjoys his dependency. Dependency is not, for the majority who are not medical cases, a social disease either, but a learned condition. Few, if any, users are unaware of the potential danger of the drug and of the legal consequences of its use, prior to involvement in the subculture. Notwithstanding the above, dependency, once established, requires both medical and social intervention.

All that I would take from the above passage is that the heroin user does not suffer from a disease in the traditional sense but, nevertheless, dependency once established requires both social intervention and medical intervention.

In discussing method the report notes that in order to avoid establishing a precedent, a detailed examination was made of existing federal and provincial legislation including the *Mental Health Act*, the *Health Act*, the *Venereal Disease Suppression Act* and the *Regulations for Control of Communicable Diseases*. The conclusion is reached that "In the British Columbia Provincial Acts and Regulations, authority is vested in specified officials to direct persons into treatment where warranted for their own or others' well-being with appropriate penalties for non-compliance" (at p. 117) and "therefore, consideration of some form of direction into treatment is NOT precedent setting", *ibid*.

The key unit envisaged in the total system of care for the heroin user would be the area co-ordinating centre where a decision would be reached by an evaluation panel as to use, type of support and duration of support required, predicated on the historical, biochemical and clinical evidence provided the evaluation panel of the centre after diagnosis. The director, acting on the advice of the panel, would make the decision as to direction into treatment or otherwise.

Depending on the examination, evaluation and findings, under the authority of the director, the patient might be channelled into support by one of the four following procedures:

– Referral to a supportive in-patient unit where committal for treatment is authorized.
– Referral to a supportive in-patient unit where voluntary admission is requested and approved.

– Referral to a community clinic where a personal history justifies such a procedure.

– Release without prejudice where the examination criteria do not indicate use or dependency.

On the subject of "Period of Control" the report reads (at p. 127):

> Subject to a satisfactory treatment and after-care record, the medical entry plan envisages the total system of treatment and after-care being three years.
>
> In cases where the user is directed to a treatment centre the time spent in treatment will be six months which may be extended for a further six-month period with the approval of the Board of Review. Where rapid response to the treatment regimen is confirmed, the Director of the treatment centre may, at the appropriate time, authorize the transfer of the patient to a community clinic or directly to community supervision.
>
> In cases where the user is committed to a community clinic the time spent in treatment may be a period of one year which may be extended for a further six months with the approval of the Board of Review.
>
> In the case of voluntary entry, the treatment phase can be omitted or the time spent in treatment materially reduced, if the initial evaluation or satisfactory progress of the patient warrants such a decision.
>
> Notwithstanding the above, the time spent in total in the system (3 years) cannot be reduced.

The report recommended that the Minister of Health set up such treatment programmes as would offer assistance to the individual, and be in conformity with the overall plan. The programmes might include: psychiatric assessment and counselling; behavioural modification, hypnosis; professional intensive individual counselling, group or family therapy; chemotherapy such as use of a narcotic antagonist, immunological techniques if developed, narcotic support in special cases; training for employment support.

IV

*The Heroin Treatment Act*

The *Heroin Treatment Act* was enacted by the Legislative Assembly of the Province of British Columbia on June 28, 1978. It was given royal assent on June 29, 1978, and came into force by proclamation on July 27, 1978.

The Act provides a comprehensive programme for the evaluation, treatment and rehabilitation of narcotic dependent persons. It makes provision for the creation and administration of treatment centres and clinics for persons dependent on narcotics as defined in the Act, essentially heroin and methadone. Extraordinary powers are given to the directors and evaluation panels of the area co-ordinating centres which are charged with the task of examining persons believed to be dependent on narcotics. The evaluation panel consists of at least two medical practitioners and one other person. The panel conducts medical and psychological examinations at the centre and reports in writing to the director "as to whether the person is or is not in need of treatment for narcotic dependency and where, in its opinion, treatment is needed, make[s] recommendations to the director respecting the treatment" (s. 4(2)). For the purpose of this examination a person may be detained at the centre for up to 72 hours and he must furnish a sample of blood and urine.

Where treatment is recommended by the panel, the person may consent to committal for treatment. Where the panel is unanimous in recommending treatment and the person does not voluntarily submit to treatment, the director of the centre may apply, *ex parte* if need be, to the Supreme Court of British Columbia for a committal order. The court must be satisfied that the person is in need of treatment for narcotic dependency.

A director is required to develop programmes for the treatment of patients generally, or for the treatment of an individual patient. A treatment programme of a patient must last for three consecutive years and may include some or all of the following (s. 5(2)):

(*a*) where a director so directs, detention in a treatment centre for a period not exceeding 6 consecutive months;

(*b*) attendance at a treatment clinic at such times and over such periods, not exceeding one year in total, as a director may require;

(*c*) supervision and direction of such kind and of such duration as a director may require.

Such a period of detention may not be shortened or rescinded but is subject to indefinite prolongation by a board of review. The board of review may also require a person who is not in detention but who is undergoing treatment to be detained in a treatment centre or clinic for up to seven days in order "to facilitate the assessment, monitoring, or review of a patient's needs . . ." (s. 7(2)).

The powers conferred are couched in language emphasizing the medical treatment aspect of the legislation. A person subject to such treatment is defined in the Act as a "patient" whether his treatment is voluntary or compulsory. The evaluation panel which recommends treatment must be composed of medical practitioners in the majority. The recommendation is based on a medical and psychological examination. The Act contains the following statutory definitions of "dependency" and of "patient" and of "treatment" from s. 1 of the Act:

"dependency" means, in relation to a narcotic, a state of psychological or physical dependence, or both, on a narcotic following its use on a periodic or continuous basis;

. . . . .

"patient" means a person who is required or voluntarily agrees to undergo treatment under this Act;

"treatment" means one, more, or all of direction, supervision, or treatment of a person for the purpose of terminating or diminishing his use of or dependency on a narcotic.

The Act contains a number of sections embodying measures which, combined with the possibility of detention for a period of at least three years, are the major concern of the appellant. Section 13(1) of the Act provides that where a peace officer believes on reasonable grounds that a person has a dependency on a narcotic, he may give the person a written notice specifying a date and time, not less than 24 hours or more than 48 hours from the time of the giving of the notice, at which the person is required to attend and submit to examination at the area co-ordinating centre specified in the notice. Where a person does not comply with such a notice the Alcohol and Drug Commission of the province may apply *ex parte* to a judge for a warrant authorizing a peace officer to take the person into custody and take him to an area co-ordinating centre.

By s. 11(1) of the Act, a peace officer is authorized, without the necessity of obtaining a warrant, to take to a treatment centre for detention a person whose detention has been authorized or required under the Act. Section 16 creates several offences for non-compliance with the Act.

There are certain safeguards built into the Act which demonstrate a concern for the protection of the individual who finds himself subject to the provisions of the Act. The evaluation panel must make a report in writing to the director within 60 hours of the admission of a person for examination and the director must "forthwith" provide the person examined with a copy. A court order of committal may be appealed to the Court of Appeal of British Columbia and nothing in the Act deprives a person of any remedies available upon judicial review. Where an application has been made for an extension of treatment or detention the patient has the right to be heard by the board of review.

. . . .

VI

*The issues*

The appellant submits that the Court of Appeal for British Columbia erred in law in four respects:

(a) In failing to hold that the *Heroin Treatment Act* is in pith and substance legislation in relation to the subject-matter of narcotics and as such falls within the exclusive power of the Parliament of Canada to make laws for the peace, order and good government of Canada.

(b) In failing to hold that the *Heroin Treatment Act* is in pith and substance legislation in relation to criminal law and as such as within the exclusive legislative authority of the Parliament of Canada under s. 91(27) of the *British North America Act, 1867*.

(c) In failing to hold that the *Heroin Treatment Act* is in pith and substance legislation in relation to the subject matter of narcotics and as such falls within the treaty-making power exercised by Parliament and as such falls within the exclusive power of Parliament to make laws for the peace, order and good government of Canada.

(d) In failing to hold that the *Heroin Treatment Act*, if valid provincial legislation, was rendered inoperative by operation of the *Narcotic Control Act*, the *Criminal Code*, the *Penitentiaries Act*, R.S.C. 1970, c. P-6, and the *Parole Act*, R.S.C. 1970, c. P-2.

[His Lordship's discussion of the POGG, treaty power and paramountcy are omitted.]

VIII

*Criminal law*

The appellant submits that the *Heroin Treatment Act* in effect creates a new crime of narcotic dependency and is a colourable attempt to "stiffen the existing criminal law", as in *Johnson v. A.-G. Alta.*, [1954] S.C.R. 127 at 165, *per* Cartwright J. I do not agree. It is true that one of the objects of the Act is the suppression of "local evils" — local conditions giving rise to crime — but this is a matter of merely local nature in the province and within s. 92(16) of the *B.N.A. Act, 1867*: see *Hodge v. The Queen* (1883), 9 App. Cas. 117 at 130-1 (P.C.); *A.-G. Ont. v. A.-G. Can.*, [1896] A.C. 348 at 365; *A.-G. Man. v. Manitoba Licence Holders' Ass'n*, [1902] A.C. 73 at 78 (P.C.). It is true that compulsory treatment under the Act may involve restraints upon freedom, including a period of treatment in a treatment centre, but such provisions do not dictate that the statute be characterized as criminal legislation. It is not an easy matter, I confess, to determine whether the *Heroin Treatment Act* is a valid provincial health law with what might be regarded as punitive features or whether the pith and substance of the Act is criminal law and therefore invalid. I think, on balance, however, it was open to the Court of Appeal of British Columbia to conclude, as it did, that the provisions of the impugned statute for the examination, apprehension and detention of dependent persons or patients are in no way intended to be punitive. They are provided for as ancillary to "treatment" as defined. The legislative plan is not to punish users of narcotics. It is to provide facilities and other means designed to assist in terminating or diminishing a "patient's" use of or dependency on the defined narcotic. I am not prepared to hold that the legislation is colourable.

Although the cases of *Re Bowack* (1892), 2 B.C.L.R. 216 (S.C.) and *Fawcett v. A.-G. Ont.*, [1964] S.C.R. 625, and *Green v. Livermore*, [1940] O.R. 381 (S.C.), are by no means a perfect analogy they do afford examples of the extent to which provincial legislation providing for the compulsory apprehension, detention and treatment of persons for health purposes has been sustained.

Recently, in *Reference re Intoxicated Persons Detention Act*, [1981] 1 W.W.R. 333, the Manitoba Court of Appeal was called upon to consider the validity of an Act which provided that a police officer could take into custody and place in a detoxication centre for a period of up to 24 hours a person who was intoxicated in a place to which the public had access. The five-judge court unanimously upheld the validity of the legislation. Huband J.A. (Freedman C.J.M. and Monnin J.A. concurring) said (at pp. 338-9 W.W.R.):

> On cannot gloss over the reality that, under the terms of the Act, a person who becomes intoxicated can be confined aginst his will in jail-like surroundings for a period of time of, and up to 24 hours. But the fact of confinement does not necessarily take this legislation into the realm of criminal law. Legislation in the field of mental diseases, and quarantine relative to communicable diseases, can involve involuntary confinement, but clearly it is dealing with the health of a citizen, as opposed to criminality. Child welfare legislation authorizes the confinement of children in protective custody — for example, to prevent harm from potentially abusive parents. That confinement is for the safety and security of the individual and does not invade the domain of criminal law.
>
> The purpose of the *Intoxicated Persons Detention Act* is made abundantly clear in s. 3(1). The purpose is to prevent an intoxicated person from being a danger either to himself or to others.

The interface between criminal law and provincial legislation which might be seen as impugning upon the federal jurisdiction in the field of criminal law has not been closely drawn. As Professor Hogg notes in *Constitutional Law of Canada* (1977), chapter 16 of his work, the dominant tendency of the case-law has been to uphold provincial penal legislation; recent cases have been generous to provincial power, and "the result is that over much of the field which may loosely be thought of as criminal law legislative power is concurrent" (at p. 292).

Examples of compatible federal and provincial legislation abound, for example, in health legislation: *Fawcett v. A.-G. Ont., supra*; in *Re Bowack, supra; Green v. Livermore, supra; Re Levkoe and The Queen* (1977), 18 O.R. (2d) 265 (Div. Ct.) in *quasi*-criminal legislation: *A.-G. Can. v. Montreal*, [1978] 2 S.C.R. 770; *Re Nova Scotia Board of Censors and McNeil*, [1978] 2 S.C.R. 662; *Smith v. The Queen*, [1960] S.C.R. 776.

. . . .

## X

### *Public health*

In ascertaining the "pith and substance" of a law in order to determine its validity under ss. 91 or 92 of the *B.N.A. Act, 1867*, "it is necessary to identify the dominant or most important characteristic of the challenged law" (Hogg, *ibid.*, at p. 80). The *Heroin Treatment Act* provides for the treatment, both voluntary and compulsory, of heroin addicts. The main contention of the provinces (British Columbia, Manitoba and Alberta) and the Attorney-General of Canada is that legislation providing for the treatment of addicts is *intra vires* the province as legislation in relation to health and thus a local and private matter. Public health falls under provincial competence as does, what is in effect, civil committal in implementation of health legislation.

Section 92, it is true, does not contain a specific head of power dealing with health and public welfare. Section 92(7) provides for the phsyical facilities of the provincial health care:

> 92(7)  The Establishment, Maintenance and Management of Hospitals . . . in and for the Province, other than Marine Hospitals.

The Royal Commission on Dominion-Provincial Relations (the Rowell-Sirois Commission) in 1938 commented on this absence of a specific head of power dealing with the administration of public health (at pp. 32-3):

> In 1867 the administration of public health was still in a very primitive stage, the assumption being that health was a private matter and state assistance to protect or improve the health of the citizen was highly exceptional and tolerable only in emergencies such as epidemics, or for purposes of ensuring elementary sanitation in urban communities. Such public health activities as the state did undertake were almost wholly a function of local and municipal governments. It is not strange, therefore, that the British North America Act does not expressly allocate jurisdiction in public health, except that marine hospitals and quarantine (presumably ship quarantine) were assigned to the Dominion, while the province was given jurisdiction over other hospitals, asylums, charities and eleemosynary institutions. But the province was assigned jurisdiction over "generally all matters of a merely local or private nature in the Province", and it is probable that this power was deemed to cover health matters, while the power over "municipal institutions" provided a convenient means for dealing with such matters.

The Rowell-Sirois Commission recommended that (at p. 34):

> Provincial responsibilities in health matters should be considered basic and residual. Dominion activities on the other hand, should be considered exceptions to the general rule of provincial responsibility, and should be justified in each case on the merit of their performance by the Dominion rather than by the province . . . Dominion jurisdiction over health matters is largely, if not wholly, ancillary to express jurisdiction over other subjects . . .

Thus historically, at least, the general jurisdiction over public health was seen to lie with the provinces under s. 92(16):

> 92(16) . . . Matters of a merely local or private Nature in the Province.

although the considerable dimensions of this jurisdiction were unlikely foreseen in 1867.

This view that the general jurisdiction over health matters is provincial (allowing for a limited federal jurisdiction either ancillary to the express heads of power in s. 91 or the emergency power under peace, order and good government) has prevailed and is now not seriously questioned: see *Rinfret v. Pope* (1886), 12 Q.L.R. 303 (Que. C.A.); *Re Bowack, supra; Labatt Breweries of Canada Ltd. v. A.-G. Can.*, [1980] 1 S.C.R. 914, *per* Estey J.

The medical treatment of drug addiction is a *bona fide* concern of the provincial Legislature under its general jurisdiction with respect to public health. The constitutional question to be answered is whether the "dominant or most important characteristic" of the *Heroin Treatment Act* is the medical treatment of drug addiction.

Narcotic addiction has been perceived to be a social evil and federal legislation has made possession of, and trafficking in, narcotics, criminal offences. Addiction itself, however, is a physiological condition the treatment of which would seem to be a medical concern to be dealt with by the provincial Legislature. In recent years there has been an increasing world-wide trend to the "medicalization" of the problem of narcotic addiction with an emphasis upon the substitution of treatment and rehabilitation programmes for conviction and punishment in drug related offences: see, for example, the Single Convention on Narcotic Drugs, 1961, *ibid.*

In my opinion, the "pith and substance" of the *Heroin Treatment Act* is the medical treatment of heroin addicts and is within the general provincial competence over health matters under s. 92(16) of the *B.N.A. Act, 1867.* I am in agreement with the LeDain Commission that narcotic addiction is not a crime but a physiological condition necessitating both medical and social intervention. This intervention is necessarily provincial. The compulsory aspects of this intervention are incidental to the effectiveness of the treatment, narcotic addiction by its very nature being a compulsive condition over which the individual loses control. Although coercion will obviously play a significant role it seems to me that the dominant or most important characteristic of the *Heroin Treatment Act* is the treatment and not the coercion. The Legislature of British Columbia in my view, has sought to treat persons found to be in a state of psychological or physical dependence on a narcotic as sick and not criminal. The Legislature is endeavouring to cure a medical condition, not to punish a criminal activity.

A factor which plays no part in the determination of the constitutional validity of the Act, but which, as a practical matter, is not negligible, is the support of both the provincial and federal authorities for the validity of the legislation. Although it does not resolve the constitutional issue it is interesting to observe that in these proceedings a provincial statute is being attacked on the ground that it falls within federal competence yet the Attorney-General of Canada is not contesting the constitutionality of the provincial statute. He would like to see the provincial legislation remain in place. The federal legislation (which is not in force) foresees co-operation with the provinces whereby a narcotic addict who has not been charged with an offence of possession, if a provincial statute provides for custody for treatment, may be confined in a federal institution and deemed to have been sentenced to custody for treatment under the *Narcotic Control Act*. The provincial statute, on the other hand, provides that a person detained under a federal law may be detained or treated under the provincial statute, if the federal law so permits.

. . . .

## XII

*Conclusion*

In the circumstances of this case, I find that the *Heroin Treatment Act* is in pith and substance legislation in relation to health in the province and as such *intra vires* the provincial Legislature in its entirety.

It should perhaps be noted, before concluding, that the *Canadian Charter of Rights and Freedoms* was not raised as an issue, nor argued in this court or in the courts of British Columbia.

I would answer the question settled by the Chief Justice in the negative. The *Heroin Treatment Act* is not *ultra vires* the Legislature of the Province of British Columbia.

I would dismiss the appeal with costs to the respondent.

ESTEY J.: — I have had the opportunity of reading the reasons for judgment of my colleague Dickson J. and concur in the disposition made therein on this appeal. Because I arrive at this conclusion by a different route something should be said in explanation.

The subject-matter of the legislation, its pith and substance, is medical treatment of the drug addict. The statute creates no offences and there is no suggestion that the "treatment" under the statute is in truth punishment for addiction. McFarlane J.A. describes the statute, [[1981] 1 W.W.R. 511]:

> the provisions of the impugned statute for the examination, apprehension and detention of dependent persons or patients are in no way intended to be punitive. They are provided for as ancillary to "treatment" as defined. The legislative plan is not to punish users of narcotics. It is to provide facilities and other means designed to assist in terminating or diminishing a "patient's" use of or dependency on the defined narcotic.

As such the legislation finds its constitutional base in s. 92(7) of the *Constitution Act 1867*:

> 92(7) The Establishment, Maintenance, and Management of Hospitals, Asylums, Charities, and Eleemosynary Institutions in and for the Province, other than Marine Hospitals.

together with paras. (13) and (16) of s. 92.

Health is not a subject specifically dealt with in the *Constitution Act* either in 1867 or by way of subsequent amendment. It is by the Constitution not assigned either to the federal or provincial legislative authority. Legislation dealing with health matters has been found within the provincial power where the approach in the legislation is to an aspect of health, local in nature: see *Fawcett v. A.-G. Ont.*, [1964] S.C.R. 625; *Re Bowack*, [1892] 2 B.C.L.R. 216; *Reference re Intoxicated*

*Persons Detention Act*, [1981] 1 W.W.R. 333 (Man. C.A.); and *Green v. Livermore*, [1940] O.R. 381 (S.C.). On the other hand, federal legislation in relation to "health" can be supported where the dimension of the problem is national rather than local in nature (see *A.-G. Ont. v. Canada Temperance Federation*, [1946] A.C. 193 at 205-6; *Toronto Electric Com'rs v. Snider*, [1925] A.C. 396 at 412), or where the health concern arises in the context of a public wrong and the response is a criminal prohibition. In *Russell v. The Queen* (1882), 7 App. Cas. 829 at 839, Sir Montague Smith suggested the illustration of a law which prohibited or restricted the sale or exposure of cattle having a contagious disease. In *Labatt Breweries of Canada Ltd. v. A.-G. Can.*, [1980] 1 S.C.R. 914 at 934, the case of adulteration provisions in a statute was cited. Health concerns are directly raised by the jurisdiction attributed to Parliament by s. 91(11) of the *Constitution Act, 1867*, and may also be raised by s. 91(7) and perhaps para. (2) as well. In sum "health" is not a matter which is subject to specific constitutional assignment but instead is an amorphous topic which can be addressed by valid federal or provincial legislation, depending in the circumstances of each case on the nature or scope of the health problem in question.

The *Narcotic Control Act*, R.S.C. 1970, c. N-1, has been found in *R. v. Hauser*, [1979] 1 S.C.R. 984, to be valid federal legislation under the general power to make laws for the peace, order and good government of Canada. But I do not read that authority as determining that narcotics addiction treatment as distinct from regulation of trafficking and use of narcotics is necessarily assigned to the peace, order and good government powers of Parliament without more and in any case as being an assignment of the field to exclusive federal authority in the absence of parliamentary action.

Part II of the *Narcotic Control Act* was enacted in 1961 (1961 (Can.), c. 35), presumably in implementation of the Single Convention on Narcotic Control, 1961, to which Canada is a signatory. Part II, which has never been proclaimed, deals with treatment as an aspect of sentencing. Section 19 of that part is of interest in this proceeding:

> 19(1) Where the legislature of a province enacts legislation that is designed to provide custody for treatment for persons who, although not charged with the offence of possession of a narcotic, are narcotic addicts, the Minister may enter into an agreement with the province, subject to the approval of the Governor in Council, for the confinement and treatment of such persons in institutions maintained and operated pursuant to the Penitentiary Act and for the release and supervision of such persons pursuant to the Parole Act.
>
> (2) A narcotic addict who is committed to custody for treatment pursuant to an Act of the legislature of a province shall be deemed, for the purposes of the Penitentiary Act and the Parole Act, to have been sentenced to custody for treatment under this Act.

Whatever may be the case should action be taken by Parliament in implementing this part, health would appear to be a divisible field according to the nature of the measure taken.

The provincial statute may therefore be valid and effective in this field in the absence of federal legislation. On the advent of federal legislation other considerations arise and the provincial statute in that case may be displaced in whole or in part. None of these matters need be settled on this appeal.

As to the criminal law no issue here arises once the British Columbia statute is characterized for constitutional purposes as being in pith and substance related to the medical treatment of addiction and not to its punishment. Where treatment involves detention, the distinction between treatment and punishment is difficult particularly where in the individual case at some periods in time no other "treatment" is administered. Punishment and treatment look very much alike in some circumstances. Here the Court of Appeal was satisfied, and I am in respectful agreement, that this is health legislation and not legislation concerning the criminal aspects of drug trafficking.

The federal criminal power is not here challenged by some new doctrine of concurrent provincial criminal authority. The power of the province to enact *quasi*-criminal legislation must be predicated upon the existence of an otherwise valid provincial legislative programme. The offences created for the enforcement or establishment of such a programme have been historically treated by the court as being ancillary to the power of the provincial Legislature invoked by the principal legislation. Without the existence of the prerequisite provincial authority independent of the offence-creating provisions, the legislation would be invalid as trenching upon the exclusive federal jurisdiction in criminal law. Thus we see that provincial enforcement provisions may be validly adopted in the context of schemes clearly provincial as for example in the field of regulation of highways or the regulation of trading in securities: see *O'Grady v. Sparling*, [1960] S.C.R. 804; *Mann v. The Queen*, [1966] S.C.R. 238, and *Smith v. The Queen*, [1960] S.C.R. 776. Where on the other hand the provincial legislation is not founded in an independent paragraph of s. 92 but is "in relation to what is conceived to be a public evil not in relation to civil rights or local matters" (see *Switzman v. Elbling*, [1957] S.C.R. 285 at 317, *per* Cartwright J.), the provincial legislation will be struck down: see *Johnson v. A.-G. Alta.*, [1954] S.C.R. 127; *Saumur v. City of Quebec*, [1953] 2 S.C.R. 299, and *Switzman v. Elbling*.

I would therefore find the British Columbia statute to be *intra vires* on the basis of the authority of the province under the paragraphs of s. 92 noted above and not being an invasion of the exclusive federal powers with reference to criminal law in s. 91(27). In reaching this conclusion, it must be emphasized that the divided or concurrent field of health legislation requires that any such interpretation or conclusion with reference to provincial legislation may come under subsequent review if and when it is joined in the field by federal legislation dealing with matters of national concern.

*Appeal dismissed.*

## Note

It is not particularly helpful to categorize the division of legislative power over health matters as Dickson J. has done in the *Schneider* case by saying that the provinces have a "general jurisdiction" whereas Parliament has a merely "limited federal jurisdiction either ancillary to the express heads of power in s. 91 or the emergency power under peace, order and good government". Both have jurisdiction as granted by their respective collocations of legislative power. In addition, it is questionable why federal jurisdiction should be limited to the emergency aspect of the general power in light of both the "new matter" holding in *R. v. Hauser*, [1979] 1 S.C.R. 984 and the re-affirmation of the existence of the national dimensions doctrine in *Labatt Breweries of Canada Limited v. A.G. Can.*, [1980] 1 S.C.R.

914, a post-*Anti-Inflation Act Reference*, [1976] 2 S.C.R. 373 case. There is no reason why a piece of federal health legislation could not be supported on one of those elements of the POGG in the appropriate case. It will be noted that Estey J. in *Schneider* contemplates the possibility of federal legislation "of national concern" entering the field. More to the point, Estey J. is clearly correct that health is not a subject which has been specifically allocated in the *Constitution Act* to either the provincial Legislatures or Parliament. The course of judicial decisions in the field, some of which are noted by Estey J., indicates that neither level of government is predominant in the area. Rather, as he notes, "health would appear to be divisible field according to the nature of the measure taken."

See *R. v. Cosman's Furniture (1972) Ltd.* (1976), 73 D.L.R. (3d) 312 (Man. C.A.) upholding the constitutional validity of regulations made pursuant to the *Hazardous Products Act*, R.S.C. 1970, c. H-3 respecting infants' cribs and cradles as safeguarding the health and security of infants, a matter which is comprehended by the criminal law power. See also *Re Canada Metal Co. and The Queen* (1982), 144 D.L.R. (3d) 124 (Man. Q.B.), upholding the emission standards of the federal *Clean Air Act*, S.C. 1970-71-72, c. 47 pursuant to both the POGG and section 91(27).

# WESTENDORP v. THE QUEEN

In the Supreme Court of Canada. [1983] 1 S.C.R. 43.

Laskin C.J.C., Ritchie, Dickson, Beetz, Estey, McIntyre, Chouinard, Lamer and Wilson JJ. January 25, 1983.

Appeal by the accused from a judgment of the Alberta Court of Appeal, [1982] 2 W.W.R. 728, allowing an appeal by the Crown from the accused's acquittal by Oliver Prov. Ct. J., [1981] 6 W.W.R. 527.

The judgment of the Court was delivered by

LASKIN C.J.C.: — This appeal, which is here by leave of this court, arises out of a charge against the appellant of being on a street for the purpose of prostitution in contravention of s. 6.1(2) of By-law 9022 of the City of Calgary, as enacted by amending By-law 25M81. The accused was acquitted at her trial on the ground, *inter alia*, that the impugned by-law was unconstitutional as invading federal authority in relation to the criminal law as well as federal legislation in that area. The acquittal was set aside by the Alberta Court of Appeal speaking through Kerans J.A., who held that there was no invasion of the federal criminal law power or of federally enacted provisions of the *Criminal Code*, and that the particular provisions of the by-law were validly enacted under ss. 152 and 169 of the *Municipal Government Act*, R.S.A. 1970, c. 246.

*The facts*

The facts are not in dispute. There is no question but that the accused and a female friend approached a plain clothes officer on a city street and solicited his interest to engage in intercourse or *fellatio* for stated payments. They moved with him to a car on a parking-lot where another plain clothes officer was waiting and both women were then arrested. The charge followed, reading that the accused Westendorp was on the street for the purpose of prostitution. . . .

## The issues

Three issues were raised in the appeal, of which only the constitutional issue need be addressed. Of the two which may be set aside, one was whether the power to enact this by-law was delegated to the municipality as allegedly conferred by the provincial Legislature. I am prepared to proceed in this respect on the supposition that the challenged by-law was authorized under provincial legislation. The second issue raised on the appeal, and extensively addressed by the appellant and by the respondent Attorney-General of Alberta and supporting intervenors representing New Brunswick, British Columbia and Saskatchewan, concerned an alleged violation of the *Canadian Charter of Rights and Freedoms* under the *Constitution Act, 1982* and in particular s. 7 thereof.

Section 7 of the Charter reads as follows:

> 7. Everyone has the right to life, liberty and security of the person and the right not to be deprived thereof except in accordance with the principles of fundamental justice.

It appeared in the course of argument that counsel for the appellant not only sought to infuse a substantive content into s. 7, beyond any procedural limitation of its terms, but also to rely on s. 7 to challenge the validity of the by-law provision without accepting as a necessary basis for the s. 7 submission that it could only apply if the by-law was to be taken as valid under the distribution of powers between the legislating authorities. In the result, counsel for the appellant abandoned the challenge under the Charter of Rights and Freedoms.

What, therefore, is left for determination by this court is whether the challenged by-law s. 6.1(1) is outside the powers assigned to the Province, invading federal legislative authority. In my opinion, for the reasons expressed below, the by-law is *ultra vires* as invading exclusive federal power in relation to the criminal law.

## The Calgary by-law and s. 6.1 thereof

By-law 9022, first enacted in 1974, and cited as the Street By-law, is an extensive regulatory and prohibitory enactment relating to the use of city streets. I shall come to some of its details shortly. As it first stood, it contained no provision respecting prostitution although it did embrace control of certain street activities such as soliciting or carrying on business, trades or occupations on any street. On June 25, 1981, city council amended By-law 9022 by enacting By-law 25M81, adding s. 6.1 to the master by-law. Clearly, it had to stand on its own terms because there was no suggestion that prior to its enactment what it encompassed could in any way be subsumed under any other terms of the master by-law.

Section 6.1 was included as the last section in a group of provisions under the heading "Use of Streets". The original sections under this heading were ss. 3, 4, 5 and 6. The following heading was "Dangerous Practices and Obstructions". The new s. 6.1 preceded this heading. It will be useful to set out ss. 3 and 4 and make reference to ss. 5 and 6 before setting out the added s. 6.1.

Sections 3 and 4 are in these terms:

3.(1) Except as otherwise provided in this By-law, in the Calgary Traffic By-law, in other by-laws of the City, or in provincial or federal statutes or regulations, all persons may use the streets for all purposes for which a public thoroughfare normally may be used.

(2) A person using a street shall comply with all provisions of the Calgary Traffic By-law applicable to him.

4. Where a sidewalk is provided no person shall walk

(a) on a border of a street that is sown with grass or other seed, or

(b) on or along the travelled portion of a street except to cross the street unless in either case he could not use the sidewalk with safety.

Section 5(1) states that subject to the provisions of s-s. (3) of this section and of s. 6 and of s. 6.1 a person shall not place or leave any wares, merchandise or chattels to display them for sale, or sell or solicit purchasers for such goods, nor leave a motor vehicle parked offering or displaying it for sale, nor conduct an auction sale. Under s. 5(2), other than a person set out in subsection (3) (and there are exceptions listed here which I need not enumerate), no person shall solicit for or carry on his business, trade or occupation on any portion of the street. Section 6 requires the approval of the city commissioners for placing newspapers on racks or stands on portions of a public street, subject to specified conditions. Then comes the new s. 6.1, a lengthy section with its own definition of terms.

Section 6.1, when separately enacted under By-law 25M81, was preceded by a heading and a lengthy recital which were as follows:

Being a By-law of The City of Calgary to Amend By-law Number 9022 to Prohibit use of City Streets by those Approaching or being Approached by Others for the Purpose of Prostitution . . .

WHEREAS subsection (3) of section 169 of *The Municipal Government Act* provides that subject to every other act, a municipal council has control and management of, among other things, the public highways, roads, streets, lanes, alleys and bridges within the municipality including the air space above;

AND WHEREAS subsection (1) of section 14 of *The Highway Traffic Act 1975* provides, among other things, that a municipal council may make by-laws controlling and regulating the use of all highways, sidewalks and other public places and delegating to the chief constable or municipal commissioner any powers in connection therewith;

AND WHEREAS there are persons who locate themselves upon, and hold themselves out on City streets for the purpose of prostitution;

AND WHEREAS there are persons who approach or are approached by others on City streets for the purpose of prostitution;

AND WHEREAS these above mentioned persons often collect in groups on City streets and attact crowds on City streets, vehicular and pedestrian;

AND WHEREAS the above mentioned activities are a source of annoyance and emabarrassment to members of the public and interfere with their right and ability to move freely and peacefully upon the City streets;

AND WHEREAS it is expedient to provide by by-law that the highways, streets, sidewalks, alleys, lanes and public places of the City shall not be used for the purpose of holding out or offering to other persons lawfully using the streets services of a prostitute and to amend by-law number 9022, The Street By-law for this purpose;

This heading and recital do not appear in s. 6.1 as it was subsumed under By-law 9022 but it was relied on to support the challenged by-law.

Section 6.1 as found in by-law 9022 reads:

6.1(1) In this section

    (a) "offering" includes but is not limited to the holding out, proposing, making available or expressing willingness to participate in a sexual service with a person for payment;

    (b) "prostitution" means the sale or offering for sale of sexual services and includes the purchase or offering to purchase sexual services;

    (c) "sexual services" include but are not limited to activities of a sexual nature for amusement, gratification, pleasure, stimulation, titillation or otherwise of any person;

(2) No person shall be or remain on a street for the purpose of prostitution.

(3) No person shall approach another person on a street for the purposes of prostitution.

(4) Any person contravening the provisions of this section is guilty of an offence and is liable on summary conviction:

    (a) for a first offence to a fine of not less than one hundred dollars ($100.00) and not more than five hundred dollars ($500.00) or in default of payment of the fine and costs, to imprisonment for not more than sixty (60) days; and

    (b) for a second or subsequent offence to a fine of not less than three hundred dollars ($300.00) and not more than five hundred dollars ($500.00) or in default of payment of the fine and costs to imprisonment for not more than six (6) months

unless in either case the fine and costs, including the cost of committal are sooner paid.

### The scope of the Calgary by-law saving s. 6.1

I have already noted that the first heading of the by-law following s. 6.1 refers to "Dangerous Practices and Obstructions". Then follows a heading entitled "Projections Over Streets" and a succeeding heading reading "Requirements for Canopies and Similar Projections". In turn this is followed by a heading "Fire Escapes" and then a succession of headings designated as "Sidewalk Chutes", "Litter and Refuse on the Streets", "Garbage and Laundry Chutes" and "Shopping Carts". By no stretch of any imagination do any of the aforementioned headings have any affinity with s. 6.1 and it is unnecessary to enter into any detail of the provisions included under the various headings.

The next heading in the by-law is entitled "Parades", which is self-explanatory. Then comes a heading called simply "Sidewalks" which restricts use of motor vehicles, bicycles and horses along a sidewalk and also prohibits parking or leaving vehicles on a sidewalk. There are exceptions which, again, I need not elaborate. The succeeding heading of the by-law is entitled "Care of Boulevards", then follows a heading "Clearing of Sidewalks" and following it a heading entitled "Protection of Street Surfaces". The next heading in this extensive by-law is "Use of Streets and Sidewalks for Building Operations" and this in turn is followed by the heading "Excavating and Breaking up Street Surfaces". Then comes a heading "Use of Space Under Streets", followed by a heading "Building Foundations Not to Encroach on Streets", a further heading entitled "Erection of Poles", then a heading reading "Alterations in Street Grades". A concluding provision deals with penalties for breach of provisions other than s. 6.1 and imposes fines ranging from $20 to $300 and imprisonment up to 10 days or 30 days or 45 days or 60 days, according to the gravity of the infractions.

I have referred, however briefly, to the types of regulations and prohibitions and accompanying penalties which the by-law encompasses beyond s. 6.1. Apart from such relevance to s. 6.1 as may be found in ss. 3 to 5, there is nothing in the by-law which has any relation to s. 6.1 or to the scale of penalties prescribed for breach of s. 6.1 compared with those in the general penalty provisions of the by-law to which I have referred. Section 6.1 stands as an intruded provision of By-law 9022 which might just as well have been left in its original form in By-law 25M81. In short, there is nothing in By-law 9022 which invigorates s. 6.1 which must stand on its own merit as a valid municipal by-law.

*Terms of s. 6.1: Its pith and substance*

It is patent, from a comparison of s. 6.1 with ss. 3, 4 and 5 of the by-law, that s. 6.1 is of a completely different order from its preceding sections and, certainly, from all those succeeding it. It is specious to regard s. 6.1 as relating to control of the streets. If that were its purpose, it would have dealt with congregation of persons on the streets or with obstruction, unrelated to what the congregating or obstructing persons say or otherwise do. As the by-law stands and reads, it is activated only by what is said by a person, referable to the offer of sexual services. For persons to converse together on a street, as did the two women and the police officer here, and to discuss a recent or upcoming sporting event or a concert or some similar event would not attract liablity. It is triggered only by an offer of sexual services or a solicitation to that end. There is no violation of s. 6.1 by congregation or obstruction *per se*; the offence arises only by proposing or soliciting another for prostitution. To remain on a street for the purpose of prostitution or to approach another for that purpose is so patently an attempt to control or punish prostitution as to be beyond question. The matter goes beyond the provincial legislation held by this court to be invalid in *Switzman v. Elbling*, [1957] S.C.R. 285, which prohibited any person to possess or occupy a house in the province to propagate communism or bolshevism. It is clearly distinguishable from *Bedard v. Dawson and A.-G. Can.*, [1923] S.C.R. 681, where the provincial legislation under attack there was justified as concerned with the control and enjoyment of property. There is no property question here, no question even of interference with the enjoyment of public property let alone private property.

Nor can any comparison be made between this case and the judgment of this court in *A.-G. Can. v. Dupond*, [1978] 2 S.C.R. 770, which related to a municipal anti-demonstration by-law which was also emphasized as being of a temporary nature. That by-law related plainly to parades and assemblies on the streets, different from s. 6.1 of the present case.

The question remains, however, whether, recognizing the differences in principle between the present case and the three cases in this court mentioned above, there is none the less constitutional scope for the valid enactment of the challenged by-law. This brings me to consider the reasons given by Kerans J.A. for upholding the by-law. He construed it as an attempt to deal with a public nuisance. This is not how the offence under the by-law is either defined or charged. The recitals in the by-law as enacted by By-law 25M81 cannot be used to justify substantive charging sections when those sections contain a different formulation and their own definition of an offence. It is these aspects that present the constitutional issue.

In examining the submission of counsel for the accused that the by-law was a colourable attempt to deal, not with a public nuisance but with the evil of prostitution, Kerans J.A. observed that the evil of prostitution is a matter of public morality and, if the pith and substance of this legislation were an attack on this evil, it might well be a matter beyond the competence of the Legislature of Alberta. He then went on to say that [at p. 743 [1982] 2 W.W.R.]:

> ... the by-law does not strike at prostitution as such; it does not seek to suppress the market for sexual favours; it seeks only to protect the citizens who use the streets from the irritation and embarrassment of being unwilling participants in that market.

This assessment of "pith and substance" is to me baffling when regard is had to the terms of s. 6.1. It becomes doubly baffling when Kerans J.A. says that [at p. 746 [1982] 2 W.W.R.]:

> I concede that the Calgary legislation makes it an offence for a prostitute simply to enter upon a street for the purpose of prostitution, *i.e.*, without yet doing anything. But this is not an attack on prostitution as such. This is an attempt, by preventative measure, to regulate the activities of the prostitutes and their customers on the streets. It is, as it were, a pre-emptive strike. And as such is troubling. But it is insufficiently troubling to change the pith and substance of the legislation.

What appears to me to emerge from Kerans J.A.'s consideration of the by-law is to establish a concurrency of legislative power, going beyond any double aspect principle and leaving it open to a Province or to a municipality authorized by a Province to usurp exclusive federal legislative power. If a Province or municipality may translate a direct attack on prostitution into street control through reliance on public nuisance, it may do the same with respect to trafficking in drugs. And, may it not, on the same view, seek to punish assaults that take place on city streets as an aspect of street control!

However desirable it may be for the municipality to control or prohibit prostitution, there has been an over-reaching in the present case which offends the division of legislative powers. I would, accordingly, allow the appeal, set aside the judgment of the Alberta Court of Appeal and restore the acquittal directed by the provincial court judge.

*Appeal allowed.*

[For an analysis of the *Westendorp* decision and its implications, see Whyte, "Prostitution: Municipal Regulation and the Domain of Criminal Law Meet Again" (1983), 32 C.R. (3d) 107. *Westendorp* was reaffirmed by the Supreme Court of Canada in *Goldwax v. Montreal*, [1984] 2 S.C.R. 525.]

### Note on Provincial Legislative Power to Regulate Morality

The issue of the extent to which a provincial Legislature may regulate morality is focussed by the apparent inconsistency between the majority of the Supreme Court of Canada's alternative holding in *Nova Scotia Board of Censors v. McNeil*, [1978] 2 S.C.R. 662, that morality has a local aspect for constitutional purposes and Laskin C.J.C.'s decision for the Court in *Westendorp v. The Queen*, [1983] 1 S.C.R. 43 striking down a municipal anti-prostitution by-law. I leave aside cases where the legislation has as its object and purpose the regulation of a business or trade, which is essentially a characterization issue, and assume that the adult entertainment regulation in question is primarily directed at morality.

The argument in favour of provincial power to regulate morality centres on the majority's alternative basis for decision in *McNeil*. Ritchie J. used the statement of

Lord Atkin in *Proprietary Articles Trade Association v. A.G. Can.*, [1931]A.C. 310 at 324 (P.C.) that "morality and criminality are far from co-extensive" as a spring-board for the proposition. . . . at 84 D.L.R. (3d) 1 at 23 that provincial legislation "which authorizes the establishment and enforcement of a local standard of morality in the exhibition of films is not necessarily 'an invasion of the federal criminal field . . .' ". Put in positive terms, Ritchie J. said at p. 28 that "the determination of what is and what is not acceptable for public exhibition on moral grounds may be viewed as a matter of a 'local and private nature in the Province' within the meaning of s. 92(16) of the [*Constitution Act, 1867*] . . .".

Juxtaposed against this holding are the unanimous judgments by the Supreme Court of Canada in *Westendorp, supra*, and *Goldwax v. Montreal*, [1984] 2 S.C.R. 525 striking down municipal anti-prostitution by-laws as an invasion of section 91(27). Laskin C.J.C.'s judgment in *Westendorp*, although somewhat ambiguous on the point, appears to be predicated on the view that morality as a "matter" of legislation uncoupled with a separate matter within provincial jurisdiction (for example, regulation of public streets, crowd control or regulation of a trade or business) is within exclusive federal authority. If so, the Supreme Court must be taken to have overruled its earlier alternative ratio in *McNeil*. Recent lower court decisions, although somewhat inconsistent, have tended to the latter view and struck down provincial legislation aimed at public morality: *Nordee Investments Ltd. v. Burlington* (1984), 48 O.R. (2d) 123 (C.A.) leave to appeal refused (1985), 9 O.A.C. 79 (S.C.C.); *Rio Hotel Ltd. v. Liquor Licensing Bd.* (1983), 47 N.B.R. (2d) 436 (C.A.); *Re Koumoudouros and Metro. Toronto* (unreported Ont. C.A. released October 17, 1985); *cf. Cal Investments Ltd. v. Winnipeg* (1978), 84 D.L.R. (3d) 699 (Man. C.A.); *Moffat v. Edmonton* (1979), 99 D.L.R. (3d) 101 (Alta. C.A.).

In *Nordee Investments Ltd., supra*, the Ontario Court of Appeal struck down a municipal by-law which provided a minimum dress code for all people performing services in victualing houses or places of lodging. There is some ambiguity in Cory J.A.'s reasons as to whether the by-law was invalid as an invasion of the federal criminal law power, on the basis of the paramountcy doctrine, or because the municipality exceeded its statutory jurisdiction. Much of Cory J.A.'s language, and the fact that he found the by-law to be *ultra vires* rather than merely inoperative, point to the first explanation. Moreover, this is the interpretation put on *Nordee* by the Ontario Court of Appeal in *Re Sherwood Park Restaurant Inc. and Markham; Re Wendy and Markham* (1984), 48 O.R. (2d) 449 (leave to appeal refused 14 D.L.R. (4th) 287n (S.C.C.)). On the section 91(27) point, Howland C.J.O. said at 450:

> The regulation of the dress or undress in an eating establishment of someone who has nothing whatever to do with the preparation, handling or serving of food or which has nothing whatever to do with any other legitimate object within principal jurisdiction is a clear attempt to regulate the public morals and therefore is an attempt to legislate in the field of criminal law.

This was reaffirmed by the Ontario Court of Appeal in *Re Koumoudouros, supra*, in striking down a municipal by-law which provided that no burlesque entertainer could offer services in a liquor licensed establishment except while wearing opaque clothing which fully covered the pubic area. The Court said at p. 3:

> In our opinion, the true object and purpose of s. 28(2) [of the by-law] is not the regulation of the trade and business of an adult entertainment parlour, but the regulation of public morals, and hence is legislation in relation to a matter coming within s. 91(27) of the *Constitution Act, 1867*.

That is not to say that the mere fact that provincial legislation makes a moral judgment is sufficient to bring it within the ambit of section 91(27). The lynchpin of validity, as always, is whether the true object and purpose of the impugned enactment is the regulation of a matter which is within the provincial catalogue of legislative powers. The presence of a moral element in the purpose is not determinative, as stated in *Information Retailers Assoc. of Metro. Toronto*, (unreported Ont. C.A. released October 17, 1985) at p. 17 citing, *inter alia*, *Montreal v. Arcade Amusement Inc.*, [1985] 1 S.C.R. 368; *Cal Investments Ltd. v. Winnipeg* (1978), 84 D.L.R. (3d) 699 (Man. C.A.) and *Moffat v. Edmonton* (1979), 99 D.L.R. (3d) 101 (Alta. C.A.). This assertion in *Information Retailers* is clearly correct in principle, although there is a problem in Robins J.A.'s assertion for the court that the legislation in *Nova Scotia Board of Censors* would not today be vulnerable to attack following *Westendorp*, or that *Cal Investments* and *Re Moffat* be decided the same way today. It seems clear that, while morality is not *necessarily* a separate constitutional value and may be regulated by either level of government depending upon the characterization of the legislation as a whole, legislation whose sole or primary purpose is the regulation of morality is legislation in relation to criminal law. There is real difficulty in accepting that the *Nova Scotia Board of Censors* legislation, or that in the *Information Retailers* case for that matter, was in its true object and purpose aimed at the regulation of a business or trade. In any event, it should be noted that Robins J.A. does not say that Ritchie J.'s alternative ratio in *Nova Scotia Board of Censors* is still correct today. He merely says that the *legislation* in the case would not be vulnerable to attack. This impliedly explains *Nova Scotia Board of Censors* as a characterization case, and says nothing about Ritchie J.'s proposition that legislation which is aimed at morality can be valid on the basis of section 92(16) of the *Constitution Act, 1867*.

While the better view following *Westendorp* and *Goldwax* is that a provincial Legislature cannot enact legislation which in pith and substance aims at the control of morality, *quaere* whether it may accomplish the same result by applying for a civil injunction to prevent a public nuisance. In *A.G. B.C. v. Couillard* (1984), 42 C.R. (3d) 273 (B.C. S.C.), *per* McEachern C.J., the Attorney General of British Columbia was successful in obtaining an interlocutory injunction, which at the date of writing is still in effect. In *A.G. N.S. v. Beaver* (1984), 31 C.C.L.T. 54, aff'd 32 C.C.L.T. 170 (N.S. C.A.), the judge at first instance refused to grant a similar injunction to have effect within the City of Halifax. The Court of appeal upheld his exercise of his discretion but held that, if granted, the injunction would have been valid. These cases point to the more basic problem of whether an injunction can be obtained to enforce the criminal law. Middleton J.A. in *Robinson v. Adams* (1924), 56 O.L.R. 217 at 224 *et seq.* (C.A.) held that such an injunction was not possible both because it ran against the constitutional division of powers in Canada and because of a lack of jurisdiction in equity. The latter statement has been put in serious doubt by the recent British case of *Gouriet v. Union of Postal Workers*, [1978] A.C. 435 (H.L.). However, Middleton J.A.'s point that in Canada such an injunction would represent an invasion of the criminal power of Parliament has never been convincingly rebutted. For some recent cases dealing with injunctions to enforce criminal law: see *League for Life in Manitoba Inc. v. Morgentaler*, [1985] 4 W.W.R. 633 (Man. Q.B.); *cf. A.G. Alta. v. Plantation Indoor Plants Ltd.*, [1982] 2 W.W.R. 167 (Alta. C.A.), granting an injunction to restrain breach of the federal *Lord's Day Act*, R.S.C. 1970, c. L-13, a statute which was subsequently struck down in *R. v. Big M Drug Mart Ltd.*, [1985] 1 S.C.R. 295 on *Charter* grounds.

# 6. Adulteration Legislation

## Note on Adulteration

In *Standard Sausage Co. v. Lee*, [1934] 1 W.W.R. 81 and [1934] 1 D.L.R. 707 (addendum judgment of Martin J.A.), referred to in *R. v. Perfection Creameries Ltd.*, [1939] 2 W.W.R. 139 (Man. C.A.) and followed in *Berryland Canning Co. v. The Queen* (1974), 44 D.L.R. (3d) 568 (Fed. T.D.), Macdonald J.A. of the British Columbia Court of Appeal, dealt with the facts and issues as follows:

In this appeal the right of the Dominion Parliament to enact the *Food and Drugs Act*, R.S.C. 1927, c. 76, and specifically ss. 3, 4 and 23 thereof and regulations thereunder is questioned. Appellant used an adulterant in the manufacture of sausages, viz., sulphur dioxide to the extent of 0.46 parts to every 2,000 parts of meat product. This quantity is not injurious to health. It is submitted that he was unlawfully enjoined from using this drug as a preservative on the ground that the sections of the Act referred to and regulations passed thereunder are *ultra vires* of the Federal Parliament.

The sample sausage, submitted for analysis, found to contain the adulterant, was sold as "fresh sausage". By spreading sulphur dioxide over it, or mixing it with the sausage, it stops fermentation and makes it fit for consumption and therefore saleable for from 12 to 18 hours longer than would otherwise be the case. [His Lordship here quoted the pertinent statutory provisions, and then continued as follows.]

It will be observed that it is an offence to use an adulterant even although it may not be injurious to health. The penalty however is greater if it is injurious in that respect. This raises the question in issue — is it within the power of the Dominion Parliament to declare that a harmless act is criminal?

By ss. 3 and 4 adulteration (the alleged criminal offence) is defined by regulations passed pursuant thereto. By Order in Council it is provided (IX(2)) that, 'Preservatives other than those mentioned in class 1 section XII, or colouring matter, shall not be used in or upon meat or meat products.

By referring to Class 1 of s. 12 of the regulations it will be found that sulphur dioxide is not included in the list of permissible preservatives. It follows therefore that unless the sections referred to and regulations are *ultra vires* of the Federal Parliament the appeal must be dismissed.

These sections (and regulations) are valid, if at all, under s. 91(27) of the *British North America Act* giving exclusive authority to the National Government to legislate in respect of 'The Criminal Law . . . including the Procedure in Criminal Matters.'

Acts of a similar nature respecting food adulteration appear in the Dominion statutes, practically since Confederation, standing often side by side with somewhat similar legislation, of a more restricted character, enacted by the Provinces. In *Reg. v. Wason* (1890), 17 O.A.R. 221, a provincial Act to provide against frauds in supplying milk to cheese or butter manufactories (held *intra vires*) was considered in its relation to the Dominion *Adulteration Act* of that day and as Rose J. stated in *Reg. v. Stone* (1893), 23 O.R. 46, at p. 49, where the Dominion *Adulteration Act* was held to be *intra vires* of the Dominion Parliament, the reported argument of Mr. Edward Blake, in the *Wason* case correctly outlined the law where the jurisdictions of the provincial and Dominion Legislatures appear to overlap.

The cases have been so often reviewed that extended references should not be necessary. The Dominion Parliament cannot acquire jurisdiction by attaching penalties to the commission of acts otherwise within the exclusive legislative control of the provinces subject to this — that it is not precluded from creating offences merely because the subject-matter, in another aspect, may fall under one of the sub-heads of s. 92. The limitation is that the Dominion Parliament cannot under the guise of criminal law legislate for the purpose of assuming, or with the object of securing, control over activities properly local and provincial in character. This however is not the avenue of approach in considering the case at bar. We start with the fact that the selling of food, not only unfit for human consumption but *dangerous* was a criminal offence at common law. If death followed, the vendor, if he knew it was unfit or 'dangerous', might be indicted for manslaughter.

Section 224 of the Code makes it a criminal offence to knowingly sell food unfit for consumption. Food may be rendered unfit or potentially dangerous by adulteration. This case arises only because the mixing of sulphur dioxide with meat to the extent disclosed in evidence is not injurious to health. But the subject of legislation is adulteration of food (properly classified as a crime) and what constitutes adulteration must, at least within reasonable limits, be left to the judgment of Parliament in the light of the best knowledge available at the time. The subject of food purity, free from adulteration by the admixture of baser ingredients, is so important and the need to preserve its purity so great to prevent widespread calamity that precautions of the most detailed character must be taken to ensure it. These restrictions may be unnecessarily wide and open to criticism but that does not affect the principle. By the regulations Parliament entrusted to the Governor in Council the power and duty to make regulations prescribing what preservatives might or might not be used in or upon meat or meat products. Eight are permitted, *viz.*, common salt, sugar, saltpetre, wood smoke, vinegar, spices, alcohol and refined sodium nitrate. Greater scientific knowledge may induce Parliament or the Goveror in Council to add sulphur dioxide to the list. In that event it would doubtless be necessary to prescribe the quantities that could safely be used. This might involve the danger that careless manufacturers would use too much or too little and for aught we know excessive quantities might be injurious to health.

In the meantime, it is reasonable to provide in dealing with a product in which it is essential to maintain purity, that with other preservatives available, sulphur dioxide may not be used at all. We may assume that the framers of the regulations were aware of the facts disclosed in evidence, *viz.*, that this preservative is used, at least in part, to enable the dealer to offer the product for sale from 12 to 18 hours later than he otherwise could if no preservatives, permissible preservatives, were used. What happens if the dealer should be careless and sell after 20 hours elapse: or if a larger quantity should be used than 0.46 to 2,000 parts? The meat inspector stated that this quantity 'so far as a poison is concerned' would be inert but he does not state possible results if by mistake or design a larger proportion should be used.

These considerations point to the conclusion that, granted the general subject of the adulteration of food may be the subject of legislation by the Dominion Parliament under the heading 'criminal law', it must follow, reasonably and necessarily, that it may define precisely the ingredients that may or may not be used. Nor is it any less a crime because it may be shown scientifically that some of the ingredients prescribed may not, if used in proper quantities, be deleterious at all. It is not a *sine qua non*, as many provisions of the Criminal Code show, that injury to property or to the person must necessarily follow the commission of the unlawful act. This contingency is recognized inasmuch as the penalty is less severe if injurious results do not follow. . . .

The primary object of this legislation is the public safety — protecting it from threatened injury. If that is its main purpose — and not a mere pretence for the invasion of civil rights — it is none the less valid because it may be open to a criticism, from which few acts are free, that its purpose would be served equally well by accepting the opinion of others, *viz.*, that sulphur dioxide might with safety be added to the list of usable preservatives. Tampering with food by the introduction of foreign matter, however good the intentions, should properly be regarded as a public evil and it may properly be regarded as highly dangerous to lower the bars, or to remove restrictions which, rightly or wrongly, Parliament in its wisdom thought fit to prescribe.

I think, too, if further support is required, the Act may be upheld because its purpose is not only to protect the consumer, but also to suppress fraud, in its criminal aspect, in the distribution of food products. The product was 'sold as fresh sausage'. It is in fact the substitution of an article treated with a preservative for one free from extraneous matter. If a dealer sold sausages as 'fresh' and then treated them in this way he would obtain money by fraud and false pretences and the customer would not be appeased by the assurance of the meat inspector that this 'keep 'em' process, as the butchers call it, is wholly effective. However it is not necessary to rely on this view. The drug in limited quantities may be safe; it is necessary to convince Parliament on that point.

Contrast the *Margarine* case, [1949] S.C.R. 1, aff'd. [1951] A.C. 179 (P.C.), and *Labatts Breweries of Canada Limited v. A.G. Can.*, [1980] 1 S.C.R. 914, reproduced in part at Chapter 8, *supra*.

The validity of federal adulteration legislation was recognized by the Privy Council in its unreported judgment in the *McCarthy Act* case, 1885, where in invalidating the Dominion *Liquor Licence Act*, 1883, it stated that the provisions of this Act as to adulteration, if separated, would be *intra vires*. For a recent illustration of adulteration legislation, see *Maple Products Industry Act*, R.S.C. 1970, c. M-2. The authority of the provinces in the matter recognized in *R. v. Wason* (1890), 17 O.A.R. 221, illustrates the aspect doctrine; Dominion legislation would govern where it "occupied the field".

If it is open to the Dominion to establish or prescribe standards of purity or wholesomeness above scientifically tested safety levels (as *Standard Sausage Co. v. Lee* indicates), would it be within its power to require the fluoridation of water?

# 15

# Legislative Power Over Civil Liberties

*Note on Civil Liberties and Legislative Power*

This chapter is not concerned with the *Canadian Charter of Rights and Freedoms*. It is concerned only with the question of the distribution of power as between Parliament and the provincial Legislatures. As noted by Laskin C.J.C. in *Westendorp v. The Queen*, [1983] 1 S.C.R. 43 when counsel attempted to argue section 7 of the *Charter*, there must be an initial judicial determination of legislative validity before the *Charter* has any application. Restated, the *Charter* does not expand the jurisdiction of either level of government (section 31) and, in the absence of an independent anchor in some other provision of the *Constitution Act* for a federal or provincial exercise of legislative power, one never reaches the *Charter*. The question of legislative validity apart from the *Charter* is therefore the first step in constitutional civil liberties adjudication.

Apart from the dictum by Abbott J. in *Switzman v. Elbling*, [1957] S.C.R. 285, there is no high authority which places civil liberties beyond the legislative reach of both Parliament and the provincial legislatures. On the contrary, there is an explicit denial that this is so in *A.G. Can. v. Dupond*, [1978] 2 S.C.R. 770, reproduced in part below. (See on this point, Cline and Finley, "Whither the Implied Bill of Rights? *A.G. Can. and Dupond v. The City of Montreal*" (1980-81), 45 Sask. L.R. 137). That being said, however, legislative supremacy is nonetheless resisted occasionally by the Courts beyond mere resort to constructional expedients for evading distasteful enactments. Thus, in *R. v. Hess (No. 2)*, [1949] 1 W.W.R. 586 (B.C.C.A.), O'Halloran J.A. denied to Parliament power to authorize the detention of a person, acquitted on an appeal, pending the determination of a further appeal by the Crown to the Supreme Court of Canada. His principal concern was with the power of the Courts, a matter underlined in *Crevier v. A.G. Que.*, [1981] 2 S.C.R. 220 denying legislative power to oust judicial review of administrative action: see Chapter 3, *supra*. But O'Halloran J.A. went farther, as brief reference to his language shows. He said, in part:

> It is part of the common law of England that Parliament shall respect the decisions of the Courts. If Parliament may assume the power to set aside a decision of the Court or interfere with the enforcement of its judgments because it does not like a decision or a judgment then there is really no use for Courts at all in our constitutional sense, for then the people would be saddled with a judiciary whose first law would be to decide a case in accordance with the wishes of the dominant party then in control of the machinery of the state. It would break down the independence of the judiciary and destroy the judicial system Canada and its common law provinces have inherited.

From this conception the learned Judge proceeded to the view that the preamble to the *Constitution Act, 1867*, expressing the desire for federal union "with a Constitution similar in principle to that of the United Kingdom", had incorporated the written constitution of the United Kingdom, as reflected in *Magna Carta*, the *Petition of Right*, the *Bill of Rights* and the *Act of Settlement*; hence the impugned federal legislation, *Criminal Code*, section 1025A, "is contrary to the Canadian Constitution and beyond the competence of Parliament or any provincial Legislature to enact so long as our Constitution remains in its present form of a constitutional democracy." To a similar effect, see *Liyanage v. The Queen*, [1967] 1 A.C. 259 where the Privy Council struck down what was effectively a legislative direction to the courts to convict an accused on the basis of a provision in Ceylon's constitution respecting the appointment of judges in similar terms to section 96 of the *Constitution Act*. The reasoning was essentially that the inclusion of an appointment power in a written constitution must import the notion of a kernel of judicial power which cannot be invaded by the legislature.

It is a measure of the political character of constitutional law, even under Canadian federalism, that both O'Halloran J.A. in *R. v. Hess (No. 2), supra*, and Abbott J. in the *Switzman* case should find inspiration for their innovations in constitutional limitations in the preamble to the *Constitution Act, 1867* — a statement which not only lacks enacting force but in substance refers to the political traditions of a unitary state possessing in law an omnipotent legislature. The "freedoms" in Great Britain are protected in the main by common law rules providing redress in civil actions against illegal governmental action, and procedural safeguards in criminal prosecutions: see Dicey, *Law of The Constitution* (10th ed. 1959), Introduction, section 3; chapters 4-7; appendix, sec. 2; Jennings, *The Law and The Constitution* (5th ed. 1959), chapter 8; Wade and Phillips, *Constitutional Law* (7th ed. 1965), Part II, chapters 35-40. The private litigation aspect of civil liberties in Canada is exemplified in such judgments of the Supreme Court of Canada as *Chaput v. Romain*, [1955] S.C.R. 834; *Lamb v. Benoit*, [1959] S.C.R. 321; and *Roncarelli v. Duplessis*, [1959] S.C.R. 121. The relation of these common law rules to superseding legislation has, at least until recent constitutional litigation, and the enactment of the *Charter of Rights*, raised political rather than legal issues, save in so far as there might be a question whether the overriding legislation was competent to the Dominion or to a Province. This is apart, of course, from rules of construction applied by the Courts to minimize the impact of the statute on the traditional common law. In this latter respect, the problem is one for the draftsman to consider in seeking to implement in words the policy which is being legislated.

Some of the common law protection of the freedoms has passed into statute law, and in Canada this is especially so in the field of criminal law and procedure. In Saskatchewan, a provincial *Bill of Rights Act*, R.S.S. 1953, c. 345 was successfully invoked to qualify a municipal by-law in so far as it purported to prohibit distribution of religious handbills: see *R. v. Naish*, [1950] 1 W.W.R. 987 (Sask. Mag. Ct.); and see Note (1941), 19 Can. Bar Rev. 49; Note (1949), 27 Can. Bar Rev. 1248. This is a parallel situation to the decision in the later *Saumur* case, reproduced below and to the judgment of the Supreme Court in *McKay v. The Queen*, [1965] S.C.R. 798. A particular example is afforded by *Donald v. Hamilton Board of Education*, [1945] O.R. 518 (C.A.), raising the question (which was decided favourably to the parents and pupils concerned) whether a statutory guarantee of freedom of religion in school legislation was being abridged by a disciplinary requirement of singing the "national anthem" and saluting the flag. The case may usefully be compared with the "flag salute" decisions in the United States: see *Minersville School District v. Gobitis*, 310 U.S. 586 (1940); *West Virginia State Board of Education v. Barnette*, 319 U.S. 624 (1943); and see Note (1944), 22 Can. Bar Rev. 840. Another comparison is provided by the respective approaches of the Courts in Canada and the United States to racially restrictive covenants. While in the United States reliance could be placed on a constitutional prohibition against judicial enforcement of such covenants — this being state action prohibited under the equal protection tems of the 14th amendment to the Constitution — in Canada the argument against enforcement of such covenants turned on conceptions of public policy and on rules of property law: see in the United States *Shelley v. Kraemer; McGhee v. Sipes*, 334 U.S. 1 (1948); *Barrows v. Jackson*, 346 U.S. 249 (1953); in Canada, see *Re Drummond Wren*, [1945] O.R. 778 (H.C.); *Noble and Wolf v. Alley*, [1951] S.C.R. 64 and see Note, "Equal Protection and the Racial Restrictive Covenant" (1955), 30 Ind. L.J. 366. It is questionable whether the *Charter* will be applied directly to racially restrictive covenants, as was done in the United States in *Shelley v. Kraemer, supra*, or whether Canadian courts will take a more restrictive view of the scope of "government action" in section 32. For a discussion of section 32 of the *Charter*, see "Note on the Application of the Charter", Chapter 24, *infra*. In any event, there is no question that the *Charter* will have at least an indirect effect on such cases as the strongest possible evidence of a public policy of equality: see Finkelstein, "The Relevance of Pre-*Charter* Caselaw to Post-*Charter* Adjudication" (1982), 4 Sup. Ct. L.R. 267 at 283.

A convenient classification of civil liberties, based on political and social experience, is to recognize four different meanings in the term. There are, *first*, the traditional political liberties, i.e. freedom of association, of assembly, of utterance, of communication and of conscience and religion. *Second*, there is legal liberty, perhaps better explained as liberty which is connected to the legal order, such as freedom from arbitrary arrest, or arbitrary search and seizure; protection from self-crimination and protection of fair and impartial adjudication. *Third*, there is economic civil liberty, involving a transfer to the economic sphere of the notion of individual rights developed in the political sphere. *Fourth*, there is civil liberty in egalitarian or human rights sense, involving not state abstention but affirmative intervention to secure such things as equality of employment opportunity or of access to services or amenities without discrimination on account of religion, colour or origin. For an elaboration of these classifications, referrable to legislative power in Canada: see Laskin, "An Inquiry into the Diefenbaker Bill of Rights" (1959), 37 Can. Bar Rev. 77. They do not all stand on the same footing so far as legislative power is concerned. While the *Dupond* case, reproduced in part below, presents a serious obstacle to the following proposition, it may be asserted that the traditional political liberties are within the legislative power of Parliament alone, at least so far as their protection is concerned if not also so far as their restriction is concerned. As has been admirably and exhaustively demonstrated by Rand, Kellock and Estey JJ. in the *Saumur* case, there is no tenable basis on which it may be said that the term "civil rights in the Province" in section 92(13) comprehends the traditional political liberties: see also Laskin, *supra*, at pp. 113 ff. The jurisprudential and constitutional difficulties with *Dupond* are fully discussed in Swinton, "Constitutional Law-Freedom of Assembly-Criminal Law Power-Provincial Power over Matters of a Merely Local or Private Nature" (1979), 57 Can. Bar Rev. 326. For further comments on some of the more questionable aspects of the case, see Finkelstein, *supra* at pp. 271-2 and 277-8, and Avary, "The Criminal Law Power in the Constitution: And then came *McNeil* and *Dupond*" (1979), 11 Ottawa L.R. 1. Unfortunately, the Supreme Court of Canada has been moving away from the civil libertarian stance of *Alberta Press, Saumur* and *Switzman* in division of powers matters to one of a denial that such liberties are even involved in a serious way. It all comes down, as it must in constitutional cases, to a question of the characterization of the pith and substance of legislation, but surely *Walter v. A. G. Alta.*, reproduced in part below, was a religion rather than a mode of landholding case (in any event, was it not as appropriate a case for reading down as *McKay v. The Queen*, [1965] S.C.R. 798?), *Dupond* was an association and expression case rather than one dealing with a local matter of street control, and *McNeil*, reproduced in part below, was an expression case rather than one dealing with regulation of a local trade. These cases indicate a clear retreat from the earlier decisions. However, based as they are upon what must be considered mischaracterizations of the pith and substance of the legislation at issue, they are ripe for reconsideration. Laskin C.J.C.'s powerful dissents in *Dupond* and *McNeil* should, in my view, form the law in this area on grounds of both logic and adherence to precedent. It is to be hoped that such a reconsideration is not lost in the shuffle of the *Charter*. From a practical point of view, the division of legislative authority in this area retains real significance in cases where, for example, a legislature enacts a restrictive law and seeks to protect it by resort to the *non-obstante* clause in section 33 of the *Charter*. Apart from the issue of whether or how section 1 of the *Charter* acts upon section 33, the only relief in such situations is in the division of powers.

It is my view that, in terms of legislative power, the reasoning and implications flowing from the *Alberta Press* case, *Saumur, Switzman* and Laskin C.J.C.'s dissents in *Dupond* and *McNeil* are persuasive that the political liberties should represent independent constitutional values which are exclusively in federal keeping. The same cannot be said of economic liberty or liberty in the egalitarian sense or even legal liberty. Whatever the content of the latter, they are respectively subject to either federal or provincial legislation, or to both concurrently, according to whether the activities or proceedings with which these classes of liberties are connected are themselves within the power of the Dominion or of a Province, or according to the aspect from which they are treated. Thus, for example, a Province is competent to enact non-discriminatory fair employment practices legislation relative to industries or establishments within provincial legislative control: see *R. v. McKay* (1956), 5 D.L.R. (2d) 403 (Ont. Co. Ct.). But Parliament is equally competent to deal with discrimination within matters of federal jurisdiction.

## 1. Association

# DISTRICT OF KENT v. STORGOFF and A.-G. B.C.

In the Supreme Court of British Columbia. (1962), 41 W.W.R. 301.

Whittaker J. Nov. 19, 1962.

Motion by the provincial Attorney-General to dissolve an interlocutory injunction restraining violation of a by-law (see 40 W.W.R. 278), and, by consent, treated as trial of the action.

WHITTAKER J.: This action is brought by the Corporation of the District of Kent (hereinafter referred to as "Kent") against Florence Storgoff and Marie Shlakoff and the class that they represent being the Sons of Freedom Sect of the Doukhobors. The Attorney-General of British Columbia is also named as a defendant.

The plaintiff's claim is for an injunction restraining the defendants (other than the Attorney-General) from violating the terms and provisions of plaintiff's By-law No. 399 passed on September 8, 1962. My brother Munroe, on October 9, 1962, granted an injunction until trial. In his reasons for judgment Munroe J., was careful to express no opinion as to the validity of the by-law. . . .

At the outset of the present hearing, Mr. Wilson, counsel for Kent, admitted that certain portions of the by-law were bad for uncertainty. Counsel for the Attorney-General conceded that those portions could properly be severed. The preamble and operative sections of the by-law, with the offending portions deleted, read:

> WHEREAS the Council of the District of Kent is reliably informed that an organized group of several hundred members of the Doukhobor sect known as Sons of Freedom is rapidly approaching the District of Kent with the intention of remaining in that District for an indefinite period.
>
> AND WHEREAS many children of school age are within the approaching group.
>
> AND WHEREAS the group has neither the financial resources necessary to enable the members to acquire dwelling houses nor the intention of acquiring or maintaining dwelling houses within the district.
>
> AND WHEREAS members of the sect are addicted to nudism, arson and the illegal use of dynamite and explosive devices.
>
> AND WHEREAS the District of Kent lacks school accommodation to take care of the children of school age with the group.
>
> AND WHEREAS the District of Kent lacks facilities for the accommodation of a group of this magnitude under healthful and sanitary conditions.
>
> AND WHEREAS the arrival of a group of this kind in the District of Kent will disorganize the educational system of the School District, will be a menace to health and is likely to lead to breaches of the peace and the possible break-down of law and order in the District.
>
> AND WHEREAS the powers and authorities vested in or conferred upon the Council are inadequate to deal with the emergency created by these conditions.

NOW THEREFORE the Council of the District of Kent in open meeting duly assembled enacts as follows:

1. The council of the District of Kent declares that by reason of the matters set forth in the preamble hereto an emergency exists.
2. No person . . . being a part of the group of Doukhobors presently moving from the Kootenay area or the Grand Forks area to Agassiz or the District of Kent with the intention of remaining close to the Mountain Prison for Doukhobors and no person who is . . . a member of . . . the Doukhobor sect known as Sons of Freedom shall enter the District of Kent during the continuance of this emergency.
3. Any person who contravenes any provision of the By-law shall be liable to arrest without warrant and on summary conviction to a fine of up to $500.00 or to imprisoment for up to six months or both together with costs.

This by-law was passed by Kent in purported exercise of the powers conferred upon municipal bodies by s. 218(2) of the Municipal Act, R.S.B.C. 1960, c. 255. The subsection is as follows:

(2) Notwithstanding any other provision of this Act, when the powers and authorities vested in or conferred upon the Council of a municipality are inadequate to deal with an emergency, the Council may, by by-law adopted by an affirmative vote of at least two-thirds of all the members thereof, declare that an emergency exists and exercise such powers as are necessary to deal effectively with the emergency.

It is not for me to say whether such an emergency existed as would justify the exercise by Kent of the rather wide powers conferred by s. 218(2). The council evidently felt that the authorities vested in them were inadequate to meet the situation and declared that an emergency existed. That would appear to conclude the question as to whether or not an emergency did in fact exist. If, however, that were a question for me to decide, I would have no hesitation in saying that Kent was, and still is, confronted with an emergency of alarming proportions. In what is known as the Mountain Prison in Kent Municipality some sixty-eight Freedomites are serving sentences for such offences as arson, bombing and possession of explosives. In August or early September of this year there was a mass migration of Freedomites, men, women and children from their homes in the Kootenays approximately 400 miles distant from Kent, with the expressed intention of "going where our destiny lies, with our fathers, husbands, brothers and sons at Buchenwald". Before leaving on this trek many burned their own homes. Eventually the trekkers arrived at Hope, only a few miles from Kent, where they are now camped. There are approximately 1,000 persons in this group, including about 160 children.

On September 10, 1962, representatives of the Freedomite marchers read the following document at a meeting of the Kent municipal council:

To GIVE THE GENERAL PUBLIC A CLEAR UNDERSTANDING OF OUR PRESENT MISSION, WE WOULD LIKE TO PUBLISH OUR SIDE OF THE PRESENT SITUATION. WE TAKE FULL RESPONSIBILITY FOR THE FOLLOWING STATEMENT.

First — Our Destination

We are going where our destiny lies, with our fathers, husbands, brothers and sons at Buchenwald.

Second — Why We Are Going

John L. Lebedoff, who has the protection of the R.C.M.P., has been threatening our people with loss of life if we did not comply with his wishes, which are: *the burning of homes voluntarily*. If this was not carried out, he stated that the homes would be levelled to the ground with bulldozers supplied by the R.C.M.P. He further stated that Krestova would be razed to the ground; the old would be destroyed, the new would be created.

This shows us how Lebedoff and the Government of British Columbia have been working hand-in-hand to create the present situation. While the Government were building the fireproof and indestructible Buchenwald of Mountain Prison at Agassiz, Lebedoff was instigating the terrorism for the complete destruction of Krestova and the other districts of Sons of Freedom.

This accomplishes the plans of Lebedoff and the Government of fulfilling the purpose of Buchenwald, which is the transplanting of the Sons of Freedom from their homes to a concentration camp.

This terrorism and the consequent use of the Mountain Prison has left us destitute and homeless.

Now, we, the mothers, wives, children, the aged are going there to complete the transplanting. Why [do] we the children follow in line with our fathers and mothers? Because we fear we will be taken again from our parents and will undergo again the same experience, cold hunger and separation as we have went through in the New Denver Dormitory.

Have you built this Buchenwald for us or for yourselves? If for us, then let us go there to join our brethren. If you find that the Mountain Prison will not be satisfactory for all of us, will not accommodate all of us, then build us a duplicate at Krestova. You make claims that the Mountain Prison is only for terrorists and wrongdoers. We ask all of you who the wrongdoers in Germany were — the Fascists and Hitlerites, those who built Buchenwald and allowed it to be built, or those who were imprisoned in it? If you judge that those who built and allowed it to be built, are the guilty party, then by comparison you likewise are the wrongdoers. By remaining silent, you share the guilt.

You consider us third-class citizens, not worthy of having homes or land, or having a family and our own way of lives, of having children and bringing them up satisfactorily according to our religious convictions. You wish to solve our problems with the complete liquidation of our group. If that is your true desire, Good! Do with us as you wish. Do with our bodies as you think necessary — soap, fertilizer, handbags, lampshades and bind your books with our hides.

The population of Kent is about 2,200. The prospect facing this small municipality was its invasion by 1,000 people belonging to a sect with a history of violence and the expressed present intention of joining those members of the sect then inmates in the Mountain Prison. These people were without housing and had no financial resources. Problems of housing and sanitation would inevitably arise. Schools would have to be provided for the children. The residents of Kent might well fear a break-down of law and order following the frustration of the Freedomites' expressed purpose of joining their imprisoned brethren. These are the urgent problems which the residents of Kent have sought to forestall by the passage of the by-law in question.

Said s. 218(2) is, in my opinion, wide enough to confer upon a municipal council the power, in an emergency, to adopt such measures as could be exercised by the Provincial Government. It cannot, however, authorize the enactment of legislation in a field assigned exclusively to the Parliament of Canada....

... it seems clear that Kent has, by ss. 2 and 3 of the by-law, made, or attempted to make it a crime for any Freedomite to enter the municipality. This is an invasion of the exclusive legislative authority of the Parliament of Canada, unless it can be said that the imposition of punishment was for the purpose of enforcing a law coming within any of the classes of subjects enumerated in ... s. 92.

It is true that in the preamble the by-law refers to anticipated problems of housing, education and health. Those are local problems, but the penalties imposed are not for the breach of any law relating to those subjects. The by-law is designed to prevent conditions arising which may lead to their breach. This is a laudable object, if it could be achieved by the exercise of powers within the jurisdiction of the municipality or the Province, but Kent has sought to meet the situation by the creation of a new crime. This is clearly beyond its powers.

The by-law is also designed to prevent conditions arising which may lead to a breach of the peace or unlawful assembly. These are matters relating to the criminal law and as such are within the exclusive legislative jurisdiction of the Parliament of Canada. Both are covered by the *Criminal Code*, 1953-54 (Can.), c. 51; breach of the peace by ss. 30 and 31, and unlawful assembly by s. 64. . . .

I am of the opinion that for the reasons mentioned the by-law must be declared invalid and the interim injunction dissolved. There were a number of other points of attack on the by-law which I need not consider. I may say that I have been greatly assisted by the able arguments of counsel on both sides.

If I am right in the decision I have given it would appear that Kent, acting alone, is helpless in the face of the emergency with which it is threatened. One does not like to think that the law is so inadequate that higher authority also finds itself powerless to come to Kent's assistance. [The learned Judge then referred to *Criminal Code*, ss. 64, 27 and 435 respecting unlawful assembly, preventive use of force, and power to arrest without warrant. He concluded as follows:]

These preventive measures could be taken as soon as the Freedomites show signs of leaving their present camping grounds for their march on Kent.

Anything I have said which is unnecesary for my decision on the validity of the by-law is said solely for consideration by the proper authorities, and is not intended as a judicial pronouncement. It is not for me to say what Government policy should be. Nevertheless, every citizen must be concerned, as I have been while writing these reasons, because of the problems facing the people of Kent if the Freedomites are permitted to enter their municipality.

*Action dismissed.*

### Note

An interesting perspective on whether having a constitutionally entrenched instrument in place always favours a civil libertarian outcome may be seen by contrasting the *Storgoff* case with the American case of *Village of Belle Terre v. Boraas*, 416 U.S. 1 (1974). In the latter case, a municipal land use ordinance restricted a certain area to single family dwellings and defined "family" to exclude three or more unrelated people. Six unrelated people living in one house, "hippies" in the parlance of the times, were ordered to move. Douglas J. held that the ordinance did not violate their First Amendment associational rights. One could argue that the decision in reality protected the associational rights of the villagers, but the same argument was implicitly rejected in *Storgoff*. In fact, one may question how well *Belle Terre* sits with *National Socialist Party v. Skokie*, 432 U.S. 43 (1977) where the Nazis were permitted to march (they later declined to do so) notwithstanding the sensibilities of the town's inhabitants, a disproportionate number of whom were Jewish concentration camp survivors. In fact, *Skokie* is an even clearer case for exclusion because the Nazis deliberately chose the town for its high Jewish population. It was, as distinct from *Belle Terre*, a deliberate psychic attack on the town's residents.

## 2. Expression and Religion

### Note on Federal Political Rights and Provincial Legislative Power

Long before the *Alberta Press Bill* reference, *infra*, Boyd C. in *Re North Perth; Hessin v. Lloyd* (1891), 21 O.R. 538 at 542 (C.A.) anticipated some of the issues that were canvassed in it. After making the obvious statement that "Ontario has no legislative power over the electoral franchise of the Dominion", he went on to discuss electoral legislation in general, whether federal or provincial, and assessed it as follows:

> The subjects of this class of legislation are of a political character, dealing with the citizen as related to the Commonwealth (whether province or Dominion), and they are kept distinct in the Federal Constitutional Act from matters of civil rights in the Provinces which regard mainly the *meum* and *tuum* as between citizens. It is in my view rather confusing to speak of the right of voting as comprehended under the 'civil rights' mentioned in sec. 92 sub-s. 13 of the B.N.A. Act. This franchise is not an ordinary civil right; it is historically and truly a statutory privilege of a political nature, being the chief means whereby the people, organized for political purposes, have their share in the functions of government. The question in hand, therefore, falls within the category not of 'civil rights in the Province', but of electoral rights in Canada.

It would be taking the case too far to see in this quotation any recognition of federal power over provincial electoral matters; but, as in the case of the *Alberta Press Bill* reference in the judgments of Duff C.J.C. (Davis J. concurring) and of Cannon J., there is the intimation that public debate on political matters, whether federal or provincial, cannot be trammelled by provincial legislation. Moreover, the contrast drawn in *Re North Perth* between political and civil rights for *Constitution Act, 1867* purposes is relevant to a consideration of the divided judgments of the Supreme Court of Canada in *Oil, Chemical & Atomic Workers International Union, Local 16-601 v. Imperial Oil Ltd.*, [1963] S.C.R. 584, and *McKay v. The Queen*, [1965] S.C.R. 798. A bare majority of a seven-Judge Court in the first of these two cases upheld provincial legislation on principles which were denied by a bare majority of the full nine-Judge Court in the second in giving a limited construction to a municipal zoning by-law.

The *Imperial Oil Ltd.* case involved the validity and, alternatively, the reach of an amendment to the British Columbia *Labour Relations Act* which prohibited a trade-union, as the beneficiary of a revocable check-off of union dues under the Act or under a collective agreement, or of dues paid as a condition of membership in the trade union, from distributing or expending any of such money to or on behalf of any political party or candidate for political office. Ancillary provisions to fortify the prohibition were included in the amendment, but it is unnecessary to detail them; and it is a sufficiently accurate characterization of the amendment for the purposes of this Note to say that it prohibited a trade union from making political contributions out of compulsory dues.

In sustaining this provincial legislation in its application both to federal and provincial political activity and elections, the majority saw it as a protection of the civil rights of individual employees, which the Province could give. The Province had undoubted power to regulate labour relations in enterprises within provincial jurisdiction and could fix the conditions upon which the certification and compulsory collective bargaining advantages of the *Labour Relations Act* would be accorded. Indeed, the assumption of the majority was that because the machinery of the Act was geared to certification so that trade unions seeking its advantages could be put on terms, it was open to the Province to limit the use of compulsory dues for "political", or non-"labour relations", purposes. In effect, trade unions operating in the Province in respect of enterprises within provincial legislative jurisdiction were held properly subject to provincial legislative control in the use of dues paid by members, a control extending to prohibition of support for federal political activity. In the view of the dissenting Judges, the fact that this interference with the relations of trade unions and employers was not conditioned on the conferment of privileges that go with certification caused the legislature to shed any nexus with labour relations. Moreover, it had legislated in general terms that were broad enough to encompass federal political activity. On this view, the challenged amendment was in relation to political activity, and invalid at least in its purported application to federal politics. This was so whether the purpose was to protect the political freedom of choice of individual employees or to limit trade union participation in federal politics through the use of union funds.

The case raised the same type of dilemma that confronted the Supreme Court in *Saumur*, reproduced in part below, which had come to an inconclusive result on the constitutional issue. With the *Switzman* case, reproduced in part below (and the earlier *Birks* case), it was arguable that the Supreme Court had shown its preference for protecting the traditional political freedoms against general restrictive provincial legislation, in line with the Rand, Kellock, Estey and Locke JJ. approach in *Saumur*. Only Taschereau, Cartwright and Fauteux JJ. of the *Saumur* Court were still on the bench when the *Imperial Oil Ltd.* and *McKay* cases were decided. Taschereau J. (later C.J.C.) alone dissented in the *Switzman* case, whereas he had the companionship of dissent by Cartwright and Fauteux JJ. in the *Saumur* case. Both he and Fauteux J. remained faithful to their *Saumur* philosophy in the *Imperial Oil Ltd.* case; Cartwright J. obviously did not feel that that philosophy had any application. In the *McKay* case, Taschereau C.J.C. by joining in Cartwright J.'s judgment for the majority, enabled the Court (with the two newest Judges, Spence and Hall JJ. dividing for the Cartwright J. and Martland J. views respectively) to return to the *Saumur* approach of Rand J. and Company.

This approach was a two-fold one; first, to view the impugned provincial legislation in terms of the reach of its language; and, second, to recognize in the political freedoms an independent constitutional value which could not be submerged in general provincial legislation merely because there was a constitutional peg on which the legislation could hang. Of the by-law in the *McKay* case it could be said, as Kellock J. said of the by-law in the *Saumur* case, that "its validity is not to be judged from the standpoint of matters to which it might be limited but upon the completely general terms in which it in fact is couched". The zoning by-law in the *McKay* case forbade the display on certain residential property of all signs except those expressly permitted. Election signs were not within the permitted class, and the simple question was whether the by-law should be construed to embrace in its prohibition signs concerned with promoting candidates for election to the federal House of Commons.

The majority saw the case as involving the well known situation where general provincial or provincially authorized enactments must be limited in their reach to objects to which provincial competence extends. The Province had no authority to regulate federal election campaigning, and hence the zoning by-law could properly be construed as not extending thereto. To sweep federal election activity into the ban of the by-law merely because of the generality of its language was to denigrate the federal constitutional value involved. A Province clearly cannot extend its legislation to federal Crown property, either in general or in specific terms; nor can it do so in respect of federal Crown enterprises.

These considerations have a bearing on the question which the dissenting Judges saw as the pivotal one. Speaking through Martland J. they considered that the effect of the zoning by-law on federal electioneering was only incidental. It is unnecessary to dwell on the thesis of the *Alberta Bank Taxation* case that the particular zoning restriction in the *McKay* case should be writ large in order to assess its constitutionality, and envisaged therefore as applicable throughout all the Provinces. It is enough to view it in the context of federal candidacy in a single constituency in which the restriction applied. The values involved in the opposing judgments emerge no less clearly on such an appraisal.

[The *Liquor Control Act*, R.S.O. 1960, c. 217 provided that "no person unless authorized by the Board, shall exhibit, publish or display any ... advertisement or any other announcement, publication or price list of or concerning liquor or where or from whom the liquor may be had, obtained or purchased." It was argued in *R. v. Toronto Magistrates; Ex parte Telegram Publishing Co.*, [1960] O.R. 518 (H.C.), that this prohibition went beyond the regulatory objects of the statute, that it would, for example, prevent publications by temperance organizations, and that it was consequently invalid as an interference with freedom of speech and freedom of the press. *Held*, the prohibition should be construed as relating to advertising of the sale of liquor, and it was consequently valid.]

# REFERENCE RE ALBERTA STATUTES

In the Supreme Court of Canada. [1938] S.C.R. 100.

Duff C.J. and Cannon, Crocket, Davis, Kerwin and Hudson JJ. March 4, 1938.

Reference to the Supreme Court of Canada to determine the validity of three bills passed by the legislative assembly of Alberta in 1937 but reserved by the Lieutenant-Governor for the signification of the Governor-General's pleasure. The three bills were: Bill No. 1, "An Act respecting Taxation of Banks"; Bill No. 8, "An Act to Amend and Consolidate the Credit of Alberta Regulation Act"; and Bill No. 9, "An Act to ensure the Publication of Accurate News and Information". The judgments as reproduced below refer only to the last mentioned bill.

DUFF C.J. (for himself and Davis J.): ... We now turn to Bill No. 9.

This Bill contains two substantive provisions. Both of them impose duties upon newspapers published in Alberta which they are required to perform on the demand of "the Chairman", who is, by the interpretation clause the Chairman of "the Board constituted by section 3 of *The Alberta Social Credit Act*."

The Board upon the acts of whose Chairman the operation of this statute depends, is, in point of law, a non-existent body (there is, in a word, no "board" in existence "constituted by section 3 of *The Alberta Social Credit Act*") and both of the substantive sections, sections 3 and 4, are, therefore, inoperative. The same indeed, may be said of sections 6 and 7 which are the enactments creating sanctions. It appears to us, furthermore, that this Bill is a part of the general scheme of Social Credit legislation, the basis of which is *The Alberta Social Credit Act*; the Bill presupposes, as a condition of its operation, that *The Alberta Social Credit Act* is validly enacted; and, since that Act is *ultra vires*, the ancillary and dependent legislation must fall with it.

This is sufficient for disposing of the question referred to us but, we think, there are some further observations upon the Bill which may properly be made.

Under the constitution established by *The British North America Act*, legislative power for Canada is vested in one Parliament consisting of the Sovereign, an upper house styled the Senate, and the House of Commons. Without entering in detail upon an examination of the enactments of the Act relating to the House of Commons, it can be said that these provisions manifestly contemplate a House of Commons which is to be, as the name itself implies, a representative body; constituted, that is to say, by members elected by such of the population of the united provinces as may be qualified to vote. The preamble of the statute, moreover, shows plainly enough that the constitution of the Dominion is to be similar in principle to that of the United Kingdom. The statute contemplates a parliament working under the influence of public opinion and public discussion. There can be no controversy that such institutions derive their efficacy from the free public discussion of affairs, from criticism and answer and counter-criticism, from attack upon policy and administration and defence and counter-attack; from the freest and fullest analysis and examination from every point of view of political proposals. This is signally true in respect of the discharge by Ministers of the Crown of their responsibilities to Parliament, by members of Parliament of their duty to the electors, and by the electors themselves of their responsibilities in the election of their representatives.

The right of public discussion is, of course, subject to legal restrictions; those based upon considerations of decency and public order, and others conceived for the protection of various private and public interests with which, for example, the laws of defamation and sedition are concerned. In a word, freedom of discussion means, to quote the words of Lord Wright in *James v. Commonwealth*, [1936] A.C. 578 at 627 (P.C.), "freedom governed by law."

Even within its legal limits, it is liable to abuse and grave abuse, and such abuse is constantly exemplified before our eyes; but it is axiomatic that the practice of this right of free public discussion of public affairs, notwithstanding its incidental mischiefs, is the breath of life for parliamentary institutions.

We do not doubt that (in addition to the power of disallowance vested in the Governor-General) the Parliament of Canada possesses authority to legislate for the protection of this right. That authority rests upon the principle that the powers requisite for the protection of the constitution itself arise by necessary implication from *The British North America Act* as a whole (*Fort Frances Pulp & Power Co. Ltd. v. Manitoba Free Press Co. Ltd.*, [1923] A.C. 695 (P.C.)); and since the subject-matter in relation to which the power is exercised is not exclusively a provincial matter, it is necessarily vested in Parliament.

But this by no means exhausts the matter. Any attempt to abrogate this right of public debate or to suppress the traditional forms of the exercise of the right (in public meeting and through the press) would, in our opinion, be incompetent to the legislatures of the provinces, or to the legislature of any one of the provinces, as repugnant to the provisions of the *British North America Act*, by which the Parliament of Canada is established as the legislative organ of the people of Canada under the Crown, and Dominion legislation enacted pursuant to the legislative authority given by those provisions. The subject-matter of such legislation could not be described as a provincial matter purely; as in substance exclusively a matter of property and civil rights within the province, or a matter private or local within the province. It would not be, to quote the words of the judgment of the Judicial Committee in *Great West Saddlery Co. v. The King*, [1921] 2 A.C. 91 at 122 (P.C.), "legislation directed solely to the purposes specified in section 92"; and it would be invalid on the principles enunciated in that judgment and adopted in *Caron v. The King*, [1924] A.C. 999 at 1005 (P.C.).

The question, discussed in argument, of the validity of the legislation before us, considered as a wholly independent enactment having no relation to the *Alberta Social Credit Act*, presents no little difficulty. Some degree of regulation of newspapers everybody would concede to the provinces. Indeed, there is a very wide field in which the provinces undoubtedly are invested with legislative authority over newspapers; but the limit, in our opinion, is reached when the legislation effects such a curtailment of the exercise of the right of public discussion as substantially to interfere with the working of the parliamentary institutions of Canada as contemplated by the provisions of *The British North America Act* and the statutes of the Dominion of Canada. Such a limitation is necessary, in our opinion, "in order" to adapt ... words ... from the judgment in *Bank of Toronto v. Lambe* (1887), 12 App. Cas. 575 (P.C.), "to afford scope" for the working of such parliamentary institutions. In this region of constitutional practice, it is not permitted to a provincial legislature to do indirectly what cannot be done directly (*Great West Saddlery Co. v. The King*).

Section 129 of *The British North America Act* is in these words:

> 129. Except as otherwise provided by this Act, all Laws in force in Canada, Nova Scotia or New Brunswick, at the Union, and all Courts of Civil and Criminal Jurisdiction, and all legal Commissions, Powers, and Authorities, and all Officers, Judicial, Administrative, and Ministerial, existing therein at the Union, shall continue in Ontario, Quebec, Nova Scotia, and New Brunswick respectively, as if the Union had not been made; subject nevertheless (except with respect to such as are enacted by or exist under Acts of the Parliament of Great Britain or of the Parliament of the United Kingdom of Great Britain and Ireland), to be repealed, abolished, or altered by the Parliament of Canada, or by the Legislature of the respective Provinces, according to the Authority of the Parliament or of that Legislature under this Act.

The law by which the right of public discussion is protected existed at the time of the enactment of *The British North America Act* and, as far as Alberta is concerned, at the date on which the Alberta Act came into force, the 1st of September, 1905. In our opinion (on the broad principle of the cases mentioned which has been recognized as limiting the scope of general words defining the legislative authority of the Dominion) the Legislature of Alberta has not the capacity under section 129 to alter that law by legislation obnoxious to the principle stated.

The legislation now under consideration manifestly places in the hands of the Chairman of the Social Credit Commission autocratic powers which, it may well be thought, could, if arbitrarily wielded, be employed to frustrate in Alberta these rights of the Crown and the people of Canada as a whole. We do not, however, find it necessary to express an opinion upon the concrete question whether or not this particular measure is invalid as exceeding the limits indicated above.

The answer to the question concerning this Bill is that it is *ultra vires*.

CANNON J.: . . . The third question put to us is the following:

Is Bill No. 9, entitled *An Act to ensure the Publication of Accurate News and Information*, or any of the provisions thereof and in what particular or particulars or to what extent *intra vires* of the legislature of the province of Alberta? . . .

The preamble of the bill, which I will hereafter call the "Press Bill" recites that it is "expedient and in the public interest that the newspapers published in the Province should furnish to the people of the Province statements made by the authority of the Government of the Province as to the true and exact objects of the policy of the Government and as to the hindrances to or difficulties in achieving such objects to the end that the people may be informed with respect thereto."

Section 3 provides that any proprietor, editor, publisher or manager of any newspaper published in the province shall, when required to do so by the Chairman of the Board constituted by section 3 of the *Alberta Social Credit Act*, publish in that newspaper any statement furnished by the Chairman which has for its object the correction or amplification of any statement relating to any policy or activity of the government of the province published by that newspaper within the next preceding thirty-one days.

And section 4 provides that the proprietor, etc., of any newspaper upon being required by the Chairman in writing shall within twenty-four hours after the delivery of the requirement "make a return in writing setting out every source from which any information emanated, as to any statement contained in any issue of the newspaper published within sixty days of the making of the requirement and the names, addresses and occupations of all persons by whom such information was furnished to the newspaper and the name and address of the writer of any editorial, article or news item contained in any such issue of the newspaper."

Section 5 denies any action for libel on account of the publication of any statement pursuant to the Act.

Section 6 enacts that in the event of a proprietor, etc., of any newspaper being guilty of any contravention of any of the provisions of the Act, the Lieutenant-Governor-in-Council, upon a recommendation of the Chairman, may by order prohibit,

(a) the publication of such newspaper either for a definite time or until further order;

(b) the publication in any newspaper of anything written by any person specified in the order;

(c) the publication of any information emanating from any person or source specified in the order.

Section 7 provides for penalties for contraventions or defaults in complying with any requirement of the Act.

The policy referred to in the preamble of the Press bill regarding which the people of the province are to be informed from the government standpoint, is undoubtedly the Social Credit policy of the government. The administration of the bill is in the hands of the Chairman of the Social Credit Board who is given complete and discretionary power by the bill. "Social Credit," according to sec. 2(b) of ch. 3,

1937, second session, of the *Alberta Social Credit Amendment Act* is "the power resulting from the belief inherent within society that its individual members in association can gain the objectives they desire;" and the objectives in which the people of Alberta must have a firm and unshaken belief are the monetization of credit and the creation of a provincial medium of exchange instead of money to be used for the purposes of distributing to Albertans loans without interest, per capita dividends and discount rates to purchase goods from retailers. This free distribution would be based on the unused capacity of the industries and people of the province of Alberta to produce goods and services, which capacity remains unused on account of the lack or absence of purchasing power in the consumers in the province. The purchasing power would equal or absorb this hitherto unused capacity to produce goods and services by the issue of Treasury Credit certificates against a Credit Fund or Provincial credit account established by the Commission each year representing the monetary value of this "unused capacity" — which is also called "Alberta credit."

It seems obvious that this kind of credit cannot succeed unless every one should be induced to believe in it and help it along. The word "credit" comes from the latin: *credere*, to believe. It is, therefore, essential to control the sources of information of the people of Alberta, in order to keep them immune from any vacillation in their absolute faith in the plan of the government. The Social Credit doctrine must become, for the people of Alberta, a sort of religious dogma of which a free and uncontrolled discussion is not permissible. The bill aims to control any statement relating to any policy or activity of the government of the province and declares this object to be a matter of public interest. The bill does not regulate the relations of the newspapers' owners with private individual members of the public, but deals exclusively with expression of opinion by the newspapers concerning government policies and activities. The pith and substance of the bill is to regulate the press of Alberta from the viewpoint of public policy by preventing the public from being misled or deceived as to any policy or activity of the Social Credit Government and by reducing any opposition to silence or bring upon it ridicule and public contempt.

I agree with the submission of the Attorney-General for Canada that this bill deals with the regulation of the press of Alberta, not from the viewpoint of private wrongs or civil injuries resulting from any alleged infringement or privation of civil rights which belong to individuals, considered as individuals, but from the viewpoint of public wrongs or crimes, *i.e.*, involving a violation of the public rights and duties to the whole community, considered as a community, in its social aggregate capacity.

Do the provisions of this bill, as alleged by the Attorney-General for Canada, invade the domain of criminal law and trench upon the exclusive legislative jurisdiction of the Dominion in this regard?

The object of an amendment of the criminal law, as a rule, is to deprive the citizen of the right to do that [which], apart from the amendment, he could lawfully do. Sections 120 to 136 of the Criminal Code deal with seditious words and seditious publications; and sect. 133(a) reads as follows:

> No one shall be deemed to have a seditious intention only because he intends in good faith, —
> (a) to show that His Majesty has been misled or mistaken in his measures; or
> (b) to point out errors or defects in the *government* or constitution of the United Kingdom, or of any part of it, or of Canada or *any province thereof*, or in either House of Parliament of the

United Kingdom or of Canada, or *in any legislature*, or in the administration of justice; or to excite His Majesty's subjects to attempt to procure, by lawful means, the alteration of any matter of state; or

     (c) to point out, in order to their removal, matters which are producing or have a tendency to produce feelings of hatred and ill-will between different classes of His Majesty's subjects.

It appears that in England, at first, criticism of any government policy was regarded as a crime involving severe penalties and punishable as such; but since the passing of *Fox's Libel Act* in 1792, the considerations now found in the above article of our Criminal Code that it is not criminal to point out errors in the Government of the country and to urge their removal by lawful means have been admitted as a valid defence in a trial for libel.

Now, it seems to me that the Alberta legislature by this retrograde Bill is attempting to revive the old theory of the crime of seditious libel by enacting penalties, confiscation of space in newspapers and prohibitions for actions which, after due consideration by the Dominion Parliament, have been declared innocuous and which, therefore, every citizen of Canada can do lawfully and without hindrance or fear of punishment. It is an attempt by the legislature to amend the Criminal Code in this respect and to deny the advantage of sect. 133(a) to the Alberta newspaper publishers.

Under the British system, which is ours, no political party can erect a prohibitory barrier to prevent the electors from getting information concerning the policy of the government. Freedom of discussion is essential to enlighten public opinion in a democratic State; it cannot be curtailed without affecting the right of the people to be informed through sources independent of the government concerning matters of public interest. There must be an untrammelled publication of the news and political opinions of the political parties contending for ascendancy. As stated in the preamble of the *British North America Act*, our constitution is and will remain, unless radically changed, "similar in principle to that of the United Kingdom." At the time of Confederation, the United Kingdom was a democracy. Democracy cannot be maintained without its foundation: free public opinion and free discussion throughout the nation of all matters affecting the State within the limits set by the Criminal Code and the common law. Every inhabitant in Alberta is also a citizen of the Dominion. The province may deal with his property and civil rights of a local and private nature within the province; but the province cannot interfere with his status as a Canadian citizen and his fundamental right to express freely his untrammelled opinion about government policies and discuss matters of public concern. The mandatory and prohibitory provisions of the Press Bill are, in my opinion, *ultra vires* of the provincial legislature. They interfere with the free working of the political organization of the Dominion. They have a tendency to nullify the political rights of the inhabitants of Alberta as citizens of Canada, and cannot be considered as dealing with matters purely private and local in that province. The federal Parliament is the sole authority to curtail, if deemed expedient and in the public interest, the freedom of the press in discussing public affairs and the equal rights in that respect of all citizens throughout the Dominion. These subjects were matters of criminal law before Confederation, have been recognized by Parliament as criminal matters and have been expressly dealt with by the Criminal Code. No province has the power to reduce in that province the political rights of its citizens as compared with those enjoyed by the citizens of other provinces of Canada. Moreover, citizens outside the province of Alberta have a vital interest in having full information and comment, favourable and unfavourable, regarding the policy of the Alberta government and concerning events in that province which would, in the ordinary course, be the subject of Alberta newspapers' news items and articles.

I would, therefore, answer the question as to Bill No. 9 in the negative.

KERWIN J. (for himself and Crocket J.): ... the Press Bill is part of the same legislative plan that, in my opinion, is outside the powers conferred upon the provinces, and ... the part must suffer the fate of the whole.

Other objections against the validity of the Press Bill were urged but I refrain from expressing any opinion upon them. They raise important constitutional questions, the consideration of which I prefer to postpone until the need to do so arises.

HUDSON J.: ... I concur in the views of the other members of the Court that the bill entitled "An Act to ensure the publication of accurate news and information" is *ultra vires*, because it is ancillary to and dependent upon the *Alberta Social Credit Act*, but refrain from expressing any views as to the boundaries of legislative authority as between the provinces and the Dominion in relation to the press. It is a problem with many facets with which I hesitate to deal until presented to us in a more concrete form.

[An appeal to the Privy Council proceeded on Bill No. 1 alone: [1939] A.C. 117 (P.C.).

See the criticism by Tollefson, "Freedom of the Press", in Lang (ed.), *Contemporary Problems of Public Law in Canada* (1968), p. 49.]

# SAUMUR v. QUEBEC AND A.-G. QUE.

In the Supreme Court of Canada. [1953] 2 S.C.R. 299.

Rinfret C.J.C, Kerwin, Taschereau, Rand, Kellock, Estey, Locke, Cartwright and Fauteux JJ. Oct. 6, 1953.

Appeal from a judgment of the Quebec Court of Queen's Bench, Appeal Side, 104 C.C.C. 106, dismissing an appeal from a judgment of the Superior Court holding a certain by-law applicable to Jehovah's Witnesses.

RINFRET C.J.C. (dissenting) (translation of reasons originally given in French):

Stripped of its extravagant build-up and reduced to its true dimensions, this case, in my opinion, is really very simple. It surely does not have the scope and importance that Jehovah's Witnesses have tried to give it through the interpretation of Mr. Laurier Saumur, the appellant, describing himself as a missionary evangelist.

It is a question of the validity of a municipal by-law and there have probably been hundreds and hundreds of cases of this kind since Confederation. If, on the other hand, this type of case has not been very frequently submitted to the Supreme Court of Canada, it is only because of its relative lack of importance and its limited application in each case to the territory of the municipality concerned.

Here is the text of the by-law attacked:

> 184(1). It is by the present by-law forbidden to distribute in the streets of the City of Quebec any book, pamphlet, booklet, circular, tract whatever, without having previously obtained for so doing the written permission of the Chief of Police.
>
> (2) Any one contravening the present by-law shall be liable to a fine, with or without costs, and in default of immediate payment of said fine, with or without costs, as the case may be, to an imprisonment to be fixed by the Recorder's Court of the City of Quebec, at its discretion, but the said fine shall not exceed one hundred dollars and the imprisonment shall not exceed three months of the calendar. Said imprisonment nevertheless shall cease at any time before the expiration of the term fixed by the said Recorder's Court, upon payment of the said fine or of the said fine and costs, as the case may be, and if said infraction is repeated, said repetition of offence shall constitute day by day, after summons or arrest, a separate offence.

The appellant, pleading his status as subject of Her Majesty the Queen and resident of the City of Quebec, and further alleging that he is a missionary-evangelist and one of Jehovah's Witnesses, declares that he considers it his duty to preach the Bible, either orally or by distributing publications in the form of books, booklets, periodicals, leaflets, etc., from house to house and in the streets.

He claims that By-law 184, reproduced above, in effect renders illegal this distribution of literature without written approval of the Chief of Police of the City of Quebec. He adds that in his capacity as a Canadian citizen he has an absolute right to the expression of his opinions, and that that flows from his right of freedom of speech, freedom of the press and free exercise of his worship of God, as guaranteed by the unwritten British Constitution, by the *B.N.A. Act* generally, and also by the statutes of the Province of Quebec, especially the *Freedom of Worship Act*, R.S.Q. 1941, c. 307.

He alleges that the City of Quebec and the Province of Quebec have no jurisdiction, either in law or constitutionally, to adopt a by-law such as the above, and that the latter is *ultra vires*, unconstitutional, illegal and void. . . .

The respondent, the City of Quebec, has pleaded that By-law 184 was a municipal law lawfully enacted in the exercise of the regulatory powers of the City and according to its incorporating statute; that the law of the Province, by virtue of which the by-law was passed is constitutional. . . .

. . . the by-law in dispute is nothing other than a police regulation; it is based primarily on the fact that the streets should not be used for the purpose of distributing documents. The normal use of the streets is that of circulation on foot or in vehicles (see Dillon on Municipal Corporations, 5th ed., p. 1083; McQuillin on Municipal Corporations, 2nd ed., vol. 3, p. 936 and following; same volume, p. 61, no. 938).

Let us note first of all that the *Charter* of the City of Quebec is anterior to Confederation (29-30 Vict., c. 57). The City is not governed by the *Cities and Towns Act*, R.S.Q. 1941, c. 233, but it is not improper to refer to this law to get a clear idea of the extent of the powers which are bestowed there for the regulation of the streets. . . .:

It is not less clear that in the distribution it makes of legislative powers, the *B.N.A. Act*, by ss. 91 and 92, confers, upon the Legislature in each Province, the exclusive power to make laws relative to the municipal institutions in the Province (s-s. (8)), to property and civil rights in the Province s-s. (13)), and generally to all matters of a purely local and private nature in the Province (s-s. (16)).

It would be really fantastic to maintain that some of the powers . . . in the *Cities and Towns Act* of the Province of Quebec, could belong to the federal field. I cannot easily picture the Federal Parliament undertaking to adopt laws on any of these matters. (See the judgment of the Privy Council in *Hodge v. The Queen* (1883), 9 App. Cas. 117 at 131, 133-4).

The difficulty that the appellant is experiencing here results from several reasons:

First: His right to distribute religious pamphlets does not constitute the exercise of worship or religious profession.

Secondly: In any event, the free exercise and enjoyment of religious profession and worship does not, by virtue of s. 2 of R.S.Q. 1941, c. 307, enjoy absolute authorization, but the worship must be exercised "so as the same be not made an excuse for acts of licentiousness, or a justification of practices inconsistent with the peace and safety of the Province."

Thirdly: Freedom of worship is a civil right and consequently falls under s-s. (13) of s. 92 of the *B.N.A. Act*. It is thus provincial domain . . .

Finally, the last point is the question whether freedom of worship is a civil right which is subject to the jurisdiction of the provincial Legislatures. That is what the Provinces of Saskatchewan and Alberta considered when they adopted laws entitled: *An Act to Protect Certain Civil Rights* (S.S. 1947, c. 35). The object of the law is declared in the preamble as being "to protect Certain Civil Rights" and s. 3 of the law stipulates: "Every person and every class of persons shall enjoy the right to freedom of conscience, opinion and belief, and freedom of religious association, teaching, practice and worship." The Province of Alberta has a similar statute.

On this point it is interesting to refer to the interpretation given by the Privy Council of the expression "civil rights" in the *Quebec Act* of 1774, in the case of *Citizens Ins. Co. of Canada v. Parsons* (1881), 7 App. Cas. 96 at 111 (P.C.): "It is to be observed that the same words, 'civil rights,' are employed in the Act of 14 Geo. 3, c. 83, which made provision for the Government of the province of Quebec. Section 8 of that Act enacted that His Majesty's Canadian subjects within the province of Quebec should enjoy their property, usages, and other civil rights, as they had before done, and that in all matters of controversy relative to property and civil rights resort should be had to the laws of Canada, and be determined agreeably to the said laws. In this statute the words 'property' and 'civil rights' are plainly used in their largest sense; and there is no reason for holding that in the statute under discussion they are used in a different and narrower one."

It is sufficient to draw attention to the contradiction of the argument of the attorney for the appellant who on one hand alleges the unconstitutionality of the *Quebec Charter*, while claiming on the other hand that it is in conflict with the *Freedom of Worship Act* of this same Province of Quebec. It is incontestible that the Legislature which has adopted c. 307 had the desired competence to adopt the Charter of the City of Quebec by virtue of which By-law 184 was enacted. . . .

KERWIN J.: — In my view the right to practise one's religion is a civil right in the Province under head (13) of s. 92 of the *B.N.A. Act* just as much as the right to strike or lockout dealt with by the Judicial Committee in *Toronto Elec. Com'rs. v. Snider*, [1925] A.C. 396 (P.C.). . . .

For the same reason I also think that freedom of the press is a civil right in the Province. [The learned judge concluded that, while the by-law was not *ultra vires*, its present application to prevent the appellant's distribution of pamphlets on the highways was not authorized by it and was subject to be enjoined.] . . .

RAND J.: — Strictly speaking, civil rights arise from positive law; but freedom of speech, religion and the inviolability of the person, are original freedoms which are at once the necessary attributes and modes of self-expression of human beings and the primary conditions of their community life within a legal order. It is in the circumscription of these liberties by the creation of civil rights in persons who may be injured by their exercise, and by the sanctions of public law, that the positive law operates. What we realize is the residue inside that periphery. Their significant relation to our law lies in this, that under its principles to which there are only minor exceptions, there is no prior or antecedent restraint placed upon them: the penalties, civil and criminal, attach to results which their exercise may bring about, and apply as consequential incidents. So we have the civil rights against defamation, assault, false imprisonment and the like, and the punishments of the criminal law; but the sanctions of the latter lie within the exclusive jurisdiction of the Dominion. Civil rights of the same nature arise also as protection against infringements of these freedoms.

That legislation "in relation" to religion and its profession is not a local or private matter would seem to me to be self-evident: the dimensions of this interest are nationwide; it is even today embodied in the highest level of the constitutionalism of Great Britain; it appertains to a boundless field of ideas, beliefs and faiths with the deepest roots and loyalties; a religious incident reverberates from one end of this country to the other, and there is nothing to which the "body politic of the Dominion" is more sensitive.

There is, finally, the implication of s. 93 of the *Confederation Act* which deals with education. In this section appear the only references in the statute to religion. Subsection (1) speaks of "Denominational Schools" and preserves their existing rights and privileges. Subsection (2) extends to the separate schools "of the Queen's Protestant and Roman Catholic Subjects" in Quebec the same "Powers, Privileges and Duties" then conferred and imposed upon the separate schools of the "Queen's Roman Catholic Subjects" in Upper Canada. Subsection (3) provides for an appeal to the Governor-General in Council from an any act or decision of a provincial authority "affecting any Right or Privilege of the Protestant or Roman Catholic Minority of the Queen's Subjects in relation to Education". Subsection (4) declares that in the event of any failure on the part of the provincial authority to observe or enforce the provincial laws contemplated by the section, Parliament may provide for the execution of the provisions of the section. On the argument advanced, and apart from the question of criminal law, these vital constitutional provisions could be written off by the simple expedient of abolishing, as civil rights and by provincial legislation, the religious freedoms of minorities, and so, in legal contemplation, the minorities themselves. . . .

I would, therefore, allow the appeal. . . .

KELLOCK J.: — . . . The question, . . . which lies at the threshold of the case is as to the true nature and character of the by-law.

It will be observed that the by-law is perfectly general in its terms and that while it prohibits in the absence of a licence, at the same time it contemplates, fully as much, distribution at the unfettered will of the municipal official to whom it is delegated the power to grant or to refuse to grant licences. The by-law affords no guide whatever for the regulation from any standpoint of the prohibition or permission for which it provides.

. . . Assuming, for the purposes of argument, that the by-law here in question might, in actual administration by the official mentioned therein, be administered solely to prevent literature reaching the streets which might cause disturbances or nuisance therein, and that a by-law expressly so limited would be within provincial competence, the present by-law is not so limited in its terms. Its validity is not to be judged from the standpoint of matters to which it might be limited, but upon the completely general terms in which it in fact is couched. . . .

It is undoubted that, under a by-law of the nature of By-law 184, the circulation of such material as the above would be impossible except with permission of the censor. This aspect of religious freedom would thereby be interfered with. The question is, therefore, as to the competency of provincial legislation in this field. In support of the by-law, it is said that this is a subject-matter within the category of "Civil Rights in the Province."

In considering this contention certain historical matters are relevant. Under the *Quebec Act* of 1774, c. 83, provision is made for the government of the Province of Canada, which included, *inter alia*, all of the present Provinces of Ontario and Quebec. By s. 8 it is provided that all His Majesty's Canadian subjects within the Province, with the exception of religious orders and communities, might hold and enjoy "their Property and Possessions, together with all Customs and Usages relative thereto, and all other their *Civil Rights*, in as large, ample and beneficial Manner" as if certain previously made proclamations, etc., had not been made. And it was further provided that in all matters of controversy "relative to *Property and Civil Rights*" resort should be had to the laws of Canada as the rule for decision of the same and that all causes which might thereafter be instituted in any of the Courts of justice should, with respect to "such Property and Rights" be determined agreeably to the said laws and customs of Canada until varied by subsequent enactment.

It is plain from other provisions of the statute that "Property and Civil Rights" do not include the right of exercise and profession of religion, as to which express provision was made elsewhere in the statute. . . .

Any contention that the right to the exercise of religion is a mere "civil right" is, therefore, for these reasons quite untenable in my opinion. Even if such a matter could be so regarded, it would not be a civil right "within the Province".

The *B.N.A. Act* itself indicates, in my opinion, that the subject-matter of religious profession is not a matter of provincial legislative jurisdiction within any of the heads of s. 92.

By s. 93 it is enacted that a provincial Legislature may legislate "in relation to" education but subject, *inter alia*, to the provision that:

> (1) Nothing in any law shall prejudicially affect any Right or Privilege with respect to Denominational Schools which any Class of Persons have by Law in the Province at the Union.

The "class" in s-s. (1) must, as stated by the Judicial Committee in *Ottawa R.C. Separate School Trustees v. Mackell*, [1917] A.C. 62 at 69 (P.C.), be a class determined "according to religious belief". The right or privilege preserved by s-s. (1) to such a class with respect to its denominational schools is such only as existed "by law" at the time of Union. It would in my opinion be absurd to say that a provincial Legislature, while it cannot strike at the right of any such class to impart religious instruction to its adherents, may nevertheless legislate so as to affect or destroy the religious faith of the denomination and thus affect or entirely do away with all necessity for religious instruction in that faith. . . .

ESTEY J.: . . . It will also be observed that in the declaration of this right in the Act of 1851 no penalty is provided for infraction thereof. That would indicate that such was left to the field of criminal law where, in principle, it would seem to belong. The right of the free exercise and enjoyment of religious profession and worship, is a personal, sacred right for which, history records, men have striven and fought. Wherever attained they have resisted restrictions and limitations thereon in every possible manner. In one sense it may be styled a civil right, but it does not follow that it would be included within the phrase "Property and Civil Rights in the Province" within the meaning of s. 92(13) of the *B.N.A. Act*. On the contrary it would rather seem that such a right should be included among those upon which the Parliament of Canada might legislate for the preservation of peace, order and good government.

Moreover, having regard to the nature and character of the right which was, by the *Treaty of Paris*, given "to the inhabitants of the countries ceded" and the legislation of 1851 where it is in the preamble thereto stated "legal equality among all Religious Denominations is an admitted principle of Colonial Legislation" and such "a fundamental principle of our civil polity" that legislative sanction should be given thereto, it would appear that if the draftsmen and those enacting the *B.N.A. Act* intended that legislation in relation to this right should be enacted by the Province and effective in a part, rather than by the Parliament of Canada and, therefore, effective in the country as a whole, that express language to that effect would have been embodied in that enactment, more particularly as by that Act "One Dominion under the Crown . . . with a Constitution similar in Principle to that of the United Kingdom" was created.

Furthermore, if such had not been the intention of those preparing and enacting the *B.N.A. Act* it would seem most unlikely that under s. 93 thereof they would have given, in relation to education, the exclusive legislative authority to the provincial Legislature and then have specifically reserved an appeal "to the Governor General in Council from any Act or Decision of any Provincial Authority affecting any Right or Privilege of the Protestant or Roman Catholic Minority of the Queen's subjects in relation to Education" and given power to the Parliament of Canada to enact legislation, in the absence of appropriate provincial legislation, requisite for the due "Execution of the Provisions" of s. 93 and necessary to give effect to its decision upon any appeal under that section.

It, therefore, appears that legislation in relation to this right comes within the description and classification referred to by Sir Montague E. Smith in *Russell v.*

*The Queen* (1882), 7 App. Cas. 829 at 839-40 (P.C.), where his Lordship, when considering the competence of the Parliament of Canada to enact the *Canada Temperance Act*, 1878, stated:

> Law of this nature designed for the promotion of public order, safety, or morals, and which subject those who contravene them to criminal procedure and punishment, belong to the subject of public wrongs rather than to that of civil rights. They are of a nature which falls within the general authority of Parliament to make laws for the order and good government of Canada, and have direct relation to criminal law, which is one of the enumerated classes of subjects assigned exclusively to the Parliament of Canada . . .

The provision of the enactment of 1851 (assented to in 1852), being legislation under s. 91 of the *B.N.A. Act*, by virtue of s. 129 thereof continued in force after Confederation and thereafter could be repealed, abolished or altered by the Parliament of Canada but not by a provincial Legislature. It has never been repealed or altered by that Parliament and, therefore, remains in force. The enactment, therefore, of s. 2 of c. 307 by the Province of Quebec, being legislation in relation to this right, could not be enacted under either heading (13) (Property and Civil Rights in the Province) or heading (16) (Generally all Matters of a merely local or private Nature in the Province) of s. 92 of the *B.N.A. Act.* . . .

CARTWRIGHT J. (dissenting): . . . In my view, legislation authorizing the City to pass this by-law is *prima facie* in relation to either or both of two subjects within the provincial power which may be conveniently described as (1) the use of highways, and (2) police regulations and the suppression of conditions likely to cause disorder. I propose to deal with these in the order mentioned.

The judgments of this Court in *O'Brien v. Allen* (1900), 30 S.C.R. 340, and in *Prov. Sec. of P.E.I. v. Egan*, [1941] S.C.R. 396, established that the use of highways in the Province is a subject-matter within the provicial power. . . .

It appears to me to follow from the judgments in *O'Brien v. Allen, supra*, and *Prov. Sec. of P.E.I. v. Egan, supra*, that the legislative authority to permit, forbid or regulate the use of the highways for purposes other than of passing and repassing belongs to the Province.

Dealing next with the subject of police regulations and the suppression of conditions likely to cause disorder, it appears that this Court has decided that the Province has power to legislate in relation to such matters. [The learned Judge referred here to *Bédard v. Dawson, Reference re Adoption Act*, and *Lymburn v. Mayland*]. . . .

It follows from these authorities that it is within the competence of the Legislature of the Province to prohibit or regulate the distribution, in the streets of the municipalities in the Province, of written matter having a tendency to insult or annoy the recipients thereof with the possible result of giving rise to disorder, and perhaps violence, in the streets.

It is said, however, if I have correctly apprehended the argument for the appellant, that even if the legislation in question appears *prima facie* to fall within the powers of the provincial Legislature under the two heads with which I have dealt above it is in reality an enactment destructive of the freedom of the press and the freedom of religion both of which are submitted to be matters as to which the Province has no power to legislate. In support of such submission counsel referred to a large number of cases decided in the Courts of the United States of America but

I am unable to derive any assistance from them as they appear to be founded on provisions in the Constitution limiting the power to make laws in relation to such matters. Under the *B.N.A. Act*, on the other hand, the whole range of legislative power is committed either to Parliament or the provincial Legislatures and competence to deal with any subject-matter must exist in one or other of such bodies. There are thus no rights possessed by the citizens of Canada which cannot be modified by either Parliament or the Legislatures, but it may often be a matter of difficulty to decide which of such bodies has the legislative power in a particular case. . . .

In my view, freedom of the press is not a separate subject-matter committed exclusively to either Parliament or the Legislatures. In some respects, Parliament, and in others, the Legislatures may validly deal with it. In some aspects it falls within the field of criminal law, but in others it has been dealt with by provincial legislation, the validity of which is not open to question, as for example the *Libel and Slander Act*, R.S.O. 1950, c. 204, and the similar Acts in the other Provinces. If the subject-matter of a provincial enactment falls within the class of subjects enumerated in s. 92 of the *B.N.A. Act* such enactment does not, in my opinion, cease to be *intra vires* of the Legislature by reason of the fact that it has the effect of cutting down the freedom of the press. The question of legislative competence is to be determined not by inquiring whether the enactment lays a previous restraint upon publication or attaches consequences after publication has occurred but rather by inquiring whether in substance the subject-matter dealt with falls within the provincial power. I have already indicated my view that the Province has power under the two headings which I have discussed above to authorize the passing of the by-law in question. . . .

It may well be that Parliament alone has power to make laws in relation to the subject of religion as such, that that subject is, in its nature, one which concerns Canada as a whole and so cannot be regarded as of a merely local or private nature in any Province or as a civil right in any Province; but we are not called upon to decide that question in this appeal and I express no opinion upon it. I think it clear that the Provinces, legislating within their allotted sphere, may affect the carrying on of activities connected with the practice of religion. For example, there are many municipal by-laws in force in cities in Ontario, passed pursuant to powers conferred by the provincial Legislature, which provide that no buildings other than private residences shall be erected on certain streets. Such by-laws are, in my opinion, clearly valid although they prevent any religious body from building a church or similar edifice on such streets. Another example of provincial legislation which might be said to interfere directly with the free exercise of religious profession is that under which the by-law considered in *Re Cribbin & Toronto* (1891), 21 O.R. 325 (Q.B.), was passed. That was a by-law of the City of Toronto which provided in part: "No person shall on the Sabbath-day, in any public park, square, garden, or place for exhibition in the city of Toronto, publicly preach, lecture or declaim." The by-law was attacked on the ground, *inter alia*, that it was unconstitutional but it was upheld by Galt C.J. and in my opinion his decision was right. No useful purpose would be served by endeavouring to define the limits of the provincial power to pass legislation affecting the carrying on of activities connected with the practice of religion. The better course is, I think, to deal only with the particular legislation now before us. . . .

To summarize, I am of opinion that it was within the competence of the Legislature to authorize the passing of the by-law in question under its power to legislate in relation to (i) the use of highways, and (ii) police regulations and the suppression of conditions likely to cause disorder; and that such legislation is not rendered invalid because it interferes to the limited extents indicated above with either the freedom of the press or the freedom of religion. It follows that I would dismiss the appeal. . . .

*Appeal allowed.*

[Locke J. read the by-law as addressed in pith and substance to censorship, hence *ultra vires* under the principles announced by Sir Lyman Duff C.J. in *Re Alberta Legislation*, [1938] S.C.R. 100 at 132; affirmed [1939] A.C. 117 (P.C.). Taschereau J., dissenting, concurred with Rinfret C.J.C. and Fauteux J., dissenting, concurred with Cartwright J. The formal judgment of the Court was as follows:

The appeal is allowed and the judgment of the Court of Queen's Bench (Appeal Side) set aside. It is declared that By-law 184 of the City of Quebec passed on October 27, 1933, does not extend so as to prohibit the appellant as a member of Jehovah's Witnesses from distributing in the streets of Quebec any book, pamphlet, booklet, circular or tract of Jehovah's Witnesses included in the exhibits. The City of Quebec, its officers and agents are restrained from in any way interfering with such actions of the appellant.
The Chief Justice, Taschereau, Cartwright and Fauteux JJ. dissenting would have dismissed the appeal.
Rand, Kellock, Estey and Locke JJ. would have declared the by-law *ultra vires*.
The appellant is entitled to his costs throughout against the City of Quebec, except that nothing is allowed for, or in connection with, his *factum* in this Court. No order is made as to costs for or against the intervenant, the Attorney-General of Quebec.
The *Saumur* case is discussed by Laskin, "Our Civil Liberties — The Role of the Supreme Court" (1955), 41 Queen's Quarterly 455.]

## Note

Following the *Saumur* decision, the *Quebec Freedom of Worship Act*, R.S.Q. 1941, c. 307 was amended by 1953-54, c. 15 to provide in effect that it is not freedom of religious profession and worship to distribute the kind of pamphlets that Jehovah's Witnesses were passing out, *i.e.* pamphlets attacking the religious beliefs of others, or to make speeches involving such attacks. The amendment created a summary conviction offence in these respects and provided for injunction proceedings. Does the amendment effectively cure in favour of the Province the situation produced by the view of Kerwin J. that the by-law in the *Saumur* case must give way before the *Freedom of Worship Act*? An attempt to obtain a ruling on the validity of the amended statute was rejected in *Saumur v. A.-G. Que.*, [1964] S.C.R. 252 on the ground that the plaintiff had no status to sue for a declaratory judgment.

The *Saumur* case, and especially the judgment of Kellock J., was relied on in *R. v. Beattie*, [1967] 2 O.R. 488 (H.C.) to invalidate a municipal by-law which purported to regulate the use of parks and prohibited the use of language likely to stir up hatred against any member of the public distinguished by colour, race, religion, ethnic or national origin. Is this decision consistent with *Re Cribbin and Toronto*, referred to on p. 931?

In *R. v. Harrold*, [1971] 3 W.W.R. 365 (B.C. C.A.) (leave to appeal to S.C.C. refused 3 C.C.C. (2d) 387n) the accused, a member of a religious group which would gather in the city streets and chant sounds to the accompaniment of a small drum and a few cymbals, was convicted of violating a City of Vancouver anti-noise by-law. The British Columbia Court of Appeal in upholding the conviction applied the dictum of Cartwright J. in *Saumur*, (see pp. 404 *et seq., supra*) and held:

> the right to freedom of religion does not permit anyone, acting under the umbrella of his religious teachings and practices, to violate the law of the land, whether that law be Federal, Provincial or Municipal.

Leave to appeal to the Supreme Court of Canada was refused.

# SWITZMAN v. ELBLING AND A.-G. QUE.

In the Supreme Court of Canada. [1957] S.C.R. 285.

Kerwin C.J.C, Taschereau, Rand, Fauteux, Abbott, Kellock, Locke, Nolan and Cartwright JJ. November 7, 1957

Appeal from a judgment of the Quebec Court of Queen's Bench (Appeal Side), [1954] Que. Q.B. 421, affirming a judgment of Collins J. and upholding the validity of the *Communistic Propaganda Act* (Que.).

KERWIN C.J.C.: — I am unable to agree with Mr. Beaulieu's contention that there is in issue the constitutional validity of only part of the statute. The order signed by the Attorney-General of the Province of Quebec, dated January 27, 1949, recites the provisions of both ss. 3 and 12 of that Act and in his intervention the Attorney-General asked the Court to declare the said Act in its entirety consti-tutional and valid and in full force and effect.

Section 1 provides: "This Act may be cited as *Act Respecting Communistic Propaganda.*"

Sections 3 and 12 read:

> 3. It shall be illegal for any person, who possesses or occupies a house within the Province, to use it or allow any person to make use of it to propagate communism or bolshevism by any means whatsoever.
>
> 12. It shall be unlawful to print, to publish in any manner whatsoever or to distribute in the Province any newspaper, periodical, pamphlet, circular, document or writing whatsoever propa-gating or tending to propagate communism or bolshevism.

Sections 4 to 11 provide that the Attorney-General, upon satisfactory proof that an infringement of s. 3 has been committed, may order the closing of the house; authorize any Peace Officer to execute such order and provide a procedure by which the owner may apply by petition to a Judge of the Superior Court to have the order revised. Section 13 provides for imprisonment of anyone infringing or participating in the infringement of s. 12. In my opinion it is impossible to separate the provisions of ss. 3 and 12.

The validity of the statute was attacked upon a number of grounds, but, in cases where constitutional issues are involved, it is important that nothing be said that is unnecessary. In my view it is sufficient to declare that the Act is legislation in relation to the criminal law over which, by virtue of head 27 of s. 91 of the *B.N.A. Act*, the Parliament of Canada has exclusive legislative authority. The decision of this Court in *Bédard v. Dawson & A.-G. Que.*, [1923] S.C.R. 681, is clearly distinguishable. As Mr. Justice Barclay points out, the real object of the Act here under consideration is to prevent propagation of Communism within the Province and to punish anyone who does so — with provisions authorizing steps for the closing of premises used for such object. The *Bédard* case was concerned with the control and enjoyment of property. I am unable to agree with the decision of Greenshields C.J. in *Fineberg v. Taub* (1939), 77 Que. S.C. 233. It is not necessary to refer to other authorities, because, once the conclusion is reached that the pith and substance of the impugned Act is in relation to criminal law, the conclusion is inevitable that the Act is unconstitutional.

The appeal should be allowed, the judgments below set aside and the action dismissed with costs. . . .

TASCHEREAU J. (dissenting) (approved translation of reasons originally given in French): . . . The appellant admitted having used the building for the propagation of Communistic doctrine, but has specifically pleaded that the law was *ultra vires* of the Legislature of Quebec, as it constitutes an infringement of the legislative power of the federal authority, who alone would be empowered to legislate on the matter. As the constitutionality of the provincial Act was challenged, notice was given to the Attorney-General of the Province of Quebec, pursuant to art. 114 of the *Code of Civil Procedure*, and the latter produced an intervention, in which he supported the total validity of the Act.

Mr. Justice Collins of the Superior Court maintained the action, as well as the intervention of the Attorney-General, cancelled the lease, and consequently upheld the validity of the legislation. This judgment was affirmed by the Court of Queen's Bench, Mr. Justice Barclay dissenting. . . .

The law called *An Act to Protect the Province against Communistic Propaganda* enacts that it is illegal for any person who possesses or occupies a house within the Province, to use it or to allow any person to make use of it to propagate Communism or Bolshevism by any means whatsoever. The law authorizes the Attorney-General, upon satisfactory proof that an infringement has been committed, to order the closing of the house for a period of not more than one year. The recourse conferred by law to the owner of the house, is to make a petition to the Court for a review of the order, by establishing that he was acting in good faith, that he was in ignorance of the house being used in contravention of the Act, or that the house had not been used for illegal purposes.

The appellant contends that this legislation is exclusively within the domain of the criminal law, and that consequently it is without the legislative competency of the provincial authority. I would willingly agree with him, if the Legislature had enacted that Communism was a crime punishable by law, because there would then be clearly an encroachment on the federal domain, which would make the legislation *ultra vires* of the Province. But such is not the case that we have before us. The Legislature did not say that any act constituted a crime, and it did not confer the character of criminalty upon the Communistic doctrine. If the provincial Legislature has no power to create criminal offences, it has the right to legislate to prevent crimes, disorders, as treason, sedition, illegal public meetings, which are crimes under the Criminal Code, and to prevent conditions calculated to favour the development of crime. In order to achieve its aims, I entertain no doubt that it may validly legislate as to the possession and use of property, as this is exclusively within the domain of civil law, and is by virtue of s. 92 of the *B. N. A. Act* (head 13) within the provincial competency.

The case of *Bédard v. Dawson (supra)*, is very similar to the present case. There again, the validity of the provincial law entitled *An Act Respecting the Owners of Houses used as Disorderly Houses*, was challenged. This law enacted that it was illegal for any person who owned or occupied any house or building of any nature whatsoever, to use or to allow any person to use the same as a disorderly house. A certified copy of any judgment convicting any person of an offence under ss. 228, 228*a*, 229 or 229*a*, of the old *Criminal Code*, was a *prima facie* proof of such use of the house in respect of which such conviction was had. After notice given to the interested parties, if such building still continued to be used as a disorderly house, an injunction could be obtained directed to the owner or the lessee, restraining them from using or permitting the use of such building for the above purposes. After the expiry of ten days, *the Court could order the closing of the house.*

The Supreme Court of Canada [[1923] S.C.R. 681], affirming the decision of the Court of King's Bench of the Province of Quebec (*Bédard v. Dawson*, 33 Que. K.B. 246) held that this law was constitutional, and that although criminal law and rules of procedure were exclusively within the authority of the Federal Parliament, the provincial Legislature had the right to legislate on all civil matters in relation to criminal law and to sanction its enactments with a penalty. . . .

[His Lordship then considered *Lymburn v. Mayland*, [1932] A.C. 318, and *Prov.-Sec. of P. E. I. v. Egan*, [1941] S.C.R. 396, and continued as follows:]

I am clearly of opinion that if a Province may validly legislate on all civil matters in relation to criminal law, *that if it may enact laws calculated to suppress conditions favouring the development of crime*, and control properties in order to protect society against any illegal uses that may be made of them, if it has the undeniable right to supervise brokers in their financial transactions in order to protect the public against fraud, if, finally, it has the right to impose civil incapacities as a consequence of a criminal offence, I cannot see why it could not also have the power to enact that all those who extol doctrines, calculated to incite to treason, to the violation of official secrets, to sedition, etc., should be deprived of the enjoyment of the properties from where are spread these theories, the object of which is to undermine and overthrow the established order.

For all these reasons, I am of opinion that this appeal must be dismissed with costs. . . .

RAND J.: By 1937, c. 11, passed by the Legislature of the Province of Quebec entitled *An Act to Protect the Province against Communistic Propaganda* (now R.S.Q. 1941, c. 52) the following provisions are enacted:

> 3. It shall be illegal for any person who possesses or occupies a house within the Province, to use it or allow any person to make use of it to propagate communism or bolshevism by any means whatsoever.
>
> 12. It shall be unlawful to print, to publish in any manner whatsoever or to distribute in the Province any newspaper, periodical pamphlet, circular, document or writing whatsoever propagating or tending to propagate communism or bolshevism.

The word "house" is defined to extend to any building or other construction whatever. By s. 4 the Attorney-General, "upon satisfactory proof that an infringement of section 3 has been committed, may order the closing of the house against its use for any purpose whatsoever for a period of not more than one year; the closing order shall be registered at the registry office of the registration division wherein is situated such house, upon production of a copy of such order certified by the Attorney-General". When a house is closed, an owner who has not been in possession may apply to the Superior Court to have the order revised upon proving that in good faith he was ignorant of the use being made in contravention of the Act or that the house has not been so used during the 12 months preceding the order. Conversely, after an order has been so modified or terminated, the Attorney-General may, on application to the same Court, obtain a decree reviving it. No remedy by resort to a Court is extended to the person in possession against whom the order has become effective. The Attorney-General may at any time permit re-occupation on any conditions thought proper for the protection of the property and its contents or he may revoke the order.

The action in this appeal was brought by an owner against a tenant to have a lease set aside and for damages on the ground of the use of the leased premises for the illegal purpose so defined and their closure under such an order. As the validity of the Act was challenged by the defence, the Attorney-General intervened and that issue became the substantial question in the proceedings.

In addition to the closure, a large quantity of documentary matter was seized and removed. In the order both ss. 3 and 12 are recited and the concluding paragraph is in these terms:

> Je, soussigné, procureur général de la province de Québec, croyablement informé des infractions et violations ci-dessus, vous enjoins de fermer pour toutes fins quelconques, pendant un an à compter de l'exécution de cet ordre, la maison portant le numéro civique 5321 de l'avenue du Parc, dans la cité de Montréal, et de plus, vous êtes par les présentes autorisé, et je vous donne les instructions en conséquence, à saisir et confisquer tout journal, revue, pamphlet, circulaire, document ou écrit quelconque imprimé, publié ou distribué en contravention à la dite loi, en particulier et sans restrictions à saisir et à détruire les exemplaires du journal 'Combat'.

From this it is clear that the order was based upon both sections. . . .

The first ground on which the validity of s. 3 is supported is head 13 of s. 92 of the *B.N.A. Act*, "Property in the Province" and Mr. Beaulieu's contention goes in this manner: by that head the Province is vested with unlimited legislative power over property; it may, for instance, take land without compensation and generally may act as amply as if it were a sovereign state, untrammelled by constitutional limitation. The power being absolute can be used as an instrument or means to effect any purpose or object. Since the objective accomplishment under the statute here is an act on property, its validity is self-evident and the question is concluded.

I am unable to agree that in our federal organization power absolute in such a sense resides in either Legislature. The detailed distribution made by ss. 91 and 92 places limits to direct and immediate purposes of provincial action. Under head 13 the purpose would, in general, be a "property" purpose either primary or subsidiary to another head of the same section. If such a purpose is foreign to powers vested in the Province by the Act, it will invade the field of the Dominion. For example, land could not be declared forfeited or descent destroyed by attainder on conviction of a crime, nor could the convicted person's right to access to provincial Courts be destroyed. These would trench upon both criminal law and citizenship status. The settled principle that calls for a determination of the "real character", the "pith and substance", of what purports to be enacted and whether it is "colourable" or is intended to effect its ostensible object, means that the true nature of the legislative act, its substance in purpose, must lie within s. 92 or some other endowment of provincial power. That a power ostensibly as here under a specific head cannot be exercised as a means directly and immediately to accomplish a purpose not within that endowment is demonstrated by the following decisions of the Judicial Committee: *Union Colliery Co. of B.C. Ltd. v. Bryden*, [1899] A.C. 580 (P.C.), holding that legislative power in relation to employment in a coal mine could not be used as a means of nullifying the civil capacities of citizenship and, specifically, of persons qualifying under head 25 of s. 91, Naturalization and Aliens; *Reference re Validity of Section 5(a) of Dairy Industry Act; Can. Federation of Agriculture v. A.-G. Que.*, [1951] A.C. 179 (P.C.), holding that the Dominion, under its power in relation to criminal law, could not prohibit the manufacture of margarine for the purpose of benefiting in local trade one class of producer as against another. The heads of ss. 91 and 92 are to be read and interpreted with each other and with the provisions of the statute as a whole; and what is then exhibited is a pattern of limitations, curtailments and modifications of legislative scope within a texture of interwoven and interacting powers.

In support of the legislation on this ground, *Bédard v. Dawson*, [1923] S.C.R. 681, was relied on. In that case the statute provided that it should be illegal for the owner or occupier of any house or building to use it or allow it to be used as a disorderly house; and procedure was provided by which the Superior Court could, after a conviction under the Criminal Code, grant an injunction against the owner restraining that use of it. If the use continued, the Court could order the building to be closed for a period of not more than one year.

This power is seen to have been based upon a conviction for maintaining a public nuisance. Under the public law of England which underlies that of all the Provinces, such an act was not only a matter for indictment but in a civil aspect the Court could enjoin its continuance. The essence of this aspect is its repugnant or prejudicial effect upon the neighbouring inhabitants and properties.

On that view this Court proceeded in *Bédard*. . . .

That the scene of study, discussion or dissemination of views or opinions on any matter has ever been brought under legal sanction in terms of nuisance is not suggested. For the past century and a half in both the United Kingdom and Canada, there has been a steady removal of restraints on this freedom, stopping only at perimeters where the foundation of the freedom itself is threatened. Apart from sedition, obscene writings and criminal libels, the public law leaves the literary, discursive and polemic use of language, in the broadest sense, free.

The object of the legislation here, as expressed by the title, is admittedly to prevent the propagation of Communism and Bolshevism, but it could just as properly have been the suppression of any other political, economic or social doctrine or theory; and the issue is whether that object is a matter "in relation to which" under s. 92 the Province may exclusively make laws. Two heads of the section are claimed to authorize it: head 13, as a matter of "Civil Rights", and head 16, "Local and Private Matters".

Mr. Tremblay in a lucid argument treated such a limitation of free discussion and the spread of ideas generally as in the same category as the ordinary civil restrictions of libel and slander. These obviously affect the matter and scope of discussion to the extent that it trenches upon the rights of individuals to reputation and standing in the community; and the line at which the restraint is drawn is that at which public concern for the discharge of legal or moral duties and government through rational persuasion, and that for private security, are found to be in rough balance.

But the analogy is not a true one. The ban is directed against the freedom or civil liberty of the actor; no civil right of anyone is affected nor is any civil remedy created. The aim of the statute is, by means of penalties, to prevent what is considered a poisoning of men's minds, to shield the individual from exposure to dangerous ideas, to protect him, in short, from his own thinking propensities. There is nothing of civil rights in this; it is to curtail or proscribe these freedoms which the majority so far consider to be the condition of social cohesion and its ultimate stabilizing force.

It is then said that the ban is a local matter under head 16; that the social situation in Quebec is such that safeguarding its intellectual and spiritual life against subversive doctrines becomes a special need in contrast with that for a general regulation by Parliament. A similar contention was made in the *Reference re Saskatchewan Farm Security Act, 1944, Section 6*, [1947] S.C.R. 394, affirmed in the Judicial Committee [1949] A.C. 110 (P.C.) (*sub nom. A.-G. Sask. v. A.-G. Can.*). What was dealt with there was the matter of interest on mortgages and a great deal of evidence to show the unique vicissitudes of farming in that Province was adduced. But there, as here, it was and is obvious that local conditions of that nature, assuming, for the purpose of the argument only, their existence, cannot extend legislation to matters which lie outside of s. 92.

Indicated by the opening words of the preamble in the Act of 1867, reciting the desire of the four Provinces to be united in a federal union with a Constitution "similar in Principle to that of the United Kingdom", the political theory which the Act embodies is that of parliamentary Government, with all its social implications, and the provisions of the statute elaborate that principle in the institutional apparatus which they create or contemplate. Whatever the deficiencies in its workings, Canadian Government is in substance the will of the majority expressed directly or indirectly through popular assemblies. This means ultimately government by the free public opinion of an open society, the effectiveness of which, as events have not infrequently demonstrated, is undoubted.

But public opinion, in order to meet such a responsibility, demands the condition of a virtually unobstructed access to and diffusion of ideas. Parliamentary Government postulates a capacity in men, acting freely and under self-restraints, to govern themselves; and that advance is best served in the degree achieved of individual liberation from subjective as well as objective shackles. Under that Government, the freedom of discussion in Canada, as a subject-matter of legislation, has a unity of interest and significance extending equally to every part of the Dominion. With such dimensions it is *ipso facto* excluded from head 16 as a local matter.

This constitutional fact is the political expression of the primary condition of social life, thought and its communication by language. Liberty in this is little less vital to man's mind and spirit that breathing is to his physical existence. As such an inherence in the individual it is embodied in his status of citizenship. Outlawry, for example, divesting civil standing and destroying citizenship, is a matter of Dominion concern. Of the fitness of this order of Government to the Canadian organization, the words of Taschereau J. in *Brassard v. Langevin* (1877), 1 S.C.R. 145 at 195 should be recalled: "The object of the electoral law was to promote, by means of the ballot, and with the absence of all undue influence, the free and sincere expression of public opinion in the choice of members of the Parliament of Canada. This law is the just sequence to the excellent institutions which we have borrowed from England, institutions which, as regards civil and religious liberty, leave to Canadians nothing to envy in other countries."

Prohibition of any part of this activity as an evil would be within the scope of criminal law, as ss. 60, 61 and 62 of the *Criminal Code* dealing with sedition exemplify. Bearing in mind that the endowment of parliamentary institutions is one and entire for the Dominion, that Legislatures and Parliament are permanent features of our constitutional structure, and that the body of discussion is indivisible, apart from the incidence of criminal law and civil rights, and incidental effects of legislation in relation to other matters, the degree and nature of its regulation must await future consideration; for the purposes here it is sufficient to say that it is not a matter within the regulation of a Province.

Mr. Scott, in his able examination of the questions raised, challenged also the validity of ss. 4 *et seq.* which vested in the Attorney-General the authority to adjudicate upon the commission of the illegal act under s. 3 and to issue the order of closure; but in view of the conclusion reached on the other grounds, the consideration of this becomes unnecessary.

I would, therefore, allow the appeal, set aside the judgments below, dismiss the action and direct a declaration on the intervention that the statute in its entirety is *ultra vires* of the Province. . . .

FAUTEUX J. (translation): . . . That the sole legal object of the Act is to prohibit, with penal sanctions, Communistic propaganda, or more precisely to make such propaganda a criminal act, could, I think, not be more manifest.

. . . In this specific instance, the subject-matter of the main provision — prohibition of Communistic propaganda — is certainly one not coming, by itself, within the class of subjects enumerated in s. 92 as being within the competence of the Legislature. Parliament alone, legislating in criminal matters, is competent to enact, define, prohibit and punish these matters of a writing or of a speech that, on account of their nature, injuriously affect the social order or the safety of the state. Such are, for example, defamatory, obscene, blasphemous or seditious libels. In such cases, the rights being encroached upon are not those of an individual entitling him to a monetary compensation. . . .

Two fundamental differences should be pointed out between this Act and the *Act Respecting the Owners of Houses used as Disorderly Houses*, the constitutionality of which was affirmed by this Court in *Bédard v. Dawson (supra)*. In the *Disorderly House Act* [now R.S.Q. 1941, c. 50], there is no provision of the nature of s. 12, as in the statute now under consideration, but merely a provision of the nature of s. 3, *i.e.*, a provision declaring illegal the use of a house as a disorderly one. Moreover, in the *Disorderly House Act*, the Legislature adopted as a definition of the expression "disorderly house", the definition of this expression in the Criminal

Code. The existence and the operation of the provincial Act was thus, in its principle and extent, fully subordinated to the existence and operation of the provisions established in the Criminal Code. It was therefore held that the Legislature had not created a crime but had simply provided for civil consequences resulting from the commission of a crime created by competent authority, and suppressed the conditions leading to the commission of that crime. That fundamental feature is obviously missing in the present case; here, the Legislature, not Parliament, created the crime. This aspect of the matter was not present in *Bédard v. Dawson (supra)*; it was present, but was not considered, in *Fineberg v. Taub* (1939), 77 Que. S.C. 233. For these reasons, neither the decision of this Court in the first case nor the decision of the Superior Court in the second case are authorities supporting the proposition that "Property and Civil Rights in the Province" is the matter in relation to which the law under consideration is enacted....

ABBOTT J.: . . . The right of free expression of opinion and of criticism, upon matters of public policy and public administration, and the right to discuss and debate such matters, whether they be social, economic or political, are essential to the working of a parliamentary democracy such as ours. Moreover, it is not necessary to prohibit the discussion of such matters, in order to protect the personal reputation or the private rights of the citizen. That view was clearly expressed by Duff C.J.C. in *Re Alberta Legislation*, [1938] S.C.R. 100 at 132-4....

This right cannot be abrogated by a provincial Legislature, and the power of such Legislature to limit it, is restricted to what may be necessary to protect purely private rights, such as for example provincial laws of defamation. It is obvious that the impugned statute does not fall within that category. It does not, in substance, deal with matters of property and civil rights or with a local or private matter within the Province and in my opinion is clearly *ultra vires*. Although it is not necessary, of course, to determine this question for the purposes of the present appeal, the Canadian Constitution being declared to be similar in principle to that of the United Kingdom, I am also of opinion that as our constitutional Act now stands, Parliament itself could not abrogate this right of discussion and debate. The power of Parliament to limit it is, in my view, restricted to such powers as may be exercisable under its exclusive legislative jurisdiction with respect to criminal law and to make laws for the peace, order and good Government of the nation.

For the reasons which I have given, I would allow the appeal....

*Appeal allowed.*

[Kellock J. agreed with Rand J. but also delivered a short concurring judgment. Locke J. concurred with Nolan J. who in a concurring judgment concluded that Parliament had exclusive authority to make Communism a crime or to forbid its propagation and hence the provincial statute (which was different from that in *Bédard v. Dawson*) was *ultra vires*. Cartwright J. agreed in a short concurring judgment that the provincial statute invaded the exclusive authority of Parliament in relation to criminal law.]

### Note

In *Oil, Chemical & Atomic Workers International Union Local 16-601 v. Imperial Oil Ltd.*, [1963] S.C.R. 584, Abbott J., dissenting, cautiously reaffirmed his views in the *Switzman* case, *supra*.

The Labour Relations Act, R.S.Q. 1941, c. 162A, s. 6, am. 1953 (2nd sess.), c. 10, s. 1 provided that an association which tolerated a communist among its organizers or officers should be denied recognition. Is this provision (now repealed; the Labour Relations Act has been replaced by the Labour Code, R.S.Q. 1964, c. 141, as amended) valid in the face of the *Switzman* case?

The *Labour Relations Act*, R.S. Nfld. 1952, c. 258, am. 160, c. 58, s. 5 provided by s. 6A that where on an application by the Attorney-General, the Supreme Court is satisfied that a substantial number of the superior officers, agents or representatives of a trade union or any body, group or organization of trade unions outside the province has been convicted of any crime such as trafficking in narcotics, manslaughter, extortion, embezzlement or perjury and any or all of them remain as officers, agents or representatives, the Court shall order that on the expiration of three months from the order any trade union in the province which is a branch, local or affiliate of that trade union or body, group or organization of trade unions shall be dissolved unless within that time it ceases to be such a branch, local or affiliate. Does this provision (which was repealed by 1963, c. 82, s. 2) offend the principles expressed by the ratio of the *Switzman* case? *Cf.* McWhinney, "Mr. Justice Rand's "rights of the Canadian citizen" — The "Padlock" case" (1958), 4 Wayne L. Rev. 115.

A municipal charter authorized suspension of a business licence for gross misconduct on an inspector's opinion. May this power be validly invoked as a matter of legislative jurisdiction to suspend the licence for publication of a newspaper at a certain address because of disapproval of its contents? See *Hlookoff v. Vancouver* (1968), 63 W.W.R. 129 (B.C.S.C.).

In the fall of 1970 the Lieutenant Governor of British Columbia approved an Order in Council which declared as public policy that no teachers in an educational institution receiving government support

> shall continue in the employment of the educational institution if they advocate the policies of Le Front de Liberation du Quebec, or the overthrow of democratically elected governments by violent means.

Is the Order in Council *ultra vires*? In *Jamieson v. A.G. B.C.*, [1971] 5 W.W.R. 600 (B.C.S.C.) an attempt to obtain such a declaration failed because it was held the plaintiffs had no status to sue.

# WALTER v. A.-G. ALTA.

In the Supreme Court of Canada. [1969] S.C.R. 383.

Cartwright C.J.C., Fauteux, Abbott, Martland, Judson, Ritchie, Hall, Spence and Pigeon JJ. October 31, 1968.

The judgment of the Court was delivered by

MARTLAND J.: — The question in issue in both these appeals is as to the constitutional validity of *The Communal Property Act*, R.S.A. 1955, c. 52, as amended, hereinafter referred to as "the Act". In each of the two actions the real purpose was to obtain a declaration that this statute was ultra vires of the Legislature of the Province of Alberta and they were consolidated for trial.

The facts are not in issue. The appellants, other than the Fletchers, are Hutterians. The Fletchers are owners of land in Alberta which their fellow plaintiffs sought to purchase. The plaintiffs in the other action also sought to purchase Alberta lands. It is conceded that the lands in each case sought to be acquired would be held in common as defined in s. 2(b)(i) of the Act and that the operation of the Act prevents the acquisition of the lands. The appellants, other than the Fletchers, in each case formed part of a religious community which based its community life and its holding of property on religious principles.

As of December 31, 1963, Hutterite colonies held approximately 480,000 acres of land in Alberta and over 10,000 acres had been added in 1964. The approximate population of Hutterites in Alberta as of December 31, 1963, was 6,000.

The Act is described as "An Act respecting Lands in the Province Held as Communal Property." "Communal Property" is defined in s. 2 of the Act, which states:

> 2. In this Act,
>   (a) "colony"
>     (i) means a number of persons who hold land or any interest therein as communal property, whether as owners, lessees or otherwise, and whether in the name of trustees or as a corporation or otherwise,
>     (ii) includes a number of persons who propose to acquire land to be held in such manner, and
>     (iii) includes Hutterites or Hutterian Brethren and Doukhobors;
>   (b) "communal property" means
>     (i) land held by a colony in such a manner that no member of the colony has any individual or personal ownership or right of ownership in the land, and each member shares in the distribution of profits or benefits according to his needs or in equal measure with his fellow members, and
>     (ii) land held by a member of the colony by personal ownership or right of ownership or under a lease, if the land is used in conjunction with and as part of other land held in the manner described in subclause (i);
>   (c) "Board" means the Communal Property Control Board established pursuant to this Act.

The general scheme of the Act for controlling the holding of land as communal property is as follows:

Unless otherwise authorized by the Lieutenant Governor in Council in the public interest (s. 5(2)) no colony existing on the 1st day of May, 1947, may increase the holdings of its land beyond its holdings on the 1st day of March, 1944 (s. 4(1)), or, if on that date the holdings were less than 6,400 acres, they may be extended thereto (s. 4(5)). The significance of the dates May 1, 1947, and March 1, 1944, referred to in the statute is as follows: The first Alberta legislation in relation to acquisition of land by Hutterites to come into force was *The Land Sales Prohibition Act*, 1944 (Alta.), c. 15, which came into force on March 1, 1944. In general that statute prohibited the selling of land to and the purchase of land by Hutterites. That Act, as amended, remained the law until it expired on May 1, 1947, and on that date *The Communal Property Act*, 1947 (Alta.), c. 16, came into force. So that between March 1, 1944, and May 1, 1947, no Hutterite could acquire any land in Alberta, but by virtue of the provisions of *The Communal Property Act* which came into force on the latter date the restrictions on the acquisition of land were lessened somewhat in relation to Hutterites and the new provisions were made applicable to all "colonies", whether Hutterite or otherwise.

The general scheme of the Act goes on to provide as follows:

No "colony" which exists or existed outside the province may acquire land without the consent of the Lieutenant Governor in Council (s. 6).

No land may be acquired for the purpose of establishing a new "colony" without the consent of the Lieutenant Governor in Council (s. 7).

By an amendment to the statute which came into force on May 1, 1951, the Lieutenant Governor in Council was authorized to divide the province into zones and to designate the number of acres a "colony" established after that date may acquire in any zone or class of zones (s. 5(1)). By virtue of an amendment made in 1960, "colonies" established after May 1, 1947, were also limited to the number of acres designated by the Lieutenant Governor for each zone (s. 9).

The Lieutenant Governor in Council is authorized to establish a Communal Property Control Board (s. 3a(1)), which is to hear applications by "colonies" for leave to acquire land. Where the application is for leave to acquire additional lands for a "colony" already holding lands, the Board may grant or refuse the application, subject to an appeal to a judge of a district court by "a person or colony not satisfied with the decision of the Board . . ." (s. 13, subss. (1) to (6)).

Where the granting of the application would result in the establishment of a new "colony", the Board is to give public notice of the application, and hold such hearings and make such inquiries as it deems necessary to determine whether the granting of the application would be in the public interest, giving consideration to the location of the lands applied for, the location of the existing "colonies", the geographical location of the lands intended for communal use in relation to the lands not so used, and any other factors which the Board may deem relevant.

Following its investigation the Board is to submit a report to the Minister of Municipal Affairs as to its recommendations in the matter. After consideration of the report the Lieutenant Governor in Council may consent or withhold consent as he deems proper in the public interest, irrespective of the Board's recommendation (s. 14).

Dispositions of land to "colonies" which would result in contravention of the provisions of the statute are prohibited (s. 11).

The submission of the appellants is that the Act is legislation in respect of religion and, in consequence, is beyond the legislative powers of a provincial legislature. The respondent contends that the Act is legislation in respect of property in Alberta, controlling the way in which land is to be held, by regulating the acquisition and disposition of land to be acquired by colonies to be held as communal land.

The learned trial judge, Milvain J. (as he then was), held that, in pith and substance, the Act relates to land tenure in the province and is, therefore, intra vires of the Legislature of the Province of Alberta under s. 92(13) of the *British North America Act*.

The judgment was sustained on appeal [(1967), 58 W.W.R. 385].

In my opinion, the Act was enacted in relation to the ownership of land in Alberta and the Legislature had jurisdiction under s. 92 (13) of the *British North America Act*, because it deals with property in the province. The scheme of the legislation indicates that the Legislature considered the use of large areas of land in Alberta for the purposes of communal living was something which, in the public interest, required to be regulated and controlled. The Act restricts, but does not prohibit, the use of land for such purposes.

It would seem to me to be clear that a provincial legislature can enact laws governing the ownership of land within the province and that legislation enacted in relation to that subject must fall within s. 92(13), and must be valid unless it can be said to be in relation to a class of subject specifically enumerated in s. 91 of the *British North America Act* or otherwise within exclusive Federal jurisdiction.

There is no suggestion in the present case that the Act relates to any class of subject specifically enumerated in s. 91.

It was on the basis that the legislation in question in the cases of *Henry Birks & Sons (Montreal) Limited v. The City of Montreal* [[1955] S.C.R. 799] and *Switzman v. Elbling* [[1957] S.C.R. 285] related to the subject of criminal law, assigned specifically to the Parliament of Canada by s. 91(27) of the *British North America Act*, that the statutes were held to be *ultra vires* of the Legislature of the Province of Quebec.

The *Birks* case involved the validity of a statute which empowered municipal councils of cities and towns to pass by-laws to compel the closing of stores on New Year's Day, the festival of Epiphany, Ascension Day, All Saints' Day, Conception Day and Christmas Day. The legislation was supported in argument on the basis that it related to the control of merchandising and the well-being of employees. It was held to be *ultra vires* of the Legislature of Quebec because it authorized the compulsion of Feast Day observance, and such legislation in England, as in the case of Sunday observance legislation, had been assigned to the domain of criminal law. Legislation in this field was held to relate to the subject of criminal law, assigned specifically to the Parliament of Canada by s. 91(27).

Rand J. went on to add that the legislation was in relation to religion, and beyond provincial competence, and he referred to the *Saumur* case. Kellock and Locke JJ. said that, even if it were not properly "criminal law", it was beyond the competence of the Legislature as being legislation with respect to freedom of religion, a matter dealt with in the statute of the Province of Canada of 1852, 14-15 Vict., c. 175, the relevant portion of which is quoted later in these reasons.

*Switzman v. Elbling* involved the validity of *The Act Respecting Communistic Propaganda*, R.S.Q. 1941, c. 52, which, *inter alia*, made it illegal for any person who possessed or occupied a house in the province to use it or to allow any person to make use of it to propagate communism or bolshevism by any means whatsoever. It was attempted to support the legislation on the ground that it dealt with property in the province.

The majority of the Court was of the opinion that the legislation was in respect of criminal law which, under s. 91(27), was within the exclusive competence of the Parliament of Canada.

It was submitted by the appellants that the Act is aimed at preventing the spread of Hutterite colonies in Alberta, that, because the maintenance of such colonies is a cardinal tenet of the Hutterite religion, the Act seeks to deal with religion, and that the subject of religion is within the exclusive jurisdiction of the Parliament of Canada. Their position is stated in the reasons of Johnson J.A., in the Court below, as follows:

> This Act then in its pith and substance is legislation restricting the acquisition by Hutterites of more land in the province.... I find it difficult to say that legislation which is aimed at the restriction of new and existing colonies and the holding of land in common as practised by these colonies when living in such colonies and holding lands in that manner are the principal tenets of Hutterian faith, does not deal with religion.

With respect, I do not share this view . . .

The purpose of the legislation in question here is to control the use of Alberta lands as communal property. While it is apparent that the legislation was prompted by the fact that Hutterites had acquired and were acquiring large areas of land in Alberta, held as communal property, it does not forbid the existence of Hutterite colonies. What it does is to limit the territorial area of communal land to be held by existing colonies and to control the acquisition of land to be acquired by new colonies which would be held as communal property. The Act is not directed at Hutterite religious belief or worship, or at the profession of such belief. It is directed at the practice of holding large areas of Alberta land as communal property, whether such practice stems from religious belief or not. The fact that Hutterites engage in that practice was the circumstance which gave rise to the necessity for the Legislature's dealing generally with the holding of land as communal property, but that does not mean that legislation controlling the holding of land in that way is not in relation to property in the Province of Alberta.

It is a function of a provincial legislature to enact those laws which govern the holding of land within the boundaries of that province. It determines the manner in which land is held. It regulates the acquisition and disposition of such land, and, if it is considered desirable in the interests of the residents in that province, it controls the extent of the land holdings of a person or group of persons. The fact that a religious group upholds tenets which lead to economic views in relation to land holding does not mean that a provincial legislature, enacting land legislation which may run counter to such views, can be said, in consequence, to be legislating in respect of religion and not in respect to property.

Religion, as the subject-matter of legislation, wherever the jurisdiction may lie, must mean religion in the sense that it is generally understood in Canada. It involves matters of faith and worship, and freedom of religion involves freedom in connection with the profession and dissemination of religious faith and the exercise of religious worship. But it does not mean freedom from compliance with provincial laws relative to the matter of property holding. There has been no suggestion that mortmain legislation by a provincial legislature is incompetent as interfering with freedom of religion . . .

In my opinion, the legislation in question here undoubtedly affects the future expansion and creation of Hutterite colonies in Alberta, but that does not mean it was enacted in relation to the matter of religion. The Act is in relation to the right to acquire land in Alberta, if it is to be used as communal property, and, in consequence, it is within provincial jurisdiction under s. 92(13).

Having reached this conclusion, it is unnecessary for me to express any opinion in respect of the submission of the respondent that legislation in relation to religious freedom falls within the exclusive jurisdiction of provincial legislatures . . .

I would dismiss the appeals with costs. No costs should be paid by or to the intervenant.

*Appeals dismissed with costs.*

[Compare the approach of the United States Supreme Court in *Wisconsin v. Yoder*, 406 U.S. 205. For a fuller discussion of the Hutterite way of life see *Hofer v. Hofer*, [1970] S.C.R. 958, where the majority of the Supreme Court of Canada (Pigeon J. dissenting) held that a member of the Hutterite colony expelled for changing his views to those of a faith incompatible with Hutterite tenets could not move to dissolve the Colony and distribute its assets rateably among the contributing members.

See, generally, Sanders, "The Hutterites: A Case Study in Minority Rights" (1964), 42 Can. Bar Rev. 225.]

# ATTORNEY-GENERAL OF CANADA v. DUPOND

In the Supreme Court of Canada. [1978] 2 S.C.R. 770.

Laskin, C.J.C., Martland, Judson, Ritchie, Spence, Pigeon, Dickson, Beetz and de Grandpré, JJ. January 19, 1978.

Appeals by the Attorney-General for Canada and a ratepayer from decisions of the Quebec Court of Appeal, [1974] Que. C.A. 402, allowing appeals of the Attorney-General for Quebec and the City of Montreal from a declaration by a trial Judge on petition by a ratepayer that a by-law and ordinance of the City of Montreal were unconstitutional.

The dissenting judgment of Laskin C.J.C. and Spence and Dickson JJ. was delivered by

LASKIN C.J.C.: — The terms of the impugned by-law and of the ordinance, passed pursuant to s. 5 thereof, are set out in the reasons of my brother Beetz which I have had the advantage of reading, and I shall not repeat them. It is obvious from the recitals as well as from the terms of the key s. 5 that the City of Montreal has enacted a mini-Criminal Code, dealing with apprehended breach of the peace, apprehended violence and the maintenance of public order, and we are urged to sustain this incursion into the field of criminal law — a matter exclusively for the Parliament of Canada — because it is a matter of local or private nature in the Province.

The only local or private aspect is, in my opinion, the territorial ambit of the by-law and of the ordinance, and this has never been a test of constitutional validity. My brother Beetz has referred to the challenged provisions as regulatory of the public domain, the reference being to public streets and parks. It is not, however, directed to that end as the recitals and central terms clearly indicate. What it does, plainly and without reference to any regulatory consideration, is to make it a punishable offence — a crime — to breach s. 5 of the by-law and the ordinance. Sections 1 and 3 of the by-law do have a relationship to traffic regulation and may be justified in themselves on that basis as provisions which may competently be authorized by provincial legislation. They are, however, integrated in other provisions which are in no sense directed to traffic considerations or to any regulatory use of public parks, and, indeed, as my brother Beetz has noted, the focus is on s. 5 of the by-law and on the ordinance passed in implementation thereof. That provision is so explicitly directed to breach of the peace and to the maintenance of public order as to fall squarely within exclusive federal authority in relation to the criminal law.

The very title of the by-law, as one "relating to exceptional measures to safeguard the free exercise of civil liberties, to regulate the use of the public domain and to prevent riots and other violations of order, peace and public safety" shows its character. The references to safeguarding the free exercise of civil liberties and to regulation of the use of the public domain are hollow references, not in any way fulfilled by the substantive terms of the by-law as are the references to riots, breach of the peace and public order. Moreover, the enactment of the by-law as an exceptional measure is itself an indicator of how far removed it is from any concern, except a consequential one, with regulation of the use of streets and public parks. The enactment of the by-law smacks of an assertion of municipal authority to legislate for the "peace, order and good government" of the City of Montreal, an authority which I do not find in the catalogue of provincial powers under the *British North America Act, 1867*.

The central s. 5 of the by-law and the ordinance are a long way from *Hodge v. The Queen* (1883), 9 App. Cas. 117 (P.C.). That case was concerned with provincial liquor licensing legislation and hence had a constitutional foundation in the local regulation of a trade or business in the Province. The legislation was, therefore, sustainable either under s. 92(13) or under s. 92(16) of the *British North America Act, 1867*, although it will be recalled that in *A.-G. Man. v. Manitoba Licence Holders' Ass'n*, [1902] A.C. 73 (P.C.), the Privy Council preferred to assign provincial regulatory liquor legislation to s. 92(16). There is no similar foundation for the by-law and especially for s. 5 thereof, which is enacted as a strict prohibitory provision unredeemed by any regulatory aspect.

No doubt a prohibition, as a matter of its impact, is regulatory but, for constitutional purposes, provincial prohibitions to be valid have to be associated with a valid scheme of regulation as enforcements or reinforcements thereof, and are not sustainable as peremptory directions against forbidden conduct or behaviour. I am far from supporting the full implications of *City of Toronto v. Virgo*, [1896] A.C. 88, where the Privy Council, at 93, said this in reference to a municipal by-law:

> . . . there is a marked distinction to be drawn between the prohibition or prevention of a trade and the regulation or governance of it, and indeed a power to regulate and govern seems to imply the continued existence of that which is to be regulated or governed.

Yet the distinction drawn in the case is apt here where there is no substratum of regulation upon which a sanction has been mounted.

Two other points are made by the proponents of the by-law. One is that it was called forth by exceptional conditions in Montreal, an assertion which in itself makes the by-law suspect. There is no accretion to provincial legislative authority to enable it to deal with apprehended riots or public disorder merely because the provincial Government or delegated municipal authorities are of the opinion that preventive measures must be taken. They may be taken under ordinary police powers and in accordance with the federal *Criminal Code*, to which I will refer later in these reasons. The second point is that there is no constitutional bar to provincial (or validly authorized municipal) legislation which complements the federal *Criminal Code*. This is a proposition which flies in the face of the scheme of distribution of legislative power; it is destructive of the principle of exclusiveness as expressed in *Union Colliery Co. of B.C. v. Bryden*, [1899] A.C. 580 at 588 (P.C.); and it is not supported by any authorities. Cases such as *O'Grady v. Sparling*, [1960]

S.C.R. 804, and *Mann v. The Queen*, [1966] S.C.R. 238, to take two of those relied upon by the proponents of the by-law, turn on a conclusion that the enactments challenged therein were independently valid as being in relation to a matter within provincial competence. Judson, J., speaking for the majority in *O'Grady v. Sparling*, at 810 S.C.R., said that: "The power of a Provincial Legislature to enact legislation for the regulation of highway traffic is undoubted ... [and] the legislation under attack here is part and parcel of this regulation." It cannot be said of the challenged s. 5 of the by-law in this case that it has any such anchorage.

Whether the apt term be "complementary" or "supplementary", it has hitherto been a mark of our constitutional jurisprudence that a Province cannot legislate to reinforce the federal criminal law: *Johnson v. A.-G. Alta.*, [1954] S.C.R. 127. The fact that it might seek to foreclose a breach of the criminal law by preventive measures did not relieve against this provincial disability: see *A.-G. Ont. v. Koynok*, [1940] O.W.N. 555 (C.A.). There may, of course, be differences as to the appropriateness of the application of this principle in particular cases but the principle itself has not, as I read the case law, been heretofore doubted.

If any reported case in the Canadian Courts has an affinity to the one now before us it is *District of Kent v. Storgoff* (1962), 41 W.W.R. 301 (B.C.S.C.). It is very much in point, and on this I differ from my brother Beetz. That case also involved a municipal by-law which was likewise passed as an exceptional measure; and the same expediency that is invoked here to support the by-law and s. 5 thereof was invoked there. Whittaker, J., of the British Columbia Supreme Court did not yield to the expediency reflected in the by-law, although he sympathized with the municipality in its problem; and he pointed out, quite properly, that preventive measures were open under provisions of the *Criminal Code* relating to unlawful assemblies, to prevention of use of force and to power to arrest without warrant.

The by-law in the *District of Kent* case purported to prohibit members of a Doukhobor sect from entering the municipality which contained a prison where a large number of members were serving sentences. Fellow members, numbering about 1,000, were intending to march on the prison and had begun to do so from their homes about 400 miles away, and the by-law was passed as an emergency measure because of concern that the facilities of the municipality, with a population of 2,200, would be overtaxed so far at least as housing and sanitation were concerned, and there was also an apprehension of a breakdown of law and order. The by-law made it an offence punishable by a fine or imprisonment or both for a member of the sect to enter the municipality during the continuance of the emergency and they were liable, if they did so, to arrest without warrant.

. . . .

There is more to be said for the validity of the by-law in the *District of Kent* case than there is for the validity of the one in the present case. There are here no considerations of health or sanitation or education but a naked concern for the public peace and about anticipated violence. The by-law is directed to these considerations and they are matters of criminal law alone. Of course, there can be only sympathetic regard for the ability of the police to handle violent demonstrators. I should have thought, however, that an internal instruction or memorandum of procedures to this end would have sufficed in invocation of the extensive police powers of arrest without warrant given by ss. 449 and 450 of the *Criminal Code* and of the power to deal with and disperse unlawful assemblies, given by ss. 64 to 69 of the *Criminal Code*. There are express supporting provisions in ss. 32 and 33 as well as general support in ss. 27 and 30. Any doubt about the actual encroachment of the by-law into the field of criminal law may easily be resolved by comparing s. 5 of the by-law with ss. 27 and 68 of the *Criminal Code*, s. 6 of the by-law with s. 69(*b*) and (*c*) of the *Criminal Code*, and s. .7 of the by-law with ss. 66 and 67 of the *Criminal Code*.

There is a distasteful part of the challenged by-law and ordinance which, surprisingly, appears to be relied on to support their validity. The prohibition of assemblies or gatherings is not limited to those from which disorder or violence is anticipated but extends to all assemblies, all gatherings for the prescribed 30-day period. I am unable to appreciate how this gives credence to the by-law as a local measure. We are left in no doubt here as to the scope of operation of the by-law. In *Saumur v. City of Quebec*, [1953] 2 S.C.R. 299, Kellock, J., noted that the challenged by-law there was "not to be judged from the standpoint of matters to which it might be limited, but upon the completely general terms in which it in fact is couched" (at 339 S.C.R.). Here, persons who might seek to associate or gather for innocent purposes are to be barred, not because of any problem as to whether certain public areas should be open at certain times or on certain days or occasions — all of which go to their ordinary regulation — but because of a desire to forestall the violent or the likely violent. This is the invocation of a doctrine which should alarm free citizens even if it were invoked and applied under the authority of the Parliament of Canada, which has very wide power to enact criminal law. To find it invoked by a delegated authority like a municipality, which is limited at the outside to those powers that are open to a Province, appears to me to be an aggravation of its intrusion into the field of criminal law.

Certainly, enforcement of the criminal law is often difficult, and where large numbers of persons may be involved the difficulties are compounded. Yet it has always been central to our criminal law that the police are expected to enforce it against violators and not against innocents, and to exercise a reasonable and honest judgment as to those who are in each of these classifications. What can be more draconian than for a municipality to ignore the distinction and then to insist that it is not legislating in relation to crime or criminal law when its prime purpose is to forestall anticipated breaches of the peace and to deal with unlawful assemblies and riots!

The by-law goes much beyond what was invalidated in *Henry Birks & Sons Ltd. v. City of Montreal*, [1955] S.C.R. 799, and in *Switzman v. Elbling*, [1957] S.C.R. 285. Of course, those cases relate to other factual issues but they reflect the scope of the federal criminal law power even in situations where there is a connection — found there to be too tenuous to support the challenged provisions — with the regulation of commercial establishments and the use of private premises.

I see nothing in *Bédard v. Dawson*, [1923] S.C.R. 681, to give any support to the by-law. It has been overtaken by later cases such as *Johnson v. A.-G. Alta., supra*, and *Switzman v. Elbling, supra*, and even if it still has any vitality, its rationale relates to the suppression of a nuisance, a matter pertaining to the enjoyment of private premises. The by-law here has nothing to do with private nuisances but only with conduct and anticipated conduct of persons in streets and public parks.

I would allow the appeal, set aside the judgment below and restore the order at trial declaring the by-law and the ordinance *ultra vires*. It is clear that if s. 5 goes, ss. 6 and 7 of the by-law must also fall, and so too must s. 4. This effectively denudes the by-law of any substance.

I would give the appellant Claire Dupond her costs throughout against the City of Montreal, but there should be no costs to or against the Attorney-General of Quebec or the Attorney-General of Canada.

The judgment of Martland, Judson, Ritchie, Pigeon, Beetz and de Grandpré JJ. was delivered by

BEETZ, J.: — Appellant Claire Dupond has attacked the constitutional validity of the City of Montreal By-law 3926 and of Ordinance No. 1 passed by the Executive Committee of the city pursuant to s. 5 of that by-law. She did so under s. 515 of the *Charter of the city of Montreal, 1960,* 1959-60 (Que.), c. 102, which provides that any ratepayer, by petition in his own name presented to the Superior Court, may demand the annulment of any by-law on the ground of illegality. The Attorney-General for Quebec and the Attorney-General for Canada were impleaded as third parties and participated in the proceedings throughout, the first to support the validity of the by-law and of the ordinance and the second to oppose it. The trial Judge having declared the by-law and the ordinance unconstitutional, the City of Montreal and the Attorney-General for Quebec both appealed to the Quebec Court of Appeal. In separate judgments on each appeal, the Court of Appeal set aside the judgment at trial and dismissed Claire Dupond's petition. These are the judgments separately appealed from by the Attorney-General for Canada and Claire Dupond. The Attorney-General for Ontario and the Attorney-General for Alberta were granted leave to intervene but only the Attorney-General for Alberta did in fact intervene; he supported the validity of the by-law and of the ordinance.

By-law 3926 reads as follows:

By-law relating to exceptional measures to safeguard the free exercise of civil liberties, to regulate the use of the public domain and to prevent riots and other violations of order, peace and public safety.

At the meeting of the Council of the City of Montreal held on November 12, 1969, Council ordained:

WHEREAS it is imperative to provide for the protection of citizens in the exercise of their liberties, safeguard public peace and prevent violence against persons and property;

WHEREAS violence, armed robberies and other criminal acts often accompany certain demonstrations;

WHEREAS it is in order to enact exceptional emergency measures for the protection of citizens and the maintenance of peace and public order;

WHEREAS it is in order to regulate the use of the public domain and safeguard the right of citizens to the peaceful enjoyment of the public domain of the City;

1.- Anyone is entitled to the use and enjoyment of the streets, public places and public domain of the City of Montreal untroubled and in peace and public order.

2.- Assemblies, parades or other gatherings that endanger tranquility, safety, peace or public order are prohibited in public places and thoroughfares, parks or other areas of the City's public domain.

3.- No person participating in or present at an assembly, parade or other gathering on the public domain of the City shall molest or jostle anyone, or act in any way so as to hamper the movement, progress or presence of other citizens also using the public domain of the City on that occasion.

4.- Any assembly, parade or gathering on the public domain which gives rise to a violation against any article of this by-law, or to any acts, behaviour or utterances which disturb the peace or public order shall ipso facto be an assembly, parade or gathering which endangers tranquility, safety, peace or public order under the terms of Article 2 of this by-law, and shall disperse forthwith.

5.- When there are reasonable grounds to believe that the holding of assemblies, parades or gatherings will cause tumult, endanger safety, peace or public order or give rise to such acts, on report of the Directors of the Police Department and of the Law Department of the City that an exceptional situation warrants preventive measures to safeguard peace or public order, the Executive Committee may, by ordinance, take measures to prevent or suppress such danger by prohibiting for the period that it shall determine, at all times or at the hours it shall set, on all or part of the public domain of the City, the holding of any or all assemblies, parades or gatherings.

6.- All persons shall immediately obey the order of a peace officer to leave the scene of any assembly, parade or gathering held in violation of this by-law.

7.- Whoever participates in an assembly, parade or gathering held in violation of this by-law or otherwise contravenes, in any way, any provision of this by-law, shall be liable to either imprisonment or a fine, with or without costs, for the term or the amount that the Municipal Court of Montreal will determine, at its discretion, and failing the immediate payment of such fine, or such fine and costs, as the case may be, to imprisonment for a term to be determined by the said Municipal Court, at its discretion; the imprisonment for failure to pay the fine or costs shall cease at any time before expiry of the term determined by the Court, upon payment of the fine or of the fine and costs, as the case may be.

Such imprisonment shall not exceed sixty (60) days nor such fine one hundred (100) dollars.

The ordinance passed by the Executive Committee of the city pursuant to s. 5 of the by-law reads as follows:

Under by-law 3926 relating to exceptional measures to safeguard the free exercise of civil liberties, to regulate the use of the public domain and to prevent riots and other violations of order, peace and public safety.

At the meeting of the Executive Committee of the City of Montreal held on November 12, 1969 (no. 38961)

the Executive Committee ordained:

ORDINANCE TO PROHIBIT THE HOLDING OF ANY ASSEMBLY, PARADE OR GATHERING ON THE PUBLIC DOMAIN OF THE CITY OF MONTREAL FOR A TIME-PERIOD OF 30 DAYS.

CONSIDERING the reports from the Directors of the Police Department and of the Law Department of the City of Montreal attached hereto as an integral part of these presents;

CONSIDERING there are reasonable grounds to believe that the holding of assemblies, parades or gatherings on the public domain of the City would endanger the safety, peace or public order or might give rise to such danger;

CONSIDERING the exceptional situation prevailing in the City of Montreal and the need to take preventive measures to safeguard peace and public order.

The holding of any assembly, parade or gathering anywhere and at any time on the public domain of the City is prohibited for a time-period of thirty (30) days to end the thirteenth (13th) day of December 1969 at midnight, except for the parades already authorized by the Director of the Police Department under By-law 1319 dealing with traffic, before the adoption of this ordinance, and provided such parades do not endanger tranquility, peace and public order.

. . . .

The only evidence tendered at trial was the brief testimony of Claire Dupond that she is a ratepayer of the City of Montreal and a Canadian citizen.

There is in the case no factual background except what is mentioned in the reports of the Directors of the Police Department and of the Law Department of the City of Montreal attached to Ordinance No. 1 and quoted above. The facts recited in those reports have not been disputed. They must be taken to be true. It was conceded at the hearing that Ordinance No. 1 was enacted on account of those facts.

The submissions made against the constitutional validity of the by-law and of the ordinance may be summarized as follows:

1. They are in relation to criminal law and *ultra vires* of the City of Montreal and of the provincial Legislature;
2. They are in relation to and in conflict with the fundamental freedoms of speech, of assembly and association, of the press and of religion which are made part of the Constitution by the preamble of the *British North America Act, 1867*, or which come under federal jurisdiction and are protected by the *Canadian Bill of Rights*.

. . . .

## II

In *Hodge v. The Queen* (1883), 9 App. Cas. 117, the Judicial Committee of the Privy Council upheld the constitutional validity of the Ontario *Liquor Licence Act* of 1877 and of regulations enacted pursuant to that Act. At p. 131, the Judicial Committee referred to those regulations as

> . . .regulations in the nature of police or municipal regulations of a merely local character . . . and such as are calculated to preserve in the municipality . . . peace . . . and repress . . . disorderly and riotous conduct.

I could not find a better description to characterize s. 5 of the by-law and the ordinance. They are on their face regulations of a merely local character. The ordinance was passed for reasons peculiar to the City of Montreal at the relevant time. Both s. 5 and the ordinance relate to the use of the municipal public domain in exceptional circumstances when there are reasonable grounds to believe that the holding of assemblies, parades or gatherings in the streets, parks and other parts of the public domain will endanger safety, peace or public order. These are not punitive but essentially preventive measures, the purpose and effect of which is the prevention of conditions conducive to breaches of the peace and detrimental to the administration of justice. This preventive character is illustrated by the fact that the ordinance prohibits the holding on the public domain of *any* assembly, parade or gathering, including those of the most innocent and innocuous kind. The temporary nature of the ordinance and of any ordinance which could be passed pursuant to s. 5 is also indicative of the preventive aspect of this legislative scheme.

In *Reference re Adoption Act*, [1938] S.C.R. 398 at 403, Sir Lyman P. Duff, C.J.C., wrote:

> . . . while, as subject-matter of legislation, the criminal law is entrusted to the Dominion Parliament, responsibility for the administration of justice and, broadly speaking, for the policing of the country, the execution of the criminal law, the suppression of crime and disorder, has from the beginning of Confederation been recognized as the responsibility of the Provinces and has been discharged at great cost to the people; so also, the Provinces, sometimes acting directly, sometimes

through the municipalities, have assumed responsibility for controlling social conditions having a tendency to encourage vice and crime.

It is now well established that the suppression of conditions likely to favour the commission of crimes falls within provincial competence: *Bédard v. Dawson*, [1923] S.C.R. 681; *Di Iorio v. Warden, Jail of Montreal and Brunet*, [1978] 1 S.C.R. 152.

It would be an over-simplification to say that ordinances which may be passed under s. 5 are purely prohibitory: demonstrations can be restricted to certain areas of the municipal public domain, to certain times of the day or the night, to certain types of assemblies, parades or gatherings; that is why, in spite of the prohibitory form of the ordinances, s. 5 can be said to be, in substance, regulatory of the use of the public domain as the by-law held *intra vires* by McRuer, C.J.H.C., in *R. v. Campbell*, [1962] O.R. 1134 (H.C.) [aff'd [1963] 2 O.R. 149 (C.A.)].

However, I would not hesitate to uphold the validity of ordinances contemplated by s. 5 even if they were strictly prohibitory:

> A provincial enactment does not become a matter of criminal law merely because it consists of a prohibition and makes it an offence for failure to observe the prohibition . . .

(*per* Judson, J., in *O'Grady v. Sparling*, [1960] S.C.R. 804 at 810).

In my view, the impugned enactments relate to a matter of a merely local nature in the Province within the meaning of s. 92(16) of the Constitution. Bearing in mind that the other heads of power enumerated in s. 92 are illustrative of the general power of the Province to make laws in relation to all matters of a merely local or private nature in the Province, I am of the opinion that the impugned enactments also derive constitutional validity from heads 8, 13, 14 and 15 of s. 92.

*Re Race Track and Betting* (1921), 49 O.L.R. 339, a judgment of the Ontario Court of Appeal, and *District of Kent v. Storgoff* (1962), 41 W.W.R. 301, a judgment of Whittaker, J., of the British Columbia Supreme Court, were cited to us as persuasive authorities to the effect that s. 5 of the by-law and the ordinance are *ultra vires*. These cases dealt with different situations and I think it better not to discuss them in order to avoid going further than necessary for the decision of the case at hand. *Johnson v. A.-G. Alta.*, [1954] S.C.R. 127, was also cited. It is entirely distinguishable: a Province had added a sanction to an offence already dealt with in the *Criminal Code*.

### III

When an enactment is in itself of a local or private nature, the onus of showing that it otherwise comes within one or more of the classes of subjects enumerated in s. 91 falls upon the party so asserting: *L'Union St-Jacques de Montréal v. Bélisle* (1874), L.R. 6 P.C. 31 at 36.' Appellants have tried to discharge the onus by submitting that s. 5 of the by-law and the ordinance relate to criminal law.

One line of argument was that the impugned enactments are anti-riot measures dealing with a field already covered by ss. 64 to 70 of the *Criminal Code* and that their essential purpose is to supplement what was thought to be a lacuna in the *Code*.

I do not agree that s. 5 and the ordinance deal with the same subject-matter as the *Code*, under the same aspect and for the same purpose. They differ in more than one way but the main difference is as follows: the *Criminal Code* forbids unlawful assemblies and riots and provides for the punishment of these offences once they have been committed; it also compels a justice, mayor or sheriff to command, in Her Majesty's name, the dispersion of an unlawful assembly which has already begun to disturb the peace tumultuously; s. 5 and the ordinance on the other hand are aimed at preventing assemblies, parades and gatherings which have not yet taken place. There are in the *Code* no preventive measures similar to s. 5 of the by-law. Counsel for the Attorney-General for Canada readily conceded this; his point was that Parliament could enact a measure such as s. 5 of the by-law and, moreover, that only Parliament could do so.

It may be that Parliament could enact measures of a preventive nature under its ancillary powers. But we are not concerned in this case with the outer limits of federal jurisdiction over criminal law and I fail to see how the fact that Parliament has not exercised a possible incidental power should sterilize provincial legislative competence and prevent a Province or a city from exercising their own powers. And, in the exercise of their own powers, the Provinces may constitutionally complement federal legislation. The reports are replete with cases where provincial legislation complementary to federal legislation was upheld as long as it did not collide with the latter: *Provincial Secretary of Prince Edward Island v. Egan*, [1941] S.C.R. 396; *Reference re s. 92(4), Vehicles Act, 1957 (Sask.)*, [1958] S.C.R. 608; *Smith v. The Queen*, [1960] S.C.R. 776; *O'Grady v. Sparling, supra; Stephens v. The Queen*, [1960] S.C.R. 823; *Lieberman v. The Queen*, [1963] S.C.R. 643; *Fawcett v. A.-G. Ont.*, [1964] S.C.R. 625; *Mann v. The Queen*, [1966] S.C.R. 238.

This part of appellants' first submission must fail.

The second line of argument with respect to appellants' first submission is that s. 5 of the by-law and the ordinance are *ultra vires* under the doctrine of *Saumur v. City of Quebec*, [1953] 2 S.C.R. 299; *Henry Birks & Sons Ltd. v. City of Montreal*, [1955] S.C.R. 799, and *Switzman v. Elbling*, [1957] S.C.R. 285.

I cannot see anything in the ordinance which interferes with freedom of religion, of the press, or of speech, or which imposes religious observances, in such a way as to bring the matter within the criminal law power of Parliament. The ordinance prohibits the holding of *all* assemblies, parades or gatherings for a time period of 30 days, irrespective of religion, ideology or political views. It does so for the reasons given in the reports of the Director of the Police Department and of the Chief Attorney of the city; the reasons have nothing to do with those for which provincial enactments were invalidated in the *Saumur, Birks* and *Switzman* cases.

Furthermore, the discretionary power to pass an ordinance under s. 5 of the by-law is not an uncontrollable discretion given to a municipal officer, as was the case in *Saumur*: it is vested in the Executive Committee of the city; it cannot be exercised except on report of the Directors of the Police Department and of the Law Department of the city; this report must give reasons why an ordinance should be passed; these reasons must be up to the standard contemplated in the preamble of the by-law and in s. 5, that is, an exceptional emergency situation must have arisen which warrants the enactment of preventive measures; finally, the prohibition must be limited in time to the period determined by the Executive Committee; it must be temporary for by their very nature exceptional emergency measures cannot be permanent.

Should the discretionary power vested in the Executive Committee by s. 5 be exercised for unconstutional purposes, or should it simply be exercised unreasonably, judicial review would be available.

I should add that, under the City Charter, the Executive Committee is not an irresponsible body and that the media are in no way muzzled by the enactment of an ordinance.

This part of the first submission must also fail.

## IV

The second submission against the constitutionality of s. 5 and of the ordinance was that they are in relation to and in conflict with the fundamental freedoms of speech, of assembly and association, of the press and of religion which were inherited from the United Kingdom and made part of the Constitution by the preamble of the *British North America Act, 1867*, or which come under federal jurisdiction and are protected by the *Canadian Bill of Rights*. The *Alberta Press Act Case, Reference re Alberta Legislation*, [1938] S.C.R. 100. Aff'd. [1939] A.C. 117 (P.C.), was relied upon.

I find it exceedingly difficult to deal with a submission couched in such general terms. What is it that distinguishes a right from a freedom and a fundamental freedom from a freedom which is not fundamental? Is there a correlation between freedom of speech and freedom of asembly on the one hand and, on the other, the right, if any, to hold a public meeting on a highway or in a park as opposed to a meeting open to the public on private land? How like or unlike each other are an assembly, a parade, a gathering, a demonstration, a procession? Modern parlance has fostered loose language upon lawyers. As was said by Sir Ivor Jennings, the English at least have no written constitution and so they may divide their law logically: W. Ivor Jennings, "The Right of Assembly in England", 9 N.Y.U. Law Q. Rev. 217 (1931-32).

I am afraid I cannot avoid answering in kind appellants' submission. I believe I can state my position in a relatively small number of propositions which require little or no development for, difficult as it is at this level of abstraction, I must try not to say more than is necessary to dispose of the submission:

1. None of the freedoms referred to is so enshrined in the Constitution as to be above the reach of competent legislation.

2. None of those freedoms is a single matter coming within exclusive federal or provincial competence. Each of them is an aggregate of several matters which, depending on the aspect, comes within federal or provincial competence.

(This proposition is postulated in s. 5(3) of "An Act for the Recognition and Protection of Human Rights and Fundamental Freedoms", 1960 (Can.), c. 44, of which the *Canadian Bill of Rights* constitutes Part I.)

3. Freedoms of speech, of assembly and association, of the press are of religion are distinct and independent of the faculty of holding assemblies, parades, gatherings, demonstrations or processions on the public domain of a city. This is particularly so with respect to freedom of speech and freedom of the press as considered in the *Alberta Press Act Case, supra*. Demonstrations are not a form of speech but of collective action. They are of the nature of a display of force rather than of that of an

appeal to reason; their inarticulateness prevents them from becoming part of language and from reaching the level of discourse.

4. The right to hold public meetings on a highway or in a park is unknown to English law. Far from being the object of a right, the holding of a public meeting on a street or in a park may constitute a trespass against the urban authority in whom the ownership of the street is vested even though no one is obstructed and no injury is done; it may also amount to a nuisance: A.L. Goodhart, "Public Meetings and Processions", 6 Cambridge Law Jo., 161 (1937); W. Ivor Jennings, *op. cit.*; E.C.S. Wade, "Police Powers and Public Meetings", 7 Cambridge Law Jo. 175 (1937); André Jodouin, "La liberté de manifester", 1 Revue Générale de Droit, U. of Ottawa 9 (1970). The state of English law is perhaps best summarized in a well known dictum of that great English Judge, Wills, J., in *Ex parte Lewis* (1888), 21 Q.B.D. 191 at 197 (P.C.):

> A claim on the part of persons so minded to assemble in any numbers, and for so long a time as they please to remain assembled, upon a highway, to the detriment of others having equal rights, is in its nature irreconcilable with the right of free passage, and there is, so far as we have been able to ascertain, no authority whatever in favour of it. It was urged that the right of public meeting, and the right of occupying any unoccupied land or highway that might seem appropriate to those of her Majesty's subjects who wish to meet there, were, if not synonymous, at least correlative. We fail to appreciate the argument, nor are we at all impressed with the serious consequences which it was said would follow from a contrary view. There has been no difficulty experienced in the past, and we anticipate none in the future, when the only and legitimate object is public discussion, and no ulterior and injurious results are likely to happen. Things are done every day, in every part of the kingdom, without let or hindrance, which there is not and cannot be a legal right to do, and not unfrequently are submitted to with a good grace because they are in their nature incapable, by whatever amount of user, of growing into a right.

Being unknown to English law, the right to hold public meetings on the public domain of a city did not become part of the Canadian Constitution under the preamble of the *British North America Act, 1867*.

5. The holding of assemblies, parades or gatherings on the public domain is a matter which, depending on the aspect, comes under federal or provincial competence and falls to be governed by federal and provincial legislation such as the *Criminal Code*, laws relating to picketing, civil laws, municipal regulations and the like including s. 5 of the impugned by-law and the ordinance passed pursuant to it.

6. The *Canadian Bill of Rights*, assuming it has anything to do with the holding of assemblies, parades or gatherings on the public domain, does not apply to provincial and municipal legislation.

Appellants' second submission must also fail.

I would therefore dismiss both appeals. This is not a case for costs.

*Appeals dismissed.*

[For a critical comment on the *Dupond* decision, see Swinton, "Comment" (1979), 57 Can. Bar Rev. 326.]

# RE NOVA SCOTIA BOARD OF CENSORS AND McNEIL

In the Supreme Court of Canada. [1978] 2 S.C.R. 662.

Laskin, C.J.C., Martland, Judson, Ritchie, Spence, Pigeon, Dickson, Beetz and de Grandpré, JJ. January 19, 1978.

Appeal by the Nova Scotia Board of Censors and the Attorney-General of Nova Scotia from a judgment of the Nova Scotia Supreme Court, Appeal Division, 78 D.L.R. (3d) 46, declaring certain sections of the *Theatres and Amusements Act*, R.S.N.S. 1967, c. 304, as amended, and certain Regulations made thereunder *ultra vires*.

The judgment of Laskin C.J.C. and Judson, Spence and Dickson JJ., concurring, dissenting, was delivered by

LASKIN, C.J.C.: — The Attorney-General of Nova Scotia appeals, with leave of this Court, from a judgment of the Appeal Division of the Nova Scotia Supreme Court declaring, by unanimous decision of the four members of the Appeal Division, that (1) it was *ultra vires* the Legislature of Nova Scotia to enact, by use of the word "prohibiting", s. 2(1)(b), (g) and s. 3(2), (3) of the *Theatres and Amusements Act*, R.S.N.S. 1967, c. 304, as amended, and (2) Regulations 4, 5(1), 13, 18 and 32, made pursuant to the Act were also *ultra vires*.

The issue in this appeal which gave rise to the declaration of invalidity was precipitated by the banning by the Amusements Regulation Board (a tribunal established under the aforementioned Act and known prior to May 15, 1972, as the Nova Scotia Board of Censors) of the film "Last Tango in Paris" from public viewing in theatres or other places in the Province. The ban was announced on or about January 8, 1974. No reasons were given for the prohibition and, indeed, it was one of the submissions of the Attorney-General of Nova Scotia that reasons were not obligatory because there was no requirement under the Act or Regulations that the Board give reasons. The Attorneys-General of Ontario, Quebec, British Columbia, Prince Edward Island and Alberta intervened to oppose the judgment in appeal and the Attorney-General of Canada and the Canadian Civil Liberties Association intervened in support of the judgment.

In this Court, following the granting of leave to appeal, the constitutional question to be considered was formulated as follows by an order of June 4, 1976, amended by an order of July 5, 1976:

> Are Sections 2(1)(b), 2(1)(g), 3(2) and 3(3) of the Theatres and Amusements Act, R.S.N.S., 1967, c. 304 and Regulations 4, 5(1), 13, 18 and 32 made under the provisions of tht Act, *intra vires* the Legislature of Nova Scotia?

Provision for interventions was also made under the order.

The present case came before this Court earlier on the question of the plaintiff's standing to challenge the constitutionality of the legislation under which the Amusements Regulation Board acted; and in sustaining the Courts below, which had rejected the challenge to the plaintiff's standing (see [1976] 2 S.C.R. 265, [aff'g 9 N.S.R. (2d) 506]) this Court noted that the *Theatres and Amusements Act* was not only a statute authorizing the licensing of theatres, film exchanges, cinematograph operators and apprentices as well as theatre performances (including, by definition, moving picture performances or exhibitions) and envisaging too regulations in connection therewith, but it was also a statute operating directly upon the public by empowering the Amusements Regulation Board to permit or prohibit the public exhibition of any film and any performance in any theatre. (The Act also provided for an amusement tax payable by members of the public attending places of amusement but nothing turns on this feature of the Act.) The licensing power operated upon those engaged in the theatre business or in the film business or who worked as motion picture projectionists. As to them, s. 2(3) of the Act is explicit that "The Board may in its absolute discretion revoke or suspend any license [*sic*] issued under the authority of this Act or of the regulations." Whether the Board's licensing control is exercisable *in terrorem* with respect to any particular film which an exhibitor or theatre operator may wish to show for public viewing is not a question that arises here. Clearly, the Board's censorship authority, given by s. 3(2), (3) of the Act, is an overriding authority, and in this respect engages the interests of members of the public beyond the interests of exhibitors or theatre owners or operators as licensees under the Act.

The following are the provisions of the Act and Regulations which are relevant to the determination of the constitutional question that arises in this case:

*Provisions of the Act*

> 1. In this Act,
>
>     . . . . .
>
> (g) "performance" means any theatrical, vaudeville, musical or moving picture performance or exhibition for public entertainment, or any other performance or exhibition for public entertainment, whether or not of the kind hereinbefore enumerated;
>
>     . . . . .
>
> 2(1) The Governor in Council from time to time make regulations for or in relation to or incidental to any one or more or to any part or parts of any one or more of the following matters:
> (a) the licensing and regulating of theatres and places of amusement;
> (b) regulating and licensing or prohibiting any performance or performances in a theatre or theatres, and any amusement or amusements or recreation or recreations in a place or places of amusement, and any amusement or amusements, recreation or recreations for participating or indulging in which by the public or some of them, fees are charged by any amusement owner;
> (c) the construction, use, safety, inspection and supervision of theatres;
> (d) the licensing, using and operating of cinematographs;
> (e) prescribing the terms and conditions under which cinematographs shall be operated;
> (f) the licensing, operating and defining of film exchanges;
> (g) prohibiting or regulating the exhibition, sale, lease, and exchange of films;
> (h) the examining, regulating and licensing of cinematograph operators and apprentices;
> (i) prescribing the terms and conditions under which films shall be exhibited, sold, leased and exchanged;
> (j) prescribing the term or period during which any class of license shall be in force;
> (k) prescribing and regulating the fees, including methods for ascertaining, calculating or determining the fees to be paid for licenses, and for examinations of cinematograph operators, and for examinations of films;
> (l) prescribing by whom licenses shall be issued;
>
>     . . . . .

(3) The Board may in its absolute discretion revoke or suspend any license issued under the authority of this Act or of the regulations.

. . . . .

3(2) The Board shall have power to permit or to prohibit

(a) the use or exhibition in Nova Scotia or in any part or parts thereof for public entertainment of any film;

(b) any performance in any theatre;

(c) any amusement in a place of amusement or any amusement or recreation for participating or indulging in which by the public or some of them fees are charged by any amusement owner.

(3) Any power mentioned in subsection (2) may be exercised by the Board, notwithstanding that the Board has previously permitted the use or exhibition of the film, or that a license respecting the theatre is in force.

(4) There shall be an appeal from the Board to the person, body or court designated, and subject to the conditions prescribed by regulation of the Governor in Council.

. . . . .

8. Any person who violates this Act or who violates any of the regulations made under this Act, shall be liable to a penalty of not less than twenty dollars or more than two hundred dollars.

. . . . .

20(1) Where the Board is satisfied after due inquiry that any film exchange or theatre owner has violated this Act or any regulations made hereunder the Board may:

(a) revoke or cancel any license of such film exchange; or

(b) revoke or cancel any license of such theatre owner, or

(c) attach to any of such licenses such terms, conditions or restrictions as it deems advisable.

## Provisions of the Regulations

2. An appeal from a decision of the Board shall be to the Governor in Council.

3(1) No theatre owner shall give any performance in his theatre unless he holds in respect of the theatre a license which is in force.

. . . . .

4. No theatre owner shall permit any performance to be given in his theatre unless the same is authorized under the Regulations.

5(1) No theatre owner shall permit the use or exhibition in his theatre of any film which has not been authorized by the Board.

. . . . .

13. No person shall advertise any performance unless the permission of the Board has first been obtained.

. . . . .

16(1) No 35mm film exchange shall carry on business in the Province unless it holds a license which is in force . . .

. . . . .

18(1) No film shall be used or exhibited in the Province unless the film has been submitted to the Board and the Board has authorized the use or exhibition thereof.

(2) The Board may authorize or prohibit the use or exhibition of any film or may authorize the use of any film with such changes as it may direct. No film shall be so changed without the consent of the film exchange.

(3) The Board shall give a certificate in respect of every film which it has authorized for use or exhibition in the Province.

(4) The Board may at any time or from time to time re-examine any film and may prohibit the use or exhibition of any film which it has previously authorized for use or exhibition or may permit its use or exhibition with such further changes as the Board may direct.

(5) No film exchange shall use, exhibit, sell, lease or exchange any film unless a certificate of the Board has been issued in respect thereof and any film which is used, exhibited, sold, leased or exchanged in violation of this regulation may be confiscated by the Board.

. . . . .

32(1) No theatre owner or amusement owner shall permit any indecent or improper performance in his theatre or place of amusement.

(2) No performer shall take part in any indecent or improper performance.

(3) The Board may from time to time define what constitutes an indecent or improper performance within the meaning of these Regulations.

. . . . .

An administrative authority like the Board, which is given unfettered and unguided power and discretion to prohibit the public exhibition of a film, and whose statutory power in that respect is challenged as being unconstitutional, cannot shield its exercise of that power by refusing to disclose the grounds upon which it has acted. Although counsel for the Attorney-General of Nova Scotia stated in the course of his submissions that there was no limit to the Board's power to prohibit, his proposition is incorrect on administrative law grounds as well as on constitutional law grounds. It is enough, on the administrative side, to offer the reminder that an administrative authority must act in good faith, however wide its powers and regardless of the ambit of its discretion: see *Roncarelli v. Duplessis*, [1959] S.C.R. 121. On the constitutional side, there is the principle laid down by Kellock, J., in *Saumur v. City of Quebec*, [1953] 2 S.C.R. 299 at 339, where, speaking in relation to a Quebec city by-law which similarly gave unfettered and unguided discretion (to the chief of police) to refuse or grant permission to distribute pamphlets in the streets of the city, he said of the by-law:

Its validity is not to be judged from the standpoint of matters to which it might be limited, but upon the completely general terms in which it in fact is couched.

A more recent instance of this approach, although not arising in a strictly constitutional context, is seen in the decision of this Court in *City of Prince George v. Payne*, [1978] 1 S.C.R. 458. There the question was whether the City could lawfully refuse a business licence to a so-called sex shop under the broad mandate of the applicable British Columbia *Municipal Act* which, as here, contained no guidelines or standards but provided only that a licence or a renewal of licence shall not be unreasonably refused. This Court held, *inter alia*, that the City exceeded its powers in exercising its licensing authority to prohibit wholesale a particular business, a particular land use.

The issues before this Court in the present case do not engage the licensing authority of the Amusements Regulation Board, they do not relate to any film classification system, they are in no way concerned with the safety or suitability of premises in which films are sought to be exhibited or presented. The only inference that can be, indeed must be, drawn from the bare facts on the record is that the Board presumes to protect the general public from exposure to certain kinds of films, to insulate members of the public from viewing those films because, in the Board's allegedly unchallengeable judgment, the general public should not see them. Put another way, the Board asserts an unlimited statutory authority to determine for the general public what films are fit for public viewing.

The challenged provisions of the Act authorize regulations for (1) regulating and licensing or prohibiting any performance (which, as defined, includes film showings), and (2) prohibiting or regulating the exhibition of films. They go on to empower the Board to permit or to prohibit the exhibition of any film and, indeed, to prohibit notwithstanding a previous permission to exhibit. The Regulations that were attacked forbid theatre owners to permit any performance unless it has been authorized under the Regulations and, similarly, forbid any theatre owner to permit exhibition of any film in his theatre which has not been authorized by the Board. These are supplementary provisions to the Board's power to permit or prohibit and are fed by Regulation 18 which requires submission of films to the Board and Board authorization for their use or exhibition. Under that Regulation, the Board may authorize or prohibit use or exhibition of a film or may authorize use with directed changes. Regulation 32 forbids any theatre owner to permit "any indecent or improper performance in his theatre", the Board being left to define what those terms mean. The sanction for any breach of the Act or Regulations by any person is a monetary penalty and also revocation or cancellation of licence if the offender is a licence holder, thus emphasizing the Board's complete control over the exhibition of films in the Province. One other Regulation was invalidated by the judgment below, namely, Regulation 13, forbidding the advertising of any performance without the prior permission of the Board. It too reinforces the prohibitory authority of the Board over the exhibition of films.

There are no criteria fixed by the statute upon which the Board is required to act, no provision distinguishing or classifying films as being fit for viewing by adults but not by children. Only Regulation 32 purports to establish criteria but they are at large, namely, "indecent or improper performance" as the Board may define; and although they are addressed to theatre owners and amusement owners they relate directly to the general public's opportunity to view films that are sought to be exhibited. All of this is by way of prior determination, by way of anticipatory control of public taste.

[His Lordship's review of the film censorship legislation in other provinces is omitted.]

What is involved, as I have already noted, is an unqualified power in the Nova Scotia Board to determine the fitness of films for public viewing on considerations that may extend beyond the moral and may include the political, the social and the religious. Giving its assertion of power the narrowest compass, related to the film in the present case, the Board is asserting authority to protect public morals, to safeguard the public from exposure to films, to ideas and images in films, that it regards as morally offensive, as indecent, probably as obscene.

The determination of what is decent or indecent or obscene in conduct or in a publication, what is morally fit for public viewing, whether in films, in art or in a live performance is, as such, within the exclusive power of the Parliament of Canada under its enumerated authority to legislate in relation to the criminal law. . . .

It was contended, however, by the appellant and by supporting intervenants that the Nova Scotia Board was merely exercising a preventive power, no penalty or punishment being involved, no offence having been created. It is true, of course, that no penalty or punishment is involved in the making of an order prohibiting the exhibition of a film, but it is ingenuous to say that no offence is created when a licensee who disobeyed the order would be at risk of a cancellation of his licence and at risk of a penalty and any one else who proposed to exhibit the film publicly would likewise be liable to a penalty. Indeed, the contention invites this Court to allow form to mask substance and amounts to an assertion that the provincial Legislature may use the injunction or prohibitory order as a means of controlling conduct or performances or exhibitions, doing by prior restraint what it could not do by defining an offence and prescribing *post facto* punishment. This was attempted in the Ontario legislation that was considered and held unconstitutional in *A.-G. Ont. v. Koynok*, [1940] O.W.N. 555 (C.A.) (judgment set aside on appeal on other grounds), legislation authorizing the Attorney-General to obtain an injunction restraining the publication of printed matter which continuously or repeatedly publishes writings that are obscene or immoral. The short answer, in any event, to the provincial contention is that given by the Privy Council in *A.-G. Ont. v. Canada Temperance Federation*, [1946] A.C. 193 at 207, where Viscount Simon noted that "to legislate for prevention appears to be on the same basis as legislation for cure", a proposition that was applied by this Court in *Goodyear Tire & Rubber Co. of Canada Ltd. et al. v. The Queen*, [1956] S.C.R. 303 at 309.

It does not follow from all of the foregoing that provincial legislative authority may not extend to objects where moral considerations are involved, but those objects must in themselves be anchored in the provincial catalogue of powers and must, moreover, not be in conflict with valid federal legislation. It is impossible in the present case to find any such anchorage in the provisions of the Nova Scotia statute that are challenged, and this apart from the issue of conflict which, I think, arises in relation to ss. 159 and 163 of the *Criminal Code*. What is asserted, by way of tying the challenged provisions to valid provincial regulatory control, is that the Province is competent to license the use of premises, and entry into occupations, and may in that connection determine what shall be exhibited in those premises. This hardly touches the important issue raised by the present case and would, if correct, equally justify control by the Province of any conduct and activity in licensed premises even if not related to the property aspect of licensing, and this is patently indefensible. Moreover, what is missing from this assertion by the appellant is a failure to recognize that the censorship of films takes place without relation to any premises and is a direct prior control of public taste. . . .

It is not enough to save the challenged prohibitory provisions of the Nova Scotia statute, if they are otherwise invalid, that they are part of a legislative scheme which embraces licensing of theatres and of motion picture projectionists. As I have already noted, the provisions now challenged go beyond the licensing provisions and engage the public directly. The position here is no different from that presented in relation to federal legislation in *MacDonald v. Vapour Canada Ltd.*, [1977] 2 S.C.R. 134, where a provision in the *Trade Marks Act* characterized as unrelated to matters within federal competence, was not saved because of its alleged affinity with the general scheme of the Act.

This is not the first time that the Courts have been faced with the problem of assessing the validity of broadly-drawn provincial legislation and of determining, in line with the preferable approach in such cases, whether it can reasonably be confined to matters within provincial competence. That can properly be done in cases like *Shannon v. Lower Mainland Dairy Products Board*, [1938] A.C. 708

(P.C.), where the marketing or other regulatory scheme, although on its face susceptible of an extra-provincial application, is restricted to intra-provincial transactions. Another illustration, more germane and still outside the present case, is
*McKay v. The Queen*, [1965] S.C.R. 798, where a municipal zoning by-law
prohibiting signs on residential property was construed by the majority of this
Court to be inapplicable to the posting of federal election signs, this being a matter
outside of provincial competence.

For all the foregoing reasons I would dismiss this appeal and answer the constitutional question in the negative. The respondent is entitled to its costs in this Court
but there will be no costs to or against any of the intervenants. In view of the
conclusion to which I have come on the basis of the federal criminal law power and
the exercise thereof, I find it unnecessary to consider the larger issue, raised but not
pressed by the intervenant the Canadian Civil Liberties Association, of the relation
of censorship to free speech and the constitutional authority in that respect of
Parliament and the provincial Legislatures.

The judgment of Martland, Ritchie, Pigeon, Beetz and de Grandpré JJ. was
delivered by

RITCHIE, J.: . . .
When the Act and the Regulations are read as a whole, I find that to be
primarily directed to the regulation, supervision and control of the film business
within the Province of Nova Scotia, including the use and exhibition of films in that
Province. To this end the impugned provisions are, in my view, enacted for the
purpose of reinforcing the authority vested in a provincially appointed Board to
perform the task of regulation which includes the authority to prevent the
exhibition of films which the Board, applying its own local standards, has rejected
as unsuitable for viewing by provincial audiences. This legislation is concerned with
dealings in and the use of property (*i.e.*, films) which take place wholly within the
Province and in my opinion it is subject to the same considerations as those which
were held to be applicable in such cases as *Shannon v. Lower Mainland Dairy
Products Board*, [1938] A.C. 708; *Home Oil Distributors Ltd. v. A.-G. B.C.*, [1940]
S.C.R. 444, and *Caloil Inc. v. A.-G. Can.*, [1971] S.C.R. 543.

In the *Shannon* case, the Natural Products Marketing legislation was put in
issue as constituting an encroachment on "the regulation of trade and commerce", a
subject assigned exclusively to the Parliament of Canada by s. 91(2), and in the
course of delivering the opinion of the Judicial Committee, Lord Atkin had
occasion to say of this ground [at p. 718 A.C.]:

> It is sufficient to say upon the first ground that it is apparent that the legislation in question is
> confined to regulating transactions that take place wholly within the Province, and are therefore
> within the sovereign powers granted to the legislature in that respect by s. 92 of the British North
> America Act.

More recently, in commenting on that case and the *Home Oil* case, *supra*, Mr.
Justice Pigeon had occasion to say in *Caloil Inc. v. A.-G. Can., supra*, at p. 549
S.C.R.:

> It is to be noted that the *Shannon* and *Home Oil* cases both dealt with the validity of provincial
> regulation of local trades. They hold that provincial authority over transactions taking place

wholly within the Province is, as a rule, applicable to products imported from another country, or brought in from another Province, as well as to local products. However, it must be borne in mind that the division of constitutional authority under the Canadian Constitution often results in over-lapping legislation.

It will be seen that, in my opinion, the impugned legislation constitutes nothing more than the exercise of provincial authority over transactions taking place wholly within the Province and it applies to the "regulating, exhibition, sale and exchange of films" whether those films have been imported from another country or not.

We are concerned, however, in this appeal with a decision of the Appeal Division of the Supreme Court of Nova Scotia in which the majority quite clearly struck down the legislation as *ultra vires* on the sole ground that it was concerned with morality and as such constituted an invasion of the criminal law field reserved to the exclusive legislative authority of Parliament under s. 91(27) of the *British North America Act, 1867.*

. . . .

Although no reasons were given by the Board for the rejection of "Last Tango in Paris", all members of the Appeal Division were satisfied that its exhibition was prohibited on moral grounds and under all the circumstances I think it to be apparent that this was the case. In any event, I am satisfied that the Board is clothed with authority to fix its own local standards of morality in deciding whether a film is to be rejected or not for local viewing.

Simply put, the issue raised by the majority opinion in the Appeal Division is whether the Province is clothed with authority under s. 92 of the *British North America Act, 1867* to regulate the exhibition and distribution of films within its own boundaries which are considered unsuitable for local viewing by a local board on grounds of morality or whether this is a matter of criminal law reserved to Parliament under s. 91(27).

In the present context, the question of whether or not the impugned legislation encroaches on the criminal law authority is, in my opinion, best approached in light of the statement made by Kerwin, C.J.C., in the course of his reasons for judgment in *Lord's Day Alliance of Canada v. A.-G. B.C.,* [1959] S.C.R. 497 at 503, where he said:

> In constitutional matters there is no general area of criminal law and in every case the pith and substance of the legislation in question must be looked at.

Under the authority assigned to it by s. 92(27), the Parliament of Canada has enacted the *Criminal Code,* a penal statute the end purpose of which is the definition and punishment of crime when it has been proved to have been committed.

On the other hand, the *Theatres and Amusements Act* is not concerned with creating a criminal offence or providing for its punishment, but rather in so regulating a business within the Province as to prevent the exhibition in its theatres of performances which do not comply with the standards of propriety established by the Board.

The areas of operation of the two statutes are therefore fundamentally different on dual grounds. In the first place, one is directed to regulating a trade or business where the other is concerned with the definition and punishment of crime; and in the second place, one is preventive while the other is penal.

As the decision of the Appeal Division depends upon equating morality with criminality, I think it desirable at this stage to refer to the definitive statement made by Lord Atkin in this regard in the course of his reasons for judgment in *Proprietary Articles Trade Ass'n v. A.-G. Can.*, [1931 A.C. 310 at 324 (P.C.) where he said:

> Morality and criminality are far from co-extensive; nor is the sphere of criminality necessarily part of a more extensive field covered by morality — unless the moral code necessarily disapproves all acts prohibited by the State, in which case the argument moves in a circle. It appears to their Lordships to be of little value to seek to confine crimes to a category of acts which by their very nature belong to the domain of "criminal jurisprudence" . . .

I share the opinion expressed in this passage that morality and criminality are far from co-extensive and it follows in my view that legislation which authorizes the establishment and enforcement of a local standard of morality in the exhibition of films is not necessarily "an invasion of the federal criminal field" as Chief Justice MacKeigan thought it to be in this case.

Even if I accepted the view that the impugned legislation is concerned with criminal morality, it would still have to be noted that it is preventive rather than penal and the authority of the Province to pass legislation directed towards prevention of crime is illustrated by the case of *Bédard v. Dawson*, [1923] S.C.R. 681, which was concerned with the validity of a statute of the Province of Quebec entitled "An Act respecting the owners of houses used as disorderly houses", by which the Judge was authorized to order the closing of a disorderly house. The legislation was held to be *intra vires* on the ground that it was concerned with property within the Province and Mr. Justice Anglin said, at p. 685 S.C.R.:

> . . . I am of the opinion that this statute in no wise impinges on the domain of criminal law but is concerned exclusively with the control and enjoyment of property and the safeguarding of the community from the consequences of an illegal and injurious use being made of it — a pure matter of civil right. In my opinion in enacting the statute now under consideration the Legislature exercised the power which it undoubtedly possesses to provide for the suppression of a nuisance and the prevention of its recurrence by civil process.

The law of nuisance was undoubtedly a factor in the reasoning of some of the Judges in this Court and in the Court of King's Bench of Quebec, but in my view the matter was not too broadly stated by Duff J., as he then was, at p. 684 S.C.R. where he said:

> The legislation impugned seems to be aimed at suppressing conditions calculated to favour the development of crime rather than at the punishment of crime. This is an aspect of the subject in respect of which the Provinces seem to be free to legislate. I think the legislation is not invalid.

As I have already said, however, I take the view that the impugned legislation is not concerned with criminality. The rejection of films by the Board is based on a failure to conform to the standards of propriety which it has itself adopted and this failure cannot be said to be "an act prohibited with penal consequences" by the Parliament of Canada either in enacting the *Criminal Code* or otherwise. This is not to say that Parliament is in any way restricted in its authority to pass laws penalizing immoral acts or conduct, but simply that the provincial Government in regulating a local trade may set its own standards which in no sense exclude the operation of the federal law.

There is, in my view, no constitutional barrier preventing the Board from rejecting a film for exhibition in Nova Scotia on the sole ground that it fails to conform to standards of morality which the Board itself has fixed notwithstanding the fact that the film is not offensive to any provision of the *Criminal Code*; and, equally, there is no constitutional reason why a prosecution cannot be brought under s. 163 of the *Criminal Code* in respect of the exhibition of a film which the Board of Censors has approved as conforming to its standards of propriety.

[His Lordship's discussion of the paramountcy issue is omitted.]

As I have said, I take the view that the legislation here in question is, in pith and substance, directed to property and civil rights and therefore valid under s. 92(13) of the *British North America Act, 1867* but there is a further and different ground on which its validity might be sustained. In a country as vast and diverse as Canada, where tastes and standards may vary from one area to another, the determination of what is and what is not acceptable for public exhibition on moral grounds may be viewed as a matter of a "local and private nature in the Province" within the meaning of s. 92(16) of the *British North America Act, 1867*, and as it is not a matter coming within any of the classes of subject enumerated in s. 91, this is a field in which the Legislature is free to act.

In the References as to the validity of "An Act to amend the *Supreme Court Act*", *Reference re Privy Council Appeals*, [1940] S.C.R. 49. Aff'd. [1947] A.C. 127, Chief Justice Duff had occasion to say at pp. 58-9 S.C.R.:

The legislative powers of the Provinces are strictly confined in their ambit by the territorial limits of the Provinces. The matters to which that authority extends are matters which are local in the provincial sense. This principle was stated in two passages in the judgment in the *Local Option* case (*A.-G. Ont. v. A.-G. Can.*), [1896] A.C. 348 delivered by Lord Watson speaking for a very powerful Board at pp. 359 and 365, respectively. I quote them . . .

The second passage to which the Chief Justice referred reads as follows:

It is not necessary for the purposes of the present appeal to determine whether provincial legislation for the suppression of the liquor traffic, confined to matters which are provincial or local within the meaning of Nos. 13 and 16, is authorized by the one or by the other of these heads. It cannot, in their Lordships' opinion, be logically held to fall within both of them. In s. 92, No. 16 appears to them to have the same office which the general enactment with respect to matters concerning the peace, order and good government of Canada, so far as supplementary of the enumerated subject, fulfils in s. 91. It assigns to the provincial legislature all matters in a provincial sense local or private which have been omitted from the preceding enumeration, and, although its terms are wide enough to cover, they were obviously not meant to include, provincial legislation in relation to the classes of subjects already enumerated.

As I indicated at the outset, I have taken note of the lengthy judgment of Mr. Justice Macdonald in the Appeal Division in which he finds that the impugned legislation is *ultra vires* as infringing on the fundamental freedoms to which he refers, which include freedom of association; of assembly; of speech; of the press; of other media in the dissemination of news and opinion; of conscience and of religion.

Mr. Justice Macdonald's approach appears to me to be illustrated by the following comment which he makes after referring to censorship legislation relating to morals in other provinces [at p. 55]:

> The foregoing criteria are of the usual "sex, morals and violence" type that are normally associated with film censorship. In the present case, however, the censorship criterion, being left to the *Board* to determine, *could* be much wider and encompass political, religious and other matters. In my opinion censorship relating to party politics cannot be tolerated in a free society where unfettered debate on political issues is a necessity, subject, of course, to the criminal law, particularly those provisions of the *Criminal Code*, relating to sedition, treason and incitement to crime.

(The emphasis is added.)

It is true that no limitations on the authority of the board are spelled out in the Act and that it might be inferred that it *could* possibly affect some of the rights listed by Macdonald, J.A., but having regard to the presumption of constitutional validity to which I have already referred, it appears to me that this does not afford justification for concluding that the purpose of the Act was directed to the infringement of one or more of those rights. With the greatest respect, this conclusion appears to me to involve speculation as to the intention of the Legislature and the placing of a construction on the statute which is nowhere made manifest by the language employed in enacting it.

For all these reasons, I would allow this appeal, set aside the judgment of the Appeal Division of Nova Scotia and substitute for the declaration made thereunder a declaration that Regulation 32 made pursuant to the *Theatre and Amusements Act* of Nova Scotia is null and void.

This does not appear to me to be a case in which costs should be awarded.

*Appeal allowed in part.*

## 3. Mobility and the Right to Pursue a Livelihood

*Note*

Although by section 91(25) of the *Constitution Act, 1867* the Dominion has exclusive legislative authority in relation to "naturalization and aliens" and by section 95 it has concurrent but overriding authority in relation to immigration, there is no specific reference in the Act to citizenship or nationality. However, the right of the Dominion, under its general power to define the national status of persons in Canada, to regulate admission into and exclusion and deportation from Canada is undeniable. *Cf.* Rand J. in *Winner v. S.M.T. (Eastern) Ltd. and A.-G. Can.*, [1951] S.C.R. 887 at 919 (aff'd [1954] A.C. 541 (P.C.)). Prior to the *Statute of Westminster*, 1931 (Imp.), s. 4, Dominion authority in relation to nationality was limited by Imperial legislation applicable to Canada; for example, see the *Naturalization Act*, 1847 (Imp.), c. 83; *Naturalization Act*, 1870 (Imp.), c. 14; *British Nationality and status of Aliens Act* 1914 (Imp.), c. 17; and see the discussion in Clement, *The Canadian Constitution*, (1916) chaps. 9 and 31. Since the *Statute of Westminster* it has become possible (in view of the power given to the Dominion to repeal British legislation applicable to Canada) to deal with and give full meaning to Canadian citizenship as opposed to British nationality; see the *Canadian Citizenship Act*, first enacted in 1946, and now R.S.C. 1970, c. C19; and see Tamaki, "The Canadian Citizenship Act, 1946" (1947), 7 Univ. of Tor. L.J. 68.

Federal power in relation to national status, and to aliens and immigration, clearly enables the Dominion to make freedom of movement throughout Canada and attribute not only of citizenship but of lawful presence in Canada: see Note

(1941), 19 Can. Bar Rev. 750, discussing the United States case of *Edwards v. People of State of California*, 314 U.S. 160 (1941). Nor is there any doubt about federal legislative power subject to the *Charter*, and in particular section 6(1) thereof, to exclude or deport either aliens ( *Re Jolly and Minister of Manpower and Immigration* (1975), 54 D.L.R. (3d) 277 (Fed. C.A.)) or naturalized persons (usually upon revocation of their naturalization under stipulated circumstances), or even natural-born persons, although this raises questions of international law relative to the reception of such persons abroad: see *A.-G. Can. v. Cain; A.-G. Can. v. Gilhula*, [1906] A.C. 542 (P.C.); *Co-operative Committee on Japanese Canadians v. A.-G. Can.*, [1947] A.C. 87 (P.C.). Any doubt about extra-territorial power has, of course, been removed by section 3 of the Statute of Westminster; see also *Croft v. Dunphy*, [1933] A.C. 156 (P.C.). Whatever the scope of provincial power to condition entry into a province under section 95 of the *Constitution Act, 1867*, it is still subordinate to federal power conferred by the same section. The question may be asked, however, whether conditions of entry related not to immigration as such but to some regulatory policy otherwise competent to a province are not similarly subject to overriding Dominion legislation. For a particular illustration of provincial legislation of this character (now repealed) aimed at national and international trade unionism; see Forsey, "The Prince Edward Island Trade Union Act, 1948" (1948), 26 Can. Bar Rev. 1159; and *cf.* Mercier, "Immigration and Provincial Rights" (1944), 22 Can. Bar Rev. 856.

Difficult questions remain which admit of no categorical answer. Is any special significance to be attached to the fact that Dominion power under section 91(25) is in relation to "naturalization", not naturalized persons; and "aliens", not alienage? Or should the courts read the terms as if they were "naturalization and naturalized persons and aliens and alienage"? What is the extent of Dominion power to legislate as to the consequences of citizenship or nationality or alienage, in the light of provincial legislative authority, especially in relation to property and civil rights in the province? How far can a provincial legislature regulate or limit the activities of or deny privileges to naturalized persons or aliens? With respect to this last question: see *Re Redline and Univ. of Alta. Gov.* (1980), 110 D.L.R. (3d) 146 (Alta. C.A.) upholding a provincial regulation establishing a fee differential for foreign students as being in relation to provincial power over education. Furthermore, the differentiation based on national origin did not violate the applicable provincial human rights legislation because foreign students do not have a right to education, merely a privilege.

[See, Head "The Stranger in Our Midst: A Sketch of the Legal Status of the Alien in Canada" in *2 Canadian Yearbook of International Law* (1964), p. 107.]

# UNION COLLIERY CO. OF BRITISH COLUMBIA LTD. v. BRYDEN

In the Privy Council. [1899] A.C. 580.

Lord Watson, Lord Hobhouse, Lord MacNaghten, Sir Richard Couch and Sir Edward Fry. July 28, 1899.

Appeal from a judgment of the British Columbia Supreme Court *en banc*, affirming a judgment of Drake J. upholding the validity of s. 4 of the *Coal Mines Regulation Act*, 1890, now s. 4 of R.S.B.C. 1897, c. 138.

LORD WATSON: The appellant company carries on the business of mining coal by means of underground mines, in lands belonging to the company, situated near to the town of Union in British Columbia. The company have hitherto employed, and still continue to employ, Chinamen in the working of these underground mines.

By s. 4 of the *Coal Mines Regulation Act*, 1890, it is expressly enacted that, "no boy under the age of twelve years, and no woman or girl of any age, *and no Chinaman*, shall be employed in or allowed to be for the purpose of employment in any mine to which the Act applies, below ground."

By the Act of 1890, the words "and no Chinaman" were added to the 4th section of the then existing *Coal Mines Regulation Act*, which was chapter 84 of the Consolidated Statutes of 1888, and now, as amended, is chapter 138 of the Revised Statutes of British Columbia, 1897. It is sufficiently plain, and it is not matter of dispute, that the provisions of the Act of 1890 were made to apply, and so far as competently enacted do apply, to the underground workings carried on by the appellant company.

The present action was instituted, in the Supreme Court of British Columbia, by the respondent, John Bryden, against the appellant company of which he is a shareholder. It concludes (1) for a declaration that the company had and has no right to employ Chinamen in certain positions of trust and responsibility, or as labourers in their mines below ground, and that such employment was and is unlawful, and (2) for an injunction restraining the company from employing Chinamen in any such position of trust and responsibility, or as labourers below ground, and from using the funds of the company in paying the wages of the said Chinamen. The respondent averred in his statement of claim that the employment of Chinamen in positions of trust and responsibility, and as labourers underground, was a source of danger and injury to other persons working in the mines, which involved the liability of the company for damages, and was also injurious and destructive to the mines. He also pleaded that the employment of Chinamen in these capacities was contrary to the statute law of the province.

The appellant company, by their statement of defence, denied that there was any risk of injury arising either to other workmen in their mines, or the mines, from the employment of Chinamen as underground miners. They pleaded that, in so far as they related to adult Chinamen, the enactments of s. 4 of the *Coal Mines Regulation Act* were void as being *ultra vires* of the legislature of the Province of British Columbia. . . .

. . . It appeared from the evidence that the appellant company, in working some of their underground seams of coal, employed no workmen except Chinamen who were of full age, and that, in those parts of their workings where miners other than Chinamen were employed, no Chinamen occupied a position of trust or responsibility, such as were alleged in the statement of claim. The consequence was that, in the subsequent conduct of the litigation, the Courts below, and their Lordships in this appeal, have only been invited to consider the conclusions of the action in so far as these bear upon the legality of employing Chinese labour in violation of the express enactments of s. 4 of the Revised Statute No. 138 of 1897. In other words, the controversy has been limited to the single question — whether the enactments of s. 4, in regard to which the appellant company has stated the plea of *ultra vires*, were within the competency of the British Columbian Legislature. . . .

There can be no doubt that, if s. 92 of the Act of 1867 had stood alone and had not been qualified by the provisions of the clause which precedes it, the provincial legislature of British Columbia would have had ample jurisdiction to enact s. 4 of the *Coal Mines Regulation Act*. The subject-matter of that enactment would clearly have been included in s. 92, sub-s. 10, which extends to provincial undertakings such as the coal mines of the appellant company. It would also have been included in s. 92, sub-s. 13, which embraces "Property and Civil Rights in the Province."

But s. 91, sub-s. 25, extends the exclusive legislative authority of the Parliament of Canada to "naturalization and aliens." Sect. 91 concludes with a proviso to the effect that "any matter coming within any of the classes of subjects enumerated in this section shall not be deemed to come within the class of matters of a local or private nature comprised in the enumeration of the classes of subjects by this Act assigned exclusively to the legislatures of the provinces."

Sect. 4 of the Provincial Act prohibits Chinamen who are of full age from employment in underground coal workings. Every alien when naturalized in Canada becomes, *ipso facto*, a Canadian subject of the Queen; and his children are not aliens, requiring to be naturalized, but are natural-born Canadians. It can hardly have been intended to give the Dominion Parliament the exclusive right to legislate for the latter class of persons resident in Canada; but s. 91, sub-s. 25, might possibly be construed as conferring that power in the case of naturalized aliens after naturalization. The subject of "naturalization" seems *prima facie* to include the power of enacting what shall be the consequences of naturalization, or, in other words, what shall be the rights and privileges pertaining to residents in Canada after they have been naturalized. It does not appear to their Lordships to be necessary, in the present case, to consider the precise meaning which the term "naturalization" was intended to bear, as it occurs in s. 91, sub-s. 25. But it seems clear that the expression "aliens" occurring in that clause refers to, and at least includes, all aliens who have not yet been naturalized; and the words "no Chinaman," as they are used in s. 4 of the Provincial Act, were probably meant to denote, and they certainly include, every adult Chinaman who has not been naturalized. . . .

The provisions of which the validity has been thus affirmed by the Courts below are capable of being viewed in two different aspects, according to one of which they appear to fall within the subjects assigned to the provincial parliament by s. 92 of the British North America Act, 1867, whilst, according to the other, they clearly belong to the class of subjects exclusively assigned to the legislature of the

Dominion by s. 91, sub-s. 25. They may be regarded as merely establishing a regulation applicable to the working of underground coal mines; and, if that were an exhaustive description of the substance of the enactments, it would be difficult to dispute that they were within the competency of the provincial legislature, by virtue either of s. 92, sub-s. 10, or s. 92, sub-s. 13. But the leading feature of the enactments consists in this — that they have, and can have, no application except to Chinamen who are aliens or naturalized subjects, and that they establish no rule or regulation except that these aliens or naturalized subjects shall not work, or be allowed to work, in underground coal mines within the Province of British Columbia.

Their Lordships see no reasons to doubt that, by virtue of s. 91, sub-s. 25, the legislature of the Dominion is invested with exclusive authority in all matters which directly concern the rights, privileges, and disabilities of the class of Chinamen who are resident in the provinces of Canada. They are also of opinion that the whole pith and substance of the enactments of s. 4 of the *Coal Mines Regulation Act*, in so far as objected to by the appellant company, consists in establishing a statutory prohibition which affects aliens or naturalized subjects, and therefore trenches upon the exclusive authority of the Parliament of Canada. The learned judges who delivered opinions in the Full Court noticed the fact that the Dominion legislature had passed a "Naturalization Act, No. 113 of the Revised Statutes of Canada, 1886," by which a partial control was exercised over the rights of aliens. Walkem J. appears to regard that fact as favourable to the right of the provincial parliament to legislate for the exclusion of aliens being Chinamen from underground coal mines. The abstinence of the Dominion Parliament from legislating to the full limit of its powers, could not have the effect of transferring to any provincial legislature the legislative power which had been assigned to the Dominion by s. 91 of the Act of 1867.

Their Lordships will therefore humbly advise Her Majesty to reverse the judgment appealed from; to find and declare that the provisions of s. 4 of the British Columbia *Coal Mines Regulation Act*, 1890, which are now embodied in chapter 138 of the Revised Statutes of British Columbia, 1897, were, in so far as they relate to Chinamen, *ultra vires* of the provincial legislature, and therefore illegal. . . .

*Appeal allowed.*

# CUNNINGHAM v. TOMEY HOMMA

In the Privy Council. [1903] A.C. 151.

The Lord Chancellor, Lord MacNaghten, Lord Davey, Lord Robertson and Lord Lindley. Dec. 17, 1902.

Appeal from a judgment of the British Columbia Supreme Court *en banc*, affirming a judgment of the County Court which reversed a decision of a collector of votes and ordered that the name of Tomey Homma be placed on the register of voters for the Vancouver electoral district to enable him to vote in a provincial election. Tomey Homma was a native of the Japanese empire not born of British parents but a naturalized British subject. Sect. 8 of the *Provincial Elections Act*,

R.S.B.C. 1897, c. 67 provided that "no Chinaman, Japanese, or Indian shall have his name placed on the register of voters for any electoral district, or be entitled to vote at any election." By s. 3 the term "Japanese" was defined to include "any native of the Japanese empire or its dependencies not born of British parents, and shall include any person of the Japanese race naturalized or not."

EARL OF HALSBURY L.C.: In this case a naturalized Japanese claims to be placed upon the register of voters for the electoral district of Vancouver City, and the objection which is made to his claim is that by the electoral law of the province it is enacted that no Japanese, whether naturalized or not, shall have his name placed on the register of voters or shall be entitled to vote. Application was made to the proper officer to enter the applicant's name on the register, but he refused to do so upon the ground that the enactment in question prohibited its being done. This refusal was overruled by the Chief Justice sitting in the county court, and the appeal from his decision to the Supreme Court of British Columbia was disallowed. The present appeal is from the decision of the Supreme Court.

There is no doubt that, if it is within the capacity of the province to enact the electoral law, the claimant is [dis]qualified by the express language of the statute; but it is contended that the 91st and 92nd sections of the British North America Act have deprived the province of the power of making any such provision as to disqualify a naturalized Japanese from electoral privileges. It is maintained that s. 91, sub-s. 25, enacts that the whole subject of naturalization is reserved to the exclusive jurisdiction of the Dominion, while the Naturalization Act of Canada enacts that a naturalized alien shall within Canada be entitled to all political and other rights, powers, and privileges to which a natural-born British subject is entitled in Canada. To this it is replied that, by s. 92, sub-s. 1, the constitution of the province and any amendment of it are placed under the exclusive control of the provincial legislature. The question which their Lordships have to determine is which of these two views is the right one, and, in determining that question, the policy or impolicy of such an enactment as that which excludes a particular race from the franchise is not a topic which their Lordships are entitled to consider.

The first observation which arises is that the enactment, supposed to be *ultra vires* and to be impeached upon the ground of its dealing with alienage and naturalization, has not necessarily anything to do with either. A child of Japanese parentage born in Vancouver City is a natural-born subject of the King, and would be equally excluded from the possession of the franchise. The extent to which naturalization will confer privileges has varied both in this country and elsewhere. From the time of William III down to Queen Victoria no naturalization was permitted which did not exclude the alien naturalized from sitting in Parliament or in the Privy Council.

In Lawrence's Wheaton, p. 903 (2nd annotated ed. 1863), it is said that "though (in the United States) the power of naturalization be nominally exclusive in the Federal Government, its operation in the most important particulars, especially as to the right of suffrage, is made to depend on the local constitution and laws." The term "political rights" used in the Canadian Naturalization Act is, as Walkem J. very justly says, a very wide phrase, and their Lordships concur in his observation that, whatever it means, it cannot be held to give necessarily a right to the suffrage in all or any of the provinces. In the history of this country the right to the franchise has been granted and withheld on a great number of grounds, conspicuously upon grounds of religious faith, yet no one has ever suggested that a person excluded from the franchise was not under allegiance to the Sovereign.

Could it be suggested that the province of British Columbia could not exclude an alien from the franchise in that province? Yet, if the mere mention of alienage in the enactment could make the law *ultra vires*, such a construction of s. 91, sub-s. 25, would involve that absurdity. The truth is that the language of that section does not purport to deal with the consequences of either alienage or naturalization. It undoubtedly reserves these subjects for the exclusive jurisdiction of the Dominion — that is to say, it is for the Dominion to determine what shall constitute either the one or the other, but the question as to what consequences shall follow from either is not touched. The right of protection and the obligations of allegiance are necessarily involved in the nationality conferred by naturalization; but the privileges attached to it, where these depend upon residence, are quite independent of nationality.

This, indeed, seems to have been the opinion of the learned judges below; but they were under the impression that they were precluded from acting on their own judgment by the decision of this Board in the case of *Union Colliery Co. v. Bryden*, [1899] A.C. 580 (P.C.). That case depended upon totally different grounds. This Board, dealing with the particular facts of that case, came to the conclusion that the regulations there impeached were not really aimed at the regulation of coal mines at all, but were in truth devised to deprive the Chinese, naturalized or not, of the ordinary rights of the inhabitants of British Columbia, and, in effect, to prohibit their continued residence in that province, since it prohibited their earning their living in that province. It is obvious that such a decision can have no relation to the question whether any naturalized person has an inherent right to the suffrage within the province in which he resides.

For these reasons their Lordships will humbly advise His Majesty that the order of the Chief Justice in the county court and the order of the Supreme Court ought to be reversed. . . .

*Appeal allowed.*

[Are *Union Colliery Co. v. Bryden* and *Cunningham v. Tomey Homma* reconcilable? See Lefroy, *Canada's Federal System* (1913), p. 308. Cf. *In re the Coal Mines Regulation Act* (1904), 10 B.C.R. 408 (C.A.), following the *Bryden* case and distinguishing the *Tomey Homma* case. Is there a tenable distinction between provincial legislation which confers a privilege, e.g. the right to vote, and provincial legislation which denies to persons advantages which are ordinarily available, e.g. work in coal mines? Is it open to a province to make distinctions or discriminate on account of race or ethnic origin and thus circumvent any limitation arising from section 91(25)?

May a provincial legislature exclude aliens, who are otherwise qualified, from practising a profession in the province simply because of alienage? It is clearly open to a provincial legislature to provide for self-regulation of a profession, but may the regulatory body, when granted a general authority, exclude persons because they are, for example, communists? See *Martin v. Law Society of British Columbia*, [1950] 3 D.L.R. 173 (B.C. C.A.) aff'g [1949] 1 D.L.R. 105 (B.C. S.C.). May it similarly exclude aliens? Would it make any difference if the Dominion purported to give aliens equal rights and privileges with all natural-born or naturalized persons? Could the Dominion validly so legislate to supersede or foreclose provincial legislation?

May a province validly enact that no one may change his name save under a prescribed procedure and then exclude aliens from any right to resort to that procedure? See *Change of Name Act*, R.S.O. 1980, c. 60; Note (1940), 18 Can. Bar Rev. 69.

How far, if at all, may a province deny to aliens access to provincial courts? Cf. Harrison J. in *S.M.T. (Eastern) Ltd. v. Winner* (1950), 26 M.P.R. 27 (N.B. C.A.) (foreign national has no status to attack constitutionality of provincial legislation), rev'd [1951] S.C.R. 887, which was varied (on other grounds), [1954] A.C. 541.

The relation of this problem to Dominion and foreign companies is discussed in Chapter 11, *supra.*]

# QUONG-WING v. THE KING

In the Supreme Court of Canada. (1914) 49 S.C.R. 440.

Fitzpatrick C.J.C., Davies, Idington, Duff and Anglin JJ. Feb. 23, 1914.

Appeal from a judgment of the Saskatchewan Supreme Court, 4 W.W.R. 1135, affirming on appeal by way of stated case, a conviction of appellant on a charge of employing white females in violation of 1912 (Sask.), c. 17.

FITZPATRICK C.J.C.: The appellant, a Chinaman and a naturalized Canadian citizen, was convicted of employing white female servants contrary to the provisions of chapter 17 of the statutes of Saskatchewan, 1912, and, for his defence, he contends that the Act in question is *ultra vires* of the provincial legislature.

It is urged that the aim of the Act is to deprive the defendant and the Chinese generally, whether naturalized or not, of the rights ordinarily enjoyed by the other inhabitants of the Province of Saskatchewan and that the subject-matter of the Act is within the exclusive legislative authority of the Parliament of Canada.

The Act in question reads as follows: —

> 1. No person shall employ in any capacity any white woman or girl or permit any white woman or girl to reside or lodge in or to work in or, save as a *bona fide* customer in a public apartment thereof only, to frequent any restaurant, laundry or other place of business or amusement owned, kept or managed by any Chinaman.
>
> 2. Any employer guilty of any contravention or violation of this Act, shall, upon summary conviction be liable to a penalty not exceeding $100 and, in default of payment, to imprisonment for a term not exceeding two months.

In terms the section purports merely to regulate places of business and resorts owned and managed by Chinese, independent of nationality, in the interest of the morals of women and girls in Saskatchewan. There are many factory Acts passed by provincial legislatures to fix the age of employment and to provide for proper accommodation for workmen and the convenience of the sexes which are intended not only to safeguard the bodily health, but also the morals of Canadian workers, and I fail to understand the difference in principle between that legislation and this.

It is also undoubted that the legislatures authorize the making by municipalities of disciplinary and police regulations to prevent disorders on Sundays and at night, and in that connection to compel tavern and saloon keepers to close their drinking places at certain hours. Why should those legislatures not have powers to enact that women and girls should not be employed in certain industries or in certain places or by a certain class of people? This legislation may affect the civil rights of Chinamen, but it is primarily directed to the protection of children and girls.

The Chinaman is not deprived of the right to employ others, but the classes from which he may select his employees are limited. In certain factories women or children under a certain age are not permitted to work at all, and, in others, they may not be employed except subject to certain restrictions in the interest of the employee's bodily and moral welfare. The difference between the restrictions imposed on all Canadians by such legislation and those resulting from the Act in question is one of degree, not of kind.

I would dismiss the appeal with costs.

DAVIES J.: The question on this appeal is not one as to the policy or justice of the Act in question, but solely as to the power of the provincial legislature to pass it. There is no doubt that, as enacted, it seriously affects the civil rights of the Chinamen in Saskatchewan, whether they are aliens or naturalized British subjects. If the language of Lord Watson, in delivering the judgment of the Judicial Committee of the Privy Council in *Union Colliery Company of British Columbia v. Bryden*, [1899] A.C. 580, was to be accepted as the correct interpretation of the law defining the powers of the Dominion Parliament to legislate on the subject-matter of "naturalization and aliens" assigned to it by item 25 of section 91 of the "British North America Act, 1867," I would feel some difficulty in upholding the legislation now under review....

But in the later case of *Cunningham v. Tomey Homma*, [1903] A.C. 151, the Judicial Committee modified the views of the construction of sub-section 25 of section 91 stated in the *Union Colliery* decision....

Reading the *Union Colliery* case, therefore, as explained in this later case, and accepting their Lordships' interpretation of sub-section 25 of section 91, that "its language does not purport to deal with the consequences of either alienage or naturalization", and that, while it exclusively reserves these subjects to the jurisdiction of the Dominion in so far as to determine what shall constitute either alienage or naturalization, it does not touch the question of what consequences shall follow from either, I am relieved from the difficulty I would otherwise feel.

The legislation under review does not, in this view, trespass upon the exclusive power of the Dominion legislature. It does deal with the subject-matter of "property and civil rights" within the province, exclusively assigned to the provincial legislatures, and so dealing cannot be held *ultra vires*, however harshly it may bear upon Chinamen, *naturalized or not*, residing in the province. There is no inherent right in any class of the community to employ women and children which the legislature may not modify or take away altogether. There is nothing in the "British North America Act" which says that such legislation may not be class legislation. Once it is decided that the subject-matter of the employment of white women is within the exclusive powers of the provincial legislature and does not infringe upon any of the enumerated subject-matters assigned to the Dominion, then such provincial powers are plenary....

I think the pith and substance of the legislation now before us is entirely different [from that in the *Bryden* case]. Its object and purpose is the protection of white women and girls; and the prohibition of their employment or residence, or lodging, or working, etc., in any place of business or amusement owned, kept or managed by any Chinaman is for the purpose of ensuring that protection. Such

legislation does not, in my judgment, come within the class of legislation or regulation which the Judicial Committee held *ultra vires* of the provincial legislatures in
the case of *The Union Collieries v. Bryden.*

The right to employ white women in any capacity or in any class of business is a
civil right, and legislation upon that subject is clearly within the power of the
provincial legislatures. The right to guarantee and ensure their protection from a
moral standpoint is, in my opinion, within such provincial powers and, if the legislation is *bona fide* for that purpose, it will be upheld even though it may operate
prejudicially to one class or race of people.

There is no doubt in my mind that the prohibition is a racial one and that it does
not cease to operate because a Chinaman becomes naturalized. It extends and was
intended to extend to all Chinamen as such, naturalized or aliens. Questions which
might arise in cases of mixed blood do not arise here. . . .

The prohibition against the employment of white women was not aimed at
alien Chinamen simply or at Chinamen having any political affiliations. It was
against "any Chinaman" whether owing allegiance to the rulers of the Chinese Empire, or the United States Republic, or the British Crown. In other words, it was not
aimed at any class of Chinaman, or at the political status of Chinamen, but at
Chinamen as men of a particular race or blood, and whether aliens or naturalized.

For these reasons I would dismiss the appeal with costs.

IDINGTON J. (dissenting): . . . The Act, by its title, refers to female labour and
then proceeds to deal with only the case of white women.

In truth, its evident purpose is to curtail or restrict the rights of Chinamen.

In view of the provisions of the "Naturalization Act," under and pursuant to
which the appellant, presumably, has become a naturalized British subject, one
must have the gravest doubt if it ever was intended to apply such legislation to one
so naturalized.

The "Naturalization Act," in force long before and at the time of the creation of
the Province of Saskatchewan, and ever since, provided by section 4 for aliens
acquiring and holding real and personal property, and by section 24, as follows: —

> 24. An alien to whom a certificate of naturalization is granted shall, within Canada, be
> entitled to all political and other rights, powers and privileges, and be subject to all obligations to
> which a natural-born British subject is entitled or subject within Canada, with this qualification,
> that he shall not, when within the limits of the foreign state of which he was a subject previously to
> obtaining his certificate of naturalization, be deemed to be a British subject unless he has ceased to
> be a subject of that state in pursuance of the laws thereof, or in pursuance of a treaty or convention
> to that effect.

These enactments rest upon the class No. 25 of the classification of subjects
assigned, by section 91 of the "British North America Act, 1867," to the exclusive
jurisdiction of the Dominion Parliament, and which reads as follows: "Naturalization and Aliens." The political rights given any one, whether naturalized or natural-
born British subjects, may in many respects be limited and varied by the legislation
of a province, even if discriminating in favour of one section or class as against
another. Some political rights or limitations thereof may be obviously beyond the
power of such legislature. But the "other rights, powers and privileges" (if meaning
anything) of natural-born British subjects to be shared by naturalized British

subjects, do not so clearly fall within the powers of the legislatures to discriminate with regard to as between classes or sections of the community. . . .

Again, it may also be well argued that, within the exclusive powers given to the Dominion Parliament over the subject of naturalization and aliens, there is implied the power to guarantee to all naturalized subjects that equality of freedom and opportunity to which I have adverted. And I ask, has it not done so by the foregoing provision of the "Naturalization Act"? . . .

The appellant having, under the "Naturalization Act" (as I think fair to infer) become a British subject, he has presumably been certified to as a man of good character and enjoying the assurance, conveyed in the section thereof which I have quoted, of equal treatment with other British subjects, I shall not willingly impute an intention to the legislature to violate that assurance by this legislation specially aimed at his fellow-countrymen in origin. Indeed, in a piece of legislation alleged to have been promoted in the interests of morality, it would seem a strange thing to find it founded upon a breach of good faith which lies at the root of nearly all morality worth bothering one's head about. . . .

Looked at from this point of view I am constrained to think that this Act must be construed as applicable only to those Chinamen who have not become naturalized British subjects, and is not applicable to the appellant who has become such.

Whether it is *ultra vires* or *intra vires* the alien Chinamen is a question with which, in this view, I have nothing to do.

DUFF J.: . . . There can be no doubt that, *prima facie*, legislation prohibiting the employment of specified classes of persons in particular occupations on grounds which touch the public health, the public morality or the public order from the "local and provincial point of view" may fall within the domain of the authority conferred upon the provinces by section 92(16). Such legislation stands upon precisely the same footing in relation to the respective powers of the provinces and of the Dominion as the legislation providing for the local prohibition of the sale of liquor, the validity of which legislation has been sustained by several well-known decisions of the Judicial Committee. . . .

I think that, on the proper construction of this Act (and this appears to me to be the decisive point), it applies to persons of the races mentioned without regard to nationality. According to the common understanding of the words "Japanese, Chinaman or other Oriental person," they would embrace persons otherwise answering the description who, as being born in British territory (Singapore, Hong Kong, Victoria or Vancouver, for instance), are natural-born subjects of His Majesty equally with persons of other nationalities. The terms Chinamen and Chinese, as generally used in Canadian legislation, point to a classification based upon origin, upon racial or personal characteristics and habits, rather than upon nationality or allegiance. The "Chinese Immigration Act," for example, R.S.C. 1906, ch. 95 (sec. 2(d) and sec. 7) particularly illustrates this; and the judgment of Mr. Justice Martin, *In re The Coal Mines Regulation Act* (1904), 10 B.C.R. 408 (C.A.), at pages 421 and 428, gives other illustrations. Indeed, the presence of the phrase "other Oriental persons" seems to make it clear, even if there could otherwise have been any doubt upon the point, that the legislature is not dealing with these classes of persons according to nationality, but as persons of a certain origin or persons having certain common characteristics and habits sufficiently indicated by the language used. *Prima facie*, therefore, the Act is not an Act dealing with aliens or with naturalized subjects as such. It seems also impossible to say that the Act is, in its practical operation, limited to aliens and naturalized subjects. . . .

Orientals are not prohibited in terms from carrying on any establishment of the kind mentioned. Nor is there any ground for supposing that the effect of the prohibition created by the statute will be to prevent such persons carrying on any such business. It would require some evidence of it to convince me that the right and opportunity to employ white women is, in any business sense a necessary condition for the effective carrying on by Orientals of restaurants and laundries and like establishments in the Western provinces of Canada. Neither is there any ground for supposing that this legislation is designed to deprive Orientals of the opportunity of gaining a livelihood.

There is nothing in the Act itself to indicate that the legislature is doing anything more than attempting to deal according to its lights (as it is its duty to do) with a strictly local situation. In the sparsely inhabited Western provinces of this country the presence of Orientals in comparatively considerable numbers not infrequently raises questions for public discussion and treatment, and, sometimes in an acute degree, which in more thickly populated countries would excite little or no general interest. One can without difficulty figure to one's self the considerations which may have influenced the Saskatchewan Legislature in dealing with the practice of white girls taking employment in such circumstances as are within the contemplation of this Act; considerations, for example, touching the interests of immigrant European women, and considerations touching the effect of such a practice upon the local relations between Europeans and Orientals; to say nothing of considerations affecting the administration of the law. And, in view of all this, I think, with great respect, it is quite impossible to apply with justice to this enactment the observation of Lord Watson in the *Bryden* case, that "the whole pith and substance of it is that it establishes a prohibition affecting" Orientals. For these reasons, I think, apart altogether from the decision in *Cunningham v. Tomey Homma*, to which I am about to refer, that the question of the legality of this statute is not ruled by the decision in *Bryden's* Case.

I think, however, that in applying *Bryden's* case we are not entitled to pass over the authoritative interpretation of that decision which was pronounced some years later by the Judicial Committee itself in *Cunningham v. Tomey Homma*, [1903] A.C. 151. The legislation their Lordships had to examine in the last mentioned case, it is true, related to a different subject-matter. Their Lordships, however, put their decision upon grounds that appear to be strictly appropriate to the question raised on this appeal. Starting from the point that the enactment then in controversy was *prima facie* within the scope of the powers conferred by section 92(1), they proceeded to examine the question whether, according to the true construction of section 91(25), the subject-matter of it really fell within the subject of "aliens and naturalization"; and, in order to pass upon that point, their Lordships considered and expounded the meaning of that article. . . .

It should not be forgotten that the very eminent judges (Lord Halsbury, Lord Macnaghten, Lord Davey, Lord Robertson and Lord Lindley), constituting the

Board which heard the appeal in *Cunningham's* case, had that case before them for something like six months after it had been very fully argued by Mr. Blake against the provincial view; and, in delivering the considered judgment of the Board, Lord Halsbury, as we have seen, examines and sums up the effect of the decision in *Bryden's* case, which the courts in British Columbia had believed themselves to be following in passing upon *Cunningham's* case. In these circumstances, whatever might otherwise have been one's view of their Lordships' judgment in *Bryden's* case, we should not be entitled to adopt and act upon a view as to the construction of item 25 of section 91 ("B.N.A. Act"), which was distinctly and categorically rejected in the later judgment.

There is one more point to be noted. Section 24 of the "Naturalization Act," ch. 77, of the Revised Statutes of Canada, 1906, provides as follows: [The section is set out in the judgment of Idington J., *supra*.]

It is unnecessary to consider whether or not this section goes beyond the powers of the Dominion in respect of the subject of naturalization, or whether "the rights, powers and privileges" referred to therein ought to be construed as meaning those only which are implied by the "protection" that is referred to as the correlative of allegiance in the . . . judgment of the Judicial Committee in *Cunningham's* case. This much seems clear: The section cannot fairly be construed as conferring upon persons naturalized under the provisions of the "Naturalization Act," a status in which they are exempt from the operation of laws passed by a provincial legislature in relation to the subjects of section 92 of the "British North America Act, 1867," and applying to native-born subjects of His Majesty in like manner as to naturalized subjects and aliens. If the enactment in question had been confined to Orientals who are native-born British subjects it would have been impossible to argue that there was any sort of invasion of the Dominion jurisdiction under section 91(25); and it seems equally impossible to say that this legislation deprives any Oriental, who is a naturalized subject, of any of "the rights, powers and privileges" which an Oriental, who is a native-born British subject, is allowed to exercise or retain.

*Appeal dismissed.*

[Anglin J. agreed with Davies J. *The Canadian Citizenship Act*, R.S.C. 1970, c. C-19, section 22 provides as follows:

A Canadian citizen other than a natural-born Canadian citizen is, subject to the provisions of this Act, entitled to all the rights, powers and privileges and is subject to all obligations, duties and liabilities to which a natural-born Canadian citizen is entitled or subject and, on and after becoming a Canadian citizen, subject to the provisions of this Act, has a like status to that of a natural-born Canadian citizen.

Consider the affirmative effect, if any, of this provision: see also section 24 which removes the property disabilities of aliens; and *cf. Re Kvasnak*, [1951] 3 D.L.R. 412 (Sask. C.A.); *Re Lukac; Hayzel v. Public Trustee* (1963), 44 W.W.R. 582 (Alta. S.C.).

The limitations on provincial legislative power arising from section 91(25) do not obtain where the provincial legislature acts in a proprietary capacity, e.g., in relation to Crown lands. However, the position may be affected by overriding competent Dominion legislation; see *Brooks-Bidlake and Whittall Ltd. v. A.-G. B.C.*, [1923] A.C. 450 and *A.-G. B.C. v. A.-G. Can.*, [1924] A.C. 203. In the former case, Lord Cave said, *inter alia*, that "sect. 91(25) reserves to the Dominion Parliament the general right to legislate as to the rights and disabilities of aliens and naturalized persons; but the Dominion is not empowered by that section to regulate the management of the public property of the province, or to determine whether a grantee or licensee of that property shall or shall not be permitted to employ persons of a particular race. These functions are assigned by s. 92, head 5, and s. 109 of the [B.N.A.] Act to the Legislature of the Province; and there is nothing in s. 91 which conflicts with that view."]

# WINNER v. S.M.T. (EASTERN) LTD. AND A.-G. CAN.

In the Supreme Court of Canada. [1951] S.C.R. 887.

Rinfret C.J.C., Kerwin, Taschereau, Rand, Kellock, Estey, Locke, Cartwright and Fauteux JJ. Oct. 22, 1951.

RAND J.: This appeal raises the question of the extent and nature of the provincial jurisdiction over highways of New Brunswick. As now constituted, the action is brought by S.M.T. (Eastern) Ltd. as relator on behalf of the Attorney-General. That company is a carrier of passengers by bus under a licence to operate on named highways which include one running from St. Stephen near the international boundary bordering the State of Maine, through the cities of Saint John and Moncton and on to the boundary with Nova Scotia. The appellant, Winner, is an American citizen of Maine, who conducts a bus line which for some time prior to 1949 had been operating between Boston and Halifax over the highway mentioned. In June, 1949, he was granted a licence under the *Motor Carrier Act* for the operation of his buses, subject to the restriction that no passengers could be set off or taken on in the Province. The result was that only an operation across the Province was authorized. In disregard of that limitation, he is taking up and setting down passengers without reference to originating point or destination. . . .

The claim made for provincial control is, in my opinion, excessive. The first and fundamental accomplishment of the constitutional Act was the creation of a single political organization of subjects of His Majesty within the geographical area of the Dominion, the basic postulate of which was the institute of a Canadian citizenship. Citizenship is membership in a state; and in the citizen inhere those rights and duties, the correlatives of allegiance and protection, which are basic to that status.

The [B.N.A.] Act makes no express allocation of citizenship as the subject-matter of legislation to either the Dominion or the Provinces; but as it lies at the foundation of the political organization, as its character is national, and by the implication of head (25), s. 91, "Naturalization and Aliens", it is to be found within the residual powers of the Dominion: *Canada Temperance case* [*A.-G. Ont. v. Can. Temperance Federation*], [1946] A.C. 193 at 205 (P.C.). Whatever else might have been said prior to 1931, the *Statute of Westminster*, coupled with the declarations of constitutional relations of 1926, out of which it issued, creating, in substance, a sovereignty, concludes the question.

But incidents of status must be distinguished from elements or attributes necessarily involved in status itself. British subjects have never enjoyed an equality in all civil or political privileges or immunities as is illustrated in *Cunningham v. Tomey Homma*, [1903] A.C. 151, in which the Judicial Committee maintained the right of British Columbia to exclude a naturalized person from the electoral franchise. On the other hand in *Bryden's* case [*Union Colliery Co. of B.C. v. Bryden*], [1899] A.C. 580 (P.C.), a statute of the same Province that forbade the employment of Chinamen, aliens or naturalized, in underground mining operations, was found to be incompetent. As explained in *Homma's* case [p. 157], that decision is to be taken as determining "that the regulations there impeached were not really aimed at the regulation of coal mines at all, but were in truth devised to deprive the Chinese, naturalized or not, of the ordinary rights of the inhabitants of British Columbia and, in effect, to prohibit their continued residence in that province, since it prohibited their earning their living in that province".

What this implies is that a Province cannot, by depriving a Canadian of the means of working, force him to leave it: it cannot divest him of his right or capacity to remain and to engage in work there: that capacity inhering as a constituent element of his citizenship status is beyond nullification by provincial action. The contrary view would involve the anomaly that although British Columbia could not by mere prohibition deprive a naturalized foreigner of his means of livelihood, it could do so to a native-born Canadian. He may, of course, disable himself from exercising his capacity or he may be regulated in it by valid provincial law in other respects. But that attribute of citizenship lies outside of those civil rights committed to the Province, and is analogous to the capacity of a Dominion corporation which the Province cannot sterilize.

It follows, *a fortiori*, that a Province cannot prevent a Canadian from entering it except, conceivably, in temporary circumstances, for some local reason as, for example, health. With such a prohibitory power, the country could be converted into a number of enclaves and the "union" which the original Provinces sought and obtained disrupted. In a like position is a subject of a friendly foreign country; for practical purposes he enjoys all the rights of the citizen.

Such, then, is the national status of embodying certain inherent or constitutive characteristics, of members of the Canadian public, and it can be modified, defeated or destroyed, as for instance by outlawry, only in Parliament.

Highways are a condition of the existence of an organized state: without them its life could not be carried on. To deny their use is to destroy the fundamental liberty of action of the individual, to proscribe his participation in that life: under such a ban, the exercise of citizenship would be at an end. A narrower constitutional consideration arises. Civil life in this country consists of inextricably intermingled activities and relations within the legislative jurisdiction of both Parliament and Legislature; and deprivation of the use of highways would confound matters appertaining to both. To prevent a person from engaging in business as a post office or a customs house or a bank by forbidding him the use of highways is, so far, to frustrate a privilege imbedded in Dominion law. These considerations are, I think, sufficient to demonstrate that the privilege of using highways is likewise an essential attribute of Canadian citizenship status.

The Province is thus seen to be the *quasi*-trustee of its highways to enable the life of the country as a whole to be carried on; they are furnished for the Canadian public and not only or primarily that of New Brunswick. Upon the Province is cast the duty of providing and administering them, for which ample powers are granted; and the privilege of user can be curtailed directly by the Province only within the legislative and administrative field of highways as such or in relation to other subject-matter within its exclusive field. The privilege of operating on the highway now enjoyed by Winner so far constitutes therefore the equivalent of a right-of-way....

[See also the judgment of Estey J., who said, in part:

> While it was contended by certain of the Attorneys-General that the Province possesses the power to prohibit an international and interprovincial bus to pass and repass upon its highways, no authority was cited to that effect. The Dominion of Canada was created by the *B.N.A. Act* as "one Dominion under the Name of Canada" (s. 3); and there shall be "one Parliament for Canada" (s. 17). Moreover, there is but one Canadian citizenship, and, throughout, the *B.N.A. Act* contemplates that citizens, and all others who may be for the time being in Canada, shall enjoy freedom of passage throughout the Dominion, subject to compliance with competent provincial legislation.

The judgment of the Privy Council in this case, reversing in part the judgment of the Supreme Court is reproduced at Chapter 9. It makes no reference to the issues raised by Rand and Estey JJ. in the portions of their judgments quoted above.

Is it competent to a Province to license associations, *e.g.*, trade unions, and to exclude from the Province or to deny existence to any that are affiliated with groups elsewhere or which admit non-residents to membership? Would it make any difference if the licence or exclusion were referable only to privileges conferred by provincial legislation? See Forsey, "The Prince Edward Island Trade Union Act, 1948" (1948), 26 Can. Bar Rev. 1159.

In view of explicit provision in section 95 of the *Constitution Act, 1867* for concurrent power in the Provinces and the Dominion (but subject to federal paramountcy) to legislate in relation to immigration, is it arguable that a Province may exclude persons holding certain opinions from entering the Province, at least where there is no superseding affirmative federal legislation? Is there a "right" of interprovincial movement of people no less than of goods which is beyond provincial restriction? *Cf. Edwards v. California*, 314 U.S. 160 (1941); Note (1942), 55 Harv. L. Rev. 873; and see Note (1941), 19 Can. Bar Rev. 750.]

# MORGAN v. ATTORNEY-GENERAL FOR PRINCE EDWARD ISLAND

In the Supreme Court of Canada. [1976] 2 S.C.R. 349.

Laskin, C.J.C., Martland, Judson, Ritchie, Spence, Pigeon, Dickson, Beetz and de Grandpré, JJ. June 26, 1975.

Appeal from the judgment of the Prince Edward Island Supreme Court, *in banco*, 5 Nfld. & P.E.I.R. 129, dismissing an action for a declaratory judgment and for a writ of *mandamus*.

The judgment of the Court was delivered by

LASKIN C.J.C.: — This appeal arises out of a declaratory action by two citizens of the United States, who are also resident there challenging the validity of s. 3 of the *Real Property Act*, c. 40, s. 1 (P.E.I.).

The challenged s. 3 reads as follows:

3(1) Persons who are not Canadian citizens may take, acquire, hold, convey, transmit, or otherwise dispose of, real property in the Province of Prince Edward Island subject to the provisions of sub-section two (2) here next following.

(2) Unless he receives permission so to do from the Lieutenant-Governor-in-Council, no person who is not a resident of the Province of Prince Edward Island shall take, acquire, hold or in any other manner receive, either himself, or through a trustee, corporation, or any such the like, title to any real property in the Province of Prince Edward Island the aggregate total of which exceeds ten (10) acres, nor to any real property in the Province of Prince Edward Island the aggregate total of which has a shore frontage in excess of five (5) chains.

(3) The grant of any such permission shall be at the discretion of the Lieutenant-Governor-in-Council, who shall notify the applicant in writing by means of a certified copy of an Order-in-Council of his decision within a reasonable time.

(4) An application for any such permission shall be in the form prescribed, from time to time, by the Lieutenant-Governor-in-Council.

(5)(a) For the purposes of this section, "Canadian citizen" means persons defined as Canadian citizens by the Canadian Citizenship Act (R.S.C. 1970, Vol. 1, Cap. C-19).

(b) For the purposes of this section "resident of the Province of Prince Edward Island" means a bona fide resident, animus et factum, of the Province of Prince Edward Island.

(c) For the purposes of this section "corporation" means any company, corporation or other body corporate and politic, and any association, syndicate or other body, and any such the like, and the heirs, executors, administrators and curators, or other legal representatives of such person, as such is defined and included by The Domiciled Companies Act (Laws of Prince Edward Island 1962).

. . . .

I view s. 3 as applying to Canadian citizens who reside outside of Prince Edward Island, whether elsewhere in Canada or outside of Canada and to aliens who reside outside of Prince Edward Island, whether elsewhere in Canada or, as here, outside of Canada. This being so, the attack on this provision was based initially on an allegedly unconstitutional discrimination between resident and non-resident Canadian citizens, at least those residing elsewhere in Canada. Citizenship, it was urged, involved being at home in every Province, it was a status that was under exclusive federal definition and protection, and it followed that a residential qualification for holding land in any Province offended against the equality of status and capacity that arose from citizenship and, indeed, inhered in it.

. . . .

Section 3 which is under challenge here does not distinguish between natural-born and naturalized Canadian citizens in making provincial residence the relevant factor for holding land. If it did, a different question would be presented, and account would have to be taken of the effect of s. 22 of the *Canadian Citizenship Act* which prescribes equality of status and equalityof rights and obligations for all citizens, whether natural-born or naturalized.

Although citizenship as such is not mentioned in the *British North America Act, 1867*, it was not doubted by anyone on this appeal that, whether by implication from s. 91(25) thereof or under the opening words thereof, it was for Parliament alone to define citizenship and to define how it may be acquired and lost. How far beyond this Parliament may go in investing citizenship with attributes that carry against provincial legislation has not been much canvassed in this Court; nor, on the other hand, is there any large body of case law dwelling on the limitation on provincial legislative power arising from a grant of citizenship or the recognition thereof in a natural-born citizen or arising from federal power in relation to naturalization and aliens under s. 91(25) of the *British North America Act, 1867*.

The well-known dictum by Rand, J., in *Winner v. S.M.T. (Eastern) Ltd. and A.-G. N.B.*, [1951] S.C.R. 887 at 920, that "a Province cannot prevent a Canadian from entering it except, conceivably, in temporary circumstances, for some local reason as, for example, health", was preceded by some observations upon which stress was laid by the appellants and by the Attorney-General of Canada. These observations engaged the decisions of the Privy Council in *Union Colliery Co. of*

*B.C., Ltd. v. Bryden*, [1899] A.C. 580, and *Cunningham v. Tomey Homma*, [1903] A.C. 151, and they are as follows (at pp. 918-20 S.C.R.):

> Citizenship is membership in a state; and in the citizen inhere those rights and duties, the correlatives of allegiance and protection, which are basic to that status.
>
> . . . . .
>
> But incidents of status must be distinguished from elements or attributes necessarily involved in status itself. British subjects have never enjoyed an equality in all civil or political privileges or immunities as is illustrated in *Cunningham v. Tomey Homma*, in which the Judicial Committee maintained the right of British Columbia to exclude a naturalized person from the electoral franchise. On the other hand, in *Bryden's* case, a statute of the same province that forbade the employment of Chinamen, aliens or naturalized, in underground mining operations was found to be incompetent. As explained in *Homma's* case, that decision is to be taken as determining, "that the regulations there impeached were not really aimed at the regulation of coal mines at all, but were in truth devised to deprive the Chinese, naturalized or not, of the ordinary rights of the inhabitants of British Columbia and, in effect, to prohibit their continued residence in that province, since it prohibited their earning their living in that province".
>
> What this implies is that a Province cannot, by depriving a Canadian of the means of working, force him to leave it: it cannot divest him of his right or capacity to remain and to engage in work there: that capacity inhering as a constituent element of his citizenship status is beyond nullification by provincial action. The contrary view would involve the anomaly that although British Columbia could not by mere prohibition deprive a naturalized foreigner of his means of livelihood, it could do so to a native-born Canadian. He may, of course, disable himself from exercising his capacity or he may be regulated in it by valid provincial law in other aspects. But that attribute of citizenship lies outside of those civil rights committed to the Province, and is analogous to the capacity of a Dominion corporation which the Province cannot sterilize.

These passages from the reasons of Rand, J., in the *Winner* case raise, by and large, the issues upon which the parties and the intervenants have made their various submissions, both in respect of the scope of the federal citizenship power and the federal power in relation to aliens. Rand, J., recognized that even a native-born citizen (to use his words) "may . . . disable himself from exercising his capacity or he may be regulated in it by valid provincial law in other aspects".

The power of a provincial Legislature to regulate the way in which land in the Province may be held, how it may be transferred, how it may be used (and this, whether the land be privately-owned or be land held by the Crown in right of the Province) is not contested. Nor, as I understand the submissions that were made, is it doubted that the provincial Legislature may limit the amount of land that may be held by any person, assuming equal opportunity to anyone to purchase. The contention is, however, that as soon as the Province moves to differentiate in this respect between classes of persons the legislation becomes suspect, and if it turns out that some citizens, and indeed some aliens, are disadvantaged as against others, that is as against those who are resident in the Province, the legislation must be regarded as in pith and substance in relation to citizenship and in relation to aliens and hence *ultra vires*.

I do not agree with this characterization, and I do not think it is supportable either in principle or under any case law. No one is prevented by Prince Edward Island legislation from entering the Province and from taking up residence there. Absentee ownership of land in a Province is a matter of legitimate provincial concern and, in the case of Prince Edward Island, history adds force to this aspect of its authority over its territory. In *Walter v. A.-G. Alta.*, [1969] S.C.R. 383, this

Court concluded that it was open to the Province of Alberta to control the extent to which groups of persons could hold land on a communal basis, and the legislation that was unsuccessfully challenged in that case flatly prohibited the acquisition of land in the Province by "colonies" outside the Province, without the consent of the Lieutenant-Governor in Council. It is true that no differentiation was expressly made on the basis of residence or citizenship or alienage, and that all who fell within the regulated groups were treated alike. Yet, it is also clear that the definition of the regulated bodies of persons was for the Province, and if the Province could determine who could hold or the extent to which land could be held according to whether a communal property regime was observed, it is difficult to see why the Province could not equally determine the extent of permitted holdings on the basis of residence. In neither case is this Court concerned with the wisdom or utility of the provincial land policy but only with whether the Province has transgressed the limits of its legislative authority. I recognize, of course, that there may be cases where the line between wisdom and validity may be difficult to draw, but I find no such difficulty here.

In the *Walter* case, Martland, J., speaking for the Court put the matter squarely in the following words [at p. 389 S.C.R]:

> It would seem to me to be clear that a provincial Legislature can enact laws governing the ownership of land within the Province and thåt legislation enacted in relation to that subject must fall within s. 92(13), and must be valid unless it can be said to be in relation to a class of subject specifically enumerated in s. 91 of the *B.N.A. Act* or otherwise within exclusive federal jurisdiction.
>
> There is no suggestion in the present case that the Act relates to any class of subject specifically enumerated in s. 91.

In the present case, as I have already observed, there is very much the suggestion that there has been an invasion of federal legislative power.

. . . .

Legislation of a Province dealing with the capacity of a person, whether alien or infant or other, to hold land in the Province is legislation in an aspect open to the Province because it is directly concerned with a matter in relation to which the Province has competence. Simply because it is for Parliament to legislate in relation to aliens does not mean that it alone can give an alien capacity to buy or hold land in a Province or take it by devise or by descent. No doubt, Parliament alone may withhold or deny capacity of an alien to hold land or deny capacity to an alien in any other respect, but if it does not, I see no ground upon which provincial legislation recognizing capacity in respect of the holding of land can be held invalid.

. . . .

In approaching this question I make nothing of the fact that s. 3(2) speaks in terms of residency and non-residency as if these words carried some connotation that set aliens and citizens apart so that the legislation did not touch them. I am prepared to treat it by extrapolation as referring expressly to resident aliens and citizens and to non-resident aliens and citizens; there are certainly no other classes so distinguishable. On this view of s. 3(2), I turn to a consideration of *Union Colliery Co. v. Bryden* and of *Cunningham v. Tomey Homma* to which Rand J., referred in the passages of his reasons in the *Winner* case that I have quoted.

The *Union Colliery Co.* case involved a preliminary question of the construction of the challenged s. 4 of the British Columbia *Coal Mines Regulation Act*, 1890 in its reference to "Chinaman" in that provision, which was as follows:

> No boy under the age of twelve years, and no woman or girl of any age, and no Chinaman, shall be employed in or allowed to be for the purpose of employment in any mine to which the Act applies, below ground.

The Privy Council construed the term "Chinaman" as embracing Chinese who were aliens or naturalized persons, and it went on from there to assess the scope of the exclusive federal power in relation to "naturalization and aliens" under s. 91(25) of the *British North America Act, 1867*. It said of this power that (1) "The subject of 'naturalization' seems prima facie to include the power of enacting what shall be the consequences of naturalization, or, in other words, what shall be the rights and privileges pertaining to residents of Canada after they have been naturalized" (at p. 586); and (2) it invested the Parliament of Canada "with exclusive authority in all matters which directly concern the rights, privileges, and disabilities of the class of Chinamen who are resident in the provinces of Canada" (at p. 587). In the result, the challenged legislation which, in the words of the Privy Council, consisted in pith and substance "in establishing a statutory prohibition which affects aliens or naturalized subjects" was *ultra vires* as invading exclusive federal authority.

I am bound to say that this result, assessed only according to the words used in reaching it, appears to be very far-reaching, especially when the Privy Council also said in the *Union Colliery Co.* case that so far as natural-born Canadians were concerned, "it can hardly have been intended to give the Dominion Parliament the exclusive right to legislate for [this] class of persons resident in Canada" (at p. 586). It is plain to me that the Privy Council receded from the literal effect of its language in the *Union Colliery Co.* case when it decided *Cunningham v. Tomey Homma*. It was said flatly in this last-mentioned case that "the truth is that the language of [s. 91(25)] does not purport to deal with the consequences of either alienage or naturalization" (at p. 156), and hence it was open to a Province to deny the provincial franchise to Japanese persons, whether naturalized or not, and this notwithstanding that so far as naturalized Japanese persons were concerned federal legislation put them on a basis of equality with natural-born persons. But even natural-born persons of Japanese descent were excluded from the franchise, and this too was held to be within provincial competence. The Privy Council stated that while it was for the Parliament of Canada to determine what constitutes alienage or naturalization, "the question as to what consequences shall follow from either is not touched. The right of protection and the obligations of allegiance are necessarily involved in the nationality conferred by naturalization; but the privileges attached to it, where these depend upon residence, are quite independent of nationality" (at p. 157).

The Privy Council regarded the electoral legislation in *Cunningham v. Tomey Homma* as validly enacted under s. 92(1) of the *British North America Act, 1867*, which authorizes legislation in relation to "the amendment from time to time, notwithstanding anything in this Act, of the Constitution of the Province, except as regards the office of Lieutenant-Governor". I am not concerned in this present case with the question whether the franchise, the right to vote, has such a special relationship to naturalization and to natural-born status as to preclude provincial discrimination against certain racial groups. The Privy Council obviously thought not. Its reasons suggested a distinction between a privilege, *e.g.*, the franchise, which the Province could grant or withhold from aliens or naturalized or even natural-born citizens, and what appeared to it to be the draconian prohibition involved in the *Union Colliery Co.* case. Of that case it said this (at p. 157):

> This Board, dealing with the particular facts of that case, came to the conclusion that the regulations there impeached were not really aimed at the regulation of coal mines at all, but were in truth devised to deprive the Chinese naturalized or not, of the ordinary rights of the inhabitants of British Columbia and, in effect, to prohibit their continued residence in that Province, since it prohibited their earning their living in that Province. It is obvious that such a decision can have no relation to the question whether any naturalized person has an inherent right to the suffrage within the Province in which he resides.

The view so taken of the *Union Colliery Co.* case is difficult indeed to discern from the reasons for judgment therein but, taking the interpretation put upon it in *Cunningham v. Tomey Homma*, it is a far different case from the present one, which does not involve any attempt, direct or indirect, either to exclude aliens from Prince Edward Island or to drive out any aliens now residing there. I would not myself have thought that the mere prohibition against employment of Chinese persons in underground mining could be taken to be a general prohibition against their earning a living in British Columbia and, however distasteful such legislation was, that it was beyond provincial competence. At any rate, what we have in the present case is not any attempt to regulate or control alien residents of Prince Edward Island in what they may do or not do therein, but rather a limitation on landholding by non-residents.

. . . .

I do not think that federal power as exercised in ss. 22 and 24 of the *Citizenship Act*, or as it may be exercised beyond those provisions, may be invoked to give aliens, naturalized persons or natural-born citizens any immunity from provincial regulatory legislation, otherwise within its constitutional competence, simply because it may affect one class more than another or may affect all of them alike by what may be thought to be undue stringency. The question that would have to be answered is whether the provincial legislation, though apparently or avowedly related to an object within provincial competence, is not in truth directed to, say, aliens or naturalized persons so as to make it legislation striking at their general capacity or legislation so discriminatory against them as in effect to amount to the same thing.

The issue here is not unlike that which has governed the determination of the validity of provincial legislation embracing federally-incorporated companies. The case law, dependent so largely on the judicial appraisal of the thrust of the particular legislation, has established, in my view, that federally-incorporated companies are not constitutionally entitled, by virtue of their federal incorporation, to any advantage, as against provincial regulatory legislation, over provincial corporations or over extra-provincial or foreign corporations, so long as their capacity to establish themselves as viable corporate entities (beyond the mere fact of their incorporation), as by raising capital through issue of shares and debentures, is not precluded by the provincial legislation. Beyond this, they are subject to competent provincial regulations in respect of businesses or activities which fall within provincial legislative power.

In the present case, the residency requirement affecting both aliens and citizens alike and related to a competent provincial object, namely, the holding of land in the Province and limitations on the size of the holdings (relating as it does to a limited resource), can in no way be regarded as a sterilization of the general capacity of an alien or citizen who is a non-resident, especially when there is no attempt to seal off provincial borders against entry. Since, in my view, s. 3(2) is valid provincial legislation in its application to aliens or citizens who reside elsewhere in Canada than in Prince Edward Island, and hence is *a fortiori* valid in respect of persons resident outside of Canada I need not consider whether the appellants would be subject to the limitations of s. 3(2) even if persons resident elsewhere in Canada would constitutionally be free of them.

I would dismiss the appeal with costs, and would make no order as to costs by or against the intervenants.

*Appeal dismissed.*

[In *Re Minister of Revenue for Ontario and Hala* (1977), 81 D.L.R. (3d) 710 (Ont. H.C.), Henry J. upheld a provincial statute which imposed a special land transfer tax on people, citizens or otherwise, residing outside Canada, and on Canadian residents who were neither citizens nor permanent residents, characterizing the legislation as being in relation to the holding of land rather than alienage. This was so notwithstanding that the purpose was to discourage these people from acquiring land in the Province.]

# PART II
## CANADIAN CHARTER OF RIGHTS AND FREEDOMS

# 16

# Introduction

*Note on the Canadian Bill of Rights, the Significance of the Constitutional Entrenchment of the Canadian Charter of Rights and Freedoms, and the Legislative Override in Section 33 of the Charter*

The profound influence of the late Chief Justice Laskin on Canadian constitutional law is nowhere more deeply felt than in the area of civil liberties. While he passed away before the Supreme Court of Canada started handing down decisions on the *Canadian Charter of Rights and Freedoms*, there is no doubt that this work and philosophy both as scholar and jurist will be considered and applied in the *Charter*'s development.

In his seminal article "An Inquiry into the Diefenbaker Bill of Rights" (1959), 37 Can. Bar Rev. 77, Professor Laskin (as he then was) enunciated the four classifications of civil liberties which have been adopted in substantially the same form in the *Charter*. He said at pp. 80-2:

> ... History and tradition have hallowed what may be termed political civil liberty which is associated with the operation of our parliamentary institutions and which make parliamentary democracy possible and tolerable. The substance of this kind of liberty is freedom of association, freedom of assembly, freedom of utterance, freedom of the press (or of the use of other media for dissemination of news and opinion) and freedom of conscience and of religion. Crucial as any of these may be to the preservation of the nature of our polity, they are not absolutes. As will be shown below, freedom of association and of assembly have been qualified by propriety (and in the result, legality) of purpose and by a duty to keep the peace. Freedom of speech does not on a level of public order and law cover incitement to crime or seditious utterances; and, on a private level, it is limited by the law of defamation. This is equally true with freedom of the press which, moreover, cannot be invoked to support publications that are in contempt of court. Freedom of religion and of conscience will not, in the views of the courts of the common-law countries, justify human sacrifice or polygamy or the practice of medicine without proper certification or refusal to obey compulsory school attendance laws.
>
> Closely associated with political liberty, if not in truth particular projections thereof, and liberties connected with the legal order. Among these are freedom of arbitrary arrest, or arbitrary search and seizure of person, premises and papers; and protection of impartial adjudication, involving notice and hearing, an independent judiciary and access to counsel; and protection against compulsory self-crimination. It is well to note that while these values emerged in the political struggles that helped fashion our basic criminal procedure, they have in recent years been adapted in part as a means of curial control of administrative adjudication.
>
> Where feasible, this has been used as a second line of defence of a third class of liberty, which may be termed economic civil liberty. Individual rights in an economic sense symbolized freedom from state regulation or intervention in economic affairs. Such a call to liberty is no longer as impressive as it once was, but it is of some interest to note that the trade unionist who was once the victim of the assertion of economic liberty is now relying on a particular version of it to defend free collective bargaining and his freedom to engage in strikes and in picketing. Public controls, in the general social interest, administered through government departments or through more or less independent statutory tribunals, have made heavy inroads upon economic individualism. In an era

of great social and economic change, it has become quite clear that economic liberty, however defined, must be more relative in its operation than either the political or the legal liberties referred to above.

A more recent call to liberty, or at least one that has more recently had some response, is liberty in a human rights or egalitarian sense. Involving, as this has, positive state intervention to secure such things as equality of employment opportunity or of access to public places without discrimination on account of colour or religion or ethnic or national origin or ancestry, it is, in a sense, the antithesis of the economic individualism that deprecated state interference in business or social relations. It would be idle to attempt an exhaustive list of the claims or interests for which protection is or might be sought under the head of human (or, perhaps, social) rights. Unemployment insurance, state provision for hospitalization and medical care, and opportunity for free education compatible with ability, are some of the better known and partly realized objectives in this class of liberty. To a considerable extent, the Universal Declaration of Human Rights embraces the kind of interests which are comprehended within my fourth class of civil liberty. As a class of social welfare benefits they appear to me to be no less relative than liberty in its economic sense and hence stand on a less exalted plane than do political or legal liberty.

There are, of course, additional rights regarding language, culture, aboriginal rights and so on enshrined in the *Charter*, but the basic structure follows the Laskin model quite faithfully.

Over the years prior to the promulgation of the *Charter*, there was considerable discussion and pressure for a constitutionally entrenched instrument: see W. Glen How "The Case for a Canadian Bill of Rights" (1948), 26 Can. Bar Rev. 759. The matter was examined in part by a Joint Parliamentary Committee on Human Rights and Fundamental Freedoms, established in 1947, in relation to Canada's obligations under the United Nations Universal Declaration of Human Rights: see (1949), 26 Can. Bar Rev. 706. A more extensive examination was made by a Senate Committee on Human Rights and Fundamental Freedoms which reported in 1950, after taking considerable evidence, on the desirability at least of the enactment by the federal Parliament of a Declaration of Human Rights covering matters within federal legislative authority. The Committee added that were it not for constitutional difficulties which existed at the time, the most desirable step would be to write basic rights into the constitution "so that they may be administered in our Courts and so that they may become binding and obligatory alike upon individuals and upon government". For similar conclusions, see Scott "Dominion Jurisdiction over Human Rights and Fundamental Freedoms" (1949), 27 Can. Bar Rev. 497.

The government of Canada initially chose a halfway house between a fully entrenched constitutional instrument and the *status quo*, moving Parliament to enact a statutory, essentially declaratory *Canadian Bill of Rights*. The *Bill of Rights*, which is preserved by section 26 of the *Charter*, has been unfortunate both in terms of its statutory reach and its subsequent judicial interpretation.

As to its statutory reach, the *Bill* is operative only on the federal level and by its terms does not extend to the provincial governments or legislatures. This is so notwithstanding that there is good ground to contend that Parliament could bind the provinces with respect to a number of areas covered by the *Bill*: see Laskin, *supra* at pp. 99-125; cf. *A.G. Can. v. Dupond*, [1978] 2 S.C.R. 770. The *Bill* is addressed to Parliament itself and to the Courts, admonishing the former not to enact, and the latter not to construe, federal legislation in derogation of the declared rights. As first presented in 1958 (and it was little changed), it was the subject of an extensive symposium examination in (1959), 37 Can. Bar Rev. 1-236, 247-262, including some comparative evaluations, especially on the position in the United States.

Section 1 of the *Bill* is declaratory of certain fundamental freedoms which are said to have existed and are to continue to exist without discrimination by reason of race, national original, colour, religion or sex. Section 1 is then given operative force by its referential incorporation into section 2 which in turn commands the courts to construe and apply federal legislation so as not to abridge the declared freedoms; and section 2 itself contains a whole set of additional guarantees. These are essentially a statement of procedural safeguards mainly, but not completely, related to the criminal trial process.

The statutory *Bill of Rights* has largely been a failure as an effective instrument for redress of grievances. *Robertson and Rosetanni v. The Queen*, [1963] S.C.R. 651, was the first decision on the *Canadian Bill of Rights* to reach the Supreme Court of Canada. In that case the Court took the narrow position that "construed and applied" in section 2 meant only that existing federal legislation was to be interpreted in a way compatible with the *Bill of Rights*, but if it could not be so interpreted then section 2 was spent and the prior federal legislation prevailed. On this basis the *Canadian Bill of Rights* could at best be an interpretation statute providing rules of construction of federal statutes, but with little, if any, substantive effect. The turning point came in *R. v. Drybones*, [1970] S.C.R. 282, rejecting an earlier decision of the British Columbia Court of Appeal in *R. v. Gonzales* (1962), 37 C.R. 56 (B.C.C.A.).

At issue in *Drybones* was a clash between the provisions of section 94 of the *Indian Act*, R.S.C. 1952, c. 149, and section 19 of the *North-West Territories Liquor Ordinance*, R.O.N.W.T. 1956, c. 60 (a law of Canada), the aggregate effect of which was that in the North-West Territories it was not an offence for anyone except an Indian to be intoxicated elsewhere than in a public place. Two important propositions resulted from the decision. First, in the language of Ritchie J., delivering the majority opinion in *R. v. Drybones*, [1970] S.C.R. 282 at 294:

> It seems to me that a more realistic meaning must be given to the words in question and the afford, in my view, the clearest indication that s. 2 is intended to mean and does mean that if a law of Canada cannot be 'sensibly construed and applied' so that it does not abrogate, abridge or infringe one of the rights and freedoms recognized and declared by the Bill, then, such law is inoperative 'unless it is expressly declared by an Act of the Parliament of Canada that it shall operate notwithstanding the *Canadian Bill of Rights*'.

While the court did not depart explicitly from its holding in *Robertson and Rosetanni*, it had nonetheless elevated the *Canadian Bill of Rights* beyond a mere interpretation statute whose terms would yield to a contrary intention; the *Bill* now had paramount force when a federal enactment conflicted with its terms and it was the incompatible federal enactment which had to give way. It is perhaps worth noting that Cartwright C.J.C., who had been unable to agree with the majority on this issue in *Robertson and Rosetanni*, now decided his earlier decision had been wrong and thereby found himself dissenting in *Drybones* as well.

The second point decided in *Drybones* (and it flowed from the first) was that the accused Indian in being convicted and punished under section 94 of the *Indian Act* was denied equality before the law contrary to section 1(b) of the *Bill of Rights* because in the words of Ritchie J., in [1970] S.C.R. 282 at 297:

> I think that s. 1(b) means at least that no individual or group of individuals is to be treated more harshly than another under that law, and I am therefore of opinion that an individual is denied

equality before the law if it is made an offence punishable at law, on account of his race, for him to do something which his fellow Canadians are free to do without having committed any offence or having been made subject to any penalty.

The cases subsequent to *Drybones* failed to live up to its promise. Two of the most significant of these are *A.G. Can. v. Lavell; Isaac v. Bedard*, [1974] S.C.R. 1349 and *Bliss v. A.G. Can.*, [1979] 1 S.C.R. 183. *Lavell* involved provisions of the *Indian Act*. Under section 12(1)(b) of that Act, an Indian woman who married a non-Indian lost her Indian status (and all the incidental rights which that status conferred) whereas no such disability was visited on an Indian man registered under section 11(1)(b) who then marries a non-Indian. In a 5-4 decision, the Supreme Court held that the impugned provision did not offend the guarantee of equality before the law. It is not easy to distill the ratio of *Lavell*; nor is it easy to see any such difference in principle between *Lavell* and *Drybones* as would yield opposite results. It would seem however that *Lavell* at least stands for these propositions:

(1) equality before the law means only equality in the administration or application of the law before the ordinary courts of the land. It is not in any way concerned with the internal regulation of the status of Indians on the reserve. This is a narrow treatment indeed, one which was specifically rejected by Laskin J. (as he then was) for the minority and which holds little prospect for a fertile application of section 1(b) of the *Bill of Rights* in the future. Indeed in *R. v. Burnshine*, [1975] 1 S.C.R. 693, the Court narrowed the guarantee even further by holding that the right to equality before the law in section 1(b) of the *Bill* did not mean that all federal statutes must apply equally to all individuals in all parts of Canada. Federal legislation which applied to a particular group of class of people (here young offenders who were differently dealt with in Ontario and British Columbia than in any of the other provinces) did not offend section 1(b) if it was enacted to achieve a valid federal objective.

(2) The *Canadian Bill of Rights* must be subject to and cannot detract from the effective exercise by Parliament of its exclusive authority to legislate in relation to Indians under section 91(24) of the *Constitution Act, 1867*. Applying this principle to *Lavell* and *Drybones*, one could say that the enactment of laws establishing qualifications for Indian status is indispensable to the exercise of legislative power under section 91(24), whereas the enactment of laws pertaining to liquor offences is not. Similarly, there may have been a concern on the part of the majority, that, were *Lavell* decided differently, it is but a short step to the conclusion that the *Bill of Rights* would render the whole *Indian Act* inoperative, thereby virtually suppressing federal legislation over Indians. The answer to that is, of course, as Laskin J. stated in the minority opinion in *Lavell*, [1974] S.C.R. 1349 at 1375 "discriminatory treatment on the basis of race or colour or sex does not inhere in that grant of legislative power" and one cannot resort to the *Constitution Act, 1867* to escape the force of the *Bill of Rights*.

In *Bliss v. A.G. Can., supra*, section 30 of the *Unemployment Insurance Act, 1971*, S.C. 1970-71-72, c. 48 (since am. 1974-75-76, c. 66, section 22(1)) established extended benefits for pregnant women provided those women had ten weeks of insurable earnings. Pursuant to section 17(2), a person needed only eight weeks' insurable earnings to be eligible for regular benefits. However section 46 provided that a pregnant claimant could not receive any benefits during the eight weeks prior to and ten weeks following confinement otherwise than pursuant to section 30. The combined result of the sections was that a pregnant woman with eight weeks insurable earnings but less than ten was not entitled to even regular benefits in the period specified by section 46, notwithstanding that she might be capable of and available for work at the time of her application. Ms. Bliss, a pregnant woman falling within the disentitlement provisions of section 46, challenged the section as contravening the equality guarantee in section 1(b) of the *Canadian Bill of Rights*.

Ritchie J., delivering the judgment of the Supreme Court of Canada upheld the legislation saying that sections 30 and 46 "form an integral part of a legislative scheme enacted for valid federal objectives and they are concerned with conditions from which men are excluded. Any inequality between the sexes in this area is not created by legislation but by nature."

Ritchie J. went on to distinguish the case before him from *Drybones* on two dubious bases; first, that the legislation in *Drybones* treated one segment of the population more harshly than another whereas here there were differences only in the entitlement to benefits; and second, that there was no inequality of treatment here "in the administration and enforcement of the law before the ordinary Courts of the land as was the case in *Drybones*".

This reasoning is extremely problematic. It is difficult to see a distinction in substance between a law which treats one group more harshly than others from one which distributes benefits unevenly on suspect racial or other grounds. Indeed one is often, possibly always, simply the flip side of the other.

An even greater difficulty with the reasoning, and the part which has virtually emasculated the equality guarantee in the *Canadian Bill of Rights* is the argument first put forward in *Lavell* and repeated here that the key to equality is equal treatment in the administration and enforcement of the legislation. This, when combined with the "valid federal objective" test enunciated in *R. v. Burnshine*, [1975] 1 S.C.R. 693 at 708 and *Prata v. Minister of Manpower and Immigration*, [1976] 1 S.C.R. 376 at 382; *MacKay v. The Queen*, [1980] 2 S.C.R. 370 and *Bliss*, effectively insulate statutory provisions from an equality rights attack. Even the most invidiously discriminatory law can be upheld provided that in the administration of the statute all the people in the disadvantaged group are equally disadvantaged. Similarly, the valid federal objective test as applied in *Burnshine*, *Prata* and *Bliss* appears to miss the point because it focusses upon validity in terms of legislative jurisdiction pursuant to section 91 of the *Constitution Act, 1867*. Any law without a valid federal purpose measured by reference to the *Constitution Act, 1867* would be unconstitutional in a division of powers sense in any event, so a resort to the statutory *Bill of Rights* would be superfluous. Since constitutionality thus presupposes a "valid" purpose in section 91 terms, law which reaches the *Bill of Rights* stage of inquiry will never fail a *Bill of Rights* attack. The "valid federal objective" test as reformulated by McIntyre J. in his minority decision in *MacKay v. The Queen*, [1980] 2 S.C.R. 370 that the test must mean more than basic constitutionality to include consistency with the *Canadian Bill of Rights* is more consonant with the legislative policy underlying the *Bill*. However his was only a minority concurrence, and goes beyond the formulation set out in the above-noted cases. For a detailed analysis of the *Bliss* case, see Gold, "Equality Before the Law in the Supreme Court of Canada: a Case Study" (1980), 18 Osgoode Hall L.J. 336.

It is worthwhile to note that the *Bill of Rights* does not only apply to situations where the provisions of two federal statutes are in conflict (e.g. *Drybones*) or to situations where various provisions of one statute may clash (e.g. *Lavell*). It may also apply where a statute or provision thereof alone must be measured against the standards of the *Bill of Rights* and conform to its guarantees. This is effectively what the court was doing in *Lowry v. The Queen*, [1974] S.C.R. 195, as well as in *Curr v. The Queen*, [1972] S.C.R. 889, and *Brownridge v. The Queen*, [1972] S.C.R. 926, and less obviously what it was also called upon to do in *A. G. Can. v. Canard*, [1976] 1 S.C.R. 170.

One situation where the *Bill of Rights* does not, of course, apply is in resolving a direct conflict between the provisions of a federal statute on the one hand and a provincial statute on the other (see e.g. *Re Birth Registration No. 67-09-022272*, [1974] 3 W.W.R. 363 (B.C. C.A.). The interesting issue which arose in *Canard* was whether the *Bill of Rights* can govern where the subject matter of the impugned federal legislation (administration of estates) was generally the subject of provincial legislation, but where the latter was not directly in issue. In principle there seems no reason why it cannot where the federal legislation operates prohibitively against a specified class and the court is simply called upon to asses whether that legislation, in view of its purpose, denies the affected class the protection of the *Bill of Rights*. More precisely it involves no more than measuring the federal legislation in its own terms against the standards of the *Bill of Rights*. This conclusion is implicit even in the reasons of Beetz J. for the majority, and explicit in the dissenting judgment of Laskin C.J.C.

There is not in the *Canadian Bill of Rights*, as there is in the *Charter*, any sanction for an infringement of its provisions, either in terms of the effect on the impugned federal legislation or on the individual who has successfully invoked one of its guarantees. Accordingly it has been left to the courts to provide the sanction. The *Canadian Bill of Rights* in no sense repeals a piece of federal legislation under attack — that is a matter for Parliament. It either renders the legislation inoperative as in *Drybones*, or, as in *Brownridge v. The Queen, supra*, federal legislation may become inapplicable in a particular fact situation while otherwise remaining operative. For an individual the relevant question, at least in the field of criminal law, is whether an infringement of the *Canadian Bill of Rights* automatically vitiates a conviction. The answer is generally no. There can be no real quarrel with that result where there is admissible evidence, apart from the evidence obtained through a violation of the *Bill*, to sustain a conviction. Conversely, in a case such as *Brownridge*, where the accused was denied the right to retain and instruct counsel contrary to section 2(c)(ii) of the *Bill* and thereupon refused to take a breathalyzer test, it was only logical that his conviction under section 253(2) of the *Criminal Code* for refusing to take the test be set aside because in the words of Laskin J., [1972] S.C.R. 926 at 955, "the violation in this case was the very basis upon which the accused was charged". A middle ground is represented by *Hogan v. The Queen*, [1975] 2 S.C.R. 574, where the accused was also denied his right to speak to his counsel before taking a breathalyzer test. Upon being told he would be charged with failing to take the test, and lacking the fortitude of Mr. Brownridge, he submitted, whereupon he was charged with and convicted of driving with a blood alcohol level greater than .08, contrary to section 236 of the *Criminal Code*. The majority of the Supreme

Court of Canada sustained the conviction essentially on the basis of the Anglo-Canadian common law position relating to the admissibility of illegally obtained evidence. The minority position reflects the importance of the *Canadian Bill of Rights* as a quasi-constitutional document, and indeed one wonders what primacy the *Bill* can really have in safeguarding the rights of the individual unless the sanction for an invasion of one of its guarantees is the exclusion of the evidence thereby obtained. This question becomes even more important in the context of section 24(2) of the *Charter*. See Chapter 24, *infra*.

Most of the unresolved issues concerning the guarantees themselves are found in section 1 of the *Bill*. In *Curr v. The Queen*, [1972] S.C.R. 889, Laskin J., in delivering the majority opinion of the Supreme Court of Canada in [1972] S.C.R. 889 at 896, considered the reach of that section:

> the prohibited discrimination is an additional lever to which federal legislation must respond. Putting the matter another way, federal legislation which does not offend s. 1 in respect of any of the prohibited kinds of discrimination may nonetheless be offensive to s. 1 if it is violative of what is specified in any of the clauses (a) to (f) of s. 1. It is *a fortiori*, offensive if there is discrimination by reason of race so as to deny equality before the law. That is what this Court decided in *R. v. Drybones* and I need to say no more on this point.

However, in *A. G. Can. v. Lavell, supra*, Ritchie J. (writing the majority judgment) explained the above passage as follows in [1974] S.C.R. 1349 at 1358:

> it follows, in my view, that those sections cannot be invoked unless one of the enumerated rights and freedoms has been denied to an individual Canadian or group of Canadians.... There is no language anywhere in the Bill of Rights stipulating that the laws of Canada are to be construed without discrimination unless that discrimination involves the denial of one of the guaranteed rights and freedoms.

It therefore now appears that a prohibited discrimination alone which does not result in a denial of equality before the law (as that phrase was denied in *Drybones* and narrowed by the majority in *Lavell*) cannot amount to an infringement of the *Bill of Rights*. In fact such a finding was essential to the majority result in *Lavell*. It is no doubt also true that the extent to which federal legislation can discriminate on grounds not enumerated in section 1, for example age or literacy, will depend solely on whether such discrimination amounts to a denial of section 1(b).

There has been fairly extensive invocation of the Bill since its enactment. Much of the jurisprudence has been given to developing the content and meaning of the specific guarantees and freedoms. A detailed discussion of that subject is beyond the scope of this book. Suffice it to say that section 1(a) and (b) has raised the most difficult questions of interpretation and warranted the most detailed examination. Section 1(c) to (f) contains the traditional "political" civil liberties and has achieved little impact beyond its purely declaratory value. Because of the similarity of section 1(a) and (b) to the language of the Fifth and Fourteenth Amendments to the United States Constitution there has been, in argument at least, frequent resort to American authority. In general the Supreme Court of Canada has been wary in *Bill of Rights* litigation (but not to the same degree in *Charter* litigation) of using American judicial experience. Rejection of the American approach can be seen in *Curr* and *Lavell, supra*, and *Smythe v. R.*, [1971] S.C.R. 680. In *Curr* the Court did leave the door open (if there were manageable standards) for future use of the American concept of the due process clause as a means of controlling substantive federal legislation, but it is not open very wide. See also the minority judgment of Laskin C.J.C. in *Morgentaler v. The Queen*, [1976] 1 S.C.R. 616 at 621.

[There is an extensive literature on the *Canadian Bill of Rights*. See for example: *McWhinney*, "A Bill of Rights and Fundamental Law: Illusion and Reality" (1958), 5 McGill L.J. 36; Laskin, "Canada's Bill of Rights: A Dilemma for the Court?" (1962), 11 Int. & Comp. Law Q. 519; Schmeiser, "Disadvantages of an Entrenched Canadian Bill of Rights" (1968), 33 Sask. L. Rev. 249; Tarnopolsky, "The Canadian Bill of Rights from Diefenbaker to Drybones" (1971), 17 McGill L.J. 437; Hogg, "The Canadian Bill of Rights: Equality Before the Law" (1974), 52 Can. Bar Rev. 263; Sanders, "The Bill of Rights and Indian Status" (1972), 7 U.B.C.L. Rev. 81; Leigh, "The Indian Act, the Supremacy of Parliament and the Equal Protection of the Laws" (1970), 16 McGill L.J. 389; Smith, "Regina v. Drybones and Equality Before the Law" (1971), 49 Can. Bar Rev. 163.]

The result of the above is that *Drybones* is the only case in which the Supreme Court of Canada used the *Canadian Bill of Rights* to render substantive, as opposed to evidentiary (*R. v. Shelley*, [1981] 2 S.C.R. 196 dealing with a reverse onus) or procedural (*Singh v. Minister of Employment and Immigration*, (1985) 1 S.C.R. 177 where 3 of the 6 judges invoked the statutory *Bill* rather than the *Charter* with respect to certain appeal provisions in the *Immigration Act*, S.C. 1976-77, c. 52), federal legislation inoperative. The subsequent course of Supreme Court decisions, and in particular the "valid federal objective" test as enunciated in *Bliss, Burnshine, Prata* and *MacKay*, has largely emasculated the *Bill*. Early indications are that the *Charter of Rights* will not suffer the same fate. In an address to the Canadian Bar Association on February 2, 1985, Dickson C.J.C. said:

... I believe it is already clear that the experience with the *Canadian Bill of Rights* will not be repeated. It was often said that, when dealing with the *Bill of Rights*, the Canadian judiciary were indecisive and unadventurous and that they 'sapped the *Bill of Rights* of necessary protection against government heavy-handedness'. I do not think that charge could be laid against the judiciary in dealing with *Charter* cases. Canadian courts, including the Supreme Court of Canada, have accepted the new responsibility which has been thrust upon them by the parliamentarians. They recognize the vital role they will play in determining the kind of society Canada is and will become under the *Charter*. I expect that in our Court, we will proceed with *Charter* cases one by one in a reasonable and principled way, guarding against excessive enthusiasm in light of the various and serious implications of striking down otherwise valid legislation, but willing to impose limits upon governmental action where warranted by the dictates of the *Charter*.

The reason for the different judicial treatments of the *Charter of Rights* and the *Bill of Rights* lies in the fact that the former is a constitutionally entrenched instrument whereas the latter is a simple statute. The comments of Laskin C.J.C. in *Morgentaler v. The Queen*, [1976] 1 S.C.R. 616 at 621 and *Curr v. The Queen*, [1972] S.C.R. 889 at 892 with respect to the distinction between a constitutional as opposed to a statutory jurisdiction were prescient on the point. In *R. v. Big M Drug Mart*, [1985] 3 W.W.R. 481 at 523, Dickson J. (as he then was), speaking for a majority of the Supreme Court of Canada, said about *Robertson and Rosetanni v. R.*, [1963] S.C.R. 651: "an examination of the majority's interpretation demonstrates that it cannot easily be transferred to a constitutional document like the *Charter* and the fundamental guarantees it enshrines". To the same effect, see Wilson J.'s judgment in *Singh v. Minister of Employment and Immigration*, [1985] 1 S.C.R. 177 at 209 and Lamer J.'s judgment in *Reference re section 94(2) of the Motor Vehicle Act* (B.C.) (unreported, released S.C.C. December 17, 1985). The legitimacy of the courts being involved in the exercise of forceful *Charter* review is strongly stated by Lamer J. in the *Motor Vehicle Reference* at p. 6 *et seq.* of the unreported judgment, reproduced *infra* at Chapter 20. Section 52 of the *Charter* provides that the Constitution of Canada, defined to include the *Constitution Act, 1982* and the statutes and orders referred to in the schedule thereto, is "the supreme law of Canada, and any law that is inconsistent with the provisions of the Constitution is, to the extent of the inconsistency, of no force and effect". This declaration of constitutional status has been taken by the courts as a direction to apply the *Charter*'s principles more forcefully than the *Canadian Bill of Rights*.

The *Charter* contains an unfortunate provison in section 33(1), included as part of the political compromise to secure passage of the *Constitution Act, 1982* through the Imperial Parliament following the *Patriation Case*, [1981] 1 S.C.R. 753, which allows Parliament or a provincial legislature to declare by statute that a statute or particular provision thereof shall operate notwithstanding sections 2 or 7 to 15 of the *Charter* for a five year period (section 33(3)) subject to re-enactment (section 33(4)). The leading case on section 33(1) is *Alliance des Professeurs de Montreal v. A.G. Que.* (1985), 21 C.C.C. (3d) 273 (Que. C.A.), leave to appeal to S.C.C. granted September 30, 1985. In *Alliance des Professeurs*, the Quebec Legislature passed an omnibus statute, Bill 62, which declared that all present or future provincial statutes (with minor exceptions) would operate notwithstanding section 2 and sections 7 to 15 of the *Charter*. The Quebec Court of Appeal summarized section 33(1) at p. 279 (C.C.C.) as requiring that the override declaration: (1) must be expressly stated; (2) must be part of the statute which is sought to be exempted; and (3) must indicate which provision of the *Charter* is to be disregarded. The Court of Appeal held that the formal requirements of section 33(1) must be strictly complied with and, since Bill 62 did not comply with the third requirement, it was invalid. Due to a quirk in the legislative drafting of the *Charter*, it is unclear whether section 33 confers an absolute power to opt out of section 2 and sections 7 to 15 or whether the exercise of this power must be reasonably and demonstrably justified in a free and democratic society pursuant to section 1. In *Alliance des Professeurs*, Jacques J.A. was the only one of the three judges who wrote reasons for decision who specifically addressed section 1. The others appeared to assume without analysis that it did not apply. Jacques J.A. opened the discussion by saying (at p. 280) that Section 33 permits the substitution of a purely political guarantee of fundamental rights for the new constitutional legal guarantee", which on its face militates against the application of section 1, but he followed up by using section 1 as what he termed a code of "rules of constitutional interpretation". He did not assess Bill 62 by reference to reasonableness, as one would have to do if one was applying section 1 to its fullest extent, but he at least went so far as to utilize the description in section 1 of Canada as a "free and democratic society" as the controlling canon of construction for section 33(1). Jacques J.A. said (at p. 282) that "One of the characteristics of a free and democratic society is therefore the resolution of disputes by means of discussion, by the free expression of opinion". He continued (at p. 283) that "The exercise of s. 33 power must therefore come within the basic principles which define our society". In essence, Jacques J.A. was willing to use section 1 at least to prescribe the setting, or constitutional context, in which section 33(1) operates. I suggest that the matter goes beyond that.

First, the inclusion of the word "only" in section 1 indicates that the section is a complete code of the limitations on *Charter* rights. Second, section 33 does not contain a *non-obstante* clause which might free it from the strictures of section 1. Third, and even more to the point, section 1 is not one of the provisions enumerated in section 33 which a legislature can opt out of in particular cases. Finally, on a more general level, section 33 should be construed in the same manner as all other *Charter* provisions, that is, in the context of the document as a whole (of which section 1 is a part). As stated by Lamer J. for a 6:1 majority in *Dubois v. The Queen*, [1986] 1 W.W.R. 193 a case dealing with the interpretation of section 13 of the Charter, at p. 220:

> Our constitutional Charter must be construed as a system where "every component contributes to the meaning as a whole, and the whole gives meaning to its parts" (P.A. Cote writing about statutory interpretation in *The Interpretation of Legislation in Canada* (1984), p. 236). The courts must interpret each section of the Charter in relation to the others . . .

These factors support the view that sections 1 and 33 can only be reconciled by interpreting section 1 as acting on section 33. Parliament or a provincial legislature must lead evidence to show that its resort to section 33 is reasonable, prescribed by law and demonstrably justified in a free and democratic society. It may be that the government's burden of justifying restrictions is less where section 33 is invoked than where it is not, given the obvious policy in section 33 of allowing legislative flexibility, but I would suggest that a burden nevertheless exists. The government should at least have to show that it has turned its mind to the consequences of each particular invocation of section 33. It clearly could not have done so with respect to Bill 62, an omnibus bill enacted for purely federal-provincial political reasons without thought of its particular applications at all.

The remainder of this work is devoted to a detailed examination of selected provisions of the *Canadian Charter of Rights and Freedoms*.

### Note on section 1: reasonable limits prescribed by law as can be demonstrably justified in a free and democratic society

Section 1 is arguably the most critical provision in the *Canadian Charter of Rights and Freedoms*. It contains the *Charter*'s code of evidence, indicating the respective burdens to be borne by the parties to *Charter* litigation, and as well is stated to be an exhaustive (by the use of the word "only") code of limitations on *Charter* rights and freedoms. The provision reads as follows:

> The *Canadian Charter of Rights and Freedoms* guarantees the rights and freedoms set out in it subject *only* to such reasonable limits prescribed by law as can be demonstrably justified in a free and democratic society. (emphasis added).

Section 1 thus prescribes a two step approach to *Charter* issues. As described by the Ontario Court of Appeal in *Re Germany and Rauca* (1983), 41 O.R. (2d) 225 at 240, the first issue is whether a guaranteed right or freedom has been infringed, breached or denied. If it has, the second issue is whether the restriction or denial is saved by the limitation provisions of section 1. See also *Re Southam and The Queen (No. 1)* (1983), 41 O.R. (2d) 113 (Ont. C.A.); *R. v. Bryant* (1984), 48 O.R. (2d) 732 at 737 (Ont. C.A.).

The initial burden is on the applicant for a *Charter* remedy to demonstrate that one of the rights or freedoms guaranteed to him (or, in the case of a corporation, to it) is implicated. As to the application of various provisions of the *Charter* to corporations: see *R. v. Big M Drug Mart Ltd.*, [1985] 3 W.W.R. 481 (S.C.C.); *R. v. Videoflicks Ltd.* (1984), 48 O.R. (2d) 395 (C.A.); *Re Southam Inc. and The Queen (No. 1)* (1983), 41 O.R. (2d) 113 (C.A.) (section 2); *R. v. Fisherman's Wharf Ltd.* (1982), 135 D.L.R. (3d) 307 (N.B.Q.B.), Aff'd on other grounds 144 D.L.R. (3d) 21 (N.B.C.A.) (section 7); *Re R.L. Crain Inc. and Couture* (1983), 6 D.L.R. (4th) 478 (Sask. Q.B.) (section 7); *Hunter v. Southam*, [1984] 2 S.C.R. 145 (section 8); *Re Panarctic Oils Ltd. and The Queen* (1982), 69 C.C.C. (2d) 393 (N.W.T.S.C.); *R. v. Corkum (H.W.) Construction Co. Ltd.* (1983), 150 D.L.R. (3d) 555 (N.S.C.A.) (section 11(b)); *Tricontinental Investments Co. v. Guarantee Co. of North America* (1982), 141 D.L.R. (3d) 741 (Ont. H.C.) (section 11(c), where the court proceeded on the implicit assumption and without raising the issue, that section 11(c) applies to corporations); cf. *Re PPG Industries Canada Ltd. and A.G. Can.* (1983), 3 C.C.C. (3d) 97 (B.C.C.A.) (section 11(f) does not apply to corporations).

In considering the applicant's burden of establishing that a *Charter* right has been *prima facie* infringed, the better view on the language of section 1, and in particular its use of the words "subject *only*" to the limitations set out therein, is that the rights and freedoms set out in the *Charter* should be interpreted in an absolute sense to the full extent of their terms. In that respect, *Re Klein and Law Society of Upper Canada* (1985), 50 O.R. (2d) 118 (Div. Ct.) is likely wrong. In that case, the majority of the Ontario Divisional Court read an internal limitation into the expression guarantee in section 2(b) to exclude commercial speech. This approach is inconsistent with the approach taken in *Re Ontario Film & Video Appreciation Society and Ontario Board of Censors* (1984), 45 O.R. (2d) 80n (C.A.) affirming 41 O.R. (2d) 583 at 590 (Div. Ct.), and *R. v. Videoflicks Ltd.* (1984), 48 O.R. (2d) 395 at 430-1. In the latter case, Tarnopolsky J.A. said for a unanimous Ontario Court of Appeal:

> As the Divisional Court said in *Re Ontario Film & Video Appreciation Society*, freedom of expression under the *Charter* must extend to all forms of expression.

American jurisprudence at this initial stage of determining whether a *prima facie* infringement has occurred may be of limited usefulness because the *U.S. Constitution* does not contain an equivalent to section 1. Its guarantees are textually absolute. Accordingly, there is a clear need for judicially imposed criterion to limit their scope. This distinction between the *Charter* and the *U.S. Constitution* was discussed by Kerans J.A. for a majority of the Alberta Court of Appeal in *Reference re Public Service Employee Relations Act, Labour Relations Act, and Police Officers Collective Bargaining Act*, [1985] 2 W.W.R. 289 at 297:

> Third, the interpretation of the Charter proceeds in two stages: one first defines the right, then one determines whether the proposed limit on the right is permissible. This is a significant difference from the approach required, for example, by the Canadian Bill of Rights or the United States Constitution. The interpreters of those documents have understandably recognized the need to balance protected rights against perceived greater good. For lack, however, of any express bargaining power such as that found in s. 1 or s. 33 (or, in the case of ss. 8 and 9, where the stated right includes an explicit qualifier such as 'unreasonable' or 'arbitrarily'), the interpreting court might

balance by means of a definitional stop. For example, a court recognizes that freedom of speech must yield to the greater good of protection from defamation. To provide this balance, one can 'define' freedom of speech to be 'speech which does not defame.' This is what I mean by balancing with a definitional stop. That solution is not necessary or desirable under the Canadian Charter. Specifically, I cannot accept the proposition that the 'harm' rule is built into the definition of each right or freedom, that being that one is free only to do that which does not harm others. The significance is that, in defining a Charter right, the court need not be troubled by arguments reciting the mischief which can arise if the right is absolute. Those problems generally are the concern of legislators and judges only on the invocation of s. 33 or s. 1.

On the same point, see *Re Soenen and Thomas* (1983), 3 D.L.R. (4th) 658 at 666-7 (Alta. Q.B.).

Interestingly, the Supreme Court of Canada has indicated recently that the government may be called upon to support the legitimacy of its interest or objective even before the inquiry reaches the section 1 stage. Dickson J. (as he then was) stated in *R. v. Big M Drug Mart Ltd.*, [1985] 3 W.W.R. 481 at 531 (S.C.C.):

At the outset, it should be noted that not every government interest or policy objective is entitled to s. 1 consideration. Principles will have to be developed for recognizing which government objectives are of sufficient importance to warrant overriding a constitutionally protected right or freedom. Once a sufficiently significant government interest is recognized then it must be decided if the means chosen to achieve this interest are reasonable — a form of proportionality test. The court may wish to ask whether the means adopted to achieve the end sought do so by impairing as little as possible the right or freedom in question.

Several points should be noted about the above quotation. First, Dickson J. appears to be making a distinction for analytical purposes between the legislative or government objective on one hand and the means used to achieve it on the other, such that the former is tested in the analysis of the substantively protected right itself. Section 1 is reserved to test legislative means used, rather than purposes, and then only for legislation whose purpose has passed the pre-section 1 hurdle. The initial stage in the two-step inquiry contemplated by *Rauca, Southam (No. 1)* and *Soenen* must therefore contemplate judicial review of both the scope of the subtantive guaranteed right and a weighing of the government's purpose. This review of the purpose of the legislation cannot by itself support the legislation — that must await the means test in section 1 — but it can, according to *Big M*, cause it to fall without recourse to section 1.

The primary difficulty with this approach is similar to that faced by cases such as *Klein* where the courts sought to circumscribe the scope of the substantive right in textually absolute gaurantees like section 2(b) without recourse to section 1, except that now the courts must circumscribe government purposes. The problem in both situations is that, having cut the inquiry adrift from section 1, there are no standards in the *Charter* by which to measure either the scope of the right, as in *Klein*, or the compellingness of the purpose, as in *Big M*. Dickson J. states that "principles must be developed", but it is legitimate to ask why that is so, when section 1 supplies those principles for both means *and* purposes: they must be reasonable, prescribed by law, and demonstrably justified in a free and democratic society. Dickson J.'s comments in *Big M* are arguably *obiter*, given that he proceeded to apply a section 1 analysis, so the matter is still open for reconsideration or clarification.

The second point to be noted from the above quotation is that Dickson J. has proposed a varying standard in cases where section 1 is applicable, but that standard leans toward a restrictive interpretation. The basic standard is one of proportionality, which I would suggest requires a balancing of the character of the protected right, the degree of the infringement and the intensity and importance of the public policy or purpose sought to be achieved. Proportionality varies with the circumstances, and even mere rationality may be sufficient in some cases depending upon what is involved. However the basic standard approaches necessity:

> The court *may* wish to ask whether the means adopted to achieve the end sought do so by impairing *as little as possible* the right or freedom in question. (Emphasis added). [1985] 3 W.W.R. 481 at 531.

The permissive use of the word "may" thus leaves open the possibility of a less strict standard in some cases. However, it also indicates that section 1 will often require the state to show that the means used was necessary to the achievement of its objective and that no less restrictive alternative was available. If a less restrictive alternative to achieving the purpose was available or (if this is different) the legislation was either over or under-inclusive, the legislation or government action would be invalid.

It should be noted that, in cases where section 1 is available to save limitations on *Charter* rights, it can only do so where at least a residue of the protected right remains after the application of section 1. Restated, section 1 cannot save legislation which purports to carve out complete exceptions to *Charter* guarantees and is, in effect, tantamount to a constitutional amendment. Thus, for example, the Supreme Court of Canada held in *A. G. Que. v. Quebec Association of Protestant School Boards* (1984), 10 D.L.R. (4th) 321 that a provincial statute could not completely eviscerate the language guarantees in section 23 of the *Charter*. The Court said at pp. 337-8 D.L.R.:

> Whatever their scope, the limits which s. 1 of the Charter allows to be placed on the rights and freedoms set out in it cannot be equated with exceptions such as those authorized by s. 33(1) and (2) of the Charter, which in any event do not authorize any exception to s. 23:
>
> > 33(1) Parliament or the legislature of a province may expressly declare in an Act of Parliament or of the legislature, as the case may be, that the Act or a provision thereof shall operate notwithstanding a provision included in section 2 or sections 7 to 15 of this Charter.
> >
> > (2) An Act or a provision of an Act in respect of which a declaration made under this section is in effect shall have such operation as it would have but for the provision of this Charter referred to in the declaration.
>
> Nor can those limits be tantamount to amendments to the Constitution of Canada, the procedure for which is prescribed in s. 38 *et seq.* of the *Constitution Act, 1982.*
>
> Now, the real effect of s. 73 of the Bill 101 is to make an exception to s. 23(1)(b) and (2) of the Charter in Quebec; yet those subsections are not provisions to which exceptions can be made under s. 33(1) and (2) of the Charter. In addition, s. 73 of Bill 101 directly alters the effect of s. 23 of the Charter of Quebec, without following the procedure laid down for amending the Constitution.
>
> The rights stated in s. 23 of the Charter are guaranteed to very specific classes of persons. This specific classification lies at the very heart of the provision, since it is the means chosen by the framers to identify those entitled to the rights they intended to guarantee. In our opinion, a legislature cannot by an ordinary statute validly set aside the means so chosen by the framers and effect this classification. Still less can it remake the classification and redefine the classes.
>
> . . . .
>
> The provisions of s. 73 of Bill 101 collide directly with those of s. 23 of the Charter, and are not limits which can be legitimized by s. 1 of the Charter. Such limits cannot be exceptions to the rights and freedoms guaranteed by the Charter nor amount to amendments of the Charter. An Act of

Parliament or of a legislature which, for example, purported to impose the beliefs of a State religion would be in direct conflict with s. 2(a) of the Charter, which guarantees freedom of conscience and religion, and would have to be ruled of no force or effect without the necessity of even considering whether such legislation could be legitimized by s. 1.

It should be noted that section 1 also applies where a substantive guarantee contains an internal modifier such as "fundamental justice" (section 7), "cruel and unusual" (section 12), "unreasonable" (sections 8, 11(b) and (e)), "arbitrarily" (section 9), "promptly" (section 10(a)), or "without delay" (section 10(b)). One view in early cases like *Re Moore and The Queen* (1984), 45 O.R. (2d) 3 (Ont. H.C.) was that the provision is self-defining as to what constitutes a reasonable limitation and, accordingly, no recourse to section 1 is necessary. This in effect reads section 1 out of the *Charter* with respect to such guarantees. This view is clearly incorrect following *R.v. Therens*, [1985] 4 W.W.R. 286 where after finding a breach of section 10 of the *Charter*, the Supreme Court of Canada reviewed section 1 to see if the infringement could be saved. See also *Singh v. Minister of Employment and Immigration*, [1985] 1 S.C.R. 177 and *Reference re section 94(2) of the Motor Vehicle Act* (B.C.) (unreported S.C.C. released December 17, 1985) where Wilson J. and Lamer J. respectively analyzed section 1 after finding in both cases that breaches of section 7 had occurred. None of the majority judgments in *Therens*, *Singh* or *The Motor Vehicle Reference* clearly enunciated the relationship between section 1 and the respective substantive provisions, but their analysis of section 1 indicates that it modifies the modifiers. *Re Soenen and Thomas* (1983), 3 D.L.R. (4th) 658 at 668 (Alta. Q.B.) is instructive, where McDonald J. said:

> Where such modifiers are used, they must be given meaning by the courts, but that meaning should not be tempered by judicially-created criteria designed to curtail judicial review and enhance judicial deference to an expression of legislative will. Where, as in the case of the fundamental freedoms and many of the legal and other rights stated in the Charter, no modifier is found, my original proposition is even more obviously the result and even the appearance is one of 'absoluteness' in the application of the right or freedom. All this, I repeat, is before proceeding to any application of the second part of s. 1.

The guarantee against unreasonable search or seizure in section 8 of the *Charter* is useful for illustrative purposes. The *Soenen* view that "reasonableness" in section 8, for example, should not be interpreted coextensively with "reasonable limits" in section 1, is buttressed by the second part of the latter provision which makes it clear that not all reasonable limits are valid. Only those reasonable limits which are also prescribed by law and demonstrably justified in a free and democratic society are saved. If reasonableness meant the same thing in sections 1 and 8, the inquiry would always be cut off before it progressed to a test of the super-added elements of legal prescription and demonstrable justification. In effect, substantive rights which contain internal modifiers would be put to a lower standard of justification than is indicated by section 1.

A better approach is to treat the modifiers as minimal thresholds without the detailed balancing of societal interests and legislative goals which is required by the reasonableness and other elements in the second part of section 1. Thus in the search or seizure example, the fact that a search or seizure is done without a warrant should be *prima facie* evidence of unreasonableness: cf. Seaton J.A. in *R. v. Collins* (1983), 33 C.R. (3d) 130 (B.C.C.A.). It will then be open to the Crown pursuant to the second part of section 1 to show that the omission was justified where either exigent circumstances existed, as in the hot pursuit cases (*Semayne's Case* (1603), 77 E.R. 194 (K.B.); *Warden v. Hayden*, 387 U.S. 294 (1967)), emergencies and "automobile cases" (*Carroll v. U.S.*, 267 U.S. 132 (1925)), or where the person searched does not have a reasonable expectation of privacy: On the importance of a reasonable expectation of privacy, see *Hunter v. Southam*, [1984] 2 S.C.R. 145. Examples of where a person lacks a reasonable expectation of privacy in the United States are: in vacated hotel rooms (*Abel v. U.S.*, 362 U.S. 217 (1960)); articles exposed to public view (*Katz v. U.S.*, 389 U.S. 347 (1967), in Ontario, see *R. v. Longtin* (1983), 41 O.R. (2d) 545 (C.A.)); open fields (*Hester v. U.S.*, 265 U.S. 57 (1924)); the exterior of an automobile (*Caldwell v. Lewis*, 417 U.S. 583 (1974)); at customs (*U.S. v. Ramsay*, 431 U.S. 606 (1977), in Ontario, see *R. v. Simmons* (1984), 11 C.C.C. (3d) 193 (Ont. C.A.)); and in dealings with a third party such as a bank (*U.S. v. Miller*, 425 U.S. 435 (1976)). For further discussion of search or seizure generally, see Chapter 21, *infra*.

Once the applicant for a *Charter* remedy has established that one of his guaranteed rights has been infringed, the onus shifts to the person seeking to justify it to demonstrate that the elements in the second part of section 1 have been satisfied. As stated by MacKinnon A.C.J.O. for the Ontario Court of Appeal in *Re Southam Inc. and The Queen (No. 1)* (1983), 41 O.R. (2d) 113 at 124:

> The wording [of s. 1] imposes a positive obligation on those seeking to uphold the limit or limits to establish to the satisfaction of the court by evidence, by the terms and purpose of the limiting law, its economic, social and political background, and, if felt helpful, by references to comparable legislation of other acknowleged free and democratic societies, that such limit or limits are reasonable and demonstrably justified in a free and democratic society.

On the same point respecting onus, see also *R. v. Bryant* (1984), 48 O.R. (2d) 732 at 739 (C.A.); *Re Germany and Rauca* (1983), 41 O.R. (2d) 225 at 241 (C.A.); *Re Cadeddu and The Queen* (1982), 4 C.C.C. (3d) 97 (Ont. H.C.); *Re Ontario Film and Video Appreciation Society and Ontario Board of Censors* (1983), 45 O.R. (2d) 80n (C.A.) affirming 41 O.R. (2d) 583 (Div. Ct.); *Re Jamieson and The Queen* (1982), 70 C.C.C. (2d) 430 (Que. S.C.); *Quebec Association of Protestant School Boards v. A.G. Que.* (1982), 140 D.L.R. (3d) 33 at 59 (Que. S.C.); *National Citizens Coalition Inc. v. A.G. Can.*, [1984] 5 W.W.R. 436 at 442-3 (Alta. Q.B.).

The first thing that the party seeking to uphold the limitation must show is that it is "prescribed by law". LeDain J., speaking for a unanimous Supreme Court of Canada on this particular point, said in *R. v. Therens*, [1985] 4 W.W.R. 286 at 311 (S.C.C.):

> The requirement that the limit be prescribed by law is chiefly concerned with the distinction between a limit imposed by law and one that is arbitrary. The limit will be prescribed by law within the meaning of s. 1 if it is expressly provided for by statute or regulation, or results by necessary implication from the terms of a statute or regulation or from its operating requirements. The limit may also result from the application of a common law rule.

The requirements that a limitation be "reasonable" and "demonstrably justified" are the real keys to section 1, and they involve a balancing of public and private interests. Restated, human rights adjudication is a search for limits. Incursions into guaranteed, private spheres, are permitted, but only to the extent necessary to promote the achievement of important state interests. The limitations on protected rights must be strictly tailored to meet the objective and proportionate to the goal sought to be achieved. The proper application of the section 1 balancing is succinctly set out by Blair J.A. in *R. v. Bryant* (1984), 48 O.R. (2d) 732 at 739 (C.A.):

> ... The standard by which the reasonableness of the limitation of the Charter right must be assessed is that the court must be satisfied that a valid legal, social or other objective is served by the limitation of the right and that the limitation is restricted to that which is necessary for the attainment of the desired objective: *Quebec Ass'n of Protestant School Boards v. A.G. Que. (No. 2)* (1982), 140 D.L.R. (3d) 33 at 77, per Deschênes C.J.S.C.; affirmed [1983] Que. C.A. 77 and (sub nom. *A.G. Que. v. Quebec Ass'n of Protestant School Boards*) (1984), 10 D.L.R. (4th) 321. This standard of justification was adopted by Chief Justice Deschênes from the pre-*Charter* decision of the Supreme Court of Canada in *MacKay v. The Queen*, [1980] 2 S.C.R. 370, which dealt with an alleged statutory infringement of the right to equality before the law under the *Canadian Bill of Rights*, S.C. 1960, c. 44 [now R.S.C. 1970, App. III]. The approach taken by McIntyre J. in that case applies, in my opinion, to the Charter. He said at p. 407 S.C.R.:
>
> > I would be of the opinion, however, that as a minimum it would be necessary to inquire whether any inequality has been created for a valid federal constitutional objective, whether it has been created rationally in the sense that it is not arbitrary or capricious and not based upon any ulterior motive or motives offensive to the provisions of the *Canadian Bill of Rights*, and whether it is a necessary departure from the general principle of universal application of the law for the attainment of some necessary and desirable social objective.
>
> He added at p. 408 S.C.R.:
>
> > It must not however be forgotten that, since the principle of equality before the law is to be maintained, departures should be countenanced only where necessary for the attainment of desirable social objectives, and then only to the extent necessary in the circumstances to make possible the attainment of such objectives.
>
> Section 1 of the Charter requires that the courts engage in a balancing process. The permissible limits of government action, on the one hand, must be measured against the rights of the individual on the other, Courts must be flexible in their approach to Charter cases, particularly in the admission of evidence of relevant facts in order to ensure that the competing interests involved are fully considered. In *Re Southam*, [(1983), 41 O.R. (2d) 113] MacKinnon A.C.J.O. described the task of the court at p. 130 O.R.:
>
> > In any event I believe the court must come back, ultimately, having derived whatever assistance can be secured from the experience of other free and democratic societies, to the facts of our own free and democratic society to answer the question whether the limit imposed on the particular guaranteed freedom has been demonstrably justified as a reasonable one, having balanced the perceived purpose and objectives of the limiting legislation, in light of all relevant considerations, against the freedom or right allegedly infringed.

In *Singh v. Minister of Employment and Immigration*, [1985] 1 S.C.R. 177 Wilson J., speaking for three out of six judges held that certain appeal procedures in the federal *Immigration Act*, S.C. 1976-77, c. 52 were contrary to the principles of fundamental justice and were not saved by section 1 of the Charter. In the course of her reasons she made it clear that considerations of cost, administrative convenience or other "utilitarian considerations" will not generally pass section 1 muster. She said at p. 218:

> Seen in this light I have considerable doubt that the type of utilitarian consideration brought forward by Mr. Bowie can constitute a justification for a limitation on the rights set out in the *Charter*. Certainly the guarantees in the *Charter* would be illusory if they could be ignored because it was administratively convenient to do so. No doubt considerable time and money can be saved

by adopting administrative procedures which ignore the principles of fundamental justice, but such an argument, in my view, misses the point of the exercise under s. 1. The principles of natural justice and procedural fairness which have long been espoused by our courts, and the constitutional entrenchment of the principles of fundamental justice in s. 7, implicitly recognize that a balance of administrative convenience does not override the need to adhere to these principles. Whatever standard of review eventually emerges under s. 1, it seems to me that the basis of the justification for the limitation of rights under s. 7 must be more compelling than any advanced in these appeals.

This point that there is a high standard of justification in s. 1 was reiterated by Lamer J. in the *Motor Vehicle Reference, supra,* where he said at p. 41 of the unreported judgment:

> Administrative expediency, absolute liability's main supportive argument, will undoubtedly under section 1 be invoked and occasionally succeed. Indeed, administrative expediency certainly has its place in administrative law. But when administrative law chooses to call in aid imprisonment through penal law, indeed sometimes criminal law and the added stigma attached to a conviction, exceptional, in my view, will be the case where the liberty or even the security of the person guaranteed under section 7 should be sacrificed to administrative expediency. Section 1 may, for reasons of administrative expediency, successfully come to the rescue of an otherwise violation of section 7, but only in cases arising out of exceptional conditions, such as natural disasters, the outbreak of war, epidemics, and the like.

The question of the kinds and extent of evidence which is necessary to enable the courts to effectively balance the competing interests is of critical importance. The previously quoted passage from *R. v. Bryant* indicates the sorts of evidence which the courts will require as to the reasonableness and demonstrable justification of a particular limiting provision. It is clear that a *pro forma* or minimal record will not be sufficient: see *Law Society of Upper Canada v. Skapinker* (1984), 9 D.L.R. (4th) 161 at 182 (S.C.C.); *R.W.D.S.U. Locs. 496, 544, 635 and 955 v. Saskatchewan,* [1985] 5 W.W.R. 97 (Sask. C.A.), leave to appeal to S.C.C. granted 61 N.R. 266n; *Singh v. Minister of Employment and Immigration,* [1985] 1 S.C.R. 177.

Interesting questions arise about the proper method of introducing such evidence. In the odd case, courts will find justification pursuant to section 1 in the scheme of the *Charter* itself, and will in effect take judicial notice of the balancing factors where these factors are constituted by the countervailing rights of others. For example, in *Re British Columbia Government Employees' Union and A.G. B.C.* (1985), 2 D.L.R. (4th) 399 (B.C. C.A.) (leave to appeal to S.C.C. granted October 1, 1985), the B.C. Supreme Court of its own motion issued an injunction to prohibit picketing of courts. The Court of Appeal refused to dissolve the injunction on an application pursuant to section 2(b) and (c) of the *Charter.* On the section 1 point, the Court took judicial notice of the value of public access to courts as an overriding consideration. At p. 406, the Court said:

> In our opinion, no limit on a Charter right could be more demonstrably justified than one which preserves the public's unfettered right to access to the courts of justice. It is implicit in the very scheme of the Charter where any citizen may apply to the courts to redress infringements of the rights enumerated. Without preservation of the public right the shield of judicial protection offered by the Charter would become an illusion.

However, such cases are relatively rare, and the courts will normally require hard evidence from the party seeking to support the limitation: see *R.W.D.S.U. v. Saskatchewan, supra,* where a majority of the Saskatchewan Court of Appeal struck down a provincial statute prohibiting strikes and lock-outs as contravening freedom of association under section 2(d) of the *Charter*, because there was no evidence on the record for the purposes of section 1 about (i) the circumstances of those who would be detrimentally affected by the legislation; (ii) the circumstances of those who would be detrimentally affected if the legislation was *not* passed, and (iii) the choices of limits which the legislators had when they made their selection.

Litigants may be tempted to present economic, political or sociological evidence to the court in "Brandeis Brief" form as is often done in the United States in constitutional cases, and which was done in Canadian constitutional references even prior to the *Charter*: see *Reference re Residential Tenancies Act*, [1981] 1 S.C.R. 714; *Reference re Amendment of Constitution of Canada* (Nos. 1, 2 and 3), [1981] 1 S.C.R. 753; *Reference re Anti-Inflation Act*, [1976] 2 S.C.R. 373. It is questionable whether the procedure used on a reference in Canada is acceptable in concrete cases in a trial situation. It is submitted that expert evidence should be tested by cross-examination as to the validity of the underlying assumptions used and conclusions reached. A trial judge would then be able to reach a more informed decision about the matter than where he was simply handed two conflicting, uncross-examined upon reports: see *Public Service Alliance of Canada v. Canada* (1984), 11 D.L.R. (4th) 337 (Fed. T.D.) where *viva voce* expert economic evidence was taken; and note that the Federal Court of Appeal expressed skepticism on appeal in that case at (1984), 11 D.L.R. (4th) 387 at 393 (Fed. C.A.), leave to appeal to the Supreme Court of Canada granted 57 N.R. 161, about the utility of economic evidence in *Charter* cases.

Another question which will no doubt be tested over time is what constitutes a "free and democratic society". In *Re Southam Inc. and The Queen (No. 1)* (1983), 41 O.R. (2d) 113 the Ontario Court of Appeal referred to comparable legislation of "acknowledged" free and democratic societies, but a litigant may refuse to make such an acknowledgment and put the opposite party to the strict proof thereof: see *R. v. Keegstra* (1984), 19 C.C.C. (3d) 254 (Alta. Q.B.). A court may brush aside such objections where countries like Britain or the United States are involved, but it may become a very real issue in other situations. Many extremely controlled societies have constitutions which purport to include all sorts of freedoms which are dishonoured in practice. Evidence of the sociological and political environment in these countries may be necessary before they are accepted as being free and democratic. Furthermore, the issue of what the law is in a particular foreign jurisdiction is always one of fact, and may be problematic. Knowledge of foreign law (which at common law includes laws enacted by other provinces) is not to be imputed to the judge (*Nelson v. Bridport* (1845), 8 Beav. 527 at 536 per Lord Langsdale, M.R.) and Canadian courts will not take judicial notice of it unless authorized to do so by statute; e.g. *Canada Evidence Act*, R.S.C. 1970, c. E-10 as amended, section 17-8; Ontario *Evidence Act*, R.S.O. 1980, c. 145, s. 25. The Supreme Court of Canada will take judicial notice of the laws of all provinces and territories in Canada as long as they were pleaded in the courts below: see *Can. National SS. Co. Ltd. v. Watson*, [1939] S.C.R. 11; *Logan v. Lee* (1907), 39 S.C.R. 311.

The general presumption is that foreign law is the same as domestic law: see McLeod, *The Conflict of Laws* (1983) at p. 39; Castel, *Canadian Conflict of Laws* (1975), Vol. 1 at p. 653. That presumption is not of much assistance in the context of section 1 where a party seeks to use the laws of another society as a yardstick to measure the demonstrable justifiability of the particular *Charter* limitation at issue.

Accordingly, in the absence of situations where the courts will take judicial notice, pleading and proof are necessary: see *R. v. Keegstra, supra*. The foreign law must be pleaded and evidence adduced to support it (*Re Brooks*, [1945] 1 D.L.R. 726 (Ont. H.C.)) usually through the expert testimony of a judge, lawyer, teacher or public office-holder from the foreign jurisdiction: see McLeod, *supra* at p. 34; *Gold v. Reinblatt*, [1929] S.C.R. 74. Ontario courts have held that affidavit evidence should not be accepted as proof of foreign law (*People's Wayne County Bank v. Killam* (1932), 41 O.W.N. 417 (H.C.); *Lear v. Lear*, [1973] 3 O.R. 935 (S.C.), rev'd 51 D.L.R. (3d) 56 (Ont. C.A.)), although this would not apply where the proper procedure for the proceeding is by originating notice of motion ("applications" pursuant to Rule 14 of the Ontario *Rules of Civil Procedure*) and proof of facts is *prima facie* done by affidavit in the absence of an order for the trial of an issue.

For further literature on section 1 of the *Charter*, see Morel, "Le Clause Limitative de l'Article 1 de la Charte Canadienne des Droits et Libertés: Une Assurance Contre le Gouvernement des Juges" (1983), 61 Can. Bar Rev. 81; Finkelstein, "Section 1: The Standard for Assessing Restrictive Government Actions and the *Charter's* Code of Procedure and Evidence" (1983), 9 Queen's L.J. 143; Marx, "Entrenchment, Limitations and Non-Obstante", *Canadian Charter of Rights and Freedoms, Commentary* (1982, Tarnopolsky and Beaudoin, eds.), pp. 61-74.

The application of section 1 is elaborated upon in the cases which follow and in succeeding chapters.

# RE SOUTHAM INC. AND THE QUEEN (No. 1)

In the Ontario Court of Appeal. 41 O.R. (2d) 113.

MacKinnon A.C.J.O., Jessup and Martin JJ.A. March 31, 1983.

Appeal by the Crown from a judgment of Smith J., 38 O.R. (2d) 748, allowing an application for a declaration that s. 12(1) of the *Juvenile Delinquents Act* (Can.) is unconstitutional by reason of s. 2(*b*) of the *Canadian Charter of Rights and Freedoms*.

The judgment of the court was delivered by

MACKINNON A.C.J.O.: — This appeal involves the issue of the right of access by the public to the work of the courts balanced against society's interest in the protection and reformation of children who fall within the definition of juvenile delinquents as defined in the *Juvenile Delinquents Act*, R.S.C. 1970, c. J-3.

Mr. Justice Smith, who heard the application in motions court, declared that s. 12(1) of the *Juvenile Delinquents Act*, which requires that all trials of children shall take place *in camera*, was *ultra vires* as infringing s. 2(*b*) of the *Canadian Charter of Rights and Freedoms*. Peripheral questions were raised as to the status of the respondent to make the application for the declaration under s. 24(1) of the Charter and the right of the appellant to appeal, but the arguments relevant to these questions were not pressed at the end.

It has become trite for courts to say that every case in which a section of the Charter is raised by way of argument is a "very important case". In my view, some are and some are not and it trivializes the Charter to give extensive notice and consideration to every extreme position raised, purportedly, in reliance on it. The question raised in the instant case is of significance as it sets out in sharp relief the conflicting interests within society and the court is now called upon to choose between such interests under the direction of the Charter.

I should say at the outset that so far as this particular matter is concerned, counsel for the respondent stated that he was not arguing that the press was in any special or privileged position. His argument was that the closing of *all* trials of juveniles to the public (which, of course, includes representatives of the press) under the present legislation is an infringement of the freedom guaranteed under s. 2(*b*) of the Charter and inconsistent with the provisions of the Constitution.

### How the issue arose

On June 11th a reporter employed by the respondent Southam Inc. attended with counsel at the Provincial Court (Family Division) in Ottawa presided over by His Honour Judge Guzzo. They were advised that reporters or other members of the general public were not permitted to be present during the hearing of proceedings under the *Juvenile Delinquents Act*. Counsel for the respondent thereupon made an application to Judge Guzzo requesting that the public and, in particular, representatives of the media, be permitted to be present at such hearings.

After hearing submissions, Judge Guzzo was of the view that the Attorneys-General of Ontario and Canada should be served with notice of the respondent's application before he considered the submissions made. The application was, accordingly, adjourned to permit respondent's counsel time to research the matter further. The respondent did not renew this particular application but the same reporter once again, on June 15th, attempted to enter Judge Guzzo's court-room. Upon being advised that the reporter was not a witness in the proceedings involving a juvenile delinquent, Judge Guzzo directed her to leave the court-room.

The respondent then moved before the learned motions court judge for an order "in the nature of *mandamus* compelling His Honour Judge Guzzo of the Provincial Court (Family Division) to permit the applicants to be present during the hearings of proceedings held in Provincial Court (Family Division) in Ottawa pursuant to the *Juvenile Delinquents Act*, R.S.C. 1970, c. J-3". It was, we were advised, a general motion to "open the Juvenile Court" not related to any specific proceedings. The application was made pursuant to "the provisions of Sec. 24 of the *Constitution Act 1982*". Initially, in its appellant's statement, the Crown argued that the respondent did not have status to bring the application and that the Supreme Court of Ontario was not "a court of competent jurisdiction" within the meaning of that phrase found in s. 24(1) of the Charter. However, as already noted that position was not pressed during the argument, the Crown agreeing that the application was properly before Mr. Justice Smith. Counsel also agreed that the Crown had a right of appeal in the instant case under s. 28 of the *Judicature Act*, R.S.O. 1980, c. 223. It is not necessary, accordingly, for me to consider these two questions further.

During the course of the argument in the court below the respondent altered its application in regard to the relief it sought and asked for a declaration that s. 12(1) of the *Juvenile Delinquents Act* was *ultra vires*. The motions court judge granted the declaration requested.

*Argument and conclusion*

In reviewing the statutes and submissions made, it must be noted that it was not a juvenile delinquent or his representative who made the application and s. 11(*d*) of the Charter, which gives to anyone charged the right to "a fair and public hearing", was not argued and is not in issue. If an alleged juvenile delinquent had been the applicant, s. 11(*d*) would have been directly in issue.

Section 12 of the *Juvenile Delinquents Act* reads:

> 12(1) The trials of children shall take place without publicity and separately and apart from the trials of other accused persons, and at suitable times to be designated and appointed for that purpose.
>
> (2) Such trials may be held in the private office of the judge or in some other private room in the court house or municipal building, or in the detention home, or if no such room or place is available, then in the ordinary court room, but when held in the ordinary court room an interval of half an hour shall be allowed to elapse between the close of the trial or examination of any adult and the beginning of the trial of a child.
>
> (3) No report of a delinquency committed, or said to have been committed, by a child, or of the trial or other disposition of a charge against a child, or of a charge against an adult brought in the juvenile court under section 33 or under section 35, in which the name of the child or of the child's parent or guardian or of any school or institution that the child is alleged to have been attending or of which the child is alleged to have been an inmate is disclosed, or in which the identity of the child is otherwise indicated, shall without the special leave of the court, be published in any newspaper or other publication.
>
> (4) Subsection (3) applies to all newspapers and other publications published anywhere in Canada, whether or not this Act is otherwise in force in the place of publication.

The Supreme Court of Canada in *C. B. v. The Queen* (1981), 62 C.C.C. (2d) 107, had before them for interpretation the words "without publicity" found in s. 12(1) of the *Juvenile Delinquents Act*. Holding that the verb "shall" found in s. 12(1) is mandatory and allows for no discretion, Chouinard J., speaking for a unanimous court, held that "without publicity" means "*in camera*". This means, of course, that except for those people specifically permitted or directed by the statute to be present, no member of the general public may be present at such hearings. The Supreme Court was not asked to interpret the applicability of the *Canadian Bill of Rights* to s. 12(1) and the decision was made prior to the coming into force of the *Constitution Act, 1982* with its *Canadian Charter of Rights and Freedoms*.

The argument which was made before us and which found favour with the motions court judge was that the exclusion of the public from such trials offends "freedom of expression, including freedom of the press", guaranteed by the Charter.

The sections of the Charter to which we were referred are the following:

*Rights and freedoms in Canada*

1. The *Canadian Charter of Rights and Freedoms* guarantees the rights and freedoms set out in it subject only to such reasonable limits prescribed by law as can be demonstrably justified in a free and democratic society.

*Fundamental freedoms*

2. Everyone has the following fundamental freedoms:

. . . . .

(*b*) freedom of thought, belief, opinion and expression, including freedom of the press and other media of communications;

*Other rights and freedoms not affected by Charter*

> 26. The guarantee in this Charter of certain rights and freedoms shall not be construed as denying the existence of any other rights or freedoms that exist in Canada.

We were also referred to s. 52 of the *Constitution Act, 1982* which establishes the supremacy of the Constitution of Canada, including the Charter, over other laws, and provides the basis for judicial review of legislation in Canada:

> 52(1) The Constitution of Canada is the supreme law of Canada, and any law that is inconsistent with the provisions of the Constitution is, to the extent of the inconsistency, of no force or effect.

This section gives to the court the necessary power to make the requested declaration if there is found to be the required inconsistency. The basic question is whether the trial of children *in camera* is a breach of freedom of "opinion and expression, including freedom of the press and other media communication". Following the wording in some American authorities the motions court judge held that freedom of expression and of the press are "adjuncts" to the concept of openness of our judicial system and the right of access to the courts.

*Is free access to the courts a fundamental right or freedom?*

*Section 2(b) of the Charter*

There can be no doubt that the openness of the courts to the public is one of the hallmarks of a democratic society. Public accessibility to the courts was and is a felt necessity; it is a restraint on arbitrary action by those who govern and by the powerful. The most recent and comprehensive review of principle in this area of the law was made by Dickson J. in this reasons for the majority in *A.-G. N.S. v. MacIntyre* (1982), 65 C.C.C. (2d) 129 (S.C.C.).

In this case, a television journalist applied for an order requiring a justice of the peace to make available to him for inspection, search warrants and informations in his possession. A Supreme Court Judge allowed the application and held that the journalist, as a member of the general public, was entitled to inspect executed search warrants and supporting informations. The Nova Scotia Court of Appeal dismissed the appeal from that judgment and did not restrict the right of access to only executed warrants. The Supreme Court dismissed the appeal but restricted the right of access, as had the Supreme Court Judge, to executed search warrants.

In the course of his reasons, Dickson J. said (pp. 144-5 C.C.C.):

> The question before us is limited to search warrants and informations. The response to that question, it seems to me, should be guided by several broad policy considerations, namely, respect for the privacy of the individual, protection of the administration of justice, implementation of the will of Parliament that a search warrant be an effective aid in the investigation of crime, and finally, a strong public policy in favour of "openness" in respect of judicial acts. The *rationale* of this last-mentioned consideration has been eloquently expressed by Bentham in these terms:
>
> > "In the darkness of secrecy, sinister interest, and evil in every shape have full swing. Only in proportion as publicity has place can any of the checks applicable to judicial injustice operate. Where there is no publicity there is no justice. Publicity is the very soul of justice. It is the keenest spur to exertion and surest of all guards against improbity. It keeps the judge himself while trying under trial."

The concern for accountability is not diminished by the fact that the search warrants might be issued by a Justice *in camera*. On the contrary, this fact increases the policy argument in favour of accessibility. Initial secrecy surrounding the issuance of warrants may lead to abuse, and publicity is a strong deterrent to potential malversation.

In short, what should be sought is maximum accountability and accessibility but not to the extent of harming the innocent or of impairing the efficiency of the search warrant as a weapon in society's never-ending fight against crime.

## And, at pp. 145-6 C.C.C.:

It is now well established, however, that covertness is the exception and openness the rule. Public confidence in the integrity of the Court system and understanding of the administration of justice are thereby fostered. As a general rule the sensibilities of the individuals involved are no basis for exclusion of the public from judicial proceedings. The following comments of Laurence J. in *R. v. Wright*, 8 T.L.R. 293, are apposite and were cited with approval by Duff J. in the *Gazette Printing Co. v. Shallow* (1909), 41 S.C.R. 339 at 359:

> " 'Though the publication of such proceedings may be to the disadvantage of the particular individual concerned, yet it is of vast importance to the public that the proceedings of courts of justice should be universally known. The general advantage to the country, in having these proceedings made public more than counterbalances the inconveniences to the private persons whose conduct may be the subject of such proceedings.' "

The leading case is the decision of the House of Lords in *Scott v. Scott*, [1913] A.C. 417. In the later case of *McPherson v. McPherson*, [1936] A.C. 177 at 200, Lord Blanesburgh, delivering the judgment of the Privy Council, referred to "publicity" as the "authentic hall-mark of judicial as distinct from administrative procedure".

It is, of course, true that *Scott v. Scott* and *McPherson v. McPherson* were cases in which proceedings had reached the stage of trial whereas the issuance of a search warrant takes place at the pre-trial investigative stage. The cases mentioned, however, and many others which could be cited, establish the broad principle of "openness" in judicial proceedings, whatever their nature, and in the exercise of judicial powers. The same policy considerations upon which is predicated our reluctance to inhibit accessibility at the trial stage are still present and should be addressed at the pre-trial stage.

## And, at pp. 146-7 C.C.C.:

*Ex parte* applications for injunctions, interlocutory proceedings, or preliminary inquiries are not trial proceedings, and yet the "open court" rule applies in these cases. The authorities have held that subject to a few well-recognized exceptions, as in the case of infants, mentally disordered persons or secret processes, all judicial proceedings must be held in public. The editor of Halsbury's Laws of England, 4th ed., vol. 10, para. 705, p. 316, states the rule in these terms:

> "In general, all cases, both civil and criminal, must be heard in open court, but in certain exceptional cases, where the administration of justice would be rendered impracticable by the presence of the public, the court may sit in camera."

At every stage the rule should be one of public accessibility and concomitant judicial accountability; all with a view to ensuring there is no abuse in the issue of search warrants, that once issued they are executed according to law, and finally that any evidence seized is dealt with according to law. A decision by the Crown not to prosecute, notwithstanding the finding of evidence appearing to establish the commission of a crime may, in some circumstances, raise issues of public importance.

In my view, curtailment of public accessibility can only be justified where there is present the need to protect social values of superordinate importance. One of these is the protection of the innocent.

He concluded that the effective administration of justice would be frustrated if individuals were permitted to be present when the warrants were issued and that the exclusion of the public from the proceedings attending the actual issuance of the warrant was justified. However, once the warrant has been executed, the need for concealment virtually disappears and "The curtailment of the traditionally uninhibited accessibility of the public to the working of the Courts should be undertaken with the greatest reluctance" (pp. 148-9 C.C.C.).

In the instant case, counsel for the Crown argued strenuously that public access to the courts was not a specific or fundamental right guaranteed by the Charter and therefore s. 24(1) could not be invoked as it had no application to the question. Further, he argued, that being so, there was no need to resort to s. 1 and determine the s. 12(1) imposed "reasonable limits .. as can be demonstrably justified in a free and democratic society".

It is true that public accessibility to the courts is not spelled out in terms as part of the fundamental freedoms. Counsel argued that "freedom of the press" is limited by s. 2(b) itself, in that it is but part of freedom of thought, belief, opinion and expression. I do not believe that it is appropriate to use the word "limited" in connection with s. 2(b) although I do accept that freedom of the press refers to the dissemination of expression of thought, belief or opinion through the medium of the press. If anything, the words "freedom of expression" would seem to have a wider or larger connotation than the words "freedom of the press".

Counsel for the Crown pointed out that the wording in the Charter with regard to "freedom of the press" differs significantly from that in the First Amendment to the United States Constitution. The First Amendment reads, in part:

> Congress shall make no law .. abridging the freedom of speech or of the press; or the right of the people peaceably to assemble ..

It can be seen that the reference is to freedom of the press, *simpliciter*, unlike the Charter which includes freedom of the press in freedom of thought, belief, opinion and expression. However, whether the American case-law on freedom of the press is of persuasive authority is of small moment in the instant case as the respondent is relying on s. 2(b) as guaranteeing to the general public free access to the courts as an integral part of the fundamental freedom of opinion and expression. It is not an issue of "freedom of the press" *per se*.

In *Richmond Newspapers, Inc. v. Commonwealth of Virginia*, 100 S. Ct. 2814 (1980), the Supreme Court of the United States considered for the first time the narrow question of whether the right of the public and the press to attend criminal trials was guaranteed under the United States Constitution. One Stevenson had been indicted for murder, three abortive trials had taken place and he was being tried in the same court for a fourth time. At the opening of that trial, counsel for the accused moved that it be closed to the public and the prosecutor stated that he had no objection. The trial judge thereupon ordered the court-room cleared. Richmond Newspapers subsequently moved to intervene and ultimately took the issue to appeal.

In delivering the lead judgment of the court, Chief Justice Burger reviewed at some length the Anglo-American history of criminal trials. This review emphasized that from time immemorial, judicial trials have been held in open court, to which the public have free access. He concluded that "from this unbroken, uncontradicted history, supported by reasons as valid today as in centuries past, we are bound to conclude that a presumption of openness inheres in the very nature of a criminal trial under our system of justice" (p. 2825). He went on to say (p. 2826):

> The First Amendment, in conjunction with the Fourteenth, prohibits governments from "abridging the freedom of speech or of the press; or the right of the people peaceably to assemble, and to petition the government for a redress of grievances". These expressly guaranteed freedoms share a common core purpose of assuring freedom of communication on matters relating to the functioning of government. Plainly it would be difficult to single out any aspect of government of higher concern and importance to the people than the manner in which criminal trials are conducted.

As stated, counsel for the Crown submits that the right of public access to the courts does not fall under the fundamental freedoms guaranteed by the Charter. I do not agree. The Charter as part of a constitutional document should be given a large and liberal construction. The spirit of this new "living tree" planted in friendly Canadian soil should not be stultified by narrow technical, literal interpretations without regard to its background and purpose; capability for growth must be recognized: *Re s. 24 of B.N.A. Act; Edwards v. A.-G. Can.*, [1930] A.C. 124 at 136 (P.C.). Although said in a very different connection, it is apposite here: "For the letter killeth but the spirit giveth life."

Trials of juveniles are not criminal trials as such and the enforcement process is "specially adapted to the age and impressibility of juveniles and fundamentally different, in pattern and purpose, from the one governing in the case of adults": *A.-G. B.C. v. Smith*, [1967] S.C.R. 702 at 710. Nevertheless, serious criminal matters are heard by juvenile courts, matters in which there is a public interest and concern, and in which in many cases, it is acknowledged by the Crown, no necessary interest of the juvenile is served by the exclusion of the public from such hearings.

It is true, as argued, that free access to the courts is not specifically enumerated under the heading of fundamental freedoms but, in my view, such access, having regard to its historic origin and necessary purpose already recited at length, is an integral and implicit part of the guarantee given to everyone of freedom of opinion and expression which, in terms, includes freedom of the press. However the rule may have had its origin, as Mr. Justice Dickson pointed out, the "openness" rule fosters the necessary public confidence in the integrity of the court system and an understanding of the administration of justice. The respondent has established that its right, as a member of the public, under s. 2(*b*) of the Charter, has, *prima facie*, been infringed.

*Is s. 12(1) a reasonable limit as can be demonstrably justified in a free and democratic society?*

### Section 1 of the Charter

I turn now to the last question to be answered: is the exclusion of the public under s. 12(1) a reasonable limit prescribed by law as can be demonstrably justified in a free and democratic society (to quote the relevant words of s. 1 of the Charter)? As a subsidiary consideration, the standard as formed by Mr. Justice Dickson would have to be met, namely: "[C]urtailment of public accessibility can only be justified where there is present the need to protect social values of superordinate importance." A preliminary question which has to be determined is: upon whom is the burden of establishing that the limit in issue is a reasonable one demonstrably justifiable in a free and democratic society?

### *"Onus" or "burden" of proof under s. 1*

The Crown takes the initial position that the freedoms granted under s. 2 of the Charter, guaranteed by s. 1, are conditioned, qualified or limited rights by virtue of the wording of s. 1 which qualifies the rights and freedoms by making them subject to reasonable limits on a particular basis. The onus or burden, the argument goes, is on him who is asserting that his particular freedom has been infringed or breached to establish that the limit imposed by the law being attacked, is an unreasonable limit which *cannot* be demonstrably justified in a free and democratic society.

It appears to me that that position and the reasoning supporting it is strained and inappropriate to the clear wording of the two sections. Section 2 states that everyone has the named fundamental freedoms. Section 1 guarantees those rights and, although the rights are not absolute or unrestricted, makes it clear that if there is a limit imposed on these fundamental rights by law, the limits must be reasonable and demonstrably justified in a free and democratic society. The wording imposes a positive obligation on those seeking to uphold the limit or limits to establish to the satisfaction of the court by evidence, by the terms and purpose of the limiting law, its economic, social and political background, and, if felt helpful, by references to comparable legislation of other acknowledged free and democratic societies, that such limit or limits are reasonable and demonstrably justified in a free and democratic society. I cannot accept the proposition urged upon us that, as the freedoms may be limited ones, the person who establishes that, *prima facie*, his freedom has been infringed or denied must then take the further step and establish, on the balance of probabilities, the negative, namely, that such infringement or limit is unreasonable and cannot be demonstrably justified in a free and democratic society. In some case, of course, the frivolous nature of the claim to protection of a freedom or right and of the submissions made in support will be immediately apparent and it will not take great effort to determine that the claim to a guaranteed freedom or right is not tenable under the Charter and under the circumstances. But that is not this case.

As part of his submission in connection with the alleged onus or burden on the respondent, counsel for the Crown pointed out that under s. 24(1) the applicant initiates the proceeding and, accordingly, the usual rules should apply, namely, that if at the end of the hearing the court is undecided and matters are left in balance, then the application must fail. He argued that the onus has always been on an applicant claiming that a Legislature has exceeded in legislation or a portion thereof, its legislative jurisdiction or competence. He submitted that, under the "presumption of constitutionality", there is a clear evidentiary burden on the applicant which includes establishing that the limit is not a reasonable one and that it is not demonstrably justified in a free and democratic society. It does not appear to me that the so-called "presumption of constitutionality" assists in this type of case. There is no conflict here between two legislative bodies, federal and provincial, claiming jurisdiction over a particular legislative subject-matter. This rather is a determination whether a portion of a law is inconsistent with the provisions of the Constitution, the supreme law of Canada. This supreme law was enacted long after the *Juvenile Delinquents Act* and there can be no presumption that the legislators intended to act constitutionally in light of legislation that was not, at that time, a gleam in its progenitor's eye. In any event, like Chief Justice Deschênes, I am of the view that the complete burden of proving an exception under s. 1 of the Charter rests on the party claiming the benefit of the exception or limitation: *Quebec Ass'n of Protestant School Boards v. A.-G. Que. (No. 2)* (1982), 140 D.L.R. (3d) 33 at 59 (Que. S.C.).

*Is the limit a "reasonable limit" as can be demonstrably justified in a free and democratic society?*

It is agreed that the limit in the instant case is "prescribed by law".

The learned motions court judge, in the course of his reasons, stated 38 O.R. (2d) 748 at 754 (*sub nom. Reference re Constitutional Validity of s. 12 of Juvenile Delinquents Act*): "That the courts possess an inherent jurisdiction to forbid access [to the courts] in certain narrow instances, is beyond dispute." If that were so I would have very little difficulty in giving effect to the respondent's position. However, a statutory court such as the provincial court (family division) has no inherent jurisdiction but has only that jurisdiction which is specifically conferred on it by statute. Both counsel before us agreed that the motions court judge was in error in this regard.

However, counsel for the respondent sought to support the position that a family court judge had a discretion under the *Juvenile Delinquents Act* to close his court by arguing that such a discretion was given under ss. 12(2) and 36(1) of that Act. Section 12(2), quoted, beginning as it does with the words, "Such trials", refers back to s. 12(1), the section under attack. That section directs that trials of children shall be held *in camera* and s-s. (2) is a permissive section dealing with the location of the trials to be held *in camera*. Section 12(1) is absolute in its terms and s. 12(2) was not intended to give and does not give an additional discretionary power to the judge to exclude the public which, in view of the wording of s. 12(1), would be quite unnecessary.

Section 36(1) reads:

> 36(1) Every juvenile court has such and like powers and authority to preserve order in the court during the sittings thereof and by the like ways and means as now by law are or may be exercised and used in like cases and for the like purposes by any court in Canada and by the judges thereof, during the sittings thereof.

The power given to the juvenile court to preserve order and cite for contempt of court has no relevance to a discriminatory power to exclude the public in order to protect the interests of the child and advance the perceived purpose and object of juvenile hearings. A juvenile judge could not use this subsection to exclude the public (and the press as part of the public) at the beginning of a hearing when there is no prospect of or concern for disorder.

We are accordingly left in the unhappy position of it being all or nothing. If s. 12(1) is allowed to stand, so long as the present Act is in existence the public is excluded from every such hearing; if s. 12(1) is struck down the public, until further amendment, can attend all such hearings without regard to any other interests.

There is no half-way house such as now exists in similar legislation actual and contemplated, where the court is given a discretion to exclude the public in the best interests of the child and ultimately of the public. The choice, accordingly, at present has to be made between the two absolutes.

The purpose of the legislation under review is effectively set out in ss. 3(2) and 38 of the Act:

> 3(2) Where a child is adjudged to have committed a delinquency he shall be dealt with, not as an offender, but as one in a condition of delinquency and therefore requiring help and guidance and proper supervision.
>
> . . . . .
>
> 38. This Act shall be liberally construed in order that its purpose may be carried out, namely, that the care and custody and discipline of a juvenile delinquent shall approximate as nearly as may be that which should be given by his parents, and that as far as practicable every juvenile delinquent shall be treated, not as criminal, but as a misdirected and misguided child, and one needing aid, encouragement, help and assistance.

As the motions court judge pointed out, the *Young Offenders Act*, 1980-81-82 (Can.), c. 110 (which will replace the *Juvenile Delinquents Act*), enacted but not yet proclaimed in force, is now based on the principle of responsibility and account-ability (s. 3(1)). Under that Act hearings are open to the public with the court having the power under certain conditions or circumstances to exclude any or all members of the public from the proceedings, with certain exceptions. It is not an automatic exclusion as under the present legislation.

Section 39 of the *Young Offenders Act* reads:

> 39(1) Subject to subsection (2), where a court or justice before whom proceedings are carried out under this Act is of the opinion
>
> (*a*) that any evidence or information presented to the court or justice would be seriously injurious or prejudicial to
>
> > (i) the young person who is being dealt with in the proceedings,
> > (ii) a child or young person who is a witness in the proceedings,
> > (iii) a child or young person who is aggrieved by or the victim of the offence charged in the proceedings, or
>
> (*b*) that it would be in the interest of public morals, the maintenance of order or the proper administration of justice to exclude any or all members of the public from the court room,
>
> the court or justice may exclude any person from all or part of the proceedings if the court or justice deems that person's presence to be unnecessary to the conduct of the proceedings.
>
> (2) A court or justice may not, pursuant to subsection (1), exclude from proceedings under this Act
>
> (*a*) the prosecutor;
> (*b*) the young person who is being dealt with in the proceedings, his parent, his counsel or any adult assisting him pursuant to subsection 11(7);
> (*c*) the provincial director or his agent; or
> (*d*) the youth worker to whom the youth person's case has been assigned.
>
> (3) The youth court, after it has found a young person guilty of an offence, or the youth court or the review board, during a review of a disposition under sections 28 to 33, may, in its discretion, exclude from the court or from a hearing of the review board, as the case may be, any person other than

(*a*) the young person or his counsel,
(*b*) the provincial director or his agent,
(*c*) the youth worker to whom the young person's case has been assigned, and
(*d*) the Attorney-General or his agent,

when any information is being presented to the court or the review board the knowledge of which might, in the opinion of the court or review board, be seriously injurious or seriously prejudicial to the young person.

When and if the *Young Offenders Act* in its present form will be proclaimed in force cannot be predicted.

Counsel for the appellant, although candidly acknowledging that not every hearing under the *Juvenile Delinquents Act* would call for the exclusion of the public, argued that to give effect to the declared purpose of the Act, it was necessary to close all juvenile court hearings to the public and this is a reasonable limit on the rights of the public to be present at trials. He pointed out that in smaller municipalities the presence of friends and curious neighbours could have a chilling and inhibiting effect on the evidence of the child and parents or guardian. The court might not have the necesary full information to be able to reach a proper understanding in order to give the necessary aid, encouragement and protection to the child. He, in substance, argued the grounds that give to the court under the proposed legislation (s. 39) the discretionary power to exclude members of the public. The difference is that the reasoning is used to support the reasonableness of mandating the total exclusion of the public in all cases, not to support the use of a discretionary power.

Counsel submitted that the interests of the public are protected in that s. 12(3) gives to the court the discretion to allow for the publication of the identity of the child. Further, it was suggested that the offensive aspects of a "private" trial are ameliorated by other parts of the governing Act. For example, there is no prohibition against speaking to those who were in attendance at the hearing nor against securing a transcript of the proceedings. The parents or guardians must be served with notice of any charge of delinquency and may be present and be heard (ss. 10 and 22(4)). The child's probation officer must be present in the court in order to represent the interests of the child when the case is heard (s. 31); the juvenile court committee, being a committee of citizens, may be present at any session of the juvenile court (ss. 27 and 28). The child is entitled to be represented by counsel. All these are factors which, counsel for the appellant argues, establish that s. 12(1), in the context of the Act, does not truly deprive the public of the right of access to the courts, and therefore it is a reasonable limit on s. 2(*b*) of the Charter.

While the argument is superficially an attractive one, it does not meet the basic objection under the Charter respecting the arbitrary nature of the operation of the section. Further, the examples of public access to the proceedings recited above (some of which are indirect at best) raise with even greater clarity and emphasis the question of the necessity and reasonableness of an absolute bar in all cases. It can be seen that under the *Young Offenders Act* although the court is given the discretionary power to exclude all members of the public, it cannot exclude the young offender, his parents, his counsel or his youth worker (probation officer). Such representation of the public does not, in my view, satisfy the required fundamental freedom of expression as earlier reviewed, or reasonably qualify the arbitrary nature of the absolute effect of the present section.

Counsel for the appellant argued that, in any event, the limit imposed on the fundamental freedom was a *reasonable limit demonstrably justified in a free and democratic society* (emphasis added). In support of his position he pointed out that the section had been on the Canadian statute books since 1908 without objection, and that Canada was a free and democratic society. It seems to me that this reasoning, by itself, has little to do with the requirements of s. 1 of the Charter. If the fact that an Act had been on our statute books without challenge for a period of years was determinative of the question and issue raised by s. 1, no statute or section of a statute in existence prior to the Charter coming into force could be effectively challenged.

We are left, at present, to a certain extent wandering in unexplored terrain in which we have to set up our own guide-posts in interpreting the meaning and effect of the words of s. 1 of the Charter. In determining the reasonableness of the limit in each particular case, the court must examine objectively its argued rational basis in light of what the court understands to be reasonable in a free and democratic society. Further, there is, it appears to me, a significant burden on the proponent of the limit or limits to demonstrate their justification to the satisfaction of the court. As I said earlier that may be easily done in a number of cases.

In determining whether the limit is justifiable, some help may be derived from considering the legislative approaches taken in similar fields by other acknowledged free and democratic societies. Presumably this may also assist in determining whether the limit is a reasonable one. It may be that some of the rights guaranteed by the Charter do not have their counterpart in other free and democratic societies and one is sent back immediately to the facts of our own society. In any event I believe the court must come back, ultimately, having derived whatever assistance can be secured from the experience of other free and democratic societies, to the facts of our own free and democratic society to answer the question whether the limit imposed on the particular guaranteed freedom has been demonstrably justified as a reasonable one, having balanced the perceived purpose and objectives of the limiting legislation, in light of all relevant considerations, against the freedom or right allegedly infringed.

In reviewing what is the practice in other free and democratic societies, it is of some interest to note that there appears, at the present time, to be no consistent rule or principle in the field we are examining in the states of the United States.

The Supreme Court of the United States, having found that the trial of a criminal case must be open to the public in *Richmond Newspapers Inc. v. Commonwealth of Virginia*, 100 S. Ct. 2814 (1980), recently dealt with a similar problem in a somewhat different context. In *Glope Newspaper Co. v. Superior Court for County of Norfolk*, 50 L.W. 4759 (1982), the Massachusetts trial court, relying on a Massachusetts statute providing for exclusion of the general public from trials of specified sexual offences involving a victim under the age of 18, ordered the exclusion of the press and public from the court-room during the trial of a defendant charged with rape of three minor girls. The Globe newspaper challenged the exclusion order and the Massachusetts Supreme Judicial Court construed the Massachusetts statute as requiring, under all circumstances, the exclusion of the press and public during the testimony of a minor victim in a sex-offence trial. The majority of the Supreme Court held that the right of access to criminal trials could not be denied generally by a mandatory closure rule but the interests of minor victims could be just as well served by requiring the trial court to determine, on a case-by-case basis, if the minor victims' well-being necessitated closure.

Chief Justice Burger, who had delivered the lead judgment in the *Richmond Newspapers Inc.* case, *supra*, dissented in the *Globe Newspaper* appeal. He opened his dissent with these words, at pp. 4763-4:

> Historically our Society has gone to great lengths to protect minors *charged* with crime, particularly by prohibiting the release of the names of offenders, barring the press and public from juvenile proceedings, and sealing the records of those proceedings. Yet today the Court holds unconstitutional a state statute designed to protect not the *accused*, but the minor *victims* of sex crimes. In doing so, it advances a disturbing paradox. Although states are permitted, for example, to mandate the closure of all proceedings in order to protect a 17-year-old charged with rape, they are not permitted to require the closing of part of criminal proceedings in order to protect an innocent child who has been raped or otherwise sexually abused.

(The italics are Burger C.J.'s)

His statement seems to indicate that in all cases the press and public are barred from juvenile proceedings. However, the statutes I have located do not bear that out. In many states it appears that the court is given a discretion to exclude the public. With the library facilities available to me it has been difficult to ascertain just what the statutes of many of the states say in regard to proceedings in juvenile courts. So far as it can be ascertained, there are some states which bar outright all public presence but there are many others which confer a discretion upon the judge to determine exclusion and others which make no mention of the question. Where there is a statutory exclusion of the public, the statutes uniformly provide for admission of individuals interested in the juvenile programme, *i.e.*, teachers, students and practitioners of social work and criminology, and there is, according to text-writers, "a growing tendency . . . to permit the newspapers access to the juvenile courts": "Rights and Rehabilitation in the Juvenile Courts", 67 Columbia Law Review 281 at p. 285 (1967). If this were so in 1967, it would not appear to be straining to feel that it would be even more so in 1983. Further, whether the states' juvenile court legislation which bars without any exercise of judicial discretion public access to all juvenile proceedings would now stand in light of the *Globe Newspaper* case is questionable.

I turn now to a direct consideration of those portions of juvenile court legislation in this area of concern in other "free and democratic" societies.

[His Lordship's review of the law in other jurisdictions is omitted.]

If any majority approach can be identified from the review of comparable legislation, it is that juvenile courts are given the discretion to exclude members of the public depending upon its view of the circumstances. There are comparatively few jurisdictions where the prohibition of access is absolute with no discretion left to the hearing judge to determine whether it is appropriate and necessary to exclude all or any of the public.

As I stated earlier, I think it is necessary to view the reasonableness of the absolute ban in light of the purpose of the ban as balanced against the fundamental right guaranteed by the Charter

Although there is a rational basis for the exclusion of the public from hearings under the *Juvenile Delinquents Act*, I do not think an absolute ban in all cases is a reasonable limit on the right of access to the courts, subsumed under the guaranteed freedom of expression, including freedom of the press. The net which s. 12(1) casts is too wide for the purpose which it serves. Society loses more than it protects by the all-embracing nature of the section. As stated earlier, counsel for the Attorney-General was quick to acknowledge (and very fairly so) that not every juvenile court proceeding would require the barring of public access. An amendment giving juris-diction to the court to exclude the public from juvenile court proceedings where it concludes, under the circumstances, that it is in the best interests of the child or others concerned or in the best interests of the administration of justice to do so would meet any residual concern arising from the striking down of the section. As Mr. Justice Martin said in *R. v. Oakes* (1983), 40 O.R. (2d) 660 (C.A.), we are not entitled to rewrite the statute under attack when considering the applicability of the provisions of the Charter. Parliament can give the necessary discretion to the court to be exercised on a case-to-case basis which, in my view, would be a prospective reasonable limit on the guaranteed right and demonstrably justifiable. The pro-tection of social values of "superordinate importance" referred to by Dickson J. in *A.-G. N.S. v. MacIntyre* (1982), 65 C.C.C. (2d) 129 (S.C.C.), does not require, in my view, an absolute bar in all cases of the public, including the press, from juvenile court proceedings.

The appellant in the present case has not demonstrably justified the limit imposed by s. 12(1) as a reasonable one in this free and democratic society and, accordingly, the appeal is dismissed.

*Appeal dismissed.*

[Similarly, it is an improper exercise of discretion for a trial judge to ban the publication of any or all evidence taken in juvenile court proceedings in perpetuity: see *Canadian Newspapers Co. v. Swail and G.M.R.* (1984), 31 Man. R. (2d) 187 (C.A.).

Is there a difference between absolute exclusion of the press from juvenile proceedings altogether, thereby effectively precluding the publication of *any* details of the proceedings, and an absolute pro-hibition only on those matters which would tend to reveal the identity of the juvenile? See *Re Southam Inc. and The Queen* (1984), 14 D.L.R. (4th) 683 (Ont. H.C.).]

# RE FEDERAL REPUBLIC OF GERMANY AND RAUCA

In the Ontario Court of Appeal. 41 O.R. (2d) 225.

Howland C.J.O., MacKinnon A.C.J.O., Brooke, Martin and Houlden JJ.A.
April 12, 1983.

Appeal by the accused fugitive from the dismissal of his application for *habeas corpus* following the decision of Evans C.J.H.C., 38 O.R. (2d) 705, that he be com-mitted to custody to await surrender to the Federal Republic of Germany.

BY THE COURT: — On June 17, 1982, the appellant was arrested pursuant to a warrant of apprehension issued by Parker A.C.J.H.C. under s. 10 of the *Extradition Act*, R.S.C. 1970, c. E-21. The warrant alleged that the appellant was accused of aiding and abetting the murder of 10,500 persons on or about October 28, 1941, in Kaunas (also known as Kowno and Kauen), Lithuania, a crime within the jurisdiction of the Federal Republic of Germany (the "Requesting State"). A warrant for the appellant's arrest on this charge had been issued by the Requesting State at Frankfurt am Main on September 21, 1961. The appellant was brought before Parker A.C.J.H.C. on June 17, 1982, and was remanded in custody for a hearing before an extradition judge.

On June 21, 1982, the appellant was brought before Griffiths J., sitting as a judge of the Supreme Court of Ontario and as a judge pursuant to the *Extradition Act*, on an application for an order for judicial interim release. Following the hearing, Griffiths J. granted the application on certain terms and conditions. The respondent appealed this order to the Federal Court of Canada, Appeal Division. The appeal was dismissed. The appellant did not, however, comply with the terms and conditions contained in the order and was, therefore, not released from custody.

On July 29, 1982, the Requesting State informed the Government of Canada that the warrant of September 21, 1961, had been replaced by a new warrant dated July 16, 1982, issued by the same court that had issued the original warrant. The new warrant charged the appellant with the murder of some 11,584 persons between August 18, 1941, and December 25, 1943. In addition to the alleged murders on October 28, 1941 (in the new warrant reduced to the murder of 9,200 persons), the new warrant charged the appellant with committing or aiding and abetting in the commission of murders on four other occasions.

On October 24, 1982, a new warrant of apprehension was issued by Evans C.J.H.C. based on the warrant of July 16, 1982. The appellant, while in custody, was arrested on this new warrant. On September 1, 1982, he was brought before Parker A.C.J.H.C. on an application for an order of judicial interim release. The application was refused.

On October 12 and 13, 1982, Evans C.J.H.C., sitting as an extradition judge, conducted a hearing in accordance with the *Extradition Act*. At the conclusion of the hearing, he reserved judgment.

On November 4, 1982, Evans C.J.H.C. delivered lengthy reasons (38 O.R. (2d) 705) in which, after a careful review of the facts and the law, he concluded that it was a proper case to issue a warrant under s. 18 of the *Extradition Act*. Accordingly, he directed that a warrant of committal issue requiring the fugitive, Helmut Rauca, to surrender into custody at the nearest convenient prison, there to remain until surrendered to the Federal Republic of Germany or until discharged by law. As required by s. 19(*a*) of the *Extradition Act*, the Chief Justice informed the appellant that he would not be surrendered to the Requesting State until after the expiration of 15 days and that he had the right to apply for a writ of *habeas corpus*.

On November 22, 1982, the appellant applied to Evans C.J.H.C., sitting as a judge of the Supreme Court of Ontario, for a writ of *habeas corpus*. The application was brought before Evans C.J.H.C. so that the matter could be disposed of expeditiously, and an appeal taken without delay to this court. Counsel for the appellant requested the Chief Justice to dismiss the application for the same reasons that he had given on November 4th. Counsel for the respondents advised the Chief Justice that he had no objection to this procedure. Accordingly, the Chief Justice, without hearing argument, dismissed the application for the same reasons that he had given on November 4th.

An appeal was then launched to this court. On January 18, 1983, an application was brought by the Canadian Jewish Congress for leave to intervene in the appeal. After hearing argument, the court granted leave to the congress to intervene, such leave being limited to the following legal issues:

1. whether the extradition order is a violation of the appellant's right as a Canadian citizen to remain in Canada under the *Canadian Charter of Rights and Freedoms*, and
2. whether the crimes charged were committed within the jurisdiction of the Federal Republic of Germany at the time when they were committed so as to entitle the Federal Republic of Germany to request extradition.

[His Lordship's detailed review of the facts, including the fact that the appellant became a naturalized citizen in 1956 and no allegations were raised in those proceedings about the validity of his citizenship, is omitted.]

*Extradition*

Before moving to consider the submissions made on behalf of the appellant, it will be helpful to discuss briefly extradition and Canada's *Extradition Act*.

Extradition, as defined by Professor G. V. LaForest (now Mr. Justice LaForest) in his helpful book *Extradition to and from Canada*, 2nd ed. (1977), at p. 1, is "the surrender by one state at the request of another of a person who is accused, or has been convicted, of a crime committed within the jurisdiction of the requesting state". The crime must be a crime in both States. The *Extradition Act* provides for the surrender, to any country with which Canada has an extradition treaty, of fugitives who have been accused of crimes set forth in the treaty. The theory of such laws is that the procedure strengthens the law enforcement agencies within the State requesting the surrender by reducing the possibility of the criminals escaping. From the point of view of the State to which the criminal escapes, that State does not become a haven for such criminals. Further, as Professor LaForest points out (at p. 16), it is better in general "that a crime be prosecuted in the country where it is committed and where the witnesses and the persons most interested in bringing the criminal to justice reside". Shearer, in his book *Extradition in International Law* (1971), describes the purpose of extradition as viewed by the majority of nations in the world community (p. 21):

> . . . as the major effective instrument of international co-operation in the suppression of crime. For extradition, as the term has been understood for many centuries, is the formal surrender, based upon reciprocating arrangements, by one nation to another of an individual accused or convicted of an offence outside its own territory and within the jurisdiction of the other which, being competent to try and punish him, demands the surrender. The two important features distinguishing extradition from the other modes of dealing with the problem are thus brought out in this definition: the conscious purpose to restore a criminal to a jurisdiction competent to try and punish him, and the principle of reciprocity secured by formal arrangements.

By s. 3, the *Extradition Act* automatically applies to implement a treaty or arrangement. If the treaty arrangement is made after the commencement of the Act, as in the instant case, it applies as soon as it becomes binding on Canada.

In summarizing the procedures set out in the *Extradition Act*, we need only quote the admirable summary of these procedures and their significance by the Chief Justice of the High Court [38 O.R. (2d) 705 at 708-9]:

> The *Extradition Act* has built-in procedural safeguards for the protection of fugitives in that action is required both at the judicial and political levels in order to complete extradition proceedings. The requesting state requisitions the Canadian Government for the surrender of the fugitive. The court orders apprehension and determines whether or not the fugitive is liable to be extradited under the appropriate treaty and statute. The fact that a court may decide there is sufficient evidence to warrant extradition does not preclude the right of the fugitive to be exempted from surrender at the political level. The executive is not required to surrender a fugitive, whether a Canadian citizen or not, even though a court may decide that a *prima facie* case has been established against the fugitive.
>
> Extradition is purely a creature of treaty and statute as at common law there was no inherent jurisdiction in the courts to send a person out of the country against his will. (*Re Insull*, [1933] O.R. 675 (S.C.)). The present *Extradition Act* provides in Part I for the apprehension and surrender of an accused to any foreign state with which there is an arrangement or treaty regarding surrender. The instant case falls under Part I, as there is a treaty between Canada and the Federal Republic of Germany concerning extradition, signed at Ottawa, July 11, 1977, and in force as of September 30, 1979.
>
> Under the *Extradition Act*, a judge of the Supreme Court of Ontario is authorized to act judicially in extradition matters within the province. The nature of the hearing and the procedural rules are set out in ss. 13 and 18 and include the requirements for the admission in evidence of depositions and statements taken in a foreign state which might not be otherwise admissible.
>
> The hearing is not a trial but rather an inquiry, similar to a preliminary hearing, held to determine whether there is a *prima facie* case that the fugitive has committed the extradition crime alleged. It is not a proceeding concerned with the determination of guilt or innocence. The ordinary technicalities of criminal procedure apply only to a limited extent and the procedure except as otherwise provided in the statute is basically the same as that on a preliminary inquiry. (*Re Armstrong and State of Wisconsin*, [1972] 3 O.R. 229 (S.C.)).
>
> The function of the extradition judge is to determine whether the evidence adduced would justify a committal for trial. He is not empowered to decide the merits of the charge or to pass upon the credibility of witnesses. He decides whether there is a *prima facie* case for the accused to meet. The trial and ultimate determination of guilt or innocence rests within the jurisdiction of some other tribunal.

A further point to be noted at this stage, to which we shall return, is that under art. 16 of the German Constitution "no German may be extradited to a foreign country". Article V of the treaty states that "neither of the contracting parties shall be bound to extradite its own nationals". Accordingly, there is an apparent lack of absolute reciprocity in the implementation of the treaty when it comes to the extradition of the Federal Republic's own nationals.

## The Canadian Charter of Rights and Freedoms

In opening his argument counsel for the appellant referred to the following statement by Herbert Weschler in his book *Principles, Politics and Fundamental Law* (1961), excerpted by the Honourable David C. McDonald in his book *Legal Rights in the Canadian Charter of Rights and Freedoms* (1982), at p. 230:

> A principled decision, in the sense I have in mind, is one that rests on reasons with respect to all the issues in the case, reasons that in their generality and their neutrality transcend any immediate result that is involved.

While it is difficult to disabuse one's mind of the horror and inhumanity of the recited allegations of fact, we agree that in considering the submissions based on fundamental rights our reasons must "transcend" the results of any particular case. We, accordingly, approach the arguments made in that light.

The attack on the warrant of committal was based on two main ground. The first argument advanced was that the provisions of s. 6(1) of the *Canadian Charter of Rights and Freedoms* rendered inoperative the provisions of the *Extradition Act* and of the Extradition Treaty. The Act (and the treaty under it) is, it was argued, inconsistent with the supreme law of Canada and is, therefore, of no force and effect (s. 52 of the *Constitution Act, 1982*). Section 6(1) reads:

> 6(1) Every citizen of Canada has the right to enter, remain in and leave Canada.

Section 52(1) reads:

> 52(1) The Constitution of Canada is the supreme law of Canada, and any law that is inconsistent with the provisions of the Constitution is, to the extent of the inconsistency, of no force or effect.

It is the appellant's desire, as a citizen of Canada, to remain in Canada and he claims the right to so remain as guaranteed to him by s. 1 and s. 6(1) of the Charter.

The Chief Justice of the High Court while accepting that extradition is "*prima facie* an infringement on the s. 6 mobility rights of a citizen" concluded that the Requesting State had established "that extradition is a procedure prescribed by law and is a reasonable limitation on one's guaranteed rights and freedoms which can be demonstrably justified in our society" [38 O.R. (2d) 705 at 717].

In this last passage he had reference to s. 1 of the Charter which reads:

> 1. The *Canadian Charter of Rights and Freedoms* guarantees the rights and freedoms set out in it subject only to such reasonable limits prescribed by law as can be demonstrably justified in a free and democratic society.

There are, in reality, two aspects to the first issue. The first aspect concerns whether the appellant's right as a citizen to remain in Canada has been (or will be) infringed by the action taken under the *Extradition Act* and the treaty. The position of the respondent is that on the clear wording of s. 1 of the Charter the right to remain is a qualified right. The *Extradition Act* and treaty prescribe a reasonable limit on the right to remain, such limit being demonstrably justifiable in a free and democratic society. Accordingly, it is incumbent upon the appellant, the argument goes, to show otherwise.

We do not agree with this approach. In our view, the issue has to be approached in two steps. First, it has to be determined whether the guaranteed fundamental right or freedom has been infringed, breached or denied. If the answer to that question is in the affirmative, then it must be determined whether the denial or limit is a reasonable one demonstrably justifiable in a free and democratic society.

We agree with the Chief Justice of the High Court and have no doubt that the order made and its consequences, *prima facie*, interfere with the appellant's guaranteed right as a citizen to remain in Canada.

Much argument revolved around the question of onus. That is, who properly bore the burden or onus of establishing that the limits, in this case the extradition laws imposed on a fundamental right or freedom, are reasonable and are demonstrably justifiable in a free and democratic society. Merely stating the question and quoting the section appear to give the answer. However, counsel for the respondents argued that as the right to remain in Canada is by definition a qualified right, that is, qualified by the words of s. 1, the applicant must demonstrate on the balance of probabilities that the limits imposed by the extradition laws on the right he claims as a Canadian citizen to remain in Canada, are unreasonable and unjustified.

This question was fully canvassed by this court in *Re Southam Inc. and The Queen (No. 1)*, 41 O.R. (2d) 113. In adopting the reasoning on this point in the case we would only add that, in our opinion, the wording of s. 1 makes it clear that he who seeks to support the limit prescribed by law has the burden of establishing on the balance of probabilities that it is reasonable and demonstrably justifiable. There is no issue that the limits in the instant case are "prescribed by law".

We turn now, accordingly, to the second aspect of the first issue: have the respondents demonstrably justified the limit to be a reasonable limit in a free and democratic society? In approaching the question objectively, it is recognized that the listed rights and freedoms are never absolute and that there are always qualifications and limitations to allow for the protection of other competing interests in a democratic society. A readily demonstrable example of this is "freedom of speech" which is limited or qualified by the laws of defamation, obscenity, sedition, etc. Lord Reid pointed out in *Attorney-General v. Times Newspapers Ltd.*, [1974] A.C. 273 at 294 (H.L.):

> Public policy generally requires a balancing of interests which may conflict. Freedom of speech should not be limited to any greater extent than is necessary but it cannot be allowed where there would be real prejudice to the administration of justice.

In the present appeal counsel for the appellant argued that leaving the ultimate determination to the Minister whether to extradite or not gives a discretion to the executive which is arbitrary and unreasonable. He also argued that the fact that the Federal Republic would not extradite its own citizens under the treaty made the extradition of Canadian citizens under the treaty unreasonable.

The discretion of the executive has been a recognized and accepted qualification in extradition treaties for over a century. Free and democratic societies have refused to extradite for "political crimes" as they determine them. It must be noted that here the discretion is entirely in favour of the "fugitive". The Minister can accept the extradition order made by the court, or he can refuse to follow it where the treaty provides for the discretionary surrender of nationals; the discretion is exercisable by the executive only and is not a question cognizable by the courts: *Re Galwey*, [1896] 1 Q.B. 230 at 236; *R. v. MacDonald; Ex parte Strutt* (1901), 11 Q.L.J. 85 at 90.

In reviewing international agreements and their history, it can be seen that there is no international convention, written or otherwise, that militates against the extradition of a State's own nationals. . . .

. . . Nations of the British Commonwealth have never favoured the practice of excluding the extradition of one's own nationals and, in considering the interpretation to be placed on s. 1 of the Charter, it must be remembered that the Charter has been placed in a fabric of existing laws to which consideration has to be given. In Ontario, Richards J., over a century ago, in dealing with a claim for extradition of a British subject to the United States, said:

> Whatever may be considered to have been the general rule in relation to a Government surrendering its own subjects to a foreign Government, I cannot say that I have any doubt, that under the Treaty and our own Statute, a British subject who is in other respects brought within the law, cannot legally demand that he ought not to be surrendered merely because he is a natural born subject of Her Majesty.

(See *Re Burley* (1865), 60 B.F.S.P. 1241 at 1261.)

The learned Chief Justice of the High Court, in the course of his reasons, spoke of "the usual presumptive canon of construction of legislative validity". We do not feel this presumption is of much assistance in construing legislation in light of the Charter which post-dates such legislation and the reasonableness of which legislation hitherto has never had to be examined or justified. Nevertheless the Charter was not enacted in a vacuum and the rights set out therein must be interpreted rationally having regard to the then existing laws and, in the instant case, to the position which Canada occupies in the world and the effective history of the multitude of extradition treaties it has had with other nations.

It is clear from the proceedings of the Joint Committee on the Constitution of Canada that the present problem was not absent from their consideration. The Deputy Minister of Justice, on being questioned about exile and deportation with relation to s. 6, made the following reply:

> *Mr. Tassé:* Perhaps I might mention that we do not see Clause 6 as being an absolute right. I will give you an example of a situation where a citizen would, in effect lose his right to remain in the country; that would be by virtue of an order under the Extradition Act; if someone committed an offence in another country and he is sought in this country, he could be surrendered to the other country.
>
> The same thing would apply in the case of countries belonging to the Commonwealth to which the Extradition Act does not apply, but the Fugitive Offenders Act does apply. In that situation a Canadian would not have the right to remain in the country by virtue of the offences he might have committed in another country and for which he is sought so that justice could be applied.
>
> *Mr. Epp:* Mr. Tassé, I do not think that is really what we are dealing with. That is not arbitrary and under the Extradition Act there is a process to which the person is entitled before that extradition order can in fact be finalized.

(See Proceedings of the Joint Committee on the Constitution of Canada, *Hansard*, January 27, 1981, pp. 46:117 to 46:118.)

Counsel for the appellant suggested that there was a possibility that the appellant could be prosecuted in Canada for the crimes with which he had been charged. If there was this alternative, the argument was that extradition was not a reasonable limit on the appellant's right as a citizen to remain in Canada. This submission was not pressed strongly and, like the Chief Justice of the High Court, we are not persuaded that there is, at present, a right to prosecute the appellant for the recited crimes in Canada. Even if there were such a right to prosecute, in light of the described purpose and reason for and lengthy history of extradition, it would not turn a reasonable limit on the citizen's right to remain in this country into an unreasonable limit.

The intervenant, who was permitted to intervene on limited grounds, and who supported the respondents, sought to take an inconsistent position on this particular issue and to argue that the appellant could be prosecuted in this country. Its interest seemed to be in what would happen to the appellant if extradition were denied. That, of course, is not a matter which is before us. This would only become a viable question if extradition is denied as would the possibility that Parliament might enact retroactive criminal legislation to cover this situation.

In this connection counsel for the appellant, while not pressing it in his oral submissions, in his statement argued that "in deciding the nature of the burden regard must be had", *inter alia*, to "the absence of evidence that no reasonable alternative exists other than to abrogate the right of the citizen to remain in Canada". He apparently relied on the *Geneva Conventions Act*, R.S.C. 1970, c. G-3, and the *War Crimes Act*, 1946 (Can.), c. 73, and the possibility of the enactment of future retroactive criminal legislation. Not only is the *Geneva Conventions Act* not a statute of general application but it is a piece of substantive law which does not have a retroactive effect. Equally, the *War Crimes Act* is not a statute of general application and by its very terms does not cover the present factual situation where the crimes were not committed against Canadian citizens. Further, a proceeding against the appellant under that Act could run afoul of s. 11(*f*) of the Charter which guarantees, except in the case of an offence under military law tried before a military tribunal, the right to a trial by jury where the maximum punishment for the offence is imprisonment for five years or more. We can only repeat that we are not persuaded that at present there is such an alternative to extradition as to make extradition an unreasonable limit not demonstrably justifiable in a free and democratic society.

It is not necessary to turn to lengthy dictionary definitions of the words "demonstrably justified". They are words of common understanding and usage and they place a significant burden on the proponents of the limiting legislation. When the *rationale* and purpose of the *Extradition Act* and treaty under it are looked at (having in mind that crime should not go unpunished), Canada's obligations to the international community considered and the history of such legislation in free and democratic societies examined, in our view, the burden of establishing that the limit imposed by the *Extradition Act* and the treaty on s. 6(1) of the Charter is a reasonable one demonstrably justified in a free and democratic society has been discharged by the respondents. . . .

*Appeal dismissed.*

### Note

The Supreme Court of Canada's decision in *R. v. Oakes*, S.C.C., February 28, 1986 (unreported) is extracted in the "Addendum" following Chapter 24 of this book.

# 17

# Fundamental Freedoms

## 1. Expression

### (a) General

*Section 1: The Standard For Assessing Restrictive Government Actions And The Charter's Code Of Procedure And Evidence*

Neil Finkelstein. (1983), 9 Queens L.J. 143 at 164-79.

. . . .

[footnotes omitted]

*Case Study #1 — Freedom of Expression*

The state's burden of demonstrably justifying laws which infringe upon freedom of expression is always heavy, but it varies in degree depending upon the context. The state may impose either content or medium-based limitations. Content-based limitations are triggered by the content of the speaker's message, prohibiting certain classes of messages but not others. Examples are laws respecting sedition, contempt of court, the content of advertising, obscenity, and censorship of books and films. On the other hand, medium-based restrictions do not focus upon the content of the message, but rather upon the medium through which the message is transmitted. Laws respecting the control of public streets for traffic circulation purposes, noise control, and election financing are illustrations of content-neutral, medium-based regulation. The state's burden of justifying medium-based limitations is not as heavy, because the fear of the propagation of a state line is not as clearly present.

### (i) *Content-based limitations*

Not all categories of speech are equally protected. The degree of constitutional protection of any given category should depend upon its importance to the functioning of society. Political speech has always been considered essential, and it accordingly has rested in the Anglo-American constitutional systems' most favoured place. Courts have always been extremely sensitive to laws purporting to regulate the content of political speech, because the notion that the free exchange of ideas is essential to the functioning of democracy is one of the fundamental premises of Western society.

It should be noted that the parameters of so-called "political speech" are very wide, and include in their ambit ideas respecting choice of lifestyle, religion, philosophy and morality. It is virtually impossible to draw clear, principled lines dividing "political" and "non-political" expression, and we should favour a flexible constitutional approach in order to preserve a tradition of vigorous public debate. One of the bases of a constitutional *Charter* is the worth and importance of the individual. Individuality in modes of self-expression must be protected in the absence of proof that it represents a real threat to a legitimate state interest.

The American courts start from the position that political speech in its widest sense is presumptively protected. The speaker does not have to demonstrate that his message has any social value. Restrictions are presumed to be invalid unless the government can show that positive harm will result from the transmission of the message. Thus in *National Socialist Party v. Skokie*, 432 U.S. 43 (1977), the Nazis did not have to show that their ideals and goals were a valuable contribution to the political ideology of the United States. They only had to demonstrate that the Village of Skokie was imposing a content-based prior restraint by refusing to allow them to parade. The burden then shifted to Skokie to show that allowing the Nazis to march would result in positive harm *which could not be prevented by less restrictive means.*

This last caveat is very important. The Nazis chose Skokie as the site for the march because the population was predominantly Jewish. As such, there would be more media attention if the parade was held there than there would be in some place where there were no Jewish people. The civil rights marchers used the same rationale in choosing Birmingham rather than Harlem as the site for their marches, albeit for a far worthier cause. Skokie argued that the image of the hated swastika was likely to provoke violent counter-demonstrations by its inhabitants. One way of preventing that violence was to halt the march, so that the unwilling listeners would not attack the unpopular speakers. The fatal flaw in this solution is that it places effective censorship power in the hands of the majority. If enough people do not like the unpopular speaker's message, they can silence him. This is precisely what a constitutional *Bill of Rights* or *Charter* is designed to prevent. Unpopular minority speech needs constitutional protection. Popular majoritarian speech does not. In this case, a less restrictive way of preventing violence would have been to provide more police supervision.

*Skokie* illustrates that the judicial starting point is often determinative of the ultimate result. If the burden had been on the Nazis to demonstrate the social utility of their message, the march would not have been permitted to proceed. A totally different outcome resulted from placing the burden on the government to show positive harm.

A similar philosophy with respect to freedom of political expression existed in Canada even before section 1 of the *Charter* made it part of our constitutional law. In *Boucher v. The King*, [1951] S.C.R. 265, a Jehovah's Witness was charged with sedition for distributing a pamphlet entitled "Quebec's Burning Hate for God and Christ and Freedom" on the streets of Quebec City. The pamphlet detailed instances of persecution of the Witnesses by both angry mobs and organized authorities, and urged people to end these injustices and return to the Bible. The pamphlet further stated that the Roman Catholic Church was influencing the courts and the administration of justice.

The pamphlet was obviously intended to disturb the recipients thereof, particularly given the Church-dominated climate in Quebec at the time. In fact, it created a real danger that members of the public would attack the pamphleteer himself. The Supreme Court of Canada did not analyse the pamphlet from the standpoint of its possible social utility although, as distinct from that of the Nazis, its message had merit, but rather examined the surrounding circumstances to see what harm could arise. Because Boucher did not intend to incite anyone to violence against the state, the Supreme Court reversed his conviction for sedition. An angry mob could not silence an unpopular speaker simply because his message disturbed them.

This is not to say that content-based restrictions are *per se* unconstitutional under the *Charter*. In some cases, suppression of the message will be the only way to preserve order. Where there is an immediate danger that the speech will lead to violence, the speech may be suppressed until the danger has passed.

Not all types of speech are accorded the same degree of protection as political speech. The place of a given category of expression on the spectrum of constitutional protection is determined by its social utility. Social utility in this context means the utility of the *category or class* of message, not the utility of the *particular* message itself. Political speech is at the top of the *Charter* hierarchy, because a democratic society cannot function without it. Commercial speech, for example, falls somewhere in the middle. On one hand, it has some social utility because it is informational. On the other, the state must be allowed a somewhat freer hand with commercial speech than with political expression, because it has a responsibility to regulate both anti-competitive practices and misleading or dangerous advertising. Obscenity is at the bottom of the scale, because it is considered to be without social value. It has therefore traditionally been unprotected in both the United States and Canada.

Purely commercial speech was initially beyond the pale of First Amendment protection in the United States, following *Valentine v. Christensen*, 316 U.S. 52 (1942). That has changed, since *Bigelow v. Virginia*, 421 U.S. 809 (1975) and *Virginia Board of Pharmacy v. Virginia Consumer Council*, 425 U.S. 748 (1976). In *Bigelow*, the defendant was convicted pursuant to a Virginia statute of advertising the availability of legal out-of-state abortions. The United States Supreme Court struck down the statute and reversed the conviction. *Bigelow* did not squarely raise the issue of whether purely commercial speech was protected, because the advertisement in question provided information about a service which was itself constitutionally protected. It went beyond advertising ordinary commercial matters.

The United States Supreme Court was faced with the issue of whether purely commercial advertising fell within the First and Fourteenth Amendments in *Virginia Board of Pharmacy v. Virginia Consumer Council*. A Virginia statute prohibited licensed pharmacists from price advertising. Since only licensed pharmacists could dispense prescription drugs, the ban effectively blocked the dissemination of price information otherwise than by consumers' word of mouth. Blackmun J. posed the issue as follows:

> Our pharmacist does not wish to editorialize on any subject, cultural, philosophical or political. He does not wish to report any particularly newsworthy fact, or to make generalized observations even about commercial matters. The 'idea' he wishes to communicate is simply this: 'I will sell you the x prescription at the y price.' Our question is whether this communication is wholly outside the protection of the First Amendment.

Blackmun J. started with two propositions. First, speech does not lose its First Amendment protection simply because money is spent to disseminate it to the public. For instance, political campaign spending to convey information about the candidate is protected, as are corporate expenditures to publicize corporate views on referendum issues. Second, speech is protected even if it is "sold" for a profit. To take an extreme example, the state could not ban the sale of Sir Winston Churchill's *The Gathering Storm* simply because he wrote it for money. Blackmun J. therefore reasoned that if some speech which is made for money is protected, the distinguishing feature between protected and unprotected speech cannot be financial, or that its speaker has an economic rationale. By way of illustration, statements on the merits by contestants in a labour dispute are constitutionally guaranteed notwithstanding that both the employer's and employees' interests are purely economic.

The social value which is protected is the free flow of commercial information:

> As to the particular consumer's interest in the free flow of commercial information, that interest may be as keen, if not keener by far, than his interest in the day's most urgent political debate. . . . Generalizing, society also may have a strong interest in the free flow of commercial information. Even an individual advertisement, though entirely "commercial", may be of general public interest.

Thus, even purely commercial information merits a degree of constitutional protection, because it is necessary for the effective functioning of a free market economy. On the other hand, state regulation of commercial speech is valid where it serves a "significant governmental interest" and leaves open alternative channels for the transmission of the information. The burden is on the state to demonstrate the nature and significance of its interest, the necessity for the restriction, and the existence of alternative channels of communication.

The United States Supreme Court has since diluted the impact of *Virginia Board of Pharmacy*, but it has left the principles stated therein intact. Commercial speech is still *prima facie* protected, and the burden remains on the state to demonstrate the existence of a "significant government interest" which justifies restrictions in particular cases.

Section 1 of the *Charter* codifies the *Virginia Board of Pharmacy* approach of requiring the government to justify laws which restrict commercial speech. Cases decided before the advent of the *Charter* are therefore suspect. A pre-*Charter* case like *Jabour v. Law Society of British Columbia* (1982), 137 D.L.R. (3d) 1 (S.C.C.) is an instance in point. In *Jabour*, a lawyer advertised his business hours and prices for routine services, without any accompanying puffery. The Law Society of British Columbia disciplined him, and he appealed up to the Supreme Court of Canada, arguing, *inter alia*, that the regulation abridged his freedom of expression.

*Jabour* is very similar on its facts to the American case of *Bates v. State Bar of Arizona*, 433 U.S. 350 (1977) where the U.S. Supreme Court struck down a state ban on lawyers' advertising. *Bates* was in fact referred to in *Jabour* on an anti-combines point, but no mention was made of it with respect to its constitutional expression principle. Estey, J. upheld the Law Society regulations, which drew their force from a provincial statute, on traditional division of powers principles without reference to the freedom of expression principles which now have to be applied.

In my view, *Jabour* would be decided differently today. Courts are now constitutionally mandated by section 1 to analyse expression cases, and indeed all cases where *Charter* guarantees are implicated, on their own terms, rather than to simply fit them into division of powers pigeon-holes. They must conduct a rigorous inquiry into the legitimacy and necessity for restrictive rules such as the ones at issue in *Jabour*. Regulations which prohibit purely informational advertising required by the public in order to make considered decisions about its choice of lawyer cannot pass section 1's test of demonstrable justification and must be struck down.

The courts must also ensure that they are in fact dealing with commercial speech, and not political speech, its more highly protected brother. For example, a cigarette manufacturer lobbying for the repeal of legislation restricting cigarette advertising has a purely economic motive, and yet, being advocacy for legislative change, it is clearly political speech worthy of the highest degree of constitutional protection. Furthermore, legislation seeking to regulate commercial speech must be narrowly tailored to meet that purpose. It must contain standards to ensure that only unprotected speech is caught in its net. By way of example, regulations promulgated pursuant to the "character of advertising" provision in s. 16 of the federal *Broadcasting Act* delegate complete authority to the C.R.T.C. to prescreen alcoholic beverage commercials without reference to any standards whatsoever. In one instance, this power was used to stop the broadcasting of beer commercials on the basis that they tended to portray religion too lightly. Provisions like these cannot meet the degree of scrutiny mandated by section 1 of the *Charter*.

At the bottom of the expression hierarchy, some types of speech are unprotected altogether. It is important to fit them into the demonstrable justification analysis to understand the true rationale for their exclusion. It has been said in the United States that "fighting words" and sedition fall outside the ambit of constitutional protection. The rationale is that such speech immediately strikes at the "ordered liberty" which society must have. It is important to recognize that fighting words and sedition are not deprived of protection by virtue of their content. They become unprotected by the immediacy of the danger which they generate, and thus fall squarely within the standard section 1 analysis.

Obscenity is the only class of speech which is truly beyond the constitutional pale, at least in the United States, and I am not aware of any convincing rationale for this. That is not to say that society does not have a legitimate interest in regulating obscenity for limited purposes, such as protecting minors or the community's collective privacy interest. However, I cannot see any reason why obscenity should be the only class of speech where the burden is on the applicant to justify the content of the speech, and demonstrate that it has "redeeming social value." In my view, Canadian constitutional law is significantly different from American law on the point in light of section 1 of the *Charter* which puts the burden on the government to enunciate a justification for restricting even obscene speech. The mere fact that the speech has no value does not deprive it of Canadian constitutional protection.

Given the presence of section 1 in the *Charter*, which puts the burden of demonstrably justifying restrictive laws on the state, the reach and rationales of our obscenity laws will have to be closely scrutinized. Neither of the two traditional justifications can support a *complete* ban on obscenity. The first proffered justification is that obscenity imposes on an unwilling community, embarrassing it by forcing it to either look or turn away. The difficulty is that the same can be said for offensive political speech. The Nazi march through Skokie "embarrassed" the

Jewish inhabitants by putting them to the choice of listening to Nazi propaganda or staying home. The only difference between the two situations is our initial position. We assume the value of even Nazi political speech in the absence of a showing of positive harm. With obscene speech, we traditionally start from the position that it is valueless and put the burden on the applicant to justify it.

The second justification for restricting obscenity is that it may corrupt the morals of the community. There are two problems with this rationale as a justification for a complete, as opposed to a partial, ban. First, the same may be said again of Nazi propaganda. Some people may be "corruptible", and find the idea appealing that their troubles are the fault of some helpless ethnic minority. Second, this rationale is based upon the same paternalistic notions that Rand J. criticized in *Switzman v. Elbling*, [1957] S.C.R. 285 at 305:

> The aim of the statute is, by means of penalties, to prevent what is considered a poisoning of men's minds, to shield the individual from exposure to dangerous ideas, to protect him, in short, from his own thinking propensities.

The demonstrable justification provision of section 1 requires the government to show that legitimate state interests are at stake, going beyond paternalistic notions of what Canadian society should see or hear. Naturally, community interests could be protected by specifically tailored legislation. The government could protect the community's collective privacy interest by prohibiting pornography outside specifically zoned areas, and it could protect children by regulating the time, place and manner in which obscene material is distributed.

This approach would force a reconsideration of cases like *R. v. Hawkshaw* (1982), 39 O.R. (2d) 571. The issue there was whether it was an offence under s. 159 of the *Criminal Code* to make a pornographic picture involving a seventeen year old minor for purely private viewing. Howland C.J.O., speaking for the majority of the Ontario Court of Appeal, held that the circumstances of the offence might constitute obscenity, because a trial judge (at p. 583):

> might be driven to conclude that the community would not tolerate, even for private viewing, a photograph depicting the commission of an act of gross indecency where one of the participants is a minor.

The problem with this test for obscenity is that it is none of the community's business what a person wants to do in private. Thus it is irrelevant whether the community will tolerate pornography for purely private use, particularly under a constitutional *Charter* which is supposed to insulate the individual from community prejudices as far as possible. Furthermore, the fact that a minor was involved here was a red herring. The statute was not directed at minors, but rather was a general anti-obscenity provision. The provision lacked constitutionally acceptable standards and was overbroad. Today it would hopefully be read down or declared to be of no force and effect. It would be different if the statute was specifically tailored to exclude minor participation in obscene acts, because it would then be keyed directly into the legitimate community interest of protecting minors.

I have assumed for the purposes of the preceding discussion that the particular speech under consideration is in fact obscene. That assumption will be at issue in most cases. The question will be whether or not the penal legislation involved contains constitutionally adequate standards for defining obscenity.

For example, as indicated recently by the Ontario Divisional Court in *Ontario Film and Video Society v. Ontario Board of Censors* (1983), 41 O.R. (2d) 583, censorship legislation such as that considered in *McNeil v. Nova Scotia Board of Censors*, [1978] 2 S.C.R. 662, a pre-*Charter* case, falls far short of the mark because it is constitutionally overbroad. Censorship legislation must be drafted in such a way that messages which convey legitimate political, moral or philosophical ideas are not caught within its ambit, notwithstanding that they may be packaged in a somewhat prurient way.

This necessity for adequate legislative standards has also arisen recently in the analogous area of press access to courts. In *R. v. Southam* (1983), 41 O.R. (2d) 113, the Ontario Court of Appeal considered the validity of s. 12 of the federal *Juvenile Delinquents Act*. The provision as judicially interpreted by the Supreme Court of Canada in *C.B. v. Kimelman* (1981), 38 N.R. 451 (S.C.C.) imposed an absolute bar on press or public attendance at juvenile trials. In a well-crafted decision, Mac-Kinnon A.C.J.O. gave a broad reading to the expression guarantee in s. 2 of the *Charter*, holding that it comprehended access to certain types of information (such as information about judicial proceedings) as well as the right to talk or write about it, and then meticulously analysed the various elements of the limitation clause in section 1. In the result, the absolute bar was struck down because *in camera* hearings were not necessary for the protection of juveniles in all cases, and the legislation did not contain adequate standards to distinguish between cases which did and cases which did not. MacKinnon A.C.J.O. suggested that an amendment to the Act giving the court discretion to decide when the public should be excluded would be one way of dealing with the problem.

## (ii) *Medium-based limitations*

The state burden of demonstrable justification is generally heavier where content-based restrictions are concerned, in order to guard against the propagation of a state line. Where "medium-based" restrictions are concerned, the concern that the state may be advancing a particular point of view, or prohibiting the dissemination of a different one, is not as clearly present. Medium-based limitations by definition are directed at some other purpose and only incidentally affect expression. The *Charter* problem is that this "incidental effect" may in certain cases be an insurmountable obstacle to the transmission of messages by poorer groups.

To illustrate, a prohibition on all demonstrations regardless of message would be content-neutral, and it would keep the streets clear for public transit. However, demonstrations are often the only medium of communication that poorer (and usually more radical) groups have available to them. A law as absolute as the one postulated above effectively silences them. Furthermore, the effect of such a law is unevenly distributed. Wealthier groups (usually with more "acceptable" messages) can afford to use expensive alternative media.

The demonstrable justification provision in section 1 requires the courts to intervene where an otherwise legitimate regulation is not sensitive enough to *Charter* concerns. Thus a complete ban on the use of streets is inappropriate, but a time, manner and place restriction such as closing only certain streets, possibly at selected busy times, might be legitimate. Furthermore section 1 requires that there be a close relationship between the legislative means and end. The state could not ban the distribution of all handbills, another medium of communication used by poorer groups, simply to reduce littering. It is true that there is a rational relationship between handbills and littering, and that the regulation would be relatively cost effective. However, given the severe effect of the law on these groups, the state would have to find a less restrictive way of maintaining clean streets. It could hire more street cleaners, albeit at greater expense.

An interesting situation, insofar as the demonstrable justification phrase in section 1 is concerned, arises where the competition is between purely private interests, as opposed to competing public against private interests. The burden on the state is not as great in these cases, because it is not furthering an interest of its own. The media access cases in election situations are a good example. The election candidate's interest in disseminating his campaign information as widely as possible confronts the press' interest in maintaining editorial discretion over what it will broadcast.

In the American case of *CBS v. FCC*, 101 S. Ct. 2813 (1981), the *Federal Election Campaign Act*, 47 U.S.C., S. 312(a)(7) provided that the Federal Communications Commission (F.C.C.) could revoke the license of any broadcaster who refused to allow "reasonable access" to any qualified federal candidate. The Carter-Mondale Presidential Committee requested thirty minutes of air time early in the campaign for the Democratic presidential nomination. All three networks refused because there was an unusually high number of candidates, and programming would be greatly disrupted if the networks had to give each of them equal access. The FCC ordered the networks to sell the time. The Supreme Court did not apply strict scrutiny to the FCC standards, but rather deferred to the FCC balancing the respective rights of the press and the candidate. It is likely that the Supreme Court of Canada will apply a similar standard of deference to legislative decisions in cases involving competing private interests. On the other hand, where the state is furthering an interest of its own, balancing a state interest against a purely private one, the demonstrable justification clause requires more.

[Is there a distinction for Charter purposes between an election-financing law that provides a scheme whereby candidates and political parties can have a portion of their election expenses reimbursed by the government and one which limits political expenditures? See *Re MacKay and Manitoba* (1985), 19 D.L.R. (4th) 185 (Man. Q.B.) upholding the former law (notwithstanding an argument that the law forced taxpayers to contribute to parties with which they disagreed), and *National Citizens Coalition Inc. v. A.G. Can.*, [1984] 5 W.W.R. 436 (Alta. Q.B.), striking down the latter law.]

In *Re Allman and Commissioner of the Northwest Territories* (1983), 8 D.L.R. (4th) 230 (N.W.T.C.A.), leave to appeal to the Supreme Court of Canada refused May 17, 1984, the Northwest Territories Court of Appeal held that freedom of expression in section 2(*b*) of the *Charter* does not comprehend the right to vote in a plebiscite. Belzil J.A., speaking for the Court at p. 236, said:

Freedom of expression is the bulwark of all fundamental freedoms and always the first to be repressed or controlled by totalitarian regimes. Its inclusion in the Canadian Charter, as in the other human rights documents referred to, is a safeguard against repression and control by ruling authority. Section 2(*b*) of the Canadian Charter guarantees that no government in Canada will act to abridge or abrogate that freedom.

> Viewed in this perspective, it becomes immediately and abundantly clear that the expression of opinion sought by a plebiscite under the *Plebiscite Ordinance* has nothing at all to do with the fundamental freedom of expression guaranteed by the Canadian Charter. It does not abridge or abrogate the fundamental freedom of expression previously enjoyed by the applicants as a guaranteed birthright. It is a supplementary forum created by the territorial government for its own information purposes. The fact that the applicants were denied the opportunity to participate in a public opinion poll did not detract from their fundamental right to speak out and express their views on the subject-matter, whether individually or through the media.

The primordinate purpose of section 2(*b*) of the *Charter*, although by no means its only purpose, is to allow the citizenry to influence government through the expression of opinion. It seems strange in that context that the right to present one's views to the government in the forum which the government has established for just that purpose on an issue which the government deems important enough to call a plebiscite on, is not comprehended by section 2(*b*) of the *Charter*. In my view, this is too narrow a reading of section 2(*b*) and it is regrettable that the Supreme Court of Canada refused to grant leave to appeal.

[A number of the areas in the above 1983 article have been dealt with in subsequent jurisprudence, some of which is reproduced below. Examples are cases dealing with commercial speech (see *Klein, infra*), and obscenity (*Red Hot Video infra*)]

[For additional commentary on section 2(*b*), see Hogg, *Constitutional Law of Canada* (2d ed. 1985), p. 712 and the references cited therein.]

## (b) Political Speech

# RE ONTARIO FILM & VIDEO APPRECIATION SOCIETY AND ONTARIO BOARD OF CENSORS

In the Ontario Court of Appeal. (1984), 45 O.R. (2d) 80.

**NOTE:** Pursuant to leave granted May 30, 1983 (MacKinnon A.C.J.O., Blair and Thorson JJ.A.), an appeal and cross-appeal from the above decision to the Ontario Court of Appeal were dismissed (MacKinnon A.C.J.O., Arnup, Dubin, Houlden and Tarnopolsky JJ.A.) February 6, 1984. The following was endorsed on the appeal record by

MACKINNON A.C.J.O.: — The Divisional Court thoroughly and carefully canvassed the issues that were raised on this appeal and cross-appeal. As we are in substantial agreement with their analysis of these issues and their reasoned conclusions, it would serve no useful purpose to repeat at any length the facts and the issues.

It is argued before us on behalf of the appellant that s. 3(2)(*a*) of the *Theatres Act*, R.S.O. 1980, c. 498, in view of its lengthy history and the manner in which it is interpreted and applied by the Ontario Board of Censors, is, in some fashion, a recognized restraint on the freedom of expression which falls outside s. 2(*b*) of the *Canadian Charter of Rights and Freedoms*. In other words, it is a pre-Charter recognized restraint on the freedom of expression, and there is no need to go to s. 1 of the Charter to salvage it.

Section 3(2)(*a*) reads:

3(2) The Board has power,
  (*a*) to censor any film and, when authorized by the person who submits film to the Board for approval, remove by cutting or otherwise from the film any portion thereof that it does not approve of for exhibition in Ontario;

We cannot accept that argument. We agree with the conclusion of the Divisional Court that s. 3(2)(*a*) clearly imposes a limitation on freedom of expression as guaranteed by s. 2(*b*) of the Charter. We also agree that ss. 35 and 38 of the *Theatres Act* are capable of being interpreted and applied as part of that limitation. The Divisional Court concluded on this point [41 O.R. (2d) 583 at 593]:

These sections, in so far as they purport to prohibit or to allow the censorship of films, may be said to be "of no force or effect . . .

We would go further than the Divisional Court on this issue. In our view, s. 3(2)(*a*), rather than being of "no force or effect" is *ultra vires* as it stands. The subsection allows for the complete denial or prohibition of the freedom of expression in this particular area and sets no limits on the Ontario Board of Censors. It clearly sets no limit, reasonable or otherwise, on which an argument can be mounted that it falls within the saving words of s. 1 of the Charter, "subject only to such reasonable limits prescribed by law". Further, like the Divisional Court, we conclude that s. 3(2)(*b*) and ss. 35 and 38 cannot be interpreted and applied in their present form to support the censorship of film although they have a valid role to play otherwise. As pointed out by the Divisional Court, there is no challenge in these proceedings to the system of film classification, nor to the general regulation of theatres and projectionists and other matters dealt with in the statute and regulations.

The Divisional Court stated that they were expressing no view whether the standards issued by the Ontario Board of Censors, if embodied in the legislation, or the regulations properly authorized by the statute, would be considered "reasonable limits" within the meaning of those words found in s. 1 of the Charter. This question is not before us and we express no opinion on whether there can be legislated guide-lines for the Ontario Board of Censors so as to be reasonable limits prescribed by law on the freedom of expression, demonstrably justified in a free and democratic society. In dealing with this point, the Divisional Court stated [at p. 591 O.R.]: "One thing is sure, however, our courts will exercise considerable restraint in declaring legislative enactments, whether they be statutory or regulatory, to be unreasonable." We do not think, if they were purporting to enunciate a principle, that there is any such principle to be applied in the determination of what is "reasonable" under s. 1 of the Charter. In approaching the question, there is no presumption for or against the legislation but there are many factors to be considered, in light of the legislation itself and its background, which have been recited in a number of authorities: *Re Federal Republic of Germany and Rauca* (1983), 41 O.R. (2d) 225 at 244 (C.A.); *Re Southam Inc. and The Queen (No. 1)* (1983), 41 O.R. (2d) 113 at 129-30 (C.A.).

The appeal by the Ontario Board of Censors is dismissed.

On the cross-appeal by the respondents, we did not feel it necessary to call on the cross-respondents to respond to the argument. We are in agreement with the

Divisional Court in their disposition of the issues in the cross-appeal and it is not necessary to add anything further. The cross-appeal is dismissed.

As success was divided there will be no order as to costs.

*Appeal dismissed.*
*Cross-appeal dismissed.*

# RE ONTARIO FILM AND VIDEO APPRECIATION SOCIETY AND ONTARIO BOARD OF CENSORS

In the Ontario Divisional Court. 41 O.R. (2d) 583.

J. Holland, Boland and Linden JJ. March 25, 1983.

Application, *inter alia*, to quash a number of decisions of the Ontario Board of Censors.

BY THE COURT: — This application raises the question of the constitutional validity of the censorship (prior restraint) provisions of the *Theatres Act*, R.S.O. 1980, c. 498, and the standards and procedures of the Ontario Board of Censors pursuant to which the board has carried out its statutory mandate relating to films to be shown *to the public or for gain*. The application was precipitated by the enactment of the *Constitution Act, 1982*, and in particular by the guarantee of the right to freedom of expression as contained in s. 2(*b*) of the *Canadian Charter of Rights and Freedoms* which provides:

> 2. Everyone has the following fundamental freedoms:
>
> . . . . .
>
> (*b*) freedom of thought, belief, opinion and expression . . .

Any limitation upon this guaranteed freedom must meet the tests set out in s. 1 of the Charter, which reads as follows:

> 1. The *Canadian Charter of Rights and Freedoms* guarantees the rights and freedoms set out in it subject only to such *reasonable limits prescribed by law as can be demonstrably justified in a free and democratic society.*

(Emphasis added.)

Section 52 provides for primacy in the following way:

> 52(1) The Constitution of Canada is the supreme law of Canada, and any law that is inconsistent with the provisions of the Constitution is, to the extent of the inconsistency, of no force or effect.

We are asked to find that the censorship (prior restraint) provisions of the *Theatres Act* and/or the standards and procedures of the board do limit the freedom of expression so guaranteed and do not successfully meet the tests set out in s. 1 and accordingly must be constitutionally invalid.

Before setting out the particular sections of the *Theatres Act* which are impugned, we should record that the right of the province to enact such legislation is not in issue: see *Nova Scotia Board of Censors v. McNeil*, [1978] 2 S.C.R. 662.

Further, there has been no challenge to the system of film classification in operation in Ontario for some time, nor of the general regulation of theatres and projectionists and other matters dealt with in the statute. Nor has there been any assault upon the provisions of the *Criminal Code* of Canada which continue to proscribe forms of expression which unduly exploit sex and violence.

What is impugned in this proceeding is the power granted to the Ontario Board of Censors to "censor any film" (s. 3(2)(*a*)), to "prohibit . . . the exhibition of any film in Ontario" (s. 3(2)(*b*)), as well as the requirement that "all film" be "submitted to the Board for approval" (s. 35) and the prohibition against exhibiting "any film that has not been approved by the Board" (s. 38). It is vigorously contended by the applicants and the intervenors that this system of censorship is a prior restraint of expression, which cannot continue in this province in the face of the new Charter. The Crown has defended, no less strenuously, the constitutionality of the present censorship scheme.

In April of 1982, immediately following the proclamation of the new Charter, the applicant submitted four films to the board of censors, seeking approval for public showings. The "Art of Worldly Wisdom" and "Rameau's Nephew" were both approved for exhibition, but only at one time and at one place. "Not A Love Story" was rejected on the ground that the National Film Board, the owners of the film, had not released it for public exhibition by the applicant on a commercial basis. The fourth film, "Amerika", was rejected by the board of censors, which gave reasons having to do with the explicit portrayal of certain sexual activity. The members of this court have not viewed the films in question, because this was not felt to be necessary in disposing of the application. (There are several administrative law issues arrising from the facts, which will be dealt with later.)

The provisions of the *Theatres Act* which are relevant include s. 3, which reads:

> 3(1) The board known as the Board of Censors is continued and shall consist of the Director who shall be chairman of the Board and the Assistant Director who shall be vice-chairman of the Board and such other persons as the Lieutenant Governor in Council may appoint.
> (2) The Board has power,
> > (*a*) *to censor any film* and, when authorized by the person who submits film to the Board for approval, remove by cutting or otherwise from the film any portion thereof that it does not approve of for exhibition in Ontario;
> > (*b*) *subject to the regulations, to approve, prohibit or regulate the exhibition of any film in Ontario*;
> > (*c*) to censor any advertising matter in connection with any film or the exhibition thereof;
> > (*d*) subject to the regulations, to approve, prohibit or regulate advertising in Ontario in connection with any film or the exhibition thereof;
> > (*e*) to classify any film as adult entertainment;
> > (*f*) to classify any film as restricted entertainment; and
> > (*g*) to carry out its duties under this Act and the regulations.

[Emphasis added.] Section 35 stipulates as follows:

> 35. All film before being exhibited in Ontario shall be submitted to the Board for approval, accompanied by the prescribed fee.

Section 38 states:

> 38. No person shall exhibit or cause to be exhibited in Ontario any film that has not been approved by the Board.

The word "exhibit" is defined by s. 1(c) as follows:

1. In this Act,

. . . . .

(c) "exhibit", when used in respect of film or moving pictures, means to show film for viewing for direct or indirect gain or for viewing by the public and "exhibition" has a corresponding meaning;

It should also be noted that s. 63(1), para. 9 of the *Theatres Act* authorizes the making of regulations "prohibiting and regulating the use and exhibition of film or any type or class thereof" but none have been prepared. Section 63(1), para. 14 authorizes the making of regulations "prescribing the terms and conditions under which film or any type or class thereof may be sold, rented, leased, exhibited or distributed", but none have been issued.

The relevant provisions of the *Theatres Act* have been in place in this province since 1911 and we are advised that the present application is the first court challenge to be made upon these provisions or upon the board's operation thereunder. This must speak well of the conduct of the board members in carrying out the board's legislated duty, which undoubtedly involves difficult and controversial matters. We should point out that the application before us did not involve criticism of the board except to the extent that it is said the statutory provisions and the standards and procedures of the board were inconsistent with the guaranteed freedom of expression and did not meet the test set out in s. 1. The issue is essentially legal and not factual.

Over the years the board has issued several versions of a document entitled "Standards for classification and/or Censorship of Films" to which it purports to adhere in exercising its authority. These standards set out descriptions of the type of material that would be classified as "general", "adult entertainment" or "restricted" as well as the type of material that it would recommend to be eliminated. It is explained that a film might be rejected altogether, something it says is "very rare", if the required eliminations were "so extensive as to ruin the continuity of the film". Most of the offensive types of material deal with sexual explicitness, violence or the exploitation of children, but "blasphemous" and "sacrilegious" matter is also mentioned. It has also circulated to the public and any interested persons several versions of a pamphlet entitled "Film Classification and Censorship", which sets out much of the same material contained in the standards. All of these publications, however, are conceded by the Crown to have no legal status; they are distributed merely for the assistance of the public in order to indicate the general approach of the board. It is clear that the standards are not legally binding on the board, although it is asserted that they are generally used by the board as guide-lines.

When Her Majesty proclaimed into force the new Charter of Rights and Freedoms, all Canadians were *guaranteed* certain fundamental freedoms set out in s. 2, such as "freedom of . . . expression, including freedom of the press and other media of communication". This section is mainly declaratory of the freedoms which have long existed in Canada (see *Nova Scotia Board of Censors v. McNeil, supra; A.-G. Can. v. Dupond*, [1978] 2 S.C.R. 770; and *A.-G. Can. v. Law Society of British Columbia; Jabour v. Law Society of British Columbia* (1982), 137 D.L.R. (3d) 1 (S.C.C.)), for we Canadians have always enjoyed a full measure of freedom of expression, as well as the other freedoms. Nevertheless, our political leaders concluded that these freedoms should be entrenched in a Charter in order to guarantee these rights for all Canadians, including future generations, and, possibly, to permit expansion over the years ahead.

These fundamental freedoms guaranteed in the Charter are not absolute. The Charter recognizes that it is sometimes necessary to restrict freedom of expression to an extent to protect the interest of society. Consequently, it is possible for our governments to circumscribe the freedoms enunciated in s. 2. They may do so by invoking the notwithstanding clause (s. 33). Alternatively, they may do so by observing the provisions of s. 1 of the Charter, which indicates that the rights and freedoms set out in it are "*subject only* to such reasonable limits prescribed by law as can be demonstrably justified in a free and democratic society" [emphasis added].

It is not in dispute that in the event that legislation is enacted which limits any of these freedoms, the government bears the onus of demonstrating that the limit comes within the language of s. 1. The presumption of constitutional validity, which generally applies in cases of ordinary legislation, is not available once it is shown that there has been an interference with one of the fundamental freedoms: see *Quebec Ass'n of Protestant School Boards v. A.-G. Quebec (No. 2)* (1982), 140 D.L.R. (3d) 33 (Que. C.A.); *Federal Republic of Germany v. Rauca* (1982), 38 O.R. (2d) 705 (H.C.); Tarnopolsky & Beaudoin, *The Canadian Charter of Rights and Freedoms: Commentary* (1982), at p. 70.

We are all of the view that ss. 3(2)(*a*) and (*b*), 35 and 38 impose a limitation on the freedom of expression of the applicant as guaranteed by s. 2(*b*) of the Charter. It is clear to us that all forms of expression, whether they be oral, written, pictorial, sculpture, music, dance or film, are equally protected by the Charter. The burden, therefore, falls upon the Attorney-General to satisfy us on the balance of probabilities that the requirements of s. 1 of the Charter have been met, and "[t]he standard of persuasion to be applied by the court is a high one if the limitation in issue is to be upheld as valid": see Evans C.J.H.C. in *Rauca, supra* [at p. 716 O.R.]. By placing such an onus on governments, the Charter inhibits the courts from permitting the dilution of the guaranteed fundamental freedoms. Hence, any limit placed on these freedoms must be shown to be *demonstrably justifiable in a free and democratic society*; it must be a *reasonable limit*; and it must be a limit that is "*prescribed by law*". Let us examine each of these three items in turn.

*Demonstrably justifiable in a free and democratic society*

As for being demonstrably justifiable in a free and democratic society, it has been held that there must be a reasonable ground upon which a limitation can be based for it to be "justifiable": see Chief Justice Evans, *Rauca, supra*. Chief Justice Deschênes has suggested that we must focus on the "validity" of the "objective" of the legislation: *Quebec Ass'n of Protestant School Boards* case, *supra*. It is obvious that the *Theatres Act* (and its predecessors back to 1911) primarily seeks, among other things, to prevent socially offensive films from being publicly shown in Ontario. Eight other provinces and many other free and democratic countries have similar legislation: see *Report of the Committee on Obscenity and Film Censorship*, U.K. Cmnd. 7772 (1979). Moreover, the federal criminal prohibition against obscenity is evidence that there is and has been sufficient concern in this country about this problem to enact legislation to combat it. We are satisfied, therefore, that some prior censorship of film is demonstrably justifiable in a free and democratic society. (No one questioned that Canada and each of its constituent provinces and territories are free and democratic.)

*Reasonable limits*

The next issue to consider is whether the limits placed on the freedom of expression by the *Theatres Act* are reasonable ones. Counsel for the Crown argued that the limits are reasonable since they curtail only the freedom of those who wish to exhibit films to the public or for gain. He points out that any one can make films, show them privately, rent them and sell them. Hence, it is said the freedom of expression is only curtailed to the extent that a person wishes to exhibit film to the public or for profit. It would be fair to assume that the prime purpose for making films is to exhibit them to the public. If a film-maker cannot show his film to the public there is little point in making it. Moreover, the profit motive cannot be a valid reason to prevent a film-maker from showing his work, for one who shows film for profit can have no less freedom of expression than one who does so not for profit. The extent of freedom of expression cannot depend on that, for there is nothing wrong with making a profit from one's art or one's ideas. In addition freedom of expression extends to those who wish to express someone else's ideas or show someone else's film. It also extends to the listener and to the viewer, whose freedom to receive communication is included in the guaranteed right.

Another argument advanced by the Crown is that a prohibition can be reasonable if it applies only to film-makers, not to authors of books, publishers of papers, performers on the stage, TV producers, etc. We cannot agree. The Charter, in allowing reasonable limits, does not countenance the total eradication of freedom of expression for those who use a particular form of expression such as film. If film is the medium in which an individual works, he could thereby be denied completely his only means of self-expression. To say that other media are available to him is no comfort at all. This argument really involves the question of fair treatment between various forms of communication. Hence, although one particular form of expression may not be prevented completely, a legislative body, acting within its jurisdiction, may place limits only upon one type of expression and not on others provided that such limits meet the test set out in s. 1.

As to whether the standards issued by the board of censors would be considered to be reasonable limits, we express no views. They may or may not be acceptable, but in the light of the position we take on the next issue, it is not necessary for us to express a view. One thing is sure, however, our courts will exercise considerable restraint in declaring legislative enactments, whether they be statutory or regulatory, to be unreasonable.

*Prescribed by law*

The next issue is whether the limits placed on the applicant's freedom of expression by the board of censors were "prescribed by law". It is clear that statutory law, regulations and even common law limitations may be permitted. But the limit, to be acceptable, must have legal force. This is to ensure that it has been established democratically through the legislative process or judicially through the operation of precedent over the years. This requirement underscores the seriousness with which courts will view any interference with the fundamental freedoms.

The Crown has argued that the board's authority to curtail freedom of expression is prescribed by law in the *Theatres Act*, ss. 3, 35 and 38. In our view, although there has certainly been a legislative grant of power to the board to censor and prohibit certain films, the reasonable limits placed upon that freedom of expression of film-makers have not been legislatively authorized. The Charter requires reasonable limits that are prescribed by law; it is not enough to authorize a board to censor or prohibit the exhibition of any film of which it disapproves. That kind of authority is not legal for it depends on the discretion of an administrative tribunal. However dedicated, competent and well-meaning the board may be, that kind of regulation cannot be considered as "law". It is accepted that law cannot be vague, undefined, and totally discretionary; it must be ascertainable and understandable. Any limits placed on the freedom of expression cannot be left to the whim of an official; such limits must be articulated with some precision or they cannot be considered to be law.

There are no reasonable limits contained in the statute or the regulations. The standards and the pamphlets utilized by the Ontario Board of Censors do contain certain information upon which a film-maker may get some indication of how his film will be judged. However, the board is not bound by these standards. They have no legislative or legal force of any kind. Hence, since they do not qualify as law, they cannot be employed so as to justify any limitation on expression, pursuant to s. 1 of the Charter. We draw comfort in this conclusion from the views of Professor Beckton, in *The Canadian Charter of Rights and Freedoms: Commentary* (1982), p. 107 (Tarnopolsky & Beaudoin, editors), where she wrote:

> Clearly statutes which create censorship boards without specific criteria would be contrary to the guarantees of free expression, since no line is drawn between objectionable and non-objectionable forms of expression. Now standards will have to be created to measure the limits to which obscene expressions may be regulated.

This does not mean that the censorship scheme set out in the *Theatres Act* is invalid. Clearly the classification scheme by itself does not offend the Charter. Nor do we find that ss. 3, 35 and 38 are invalid, but the problem is that standing alone they cannot be used to censor or prohibit the exhibition of films because they are so general, and because the detailed criteria employed in the process are not prescribed by law. These sections, in so far as they purport to prohibit or to allow censorship of films, may be said to be "of no force or effect", but they may be rendered operable by the passage of regulations pursuant to the legislative authority or by the enactment of statutory amendments, imposing reasonable limits and standards.

We turn now to the several other constitutional and administrative law issues to be addressed relating to the specific request made to the board. The decision of the board that the two films could be shown at one time and one place is a valid exercise of the board's power to "regulate" pursuant to s. 3(2)(*b*).

The decision concerning "Not A Love Story" is defensible as a refusal by the board to engage in an academic exercise. The applicants were seeking permission to show a film they did not own and which they had no right to exhibit. The board does not have to spend its time engaging in theoretical activity. Although no copy of the film was submitted to the board as required by the Act, this ground was not relied upon by the board. While it is said that the reason the board gave, that the National Film Board had not released the film for public commercial showing, was an improper interference with freedom of expression because there is no specific legislative authority for doing so, in view of the above, we need not decide this issue.

The decision to prohibit the public exhibition of "Amerika" must be quashed because it was an interference with the freedom of expression of the applicant that was not based on a legally binding standard.

As for the denial of natural justice, procedural fairness, and the need for a hearing pursuant to the *Statutory Powers Procedure Act*, R.S.O. 1980, c. 484, this much can be said. It is not clear on the evidence before us that there was any infringement of the right to be heard. The Standard Procedures for Classification and Censorship of Film distributed by the board provides for a written report by the board without a hearing. However, if there is an objection, the distributor may, within 15 days, make submissions in writing, which the board will consider. The board may request a meeting with the distributor to discuss the submission. After that another report will be made by the board. In this case, following the reports of the board on the four films, the applicant did not object in writing or request a hearing, but commenced legal proceedings immediately. We are of the view that the applicant has not exhausted its remedies and hence we decline to exercise our discretion to invoke any prerogative remedy that may be available.

The decision of the board of censors concerning "Amerika", therefore, is quashed. The application in all other respects is dismissed.

Counsel have agreed that there should be a stay of execution of this decision pending the time limited for appeal and we so direct. In the event that no appeal is to be taken, we may be spoken to, before the time for appeal lapses, about a further stay of execution.

We make no order as to costs to any party.

*Application granted in part.*

# RE INFORMATION RETAILERS ASSOCIATION OF METROPOLITAN TORONTO INC. AND MUNICIPALITY OF METROPOLITAN TORONTO

In the Ontario Court of Appeal. (1985), 52 O.R. (2d) 449.

Houlden, Cory and Robins JJ.A. Oct. 17, 1985.

The judgment was delivered by

ROBINS J.A.: —

The Municipality of Metropolitan Toronto appeals, with leave, from a judgment of the Divisional Court (now reported in 48 O.R. (2d) 290), declaring: (1) that it was *ultra vires* the Legislature of Ontario to legislate in relation to "books", "magazines" and "other reading . . . matter" pursuant to s. 222(9)(*b*) of the *Munici-*

*pal Act*, R.S.O. 1980, c. 302, and (2) that ss. 1(1a)(a) and 2(27a) of By-law 107-78 of the municipality regulating the sale of "adult books or magazines" were void and of no force and effect.

The issues which gave rise to these declarations of invalidity were precipitated by amendments made by the appellant municipality in 1983 to By-law 107-78, the general licensing by-law of Metropolitan Toronto. These amendments were designed to regulate the sale and display of books and magazines of which a principal feature is the portrayal or depiction of specified body areas and which appeal to or are designed to appeal to erotic or sexual appetites or inclinations. Under the terms of the amended by-law retailers of such publications must be licensed and the publications must be displayed at a height of at least 1.5m. (5 ft.) above the floor and behind an opaque barrier which permits only the names of the books or magazines to be visible to the public. The principal purpose of the by-law, as stated by the municipality, is "to restrict physical and visual access by children to certain publications, particularly what are known as 'adult' or 'skin' magazines, on sale in stores in Metropolitan Toronto". The licensing requirement applies to all stores selling such publications and is intended to facilitate the enforcement of the restriction.

Section 222 of the *Municipal Act* authorizes municipal councils to pass by-laws relating to "adult entertainment parlours". However, in so far as the section purports to authorize municipal regulation of the sale of books and magazines with erotic content, the Divisional Court held that it intrudes upon federal jurisdiction over criminal law and is thus beyond provincial legislative competence. Since the appellant municipality's power to enact the by-law in question is predicated on the validity of the authority conferred by the impugned provisions of s. 222, the licensing requirements imposed by the by-law on retailers of adult books and magazines and the clause defining those publications were also held invalid. In addition, the Divisional Court found the by-law invalid on the ground that its definition of "adult book or magazine" was so vague and uncertain as in itself to render the by-law unenforceable.

The respondents on this appeal are the Information Retailers Association of Metropolitan Toronto Inc. ("Retailers"), an incorporated association of individuals and corporations who are engaged in the distribution and sale of books and magazines, and the Canadian Periodical Publishers Association ("Publishers"), an incorporated association of publishers of Canadian periodicals. The proceedings originated with their applications, separately brought, challenging by way of judicial review the validity of the 1983 amendments by By-law 107-78 and the enabling provincial statute. The applications were heard together by the Divisional Court as were these appeals from its decision. The standing of the respondents to bring the proceedings is not in issue. The Attorney-General of Ontario has intervened in this Court in support of the appellant's position that the impugned provisions of s. 222 of the *Municipal Act* are within the jurisdiction of the provincial Legislature.

*The legislation in issue*

Section 222 was added to the *Municipal Act* in 1978, as s. 368(*b*) (1978, c. 17, s. 2) for the purpose of vesting authority in municipalities to regulate and control certain sex-oriented trades and businesses not covered by the Act as it then stood. The section, in so far as it is relevant to this appeal, reads as follows:

> 222(1) By-laws may be passed by the concils of all municipalities for licensing, regulating, governing, classifying and inspecting adult entertainment parlours or any class or classes thereof and for revoking or suspending any such licence for limiting the number of such licences to be granted, in accordance with subsection (3).
>
> . . . . .
>
> (9) In this section,
>
> > (a) "adult entertainment parlour" means any premises or part thereof in which is provided, in pursuance of trade, calling, business or occupation, goods or services appealing to or designed to appeal to erotic or sexual appetites or inclinations;
> >
> > (b) "goods" includes books, magazines, pictures, slides, film, phonograph records, prerecorded magnetic tape and any other reading, viewing or listening matter;
> >
> > (c) "to provide" when used in relation to goods includes to sell, offer to sell or display for sale, by retail or otherwise such goods, and "providing" and "provision" have corresponding meanings;

It is to be noted that the regulatory power granted to municipal councils over adult entertainment parlours is applicable to all premises in which goods appealing to or designed to appeal to erotic or sexual appetites or inclinations are provided in pursuance of a trade or business; that "goods" is defined to include books, magazines and other reading matter; and that the provision of goods includes the sale and the display for sale of goods by retail or otherwise.

By-law 107-78, as I indicated earlier, is the general licensing by-law of Metropolitan Toronto and deals with the licensing, regulating and governing of a wide variety of trades, callings, businesses and occupations in the metropolitan area. Its scheme is such that persons engaged in specified trades or businesses must be licensed by the Metropolitan Licensing Commission and comply with the regulations pertaining to their trade or business as provided for in a series of schedules forming part of the by-law. The by-law contains provisions dealing with applications for licenses, the authority of the licensing commission to grant, refuse or revoke licences, licence fees, and offences and penalties for contravention of the by-law.

In March, 1983, the appellant passed By-law 41-83 which amended By-law 107-78 by adding provisions that required retail sellers of "adult books or magazines" to be licensed and to comply with specified display regulations. The amendment was enacted on the purported authority of s. 222 of the *Municipal Act*. Although By-law 107-78 contained regulations with respect to "adult entertainment parlours", prior to this amendment its definition of that term was limited to the provision of "services" and did not apply to "goods". Sellers of books and magazines, adult or otherwise, were not previously governed by this by-law and, it follows, were not required to be licensed. The March, 1983 amendments compelled the licensing of:

> 2(27a) Every person who provides in any premises or part thereof, in pursuance of a trade, calling, business or occupation, adult books or magazines, or who operates any premises or part thereof in which such books or magazines are so provided.

The corresponding definitions are set forth in ss. 1(1a)(a) of By-law 107-78 as amended. The definition of "adult book or magazine" was further amended in May,

1983, but it may none the less be helpful to reproduce the original definition section in its entirety:

1. (1a)(a) "Adult book or magazine", means any book or magazine appealing to or designed to appeal to sexual or erotic appetites or inclinations.

(b)(i) "Book or magazine appealing to or designed to appeal to sexual or erotic appetites or inclinations" means any book or magazine of which a feature or characteristic is the portrayal or depiction, by means of photographs, drawings, or otherwise, of the specified body areas of any person or persons or of which a feature or characteristic of a substantial part thereof is such portrayal or depiction.

(ii) Notwithstanding the generality of sub-paragraph (i), nothing contained therein shall be deemed to apply to any book or magazine other than those referred to in section 222 of the Municipal Act.

(c) "To provide", when used in relation to any book or magazine, means to sell, offer to sell or display for sale by retail or otherwise such book or magazine, and "provider", "providing" and "provision" have corresponding meanings.

(d) "Specified body areas" means:

(a) in the case of a female person, her breasts; and

(b) in the case of all person, the pubic, perineal and perianal areas and the buttocks.

Schedule 41 was also added to By-law 107-78. The regulations contained in this schedule demand that every operator who provides adult books or magazines in any premises or part thereof comply with certain display requirements. Operators of "adult entertainment parlour stores" are excepted, that term being defined to cover the relatively small number of stores in which the *principal* business is the provision of books or magazines or other goods or services appealing to or designed to appeal to sexual or erotic appetites or inclinations. The sections of the by-law applicable to operators of such stores are not in issue in this case. The relevant display restrictions are set forth in sch. 41 as follows:

3. (1) Every operator who provides adult books or magazines in any premises or part thereof other than an adult entertainment parlour store, or who operates such premises or part thereof, shall comply with the following regulations in respect of such premises or part:

(a) No adult book or magazine shall be displayed at a height of less than 1.5 metres above floor level, unless such book or magazine is in a part of the premises to which the public is not permitted physical access.

(b) All adult books or magazines offered for sale or displayed in such premises or part shall be placed behind an opaque barrier of a size and nature which shall ensure that the cover of every such book or magazine while so displayed, except for the name thereof, may not be seen by any member of the public.

Shortly following the enactment of the amending by-law in March, 1983, the municipality referred the by-law to the legislation and licensing committee requesting that it be given further consideration by the committee. This request was prompted by a concern that the definition of "adult book or magazine" was broad enough to bring legitimate works of art and photography within its purview and, as well, by a concern that, given the option of enforcement by prosecution, the licensing requirement and annual fee imposed by the by-law constituted unnecessary impositions on the small businesses effected by the by-law. On May 10, 1983, the appellant enacted By-law 82-83 which changed the definition of "adult book or magazine" but left the licensing requirement and other provisions of the March amendment in place. The amended definition of "adult book or magazine", and it is this definition that the Divisional Court declared void for vagueness, reads:

1(1a)(a) "Adult book or magazine" means any book or magazine:

(i) of which a principal feature or characteristic is the portrayal or depiction, by means of photographs, drawings or otherwise, of one or more of the specified body areas of any person or persons; and

(ii) which appeals to or is designed to appeal to erotic or sexual appetites or inclinations.

Before turning to the legal issues, it is important to appreciate the reasons underlying the municipality's enactment of these 1983 amendments. For many years members of council had received complaints from the public about the display of "skin" magazines in variety and convenience stores normally frequented by children in or near family-oriented neighbourhoods. Since 1976, the major supplier of magazines to retailers in Metropolitan Toronto has categorized such magazines and requested merchants to display them, on a voluntary basis, in such a way as to restrict their access by children, but with limited success. While many submissions were received by the municipality with respect to the offensiveness and public indecency of these publications and the damaging effects of pornography, there is no reason to doubt its assertion that the display restrictions were imposed primarily to keep adult publications out of the ready reach of youngsters and to limit their exposure to them. The by-law does not, as counsel for the appellant stresses, impose any prohibition on the sale of the books or magazines covered by it, nor does it purport to deal with obscenity.

. . . .

## The Charter Issue

Freedom of expression is a fundamental freedom protected by section 2(b) of the *Charter*. The protection applies to all phases of expression from writer, artist and photographer through to distributor and retailer and on to reader and viewer. *R. v. Videoflicks Ltd.* (1984), 48 O.R. (2d) 395 at 431 (C.A.); *Re Ontario Film & Video Appreciation Society and Ontario Board of Censors* (1984), 45 O.R. (2d) 80 (C.A.). The freedom to distribute and sell is as essential to the exercise of the freedom as the freedom to publish, for without the means of disseminating expression, the publication would be of little value. Non-obscene "adult books and magazines", no matter how tasteless or tawdry they may be, are entitled to no less protection than other forms of expression; the constitutional guarantee extends not only to that which is pleasing, but also to that which to many may be aesthetically distasteful or morally offensive; it is indeed often true that "one man's vulgarity is another's lyric".

In this case the appellant acknowledges that section 2(b) of the *Charter* "guarantees the fundamental freedom to sell and display adult magazines or books to the public", but it asserts that the display restriction merely regulates the place and manner of display and neither adversely interferes with access to these publications nor adversely impacts on their content and, hence, cannot be said to constitute an infringement of the freedom. The respondents, on the other hand, concede that, assuming a properly drawn by-law, a restriction on the manner of display imposed for the purpose of protecting the welfare of children may not of itself be unreasonable and can be demonstrably justified within the meaning of section 1 of the *Charter*. They submit however that as this by-law is drafted it unreasonably limits freedom of expression in that the scope of the by-law is defined in terms so vague or overbroad that, in either case, its operation extends well beyond the bounds necessary to attain the desired purpose. The respondents object particularly to the by-law's inclusion of "books" and its imposition of a licensing scheme on vendors of books.

While the supervision of children's reading may best be left to their parents, parental control cannot always be provided. The transcendent interest of society in the well-being of children clearly justifies reasonable municipal regulation designed to discourage or limit their exposure to sexually-oriented pictorial material. The regulatory scheme must not however be out of proportion to that objective; the net, in other words, must not be cast too wide. As Chief Justice Dickson noted in *R. v. Big M Drug Mart Ltd.*, [1985] 1 S.C.R. 295 at 352:

> . . . it should be noted that not every government interest or policy objective is entitled to s. 1 consideration. Principles will have to be developed for recognizing which government objectives are of sufficient importance to warrant overriding a constitutionally protected right or freedom. Once a sufficiently significant government interest is recognized then it must be decided if the means chosen to achieve this interest are reasonable — a form of proportionality test. *The court may wish to ask whether the means adopted to achieve the end sought do so by impairing as little as possible the right or freedom in question.*

[Emphasis added]

The means adopted will not be reasonable if the infringement on the fundamental freedom is disproportionate to the societal good which is to be achieved through the enactment. *MacKay v. The Queen*, [1980] 2 S.C.R. 370 at 408; *Quebec Association of Protestant School Boards v. Attorney General of Quebec (No. 2)* (1982), 140 D.L.R. (3d) 33 at 77, aff'd (1983), 1 D.L.R. (4th) 573 (Que. C.A.), aff'd [1984] 2 S.C.R. 66 (S.C.C.).

The question then becomes one of determining whether the steps taken by this municipal council have in fact been kept within the bounds required by the situation so as not to impinge on the protected freedom to a degree greater than is necessary to achieve the legitimate governmental interest. This by-law, in my opinion, fails that test. Rather than being narrowly tailored to further the objective legitimately sought to be advanced, the by-law defines its coverage in terms so wide as to sweep within its ambit material which is not necessary to further the desired objective.

By definition, the by-law covers all nude and some partially nude photographs or depictions so long as they appeal to or are designed to appeal to erotic or sexual appetites or inclinations and constitute a principal feature or characteristic of a book or magazine. This encompasses a very large area of visual erotica. However, on the Municipality's own evidence, the by-law was enacted out of a concern about the open display of so-called "girlie" or "skin" magazines in neighbourhood variety and convenience stores frequented by children. It was not enacted because of erotic pictorial material in books or magazines generally. The use of so wide a definition, in my opinion, manifestly renders the by-law broader in its application than is necessary to effect its avowed and legitimate purpose.

Books were included in the by-law notwithstanding the apprehension of some members of council that the by-law could have the effect of prohibiting the open display of legitimate works of art and photography. The May, 1983 revision of the definition of "adult book or magazine" did not, in my view, succeed in narrowing the then existing definition so as to avoid the likelihood of that consequence. There is no denying that many books sold in bookstores (and several have been filed in evidence to illustrate the point) contain as a principal feature or characteristic nudity or partial nudity and, regardless of the dignity of presentation, can fairly be said to appeal to or be designed to appeal to sexual inclinations. On the wording of the definition, these books would fall within its purview requiring that they be displayed in the same manner as "skin" magazines, in this case behind an opaque barrier but potentially, as some similar by-laws require, in sealed packages or wrappings.

It is no answer for the Municipality, having prescribed a definition broad enough to encompass these books, to say that booksellers would, as a matter of common understanding, be aware of the type of publication the by-law is designed to regulate or that the by-law can be subjected to a narrowing construction; nor is it any answer to say that the Municipality can be relied on not to enforce the by-law with respect to "legitimate" books. Booksellers should not be left to guess whether or not it is intended that a particular book be within the purview of the by-law; nor should they be left to the vagaries of bureaucratic enforcement or, indeed, to the popular pressures that may arise to influence enforcement. "Bookselling", as Mr. Justice Fortas once observed, "should not be a hazardous profession". *Ginsberg v. State of New York*, 390 U.S. 629 at 674.

As the by-law stands, a bookseller is obliged by s. 2(27a) to make important daily decisions as to whether he must have a licence for the sale of a particular book or whether a book must be placed behind a blinder. Without detailing the licensing scheme, which was amended shortly before this appeal, it confers a discretion on the Licensing Commission to refuse or revoke a licence on the basis of whether the applicant's conduct affords reasonable grounds for a belief that he will not carry on the business "in accordance with law and with integrity and honesty"; previously the Licensing Commission was empowered to take an applicant's "character" into account in determining whether his carrying on of the business may be in any way adverse to the "public interest". Licensed booksellers are subject to municipal inspection. Contravention of the by-law can result in serious consequences including not only the imposition of a fine but, by virtue of s. 329 of the *Municipal Act*, [R.S.O. 1980, c. 302] the premises may be ordered closed for a period not exceeding two years for failure to obtain a licence and, by virtue of the *Landlord & Tenant Act*, R.S.O. 1980, c. 232, a tenant engaged in a business for which a licence is required under a by-law passed under s. 222 may have his lease forfeited if the licence is not obtained.

It is to be noted that shortly before the by-law's enactment the Mayor of Toronto, one of its leading proponents, in a memorandum to the Metropolitan Council expressed his reservations about both the inclusion of "books" and the proposed licensing requirement. With respect to the latter he wrote, with some clairvoyance:

> ... I feel very strongly that the proposed licensing mechanism is not necessary to achieve compliance, and that prosecution of violators of the by-law is a preferable route to take. *The licensing mechanism seems to me to be an over-regulation* which was not contemplated in my original proposal of September 14, 1982. Such a requirement might well result in a challenge to the by-law and frustrate my original intention of requiring *magazines* to be placed 1.5 metres (5 feet) above the floor and behind an opaque barrier. [Emphasis added].

It seems to me also that the licensing scheme is an "over-regulation" and, like the scope of the by-law, goes beyond the bounds required to achieve the objective. I am not persuaded that it can be justified on the basis that it provides "a simpler, more effective and speedier" means of enforcing the regulation than prosecution in the courts. Without questioning the good faith of the appellant, licensing schemes clearly can operate and historically have operated as a form of prior restraint on the free flow of expression. While the scheme here relates to what would seem to be a rather minor display restriction, concern about its potential effect has been voiced in these proceedings by the organized Canadian book publishing and book selling industries. Affidavits objecting to the by-law have been filed not only on behalf of the respondents, Retailers and Publishers, but also on behalf of the Canadian Book Publishers Council, the Book and Periodical Development Council and the Association of Canadian Publishers. They, in short, are apprehensive that, to avoid problems with licensing inspectors, booksellers will tend to assign books with erotic content which may conceivably be covered by the by-law's "unworkable definition" to a "ghetto" or special area in the store; that in the long run the number of such books carried in stock will be reduced; that experimental and non-traditional books will be the most affected; and that editorial selection of material will respond by seeking to ensure that material accepted for publication will be such, or presented as such, that it will not be subject to regulation.

In my opinion, these concerns are not without foundation and represent a risk which ought not to be run. Having regard to the broadly phrased scope of the by-law, the consequences of non-compliance, the perception of at least some booksellers that a "social stigma" attaches to a licence issued pursuant to legislation designed to control "adult entertainment parlours", and the nuisance involved in satisfying the licensing and display requirements, there may be a tendency on the part of some booksellers to comply with the law by not selling books which by any stretch of the interpretive imagination can be said to fall within the ambit of the by-law. The resulting self-censorship would limit or impede the marketing of a protected form of expression and interfere with the public's right of access to non-obscene books with erotic pictorial content. Legal over-kill is ill-suited to the delicate sphere of free expression and, here, is fatal to the by-law.

Returning more specifically to magazines, as I have already indicated, so long as the regulation is sufficiently limited in its reach and sufficiently precise in its terms to enable retailers to know with reasonable certainty what magazines are covered, reasonable regulation as to manner and place of display will not infringe the protected freedom. In the case of this by-law, whether it be seen as overbroad or vague (and an element of vagueness is intrinsic in overbroad legislation) the vice is essentially the same: it lacks a definition proportionate to its aim which would give those governed by it and those who administer it a reasonable opportunity to know what is covered by it, and to act accordingly.

It would appear from the magazines tendered as representative of the type at which the display regulation is directed, that these publications are characterized by content featuring the depiction or portrayal of the nude human body, generally female, in such a pose or posture that the viewers' attention or concentration is focussed on the breasts or genital areas or in which the breasts or genital areas are exposed and provocatively emphasized. If, under s. 222, the Municipality wishes to pass a by-law with respect to magazines "appealing to or designed to appeal to erotic or sexual appetites or inclinations", a form of words can doubtless be devised which will make abundantly clear the distinguishing characteristics of the publications meant to be included in the general words of the Act. . . .

## Note on Hate Propaganda

The Ontario Divisional Court's comments in *Ontario Film & Video Appreciation Society, supra* about the scope of the freedom of expression guarantee in section 2(b) of the *Charter* were approved by the Ontario Court of Appeal in *R. v. Videoflicks Ltd.* (1984), 48 O.R. (2d) 395 where Tarnopolsky J.A. speaking for the Court, said at pp. 430-2:

> [Counsel for Videoflicks Ltd.] contends that s. 2(b) takes into account the type of activity Videoflicks Ltd. is engaged in, namely the providing of video tapes — 99% rental and only about 1% sales — to subscribing members and to the public at large for use in the home on videoplayers. I agree. As the Divisional Court held in *Re Ontario Film & Video Appreciation Society and Ontario Board of Censors* (1983), 41 O.R. (2d) 583 at 590, freedom of expression under the *Charter* must extend to all forms of expression. I would add that this applies to all phases of expression from maker or originator through supplier, distributor, retailer, renter or exhibitor to receiver, whether as a listener or a viewer. This view of the ambit of s. 2(b) of the *Charter* is supported by the more fully defined but comparable art. 19(2) of the *Covenant on Civil and Political Rights*:
>
> Article 19
> (2) Everyone shall have the right to freedom of expression; this right shall include freedom to seek, receive and impart information and ideas of all kinds, regardless of frontiers, either orally, in writing or in print, in the form of art, or through any other media of his choice.
>
> The matter does not end there however. Counsel for the Attorney-General makes clear that the central question is whether the regulation of sales or rentals through prohibitions of such on the holidays named in the *Act* really amounts to a limit on freedom of expression. To answer in the affirmative, she argues, would effectively prohibit the government from adopting any type of regulation in this area since all regulation implies restriction. I agree. Under the *Act*, there is no regulation of content which, in the absence of justification under s. 1 of the *Charter*, would constitute contravention of s. 2 thereof: *Ontario Film & Video Appreciation Society* case, *supra*. Nor is there a restriction on who can produce, distribute, sell or rent video tapes. Similarly, the *Act* does not impose restrictions on who may view or hear them, or where or when. In fact, the tapes may be viewed or listened to even on the holidays named in the *Act*. In short, there is not such a regulation of time as to sales or rentals as to amount to a serious interference with access to these tapes. I would agree with the analogy of the use of videotapes with the watching of television or the seeing and hearing of movies in a cinema. However, television sales and rentals are regulated as to time and cinemas are regulated as to time and place. For a whole number of public policy reasons of health or noise-abatement or hours of rest, entertainment is regulated as to time and place. One may not be able to buy or rent books or records or attend public entertainment at just any time. Mere regulation as to time and place, however, cannot be considered an infringement of freedom of expression, unless there is evidence that such regulation in intent or effect adversely impacts upon content or adversely interferes with production, availability and use or determines who can be involved in these. No such evidence was provided in this case.
>
> If what I have suggested is more applicable to the test of what is a reasonable limit under s. 1 of the *Charter*, rather than to what is the essence of an infringement of s. 2, then I would have no difficulty in concluding that the regulation under the *Act* is so obviously such a reasonable limit that there is no need to require proof thereof by the Attorney-General.
>
> As a result, the appeal of Videoflicks Ltd., based upon the allegation that the *Act* contravenes the freedom of expression under s. 2(b) of the *Charter* is dismissed.

It is interesting to note that Tarnopolsky J.A. found that article 19(2) of the *Covenant on Civil and Political Rights* is "comparable" to section 2(b), albeit "more fully defined". If it is indeed comparable, the scope of section 2(b) is far wider than envisaged by *Re Klein and Law Society of Upper Canada* (1985), 50 O.R. (2d) 118 (Div. Ct.), where the majority of the Divisional Court read an internal limitation into section 2(b) which does not appear anywhere in the text of the provision to exclude "commercial speech" from its ambit. See also *Grier v. Alberta Optometric Association*, [1985] 5 W.W.R. 436 (Alta. Q.B.) to the same effect as *Klein*. In my view, a far preferable approach to that taken in *Klein*, and one which is more consistent with the text of section 2(b), and its interaction with section 1, previous authority in *Ontario Film & Video Appreciation Society* (1984), 45 O.R. (2d) 80n (C.A.) and *Videoflicks* (1984), 48 O.R. (2d) 395 (C.A.), is to give an expansive interpretation to section 2(b) and to leave it to section 1 to set limitations.

The above approach was followed in *Canadian Human Rights Commission v. Taylor and the Western Guard Party* (1984), 6 C.H.R.R. D/2595 (Fed. T.D.). Section 2 of the *Canadian Human Rights Act*, S.C. 1976-77, c. 33 provided that the purpose of the Act was to ensure individuals would not be subjected to or hindered by "discriminatory practices" based upon prohibited grounds of discrimination such as religion. Section 13(1) of the Act made it a discriminatory practice to "communicate telephonically . . . any matter that is likely to expose a person or persons to hatred or contempt" on the basis of prohibited grounds of discrimination. A tribunal was appointed under the Act to investigate complaints that the respondents were sending anti-semitic tape recorded messages over the telephone. After a hearing, the tribunal found that "the messages in question not only expose identified individuals but persons generally to hatred or contempt by reason of the fact that those persons are identifiable as Jews." The tribunal accordingly ordered the respondents to cease the discriminatory practice. The order was filed in Federal Court pursuant to the Act. After numerous repeated violations of the order and various contempt proceedings in Federal Court, the respondents were found in contempt and punishment imposed by Jerome A.C.J. On the issue of constitutionality of the restrictions in the Act on freedom of expression, Jerome A.C.J. said at p. D/2597 (C.H.R.R.) that:

> the test to be applied here is whether the sacrifice of the right is in proportion to the objective of achieving the elimination of the evil under attack from the Canadian way of life.

The "evil" in this case was racial discrimination and Jerome A.C.J. found at p. D/2597 that "freedom of speech must give way to certain restrictions and one of them must be upon the use of it to incite hatred or contempt upon racial grounds". Jerome A.C.J. found at p. D/2598 that:

> It is appropriate that Parliament express the principle that communications which have as their purpose incitement of racial hatred are unacceptable in Canadian society. That is the evil which the relevant sections of the *Canadian Human Rights Act* endeavour to combat and for the reasons given, I am not persuaded that the resulting restriction upon freedom of speech is out of proportion to that objective. There is therefore no basis for finding that these legislative provisions exceed 'reasonable limits . . . demonstrably justified in a free and democratic society'.

The difficulty with *Western Guard* is that there is a dearth of reasoning at critical points. There is no question that the elimination of racial discrimination is a legitimate governmental purpose, as indeed was found by Jerome A.C.J. The real issue is whether the means used and the standards applied are sufficiently sensitive to *Charter* concerns. In the case of the *Canadian Human Rights Act* restrictions at issue in *Western Guard*, it is legitimate to ask whether incitement to hatred which falls short of potential physical danger can be constitutionally proscribed given the freedom of expression guarantee in section 2. Restated, one may ask whether the harm of hatred or contempt short of a threat to order outweighs an individual's expression interest. While one must be cognizant of the admonition in both *Hunter v. Southam*, [1984] 2 S.C.R. 145 and *Reference re Section 94(2) of the Motor Vehicle Act (B.C.)* (unreported, S.C.C., released Dec. 17, 1985), that American jurisprudence cannot be accepted without care, it is nevertheless useful and often highly instructive: see, for example, *Hunter v. Southam, supra; R. v. Big M Drug Mart Ltd.*, [1985] 1 S.C.R. 295; *Singh v. Minister of Employment and Immigration*, [1985] 1 S.C.R. 177; and *Operation Dismantle Inc. v. The Queen*, [1985] 1 S.C.R. 441.

Given the long experience that American courts have had with an entrenched guarantee of free speech and, as well, the common British legal heritage which Canada shares with the United States, American First Amendment jurisprudence should be carefully considered in Canadian cases decided pursuant to section 2(b) of the *Charter*.

A thumbnail sketch of the relevant American law is in order. Cases dealing with the tests for restricting advocacy of lawless action and "fighting words" cases provide the closest analogy to the issues raised in *Western Guard*. In *Schenck v. United States*, 214 U.S. 47 (1919) the conventional wisdom of the day had been that speech was punishable if the natural and reasonable tendency was to bring about a forbidden effect: see Gunther, "Learned Hand and the Origins of Modern First Amendment Doctrine: Some Fragments of History", 27 Stan. L. Rev. 719 at 724 (1975); Tribe, *American Constitutional Law* (1978), pp. 608-17. The government did not argue that the defendant's circulars to draftees about the unconstitutionality of the draft actually interfered with the war effort. The issue was whether the circulars were sufficient evidence of an attempt to interfere. Mr. Justice Holmes stated at p. 52:

> The question in every case is whether the words used are used in circumstances and are of such a nature as to create a clear and present danger that they will bring about the substantive evils that Congress has a right to prevent.

The conviction was upheld on the basis that the jury, having been properly charged, had not acted unreasonably in finding that the circulars could be expected to persuade recipients to refuse induction.

The clear and present danger test was refined in *Brandenburg v. Ohio*, 395 U.S. 444 (1969) where the U.S. Supreme Court reversed the conviction of a Ku Klux Klansman under a state statute which forbade advocating terrorism to achieve political reform. The Court held that mere advocacy was not enough unless it was 1) "directed to inciting or producing imminent lawless action" and 2) "likely to incite or produce such action": see 395 U.S. 444 at 447. The first criterion treats only words of incitement as unprotected, and the second focusses on likely harm. For a general discussion of *Brandenburg* see Comment, "*Brandenburg v. Ohio*: A Speech Test for all Seasons", 43 U. Chi. L. Rev. 151 (1975).

The "fighting words" cases are also relevant to the issues raised by *Western Guard*. The cases arise where offensive speech is spoken before a hostile audience. In *Chaplinsky v. New Hampshire*, 315 U.S. 568 (1942), a Jehovah's Witness was convicted of disorderly conduct for calling a city marshall a "damn fascist" and "God damned racketeer". The U.S. Supreme Court upheld the conviction on the theory that fighting words, which "by their very utterance inflict injury or tend to incite an immediate breach of the peace" (315 U.S. 568 at 572), are unprotected. Recent U.S. Supreme Court decisions indicate that the fighting words exception to the First Amendment is to be narrowly construed. The words must have a direct tendency to cause the person to whom they are addressed to resort to violence. See, for example, *Gooding v. Wilson*, 405 U.S. 518 (1972); *Terminiello v. Chicago*, 337 U.S. 1 (1949); *Cohen v. California*, 403 U.S. 15 (1971). In *Cohen*, the U.S. Supreme Court refused to classify the words "Fuck the Draft" sewn onto the back of a jacket and worn into the Los Angeles County Courthouse as "fighting words". Justice Harlan said that the words were not directed at any particular person, and there was no evidence that "substantial numbers of citizens are standing ready to strike out physically at whoever may assault their sensibilities . . ." Similarly in *Terminiello v. Chicago, supra*, the defendant was convicted for breach of the peace for making a racist speech which caused anger in the crowd. The statute prohibited expression which "stirs the public to anger [or] invites dispute". The U.S. Supreme Court refused to even consider whether the particular speech would have been punishable under a more narrowly drawn statute, and held that the statute in question was overbroad and therefore void on its face. Douglas J. said at 337 U.S. 4:

> [a] function of free speech under our system of government is to invite dispute. It may indeed best serve its high purpose when it induces a condition of unrest, creates dissatisfaction with conditions as they are, or even stirs people to anger.

A particular point is put upon the issues in *Western Guard* when one considers the conflicting results the group defamation cases of *National Socialist Party v. Skokie*, 432 U.S. 43 (1977) and *Beauharnais v. Illinois*, 343 U.S. 350 (1952). In *Beauharnais*, the speaker was convicted pursuant to an Illinois group libel law for making defamatory remarks against blacks. The U.S. Supreme Court upheld the law on the basis that the First Amendment does not prevent the state from punishing group defamatory utterances which are calculated to have a powerful emotional impact. Some 25 years later, in *Skokie*, the Nazis chose Skokie, Illinois as the site for a proposed march. The town was predominantly Jewish, and accordingly the march would attract significant media attention. A state trial court issued an injunction prohibiting the Nazis from "parading the [Nazi] uniform"; "displaying the swastika"; and "distributing pamphlets [that] incite or promote hatred against persons of Jewish faith or ancestry or hatred against any persons of any faith or ancestry, race or religion". The Illinois appellate courts denied stays of the injunction pending appeal. The U.S. Supreme Court reversed and granted the stays. The Supreme Court did not reach the merits but rather rested its decision on the grounds that in the absence of an expedited appeal process, the injunction would deprive the petitioners of possible First Amendments rights for too long a period.

Following this decision, Skokie promulgated three ordinances which would have the combined effect of halting the march. One of these ordinances prohibited the dissemination of materials which intentionally "promotes and incites hatred against persons by reason of their race, national origin or religion". In *Collin v. Smith*, 578 F. 2d 1197 (1978, 7th Circ.), the Seventh Circuit Court of Appeals invalidated the ban on the dissemination of materials promoting and inciting hatred, saying: "It may be questioned, after cases such as *Cohen v. California, Gooding v. Wilson*, and *Brandenburg v. Ohio*, whether the tendency to induce violence approach sanctioned implicitly in [*Beauharnais v. Illinois*] would pass constitutional muster today". Skokie sought a stay of the Court of Appeals ruling pending review, but it was denied by the U.S. Supreme Court in *Smith v. Collin*, 436 U.S. 953. Justice Blackmun, joined by Justice Rehnquist in dissent, would have allowed the stay on the basis that there was "some tension [between the Court of Appeal's ruling and] this Court's decision, 25 years ago, in *Beauharnais*". The two cases therefore stand at odds with one another. While the matter was dropped before the Supreme Court ever reached the merits of the First Amendment issue, the Court's refusal to grant a stay clearly signals a willingness to reconsider the *Beauharnais* decision.

Returning to *Western Guard*, it is clear that a discussion of permissible standards was clearly in order. I would submit that the problem is not one of vagueness, as a proscription against expression which is "likely to expose a person or persons to hatred or contempt" is arguably sufficiently certain, but rather one of balancing the competing interests of society's needs on the one hand and the *Charter's* command in section 2(b) on the other. We need to know the reasons why the state's interest in preventing the dissemination of racial hatred in a situation where there was no evidence of a danger to public order, or even that anyone was in fact incited to hatred outweighs the speaker's expression interest. That is particularly so in *Western Guard* where it appears from the rather brief rendition of the facts that the offending statements were on taped telephone messages, some of which were even found to be "innocuous". It does not appear from the facts as recited by Jerome A.C.J. that the speaker was actively making phone calls. Those who wished to hear the message would telephone a particular number of their own motion and listen to it. In my view, the extent and quality of the government's interest in dictating what sort of taped messages can be piped over telephone wires to interested callers, should have been more fully explored. Far more analysis should have been devoted to an examination of the underpinnings of the section 1 rationalization in *Western Guard*. The issues are more carefully canvassed in the case which follows:

## R. v. KEEGSTRA

In the Alberta Court of Queen's Bench. 19 C.C.C. (3d) 254.

Quigley J. November 5, 1984.

QUIGLEY J. (orally): — The accused, James Keegstra stands charged that he,

between the 1st day of September, A.D. 1978 and the 31st day of December A.D. 1982, inclusive at or near the Town of Eckville in the Province of Alberta, did unlawfully promote hatred against an identifiable group, to wit: the Jewish people, by communicating statements while teaching to students at Eckville High School contrary to the provisions of the Criminal Code.

Counsel for the applicant submits that s. 281.2(2) of the [Criminal] *Code* offends against the fundamental freedoms guaranteed by the Charter, namely, s. 2(*b*) which states:

> 2. Everyone has the following freedoms:
>
> .   .   .   .   .
>
> > (*b*) freedom of thought, belief, opinion and expression, including freedom of the press and other media of communication.

and therefore urges that the *Criminal Code* section is of no force and effect.

Section 281.2(2) of the *Code* is not a proscription against the freedom to publicly criticize any of our nation's fundamental values or institutions. The section deals with a social value, specifically the recognition of the right of a particular group of individuals characterized by colour, race, religion, or ethnic origin to be protected from wilfully promoted hatred at the public level.

[His Lordship's review of a number of American authorities is omitted.]

The elected parliamentary representatives of the Canadian people have already proclaimed the principles from which freedom of speech and freedom of expression derive their meaning and justification. The *Canadian Bill of Rights* contains the following preamble:

> The Parliament of Canada *affirming* that the Canadian Nation is founded upon principles that acknowledge the Supremacy of God, the dignity and worth of the human person and the position of the family in a society of free men and free institutions;
>
> *Affirming* also that men and institutions remain free only when freedom is founded upon respect for moral and spiritual values and the rule of law;
>
> And *being desirous of enshrining these principles and the human rights and fundamental freedoms derived from them* in a Bill of Rights *which shall* reflect the respect of Parliament for its constitutional authority and *which shall ensure the protection of these rights and freedoms in Canada*;
>
> Therefore Her Majesty, by and with the advice and consent of the Senate and House of Commons of Canada, enacts as follows:

(Emphasis mine.)

The preamble to the *Bill of Rights* is a clear proclamation and affirmation by the Canadian people of the source principles upon which our concept of freedom is founded. As a sovereign nation, we have not only declared to ourselves, but to the world as well, the nature and meaning of our concept of freedom. Those beyond our borders who contemplate emigrating to Canada may assess the clear pronouncement citing the freedoms and rights we espouse, reflect upon the principles from which such freedoms and rights are derived and determine the meaning and consequent extent of such freedoms and rights. The nature and extent of these rights and freedoms may attract or repel potential immigrants but at the very least they should prevent anyone from harbouring a misguided belief that the Canadian concept of "freedom and rights" is an absolute one. Whatever meanings these expressions may convey when used in other nations, it is my view that in relation to Canada they are not to be equated to meaning unlimited licence.

We have declared as a nation that our human rights and fundamental freedoms are derived from:

(1)  An acknowledgment of the Supremacy of God.

(2)  An acknowledgment of the dignity and worth of the human person.

(3) An acknowledgment of a respect for moral and spiritual values.

(4) An acknowledgment of the rule of law.

By s. 1 of the *Bill of Rights* we have made a further declaration concerning the historical, present and future existence of our fundamental rights and freedoms. It provides:

> 1. It is hereby *recognized and declared* that in Canada *there have existed* and *shall continue to exist* without discrimination by reason of race, national origin, colour, religion or sex the following human rights and fundamental freedoms . . .

(Emphasis mine.)

We compel no one to profess or accept that God is Supreme, nor to believe that He exists. There is no requirement to accept our assertion that moral and spiritual values exist, nor even to accept that if such do exist they are conducive to promoting the common good. The same freedom remains in regard to upholding or rejecting the affirmation concerning the dignity and worth of the human person. One need not champion the rule of law. One is free to express criticisms of all these principles. Indeed, it is conceivable that there are those who do not accept any of these declared principles yet are anxious to avail themselves of the protection afforded by the rights and freedoms generated by these principles. As a nation, we have said that our concept of freedom flows from these principles, and while one may choose not to accept or espouse them, he or she must abide by the rule of law that reflects them.

In my view, for the purpose of interpreting and comprehending the meaning of the word "freedom" as used in the phrase "freedom of speech" (s. 1(*d*) of the *Bill of Rights* and "freedom of expression" (s. 2(*b*) of the *Canadian Charter of Rights and Freedoms*) the proclaimed principles from which these freedoms are derived cannot be ignored or laid aside. I do not perceive the preamble to the *Bill of Rights* nor the declaration in s. 1 of that statute as being mere hollow pious platitudes. They are clear and strong affirmations of historical and continuing beliefs enunciated by Parliament on behalf of the Canadian people.

Having regard to those principles that we as a nation recognize and affirm, does the Canadian concept of freedom of expression include in it the freedom to wilfully and publicly promote hatred against a section of the populace distinguished by colour, race, religion or ethnic origin? To determine the answer to this question one must examine whether or not the principles to which we have referred rationally support such an interpretation.

Is it in accord with the acknowledgment of the Supremacy of God that freedom of expression derived from such an acknowledgment should include the freedom to publicly and wilfully promote hatred against a section of the Canadian public distinguished by colour, race, religion or ethnic origin?

Is it in accord with the acknowledgment of the dignity and worth of the human person that freedom of expression derived from such an acknowledgment should include the freedom to publicly and wilfully promote hatred against a section of the Canadian public distinguished by colour, race, religion or ethnic origin?

Is it in accord with the acknowledgment that freedom is founded upon respect for moral and spiritual values that freedom of expression derived from such an acknowledgment should include the freedom to publicly and wilfully promote hatred against a section of the Canadian public distinguished by colour, race, religion or ethnic origin?

Is it in accord with the acknowledgment that freedom is founded upon respect for the rule of law that freedom of expression derived from such an acknowledgment should include the freedom to publicly and wilfully promote hatred against a section of the Canadian public distinguished by colour, race, religion or ethnic origin?

While the questions are posed separately, the principles referred to in each, are not contradictory of one another. The acknowledgment of the Supremacy of God, the dignity and worth of the human person, and respect for moral and spiritual values and the rule of law, having regard to the context in which they are found, are principles which must be regarded as being harmoniously interwoven for the single purpose of giving a particular and efficacious meaning to the words "rights" and "freedoms" as used in the *Bill of Rights* and the Charter.

I am satisfied that there is clear and compelling evidence that we do not only honour these principles in the abstract. It is to be found in the Charter itself. Section 15(1) of the Charter provides:

> 15(1) Every individual is equal before and under the law and has the right to the equal protection and equal benefit of the law without discrimination and, in particular, without discrimination based on race, national or ethnic origin, colour, religion, sex, age or mental or physical disability.

While this section does not come into force until April 17, 1985, it is part of the law of Canada and of the Charter itself.

Section 15 of the Charter guarantees a right which rationally flows from our affirmation that men remain free only when freedom is founded upon respect for moral and spiritual values. We have recognized that Canadians have a moral sense, that is a sense of what is good and what is evil. Section 15 also manifests in the concrete as opposed to the abstract, our affirmation that each human person has dignity and worth.

Finally reference should also be made to s. 27 of the Charter which provides:

> 27. This Charter shall be interpreted in a manner consistent with the preservation and enhancement of the multicultural heritage of Canadians.

This section compels an interpreter of the Charter to do so in a particular way. Is it in accord with a requirement to interpret the Charter in a manner consistent with the preservation and enhancement of the multicultural heritage of Canadians to interpret the phrase "freedom of expression" as including the freedom to publicly and wilfully promote hatred against a section of the Canadian public distinguished by colour, race, religion or ethnic origin? In my view, the only rational answer is "No".

In my view, the wilful promotion of hatred under circumstances which fall within s. 281.2(2) of the *Criminal Code* of Canada clearly contradicts the principles which recognize the dignity and worth of the members of identifiable groups, singly and collectively; it contradicts the recognition of moral and spiritual values which impels us to assert and protect the dignity of each member of society; and it negates or limits the rights and freedoms of such target groups; and in particular denies them the right to the equal protection and benefit of the law without discrimination.

Under these circumstances, it is my opinion that s. 281.2(2) of the *Code* cannot rationally be considered to be an infringement which limits "freedom of expression", but on the contrary it is a safeguard which promotes it. The protection afforded by the proscription tends to banish the apprehension which might otherwise inhibit certain segments of our society from freely expressing themselves upon the whole spectrum of topics, whether social, economic, scientific, political, religious, or spiritual in nature. The unfettered right to express divergent opinions on these topics is the kind of freedom of expression the Charter protects.

In my opinion, the words "freedom of expression" as used in s. 2(*b*) of the Charter does not mean an absolute freedom permitting an unbridged right of speech or expression. In particular, I hold that s. 281.2(2) of the *Criminal Code* does not infringe upon the freedom of expression granted by s. 2(*b*) of the Charter.

This does not end the matter, for if I have erred in my view and *prima facie* s. 281.2(2) does infringe the guaranteed fundamental right of freedom, it is appropriate to determine in that circumstance, whether the denial or limit is a reasonable one demonstrably justified in a free and democratic society.

Section 1 of the Charter provides as follows:

> 1. The *Canadian Charter of Rights and Freedoms* guarantees the rights and freedoms set out in it subject only to such reasonable limits prescribed by law as can be demonstrably justified in a free and democratic society.

The burden of proof lies with the party claiming the benefit of s. 1 of the Charter. . . .

It seems clear that a cautious approach should be used to determine whether legislation limiting a fundamental freedom is reasonable as can be demonstrably justified in a free and democratic society. The factors to be considered are:

(a) Rationality
(b) Proportionality
(c) Comparison

(A) *Rationality*

The object of the legislation is obviously to control hatemongers from spreading their hatred to others and to give some protection to the target groups that the law heretofore did not protect. In effect it is a law to control those who publicly defame groups as opposed to an individual. There have always been laws to protect the individual from defamatory libel, blasphemous libel and seditious libel whereas groups distinguished by race or a religion had no protection. The object of this law is to give "the group" the same protection as the individual in view of the harm that such hatemongering is capable of causing. The purpose of the legislation is to protect the rights of members of the defamed group from the promotion of hatred against them.

The *Special Committee on Hate Propaganda in Canada* addressed itself to determining how extensive the hate propaganda problem was in Canada. They found clear evidence of the existence of individuals and groups of individuals who were actively involved in communicating hate propaganda, both from within and without our borders.

The committee found that not only were their activities and materials deeply offensive to many Canadians, whether targets of the material or not, but that it would be a mistake to ignore the potential of prejudice developed by these groups and their continuing hate activities.

In its report to the Minister of Justice, the committee then said at p. 24:

> The Committee firmly believes that Canadians who are members of any identifiable group in Canada are entitled to carry on their lives as Canadians without being victimized by the deliberate vicious promotion of hatred against them. In a democratic society freedom of speech does not mean the right to vilify. The number of organizations involved and the number of persons hurt is no test of the issue; the arithmetic of a free society will not be satisfied with over simplified statistics demonstrating that few are casting stones and not many are receiving hurts. What matters is that incipient malevolence and violence, all of which are inherent in "hate" activity deserves national attention. However small the actors may be in number the individuals promoting hate in Canada constitute a "clear and present danger" to the functioning of a democratic society. For in times of social stress such "hate" could mushroom into a real and monstrous threat to our way of life. . . .
>
> In the Committee's view the "hate" situation in Canada, although not alarming, clearly is serious enough to require action. It is far better for Canadians to come to grips with this problem now before it attains unmanageable proportions rather than deal with it at some future date in an atmosphere of urgency, of fear, and perhaps even of crisis. The Canadian community has a duty not merely the right to protect itself from the corrosive effects of propaganda that tends to under-mine the confidence that various groups in a multicultural society must have in each other. The Committee therefore concludes that action by Government is necessary . . .

The hurt or harm that is caused by the evil and is in need of protection must also be examined as part of the rationality for the legislation.

The purpose of criminal law is not only to establish sanctions against criminal behaviour but is also to create a public conscience or a minimum standard for expected behaviour in Canadian society. This legislation manifests such a purpose and has as its objective the protection of certain segments of society from the wilful promotion of hatred and the injurious consequences thereof.

The actual hurt or harm that flows from the danger of hatemongering, is sustained by two groups.

1. Those to whom the hate propaganda is communicated.
2. Those who, as an identifiable group, constitute the target of the promoter of hatred.

The effect of hatred on prospective converts can be serious. These effects have been documented throughout history and are self-evident. It does not take an expert in the field of psychology to inform the court that hate breeds hate. One has only to look at the major conflicts throughout history and the major racial uprisings and riots that have occurred. In my view, it is beyond doubt that breeding hate is detrimental to society for psychological and social reasons and that it can easily create hostility and aggression which leads to violence. Hatred is the antithesis of love. While the latter promotes goodwill and unity the former is divisive and calculated to injure and ultimately destroy those against whom it is directed. The inherent danger of an aggressive response by target groups is self-evident with history supplying us with many illustrations. Avoidance of the issue or acceptance of the prejudice can have cruel economic, social and psychological consequences. Such degradation and demoralization should not have to be accepted by any minority group in Canadian society. In my view, such kind of expression must be modified and any bias in favour of maximum rhetoric must give way in view of the serious injury to the community itself and to individual members of identifiable groups innocently caught by such prejudice.

As Professor Graham Hughes, Professor of Law, New York University said in an article in 16 U.T. Law Jo. (1966), entitled "Prohibiting Incitement to Racial Discrimination" at p. 364:

> There is something too enticingly simple about the view that free speech is an "absolute" value, an invasion of which is insupportable. Those who seem inclined to dispute never offer convincing reasons why keeping one's mouth shut under pain of punishment should also be considered a greater evil than any mischief which may result from publishing the words in question.

It is commonplace that the demeaning self-image ultimately accepted by some members of such target groups as a result of such propaganda often strips them of any real sense of personal dignity and self-worth.

Reference is again made to what I have already said in relation to the principles espoused by us as a nation. Hate propaganda is an attempt to achieve the antithesis of those principles. In my view, the Canadian Charter does not guarantee anyone the right to promote the degradation of others because of their race, religion or ethnic origin.

### (B) *Proportionality*

The second factor the court must look at to determine the reasonableness of the limit is proportionality or how wide is the limit on the right in proportion to the full extent of the right itself. In other words, is it an extensive limitation that takes away a substantial proportion of the right? An example of where the proportionality of the limitation on the Charter right was too wide was Bill 101 of the Quebec statutes in relation to s. 23 of the Charter since the limitation was almost a complete denial of the right: see *A.-G. Que. v. Quebec Ass'n of Protestant School Boards*, Supreme Court of Canada, July 26, 1984 [since reported 10 D.L.R. (4th) 321, [1984] 2 S.C.R. 66, 54 N.R. 196].

The limitation imposed by s. 281.2(2) of the *Code* has a very minimal effect on the over-all right of freedom of expression. It limits only those expressions in the form of communicated statements that promote hatred against identifiable groups. There are built in defences and restrictions on the application of the law and to the successful prosecution thereof. These restrictions and defences are as follows:

1. The expression must be made in a public place. The limitation does not apply to private conversation.
2. Identifiable group is defined and restricted to a section of the public distinguished by colour, race, religion or ethnic origin (s. 281.1(4) of the *Criminal Code*).
3. The promotion of hatred must be "wilful".
4. Truth of the statements. If the defence establishes that the statements were true, this is an absolute statutory defence (s. 281.2(3)(*a*)).
5. *Bona fide* opinions on a religious subject (s. 281.2(3)(*b*)).

6. Statements made for the public benefit. If the expressions are made for the public benefit they could not be successfully prosecuted if the statements are made in the reasonable belief of their veracity (s. 281.2(3)(*c*)).
7. *Bona fide* pointing out for the purpose of removal matters tending to produce ill will towards an identifiable group. This defence would remove statements which reproduce hate literature but only for the purpose of inquiring as to how best to deal with it as a problem (s. 281.2(3)(*d*)).
8. The necessity of the consent of the Attorney-General pursuant to s. 281.2(6)).

In addition in determining the extent of the limitation balanced against the rationality of the legislation as set out above, the court should attempt to balance the limitation of the right with the evil or harm done to others. In my view, if there is a restriction it is exceedingly slight when compared to the over-all right of freedom of expression and particularly when set against the evil or harm that results from hatemongering. In this situation the individual's freedom of expression must give way to the broader interests of social cohesion and the common good.

[His Lordship's comparison with similar legislation elsewhere is omitted.]

The factors of rationality, proportionality and comparison need not be weighed separately nor need such factor contribute an equal measure of support to the determination of whether a limit prescribed by law is reasonable and can be demonstrably justified in a free and democratic society. Indeed, I am satisfied there will be circumstances in which the onus to establish such requirements will be amply discharged without the need of looking at legislation or case-law beyond our own borders.

In the present case, reference to the preamble to the *Bill of Rights* and ss. 15 and 27 of the Charter itself, precludes the necessity for any extensive review of legislation or policy commitments in foreign jurisdictions.

The Crown has persuaded me that there is a compelling, rational and objective basis for whatever limitation there is in s. 281.2(2) of the *Code* to the freedom of expression guaranteed by the Charter. I am satisfied that such limitation would be regarded as being within the bounds of reason by fair-minded people accustomed to the norms of a free and democratic society. I therefore hold that the limitation, if there is one, is reasonable, is prescribed by law and is demonstrably justified in a free and democratic society and in particular in our own Canadian society.

· · · ·

*Ruling accordingly.*

### Note on Contempt of Court

In Britain and Canada, the law respecting contempt of court has generally favoured the administration of justice over press freedom. Accordingly, contempt law has imposed prior restraints over the publication of any judicial information in order to ensure a fair trial: McRuer, "Criminal Contempt of Court Procedure: Protection of the Rights of the Individual" (1952) 30 Can. Bar Rev. 225 at 226; Miller, *Contempt of Court* (1976); Borrie and Love, *The Law of Contempt* (1973); Watkins,

"The Enforcement of Conformity to Law through Contempt Proceedings" (1967) Osgoode Hall L.J. 125. An article or statement which may be prejudicial to the merits of a case constitutes contempt — *A. G. v. Times Newspapers*, [1974] A.C. 273 (H.L.) — although the current status of this principle is somewhat in doubt given the subsequent disposition of this case by the European Court on Human Rights: see *Sunday Times Case*, European Court of Human Rights (1979), where the Court held that merely discussing pending litigation in a moderate manner is not contempt.

The second type of contempt is that of "scandalizing the court" by directing insulting or slanderous remarks at a judge in his official capacity, or impugning his impartiality. However, reasonable criticism is not contempt. In Canada, see *Hebert v. A.G. Que.*, [1967] 2 C.C.C. 111 (Que.S.C.), and in the United Kingdom, see *R. v. Metropolitan Police Commissioners; Ex parte Blackburn (No. 2)*, [1968] 2 Q.B. 150 at 155 (C.A.). By contrast, the Americans take the position that prior restraints are impermissible even in trial situations, and have favoured freedom of the press: *Nebraska Press Association v. Stuart*, 427 U.S. 539 (1976) (adopting a clear and present danger test). Outside the courtroom, the judiciary are no more immune to criticism than anyone else: *Pennekamp v. Florida*, 328 U.S. 331 (1946).

With regard to "scandalizing the court", it is open to question whether the courts need as much protection as they are given in Canada. I would suggest that, even if we do not move all the way to the American position, we should at least move to a halfway house where the state must establish that the impugned remarks do positive harm to the administration of justice. Mere insult to a judge in his official capacity, no matter how offended that judge or even the judges as a collectivity may be, and no matter how serious the insult, should not be enough. In my view, the demonstrable justification element in section 1 of the *Charter* requires the state to lead evidence showing that positive, concrete harm to the administration of justice will result from the impugned expression. A mere recital that such expression may tend in an abstract way to bring the administration of justice into disrepute should be insufficent to sustain a contempt conviction for "scandalizing the court".

### (c) Obscenity

# R. v. RED HOT VIDEO LTD.

In the British Columbia Court of Appeal. 45 C.R. (3d) 36.

Nemetz C.J.B.C., Hinkson and Anderson JJ.A.. March 18, 1985.

The judgment of Nemetz C.J.B.C. and Hinkson J.A. was delivered by

NEMETZ C.J.B.C. — After a trial before Collins Prov. J. in the Provincial Court at Victoria, Red Hot Video Limited (the appellant) was convicted of three counts of possession for the purpose of distribution of three obscene videotapes, "Bad Girls", "The Filthy Rich", and "Candy Stripers" [[1983] B.C.W.L.D. 1626]. The convictions were appealed to Melvin Co. Ct. J. of the County Court of Vancouver Island, who on 6th March 1984 dismissed the appeal and affirmed the convictions [38 C.R. (3d) 275]. The appellant now seeks leave to appeal to this court.

The Criminal Code provides in part:

> 159. (1) Every one commits an offence who
> (*a*) makes, prints, publishes, distributes, circulates, or has in his possession for the purpose of publication, distribution or circulation any obscene written matter, picture, model, phonograph record or other thing whatsoever, or
> (*b*) makes, prints, publishes, distributes, sells or has in his possession for the purpose of publication, distribution or circulation, a crime comic
>
> . . .
>
> (8) For the purposes of this Act, any publication a dominant characteristic of which is the undue exploitation of sex, or of sex and any one or more of the following subjects, namely, crime, horror, cruelty and violence, shall be deemed to be obscene.

Counsel for the appellant concedes that Parliament is entitled to legislate against obscenity or pornography. He further concedes that all three films are obscene. He acknowledges that "Bad Girls" and "The Filthy Rich" are concerned solely with sex and violence, and that "Candy Stripers" is concerned solely with sex sans violence.

However, it is submitted that:

1. Section 159 is so "vague and overbroad" that it violates the principles of fundamental justice guaranteed by s. 7 of the Canadian Charter of Rights and Freedoms, i.e., that "Everyone has the right to life, liberty and security of the person and the right not to be deprived thereof except in accordance with the principles of fundamental justice."

2. Section 159 is not a "reasonable limit" upon freedom of expression within the meaning of s. 1 and s. 2(*b*):

> 1. The *Canadian Charter of Rights and Freedoms* guarantees the rights and freedoms set out in it subject only to such reasonable limits prescribed by law as can be demonstrably justified in a free and democratic society.
> 2. Everyone has the following fundamental freedoms: . . .
> (*b*) freedom of thought, belief, opinion and expression, including freedom of the press and other media of communication.

By way of preface, it is to be noted that historically Canadian courts have been disinclined to act as censors of depictions or writings which allegedly are obscene. To the contrary, it is only if it is shown that such writings or depictions are clearly obscene that the courts will act: *R. v. Dom. News & Gifts (1962) Ltd.*, 40 C.R. 109, reversed [1964] S.C.R. 251 (accepting the dissent of Freedman J.A. in its entirety). Eroticism contained in a written or visual artistic matrix is one thing, obscenity is another.

Here, we are not faced with having to determine whether the films before us are obscene. They are conceded to be obscene. For centuries democratic societies have set certain limits to freedom of expression. Libel and slander are two such limitations. Obscenity is also a limitation. As Dickson J.A. (now C.J.C.) said in *R. v. Great West News Ltd.*, [1970] 4 C.C.C. 307 at 309 (Man. C.A.):

> . . . all organized societies have sought in one manner or another to suppress obscenity. The right of the state to legislate to protect its moral fibre and well-being has long been recognized, with roots deep in history. It is within this frame that the courts and judges must work.

Again, in *R. v. Prairie Schooner News Ltd.* (1970), 75 W.W.R. 585 (Man. C.A.), the learned Chief Justice considered the scope of free speech under the old Canadian Bill of Rights and said this in part:

> Freedom of speech is not unfettered either in criminal law or civil law. The *Canadian Bill of Rights* was intended to protect, and does protect, basic freedoms of vital importance to all Canadians. It does not serve as a shield behind which obscene matter may be disseminated without concern for criminal consequences. *The interdiction of the publications which are the subject of the present charges in no way trenches upon the freedom of expression which the Canadian Bill of Rights assures.* [The italics are mine.]

It is my view that these words apply equally to the new Charter of Rights and Freedoms, s. 2(*b*) and s. 7. If we look at American decisions one must take care to consider the basic difference between their Bill of Rights and our Charter. Section 1 of the Canadian Charter provides that the rights and freedoms set out in the Charter are guaranteed "subject only to such reasonable limits prescribed by law as can be demonstrably justified in a free and democratic society". The American Bill of Rights does not have such a limitation. This Canadian proviso is of paramount importance when one examines American case law for assistance in interpreting our Charter. Even with the lack of such limitation, the Supreme Court of the United States, in considering their First Amendment, has held that "obscenity is not within the area of protected speech or press": *Ginsberg v. New York*, 390 U.S. 629 at 635 (1968, U.S.S.C.), rehearing denied 391 U.S. 971 (1968), per Brennan J. Also see *New York v. Ferber*, 484 U.S. 747 (1982), where White J. adopted this tenet from *Chaplinsky v. New Hampshire*, 315 U.S. 568 at 571-72 (1942):

> There are certain well-defined and narrowly limited classes of speech, the prevention and punishment of which have never been thought to raise any Constitutional problem. These include the lewd and obscene . . . It has been well observed that such utterances are no essential part of any exposition of ideas, and are of such slight social value as a step to truth that any benefit that may be derived from them is clearly outweighed by the social interest and morality . . .

Accordingly, the first question is whether the definition of obscenity contained in s. 159(8) is so "vague and overbroad" that persons of ordinary intelligence are unable to ascertain its meaning and thus have their rights under s. 7 of the Charter negated.

I agree with counsel for the appellant that the laws must not be vague. In particular, a criminal statute must delineate with certitude an understandable and ascertainable standard. I turn, therefore, as a guide for the citizen, to examine s. 159. Subsection (8) was first enacted in 1959 [by S.C. 1959, c. 41, s. 11]. It was considered by the Supreme Court of Canada in *Brodie v. R.; Dansky v. R.; Rubin v. R.*, [1962] S.C.R. 681. Speaking of s. 159(8) [then s. 150(8) of the Criminal Code, S.C. 1953-54, c. 51], Judson J., speaking for himself and Cartwright, Abbott and Martland JJ., said [at p. 702]:

> . . . I think that the new statutory definition does give the Court an opportunity to apply tests which have some certainty of meaning and are capable of objective application and which do not so much depend *as before* upon the idiosyncracies and sensitivities of the tribunal of fact, whether judge or jury. [The italics are mine.]

Of course, "as before" referred to the old *Hicklin* test (*R. v. Hicklin* (1868), L.R. 3 Q.B. 360), which the learned justice considered "vague, difficult and unsatisfactory to apply" [p. 702]. This statement of Judson J. was referred to with approval 16 years later by Laskin C.J.C. and Spence and Dickson JJ. in *Dechow v. R.*, [1978] 1 S.C.R. 951.

Mr. Henderson, for the appellant, submits that the vagueness in s. 159 lies in the use of the "community standard" test to determine what is obscene under s. 159(8). That proviso states that a publication is obscene if a dominant characteristic of it is the "undue exploitation" of sex or sex with other elements stated therein such as violence. The Supreme Court of Canada has held that there is undue exploitation when the accepted standards of tolerance in the contemporary Canadian community have been exceeded: *Brodie v. R.*, supra. First it is argued that the community tolerance standard is such a difficult and elusive concept that it leaves citizens unable to predict with any certainty whether they are partaking in proscribed activity.

I cannot accept this submission. The fact of the matter is that in all the cases cited to us by both counsel the courts found no difficulty in applying the community standards rule. As was pointed out by Dickson J.A. in *R. v. Great West News Ltd.*, supra, at p. 315:

> If any inference can be drawn from *Brodie* it is that the Judge must, in the final analysis, endeavour to apply what he, in the light of his experience, regards as contemporary standards of the Canadian community. In so doing he must be at pains to avoid having his decision simply reflect or project his own notions of what is tolerable.

What, then, are the standards to be considered? These standards were eloquently articulated by Freedman J.A. (as he then was) in *Dom. News*, supra, and I quote him in part [p. 116]:

> Those standards are not set by those of lowest taste or interest. Nor are they set exclusively by those of rigid, austere, conservative, or puritan taste and habit of mind. Something approaching a general average of community thinking and feeling has to be discovered.

He went on to state that the standards must be of the Canadian contemporary community, since the mores of society change.

Having these tenets in mind, what can be said of the films under consideration? Of "Bad Girls" there is nothing that can be said to have it escape the sanction set out in the understandable and certain language of s. 159(8), which states that any publication a dominant characteristic of which is the undue exploitation of sex *or of sex and* any one or more of the following subjects, namely, crime, horror, *cruelty and violence*, shall be deemed to be obscene. A reading of Collins Prov. J.'s description leaves me in no doubt whatsoever that "Bad Girls" is wholly destitute of a literary plot, but consists in not only repetitive depictions of a sexual orgy including cunnilingus, fellatio and buggery, but also a belt beating of a naked woman. It portrays dehumanizing and degrading sexual behaviour accompanied with violence, behaviour unacceptable by any Canadian community standard.

As for "Filthy Rich", the film falls into the same category as "Bad Girls", since the scenes depicted include violence (rape), and cunnilingus, fellatio, buggery and group sex. I see very little difference in "Candy Stripers". While the sexual behaviour may not be as overtly violent as in the other two films, we have here a visual depiction of the undue exploitation of sex together with cruelty.

As Shannon J. noted in *R. v. Wagner* (1985), 43 C.R. (3d) 318 (Alta. Q.B.), such unduly exploitative films, even if devoid of acts of violence, degrade men and women by portraying them as having animal characteristics. "Women, particularly, are deprived of unique human character or identity and are depicted as sexual playthings, hysterically and instantly responsive to male sexual demands." I agree and add that this type of degrading vilification of women is unacceptable by any reasonable Canadian community standard.

Accordingly, it is my opinion that s. 159 and the use of the community standard test in its interpretation is not so "vague and overbroad" as to impinge on the right set out in s. 7 of the Charter.

If s. 159 is a limitation upon the rights set out in s. 7 and s. 2, is it a reasonable limitation that can be demonstrably justified in a free and democratic society? In my opinion it is. Judges are not so insulated from observing community standards that they have failed to notice the growing concern expressed by the Canadian community at large that the undue sexual exploitation of women and children depicted in certain publications and films can, in certain circumstances, lead to abject and servile victimization. To protect these classes of our society, Parliament has enacted s. 159, a precise and understandable standard for the guidance of those who would contravene contemporary Canadian community standards.

Melvin Co. Ct. J. was right in upholding the decision of the learned trial judge. I would dismiss this appeal.

ANDERSON J.A.: — After a trial before Collins Prov. J. the appellant was convicted pursuant to s. 159(1)(*a*) of the Code of three counts of possession of obscene videotapes for the purpose of distribution [[1983] B.C.W.L.D. 1626]. An appeal was taken to Melvin Co. Ct. J., who affirmed the convictions [38 C.R. (3d) 275], and the appellant now seeks leave to appeal from the judgment of Melvin Co. Ct. J.

The videotapes in question were described by the learned trial judge as follows:

> I viewed the three videotapes in court. "Bad Girls" contains scenes showing close-up and explicit views of female and male genitalia, erection, cunnilingus, sexual intercourse, fellatio and buggery. There are scenes of women masturbating, of a man ejaculating in the face of a woman, of lesbian love-making, again showing close-up and explicit views of female genitalia. A naked woman in chains is ordered to urinate on a man. Women are made to watch acts of fellatio and ejaculation on the naked body of a woman. An act of cunnilingus is performed on a woman while she is bound. A naked woman, while in chains, is beaten with a belt and asked if she wants the assailant's penis. When she agrees, she is required to commit fellatio while other persons watch. This conduct arouses the others and soon there is a sex orgy with lesbian love-making, cunnilingus, fellatio, sexual intercourse and ejaculation. The film from beginning to end portrays prolonged and close-up scenes of sexual activity in the most explicit manner. Nothing is left to one's imagination and the sexual activity is not simulated.
>
> "The Filthy Rich" opens with scenes of cunnilingus by two couples. Then both couples engage in sexual intercourse. In each case there are prolonged and vivid close-up views of male and female genitalia. The film, like "Bad Girls", continues with almost unending scenes of cunnilingus, both male and female masturbation, sexual intercourse in various positions, male ejaculation, fellatio, fellatio and cunnilingus together, erections, rape, buggery and group sex. As in "Bad Girls", the sex acts are not simulated.
>
> "Candy Stripers" opens with a vivid and explicit scene of sexual intercourse, culminating in the man ejaculating in the woman's face. Thereafter the film for the most part has an almost continuous string of scenes depicting explicit acts of lesbianism, with women performing what might

best be described as "female cunnilingus" on one another and inserting fingers in one another's anus. In all cases there are prolonged close-up views of female genitalia. In several scenes a woman is shown masturbating with a banana. In other scenes a man places a finger in a woman's vagina, then two fingers, then three fingers and eventually his whole hand up to his wrist. When he withdraws his hand a woman takes over and eventually places both of her hands in the vagina of the same woman. These scenes are prolonged and extremely explicit. There are scenes showing acts of cunnilingus, sexual intercourse, buggery, ejaculation in the face of women, and fellatio. Towards the end of the film a party deteriorates into what can best be described as a sex orgy. As in the other films, the acts I have described are not simulated.

It is conceded by counsel for the appellant that all three videotapes are "obscene". It is agreed that "Bad Girls" and "Filthy Rich" are concerned solely with sex and elements of violence. It is also agreed that "Candy Stripers" is concerned solely with sex not involving violence. The grounds upon which the application for leave to appeal is founded are:

(1) that s. 159(8) of the Criminal Code is so vague, uncertain, overbroad and incapable of definition that it violates the principles of fundamental justice guaranteed by s. 7 of the Charter; and

(2) that s. 159(8) of the Criminal Code is not a "reasonable limit" upon freedom of expression within the meaning of ss. 1 and 2(b) of the Charter.

Section 159(8) of the Criminal Code reads as follows:

(8) For the purposes of this Act, any publication a dominant characteristic of which is the undue exploitation of sex, or of sex and any one or more of the following subjects, namely, crime, horror, cruelty and violence, shall be deemed to be obscene.

The relevant sections of the Charter are:

1. The Canadian Charter of Rights and Freedoms guarantees the rights and freedoms set out in it subject only to such reasonable limits prescribed by law as can be demonstrably justified in a free and democratic society.

2. Everyone has the following fundamental freedoms: . . .

(b) freedom of thought, belief, opinion and expression, including freedom of the press and other media of communication . . .

7. Everyone has the right to life, liberty and security of the person and the right not to be deprived thereof except in accordance with the principles of fundamental justice.

In his factum, counsel for the Crown makes the following concession:

The respondent agrees that:

"It is accepted that law cannot be vague, undefined, and totally discretionary; it must be ascertainable and understandable. Any limits placed on the freedom of expression cannot be left to the whim of an official; such limits must be articulated with some precision or they cannot be considered to be law."

Re Ontario Film & Video Appreciation Society and Ontario Board of Censors, supra 41 O.R. (2d) at p. 592.

In view of the concession made by counsel for the Crown, the major issue in this appeal is whether or not s. 159(8) of the Criminal Code is so vague "that men of common intelligence must necessarily guess at its meaning and differ as to its application": see *Hamilton Independent Variety & Confectionery Stores Inc. v. Hamilton* (1983), 20 M.P.L.R. 241 (Ont. C.A.).

The argument of counsel for the appellant with respect to this issue may be summarized as follows:

(a) The courts have encountered great difficulty in defining national standards of "undueness".

(b) Section 159(8) of the Code does not describe the sexual acts the depiction of which constitutes an offence.

(c) Section 159(8) does not contain any definition of the words "exploitation", "undueness" or "sex".

(d) While the courts have held that "undueness"is to be determined by national community standards, such standards do not enable a citizen to ascertain what may or may not be depicted.

(e) National community standards are virtually impossible to ascertain or define.

(f) Community standards vary from time to time.

(g) It is much more difficult to ascertain the national level of tolerance than the national level of approval.

(h) The expert evidence adduced in this case shows that there can be no true national standard.

(i) There is no mechanism by which a citizen can obtain "prior approval" of material which he desires to publish.

(j) The decision as to whether or not to prosecute depends on the arbitrary determination by police and prosecutors that published material does or does not offend against national community standards.

The argument of counsel for the appellant has considerable merit but must, in my opinion, fail for the following reasons:

(1) The fact that the terms of a statute are not capable of precise definition is not in itself a reason for holding that the statute does not disclose an offence known to the law.

(2) The standards fixed by the courts are not so lacking in precision as not to enable a citizen "to foresee, to a degree that is reasonable in the circumstances, the consequences which a given action may entail".

(3) The standards fixed by the courts are rendered more precise by the constitutional limitations on Parliament set out in s. 2 of the Charter of Rights because all limitations on freedom of expression must, in accordance with s. 1 of the Charter, be "reasonable" and "demonstrably justified in a free and democratic society".

As to the first issue, the judgment of the European Court of Human Rights in *Sunday Times v. U.K.* (1979), 2 E.H.H.R. 245 at 271, is directly on point:

49. In the Court's opinion, the following are two of the requirements that flow from the expression "prescribed by law". First, the law must be adequately accessible: the citizen must be able to have an indication that is adequate in the circumstances of the legal rules applicable to a given case. *Secondly, a norm cannot be regarded as a "law" unless it is formulated with sufficient precision to enable the citizen to regulate his conduct: he must be able — if need be with appropriate advice — to foresee, to a degree that is reasonable in the circumstances, the consequences which a given action may entail. Those consequences need not be foreseeable with absolute certainty: experience shows this to be unattainable. Again, whilst certainty is highly desirable, it may bring in its*

*train excessive rigidity and the law must be able to keep pace with changing circumstances. Accordingly, many laws are inevitably couched in terms which, to a greater or lesser extent, are vague and whose interpretation and application are questions of practice.* [The italics are mine.]

See also the judgment of Zuber J.A. in *Popert v. R.* (1981), 19 C.R. (3d) 393 (Ont. C.A.), as follows:

I concede that the term "immoral" is a word of imprecise meaning and that it may be difficult to apply. However, the problem is not unique. Often the law, whether a product of case law or statute, expresses itself in imprecise terms such as "reasonable", "undue", and "dangerous". It is through such words that the values of the community find expression in the court-room. It is the function of the Courts to work as best as they can with the tools in hand.

Regard should also be had to the judgment of Judson J. in *Brodie v. R.; Dansky v. R.; Rubin v. R.,* [1962] S.C.R. 681 at 702:

In contrast, I think that the new statutory definition does give the court an opportunity to apply tests which have some certainty of meaning and are capable of objective application and which do not so much depend as before upon the idiosyncracies and sensitivities of the tribunal of fact, whether judge or jury. We are now concerned with a Canadian statute which is exclusive of all others.

Counsel for the appellant submits that the issue here has been determined in his favour in the United States Supreme Court by the judgment of the majority in *Miller v. California*, 413 U.S. 15 (1973), rehearing denied 414 U.S. 881 (1973). It is argued that, because of vagueness and overbreadth, the Supreme Court required state legislatures to specify the sort of depiction of sexual conduct that was prohibited. The portion of the judgment of Burger C.J. relied upon reads as follows (at pp. 23-24):

We acknowledge, however, the inherent dangers of undertaking to regulate any form of expression. State statutes designed to regulate obscene materials must be carefully limited. See Interstate Circuit, Inc. v. Dallas, supra, at 682-685, 20 L Ed 2d 225. As a result, we now confine the permissible scope of such regulation to words which depict or describe sexual conduct. That conduct must be specifically defined by the applicable state law, as written or authoritatively construed.

The footnote to the quoted extract reads in part as follows:

We do not hold, as Mr. Justice Brennan intimates, that all States other than Oregon must now enact new obscenity statutes. Other existing state statutes, as construed heretofore or hereafter, may well be adequate. See United States v. 12 200-Ft. Reels of Film, 413 US, p. 130 n 7.

The distinguishing words are "or authoritatively construed" and "as construed heretofore or hereafter".

In Canada, s. 159(8) has been authoritatively construed and defined by the Supreme Court of Canada and the appellate courts. These judgments are extensively reviewed by Borins Co. Ct. J. in *R. v. Doug Rankine Co.* (1983), 36 C.R. (3d) 154 (Ont. Co. Ct.), as follows:

[His Lordship's lengthy quotation from *Rankine* is omitted.]

The principles enunciated in the above authorities may be summarized as follows:

1. The test to be applied in determining what is undue exploitation within s. 159(8) is whether the accepted standards of tolerance in the contemporary Canadian scene have been exceeded.

2. The standard is a national standard.

3. While expert evidence may be helpful, it is for the judge, in the final analysis, to endeavour to apply what he, in the light of his experience, regards as contemporary standards of the Canadian community.

4. Something approaching a general average of community thinking has to be discovered.

5. The manner and circumstances of distribution are relevant in determining whether or not a publication is obscene (distribution to a private adult audience or otherwise).

6. In determining "undueness" the artistic and literary purposes of the author must be considered.

7. No material will be condemned unless it is clearly "undue".

8. "Undueness" is to be measured by the "tolerance" of the average Canadian and not by the "tastes" of the average Canadian.

"Men of common intelligence" would also know that the words "undue exploitation of sex" will be construed in the context of "obscenity". The word "obscene" is defined in the Shorter Oxford English Dictionary, 3rd ed. (1944), as follows:

> (-Fr. *obscène* or L. obscenus, obscaenus ill-omened, abominable, disgusting, indecent, orig. a term of augury.) 1. Offensive to modesty or decency; expressing or suggesting lewd thoughts 1598; 2. Offensive to the senses or the mind; disgusting, filthy. *arch.*

The word "obscenity" is defined as follows:

> Obscene quality or character: a. Indecency, lewdness (esp. of language); in *pl.* obscene words or matters; b. Foulness, loathsomeness; in *pl.* foul acts, dirty work — 1807.

It will be seen, therefore, that material will not be classed as obscene unless the material falls within the above definitions. The material must be so "filthy or disgusting" as not to be tolerated by the average Canadian.

The words "undue exploitation of sex" are also used in a pejorative sense. Thus there must be an excessive emphasis on sex for a base or selfish purpose.

It is said, however, that it is impossible for "men of common intelligence" to ascertain contemporary national standards of tolerance. This argument cannot, in my opinion, prevail. "Men of common intelligence" can seek guidance as to the "national standard of tolerance" from the decided cases. While the decided cases do deal with questions of fact, which differ to some degree in each case, these cases do offer, when viewed as a whole, a national consensus as to the "Canadian standard of tolerance".

Another case dealing with "national standards of tolerance" is *R. v. Wagner* (1985), 43 C.R. (3d) 318 (Alta. Q.B.) where after reviewing the videotapes in question, including "Candy Stripers", Shannon J. had this to say [at 331-32 (C.R.)]:

> Dr. Check testified that in the past pornography was classified as either violent or non-violent; however, modern research establishes three types. They are:
>
> (a) sexually explicit with violence;
> (b) sexually explicit without violence, but dehumanizing or degrading; and
> (c) explicit erotica.

In sexually violent pornography one finds the overt infliction of pain and the overt use of force, or the threat of either of them.

In sexually explicit pornography that is free of violence, but is degrading or dehumanizing, men and women are often verbally abused and portrayed as having animal characteristics. Women, particularly, are deprived of unique human character or identity and are depicted as sexual playthings, hysterically and instantly responsive to male sexual demands. They worship male genitals and their own value depends upon the quality of their genitals and breasts. Thus in such films professional women, such as nurses and secretaries, are hired solely for the purpose of sexual gratification, without regard for their professional qualifications and abilities.

On the other hand, sexually explicit erotica portrays positive and affectionate human sexual interaction, between consenting individuals participating on a basis of equality. There is no aggression, force, rape, torture, verbal abuse or portrayal of humans as animals.

This court accepts that classification. Furthermore, it holds that the contemporary Canadian community will not tolerate either of the first two classes. It will tolerate erotica no matter how explicit it may be. It is the message that counts, not the degree of explicitness. In addition, this court is convinced that Dr. Check was right when he said that the seven cassette films that he viewed, for the most part, fall into the category of non-violent but degrading and dehumanizing , with some episodes in the sexually violent class.

He did not view the film "Greenhorn". It is painfully boring, as it presents scene after scene of homosexual activities, but it is free of violence, crime, horror, and cruelty. All of the participants are willing, consenting adults. No one is degraded or dehumanized. It qualifies as erotica.

The eight video cassette films that I viewed are popularly referred to as "skin-flicks". Freedman C.J.M. accurately described them in *R. v. Odeon Morton Theatres Ltd.*, [1974] 3 W.W.R. 304 (Man. C.A.):

"The basic characteristic of "skin-flicks" is that they are wholly destitute of plot or, if they do have anything resembling a story line, it is one that is transparently thin, a palpably meagre framework on which to hang one erotic episode after another."

In such films a dominant characteristic is the exploitation of sex; indeed, it is the dominant characteristic. That exploitation becomes undue and the films consequently obscene:

(1) if any such episode or episodes present crime, horror, violence, or cruelty in association with the sexually explicit activities; or

(2) if any such episode or episodes portray the participants in a manner that is degrading or dehumanizing.

In my view, having regard to the guidelines spelled out by the courts and to the contemporary Canadian standards held to apply by the learned judges in the above cases, it cannot be said that "men of common intelligence" cannot ascertain the prevailing "national standard of tolerance". To summarize, while difficulties may arise from time to time in rare cases, making it difficult for a prosecutor, a policeman or a citizen to ascertain whether certain material does or does not offend against s. 159(8), the definition of "obscenity" enunciated by the Supreme Court of Canada, when read together with the decided cases, makes it possible for any person to ascertain with reasonable certainty whether the material proposed to be published is or is not within the purview of s. 159(8). To give a precise definition is impossible. The law is not perfect. We cannot do perfect justice. The courts have, however, devised a reasonable, workable standard in this area of the law.

While, as I have said, it is not wise or possible to give a precise definition of "obscenity", it is possible to illustrate the type of material that does not fall within contemporary Canadian standards of tolerance.

Material lacking serious literary, artistic, political or scientific value dealing to an excessive degree with explicit sex involving violence will be prohibited. Likewise, similar material dealing with explicit sex involving the participation of children will be prohibited. Similar sexually explicit material portraying men and women as having animal characteristics will also be prohibited, even though there is an absence of physical violence. This type of material was described by Shannon J. in *R. v. Wagner*, supra, as follows [at p. 331]:

> In sexually explicit pornography that is free of violence, but is degrading or dehumanizing, men and women are often verbally abused and portrayed as having animal characteristics. Women, particularly, are deprived of unique human character or identity and are depicted as sexual playthings, hysterically and instantly responsive to male sexual demands. They worship male genitals and their own value depends upon the quality of their genitals and breasts.

I wish to emphasize that the word "undue" denotes excessive emphasis on sex and that the presence of isolated depictions of explicit sex will not be prohibited. I would also emphasize that "sex" must be a dominant characteristic and that even if, for example, the material dealt to a substantial degree with explicit sex and violence if the material was of serious literary, artistic, political or scientific value it would not, except in rare cases, be subject to condemnation. It is my view that, while the mterial might be devoted almost entirely to explicit sex, explicit sex could not be said to be a dominant characteristic if the theme, plot or purpose had serious literary, artistic, political or scientific merit. The only dominant characteristic would be the theme, plot or purpose and all other characteristics, including explicit sex, would be subservient to the theme, plot or purpose. It will be observed that the videotapes condemned by the judges in the *Doug Rankine, Ramsingh* and *Wagner* cases, all supra, were all without merit of any kind, literary, artistic or otherwise. "Men of common intelligence" could easily ascertain that they were entirely without merit and were clearly contrary to "national standards of tolerance".

It will also be observed that s. 2(*b*) of the Charter narrows the scope of s. 159(8) of the Code. Any limitation on freedom of expression must meet the strict requirements of s. 1 of the Charter, namely, that the limitation is reasonable and such "as can be demonstrably justified in a free and democratic society". We must be careful, therefore, not to prohibit the publication of materials for the sole reason that the materials do not meet with popular approval or do not appeal to popular tastes. In my view, a restriction on freedom of expression can be "demonstrably justified" only if it can be shown that the material sought to be banned from publication causes or threatens to cause real and substantial harm to the community. In this respect it is my opinion that publication of material placing excessive emphasis on explicit sex with violence, explicit sex involving children and explicit sex portraying human beings as having animal characteristics results in substantial harm to the community and we are thus justified in prohibiting the publication of such material.

It has been said that videotapes of the type condemned by the courts are not a threat to society because they are seen only in private by a consenting adult audience. Quite apart from the risk that these videotapes may fall into the hands of children, it is my opinion that such materials are clearly a threat to society. They constitute a threat to society because they have a tendency to create indifference to violence insofar as women are concerned. They tend to dehumanize and degrade both men and women in an excessive and revolting way. They exalt the concept that in some perverted way domination of women by men is accepted in our society.

I would add that, in determining whether or not the requirements of s. 1 of the Charter have been satisfied, it seems to me that we should not decide these matters in a vacuum but should have regard to the provisions of the Charter as a whole, including s. 28, reading as follows:

> 28. Notwithstanding anything in this Charter, the rights and freedoms referred to in it are guaranteed equally to male and female persons.

If true equality between male and female persons is to be achieved it would be quite wrong in my opinion to ignore the threat to equality resulting from the exposure to male audiences of the violent and degrading material described above. As I have said, such material has a tendency to make men more tolerant of violence to women and creates a social climate encouraging men to act in a callous and discriminatory way towards women.

Apart from such harmful and offensive material involving the subject of sex, we are not justified in restricting free expression in this area in any way. It must be remembered that freedom of expression includes the freedom to receive all material which is not harmful to others. It follows that in the privacy of his home every citizen is entitled to read, see or hear all material involving the subject of sex which is not harmful to others.

In conclusion, I would stress that we must be careful not to restrict freedom of expression beyond what is clearly required for the protection of society. We cannot ban the publication of all harmful or offensive material involving the subject of sex. At the expense of repetition, the only material that can be banned is material which is clearly offensive, explicit, excessive and substantially harmful, in the manner described above.

I adopt the remarks of Clare Beckton in "Freedom of Expression (S. 2(b))", c. 5 of Tarnopolsky and Beaudoin (eds.), Canadian Charter of Rights and Freedoms: Commentary (1982), at p. 107:

> With the entrenchment of s. 2(b) of the Charter the Supreme Court will have to face squarely the limits of censorship. Clearly statutes which create censorship boards without specific criteria would be contrary to the guarantees of free expression, since no line is drawn between objectionable and non-objectionable forms of expression. Now standards will have to be created to measure the limits to which obscene expression may be regulated.
>
> Although the American approach does not offer much assistance for Canadian courts, it is submitted that the overbreadth approach or even a test similar to the clear and present danger standard should be used. It is not enough to say merely that moral standards are offended by the proliferation of obscene material, without demonstrating that harm is caused by the dissemination of objectionable material. If freedom of expression is to be a valuable right, a moral sense of indignity is not a sufficient reason for prohibiting access to allegedly obscene material. Any censorship which is not clearly justifiable interferes with the right of free expression. Clearly there are legitimate interests to be protected, particularly as they pertain to access by minors to material described as obscene or pornographic, but the danger is ever present from legislation that is overbroad, and from the lack of clear standards against which to measure the material.

To apply the points made in the above-quoted passage to the case on appeal:

1. Section 2(b) of the Charter prevents Parliament from enacting legislation to prohibit the publication of any materials unless it can be demonstrably justified that

the publication of such materials will clearly cause substantial harm to the community.

2. As exemplified in these reasons, clear standards have been established in respect of s. 159(8) and "men of common intelligence" can ascertain whether or not the material sought to be published comes within the prohibited area.

The materials in question offend against the standard enunciated in s. 159(8) because they constitute a threat of real and substantial harm to the community. They have no literary or artistic merit and in a revolting and excessive way create an attitude of indifference to violence insofar as women are concerned and tend to dehumanize both men and women. They approve the domination of women by men as an acceptable social philosophy.

For the above reasons, I would dismiss the appeal.

*Appeal dismissed.*

## Note

In *Re Luscher and Deputy Minister of National Revenue, Customs and Excise* (1985), 45 C.R. (3d) 81 Hugessen J., speaking for the Federal Court of Appeal, struck down a prohibition in the schedule to the Customs Tariff (Canada) against importation of books and other materials "of an immoral or indecent character". First, as distinguished from the obscenity provisions in the *Criminal Code* which Hugessen J. said were described in section 159(8) in "words which might be thought to give those provisions sufficient certainty and particularity," the words "moral" and "indecent" were not defined in the customs legislation before him. They were accordingly too vague on their own to be "reasonable limits" within the meaning of section 1. Second, although related, the words "moral" and "indecent" were "highly subjective and emotional in their content. Opinions honestly held by reasonable people will vary". While the *Criminal Code* definition of obscenity is restricted to matters which are predominantly sexual, there was no such statutory limitation in the legislation at issue here. To use Hugessen J.'s example, both sides of the abortion debate argue that their view alone is "moral", and material espousing the contrary position might be comprehended on a wide interpretation of the legislation. This difficulty of definition, of not allowing a person to know whether he fell within or without the proscription, was a fatal flaw in the legislation. Hugessen J. said at p. 85:

> ... a limit which is vague, ambiguous, uncertain, or subject to discretionary determination is, by that fact alone, an unreasonable limit. If a citizen cannot know with tolerable certainty the extent to which the exercise of a guaranteed freedom may be restrained, he is likely to be deterred from conduct which is, in fact, lawful and not prohibited. ... While there can never be absolute certainty, a limitation of a guaranteed right must be such as to allow a very high degree of predictability of the legal consequences.

In response to the argument that the material before him would be prohibited on any view of the legislation, narrow or wide, and that therefore there should be no vagueness problem as regards the particular material in question, Hugessen J. said at p. 89:

I would add that it is, of course, no answer to the argument that a limitation on freedom is so vague as to be unreasonable to say that this publication or that is so immoral or indecent that it clearly falls afoul of the prohibition . . . Even the most defective provision is unlikely to be so vague as not to permit the placing of some cases on one side of the line or the other. What is significant is the size and importance of the grey area between the two extremes. Vagueness or uncertainty, like unreasonableness, are not themselves absolute but tests by which the courts must measure the acceptability of limits upon Charter-protected freedoms.

## (d) Commercial Speech

# RE KLEIN AND LAW SOCIETY OF UPPER CANADA; RE DVORAK AND LAW SOCIETY OF UPPER CANADA

In the Ontario Divisional Court. 50 O.R. (2d) 118.

Henry, Eberle and Callaghan JJ. Feb. 4, 1985.

Applications seeking declarations that the Rules of Professional Conduct of the Law Society of Upper Canada relating to fee advertising and communications with the media are of no force or effect.

HENRY J. (dissenting): — [the facts are set out in the decision of CALLAGHAN J.]

I have had the opportunity of reading the reasons for judgment in these proceedings of my brethren. With due deference to their skill and learning I am unable to agree entirely with their *rationale* and conclusion and must, as a result, expound my own.

The two applicant solicitors, members of the Law Society of Upper Canada, apply to this court for judicial review pursuant to the *Judicial Review Procedure Act*, R.S.O. 1980, c. 224, and for a declaration that the Law Society's Rules of Professional Conduct and commentaries thereto, and the decisions of Convocation as they relate to advertising by solicitors, are of no force or effect as being inconsistent with the *Canadian Charter of Rights and Freedoms*.

Mr. Klein seeks only the modest right to make available to clients awaiting an interview in his reception room brochures describing particular legal services and the fees that he will charge therefor — information that he will give orally to the client at the interview in accordance with the policy of the Law Society.

Mr. Dvorak seeks the right to advertise his services and fees charged therefor in the press; he also has circulated a form letter to a group of chartered accountants soliciting their business for the purpose of incorporation, and stating the fees to be charged at reduced rates.

Both solicitors face the proscription of these activities by the Law Society's rules as published by the Professional Conduct Committee of Convocation in its handbook called "The Code of Professional Conduct". Disciplinary proceedings have been commenced against Mr. Dvorak; none has been commenced against Mr. Klein.

In addition, Mr. Dvorak seeks the right to communicate with the news media to open a discussion on the Law Society's prohibition of advertising by solicitors to the public. He took this step and faces disciplinary proceedings as a result for using the media to publicize himself.

. . . .

I turn first to the question of the advertising by a solicitor of the services that he can provide and the fees he charges therefor. The issues here are as follows:

(1) Does freedom of expression as guaranteed by the Charter include commercial speech and expression?
(2) Does the Charter apply to the Law Society of Upper Canada?
(3) Can the Law Society's prohibition against advertising be demonstrably justified as a reasonable limit on freedom of expression in a free and democratic society within the meaning of s. 1 of the Charter?

I say at once with respect to the second issue that I am entirely in agreement with the views expressed by my brother Callaghan, concurred in by my brother Eberle, that the Charter applies to the rules of professional conduct and the commentaries thereto, and the decisions of Convocation as they relate to the impugned conduct of the applicants before us. I therefore need not deal with this issue further.

. . . .

In dealing with the two issues left to me to consider, the starting point is s. 2 of the Charter which prescribes the following fundamental freedoms:

> 2. Everyone has the following *fundamental* freedoms:
> (a) freedom of conscience and religion;
> (b) freedom of thought, belief, opinion and expression, including freedom of the press and other media of communication;
> (c) freedom of peaceful assembly; and
> (d) freedom of association.

(Emphasis added.)

Section 1 of the Charter then provides:

> 1. The *Canadian Charter of Rights and Freedoms* guarantees the rights and freedoms set out in it subject only to such reasonable limits prescribed by law as can be demonstrably justified in a free and democratic society.

Mr. Scott, on behalf of Mr. Klein, in his usual lucid and reasonable presentation, puts the case thus:

> The fundamental right to freedom of expression guaranteed to every person is absolute in the sense that it *prima facie* embraces all modes of expression by the individual; it includes economic free speech of which commercial advertising is a part. The only restraints that may be imposed upon it are such as fall within s. 1 of the Charter in the form of reasonable limits prescribed by law; those limits must be demonstrably justified in a free and democratic society. The limits placed by the Law Society in its code are not so justified.

A similar position is taken by Mr. Kopyto, on behalf of Mr. Dvorak, who adopts Mr. Scott's presentation.

On behalf of the Law Society, Mr. O'Brien submits that s. 2 of the Charter does not embrace economic freedom of expression; that the Law Society, like other professional bodies, has always been accorded the right to regulate advertising by its members (a right which is preserved by s. 26 of the Charter); that by choosing to join the profession, a solicitor accepts the Law Society's limitations on his conduct by implied contract or waiver, and that this exception is inherent in s. 2 of the Charter, so that resort to s. 1 is neither necessary nor appropriate.

I have reached the conclusion that the position taken by the applicants must prevail. In my opinion it is sound for the following reasons:

In my opinion, s. 2 of the Charter is on its face and on its plain, ordinary meaning of universal application. First, the Charter is a uniquely Canadian document which, when it came into force, enacted a new regime of law guaranteeing fundamental rights and freedoms as part of the Constitution, overriding conflicting legislation of Parliament and the Legislatures and their delegates. Those freedoms are expressed in s. 2 as absolutes because they are the fundamental heritage as we see it of every individual. They can only be impaired within the latitude permitted by the Charter itself and any attempt to impair them must pass the acid test of s. 1. At that stage it must be determined whether a limitation on the freedom is prescribed by law and if so whether it is, by democratic standards, reasonable. There are two ways in which such a limitation can be prescribed; it may be one derived from the common law or it may be one prescribed by statute. In either case the Charter, while not relieving Parliament and the Legislatures of the obligation to conform to its principles, ultimately imposes on the courts the duty of deciding whether the limitation is "demonstrably justified in a free and democratic society".

In determining what is demonstrably justified in a free and democratic society, the courts will have regard to standards accepted in Canada (which is characterized by free parliamentary institutions)' and also those accepted in other democratic polities of the free world. In each case it is, however, a matter of judgment. In each case the courts, in applying the exception in s. 1, must evaluate the common law principles that have traditionally limited the freedom in question, and perhaps more usually, the legislative restraints upon it, in the light of the test prescribed.

In the pre-Charter era the common law approach was to identify a freedom such as freedom of speech or expression as "freedom under the law", to use the concept expressed by Duff C.J.C. in the *Alberta Press* case (*Reference re Alberta Statutes*, [1938] S.C.R. 100 at pp. 132-3, [1938] 2 D.L.R. 81 at p. 107), a principle adopted by the courts to reflect parliamentary sovereignty or the gloss of judicial pronouncement. In the Charter era "freedom under the law" raises the inevitable question, "what kind of law?", and the response is a law that meets the test of s. 1, whether it be common law or statute. Freedom under the law becomes freedom subject only to a law that can stand the scrutiny of s. 1.

In applying this principle I think it appropriate to return to fundamentals, perhaps trite to state. What is meant by "freedom of expression"?

(a) Freedom is an absence of restraint. In the democratic tradition as expounded by the courts, a person is free to express himself orally or in writing so long as he does not contravene some law. In general, apart from oppressive laws, the approach of the legislator and of the courts has been to permit the individual to speak freely unless in so doing he is injuring another person or the general public.

(b) In a democratic society as we conceive it, no freedom is absolute, including freedom of expression. This acknowledged limitation springs from the common law itself, some of which has been codified in Canada by statute. The limitation on freedom of expression (as is true of other freedoms mentioned in s. 2 of the Charter) reflects a necessary balancing of the absolute freedom of the individual and its conflict with the rights of other individuals or of the public at large. Hence the law has evolved and has been accepted as reasonable, to declare that a person may express himself freely so long as, for example, he does not offend against the criminal and civil laws relating to treason, sedition, libel, obscenity, blasphemy and perjury.

(c) It is inherent in the characteristics of a free and democratic society that ideas as to the appropriateness or tolerability of such restraints may change from one generation to the next as witness the current rethinking of the meaning and proper scope of the laws restraining obscenity.

(d) There can surely be no difference in principle in applying the fundamentals of freedom of expression to people engaged in trade, commerce and the professions. They too are free to speak and communicate to others but subject to the laws such as those protecting their neighbours from defamation, slander of title, slander of goods, fraud and misrepresentation.

(e) The observe of the concept of freedom of expression is the right of the person to receive the message expressed; the right of the public and individuals to know what is being expressed by others with a message to communicate applies equally to the democratic political process (it is the breath of life of parliamentary institutions as Duff C.J.C. so well put it in the *Alberta Press* case) and in my opinion to the pith and thrust of economic competition in a free market economy.

(f) Some risk must be accepted that free expression by one person may cause offence to others. A person may be harmed in his reputation by a blunt and ruthless criticism but may have to suffer it if the message published is the truth or is fair comment, or is privileged, as would be a statement made in Parliament or the Legislature. The risk is accepted as an incident of the more fundamental freedom to communicate ideas and information. There is a risk that expressions may be offensive because they are in poor taste, crude or undignified, or that criticism may offend the rulers of the day; but the scale in a democratic society tips in favour of the freedom to speak rather than its curtailment.

(g) Lack of manners, lack of good taste and lack of consideration are qualities which are very difficult to legislate, although their practice may be extremely offensive to others; in the case of a profession such conduct may call in question the integrity and the calibre of the profession as a whole in the eyes of the public which is a plain detriment. To attempt to instil these qualities in adult persons by legislation is, generally speaking, futile; adults either have these qualities inherently or as a matter of training or they have not.

To conclude this first point, the Charter, in my opinion, makes no distinction in principle between freedom of expression as it may relate to political expression or economic activity.

Second, the dictates of the private enterprise economy to which this country is dedicated (despite legislative inroads on its functioning) require that the Charter, according to its plain meaning, be applied to freedom of economic expression.

Freedom to advertise one's goods or services is fundamental to the private enterprise system. The freedom to "build a better mousetrap" is not only an essential part of the dynamics of the system but is made effective only in this era of mass marketing by the freedom to advertise in the mass media, both in the domestic market and abroad.

(To be clear, I am not here concerned with the exploitation of private property and bargaining power which led to State intervention as a result of the industrial revolution of the 19th century; that is another matter. I am concerned only with the freedom to advertise in a private enterprise economy.)

Reverting then to the fundamental concept of freedom of expression, a man is free to inform the public of his goods and services, their quality and price, so long as he is not restrained by law. This I believe to be the effect of s. 2 of the Charter which, as I have said, is subject to restraint by laws that meet the test of s. 1. It follows that I do not accept Mr. O'Brien's submission that the freedoms guaranteed by s. 2 are already curtailed by the limitations impressed on them by laws existing when the Charter came into force. The Charter is a new regime superimposed on the political, economic and legal fabric of Canadian society. Its enactment provides not only the opportunity, but the duty of legislators, governments and the courts to review and where necessary to redefine the limits to be imposed by law on the freedoms guaranteed, and to winnow out those laws that do not meet the test of s. 1. . . .

The Charter differs from the U.S. First Amendment in that freedom of speech was there entrenched and the Supreme Court was faced with the necessity of defining the liberal language as importing limits to the freedoms recognized by existing law. Under the Charter, however, the freedoms in s. 2 are to be taken as absolute because they are subject to the flexibility provided in s. 1. It is under that provision that reasonable and justifiable inroads can be made by law in the absence of which the freedom is absolute.

The Ontario Court of Appeal has said in *Re Federal Republic of Germany and Rauca* (1983), 41 O.R. (2d) 225 at 244, that: ". . . the Charter was not enacted in a vacuum and the rights set out therein must be interpreted rationally having regard to the then existing laws . . .".

As I see it, however, the pre-existing laws may well be left undisturbed but to do so must survive the test of s. 1. The Court of Appeal does not limit the scope of s. 2 — what it means is that pre-existing limiting laws may ordinarily be accepted as meeting the test of s. 1, but the Charter does not entrench the limitations; to say that would mean that the pre-Charter limits cannot be challenged by the Charter tests at all, which cannot have been intended by the legislators.

Nor do I accept Mr. O'Brien's submission that the Law Society of Upper Canada has always had the right to regulate advertising by its members which right, he says, "has been recognized traditionally and by the Law Society Act and by the cases, and it was never intended that the Charter should interfere with such well-established rights". Whatever the original position of the Law Society, the contemporary enactment of the *Law Society Act* brought the Society into the public domain by conferring on it the authority to regulate the profession. The statute does not confer rights; it confers powers (and corresponding duties) to regulate the profession in the public interest. Its powers to make regulations are the delegation of legislative authority which is subject to the approval of the Lieutenant-Governor in Council. Its disciplinary powers are subject to the procedural safeguards in the *Statutory Powers Procedure Act*, R.S.O. 1980, c. 484. As I understand Mr. O'Brien's submission, it is that the right contended for is preserved by s. 26 of the Charter which provides:

> 26. The guarantee in this Charter of certain rights and freedoms shall not be construed as denying the existence of any other rights or freedoms that exist in Canada.

The powers of the Law Society conferred by statute are not in my opinion rights within the meaning of s. 26. An example of the application of s. 26 is, I suggest, in the context the right of a person not to be libelled by another by advertising or otherwise. That is no doubt a reasonable right prescribed by law that meets the test of s. 1.

Mr. O'Brien then relies on the decision of the Supreme Court of Canada in the pre-Charter case of *A.-G. Can. v. Law Society of British Columbia; Jabour v. Law Society of British Columbia*, [1982] 2 S.C.R. 307, which upheld the authority of the Law Society to regulate advertising by its members. The court, in a unanimous and comprehensive judgment, held that the regulation of advertising by members was an ongoing function of the Benchers whose policy was not to be interfered with by the courts; moreover, the concept of freedom of expression did not extend to commercial advertising. This latter point appears succinctly in the following passage from the judgment at p. 364 S.C.R.:

> The freedom of expression with which the Court is here concerned of course has nothing to do with the elective process and the operations of our democratic institutions, the House of Commons and the provincial Legislature. We are indeed speaking about the right of economic free speech, the right to commercial advertising. It can hardly be contended that the province by proper legislation could not regulate the ethical, moral and financial aspects of a trade or profession within its boundaries.

That case was decided initially in 1977 when the solicitor, Mr. Jabour, challenged the power of the Law Society to restrict his right to advertise. Among other grounds, he raised his right of free speech and relied on the opinion of Duff C.J.C. in the *Alberta Press* case to the effect that the *British North America Act, 1867* by necessary implication gave certain rights of free speech in Canada. This argument was rejected by the Supreme Court on two grounds:

(a) The *Alberta Press* reference was concerned with "the need in the operations of the democratic community organized under *The British North America Act* for the freest possible discussion in order that Parliament would be constantly working under the influence of public opinion and public discussion" [p. 363 S.C.R.]. But in the passage I have cited above, it said that *Jabour* was by contrast contending for the right of economic free speech to which the *Alberta Press* case did not apply.

(b) When the right of free speech is not entrenched beyond the reach of Parliament or the Legislature, or as has been done, for example, in the First Amendment to the U.S. Constitution, the right is subject to curtailment by valid statute law.

The Supreme Court of Canada did not, of course, apply the Charter as we are bound to do in the cases at bar, and I am constrained with respect to approach the issues here in a different light under the imperatives of the Charter which is now in place. The difference is that whereas the pre-Charter philosophy, as expressed by the Supreme Court, confines freedom of expression to the political sector, the Charter, by s. 2, does not so confine it as I have said. The freedom is not entrenched absolutely beyond the reach of Parliament and the Legislatures (as in the U.S. *Bill of Rights*) but is subject to be limited by reasonable laws that pass the test of s. 1. The issue becomes in the context what limits on communication by advertising prescribed by law can be viewed as reasonable and demonstrably justified in a free and democratic society. The onus of showing these elements is on the authorities applying the law; in this case the Law Society of Upper Canada.

I venture to say that, in a free market economy (which is an attribute of a democratic society), freedom of communication in economic affairs is no less important to the proper functioning of society than freedom of political communication. I recognize that in Canada we do not have the classic ideal of a free market economy. There are many barriers to trade internally and internationally, and to the freedom of newcomers to enter the market which is the catalyst in a dynamic market economy. These barriers are partly the result of government intervention and partly the effect of countervailing economic power by private entrepreneurs. But the essential characteristic of the system underlies the whole — the free choice of the individual to risk his capital and labour in the market for gain.

Notwithstanding the many inroads on the operation of the market by governments, it is still the policy in this society to encourage the operation of underlying market forces to bring about the best allocation of economic resources in the interests of producers, consumers and labour alike. That is the policy of the law and of Canadian society up to the present, and a measure of deregulation of commercial activity by all indications is at present beginning to emerge.

Given then a dedication to an economy functioning by private enterprise in a reasonably competitive market, which is the mainspring of the economic machine, it is inconceivable that the system can work without advertising by entrepreneurs. The individual entering the market, as well as the established enterprise, must make known essential information about his goods and services. The consumer who needs what he has to offer must be informed of the choices available. The proper functioning of the market therefore requires that the best possible information be communicated by producers and distributors to users of their products who are seeking the best combination of price, quality and volume. But the matter does not end there. The health of the economy is of critical importance to all members of society whose access to products is essential to their life-styles, and whose very livelihood depends in the long run on a healthy economy. The general public are thus directly concerned with performance of the market economy and their governments are of necessity drawn into a continuing concern with the state of the economy and the need to develop and maintain an economic or industrial policy. The performance of the economy thus becomes a political issue. The interface between political and economic activity is inescapable.

In a society where free and full communication between producers and users of information concerning products and services and their prices is an essential component of a viable market system, it seems to me impossible to say that freedom to communicate price information about goods and services can be placed in a category divorced from political free speech.

Is a distinction to be made between professional entrepreneurs and those engaged in trade? Patently not. To be realistic about it a lawyer is just as much in business to earn a livelihood  as is a manufacturer, distributor, banker or stockbroker. His is essentially an economic activity and in so saying I do not in any way detract from his contribution to the fundamental cause of citizens in need of legal services, or in some cases to providing his services without charge to needy persons; nor do I overlook the role of the barrister and solicitor as an officer of the court, without which the justice system would be seriously impaired. The simple fact for present purposes is that, a member of the Law Society, notwithstanding his dedication to the cause of justice and his clients, performs the entrepreneurial role of providing services for which he charges a fee. The profession, collectively, makes an economic input into society for which it receives an economic return, which I suggest should be governed, so far as advertising is concerned, by principles similar to those applying to other segments of the market system. The freedom to communicate his charges for services is both a protection to the solicitor and to the public who receive the information upon which they make a rational choice as to which solicitor to retain.

Why should a lawyer not be permitted to advertise at least in the manner sought by the applicants before us? We are concerned with the communication by the applicants of simple basic information as to the services they can provide and the fees to be charged. We are not concerned here with misleading advertising, denigrating other members of the profession, or use of advertising media and content that in the present climate of public opinion may bring the profession into disrepute by its obvious poor taste. We are concerned only with communication by solicitors to members of the public of factual information untrammelled by rhetoric or hard-sell techniques. The rest are matters for another occasion.

Although a great deal of material was placed before us, we did not receive from Mr. O'Brien, in my opinion, any cogent, practical or policy reasons why a solicitor ought to be restrained, on pain of disciplinary penalty, from doing as the applicants seek to do. Perhaps I can put the Law Society's position this way: first, price advertising leads to price cutting which in turn leads to impairment of the quality of services rendered; second, it is unprofessional; moreover the Law Society should be left a free hand to govern its members in its own (subjective) judgment in accordance with the views of the Supreme Court of Canada in the *Jabour* case, and the member by joining the profession accepts the rules and has waived his right to challenge them.

The first of these propositions has not been demonstrated before us. It has been argued for generations in the profession as well as in the commercial market-place. The solution lies in the maintaining of proper educational standards and continuing standards of performance by continuing practitioners. Any tendency towards shoddy performance is to a degree self-correcting as the client who receives less than he pays for may be expected to complain to the Law Society or take the solicitor to court.

The second proposition is in part valid. There is a line to be drawn beyond which anyone would consider it unreasonable that a member of an honourable and highly intellectual profession should go. This is principally a question of applying a standard of propriety and good taste in the interests of preserving the self-worth of the member and the public perception of the member as a representative of what ought to be a dignified and responsible profession. The Law Society clearly has a role in ensuring that its members are not seen as buffoons or hucksters.

Among the material furnished to us by counsel is a transcript of the testimony of George Finlayson, Q.C., at the trial in the *Jabour* case in British Columbia; he was then the treasurer of the Law Society. Mr. Finlayson explained why the Law Society has by its rules of professional conduct placed limitations on advertising by its members. The gist of his evidence on points mentioned here is:

(a) Promotional advertising is prohibited because it seeks to persuade potential clients among the public to use the lawyers' services. Touting and soliciting are likewise prohibited. Those activities are prohibited because they are unprofessional, unethical and misleading.

(b) Informational advertising is permitted to a limited degree, which is narrowly defined. That type of permitted advertising is confined to non-promotional information to assist the public (particularly the unsophisticated and occasional user of legal services) by a listing of his professional "card" in the telephone book, the classified sections of the newspapers and in legal periodicals. It may include a fee to be charged for the initial consultation; he knows what he will have to pay for that service during which the lawyer can assess his legal problem, and advise him of the likely cost of proceeding further. That initial service and fee can be clearly defined.

(c) An advertisement that prescribes a fee for an apparently simple service such as "Uncontested Divorces $200" is misleading because it puts the burden on the potential client of deciding whether he fits into that category which the client is not competent to do; he may in fact be faced with issues under the *Family Law Reform Act* which such an advertisement does not reflect. "It is obviously designed to get people to come into the office on the misleading assumption that this is the type of legal service they require."

(d) In response to a question as to the propriety of a solicitor advertising the hourly rate he charges for his services, Mr. Finlayson said he did not consider that should be allowed:

Q. ... Now would that in your view be the kind of advertising that should be allowed or not?

A. I don't think it should. I am only speaking for myself because I don't think that type of information is of any assistance to the public. They don't care how much money you are making in an hour. What they want to know is how much you are going to charge them for a particular legal service, and hourly rates by themselves don't mean anything.

Q. All right. Your objection to that is that it only gives an hourly rate and not a price for the actual product, a price for the actual service, the total service?

A. That's right.

Q. But if a person tries to advertise the total service your objection to that is that it might not include everything?

A. No, it might not be appropriate.

Q. Yes.

A. You see, what is appropriate is when you know what the client's problem is. He wants to know how much is this going to cost and there are a lot of things in this that you really should tell him. First of all, if it is a piece of litigation he should know that if you are successful that you are going to receive party and party costs from the defendant. Secondly he ought to know that if it is a fairly open and shut case involving somebody's insured that in all probability the case will be settled and that you will be paid by the insurer and there will be no legal fees for your services. Thirdly he ought to know in a particular case that it is a very bad case and that in all probability not only will he have to pay you but he in turn will have to pay party and party costs.

Now those are the kinds of things that a client is entitled to know, and I don't see how you can put out any kind of advertisement which tells him that type of information. That is what concerns me. I am not saying you are wrong about this. This is an ongoing thing that we are considering. But I can tell you that to the propositions that you put to me, my response is that the concern of a great number of people in our profession is that we are not doing any kind of a service at all if we attempt to put a price in the media and attach it to a specific legal service.

I am not persuaded that these objections are insurmountable. Other jurisdictions have set standards to avoid misleading the potential client. As I see it, it is a matter of precise drafting of the advertisement, and after subsequent consultation with the client, of preparing and agreeing to the terms of the resulting retainer.

The third proposition based on the *Jabour* rationale I have already considered.

The final proposition is not tenable for the simple reason that a person ought not to be taken by implication to have surrendered or waived a fundamental freedom.

I conclude this part of my reasons by a brief reference to other jurisdictions. We are informed by counsel that fee advertising for basic services is now permitted in parts of the United States and in four provinces of Canada, and that the United Kingdom has done likewise as of this new year. I do not say that we should slavishly follow suit; I say only that presumably those jurisdictions have thought the freedom to advertise sufficiently important to outweigh the feared disadvantages. In particular I refer to the recent U.S. decision (made in the context of the First Amendment) as found in *Virginia State Board of Pharmacy v. Virginia Citizens Consumer Council*, 425 U.S. 748 at 758 and 761 (1976) (which involved sale of products as well as services), and *Bates v. State Bar of Arizona*, 433 U.S. 350 at 363-5, 384 (1977).

I am not concerned whether these are the final words of the United States Supreme Court; they are in fact decisions of that court. I refer to the following passages.

The United States Supreme Court upheld the pharmacist's right to advertise prices, pointing out that freedom of speech protects the rights of both speaker and listener:

Freedom of speech presupposes a willing speaker. But where a speaker exists, as in the case here, the protection afforded is to the communication, to its source and to its recipients both.

*Virginia State Board of Pharmacy v. Virginia Citizens Consumer Council, supra*, at p. 756.

The court went on to explain that the speaker, the individual consumer, and the public generally, all have vital interests in protecting the right of economic free speech:

Focusing first on the individual parties to the transaction that is proposed in the commercial advertisement, we may assume that the advertiser's interest is a purely economic one. That hardly disqualifies him from protection under the First Amendment.

. . . . .

As to the particular consumer's interest in the free flow of commercial information, that interest may be as keen, if not keener by far, than his interest in the day's most urgent political debate.

. . . . .

Generalizing, society also may have a strong interest in the free flow of commercial information. Even an individual advertisement, though entirely "commercial", may be of general public interest.

. . . . .

Advertising, however tasteless and excessive it sometimes may seem, is nonetheless dissemination of information as to who is producing and selling what product, for what reason, and at what price. So long as we preserve a predominately free enterprise economy, the allocation of our resources in large measure will be made from numerous private economic decisions. It is a matter of public interest that those decisions, in the aggregate, be intelligent and well-informed. To this end the free flow of commercial information is indispensable ... And if it is indispensable to the proper allocation of resources in a free enterprise system, it is also indispensable to the formation of intelligent opinions as to how that system ought to be regulated or altered. Therefore, even if the First Amendment were thought to be primarily an instrument to enlighten public decision-making in a democracy, we could not say that the free flow of information does not serve that goal.

One year later, in *Bates v. State Bar of Arizona, supra*, the United States Supreme Court dealt with fee advertising by lawyers. The court expressly reiterated the principles on which it relied in *Virginia Pharmacy Board*, and held that because of the First Amendment, a bar association could not prohibit publication of a "truthful advertisement concerning the availability and terms of routine legal services".

In the *Bates* decision Justice Blackmun stated as follows:

> The consumer's concern for the free flow of commercial speech often may be far keener than his concern for urgent political dialogue. Moreover, significant societal interests are served by such speech. Advertising though entirely commercial may often carry information of import to significant issues of the day.
>
> And commercial speech serves to inform the public of the availability, nature and prices of products and services and thus performs an indispensable role in the allocation of resources in a free enterprise system.
>
> In short, such speech serves individual and societal interests in assuring informed and reliable decision-making.

I find the *rationale* of these decisions persuasive and apt in considering the scope of ss. 1 and 2 of the Charter.

On the first and third issues, as I have defined them, I therefore conclude that the freedom of expression as defined in s. 2 of the Charter includes freedom of commercial expression. I further am of the opinion that the Law Society has not satisfied the onus of showing that the limitation of the applicants' freedom to advertise fees as they propose is reasonable and demonstrably justified within the meaning of s. 1 of the Charter.

I add that I make no comment on the question of charging reduced fees. If a lawyer is permitted to charge at reduced or competitive rates for his services, he should be free to advertise them; that is all that is to be decided on these applications.

. . . .

[His Lordship's dissenting opinion respecting the Law Society's rule against members initiating contact with the press in relation to the Dvorak application is omitted.]

The judgment of Eberle and Callaghan JJ. was delivered by

CALLAGHAN J: — The applicants herein seek an order declaring the Rules of Professional Conduct of the Law Society of Upper Canada ("Law Society"), the commentaries thereunder and all decisions of Convocation as they relate to fee advertising for information as to fees to be of no force or effect upon the ground that the said Rules, commentaries and decisions are in contravention of the freedom of expression guaranteed in the *Canadian Charter of Rights and Freedoms*.

. . . .

In addition, the applicant, Dvorak, sought a similar order respecting the Law Society's Rules, commentaries and decisions respecting the provision of information regarding his law practice to the press. Dvorak, in his application, advanced an additional Charter ground, namely, that the aforesaid Rules, commentaries and decisions violated the right of very citizen of Canada to pursue the gaining of a livelihood as set out in s. 6 of the Charter. However, the applicant abandoned this ground in view of the Supreme Court of Canada's decision in *Law Society of Upper Canada v. Skapinker*, [1984] 1 S.C.R. 357.

*Facts re Klein application*

The applicant, Klein, was called to the Ontario Bar in 1980 and since that time has been a member in good standing of the Law Society. As part of his practice, he makes available to the public a number of brochures on various legal matters, including such topics as "Uncontested Divorce", "Separation Agreements", "Contested Family Matters" and "Buying and Selling a Home". These brochures were available to anyone who walked into Mr. Klein's office, but were not otherwise generally available to the public. One of these brochures, on "Uncontested Divorce", was filed as part of the record. The brochure describes in a very straightforward way what an uncontested divorce is, how long it will take, whether or not the client would have to go to court and, most importantly, how much it would cost. The fee for an uncontested divorce — $350 plus disbursements — was set out in the brochure.

In September, 1983, the Law Society met in Convocation to discuss, *inter alia*, the issue of professional advertising by members of the Society. In a communiqué to its members, dated September 23, 1983, the Law Society reported that Convocation had voted not to permit fee advertising. A more detailed report of the meeting of Convocation was set out in the January 13, 1984 edition of the Ontario Lawyer's Weekly. The report noted that a special committee had recommended to Convocation that fee advertising be permitted on cards available in a member's office and on signs within the premises, placed so as not to be visible from outside. Convocation, however, rejected this recommendation. It was reported that Convocation felt that the printed material respecting a member's fees might find its way into the hands of the general public. This would, it was thought, result in price competition among members of the profession which could, in turn, result in a deterioration in the quality of legal services performed in the province.

Following the publication of the report, Mr. Klein made this application on January 16, 1984. It is to be noted that Mr. Klein was not at that time under the threat of any disciplinary proceedings by the Law Society stemming from his brochures and the fee advertising contained therein.

### Facts re Dvorak application

The applicant, Dvorak, was called to the Ontario Bar in April, 1983, and is presently a member in good standing of the Law Society, although he is currently the subject of disciplinary proceedings arising out of the facts that give rise to this application. In 1983, notwithstanding numerous applications to law firms, banks and other institutions, he was unable to secure employment. He accordingly commenced the general practice of law in July, 1983, operating out of his own residence. In an attempt to bring his services to the attention of the public, he placed advertisements in the Toronto Star. These advertisements, in the classified section, were headed with the word "lawyer" and gave the prices for noted services. One of these advertisements stated: "Incorporations — $150 plus costs" and "Divorces — $200 plus costs". Another advertisement was similarly headed and stated that he would "incorporate Ontario and Federal companies for $200 plus costs".

The advertisements came to the attention of the Law Society and on July 28, 1983, it wrote Dvorak to direct his attention to Commentary 14(a) of Rule 13 of the Law Society's Rules of Professional Conduct ("the Rules"), which provide as follows:

RULE 13
   Lawyers should make legal services available to the public in an efficient and convenient manner which will command respect and confidence and by means which are compatible with the integrity, independence and effectiveness of the profession.

*Commentary*

. . . . .

14.(a) A lawyer may publish a professional card in any publication provided that the publication will accept cards from all lawyers without restriction. The professional card may contain information that he is in General Practice, or in General Practice and in up to three of the preferred areas of practice defined by Convocation, or in up to three of the preferred areas other than General Practice, provided that he complies with the requirements respecting those areas approved from time to time by Convocation; it may also contain information concerning the languages in which he is proficient and capable of conducting his practice, his addresses, telephone numbers and office hours and his fee for an initial consultation. The card shall be no larger than 12 square inches or approximately 72 square centimetres in size. A lawyer may also publish as aforesaid and circulate among the profession or among his clients announcements containing information pertaining to his practice such as change of office hours, change of address or change of personnel.

In its letter to this applicant, the Law Society stated: "It is clear that only the fee for an initial consultation may be placed in an announcement in a newspaper. Thus, your advertisements breach the above-noted rule."

Dvorak responded to the Law Society's letter on August 31st. In that response he took the position that he was within his legal rights in placing those advertisements and any future advertisements. He claimed that the Law Society was abridging his constitutional rights.

On October 30th, Dvorak sent a form letter to various persons setting out what he characterized as his "incorporation package". The letter in its entirety is set out below:

> Dear Sir:
>
> I received my call to the Bar just last spring and since July, I have been practicing law on my own. I wanted to practice in the area of corporate, commercial, and general business law as it affects and relates to small businesses and at this time I have developed my practice to the point where approximately 90% of my clients are small businesses or small businessmen.
>
> So as to attract clients, I offer an incorporation package for the amount of $470.00 which covers the government registration fee, all of the corporate supplies, (that is, the minute book, the share certificates, etc.) and my fee for preparing the articles, the by-laws, the banking documents, and the minutes of the organizational meeting. For the other services which I perform for my clients I charge $40.00/hr.
>
> If your small business clients are anything like mine in that they would prefer to spend as little money as possible when they need professional advice on something, then they may be interested in my services.
>
> I am writing to you with the belief that by informing your clients of the availability of my services you would be enhancing your own image with your client in that by spending less for a lawyer than your client expected to pay, your client would have a healthier business for which he'd have you to thank.
>
> Yours very truly,
> (signed)
> Robert Dvorak

The letters came to the attention of the Law Society, and on November 16th it again wrote Dvorak. It requested his reason for believing that there was nothing improper in forwarding this type of letter to prospective clients. Dvorak responded on December 2nd. He stated that s. 6 of the Charter permitted him to engage in the course of conduct that he had undertaken. He stated further that he had "the right to make the services which I have to offer to the public known to the public" and went on to say that:

> If no one knows that you are alive and if you have no means of making your existence known to anyone, then how can it be said that the person is free to pursue his livelihood. I believe that such is the case in this situation.

The Law Society filed a complaint with the disciplinary committee on December 22nd alleging that Dvorak was guilty of professional misconduct. Dvorak contacted the Toronto Star in early January, 1984. He recounted to the newspaper the facts that had led up to the Law Society's complaint, and went on to state that he intended to challenge the Law Society's Rules on constitutional grounds in the courts. This contact resulted in a news article in the Sunday Star on January 15, 1984. The Law Society, on January 16th, amended its complaint to include a charge that he had initiated contact with the news media and used that opportunity to publicize himself. On January 23rd Dvorak launched this application. The Law Society undertook not to proceed with the pending disciplinary hearing until the disposition of this application for judicial review.

*Status of the Rules and commentaries*

Counsel on behalf of the Law Society took the position that the commentaries, and possibly the Rules, were not subject to the Charter because they lacked statutory force. He sought to differentiate between the Rules and the commentaries. It appears, however, on the material before this court that the Law Society in Convocation treats both the commentaries and the Rules in the same manner. For example, Communiqué No. 139, dated September 23, 1983, part of the record in the Klein application, states that Convocation decided that as of June 30, 1984, the existing provisions of the Rules respecting the preferred areas of practice should be rescinded. The "Rules" which deal with preferred areas of practice are, in fact, Commentary 14(a) to Rule 13. Rule 13 itself is silent as to the question of preferred areas of practice. Convocation considered the commentaries part and parcel of the Rules. Indeed, the same position was taken in the letter of July 28, 1983, to the applicant, Dvorak, above-noted. It is also clear that the practising members of the Bar feel bound, both by the commentaries and the Rules. Both can form the basis for an exercise by the Law Society of its disciplinary power. In my view, there is no basis for differentiating between the rules and the commentaries for the purpose of these applications.

Section 32 of the Charter provides that it applies to the Legislature and government of each province in relation to all matters within the authority of the Legislature of each province. The Law Society's mandate under the *Law Society Act*, R.S.O. 1980, c. 233, is to regulate the affairs of the legal profession in the public interest. It is part of a regulatory scheme established by the Ontario Legislature to govern the affairs and activities of the various professions. That scheme includes the establishment of similar authorities under statutes such as the *Architects Act*, R.S.O. 1980, c. 26, the *Health Disciplines Act*, R.S.O. 1980, c. 196, the *Professional Engineers Act*, R.S.O. 1980, c. 394, the *Public Accountancy Act*, R.S.O. 1980, c. 405, and the *Surveyors Act*, R.S.O. 1980, c. 492. The Law Society is a statutory authority exercising its jurisdiction in the public interest and is not, as was suggested in argument, a private body whose powers derive from some vague form of contract or articles of association found in the mists of antiquity. In promulgating rules relating to legal advertising or relations between the press and Bar, the Law Society is performing a regulatory function on behalf of the "Legislature and government" of Ontario within the meaning of s. 32 of the Charter. In so doing it is regulating not only the rights of the lawyer to speak, but also the rights of the potential client and the public at large to be informed. In my view, the fact that the Rules and commentaries in the Code of Professional Conduct have not been adopted as regulations under the *Law Society Act* does not prevent them from falling within the ambit of the Charter. As was said by Lord Denning M.R. in *Dickson v. Pharmaceutical Society of Great Britain*, [1967] 2 All E.R. 558 at 567 (C.A.) (affirmed [1968] 2 All E.R. 686 (H.L.)), in a passage that was described by Estey J. in *A.-G. Can. v. Law Society of British Columbia*, [1982] 2 S.C.R. 307 at 359 (S.C.C.) (the "*Jabour* case"), as being as true in Canada as it was in the United Kingdom: "If the council of a professional body should make a rule which is in restraint of trade, it is as much subject to the law of the land as anyone else." In enforcing the prohibitions against fee advertising and commenting to the press through the discipline process, the Law

Society effectively makes these prohibitions part of the law of Ontario and subject to the constitutional restraint of the Charter.

The fact that the Supreme Court of Canada in the *Jabour* case, *supra*, held that the "no advertising" policy of the Law Society of British Columbia did not violate its members' right of economic free speech (the right to commercial advertising) does not in my opinion assist the respondent in these applications. *Jabour* was decided without recourse to the Charter. Mr. Justice Estey, in delivering the reasons of the court, quite clearly reached his decision on the footing that where a right

> . . . is not entrenched beyond the reach of Parliament or Legislature, as has been done for example in the First Amendment to the United States Constitution, the right is subject to curtailment by valid statute law.

Page 363 S.C.R., and see p. 364 S.C.R., citing Beetz J. in *A.-G. Can. v. City of Montreal; Dupond v. City of Montreal*, [1978] 2 S.C.R. 770 at 796. We are faced here, however, with rights that have been entrenched, and so must begin our deliberations anew.

## Fee advertising and freedom of expression

The threshold problem in these two applications is the meaning of the word "expression" in s. 2(*b*) of the Charter. The entirety of s. 2 of the Charter reads as follows:

> *Fundamental freedoms*
> 2. Everyone has the following fundamental freedoms:
>    (*a*) freedom of conscience and religion;
>    (*b*) freedom of thought, belief, opinion and expression, including freedom of the press and other media of communication;
>    (*c*) freedom of peaceful assembly; and
>    (*d*) freedom of association.

It is submitted on behalf of the applicants that the words "freedom of expression" in s. 2(*b*) should be given their ordinary meaning and should be read as protecting all forms of "expression", including commercial speech. Commercial speech includes truthful and non-misleading fee advertising, such as "I will sell you X at Y price". Such advertising is clearly an "expression". The question is whether it is an expression within the meaning of s. 2(*b*) of the Charter.

Counsel on behalf of Klein argues that it is enough that the statement be found an expression to place it within the protection afforded by s. 2(*b*) and that the court's attention should then be directed to s. 1 of the Charter. I do not agree that such a literal and purposeless interpretation of the Charter is proper.

Simply because commercial speech involves an expression does not mean that it must, somehow, be accounted for under s. 2(*b*). In my view, this is to confuse form with substance. Pure commercial speech mimics political speech in form (both involve an expression), but not in substance or function. Commercial speech flows from the realm of economic activity; political speech from that of politics and government. In a democratic society the economic realm must be subordinate to the political realm. The people may determine through their elected representatives and properly so, how to regulate their economic affairs and through that, their economic speech. In doing so, their only concern need be with the process which generates the regulation. For so long as the regulation is the result of the democratic process and so long as the well-springs of that process are kept pure, through the protections afforded it by a Constitution, then there can be no valid complaint by the regulated. Complex economies are possible only under the shelter afforded them by the State and its institutions. Political regulation of individuals, however, is a different matter. Even if such regulation flows from a pure democratic process, it may be struck down, for in regulating the political activities of individuals a government may fetter the democratic process itself and, hence, bring democracy into jeopardy. Political speech is related to and prevents the fettering of the democratic process. It, of necessity, must fall within s. 2(*b*). The Charter, to a certain extent, inferentially recognizes a separation of the realms of economic and political activity and the subordination of the former to the latter. Nowhere does it speak expressly of economic rights. Section 6(2)(*b*), which provides for a right "to pursue the gaining of a livelihood", was interpreted in the Supreme Court of Canada in the *Skapinker* case to refer to mobility rights, rather than a pure economic right to work. Section 7, in speaking of a right "to life, liberty and security of the person" is placed under the heading "Legal Rights" and is grouped with those rights that deal with the rights of an accused person. The Charter reflects a concern with the political rights of the individual and does not, in my view, reflect a similar concern with the economic sphere nor with its incidents such as commercial speech.

*Prima facie* then, the freedom of expression guaranteed by s. 2(*b*) of the Charter would appear to apply to the expression of ideas and opinions relating to the political and governmental domains of the country. (I leave aside the question of whether or not artistic expression falls within s. 2(*b*)). Indeed, this is the interpretation suggested by my brother Eberle J. in this court in *Re Koumoudouros and Municipality of Metropolitan Toronto* (1984), 45 O.R. (2d) 426 at 435, where he said:

> The close linking in s. 2(*b*) of the Charter of the freedoms of thought, belief, opinion and expression, suggests rather that freedom of expression refers to the freedom of communication of ideas and opinions among the citizens of Canada, so that, in broad terms, those citizens may continue to live in the free and democratic society referred to in s. 1 of the Charter. Furthermore, s. 2(*b*) goes on, after providing for "freedom of expression", with the following words "including freedom of the press and other media of communication", these words reinforce the view that the thrust of s. 2(*b*) is in the political and governmental domain, a domain in which the freedoms of thought, belief, opinion and expression are inseparable from a free and democratic society. Further, it must not be forgotten that the Charter is found in the *Constitution Act, 1982*, which is one of Canada's principal constitutional documents, concerned with the fundamental political and governmental structures of the nation.

But, as already noted, the applicants urge upon the court a broader and more expansive interpretation of "expression", one broad enough to cover the words "I will sell you X for Y price". In doing so, they relied heavily on the United States Supreme Court decisions in *Virginia State Board of Pharmacy v. Virginia Citizens Consumer Council*, 425 U.S. 748 (1976), and in *Bates v. State Bar of Arizona*, 433 U.S. 350 (1977). In the *Virginia Citizens* case, the court held that truthful, non-misleading advertising of the prices for standardized, pre-packaged medical products and drugs was a protected form of speech under the First Amendment. In the *Bates* case, the court applied the *Virginia Citizens* case to lawyers and held that price advertising for "routine" legal services, such as uncontested divorces, was also a form of protected speech under the First Amendment.

The traditional view in the United States had been that pure commercial speech was not protected under the First Amendment. This view was best exemplified by the Supreme Court's decision in *Valentine v. Crestenson*, 316 U.S. 52 (1942), where in a short four-page decision, Mr. Justice Roberts, on behalf of the court, stated unequivocally at p. 54:

> This court has unequivocally held that the streets are proper places for the exercise of the freedom of communicating information and disseminating opinion and that though the state and munici-palities may appropriately regulate the privilege in the public interest, they may not unduly burden or prescribe its employment in these public thoroughfares. *We are equally clear that the Constitution imposes no such restraint on government as respects purely commercial advertising.*

(Emphasis added.)

The Supreme Court in the *Virginia Citizens* case disparaged *Crestenson* as "casual, almost off-hand": *Virginia Citizens, supra*, n. 16, p. 759. Mr. Justice Stewart, in his concurring judgment, stated at p. 776 that the court in reaching its decision was ending the "anomalous situation" that had been created by *Crestenson*.

It is to be noted, however, that *Crestenson* had been firmly rooted in the well-established First Amendment jurisprudence that had existed at that time and which had protected freedom of speech as the "matrix, the indispensable condition of nearly every other form of freedom": see *Talko v. Connecticut*, 302 U.S. 319 (1937), Cardozo J. for the court, at p. 327. Its centrality flowed from its function in a democratic state, a function which both justified its constitutional protection and provided the criterion by which any "speech" or "expression's" claim to such protection was measured. In a long line of authority (*Republica v. Oswald*, 1 Dall. 319 (1788); *Commonwealth v. Blanding*, 3 Pick. 304 (1825); *Grosjean v. American Press Co.*, 297 U.S. 233 (1936)) it was established that the predominant purpose of the First Amendment freedoms was to preserve speech and press as a vital source of public information in relation to public matters and those entrusted with the public business.

Given such jurisprudence, it is not surprising that the Supreme Court came to the decision it did in *Crestenson*. If its decision seemed casual in its brevity, it was only because it stood four square with the *rationale* that underlay the First Amendment. Pure commercial speech says nothing about how people are governed, or how they should govern themselves. Indeed, it stands outside of public discourse: it could be said in a tyranny or a democracy, a monarchy or a society without a government at all. Providing no support to a democracy, it did not claim constitutional protection until *Bigelow v. Virginia*, 421 U.S. 809 (1975), and then the *Virginia Citizens* case in 1976.

To justify its abrupt about-face in these cases, the Supreme Court offered two *rationales* for extending First Amendment protection to pure commercial speech. The first was to say that the nature of the information conveyed — and the strength of the public's interest in such information — justified its protection under the First Amendment: *Virginia Citizens, supra*, pp. 764-5 and 780. In the court's opinion, the value of the information conveyed, and what justified its constitutional protection, lay in its contribution to informed decision-making by the public: *ibid.*, and see *Bates, supra*, at p. 364.

The second *rationale* attempted to forge a link between commercial and non-commercial (*i.e.*, political) speech. It did this by creating a formula wherein price advertising supported a free market, which, in turn, supported a free or democratic society. Thus, in the *Virginia Citizens* case, *supra*, at p. 765, the court states:

> Moreover, there is another consideration that suggests no line between publicly "interesting" or "important" commercial advertising and the opposite kind could ever be drawn. Advertising, however tasteless and excessive it sometimes may seem, is nonetheless dissemination of information as to who is producing and selling what product, for what reason, and at what price. So long as we preserve a predominantly free enterprise economy, the allocation of our resources in large measure will be made through numerous private economic decisions. It is a matter of public interest that those decisions, in the aggregate, be intelligent and well-informed. To this end, the free flow of commercial information is indispensable. ... And it is indispensable to the proper allocation of resources in a free enterprise system, it is also indispensable to the formation of intelligent opinions as to how that system ought to be regulated or altered. Therefore, even if the First Amendment were thought to be primarily an instrument to enlighten public decision-making in a democracy, we could not say that the free flow of information does not serve that goal.

It can be said that this second *rationale*, with respect, is not convincing on its face. First, as already suggested, commercial speech is independent of and stands outside of political discourse. Information about the price at which a seller will sell his goods, and the decisions to purchase those goods that are made on the basis of that information, have absolutely nothing to say about, and no impact on, political discourse. Second, the "free market" is itself only an idea, one particular idea, about how goods should be distributed in society. It being only an idea about how goods should be allocated among citizens, there is nothing to prevent society from deciding that some other method of allocation is better. As Rehnquist J. noted in dissent in the *Virginia Citizens* case, *supra*, at p. 784:

> While there is again much to be said for the court's observation as a matter of desirable public policy, there is certainly nothing in the United States Constitution which requires the Virginia Legislature to hew to the teachings of Adam Smith in its legislative decisions regulating the pharmacy profession.

Indeed, this *rationale* was not subsequently repeated by the court. Rather, the court came to rest its protection of commercial speech on its informational content alone. This came to be the sole *rationale*: see Mr. Justice Powell in *Central Hudson Gas & Electric Corp. v. Public Service Com'n of New York*, 447 U.S. 557 at 563 (1980): "The First Amendment's concern for commercial speech is based on the informational function of advertising."

The court in *Virginia Citizens* attempted to downplay the novelty of this *rationale* by citing prior decisions which had characterized the First Amendment protections as extending to information. In particular, both Blackmun J., for the court, and Stewart J., in his concurring decision, cited *Bigelow v. Virginia, supra*, at pp. 762 and 780, respectively; Mr. Justice Blackmun (at p. 762) also cited *Thornhill v. Alabama*, 310 U.S. 88 (1940). Yet close analysis of these cases supports the observations of Rehnquist J. in dissent, who argued that the information protected had always and only related to political discussion: *Virginia Citizens, supra*, at p. 787.

The major problem with the decision in the *Virginia Citizens* case, one ignored then but subsequently acknowledged, was that the *rationales* which justified the constitutional protection of non-commercial (political and cultural) speech on the one hand, and commercial speech on the other, were fundamentally different. Indeed, they were antagonistic. As Mr. Justice Powell, for the court, emphasized in *Ohralik v. Ohio State Bar Ass'n*, 436 U.S. 447 at 456 (1978):

> To require a parity of constitutional protection for commercial and non-commercial speech alike could invite dilution, simply by a leveling process, of the force of the Amendment's guarantee with respect to the latter kind of speech. Rather than subject the First Amendment to such a devitalisation, we instead have afforded commercial speech a limited measure of protection, commensurate with its subordinate position in the scale of First Amendment values, while allowing modes of regulation that might be impermissible in the realm of non-commercial expression.

Indeed, commercial speech was afforded not just a "limited measure" of protection; it was provided "a lesser protection": *Central Hudson Gas & Electric Corp. v. Public Service Com'n of New York*, 447 U.S. 557 at 563 (1980). The lesser protection that was afforded commercial speech was founded on the premise that such speech, "although meriting some protection, is of less constitutional moment than other forms of speech": *Central Hudson Gas, supra*, at n. 5, p. 563. It was this lack of identity in the natures of commercial and non-commercial speech, if not the outright antagonism between the two, which justified "less precision" in the regulation of commercial speech than of political speech by the government: *Re Primus*, 436 U.S. 412 at 434 and 438 (1978). As the court itself noted in *Friedman v. Rogers*, 440 U.S. 1 (1979), the decision in *Virginia Citizens* represented "a substantial extension of traditional free-speech doctrine which poses special problems not presented by other forms of protected speech": n. 9, pp. 10-1. The court went on in the same note to say that because of the

> ... special character of commercial speech and the relative novelty of First Amendment protection of such speech, we act with caution in confronting First Amendment challenges to economic legislation that serves legitimate regulatory interests. Our decisions dealing with more traditional First Amendment problems do not extend automatically to this as yet uncharted area.

But if commercial speech serves a function completely different from that associated with non-commercial speech; if its too-close association with political speech threatens to devalue the latter and the First Amendment; if it is of less moment; if it is entitled to less protection, and to regulations formulated with less precision, than that to which non-commercial speech is entitled, then surely the question arises, why protect it at all? This question is all the more pertinent in Canada's case, where we are asked to embark on a voyage that the U.S. Supreme Court, with 200 years of experience in attempting to define the ambit of non-commercial speech has characterized as being on uncharted seas. As we are not bound to follow the decisions of that court there is, in my view, no sound reason for doing so in the present case.

Counsel for the applicant, Klein, suggests that some of this judicial hesitancy may be put down to the absence in the U.S. Constitution of any equivalent of the Charter's s. 1. Lacking any recourse to an express constitutional limit, the Supreme Court must create its own, while, at the same time, defining the substantive nature of the rights to be protected. According to counsel's argument then, the court need not concern itself when interpreting s. 2(b) with the "commonsense differences" (the words are those of the Supreme Court in the *Virginia Citizens* case, *supra*, at n. 24, p. 771) between commercial speech and non-commercial speech, or with the problem of how that difference should or should not be reflected in the regulation to which each form of speech is subject. Rather, the court can leave that issue to its s. 1 analysis.

But, with respect, this argument misconstrues what the United States Supreme Court was doing. The court is not simply saying that a free and democratic society may tolerate more regulation of free speech when it takes the form of pure commercial speech. Rather, it was also saying, and emphasizing, that pure commercial speech was substantively different from political speech. Thus, the fact that it fell under the First Amendment did *not* justify the application of the same criteria and tests when judging the legitimacy of its regulation by the government. In other words, the Supreme Court developed a new set of criteria, unique to commercial speech, to evaluate such regulation. The Supreme Court can do that precisely because the reasonable limits that are built into the U.S. Constitution are judge-made limits. The Charter, on the other hand, with its express provision of a reasonable limits clause in s. 1, must of necessity preclude such a course of action. The alternative is for the Canadian Courts to develop two separate and different interpretations of s. 1, one to be used where political speech is involved, the other where commercial speech is involved. That approach surely invites chaos.

Such an approach would also draw Canadian courts into a case-by-case review of regulation of most forms of commercial expression, a task better left to the people's elected representatives. For it is clear from subsequent developments in the U.S. jurisprudence that the effect of the decision in *Virginia Citizens* was to throw open to doubt the vast regulatory system governing commercial speech that had developed over the years. As a result, the Supreme Court has, inexorably, been drawn into a continuous judicial review of regulatory policy. In spite of its protest that *Virginia Citizens* did not mean that commercial speech could not be regulated, the Supreme Court has been forced to evaluate a number of various regulatory schemes already. Since the nature of such schemes depends on the nature of the product or service or industry to be regulated, the purpose of the regulation, and the parties involved, each scheme has had to be the subject of judicial scrutiny.

The court has heard cases involving questions of whether or not it was permissible under the First Amendment to prohibit promotional advertising by an electrical utility (maybe): *Central Hudson, supra*; promotional advertising by chiropractors (yes): *Talsky v. Department of Registration & Education*, 370 N.E. 2d 173; *certiorari* denied 99 S. Ct. 84; the use of trade names by a practising optometrist (yes): *Friedman, supra*; solicitation of clients by mail, by a lawyer for a political cause (no): *Primus, supra*; solicitation of clients in person where the lawyer approaches the client for reasons of self-interest (yes): *Ohralik, supra*; solicitation of clients by a lawyer when the client approaches the lawyer (maybe): *Ohralik, supra*; commercial billboards (probably): *Metromedia, Inc. v. City of San Diego*, 453 U.S. 490 (1981), and active, as opposed to passive, solicitation of former clients by a lawyer who has left his former firm (yes): *Adler, Barish, Daniels, Levin v. Epstein*, 393 A. 2d 1175 (1978); appeal dismissed, *certiorari* denied 442 U.S. 907.

This case-by-case review of all such regulatory legislation has led to no clear test as to the extent that commercial speech is protected. It also highlights the irony of the *Virginia Citizens* case, for it demonstrates that legal effect is still being given to a distinction — that between commercial and non-commercial speech — which was supposedly erased by that case. It is clear, however, that commercial speech is of less moment that political speech within the First Amendment. It would appear that its inclusion thereunder threatens to devalue the latter unless the court is eternally vigilant.

The present American situation is well-expressed by Mr. Justice Rehnquist in dissent in *Central Hudson, supra,* at pp. 598-9:

> I remain of the view that the Court unlocked a Pandora's box when it "elevated" commercial speech to the level of traditional political speech by according it First Amendment protection in *Virginia Pharmacy Board v. Virginia Citizens Consumer Council* 425 U.S. 748 (1976). The line between "commercial speech", and the kind of speech that those who drafted the First Amendment had in mind, may not be a technically or intellectually easy one to draw, but it surely produced far fewer problems than has the development of judicial doctrine in this area since *Virginia Pharmacy Board.* For in the world of political advocacy and its market place of ideas, there is no such thing as a "fraudulent" idea: there may be useless proposals, totally unworkable schemes, as well as very sound proposals that will receive the imprimatur of the "marketplace of ideas" through our majoritarian system of election and representative government. The free flow of information is important in this context not because it will lead to the discovery of any objective "truth", but because it is essential to our system of self-government.
>
> The notion that more speech is the remedy to expose falsehood and fallacies is wholly out of place in the commercial bazaar, where if applied logically the remedy of one who was defrauded would be merely a statement available upon request, reciting the Latin maxim *"caveat emptor".* But since "fraudulent speech" in this area is to be remediable under *Virginia Pharmacy Board, supra,* the remedy of one defrauded is a lawsuit or an agency proceeding based on common-law notions of fraud that are separated by a world of difference from the realm of politics and government. What time, legal decisions, and common sense have so widely severed, I declined to join in *Virginia Pharmacy Board* and regret now to see the court reaping the seeds that it there sowed. *For in a democracy, the economic is subordinate to the political, a lesson that our ancestors learned long ago, and that our descendants will undoubtedly have to learn many years hence.*

(Emphasis added.)

I would conclude that there is no reason to expand the meaning of the word "expression" in s. 2(*b*) of the Charter to cover pure commercial speech. Commercial speech contributes nothing to democratic government because it says nothing about how people are governed or how they should govern themselves. It does not relate to government policies or matters of public concern essential to a democratic process. It pertains to the economic realm and is a matter appropriate to regulation by the Legislature. Accordingly, the Rules of Professional Conduct, the commentaries thereunder and all decisions of Convocation as they relate to fee advertising, are within the jurisdiction of the Law Society. Having said this, I do not want to be taken as saying Klein could be disciplined for his brochures. The Law Society's power here is to discipline for professional misconduct or conduct unbecoming a barrister and solicitor. I do not see how Klein could be disciplined for doing in print that which he is under an obligation to do verbally: that is, inform his clients or potential clients fairly and in a non-misleading fashion what to expect regarding both his services and his prices. That, however, is a matter for the determination of the Law Society, as is the complaint in relation to advertising against Dvorak.

*Conversations with the press — s. 2(b) of the Charter*

The applicant, Dvorak's, contacting of the press is entitled to the protection of s. 2(*b*). I adopt, without repeating, my discussion of the purpose and function of s.

2(*b*) of the Charter and of the jurisprudence in both Canada and the United States respecting freedom of expression. The applicant's expression here was precisely the kind intended to be protected by the Charter. It serves a social purpose and provides information on a matter of potential public interest and debate, namely, the manner of fee advertising for lawyers.

Rule 13, Commentary 18, provides as follows:

RULE 13

Lawyers should make legal services available to the public in an efficient and convenient manner which will command respect and confidence and by means which are compatible with the integrity, independence and effectiveness of the profession.

*Commentary*

. . . . .

18.(a) A lawyer should not initiate contact with the news media on behalf of himself in respect of any cause or matter in which he is involved in his professional capacity. Furthermore, a lawyer should not, whether he initiates contacts with the news media or is contacted by them, use that opportunity to publicize himself. The lawyer may initiate contact with the media for the purpose of requesting a correction of any published error relating to his conduct, the conduct of his client or the cause or matter involved. The lawyer should be careful not to make any statement to the media which would constitute contempt of court.

(b) A lawyer contacted by the media for a personal interview concerning his own career may grant such an interview provided that he conducts himself in such interview in a manner consistent with the Rules of Professional Conduct.

A lawyer has a moral, civic and professional duty to speak out where he sees an injustice. Furthermore, lawyers are, by virtue of their education, training and experience, particularly well-equipped to provide information and stimulate reason, discussion and debate on important current legal issues and professional practices: see Rule 12. Speech of this kind surely lies at the core of the constitutional right guaranteed by s. 2(*b*). Rule 13, Commentary 18, restricts such right. Again, a client's interest in many situations and, more particularly, a client's freedom of expression may be legitimately served by having his lawyer initiate contact with the news media. The effect of this Rule is to prevent or impede the client through his lawyer from exercising his constitutionally-guaranteed right. In addition, the public has a constitutional right to receive information with respect to legal issues and matters pending in the courts and in relation to the profession and its practices. This right is substantially impaired by the said Rule in that it significantly restricts the right of the press and other media to offer — and the right of the public to receive and discuss — information of important public issues relating to the law and the operation of legal institutions. A threat of discipline by one's governing professional body is a grave and weighty one which will substantially restrict the willingness to speak out on matters of public interest. The effect of the Rule, in my view, is to impair the right of the lawyer, client and the public to disseminate and receive information to an extent which greatly exceeds any legitimate legislative or regulatory purpose of the respondent Law Society. This Rule, in my view, will have an unjustifiable chilling effect on the exercise of the freedom of expression. Even lawyers who do not "initiate" contact with the news media or who "initiate" contact for a purpose will be dissuaded from exercising their freedom of expression as the Law Society itself has taken the position that:

... any interview with the media about court proceedings invites the inference that it was given to publicize a lawyer and carries the danger of being a contempt of court. The Society intends to institute discipline proceedings where appropriate to ensure that the Rule is observed.

(See Law Society communiqué No. 145, March 22 and 23, 1984.)

It may be that to initiate contact with the press will, in some circumstances, invite the inference of self-aggrandizement, but such circumstances must in my mind, be rare, if only because the press, in all likelihood, will be unwilling to print stories whose only relevance is to the lawyer's ego. It is true that in many cases public attention on the lawyer will flow from a story concerning his case or his client. Such attention is an inherent part of political and social discussion in this country: open debate will always result in someone being in the limelight. Indeed, that is how it should be, for someone who sparks a public debate must be there to take responsibility for any conflagration that results. On the other hand, a lawyer who contacts the media for the purpose of self-promotion or self-aggrandizement may be engaging in conduct which the Law Society may well find to constitute conduct unbecoming a barrister and solicitor and which conduct might well be the appropriate subject-matter of a precisely formulated Rule or commentary thereunder.

If the concern is that a lawyer may disparage the courts, the Law Society or a fellow lawyer, then adequate safeguards already exist. To contact the press and denigrate improperly a fellow lawyer or the Law Society would surely be conduct unbecoming a barrister and a solicitor and it would not be protected by the Charter since its purpose was one for which the Charter was not designed. And as to a contact made in contempt of court, that is a matter for the court, not the Law Society, to regulate (though such a judicial finding might be grounds for further discipline by the Society).

I can therefore see no valid regulatory purpose which justifies the broad restriction on freedom of expression contained in Rule 13, Commentary 18 and, accordingly, I would issue an order declaring Commentary 18 of Rule 13 of no force or effect and quash the complaint of the Law Society filed against the applicant, Dvorak, on January 16, 1984, in so far as it includes a charge that he initiated a contact with news media and used the opportunity to publicize himself. In all other respects the application will be dismissed. As this is a matter of some public importance, it is not a proper case for costs.

*Application of applicant Klein dismissed;*
*application of applicant Dvorak granted in part.*

### Note

*Klein* was followed by the Alberta Court of Queen's Bench in *Grier v. Alberta Optometric Association*, [1985] 5 W.W.R. 436 in dismissing an application by an optometrist for an order striking down the respondent association's rule prohibiting the circulation of a price list for optometric services and equipment. Matheson J. held that commercial speech was not comprehended by section 2(*b*) of the *Charter* and, notwithstanding his characterization of the association's rule as "archaic" at p. 448, he refused to strike it down.

Is not Henry J.'s analysis in *Klein* more persuasive than that of the majority or of Matheson J. in *Grier*, given the difficulty in many cases of separating "political" and "commercial" speech? Furthermore, is there any justification in the text of section 2(*b*) for cutting down its scope without resort to section 1? In any event, it is submitted that *Klein* is inconsistent with the scope that Tarnopolsky J.A. was willing to give to section 2(*b*) in *Videoflicks, supra*: see "Note on Hate Propaganda", *supra*, for the relevant extract from *Videoflicks*, and the discussion following. For further discussion of commercial speech, see Finkelstein, "Section 1: The Standard for Assessing Restrictive Government Actions and the Charter's Code of Procedure and Evidence" (1983), 9 Queen's L.J. 143 at 164-79, *supra; cf. Re Law Society of Manitoba and Savino* (1983), 1 D.L.R. (4th) 285 (Man. C.A.) holding that Law Society rules prohibiting advertising by lawyers of areas of practice and requiring certain advertisements to be submitted to the Law Society in advance of publication are saved by section 1 of the *Charter*.

## (e) Freedom of Speech for Public Servants

# RE FRASER AND PUBLIC SERVICE STAFF RELATIONS BOARD

In the Supreme Court of Canada. (Unreported, December 10, 1985)

Dickson C.J.C. and Beetz, Estey, McIntyre, Chouinard, Lamer, Wilson, LeDain and LaForest JJ.

Appeal from a judgment of the Federal Court of Appeal, [1983] 1 F.C. 372, dismissing an application made under s. 28 of the *Federal Court Act* for the review and setting aside of a decision of the Public Service Staff Relations Boad. Appeal dismissed.

The judgment of the Court was delivered by

DICKSON C.J.C.:

Does an adjudicator err in law, for the purpose of section 28 of the *Federal Court Act*, R.S.C. 1970, c. 10 (2nd. Supp.) when he or she confirms the discharge of a federal public servant who has expressed views highly critical of the Government? Central to that issue is the proper legal balance between (i) the right of an individual, as a member of the Canadian democratic community, to speak freely and without inhibition on important public issues and (ii) the duty of an individual, *qua* federal public servant, to fulfil properly his or her functions as an employee of the Government of Canada.

I

FACTS

On February 23, 1982 the appellant, Mr. Neil Fraser, was discharged from his job with the Department of Revenue Canada. Prior to his discharge, he had worked for the department for ten years. For the five years immediately preceding the discharge he had been Group Head of the Business Audit Division of the Kingston District Office. In this position he supervised four to six auditors and was responsible for selecting large corporations and similar undertakings and auditing their financial statements to determine whether an appropriate amount of taxes had been paid.

On January 18, 1982 the Kingston Whig-Standard published a letter to the editor written by Mr. Fraser criticizing the Government's policy on metric conversion, a major topic of national debate at that time. On January 25, 1982 Mr. Fraser attended a meeting of the Kingston City Council at which a motion was presented opposing the federal Government's policy on metric conversion. The next day an article appeared in the Kingston Whig-Standard in which Mr. Fraser's views on mandatory metric conversion were briefly quoted. Beside the article was a photograph of Mr. Fraser holding a placard bearing the slogan: "Your freedom to measure is a measure of your freedom."

Mr. Fraser's supervisor, Mr. Bruce Lowe, Director of the Kingston District Office, decided that Mr. Fraser's activities warranted a disciplinary response. On January 19, 1982 Mr. Lowe suspended him for three days without pay for having "exceeded the bounds of acceptable conduct of a public servant." He was directed "to refrain from any further public statements that criticize a Government department or agency, its officials, or its rules and regulations".

Mr. Fraser was greatly concerned about the implications of this restraint on his freedom of speech. On February 1, 1982 he attended another meeting of the Kingston City Council and expressed these concerns. This time he criticized not only the Government's metric conversion program but also its intention to proceed with a constitutional *Charter of Rights and Freedoms*. Like its metric policy, the Government's policy concerning a *Charter of Rights and Freedoms* was a major, highly visible and divisive issue at that time.

On February 5, 1982 Mr. Fraser agreed to appear on an open-line radio talk show for a local Kingston radio station. He stated he would not discuss anything related to Revenue Canada but continued to voice his criticisms of the Government's metric and *Charter* policies. Among other things, he compared Prime Minister Trudeau's manner of governing to that of the dictatorship in Poland.

On February 8, 1982 Mr. Fraser met twice with senior departmental staff who advised him that further disciplinary action would be taken if he did not cease his activities. In between these two meetings he appeared on an open-line television program. At these meetings he was asked to refrain from further criticisms of Government policy until the matter had been dealt with through normal grievance channels. Senior departmental staff promised to try and expedite the grievance process. Mr. Fraser was not receptive to this proposal. He maintained his position that any criticism he made of Government policy, unrelated to the policies of his department, was consistent with his right to engage in free speech.

At the second meeting on February 8, 1982 Mr. Fraser was given a second suspension, this time for ten days. During the course of this suspension, from February 9th to 22nd, he made a number of local and national media appearances. He criticized, more broadly and more fervently than ever, the policies of the Government. He continued his campaign against British approval of the Government's constitutional proposals and against the Government's alleged abuse of the democratic process. He tried to organize a national pamphlet and telegram campaign to protest these matters. He began to make vicious personal attacks against the Prime

Minister and compared him and the Canadian Government to the Nazi regime. He was working, by his own admission, eighteen hours a day in opposition to the Government and its policies.

By letter dated February 22, 1982 Mr. Fraser was advised that as a consequence of the statements he had made to both local and national media he was being discharged from the Department of Revenue Canada, effective February 23, 1982.

Mr. Fraser grieved his two suspensions and the discharge. These grievances were referred to adjudication pursuant to s. 91(1) of the *Public Service Relations Act*, R.S.C. 1970, c. P-35. This section provides an employee covered by the *Act* the right to refer a grievance to arbitration if the employee has grieved to the final level in the process in relation to, *inter alia*, "disciplinary action resulting in discharge" and "his grievance has not been dealt with to his satisfaction."

II

## JUDGMENTS

### Public Service Staff Relations Board

Mr. Fraser's grievances were heard by an adjudicator, Deputy Chairman Kates of the Public Service Staff Relations Board. The Adjudicator reviewed carefully and in detail the relevant principles and authorities. He recognized that a line had to be drawn, or a balance reached, between Mr. Fraser's freedom of expression and the desire of the Government to maintain a public service characterized by professionalism and impartiality.

The Adjudicator decided that the first suspension of Mr. Fraser was not justified. It followed Mr. Fraser's first letter to the editor and his fairly passive attendance at one meeting of Kingston City Council. These activities, the Adjudicator concluded, were not deserving of disciplinary action on the part of the employer.

The Adjudicator then considered the second suspension and the discharge. He found that Mr. Fraser's activities after February 8, 1982 — prolonged and highly visible criticism of major governmental policies and personalities — jeopardized his ability to perform his duties at his department. Specifically, he found Mr. Fraser's conduct unlikely to instil confidence in a clientele (persons subject to tax audits) that had a right to expect impartial and judicious treatment. In these circumstances, concluded the Adjudicator, *some* disciplinary action was appropriate. The specific disciplinary measures taken, first a ten-day suspension and then the discharge, were also appropriate in light of the history of the relations between the parties and Mr. Fraser's express intention to continue his activities critical of the Government.

### Federal Court of Appeal

The Federal Court of Appeal dismissed the appeal, taken by Mr. Fraser under s. 28 of the *Federal Court Act*. See [1983] 1 F.C. 372. Pratte J. held that the Adjudicator had made no error of law. He had considered the relevant facts and law. His conclusion that the behaviour of Mr. Fraser constituted misconduct was a question of fact, not reviewable by the Federal Court of Appeal. Furthermore, it was not necessary that there be evidence before the Adjudicator to permit him to make a finding that Mr. Fraser's activities impaired his ability to do his job; this is a finding the Adjudicator is entitled to make, in assessing Mr. Fraser's conduct and its relationship to the requirements of the public service.

Thurlow C.J. and Ryan J. wrote concurring reasons. They do not differ in substance from the reasons of Pratte J.: essentially they reiterate that the Adjudicator considered the relevant factors and legal principles and applied them in a correct fashion.

III

## The Issues

There is really only one issue in this appeal: was the Federal Court of Appeal correct in concluding that the Adjudicator did not err in law in reaching his decision?

Mr. Fraser alleges two errors of law. First, he says the Adjudicator erred in holding that his criticism of Government policies, unrelated to the work of his department, could form the basis for disciplinary action. Secondly, he contends the Adjudicator erred in finding, without any evidence to that effect, that his effectiveness as a public servant was impaired by his public statements.

Before dealing with these arguments, it is necessary to discuss some general legal considerations, including the principles relevant in a review application under s. 28 of the *Federal Court Act*.

IV

## General Legal Considerations

This appeal is *not* about certain things. It does not arise under either the *Canadian Charter of Rights and Freedoms* (which had not been proclaimed when the events in this case arose) or the *Canadian Bill of Rights* (because no federal law is being challenged). Accordingly, the 'freedom of expression' and 'freedom of speech' provisions of these watershed documents are not in issue.

That is not to say, however, that this is not, at least in part, a 'freedom of speech' case. It is. As Mr. Fraser correctly points out, 'freedom of speech' is a deep-rooted value in our democratic system of government. It is a principle of our common law Constitution, inherited from the United Kingdom by virtue of the preamble to the *Constitution Act, 1867*.

But it is not an absolute value. Probably no values are absolute. All important values must be qualified, and balanced against, other important, and often competing, values. This process of definition, qualification and balancing is as much required with respect to the value of 'freedom of speech' as it is for other values. In the present case, the Adjudicator determined that the value of freedom of speech must be qualified by the value of an impartial and effective public service.

Before going on to answer whether the Adjudicator erred in law, it is necessary to understand the principles relating to s. 28(1)(b) of the *Federal Court Act*. The section provides:

> 28.(1) Notwithstanding section 18 or the provisions of any other Act, the Court of Appeal has jurisdiction to hear and determine an application to review and set aside a decision or order, other

than a decision or order of an administrative nature not required by law to be made on a judicial or
quasi-judicial basis, made by or in the course of proceedings before a federal board, commission or
other tribunal, upon the ground that the board, commission or tribunal

    (a) failed to observe a principle of natural justice or otherwise acted beyond or refused to
        exercise its jurisdiction;

    (b) erred in law in making its decision or order, whether or not the error appears on the face of
        the record; or

    (c) based its decision or order on an erroneous finding of fact that it made in a perverse or
        capricious manner or without regard for the material before it.

There is no question in this case of failure to observe the principles of natural
justice or of any other jurisdictional error. As stated above, Mr. Fraser alleges two
errors on the part of the Adjudicator. Both alleged errors raise issues of law and
thereby fall within s. 28(1)(b).

. . . .

## V

*Extent of Permissible Criticism of Government by Public Servants*

Mr. Fraser's primary submission is that there is a fundamental distinction
between job-related criticism and non-job-related criticism. A public servant must
exercise restraint, he concedes, where his or her public statements relate to the duties
of the position or the policies and programs of the department in which he or she is
employed. A governmental employee is as free as a private citizen, however, to
criticize government policies unrelated to his or her job or department. Mr. Fraser
contends that his statements, critical of the Government's metric conversion
program and its constitutional policies, were so remotely related to his duties as a
tax audit manager as not to constitute misconduct.

The respondent does not accept the line Mr. Fraser seeks to draw. The
respondent agrees that a public servant cannot publicly criticize policies relating
directly to his or her job or department, but goes further, contending that a public
servant must not criticize other government policies. The reason for this limitation,
says the respondent, is the need to preserve the neutrality and impartiality, both
actual and perceived, of the public service.

The Adjudicator recognized that a balance had to be struck between the
employee's freedom of expression and the Government's desire to maintain an
impartial and effective public service. He said:

    [It is] incumbent upon the public servant to exercise some restraint in the expression of his views in
    opposition to Government policy. Underlying this notion is the legitimate concern that the Public
    Service and its servants should be seen to serve the public in the administration and implemen-
    tation of Government policies and programs in an impartial and effective manner. Any individual
    upon assuming employment with the Public Service knows or ought to be deemed to know that in
    becoming a public servant he or she has undertaken an obligation to exercise restraint in what he or
    she says or does in opposition to Government policy. Moreover, it is recognized that the exercise of
    such restraint may very well not be a requirement of employees who work in less visible sectors of
    Canadian society.

In other words, a public servant is required to exercise a degree of restraint in his or
her actions relating to criticism of Government policy, in order to ensure that the
public service is perceived as impartial and effective in fulfilling its duties. It is

implicit throughout the Adjudicator's reasons that the degree of restraint which must be exercised is relative to the position and visibility of the civil servant.

In my opinion, the Adjudicator was correct in identifying the applicable principles and in applying them to the circumstances of the case. The act of balancing must start with the proposition that *some* speech by public servants concerning public issues is permitted. Public servants cannot be, to use Mr. Fraser's apt phrase, "silent members of society". I say this for three reasons.

First, our democratic system is deeply rooted in, and thrives on, free and robust public discussion of public issues. As a general rule, all members of society should be permitted, indeed encouraged, to participate in that discussion.

Secondly, account must be taken of the growth in recent decades of the public sector — federal, provincial, municipal — as an employer. A blanket prohibition against all public discussion of all public issues by all public servants would, quite simply, deny fundamental democratic rights to far too many people.

Thirdly, common sense comes into play here. An absolute rule prohibiting all public participation and discussion by all public servants would prohibit activities which no sensible person in a democratic society would want to prohibit. Can anyone seriously contend that a municipal bus driver should not be able to attend a town council meeting to protest against a zoning decision having an impact on her residential street? Should not a provincial clerk be able to stand in a crowd on a Sunday afternoon and protest a provincial government decision cutting off funding for a daycare centre or a shelter for single mothers? And surely a federal commissionaire could speak out at a Legion meeting to protest against a perceived lack of federal support for war veterans. These examples, and many others could be advanced, demonstrate that an absolute prohibition against public servants criticizing government policies would not be sensible.

On the other side, however, it is equally obvious that free speech or expression is not an absolute, unqualified value. Other values must be weighed with it. Sometimes these other values supplement, and build on, the value of speech. But in other situations there is a collision. When that happens the value of speech may be cut back if the competing value is a powerful one. Thus, for example, we have laws dealing with libel and slander, sedition and blasphemy. We also have laws imposing restrictions on the press in the interests of, for example, ensuring a fair trial or protecting the privacy of minors or victims of sexual assaults.

A similar type of balancing is required in the present appeal. Public servants have some freedom to criticize the government. But it is not an absolute freedom. To take but one example, whereas it is obvious that it would not be 'just cause' for a provincial Government to dismiss a provincial clerk who stood in a crowd on a Sunday afternoon to protest provincial day-care policies, it is equally obvious that the same Government would have 'just cause' to dismiss the Deputy Minister of Social Services who spoke vigorously against the same policies at the same rally.

That brings me to the crucial question: did the Adjudicator err in where he drew the line in this case? Mr. Fraser would have a clear line drawn between job-related and non-job-related criticisms. He then asserts that his criticisms fall on the non-job-related side of the line. The Adjudicator concluded that Mr. Fraser's criticisms were job-related. Accordingly, even if there is, as Mr. Fraser contends, a valid distinction between criticism which is job-related and criticism which is non-job-related, the Adjudicator concluded that Mr. Fraser's criticisms were related to his job and that, therefore, the discharge was justified. Mr. Fraser would not succeed even on the test for which he contends.

It is true that Mr. Fraser's major criticisms were directed against two policies, the metric conversion program and the *Charter*. It is also true that his job and the policies of his department did not bear on these two policies. But it does not follow that the Adjudicator erred in law in finding that Mr. Fraser's criticisms were related to his job. A job in the public service has two dimensions, one relating to the employee's tasks and how he or she performs them, the other relating to the perception of a job held by the public. In my opinion, the Adjudicator appreciated these two dimensions. His discussion on this point is in these terms:

> When Mr. Fraser suggested on the Floyd Patterson radio hot-line program on February 5, 1982 that the Prime Minister in the conduct of the nation would prefer to act in a similar manner to the present regime in Poland, he adversely affected his own ability to conduct the affairs of the department in which he worked. For example, a corporate taxpayer who is selected as the subject of an audit by Mr. Fraser who also assigns the auditor to examine his records might well speculate about the reasons for having been selected and be concerned about the professionalism of the exercise. Surely a relatively influential official of Revenue Canada who publicly and vehemently accuses his employer, the Government of Canada, and the Prime Minister of autocratic and coercive behaviour is unlikely to instil confidence in a clientele that has a right to expect impartial and judicious treatment. And if a taxpayer's reservations were to be perceived by an auditor as an obstacle to an effective investigation, Revenue Canada officials could then rely on the widest and most far-reaching instruments of search and seizure. In this context Mr. Lowe's concern about the public's perception of Revenue Canada merits some attention. A public servant simply cannot be allowed under the rubric of free speech to cultivate distrust of the employer amongst members of the constituency whom he is obliged to serve. I am satisfied that Mr. Fraser cast doubt on his effectiveness as a Government employee once he escalated his criticism of Government policy to a point and in a form that far exceeded the issues of general public interest that he espoused before February 1, 1982. Or, more succinctly, his incipient and persistent campaign in opposition to the incumbent Government conflicted with the continuation of his employment relationship. Once that situation arose he either had to cease his activities or resign from the position he occupied.

This analysis and conclusion, namely that Mr. Fraser's criticisms were job-related, is, in my view, correct in law. I say this because of the importance and necessity of an impartial and effective public service. There is in Canada a separation of powers among the three branches of government — the legislature, the executive and the judiciary. In broad terms, the role of the judiciary is, of course, to interpret and apply the law; the role of the legislature is to decide upon and enunciate policy; the role of the executive is to administer and implement that policy.

The federal public service in Canada is part of the executive branch of government. As such, its fundamental task is to administer and implement policy. In order to do this well, the public service must employ people with certain important characteristics. Knowledge is one, fairness another, integrity a third.

As the Adjudicator indicated, a further characteristic is loyalty. As a general rule, federal public servants should be loyal to their employer, the Government of Canada. The loyalty owed is to the Government of Canada, not the political party in power at any one time. A public servant need not vote for the governing party. Nor need he or she publicly espouse its policies. And indeed, in some circumstances a public servant may actively and publicly express opposition to the policies of a government. This would be appropriate if, for example, the Government were engaged in illegal acts, or if its policies jeopardized the life, health or safety of the public servant or others, or if the public servant's criticism had no impact on his or her ability to perform effectively the duties of a public servant or on the public perception of that ability. But, having stated these qualifications (and there may be others), it is my view that a public servant must not engage, as the appellant did in the present case, in sustained and highly visible attacks on major Government policies. In conducting himself in this way the appellant, in my view, displayed a lack of loyalty to the Government that was inconsistent with his duties as an employee of the Government.

As the Adjudicator pointed out, there is a powerful reason for this general requirement of loyalty, namely the public interest in both the actual, and apparent, impartiality of the public service. The benefits that flow from this impartiality have been well-described by the MacDonnell Commission. Although the description relates to the political activities of public servants in the United Kingdom, it touches on values shared with the public service in Canada:

> Speaking generally, we think that if restrictions on the political activities of public servants were withdrawn two results would probably follow. The public might cease to believe, as we think they do now with reason believe, in the impartiality of the permanent Civil Service; and Ministers might cease to feel the well-merited confidence which they possess at present in the loyal and faithful support of their official subordinates; indeed they might be lead to scrutinise the utterances or writings of such subordinates and to select for positions of confidence only those whose sentiments were known to be in political sympathy with their own.
>
> If this were so, the system of recruitment by open competition would prove but a frail barrier against Ministerial patronage in all but the earlier years of service; the Civil Service would cease to be in fact an impartial, non-political body, capable of loyal service to all Ministers and parties alike; the change would soon affect the public estimation of the Service, and the result would be destructive of what undoubtedly is at present one of the greatest advantages of our administrative system, and one of the most honourable traditions of our public life.
>
> See: Paras 10-11 of c. 11 of MacDonnell Committee quoted in *Re Ontario Service Employees Union et al. and Attorney General of Ontario* (1980), 31 O.R. (2d) 321 (C.A.), at p. 329.

There is in Canada, in my opinion, a similar tradition surrounding our public service. The tradition emphasizes the characteristics of impartiality, neutrality, fairness and integrity. A person entering the public service or one already employed there must know, or at least be deemed to know, that employment in the public service involves acceptance of certain restraints. One of the most important of those restraints is to exercise caution when it comes to making criticisms of the Government.

For the reasons outlined, I conclude that the Adjudicator did not err in law and that the Federal Court of Appeal was right in not reversing his decision on this point.

· · · ·

*Appeal dismissed.*

[*Fraser* is not, strictly speaking, a constitutional case as it arose prior to the *Charter's* proclamation. However, it is beyond question that the considerations which were determinative here are the same as those which would be controlling should a similar case arise in the context of section 2 of the *Charter*.]

## 2. Conscience and Religion

# R. v. BIG M DRUG MART LTD.

In the Supreme Court of Canada. [1985] 3 W.W.R. 481.

Ritchie, Dickson, Beetz, McIntyre, Chouinard, Lamer and Wilson JJ.
April 24, 1985.

The judgment of Dickson, Beetz, McIntyre, Chouinard and Lamer JJ. was delivered by

DICKSON J.: —

Big M Drug Mart Ltd. was charged with unlawfully carrying on the sale of goods, on Sunday, 30th May 1982, in the city of Calgary, Alberta, contrary to the Lord's Day Act, R.S.C. 1970, c. L-13.

Big M has challenged the constitutionality of the Lord's Day Act, both in terms of the division of powers and the Canadian Charter of Rights and Freedoms. Such challenge places in issue before this court, for the first time, one of the fundamental freedoms protected by the Charter, the guarantee of "freedom of conscience and religion" entrenched in s. 2.

The constitutional validity of Sunday observance legislation has in the past been tested largely through the division of powers provided in ss. 91 and 92 of the Constitution Act, 1867. Freedom of religion has been seen to be a matter falling within federal legislative competence. Today, following the advent of the Constitution Act, 1982, we must address squarely the fundamental issues raised by individual rights and freedoms enshrined in the Charter, as well as those concerned with legislative powers.

I

THE FACTS AND THE LEGISLATION

On Sunday, 30th May 1982, police officers of the city of Calgary attended at the premises owned by Big M and open to the public. They witnessed several transactions including the sale of groceries, plastic cups and a bicycle lock. Big M was charged with a violation of s. 4 of the Lord's Day Act.

### (A) The Lord's Day Act

An understanding of the scheme of that Act and its basic purpose and effect is integral to any analysis of its constitutional validity. Section 2 defines, inter alia, the Lord's Day:

'Lord's Day' means the period of time that begins at midnight on Saturday night and ends at midnight on the following night . . .

Section 4 contains the basic prohibition against any work or commercial activity upon the Lord's Day:

4. It is not lawful for any person on the Lord's Day, except as provided herein, or in any provincial Act or law in force on or after the 1st day of March 1907, to sell or offer for sale or purchase any goods, chattels, or other personal property, or any real estate, or to carry on or transact any business of his ordinary calling, or in connection with such calling, or for gain to do, or employ any other person to do, on that day, any work, business or labour.

Section 5 provides that any worker, required to work by an employer operating on Sunday in conformity with the Act, be given a substitute day of rest; s. 6 prohibits any games or performances where an admission fee is charged; s. 7 prohibits any transportation operated for pleasure where a fee is charged; s. 8 prohibits any advertisement of anything prohibited by the Act; s. 9 prohibits any shooting of fire-arms; s. 10 prohibits any sale or distribution of a foreign newspaper.

It is important to note that any person may be exempted from the operation of ss. 4, 6, and 7 by provincial legislation or municipal charter. The following exemptions are also contained in the legislation: s. 3 — the railways may be operated for passenger traffic; s. 11 — any person may do any work of necessity or mercy which covers a broad range of activities listed in paras. (a) to (x).

The Act makes it an offence punishable on summary conviction for: any person to violate the Act (s. 12); any employer to direct any violation of the Act (s. 13); any corporation to authorize, direct or permit any violation of the Act (s. 14).

Section 16 requires the Attorney General's fiat before any prosecution may be commenced for a violation of the Act. The Attorney General of Alberta granted his fiat before commencement of proceedings against Big M.

. . . .

## III

THE CONSTITUTIONAL QUESTIONS

The constitutional questions stated by this court are:

1. Does the *Lord's Day Act*, R.S.C. 1970, c. L-13 and especially s. 4 thereof infringe upon the freedom of conscience and religion guaranteed in s. 2(a) of the *Canadian Charter of Rights and Freedoms*?
2. Is the *Lord's Day Act*, R.S.C. 1970, c. L-13 and especially s. 4 thereof justified on the basis of s. 1 of the *Canadian Charter of Rights and Freedoms*?
3. Is the *Lord's Day Act*, R.S.C. 1970, c. L-13 and especially s. 4 thereof enacted pursuant to the criminal law power under s. 91(27) of the *Constitution Act, 1867*?

The Attorney General of Canada and the Attorneys General of New Brunswick and of Saskatchewan have intervened in support of the appellant Attorney General of Alberta.

. . . .

[His Lordship's discussion of standing and jurisdiction is extracted at Chapter 3, *supra*.]

## V

THE CHARACTERIZATION OF THE LORD'S DAY ACT

(A) *The Problem*

There are obviously two possible ways to characterize the purpose of Lord's Day legislation, the one religious, namely securing public observance of the

Christian institution of the Sabbath, and the other secular, namely providing a uniform day of rest from labour. It is undoubtedly true that both elements may be present in any given enactment, indeed it is almost inevitable that they will be, considering that such laws combine a prohibition of ordinary employment for one day out of seven with a specification that this day of rest shall be the Christian Sabbath — Sunday. In the Anglo-Canadian tradition this intertwining is to be seen as far back as early Saxon times in such laws as that promulgated by Ine, King of Wessex from 688 to 725:

> If the theoman [slave] work on Sunday by his lord's command, let him be free; and let the lord pay thirty shillings as a fine. But if the theow work without his knowledge, let him suffer in his hide, or in hide-gild [money paid in lieu of corporal punishment]. But if a freeman work on that day without his lord's command, let him forfeit his freedom, or sixty shillings; and be a priest doubly liable.

The presence of both secular and religious elements in Sunday observance legislation was noted by Blackstone, Commentaries (1897 ed. Lewis), vol. IV, at p. 63:

> [B]esides the notorious indecency and scandal of permitting any secular business to be publicly transacted on that day in a country professing Christianity, and the corruption of morals which usually follows its profanation, the keeping one day in the seven holy, as a time of relaxation and refreshment as well as for public worship, is of admirable service to a state, considered merely as a civil institution. It humanizes, by the help of conversation and society, the manners of the lower classes, which would otherwise degenerate into a sordid ferocity and savage selfishness of spirit; it enables the industrious workman to pursue his occupation in the ensuing week with health and cheerfulness; it imprints on the minds of the people that sense of their duty to God so necessary to make them good citizens, but which yet would be worn out and defaced by an unremitted continuance of labour, without any stated times of recalling them to the worship of their Maker.

Despite this inevitable intertwining, it is necessary to identify the "matter" in relation to which such legislation is enacted and thereby to decide within which of the heads of s. 91 or s. 92 of the Constitution Act, 1867, such legislation falls.


### (B) *The Historic Underpinnings*

Historically, there seems little doubt that it was religious purpose which underlay the enactment of English Lord's Day legislation. From early times the moral exhortation found in the Fourth Commandment (Exodux 20: 8-11) "Remember the Sabbath day, to keep it holy" increasingly became a legislative imperative. The first major piece of legislation, the Sunday Fairs Act, 1448 (27 Hen. 6, c. 5), prefaced its prohibition of fairs and markets on Sunday with a recital of "abominable injuries and offences done to Almighty God, and to his Saints" because of bodily labour, deceitful bargaining, drunkenness and religious non-observance associated with fairs. Following the Reformation under Henry VIII, religious observance acquired an added political significance and a number of statutes aimed at securing religious conformity were promulgated, including the Act of Uniformity, 1552 (5 & 6 Edw. 6, c. 1), the Act for the Keeping of Holy-Days and Fasting-Days, 1552 (5 & 6 Edw. 6, c. 3), and the Act of Uniformity, 1558 (1 Eliz. 1, c. 2). All these Acts contained provisions making Sunday worship and observance compulsory obligations, as did the later Act against Sectaries, 1593 (35 Eliz. 1, c. 1), and Act against Papists, 1593 (35 Eliz. 1, c. 2), which, as their names suggest, were designed not only to enforce mandatory religious observance as provided for by the Church of England, but also to prohibit religious observance as practised by other Christian denominations.

Under Charles I the first modern Sunday observance statutes were enacted and their religious purpose is reflected in their titles, An Act for Punishing Divers Abuses Committed on the Lord's Day called Sunday, 1625 (1 Car. 1, c. 1), and An Act for the Further Reformation of Sundry Abuses Committed on the Lord's Day commonly called Sunday, 1627 (3 Car. 1, c. 2). During the Commonwealth or Interregnum period, the Puritan Parliament passed strict laws prohibiting the profanation of the Lord's Day by any form of marketing, travel, worldly labour, sports or recourse to taverns, tobacco shops or restaurants. With the Restoration came An Act for the Better Observation of the Lord's Day commonly called Sunday, 1676 (26 Car. 2, c. 7), also known as the Sunday Observance Act. As its full title indicates, the primary object of this legislation, like that of its predecessors, was clearly religious rather than secular. It aimed at securing observance of the Lord's Day by prohibiting all persons from engaging on a Sunday in "any worldly labour or business or work of their ordinary calling" except "works of necessity or charity".

The Sunday Observance Act of 1677 served as a model for Canadian pre-Confederation legislation, especially An Act to prevent the Profanation of the Lord's Day, commonly called Sunday, 1845 (8 Vict. c. 45) (U.C.), which substantially re-enacted the English law with only minor alterations designed to suit it to the specific conditions and activities of Upper Canada. It was this statute, as re-enacted by the post-Confederation legislature of Ontario ([An Act to prevent the Profanation of the Lord's Day] R.S.O. 1897, c. 246) that the Privy Council found to be beyond the competence of the province to enact in *A.G. Ont. v. Hamilton Street Ry. Co.*, [1903] A.C. 524, a decision which lay behind the passage in 1906 of the federal Lord's Day Act. Like the Ontario Act, the federal Act embodied the basic framework and much of the language of the English Sunday Observance Act of 1677. After four consolidations, it still exhibits the same essential characteristics in its present form.

[His Lordship's review of the Canadian and American caselaw is omitted.]

VI

PURPOSE AND EFFECT OF LEGISLATION

A finding that the Lord's Day Act has a secular purpose is, on the authorities, simply not possible. Its religious purpose, in compelling sabbatical observance, has been long established and consistently maintained by the courts of this country.

The Attorney General for Alberta concedes that the Act is characterized by this religious purpose. He contends, however, that it is not the purpose but the effects of the Act which are relevant. In his submission, *Robertson*, supra, is support for the proposition that it is effects alone which must be assessed in determining whether legislation violates a constitutional guarantee of freedom of religion.

I cannot agree. In my view, both purpose and effect are relevant in determining constitutionality; either an unconstitutional purpose or an unconstitutional effect can invalidate legislation. All legislation is animated by an object the legislature intends to achieve. This object is realized through the impact produced by the operation and application of the legislation. Purpose and effect respectively in the sense of the legislation's object and its ultimate impact are clearly linked, if not indivisible. Intended and actual effects have often been looked to for guidance in assessing the legislation's object and thus, its validity.

Moreover, consideration of the object of legislation is vital if rights are to be fully protected. The assessment by the courts of legislative purpose focuses scrutiny upon the aims and objectives of the legislature and ensures they are consonant with the guarantees enshrined in the Charter. The declaration that certain objects lie outside the legislature's power checks governmental action at the first stage of unconstitutional conduct. Further, it will provide more ready and more vigorous protection of constitutional rights by obviating the individual litigant's need to prove effects violative of Charter rights. It will also allow courts to dispose of cases where the object is clearly improper, without inquiring into the legislation's actual impact.

This approach to the relevance of purpose and effect is explicit in the American cases. In *McGowan v. Maryland*, supra, Warren C.J. stated at p. 453:

> We do not hold that Sunday legislation may not be a violation of the 'Establishment' Clause if it can be demonstrated that its purpose — evidenced either on the face of the legislation, in conjunction with its legislative history, or in its operative effect — is to use the State's coercive power to aid religion.

Similarly, in *Braunfeld v. Brown*, he wrote at p. 607:

> Of course, to hold unassailable all legislation regulating conduct which imposes solely an indirect burden on the observance of religion would be a gross oversimplification. If the purpose or effect of a law is to impede the observance of one or all religions or is to discriminate invidiously between religions, that law is constitutionally invalid even though the burden may be characterized as being only indirect. But if the State regulates conduct by enacting a general law within its power, the purpose and effect of which is to advance the State's secular goals, the statute is valid despite its indirect burden on religious observance unless the State may accomplish its purpose by means which do not impose such a burden.

I would note that this approach would seem to have been taken by this court, in its unanimous decision in *A.G. Que. v. Que. Assn. of Protestant Sch. Bd.*, [1984] 2 S.C.R. 66. When the court looked for an obvious example of legislation that constituted a total negation of a right guaranteed by the Charter, and therefore one to which the limitation in s. 1 of the Charter could not apply, it recited the following hypothetical at p. 88:

> An Act of Parliament or of a legislature which, for example, purported to impose the beliefs of a State religion would be in direct conflict with s. 2(*a*) of the *Charter*, which guarantees freedom of conscience and religion, and would have to be ruled of no force or effect without the necessity of even considering whether such legislation could be legitimized by s. 1.

If the acknowledged purpose of the Lord's Day Act, namely, the compulsion of sabbatical observance, offends freedom of religion, it is then unnecessary to consider the actual impact of Sunday closing upon religious freedom. Even if such effects were found inoffensive, as the Attorney General of Alberta urges, this could not save legislation whose purpose has been found to violate the Charter's guarantees. In any event, I would find it difficult to conceive of legislation with an unconstitutional purpose, where the effects would not also be unconstitutional.

*Robertson* cannot be of assistance for the simple reason that, in applying an interpretive standard of statutory weight, the application and not the constitutionality of the legislation was in issue. This was recognized by the majority when, at p.

657, it held that the effect rather than the purpose of legislation fell to be assessed, because it was testing not the vires of the legislation, but whether its "application" offended religious freedom.

Furthermore, the reliance upon effect to the exclusion of purpose in *Robertson* has been severely criticized: see for example, Laskin, "Freedom of Religion and the Lord's Day Act" (1964), 42 Can. Bar Rev. 147; Finkelstein, "The Relevance of Pre-Charter Case Law for Post-Charter Adjudication" (1982), 4 Sup. Ct. L. Rev. 267; and Cotler, "Freedom of Assembly, Association, Conscience and Religion", Tarnopolsky and Beaudoin (eds.) (1982), p. 123, at pp. 201-207. Many of these criticisms are telling.

In short, I agree with the respondent that the legislation's purpose is the initial test of constitutional validity and its effects are to be considered when the law under review has passed or, at least, has purportedly passed the purpose test. If the legislation fails the purpose test, there is no need to consider further its effects, since it has already been demonstrated to be invalid. Thus, if a law with a valid purpose interferes by its impact with rights or freedoms, a litigant could still argue the effects of the legislation as a means to defeat its applicability and possibly its validity. In short, the effects test will only be necessary to defeat legislation with a valid purpose; effects can never be relied upon to save legislation with an invalid purpose.

A second related submission is made by the Attorney General of Saskatchewan with respect to the characterization of the Lord's Day Act. Both Stevenson Prov. J., at trial, and the American Supreme Court, in its quartet on Sunday observance legislation, suggest that the purpose of legislation may shift, or be transformed over time by changing social conditions. This submission is related to the argument that the emphasis should be on "effects" rather than "purposes". It is urged that courts, in ignoring the religious motivation for the legislation as well as its religious terminology, are implicitly assessing the legislation's effects rather than the purposes which originally underlay its enactment: see, for example, Frankfurter J. in *McGowan v. Maryland*, supra, at p. 466. A number of objections can be advanced to this "shifting purpose" argument.

First, there are the practical difficulties. No legislation would be safe from a revised judicial assessment of purpose. Laws assumed valid on the basis of persuasive and powerful authority could, at any time, be struck down as invalid. Not only would this create uncertainty in the law, but it would encourage relitigation of the same issues and, it could be argued, provide the courts with a means by which to arrive at a result dictated by other than legal considerations. It could effectively end the doctrine of stare decisis in division of power cases. This concern underlay the judgment of Viscount Simon L.C. in *A.G. Ont. v. Can. Temperance Fed.*, [1946] A.C. 193 (P.C.), wherein he refused to re-characterize the Canada Temperance Act, R.S.C. 1927, c. 196 (at p. 206):

> ... on constitutional questions it must be seldom indeed that the Board would depart from a previous decision which it may be assumed will have been acted on both by governments and subjects. In the present case the decision now sought to be overruled has stood for over sixty years; the Act has been put into operation for varying periods in many places in the Dominion; under its provisions businesses must have been closed, fines and imprisonments for breaches of the Act have been imposed and suffered.

Furthermore, the theory of shifting purpose stands in stark contrast to fundamental notions developed in our law concerning the nature of "Parliamentary intention". Purpose is a function of the intent of those who drafted and enacted the legislation at the time, and not of any shifting variable.

As Laskin C.J.C. has suggested in *R. v. Zelensky*, [1978] 2 S.C.R. 940 at 951, "new appreciations" and "re-assessments" may justify a reinterpretation of the scope of legislative power. While this may alter over time the breadth of the various heads of power and thereby affect the classification of legislation, it does not affect the characterization of the purpose of legislation, in this case the Lord's Day Act. As the Law Reform Commission of Canada observed in its Report on Sunday Observance (1976) (at p. 42):

> While the Supreme Court has never said so explicitly, it would seem apparent that any recharacterization of the *Lord's Day Act* in a modern context so as to provide a clarification of the province's role with respect to Sunday legislation is a task the Parliament of Canada and the provincial legislatures will have to take up directly.

While the effect of such legislation as the Lord's Day Act may be more secular today than it was in 1677 or in 1906, such a finding cannot justify a conclusion that its purpose has similarly changed. In result, therefore, the Lord's Day Act must be characterized as it has always been, a law the primary purpose of which is the compulsion of sabbatical observance.

## VII

### FREEDOM OF RELIGION

A truly free society is one which can accommodate a wide variety of beliefs, diversity of tastes and pursuits, customs and codes of conduct. A free society is one which aims at equality with respect to the enjoyment of fundamental freedoms and I say this without any reliance upon s. 15 of the Charter. Freedom must surely be founded in respect for the inherent dignity and the inviolable rights of the human person. The essence of the concept of freedom of religion is the right to entertain such religious beliefs as a person chooses, the right to declare religious beliefs openly and without fear of hindrance or reprisal, and the right to manifest religious belief by worship and practice or by teaching and dissemination. But the concept means more than that.

Freedom can primarily be characterized by the absence of coercion or constraint. If a person is compelled by the state or the will of another to a course of action or inaction which he would not otherwise have chosen, he is not acting of his own volition and he cannot be said to be truly free. One of the major purposes of the Charter is to protect within reason from compulsion or restraint. Coercion includes not only such blatant forms of compulsion as direct commands to act or refrain from acting on pain of sanction, coercion includes indirect forms of control which determine or limit alternative courses of conduct available to others. Freedom in a broad sense embraces both the absence of coercion and constraint, and the right to manifest beliefs and practices. Freedom means that, subject to such limitations as are necessary to protect public safety, order, health, or morals or the fundamental rights and freedoms of others, no one is to be forced to act in any way contrary to his beliefs or his conscience.

What may appear good and true to a majoritarian religious group, or to the state acting at their behest, may not, for religious reasons, be imposed upon citizens who take a contrary view. The Charter safeguards religious minorities from the threat of "the tyranny of the majority".

To the extent that it binds all to a sectarian Christian ideal, the Lord's Day Act works a form of coercion inimical to the spirit of the Charter and the dignity of all non-Christians. In proclaiming the standards of the Christian faith, the Act creates a climate hostile to, and gives the appearance of discrimination against, non-Christian Canadians. It takes religious values rooted in Christian morality and, using the force of the state, translates them into a positive law binding on believers and non-believers alike. The theological content of the legislation remains as a subtle and constant reminder to religious minorities within the country of their differences with, and alienation from, the dominant religious culture.

Non-Christians are prohibited for religious reasons from carrying out activities which are otherwise lawful, moral and normal. The arm of the state requires all to remember the Lord's day of the Christians and to keep it holy. The protection of one religion and the concomitant non-protection of others imports disparate impact destructive of the religious freedom of the collectivity.

I agree with the submission of the respondent that to accept that Parliament retains the right to compel universal observance of the day of rest preferred by one religion is not consistent with the preservation and enhancement of the multi-cultural heritage of Canadians. To do so is contrary to the expressed provisions of s. 27, which as earlier noted reads:

> 27. This Charter shall be interpreted in a manner consistent with the preservation and enhancement of the multicultural heritage of Canadians.

As Laycraft J.A. wrote (at p. 642):

> Whatever the origins of the division of belief, it is indisputable that there can now be seen among Canadians different deeply held beliefs of religion and conscience on this subject. One group, probably the majority, accepts Sunday as the Lord's Day. Another group consisting of those of the Jewish faith, and Sabbatarians whose religious beliefs do not accept Sunday as the Lord's Day distinct from Sabbath on the seventh day of the week, believe in Saturday as their holy day. Canadians of the Muslim religion observe Friday as their holy day. Some Canadians who have no theistic belief, while perhaps accepting the concept of a day for rest and recreation, object to the enforcement of a Christian Sunday.

If I am a Jew or a Sabbatarian or a Muslim, the practice of my religion at least implies my right to work on a Sunday if I wish. It seems to me that any law purely religious in purpose, which denies me that right, must surely infringe my religious freedom.

Professor Barron, in the Harvard Law Review article to which I have referred, speaks, at p. 53, of the dissent of Cartwright J. in *Robertson*:

> For the Justice, Sunday has a very special and ceremonial significance in our culture, because of the religious meaning that has historically attached to the day. It is the enforced homage to that religious Sunday of history that constitutes a forced abandonment of one of the precepts of the Sabbatarian's religion: the belief that only the Sabbath is a day of rest proclaimed by God. It is this

homage that constitutes a burden on the free exercise of his religion. The Sabbatarian, the agnostic, and the indifferent Christian may not be required to observe Sunday in church; neither should they be compelled to acknowledge that day as a religious idea. The legislature may be able to divorce the secular Sunday from the religious Sunday of history, but the Orthodox Jew, the Seventh Day Adventist, and the atheist cannot.

The main submission of the Attorney General of Alberta, and the federal and provincial Attorneys General who intervened in his support, is that, regardless of the religious purpose of the Lord's Day Act, none of its provisions offends the freedom of conscience and religion guaranteed by s. 2(a) of the Charter. This argument draws on several sources.

### (i) The Absence of an "Establishment Clause"

Much of the argument before this court on the issue of the meaning of freedom of conscience and religion was in terms of "free exercise" and "establishment". These categories derive from the guarantee of freedom of religion in the First Amendment to the Constitution of the United States. The relevant part of the First Amendment reads:

> Congress shall make no law respecting an establishment of religion, or prohibiting the free exercise thereof . . .

It is the appellant's argument that, unlike the American Bill of Rights, the Canadian Charter of Rights and Freedoms does not include an "establishment clause". He urged therefore that the protection of freedom of conscience and religion extends only to the "free exercise" of religion. In the American cases to which I have referred, McGowan v. Maryland; Braunfeld v. Brown; Gallagher v. Crown Kosher Super Market of Massachusetts; and Two Guys from Harrison-Allentown v. McGinley, all supra, Sunday observance legislation has been deal with by a majority of the court as only presenting a potential violation of the anti-establishment principle. It is said to follow from the purported absence of such a principle in the Charter that the Lord's Day Act does not in any way affect the guarantee in s. 2(a).

In my view this recourse to categories from the American jurisprudence is not particularly helpful in defining the meaning of freedom of conscience and religion under the Charter. The adoption in the United States of the categories "establishment" and "free exercise" is perhaps an inevitable consequence of the wording of the First Amendment. The cases illustrate, however, that these are not two totally separate and distinct categories, but rather, as the Supreme Court of the United States has frequently recognized, in specific instances "the two clauses may overlap". Indeed, according to Professor Tribe in his leading textbook, American Constitutional Law (1978), at p. 815, Sunday closing cases are paradigmatic examples of such overlap. Perhaps even more important is the fact that neither "free exercise" nor "anti-establishment" is a homogeneous category; each contains a broad spectrum of heterogeneous principles. This heterogeneity is reflected in the not infrequent conflict that arises between the two clauses, evident in the opposing views of Harlan J. and Stewart J. in Sherbert v. Verner, supra. Another recent and particularly telling example of this conflict is Widmar v. Vincent, 454 U.S. 263 (1981).

Thus while it is true that in its four Sunday closing cases the United States Supreme Court does categorize compulsory religious observance as a potential violation of the "anti-establishment" principle, more frequently and more typically these same words signify the very different principle of the prohibition of preferential treatment of, or state financial support to, particular religions or religious institutions.

In further support for this line of argument the appellant cites s. 29 of the Charter quoted earlier, and s. 93 of the Constitution Act, 1867. These provisions were cited as proof of the non-existence of an anti-establishment principle because they guarantee existing rights to financial support from the state for denominational schools. The respondent replies that these express provisions constitute specific and limited exceptions to the general principle of religious freedom which would otherwise prohibit any support or preference to denominational schools. Subsequent cases will decide the extent to which the Charter allows for state financial support for, or preferential treatment of, particular religions or religious institutions. That issue is not before us in the present case.

Nonetheless, even assuming arguendo that the appellant were correct, it does not follow that s. 2(a) is not offended by Sunday observance laws. If I were to accept the notion that the sections cited are proof that there is no constitutional obstacle to such support or preference, that conclusion has no necessary implications for the question of whether the state may constitutionally compel religious behaviour or observance. The fact that both practices are prohibited by the American "anti-establishment" principle offers no support for the contention that the putative lack of prohibition of the one in the Canadian Constitution necessarily imports at the same time permission to do the other.

In my view the applicability of the Charter guarantee of freedom of conscience and religion does not depend on the presence or absence of an "anti-establishment principle" in the Canadian Constitution, a principle which can only further obfuscate an already difficult area of the law. The acceptability of legislation or governmental action which could be characterized as state aid for religion or religious activities will have to be determined on a case by case basis.

### (ii) *"Freedom of Religion" under the Canadian Bill of Rights*

The Attorney General for Alberta draws support for his restrictive reading of freedom of conscience and religion from the majority judgment in *Robertson v. R.*, [1963] S.C.R. 651. It was the view of Ritchie J. that the meaning of freedom of religion, as recognized by the Bill of Rights, was well described in two excerpts which he set forth, quoted earlier in these reasons, the first from the judgment of Taschereau J. in *Chaput v. Romain*, [1955] S.C.R. 834, the second from the judgment of Rand J. in *Saumur v. Quebec (City)*, [1953] 2 S.C.R. 299.

Ritchie J. was of opinion that it was this "complete liberty of religious thought" and "untrammelled affirmation of 'religious belief' and its propagation, personal or institutional" which the Bill of Rights recognized under the rubric of "freedom of religion". On testing the provisions of the Lord's Day Act against this definition he concluded at p. 657:

... I can see nothing in that statute which in any way affects the liberty of religious thought and practice of any citizen of this country. Nor is the 'untrammelled affirmations [sic] of religious belief and its propagation' in any way curtailed.

It was his view therefore that the Lord's Day Act did not abrogate, abridge or infringe "freedom of religion" as guaranteed by the Canadian Bill of Rights.

The appellant contends that "freedom of conscience and religion" as guaranteed by s. 2(a) of the Charter has the same meaning as "freedom of religion" as recognized by the Canadian Bill of Rights and that Ritchie J. was correct in restricting it to "liberty of religious thought" and untrammelled affirmation of religious belief and its propagation. It follows therefore, in the appellant's submission, that the Lord's Day Act no more violates the guarantee in s. 2(a) of the Charter than it did the analogous guarantee in the Canadian Bill of Rights.

I cannot agree with these submissions. In my view the meaning attributed by the majority in *Robertson v. R.* to the concept of "freedom of religion" under the Canadian Bill of Rights depends on the majority's view of the distinctive nature and status of that document. An examination of the reasoning that underlies the majority's interpretation demonstrates that it cannot easily be transferred to a constitutional document like the Charter and the fundamental guarantees it enshrines.

The basis of the majority's interpretation in *Robertson* [supra] is the fact that the language of the Bill of Rights is merely declaratory: by s. 1 of the Bill of Rights, certain existing freedoms are "recognized and declared", including freedom of religion. For Ritchie J. this language dramatically narrowed the possible interpretation of the rights and freedoms enunciated by the Canadian Bill of Rights (at p. 654):

> It is to be noted at the outset that the *Canadian Bill of Rights* is not concerned with 'human rights and fundamental freedoms' in any abstract sense, but rather with such 'rights and freedoms' as they existed in Canada immediately before the statute was enacted ... It is therefore the 'religious freedom' then existing in this country that is safe-guarded by the provisions of s. 2. ...

It is on this basis that the excerpts from *Chaput v. Romain* and *Saumur v. Quebec* were seen to be significant, since they articulate descriptions of religious freedom that, in the words of the majority "were recognized by this Court as existing in Canada before the *Canadian Bill of Rights* and notwithstanding the provisions of the *Lord's Day Act*" (at p. 655).

It is not necessary to reopen the issue of the meaning of freedom of religion under the Canadian Bill of Rights, because whatever the situation under that document, it is certain that the Canadian Charter of Rights and Freedoms does not simply "recognize and declare" existing rights as they were circumscribed by legislation current at the time of the Charter's entrenchment. The language of the Charter is imperative. It avoids any reference to existing or continuing rights but rather proclaims in the ringing terms of s. 2 that:

> 2. Everyone has the following fundamental freedoms:
> (a) Freedom of conscience and religion ...

I agree with the submission of the respondent that the Charter is intended to set a standard upon which *present as well as future* legislation is to be tested. Therefore the meaning of the concept of freedom of conscience and religion is not to be determined solely by the degree to which that right was enjoyed by Canadians prior to the proclamation of the Charter. For this reason, *Robertson*, supra, cannot be determinative of the meaning of "freedom of conscience and religion" under the Charter. We must look, rather, to the distinctive principles of constitutional interpretation appropriate to expounding the supreme law of Canada.

### (iii)  *The Purpose of Protecting Freedom of Conscience and Religion*

This court has already, in some measure, set out the basic approach to be taken in interpreting the Charter. In *Hunter, Dir. of Investigation & Research, Combines Investigation Branch v. Southam Inc.*, [1984] 2 S.C.R. 145, this court expressed the view that the proper approach to the definition of the rights and freedoms guaranteed by the Charter was a purposive one. The meaning of a right or freedom guaranteed by the Charter was to be ascertained by an analysis of the *purpose* of such a guarantee; it was to be understood, in other words, in the light of the interests it was meant to protect.

In my view this analysis is to be undertaken, and the purpose of the right or freedom in question is to be sought, by reference to the character and the larger objects of the Charter itself, to the language chosen to articulate the specific right or freedom, to the historical origins of the concepts enshrined, and where applicable, to the meaning and purpose of the other specific rights and freedoms with which it is associated within the text of the Charter. The interpretation should be, as the judgment in *Southam* emphasizes, a generous rather than a legalistic one, aimed at fulfilling the purpose of the guarantee and securing for individuals the full benefit of the Charter's protection. At the same time it is important not to overshoot the actual purpose of the right or freedom in question, but to recall that the Charter was not enacted in a vacuum, and must therefore, as this court's decision in *L.S.U.C. v. Skapinker*, [1984] 1 S.C.R. 357, illustrates, be placed in its proper linguistic, philosophic and historical contexts.

With regard to freedom of conscience and religion, the historical context is clear. As they are relevant to the Charter, the origins of the demand for such freedom are to be found in the religious struggles in post-Reformation Europe. The spread of new beliefs, the changing religious allegiance of kings and princes, the shifting military fortunes of their armies and the consequent repeated redrawing of national and imperial frontiers led to situations in which large numbers of people — sometimes even the majority in a given territory — found themselves living under rulers who professed faiths different from, and often hostile to, their own and subject to laws aimed at enforcing conformity to religious beliefs and practices they did not share.

English examples of such laws, passed during the Tudor and Stuart periods, have been alluded to in the discussion above of the criminal law character of Sunday observance legislation. Opposition to such laws was confined at first to those who upheld the prohibited faiths and practices, and was designed primarily to avoid the disabilities and penalties to which these specific adherents were subject. As a consequence, when history or geography put power into the hands of these erstwhile victims of religious oppression the persecuted all too often became the persecutors.

Beginning, however, with the Independent faction within the Parliamentary party during the Commonwealth or Interregnum, many, even among those who shared the basic beliefs of the ascendant religion, came to voice opposition to the use of the state's coercive power to secure obedience to religious precepts and to extirpate non-conforming beliefs. The basis of this opposition was no longer simply a conviction that the state was enforcing the wrong set of beliefs and practices but rather the perception that belief itself was not amenable to compulsion. Attempts to compel belief or practice denied the reality of individual conscience and dishonoured the God that had planted it in His creatures. It is from these antecedents that the concepts of freedom of religion and freedom of conscience became associated, to form, as they do in s. 2(*a*) of our Charter, the single integrated concept of "freedom of conscience and religion".

What unites enunciated freedoms in the American First Amendment, s. 2(*a*) of the Charter and in the provisions of other human rights documents in which they are associated is the notion of the centrality of individual conscience and the inappropriateness of governmental intervention to compel or to constrain its manifestation. In *Hunter v. Southam*, supra, the purpose of the Charter was identified, at p. 13 [p. 155 S.C.R.], as "the unremitting protection of individual rights and liberties". It is easy to see the relationship between respect for individual conscience and the valuation of human dignity that motivates such unremitting protection.

It should also be noted, however, that an emphasis on individual conscience and individual judgment also lies at the heart of our democratic political tradition. The ability of each citizen to make free and informed decisions is the absolute prerequisite for the legitimacy, acceptability, and efficacy of our system of self-government. It is because of the centrality of the rights associated with freedom of individual conscience both to basic beliefs about human worth and dignity and to a free and democratic political system that American jurisprudence has emphasized the primacy or "firstness" of the First Amendment. It is this same centrality that in my view underlies their designation in the Canadian Charter of Rights and Freedoms as "fundamental". They are the sine qua non of the political tradition underlying the Charter.

Viewed in this context, the purpose of freedom of conscience and religion becomes clear. The values that underlie our political and philosophic traditions demand that every individual be free to hold and to manifest whatever beliefs and opinions his or her conscience dictates, provided inter alia only that such manifestations do not injure his or her neighbours or their parallel rights to hold and manifest beliefs and opinions of their own. Religious belief and practice are historically prototypical and, in many ways, paradigmatic of conscientiously held beliefs and manifestations and are therefore protected by the Charter. Equally protected, and for the same reasons, are expressions and manifestations of religious non-belief and refusals to participate in religious practice. It may perhaps be that freedom of conscience and religion extends beyond these principles to prohibit other sorts of governmental involvement in matters having to do with religion. For the present case it is sufficient in my opinion to say that whatever else freedom of conscience and religion may mean, it must at the very least mean this: government may not coerce individuals to affirm a specific religious belief or to manifest a specific religious practice for a sectarian purpose. I leave to another case the degree, if any, to which the government may, to achieve a vital interest or objective, engage in coercive action which s. 2(*a*) might otherwise prohibit.

It is the contention of the respondent that the Lord's Day Act violates freedom of conscience and religion by coercing the observance of the religious institution of the Christian Sabbath. It is, therefore, important to the appellant's argument that freedom from such coercion forms no part of "freedom of religion" as it has been articulated in the Canadian jurisprudence. The definition of freedom of conscience and religion proposed above, including freedom from compulsory religious observance, corresponds precisely to the description of religious freedom in Canada offered by Taschereau J. in the passage in *Chaput v. Romain*, supra, when he noted that all adherents of various religious faiths are entirely free to think as they wish. This is not to endorse that part of the passage from the judgment of Taschereau J. where he states that religions are on a footing of equality. The equality necessary to support religious freedom does not require identical treatment of all religions. In fact, the interests of true equality may well require differentiation in treatment.

. . . .

Two bases for restricting the scope of s. 2(*a*) have been suggested by the appellant and his supporting interveners. First was the approach, adopted by Belzil J.A. in the court below, which maintained that there is no compulsion of religion. Abstention from work on Sunday does not, in itself, have any religious significance. Its effect is, therefore, merely secular.

This argument cannot be accepted for reasons already outlined. Once the purpose has been classified as offensive, then the legislation cannot be saved by permissible effect. As a result it is unnecessary to determine whether the secular effect here in issue is sufficient, or whether a secular effect could ever be relevant, once a finding has been made that the legislation is invalid by reason of an impermissible purpose.

A second basis for urging a more restricted reading of freedom of conscience and religion was the position of the American courts on Sunday observance legislation. Such legislation has been sustained by the United States Supreme Court, though it has been recognized that such legislation might offend the non-establishment clause of the First Amendment. The absence of such a clause in the Charter, it was submitted, indicated that this court should sustain the Lord's Day Act.

Such a finding is not possible, in light of the earlier discussion in these reasons on the relevance of the absence of an anti-establishment provision in s. 2(*a*) of the Charter.

In my view, the guarantee of freedom of conscience and religion prevents the government from compelling individuals to perform or abstain from performing otherwise harmless acts because of the religious significance of those acts to others. The element of religious compulsion is perhaps somewhat more difficult to perceive (especially for those whose beliefs are being enforced) when, as here, it is non-action rather than action that is being decreed, but in my view compulsion is nevertheless what it amounts to.

I would like to stress that nothing in these reasons should be read as suggesting any opposition to Sunday being spent as a religious day; quite the contrary. It is recognized that for a great number of Canadians, Sunday is the day when their souls rest in God, when the spiritual takes priority over the material, a day which, to them, gives security and meaning because it is linked to Creation and the Creator. It is a day which brings a balanced perspective to life, an opportunity for man to be in communion with man and with God. In my view, however, as I read the Charter, it mandates that the legislative preservation of a Sunday day of rest should be secular, the diversity of belief and non-belief, the diverse socio-cultural backgrounds of Canadians make it constitutionally incompetent for the federal Parliament to provide legislative preference for any one religion at the expense of those of another religious persuasion.

In an earlier time, when people believed in the collective responsibility of the community toward some deity, the enforcement of religious conformity may have been a legitimate object of government, but since the Charter, it is no longer legitimate. With the Charter, it has become the right of every Canadian to work out for himself or herself what his or her religious obligations, if any, should be and it is not for the state to dictate otherwise. The state shall not use the criminal sanctions at its disposal to achieve a religious purpose, namely, the uniform observance of the day chosen by the Christian religion as its day of rest.

On the authorities and for the reasons outlined, the true purpose of the Lord's Day Act is to compel the observance of the Christian Sabbath and I find the Act, and especially s. 4 thereof, infringes upon the freedom of conscience and religion guaranteed in s. 2(a) of the Charter. The answer to the first constitutional question will be in the affirmative.

## VIII

SECTION 1 OF THE CHARTER

Is the Lord's Day Act, and especially s. 4 thereof, justified on the basis of s. 1 of the Canadian Charter of Rights and Freedoms? That is the second question posed.

The appellant submits that even if the Lord's Day Act does involve a violation of freedom of conscience and religion as guaranteed by s. 2(a) of the Charter, the provisions of the Act constitute a reasonable limit, demonstrably justifiable in a free and democratic society on that right and that therefore the Act can be saved pursuant to s. 1 of the Charter. In support of this submission the Attorney General for Alberta maintains that public convenience, order and health necessitate standardized working hours and a standardized day of rest. As evidence he cites a study undertaken for the United Nations by Professor Arcot Kreshnaswami. The Attorney General for Canada supplements these arguments with submissions as to the venerable history of the "secondary principle" underlying Sunday observance legislation, namely the provision of a uniform day of rest for labouring people. He also cites numerous statutes enacted in such free and democratic societies as Great Britain, Australia and New Zealand whose purpose is to mandate a compulsory day of rest on Sunday.

At the outset, it should be noted that not every government interest or policy objective is entitled to s. 1 consideration. Principles will have to be developed for recognizing which government objectives are of sufficient importance to warrant overriding a constitutionally protected right or freedom. Once a sufficiently significant government interest is recognized then it must be decided if the means chosen to achieve this interest are reasonable — a form of proportionality test. The court may wish to ask whether the means adopted to achieve the end sought do so by impairing as little as possible the right or freedom in question.

Two reasons have been advanced to justify the legislation here in issue as a reasonable limit. It can be urged that the choice of the day of rest adhered to by the Christian majority is the most practical. This submission is really no more than an argument of convenience and expediency and is fundamentally repugnant because it would justify the law upon the very basis upon which it is attacked for violating s. 2(*a*).

The other more plausible argument is that everyone accepts the need and value of a universal day of rest from all work, business and labour and it may as well be the day traditionally observed in our society. I accept the secular justification for a day of rest in a Canadian context and the reasonableness of a day of rest has been clearly enunciated by the courts in the United States of America. The first and fatal difficulty with this argument is, as I have said, that it asserts an objective which has never been found by this court to be the motivation for the legislation. It seems disingenuous to say that the legislation is valid criminal law and offends s. 2(*a*) because it compels the observance of a Christian religious duty, yet is still a reasonable limit demonstrably justifiable because it achieves the secular objective the legislators did not primarily intend. The appellant can no more assert under s. 1 a secular objective to validate legislation which in pith and substance involves a religious matter than it could assert a secular objective as the basis for the argument that the legislation does not offend s. 2(*a*). While there is no authority on this point, it seems clear that Parliament cannot rely upon an ultra vires purpose under s. 1 of the Charter. This use of s. 1 would invite colourability, allowing Parliament to do indirectly what it could not do directly.

The characterization of the purpose of the Act as one which compels religious observance renders it unnecessary to decide the question of whether s. 1 could validate such legislation whose purpose was otherwise or whether the evidence would be sufficient to discharge the onus upon the appellant to demonstrate the justification advanced.

If a court or tribunal finds any statute to be inconsistent with the Constitution, the overriding effect of the Charter, s. 52(1), is to give the court not only the power, but the duty, to regard the inconsistent statute, to the extent of the inconsistency, as being no longer "of force or effect". That, in my view, is the position in respect of the Lord's Day Act. The answer to the second question will be in the negative.

[His Lordship's discussion of whether the *Lord's Day Act*, and in particular section 4 thereof, was enacted pursuant to section 91(27) is omitted.]

*Appeal dismissed.*

[Ritchie J. took no part in the judgment, and Wilson J.'s concurring judgment is omitted.]
[In *R. v. Videoflicks Ltd.* (1984), 48 O.R. (2d) 395 (Ont. C.A.), a case which is currently on appeal to the Supreme Court of Canada, the Ontario Court of Appeal upheld provincial Sunday closing legislation which was enacted for the secular purpose of providing a uniform day of rest. However, the Court of Appeal held that the legislation could not apply to a corporation controlled by Orthodox Jewish people whose religious day of rest was Saturday. The effect of the legislation was to penalize those whose

Sabbath was not Sunday and accordingly, only insofar as those with a sincerely held religious belief were concerned, the legislation had to be read down as a consequence of section 2(a) of the *Charter*.]

## Note on Freedom of Religion

On the point of parental rights to raise their children according to the tenets of their religious beliefs, see Finkelstein, "Legal and Constitutional Aspects of Public Funding for Private Schools in Ontario" *infra* at chapter 23; *Wisconsin v. Yoder*, 406 U.S. 250 (1972). Naturally, this right is limited where countervailing interests are involved. For example, state interests in safety regulations, child labour laws and its interest in ensuring that children do not grow up to be a burden on the state support a degree of regulation even as against a parent's religious interest: see discussion and citations in Finkelstein, *infra*. Similarly, a parent cannot rely on section 2(a) of the *Charter* to excuse him from providing the necessaries of life to his child. Thus in *R. v. Tutton* (1985), 44 C.R. (3d) 193 (Ont. C.A.), Dubin J.A., speaking for the Ontario Court of Appeal, said at p. 227:

> As previously noted, the learned trial judge instructed the jury in part as follows:
>
> 'It is not a lawful excuse for a person to have religious beliefs that say it is wrong to give insulin or that God has told them that it is not necessary to give insulin to a child. The law of this country is paramount and must be obeyed by everyone without exception.'
>
> Counsel for the appellants submitted that the above instruction offends s. 2(a) of the *Canadian Charter of Rights and Freedoms* which proclaims freedom of conscience and religion as a fundamental freedom.
>
> With respect, I find no merit in this argument. The duty imposed by statute to provide necessaries of life is applicable to all parents. It is not a lawful excuse for a parent who, knowing that a child is in need of medical assistance, refuses to obtain such assistance because to do so would be contrary to a tenet of their own particular faith. The guarantee of freedom of conscience and religion as enshrined in the *Charter* has nothing to do with this issue.

Is Dubin J.A. correct in saying that section 2(a) of the *Charter* has "nothing to do with this issue"? Is it not more correct to say that section 2(a) is implicated as long as there is a *bona fide* religious belief but that it is overridden in the *Tutton* case by section 1 of the *Charter*? Similarly, the court is entitled to consider the effect on the child of the father's religious beliefs and practices in awarding custody and access, and to limit access by prohibiting him from taking the children to religious services: see *Brown v. Brown* (1983), 3 D.L.R. (4th) 283 (Sask. C.A.).

The courts generally have been more restrictive than I would argue is desirable on the scope of the freedom of religion guarantee, cutting down its parameters notwithstanding the textual breadth of section 2(a). They should be relying more upon section 1. For example, in *Baxter v. Baxter* (1983), 45 O.R. (2d) 348 (Ont. H.C.), the Ontario High Court held that the granting of a decree absolute pursuant to the *Divorce Act* does not violate a person's freedom of religion because section 2(a) protects individual interests by prohibiting government interference. The Court said that section 2(a) does not speak to the question of what an individual can exact from the state where, as in this case, the petitioner sought a divorce. The concern with this reasoning is, at first, that there may well be cases where there is an affirmative duty on the part of government to act as for example to grant police protection to religious institutions pursuant to section 2(a) as part of a programme of general application. In cases like these, there *is* a *Charter* claim based upon what an individual can exact from the state. Second, as a matter of principle I would suggest that the courts should accept religious claims at face value in the absence of proof of bad faith instead of creating an interference/permissive dichotomy for the purposes of section 2(a), and then proceed to section 1 to support limitations. In *Baxter v. Baxter*, the issue could have been dealt with in section 1 terms on the basis of the reasonableness of society's interest in marriage and divorce and, further, that the government is entitled to balance competing private interests (e.g. that of petitioner and respondent in divorce cases) on a reasonable and demonstrably justifiable basis.

For further commentary on section 2(a) of the *Charter*, see Hogg, *Constitutional Law of Canada* (2d ed. 1985), p. 710, which includes a number of references.

## 3. Press

### (a) General

## GAY ALLIANCE TOWARD EQUALITY v. VANCOUVER SUN; BRITISH COLUMBIA HUMAN RIGHTS COMMISSION v. VANCOUVER SUN

In the Supreme Court of Canada. [1979] 2 S.C.R. 435.

Laskin C.J.C., Martland, Ritchie, Spence, Pigeon, Dickson, Beetz, Estey and Pratte JJ. May 22, 1979.

Appeal from a decision of the British Columbia Court of Appeal allowing an appeal from the judgment of MacDonald J. upholding a decision of a board of inquiry constituted pursuant to the *Human Rights Code of British Columbia* that the Vancouver Sun newspaper failed to show reasonable cause for refusing to publish an advertisement submitted by the Gay Alliance Toward Equality, a homosexual association.

The Gay Alliance Toward Equality, a homosexual association, whose object was to protect the social and legal interests of its members and to advance the cause of homosexual equality with other members of society, submitted an advertisement for its "Gay Tide" paper to the Vancouver Sun newspaper for publication. The Vancouver Sun refused to print the advertisement, stating as its only reason that it "was not acceptable for publication in this newspaper." This was so notwithstanding that there was no suggestion that the contents of the proposed advertisement were unlawful.

Section 3 of the *Human Rights Code of British Columbia* reads as follows:

> 3(1) No person shall
> (a) deny to any person or class of persons any accommodation, service, or facility, customarily available to the public; or
> (b) discriminate against any person or class of persons with respect to any accommodation, service, or facility customarily available to the public,
> unless reasonable cause exists for such denial or discrimination.

(2) For the purposes of subsection (1),

    (a) the race, religion, colour, ancestry, or place of origin of any person or class of persons shall not constitute reasonable cause; and

    (b) the sex of any person shall not constitute reasonable cause unless it relates to the maintenance of public decency . . .

A board of inquiry was appointed pursuant to the Code to inquire into the matter and found that the publication of advertisements in the Vancouver Sun was a "service or facility customarily available to the public" and that its refusal to publish was without reasonable cause. The board stated a case as required by the Code which included the following:

10.  The refusal by the Appellant to publish the advertisement in question was stated to be the result of a policy which the paper has in its advertising department (as distinct from its editorial department) to avoid any advertising material dealing with homosexuals or homosexuality, and the Appellant argued that this policy was justified on three grounds:

    (1) That homosexuality is offensive to public decency and that the advertisement would offend some of its subscribers;

    (2) That the Code of Advertising Standards, a Code of Advertising Ethics subscribed to by most of the daily newspapers in Canada includes the following section:

        "Public decency — no advertisement shall be prepared, or be knowingly accepted which is vulgar, suggestive or in any way offensive to public decency."

    and that the advertisement in question did not conform to the standards therein set out; and

    (3) That the Appellant newspaper had a duty to protect the morals of the community.

11.  This Board of Inquiry found that the central theme of the Appellant's argument was that the policy in question was predicated on a desire to protect a reasonable standard of decency and good taste.

12.  Assessing all the evidence offered on the question of the cause or motivation behind the Appellant's refusal to publish the Respondent's advertisement, the majority of the Board of Inquiry found the inevitable conclusion to be that the real reason behind the policy was not a concern for any standard of public decency, but was, in fact, a personal bias against homosexuals and homosexuality on the part of various individuals within the management of the Appellant newspaper. Board Member Dr. Dorothy Smith dissented on this point and held that there was no evidence whatsoever on which the Board could make such a finding; and that, in particular there was no evidence to rebut the Appellant's repeated statements that its policy was predicated on a desire to protect a reasonable standard of decency and good taste.

The questions of law were stated as follows:

The appellant desires to question the finding that a violation did take place on the grounds that the said Judgment was erroneous in point of law or in excess of jurisdiction, the questions submitted being:

    1. Was the Board of Inquiry correct in law in holding that pursuant to Section 3(1) of the Human Rights Code of British Columbia that classified advertising was a service or facility customarily available to the public.

    2. Was the Board of Inquiry correct in law in holding that the Appellant herein denied to any person or class of persons any accommodation, service or facility customarily available to the public or discriminated against any person or class of persons with respect to any accommodation, service or facility customarily available to the public pursuant to Section 3(1) of the Human Rights Code of British Columbia.

3. Was the Board of Inquiry correct in law in holding that pursuant to Section 3(1) of the Human Rights Code of British Columbia that the Appellant herein did not have reasonable cause for the alleged denial and did not have reasonable cause for the alleged discrimination.

On appeal to the Supreme Court of Canada, Laskin C.J.C., dissenting, held that the board's findings were conclusions of fact with which the Court had no jurisdiction to interfere. He therefore did not find it necessary to reach the substantive issues of editorial discretion or the right to express one's views through certain media of communication. The other members of the Court had this to say on these issues:

The judgment of Martland, Ritchie, Spence, Pigeon, Beetz and Pratte JJ., was delivered by

MARTLAND J.: . . .

The first two questions of law stated in the stated case raise a serious issue as to the extent to which the discretion of a newspaper publisher to determine what he wishes to publish in his newspaper has been curtailed by the *Human Rights Code*. Is his decision not to publish some item in his newspaper subject to review by a board of inquiry set up under the Act, with power, if it considers his decision unreasonable, to compel him to publish that which he does not wish to publish?

The Supreme Court of the United States, in 1974, in *Miami Herald Publishing Co. v. Tornillo*, 418 U.S. 241, had to consider whether a Florida statute violated the First Amendment's guarantee of freedom of the press. This statute granted to a political candidate the right to equal space in a newspaper to answer criticism and attacks on his record by a newspaper. This right is somewhat similar to that defined in s. 3 of Bill No. 9 entitled "An Act to ensure the Publication of Accurate News and Information", which had been reserved by the Lieutenant-Governor of Alberta, and which was under consideration in this Court: see *Reference re Alberta Legislation*, [1938] S.C.R. 100 [aff'd [1939] 117 (*sub nom. A.-G. Alta. v. A.-G. Can.*) (P.C.) (the *Alberta Press* case)].

The Supreme Court of the United States held that the statute under consideration was a violation of the First Amendment. In the course of his reasons for judgment, Chief Justice Burger, who delivered the opinion of the Court, said that the statute failed to clear the barriers of the First Amendment because of its intrusion into the function of editors. He went on to say at p. 258:

A newspaper is more than a passive receptacle or conduit of news, comment, and advertising. The choice of material to go into a newspaper, and the decisions made as to limitations on the size and content of the paper, and treatment of public issues and public officials — whether fair or unfair — constitute the exercise of editorial control and judgment. It has yet to be demonstrated how governmental regulations of this crucial process can be exercised consistent with First Amendment guarantees of a free press as they have evolved at this time.

The *Canadian Bill of Rights*, s. 1(*f*), recognizes freedom of the press as a fundamental freedom.

While there is no legislation in British Columbia in relation to freedom of the press, similar to the First Amendment or to the *Canadian Bill of Rights*, and while there is no attack made in this appeal on the constitutional validity of the *Human Rights Code*, I think that Chief Justice Burger's statement about editorial control and judgment in relation to a newspaper is of assistance in considering one of the essential ingredients of freedom of the press. The issue which arises in this appeal is as to whether s. 3 of the Act is to be construed as purporting to limit that freedom.

Section 3 of the Act refers, in paras. (a) and (b), to "service . . . customarily available to the public". It forbids the denial of such a service to any person or class of persons and it forbids discrimination against any person or class of persons with respect to such a service, unless reasonable cause exists for such denial or discrimination.

In my opinion the general purpose of s. 3 was to prevent discrimination against individuals or groups of individuals in respect of the provision of certain things available generally to the public. The items dealt with are similar to those covered by legislation in the United States, both federal and state. "Accommodation" refers to such matters as accommodation in hotels, inns and motels. "Service" refers to such matters as restaurants, bars, taverns, service stations, public transportation and public utilities. "Facility" refers to such matters as public parks and recreational facilities. These are all items "customarily available to the public". It is matters such as these which have been dealt with in American case law on the subject of civil rights.

The case in question here deals with the refusal by a newspaper to publish a classified advertisement, but it raises larger issues, which would include the whole field of newspaper advertising and letters to the editor. A newspaper exists for the purpose of disseminating information and for the expression of its views on a wide variety of issues. Revenues are derived from the sale of its newspapers and from advertising. It is true that its advertising facilities are made available, at a price, to the general public. But Sun reserved to itself the right to revise, edit, classify or reject any advertisement submitted to it for publication and this reservation was displayed daily at the head of its classified advertisement section.

The law has recognized the freedom of the press to propagate its views and ideas on any issue and to select the material which it publishes. As a corollary to that, a newspaper also has the right to refuse to publish material which runs contrary to the views which it expresses. A newspaper published by a religious organization does not have to publish an advertisement advocating atheistic doctrine. A newspaper supporting certain political views does not have to publish an advertisement advancing contrary views. In fact, the judgments of Duff, C.J.C., Davis and Cannon, JJ., in the *Alberta Press* case, previously mentioned, suggest that provincial legislation to compel such publication may be unconstitutional.

In my opinion, the service which is customarily available to the public in the case of a newspaper which accepts advertising is a service subject to the right of the newspaper to control the content of such advertising. In the present case, the Sun had adopted a position on the controversial subject of homosexuality. It did not wish to accept an advertisement seeking subscription to a publication which propagates the views of the Alliance. Such refusal was not based upon any personal characteristic of the person seeking to place that advertisement, but upon the content of the advertisement itself.

Section 3 of the Act does not purport to dictate the nature and scope of a service which must be offered to the public. In the case of a newspaper, the nature and scope of the service which it offers, including advertising service, is determined by the newspaper itself. What s. 3 does is to provide that a service which is offered to the public is to be available to all persons seeking to use it, and the newspaper cannot deny the service which it offers to any particular member of the public unless reasonable cause exists for so doing.

In my opinion the Board erred in law in considering that s. 3 was applicable in the circumstances of this case. I would dismiss the appeal with costs.

The dissenting judgment of Dickson and Estey JJ. was delivered by

DICKSON, J. (dissenting): . . .

### III

Counsel for the Vancouver Sun strongly contended for the traditional right of editorial control over newspaper content, including advertising. English law is remarkably bereft of guidance on the subject of editorial control over advertising. But in the United States, the common law is clear. Perhaps the best statement of the law is found in *Approved Personnel Inc. v. The Tribune Co.* (1965), 177 So. 2d 704 (Dist. C.A. Fla.) at 706:

> In the absence of any statutory provisions to the contrary, the law seems to be uniformly settled by the great weight of authority throughout the United States that the newspaper publishing business is a private enterprise and is neither a public utility nor affected with the public interest. The decisions appear to hold that even though a particular newspaper may enjoy a virtual monopoly in the area of its publication, this fact is neither unusual nor of important significance. The courts have consistently held that in the absence of statutory regulation on the subject, a newspaper may publish or reject commercial advertising tendered to it as its judgment best dictates without incurring liability for advertisements rejected by it.

In "Annotation — Right of Publisher of Newspaper or Magazine, in Absence of Contractual Obligation, to Refuse Publication of Advertisement", by E.L. Kellett, 18 A.L.R. 3d 1286 at 1287-8, the following summary is provided:

> With the exception of one case, it has universally been held that the absence of circumstances amounting to an illegal monopoly or conspiracy, the publisher of a newspaper or magazine is not required by law to accept and publish an advertisement, even where the advertisement is a proper one, and the regular fee for publication has been paid or tendered. . . .
>
> The reasons for refusing to compel publication of an advertisement are that at common law a newspaper is strictly a private enterprise, is not a business clothed or affected with a public interest as is a public utility, innkeeper, or railroad, and that newspaper publishers are accordingly free to contract and deal with whom they please in conformity with the inherent right of every person to refuse to maintain trade relations with any individual.

In the British Royal Commission on the Press, 1947-49, Report (Cmd. 7700, 1949), there is a brief discussion of the "right of newspapers to reject advertisements" at p. 144:

> We have received evidence that some newspapers refuse all advertisements of a particular class. This is a different matter. We consider that a newspaper has a right to refuse advertisements of any kind which are contrary to its standards or may be objectionable to its readers. This right, however, should not be exercised arbitrarily.

I think it would be correct to state that a newspaper has a right to reject advertising at common law.

## IV

Apart from the common law position, counsel for the Vancouver Sun also cast his argument in terms of press freedom. This raises issues which have not been satisfactorily resolved, either in Canada, in Britain or in the United States. These issues which can be defined broadly as (1) the content of the term "freedom of the press"; (2) the distinction between "political" and "commercial" speech; and (3) the vexed issue of access to the press. The discussion which follows is not for the purpose of resolving any constitutional issue. There is no constitutional challenge to s. 3(1) of the *Human Rights Code of British Columbia*. I wish merely to sketch the broad and important judicial background to the question posed in the case at bar.

As a starting point, I can do no better than quote from the British Royal Commission on the Press, Final Report (Cmd. 6810, 1977), pp. 8-9:

> Freedom of the press carries different meanings for different people. Some emphasize the freedom of proprietors to market their publications, others the freedom of individuals, whether professional journalists or not, to address the public through the press; still others stress the freedom of editors to decide what shall be published. These are all elements in the right to freedom of expression. But proprietors, contributors and editors must accept the limits to free expression set by the need to reconcile claims which may often conflict. The public, too, asserts a right to accurate information and fair comment which, in turn, has to be balanced against the claims both of national security and of individuals to safeguards for their reputation and privacy except when these are overridden by the public interest. But the public interest does not reside in whatever the public may happen to find interesting, and the press must be careful not to perpetrate abuses and call them freedom. Freedom of the press cannot be absolute. There must be boundaries to it and realistic discussion concerns where those boundaries ought to be set.
>
> We define freedom of the press as that degree of freedom from restraint which is essential to enable proprietors, editors and journalists to advance the public interest by publishing the facts and opinions without which a democratic electorate cannot make responsible judgments.

Later in their report, the Commissioners discuss legal constraints on the press and make the following general comment which, save for the freedom of the press assured by the *Canadian Bill of Rights*, is equally applicable to Canada (at p. 183):

> This country is unlike many others in having no laws which relate specifically to the press. There is no constitutional guarantee of the freedom of the press, as there is in the United States, and no judicial surveillance of the contents of the newspapers, as there is in Sweden. Nevertheless, there are areas of general law which relate predominantly, and in some cases almost exclusively, to the activities of the press. In important ways, legal provisions help to maintain the delicate balance between freedom of the press and the public interest.

In Canada, as in Britain, much of the protection of the freedom of the press must derive from the interpretation of the "general law" rather than from a constitutional guarantee, and from the interpretation of statutes such as the British Columbia *Human Rights Code* as they may affect the press. While admittedly the *Alberta Press* case, *Reference re Alberta Legislation*, [1938] S.C.R. 100 [aff'd [1939] A.C. 117 (*sub nom. A.-G. Alta. v. A.-G. Can.*) (P.C.)], dealt with the constitutional validity of the "Alberta Press bill", as it was termed, the comments of Chief Justice Duff and Mr. Justice Cannon in that case are important in defining the notion of freedom of the press in the Canadian context.

In the United States, freedom of the press rests upon the First Amendment, which reads:

> Congress shall make no law respecting an establishment of religion, or prohibiting the free exercise thereof; or abridging the freedom of speech, or of the press, or the right of the people peaceably to assemble, and to petition the Government for redress of grievances.

The framers of the United States Constitution linked freedom of speech in the First Amendment to freedom of the press to provide an effective forum for such expression: "Conflict Within the First Amendment: A Right to Access to Newspapers", 48 N.Y.U.L.R. 1200 (1973). In the result, there would appear to be general agreement in Britain, Canada, and the United States, as to the "free public discussion" rationale for freedom of the press.

## V

Within the First Amendment in the United States two issues have been much discussed: whether the First Amendment mandates equal protection for "commercial" as opposed to "political" speech, and whether the First Amendment not only protects expression once it comes to the fore, but also serves to ground an affirmative right of access to the media. In response to these issues two trends can be discerned in the American cases. The first is the obliteration of any meaningful distinction between "political" and "commercial" speech within the First Amendment. The second is the rejection of a right of access to the press based upon the First Amendment.

The so-called "commercial speech" doctrine finds its origin in the case of *Valentine v. Chrestensen*, 316 U.S. 52 at 54 (1942), where Mr. Justice Roberts, on behalf of the Court, stated unequivocally: "We are equally clear that the Constitution imposes no such restraint [the First Amendment] on government as respects purely commercial advertising." I do not intend any detailed canvas of the American authorities other than to say that the "commercial" exception appeared to retain its virility as recently as the case of *Pittsburgh Press Co. v. Pittsburgh Commission on Human Relations*, 413 U.S. 376 (1973), but the ambit of that case was shortly thereafter cut down in *Bigelow v. Virginia*, 421 U.S. 809 (1975), and further narrowed the following year in *Virginia State Board of Pharmacy v. Virginia Citizens Consumer Council Inc.*, 425 U.S. 748 (1976), where the Court struck down the restrictions on prescription drug advertising found in Virginia law as violating the First Amendment. Nor has this wave receded: see *Bates v. State Bar of Arizona*, 97 S. Ct. 2691 (1977), where State bar restrictions on advertising by lawyers were struck down.

A separate line of cases has upheld the view that the First Amendment serves no affirmative function, *i.e.*, it does not mandate any right of access, however limited, to the media: see *Chicago Joint Board, Amalgamated Clothing Workers of America A.F.L.-CLO v. Chicago Tribune Co.*, 307 F. Supp. 422 (1969 N.D. Ill); aff'd 435 F.2d 470 (7th Cir.); *certiorari* denied 402 U.S. 973. Any doubts, so far as the United States is concerned, as to a right of access to newspapers, would appear to be settled by the Supreme Court in *Miami Herald Publishing Co. v. Tornillo*, 418 U.S. 241 (1974). The newspaper had refused to print Tornillo's replies to editorials critical of his candidacy for State office and Tornillo brought suit seeking injunctive and declaratory relief under Florida's "right of reply" statute. That statute provided that:

... if a candidate for nomination or election is assailed regarding his personal character or official record by any newspaper, the candidate has the right to demand that the newspaper print, free of cost to the candidate, any reply the candidate may make to the newspaper's charges. The reply must appear in as conspicuous a place and in the same kind of type as the charges which prompted the reply, provided it does not take up more space than the charges. Failure to comply with the statute constitutes a first-degree misdemeanour.

While the Circuit Court held the statute unconstitutional as an infringement on the freedom of the press under the First and Fourteenth Amendments, the Florida Supreme Court found no such violation, free speech being enhanced and not abridged by the statute, which furthered the "broad societal interest in the free flow of information to the public". This view was rejected by the Supreme Court on the ground that it constituted interference by the Government with the exercise of editorial control and judgment, and hence with First Amendment guarantees of a free press. See also *Columbia Broadcasting System Inc. v. Democratic National Committee*, 412 U.S. 94 (1973).

Before leaving the American cases it is, I think, appropriate to note that these cases were decided in light of a strong First Amendment constitutional underpinning, and legislation such as that found in the British Columbia *Human Rights Code* was not in issue. Our limited jurisprudence, to which I will shortly refer, would appear to accept a greater degree of regulation in respect of newspaper advertising than is apparent in the United States.

## VI

Although freedom of the press is one of our cherished freedoms, recognized in the *quasi*-constitutional *Canadian Bill of Rights*, the freedom is not absolute. Publishers of newspapers are amenable to civil and criminal laws which bear equally upon all businessmen and employers, generally, in the community, for example, those regulating labour relations, combines, or imposing non-discriminatory general taxation. False and misleading advertising may properly be proscribed. In *Cowen v. A.-G. B.C.*, [1941] S.C.R. 321, the central question was whether a 1939 amendment to the British Columbia *Dentistry Act*, which barred any person not registered under the Act from practising or offering to practise dentistry in the Province, was limited to acts within the Province, and press freedom was not raised. The result of the decision, however, was the maintenance of an injunction to prevent the publication of certain advertisements in a daily newspaper. In *Benson & Hedges (Canada) Ltd. et al. v. A.-G. B.C.*, [1972] 5 W.W.R. 32 (B.C.S.C.), an Act, the effect of which was "to prohibit advertising by any person of tobacco products", was upheld, although press freedom does not appear to have been in issue or argued. In *R. v. Toronto Magistrates; Ex parte Telegram Publishing Co.*, [1960] O.R. 518 (Ont. H.C.), Mr. Justice Schatz held that a section of the *Liquor Control Act* of Ontario prohibiting the publication of any announcement concerning liquor was not an encroachment on the freedom of the press, or upon freedom of speech.

Newspapers occupy a unique place in western society. The press has been felicitously referred to by de Toqueville as "the chief democratic instrument of freedom". Blackstone wrote, "The liberty of the press is indeed essential to the nature of a free state." Jefferson went so far as to assert, "Were it left for me to decide whether we should have a government without newspapers, or newspapers without a government, I should not hesitate a moment to prefer the latter." There is a direct and vital relationship between a free press and a free society. The right to speak freely, publish freely, and worship freely, are fundamental and indigenous rights, but it is "freedom governed by law", as Lord Wright observed in *James v. Commonwealth of Australia*, [1936] A.C. 578 at 627. In the *Alberta Press* case, *supra*, we find these words of Sir Lyman P. Duff, C.J.C. at p. 134 S.C.R.:

> Some degree of regulation of newspapers everybody would concede to the Provinces. Indeed, there is a very wide field in which the Provinces undoubtedly are invested with legislative authority over newspapers; but the limit, in our opinion, is reached when the legislation effects such a curtailment of the exercise of the right of public discussion as substantially to interfere with the working of the parliamentary institutions of Canada. . . .

Governments in Canada have generally respected press independence and have followed a policy of non-intervention.

There is an important distinction to be made between legislation designed to control the editorial content of a newspaper, and legislation designed to control discriminatory practices in the offering of commercial services to the public. We are dealing in this case with the classified advertising section of a newspaper. The primary purpose of commercial advertising is to advance the economic welfare of the newspaper. That part of the paper is not concerned with freedom of speech on matters of public concern as a condition of democratic polity, but rather with the provision of a "service or facility customarily available to the public" with a view to profit. As such, in British Columbia a newspaper is impressed with a statutory obligation not to deny space or discriminate with respect to classified advertising, unless for reasonable cause. It should be made clear that the right of access with which we are here concerned has nothing to do with those parts of the paper where one finds news or editorial content, parts which can in no way be characterized as a service customarily available to the public. The effect of s. 3 of the British Columbia *Human Rights Code* is to require newspapers within the Province to adopt advertising policies which are not in violation of the principles set out in the *Code*.

. . . .

I would allow the appeal, set aside the judgment of the British Columbia Court of Appeal and restore the judgment of MacDonald, J., and the order of the board of inquiry, with costs throughout.

*Appeal dismissed.*

# RE NEW BRUNSWICK BROADCASTING CO. LTD. AND CANADIAN RADIO-TELEVISION & TELECOMMUNICATIONS COMMISSION*

In the Federal Court of Appeal. [1984] 2 F.C. 410.

Thurlow C.J., Pratte and Ryan JJ. July 27, 1984.

Appeal from and application for judicial review of a decision of the Canadian Radio-television and Telecommunications Commission.

The judgment of the court was delivered by

THURLOW C.J.: — This is a joint proceeding consisting of an appeal under s. 26 of the *Broadcasting Act*, R.S.C. 1970, c. B-11, and an application under s. 28 of the *Federal Court Act*, R.S.C. 1970, c. 10 (2nd Supp.). What is attacked by both the appeal and the review application is a decision of the Canadian Radio-television and Telecommunications Commission dated August 11, 1983, which limited the renewal of the television broadcasting licences of the appellant and its rebroadcasters to a term expiring on January 1, 1986. It is common ground that but for a direction to the commission given by Order in Council dated July 29, 1982, and purporting to be made pursuant to s. 22 of the *Broadcasting Act*, which the commission took into account in reaching its decision, the period for which the renewal of the licences was granted by the commission would have been at least somewhat longer, though, for reasons appearing in the decision, it would not have been for the full five-year period for which the commission has, under s. 17, authority to grant or renew broadcasting licences.

The appellant's case is that the direction was illegal and void and should not have been taken into account by the commission because: . . .

(2) it deprived the appellant and the public of the right under para. 2(*b*) of the *Canadian Charter of Rights and Freedoms* to freedom of thought, belief, opinion and expression including freedom of the press and other media of communication; and

. . . .

*The Charter of Rights point*

The appellant's submission on the Charter proceeds thus:

(1) Since freedom of the press and other media of communication is constitutionally guaranteed, the requirement of a licence for the operation of a broadcasting undertaking is in breach of s-s. 2(*b*) of the Charter;
(2) It is acknowledged, however, that the requirement of a licence is a limit which can be demonstrably justified in a free and democratic society because:
    (a) as set out in s. 3 of the *Broadcasting Act* radio frequencies are a public property which have to be allotted according to agreement in order to ensure a fair allocation of available frequencies, and

---

*Leave to appeal to the Supreme Court of Canada (Estey, McIntyre and Wilson JJ.) granted December 3, 1984.

   (b) there has to be an individual (company) responsible for civil and criminal liability.

(3) However, the direction, in so far as it denies broadcasting licences to "newspaper proprietors", is inconsistent with and in violation of the appellant's right of freedom of the press and other media of communication guaranteed to everyone by s-s. 2(b) of the Charter. Further, in so far as the direction denies to the public broadcasting service because a newspaper proprietor controls a broadcasting undertaking, it is inconsistent with and in violation of the rights and freedoms guaranteed to everyone by s-s. 2(b) of the Charter.

   In my opinion, the argument confuses the freedom guaranteed by the Charter with a right to the use of property and is not sustainable. The freedom guaranteed by the Charter is a freedom to express and communicate ideas without restraint, whether orally or in print or by other means of communication. It is not a freedom to use someone else's property to do so. It gives no right to anyone to use someone else's land or platform to make a speech, or someone else's printing press to publish his ideas. It gives no right to anyone to enter and use a public building for such purposes. And it gives no right to anyone to use the radio frequencies which, before the enactment of the Charter, had been declared by Parliament to be and had become public property and subject to the licensing and other provisions of the *Broadcasting Act*. The appellant's freedom to broadcast what it wishes to communicate would not be denied by the refusal of a licence to operate a broadcasting undertaking. It would have the same freedom as anyone else to air its information by purchasing time on a licensed station. Nor does the Charter confer on the rest of the public a right to a broadcasting service to be provided by the appellant. Moreover, since the freedom guaranteed by para. 2(b) does not include a right for anyone to use the property of another or public property, the use of which was subject to and governed by the provisions of a statute, there is, in my opinion, no occasion or need to resort to s. 1 of the Charter to justify the licensing system established by the *Broadcasting Act*.

   Accordingly, I would reject the appellant's submission.

### Note on the Print and Broadcast Media

   The print and broadcast media are treated differently in the United States for First Amendment purposes. The print media has unfettered editorial discretion, subject to properly drawn laws respecting matters such as sedition, obscenity, and defamation (but see *New York Times v. Sullivan*, 376 U.S. 254 (1963) where Alabama's overbroad common law of libel was held to be an impermissible clog on a newspaper's First Amendment rights). Thus no person may claim a "right of reply" or access to a newspaper even to respond to a personal attack: *Miami Herald Publishing Co. v. Tornillo*, 418 U.S. 241 (1974). On the other hand, the U.S. Supreme Court has been more tolerant of government restrictions on the broadcast media. Admittedly no person may claim a generalized right of access apart from government regulation (*Columbia Broadcasting System v. Democratic National Committee*, 412 U.S. 94 (1973)), and even publicly funded broadcasters have a constitutional right to editorialize (*FCC v. League of Women Voters*, 104 S. Ct. 3106 (1984)). However, FCC regulations which provide a "limited right to 'reasonable' access" for federal political candidates where a campaign has begun (*CBS v. FCC*, 101 S. Ct. 2813 (1981)) and a right of reply to those who have been personally attacked by a broadcaster (*Red Lion Broadcasting Co. v. FCC*, 395 U.S. 367 (1969)) have been upheld.

A variety of rationales have been advanced in the caselaw and commentary to support the different constitutional treatment. The most important of these is the spectrum scarcity rationale. The argument is that, given the current state of receiving and transmitting technology, there is a finite number of commercially useable frequencies available. As there is accordingly limited access by broadcasters to the airwaves, a governmental authority (the CRTC in Canada and the FCC in the U.S.) is entitled to allocate licences and exercise a limited degree of content control over broadcasters in the public interest to ensure, *inter alia*, that all points of view are presented. With respect to newspapers, on the other hand, the theory is that anyone can buy a printing press and start cranking out handbills. There is therefore unlimited access to the medium and accordingly less justification for government control. Among the other rationales given in support of government regulation of broadcast are i) the impact doctrine, which alleges that the broadcast media is so all-pervasive and credible that it has a disproportionate impact on the public's consciousness and ideas, and ii) the privacy theory, which alleges that the medium is extremely intrusive, to the point of entering one's living room without warning about the sorts of messages that are about to be broadcast: see *FCC v. Pacifica Foundation*, 438 U.S. 726 (1978). These rationales and others for distinguishing between the print and broadcast media have been criticized: For excellent analyses and collections of references, see "Note", (1981), 95 Harv. L.R. 221; "Note", (1984), 98 Harv. L.R. 205; Tribe, *American Constitutional Law* (1978), p. 697 *et seq.*; Marie Finkelstein, "The Regulation of Sex-Role Stereotyping in Broadcasting under the Freedom of Expression Guarantee in the Charter of Rights" (unpublished LL.M. thesis, Osgoode Hall Law School, 1985).

The most unsettling aspect of *Re New Brunswick Broadcasting Co. and C.R.T.C., supra*, is that it appears to refuse to recognize any freedom of expression interest at all in broadcasters, stating that because radio frequencies have been declared by Parliament to be public property, the applicant's argument with respect to section 2(b) of the *Charter* "confuses the freedom guaranteed by the *Charter* with a right to the use of property". To put a point on it, the Federal Court of Appeal goes on to say that:

> Since the freedom guaranteed by paragraph 2(b) does not include a right for anyone to use the property of another or public property, the use of which was subject to and governed by the provisions of a statute, there is, in my opinion, no occasion or need to resort to s. 1 of the *Charter* to justify the licensing system established by the *Broadcasting Act*.

If taken literally, the Court of Appeal's reasoning has the potential to eliminate a great deal of expression from the scope of section 2(b) of the *Charter*. Parades and demonstrations take place on public streets. Handbills are distributed in public places. Surely the freedom of expression guaranteed by section 2(b) includes more than the right to speak freely in the privacy of one's own property. That is not to say that freedom to speak in public on public property is not subject to restrictions, but those restrictions must be tested against the crucible of section 1 of the *Charter*. The mere fact that the speaker seeks to address a crowd in a public park cannot exclude the speech altogether from the scope of section 2(b) just because the park is govern-ment-owned.

No doubt the Court of Appeal did not intend to cast such a broad net. However, its language is unrestricted, and the Court does not say anywhere that the airwaves are any different from any other form of public property. *Re New Brunswick Broadcasting* is accordingly an extremely unsatisfactory precedent. It is to be hoped that the Supreme Court of Canada (which at the time of this writing has granted leave to appeal) will evaluate the real justifications of broadcast licence requirements (e.g. spectrum scarcity, impact, privacy, etc.). Surely the fact that Parliament has declared the airwaves to be public property is not enough.

## (b) Access to and Publication of Judicial Proceedings

# CANADIAN NEWSPAPERS COMPANY LIMITED v. A.G. CAN.

In the Ontario Court of Appeal. 49 O.R. (2d) 557.

Howland C.J.O., Lacourcière and Goodman JJ.A. February 12, 1985.

The judgment of the court was delivered by HOWLAND C.J.O.

*Is s. 442(3) of the Code of no force and effect as it contravenes s. 2(b) and s. 11(d) of the Charter?*

On the appeal counsel for the appellant raised two grounds of appeal relating to the Charter:

(a) that Osborne J. erred in finding that s. 442(3) was a reasonable limit demon-strably justified in a free and democratic society on the freedom of the press under s. 2(*b*) of the Charter, and particularly in so far as an order under s. 442(3) is mandatory upon the application of the complainant or the prosecutor.
(b) that Osborne J. erred in concluding that s. 442(3) does not *prima facie* infringe the right to a public hearing under s. 11(*d*) of the Charter.

*Section 2(b) — Freedom of the press*

Section 2(*b*) of the Charter provides that:

2. Everyone has the following fundamental freedoms:

. . . . .

(*b*) freedom of thought, belief, opinion and expression, including freedom of the press and other media of communication;

The freedom of the press to report what transpires in our courtrooms is one of the fundamental safeguards of our democratic society. Justice is not a cloistered virtue and judicial proceedings must be subjected to careful scrutiny in order to ensure that every person is given a fair trial. The presence of the public, including representa-tives of the media, ensures the integrity of judicial proceedings. Openness of the courts is essential for the maintenance of public confidence in the administration of justice and to further a proper understanding of the judicial system. It reassures the public that all persons regardless of race, colour or creed are equal before the law and that there is no arbitrary action or abuse of power. It gives the public an opportunity to see that justice is done. There is necessarily implicit in the concept of an open court the concept of publicity; the right of the media to report what they have heard in the court-room so that the public can be informed about court proceedings, and public criticism, if necessary, engendered should any impropriety occur. As MacKinnon A.C.J.O. said in delivering the judgment of this Court in *Re Southam Inc. and The Queen (No. 1)* (1983), 41 O.R. (2d) 113 at 121-2: ". . . freedom of the press refers to the dissemination of expression of thought, belief or opinion through the medium of the press."

In *F.P. Publications (Western) Ltd. v. Conner, Prov. J.*, [1980] 1 W.W.R. 504 (Man. C.A.), an order was made barring a newspaper reporter from being present at a trial in provincial court where charges of keeping a common bawdy-house were being heard. The newspaper had refused to undertake not to publish the names of witnesses who were former customers of the massage parlours. It was held by the Manitoba Court of Appeal that the exclusion order should be quashed. It was contrary to the concept of an open court and the freedom of the press.

In *Re Southam Inc. and the Queen (No. 1), supra*, this Court held that the mandatory exclusion of the public from the trial of juveniles under s. 12(1) of the *Juvenile Delinquents Act* had not been demonstrably justified as a reasonable limit prescribed by law on the right of access to the courts subsumed under the guaranteed freedom of expression, including freedom of the press, within s. 1 of the Charter. It was therefore unconstitutional.

There are a few well-recognized exceptions where proceedings *in camera* are justified because the presence of the public would be impracticable as in the case of infants, mentally disordered persons or secret processes. Section 442(1) of the *Code* provides for proceedings against the accused being held in open court. Where the presiding judge is of the opinion that it is in the interest of public morals, the maintenance of order or the proper administration of justice, he may order all or any members of the public be excluded from the court-room for all or part of the proceedings.

The basic test to be applied in determining whether banning public accessibility to court proceedings can be justified was laid down by Dickson J. (as he then was) in delivering the judgment of the majority of the Supreme Court of Canada in *A.-G. N.S. v. MacIntyre*, [1982] 1 S.C.R. 175. In that case a journalist sought a declaration that he was entitled to inspect search warrants and the informations used to obtain them. The Supreme Court of Canada held that a member of the public has such a right after the search warrant has been executed and objects found as a result of the search are brought before a justice pursuant to s. 446 of the *Code*. In considering the matter of public accessibility in light of a strong public policy in favour of "openness" in respect of judicial acts he stated at pp. 186-7 S.C.R.: ". . . curtailment of public accessibility can only be justified where there is present the need to protect social values of superordinate importance." The sensibilities of an adult person, whether he or she is the accused or a witness, is not a valid basis for limiting the publication of criminal proceedings or excluding the public from the court-room:

*A.-G. N.S. v. MacIntyre, supra*, at p. 185 S.C.R.; *Re R. and Several Unnamed Persons* (1983), 44 O.R. (2d) 81 at 84-5 (H.C.).

I am in agreement with Osborne J. that s. 442(3) of the *Code* in providing for an order prohibiting the publication of the identity of the complainant and of any information that could disclose her identity *prima facie* infringed the freedom of the press under s. 2(b) of the Charter to report what transpired at a public trial. It then becomes necessary to consider whether s. 442(3) imposed such reasonable limits prescribed by law as can be reasonably justified in a free and democratic society within s. 1 of the Charter. The onus falls on the Attorney-General for Canada who is seeking to uphold the limits in s. 442(3) to establish on the balance of probabilities that the limits are reasonable. In accordance with the test laid down in *A.-G. N.S. v. MacIntyre, supra*, it must be shown that the limits imposed are not more extensive than are necessary to protect social values of superordinate importance.

What is the social value to be protected by s. 442(3)? It is to facilitate the prosecution of persons charged with serious sexual offences within s. 246.4 of the *Code*, and for that purpose to encourage the victims to come forward and complain, and to be prepared to testify at the trial of the accused. In satisfying the onus which lies upon it the Attorney-General for Canada is entitled to tender extrinsic evidence.

In this case the extrinsic evidence consisted solely of the testimony of Doreen Carole Boucher, the co-ordinator of the centre. It was apparent from her evidence that the victims of such offences are often very reluctant to come forward and report what was done to them. They are suffering from the trauma of the assault and do not want to relive the experience. They are embarrassed by what has happened to them and are concerned about their privacy. They do not want others to know what happened to them and they are afraid of retribution by the accused. I consider that it has been clearly established that the social value to be protected, namely, the bringing of those who commit such sexual offences to justice, is of superordinate importance and can merit a prohibition against publication of the victims' identity or of any information that could disclose it. It is a reasonable limitation on the freedom of the press. The representatives of the media still have the right of access to the courtroom and to publish everything that transpires, with the exception only of the identity of the complainant and information which could disclose that identity. The Attorney-General for Canada has demonstrably justified the reasonableness of such a limitation on a balance of probabilities, subject only to the question whether such a prohibition order should be mandatory on the application of the complainant or of the prosecutor.

When s. 442(3) was first enacted by S.C. 1974-75-76, c. 93, the order was only to be made by the trial judge if the prosecutor applied for it, but if he did, then it was mandatory for the trial judge to make it. When s. 442(3) was amended by S.C. 1980-81-82-83, c. 125, the presiding judge could make the order on his own initiative and in his discretion, but it was mandatory for him to make the order if the complainant or the prosecutor applied for it. By s-s. (3.1) the presiding judge was under an obligation to inform the complainant at the first reasonable opportunity of the right to make such an application.

Has the Attorney-General for Canada demonstrably justified that it is a reasonable limitation for the order to be mandatory in every instance where the complainant or the prosecutor applies for it? Doreen Carole Boucher testified that she was aware of some instances where a rape was imagined and the alleged victim wanted to humiliate a person. There may also be instances where an alleged victim has accused a number of persons previously of sexual offences without justification. The publication of the name of the complainant may in some cases bring forth other witnesses whose testimony may be helpful.

In this connection it is pertinent to consider whether legislation similar to s. 442(3) in other free and democratic societies provides for a mandatory prohibition against identifying the complainant.

[His Lordship's review of the law in the United Kingdom, Australia and New Zealand is omitted.]

(d)  *United States*

The provisions of the United States Constitution are somewhat different from those of the Charter. However, there are some similarities in the approach which the Supreme Court of the United States has taken to the problem.

The First Amendment to the United States Constitution provides that:

> Congress shall make no law ... abridging the freedom of speech, or of the press ...

The Fourteenth Amendment provides in s. 1:

> All persons born or naturalized in the United States, and subject to the jurisdiction thereof, are citizens of the United States and the State wherein they reside. No State shall make or enforce any law which shall abridge the privileges or immunities of citizens of the United States; nor shall any State deprive any person of life, liberty, or property, without due process of law; nor deny to any person within its jurisdiction the equal protection of the laws.

The United States Supreme Court in dealing with the subject of freedom of the press has held state legislation to be unconstitutional unless the limitation which it placed on the openness of criminal proceedings was justified by an overriding state interest and was narrowly tailored to meet that interest.

In *Richmond Newspapers Inc. v. Virginia*, 448 U.S. 554 (1980), the United States Supreme Court upheld the right of the public, including representatives of the media, to attend a criminal trial, as against an order of closure under state law. In *Globe Newspaper Co. v. Superior Court for County of Norfolk*, 102 S. Ct. 2613 (1982), the Supreme Court of the United States had to consider the validity of a Massachusetts statute excluding the press and the general public during the testimony of a victim under 18 years of age at the trial of a sex offence. The majority of the court concluded that the mandatory closure rule was not valid. Closure might well have been deemed unnecessary if the trial court had been permitted to exercise its discretion.

The right to publish what is in the official record of court proceedings has similarly been protected. In *Cox Broadcasting Corp. v. Cohn*, 95 S. Ct. 1029 (1979), the constitutional validity of state legislation forbidding the publication of the name or identity of a witness in a rape case was not upheld. The Supreme Court of the United States concluded that the press cannot be liable for truthfully publishing information released to the public in the official court records. The interest of privacy was considered to fade where the information appears on the public record. Some years earlier in *State of Wisconsin v. Evjue*, 13 A.L.R. 2d 1201 (1948), the Wisconsin

Supreme Court had upheld the validity of a similar provision in a Wisconsin statute. In *Smith v. Daily Mail Publishing Co.*, 99 S. Ct. 2667 (1979), state legislation banning the publication of the name of a juvenile offender without the approval of the juvenile court was held by the Supreme Court of the United States to violate the First and Fourteenth Amendments.

## Other mandatory provisions

The situation in this case is quite different from that in *Re Global Communications Ltd. and A.-G. Can.* (1984), 44 O.R. (2d) 609. There, this Court had to consider the constitutional validity of s. 457.2 of the *Code* which it held applied to the granting of bail to a fugitive pending the extradition hearing under the *Extradition Act*, R.S.C. 1970, c. E-21. Under s. 457.2 it is mandatory for the justice upon application by the accused to make an order that the evidence taken, the information given, or the representations made, and the reasons given by the justice shall not be published in any newspaper or broadcast until the accused is discharged, if a preliminary inquiry is held, or until the trial of the accused is ended. This Court held that the right of the press to publish what transpired at the bail hearing had to yield to the public interest in order to ensure that the fugitive would have a fair trial. Without this prohibition the risk of prejudice to the accused through the dissemination of the evidence was severe. The right to the prohibition order under s. 457.2 was a reasonable limitation of the freedom of the press under s. 2(*b*) of the Charter which had been demonstrably justified.

I am not persuaded that the Attorney-General for Canada has demonstrably justified that the mandatory prohibition order under s. 442(3) upon the application of the complainant or the prosecutor is a reasonable limitation. It is not required as it was in the *Global Communications* case to ensure that the accused received a fair trial. There is no evidence that the needs of Canada for such legislation are greater than the needs of other free and democratic societies to whose legislation I have referred. The administration of justice is dependent on public confidence in the judiciary. The discretion given to the trial judge under s. 442(3) to make a prohibition order is a sufficient safeguard for the protection of the identity of the complainant. In most cases it will no doubt be made as a matter of course. However, in an exceptional case where it is not merited the presiding judge should have an opportunity to refuse to make it.

Under s. 52(1) of the *Constitution Act, 1982*, s. 442(3) of the *Code* is, to the extent that it requires the making of a mandatory order, inconsistent with the Charter and of no force and effect. This does not result in s. 442(3) being declared invalid in its entirety. The offending portion of s. 442(3) can be severed. The test to be applied as to severability is set forth in *Reference re Alberta Bill of Rights Act; A.-G. Alta. v. A.-G. Can.*, [1947] A.C. 503, where Viscount Simon in delivering the judgment of the Judicial Committee of the Privy Council stated at p. 518 A.C.:

> The real question is whether what remains is so inextricably bound up with the part declared invalid that what remains cannot independently survive or, as it has sometimes been put, whether on a fair review of the whole matter it can be assumed that the legislature would have enacted what survives without enacting the part that is *ultra vires* at all.

Here, if the offending clause is deleted, the remainder of the subsection, which simply gives the presiding judge a discretion to make the order, can stand. The valid portion of the subsection is not inextricably bound up with the invalid portion. Parliament clearly intended that the presiding judge should have the discretionary power to make a prohibitory order quite apart from having the obligation to make such an order if requested by the complainant or the prosecutor to do so. Accordingly, the offending portions of s. 442(3) can be severed: see Barry L. Strayer, *The Canadian Constitution and the Courts*, 2nd ed. (1983), at pp. 262-4.

I do not consider that it is necessary to sever s-s. (3.1). It would seem appropriate that the presiding judge should inform the complainant of her right to make an application requesting him to make a prohibitory order.

*Right to a public hearing — s. 11(d) of the Charter*

Counsel for the appellant also contended that s. 442(3) *prima facie* infringed the right to a public hearing under s. 11(*d*) of the Charter which provides:

> 11. Any person charged with an offence has the right
>
>  . . . . .
>
> (*d*) to be presumed innocent until proven guilty according to law in a fair and public hearing by an independent and impartial tribunal;

As I have already pointed out, a public hearing is one in open court which the public, including representatives of the media, are entitled to attend. The right which is protected by s. 11(*d*) of the Charter is the right of a person charged with an offence to a fair and public hearing, not the right of the public generally or of representatives of the press. In so far as the press are limited in their right to publish the proceedings then freedom of the press is involved and I have dealt with this when considering s. 2(*b*) of the Charter. I have also pointed out in dealing with *Re Global Communications and A.-G. Can., supra*, that the mandatory order under s. 442(3) is very different from the mandatory order under s. 457.2 which is required to ensure that the accused receives a fair trial. In my opinion Osborne J. was correct in concluding that the order under s. 442(3) of the *Code* did not *prima facie* infringe s. 11(*d*) of the Charter.

*Conclusion*

In summary I would grant the application to quash the appeal in the criminal proceeding and quash that appeal. I would dismiss the application to quash the appeal in the civil proceeding. I would allow the appeal in the civil proceeding and vary the order of Osborne J. by declaring that s. 442(3) is valid with the exception of the words "or if application is made by the complainant or prosecutor, shall". I would make no order as to the costs of this appeal or of the application to quash it.

*Appeal in criminal case quashed;*
*appeal in civil proceeding allowed.*

## Note on Fair and Public Trial

The general rule in both Canada and the United States is that judicial proceedings are open to the public. The reasons for the rule are discussed in the pre-*Charter* case of *A.G.-N.S. v. MacIntyre* (1982), 65 C.C.C. (2d) 129 at 145 *et seq.* (S.C.C.). They centre on the notion that justice is best preserved where its proceedings are carried out in the light of day. Publicity ensures that those in authority will proceed in a fair manner, knowing that their activities will be seen and criticized, and public confidence in the integrity of the justice system will thereby be preserved.

The publicity rule is strictly applied in the United States. There can be no prior restraints or closure of courts unless it is proved that publication creates an imminent danger to a pending adjudication or an imminent interference with the administration of justice: see *Richmond Newspapers Inc. v. Virginia*, 448 U.S. 555 (1980); *Nebraska Press Association v. Stuart*, 427 U.S. 539 (1976); cf. *Garnett Co. Inc. v. De Pasquale*, 443 U.S. 368 (1979) and see generally Tribe, *American Constitutional Law* (1978), p. 623 *et seq.*; "The Rights of the Public and the Press to Gather Information" (1974), 87 Harv. L.R. 1505. In the absence of evidence that other safeguards to ensure a fair trial are insufficient, such as a change of venue, sequestration, instructions to the jury, or a *voir dire* to determine whether a juror is biased, restrictions on publication are invalid.

A general right of access to judicial proceedings and freedom to publish about them is entrenched in Canada pursuant to sections 2(b) and 11(d) of the *Charter: Re Southam and The Queen (No. 1)* (1983), 41 O.R. (2d) 113 (Ont. C.A.); *R. v. Robinson* (1983), 34 C.R. (3d) 92 (Ont. H.C.); *Re Edmonton Journal and A.G. Alta.* (1983), 4 C.C.C. (3d) 59 (Alta. Q.B.); *R. v. Sophonow* (1983), 150 D.L.R. (3d) 590 (Man. C.A.), aff'd (1984), 31 Man. R. (2d) 8 (S.C.C.). However the standards in Canada for imposing restrictions on access or publication do not appear to be as strict as the American "imminent danger" test. Admittedly this last statement may be premature, since no Canadian standards have been clearly articulated as yet, however the practice has been more lenient in Canadian courts. To date the cases have not demanded positive evidence of harm in the manner of the American *Richmond Newspapers* case to support restraints: see *Canadian Newspapers Co. v. A.G. Can.* (1985), 49 O.R. (2d) 557 (C.A.); *Re Global Communications Ltd. and A.G. Can.* (1984), 44 O.R. (2d) 609 (C.A.); *R. v. C.R.B.* (1982), 30 C.R. (3d) 80 (Ont. H.C.); *Re Southam and The Queen (No. 2)* (1982), 38 O.R. (2d) 549 (Ont. H.C.); *Re Southam Inc. and The Queen* (1984), 14 D.L.R. (4th) 683 (Ont. H.C.); *Canadian Newspapers Co. v. Swail* (1984), 31 Man. R. (2d) 187 (C.A.); *Lortie v. The Queen* (1985), 46 C.R. (3d) 322 (Que. C.A.). Canadian courts have permitted restraints on the press with respect to judicial proceedings where the courts have felt them to be necessary to ensure a fair trial (*Canadian Newspapers Co. v. Swail, supra; R. v. C.R.B., supra*), to protect a complainant in a rape or sexual assault case (*Canadian Newspapers Co. v. A.G. Can., supra*; in the United States, see *Geise v. United States*, 262 F. 2d 151 (9th Circ. 1958), cert. denied 361 U.S. 842 (1959) to the same effect), to protect the identities of juvenile offenders (*Re Southam Inc. and the Queen* (1984), 14 D.L.R. (4th) 683 (Ont. H.C.)), to protect the identities of people the accused tried to blackmail on the basis that the trial process should not serve as a springboard for the publication of embarrassing or unfounded allegations about people's private lives

(*Toronto Sun Publishing Corp. v. A.G. Alta.*, [1985] 6 W.W.R. 36 (Alta. C.A.)) and to protect witnesses in proceedings before provincial disciplinary tribunals (*Hirt v. College of Physicians and Surgeons of British Columbia*, [1985] 3 W.W.R. 350 (B.C.C.A.)). For further examples of allowable restraints in American decisions, see *United States ex. re. Lloyd v. Vincent*, 520 F. 2d 1272 (2d Circ. 1975), cert. denied 423 U.S. 937 (1975) (preventing revelation of the identity of an undercover agent); *Starnicarbon v. American Cyanamid Co.*, 506 F 2d 532 (2d Cir. 1974) (avoid disclosure of trade secrets); *U.S. v. Bell*, 464 F 2d 667 (2d Circ. 1972), cert. denied 409 U.S. 991 (1972) (preserving confidentiality of skyjacking security procedures).

On press access to and publication of proceedings before health discipline tribunals and fatality inquiries, see *Hirt v. The College of Physicians and Surgeons of British Columbia, supra*, and *Re Edmonton Journal and A.G. Alta.* (1984), 13 D.L.R. (4th) 479 (Alta. C.A.).

For additional cases decided to date on press access to judicial proceedings, see *R. v. Banville* (1983), 3 C.C.C. (3d) 312 (N.B.Q.B.) (section 467 *Criminal Code* prohibiting the publication of evidence at a preliminary inquiry until the accused is discharged or his trial completed upheld); *R. v. Thomson Newspapers Ltd.*, Ont. S.C., December 8, 1983 (unreported) (no constitutionally guaranteed right of access to trial exhibits in section 2(b) of the *Charter*).


## 4. Association

### Note on Freedom of Association

The boundaries of freedom of expression in section 2(b) of the *Charter* have generally been assumed by the courts to be wide, and the courts have proceeded easily to section 1. The critical problem with respect to the freedom of association guarantee in section 2(d) has been the narrow scope given to the guarantee itself. Put in simple terms, the issue has been whether section 2(d) merely protects the bare right to associate or extends to protect the objects of the association as well. In analyzing this question, it is useful to examine section 2 of the *Charter* in its entirety and, as well, the First Amendment to the *U.S. Constitution*:

2. Everyone has the following fundamental freedoms:
   (a) freedom of conscience and religion;
   (b) freedom of thought, belief, opinion and expression, including freedom of press and other media of communication;
   (c) freedom of peaceful assembly; and
   (d) freedom of association.

#### AMENDMENT I

Congress shall make no law respecting an establishment of religion, or prohibiting the free exercise thereof; or abridging the freedom of speech, or of the press; or the right of the people peaceably to assemble, and to petition the Government for a redress of grievances.

Two factors should be noted from a reading of the above provisions. First, while there is overlap between the various provisions of section 2, the provisions are enumerated disjunctively. Accordingly, as a matter of statutory interpretation there

1148 FUNDAMENTAL FREEDOMS

should be a presumption against any of the guarantees being completely concurrent with any other. Each of the clauses of section 2 should be interpreted as having a discrete area within its ambit which is exclusively covered by that clause and which marks that provision's special contribution to the *Charter of Rights*. Thus, for example, the freedom of association guarantee should not be read coextensively with freedom of peaceful assembly in section 2(c) of the *Charter*.

Second, a comparison with the First Amendment indicates that section 2 of the *Charter* goes farther than the First Amendment with respect to freedom of association. The First Amendment does not contain a specific associational guarantee, and it is unclear whether freedom of association exists in the United States apart from the right to exercise other First Amendment rights through a group: see Raggi, "An Independent Right to Freedom of Association", 12 Harv. C.R.C.L. L. 1, 1-2 (1977).

Freedom of association was first clearly identified as a First Amendment interest in the United States and applied to the states through the due process clause of the Fourteenth Amendment in *NAACP v. Alabama ex rel Patterson*, 357 U.S. 449, 460-1 (1958). This approach was followed in *Anderson v. Celebrezze*, 103 S. Ct. 1564 (1983) and *Brown v. Socialist Workers '74 Campaign Committee (Ohio)*, 103 S. Ct. 416 (1982). The Supreme Court has also held that state action which infringes upon freedom of association is reviewable under the fundamental rights component of the equal protection clause: *Williams v. Rhodes*, 393 U.S. 23, 30 (1968).

Freedom of association has been viewed in "two distinct senses" in the United States, these being freedom of intimate association and freedom of expressive association: see *Roberts v. United States Jaycees*, 104 S. Ct. 3244 at 3249 (1984). Freedom of intimate association is part of the right of privacy drawn from such cases as *Griswold v. Connecticut*, 381 U.S. 479, 483-5 (1965) (state anti-contraception laws invalid). It protects close personal affiliations in order to protect the independent development of one's identity. As stated by Brennan J., writing the Opinion of the Court in *Roberts v. United States Jaycees, supra* at p. 3250 S. Ct., the relationships that "attend the creation and sustenance of the family" exemplify protected intimate associations, and are characterized by "such attributes as relative smallness, a high degree of selectivity in decisions to begin and maintain the affiliation, and seclusion from others in critical aspects of the relationship". See generally with respect to intimate association Tribe, *American Constitutional Law*, pp. 974-80 (1978); Karst, "The Freedom of Intimate Association", 89 Yale L.J. 624 (1980).

Freedom of expressive association protects individuals who are associating "for the purpose of engaging in those activities protected by the First Amendment — speech, assembly, petition for the redress of grievances, and the exercise of religion": *Roberts v. United States Jaycees, supra* at p. 3249. It is facilitative of other rights such as freedom of speech rather than an independent right. Freedom of expressive association does not enjoy the same degree of protection as intimate association, and infringements "may be justified by regulations adopted to serve compelling state interests, unrelated to the suppression of ideas, that cannot be achieved through means significantly less restrictive of associational freedoms": *Jaycees, supra* at p. 3252. For an excellent discussion of the *Jaycees* case and the issues which it raises: see Note, 98 Harv. L.R. 195 (1984). For two other recent American cases which illustrate the expressive association rationale of protecting freedom of association to secure specifically enumerated First Amendment rights, see *Anderson v. Celebrezze*, 103 Ct. 1564 (1983) (right of political minorities "to associate in the electoral arena to enhance their political effectiveness as a group", striking down a law requiring independent candidates to declare their candidacy by a specified date); *Brown v. Socialist Workers' 74 Campaign Committee (Ohio)*, 103 S. Ct. 416 (1982) (right to privacy in political association; exemption of minor party from required disclosure of identities of contributors to and recipients of campaign funds). For discussion of these cases, see Note, 97 Harv. L.R. 156 (1983).

While American cases on freedom of association may be useful in Canada where section 2(d) of the *Charter* is merely called in aid of other *Charter* guarantees, they are not particularly helpful in determining the outer limits of section 2(d) itself. The *U.S. Constitution* does not contain an explicit associational guarantee. It is therefore consonant with the text of the *U.S. Constitution* to limit freedom of association, a judicial creation, to the concept of privacy in intimate relationships drawn from the penumbras of various rights enumerated in the Bill of Rights (*Griswold v. Connecticut, supra*), and to use it as a tool to facilitate the exercise by individuals of specifically guaranteed First Amendment rights when individuals seek to assert those rights in a group. Such a restricted interpretation is not useful in the context of the *Charter* where freedom of association is a separately enumerated, independent constitutional guarantee.

There are two lines of authority to date in Canada on the scope of freedom of association in section 2(d). The first would give it a wide meaning, extending it to the objects of the association and then leaving it to section 1 to save government restrictions which are reasonable and demonstrably justified. The second line of authority would limit section 2(d) to the bare right to associate, although even in this line of cases there are some hints that the courts might be prepared to go somewhat farther in a proper case.

Freedom of association has been given a wide meaning in Ontario. In *Re Service Employees International Union, Local 204 and Broadway Manor Nursing Home* (1983), 44 O.R. (2d) 392 (Div. Ct.) affirmed on other grounds 48 O.R. (2d) 225 (C.A.), the Divisional Court struck down section 13(b) of the *Inflation Restraint Act*, S.O. 1982, c. 55.

As Galligan J. described section 13(b) at page 404 O.R., the provision deprived workers of the right to choose their own union and, through that union, to obtain expeditious and in-good-faith bargaining. It further deprived them of the right to strike. Galligan J. described the right of association as follows at 409 O.R.:

But I think that freedom of association if it is to be a meaningful freedom must include freedom to engage in conduct which is reasonably consonant with the lawful objects of an association. And I think a lawful object is any object which is not prohibited by law. It seems to me that to give to 'freedom of association' in a labour relations sense the interpretation given to it by the Judicial Committee in *Collymore v. A.G. Trinidad and Tobago*, [1969] 2 All E.R. 1207, would violate the requirement laid down by the Court of Appeal in *Re Southam Inc. and The Queen (No. 1)* (1983), 41 O.R. (2d) 113 that the Charter as part of a constitutional document should be given a large and liberal construction.

The purpose of an association of workers in a union is clear — it is to advance their common interests. If they are not free to take such lawful steps that they see as reasonable to advance those interests, including bargaining and striking, then as a practical matter their association is a barren and useless thing. I cannot imagine that the Charter was ever intended to guarantee the freedom of association without also guaranteeing the freedom to do that for which the association is intended. I have no hesitation in concluding that in guaranteeing workers' freedom of association the Charter also guarantees at the very least their freedom to organize, to choose their own union, to bargain and to strike.

O'Leary J. reviewed various authorities in relation to the scope of the freedom of association guarantee in arriving at the conclusion that (at 440 O.R.) "freedom of association for labour relations purposes in Canada has historically involved the combination of employees acting in concert to organize, collectively bargain and strike". Of special interest, he noted the intention of the draftsman where, in proceedings before the Canadian Parliamentary Special Joint Committee of the Senate and the House of Commons on the Constitution of Canada, Acting Minister of Justice Kaplan said:

> Our position on the suggestion that there be specific reference to freedom to organize and bargain collectively is that that is already covered by the freedom of association that is provided already in the declaration or in the Charter; and that by singling out association for bargaining one might tend to diminish all the other forms of association contemplated — church association; association of fratrunal organizations or community organizations. (Canadian Parliamentary Special Joint Committee of the Senate and House of Commons on the Constitution of Canada, *Minutes of Proceedings and Evidence* page 43:69-70)

Smith J. expressed the same view at pp. 462-3 that freedom of association includes both the bare right to associate and, in addition, at least some constitutional protection to shield the association in the performance of its lawful objects.

In *Re Retail, Wholesale & Dept. Store Union and Saskatchewan* (1985), 19 D.L.R. (4th) 609, a majority of the Saskatchewan Court of Appeal took a broad view of the scope of section 2(d) of the *Charter*. Bayda C.J.S. said at 619-620:

> I turn now to "defining the regulated area" relating to the freedom of association, that is, to fixing the scope of the inherent limits of the freedom of association (and thereby, using Professor Lederman's approach, to defining the freedom of association). The scope has two aspects. The first is this: Where an act is capable of being performed by a person alone or in association, then only if a person acting alone is forbidden to perform the act, is the person acting in association forbidden. The freedom of association is but an extension of a person's "right of personal liberty", to use de Toqueville's words. Unlike in the United States of America where the freedom of association is umbilically dependent upon the freedom of expression and the freedom of assembly, in Canada, under the Charter, the freedom of association, enumerated separately, is an independent freedom, independent of the freedom of expression and the freedom of peaceful assembly. It is fundamental to the constitution and the function of that independent freedom that, as Reena Raggi in an article "An Independent Right to Freedom of Association", 12 Harvard Civil Rights-Civil Liberties Law Review, No. 1 (1977), p. 15, put it:
>
> > . . . whatever action a person can pursue as an individual, freedom of association must ensure he can pursue with others. Only such a principle assures man that, in his struggle to be independent of government control, he will not be crippled simply because on occasion he strives to achieve that independence with the help of others.
>
> Professor Thomas I. Emerson in his article "Freedom of Association and Freedom of Expression", 74 Yale Law Jol., No. 1 (1964), says much the same thing (at p. 4):
>
> > Association is an extension of individual freedom. It is a method of making more effective, of giving greater depth and scope to, the individual's needs, aspirations and liberties. Hence, as a general principle, the right of individuals to associate or to refrain from association ought to be protected to the same extent, and for the same reasons, as individual liberty is protected.

Thus, as a starting point, an association should be entitled to do whatever an individual can do; conversely, conduct prohibited to an individual by a state can also be prohibited to an association. And the extent of the power of government to compel association should be limited to accomplishing such control of the individual as the government could impose directly.

The second aspect pertains to those acts which by definition cannot be performed by an individual but can only be performed in association (as, for example, a riot or price fixing), or if they can be performed by an individual, are qualitatively different when performed in association. What standard does one use here to identify the acts inherently prohibited? I answer that question this way. Every human act is the external manifestation of the will. An act has two elements, the physical and the mental. In criminal law, for example, we speak of the *actus reus* and the *mens rea*. Where the second of those elements, the mental element, common to those acting in association consists of an intention or a purpose of inflicting harm to society generally, or to one of society's members specifically, then the act is inherently prohibited. It is fundamental to our society, as I noted earlier, that the freedom of association of its members not be so broad as to permit the members to intentionally or purposely inflict harm or destruction upon society or any of the members. It is fair, I think, to say that in the end the species of the inherently prohibited acts under the second aspect falls into the same genus as the species of the prohibited acts under the first aspect. That is as it should be.

To summarize, a person asserting the freedom of association under para. 2(*d*) is free (apart from s. 1 of the Charter) to perform in association without governmental interference any act that he is free to perform alone. Where an act by definition is incapable of individual performance, he is free to perform the act in association provided the mental component of the act is not to inflict harm.

Cameron J.A. gave separate concurring reasons in *Re Retail, Wholesale & Department Store Union, supra* and agreed with Bayda C.J.S. that freedom of association includes the right to form a trade union, bargain collectively and, as a necessary incident, the right to withhold services through a strike, all subject to the limits imposed by section 1 of the *Charter*.

Thus *Broadway Manor* and *Re Retail, Wholesale & Department Store Union, supra* support the proposition that the constitutional guarantee of freedom of association protects not only the bare right to associate but the objects of the association as well. There is, however, a more restrictive line of cases.

In *Dolphin Delivery Ltd. v. Retail, Wholesale and Department Store Union, Local 580* (1984), 10 D.L.R. (4th) 198 (B.C.C.A.), leave to appeal to S.C.C. granted 56 N.R. 155, the British Columbia Court of Appeal refused to follow *Broadway Manor* and held that freedom of association was not broad enough to include a protection for picketing. Esson J.A., speaking for himself and Taggart J.A. (Hutcheon J.A. concurred in the result on other grounds), took a narrow view of the scope of section 2(d). He said at page 207:

The freedom is that of the individual (i.e. in the words of s. 2, of 'everyone'). It is the freedom to unite, to combine, to enter into union, to create and maintain an organization of persons with a common purpose. One of the classes of association guaranteed by s. 2 is undoubtedly the trade union. Everyone has the right to join a trade union and to pursue, with the other members, the collective interests of the membership. It does not follow that the Charter guarantees the objects and purposes of the union, or the means by which those can be achieved.

Esson J.A. went on at 209 (D.L.R.) to criticize the Divisional Court's judgment in *Broadway Manor* as follows:

In none of the judgments does there appear to be any consideration given to the ordinary meaning of 'association'. It is not clear whether the members of the court consider that freedom of association extends to any form of association other than trade unions but the reasoning implies an assumption that 'freedom of association' is a kind of code referring to trade unions, their purposes, objects and means of obtaining their purposes and objects. That assumption cannot be right. The freedom must be intended to protect the right of 'everyone' to associate as they please, and to form associations of all kinds, from political parties to hobby clubs. Some will have objects, and will be in favour of means of achieving those objects, which the framers of the Charter cannot have intended to protect. The freedom to associate carries with it no constitutional protection of the purposes of the association, or means of achieving those purposes.

The Federal Court of Appeal took a similar position in *Public Service Alliance of Canada v. Canada* (1984), 11 D.L.R. (4th) 387 (Fed. C.A.), leave to appeal to the Supreme Court of Canada granted 57 N.R. 161, holding that freedom of association is the freedom to enter into consensual arrangements to promote common interests or objects, but does not protect either the objects themselves or the means of attaining them. Accordingly, the Federal Court of Appeal upheld federal legislation which had the effect of prohibiting strikes in the federal public sector for a two year period. In delivering the principal judgment on behalf of the Court, Mahoney J. said at 391:

> The present issue is even more basic than those considered in the *Broadway Manor* and *Dolphin Delivery* cases which, respectively, dealt with the right to strike and the right to picket as essential incidents of collective bargaining and, indirectly, a freedom of association. Here it was the right to bargain collectively that was directly abrogated.
>
> . . . .
>
> The right of freedom of association guaranteed by the Charter is the right to enter into consensual arrangements. It protects neither the objects of the association nor the means of attaining those objects.
>
> The learned trial judge held [at 11 D.L.R. (4th) 337 at 358]:
>
>> 'In my view the clause 'freedom of association' guarantees to trade unions the right to join together, to pool economic resources, to solicit other members to choose their own internal organizational structures, to advocate to their employees and the public at large their views and not suffer any prejudice or coercion by the employer or State because of such union activities. But it does not include the economic right to strike'.
>
> I do not think it desirable to attempt to catalogue the rights and immunities inherent in a trade union's guaranteed freedom of association. Clearly, collective bargaining is, or should be, the primary means by which organized labour expects to attain its principal object: the economic betterment of its membership. However fundamental, it remains a means and, as such, the right to bargain collectively is not guaranteed by s. 2(d) of the Charter, which guarantees freedom of association.

For a review of some of the European law on freedom of association, see *Re Pruden Building Ltd. and Construction General Workers' Union Local 92* (1984), 13 D.L.R. (4th) 584 (Alta. Q.B.). This latter line of authority is consistent with the Privy Council's decision in *Collymore v. A. G. Trinidad and Tobago,* [1969] 2 All E.R. 1207 (P.C.), a case which was approved in *Dolphin Delivery* and *Public Service Alliance of Canada* but expressly rejected in *Broadway Manor* and *Re Retail, Wholesale and Department Store Union, supra.*

The Alberta Court of Appeal's decision in *Reference re Public Service Employee Relations Act, Labour Relations Act, and Police Officers Collective Bargaining Act,*

[1985] 2 W.W.R. 289 (*"Alberta Reference"*) may represent a halfway house between the two positions. The basic question in the *Alberta Reference* was whether the imposition by statute of compulsory arbitration in place of strikes and lockouts violated the freedom of association of the workers involved. Kerans J.A. carefully reviewed the contrary positions taken by the British Columbia Court of Appeal and the Ontario Divisional Court in *Dolphin Delivery* and *Broadway Manor*, respectively, but did not specifically endorse either one. Rather he left open the possibility, without deciding the point, that freedom of association in section 2(d) could extend to those actions which are essential to the core purposes of the organization. Here, as distinguished from *Broadway Manor* where the right to strike was abolished *in vacuo*, the worker was protected by compulsory arbitration which bound both the employer and employee. Kerans J.A. therefore said at 312-3:

> . . . I cannot accept that devastating harm to the vital interests of the union or members is here self-evident. On the contrary, there are other forms of action by or for workers which might be available and which might be as effective as, or more effective than, the right to strike. Compulsory arbitration might be one of them . . .
>
> No charge has been made before us that the legislation under review does not leave substantial room for the free play of collective bargaining. It has not been suggested, let alone proved, that the legislation scheme before us in pith and substance intends to or does destroy or render impotent the trade union movement among the public service employees in Alberta. Therefore, even assuming (without deciding) that we ought to extend freedom of association to protect the vitality of the trade union movement, it simply has not been shown that that vitality is at risk under this legislation.

It may be argued that the above matters are more properly considered under section 1 than section 2(d), given that the real issue raised is the extent of the impairment. Restated in section 1 terms, the question of whether the organization's vitality is at risk can be framed as whether the limitation is reasonable. On the other hand, there is some merit in focussing the analysis on section 2(d) as Kerans J.A. has done, thereby placing the onus of demonstrating the extent of the impairment on the applicant. The applicant will usually be in a better position to lead evidence of how, why and to what degree the impugned government action affects the association. If the "vitality" test is the correct test, it is not unreasonable to put the onus on the applicant to establish at least a *prima facie* case that the impugned regulation imposes a serious burden on the organization's ability to carry out its objectives.

The Alberta Court of Appeal will shortly have an opportunity to deal with the correctness of the vitality test in *Black v. Law Society of Alberta*, [1984] 6 W.W.R. 385 (Alta. Q.B.) which is currently before it on appeal. At issue in *Black* is a Law Society rule which prohibits any member from being a partner in or being associated with more than one law firm for the practice of law. The rule was upheld by Dea J. at trial on debatable grounds and is susceptible to attack both as infringing upon the bare right to associate and as completely sterilizing the association in performing its function of carrying on the practice of law.

# 18

# Democratic Rights

## RE REYNOLDS AND ATTORNEY-GENERAL OF BRITISH COLUMBIA*

In the British Columbia Court of Appeal. 11 D.L.R. (4th) 380.

Nemetz C.J.B.C., Carrothers and Craig JJ.A. May 25, 1984.

Appeal by the Attorney-General of British Columbia from a judgment of Macdonnell J., 143 D.L.R. (3d) 365, 41 B.C.L.R. 258, [1983] 2 W.W.R. 413, 32 C.R. (3d) 273, 4 C.R.R. 332, holding that s. 3(1)(*b*) of the *Election Act*, R.S.B.C. 1979, c. 103, is invalid to the extent that it prohibits a person who is on probation, following a conviction for an indictable offence, from voting.

The judgment of Nemetz C.J.B.C. and Carrothers J. was delivered by

NEMETZ C.J.B.C.: — The issue in this appeal is whether pursuant to s. 1 of the *Canadian Charter of Rights and Freedoms* it is a reasonable limit demonstrably justified in a free and democratic society to deny a citizen serving a term of probation his right to vote as provided for in section 3 of the Charter.

The facts, briefly, are that on September 8, 1980, the respondent Robert Edward Reynolds was convicted of causing bodily harm with intent to wound, which by s. 228 of the *Criminal Code*, R.S.C. 1970, c. C-34, is an indictable offence. He was sentenced to 18 months' imprisonment plus two years' probation to follow. On March 12, 1981, after serving approximately six months of the imprisonment portion of his sentence, he was released from prison. His term of probation took effect at the end of the 18 months' sentence.

In the fall of 1982, while he was still on probation, the respondent inquired of the Vancouver Registrar of Voters as to his qualifications to stand as a candidate in an election to the Legislative Assembly of this province. By letter dated October 8, 1982, the registrar informed him that he was disqualified from voting and therefore unable to stand for nomination as a candidate. The registrar based his decision on s. 3(1) of the *Election Act*, R.S.B.C. 1979, c. 103, as amended, which provides in part:

> 3(1) A person is disqualified from voting at any election, and shall not make application to have his name inserted in a list of voters, who
>
> . . . . .
>
> (*b*) has been convicted of treason or an indictable offence, unless he has secured a free of conditional pardon for the offence or has undergone the sentence imposed for the offence . . .

*Leave to appeal to the Supreme Court of Canada (Estey, McIntyre and Wilson JJ.) granted October 22, 1984.

The registrar must also have relied on s. 55 of the Act which requires, inter alia, that a person must be qualified as a voter in order to qualify as a candidate.

Faced with the registrar's decision, the respondent applied to the Supreme Court of British Columbia for an order that s. 3(1)(*b*) of the *Election Act* is null and void on the grounds that the Act contravened the provisions of the *Canadian Charter of Rights and Freedoms*. The petition came before Mr. Justice Macdonnell on November 5, 1982. In a judgment given on December 23, 1982 [[1983] 2 W.W.R. 413], he found the impugned section of the *Election Act*, to be of no force and effect to the extent that it purported to affect a person who had completed his term of imprisonment but was serving only the probationary portion of the sentence. The Attorney-General appealed that decision of this court.

On the appeal, as was done below, counsel for the Attorney-General conceded that there is a manifest conflict between s. 3(1)(*b*) of the *Election Act* and s. 3 of the Charter, which provides:

> 3. Every citizen of Canada has the right to vote in an election of members of the House of Commons or of a legislative assembly and to be qualified for membership therein.

However, Mr. Eddy, counsel for the Attorney-General, relying on s. 1 of the Charter, took the position that the disqualification imposed on persons serving a period of probation is a "reasonable limit prescribed by law" that can be "demonstrably justified in a free and democratic society." He acknowledged that the Attorney-General has the onus of establishing that the disqualification of probationers meets the test of s. 1. Section 1 of the Charter provides:

> 1. The *Canadian Charter of Rights and Freedoms* guarantees the rights and freedoms set out in it subject only to such reasonable limits prescribed by law as can be demonstrably justified in a free and democratic society.

Counsel for the Attorney-General submits that disqualification of persons serving a sentence for an indictable offence is, despite the affirmative right to vote set out in s. 3 of the Charter, a demonstrably justifiable limitation available for enactment by the Legislature. He points to disqualification on the basis of age as an example of an analogous limitation. However, it is my view that one cannot take that example as establishing a general rationale for creating further categories of disqualified persons. In each case the disqualification must be shown to be demonstrably justified in a free and democratic society as we know it in Canada today. It is not so long ago that women and certain racial minorities were also placed in disqualified categories by both the federal as well as the provincial authorities. The Charter has legally put an end to the enactment of such disqualifications. The guaranteed rights are the fundamental elements of the Charter. Any restriction must be presumed to be unconstitutional unless it can be established that the restriction is a reasonable limit as described in s. 1 of the Charter.

It is to be remembered that in no other province in Canada nor in federal elections are persons on probation disqualified from voting. The *Canada Elections Act*, R.S.C. 1970, c. 14 (1st Supp.), s. 14(4)(*e*), disqualifies only inmates of penal institutions. Similar language is found in the elections legislation of Alberta (*Election Act*, R.S.A. 1980, c. E-2, s. 41(*d*)); Manitoba (*Elections Act*, 1980 (Man.), c. 67 (C.C.S.M., c. E30), s. 31(*d*)); New Brunswick (*Elections Act*, R.S.N.B. 1973, c. E-3, s. 43(2)); Newfoundland (*Election Act*, R.S.N. 1970, c. 106, s. 4(*d*)); Nova Scotia

(*Election Act*, R.S.N.S. 1967, c. 83, s. 27(*d*)); Ontario (*Election Act*, R.S.O. 1980, c. 133, s. 13); Prince Edward Island (*Election Act*, R.S.P.E.I. 1970, c. E-1, s. 21(*d*)); and Saskatchewan (*Election Act*, R.S.S. 1978, c. E-6, s. 27(*c*)). In Quebec the disqualification does not even extend to inmates (*Election Act*, 1979 (Que.), c. 56, ss. 2, 51-64). Furthermore, in British Columbia, we were informed that persons in custody for summary conviction offences can and do vote.

I will assume that a citizen convicted of serious crimes may be disqualified from voting while serving a sentence in prison (see Taylor J.'s reasons in *Jolivet and Barker and The Queen and Solicitor-General of Canada* (1983), 48 B.C.L.R. 121 (S.C.)). However, the question as to whether prisoners may be disqualified from voting is *not* the issue here. This case deals with convicted persons who are no longer in actual custody or serving the custodial portion of their sentence, but are serving the probationary portion of their sentence. Section 52(1) of the *Constitution Act, 1982* allows an order to be made to the extent of any inconsistency between provisions of the *Charter* and the impugned legislative provisions. Section 52(1) provides:

> 52(1)  The Constitution of Canada is the supreme law of Canada, and any law that is inconsistent with the provisions of the Constitution is, *to the extent of the inconsistency*, of no force or effect.

(My emphasis.) Here, on the facts and in my opinion, the inconsistency in the impugned provincial legislation is the denial of the right to vote to persons serving a sentence of probation. That being the only inconsistency before this court, it is, therefore, to that extent that s. 3(1)(*b*) of the *Election Act* is of no force and effect.

In my view, one of the purposes of breaking sentences into custodial and non-custodial parts is to provide a probationary milieu under which the incarcerated person will be free and thus be given the opportunity of starting his reintegration into society. Furthermore, it is manifest that, in a democratic society, participating in the electoral process is one of the paths leading to a return to full integration in the community.

For these reasons, a probationer should be entitled to vote and any such limitation contained in the provincial legislation is of no force and effect. I would, therefore, affirm Macdonnell J.'s order and dismiss the appeal.

CRAIG J.A. (dissenting): — Chief Justice Nemetz has set out the circumstances in his judgment. While I find his reason for dismissing the appeal persuasive, I am not able to accede to it because I think that s. 1 of the *Canadian Charter of Rights and Freedoms* sanctions s. 3(1)(*b*) of the *Election Act*, R.S.B.C. 1979, c. 103, which disqualifies a person from voting at any election if he has been convicted of an indictable offence unless he has "undergone the sentence imposed for the offence". Provincial legislation dealing with the qualification of voters has contained this provision, although not precisely in its present form, since 1874. Obviously at that time, "sentence" meant imprisonment because parole and probation were not then a part of our legal system. Now, the word "sentence" includes probation — see s. 601, definition "sentence" of the *Criminal Code*. The federal legislation (*Canada Elections Act*, R.S.C. 1970, c. 14 (1st Supp.)) and the legislation in the other common law provinces dealing with voter qualifications have a somewhat similar provision, differing, however, in two respects: (a) it disqualifies a person who has been convicted of any offence — whether it be summary conviction or indictable; (b) but only while he is serving his sentence in a penal institution. In one aspect, therefore, the British Columbia legislation is narrower than the legislation in these other jurisdictions, but in the other aspect is broader than it is.

In any event, s. 3(1)(*b*) is contrary to s. 3 of the Charter and is valid only if it comes within s. 1 of the Charter.

Counsel for the respondent submits that while the limitation in s. 3(1)(*b*) may be a "reasonable limitation", it is not "demonstrably justified . . . in so far as it applies to persons who are not actually inmates of penal institutions". He submits that the phrase "demonstrably justified" obligates the Crown to establish that the objective of the legislation is (a) to provide "some legitimate benefit to the public", or (b) to prevent "some evil or injustice from occurring which would be contrary to the public welfare". He contends that the only way that the Crown should establish the legislation comes within (a) or (b) is to show that a person coming within s. 3(1)(*b*) is "somehow unfit" to vote and that the Crown cannot possibly establish that every person on parole or probation is "unfit" to vote.

If the basis for this legislation were that all parolees and probationers were mentally or morally "unfit" to vote while undergoing their sentence, I would agree that the Crown could not show that the limitation was "demonstrably justified" in a free and democratic society, but I do not think that this is the rationale of the legislation. I think that the rationale of the legislation is that society is entitled to suspend the voting right of a person who has breached certain laws of society, in addition to authorizing the imposition of a punishment pursuant to the criminal law. It is on this premise that I can consider whether s. 3(1)(*b*) comes within s. 1 of the Charter. In enacting s. 3(1)(*b*), the representatives of society have prescribed that the voting right of a citizen who has been convicted of an indictable offence shall be suspended until he has served his sentence. Is this a reasonable limitation on a citizen's right to vote which is guaranteed by s. 3 of the Charter that can be "demonstrably justified in a free and democratic society"?

In considering this issue, I am unable to see a valid reason for distinguishing between a limitation which is applicable only when a person is serving his sentence in a penal institution and a limitation which is applicable also when a person is serving a portion of a sentence on parole or on probation. If one is valid, the other should be valid. Conversely, if one is invalid, the other should be invalid. If society has the right to place some limitation on a citizen's right to vote, I think that the limitation in s. 3(1)(*b*) is a reasonable one: it is applicable only if the person has committed an indictable offence and only while he is serving a sentence for the commission of that offence. Can this limitation be "demonstrably justified in a free and democratic society"? As I have said, I think that the rationale of the legislation is that society is entitled to suspend the voting rights of an individual in certain circumstances. Should it have this right? More particularly, should it have the right to impose the limitation found in s. 3(1)(*b*)? The Charter deals with the rights and freedoms of citizens, including the right of a citizen to vote in a federal or provincial election. It does not specifically mention the obligations of a citizen. Obviously, however, its premise is that a citizen who has rights also has obligations. The preamble preceding s. 1 of the Charter states that "Canada is founded upon principles that recognize the supremacy of God and the rule of law". A citizen must obey the law. If he does not, he is in breach of his duty as a citizen. Society should have the right to impose reasonable sanctions on a citizen who commits a crime, other than the sanctions authorized by the criminal law. Suspending his right to vote while he is serving his sentence for the commission of an indictable offence, whether in custody or on parole or probation, is a reasonable limitation on a citizen's right to vote. I think that this is a limitation which is demonstrably justified in a free and democratic society. That being so, I would allow the appeal.

*Appeal dismissed.*

### Note on Democratic Rights

It is submitted that Craig J.A. in *Re Reynolds, supra,* is correct that there is no distinction between limitations on the right to vote while a convict is serving the custodial portion of his sentence and while he is serving his probationary term. While Nemetz C.J.B.C. assumed without deciding that *Jolivet and Barker and The Queen and Solicitor-General of Canada* (1983), 48 B.C.L.R. 121 (S.C.) was correct, the holding in *Reynolds* casts considerable doubt on the point.

Craig J.A. framed the issue as being whether "society is entitled to suspend the voting right of a person who has breached certain laws of society, *in addition to* authorizing the imposition of a punishment pursuant to the criminal law" (emphasis added). The difficulty is that both he and Nemetz C.J.B.C. for the majority held that the Crown could *not* establish that parolees or probationers were somehow unfit to vote. If that is so, the issue is slightly different from that formulated by Craig J.A. The real question, which was not addressed by either Nemetz C.J.B.C. or Craig J.A., is whether a provincial Legislature may suspend voting rights *as part of the punishment* for the breach of federal criminal law.

If that is the issue, it is highly arguable that section 3(1)(b) of the *Election Act*, R.S.B.C. 1979, c. 103 is unconstitutional on a division of powers basis without resort to sections 1 and 3 of the *Charter*. Neither level of government has the power to enforce or enact additional punishments for violation of the other's legislation, unless it could enact the substantive law on its own: see *Boggs v. The Queen*, [1981] 1 S.C.R. 49 (denial of federal power to criminalize violations of provincial law). Section 3(1)(b) of the provincial *Elections Act* does not distinguish between those indictable offences which the British Columbia Legislature could have enacted independently and those which it could not and, accordingly, is arguably unconstitutional on the *Boggs* principle.

The issue of whether even Parliament can suspend a convict's right to vote as part of his punishment is more difficult. Parliament has a wide discretion pursuant to section 91(27) to fashion punishments for breaches of criminal law and one could argue that section 13 of the *Charter*, which prohibits cruel and unusual punishments, is a complete code of the restrictions on federal power in that regard. As long as the punishment is not cruel and unusual, and a suspension of voting rights is likely not, it is valid. It is submitted that the better view is that section 13 of the *Charter* is not a complete code. Section 3 is a specific guarantee of the right to vote, and section 1 of the *Charter* should save only those restrictions which are aimed at protecting the integrity of the vote itself.

In *Re Jolivet* (1983), 48 B.C.L.R. 121 (S.C.), which upheld the ban in section 14(4)(e) of the *Canada Elections Act*, R.S.C. 1970, c. 14 (1st Supp.) on inmate voting,

Taylor J. held that disenfranchisement could *not* be justified by a need to prohibit "unfit" voters or by any deterrent or reforming value it might have. He said at 122:

> While emphasizing that he [the trial judge in Re *Reynolds*, who came to the same conclusion as the majority of the Court of Appeal in striking down the prohibition against probationers' voting] was dealing only with the voting rights of convicted persons while at large on probation, Mr. Justice MacDonell expressed a tentative opinion with respect to the position of those serving a sentence of imprisonment. He said:
>
> > It is my view on the evidence before me and the arguments addressed to me that prohibiting a prisoner from voting is a reasonable sanction, justified in a free and democratic society.
>
> The learned judge found the 'it requires little imagination to see the practical reasons why a prisoner in custody should not be entitled to vote.'
>
> Since that question was not before Mr. Justice MacDonell, his observations are not binding on me. But I accept the reasoning on which his decision in that case is based. It rests on the conclusion that disenfranchisement of criminal offenders is not justifiable by any supposed need to protect society from the votes of 'unfit persons'. In this connection the learned judge was impressed by the opinion of Mr. Justice Marshall in *Richardson v. Ramirez*, 418 U.S. 24, 41 L. Ed. 2d 551 (1974) (U.S.S.C.), particularly the observation (at p. 587):
>
> > This Court's holding in *Davis v. Beason*, 133 U.S. 333 (1890) and *Murphy v. Ramsey*, 114 U.S. 15 (1885) that a State may disenfranchise a class of voters to 'withdraw all political influence from those who are practically hostile' to the existing order, strikes at the very heart of the democratic process.
>
> Since the disenfranchisement of convicted persons cannot be justified for the protection of society, it seems that any use of disenfranchisement for punitive purposes must be unconstitutional. The prospect of loss of voting rights is hardly likely to operate as a deterrent to the commission of criminal offences, and disenfranchisement holds no hope of reforming offenders.

Taylor J. went on to uphold the disqualification in section 14(4)(e) because "the exercise of the right to vote by prisoners would be impossible for practical reasons". He said at p. 123 *et seq.*:

> To assess the seriousness of any difficulties likely to be involved in allowing the franchise to prison inmates, it is necessary to decide what is meant by 'the right to vote' guaranteed by the *Charter*. If it is simply the right to mark a ballot paper and have it counted, one would think that it could be assured to prison inmates with no great difficulty.
>
> The context in which the expression is used suggests there may be more involved in the right to vote than that.
>
> Referring to the former *British North America Act, 1867* [renamed the *Constitution Act, 1867*, by the *Constitution Act, 1982*, s. 53(1) and Schedule item 1], Mr. Justice Rand spoke in *Saumur v. City of Quebec and A.G. Que*, [1953] 2 S.C.R. 299, in memorable terms of the system of government for which it provides:
>
> > The Confederation Act recites the desire of the three Provinces to be federally united into one Dominion "with a constitution similar in principle to that of the United Kingdom". Under that constitution, Government is by parliamentary institutions, including popular assemblies elected by the people at large in both Provinces and Dominion: Government resting ultimately on public opinion reached by discussion and the interplay of ideas.
>
> That "discussion and the interplay of ideas" are to form the basis of our electoral process is confirmed, I think, by the *Charter*, in particular by adoption in s. 1 of the "free and democratic society" as its constitutional model.
>
> I conclude that the expression "right to vote in an election of members of the House of Commons or of a legislative assembly" as used in s. 3 of the Charter means more than the right to cast a ballot. It means the right to make an informed electoral choice reached through freedom of

belief, conscience, opinion expression, association and assembly — that is to say, with complete freedom of access to the process of "discussion and the interplay of ideas" by which public opinion is formed. Denial by the State of the freedoms necessary for the making of a free and democratic electoral choice involves denial also of the sort of right to vote contemplated by the Charter.

In opposition to the present petition, the Crown has filed an affidavit sworn by Marcel Sauve, Deputy Commissioner/Security for the Canadian Penitentiary Service, which suggests that certain serious problems would be created if voting were permitted in penitentiaries.

Mr. Sauve foresees in the publication of voters' lists a danger to the safety of inmates whose anonymity has until now been preserved from others. He attests to the explosive, or inflammatory, personalities of certain prisoners and of the danger which he believes would be created if election-eering activities were permitted among such persons in the prison setting. He mentions serious difficulties which he foresees resulting from the presence of canvassers — or persons claiming to be canvassers — within the prisons. He says there would inevitably be 'allegations or counter-allegations of interference with the political process' if electioneering were conducted in such a setting.

It must, I think, have been difficulties of this sort to which Mr. Justice Macdonnell referred, in the *Reynolds* decision, as the justification for denial of the franchise to prison inmates.

The petitioners say that greater difficulties are involved in conducting elections in the Northern Territories than would be encountered in extending the vote to prisoners. They point to the fact that the Province of Quebec permits prisoners to vote in provincial elections. They say that elections are now conducted in prisons, under Directive 600-4-12 of the Commissioner of Correc-tions, for the election of inmate committees. Through these elections, they say, prisoners are already involved in a form of self-government, and they accept responsibilities of participation in the democratic process. While agreeing that 'certain restrictions on the corpus of rights available to the free members of the larger society are basic to incarceration' they contend that the right to vote is not one which need be curtailed. It cannot be equated, they say, with 'such rights as mobility, liberty and association' on which they concede that there are 'obvious imposed limits' in a prison setting.

I think the petitioners have stated here the critical question on which the outcome of their application turns. They say the right to vote for the present purpose, can be put into a different category from such freedoms as the liberty of the person and the freedom of association.

I do not think it can.

It seems to me that the restrictions imposed by imprisonment on freedom of the person, the close control which must be maintained by the State over association, assembly and discussion there, and inevitable interference in free inflow and circulation of information and ideas, all of which are necessary to preservation of prison order and discipline, render it impossible for prisoners to make the free and democratic electoral choice contemplated by the Constitution. The casting of a ballot under such conditions could not, in the context of the Charter, be described as an exercise of the 'right to vote'.

Imprisonment, as a punishment for breach of the criminal law, is clearly justifiable in a free and democratic society. It follows that denial to prisoners of those constitutional rights which, of necessity, cannot be exercised by persons serving a sentence of imprisonment is also justifiable and must be taken to be authorized by s. 1 of the Charter. I have concluded that the right to vote guaranteed by s. 3 is indeed one of them.

This reasoning is highly problematic. First, the evidence reviewed by Taylor J. of the "explosive" situation which might be caused by political canvassing and elec-tioneering was thin in the extreme. Indeed, it appears to be rebutted by the evidence that i) prisoners in Quebec are entitled to vote in provincial elections; and ii) internal elections for prisoner self-government are held in federal prisons.

Second, there was no evidence before the court that it was "impossible" for prisoners to make free and informed electoral choices. It is true that restrictions on association, assembly and discussion which are made necessary by security require-ments restrict the flow of information to a certain extent. However there was no evidence that prisoners could not read newspapers or obtain information about public affairs in other ways. On the contrary, the fact that prisoners in Quebec are entitled to vote in provincial elections suggests that at least one democratically elected government believes that inmates are capable of making informed choices.

Third, the holding in *Jolivet* presupposes that the government has the authority to decide who has *enough* information to vote intelligently. This sets a dangerous precedent which may have serious consequences in other voting rights contexts. On the validity of literacy tests in the United States, see *Lassiter v. Northhampton Election Board*, 360 U.S. 45 (a state may apply a literacy test in selecting qualified voters provided the test is not discriminatory); *Oregon v. Mitchell*, 400 U.S. 112 at 131-4 (1970) (discriminatory impact of literacy tests).

Outside the prison context, the courts have given section 3 of the *Charter* a relatively limited meaning, confining it to the right to vote in federal and provincial elections. It requires that a mechanism be provided to allow absentee provincial residents from voting (*Hoogbruin and A.G.B.C.* (1984), 54 B.C.L.R. 177 (S.C.) affirmed B.C.C.A., December 9, 1985 (*infra*)) but does not secure the right to vote in plebiscites (Re *Allman and Commissioner of the Northwest Territories* (1983), 8 D.L.R. (4th) 230 (N.W.T.C.A.)). Furthermore it does not prohibit provincial Legislatures from establishing reasonable residency requirements as conditions of eligibility to vote in provincial elections. In *Re Storey and Zazelenchuk* (1984), 36 Sask. R. 103 (Sask. C.A.), Bayda C.J.S. and Cameron J.A., speaking for two of the four judges who participated in the judgment (Woods J.A. did not participate and Hall and Macdonald JJ.A. concurred in the result without reaching the *Charter*), upheld a six-month residency requirement as reasonable. They noted that Ontario, Quebec and Prince Edward Island maintain 12-month residency requirements and all of the other provinces have six-month requirements. Bayda C.J.S. and Cameron J.A. described the rationales for residency requirements as follows (at 133):

> To some extent that depends, of course, on what are the legitimate objectives of an advance residency requirement. No doubt they include protecting the integrity of provincial elections by requiring genuine ordinary residence in the province. And, since ordinary residence is such an elusive business, it is not unreasonable to define it with reference to a fairly lengthy period of time in order to avoid any argument over the issue.
>
> Moreover, a period of advance residence may be required, having regard for the nature and content of a vote. While its most basic purpose is to elect, within a constituency, a representative to the Legislative Assembly, it is not confined to that. And even though it is basically prospective in nature — the Assembly is being elected to govern for a period ahead — a vote has, in practice, a decidedly retrospective aspect to it: it often constitutes a means of passing judgment upon the performance, during their preceding terms of office, of the incumbent member as well as the government. And since today's political issues are many in number, diverse in nature and increasingly complex (and often local) it is not unreasonable to require a person to be resident in the province for a period of some months before being entitled to vote.

In the United States, see *Dunn v. Blumstein*, 405 U.S. 330 (1972).

# HOOGBRUIN v. A.G. B.C.

In the British Columbia Court of Appeal. (Unreported)

Nemetz C.J.B.C., Aikins and Macdonald JJ., December 9, 1985

BY THE COURT:

In the spring of 1983, Hoogbruin and Raffa were temporarily absent from British Columbia attending Osgoode Hall Law School in Ontario. Both are citizens of Canada and permanent residents of British Columbia. Both were provincially registered voters. In April of that year, Hoogbruin telephoned the Deputy Registrar of Voters of British Columbia on behalf of both appellants enquiring as to what provisions existed for absentee voting. He was informed that no such provisions existed and the only way the appellants could vote was by attending an advance poll in British Columbia or, on election day attending an established poll in the province. Because their studies were to continue until after the date of the election (May 5, 1983), this was not a viable option. Accordingly, they applied to a judge of the Supreme Court of British Columbia for a declaration that their constitutional right to vote was infringed because the provincial *Election Act*, R.S.B.C. 1979, c. 103 failed to provide for an absentee ballot. The judge ruled against them finding that they had failed to prove that their right to vote was so infringed. It is from the judge's decision that they appeal to this Court.

The *Canadian Charter of Rights and Freedoms* provides:

> S.3   Every citizen of Canada has the right to vote in an election of members of the House of Commons or of a legislative assembly. . . .

The B.C. *Election Act* provides:

> S.2(1)   Every person who is not disqualified by this Act or by any other law in force in the Province is entitled to be registered as a voter, and being duly registered as a voter under this Act is entitled to vote at any election. . . .

The *Constitution Act, 1982* of Canada provides:

> S.52(1)   The Constitution of Canada is the supreme law of Canada, and any law that is inconsistent with the provisions of the Constitution is, to the extent of the inconsistency, of no force or effect.

The *Charter* guarantees the "right to vote." The *Election Act* provides the appellants an "entitlement to vote." The issue is whether an entitlement to vote without creating the added statutory mechanism of an absentee ballot to implement that entitlement to vote is an infringement on the constitutional right to vote.

By way of preface it is to be noted that the right to vote is a democratic right so strongly entrenched in the Charter that unlike the fundamental freedoms set out in section 2, and the legal rights set forth in sections 7 to 15, it is not subject to the override clause afforded the Legislature by section 33(1). Accordingly, subject only to obvious exclusions such as minors or mental incompetents, the right to vote is firmly entrenched in our Constitution.

In *A.G. v. Ryan*, [1980] A.C. 718, the judgment of the Privy Council was delivered by the late Lord Diplock. In that case their Lordships were considering the written constitution of the Bahamas which, like our Constitution, confers upon a citizen rights which cannot be withdrawn or limited by any action of the Executive or Legislature in the absence of amendment. Lord Diplock, at 728, said, in part:

> A provision . . . which permits Parliament, by legislation . . . to impose limitations or qualifications upon any of those entrenched rights, is not to be construed expansively so as to authorise it to deprive the individual of the *substance* [our emphasis] of the right which prima facie is conferred upon him by the Constitution, under the guise of imposing limitations or qualifications upon it.

We are in respectful agreement with this view of entrenched rights. Furthermore, it is my opinion that it matters little whether the individual is deprived of the substance of the right to vote by commission (an express statutory limitation) or by omission (the failure of the statute to provide a mechanism to vote and thus creating a limitation to the right to vote).

We also agree with what Mr. Justice Sirois said in *Maltby v. A. G. Saskatchewan* (1982), 2 C.C.C. (3d) 153 (Sask. Q.B.) [aff'd (1984), 13 C.C.C. (3d) 308 (Sask. C.A.)], where the Legislature had failed to provide a mechanism for certain persons to vote: "To the extent that the statute makes no exception in their case, their rights as guaranteed by s. 3 of the Canadian Charter of Rights and Freedoms to my mind have been violated." In our opinion, although section 2(1) of the *Election Act* of B.C. states that these appellants have an entitlement to vote, by failing to provide a mechanism to implement that right, the statute has deprived them of the substance of that right and thus infringed their *Charter* right to vote.

That is not, of course, the end of the matter. Section 1 of the *Charter* provides

> 1. The *Canadian Charter of Rights and Freedoms* guarantees the rights and freedoms set out in it subject only to such reasonable limits prescribed by law as can be demonstrably justified in a free and democratic society.

Once it is found that the right is infringed, the onus is on the respondents to show that:

1. Any limit placed on the guaranteed right is demonstrably justifiable in a free and democratic society.
2. It is a reasonable limit.
3. It is prescribed by law.

We will deal with these prerequisites together. It is our view that the effective limitation should not be construed expansively (*A. G. v. Ryan, supra*). Furthermore, no reasonable ground upon which such a limitation can be based was shown to obtain. To the contrary, the result of the omission of provision for an absentee ballot is clearly without the legislative objective of the Act.

In 1903 the Full Court of this province (the predecessor tribunal to this Court) had to consider questions put to it arising out of the B.C. *Elections Act*. In *Re Provincial Elections Act* (1903), 10 B.C.R. 114 (C.A.) Mr. Lyman Duff K.C. (later Chief Justice of Canada) argued for a liberal interpretation of the Act submitting that it was "notorious that large numbers of voters are outside [the province] during different portions of the year." Chief Justice Hunter said, in part:

> . . . I am of the opinion that it is quite clear in the first place, that the Legislature did not intend to disfranchise *any* [our emphasis] person simply because he might be temporarily absent from the province.

The Chief Justice and the three other judges who sat on this appeal all gave a liberal interpretation to that Act to enable absentees to exercise their right to vote although absent from the province. Walkem J. went even further and stated that

> It is a rule that franchise acts should be liberally construed. The object of the Elections Act is to enfranchise and not disfranchise, persons who possess the necessary qualification for being placed on the Voters' List; and hence the Act should, if possible, be so construed as to forward that object: *Colquhoun v. Brooks* (1889), 14 App. Cas. 493.

Absentee voting exists in Canada federally and in seven of the 10 provinces and the Yukon. Aside from British Columbia, only Newfoundland and Quebec do not provide for some form of absentee voting. An absentee voting system exists in Great Britain as well as in the United States federally and every state of the United States of America. Under the Canada *Elections Act*, fishermen, mariners, air crews, forestry crews, topographical survey crews, prospectors, trappers, those suffering from illness or physical incapacities, and post-secondary students absent from the polling division are entitled to vote by proxy. These categories are similar to those listed in the Ontario, Nova Scotia and Prince Edward Island proxy regulations. In fact, the report of the *B.C. Royal Commission on Electoral Reform* (1978), which was before the judge, recommended the adoption of proxy voting procedures. Accordingly, we conclude that the resulting limitation on the right to vote created by the omission has not been shown to be a reasonable limit and therefore section 1 of the *Charter* is not applicable.

Mr. Edwards, for the respondents, in urging that no remedial action be taken by this Court, has raised the spectre of the danger of the court "subsuming or directing" the functions of the Executive or Legislature if a declaration were to be made. In our opinion there is no merit in this argument. If any law is inconsistent with the provisions of the Charter, it is the Court's duty, to the extent of such inconsistency, to declare it to be of no force or effect (section 52(1), *supra*).

Before the *Charter*, the courts could and did declare legislation invalid on division of powers grounds. When they did so, we know of no recent occasion when the legislative branch of government did not faithfully attempt to correct the impugned legislation. Likewise, when this Court declares a statute or portion thereof to be "of no force and effect" where it is inconsistent with the *Charter*, it is for the Legislature to decide what remedial steps should be taken in view of the declaration. Section 24(1) of the *Charter* empowers the courts to grant citizens remedies where their guaranteed rights are infringed or denied. The *Charter* provides:

> 24(1)   Anyone whose rights or freedoms, as guaranteed by this Charter, have been infringed or denied may apply to a court of competent jurisdiction to obtain such remedy as the court considers appropriate and just in the circumstances.

It would be anomalous, indeed, if such powers were reserved only for cases where limitations are expressly enacted and not for cases where an unconstitutional limitation results because of omission in a statute.

Mr. Edwards further submitted that the appellants' volitional absence from the province at the time that the right to vote might be exercised amounted to a non-exercise of that right and in essence resulted in a waiver of the right. In our opinion there is no reality to that submission. The exigencies of pursuing a course of education out of the province are such that students have no real choice between exercising or not exercising their right to vote. Furthermore, students, together with other citizens who must travel outside of the province to earn their livelihood, even if they wished to re-arrange their travel in order to stay in B.C. on voting day, are faced with a further hurdle. We operate under the Westminster form of government with no fixed dates set for elections. Where a fixed election date system subsists some re-arrangement might be possible. Where none exists until announced at random, the volitional return or re-arrangement becomes highly impractical.

Finally, it is to be observed that the evidence is that the absentee voting by proxy that is provided in so many places remains a relatively inexpensive means of complying with the *Charter*.

Mr. Welsh, for the appellants, at first asked that we "direct" the Legislature to enact provisions for absentee voting. Under questioning by the Court he amended his submission asking only for a declaration. In our view it would be "appropriate and just in the circumstances" to declare (see *Quebec Association of Protestant School Boards v. A.G. of Quebec (No. 2)* (1982), 140 D.L.R. (3d) 33, affirmed (1983), 1 D.L.R. (4th) 573 (Que. C.A.), as well as *Maltby (supra)*) that in the Court's view the right to vote as guaranteed by section 3 of the *Charter* is denied to B.C. registered voters where the sole reason they are unable to exercise their right to vote is that no procedural mechanism exists which would reasonably enable them to do so.

*Appeal allowed.*

# 19

# Mobility Rights, and the Right to Pursue a Livelihood

## LAW SOCIETY OF UPPER CANADA v. SKAPINKER

In the Supreme Court of Canada. 9 D.L.R. (4th) 161.

Ritchie, Dickson, Beetz, Estey, McIntyre, Lamer and Wilson JJ. May 3, 1984.

Appeal by the Law Society of Upper Canada from a judgment of the Ontario Court of Appeal, 40 O.R. (2d) 481, allowing an appeal from a judgment of Carruthers J., 38 O.R. (2d) 116, dismissing an application for a declaration that s. 28(*c*) of the *Law Society Act* (Ont.), is inoperative by reason of the *Canadian Charter of Rights and Freedoms*.

The judgment of the Court was delivered by

ESTEY J.: — By s. 28(*c*) of the *Law Society Act*, R.S.O. 1980, c. 233, the Legislature of Ontario required all members of the Bar of the province to be Canadian citizens. At the outset, let it be emphasized in the clearest possible language that the issue before this Court in this appeal is not whether it is or is not in the interest of this community to require Canadian citizenship as a pre-condition to membership in the Bar. Rather, the only issue is whether s. 28(*c*) of the *Law Society Act* is inconsistent with s. 6(2)(*b*) of the *Canadian Charter of Rights and Freedoms*.

The intervener Richardson is an American citizen and a member of the Bar of the State of Massachusetts. As we shall see, these proceedings were commenced by the respondent, Skapinker, who later was, for all practical purposes, replaced (when he became a member of the Law Society) by Richardson, who was labelled an intervener when he joined the proceedings. Richardson, by the time the appeal came on for hearing in this Court, was the only person who actually had the status of a respondent in the *Law Society* appeal. In these reasons, it is convenient simply to identify him as Richardson. He is also a permanent resident of Canada, received his LL.B. from Queen's University, Kingston, Ontario in 1980, articled in a law firm in the province for the year ending June, 1981, and has now successfully completed the Bar Admission Course of the Law Society of Upper Canada. He has candidly expressed his intention not to become a citizen of Canada. As a result, the appellant has advised Richardson that he will not be accepted as a member of the Law Society. The respondent Skapinker was in the same position but became a Canadian citizen in the course of these proceedings and has been admitted to the Bar of Ontario. By order of the High Court of Ontario made April 13, 1983, the respondent Skapinker was given leave to withdraw from these proceedings, but did not do so. Although his application has become moot, he appeared by counsel in this Court, without any objection from the other parties, on the hearing of the appeal. In the meantime, John Calvin Richardson was added as an intervener by order of the Ontario courts, and the case has proceeded as though Richardson was the initiating party to these proceedings. All this is noted at the outset as a warning to those who may seek to emulate this course in like applications in the future. The current practice of this Court is to require any person seeking to participate in an appeal here either to continue as a party with full status as such, or to be brought in as an intervener by order of this Court (references and status of the provinces therein and cases raising constitutional issues being dealt with separately in the court rules). Because this appeal raised important and novel issues under the Charter of Rights the matter was permitted to proceed as presently constituted.

The originating notice of motion initiating this matter sought a declaration that s. 28(c) of the *Law Society Act* is "inoperative and of no force and effect to the extent that it discriminates between Canadian citizens and permanent residents of Canada and, in particular, because this is inconsistent with s. 6(2)(b) of the *Constitution Act, 1982*". . . .

The respondent submits that paras. (a) and (b) are two separate rights and that the heading "Mobility Rights" does not dictate a narrow interpretation of the para. (b) right. The appellant and all interveners, including the Attorney-General of Canada, the Attorney-General of Ontario, the Attorney-General of Quebec, the Attorney-General of Saskatchewan and the Federation of Law Societies of Canada, take the position that para. (b) is not simply a "right to work" clause but is predicated on a mobility element. Within the group espousing this view, there are some differences as to the meaning properly to be attributed to para. (b).

After leave was granted for appeal to this Court, the Chief Justice framed the following constitutional question:

> Is Section 28(c) of *The Law Society Act*, R.S.O. 1980, Chapter 233, insofar as it excludes from its benefit persons having the status of permanent residents of Canada, inoperative and of no force and effect by reason of Section 6 of *The Constitution Act 1982*?

It will facilitate matters to set out s. 6 of the Charter and s. 28(c) of the *Law Society Act.*

*Canadian Charter of Rights and Freedoms:*

> 6(1) Every citizen of Canada has the right to enter, remain in and leave Canada.
>
> (2) Every citizen of Canada and every person who has the status of a permanent resident of Canada has the right
>
> > (a) to move to and take up residence in any province; and
> >
> > (b) to pursue the gaining of a livelihood in any province.
>
> (3) The rights specified in subsection (2) are subject to
>
> > (a) any laws or practices of general application in force in a province other than those that discriminate among persons primarily on the basis of province of present or previous residence; and
> >
> > (b) any laws providing for reasonable residency requirements as a qualification for the receipt of publicly provided social services.
>
> (4) Subsections (2) and (3) do not preclude any law, program or activity that has as its object the amelioration in a province of conditions of individuals in that province who are socially or economically disadvantaged if the rate of employment in that province is below the rate of employment in Canada.

The *Law Society Act*, s. 28(*c*):

> (*c*) the persons, being Canadian citizens or other British subjects,
>> (i) who are members on the 31st day of December, 1980, or
>> (ii) who after that day successfully complete the Bar Admission Course and are called to the bar and admitted and enrolled as solicitors, or
>> (iii) who after that day transfer from a jurisdiction outside Ontario and are called to the bar and admitted and enrolled as solicitors,
>
> are members and entitled to practise law in Ontario as barristers and solicitors;

We are here engaged in a new task, the interpretation and application of the *Canadian Charter of Rights and Freedoms* as adopted first as an appendage to the Resolution of Parliament on December 8, 1981, and then as an appendix to the *Canada Act, 1982*, 1982 (U.K.), c. 11. This is not a statute or even a statute of the extraordinary nature of the *Canadian Bill of Rights*, R.S.C. 1970, App. III, c. 44. It is a part of the Constitution of a nation adopted by constitutional process which, in the case of Canada in 1982, took the form of a statute of the Parliament of the United Kingdom. The adoptive mechanisms may vary from nation to nation. They lose their relevancy or shrink to mere historical curiosity value on the ultimate adoption of the instrument as the Constitution. The *British North America Act, 1867* was such a law, albeit but a statute of the Parliament of the United Kingdom and albeit incomplete in the absence of an intra-national amending mechanism. In the interpretation and application of this document the Judicial Committee of the Privy Council of the United Kingdom, which until 1949 was the highest level of the judicial branch engaged in resolving constitutional issues, said: "The British North America Act planted in Canada a living tree capable of growth and expansion within its natural limits": *Edwards v. A.-G. Can.*, [1930] A.C. 124 at 136, *per* Viscount Sankey L.C., who reiterated this judicial attitude towards a "constituent or organic statute such as the [*B.N.A.*] Act" in *British Coal Corp. v. The King*, [1935] A.C. 500 at 518 (P.C.). This Court recognized the distinction between simple "statutory interpretation" and "a constitutional role" when the court was called upon to determine the effect of the *Canadian Bill of Rights: Curr v. The Queen*, [1972] S.C.R. 889 at 899, *per* Laskin J., as he then was. The *Canadian Bill of Rights* is, of course, in form, the same as any other statute of Parliament. It was designed and adopted to perform a more fundamental role than ordinary statutes in this country. It stands, perhaps, somewhere between a statute and a constitutional instrument. Nevertheless, it attracted the principles of interpretation developed by the courts in the constitutional process of interpreting and applying the Constitution itself.

There are some simple but important considerations which guide a court in construing the Charter, and which are more sharply focused and discernible than in the case of the federal *Bill of Rights*. The Charter comes from neither level of the legislative branches of government but from the Constitution itself. It is part of the fabric of Canadian law. Indeed, it "is the supreme law of Canada": s. 52, *Constitution Act, 1982*. It cannot be readily amended. The fine and constant adjustment process of these constitutional provisions is left by a tradition of necessity to the judicial branch. Flexibility must be balanced with certainty. The future must, to the extent foreseeably possible, be accommodated in the present. The Charter is designed and adopted to guide and serve the Canadian community for a long time. Narrow and technical interpretation, if not modulated by a sense of the unknowns of the future, can stunt the growth of the law and hence the community it serves. All this has long been with us in the process of developing the institutions of government under the *B.N.A. Act, 1867* (now the *Constitution Act, 1867*). With the *Constitution Act, 1982* comes a new dimension, a new yardstick of reconciliation between the individual and the community and their respective rights, a dimension which, like the balance of the Constitution, remains to be interpreted and applied by the court.

The courts in the United States have had almost 200 years' experience at this task and it is of more than passing interest to those concerned with these new developments in Canada to study the experience of the United States courts. When the United States Supreme Court was first concerned with the supervision of constitutional development through the application of the recently adopted Constitution of the United States, the Supreme Court of the United States, speaking through Chief Justice Marshall, stated (*Marbury v. Madison*, 5 U.S. 137 at 176 (1803)):

> The question, whether an act, repugnant to the constitution, can become the law of the land, is a question deeply interesting to the United States; but, happily, not of any intricacy proportioned to its interest. It seems only necessary to recognise certain principles, supposed to have been long and well established, to decide it.

There followed a lengthy discussion not dissimilar to that engaged in by the Privy Council and by this Court in considering the allocation of powers and institutional provisions in the Constitution as it existed, at least to 1981. As to the nature of a written Constitution in relation to the component governments, the Chief Justice continued (at p. 177):

> Certainly all those who have framed written constitutions contemplate them as forming the fundamental and paramount law of the nation, and, consequently, the theory of every such government must be, that an act of the legislature, repugnant to the constitution, is void.
>
> This theory is essentially attached to a written constitution, and is consequently to be considered, by this court, as one of the fundamental principles of our society. It is not therefore to be lost sight of in the further consideration of this subject.

The court then turned to the role of the court (at pp. 177-8):

> It is emphatically the province and duty of the judicial department to say what the law is. Those who apply the rule to particular cases, must of necessity expound and interpret that rule. If two laws conflict with each other, the courts must decide on the operation of each.
>
> So if a law be in opposition to the constitution; if both the law and the constitution apply to a particular case, so that the court must either decide that case conformably to the law, disregarding the constitution; or conformably to the constitution, disregarding the law; the court must determine which of these conflicting rules governs the case. This is of the very essence of judicial duty.

The court having staked out its constitutional ground then moved on in *M'Culloch v. State of Maryland* (1819), 17 U.S. 316, to consider the techniques of interpretation to be applied in construing a Constitution. Again, speaking through Chief Justice Marshall (at p. 407):

> A constitution, to contain an accurate detail of all the subdivisions of which its great powers will admit, and of all the means by which they may be carried into execution, would partake of the prolixity of a legal code, and could scarcely be embraced by the human mind. It would probably never be understood by the public. Its nature, therefore, requires, that only its great outlines should be marked, its important objects designated, and the minor ingredients which compose those objects be deduced from the nature of the objects themselves . . . In considering this question, then, we must never forget, that it is *a constitution* we are expounding.

In recognizing that both legislative and judicial power under the Constitution is limited, the Chief Justice observed that the court must allow the legislative branch to exercise that discretion authorized by the Constitution which will (at p. 421):

> ... enable that body to perform the high duties assigned to it, in the manner most beneficial to the people. Let the end be legitimate, let it be within the scope of the constitution, and all means which are appropriate, which are plainly adapted to that end, which are not prohibited, but consist with the letter and spirit of the constitution, are constitutional.

I come back to the key issue in this appeal, the meaning of para. (*b*) in s. 6(2) of the Charter. There are at least three arguably applicable readings of s-s. (2) of s. 6 of the *Canadian Charter of Rights and Freedoms* as adopted in the *Constitution Act, 1982*, and as now incorporated in the *Constitution Acts, 1867 to 1982*:

1. The conjunction "and" appearing between paras. (*a*) and (*b*) in the English version (absent in the French version), and the heading "Mobility Rights" over the whole of s. 6, enables one to read the subsection with the word "then" understood to follow the conjunction "and" so that paras. (*a*) and (*b*) would read as follows:

   > 6(2) Every citizen ... and ... permanent resident ... has the right
   > (*a*) to move to and take up residence in any province; and [then]
   > (*b*) to pursue the gaining of a livelihood in any province.

2. A disjunctive reading may be given to s-s. (2) by deleting the conjunction "and" between paras. (*a*) and (*b*) and by assigning no interpretative value to the heading "Mobility Rights"; and further by taking into account the presence of s-s. (4) which may indicate that "mobility" is not a necessary element in each segment of s. 6. Such an approach may be said to lead to a recognition of two unrelated "free standing" rights in paras. (*a*) and (*b*), the first being a right to move and to reside in any province; the second being the right of a permanent resident to work in any province unrestricted by any law of that province which, in effect, is directed to restricting the right of the permanent resident to do so.

3. The third approach to the reading of s-s. (2)(*b*) is to separate the two paras. (*a*) and (*b*) as though the conjunction "and" were absent, but to read para. (*b*) as requiring a mobility aspect. Paragraph (*b*) would then assure to the permanent resident the right to work "in any province" whether or not he has exercised the right under para. (*a*) to move to and to take up residence "in any province". It may be said that such a reading separates but does not divorce the two paragraphs one from the other or from the balance of the section. This is the view advanced by Mr. MacPherson on behalf of the Attorney-General of Saskatchewan. The paragraph would cover the additional circumstance of transborder commuting to perform work in the province adjoining the province of residence whether or not the permanent resident has previously or subsequently moved to the second province for the purpose of undertaking or continuing to undertake the work in question.

[His Lordship's discussion of the use of headings as an aid to interpretation of substantive sections of the *Charter* is omitted.]

For the purpose of examining the meaning of the two paragraphs of s. 6(2), I conclude that an attempt must be made to bring about a reconciliation of the heading with the section introduced by it. If, however, it becomes apparent that the section when read as a whole is clear and without ambiguity, the heading will not operate to change that clear and unambiguous meaning. Even in that midway position, a court should not, by the adoption of a technical rule of construction, shut itself off from whatever small assistance might be gathered from an examination of the heading as part of the entire constitutional document. This general approach I take to be consonant with the thinking expressed in the Canadian, British and United States authorities and texts discussed above.

I return, therefore, to the words of the section itself. "Mobility Rights" has a common meaning until one attempts to seek its outer limits. In a constitutional document relating to personal rights and freedoms, the expression "Mobility Rights" must mean rights of the person to move about, within and outside the national boundaries. Subsection (1), for example, refers to a citizen's right to leave and return to Canada. Subsection (3)(a) makes reference to the exclusion of provincial laws which discriminate between persons on the basis of past or present provincial residence; and para. (b) of s-s. (3) permits the application of provincial laws which impose reasonable residency qualifications for the receipt of social services. Subsection (4) either relates to mobility of people within the country or it simply clarifies s-s. (3), which does relate to mobility, and s-s. (2) whose relationship to mobility we must determine. Thus, s-s. (4) is neutral as regards the clarification of s-s. (2) by reason of the presence of the heading "Mobility Rights".

I return to s-s. (2) itself. Paragraph (a) is pure mobility. It speaks of moving to any province and of residing in any province. If para. (b) is caught up with para. (a), it is likewise a mobility provision. If it is separate when properly construed, then it may, as the respondent urges, be a "right to work" clause without reference to movement as a prerequisite or otherwise. The presence of the conjunction "and" in the English version is not sufficient, in my view, to link para. (a) to para. (b) so as to create a single right. Conversely, the absence of the conjunctive link in the French-language version is not sufficient to separate the two paragraphs completely. In the first alternative interpretation, if only one right is created by s-s. (2), then a division into paras. (a) and (b) is superfluous. Moreover, this suggested interpretation of s. 6(2) is inconsistent with s. 6(3), which subjects the "*rights* specified in subsection (2)" to certain limitations (my emphasis).

In the second alternative meaning, the complete isolation of the two paras. (a) and (b), which is necessary to create a free-standing "right to work" provision out of para. (b), fails to account for the presence of the phrase "in any province" in para. (b). That paragraph, subject to one further consideration, would announce such a right if these words were omitted. Such a reading out of the phrase "in any province" from para. (b) creates a result verging on the absurd. Paragraph (b) would, alone amongst its neighbours, be out of context under the heading "Mobility Rights". While that heading is not of controlling interest and importance, it none the less must have a taint of relevancy. Perhaps its relevance is limited to the elimination of a meaning which, in a range of two possible interpretations, is out of sympathy with the clear meaning of the heading itself. In the interpretative result urged by the respondent, para. (b) would be a provision of singular impact and one most unlikely to be inserted as a subparagraph to a provision dealing with the movement of people. Furthermore, it would simply proclaim the historic and the obvious in the case of a Canadian citizen, and would result in the constitutional freezing of the classification of "permanent resident" which was only recently introduced into the federal immigration statute. If para. (b) were reduced by the deletion of the phrase "in any province", then the citizen or permanent resident would not have a clear and unambiguous right to commute across a provincial boundary to engage in regular work. It should be noted that the qualifying words "in any province" are not employed elsewhere in the Charter, and should not be lightly discarded from s. 6(2). No such limiting circumstance occurs, for example, in s. 2(d) or in s. 8.

It is reasonable to conclude, therefore, that s. 6(2)(b) should not be read in isolation from the nature and character of the rights granted in s-ss. (1) and (2)(a). Indeed, the repeated appearance of the expression "in any province" in each of the subprovisions of s-s. (2) would appear to make relevant the heading "Mobility Rights". The phrase "in any province" would appear to be one more link between the heading and the rights granted in s-s. (2) read as a whole. Nor should s. 6(2) be construed as a discrete section entirely separate from s. 6(3). As I have already mentioned, s. 6(3) refers to the "rights", plural, granted in s. 6(2) and provides an exception to the paramountcy of those rights. In my opinion, s. 6(3)(a) further evinces the intention to guarantee the opportunity to move freely within Canada unimpeded by laws that "discriminate ... primarily on the basis of province of present or previous residence". The concluding words of s. 6(3)(a), just cited, buttress the conclusion that s. 6(2)(b) is directed towards "Mobility Rights", and was not intended to establish a freestanding right to work. Reading s. 6(2)(b) in light of the exceptions set out in s. 6(3)(a) also explains why the words "in any province" are used: citizens and permanent residents have the right, under s. 6(2)(b), to earn a living in any province subject to the laws and practices of "general application" in that province which do not discriminate primarily on the basis of provincial residency.

There are many considerations which lead one to adopt the third interpretation of para. (b). Paragraph (b) is thereby accorded a meaning consistent with the heading of s. 6. The transprovincial border commuter is accorded the right to work under para. (b) without the need of establishing residence in the province of employment in exercise of the right under para. (a). There is a separation of function and purpose between paras. (a) and (b), and the need for separate paragraphs is demonstrated. The presence of s. 6(3)(a), already discussed, is another supporting consideration.

This interpretation finds some support in the judgment of Mr. Justice Arnup below where he says [3 C.C.C. (3d) 213 at 226]:

> It is a paragraph intended to prevent the erection by any province of barriers established to keep out persons from another province seeking to enter its work-force as part of a provincial policy to establish or preserve a preference for its own residents. The permanent resident who goes to another province has a right to pursue the gaining of a livelihood there, whether that person is a lawyer or a Class "A" mechanic ...

Shortly thereafter in his reasons, His Lordship stated [3 C.C.C. (3d) 213 at 226]:

> In my view, the right is a right not to have provincial barriers thrown up against one who wants to work.
>
> . . . . .
>
> He is not faced with a provincial barrier preventing him, a permanent resident of Canada, from moving freely within Canada to pursue the gaining of a livelihood.

*Malartic Hygrade Gold Mines Ltd. v. The Queen in right of Quebec* (1982), 142 D.L.R. (3d) 512 (Que. S.C.), a judgment of Chief Justice Deschênes, is also instructive. The Chief Justice was there faced with determining the meaning and extent of s. 6(2)(*b*) in relation to the asserted right of a member of the Bar of Ontario to participate in a judicial proceeding in Quebec without a licence or permit from the Barreau du Québec under the Quebec statute. With reference to para. (*b*), the Chief Justice said: "The purpose of this provision is undoubtedly to give Canadian citizenship its true meaning and to prevent artificial barriers from being erected between the provinces"; and later in his reasons adds, in connection with s. 6: "In principle the Charter thus intends to ensure interprovincial mobility." (The foregoing is taken from the English version of the judgment as found at pp. 520-1. The translation is obviously different than that included in the judgments of the majority and the dissent below in the Court of Appeal but the essential meaning is the same.) The principal thrust of the judgment of the Chief Justice is, however, s. 6(3) with which we are only tangentially concerned.

This conclusion as to the meaning and purpose of s. 6(2)(*b*) finds further support in the writings of all the authors whose works were brought to the attention of the court: see "Mobility Rights under the Charter", Professor John Laskin, 4 Supreme Court L.R. 89 at pp. 97-8 (1982); *Canadian Charter of Rights and Freedoms: Commentary* (1982), Tarnopolsky and Beaudoin, in particular Pierre Blache at p. 247; *Canada Act 1982, Annotated*, Peter Hogg, at p. 25.

. . . .

I conclude, for these reasons, that para. (*b*) of s-s. (2) of s. 6 does not establish a separate and distinct right to work divorced from the mobility provisions in which it is found. The two rights (in paras. (*a*) and (*b*)) both relate to movement into another province, either for the taking up of residence, or to work without establishing residence. Paragraph (*b*), therefore, does not avail Richardson of an independent constitutional right to work as a lawyer in the province of residence so as to override the provincial legislation, the *Law Society Act*, s. 28(*c*), through s. 52 of the *Constitution Act, 1982*.

Having reached this conclusion, it is not necessary to examine the submissions made by all parties and interveners with reference to ss. 6(3) and 1 of the Charter of Rights. Richardson has failed to demonstrate that s. 28(*c*) of the *Law Society Act* is inconsistent with s. 6(2)(*b*) of the Charter. Consequently, I need not determine whether the Act is none the less saved by s. 6(3) or s. 1 of the Charter.

The development of the Charter as it takes its place in our constitutional law, must necessarily be a careful process. Where issues do not compel commentary on these new Charter provisions, none should be undertaken. There will be occasion when guidance by *obiter* or anticipation of issues will serve the Canadian community, and particularly the evolving constitutional process. On such occasions, the court might well enlarge its reasons for judgment beyond that required to dispose of the issues raised. Such an instance might, in a small way, arise here. The appellant has, from the outset of these proceedings, relied upon s. 1 of the Charter as the final constitutional test supporting the validity of s. 28(*c*) of the *Law Society Act*. To that end, a minimal record was established to demonstrate the justification of the citizenship requirement as a "reasonable limit" on the rights granted by the Charter. The appellant's material supporting this part of its response to the application by the respondent was the report of a committee established by the province to study professional organizations in Ontario and which report in turn incorporated the findings of an earlier commission of inquiry. The intervener, the Federation of Law Societies of Canada, added other reports and documents concerning requirements in other professions and in other jurisdictions. Counsel for the appellant Law Society, Mr. O'Brien, very candidly admitted that because s. 1 and this very process were new to all, the record introduced by the appellant was rather slim. The originating notice which started these proceedings was one of the first under the Charter. As experience accumulates, the law profession and the courts will develop standards and practices which will enable the parties to demonstrate their position under s. 1 and the courts to decide issues arising under that provision. May it only be said here, in the cause of being helpful to those who come forward in similar proceedings, that the record on the s. 1 issue was indeed minimal, and without more, would have made it difficult for a court to determine the issue as to whether a reasonable limit on a prescribed right had been demonstrably justified. Such are the problems of the pioneer and such is the clarity of hindsight.

. . . .

*Appeal allowed.*

## Note

On the question of the desirability of conditioning membership in a provincial Law Society on Canadian citizenship, see the pre-*Charter* case of *Re Dickenson and Law Society of Alberta* (1978), 84 D.L.R. (3d) 189 (Alta. S.C.). Having held that such a rule was constitutionally valid in the pre-*Charter* context and not in contravention of the relevant provincial human rights legislation, McDonald J. added the following at 195:

> Having so held, I venture to offer a remark or two about the restriction of enrolment in the Law Society of Alberta to Canadian citizens and British subjects. What is the rationale of the restriction? Some persons have argued that, since a member of the Society is, by virtue of s. 89(2) of the *Legal Profession Act* [R.S.A. 1970, c. 203], an 'officer of the Supreme Court and all other courts of record in the Province', he should owe an allegiance to the Sovereign in whose name the Courts exercise their jurisdiction. It seems to me that he owes allegiance if he swears the oath of allegiance. An alien may swear that oath. In any event, an alien *amy* (a friendly alien) owes allegiance to the Crown if he is resident within this country or the dominions of the Queen, even if he does not take an oath of allegiance: see *Markwald v. A.G.*, [1920] 1 Ch. 348 at 363 (C.A.); *Joyce v. Director of Public Prosecutions*, [1946] A.C. 347 at 363; 1 Hals., 3rd ed., p. 501, para. 965; 7 Hals. 3rd ed., p. 209.
>
> Perhaps, however, the objection is that a person who is not a Canadian citizen or a British subject is unlikely to appreciate the constitutional history and laws of the United Kingdom and Canada, and therefore is less likely to be conscious of the fundamental rights of Canadian citizens before the Courts or of the traditions of our Courts. If that is the objection, in my view, the distinction between Canadian citizens and British subjects on the one hand, and all other persons on the other, is arbitrary in that it affords no assurance that those who are enrolled are conscious of those matters. If the object is as stated, it could better be achieved by an examination of the particular qualifications of the applicant, whether he is a Canadian citizen, a British subject, or something else.
>
> It is not without significance to me that in England at present neither the Bar nor the Law Society contains any limitation of membership to British subjects or citizens of the United Kingdom.

No doubt this is a matter which deserves even more careful consideration as to the governing principle. I would hope that the Benchers of the Law Society of Alberta and the Attorney-General would give consideration to whether the arbitrary distinction now drawn by statute is desirable.

## Note on Mobility Rights

The courts have given a wide meaning to section 6(1) of the *Charter*, which guarantees to every citizen the right to enter, remain in and leave Canada. *Re Germany and Rauca* (1983), 41 O.R. (2d) 225 (C.A.) (*supra* at Chapter 16) indicates that an applicant bears only a minimal burden under section 6(1) and that, once he has discharged that burden, the onus shifts to the state pursuant to section 1 to uphold the limitations. In *Rauca*, the Ontario Court of Appeal held that extradition was a reasonable limit prescribed by law which can be demonstrably justified in a free and democratic society, and a committal order was accordingly issued. For a Comment on the decision of Evans C.J.H.C. at first instance in *Rauca*, see Finkelstein, "A Question of Emphasis: The State's Burden in *Federal Republic of Germany v. Rauca*" (1983), 30 C.R. (3d) 112. *Rauca* has been followed in *Voss v. The Queen* (1984), 12 C.C.C. (3d) 538 (B.C.C.A.); *Re Decter and U.S.* (1983), 5 C.C.C. (3d) 364 (N.S.S.C.), aff'd 5 C.C.C. (3d) at 381 (N.S.C.A.); and *United States of America v. Cotroni (No. 2)* (1984), 11 W.C.B. 440 (Que. S.C.).

Section 6(2) guarantees the right of every citizen and permanent resident of Canada to a) move to and take up residence in any province; and b) pursue the gaining of a livelihood, subject to the qualifications in section 6(3) and (4) and section 1 of the *Charter*. Where section 121 of the *Constitution Act, 1867* provides for free movement of goods between provinces within the limits of the provision (see Chapter 8 *supra* for further discussion of section 121), section 6(2) of the *Charter* is its counterpart with respect to the free movement of people.

There were limits on provincial power to restrict personal mobility even prior to the Charter's enactment. As stated by Rand J. in *Winner v. S.M.T. (Eastern) Ltd.*, [1951] S.C.R. 887 (aff'd [1954] A.C. 541 (P.C.)):

... [a Province] cannot divest [a Canadian] of his right or capacity to remain and to engage in work there: that capacity inhering as a constituent element of his citizenship status is beyond nullification by provincial action ...

It follows, *a fortiori*, that a Province cannot prevent a Canadian from entering it except, conceivably, in temporary circumstances, for some local reason as, for example, health.

However Parliament clearly had jurisdiction to restrict the movement of people pursuant to section 91(25) of the *Constitution Act, 1867* and the general power. Section 6(2) of the *Charter* acts as a withdrawal of power from both levels of government.

The corresponding provisions in the *U.S. Constitution* are as follows:
Article IV, s. 2:

The citizens of each State shall be entitled to all privileges and immunities of citizens of the several States.

Fourteenth Amendment, s. 1:

No State shall make or enforce any law which shall abridge the privileges or immunities of citizens of the United States

These "privileges and immunities" clauses clearly protect the right to travel and take up residence in any state: see *Shapiro v. Thompson*, 394 U.S. 618 (1969); *Memorial Hospital v. Maricopa County*, 415 U.S. 250 (1974). *Shapiro* establishes that residency requirements as a condition of receiving public assistance are an impermissible clog on the right to interstate travel in the absence of evidence that they promote some "compelling" state interest: *cf.* section 6(3)(b), which merely requires proof that the requirement is "reasonable". In the United States, the state's burden varies with the interests at stake. Where vital rights and privileges are involved, such as the right to receive welfare (*Shapiro, supra*) or non-emergency medical care at government expense (*Memorial Hospital, supra*), a one year residency requirement has been held unconstitutional. On the other hand, the U.S. Supreme Court has upheld one year residency requirements for bringing a divorce action (*Sosna v. Iowa*, 419 U.S. 393 (1975)) and for entitlement to lower tuition fees charged to state residents at a state university (*Sturgis v. Washington*, 414 U.S. 1057 (1973) affirming 368 F. Supp. 38 (D.C. W.D. Wash. 1973)) and a six month residency requirement for admission to a state bar (*Rose v. Bondurant*, 409 U.S. 1020 (1972) affirming 339 F. Supp. 257 (D.C.N.M. 1972)).

The only cases in Canada to date on residency requirements pursuant to section 6(2) have excluded voting rights from the ambit of the provision: see *Re Storey and Zazelenchuk* (1982), 21 Sask. R. 158 (Sask. Q.B.), aff'd (1984), 36 Sask. R. 103 (C.A.); *Re Allman and Commissioner of the Northwest Territories* (1983), 8 D.L.R. (4th) 230 (N.W.T. C.A.) (leave to appeal to Supreme Court of Canada refused (1984), 55 N.R. 394 (S.C.C.)). In *Re Allman*, a Northwest Territories ordinance imposed a three year residency requirement as a qualification to vote in a plebiscite. The stated purpose of the rule was to ensure that only long term residents could cast their ballots on questions of long term public policy.

One would have thought that the right to vote in referendums or plebiscites is such an integral element of residence in a place that an ordinance like the one at issue in *Allman* would at least *prima facie* violate section 6(2) of the *Charter*. It would then have been incumbent upon the court to decide whether the restriction fell within the exception in section 6(3) and, if not, to weigh the rationale for the restriction against the factors listed in section 1 of the *Charter*. Instead, Belzil J.A., speaking for the Northwest Territories Court of Appeal, rejected the section 6(3) argument as "sophistry" and, further, approved the trial Judge's conclusion that the ordinance was not even a *prima facie* infringement of section 6(2). The sum total of the trial Judge's reasoning on the point, which was quoted and agreed with in full by Belzil J.A., is contained in the following paragraph at 8 D.L.R. (4th) 230 at 237:

> The applicants rely on s-s. 6(2), italicized above. The fact is, however, as shown in their affidavits, that each of them has moved to and has taken up residence in the Northwest Territories, and has been pursuing his or her livelihood within the Northwest Territories notwithstanding any disadvantage which he or she may suffer under the *Plebiscite Ordinance*. There is nothing before me to show that any of their rights under s-s. 6(2) of the Charter have been or are about to be infringed or denied in any way by reason of the Ordinance or by anything done by the respondent pursuant to the Ordinance.

The Court of Appeal did not add anything to the above passage in support of its conclusion that section 6(2) was inapplicable.

In my view, this puts too narrow a construction on section 6(2). The provision must guarantee more than a bare right to move to a province and get a job. What is intended is that a citizen or permanent resident of Canada be entitled to "take up residence"; that is, subject to section 6(3) and section 1, have all the attributes of residency enjoyed by other provincial residents. The American cases previously discussed certainly point in that direction. Furthermore section 6(3)(b) shows by implication that access to services and, presumably, other amenities are comprehended within the section 6(2) guarantee. In my view, *Re Allman* should be reconsidered when the issue arises again.

The most critical aspect of section 6(2) is the extent of the economic rights contained therein. It is clear from *Skapinker, supra*, that section 6(2)(b) does not contain a free-standing right to work, but rather should be "separated but not divorced" from the mobility right in section 6(2)(a). As stated by Estey J. (9 D.L.R. (4th) 181):

> The two rights (in clause (a) and in clause (b)) both relate to movement into another province, either for the taking up of residence, or to work without establishing residence.

It is therefore directed primarily to the economic theory of Canada as a national common market, and is designed to catch cases like *Basile v. A.G.N.S.* (1984), 62 N.S.R. (2d) 410 (C.A.).

In *Basile*, a provincial regulation excluded non-residents of Nova Scotia essentially from engaging in direct selling in the province. The Nova Scotia Court of Appeal struck down the regulation, holding that section 6(2) does not permit a province to condition the earning of a livelihood on residence therein. In the United States, see *Toomer v. Witsell*, 334 U.S. 385 (1948) (right of non-residents to do business outside their home states without discrimination is guaranteed in the absence of proof that non-residents are a peculiar cause of the problem at which the statute is directed); *Hicklin v. Orbeck*, 437 U.S. 518 (1978) (statute requiring preference in employment to be given to residents over non-residents is unconstitutional, even if the state suffers from uniquely high unemployment. *Cf.* section 6(4) of the *Charter*).

The three basic government escape hatches from section 6(2) are contained in sections 6(4), 6(3) and 1. Section 6(4) exempts employment programs whose object is to ameliorate the conditions of socially or economically disadvantaged individuals in a province where the rate of employment in that province is below the national employment rate.

The leading case on section 6(3) is *Re Demaere and The Queen*, [1983] 2 F.C. 755 (C.A.). In *Re Demaere*, a closed competition was held for a federal air traffic controller's position in Vancouver. The competition was limited essentially to employees in the Pacific region of the Canadian Air Traffic Administration. Demaere, a resident of northeast British Columbia, was excluded by the geographical conditions for eligibility. His application for review pursuant to section 21 of the *Public Service Employment Act*, R.S.C. 1970, c. P-32 was dismissed. He applied to quash the decision pursuant to section 28 of the *Federal Court Act* on the grounds that, by restricting the competition the way it did, the Administration violated section 6(2).

The first problem faced by Hugessen J., speaking for the Federal Court of Appeal, was whether section 6(2) was applicable at all given that intraprovincial rather than interprovincial mobility was at issue. Demaere was claiming the right to be eligible to move from north to south British Columbia. The reference in the

English version of section 6(2) is to "in any province", and thereby leaves the implication that it is directed at interprovincial movement. The French version provides that the right is "de se deplacer dans tout le pays", and is therefore not bounded by reference to provincial boundaries. Hugessen J. stated [in [1983] 2 F.C. 755 at 762]:

> In my opinion, the interpretation of s. 6(2) which comes the closest to reconciling the versions in both official languages and to respecting the context in which it is found is that it conveys the right to move to, reside and pursue work in any part of the country. In other words, while, on the one hand, I would not see the section as granting a right to work, I also would not, on the other hand, limit it to interprovincial mobility rights.

The difficulty is that Estey J.'s previously quoted language in *Skapinker* appears to tie the section 6(2)(a) and (b) rights to interprovincial lines ("both relate to movement into another province"), thereby having application, for example, in transprovincial border commuter cases such as *Basile* or situations where a person moves into the province and establishes residence. On the face of it, Estey J.'s language appears to exclude *Demaere* from the ambit of section 6(2). However the question of whether intraprovincial movement is comprehended by section 6(2) was not before Estey J. and, accordingly, he did not have to turn his mind to it or reconcile the English and French texts on the point. Hugessen J.'s treatment of the issue is consistent with the common market notion which underlies section 6(2). Furthermore, it contains the link to mobility which the Supreme Court of Canada in *Skapinker* held was essential. Hopefully his conclusion on the point will be followed in the future.

Having found a *prima facie* violation of section 6(2), Hugessen J. next had to consider whether the breach could be saved by section 6(3)(a). He summarized the conditions of applicability of section 6(3)(a) as follows [at p. 763]:

> ... The overriding provision must be contained:
>   i. in a law or practice;
>   ii. of general application;
>   iii. in force in a province; and
>   iv. such law or practice must not discriminate amongst persons primarily on the basis of province of present or previous residence.

Clearly no problem existed as to conditions i or iv. The practice in question was performed by a federal agency and authority for it was derived from a statute, the *Public Service Employment Act*. Equally, the practice did not discriminate primarily on the basis of province of residency. Rather, it differentiated by reference to where within a province the applicant resided.

As to whether the practice was one of general application pursuant to condition ii, Hugessen J. relied upon the double test set out by Dickson J. (as he then was) in *Kruger v. The Queen*, [1978] 1 S.C.R. 104 at 110 as conclusive for both federal and provincial laws:

> There are two *indicia* by which to discern whether or not a provincial enactment is a law of general application. It is necessary to look first to the territorial reach of the Act. If the Act does not extend uniformly throughout the territory, the inquiry is at an end and the question is answered in the negative. If the law does extend uniformly throughout the jurisdiction the intention and effects of the enactment need to be considered. The law must not be 'in relation to' one class of citizens in object and purpose. But the fact that a law may have graver consequences to one person than to another does not, on that account alone, make the law other than one of general application. There

are few laws which have a uniform impact. The line is crossed, however, when an enactment, though in relation to another matter, by its effect, impairs the status or capacity of a particular group. The analogy may be made to a law which in its effect paralyzes the status and capacities of a federal company; see *Great West Saddlery Co. v. The King*, [1921] 2 A.C. 91. Such an act is no "law of general application". See also *Cunningham v. Tomey Homma*, [1903] A.C. 151.

In my view, there is no doubt that the above passage from *Kruger* sets out the proper test for a law or practice of general application for the purposes of section 6(3)(a), notwithstanding that *Kruger* was a pre-*Charter* case, and Hugessen J. was correct to apply it. The difficulty is that, in my opinion, he applied the test wrongly. Hugessen J. held, without elaboration, that it is "plain beyond dispute that the *Public Service Employment Act* satisfies both branches of the test". That may be so, however by focussing on the statute he directed his attention to the wrong target. The real question was not whether the *statute* was of general application, but rather whether the *practice* arising under it of closing the competition to non-residents of specified areas was one of general application. When the issue is framed this way, the practice fails both branches of the *Kruger* test. First, the practice did not extend uniformly throughout the territory. On the contrary, it was specifically conditioned upon geographical differentiation. Second, it went beyond merely impairing the status or capacity of non-residents of the specified areas to qualify for consideration for the Vancouver air traffic controller's job: it paralyzed their ability to do so. Section 6(3)(a) should therefore have been held not to save impugned practice in this case.

The final question before Hugessen J. was whether a federal law could be "in force in a province" pursuant to condition iii, and he held that it could [at p. 765]:

... The words used, 'laws ... in force in a province', are certainly broad enough to include federal laws. The words are not useless since it is not uncommon for federal laws to be in force in only some of the provinces ... In the absence of any words of restriction in paragraph 6(3)(a), I am unable to say that a federal law which is in force in any or all of the provinces is not a law 'in force in a province' for the purposes of the Charter.

Hugessen J. is undoubtedly correct on the point. If section 6(2) is in fact directed at mobility and breaking down provincial barriers for certain purposes, as *Skapinker* says it is, clogs in these interests will more likely arise as a consequence of provincial rather than federal balkanizing legislation. It follows that if section 6(3)(a) is available to exempt provincial legislation, by hypothesis the greater danger, from the operation of section 6(2), it should be available for federal legislation as well.

*Malartic Hygrade Gold Mines Ltd. v. Quebec* (1982), 142 D.L.R. (3d) 512 (Que. S.C.) is a good example of the proper application of section 6(3)(a). In *Malartic*, section 59 of the *Act Respecting the Barreau du Quebec*, R.S.Q. 1977, c. B-1 did not permit members of other provincial Bars to practise occasionally in Quebec except in matters of federal jurisdiction. A member of the Ontario Bar challenged the legislation, asserting a right pursuant to section 6(2) of the *Charter* to participate in a judicial proceeding in Quebec without a licence. Chief Justice Deschênes upheld the legislation. While it *prima facie* infringed section 6(2), it was saved by section 6(3)(a) as a law of general application, applying uniformly throughout the province and imposing the same qualifications for membership in the Bar on everyone, and did not discriminate primarily on the basis of province of residence. Rather, it was based upon fulfilment of the requirements respecting education, successful completion of Bar entrance examinations and criteria respecting experience. Furthermore, the differentiation was not created as an artificial barrier between the provinces. It was based upon principles of sound administration of justice since, in respect of matters outside federal competence, Quebec is a civil rather than a common law jurisdiction.

*Black v. Law Society of Alberta*, [1984] 6 W.W.R. 385 (Alta. Q.B.) is more problematic. The Alberta Law Society Rules prohibited resident members from practising jointly with non-resident members of the Law Society or from practising in association with more than one law firm. The rules were essentially a protectionist device to prevent competition from out-of-province law firms. Dea J. upheld the rules on the basis that although they constituted a *prima facie* infringement of the rights guaranteed by section 6(2), they were saved by sections 6(3)(a) and 1 of the *Charter*. The rule prohibiting a member from carrying on the practice of law in partnership with more than one law firm was a law of general application within the meaning of section 6(3)(a) which was not (at least on its face) conditioned on residency. The rule prohibiting resident and non-resident members from practising jointly in the province was saved by section 1, on the grounds that the Law Society's ability to control or influence member conduct in pursuance of its statutory obligations to the public was effectively restricted to those resident in Alberta.

There is a qualitative difference between *Malartic* and *Black*. Section 1 of the *Charter* makes it clear that the courts are not to turn a blind eye to legitimate differences or characteristics which may require a limitation on *Charter* rights. Thus, for example, real and significant regional characteristics support the result in *Malartic*. In *Black*, the difficulties which the Law Society might have in policing out of province members, if they exist at all, can likely be combatted by far less drastic measures than were taken here. Far more evidence should have been led by the Law Society to prove otherwise. In any event, it is highly questionable whether special policing difficulties exist at all with respect to non-residents. As to competence, the Law Society sets stringent academic and practical entrance requirements for residents and non-residents alike. If a problem develops after members are admitted to the Bar, there is nothing to prevent the Law Society from instituting continuing education requirements *on a non-discriminatory basis*. As to the financial responsibility of its members, the Law Society can and does require a periodic accounting. The sanction in all cases of non-compliance with Law Society standards of competence, ethics and financial responsibility is expulsion. Section 1 should not have saved the discriminatory regulations given the absence of substantial evidence that qualified non-residents are a peculiar cause of regulatory problems which could not be cured by non-discriminatory procedures.

For further cases of interest involving section 6 of the *Charter*, see *R. v. Puzzella* (1983), 22 M.P.L.R. 201 (Ont. C.A.) (early closing by-laws are valid) and *Re Groupe des Eleveurs de Volailles de l'Est de l'Ontario and Canadian Chicken Marketing Agency* (1984), 14 D.L.R. (4th) 151 (Fed. T.D.) (inter-provincial farm products marketing quotas do not contravene section 6); *Mia v. Medical Services Comm. of B.C.* (1985), 61 B.C.L.R. 273 (S.C.) (decision to refuse a billing number for regular practice for a doctor moving to the province contravenes preference for doctors who had previously practised in the province).

*Quaere* whether the result in *Morgan v. A.G.P.E.I.*, [1976] 2 S.C.R. 349, would be different today, at least insofar as Canadian citizens and permanent residents are concerned, in light of section 6(2) of the *Charter*. Where the provincial non-resident citizen or permanent resident of Canada earned his livelihood in some way connected with land ownership, it is arguable that notwithstanding the legislative history of section 6(2) he would be brought within the ambit of the provision by the *Skapinker* test. The law would not be saved by section 6(3), discriminating as it does primarily on the basis of province of residence, and a heavy burden of justification would be placed on the provincial Legislature before section 1 could save the law. The Legislature would have to show that non-residents of the province were a peculiar cause of whatever evil the statute sought to correct. If the only evil is non-resident landholding in and of itself, the legislative purpose is itself open to question given the constitutional value of mobility expressed in section 6. The contrary argument is, of course, that section 6(2) in its terms protects the movement of people, not capital. In fact, the original federal proposal for promoting the Canadian economic union was to amend section 121 of the *Constitution Act, 1867* to prohibit federal or provincial laws or practices, with several exceptions, which discriminated against persons, goods, services or capital on the basis of province of origin or destination. See "Federal-Provincial Conference of First Ministers on the Constitution, September 8-12, 1980, Documents 80-14/061 and 80-14/064". See also Laskin, "Mobility Rights under the Charter" (1982), 4 Supreme Court L.R. 89 at 95. These proposals were rejected. Furthermore a reference to the right to acquire and hold property was omitted from the final version of section 6(2) at the urging of Prince Edward Island. See "Federal-Provincial Conference of First Ministers on the Constitution", *supra*, Verbatim Transcript at p. 600-4.

*Quaere* whether section 6(1) is available to corporations or other legal entities. Can corporations be "citizens" or "permanent residents" within the meaning of section 6(2)? As noted in Laskin, "Mobility Rights under the Charter", *supra* at 90: "Recourse to the *Citizenship Act* would also have the effect of excluding corporations from the ambit of s. 6(1), because it is only natural persons who may qualify under the statute as citizens of Canada". See also section 2(1) of the *Immigration Act, 1976*, S.C. 1976-77, c. 52 limiting the definition of "permanent resident" to natural persons. The counter-argument is that there is an international law concept of corporate nationality which might be applied to bring certain corporations within the ambit of section 6. See Brownlie, *Principles of Public International Law* (3d, 1979) at pp. 488-90. This approach has the advantage that entitlement to constitutional guarantees are not conditioned exclusively on definitions in easily amended federal statutes.

# 20

# Life, Liberty and Security of the Person

## 1. Substantive Content

### RE CONSTITUTIONAL QUESTION ACT, B.C.; REFERENCE RE SECTION 94(2) OF THE MOTOR VEHICLE ACT, B.C.

In the Supreme Court of Canada. [1986] 1 W.W.R. 481.

Dickson C.J.C., Beetz, McIntyre, Chouinard, Lamer, Wilson and LeDain JJ. Dec. 17, 1985.

Appeal from a judgment of the British Columbia Court of Appeal (1983), 42 B.C.L.R. 364, 147 D.L.R. (3d) 539, 4 C.C.C. (3d) 243, 33 C.R. (3d) 22, 5 C.R.R. 148, 19 M.V.R. 63, [1983] 3 W.W.R. 756, in the matter of a reference concerning the constitutional validity of s. 94(2) of the *Motor Vehicle Act* of British Columbia. Appeal dismissed.

The judgment of Dickson C.J.C. and Beetz, Chouinard, Lamer and LeDain JJ. was delivered by

LAMER J.:

*Introduction*

A law that has the potential to convict a person who has not really done anything wrong offends the principles of fundamental justice and, if imprisonment is available as a penalty, such a law then violates a person's right to liberty under section 7 of the *Charter of Rights and Freedoms* (*Constitution Act, 1982*, as enacted by the *Canada Act*, 1982, c. 11 (U.K.)).

In other words, absolute liability and imprisonment cannot be combined.

*The Facts*

On August 16, 1982, the Lieutenant-Governor in Council of British Columbia referred the following question to the Court of Appeal of that province, by virtue of section 1 of the *Constitutional Question Act*, R.S.B.C. 1979, c. 63:

Is s. 94(2) of the *Motor Vehicle Act*, R.S.B.C. 1979, as amended by the *Motor Vehicle Amendment Act*, 1982, consistent with the *Canadian Charter of Rights and Freedoms*?

On February 3, 1983, the Court of Appeal handed down reasons in answer to the question in which it stated that section 94(2) of the *Act* is inconsistent with the

*Canadian Charter of Rights and Freedoms*: (1983), 42 B.C.L.R. 364. The Attorney General for British Columbia launched an appeal to this Court.

## The Legislation

*Motor Vehicle Act*, R.S.B.C. 1979, c. 288, s. 94, as amended by the *Motor Vehicle Act Amendment Act, 1982*, S.B.C. 1982, c. 36, s. 19:

94.(1) A person who drives a motor vehicle on a highway or industrial road while
  (a) he is prohibited from driving a motor vehicle under sections 90, 91, 92 or 92.1, or
  (b) his driver's licence or his right to apply for or obtain a driver's licence is suspended under s. 82 or 92 as it was before its repeal and replacement came into force pursuant to the *Motor Vehicle Amendment Act*, 1982,
  commits an offence and is liable,
  (c) on a first conviction, to a fine of not less than $300 and not more than $2000 and to imprisonment for not less than 7 days and not more than 6 months, and
  (d) on a subsequent conviction, regardless of when the contravention occurred, to a fine of not less than $300 and not more than $2000 and to imprisonment for not less than 14 days and not more than one year.
  (2) Subsection (1) creates an absolute liability offence in which guilt is established by proof of driving, whether or not the defendant knew of the prohibition or suspension.

## Canadian Charter of Rights and Freedoms: Constitution Act, 1982:

S.1   The *Canadian Charter of Rights and Freedoms* guarantees the rights and freedoms set out in it subject only to such reasonable limits prescribed by law as can be demonstrably justified in a free and democratic society.

S.7   Everyone has the right to life, liberty and security of the person and the right not to be deprived thereof except in accordance with the principles of fundamental justice.

S.11 Any person charged with an offence has the right
  (d) to be presumed innocent until proven guilty according to law in a fair and public hearing by an independent and impartial tribunal;

S.52 The Constitution of Canada is the supreme law of Canada and any law that is inconsistent with the provisions of the Constitution is, to the extent of the inconsistency, of no force or effect.

## The Judgment of The Court of Appeal of British Columbia

The Court was of the view that the phrase "principles of fundamental justice" was not restricted to matters of procedure, but extended to substantive law, and that the courts were "therefore called upon, in construing the provisions of section 7 of the *Charter*, to have regard to the content of legislation".

Relying on the decision of this Court in *R. v. Sault Ste-Marie*, [1978] 2 S.C.R. 1299, the Court of Appeal found "that s. 94(2) of the *Motor Vehicle Act* is inconsistent with the principles of fundamental justice." They did not heed the invitation of counsel opposing the validity of section 94(2) to declare that, as a result of that decision by our Court, all absolute liability offences violated section 7 of the *Charter* and could not be salvaged under section 1. Quite the contrary, the Court of Appeal said that "there are, and will remain, certain public welfare offences, *e.g.* air and water pollution offences, where the public interest requires that the offences be absolute liability offences." Their finding was predicated on the following reasoning:

The effect of s. 94(2) is to transform the offence from a mens rea offence to an absolute liability offence hence giving the defendant no opportunity to prove that his action was due to an honest and reasonable mistake of fact or that he acted without guilty intent. Rather than placing the burden to establish such facts on the defendant and thus making the offence a strict liability offence, the legislature has seen fit to make it an absolute liability offence coupled with a mandatory term of imprisonment.

It can therefore be inferred with certainty that, in the Court's view, the combination of mandatory imprisonment and absolute liability was offensive to section 7. It cannot however be ascertained from their judgment whether the violation was triggered by the requirement of minimum imprisonment or solely by the availability of imprisonment as a sentence.

## Section 7

### 1. *Introduction*

The issue in this case raises fundamental questions of constitutional theory, including the nature and the very legitimacy of constitutional adjudication under the *Charter* as well as the appropriateness of various techniques of constitutional interpretation. I shall deal first with these questions of a more general and theoretical nature as they underlie and have shaped much of the discussion surrounding section 7.

### 2. *The nature and legitimacy of constitutional adjudication under the Charter*

The British Columbia Court of Appeal has written in the present case that the *Constitution Act* has added a new dimension to the role of the courts in that the courts have now been empowered by s. 52 to consider not only the *vires* of legislation but also to measure the content of legislation against the constitutional requirements of the *Charter*.

The novel feature of the *Constitution Act, 1982*, however, is not that it has suddenly empowered courts to consider the content of legislation. This the courts have done for a good many years when adjudicating upon the *vires* of legislation. The initial process in such adjudication has been characterized as "a distillation of the constitutional value represented by the challenged legislation" (Laskin, *Canadian Constitutional Law* (3d ed. rev. 1969), p. 85), and as identifying "the true meaning of the challenged law" (Lederman (ed.), *The Courts and the Canadian Constitution* (1966), p. 186), and "an abstract of the statute's content" (Professor Abel (1969), 19 U. of Toronto L.J. 487 at 490). This process has of necessity involved a measurement of the content of legislation against the requirements of the Constitution, albeit within the more limited sphere of values related to the distribution of powers.

The truly novel features of the *Constitution Act, 1982* are that it has sanctioned the process of constitutional adjudication and has extended its scope so as to encompass a broader range of values. Content of legislation has always been considered in constitutional adjudication. Content is now to be equally considered as regards new constitutional issues. Indeed, the values subject to constitutional adjudication now pertain to the rights of individuals as well as the distribution of governmental powers. In short, it is the scope of constitutional adjudication which has been altered rather than its nature, at least, as regards the right to consider the content of legislation.

In neither case, be it before or after the *Charter*, have the courts been enabled to decide upon the appropriateness of policies underlying legislative enactments. In both instances, however, the courts are empowered, indeed required, to measure the content of legislation against the guarantees of the Constitution. The words of Dickson J. (as he then was) in *Amax Potash Ltd. v. Saskatchewan*, [1977] 2 S.C.R. 576 at 590, continue to govern:

> The Courts will not question the wisdom of enactments . . . but it is the high duty of this Court to insure that the Legislatures do not transgress the limits of their constitutional mandate and engage in the illegal exercise of power.

In this respect, section 7 is no different from other *Charter* provisions. As the Attorney General for Ontario has noted in his factum:

> Section 7, like most of the other sections in the *Charter*, limits the bounds of legislative action. It is the function of the Court to determine whether the challenged legislation has honoured those boundaries. This process necessitates judicial review of the content of the legislation.

Yet, in the context of section 7, and in particular of the interpretation of "principles of fundamental justice", there has prevailed in certain quarters an assumption that all but a narrow construction of section 7 will inexorably lead the courts to "question the wisdom of enactments", to adjudicate upon the merits of public policy.

From this have sprung warnings of the dangers of a judicial "super-legislature" beyond the reach of Parliament, the provincial legislatures and the electorate. The Attorney General for Ontario, in his written argument, stated that,

> . . . the judiciary is neither representative of, nor responsive to the electorate on whose behalf, and under whose authority policies are selected and given effect in the laws of the land.

This is an argument which was heard countless times prior to the entrenchment of the *Charter* but which has in truth, for better or for worse, been settled by the very coming into force of the *Constitution Act, 1982*. It ought not to be forgotten that the historic decision to entrench the *Charter* in our Constitution was taken not by the courts but by the elected representatives of the people of Canada. It was those representatives who extended the scope of constitutional adjudication and entrusted the courts with this new and onerous responsibility. Adjudication under the *Charter* must be approached free of any lingering doubts as to its legitimacy.

The concerns with the bounds of constitutional adjudication explain the characterization of the issue in a narrow and restrictive fashion, *i.e.*, whether the terms "principle of fundamental justice" have a substantive or merely procedural content. In my view, the characterization of the issue in such fashion preempts an open-minded approach to determining the meaning of "principles of fundamental justice".

The substantive/procedural dichotomy narrows the issue almost to an all-or-nothing proposition. Moreover, it is largely bound up in the American experience with substantive and procedural due process. It imports into the Canadian context American concepts, terminology and jurisprudence, all of which are inextricably linked to problems concerning the nature and legitimacy of adjudication under the

U.S. Constitution. That Constitution, it must be remembered, has no s. 52 nor has it the internal checks and balances of sections 1 and 33. We would, in my view, do our own Constitution a disservice to simply allow the American debate to define the issue for us, all the while ignoring the truly fundamental structural differences between the two constitutions. Finally, the dichotomy creates its own set of difficulties by the attempt to distinguish between two concepts whose outer boundaries are not always clear and often tend to overlap. Such difficulties can and should, when possible, be avoided.

The overriding and legitimate concern that courts ought not to question the wisdom of enactments, and the presumption that the Legislator could not have intended same, have to some extent distorted the discussion surrounding the meaning of "principles of fundamental justice". This has led to the spectre of a judicial "super-legislature" without a full consideration of the process of constitutional adjudication and the significance of sections 1, 33 and 52 of the *Constitution Act, 1982*. This in turn has also led to a narrow characterization of the issue and to the assumption that only a procedural content to "principles of fundamental justice" can prevent the courts from adjudicating upon the merits or wisdom of enactments. If this assumption is accepted, the inevitable corollary, with which I would have to then agree, is that the Legislator intended that the words "principles of fundamental justice" refer to procedure only.

But I do not share that assumption. Since way back in time and even recently the courts have developed the common law beyond procedural safeguards without interfering with the "merits or wisdom" of enactments (*e.g., Kienapple v. The Queen*, [1975] 1 S.C.R. 729, entrapment, non-retrospectivity of offences, presumptions against relaxing the burden of proof and persuasion, to give a few examples).

The task of the Court is not to choose between substantive or procedural content *per se* but to secure for persons "the full benefit of the *Charter's* protection" (Dickson C.J.C. in *R. v. Big M Drug Mart Ltd.*, [1985] 1 S.C.R. 295 at 344), under section 7, while avoiding adjudication of the merits of public policy. This can only be accomplished by a purposive analysis and the articulation (to use the words in *Curr v. The Queen*, [1972] S.C.R. 889 at 899) of "objective and manageable standards" for the operation of the section within such a framework.

I propose therefore to approach the interpretation of section 7 in the manner set forth by Dickson C.J.C. in *Hunter v. Southam Inc.*, [1984] 2 S.C.R. 145; *R. v. Big M Drug Mart Ltd., supra*, and by LeDain J. in *R. v. Therens*, [1985] 1 S.C.R. 613. In *Big M Drug Mart Ltd.*, Dickson C.J.C. wrote at 344:

> In *Hunter v. Southam Inc.*, [1984] 2 S.C.R. 145, this Court expressed the view that the proper approach to the definition of the rights and freedoms guaranteed by the *Charter* was a purposive one. The meaning of a right or freedom guaranteed by the Charter was to be ascertained by an analysis of the *purpose* of such a guarantee; it was to be understood, in other words, in the light of the interests it was meant to protect.
>
> In my view this analysis is to be undertaken, and the purpose of the right or freedom in question is to be sought by reference to the character and the larger objects of the *Charter* itself, to the language chosen to articulate the specific right or freedom, to the historical origins of the concepts enshrined, and where applicable, to the meaning and purpose of the other specific rights and freedoms with which it is associated within the text of the *Charter*. The interpretation should be, as the judgment in *Southam* emphasizes, a generous rather than a legalistic one, aimed at fulfilling the purpose of the guarantee and securing for individuals the full benefit of the *Charter*'s protection.

### 3. The Principles of Fundamental Justice

I would first note that I shared the views of Wilson J. in her statement in *Singh v. Minister of Employment and Immigration*, [1985] 1 S.C.R. 177 at 205, that "it is incumbent upon the Court to give meaning to each of the elements, life, liberty and security of the person, which make up the 'right' contained in s. 7". Each of these, in my view, is a distinct though related concept to be construed as such by the courts. It is clear that section 7 surely protects the right not to be deprived of one's life, liberty and security of the person when that is done in breach of the principles of fundamental justice. The outcome of this case is dependent upon the meaning to be given to that portion of the section which states "and the right not to be deprived thereof except in accordance with the principles of fundamental justice". On the facts of this case it is not necessary to decide whether the section gives any greater protection, such as deciding whether, absent a breach of the principles of fundamental justice, there still can be, given the way the section is structured, a violation of one's rights to life, liberty and security of the person under section 7. Furthermore, because of the fact that only deprivation of liberty was considered in these proceedings and that no one took issue with the fact that imprisonment is a deprivation of liberty, my analysis of section 7 will be limited, as was the course taken by all, below and in this Court, to determining the scope of the words "principles of fundamental justice", I will not attempt to give any further content to liberty nor address that of the words life or security of the person.

In the framework of a purposive analysis, designed to ascertain the purpose of the section 7 guarantee and "the interests it was meant to protect" (*R. v. Big M Drug Mart Ltd., supra*), it is clear to me that the interests which are meant to be protected by the words "and the right not to be deprived thereof except in accordance with the principles of fundamental justice" of section 7 are the life, liberty and security of the person. The principles of fundamental justice, on the other hand, are not a protected interest, but rather a qualifier of the right not to be deprived of life, liberty and security of the person.

Given that, as the Attorney General for Ontario has acknowledged, "when one reads the phrase 'principles of fundamental justice', a single incontrovertible meaning is not apparent", its meaning must, in my view, be determined by reference to the interests which those words of the section are designed to protect and the particular role of the phrase within the section. As a qualifier, the phrase serves to establish the parameters of the interests but it cannot be interpreted so narrowly as to frustrate or stultify them. For the narrower the meaning given to "principles of fundamental justice" the greater will be the possibility that individuals may be deprived of these most basic rights. This latter result is to be avoided given that the rights involved are as fundamental as those which pertain to the life, liberty and security of the person, the deprivation of which "has the most severe consequences upon an individual". (*R. v. Cadeddu* (1982), 40 O.R. (2d) 128 (H.C.) at 139).

For these reasons, I am of the view that it would be wrong to interpret the term "fundamental justice" as being synonymous with natural justice as the Attorney-General of British Columbia and others have suggested. To do so would strip the protected interests of much, if not most, of their content and leave the "right" to life, liberty and security of the person in a sorely emaciated state. Such a result would be inconsistent with the broad, affirmative language in which those rights are expressed and equally inconsistent with the approach adopted by this Court toward the interpretation of Charter rights in *Skapinker v. Law Society of Upper Canada*, [1984] 1 S.C.R. 357 *per* Estey J. and *Hunter v. Southam Inc., supra*.

It would mean that the right to liberty would be narrower than the right not to be arbitrarily detained or imprisoned (section 9), that the right to security of the person would have less content than the right to be secure against unreasonable search or seizure (section 8). Such an interpretation would give the specific expressions of the "right to life, liberty and security of the person" which are set forth in sections 8 to 14 greater content than the general concept from which they originate.

Sections 8 to 14, in other words, address specific deprivations of the "right" to life, liberty and security of the person in breach of the principles of fundamental justice, and as such, violations of section 7. They are designed to protect, in a specific manner and setting, the right to life, liberty and security of the person set forth in section 7. It would be incongruous to interpret section 7 more narrowly than the rights in sections 8 to 14. The alternative, which is to interpret all of sections 8 to 14 in a "narrow and technical" manner for the sake of congruity, is out of the question. (*Skapinker v. Law Society of Upper Canada, supra,* at 366).

Sections 8 to 14 are illustrative of deprivations of those rights to life, liberty and security of the person in breach of the principles of fundamental justice. For they, in effect, illustrate some of the parameters of the "right" to life, liberty and security of the person; they are examples of instances in which the "right" to life, liberty and security of the person would be violated in a manner which is not in accordance with the principles of fundamental justice. To put matters in a different way, sections 7 to 14 could have been fused into one section, with inserted between the words of section 7 and the rest of those sections, the oft utilised provision in our statutes, "and, without limiting the generality of the foregoing (section 7) the following shall be deemed to be in violation of a person's rights under this section". Clearly, some of those sections embody principles that are beyond what could be characterized as "procedural".

Thus, sections 8 to 14 provide an invaluable key to the meaning of "principles of fundamental justice". Many have been developed over time as presumptions of the common law, others have found expression in the international conventions on human rights. All have been recognized as essential elements of a system for the administration of justice which is founded upon a belief in "the dignity and worth of the human person" (preamble to the *Canadian Bill of Rights*, R.S.C. 1970, App. III) and on "The Rule of Law" (preamble to the *Canadian Charter of Rights and Freedoms*).

It is this common thread which, in my view, must guide us in determining the scope and content of "principles of fundamental justice". In other words, the principles of fundamental justice are to be found in the basic tenets of our legal system. They do not lie in the realm of general public policy but in the inherent domain of the judiciary as guardian of the justice system. Such an approach to the interpretation of "principles of fundamental justice" is consistent with the wording and structure of section 7, the context of the section, *i.e.*, sections 8 to 14, and the character and larger objects of the *Charter* itself. It provides meaningful content for the section 7 guarantee all the while avoiding adjudication of policy matters.

Thus, it seems to me that to replace "fundamental justice" with the term "natural justice" misses the mark entirely. It was, after all, clearly open to the Legislator to use the term natural justice, a known term of art, but such was not done. We must, as a general rule, be loath to exchange the terms actually used with terms so obviously avoided.

Whatever may have been the degree of synonymy between the two expressions in the past, (which in any event has not been clearly demonstrated by the parties and intervenants), as of the last few decades this country has given a precise meaning to the words natural justice for the purpose of delineating the responsibility of adjudicators (in the wide sense of the word) in the field of administrative law.

It is, in my view, that precise and somewhat narrow meaning that the Legislator avoided, clearly indicating thereby a will to give greater content to the words "principles of fundamental justice", the limits of which were left for the courts to develop but within, of course, the acceptable sphere of judicial activity.

. . . . .

[His Lordship's discussion of the admissibility and weight of the Proceedings and Evidence of the Special Joint Committee of the Senate and House of Commons on the Constitution of Canada is extracted at chapter 5, *supra*. He then went on to reject the argument that *Duke v. The Queen*, [1972] S.C.R. 917, a *Bill of Rights* case, was of assistance in interpreting s. 7 of the *Charter*, and continued:]

## Conclusion

I have, in this judgment, undertaken a purposive analysis of the term "principles of fundamental justice" in section 7 of the *Charter* in accordance with the method established by this Court in *Big M Drug Mart Ltd., supra*. Accordingly, the point of departure for the analysis has been a consideration of the general objectives of the *Charter* in the light of the general principles of *Charter* interpretation set forth in *Skapinker, supra*, and *Southam, supra*. This was followed by a detailed analysis of the language and structure of the section as well as its immediate context within the *Charter*.

The main sources of support for the argument that "fundamental justice" is simply synonymous with natural justice have been the Minutes of the Proceedings and Evidence of the Special Joint Committee on the Constitution and the *Bill of Rights* jurisprudence. In my view, neither the Minutes nor the *Bill of Rights* jurisprudence are persuasive or of any great force. The historical usage of the term "fundamental justice" is, on the other hand, shrouded in ambiguity. Moreover, not any one of these arguments, taken singly or as a whole, manages to overcome in my respectful view the textual and contextual analyses.

Consequently, my conclusion may be summarized as follows:

The term "principles of fundamental justice" is not a right, but a qualifier of the right not to be deprived of life, liberty and security of the person; its function is to set the parameters of that right.

Sections 8 to 14 address specific deprivations of the "right" to life, liberty and security of the person in breach of the principles of fundamental justice, and as such, violations of section 7. They are therefore illustrative of the meaning, in criminal or penal law, of "principles of fundamental justice"; they represent principles which have been recognized by the common law, the international conventions and by the very fact of entrenchment in the Charter, as essential elements of a system for the administration of justice which is founded upon a belief in the dignity and worth of the human person and the rule of law.

Consequently, the principles of fundamental justice are to be found in the basic tenets and principles, not only of our judicial process, but also of the other components of our legal system.

We should not be surprised to find that many of the principles of fundamental justice are procedural in nature. Our common law has largely been a law of remedies and procedures, and as Frankfurter J. wrote in *McNabb v. U.S.*, 318 U.S. 332 (1942) at 347, "the history of liberty has largely been the history of observance of procedural safeguards". This is not to say, however, that the principles of fundamental justice are limited solely to procedural guarantees. Rather, the proper approach to the determination of the principles of fundamental justice is quite simply one in which, as Professor Tremblay has written, "future growth will be based on historical roots". ((1984), 18 U.B.C.L. Rev. 201 at 254).

Whether any given principle may be said to be a principle of fundamental justice within the meaning of section 7 will rest upon an analysis of the nature, sources, rationale and essential role of that principle within the judicial process and in our legal system, as it evolves.

Consequently, those words cannot be given any exhaustive content or simple enumerative definition, but will take on concrete meaning as the courts address alleged violations of section 7.

I now turn to such an analysis of the principle of *mens rea* and absolute liability offences in order to determine the question which has been put to the Court in the present Reference.

### Absolute Liability and Fundamental Justice in Penal Law

It has from time immemorial been part of our system of laws that the innocent not be punished. This principle has long been recognized as an essential element of a system for the administration of justice which is founded upon a belief in the dignity and worth of the human person and on the rule of law. It is so old that its first enunciation was in latin *actus non facit reum nisi mens sit rea*.

As Glanville Williams said:

> There is no need here to go into the remote history of *mens rea*; suffice it to say that the requirement of a guilty state of mind (at least for the more serious crimes) had been developed by the time of Coke, which is as far back as the modern lawyer needs to go. 'If one shoot at any wild fowl upon a tree, and the arrow killeth any reasonable creature afar off, without any evil intent in him, this is *per infortunium*.'

(Glanville Williams, *Criminal Law, The General Part*, 2nd Edition, London, Stevens and Sons Limited, 1961, p. 30.)

One of the many judicial statements on the subject worth mentioning is of the highest authority, *per* Goddard C.J. in *Harding v. Price*, [1948] 1 K.B. 695 at 700, where he said:

> The general rule applicable to criminal cases is actus non facit reum nisi mens sit rea, and I venture to repeat what I said in *Brend v. Wood* (1946), 62 T.L.R. 462, 463: 'It is of the utmost importance for the protection of the liberty of the subject that a court should always bear in mind

that, unless a statute either clearly or by necessary implication rules out mens rea as a constituent part of a crime, the court should not find a man guilty of an offence against the criminal law unless he has a guilty mind'.

This view has been adopted by this Court in unmistakable terms in many cases, amongst which the better known are *Beaver v. The Queen*, [1957] S.C.R. 531, and the most recent and often quoted judgment of Dickson J. (as he then was), writing for the Court in *R. v. Sault Ste. Marie, supra.*

This Court's decision in the latter case is predicated upon a certain number of postulates one of which, given the nature of the rules it elaborates, has to be to the effect that absolute liability in penal law offends the principles of fundamental justice. Those principles are, to use the words of Dickson J., to the effect that "there is a generally held revulsion against punishment of the morally innocent". He also stated that the argument that absolute liability "violates fundamental principles of penal liability" was the most telling argument against absolute liability and one of greater force than those advanced in support thereof.

In my view it is because absolute liability offends the principles of fundamental justice that this Court created presumptions against legislatures having intended to enact offences of a regulatory nature falling within that category. This is not to say, however, and to that extent I am in agreement with the Court of Appeal, that, as a result, absolute liability *per se* offends section 7 of the *Charter*.

A law enacting an absolute liability offence will violate section 7 of the *Charter* only if and to the extent that it has the potential of depriving of life, liberty, or security of the person.

Obviously, imprisonment (including probation orders) deprives persons of their liberty. An offence has that potential as of the moment it is open to the judge to impose imprisonment. There is no need that imprisonment, as in section 94(2), be made mandatory.

I am therefore of the view that the combination of imprisonment and of absolute liability violates section 7 of the *Charter* and can only be salvaged if the authorities demonstrate under section 1 that such a deprivation of liberty in breach of those principles of fundamental justice is, in a free and democratic society, under the circumstances, a justified reasonable limit to one's rights under section 7.

As no one has addressed imprisonment as an alternative to the non-payment of a fine, I prefer not to express any views in relation to section 7 as regards that eventuality as a result of a conviction for an absolute liability offence; nor do I need to address here, given the scope of my finding and the nature of this appeal, minimum imprisonment, whether it offends the *Charter per se* or whether such violation, if any, is dependent upon whether it be for a *mens rea* or strict liability offence. Those issues were not addressed by the Court below and it would be unwise to attempt to address them here. It is sufficient and desirable for this appeal to make the findings I have and no more, that is, that no imprisonment may be imposed for an absolute liability offence, and, consequently, given the question put to us, an offence punishable by imprisonment cannot be an absolute liability offence.

Before considering section 94(2) in the light of these findings, I feel we are however compelled to go somewhat further for the following reason. I would not want us to be taken by this conclusion as having inferentially decided that absolute liability may not offend section 7 as long as imprisonment or probation orders are not available as a sentence. The answer to that question is dependent upon the content given to the words "security of the person". That issue was and is a live one. Indeed, though the question as framed focuses on absolute liability (section 94(2)) in relation to the whole *Charter*, including the right to security of the person in section 7, because of the presence of mandatory imprisonment in section 94(1) only deprivation of liberty was considered. As the effect of imprisonment on the right to liberty is a foregone conclusion, *a fortiori* minimum imprisonment, everyone directed their arguments, when discussing section 7 to considering whether absolute liability violated the principles of fundamental justice, and then subsidiarily argued pro or contra the effect of section 1 of the *Charter*.

Counsel for those opposing the validity of section 94(2) took the position in this Court that absolute liability and severe punishment, always referring to imprisonment, violated section 7 of the *Charter*. From the following passage of the judgment in the Court of Appeal it would appear that counsel for those opposing the validity of the section took the wider position in that Court that all absolute liability offences violated section 7 because of "punishment of the morally innocent":

> In seeking to persuade the court to that conclusion counsel opposing the validity of s. 94(2) contended all absolute offences are now of no force and effect because of s. 7 of the Charter and that the provisions of s. 1 of the Charter should not be invoked to sustain them. In support of this submission counsel relied upon the view expressed by Dickson J. in *Sault Ste Marie* that there was 'a generally held revulsion against punishment of the morally innocent'. They contended that had the Charter been in effect when *Sault Ste. Marie* was decided all absolute liability offences would have been struck down.
>
> We accept without hesitation the statement expressed by the learned justice but do not think it necessarily follows that because of s. 7 of the Charter this category of offence can no longer be legislated. To the contrary, there are, and will remain, certain public welfare offences, e.g., air and water pollution offences, where the public interest requires that the offences be absolute liability offences.

While I agree with the Court of Appeal, as I have already mentioned, that absolute liability does not *per se* violate section 7 of the *Charter*, I am somewhat concerned with leaving without comment the unqualified reference by the Court of Appeal to the requirements of the "public interest".

If, by reference to public interest, it was meant that the requirements of public interest for certain types of offences is a factor to be considered in determining whether absolute liability offends the principles of fundamental justice, then I would respectfully disagree; if the public interest is there referred to by the Court as a possible justification under section 1 of a limitation to the rights protected at section 7, then I do agree.

Indeed, as I said, in penal law, absolute liability always offends the principles of fundamental justice irrespective of the nature of the offence; it offends section 7 of the *Charter* if as a result, anyone is deprived of their life, liberty or security of the person, irrespective of the requirement of public interest. In such cases it might only be salvaged for reasons of public interest under section 1.

In this latter regard, something might be added.

Administrative expediency, absolute liability's main supportive argument, will undoubtedly under section 1 be invoked and occasionally succeed. Indeed, administrative expediency certainly has its place in administrative law. But when administrative law chooses to call in aid imprisonment through penal law, indeed sometimes criminal law and the added stigma attached to a conviction, exceptional, in my view, will be the case where the liberty or even the security of the person guaranteed under section 7 should be sacrificed to administrative expediency. Section 1 may, for reasons of administrative expediency, successfully come to the rescue of an otherwise violation of section 7, but only in cases arising out of exceptional conditions, such as natural disasters, the outbreak of war, epidemics, and the like.

Of course I understand the concern of many as regards corporate offences, specially, as was mentioned by the Court of Appeal, in certain sensitive areas such as the preservation of our vital environment and our natural resources. This concern might well be dispelled were it to be decided, given the proper case, that section 7 affords protection to human persons only and does not extend to corporations.

Even if it be decided that section 7 does extend to corporations, I think the balancing under section 1 of the public interest against the financial interests of a corporation would give very different results from that of balancing public interest and the liberty or security of the person of a human being.

Indeed, the public interest as regards "air and water pollution offences" requires that the guilty be dealt with firmly, but the seriousness of the offence does not in my respectful view support the proposition that the innocent *human* person be open to conviction, quite the contrary.

*Section 94(2)*

No doubt section 94(2) enacts in the clearest of terms an absolute liability offence, the conviction for which a person will be deprived of his or her liberty, and little more, if anything, need be added. However, I should not want to conclude without addressing an argument raised by the appellant in this Court and considered by the British Columbia Court of Appeal.

The appellant argues that, as a result of the case of *R. v. MacDougall*, [1982] 2 S.C.R. 605, section 94(2) (the absolute liability provision) is of limited effect. Hence, the section raises "a false impression of a potential for wholesale injustice," says the appellant. In my view, this argument is of little relevance to the determination of this appeal. Whether the provision is of broad or of "limited" effect does not change its nature nor lead to a different characterization for the purpose of determining a violation of section 7. The question is whether the provision offends section 7 of the *Charter at all*, rather than whether it does so in "limited" or "wholesale" fashion. At best, this argument may be considered under section 1.

The appellant summarizes the decision in *MacDougall* as establishing that

> where an accused is charged with driving a motor vehicle while his licence was cancelled (contrary to a provincial statute), ignorance by the accused of the fact that his licence was revoked is ignorance of law and cannot provide the basis for an acquittal.

The respondent, however, distinguishes the *MacDougall* case from the case at bar on two grounds. First, the offence under consideration in *MacDougall* was one of strict liability rather than absolute liability. Secondly, while *MacDougall* "dealt only with the suspension by operation of law, section 94(2) encompasses Court imposed suspensions (section 90(2)), suspensions arising under the 'old law' in the absence of the accused, and suspensions imposed by administrative review by the Superintendent of Motor Vehicles requiring delivery of notice ('old' act, section 82(3))". Thus, the respondent concludes that there are "at least three classes of morally innocent persons who are, by section 94(2) deprived of the opportunity to present a defence of the type outlined by Dickson J. in *R. v. Sault Ste. Marie*, [1978] 2 S.C.R. 1299 at 1326:

> The defence will be available if the accused reasonably believed in a mistaken set of facts which, if true, would render the act or omission innocent, or if he took all reasonable steps to avoid the particular event.

In the final analysis, it seems that both the appellant and the respondent agree that section 94 will impact upon the right to liberty of a limited number of morally innocent persons. It creates an absolute liability offence which effects a deprivation of liberty for a limited number of persons. To me, that is sufficient for it to be in violation of section 7.

## Section 1

Having found that section 94(2) offends section 7 of the *Charter*, there remains the question as to whether the appellants have demonstrated that the section is salvaged by the operation of section 1 of the *Charter*. No evidence was adduced in the Court of Appeal or in this Court. The position in that regard and the argument in support of the operability of section 94(2) is as follows in appellant's factum:

> If this Court rules that s. 94(2) of the Motor Vehicle Act is inconsistent with s. 7 (or s. 11(d)) of the Charter, then it is submitted that s. 1 of the Charter is applicable. It is submitted that Laskin J. (as he then was) made it clear in *Curr v. The Queen*, supra, that it is within the scope of judicial notice for this Court to recognize that a statutory provision was enacted as part of a legislative scheme aimed at reducing the human and economic cost of bad driving. S. 94 is but part of the overall scheme laid out in the Motor Vehicle Act by which the Legislature is attempting to get bad drivers off the road. S. 94 imposes severe penalties on those who drive while prohibited from driving and those who drive while their driver's licence is suspended.
>
> It is submitted that if s. 94(2) is inconsistent with one of the above-noted provisions of the Charter, then s. 94(2) contains a 'reasonable limit, etc.' within the meaning of s. 1 of the Charter.

I do not take issue with the fact that it is highly desirable that "bad drivers" be kept off the road. I do not take issue either with the desirability of punishing severely bad drivers who are in contempt of prohibitions against driving. The bottom line of the question to be addressed here is: whether the Government of British Columbia has demonstrated as justifiable that the risk of imprisonment of a few innocent is, given the desirability of ridding the roads of British Columbia of bad drivers, a reasonable limit in a free and democratic society. That result is to be measured against the offence being one of strict liability open to a defence of due diligence, the success of which does nothing more than let those few who did nothing wrong remain free.

As did the Court of Appeal, I find that this demonstration has not been satisfied, indeed, not in the least.

In the result, I would dismiss the appeal and answer the question in the negative, as did the Court of Appeal, albeit for somewhat different reasons, and declare section 94(2) of the *Motor Vehicle Act*, R.S.B.C. 1979, as amended by the *Motor Vehicle Amendment Act*, 1982, inconsistent with section 7 of the *Canadian Charter of Rights and Freedoms*.

Having come to this conclusion, I choose, as did the Court of Appeal, not to address whether the section violates the rights guaranteed under sections 11(d) and 12 of the *Charter*.

McINTYRE J.:

I agree with Lamer J. that section 94(2) of the *Motor Vehicle Act*, R.S.B.C. 1979, c. 288, as amended by the *Motor Vehicle Amendment Act 1982*, S.B.C. 1982, c. 36, s. 19, is inconsistent with s. 7 of the *Canadian Charter of Rights and Freedoms*. I agree that fundamental justice, as the term is used in the *Charter*, involves more than natural justice (which is largely procedural) and includes as well a substantive element. I am also of the view that on any definition of the term 'fundamental justice' the imposition of minimum imprisonment for an offence in respect of which no defence can be made, and which may be committed unknowingly and with no wrongful intent, deprives or may deprive of liberty and it offends the principles of fundamental justice.

I would accordingly dismiss the appeal and answer the Constitutional Question in the negative.

WILSON J.:

I agree with my colleague, Mr. Justice Lamer, that section 94(2) of the *Motor Vehicle Act* violates section 7 of the *Charter* and is not saved by section 1. I reach that result, however, by a somewhat different route.

I start with a consideration of statutory "offences". These are divisible into offences for which *mens rea* is required and those for which it is not. Statutory offences are subject to a presumption in favour of a *mens rea* requirement as a matter of interpretation, but the courts have increasingly come to accept the proposition that legislatures may create non *mens rea* offences provided they make it clear that the *actus reus* itself is prohibited. This is typically so in the case of the so-called "regulatory" or "public welfare" offences. There is no moral delinquency involved in these offences. They are simply designed to regulate conduct in the public interest.

Two questions, therefore, have to be answered on this appeal. The first is do absolute liability offences created by statute *per se* offend the *Charter*? The second is, assuming they do not, can they be attended by mandatory imprisonment or can such a sanction only be attached to true *mens rea* offences? Certainly, in the absence of the *Charter*, legislatures are free to create absolute liability offences and to attach to them any sanctions they please. Does section 7 of the *Charter* circumscribe their power in this regard?

### 1. *Absolute liability offences*

Section 7 affirms the right to life, liberty and security of the person while at the same time indicating that a person may be deprived of such a right if the deprivation is effected "in accordance with the principles of fundamental justice". I do not view the latter part of the section as a qualification on the right to life, liberty and security of the person in the sense that it limits or modifies that right or defines its parameters. Its purpose seems to me to be the very opposite, namely to protect the right against deprivation or impairment unless such deprivation or impairment is effected in accordance with the principles of fundamental justice.

Section 7 does not, however, affirm a right to the principles of fundamental justice *per se*. There must first be found an impairment of the right to life, liberty or security of the person. It must then be determined whether that impairment has been effected in accordance with the principles of fundamental justice. If it has, it passes the threshold test in section 7 itself but the Court must go on to consider whether it can be sustained under section 1 as a limit prescribed by law on the section 7 right which is both reasonable and justified in a free and democratic society. If, however, the limit on the section 7 right has been effected through a violation of the principles of fundamental justice, the enquiry, in my view, ends there and the limit cannot be sustained under section 1. I say this because I do not believe that a limit on the section 7 right which has been imposed in violation of the principles of fundamental justice can be either "reasonable" or "demonstrably justified in a free and democratic society". The requirement in section 7 that the principles of fundamental justice be observed seems to me to restrict the legislature's power to impose limits on the section 7 right under section 1. It can only limit the section 7 right if it does so in accordance with the principles of fundamental justice and, even if it meets that test, it still has to meet the tests in section 1.

Assuming that I am correct in my analysis of section 7 and its relationship to section 1, an absolute liability offence cannot violate section 7 unless it impairs the right to life, liberty or security of the person. It cannot violate section 7 because it offends the principles of fundamental justice because they are not protected by section 7 absent an impairment of the section 7 right. Leaving aside for the moment the mandatory imprisonment sanction, I cannot find an interference with life, liberty or security of the person in section 94 of the *Motor Vehicle Act*. It is true that the section prevents citizens from driving their vehicles when their licences are suspended. Citizens are also prevented from driving on the wrong side of the road. Indeed, all regulatory offences impose some restriction on liberty broadly construed. But I think it would trivialize the *Charter* to sweep all those offences into section 7 as violations of the right to life, liberty and security of the person even if they can be sustained under section 1. It would be my view, therefore, that absolute liability offences of this type do not *per se* offend section 7 of the *Charter*.

## 2. *Absolute liability plus mandatory imprisonment*

The real question, as I see it, is whether section 7 of the *Charter* is violated by the attachment of a mandatory imprisonment sanction to an absolute liability offence. Clearly a section 7 right is interfered with here in that a person convicted of such an offence automatically loses his liberty.

In what circumstances then may the citizen be deprived of his right to liberty? Clearly not if he was deprived of it through a process which was procedurally unfair. But is section 7 limited to that?

I would assume that one of the reasons for the rider attached to the right to liberty affirmed in section 7 is to accommodate the criminal justice system. It will be through the criminal justice system that citizens will typically lose their liberty at the hands of government. The system must not, therefore, cause them to lose their liberty in violation of the principles of fundamental justice. The system must reflect those principles and the validity of the penal provisions must be assessed in relation to them.

Since section 94(2) of the *Motor Vehicle Act* imposes a limit prescribed by law on the section 7 right, we must determine whether fundamental justice is offended by attaching mandatory imprisonment to an absolute liability offence. Given that we can have statutory non *mens rea* offences, what is repugnant to fundamental justice in imprisoning someone for their commission?

At common law imprisonment was reserved for the more serious *mens rea* offences. However, we are dealing here with statutory offences and the legislation must stand unless it violates section 7. We cannot, in my view, simply state as a bald proposition that absolute liability and imprisonment cannot co-exist in a statutory context. Legislatures can supersede the common law. The legislature may consider it so important to prevent a particular act from being committed that it absolutely forbids it and, if it is committed, may subject the offender to a penalty whether he has any *mens rea* or not and whether or not he had any intention of breaking the law. Prior to the *Charter* such legislation would have been unassailable. Now it must meet the test of section 7. Where the legislature has imposed a penalty in the form of mandatory imprisonment for the commission of an absolute liability offence and has done so in clear and unambiguous language, can the legislation survive an attack under section 7? It is suggested that such legislation cannot survive because it offends the principles of fundamental justice and, in particular, the principle that punishment is inappropriate in the absence of moral culpability.

The common law distinguished sharply the conduct of the wrongdoer from his state of mind at the time. Hence the famous maxim referred to by my colleague — *actus non facit reum nisi mens sit rea*. The important thing to note, however, is that while the maxim has always been viewed as identifying the essential ingredients of a crime at common law, its meaning has been subject to a process of historical and juridical development, particularly the concept of *mens rea*. In the earliest beginnings of criminal liability the mental state of the wrongdoer was not considered at all; it was enough that he had done the fell deed: see Holdsworth, *A History of English Law* (1923-1938), vol. II, p. 50 *et seq*. At a later stage the accused's state of mind was considered for two distinct purposes, namely (1) to determine whether his conduct was voluntary or involuntary; and (2) to determine whether he realized what the consequences of his conduct might be. But the first purpose was viewed as the key one. It was considerably later in the development of the law of criminal responsibility that the emphasis changed and an appreciation of the consequences of his act became the central focus. The movement towards the concept of the "guilty mind" was not, however, a sudden or dramatic one. This is understandable. The judges of the day found the new rule hard to apply because it was difficult to look into the state of a man's mind. The ecclesiastical authorities, however, had no such problem and legal historians seem to agree that the ecclesiastical influence was largely responsible for moving the focus to the mental element in common law crime: see Holdsworth, (*supra*), p. 259.

The introduction of concepts of morality into criminal responsibility inevitably led to a sharp distinction between crimes which were *mala in se* and crimes which were merely *mala prohibita*. Blackstone describes crimes which were *mala in se* as offences against "those rights which God and nature have established" (Blackstone, *Commentaries on the Laws of England* (17th ed., by E. Christian, 1830)), p. 53 and crimes which were *mala prohibita* as breaches of "those laws which enjoin only positive duties, and forbid any such things as are not *mala in se* ... without any intermixture of moral guilt" (Blackstone, *ibid*, p. 57). This distinction is now pretty well discredited: see Archbold's *Criminal Pleading, Evidence & Practice*, 30th ed. (1938), p. 900; Allen, *Legal Duties* (1931), p. 239. While it is undoubtedly a fact that certain crimes evoke feelings of revulsion and condemnation in the minds of most people, those feelings are now generally perceived as dependent upon a number of variable factors such as environment, education and religious prejudice and are no longer seen as providing a secure basis for the segregation of crimes into two different categories. Quoting from Kenny's *Outlines of Criminal Law*, 1952, ed. J.W.C. Turner, at pp. 22-23:

> Among the members of any community at a given period, certain offences are by general agreement regarded as especially serious and excite deep moral reprobation, whereas other transgressions are regarded as venial and are more or less condoned, especially when they infringe rules of law which are unpopular. It is indeed inevitable that this apportionment of blame should be made. Yet the vague and fluctuating line which in everyday life is drawn between the one group and the other only marks a variation in degree; it is not a boundary which separates things fundamentally alien in kind. Ethical reprobation of homicide, homosexuality, libel, adultery, bigamy and slave trading, to take a few examples, is not the same in all countries, and indeed may vary from section to section of the people in the same country.
>
> . . .
>
> This defective classification of crimes clearly formed an unsound premise from which to draw any jurisprudential conclusion but it has an insidious attraction, and in the form of English phrases such as "in itself unlawful" it has penetrated into one or two modern judgments with vitiating effects upon the logic and clarity of the argument.

Accepting that a guilty mind was an essential ingredient of a crime at common law, it does not, of course, follow that the same is true of a "crime" created by statute. I have already referred to the presumption against absolute liability as a matter of statutory interpretation. This undoubtedly reflects the common law approach to the nature of crime. It is, however, only a presumption. Provided it does so in clear and unambiguous terms the legislature is free to make a person liable for the *actus reus* with or without *mens rea*.

In Kenny's *Outlines of Criminal Law*, (*supra*), p. 4 the author highlights the difficulty in identifying any essential characteristics of crimes created by statute. He points out that such crimes originate in the government policy of the day and that, so long as crimes continue to be created by government policy, the nature of statutory crime will elude definition. Lord Atkin adverted to the same difficulty in *Proprietary Articles Trade Association and others v. Attorney General for Canada and others*, [1931] A.C. 310. He stated at 324:

> ... the domain of criminal jurisprudence can only be ascertained by examining what acts at any particular period are declared by the State to be crimes, and the only common nature they will be found to possess is that they are prohibited by the State and that those who commit them are punished.

In *R. v. Pierce Fisheries Ltd.*, [1970] 5 C.C.C. 193, Ritchie J., speaking for the majority of this Supreme Court of Canada, said at 199:

> Generally speaking, there is a presumption at common law that *mens rea* is an essential ingredient
> of all cases that are criminal in the true sense, but a considerable body of case law on the subject
> satisfies me that there is a wide category of offences created by statutes enacted for the regulation of
> individual conduct in the interests of health, convenience, safety, and the general welfare of the
> public which are not subject to any such presumption.

There seems to be no doubt that in section 94 of the *Motor Vehicle Act* the legislature of British Columbia has created such an offence. Subsection (2) expressly precludes the application of any presumption in favour of a *mens rea* requirement. However, as already indicated, I do not believe that any principle of fundamental justice is offended by the creation of an absolute liability offence absent an impairment of the section 7 right.

Is fundamental justice offended then by the attachment of a mandatory term of imprisonment to the section 94 offence? Is there something repugnant about imprisoning a person for the commission of an absolute liability offence? Presumably no objection can be taken to attaching penal consequences such as a fine to a validly enacted absolute liability offence, only to penal consequences in the form of imprisonment if this gives rise to a violation of section 7 of the *Charter*. If it does, then the Court is not only empowered, but obligated by the constitution, to strike the section down.

I have already indicated that in my view a law which interferes with the liberty of the citizen in violation of the principles of fundamental justice cannot be saved by section 1 as being either reasonable or justified. The concepts are mutually exclusive. This is not, of course, to say that no limits can be put upon the right to life, liberty and security of the person. They clearly can, but only if they are imposed in accordance with the principles of fundamental justice and survive the tests in section 1 as being reasonable and justified in a free and democratic society. Nor is the government precluded from resort to section 33 of the *Charter* in order to dispense with the requirements of fundamental justice when, in a case of emergency, it seeks to impose restrictions on the section 7 right. This, however, will be a policy decision for which the government concerned will be politically accountable to the people. As it is, section 94 cannot, in my view, be saved by section 1 if it violates section 7. The sole question is whether it violates section 7.

My colleague, in finding that section 94 offends the principles of fundamental justice, has relied heavily upon the common law which precluded punishment in the absence of a guilty mind. We are not, however, dealing with a common law crime here. We are dealing with a statutory offence as to which the legislature has stated in no uncertain terms that guilt is established by proof of the act itself.

Unlike my colleague, I do not think that sections 8 to 14 of the *Charter* shed much light on the interpretation of the phrase "in accordance with the principles of fundamental justice" as used in section 7. I find them very helpful as illustrating facets of the right to life, liberty and security of the person. I am not ready at this point, however, to equate unreasonableness or arbitrariness or tardiness as used in some of these sections with a violation of the principles of fundamental justice as used in section 7. Delay, for example, may be explained away or excused or justified on a number of grounds under section 1. I prefer, therefore, to treat these sections as self-standing provisions, as indeed they are.

I approach the interpretive problem raised by the phrase "the principles of fundamental justice" on the assumption that the legislature was very familiar with the concepts of "natural justice" and "due process" and the way in which those phrases had been judicially construed and applied. Yet they chose neither. Instead they chose the phrase "the principles of fundamental justice". What is "fundamental justice"? We know what "fundamental principles" are. They are the basic, bedrock principles that underpin a system. What would "fundamental principles of justice" mean? And would it mean something different from "principles of fundamental justice"? I am not entirely sure. We have been left by the legislature with a conundrum. I would conclude, however, that if the citizen is to be guaranteed his right to life, liberty and security of the person — surely one of the most basic rights in a free and democratic society — then he certainly should not be deprived of it by means of a violation of a fundamental tenet of our justice system.

It has been argued very forcefully that section 7 is concerned only with procedural injustice but I have difficulty with that proposition. There is absolutely nothing in the section to support such a limited construction. Indeed, it is hard to see why one's life and liberty should be protected against procedural injustice and not against substantive injustice in a *Charter* that opens with the declaration:

> Whereas Canada is founded upon principles that recognize the supremacy of God and the rule of law:

and sets out the guarantee in broad and general terms as follows:

> 1. The *Canadian Charter of Rights and Freedoms* guarantees the rights and freedoms set out in it subject only to such reasonable limits prescribed by law as can be demonstrably justified in a free and democratic society.

I cannot think that the guaranteed right in section 7 which is to be subject *only* to limits which are reasonable and justifiable in a free and democratic society can be taken away by the violation of a principle considered fundamental to our justice system. Certainly the rule of law acknowledged in the preamble as one of the foundations on which our society is built is more than mere procedure. It will be for the courts to determine the principles which fall under the rubric "the principles of fundamental justice". Obviously not all principles of law are covered by the phrase; only those which are basic to our system of justice.

I have grave doubts that the dichotomy between substance and procedure which may have served a useful purpose in other areas of the law such as administrative law and private international law should be imported into section 7 of the *Charter*. In many instances the line between substance and procedure is a very narrow one. For example, the presumption of innocence protected in section 11(d) of the *Charter* may be viewed as a substantive principle of fundamental justice but it clearly has both a substantive and a procedural aspect. Indeed, any rebuttable presumption of fact may be viewed as procedural, as going primarily to the allocation of the burden of proof. Nevertheless, there is also an interest of substance to be protected by the presumption, namely the right of an accused to be treated as innocent until proved otherwise by the Crown. This right has both a societal and an individual aspect and is clearly fundamental to our justice system. I see no particular virtue in isolating its procedural from its substantive elements or vice versa for purposes of section 7. A similar analysis may be made of the rule against double jeopardy protected in section 11(h).

How then are we to decide whether attaching a mandatory term of imprisonment to an absolute liability offence created by statute offends a principle of fundamental justice? I believe we must turn to the theory of punishment for the answer.

### 3. *Punishment and fundamental justice*

It is now generally 'accepted among penologists that there are five main objectives of a penal system: see Nigel Walker, *Sentencing in a Rational Society*, 1969. They are:

1) to protect offenders and suspected offenders against unofficial retaliation;
2) to reduce the incidence of crime;
3) to ensure that offenders atone for their offences;
4) to keep punishment to the minimum necessary to achieve the objectives of the system; and
5) to express society's abhorrence of crime.

Apart from death, imprisonment is the most severe sentence imposed by the law and is generally viewed as a last resort *i.e.* as appropriate only when it can be shown that no other sanction can achieve the objectives of the system.

The Law Reform Commission of Canada in its Working Paper 11 — Imprisonment and Release (*Studies on Imprisonment*, 1976) states at p. 10:

> Justice requires that the sanction of imprisonment not be disproportionate to the offence, and humanity dictates that it must not be heavier than necessary to achieve its objective.

Because of the absolute liability nature of the offence created by section 94(2) of the *Motor Vehicle Act* a person can be convicted under the section even although he was unaware at the time he was driving that his licence was suspended and was unable to find this out despite the exercise of due diligence. While the legislature may as a matter of government policy make this an offence, and we cannot question its wisdom in this regard, the question is whether it can make it mandatory for the courts to deprive a person convicted of it of his liberty without violating section 7. This, in turn, depends on whether attaching a mandatory term of imprisonment to an absolute liability offence such as this violates the principles of fundamental justice. I believe that it does. I think the conscience of the court would be shocked and the administration of justice brought into disrepute by such an unreasonable and extravagant penalty. It is totally disproportionate to the offence and quite incompatible with the objective of a penal system referred to in paragraph (4) above.

It is basic to any theory of punishment that the sentence imposed bear some relationship to the offence; it must be a "fit" sentence proportionate to the seriousness of the offence. Only if this is so can the public be satisfied that the offender "deserved" the punishment he received and feel a confidence in the fairness and rationality of the system. This is not to say that there is an inherently appropriate relationship between a particular offence and its punishment but rather that there is a scale of offences and punishments into which the particular offence and punishment must fit. Obviously this cannot be done with mathematical precision and many different factors will go into the assessment of the seriousness of a particular offence for purposes of determining the appropriate punishment but it does provide a workable conventional framework for sentencing. Indeed, judges in the exercise of their sentencing discretion have been employing such a scale for over a hundred years.

I believe that a mandatory term of imprisonment for an offence committed unknowingly and unwittingly and after the exercise of due diligence is grossly excessive and inhumane. It is not required to reduce the incidence of the offence. It is beyond anything required to satisfy the need for "atonement". And society, in my opinion, would not be abhorred by an unintentional and unknowing violation of the section. I believe, therefore, that such a sanction offends the principles of fundamental justice embodied in our penal system. Section 94(2) is accordingly inconsistent with section 7 of the *Charter* and must, to the extent of the inconsistency, be declared of no force and effect under section 52. I express no view as to whether a mandatory term of imprisonment for such an offence represents an arbitrary imprisonment within the meaning of section 9 of the *Charter* or "cruel and unusual treatment or punishment" within the meaning of section 12 because it is not necessary to decide those issues in order to answer the constitutional question posed.

I would dismiss the appeal and answer the constitutional question in the negative.

## 2. Procedural Content

### SINGH v. MINISTER OF EMPLOYMENT AND IMMIGRATION

In the Supreme Court of Canada. 58 N.R. 1.

Dickson, C.J.C., Ritchie, Beetz, Estey, McIntyre, Lamer and Wilson, JJ. April 4, 1985.

[The opinion of Beetz J., Estey and McIntyre JJ. concurring, concurred with Wilson J. in the result. However his decision was based upon section 2(e) of the statutory federal *Bill of Rights* and he declined to express an opinion on the applicability of section 7 of the *Charter of Rights*. The opinion of Beetz J. is accordingly omitted.]

WILSON J.: The issue raised by these appeals is whether the procedures set out in the *Immigration Act, 1976*, S.C. 1976-77, c. 52 as amended, for the adjudication of the claims of persons claiming refugee status in Canada deny such claimants rights they are entitled to assert under s. 7 of the *Canadian Charter of Rights and Freedoms*.

On February 16, 1984, the court granted leave to appeal in these seven cases and they were consolidated for hearing on April 30, 1984. Six of the appellants were unrepresented by counsel when they made their applications for leave to appeal and counsel was appointed to represent them at the hearing of the appeal. The seventh appellant, Mr. Satnam Singh, was represented by his own counsel both at the hearing of the leave application and at the hearing of the appeal. The court also had the benefit of a joint submission by counsel for two intervenors, the Federation of Canadian Sikh Societies and the Canadian Council of Churches. During the hearing on April 30 and May 1, 1984, counsels' submissions were confined to the application of the *Charter of Rights and Freedoms*. On December 7, 1984, counsel were invited to make written submissions to the court on the application of the *Canadian Bill of Rights*.

At the hearing of the appeals in April and May 1984 counsel took somewhat different approaches to the presentation of the issues, but I think it is fair to say that in substance the appeals were argued on the basis that the court should approach the appeals in three stages. First, the court should decide whether refugee claimants physically present in Canada are entitled to the protection of s. 7 of the *Charter*. If the answer to this question is yes, then the court should consider whether the relevant provisions of the *Immigration Act*, in particular s. 71(1), deny the appellants' rights under s. 7 of the *Charter*. Finally, if the court answers the second question in the affirmative, it should determine whether any limitation on the appellants' rights imposed by the *Act* is justified within the meaning of s. 1 of the *Charter*.

In the written submissions presented in December 1984 counsel considered whether the procedures for the adjudication of refugee status claims violated the *Canadian Bill of Rights*, in particular s. 2(e). There can be no doubt that this statute continues in full force and effect and that the rights conferred in it are expressly preserved by s. 26 of the *Charter*. However, since I believe that the present situation falls within the constitutional protection afforded by the *Charter of Rights and Freedoms*, I prefer to base my decision upon the *Charter*.

I think the suggestion of counsel that the appeals should be approached in three stages is a good one and I am adopting it in the analysis which follows. First, however, it is important to present the facts and the legislative context within which the appeals have arisen.

## 1. *The facts*

The facts and procedural history of the seven appeals have a great deal in common and it was because of these similarities that the court felt it appropriate to consolidate the hearing. Each appellant, in accordance with the procedures set out in the *Immigration Act*, asserted a claim to Convention refugee status as defined in s. 2(1) of the *Act*. The Minister of Employment and Immigration acting on the advice of the Refugee Status Advisory Committee, made determinations pursuant to s. 45 of the *Act* that none of the appellants were Convention refugees. Each of the appellants then made an application for redetermination of his or her refugee claim by the Immigration Appeal Board pursuant to s. 70 of the *Act*. In accordance with s. 71(1) of the *Act* the Immigration Appeal Board in each case refused to allow the application to proceed on the basis that it did not believe that there were "reasonable grounds to believe that a claim could, upon the hearing of the application, be established . . .". Each applicant then sought judicial review of the Board's decision pursuant to the provisions of s. 28 of the *Federal Court Act*, R.S.C. 1970 (2nd Supp.), c. 10. These applications were denied by the Federal Court of Appeal.

:  . . . .

## 2. The Scheme of the Immigration Act

The appellants allege that the procedural mechanisms set out in the *Immigration Act*, as opposed to the application of those procedures to their particular cases, have deprived them of their rights under the *Charter*. It is important, therefore, to understand these provisions in the context of the *Act* as a whole. If, as a matter of statutory interpretation, the procedural fairness sought by the appellants is not excluded by the scheme of the *Act*, there is, of course, no basis for resort to the *Charter*. The issue may be resolved on other grounds. In *City of Toronto v. Outdoor Neon Displays Ltd.*, [1960] S.C.R. 307 at 314, this court refused counsel's invitation to express an opinion as to the constitutional validity of a statute in a situation in which it was not necessary to the court's decision to do so. I note as well that the United States Supreme Court has on many occasions articulated a policy of not deciding constitutional issues in a context where it was not strictly necessary to do so: see *Rescue Army v. Municipal Court*, 331 U.S. 549 at 568-575 (1947) and cases cited therein. Accordingly, I believe that the court should scrutinize closely:

(a) the rights which Convention refugees are accorded under the *Act*; and
(b) the procedures the *Act* sets out for adjudicating claims for refugee status

before turning to the application of the *Charter* in this context.

### (a) The Rights of Convention Refugees under the Immigration Act

The appellants make no attempt to assert a constitutional right to enter and remain in Canada analogous to the right accorded to Canadian citizens by s. 6(1) of the *Charter*. Equally, at common law an alien has no right to enter or remain in Canada except by leave of the Crown: *Prata v. Minister of Manpower and Immigration*, [1976] 1 S.C.R. 376. As Martland J., expressed the law in *Prata* at p. 380 "The right of aliens to enter and remain in Canada is governed by the *Immigration Act*" and s. 5(1) states that "No person, other than a person described in s. 4, has a right to come into or remain in Canada".

However, the *Immigration Act* does provide Convention refugees with certain limited rights to enter and remain in Canada. The *Act* envisages the assertion of a refugee claim under s. 45 in the context of an inquiry, which presupposes that the refugee claimant is physically present in Canada and within the jurisdiction of the Canadian authorities. The *Act* and Regulations do envisage the resettlement in Canada of refugees who are outside the country but the following observations are not made with reference to these individuals. When a person who is in Canada has been determined to be a Convention refugee, s. 47(1) requires the adjudicator to reconvene the inquiry held pursuant to s. 23 or s. 27 in order to determine whether the individual is a person described in s. 4(2) of the *Act*. Section 4(2) provides that a Convention refugee "while lawfully in Canada [has] a right to remain in Canada . . ." except where it is established that he or she falls into the category of criminal or subversive persons set out in s. 4(2)(b). If it is determined that the person is a Convention refugee described in s. 4(2), s. 47(3) requires the adjudicator to allow the person to remain in Canada notwithstanding any other provisions of the *Act* or Regulations.

The scope of the refugee's right to remain in Canada is made problematic by the existence in s. 4(2) of the phrase "while lawfully in Canada". Since it is a prerequisite to the holding of an examination under s. 45 that a refugee claimant be a person against whom a removal order or departure notice may be made (see *Singh v. Minister of Employment and Immigration*, [1982] 2 F.C. 689 (T.D.)), it is apparent that nobody who is determined to be a Convention refugee will, in one sense, be lawfully in Canada. In practice this circularity is avoided by the issuance of a Minister's permit pursuant to s. 37 at the time a person is determined to be a Convention refugee, thus regularizing the individual's status for purposes of s. 4(2). The case of *Boun-Leua v. Minister of Employment and Immigration*, [1981] 1 F.C. 259 (C.A.), is illustrative of the difficulties which can arise where a Minister's permit is not issued.

. . . .

In the *Boun-Leua* case, as Urie, J., pointed out, the applicant was able to return to France where his life or liberty would not be threatened and it would not be inconsistent with Canada's obligations to refugees to require him to return there. On the other hand, s. 2(2) and s. 3(g) of the *Immigration Act* envisage that the *Act* will be administered in a way that fulfils Canada's international legal obligations. These provisions read as follows:

> 2.(2) The term 'Convention' in the expression 'Convention refugee' refers to the United Nations Convention Relating to the Status of Refugees signed at Geneva on the 28th day of July, 1951 and includes the Protocol thereto signed at New York on the 31st day of January, 1967.
> 3. It is hereby declared that Canadian immigration policy and the rules and regulations made under this *Act* shall be designed and administered in such a manner as to promote the domestic and international interests of Canada recognizing the need
> (g) to fulfil Canada's international legal obligations with respect to refugees and to uphold its humanitarian tradition with respect to the displaced and the persecuted;

The Preamble to the Convention and Protocol provides:

> *Considering* that the *Charter* of the United Nations and the Universal Declaration of Human Rights approved on 10 December 1948 by the General Assembly have affirmed the principle that human beings shall enjoy fundamental rights and freedoms without discrimination.

> *Considering* that the United Nations has, on various occasions, manifested its profound concern for refugees and endeavoured to assure refugees the widest possible exercise of these fundamental rights and freedoms, . . .

The term "refugee" is defined in the Convention as follows:

> A. For the purposes of the present Convention, the term 'refugee' shall apply to any person who:

> . . . owing to well-founded fear of being persecuted for reasons of race, religion, nationality, membership of a particular social group or political opinion, is outside the country of his nationality and is unable or, owing to such fear, is unwilling to avail himself of the protection of that country; or who, not having a nationality and being outside the country of his former habitual residence as a result of such events, is unable or, owing to such fear, is unwilling to return to it. . . .

> (*United Nations Convention relating to the Status of Refugees*. HCR/INF/29/Rev. 2, Chap. 1, Article 1, paragraph A(2)).

I believe therefore that a Convention refugee who does not have a safe haven elsewhere is entitled to rely on this country's willingness to live up to the obligations it has undertaken as a signatory to the United Nations Convention Relating to the Status of Refugees: (see *Ernewein v. Minister of Employment and Immigration*, [1980] 1 S.C.R. 639 at 657-662 (per Pigeon, J., dissenting); *Hurt v. Min. of Manpower and Immigration*, [1978] 2 F.C. 340 (C.A.)).

(b) *The Procedures for the Determination of Convention Refugee Status*

The term "Convention refugee" is defined in s. 2(1) of the *Act* as follows:

'Convention refugee' means any person who, by reason of a well-founded fear of persecution for reasons of race, religion, nationality, membership in a particular social group or political opinion,
 (a) is outside the country of his nationality and is unable or, by reason of such fear, is unwilling to avail himself of the protection of that country, or
 (b) not having a country of nationality, is outside the country of his former habitual residence and is unable or, by reason of such fear, is unwilling to return to that country;

As noted above, the procedures for determination of whether an individual is a Convention refugee and for redetermination of claims by the Immigration Appeal Board are set out in ss. 45 to 48 and 70 to 71 respectively. Focussing first on the initial determination, s. 45 provides as follows:

45.(1) Where, at any time during an inquiry, the person who is the subject of the inquiry claims that he is a Convention refugee, the inquiry shall be continued and, if it is determined that, but for the person's claim that he is a Convention refugee, a removal order or a departure notice would be made or issued with respect to that person, the inquiry shall be adjourned and that person shall be examined under oath by a senior immigration officer respecting his claim.

(2) Where a person who claims that he is a Convention refugee is examined under oath pursuant to subsection (1), his claim, together with a transcript of the examination with respect thereto, shall be referred to the Minister for determination.

(3) A copy of the transcript of an examination under oath referred to in subsection (1) shall be forwarded to the person who claims that he is a Convention refugee.

(4) Where a person's claim is referred to the Minister pursuant to subsection (2), the Minister shall refer the claim and the transcript of the examination under oath with respect thereto to the Refugee Status Advisory Committee established pursuant to s. 48 for consideration and, after having obtained the advice of that Committee, shall determine whether or not the person is a Convention refugee.

(5) When the Minister makes a determination with respect to a person's claim that he is a Convention refugee, the Minister shall thereupon in writing inform the senior immigration officer who conducted the examination under oath respecting the claim and the person who claimed to be a Convention refugee of his determination.

(6) Every person with respect to whom an examination under oath is to be held pursuant to subsection (1) shall be informed that he has the right to obtain the services of a barrister or solicitor or other counsel and to be represented by any such counsel at his examination and shall be given a reasonable opportunity, if he so desires and at his own expense, to obtain such counsel.

It is difficult to characterize this procedure as a "hearing" in the traditional sense: see *Brempong* (supra) at 217-218. As Urie, J., noted in *Brempong* at 217, n. 7, the procedure is technically "non-adversarial", since only the claimant is entitled to be represented by counsel. Urie, J., described the procedure as "purely administrative in nature" and this characterization was adopted by counsel for the respondent Minister in the course of argument on these appeals.

. . . .

The refugee claimant's status, however, need not be conclusively determined by the Minister's decision on the advice of the Refugee Status Advisory Committee made pursuant to s. 45. Under s. 70(1) of the Act a person whose refugee claim has been refused by the Minister may, within a period prescribed in Regulation 40(1) as fifteen days from the time he is so informed, apply for a redetermination of his claim by the Immigration Appeal Board. Section 70(2) requires the refugee claimant to submit with such an application a copy of the transcript of the examination under oath which was conducted pursuant to s. 45(1) and a declaration under oath setting out the basis of the application, the facts upon which the appellant relies and the information and evidence the applicant intends to offer at a redetermination hearing. The applicant is also permitted pursuant to s. 70(2)(d) to set out in his declaration such other representations as he deems relevant to his application.

The Immigration Appeal Board's duties in considering an application for redetermination of a refugee status claim are set out in s. 71 which reads as follows:

> 71.(1) Where the Board receives an application referred to in subsection 70(2), it shall forthwish consider the application and if, on the basis of such consideration, it is of the opinion that there are reasonable grounds to believe that a claim could, upon the hearing of the application, be established, it shall allow the application to proceed, and in any other case it shall refuse to allow the application to proceed and shall thereupon determine that the person is not a Convention refugee.
>
> (2) Where pursuant to subsection (1), the Board allows an application to proceed, it shall notify the Minister of the time and place where the application is to be heard and afford the Minister a reasonable opportunity to be heard.
>
> (3) Where the Board has made its determination as to whether or not a person is a Convention refugee, it shall, in writing, inform the Minister and the applicant of its decision.
>
> (4) The Board may, and at the request of the applicant or the Minister shall, give reasons for its determination.

If the Board were to determine pursuant to s. 71(1) that the application should be allowed to proceed, the parties are all agreed that the hearing which would take place pursuant to s. 71(2) would be quasi-judicial, one to which full natural justice would apply. The Board is not, however, empowered by the terms of the statute to allow a redetermination hearing to proceed in every case. It may only do so if "it is of the opinion that there are reasonable grounds to believe that a claim could, upon the hearing of the application, be established . . .". In *Kwiathkowsky v. Minister of Employment and Immigration*, [1982] 2 S.C.R. 856, this court interpreted those words as requiring the Board to allow the claim to proceed only if it is of the view that "it is more likely than not" that the applicant will be able to establish his claim at the hearing, following the test laid down by Urie, J., in *Lugano v. Minister of Manpower and Immigration*, [1976] 2 F.C. 438.

. . . .

. . . it seems to me that s. 71(1) is precisely the type of express provision which prevents the courts from reading the principles of natural justice into a statutory scheme for the adjudication of the rights of individuals.

The substance of the appellants' case, as I understand it, is that they did not have a fair opportunity to present their refugee status claims or to know the case they had to meet. I do not think there is any basis for suggesting that the procedures set out in the *Immigration Act* were not followed correctly in the adjudication of these individuals' claims. Nor do I believe that there is any basis for interpreting the relevant provisions of the *Immigration Act* in a way that provides a significantly greater degree of procedural fairness or natural justice than I have set out in the preceding discussion. The *Act* by its terms seems to preclude this. Accordingly, if the appellants are to succeed, I believe that it must be on the basis that the *Charter* requires the court to override Parliament's decision to exclude the kind of procedural fairness sought by the appellants.

### 3. *The Application of the Charter*

1) *Are the Appellants Entitled to the Protection of s. 7 of the Charter?*

Section 32(1)(a) of the *Charter* provides:

> 32.(1) This *Charter* applies
> (a) to the Parliament and government of Canada in respect of all matters within the authority of Parliament....

Since immigration is clearly a matter falling within the authority of Parliament under s. 91(25) of the *Constitution Act, 1867*, the *Immigration Act* itself and the administration of it by the Canadian government are subject to the provisions of the *Charter*.

Section 7 of the *Charter* states that "Everyone has the right to life, liberty and security of the person and the right not to be deprived thereof except in accordance with the principles of fundamental justice". Counsel for the appellants contrasts the use of the word "Everyone" in s. 7 with language used in other sections, for example, "Every citizen of Canada" in s. 3, "Every citizen of Canada and every person who has the status of a permanent resident of Canada" in s. 6(2) and "Citizens of Canada" in s. 23. He concludes that "Everyone" in s. 7 is intended to encompass a broader class of persons than citizens and permanent residents. Counsel for the Minister concedes that "everyone" is sufficiently broad to include the appellants in its compass and I am prepared to accept that the term includes every human being who is physically present in Canada and by virtue of such presence amenable to Canadian law.

That premise being accepted, the question then becomes whether the rights the appellants seek to assert fall within the scope of s. 7. Counsel for the Minister does not concede this. He submits that the exclusion or removal of the appellants from Canada would not infringe "the right to life, liberty and security of the person". He advances three main lines of argument in support of this submission.

The first may be described as a reliance on the "single right" theory articulated by Marceau, J., in *R. v. Operation Dismantle Inc.*, [1983] 1 F.C. 745 (C.A.). In counsel's submission, the words "the right to life, liberty and security of the person" form a single right with closely inter-related parts and this right relates to matters of death, arrest, detention, physical liberty and physical punishment of the person. Moreover, counsel says, s. 7 only protects persons against the deprivation of that type of right if the deprivation results from a violation of the principles of fundamental justice. This argument by itself does not advance the Minister's case very far, since the appellants submit that, even on this restrictive interpretation of s. 7, their rights in relation to matters of death, arrest, detention, physical liberty and physical punishment are indeed affected. Counsel for the appellants took two different approaches in their attempt to demonstrate this.

Mr. Coveney, for the appellant Satnam Singh, and Ms. Jackman for the intervenors who supported the position of the appellants, took his position that it was inherent in the definition of a Convention refugee that rejection of his right to stay in Canada would affect his right to life, liberty and security of the person in the sense articulated by counsel for the Minister. In other words, because a Convention refugee is, by definition, a person who has a "well-founded fear of persecution", the refusal to give him refuge exposes him to jeopardy of death, significant diminution of his physical liberty or physical punishment in his country of origin.

Mr. Scott, for the other six appellants, took a different approach. He noted that the *Act* empowers immigration officials physically to detain the appellants both for purposes of examination pursuant to s. 23 or s. 27 and for purposes of removal: see ss. 20(1); 23(3); 23(5); and 104 to 108. He argued that the detention of the appellants by Canadian immigration officials would itself deprive them of personal liberty in this country and it would be a violation of s. 7 to deprive them of this liberty except in accordance with the principles of fundamental justice.

Counsel for the Minister, Mr. Bowie, sought to counter both these arguments. With respect to the first argument, he took the position that s. 7 of the *Charter* affords individuals protection from the action of the legislatures and governments in Canada and its provinces and territories, but that it affords no protection against the acts of other persons or foreign governments. He relied on the decision of Pratte, J., in *Singh v. Minister of Employment and Immigration*, [1983] 2 F.C. 347 (C.A.) who said at 349 F.C.:

> The decision of the [Immigration Appeal] Board did not have the effect of depriving the applicant of his right to life, liberty and security of the person. If the applicant is deprived of any of those rights after his return to his own country, that will be as a result of the acts of the authorities or of other persons of that country, not as a direct result of the decision of the Board. In our view, the deprivation of rights referred to in s. 7 refers to a deprivation of rights by Canadian authorities applying Canadian laws.

With respect to the second line of argument, Mr. Bowie noted that the procedures for detention and removal of individuals under the *Act* were no different for those claiming refugee status than they were for any other individuals and he argued that those provisions were consistent with the principles of fundamental justice.

It seems to me that in attempting to decide whether the appellants have been deprived of the right to life, liberty and security of the person within the meaning of s. 7 of the *Charter*, we must begin by determining what rights the appellants have under the *Immigration Act*. As noted earlier, s. 5(1) of the *Act* excludes from persons other than those described in s. 4 the right to come into or remain in Canada. The appellants therefore do not have such a right. However, the *Act* does accord a Convention refugee certain rights which it does not provide to others, namely the right to a determination from the Minister based on proper principles as to whether a permit should issue entitling him to enter and remain in Canada (ss. 4(2) and 37); the right not to be returned to a country where his life or freedom would be threatened (s. 55); and the right to appeal a removal order or a deportation order made against him (s. 72(2)(a), 72(2)(b) and 72(3)).

We must therefore ask ourselves whether the deprivation of these rights constitutes a deprivation of the right to life, liberty and security of the person within the meaning of s. 7 of the *Charter*. Even if we accept the "single right" theory advanced by counsel for the Minister in interpreting s. 7, I think we must recognize that the "right" which is articulated in s.7 has three elements: life, liberty and security of the person. As I understand the "single right" theory, it is not suggested that there must be a deprivation of all three of these elements before an individual is deprived of his "right" under s. 7. In other words, I believe that it is consistent with the "single right" theory advanced by counsel to suggest that a deprivation of the appellants' "security of the person", for example, would constitute a deprivation of their "right" under s. 7, whether or not it can also be said that they have been deprived of their lives or liberty. Rather, as I understand it, the "single right" theory is advanced in support of a narrow construction of the words "life", "liberty" and "security of the person" as different aspects of a single concept rather than as separate concepts each of which must be construed independently.

Certainly, it is true that the concepts of the right to life, the right to liberty, and the right to security of the person are capable of a broad range of meaning. The Fourteenth Amendment to the *United States Constitution* provides in part ". . . nor shall any State deprive any person of life, liberty, or property, without the due process of law . . .". In *Board of Regents of State Colleges v. Roth*, 408 U.S. 564 at 572 (1972), Stewart, J., articulated the notion of liberty as embodied in the Fourteenth Amendment in the following way:

> While this court has not attempted to define with exactness the liberty . . . guaranteed (by the Fourteenth Amendment), the term has received much consideration and some of the included things have been definitely stated. Without doubt, it denotes not merely freedom from bodily restraint but also the right of the individual to contract, to engage in any of the common occupations of life, to acquire useful knowledge, to marry, establish a home and bring up children, to worship God according to the dictates of his own conscience, and generally to enjoy those privileges long recognized . . . as essential to the orderly pursuit of happiness by free men. *Meyer v. Nebraska*, 262 U.S. 390, 399. In a Constitution for a free people, there can be no doubt that the meaning of 'liberty' must be broad indeed. See, e.g., *Bolling v. Sharpe*, 347 U.S. 497, 499-500; *Stanley v. Illinois*, 405 U.S. 645.

The "single right" theory advanced by counsel for the Minister would suggest that this conception of "liberty" is too broad to be empowered in our interpretation of s. 7 of the *Charter*. Even if this submission is sound, however, it seems to me that it is incumbent upon the court to give meaning to each of the elements, life, liberty and security of the person, which make up the "right" contained in s. 7.

To return to the facts before the court, it will be recalled that a Convention refugee is by definition a person who has a well-founded fear of persecution in the country from which he is fleeing. In my view, to deprive him of the avenues open to him under the *Act* to escape from that fear of persecution must, at the least, *impair* his right to life, liberty and security of the person in the narrow sense advanced by counsel for the Minister. The question, however, is whether such an impairment constitutes a "deprivation" under s. 7.

It must be acknowledged, for example, that even if a Convention refugee's fear of persecution is a well-founded one, it does not automatically follow that he will be deprived of his life or his liberty if he is returned to his homeland. Can it be said that Canadian officials have deprived a Convention refugee of his right to life, liberty and security of the person if he is wrongfully returned to a country where death, imprisonment or another form of persecution *may* await him? There may be some merit in counsel's submission that closing off the avenues of escape provided by the *Act* does not per se deprive a Convention refugee of the right to life or to liberty. It may result in his being deprived of life or liberty by others, but it is not certain that this will happen.

I cannot, however, accept the submission of counsel for the Minister that the denial of the rights possessed by a Convention refugee under the *Act* does not constitute a deprivation of his security of the person. Like "liberty", the phrase "security of the person" is capable of a broad range of meaning. The phrase "security of the person" is found in s. 1(a) of the *Canadian Bill of Rights* and its interpretation in that context might have assisted us in its proper interpretation under the *Charter*. Unfortunately no clear meaning of the words emerges from the case law, although the phrase has received some mention in cases such as *Morgentaler v. R.*, [1976] 1 S.C.R. 616 at 628-634 (per Laskin, C.J., dissenting); *Curr v. R.*, [1972] S.C.R. 889; and *R. v. Berrie* (1975), 24 C.C.C. (2d) 66 at 70 (B.C.S.C.). The Law Reform Commission, in its Working Paper No. 26 *Medical Treatment and Criminal Law* (1980) suggested at p. 6 that:

> The right to security of the person means not only protection of one's physical integrity, but the provision of necessaries for its support.

The Commission went on to describe the provision of necessaries in terms of Art. 25, para. 1 of the *Universal Declaration of Human Rights* (1948) which reads:

> Every one has the right to a standard of living adequate for the health and well-being of himself and of his family, including food, clothing, housing and medical care and necessary social services, and the right to security in the event of unemployment, sickness, disability, widowhood, old age, or other lack of livelihood in circumstances beyond his control.

Commentators have advocated the adoption of a similarly broad conception of "security of the person" in the interpretation of s. 7 of the *Charter*: see Garant "Fundamental Freedoms and Natural Justice" in Tarnopolsky and Beaudoin (eds.) *The Canadian Charter of Rights and Freedoms* (1982) at pp. 264-265, 271-274; Manning, *Rights, Freedoms and the Courts: A Practical Analysis of the Constitution Act, 1982* (1983), at pp. 249-254.

For purposes of the present appeal it is not necessary, in my opinion, to consider whether such an expansive approach to "security of the person" in s. 7 of the *Charter* should be taken. It seems to me that even if one adopts the narrow approach advocated by counsel for the Minister, "security of the person" must encompass freedom from the threat of physical punishment or suffering as well as freedom from such punishment itself. I note particularly that a Convention refugee has the right under s. 55 of the *Act* not to ". . . be removed from Canada to a country where his life or freedom would be threatened . . .". In my view, the denial of such a right must amount to a deprivation of security of the person within the meaning of s. 7.

This approach receives support from at least one lower court decision applying s. 7 of the *Charter*. In *Collin v. Lussier*, [1983] 1 F.C. 218 (T.D.) the applicant before the Trial Division of the Federal Court applied for certiorari to quash a decision made by the respondent to have him transferred from a medium security to a maximum security prison. He argued that the transfer endangered his "security of the person" and since it was not made in accordance with the principles of fundamental justice, his rights under s. 7 had been infringed. At p. 239, Décary, J., stated:

... such detention, by increasing applicant's anxiety as to his state of health, is likely to make his illness worse and, by depriving him of access to adequate medical care, it is in fact an impairment of the security of his person.

It is noteworthy that the applicant had not demonstrated that his health had been impaired; he merely showed that it was likely that his health would be impaired. This was held to be sufficient to constitute a deprivation of the right to security of the person under the circumstances.

It must be recognized that the appellants are not at this stage entitled to assert rights as Convention refugees; their claim is that they are entitled to fundamental justice in the determination of whether they are Convention refugees or not. From some of the cases dealing with the application of the *Canadian Bill of Rights* to the determination of the rights of individuals under immigration legislation it might be suggested that whatever procedures the legislation itself sets out for the determination of rights constitute "due process" for purposes of s. 1(a) and "fundamental justice" for purposes of s. 2(e) of the *Canadian Bill of Rights*: see *Prata v. Minister of Manpower and Immigration*, [1976] 1 S.C.R. 376 at 383; *Rebrin v. Bird and Minister of Citizenship and Immigration*, [1961] S.C.R. 376 at 381-83; *Louie Yuet Sun v. R.*, [1961] S.C.R. 70; Cf. *U.S. ex rel. Knauff v. Shaughnessy*, 338 U.S. 537 at 544 (1950). As Professor Tarnopolsky (as he then was) observed in his text *The Canadian Bill of Rights* (2nd Ed. 1975) at p. 273:

> The courts have consistently held that immigration is a privilege, and not a right.

The creation of a dichotomy between privileges and rights played a significant role in narrowing the scope of the application of the *Canadian Bill of Rights*, as is apparent from the judgment of Martland, J., in *Mitchell v. R.*, [1976] 2 S.C.R. 570. At 588, Martland, J., said:

> The appellant also relies upon s. 2(e) of the *Bill of Rights*, which provides that no law of Canada shall be construed or applied so as to deprive a person of the right to a fair hearing in accordance with the principles of fundamental justice for the determination of his rights and obligations. In [*Re McCaud*, [1965] 1 C.C.C. 168 (Ont. C.A.)] Spence, J., whose view was adopted unanimously on appeal, held that the provisions of s. 2(e) do not apply to the question of the revocation of parole under the provisions of the *Parole Act*.
>
> The appellant had no right to parole. He was granted parole as a matter of discretion by the Parole Board. He had no right to remain on parole. His parole was subject to revocation at the absolute discretion of the Board.

I do not think this kind of analysis is acceptable in relation to the *Charter*. It seems to me rather that the recent adoption of the *Charter* by Parliament and nine of the ten provinces as part of the Canadian constitutional framework has sent a clear message to the courts that the restrictive attitude which at times characterized their approach to the *Canadian Bill of Rights* ought to be re-examined. I am accordingly of the view that the approach taken by Laskin, C.J., dissenting in *Mitchell* is to be preferred to that of the majority as we examine the question whether the *Charter* has any application to the adjudication of rights granted to an individual by statute.

In *Mitchell* the issue was whether the *Canadian Bill of Rights* required s. 16(1) of the *Parole Act* to be interpreted so as to require the Parole Board to provide a parolee with a fair hearing before revoking his parole. Laskin, C.J., focussed on the consequences of the revocation of parole for the indivual and concluded that parole could not be characterized as a "mere privilege" even although the parolee had no absolute right to be released from prison. He said at p. 585:

> Between them, s. 2(c)(i) and s. 2(e) [of the *Canadian Bill of Rights*] call for at least minimum procedural safeguards in parole administration where revocation is involved, despite what may be said about the confidentiality and sensitiveness of the parole system.

It seems to me that the appellants in this case have an even stronger argument to make than the appellant in *Mitchell*. At most Mr. Mitchell was entitled to a hearing from the Parole Board concerning the revocation of his parole and a decision from the Board based on proper considerations as to whether to continue his parole or not. He had no statutory right to the parole itself; rather he had a right to proper consideration of whether he was entitled to remain on parole. By way of contrast, if the appellants had been found to be Convention refugees as defined in s. 2(1) of the *Immigration Act* they would have been entitled as a matter of law to the incidents of that status provided for in the *Act*. Given the potential consequences for the appellants of a denial of that status if they are in fact persons with a "well-founded fear of persecution", it seems to me unthinkable that the *Charter* would not apply to entitle them to fundamental justice in the adjudication of their status.

Given this conclusion, it is perhaps unnecessary to address Mr. Scott's line of argument in detail. I must, however, acknowledge some reluctance to adopt his analogy from American law that persons who are inside the country are entitled to the protection of the *Charter* while those who are merely seeking entry to the country are not. In the first place, it should be noted that the presence in this country of four of the appellants who were refused entry when they arrived in Canada is due only to the fact that the *Act* provides for a mechanism for their release from detention. As Ms. Jackman pointed out, a rule which provided *Charter* protection to refugees who succeeded in entering the country but not to those who were seeking admission at a port of entry would be to reward those who sought to evade the operation of our immigration laws over those who presented their cases openly at the first available opportunity.

An equally serious objection, it seems to me, is that the American rule does not differentiate between the special status statutorily accorded to Convention refugees who are present in this country and the status of other individuals who are seeking to enter or remain in Canada. As I understand the American law, the constitutional protection of the Fifth and Fourteenth Amendments has long been available to aliens whom the government is seeking to remove from the United States (The *Japanese Immigrant Case* (1903), 189 U.S. 86) but such protection is not available to those seeking entry which the government has decided to refuse (*U.S. ex. rel. Knauff v. Shaughnessy*) (supra). The rationale of this distinction as articulated in *Knauff* and more fully in *Shaughnessy v. U.S. ex. rel. Mezei*, 345 U.S. 206 at 210 (1953), is that "Courts have long recognized the power to expel or exclude aliens as a fundamental sovereign attribute exercised by the Government's political departments largely immune from judicial control". Seen in this sense, the deference which American courts have shown to the political branches of government in the field of immigration has been described as one aspect of the political questions doctrine: see Scharpf, *Judicial Review and the Political Question: A Functional Analysis* (1966), 75 Yale. L.J., 517 at 578-583.

Two observations about this approach will suffice for present purposes. The first is that recently the United States Supreme Court has been more reluctant to employ the political questions doctrine to provide the executive and legislative branches of government with an unreviewable authority over the regulation of aliens: see *Immigration and Naturalization Service v. Chadha*, 77 L. Ed. (2d) 317 at 338-340 (1983), (per Burger, C.J.). Second, and more importantly, it seems to me that in the Canadian context Parliament has in the *Immigration Act* made many of the "political" determinations which American courts have been justifiably reluctant to attempt to get involved in themselves. On these appeals this court is being asked by the appellants to accept that the substantive rights of Convention refugees have been determined by the *Immigration Act* itself and the court need concern itself only with the question whether the procedural scheme set up by the *Act* for the determination of that status is consistent with the requirements of fundamental justice articulated in s. 7 of the *Charter*. I see no reason why the court should limit itself in this inquiry or establish distinctions between classes of refugee claimants which are not mandated by the *Act* itself. It is unnecessary for the court to consider what it would do if it were asked to engage in a larger inquiry into the substantive rights conferred in the *Act*.

In summary, I am of the view that the rights which the appellants are seeking to assert are ones which entitle them to the protection of s. 7 of the *Charter*. It is necessary therefore to consider whether the procedures for the determination of refugee status as set out in the *Act* accord with fundamental justice.

## 2) *Is Fundamental Justice Denied by the Procedures for the Determination of Convention Refugee Status set out in the Act?*

All counsel were agreed that at a minimum the concept of "fundamental justice" as it appears in s. 7 of the *Charter* includes the notion of procedural fairness articulated by Fauteux, C.J., in *Duke v. R.*, [1972] S.C.R. 917. At 923 he said:

> Under s. 2(e) of the *Bill of Rights* no law of Canada shall be construed or applied so as to deprive him of 'a fair hearing in accordance with the principles of fundamental justice'. Without attempting to formulate any final definition of those words, I would take them to mean, generally, that the tribunal which adjudicates upon his rights must act fairly, in good faith, without bias and in a judicial temper, and must give to him the opportunity adequately to state his case.

Do the procedures set out in the *Act* for the adjudication of refugee status claims meet this test of procedural fairness? Do they provide an adequate opportunity for a refugee claimant to state his case and know the case he has to meet? This seems to be the question we have to answer and, in approaching it, I am prepared to accept Mr. Bowie's submission that procedural fairness may demand different things in different contexts: see *Martineau v. Matsqui Institution Disciplinary Bd. (No. 2)*, [1980] 1 S.C.R. 602 at 630. Thus it is possible that an oral hearing before the decision-maker is not required in every case in which s. 7 of the *Charter* is called into play. However, I must confess to some difficulty in reconciling Mr. Bowie's argument that an oral hearing is not required in the context of this case with the interpretation he seeks to put on s. 7. If "the right to life, liberty and security of the person" is properly construed as relating only to matters such as death, physical liberty and physical punishment, it would seem on the surface at least that these are matters of such fundamental importance that procedural fairness would invariably require an oral hearing. I am prepared, nevertheless, to accept for present purposes that written submissions may be an adequate substitute for an oral hearing in appropriate circumstances.

I should note, however, that even if hearings based on written submissions are consistent with the principles of fundamental justice for some purposes, they will not be satisfactory for all purposes. In particular, I am of the view that where a serious issue of credibility is involved, fundamental justice requires that credibility be determined on the basis of an oral hearing. Appellate courts are well aware of the inherent weakness of written transcripts where questions of credibility are at stake and thus are extremely loath to review the findings of tribunals which have had the benefit of hearing the testimony of witnesses in person: see *Stein v. The Ship "Kathy K"*, [1976] 2 S.C.R. 802 at 806-808 (per Ritchie, J.). I find it difficult to conceive of a situation in which compliance with fundamental justice could be achieved by a tribunal making significant findings of credibility solely on the basis of written submissions.

As I have suggested, the absence of an oral hearing need not be inconsistent with fundamental justice in every case. My greatest concern about the procedural scheme envisaged by ss. 45 to 58 and 70 and 71 of the *Immigration Act* is not, therefore, with the absence of an oral hearing in and of itself, but with the inadequacy of the opportunity the scheme provides for a refugee claimant to state his case and know the case he has to meet. Mr. Bowie argued that since the procedure under s. 45 was an administrative one, it was quite proper for the Minister and the Refugee Status Advisory Committee to take into account policy considerations and information about world affairs to which the refugee claimant had no opportunity to respond. However, in my view the proceedings before the Immigration Appeal Board were quasi-judicial and the Board was not entitled to rely on material outside the record which the refugee claimant himself submitted on his application for redetermination: see *Permaul v. Minister of Employment and Immigration* (1983), 53 N.R. 323 (Fed. C.A.); *Saraos v. Minister of Employment and Immigration*, [1982] 1 F.C. 304 at 308-309 (T.D.). Mr. Bowie submitted that there was no case against the refugee claimant at that stage; it was merely his responsibility to make a written submission which demonstrated on the balance of probabilities that he would be able to establish his claim at a hearing. If the applicant failed to bring forward the requisite facts, his claim would not be allowed to proceed, but there was nothing fundamentally unfair in this procedure.

It seems to me that the basic flaw in Mr. Bowie's characterization of the procedure under ss. 70 and 71 is his description of the procedure as non-adversarial. It is in fact highly adversarial, but the adversary, the Minister, is waiting in the wings. What the Board has before it is a determination by the Minister based in part on information and policies to which the applicant has no means of access that the applicant for redetermination is not a Convention refugee. The applicant is entitled to submit whatever relevant material he wishes to the Board, but he still faces the hurdle of having to establish to the Board that on the balance of probabilities the Minister was wrong. Moreover, he must do this without any knowledge of the Minister's case beyond the rudimentary reason which the Minister has decided to give him in rejecting his claim. It is this aspect of the procedures set out in the *Act* which I find impossible to reconcile with the requirements of "fundamental justice" as set out in s. 7 of the *Charter*.

It is perhaps worth nothing that if the Immigration Appeal Board allows a redetermination hearing to proceed pursuant to s. 71(1), the Minister is entitled pursuant to s. 71(2) to notice of the time and place of the hearing and a reasonable opportunity to be heard. It seems to me that, as a matter of fundamental justice, a refugee claimant would be entitled to discovery of the Minister's case prior to such a hearing. It must be acknowledged, of course, that some of the information upon which the Minister's case would be based might be subject to Crown privilege. But the courts are well able to give the applicant relief if the Minister attempts to make an overly broad assertion of privilege: see *Canada Evidence Act*, S.C. 1980-81-82-83, c. 111, Schedule III, s. 36.1.

Under the *Act* as it presently stands, however, a refugee claimant may never have the opportunity to make an effective challenge to the information or policies which underlie the Minister's decision to reject his claim. Because s. 71(1) requires the Immigration Appeal Board to reject an application for redetermination unless it is of the view that it is more likely than not that the applicant will be able to succeed, it is apparent that an application will usually be rejected before the refugee claimant has had an opportunity to discover the Minister's case against him in the context of a hearing. Indeed, given the fact that s. 71(1) resolves any doubt as to whether or not there should be a hearing against the refugee claimant, I find it difficult to see how a successful challenge to the accuracy of the undisclosed information upon which the Minister's decision is based could ever be launched.

I am accordingly of the view that the procedures for determination of refugee status claims as set out in the *Immigration Act* do not accord refugee claimants fundamental justice in the adjudication of those claims and are thus incompatible with s. 7 of the *Charter*. It is therefore necessary to go forward to the third stage of the inquiry and determine whether the shortcomings of these procedures in relation to the standards set out by s. 7 constitute reasonable limits which can be demonstrably justified in a free and democratic society within the meaning of s. 1 of the *Charter*.

### 3) *Can the Procedures be Saved under s. 1 of the Charter?*

Section 1 of the *Charter* reads:

> The *Canadian Charter of Rights and Freedoms* guarantees the rights and freedoms set out in it subject only to such reasonable limits prescribed by law as can be demonstrably justified in a free and democratic society.

It follows, accordingly, that if the limitations on the rights set out in the *Charter* meet the test articulated in s. 1, the *Charter* has not been violated and the court's remedial powers thereunder are not called into play.

The question of the standards which the court should use in applying s. 1 is, without a doubt, a question of enormous significance for the operation of the *Charter*. If too low a threshold is set, the courts run the risk of emasculating the *Charter*. If too high a threshold is set, the courts run the risk of unjustifiably restricting government action. It is not a task to be entered upon lightly.

Unfortunately, counsel devoted relatively little time in the course of argument to the principles the court should espouse in applying s. 1. This is certainly understandable given the complexity of the other issues which are in one sense preliminary to the application of s. 1. It is nevertheless to be regretted. A particular disappointment is the limited scope of the factual material brought forward by the respondent in support of the proposition that the *Immigration Act's* provisions constitute a "reasonable limit" on the appellants' rights. It must be acknowledged that counsel operated under considerable time pressure in the preparation of these appeals and I do not intend these remarks as a criticism of the presentation made to the court by counsel which was, indeed, extremely valuable. On the other hand, I feel constrained to echo the observations made by Estey, J., in *The Law Society of Upper Canada v. Skapinker*, [1984] 1 S.C.R. 357 at 384 where he said:

> As experience accumulates, the law profession and the courts will develop standards and practices which will enable the parties to demonstrate their position under s. 1 and the courts to decide issues arising under that provision. May it only be said here, in the cause of being helpful to those who come forward in similar proceedings, that the record on the s. 1 issue was indeed minimal, and without more, would have made it difficult for a court to determine the issue as to whether a reasonable limit on a prescribed right had been demonstrably justified.

Mr. Bowie's submissions on behalf of the Minister with respect to s. 1 were that Canadian procedures with respect to the adjudication of refugee claims had received the approbation of the office of the United Nations High Commissioner for Refugees and that it was not uncommon in Commonwealth and Western European countries for refugee claims to be adjudicated administratively without a right to appeal. He further argued that the Immigration Appeal Board was already subjected to a considerable strain in terms of the volume of cases which it was required to hear and that a requirement of an oral hearing in every case where an application for redetermination of a refugee claim has been made would constitute an unreasonable burden on the Board's resources.

One or two comments are in order respecting this approach to s. 1. It seems to me that it is important to bear in mind that the rights and freedoms set out in the *Charter* are fundamental to the political structure of Canada and are guaranteed by the *Charter* as part of the supreme law of our nation. I think that in determining whether a particular limitation is a reasonable limit prescribed by law which can be "demonstrably justified in a free and democratic society" it is important to remember that the courts are conducting this inquiry in light of a commitment to uphold the rights and freedoms set out in the other sections of the *Charter*. The issue in the present case is not simply whether the procedures set out in the *Immigration Act* for the adjudication of refugee claims are reasonable; it is whether it is reasonable to deprive the appellants of the right to life, liberty and security of the person by adopting a system for the adjudication of refugee status claims which does not accord with the principles of fundamental justice.

Seen in this light I have considerable doubt that the type of utilitarian consideration brought forward by Mr. Bowie can constitute a justification for a limitation on the rights set out in the *Charter*. Certainly the guarantees of the *Charter* would be illusory if they could be ignored because it was administratively convenient to do so. No doubt considerable time and money can be saved by adopting administrative procedures which ignore the principles of fundamental justice, but such an argument, in my view, misses the point of the exercise under s. 1. The principles of natural justice and procedural fairness which have long been espoused by our courts, and the constitutional entrenchment of the principles of fundamental justice in s. 7, implicitly recognize that a balance of administrative convenience does not override the need to adhere to these principles. Whatever standard of review eventually emerges under s. 1, it seems to me that the basis of the justification for the limitation of rights under s. 7 must be more compelling than any advanced in these appeals.

Moreover, I am not convinced in light of the submissions made by the appellants that the limitations on the rights of refugee claimants which are imposed by the adjudication procedures of the *Immigration Act* are reasonable even on the respondent's own terms. It is obvious that there is a considerable degree of dissatisfaction with the present system even on the part of those who administer it. In an address given in Toronto on October 25, 1980, Janet Scott, Q.C., the Chairman of the Immigration Appeal Board, made the following remarks:

> There is no blinking at the fact that the sections dealing with the Board's jurisdiction in refugee re-determination are highly unsatisfactory. Leaving aside any consideration of natural justice, the system is extremely cumbersome and when we enter into the sphere of natural justice, open to criticism as unjust.

In September 1980 the Minister of Employment and Immigration established a Task Force on Immigration Practices and Procedures and in November 1981 the Task Force issued a report entitled The Refugee Status Determination Process. The Task Force recommended wholesale changes in the procedures employed in the determination of refugee claims, including a recommendation that "A refugee claimant should be entitled to a hearing in every case where the [Refugee Status Advisory Committee] is not prepared to make a positive recommendation on the basis of the transcript" (Report p. xvi). In its conclusion, the Task Force discussed the impact of its recommendation that an oral hearing be given in each case. At p. 103 the Report states:

> In the end, then, the question is one of resources. Would the additional expenditures be warranted? How does one do a cost-benefit analysis where the 'benefit' is to be found in vague concepts, such as 'fairness' and 'justice'? One approach may be to canvass other forms of adjudication by federal tribunals and compare the significance of their decisions and the kinds of hearings which they offer with those of the refugee determination process. Without referring to specific bodies or in any way denigrating the importance of their work, the impact of their decisions often pales in comparison to refugee determination. Yet they generally offer far more in the way of procedural fairness.

Even if the cost of compliance with fundamental justice is a factor to which the courts would give considerable weight, I am not satisfied that the Minister has demonstrated that this cost would be so prohibitive as to constitute a justification within the meaning of s. 1. Though it is tempting to make observations about what factors might give rise to justification under s. 1, and on the standards of review which should be applied with respect to s. 1, I think it would be unwise to do so. I therefore confine my observations on the application of s. 1 to those necessary for the disposition of the appeals.

To recapitulate, I am persuaded that the appellants are entitled to assert the protection of s. 7 of the *Charter* in the determination of their claims to Convention refugee status under the *Immigration Act*. I am further persuaded that the procedures under the *Act* as they were applied in these cases do not meet the requirements of fundamental justice under s. 7 and that accordingly the appellants' rights under s. 7 were violated. Finally, I believe that the respondent has failed to demonstrate that the procedures set out in the *Act* constitute a reasonable limit on the appellants' rights within the meaning of s. 1 of the *Charter*. I would accordingly allow the appeals. In so doing I should, however, observe that the acceptance of certain submissions, particularly concerning the scope of s. 7 of the *Charter* in the context of these appeals, is not intended to be definitive of the scope of the section in other contexts. I do not by any means foreclose the possibility that s. 7 protects a wider range of interests than those involved in these appeals.

## 4. *Remedies*

I turn now to the issue of the remedy to which the appellants are entitled. Sections 24(1) and 52(1) of the *Charter* both apply. Section 52(1) requires a declaration that s. 71(1) of the *Immigration Act* is of no force and effect to the extent it is inconsistent with s. 7. The appellants who have suffered as a result of the application of an unconstitutional law to them are entitled under s. 24(1) to apply to a court of competent jurisdiction for "such remedy as the court considers appropriate and just in the circumstances". What remedy is available in the context of this case?

The court's jurisdiction is invoked in two contexts. In the first, these are appeals from dismissals by the Federal Court of Appeal of applications for judicial review under s. 28 of the *Federal Court Act*. In this context the court is limited to the powers the Federal Court is entitled to exercise pursuant to s. 28. In the other context, however, the court's broad remedial powers under s. 24 of the *Charter* are invoked.

The significance of the limitation of the court's judicial review power under s. 28 of the *Federal Court Act* is apparent from the decision of Urie, J., in *Brempong v. Minister of Employment and Immigration*, [1981] 1 F.C. 211 (C.A.). In that case, Urie, J., observed that s. 28 provided the Federal Court of Appeal with supervisory powers only over decisions made on a "judicial or quasi-judicial basis" and that accordingly the court had no jurisdiction to review what he characterized as an "administrative" decision by the Minister under s. 45 of the *Immigration Act*. The Board is a quasi-judicial body and without doubt its determinations are subject to review under s. 28. The question the court faces, as I see it, is whether the broader remedial power which it possesses under s. 24(1) of the *Charter* entitles it to extend its review of possible violations of the *Charter* to the Ministerial determinations made pursuant to s. 45 of the *Immigration Act*. In my view it does not.

Section 24(1) of the *Charter* provides remedial powers to "a court of competent jurisdiction". As I understand this phrase, it premises the existence of jurisdiction from a source external to the *Charter* itself. This court certainly has jurisdiction to review the decisions of the Immigration Appeal Board in these cases pursuant to s. 28 of the *Federal Court Act*. If the appeals originated as petitions for certiorari brought in the Trial Division of the Federal Court pursuant to s. 18 of the *Federal Court Act*, the Ministerial decisions made pursuant to s. 45 of the *Immigration Act* would be subject to review. In my view, however, any violations of the *Charter* which arose out of Ministerial decisions under s. 45 are not subject to review on these appeals because of the judicial limitations on the Federal Court of Appeal under s. 28 of the *Federal Court Act*. I would accordingly make no observations with respect to them or with respect to the question of whether or to what extent s. 45 of the *Immigration Act* is of no force and effect as a result of any inconsistency with the *Charter*.

Confining myself to the decisions of the Immigration Appeal Board which are under review, I would allow the appeals, set aside the decisions of the Federal Court of Appeal and of the Immigration Appeal Board and remand all seven cases for a hearing on the merits by the Board in accordance with the principles of fundamental justice articulated above. Since s. 71(1) of the *Immigration Act*, which restricts the Board's power to allow hearings to proceed to cases in which it is of the opinion that the applicant for redetermination is more likely than not to succeed upon a hearing of his claim, is inconsistent with the principles of fundamental justice set out in s. 7 of the *Charter*, the appellants are also entitled to a declaration that s. 71(1) is of no force and effect to the extent of the inconsistency.

*Appeal allowed.*

# 21

# Unreasonable Search or Seizure

## DIRECTOR OF INVESTIGATION AND RESEARCH OF THE COMBINES INVESTIGATION BRANCH v. SOUTHAM INC.

In the Supreme Court of Canada. [1984] 2 S.C.R. 145.

Laskin C.J.C.*, Ritchie, Dickson, Beetz, Estey, McIntyre, Chouinard, Lamer and Wilson JJ. September 17, 1984.

*The Chief Justice did not take part in the judgment.

Appeal from judgment of Alberta Court of Appeal, [1983] 3 W.W.R. 385, dismissing application for interim injunction pending trial. (For related proceedings, see [1982] 4 W.W.R. 673, affirmed 65 C.P.R. (2d) 116.)

The judgment of the Court was delivered by

DICKSON J.: — The Constitution of Canada, which includes the *Canadian Charter of Rights and Freedoms, Constitution Act, 1982, Pt. I*, is the supreme law of Canada. Any law inconsistent with the provisions of the Constitution is, to the extent of the inconsistency, of no force or effect. Section 52(1) of the Constitution Act, 1982, so mandates. The constitutional question posed in this appeal [from [1983] 3 W.W.R. 385] is whether s. 10(3), and by implication s. 10(1), of the *Combines Investigation Act*, R.S.C. 1970, c. C-23 ("the Act"), are inconsistent with s. 8 of the *Charter* by reason of authorizing unreasonable searches and seizures and are therefore of no force and effect.

## I. BACKGROUND

Subsections 10(1) and 10(3) of the *Combines Investigation Act* provide:

10.(1) Subject to subsection (3), in any inquiry under this Act the Director [of Investigation and Research of the Combines Investigation Branch] or any representative authorized by him may enter any premises on which the Director believes there may be evidence relevant to the matters being inquired into and may examine any thing on the premises and may copy or take away for further examination or copying any book, paper, record or other document that in the opinion of the Director or his authorized representative, as the case may be, may afford such evidence ...

(3) Before exercising the power conferred by subsection (1), the Director or his representative shall produce a certificate from a member of the [Restrictive Trade Practices] Commission, which may be granted on the *ex parte* application of the Director, authorizing the exercise of such power.

On 13th April 1982, in the course of an inquiry under the Act, the appellant Lawson A. W. Hunter, Director of Investigation and Research of the Combines Investigation Branch, authorized the other appellants, Messrs. Milton, Murphy, McAlpine and Marroco, all combines investigation officers, to exercise his authority under s. 10 of the Act to enter and examine documents and other things at the business premises of the Edmonton Journal, a division of the respondent corporation, Southam Inc.

On 16th April 1982, in fulfilment of the requirement in s. 10(3) of the Act, Dr. Frank Roseman, a member of the Restrictive Trade Practices Commission ("the R.T.P.C."), certified his authorization of this exercise of the director's powers.

On 17th April 1982 the *Constitution Act, 1982*, incorporating the *Canadian Charter of Rights and Freedoms*, was proclaimed. Section 8 of the *Charter* provides:

> 8. Everyone has the right to be secure against unreasonable search and seizure.

On 19th April 1982 the officers presented their certified authorization at the premises of the Edmonton Journal. The English version of this certificate reads as follows:

> In the matter of the *Combines Investigation Act* and section 33 and section 34(1)(c) thereof and
>
> in the matter of an Inquiry relating to the Production, Distribution and Supply of Newspapers and Related Products in Edmonton
>
> To:  M.J. Milton
> M.L. Murphy
> J.A. McAlpine
> A.P. Marrocco [sic]
> being my representatives under section 10 of the *Combines Investigation Act*
>
> You are hereby authorized to enter upon the premises hereinafter mentioned, on which I believe there may be evidence relevant to this inquiry, and examine anything thereon and copy or take away for copying any book, paper, record or other document that in your opinion may afford such evidence.
>
> The premises referred to herein are those occupied by or on behalf of
>
> Southam Inc,
> 10006-101 Street
> Edmonton, Alberta
>
> and elsewhere in Canada
>
> This authorization is not valid after May 31, 1982.
>
> Dated in Hull, in the Province of Quebec this 13th day of April 1982.
>
> Lawson A.W. Hunter
> Director D1 Investigation and Research
> Combines Investigation Act
>
> I hereby certify that the above exercise of powers is authorized pursuant to Section 10 of the *Combines Investigation Act*.
>
> Dated in Ottawa, in the Province of Ontario, this 16th day of April, 1982.
>
> Frank Roseman, Member,
> Restrictive Trade Practices Commission

The authorization has a breathtaking sweep; it is tantamount to a licence to roam at large on the premises of Southam Inc. at the stated address "and elsewhere in Canada".

On 20th April the officers commenced the search. They said they wished to search every file of Southam Inc. at 10006 101 Street, Edmonton, except files in the newsroom but including all files of J. Patrick O'Callaghan, publisher of the Edmonton Journal. They declined to give the name of any person whose complaint had initiated the inquiry, or to say under which section of the Act the inquiry had been begun. They also declined to give more specific information as to the subject matter of the inquiry than that contained in the authorization to search.

At noon on 20th April Southam Inc. served upon the officers of the Combines Investigation Branch a notice of motion for an interim injunction. The application was heard by Cavanagh J., who held that, although Southam had raised a serious question as to whether the search was in violation of s. 8 of the *Charter*, the balance of convenience militated in favour of denying the interlocutory injunction pending trial of the matter. At the hearing, the appellants maintained, unsuccessfully, that the Director of Investigation and Research and his authorized representatives, acting pursuant to s. 10 of the Act, were a "federal board, commission or other tribunal" within s. 2(g) of the *Federal Court Act*, R.S.C. 1970, c. 10 (2nd Supp.), and that the Federal Court, not the provincial courts of Alberta, had jurisdiction.

Southam appealed to the Alberta Court of Appeal. The appellants also appealed, from that part of the judgment which held that the Alberta Court of Queen's Bench had jurisdiction. As an interim provision the Court of Appeal ordered that the documents taken from the premises of the Edmonton Journal be sealed pending resolution of the appeal. After hearing the parties, the court held that the case was a proper one to have been treated at first instance as an application for summary judgment on the issues of: (1) whether the Alberta courts or the Federal Court had jurisdiction to make the orders requested; and (2) whether s. 10 of the Act was in whole or in part inconsistent with the provisions of the Constitution. The court therefore directed that the appeal itself be heard on this basis. At the subsequent hearing, the judgment of this court in *A. G. Can. v. Law Soc. of B.C.; Jabour v. Law Soc. of B.C.*, [1982] 2 S.C.R. 307, having by then been delivered, the present appellants abandoned their challenge to the jurisdiction of the Alberta courts and addressed their arguments solely to the substantive issue of the constitutionality of s. 10 of the Act. A unanimous five-judge panel of the Alberta Court of Appeal, speaking through Prowse J.A., held that s. 10(3), and by implication s. 10(1), of the Act were inconsistent with the provisions of s. 8 of the *Charter* and therefore of no force or effect. It is from this ruling that the present appellants bring their appeal before this court.

II. THE POSITIONS OF THE PARTIES

(a) *The Respondent, Southam Inc.*

In alleging that ss. 10(1) and 10(3) of the *Combines Investigation Act* are inconsistent with the right to be secure against unreasonable search and seizure, Southam

Inc. relies heavily on the historic protections afforded by common law and by statute as defining the correct standard of reasonableness for purposes of s. 8 of the *Charter*. This was essentially the approach taken by Prowse J.A. when he said [p. 148 (C.R.)]:

> The roots of the right to be so secure are embedded in the common law and the safeguards according that right are found in the common law, in statutes subsequently enacted, and in decisions of the courts made as the society in which we live has evolved. The expression of the right in a constitutional document reminds us of those roots and the tradition associated with the right. One would be presumptuous to assume that we have attained the zenith of our development as a civilization and that the right accorded an individual is frozen for eternity. Section 8, however, requires us to be ever mindful of some of the criteria that have been applied in the past in securing the right.

Applying this approach, Prowse J.A. concluded — correctly, in Southam Inc.'s submission — that, absent exceptional circumstances, the provisions of s. 443 of the *Criminal Code*, R.S.C. 1970, c. C-34, which extends to investigations of *Criminal Code* offences the procedural safeguards the common law required for entries and searches for stolen goods, constitute the minimal prerequisites for reasonable searches and seizures in connection with the investigation of any criminal offence, including possible violations of the *Combines Investigation Act*. Prowse J.A. summarized these procedural safeguards in the following propositions [p. 151 (C.R.)]:

> (a) that the power to authorize a search and seizure is given to an impartial and independent person (at common law a justice) who is bound to act judicially in discharging that function;
> (b) that evidence must satisfy the justice that the person seeking the authority has reasonable ground to suspect that an offence had been committed;
> (c) that evidence must satisfy the justice that the person seeking the authority has reasonable grounds to believe, at common law, that stolen property may be on the premises or, under s. 443(1)(*b*), that something that will afford evidence of an offence may be recovered; and
> (d) that there must be evidence on oath before him . . .

Southam Inc. contends that ss. 10(1) and 10(3) fail to provide any of these safeguards. In its submission, the approval by a member of the R.T.P.C. of the director's decision to authorize search and seizure is not approval by an independent arbiter or neutral and impartial person. It argues further that ss. 10(1) and 10(3) do not require that the R.T.P.C. member be satisfied that the director has reasonable grounds to suspect that an offence has been committed or to believe that there may be evidence at the place at which the director wishes to search, nor does it require evidence under oath about these matters. In fact, Southam Inc. contends, as these subsections have been judicially interpreted in cases such as *Petrofina Can. Ltd. v. Chairman of Restrictive Trade Practices Comm.*, [1980] 2 F.C. 386 (C.A.), they *prevent* the R.T.P.C. member from ascertaining or passing judgment on anything except that there is de facto an inquiry in progress under the Act, an interpretation which, in Southam's submission, constitutes the R.T.P.C. member as merely a "rubber stamp" for the director's decision to authorize a search. For all these reasons, Southam submits, giving effect to ss. 10(1) and 10(3) could yield no other result than an unreasonable search and seizure.

### (b) *The Appellants*

The appellants take a different view. In their submission, the constitutionality of s. 10 ought to be considered on the basis of whether its provisions *could be* applied consistently with the Charter. It is their contention that they can. In their view, approval by the R.T.P.C. member *does* constitute authorization by a neutral and impartial arbiter. They deny that there is any reasonable apprehension of bias attaching to him or to his function in approving the director's authorizations to enter and search premises. As to the further requirements cited by Prowse J.A. and amplified on by Southam Inc., the appellants implicitly deny that an easy parallel can be drawn between the offences set out in the *Criminal Code* and those created by the *Combines Investigation Act* so as to justify invoking the procedural safeguards in s. 443 as the proper standard of reasonableness for searches and seizures by the authorities in connection with these latter offences. In their submission, combines offences require specialized techniques for their detection and suppression. They say that for such offences, as compared to most other criminal offences, there is inherently less basis for certainty and specificity, both as to the commission of an offence and as to the existence of specific physical evidence in relation to such an offence. In this context, they contend, s. 10 does not authorize "unreasonable" search or seizure. Further, the appellants argue, the wording of s. 10 does not prevent the R.T.P.C. member in appropriate cases from requiring, for instance, evidence under oath before he approves the director's authorization. In any event, they maintain, it cannot be said that s. 10 is incapable of being applied in a manner which does not offend the Constitution, and it ought not therefore to be struck down. At most, it ought to be read down so as to include any necessary procedural safeguards. In support, they cite the decision of Van Camp J. in *R. v. Metro Toronto Pharmacists' Assn.*, Ont. H.C., 4th May 1983 (not yet reported).

### III. "UNREASONABLE" SEARCH OR SEIZURE

At the outset it is important to note that the issue in this appeal concerns the constitutional validity of a statute authorizing a search and seizure. It does not concern the reasonableness or otherwise of the manner in which the appellants carried out their statutory authority. It is not the conduct of the appellants, but rather the legislation under which they acted, to which attention must be directed.

As is clear from the arguments of the parties as well as from the judgment of Prowse J.A., the crux of this case is the meaning to be given to the term "unreasonable" in the s. 8 guarantee of freedom from unreasonable search or seizure. The guarantee is vague and open. The American courts have had the advantage of a number of specific prerequisites articulated in the Fourth Amendment to the *United States Constitution*, as well as a history of colonial opposition to certain Crown investigatory practices, from which to draw out the nature of the interests protected by that amendment and the kinds of conduct it proscribes. There is none of this in s. 8. There is no specificity in the section beyond the bare guarantee of freedom from "unreasonable" search and seizure; nor is there any particular historical, political or philosophic context capable of providing an obvious gloss on the meaning of the guarantee.

It is clear that the meaning of "unreasonable" cannot be determined by recourse to a dictionary, nor, for that matter, by reference to the rules of statutory construction. The task of expounding a constitution is crucially different from that of construing a statute. A statute defines present rights and obligations. It is easily enacted and as easily repealed. A constitution, by contrast, is drafted with an eye to the future. Its function is to provide a continuing framework for the legitimate exercise of governmental power and, when joined by a bill or a charter of rights, for the unremitting protection of individual rights and liberties. Once enacted, its provisions cannot easily be repealed or amended. It must therefore be capable of growth and development over time to meet new social, political and historical realities often unimagined by its framers. The judiciary is the guardian of the constitution and must, in interpreting its provisions, bear these considerations in mind. Professor Paul Freund expressed this idea aptly when he admonished the American courts "not to read the provisions of the Constitution like a last will and testament lest it become one".

The need for a broad perspective in approaching constitutional documents is a familiar theme in Canadian constitutional jurisprudence. It is contained in Viscount Sankey L.C.'s classic formulation in *Edwards v. A.G. Can.*, [1930] A.C. 124 at 136-37 (P.C.), cited and applied in countless Canadian cases:

> The *British North America Act* planted in Canada a living tree capable of growth and expansion within its natural limits. The object of the Act was to grant a Constitution to Canada ...
> Their Lordships do not conceive it to be the duty of this Board — it is certainly not their desire — to cut down the provisions of the Act by a narrow and technical construction, but rather to give it a large and liberal interpretation.

More recently, in *Min. of Home Affairs v. Fisher*, [1980] A.C. 319 (P.C.), dealing with the Bermudian constitution, Lord Wilberforce reiterated at p. 329 that a constitution is a document "sui generis, calling for principles of interpretation of its own, suitable to its character", and that as such a constitution incorporating a bill of rights calls for [p. 328]:

> ... a generous interpretation avoiding what has been called 'the austerity of tabulated legalism', suitable to give individuals the full measure of the fundamental rights and freedoms referred to.

Such a broad, purposive analysis, which interprets specific provisions of a constitutional document in the light of its larger objects, is also consonant with the classical principles of American constitutional construction enunciated by Marshall C.J. in *McCulloch v. Maryland*, 17 U.S. (4 Wheat.) 316 (1819). It is, as well, the approach I intend to take in the present case.

I begin with the obvious. The *Canadian Charter of Rights and Freedoms* is a purposive document. Its purpose is to guarantee and to protect, within the limits of reason, the enjoyment of the rights and freedoms it enshrines. It is intended to constrain governmental action inconsistent with those rights and freedoms; it is not in itself an authorization for governmental action. In the present case this means, as Prowse J.A. pointed out, that in guaranteeing the right to be secure from unreasonable searches and seizures s. 8 acts as a limitation on whatever powers of search and seizure the federal or provincial governments already and otherwise possess. It does not in itself confer any powers, even of "reasonable" search and seizure, on these governments. This leads, in my view, to the further conclusion that an assessment of the constitutionality of a search and seizure, or of a statute authorizing a search or seizure, must focus on its "reasonable" or "unreasonable" impact on the subject of the search or the seizure, and not simply on its rationality in furthering some valid government objective.

Since the proper approach to the interpretation of the *Charter of Rights and Freedoms* is a purposive one, before it is possible to assess the reasonableness or unreasonableness of the impact of a search or of a statute authorizing a search, it is first necessary to specify the purpose underlying s. 8: in other words, to delineate the nature of the interests it is meant to protect.

Historically, the common law protections with regard to governmental searches and seizures were based on the right to enjoy property and were linked to the law of trespass. It was on this basis that in the great case of *Entick v. Carrington* (1765), 19 State Tr. 1029, the court refused to countenance a search purportedly authorized by the executive, to discover evidence that might link the plaintiff to certain seditious libels. Lord Camden C.J. prefaced his discussion of the rights in question by saying, at p. 1066:

> The great end, for which men entered into society, was to preserve their property. That right is preserved sacred and incommunicable in all instances where it has not been taken away or abridged by some public law for the good of the whole.

The defendants argued that their oaths as Kings' messengers required them to conduct the search in question and ought to prevail over the plaintiff's property rights. Lord Camden C.J. rejected this contention, at p. 1067:

> Our law holds the property of every man so sacred, that no man can set his foot upon his neighbour's close without his leave: if he does he is a trespasser though he does no damage at all; if he will tread upon his neighbour's ground he must justify it by law.

Lord Camden C.J. could find no exception from this principle for the benefit of Kings' messengers. He held that neither the intrusions nor the purported authorizations were supportable on the basis of the existing law. That law would have countenanced such an entry only if the search were for stolen goods and if it were authorized by a justice on the basis of evidence upon oath that there was "strong cause" to believe that the goods were concealed in the place sought to be searched. In view of the lack of proper legal authorization for the governmental intrusion, the plaintiff was protected from the intended search and seizure by the ordinary law of trespass.

In my view the interests protected by s. 8 are of a wider ambit than those enunciated in *Entick v. Carrington*, supra. Section 8 is an entrenched constitutional provision. It is not therefore vulnerable to encroachment by legislative enactments in the same way as common law protections. There is, further, nothing in the language of the section to restrict it to the protection of property or to associate it with the law of trespass. It guarantees a broad and general right to be secure from unreasonable search and seizure.

The Fourth Amendment of the *United States Constitution* also guarantees a broad right. It provides:

> The right of the people to be secure in their persons, houses, papers, and effects, against unreasonable searches and seizures, shall not be violated and no Warrants shall issue, but upon probable cause, supported by Oath or affirmation, and particularly describing the place to be searched, and the persons or things to be seized.

Construing this provision in *Katz v. U.S.*, 389 U.S. 347 (1967), Stewart J., delivering the majority opinion of the United States Supreme Court, declared at p.

351 that "the Fourth Amendment protects people, not places". Stewart J. rejected any necessary connection between that amendment and the notion of trespass. With respect, I believe this approach is equally appropriate in construing the protections in s. 8 of the Charter of Rights and Freedoms.

In *Katz*, Stewart J. discussed the notion of a right to privacy, which he described at pp. 350-51 as "the right to be let alone by other people". Although Stewart J. was careful not to identify the Fourth Amendment exclusively with the protection of this right, nor to see the amendment as the only provision in the Bill of Rights relevant to its interpretation, it is clear that this notion played a prominent role in his construction of the nature and the limits of the American constitutional protection against unreasonable search and seizure. In the Alberta Court of Appeal, Prowse J.A. took a similar approach to s. 8, which he described [at p. 148 (C.R.)] as dealing "with one aspect of what has been referred to as the 'right of privacy', which is the right to be secure against encroachment upon the citizens' reasonable expectation of privacy in a free and democratic society".

Like the Supreme Court of the United States, I would be wary of foreclosing the possibility that the right to be secure against unreasonable search and seizure might protect interests beyond the right of privacy, but for purposes of the present appeal I am satisfied that its protections go at least that far. The guarantee of security from *unreasonable* search and seizure protects only a *reasonable* expectation. This limitation on the right guaranteed by s. 8, whether it is expressed negatively, as freedom from "unreasonable" search and seizure, or positively, as an entitlement to a "reasonable" expectation of privacy, indicates that an assessment must be made as to whether in a particular situation the public's interest in being left alone by government must give way to the government's interest in intruding on the individual's privacy in order to advance its goals, notably those of law enforcement.

The question that remains, and the one upon which the present appeal hinges, is how this assessment is to be made. When is it to be made, by whom and on what basis? Here again I think the proper approach is a purposive one.

(a) *When is the balance of interests to be assessed?*

If the issue to be resolved in assessing the constitutionality of searches under s. 10 were whether *in fact* the governmental interest in carrying out a given search outweighed that of the individual in resisting the governmental intrusion upon his privacy, then it would be appropriate to determine the balance of the competing interests *after* the search had been conducted. Such a post facto analysis would, however, be seriously at odds with the purpose of s. 8. That purpose is, as I have said, to protect individuals from unjustified state intrusions upon their privacy. That purpose requires a means of *preventing* unjustified searches before they happen, not simply of determining, after the fact, whether they ought to have occurred in the first place. This, in my view, can be accomplished only by a system of *prior authorization*, not one of subsequent validation.

A requirement of prior authorization, usually in the form of a valid warrant, has been a consistent prerequisite for a valid search and seizure both at common law and under most statutes. Such a requirement puts the onus on the state to demonstrate the superiority of its interest to that of the individual. As such it accords with the apparent intention of the *Charter* to prefer, where feasible, the right of the individual to be free from state interference to the interests of the state in advancing its purposes through such interference.

I recognize that it may not be reasonable in every instance to insist on prior authorization in order to validate governmental intrusions upon individuals' expectations of privacy. Nevertheless, where it is feasible to obtain prior authorization, I would hold that such authorization is a precondition for a valid search and seizure.

Here also, the decision in *Katz*, supra, is relevant. In *U.S. v. Rabinowitz*, 339 U.S. 56 (1950), the Supreme Court of the United States had held that a search without warrant was not ipso facto unreasonable. 17 years later, however, in *Katz*, Stewart J. concluded that a warrantless search was prima facie "unreasonable" under the Fourth Amendment. The terms of the Fourth Amendment are not identical to those of s. 8 and American decisions can be transplanted to the Canadian context only with the greatest caution. Nevertheless, I would in the present instance respectfully adopt Stewart J.'s formulation as equally applicable to the concept of "unreasonableness" under s. 8, and would require the party seeking to justify a warrantless search to rebut this presumption of unreasonableness.

In the present case the appellants make no argument that it is infeasible or unnecessary to obtain prior authorization for the searches contemplated by the *Combines Investigation Act*, and in my view no such argument could be made. I would therefore conclude that, in the absence of a valid procedure for prior authorization, searches conducted under the Act would be unreasonable. In the event, s. 10(3) *does* purport to establish a requirement for prior authorization, specifying as it does that searches and seizures conducted under s. 10(1) must be authorized by a member of the R.T.P.C. The question then becomes whether s. 10(3) provides for an acceptable prior authorization procedure.

(b) *Who must grant the authorization?*

The purpose of a requirement of prior authorization is to provide an opportunity, before the event, for the conflicting interests of the state and the individual to be assessed, so that the individual's right to privacy will be breached only where the appropriate standard has been met, and the interests of the state are thus demonstrably superior. For such an authorization procedure to be meaningful it is necessary for the person authorizing the search to be able to assess the evidence as to whether that standard has been met in an entirely neutral and impartial manner. At common law the power to issue a search warrant was reserved for a justice. In the recent English case of *R. v. Inland Revenue Commrs.; Ex parte Rossminster*, [1980] 2 W.L.R. 1 (H.L.), Viscount Dilhorne suggested at p. 87 that the power to authorize administrative searches and seizures be given to "a more senior judge". While it may be wise, in view of the sensitivity of the task, to assign the decision whether an authorization should be issued to a judicial officer, I agree with Prowse J.A. that this is not a necessary precondition for safeguarding the right enshrined in s. 8. The person performing this function need not be a judge, but he must at a minimum be capable of acting judicially.

In *M.N.R. v. Coopers & Lybrand*, [1979] 1 S.C.R. 495, this court had occasion to discuss the difference between an administrative and a judicial function in the authorization of a search and seizure. The *Income Tax Act*, S.C. 1970-71-72, c. 63, confers upon the minister a number of powers, including, in s. 231(4), the power under certain conditions to authorize the entry and search of buildings. At p. 507 the court described the minister's powers as "fundamentally administrative", going on to explain [pp. 507-508]:

> The power he exercises under s. 231(4) is properly characterized as investigatory rather than adjudicatory. He will collect material and advice from many sources. In deciding whether to exercise the right [to authorize entry and search], he will be governed by many considerations, dominant among which is the public interest and his duty as an executive officer of the government to administer the Act to the best of his ability. The decision to seek authority to enter and search will be guided by public policy and expediency, having regard to all the circumstances.

The court contrasted these powers with the judicial powers which s. 231(4) conferred on a judge of the superior or county court to approve the minister's authorization.

Under the scheme envisaged by s. 10 of the *Combines Investigation Act* it is clear that the director exercises administrative powers analogous to those of the minister under s. 231(4) of the *Income Tax Act*. They too are investigatory rather than adjudicatory, with his decision to seek approval for an authorization to enter and search premises equally guided by considerations of expediency and public policy. But what of the member of the R.T.P.C. whom s. 10(3) empowers to approve the director's authorization? Is his function investigatory or adjudicatory? In the Alberta Court of Appeal Prowse J.A. carefully reviewed the respective powers of the director and the commission and concluded that the Act was not entirely successful in separating the role of the director as investigator and prosecutor from that of the commission as adjudicator. In his view [p. 154(C.R.)] circumstances may arise under the Act where "the director is acting as investigator and prosecutor and the commission is acting as investigator and judge with respect to breaches of the Act". Southam Inc. summarizes and enlarges upon Prowse J.A.'s analysis, producing the following list of investigatory functions bestowed upon the commission or one of its members by the Act:

> i) The power in s. 47 to instruct the Director to commence a s. 8 inquiry.
> ii) The power to cause evidence to be gathered pursuant to ss. 9, 10, 12 and 17.
> iii) The power to issue a s. 17 order.
> iv) The power under ss. 17, 22(2)(*b*) to seek further or better evidence after the Commission has commenced a hearing.
> v) the power under s. 22(2)(*b*) after commencing a hearing and receiving evidence to direct the Director to make further inquiry and, in effect, to go back to the investigatory stage;
> vi) the power under s. 22(2)(*c*) to compel the Director to turn over to the R.T.P.C. copies of all books, papers, records or other documents obtained by the Director in such further inquiry;
> vii) the power under s. 27.1 to order the Director to give evidence before any other federal board, commission or other tribunal;
> viii) the power under s. 45.1 to seek production of statistics for evidence in an inquiry;
> ix) the power to deliver to the Director all books, papers, records of other documents produced on a s. 17 hearing;
> x) the power under s. 13 to request the appointment and instruction of counsel to assist in the inquiry.

In my view, investing the commission or its members with significant investigatory functions has the result of vitiating the ability of a member of the commission to act in a judicial capacity when authorizing a search or seizure under s. 10(3). This is not, of course, a matter of impugning the honesty or good faith of the commission or its members. It is rather a conclusion that the administrative nature of the commission's investigatory duties (with its quite proper reference points in considerations of public policy and effective enforcement of the Act) ill accords with the neutrality and detachment necessary to assess whether the evidence reveals that the point has been reached where the interests of the individual must constitutionally give way to those of the state. A member of the R.T.P.C. passing on the appropriateness of a proposed search under the *Combines Investigation Act* is caught by the maxim "Nemo judex in sua causa". He simply cannot be the impartial arbiter necessary to grant an effective authorization.

On this basis alone I would conclude that the prior authorization mandated by s. 10(3) of the *Combines Investigation Act* is inadequate to satisfy the requirements of s. 8 of the *Charter* and consequently a search carried out under the authority of ss. 10(1) and 10(3) is an unreasonable one. Since, however, the Alberta Court of Appeal found other, perhaps even more serious, defects in these provisions, I pass on to consider whether, even if s. 10(3) did specify a truly neutral and detached arbiter to authorize searches, it would nevertheless remain inconsistent with s. 8 of the *Charter*.

### (c) *On what basis must the balance of interests be assessed?*

Section 10 is terse in the extreme on the subject of criteria for issuing an authorization for entry, search and seizure. Section 10(3) merely states that an R.T.P.C. member may grant an authorization ex parte. The only explicit criteria for granting such an authorization are those mentioned in s. 10(1), namely: (1) that an inquiry under the Act must be in progress; and (2) that the director must believe that the premises may contain relevant evidence.

In cases argued before a passage of the Charter of Rights and Freedoms the courts took a narrow view of what s. 10 required or permitted the R.T.P.C. member to consider when asked to authorize search and seizure. In *Petrofina Can. Ltd. v. Chairman of Restrictive Trade Practices Comm.*, supra, the applicant challenged authorizations under ss. 9(2) and 10(3) of the Act on the grounds, inter alia, that the members who gave their authorizations did not show that they had before them sufficient information to enable them to determine the legality of the inquiry then in progress or the reasonableness of the director's belief that circumstances warranted the exercise of his powers. The Federal Court of Appeal rejected the relevance of such considerations to the members' decisions, at p. 391:

> In making the decisions that sections 9 and 10 require them to make, the Members must act judicially ... However, that duty to act judicially applies only to the decisions that the Members are required to make under sections 9(2) and 10(3). Under those provisions, the Members are neither required nor authorized to determine the legality of the Director's decision to hold an inquiry: they are merely required to ascertain that there is, *de facto*, an inquiry in progress under the Act. The Members are not required or authorized, either to pass judgment on the reasonableness of the motives prompting the Director to exercise his powers under sections 9 and 10. As the Members did not have to make decisions on those two points, they cannot, in my opinion, be blamed for not having required information on those points.

As Prowse J.A. pointed out, if the powers of a commission member are as the Federal Court of Appeal found them to be, then it follows that the decision of the director in the course of an inquiry to exercise his powers of entry, search and seizure is effectively unreviewable. The extent of the privacy of the individual would be left to the discretion of the director. A provision authorizing such an unreviewable power would clearly be inconsistent with s. 8 of the *Charter*.

Assuming, arguendo, that the Federal Court of Appeal was wrong, and the member *is* authorized, or even required, to satisfy himself as to (1) the legality of the inquiry, and (2) the reasonableness of the director's belief that there may be evidence relevant to the matters being inquired into, would that remove the inconsistency with s. 8?

To read ss. 10(1) and 10(3) as simply *allowing* the authorizing party to satisfy himself on these questions, without requiring him to do so, would in my view be clearly inadequate. Such an amorphous standard cannot provide a meaningful criterion for securing the right guaranteed by s. 8. The location of the constitutional balance between a justifiable expectation of privacy and the legitimate needs of the state cannot depend on the subjective appreciation of individual adjudicators. Some objective standard must be established.

Requiring the authorizing party to satisfy himself as to the legality of the inquiry and the reasonableness of the director's belief in the possible existence of relevant evidence would have the advantage of substituting an objective standard for an amorphous one, but would, in my view, still be inadequate. The problem is with the stipulation of a reasonable belief that evidence *may* be uncovered in the search. Here again it is useful, in my view, to adopt a purposive approach. The purpose of an objective criterion for granting prior authorization to conduct a search or seizure is to provide a consistent standard for identifying the point at which the interests of the state in such intrusions come to prevail over the interests of the individual in resisting them. To associate it with an applicant's reasonable belief that relevant evidence *may* be uncovered by the search would be to define the proper standard as the *possibility* of finding evidence. This is a very low standard, which would validate intrusion on the basis of suspicion, and authorize fishing expeditions of considerable latitude. It would tip the balance strongly in favour of the state, and limit the right of the individual to resist to only the most egregious intrusions. I do not believe that this is a proper standard for securing the right to be free from unreasonable search and seizure.

Anglo-Canadian legal and political traditions point to a higher standard. The common law required evidence on oath which gave "strong reason to believe" that stolen goods were concealed in the place to be searched before a warrant would issue. Section 443 of the *Criminal Code* authorizes a warrant only where there has been information upon oath that there is "reasonable ground to believe" that there is evidence of an offence in the place to be searched. The *American Bill of Rights* provides that "no warrants shall issue, but upon probable cause, supported by oath or affirmation". The phrasing is slightly different but the standard in each of these formulations is identical. The state's interest in detecting and preventing crime begins to prevail over the individual's interest in being left alone at the point where credibly-based probability replaces suspicion. History has confirmed the appropriateness of this requirement as the threshold for subordinating the expectation of privacy to the needs of law enforcement. Where the state's interest is not simply law enforcement, as, for instance, where state security is involved, or where the individual's interest is not simply his expectation of privacy, as, for instance, where the search threatens his bodily integrity, the relevant standard might well be a different one. That is not the situation in the present case. In cases like the present, reasonable and probable grounds, established upon oath, to believe that an offence has been committed and that there is evidence to be found at the place of the search constitutes the minimum standard consistent with s. 8 of the *Charter* for authorizing search and seizure. Insofar as ss. 10(1) and 10(3) of the *Combines Investigation Act* do not embody such a requirement, I would hold them to be further inconsistent with s. 8.

## IV. READING IN AND READING DOWN

The appellants submit that, even if ss. 10(1) and 10(3) do not specify a standard consistent with s. 8 for authorizing entry, search and seizure, they should not be struck down as inconsistent with the *Charter*, but rather the appropriate standard should be read into these provisions. An analogy is drawn to the case of *MacKay v. R.*, [1965] S.C.R. 798, in which this court held that a local ordinance regulating the use of property by prohibiting the erection of unauthorized signs, though apparently without limits, could not have been intended unconstutionally to encroach on federal competence over elections, and should therefore be "read down" so as not to apply to election signs. In the present case, the overt inconsistency with s. 8 manifested by the lack of a neutral and detached arbiter renders the appellants' submissions on reading in appropriate standards for issuing a warrant purely academic. Even if this were not the case, however, I would be disinclined to give effect to these submissions. While the courts are guardians of the Constitution and of individuals' rights under it, it is the legislature's responsibility to enact legislation that embodies appropriate safeguards to comply with the Constitution's requirements. It should not fall to the courts to fill in the details that will render legislative lacunae constitutional. Without appropriate safeguards, legislation authorizing search and seizure is inconsistent with s. 8 of the *Charter*. As I have said, any law inconsistent with the provisions of the Constitution is, to the extent of the inconsistency, of no force or effect. I would hold ss. 10(1) and 10(3) of the *Combines Investigation Act* to be inconsistent with the *Charter* and of no force and effect, as much for their failure to specify an appropriate standard for the issuance of warrants as for their designation of an improper arbiter to issue them.

## V. SECTION 1

Section 1 of the *Charter* provides:

> 1. The *Canadian Charter of Rights and Freedoms* guarantees the rights and freedoms set out in it subject only to such reasonable limits prescribed by law as can be demonstrably justified in a free and democratic society.

The phrase "demonstrably justified" puts the onus of justifying a limitation on a right or freedom set out in the *Charter* on the party seeking to limit. In the present case the appellants have made no submissions capable of supporting a claim that, even if searches under ss. 10(1) and 10(3) are "unreasonable" within the meaning of s. 8, they are nevertheless a reasonable limit, demonstrably justified in a free and democratic society, on the right set out in s. 8. It is therefore not necessary in this case to consider the relationship between s. 8 and s. 1. I leave to another day the difficult question of the relationship between those two sections and, more particularly, what further balancing of interests, if any, may be contemplated by s. 1, beyond that envisaged by s. 8.

## VI. CONCLUSION

By order of Laskin C.J.C. the constitutional question was stated as follows:

> Did the Alberta Court err in holding that subsection 10(3), and by implication subsection 10(1), of the *Combines Investigation Act*, R.S.C. 1970, c. C-23 are inconsistent with the provisions of Section 8 of the *Canadian Charter of Rights and Freedoms* and that they are therefore of no force or effect?

I would answer that question in the negative. I would dismiss the appeal with costs to the respondent.

*Appeal dismissed.*

# CONSTITUTIONAL LAW — SEARCH AND SEIZURE AFTER SOUTHAM

Finkelstein. (1985), 63 Can. Bar Rev. 178 (footnotes omitted).

. . . .

To summarize, after [*Hunter v.*] *Southam* [[1984] 2 S.C.R. 145] the applicant for a remedy must establish that he has a reasonable expectation of privacy. Once he has done that, the onus shifts to the government. According to *Southam*, enabling legislation is unreasonable, and therefore inconsistent with section 8, unless it contains at least the following minimum safeguards:

(1) a requirement of prior authorization by a neutral and detached arbiter who, while not necessarily a judicial officer, is capable of acting judicially;
(2) a requirement that there be reasonable and probable ground established on oath to believe that an offence has occurred *and* that evidence thereof is on the premises; and
(3) a requirement that the geographical area to be searched must be clearly described and limited to those areas where there is probable cause to believe the evidence is situated.

The Supreme Court in *Southam* only had to deal with the minimum constitutional requirements for a valid statutory authorization. It did not have to address the procedural requirements in any particular warrant. It should be borne in mind that a given warrant may be subject to attack even apart from the validity of the enabling legislation. While the procedural requirements of search warrants is beyond the scope of this paper, the following may be usefully noted from the general law on the sufficiency of warrants:

(1) the items sought must be described in the warrant with particularity in order to avoid fishing expeditions;

(2) the nature of the offence must be detailed in the warrant sufficiently to allow the person whose premises are subject to the search to know the reasons therefor;

(3) the grounds for the informant having probable cause to believe that an offence has been committed and that evidence thereof is on the premises must be set out in the information in sufficient detail.

## Implications of Southam for other Statutes

*Southam* has serious implications for a number of federal and provincial statutes beyond the *Combines Investigation Act*. Portions of section 231 of the *Income Tax Act*, S.C. 1970-71-72, c. 63, as amended are a prime example. Following *Southam*, the test for validity of a search or seizure provision is whether it properly balances the competing individual and state interests. In the tax context, this involves a determination of the point at which the state interest in tax collection outweighs the individual privacy interest and, flowing from that, the legislative safeguards which are necessary to ensure that both of these interests are accorded their proper weight.

It should be noted that the *Income Tax Act* is different from the *Combines Investigation Act* in an important respect. Whereas the latter is a penal statute and has been traditionally upheld on the basis of the federal criminal law power, the primary thrust of the *Income Tax Act* is to raise revenue for federal purposes. Tax audits are not necessarily, or even primarily, to discover or assist in the prosecution of criminal violations. They are to ensure that every person pays his fair share of tax. An audit will often disclose that a taxpayer has understated his tax liability for reasons having nothing to do with criminality. The taxpayer may simply have taken a different but good faith view about the application of the Act or about the characterization of a particular item of revenue or expense. Alternatively, he may have failed to declare income through oversight without criminal intent. In my view, a court is likely to hold that the audit function is a necessary adjunct to the administration of the *Income Tax Act* to catch cases like these. If so, the investigative machinery of the Act would be greatly hampered if the Minister had to lead evidence of probable tax violations as a precondition to auditing because often no violations will have occurred or even been alleged. The Ontario Court of Appeal has already signalled in *R. v. Rao* (1984), 46 O.R. (2d) 80 at 96, albeit in *obiter*, that search or seizure standards in connection with the inspection and audit of business activities for regulatory purposes may be lower than where a criminal offence has likely been committed.

However it follows from *Southam* that the balance shifts as soon as the auditor has probable cause to believe that an offence has been committed. Once the audit turns up evidence of criminality, the *Southam* protections should become operative. If so, the Minister must go to a neutral and impartial officer at that point for a warrant before proceeding further with the investigation. Nice questions may arise in particular cases as to whether the auditor should have gone for a warrant earlier, but that is a question of fact to be decided by a trial judge on a case by case basis.

The *Income Tax Act* does not contain the appropriate *Southam* standards. Section 231(1)(d) of the Act reads as follows:

> (1) Any person thereunto authorized by the Minister, for any purpose related to the administration or enforcement of this Act, may, at all reasonable times, enter into any premises or place

where any business is carried on or any property is kept or anything is done in connection with any business or any books or records are or should be kept, and . . .

(d) if during the course of an audit or examination, it appears to him that there has been a violation of this Act or a regulation, seize and take away any of the documents, books, records, papers or things that may be required as evidence as to the violation of any provision of this Act or a regulation.

The provision permits an auditor to seize documents or records during the course of an audit if it appears *to him* that there has been a violation of the Act. *Southam* requires that, once the auditor finds sufficient evidence to create a reasonable belief that an offence has been committed and that evidence thereof is on the premises, he must go before a neutral officer for authorization to seize or proceed further.

It follows that *New Garden Restaurant and Tavern Limited v. M.N.R.* (1983), 43 O.R. (2d) 417 (H.C.) must be reconsidered. In that case, the tax auditor seized documents pursuant to section 231(1)(d) on four separate non-successive days without a warrant. White J. upheld the section on the basis that:

> . . . the public interest in a reasonably efficient system of collecting tax revenue outweighs the tax-payer's expectation of privacy in the circumstances contemplated by s. 231(1)(d) of the Act which I interpret as specifically authorizing a seizure without a warrant in cases where the tax investigator comes upon incriminating evidence in the course of his audit without having formulated prior to the audit any belief of guilt of the party searched.

This reasoning does not give sufficient weight to the individual privacy interest. The state's efficiency interest remains paramount only to that point in the audit where evidence of an offence surfaces. At that point, the balance shifts in favour of the individual. A neutral officer, not the investigator, must assess the evidence of probable cause, satisfy himself that evidence is on the premises, and put meaningful limits on the search.

It should be noted that even section 231(4) of the Act, which empowers the Minister to go before a judge where he has reasonable grounds to believe that a violation has been or will be committed, is substantially overbroad. As a matter of statutory interpretation, the weight of authority is that the Minister's belief that a *particular* tax violation has occurred will support an authorization to seize evidence of *any* violation, not just the one detailed in the supporting affidavit. The presiding judge may authorize the broadest sort of fishing expedition. On this interpretation, the Federal Court of Appeal was clearly correct in holding in *M.N.R. v. Kruger Inc.*, [1984] 2 F.C. 535 (C.A.) that section 231(4) is constitutionally overbroad. Unfortunately, the court does not clearly specify whether the legislation is thereby wholly invalid or may be read down. In my view, the section is a potential candidate for the application of the reading down doctrine because it does not require a wholesale reading in of safeguards in the same way as section 10 of the *Combines Investigation Act* in *Southam*. Section 231(4) should be read to mean that the authorization referred to therein must be limited to seizures related to the offence described in the supporting affidavit. [Cf. *R. v. Print Three Inc.* (1985), 51 O.R. (2d) 321 (C.A.), refusing to apply the reading down doctrine to section 231(4) and striking it down altogether.]

The second problem with section 231(4) is that it does not require the Minister to lead evidence of a belief that evidence of the offence is on the premises. The Minister might not even have such a belief. The judge is empowered to grant a licence to roam in the hope that the Minister will find something. Section 231(4) is therefore unconstutionally overbroad.

Another likely candidate for a declaration of unconstitutionality is section 11(6) of the *Ontario Securities Act*, R.S.O. 1980, c. 466. Section 11 establishes the Act's investigative machinery. Section 11(1) empowers the Ontario Securities Commission to appoint an investigator whenever it appears probable to the Commission, based upon a statement on oath, that a violation of the Act, its regulations or the federal *Criminal Code*, R.S.C. 1970, c. C-34 in connection with a trade in securities has occurred. The investigator's appointment authorizes him to investigate the affairs of the subject person, compel witnesses to produce documents or give evidence under oath, and provide the Commission with a full report and transcripts of evidence. Most important for our purposes, section 11(6) authorizes him to seize any records or property of the person whose affairs are being investigated. The provision reads as follows:

> Where an investigation is ordered under this section, the person appointed to make the investigation may seize and take possession of any documents, records, securities or other property of the person or company whose affairs are being investigated.

As with the Restrictive Trade Practices Commission in *Southam*, the Ontario Securities Commission is not an exclusively adjudicative body. It holds hearings into various matters under the Act, but its functions are by no means limited to that. The Commission initiates investigations where it believes an offence has occurred, appoints investigators and, where it feels necessary, retains accountants and other experts to report on various aspects of the affairs of the person being investigated. Following an investigation, the Commission reports to the Minister of Consumer and Commercial Relations if it believes that an offence has been committed. The Commission is also empowered in certain circumstances to apply to a judge for the appointment of a receiver or liquidator. Thus, as in *Southam*, there is an unconstitutional intermingling of investigatory and adjudicative responsibilities.

There are further problems with the search and seizure authorization in section 11(6). The investigator's authorization is open-ended in all relevant respects. He may seize any documents or property of the person being investigated without restriction. He never has to prove to a neutral arbiter, or even to the Commission for that matter, that evidence of the offence is on any particular premises. The documents susceptible to seizure pursuant to the statute do not even have to relate to the suspected offence. The investigator has *carte blanche* both as to documents and place. In my view, this sort of enabling legislation is inconsistent with the principles enunciated in *Southam* and is unconstitutional.

*Southam* also sounds the death knell of writs of assistance issued under section 10 of the *Narcotic Control Act*, R.S.C. 1970, c. N-1. The section allowed a police officer to enter and search premises other than a dwelling house, on the authority of a writ of assistance, based only upon the officer's reasonable belief. In *R. v. Hamill*, [1984] 6 W.W.R. 530, a pre-*Southam* decision, the British Columbia Court of Appeal upheld the validity of section 10. *Hamill* is based upon the now-repudiated proposition that Parliament is entitled to decide whether the initial arbiter should be an administrative or quasi-judicial officer. After *Southam*, a person capable of acting judicially is required. As such, the Ontario Court of Appeal's decision in *R. v.*

*Noble* (1984), 48 O.R. (2d) 645, a post-*Southam* decision striking down writs of assistance in section 10, is clearly a correct statement of the law and is to be preferred over *Hamill*. In my view, section 10 is invalid and cannot be saved by the application of the reading down doctrine.

### Warrantless Searches

*Southam* dealt with the validity of a statutory authorization to search or seize, as opposed to the validity of any particular search. Nevertheless, certain inferences may be drawn from the case about when a warrantless search may be justified. Given the Supreme Court's emphasis on an individual's reasonable expectation of privacy and its requirement that prior authorizations be obtained "where it is feasible", the government will likely be able to justify warrantless searches in two kinds of situations.

The first is where the subject of the search has a diminished or non-existent expectation of privacy. Thus an individual standing on the threshold of her house in public view is liable to arrest without a warrant on a showing of probable cause. Similarly there is probably little or no reasonable expectation of privacy in vacated hotel rooms, articles exposed to public view, open fields, the exterior of an automobile, at customs, or in dealings with third parties such as banks. The rationale for the latter exclusion, at least in the United States, is that a person should expect his bank records to be amenable to subpoena. He therefore cannot expect the same degree of confidentiality with his bank as he can with his lawyer or priest. This rationale is not particularly convincing, notwithstanding the American jurisprudence. One should reasonably be able to expect confidentiality in one's dealing with a bank, and a neutral arbiter should be required to pass upon the sufficiency of the state's grounds for wanting to examine those dealings. It is to be hoped that this will be the law in Canada under the Charter.

The second category of cases where warrantless searches will likely be permissible is where the administration of justice would be unduly hampered if a warrant was required. This category of exception to the warrant requirement is based upon what may be compendiously called the "necessity rationale". Examples are searches of automobiles stopped with probable cause and searches after hot pursuit or in emergencies. The "automobile exception" to the warrant rule is a good illustration of the necessity rationale. It is also a useful admonition to the Canadian courts about the importance of grounding exceptions in a sound theoretical base. Recent American automobile cases have strayed from their origin, and we must be wary of importing them into Charter law.

In *Carroll v. United States*, 267 U.S. 132 (1925), the genesis of the automobile exception, the United States Supreme Court upheld warrantless automobile searches where there was probable cause to believe that evidence of an offence was in the car. The rationale was that the car could be driven away in the time it would take the police to obtain a proper warrant. Unfortunately, the court has since extended *Carroll* to the point where its original rationale has been left behind. In *Chambers v. Maroney*, 399 U.S. 42 (1970), the court upheld a warrantless search made after the police had impounded a car and driven it to the police station. The practical concerns supporting *Carroll* were thus not present in *Chambers*. The car was in police custody so it could not be driven away, and no substantial efficiency loss would have resulted from taking the time to get a warrant.

More recent decisions have gone even farther astray. Search warrants have generally been required for searches of luggage. Since it is easier to bring luggage than cars into police control, given space and storage constraints, there is arguably an efficiency rationale which distinguishes the two cases. Furthermore, a person has a greater expectation of privacy in his luggage. Inevitably, the question arose as to whether a warrant was needed where luggage was found in a car. One would have thought the Supreme Court would follow the luggage rather than the automobile line of cases. None of the justifications respecting warrantless searches are present whether luggage is found inside or outside a car. Luggage is relatively easy to secure pending issuance of the warrant so there are no urgent circumstances, and a person retains an equally reasonable expectation of privacy wherever it is found.

At first, the Supreme Court followed the luggage line of cases and held that search warrants were required for closed containers found in cars. It reversed itself in *United States v. Ross*, 102 S. Ct. 2157 (1982), holding that police may search closed containers where they have a general suspicion that contraband is in the car but do not know where. If the police specifically believe that the contraband is in the container, they need a warrant. The problem is that one never knows after the fact whether the police suspicion was specific or general, because the evidence of probable cause does not have to be submitted to a neutral magistrate prior to the search. Afterwards, it is easy to fit the evidence to the facts where the test is as susceptible to manipulation as the one enunciated by the court. Furthermore, *Ross* gives rise to a constitutional absurdity: why should the issue of whether luggage is found inside or outside a car have attained constitutional significance? The warrant rule should be the same wherever the luggage is found. The lesson to be learned from cases like *Chambers* and *Ross* is that while American cases are often useful in enunciating the policies underlying our similar constitutional guarantees, they should not always be followed. Each case must be assessed on its merits and followed only when it is based upon a sound rationale.

An interesting Canadian automobile example is *R. v. Esau* (1983), 147 D.L.R. (3d) 561 (Man. C.A.). The police received information that a vehicle of a particular description was being used in the sale of drugs at a particular place, and they observed it there three times. The Manitoba Court of Appeal held that even though the police were not "sure" they were stopping the right car, they had ample reason to search it without a warrant. It is, of course, arguable that since the car was in the same location three times it would return a fourth time, so the police should have obtained a warrant in the interval. However the counter-argument is that the police never knew from one time to the next whether the car would be back and, after observing the car three times in suspicious circumstances, they were not constitutionally required to gamble on it returning once more. While *Esau* is a difficult case on the facts, it can likely be justified on the exigency rationale for warrantless searches.

Another Manitoba case of interest is *R. v. Moretto* (1984), 28 M.V.R. 290 (Man. Q.B.). In *Moretto*, the police set up a "routine checkpoint" on the highway and stopped each vehicle coming through to check for licences and other automobile documentation. The police stopped the accused, examine his driver's licence and vehicle registration and transmitted the name and number to headquarters for a computer search. After a cursory visual search, the accused was released and continued on his way. Shortly thereafter the computer report came back indicating that the accused was listed as a "suspected cocaine trafficker". On the basis of this information, the police overtook the accused's vehicle, stopped his car a second time and searched. Drugs were found in a sports bag in the car.

Schwartz J. held that the first stop was valid as part of a routine check:

> The right to drive a motor vehicle on the Queen's Highways has been defined [by statute] to mean that the right is, in fact, a privilege to be exercised subject to certain restrictions contained in the *Highway Traffic Act*. Included in those restrictions are the obligations on the part of a prospective driver to be qualified; to hold an operator's permit; to carry same; to carry the registration card of the motor vehicle owner; and to produce them when required. The enforcement of these provisions do not constitute an unlawful search and seizure.

Unfortunately, Schwartz J. did not say why these provisions of the *Highway Traffic Act*, C.C.S.M., c. H60 were reasonable within the meaning of section 8 of the *Charter*. He merely asserted that they were. Given the decision in *Southam*, it is certainly arguable that statutory stop and search provisions are *prima facie* unconstitutional after *Southam*.

Schwartz J. went on to hold in the alternative, again without reasons, that even if the stop and check provisions of the *Highway Traffic Act* violated section 8 of the *Charter*, they were saved by section 1 as reasonable limits which are demonstrably justified in a free and democratic society. That is a justifiable result, though the Crown ought to have been required to lead evidence in support of its reliance on section 1. However, that aside, the case, with respect, correctly assesses the relationship between sections 1 and 8. On the face of it, one may ask how a search which is "unreasonable" within the meaning of section 8 may be "reasonable" for the purposes of section 1. It is a conundrum until one considers the *Southam* principle that the lack of a prior authorization requirement is *prima facie* unreasonable. Section 1 must then become operative to allow the Crown to lead evidence of reasonableness and demonstrable justification to support the search or seizure. It should be noted that the Supreme Court of Canada in *Southam* did not have to address the interrelationship between the two sections because no submissions were addressed to it on section 1.

Schwartz J. found that the second stop and search by the police was invalid. He held that a suspicion turned up by a computer search was not sufficient to constitute reasonable and probable grounds for believing that the accused had committed an offence or was in the process of doing so. However, having found a violation of section 8 in the second stop, Schwartz J. then refused to exclude the evidence pursuant to section 24(2). The scope and application of that section is beyond the bounds of this comment; however it is to be hoped that it will not develop into an emasculation of the protection in section 8 of the *Charter* through a too permissive reading of its concluding phrase, "bring[ing] the administration of justice into disrepute".

However the Canadian law on the search of automobiles develops, it is clear that in these and other cases warrantless searches are *prima facie* invalid and the burden of justifying them is heavy. Thus, cases such as *R. v. Burton* (1983), 1 D.L.R. (4th) 152 (Nfld. C.A.) must now be taken to have been wrongly decided. The Newfoundland Court of Appeal there upheld a warrantless search of lobster boxes anchored offshore, notwithstanding the fact that there were no exigent circumstances and there was ample time to acquire a search warrant.

A case like *R. v. Heisler* (1984), 8 D.L.R. (4th) 764 (Alta. C.A.) is more problematic. In *Heisler*, uniformed constables on special duty at a rock concert were instructed to deny entry to those who refused to submit to a check for drugs or alcohol. The accused purchased a ticket and, as she entered the concert, a constable asked to look in her purse. He did not give her the choice of either submitting to the search or leaving the premises. It was common ground that the constable did not have reasonable and probable grounds prior to the search to believe that the accused was carrying drugs. Upon finding a bag of marijuana in her purse, the constable took the accused to a security room where she voluntarily pulled another bag of marijuana out of her jeans and handed it to him. The trial judge excluded the evidence pursuant to sections 8 and 24(2) of the *Charter* and acquitted her. The Alberta Court of Appeal ordered a new trial.

The Court of Appeal agreed that the original search at the door was illegal, but it held that legality was not co-extensive with reasonableness. Lieberman J.A., speaking for the Court, approved Rehnquist J.'s decision in *Bell v. Wolfish*, 441 U.S. 520 at 559 (1979) that what is required is a balancing of the need for the search against the invasion of personal rights which it entails. One must look at the scope of the intrusion, the manner in which the search is conducted, the justification for initiating it and the place where it is done. In this case, the Court of Appeal held that the trial judge erred in not considering the nature of the event, a rock concert, or the duty of the occupier to ensure the safety of the persons attending it.

In my view, the Court of Appeal's approach was correct but its decision on the facts may be wrong. The court was right in holding that where the conduct of a search is impugned the test of reasonableness is a balancing of interests. In a rock concert situation, given the usual crush of people and the need for orderliness, it is not unreasonable to take steps to exclude alcohol or drugs for the protection of those in attendance. However, the search was not necessary to protect that interest in *Heisler*. The accused could simply have been informed of her option to leave. The constable's failure to do so should have vitiated the search. The Court of Appeal should have found section 8 to have been violated and proceeded to the question of the admissibility of the evidence pursuant to section 24(2).

## Production of Documents

*Southam* does not deal with the interesting question of whether the guarantee against unreasonable seizure comprehends compulsory production of documents. For example, section 17(1) of the *Combines Investigation Act* authorizes a member of the Restrictive Trade Practices Commission to require a corporate officer to make virtually unlimited production of corporate records. Similarly, section 11(4) of the *Ontario Securities Act* empowers an investigator to compel the attendance of witnesses and the production of documents. No independent arbiter is required to make a prior assessment of the reasonableness or relevance of the material sought. A person who fails to comply with the investigator's order may be committed for contempt by a Supreme Court judge. The judge is not authorized to inquire into the reasonableness of the investigator's order as a term of validity even after the fact, although the reasonableness of the order, or lack thereof, may be a factor in his decision about whether to commit for contempt.

The obvious distinction between entry and search on one hand and demand for production on the other is that in the former case there is an actual entry and concomitant physical invasion of privacy. There is no such direct intrusion with compulsory production of documents. While this distinction is superficially attractive, its dificulty is that if the purpose of section 8 is to protect privacy, it should apply where the state can accomplish the same result by ordering a person to produce all his records without apparent limitation. Pursuant to provisions like section 17(1) of the *Combines Investigation Act* or section 11(4) of the *Securities Act*, the public official wears the twin hats of investigator and adjudicator and performs a "constructive seizure" without the necessity of physical entry.

Canadian courts to date have been divided on whether section 8 covers compulsory production of documents. In *Attorney-General for Ontario v. Bear Island Foundation* (1982), 138 D.L.R. (3d) 683 (Ont. H.C.), Steele J. held, without reasons, that it does not, at least in a validly constituted action. It is not clear whether this was because compulsory production is not a "seizure" or because it was reasonable in the context of an action. In *Re Ziegler and Hunter* (1983), 8 D.L.R. (4th) 648 (Fed. C.A.), the applicants sought to prohibit the Director from acting upon certain orders for production issued pursuant to s. 17(1) of the *Combines Investigation Act*. A majority of the Federal Court of Appeal clearly took the position that section 8 of the *Charter* did not apply to production of documents because there was no uninvited entry or forcible seizure. The majority's decision has been followed in Ontario by the Divisional Court in *Belgoma Transportation Limited v. Director of Employment Standards* (1984), 47 O.R. (2d) 309 (Div. Ct.) [since approved by the Ontario Court of Appeal at 51 O.R. (2d) 509].

In *Re Alberta Human Rights Commission and Alberta Blue Cross Plan*, [1983] 6 W.W.R. 758 (Alta. C.A.), which the majority in *Ziegler* refused to follow, the Alberta Court of Appeal took the opposite position and held that compulsory production is indeed a seizure. The *Blue Cross* case involved a request for records belonging to an employer in connection with a preliminary investigation into a sex discrimination complaint. If proved, the alleged breach carried only civil consequences and the rules for production were analogous to those in civil proceedings. The Court therefore indicated that, while section 8 could be called in aid in an appropriate case, on the facts the demand for production was reasonable and valid. *Alberta Blue Cross* was followed in *Re Reich and College of Physicians and Surgeons of Alberta (No. 2)* (1984), 8 D.L.R. (4th) 696 (Alta. Q.B.).

In *Gershman Produce Co. Ltd. v. The Motor Transport Board*, [1985] 2 W.W.R. 63 (Man. Q.B.), Kroft J. of the Manitoba Court of Queen's Bench struck down a compulsory production statute pursuant to section 8 of the Charter. The applicant in *Gershman* held a commercial/public service vehicle licence and was alleged to have committed certain infractions thereof. The Motor Transport Board sent the applicant a notice to show cause why its licence should not be amended or revoked, followed by a demand pursuant to section 255(1)(n) of *The Highway Traffic Act* to produce all its accounting records for an eleven month period. The demand was in no way limited to the alleged infractions.

Section 255(1)(n) of *The Highway Traffic Act* incorporated by reference *mutatis mutandis* the provisions of section 27(2) of *The Public Utilities Board Act*, C.C.S.M. c. P280 which read as follows:

> The board, or any person authorized by the board to make inquiry or report, may, where it appears expedient,
> (a) enter upon and inspect any place, building, works or other property;
> (b) require the attendance of all such persons as it or he thinks fit to summon and examine and take the testimony of the persons;
> (c) administer oaths, affirmations, or declarations, and summon witnesses, enforce their attendance, and compel them to give evidence and produce the books, plans, specifications, drawings, and documents, which it or he may require them to produce.

Kroft J.'s analysis of the validity of section 255(1)(n) commenced with the obvious but apt to be overlooked point that section 8 guarantees the right to be secure against "unreasonable search *or* seizure". The phrase is disjunctive. A search is therefore not a necessary concomitant to the invocation of the section. After reviewing the *Blue Cross, Reich* and *Ziegler* cases, Kroft J. said:

> Under the legislation which I must consider, the Board, or a person designated by it, has the power to enter and inspect any place without prior approval, although that power is not specifically now under consideration. It also has the unrestricted right to require the production of documents, and by virtue of s. 24(4) of *The Public Utilities Board Act*, has all the powers vested in the Court of Queen's Bench or a judge thereof.
>
> It must also be remembered that the Board has more than an administrative and investigative function. The documents which it has the power to demand be produced may be used during the show cause hearing. That hearing can result in the imposition of very real penalties. Furthermore, pursuant to s. 290 of *The Highway Traffic Act*, there can also be a prosecution and, on summary conviction, a fine of up to $2,000.00.
>
> Within the context of *The Highway Traffic Act* I have concluded that the right of the Board or its appointee to require unrestricted production is in fact a power of seizure within the contemplation of s. 8 of the *Charter*.

Kroft J. went on to hold that, in light of *Southam*, a forced production of documents which is not reviewed prior to issuance by a neutral arbiter and is unrestricted by relevance is unreasonable and inconsistent with section 8. Unfortunately, he did not specifically address the majority argument in *Ziegler* that uninvited entry is a necessary element of section 8. He simply agreed with the Alberta cases that compulsory production is a seizure and applied the *Southam* criteria to determine reasonableness. The difficulty with Kroft J.'s reasoning is that it contains a quantum leap. It is possible to admit that forced production is a "seizure" within the meaning of section 8 while still denying that it can ever be "unreasonable" in constitutional terms. Restated, *Ziegler* and *Southam* can be reconciled if one takes the position, which did not have to be addressed in *Southam*, that actual entry is a necessary element of "privacy" as that word is constitutionally understood. Kroft J.'s decision does not address that fundamental issue.

In my opinion, the *Ziegler* view of the scope of section 8 is too narrow and Kroft J.'s ultimate conclusion that forced production can be unreasonable is correct. A person's private papers are private whether someone comes in and takes them or one is forced to hand them over. The fact that there is no actual uninvited entry by a public official certainly goes to the issue of reasonableness, and the standards of reasonableness may be higher for an entry and search than a demand for production. However, an open-ended demand for documents backed up by the power of the state is certainly a seizure as that word is generally understood. The guarantee in section 8 of the Charter should be available to cover it.

### Conclusion

The protection afforded by the constitutional guarantee against unreasonable search or seizure has taken a long step forward with the Supreme Court of Canada's decision in *Southam*. The Supreme Court has adopted what Dickson J. termed a "purposive" test. The courts must inquire into the underlying purposes of the particular constitutional guarantee at issue and be prepared to give it a broad inter-pretation consistent with its goals. It is to be hoped that in other *Charter* cases currently before it the court will apply the same broad reasoning and philosophy to other constitutional guarantees that it has to search and seizure.

[The *Gershman* case was subsequently overruled by the Manitoba Court of Appeal on the basis of the *Ziegler* reasoning.]

# 22

# Equality Rights

## A PRINCIPLED APPROACH TO EQUALITY RIGHTS: A PRELIMINARY ENQUIRY

Marc Gold (1982), 4 Sup. Ct. L.R. 131 (footnotes omitted)

. . . .

### I. THE SEARCH FOR A PRINCIPLED DECISION

How are we to understand the claim that section 15 can be interpreted in a principled way? At the outset, let us be clear as to what the claim does not involve.

Every legal decision involves the exercise of judgment. Even the most uncontroversial norm (of which equality is *not* an example) is not self-applying. In the context of constitutional adjudication, the final judgment usually rests with the courts, and in this sense, Justice Hughes' well-known dictum is correct. But this commonplace about the courts' power of decision-making should not be confused with the claim that the judiciary should be free to decide a case any way it chooses, unencumbered by doctrinal and institutional constraints. Judicial power is limited by judicial duty — the duty to take into consideration certain basic principles that inform the enterprise upon which the court is embarked. The crucial questions are whether these principles are defensible as standards to guide a court in its deliberations, and whether they are determinate enough to provide such guidance.

By definition, a principle does not apply in an all or nothing fashion. It may point towards a given decision, but it does not determine the decision in the way in which it is said that a rule does. It follows that the particular weight that a given judge may give a particular principle will be the subject of controversy, and judges will differ as amongst themselves. To speak of the resulting decisions as either right or wrong may be to use language inappropriate to the art of adjudication. Nevertheless, there may be principles upon which judges can rely in a hard case that allow us to say of the decision that it is or it is not the appropriate or proper decision given the circumstances of the particular case.

One must keep in mind the limitations of the inquiry herein pursued. The focus is not on what equality might mean as an abstract political idea. Our concern is with how the courts should interpret the equality rights provisions of the *Charter*. As such, the starting point must be the text and structure of the constitution itself. The court must accept as valid the system of rights and freedoms that are set out in it.

What are the principles that can guide a court in interpreting the equality rights provisions? The first is that of fidelity to the text of the constitution itself. The court must take the language employed seriously, keeping within the terms of reference provided by the text. This is not to suggest that it is desirable, or even possible, to restrict the judicial inquiry to a parsing of constitutional language. As Charles Black Jr. wrote: "The precision of textual explication is nothing but specious in the areas that matter." This is especially so with respect to the equality rights provisions of the *Charter*, for, as the following section will suggest, the judiciary has the power to choose how it resolves issues arising under section 15. To cite Black again: "The question is not whether the text shall be respected, but rather how one goes about respecting a text of that high generality and consequent ambiguity which marks so many crucial constitutional texts." Nevertheless, the text is the appropriate starting point for the judicial inquiry. It is only by exploring the text that one can appreciate both the guidance it may provide and its inherent limitations.

The second principle is that of fidelity to the structure of the constitution as a whole, and to the relationships it contemplates both between individuals and government, and between various institutions of government. Although this may appear to be saying no more than that a specific constitutional provision must be interpreted in context, the implications of this principle are significant. It may turn out that, when viewed as a whole, the constitution will suggest the appropriate role for the court to take.

The third principle follows from the second. We might call it the principle of the institutional division of labour. It speaks to the necessity of the court respecting the legitimate domains of other governmental institutions seized with issues of rights and freedoms. More about this below.

## II. The Language of Section 15

The text of section 15 must be understood as the end product of a process which began with the *Canadian Bill of Rights* [R.S.C. 1970, App. III]. Section 1(b) of the *Bill of Rights* referred to equality before the law and the protection of the law. The original draft of section 15 spoke in terms of equality before the law and equal protection of the law, and listed a number of grounds on the basis of which discrimination was enjoined. In response to a large number of representations before the special Joint Committee of The Senate and House of Commons, the language of section 15 was changed to include the concepts of equality under the law and the equal benefit of the law. In addition, the list of prohibited grounds was expanded by the inclusion of mental and physical disability. The legislative history of section 15 supports the view that the intention was to overcome some of the narrow interpretations of equality before the law that had developed under the *Bill of Rights*.

### 1. Equal Benefit of the Law

The concept of equal benefit admits of a variety of conceptions. If unconstrained by its context and legislative history, it could prove to be a very intrusive and expansive norm. Such a role for the concept was not intended by the drafters of section 15. The inclusion of this concept was a response to a perceived implication of the *Bliss* case [[1979] 1 S.C.R. 183]: it was intended to ensure that the provision of governmental benefits (like unemployment insurance) was not insulated from judicial review merely because such benefits are creations of the legislature.

It must be acknowledged that a court may take a wider view of the concept and deviate from the original intention. Nonetheless, the interpretation given to any concept must be consistent with the overall structure of the constitution and the political ideology of which it is a part. In the third section of this paper, I suggest that the Charter is best viewed as a post-liberal compromise of rights, a characterization which, if accurate, should suggest certain limits to the concept of equal benefit.

## 2. Equality Before and Under the Law

The other concept which was added as a result of the work of the Special Joint Committee was that of equality under the law. The legislative history makes it clear that this concept was intended to ensure that judicial review extended to the content of the law, and not just to the manner in which the law is administered.

This latter restrictive interpretation was said to have been the way in which the concept of equality before the law had been interpreted under the *Canadian Bill of Rights*. To be sure, Ritchie J. had invoked such a conception in both *Lavell* [[1974] S.C.R. 1349] and *Bliss*, but it is inaccurate to say that this conception exhausted the concept of equality before the law as it has been applied. *R. v. Drybones* [[1970] S.C.R. 282] was a case where the content of the law was challenged successfully, and the valid federal objective test, as it has evolved, also speaks to the question of the law's substantive content. As such, this changed terminology appears to have been unnecessary from an analytical perspective, but it can be defended as a harmless (and perhaps salutary) signal to the courts to pay attention to the various ways in which equality rights can be infringed.

To assert that section 15 applies to both the content of the law and the way in which it is administered tells us nothing about what equality demands in these contexts. The issues respecting challenges to the administration of the law are beyond the scope of this essay. Suffice it to say here that, if the American experience is any guide in these matters, the virtually unrestricted privileges of prosecution afforded to provincial attorneys-general might come to be constrained by the equality rights provisions. With respect to challenges to the content of the law, the starting point should be the principles which have been developed under the *Canadian Bill of Rights* respecting equality before the law.

The most general, and most promising, conception of equality before the law was enunciated by McIntyre J. in *MacKay v. R.* [[1980] 2 S.C.R. 370] where the nature of the judicial inquiry was described as follows:

> [A]s a minimum it would be necessary to inquire whether an inequality has been created for a valid federal constitutional objective, whether it has been created rationally in the sense that it is not arbitrary or capricious and not based upon any ulterior motive or motives offensive to the provisions of the *Canadian Bill of Rights*, and whether it is a necessary departure from the general principle of universal application of the law for the attainment of some necessary and desirable social objective.

A number of features of this conception should be noted here. First, the concept of invalidity refers not only to the division of powers in the constitution, but also to the compatibility of the law with the Bill of Rights (and now the Charter). This suggests that laws that appear to offend a right or freedom guaranteed in the Charter are vulnerable to challenges under section 15, as well as under the specific provisions at issue, a position consistent with the interpretation of the equal protection clause of the Fourteenth Amendment to the American Constitution.

Second, this conception of equality makes explicit that the impugned inequality must have a rational connection to the purposes ostensibly served by the law. The demand of rationality taken literally is exceedingly easy to satisfy. For the requirement of rationality to be more than tautological, the court must impose some limits on the objectives pursued by legislation, and require that the purposes invoked in legal argument before the court actually be the purposes that informed the enactment of the legislation. More generally, the efficacy of this conception of equality will depend largely upon who has the burden of demonstrating that the law is or is not rationally related to its stated or implicit purpose, an issue not addressed by McIntyre J. in *MacKay*.

Finally, this conception of equality before the law requires the court to assess the means employed by the law in light of the objectives desired. Although McIntyre J. spoke in terms of a "necessary departure from the general principles of uniform application of law" and of "social objectives" being both desirable and necessary, one should not attach too much weight to the form of words employed. In certain cases, the standard of necessity might be appropriate, whereas it might be inappropriate in others. Indeed, in the *MacKay* case itself, the strong language employed by McIntyre J. concealed the deferential way in which the test was actually applied. The point to be retained here is that the Court is called upon to pass judgment on both the means employed and the ends pursued by law. This it should be noted, is the same kind of judgment that is contemplated by section 1 of the Charter.

Although this conception of equality before the law appears to provide the outlines of the judicial inquiry, it fails to provide guidance in certain fundamental respects. It is silent as to who bears the burden of demonstrating that the impugned law is or is not reasonable and justified, and by what measure that burden can be satisfied. Moreover, this conception was developed under the *Canadian Bill of Rights*, and therefore does not address certain questions that are unique to section 15 of the Charter. Should the court apply one standard of review to all legislation that employs the classifications listed in section 15, and a different standard to legislation employing other bases of classification? Should the court employ a different standard when evaluating a racially-based legislative classification than it would in the face of, say, an age-based classification? What is the significance of the concept of discrimination set out in section 15? What is the relationship between these questions and the nature of the inquiry contemplated by section 1?

These questions will be addressed below. First, let us consider the last conception of equality rights appearing in section 15, that of equal protection of the law.

## 3. Equal Protection of the Law

Inasmuch as section 15 borrowed the concept from the Fourteenth Amendment to the American Constitution, the relevance of the American experience to adjudication under the Charter of Rights need not be debated. But while it is clear that our courts will get some guidance from American jurisprudence in this area, one should not expect instant answers to the questions identified above.

First, all legal doctrine must be understood as the product of the society (and its ideologies) of which it is a part. This is a commonplace amongst comparative lawyers, but it can be overlooked in the search for answers to hard questions. The Canadian historical experience is quite different from the American, as are the respective political cultures and these differences may prove important when deciding how our courts ought to approach the evaluation of certain kinds of legislative activity.

Second, equal protection analysis itself is in a state of disarray and confusion. American judges admit that the search for the proper meaning to be attached to that concept has been almost metaphysical in its scope, and concede that their judicial opinions often lack "consistency and clarity." This judgment is shared by the academic community as well. Nonetheless, some guidance from American jurisprudence may be available.

On the surface, the elements of equal protection analysis are easy to state. The general rule is that a legislative classification need only be related rationally to a legitimate governmental end, the burden of demonstrating that is not lying on the person challenging the law. This "minimal scrutiny", incorporated into McIntyre J.'s conception of the valid federal objective test, lies at one extreme of equal protection analysis. It almost never results in the law being declared unconstitutional.

An exception to this deferential standard of review is made in cases where the law employs a basis of classification deemed suspect or invidious, or where the law impinges upon a right deemed fundamental. In such cases, strict scrutiny is applied and the law must be justified as being necessary to achieve a compelling governmental interest. The burden of justification lies on the person seeking to uphold the law; virtually no law survives this degree of judicial scrutiny.

In between these two extremes, American courts are practising, if not always admitting, an intermediate standard of review. This standard is triggered when laws impinge upon interests deemed important, though not fundamental, or when the law employs a basis of classification deemed sensitive, though not suspect. In such cases, the law must be substantially related to an important governmental interest, with the burden of justification sometimes, but not always, resting upon the person seeking to uphold the law.

This brief outline reveals that the first step is one of characterizing both the nature of the interest affected and the legislative classification employed. As in all questions of characterization, there is no mechanical way to make the choice. It is a choice which reflects the principles and policies underlying the constitutional order itself, a choice which reflects the judges' sense of what that order entails. Consider first the fundamental rights strand of equal protection analysis in the United States.

The rights deemed fundamental, and therefore attracting strict scrutiny, have been held to include the right to marry, to control one's own reproductive system, to travel throughout the country, to vote, and to litigate in the courts. On the other hand, the U.S. Supreme Court has refused to expand the concept of fundamental rights to include, among others, the right to decent housing or the right to a decent education. What underlies this taxonomy? To what extent can it provide guidance to Canadian courts?

Regarding the first question, one can identify a reluctance on the part of the judiciary to impose affirmative obligations on government, even when such an obligation would be necessary to guarantee the equal value of formally equal rights. However understandable is this reluctance, it cannot be controlling in the Canadian context. The *Charter* itself imposes such obligations on government with respect to language rights, and the constitution speaks to a governmental commitment to the provision of essential public services to all Canadians. Nevertheless, we can expect our courts to be resistant to a role that would have them impose positive obligations on government, if for no other reason than that it seems inconsistent with the institutional division of labour implied by the existence of democratic institutions charged with these responsibilities.

Can (and should) those rights deemed fundamental be confined to those expressly protected by the constitution? The American judiciary has not confined them in this way, as the abortion and travel cases reveal. What has informed the court in this area is a sense of what values are pre-supposed by the constitution itself. It is here that the American experience may prove valuable.

If we step back from the details of American jurisprudence in this area, we can identify three values which underlie the courts' doctrine, values which have their counterpart in the Canadian constitutional order. The first is the value of democratic government. Some of the rights deemed fundamental in American constitutional law are those which are thought necessary for the proper functioning of democratic institutions. This link between fundamental rights and democracy is a theme which has played a role in our constitutional history, and is one which finds expression in the *Charter* itself.

The second value attaches to the concept of nationhood and the corresponding idea of national citizenship. This, it has been suggested, explains not only the importance attached to the right to travel, but the extent to which federal courts have protected individuals against state attempts to limit court access. In Canada, these ideas of nationhood and citizenship have had a limited impact on the fabric of our law. Centralizing as they are, such concepts have been tempered in light of the powerful role played by the provinces in Canadian federalism. Nevertheless, these ideas to a large extent underlie the mobility rights provisions of the *Charter* itself.

Since conceptions of nationhood and citizenship vary from society to society, it is appropriate for our courts to pay careful attention to those elements unique to Canada. These include the following: (1) the concept of two founding nations — more myth than reality perhaps, but a powerful myth which finds expression in our constitutional documents; (2) the recognition given to the position of Canada's aboriginal peoples; and (3) the commitment to multi-culturalism. Interests bound up with these values — like educational opportunities and other governmental benefits — ought to be deemed sufficiently fundamental to the concepts of Canadian nationhood and citizenship to deserve special protection at the hands of the judiciary.

Finally, and most problematic, is the value of individual liberty. American jurisprudence reflects a concern for limiting governmental coercion over individuals, and the entire range of cases that turned on a substantive conception of the due process clause can only be understood in these terms. In Canada, references to individual liberty appear in the *Charter*, and whatever are the differences in political culture between the United States and Canada, burdens on individual liberty which are distributed unequally will tend to attract a significant degree of judicial scrutiny.

None of this is to suggest that there is an easy way for the courts to discover and apply so-called fundamental values. Indeed, some would argue that such a search is bound to fail, with the result being the imposition of the judges' own values. This may be too blunt. In determining the importance of various interests affected by the law, courts will get clues from both the text of the *Charter* and the values implied by the text. At the end of the day, however, the courts will have to develop some theory of the underlying purposes which inform the enterprise upon which they are embarked. The point to be emphasized here is the significance of the courts' evaluation of the importance of the interests affected by the law under review; the more important is deemed the interest, the greater will be the degree of judicial scrutiny.

The question of characterization also arises with respect to the basis of the classification employed in the law. Issues analogous to those considered above also underlie the choice of the appropriate standard of review. In this area, great care must be taken with respect to the applicability of American doctrine for purposes of interpreting section 15 of the *Charter*.

Section 15 lists a number of grounds, not all of which have attracted the same level of scrutiny under the equal protection clause. For example, racially-based classifications attract strict scrutiny, gender-based ones intermediate scrutiny, and age-based classifications only minimal scrutiny. Moreover, the differences between Canadian and American society, both in their historical experiences and present structures, may make it problematic to adopt American doctrine without qualification. More about this below. It also seems appropriate to consider the reasons why American doctrine singles out certain groups for extraordinary protection. Once again, we can identify three considerations underlying American doctrine in this area, all of which are potentially appropriate for consideration by Canadian courts.

The first consideration is that of relevancy. It has been noted that some bases of classification are virtually never relevant to legitimate governmental purposes, whereas others are. Consider the following remarks of Justice Stevens:

> Equal protection analysis is often said to involve different 'levels of scrutiny'. It may be more accurate to say that the burden of sustaining an equal protection challenge is much heavier in some cases than in others. Racial classifications, which are subjected to 'strict scrutiny', are presumptively invalid because there is seldom, if ever, any legitimate reason for treating citizens differently because of their race. On the other hand, most economic classifications are presumptively valid because they are a necessary component of most regulatory programmes. . . .

The second consideration is the presence or absence of a historical pattern of discrimination directed at the group in question. The paradigmatic case is that of race, and in particular the treatment of black Americans — the institution of slavery and decades of legally sanctioned discrimination and segregation.

The third consideration is related to the second, and it speaks to the possibility that the political process might disregard the interests of particular groups. Where a group is politically powerless — especially where that is a function of a historical pattern of discrimination — it may signal that its interests have been overlooked in the legislative calculus. This is said to explain the measures of protection afforded to aliens in American law, as it does to some degree explain the suspicion with which racially-based laws are viewed.

These considerations suggest that what really concerns the American courts is the possibility that certain kinds of laws have been motivated by an improper desire to discriminate against a certain group. Inasmuch as McIntyre J. alluded to the question of legislative motive in his conception of equality before the law, and considering that section 15 speaks expressly of discrimination, it is appropriate to consider this concept further.

### 4. Discrimination

Two questions arise with respect to the concept of discrimination. First, must one establish discrimination before one can argue that one's equality rights have been infringed? Second, in cases where discrimination is relevant, what does the concept mean?

The first question arose under the *Canadian Bill of Rights* and was resolved by the Supreme Court holding that (1) equality before the law could be violated (in principle) absent discrimination on one of the grounds set out in section 1 and (2) that a law which does discriminate on the basis of an enumerated ground is not inoperative *per se*, but must be shown to have violated equality before the law. This position is consistent with American jurisprudence under the equal protection clause: a law may violate equal protection absent discrimination if it burdens a so-called fundamental right.

A similar interpretation is available under the *Charter*. First, one can read the concepts of equality before and under the law as being free-standing, that is, not tied grammatically to the concept of discrimination set out in section 15. Insofar as these concepts of equality incorporate McIntyre J.'s conception of equality before the law, which itself incorporates the outlines of American equal protection doctrine, it seems clear that the establishment of discrimination is not a necessary element in a claim under section 15. Nonetheless, most issues will involve allegations of discrimination. What then is discrimination?

It seems fairly clear that it means something more than classification. At a minimum it entails that the particular group identified in the law must suffer adversely by virtue of the law. This is the dominant position taken with respect to the concept of discrimination as it appears in provincial human rights codes, and it finds support in the case law decided under the *Canadian Bill of Rights*. This, however, is only the beginning of the inquiry, for unless discrimination involves something more than an adverse effect, it is redundant in light of the practical realities of litigation under the *Charter*.

No person will challenge a law on the basis that he or she receives a benefit where others do not; real-world cases will concern claims that a person has been adversely affected by the law. If section 15 is designed to enjoin, at least potentially, legislative burdens defined in terms, say, of race, the concept of discrimination becomes the functional equivalent of the concept of classification, at least in practical terms. Moreover, section 15(2) is designed to insulate from judicial review those programmes designed to benefit disadvantaged individuals or groups. It would seem, therefore, that section 15(1), by its own logic, presupposes an adverse impact on the person challenging the law.

The key to understanding the concept of discrimination inheres in the process of justification that is central to any claim raised under section 15. Recall McIntyre J.'s allusion to the relevance of legislative motive. If the only justification offered in defence of a law was that the law was designed to take away rights from the group specified in the law, the defence of the law would fail. To be sure, the judicial inquiry is never rendered so simple, but this rather fanciful case illustrates the evil that section 15, and the concept of discrimination, was intended to combat.

Discrimination involves not only burdening a particular individual or group *per se*; it involves the imposition of burdens for particular kinds of reasons. These reasons involve a denial of the essential worth and dignity of the class against whom the law is directed, a denial based upon unwarranted stereotypes about the capacities and roles of the members of that class. When legislation is enacted with these as motivating reasons, that legislation is discriminatory. As such, unless the person defending the law can justify the law in other terms, the law will offend the equality rights provisions of the *Charter*.

It is important to appreciate the role that the standard of review plays in bringing to light a discriminatory purpose on the part of the legislature. It has been suggested that the key issue in equality rights adjudication is one of justifying the impugned law. Given that a motive to discriminate is no justification at all, the court might be able to infer a discriminatory motive from the fact that the reasons advanced in justification do not explain adequately the means chosen to achieve the stated purpose of the law.

This, it has been suggested, is the function of the strict scrutiny doctrine in the United States. By requiring both a compelling state interest and a necessary connection between means and ends, strict scrutiny will invalidate a law passed with a discriminatory intent. If the person defending the law articulates the real motivation behind the law, that is, a discriminatory intent, the law will be struck down as unsupported by a valid governmental interest. If the defender of the law submits a legislative purpose independent of the discriminatory intent, but that purpose was not the motivating force behind the law, the law will tend not to satisfy the rigours of the means-end test demanded by strict scrutiny.

## 5. What Standard(s) of Review?

What standard or standards of review should our courts apply under section 15? As noted elsewhere in this Volume, the answer to this question will determine the legal effectiveness of the equality rights provisions. Is there a principled way to answer this question?

At the outset, we confront a set of conflicting signals emanating from the *Charter*. Section 15 adopts the American concept of equal protection of the law. Does it also incorporate the particular doctrines that have developed under this concept? If so, section 15 would embody the idea of classifications which are suspect, semi-suspect and (presumably) above suspicion, with the three standards of review that follow from these characterizations. On the other hand, section 15 lists a number of grounds explicitly — grounds on the basis of which discrimination is enjoined. Furthermore, these grounds do not exhaust the prohibition against discrimination. This might suggest that the same standard of review should be applied to laws that classify on the basis of one of the grounds enumerated, and that such a standard should be a rigorous one.

To add to the confusion is the presence of section 1. If the standard or standards of review are a function exclusively of the concepts embodied in section 15, it would appear as if section 1 has no independent function in relation to section

15. This would be undesirable given the presumption that a provision in a constitution (or indeed, in any law) ought to be given some operative meaning if possible. On the other hand, if section 1 is an integral part of every issue arising under section 15, the idea of a discrete number of standards of review becomes problematic. Since section 1 is silent as to what constitutes "reasonable limits" or counts as a justification in "a free and democratic society", it will be impossible to articulate one, or even three, standards of review; in truth, there may be as many standards as there are cases arising under section 15.

Whatever approach is adopted by the courts, it should ensure four things. First, it should permit section 1 to have some operative meaning. Second, it should accommodate the fact that various grounds were listed explicitly in section 15. Third, it should attempt to be faithful to the conceptions of equality rights set out in the *Charter*. Finally, the courts must be sensitive to the unique features of our political and legal culture.

Adherence to these principles would render certain approaches problematic. For example, assume that a court adopted the American standards of review, and applied strict scrutiny where laws classified on the basis of race, national or ethnic origin, or religion. In addition to creating problems associated with section 1 and with the fact that other grounds are prohibited explicitly, such an approach appears inconsistent with certain aspects of our legal culture as exemplified in our constitution itself.

Consider first the issue of the native peoples of Canada. Our courts already have recognized the tension between the concept of equality in the *Canadian Bill of Rights* and the express authority over Indians granted to Parliament by virtue of the constitution. This tension may be aggravated by whatever content is given to section 35 of the *Constitution Act, 1982*. Quite apart from any considerations pertaining to affirmative action programmes for native peoples, their unique position in Canadian law makes strict scrutiny untenable as a standard of review. Our legal culture simply is not status-blind in this area.

Similar considerations are relevant to the concept of national and ethnic origin. Historically, some of the worst discrimination in Canadian legal history has been directed against groups because of their national or ethnic origin. On the other hand, section 27 directs the court to interpret the *Charter* "in a manner consistent with the preservation and enhancement of the multicultural heritage of Canadians." Were a law to classify on the basis of national or ethnic origin, say, in relation to some aspect of education, could strict scrutiny be justified as the standard of review?

The same problem arises in connection with religion. Section 93 of the *Constitution Act, 1867* contemplates the existence of educational systems designed on the basis of religion, and section 29 of the *Charter* purports to insulate such systems from challenges under the *Charter*. Given this acceptance of religion as an appropriate basis of legislative classification in this context, does strict scrutiny make much sense as a general standard of review? If the adoption of the American standards of review appears problematic in light of these considerations, similar difficulties surround an approach that would have a rigorous standard apply uniformly to laws that classify on the basis of one of the listed grounds. Recall again the three reasons underlying the special protections afforded certain groups in American law.

In terms of historical patterns of discrimination, all of the groups listed in section 15 may have been victimized by public and private acts of discrimination, but not to the same degree. In terms of relevance, some of the grounds listed appear to be less relevant to the achievement of a legitimate governmental purpose than do others. Is the range of such relevant race-based distinctions the same as the range of relevant age-based distinctions? Finally, it is hard to see some of the groups as politically powerless, assuming that this is a relevant factor for a court to entertain in determining the appropriate standard(s) of review.

The language of section 15 is the result of intensive and successful lobbying on the part of representatives of some of the groups listed in the section. For example, the inclusion of mental and physical disability as a listed ground would appear to have been a consequence of the lobbying done by and on behalf of the disabled. In the International Year of the Handicapped could the government have resisted the political pressure that was brought to bear on this issue? Concerning sex discrimination, it is arguable that the representatives of women's organizations had the greatest impact on the equality rights provisions: the language of section 15 (to say nothing of section 28) was undoubtedly and directly influenced by their political efforts. In this respect, Professor Russell's remarks, although blunt, seem accurate:

> Section 15 was developed primarily on public relations grounds as a means of co-opting highly visible and vocal interest groups in supporting the Trudeau government's unilateral constitutional restructuring.

These considerations seem to point towards the need for a more flexible approach by the courts, one that could accommodate the complexities of the issues involved in contemporary disputes about equality rights. One such approach might be as follows. The court could treat section 15 as if it provided for the universal application of the law. Once an inequality in the law had been established, the inquiry would shift to section 1, and the court would determine whether or not the law was justified. The virtues of such an approach are three-fold.

First, it would provide for a more flexible judicial inquiry, allowing courts to recognize the differences that may obtain between, say, race and age as a basis for legislative classification. It would also enable a court to resolve some of the issues noted in the discussion of the problems with strict scrutiny. Wherever the constitution either grants jurisdiction over a group or activity defined in terms of one of the grounds listed in section 15 (*e.g.*, Indians or denominational schools), or expressly contemplates that certain status-based differences are of value (*e.g.*, multiculturalism), legislative action necessary to promote these constitutional values could be justified under section 1.

Second, such an approach would be consistent with the conception of equality before the law as articulated by McIntyre J. in *MacKay*. In the uncertainty that surrounds the scope and impact of the *Charter*, a measure of continuity between the pre-*Charter* and post-*Charter* era is not to be disparaged. Finally, the approach has the virtue of giving operative effect to section 1. As such, it is to be preferred to an approach that would render such a provision superfluous.

Notwithstanding the allure of this approach, there are conceptual and practical problems which suggest that further refinements are necessary. At the conceptual level, such an approach would be inconsistent with the notion of the equal protection of the law as it has evolved in American jurisprudence. Had the drafters of the *Charter* intended to treat section 15 rights as the equivalent of the right to have all laws apply equally to everyone, subject to limitations flowing from section 1, they could easily have done so. Can we ignore the fact that they did otherwise?

The practical problem is a function of section 28 of the *Charter* as it may relate to affirmative action programmes designed for the benefit of women. Section 15(2) of the *Charter* is an attempt to insulate affirmative action programmes from challenges under section 15(1); it is assumed that it would preclude a male from arguing that his equality rights were abridged by a programme designed for the benefit of women. The problem then arises with respect to section 28, which provides that : "[N]otwithstanding anything in this *Charter*, the rights and freedoms referred to are guaranteed equally to male and female persons."

The following should be noted about section 28. First, it is intended to operate notwithstanding anything in the *Charter*. It is fair to assume that this includes section 1. Second, section 15(2) does not appear to be a rights-conferring provision; it is thus doubtful whether it could be termed a right "referred to" in the *Charter*. What is the situation then, when a male challenges an affirmative action programme on the combined basis of sections 15(1) and 28? If section 15(1) is read to mean the universal application of the law and if sections 1 and 15(2) are omitted in the analysis, such an affirmative action programme presumably would fail. But this, for better or for worse, flies on the face of the extraordinary measures taken through section 15(2) to insulate such programmes from judicial review.

The way out of this apparent dilemma is to accept that the various equality rights in section 15 contain within them the idea that they are subject to reasonable limits which can be justified by the purposes of the law. As such, a challenge to an affirmative action programme under section 28 might not succeed were the court to conclude that the programme itself was reasonable and justifiable. In other words, the equality rights referred to in the *Charter* contain within them a non-absolutist conception. Such an approach would be consistent with the point made earlier, that the court must try to remain faithful to the conception of rights set out in the *Charter* as a whole.

We are not out of the woods yet, for the approach just outlined appears to make section 1 redundant again. This is not desirable in principle, and in practice it would weaken the protection that section 15 is intended to provide. Where an American court applies the standard of minimal scrutiny, or where a Canadian court applies the valid federal objective test, the onus of demonstrating the law was not justified lies on the challenger. As noted above, this also obtains in some of the American cases employing an intermediate standard of review. On the assumption that section 1 puts the burden of justification on the person defending the law, it seems as if greater protection is afforded by using section 1 as the guide, rather than remaining faithful to the doctrines associated with the equality rights set out in section 15.

The solution is to allow section 1 to alter the doctrine respecting who has the burden of justification. In other words, section 1 can be seen to exercise a modifying effect on the contours of doctrine within section 15 itself. This, I suggest, would constitute an improvement over the minimal scrutiny and valid federal objective test that courts traditionally apply.

We are still left with the problem of giving effect to the grounds listed in section 15. At least with respect to who has the initial burden of justification, this can be accomplished in the following way. Where a law classifies on the basis of one of the grounds listed in section 15, the burden shifts to the person defending the law to justify it. For example, whereas American courts would treat an age-based classification as appropriate for minimal scrutiny and therefore impose the burden on the person challenging the law, a Canadian court, using section 1 as a modifying provision, could put the burden on the person defending the law in such a case. However, where the law classifies on a ground not listed in section 15, the traditional rules with respect to burdens of justification in minimal scrutiny situations would apply.

### 6. The Structure of the Inquiry

In general terms, the structure of the inquiry would be as follows. Where a law does not classify on the basis of one of the grounds listed in section 15, the person challenging the law has the burden of making out a *prima facie* case of a denial of equality rights. Such a case would be established if the classification appears irrelevant to the purpose that one could infer underlies the law. If such a case were made out, the burden shifts to the person defending the law to demonstrate the relevance of the classification to the purposes of the law. Where a law does classify on the basis of a ground listed in section 15 (or has an impact on an interest deemed fundamental or close to it), the burden shifts automatically to the person defending the law.

At this stage, the person defending the law need only show that the classification is relevant to a legitimate governmental purpose. As Professor Conklin suggests, the purpose should be the one that actually informed the enactment of the law, not one invented *ex post facto* for the purposes of litigation.

Assuming that the person defending the law has made out a *prima facie* case that the classification is relevant, the onus shifts back to the person challenging the law to refute the claim of relevance. To discharge the onus, one must offer a rationale for the law which is more plausible than the one tendered in argument by the other side. Such a claim would be established when the purpose offered better explains the over- or under-inclusiveness that characterizes the impugned law. (Virtually all laws will exhibit some degree of "misfit".) The person challenging the law must establish that the real purpose underlying the law is somehow impermissible — for example, a discriminatory purpose or a desire to punish some individual or group for having exercised their constitutional rights. Logically, evidence of such an impermissible purpose could be completely circumstantial. Direct evidence, of course, would be even stronger, assuming it was available.

Finally, if the person challenging the law has made out a *prima facie* case that there is a more plausible rationale for the law than that which was articulated by the person defending the law, or if the suggested rationales are equally plausible, the burden should shift to the person defending the law to demonstrate that the articulated purpose justifies the law.

If this is a plausible account of the structure of the judicial inquiry under section 15, it is clear that some very hard questions remain unanswered. What counts as a justification for a law? How closely related must the means employed and the ends pursued for a court to uphold a law? How necessary need it have been for the law to have been designed as it was? How important must the governmental purpose be? By what criteria can one assess the relative importance of governmental pursuits? How does a court balance the burden imposed upon an individual against the importance of the governmental interests at stake?

There is no way around these questions. To assert, as I have done here and elsewhere, that a court ought to apply a flexible standard of review, is to require the court to confront all of these issues in every case that comes before it. In so doing, a court will get no real guidance from rules of law. If such an approach appears inconsistent with our traditional ideas of how courts ought to decide cases, it speaks to the difference that may obtain between constitutional and other forms of adjudication. It certainly speaks to the need to explore further the possibility of a principled decision under the *Charter of Rights*.

. . . .

# THE EQUALITY RIGHTS IN THE CANADIAN CHARTER OF RIGHTS AND FREEDOMS

W.S. Tarnopolsky (1983), 61 Can. Bar Rev. 242 (footnotes omitted)

There are three "equality rights" provisions in the *Canadian Charter of Rights and Freedoms* — sections 15, 27 and 28:

15.(1) Every individual is equal before and under the law and has the right to the equal protection and equal benefit of the law without discrimination and, in particular, without discrimination based on race, national or ethnic origin, colour, religion, sex, age or mental or physical disability.

(2) Subsection (1) does not preclude any law, program or activity that has as its object the amelioration of disadvantaged individuals or groups including those that are disadvantaged because of race, national or ethnic origin, colour, religion, sex, age or mental or physical disability.

27. This Charter shall be interpreted in a manner consistent with the preservation and enhancement of the multicultural heritage of Canadians.

28. Notwithstanding anything in this Charter, the rights and freedoms referred to in it are guaranteed equally to male and female persons.

These are the provisions which probably received the greatest attention from lobbying groups both before and after the November Accord of 1981. In addition, if the experience in Canada since 1960 under the *Canadian Bill of Rights*, and in the United States since 1954 under the Fourteenth Amendment, are any guide, these are the provisions that are most likely to be raised most frequently in litigation under the new Charter. This prediction, however, cannot be tested until after April 17th, 1985 because, by section 32(2) of the *Charter*, section 15, the foundation provision, does not come into effect until three years after the *Charter* came into force. Although there is no similar delay with respect to sections 27 and 28, most of the impact of these will be determined within the context of the equality rights in section

15. Further, since sections 15 and 28 are "individual rights" provisions, while section 27 is a "group rights" provision, section 27 will be dealt with separately at the end, after a discussion of the other two.

## I. *Historical and Comparative Setting*

Although equality rights provisions in basic constitutional documents began appearing only within the last two hundred years, the notion of "equality" dates at least as far back as the time of the Greek city-states, in the arguments of the Aristoteleans. Later, it was revived as a religious concept, pursuant to which it was preached that all men were equal in the eyes of God, despite their earthly inequality. Another dimension to the concept, namely that it derived from "the state of nature", was added by philosophers like Locke, near the end of the seventeenth century, and Rousseau, in the eighteenth century. The spirit of all of these historical antecedents were combined by Jefferson into the justification for the American Declaration of Independence:

> We hold these truths to be self-evident, That All Men Are Created Equal. . . .

Similarly, and just a few years later, the French Declaration of the Rights of Man and of the Citizen, 1789, proclaimed:

> Men are born and remain free and equal in respect of rights.

And, it will be recalled, one of the three slogans of the French Revolution was "égalité".

At this point, two observations must be made. The first is that in the Greek city-states the equality of "citizens" was not shared with slaves, that for almost ninety years after the American Declaration of Independence slavery was practised in the United States and, further, that in all countries at various times the reference to the rights of "men" meant just that, and to a large extent did not include women. The second is that strict numerical or absolute equality of treatment was never contemplated. The argument of Aristotle that "equality consists of treating equals equally and unequals unequally", has been accepted as an obvious fact. The acute question, of course, is how to identify unequals and how to evaluate when unequal treatment is justified and when it is not. This is a subject to which it is necessary to return later.

As mentioned previously, despite the American Declaration of Independence proclamation that "all men are created equal", it was not until after the American Civil War that practical effect was given to this aim through the "equal protection of the laws" clause in the Fourteenth Amendment. This amendment has been described, together with the Thirteenth and Fifteenth, as "the new constitution which emerged from the Second American Revolution". Although these amendments were added to the Constitution to guarantee the emancipated black population a full and equal status in American society, the United States Supreme Court decided soon after their adoption that the protection therein granted was to extend to all races, and not just to blacks. However, when Congress passed the *Civil Rights Act*, 1875, which, *inter alia*, forbade denial of equal facilities in transportation and hotels, the Supreme Court invalidated important parts of it. Perhaps the most significant means of getting around the requirements of the Fourteenth Amendment was that of "segregation", approved of by the Supreme Court in *Plessy v. Ferguson*, [163 U.S. 537 (1896)] where the doctrine was rationalized as permitting "separate but equal" facilities.

It was not until 1954, in the famous case of *Brown v. Board of Education*, [347 U.S. 483 (1954)] that the Supreme Court finally held that separate facilities were inherently unequal and so unconstitutional. It has been suggested that in the decade following *Brown v. Board of Education* the dominant movement in the American Supreme Court was "the emerging primacy of equality as a guide to constitutional decision" and that this "egalitarian revolution in the judicial doctrine" made the equal protection principles of the Fourteenth Amendment dominant even over the "due process" clause.

At this point it should be noted that, unlike the Americans and the French, the British never did formally proclaim "equality" as a fundamental principle of their Constitution. Nevertheless, in his classic definition of the United Kingdom Constitution, Dicey suggested that "equality before the law" was one of three meanings of the fundamental principle of the United Kingdom Constitution known as the "Rule of Law". He defined "equality before the law" as follows:

> . . . [T]he equal subjection of all classes to the ordinary law of the land administered by the ordinary law courts. . . .

Although Dicey's definition was intended to serve his argument that, unlike the continental situation, the United Kingdom knew nothing of "administrative law" or "administrative tribunals", and although the subsequent development of "administrative law", both in the United Kingdom and in Canada, have disproved this distinction, his limitation on the "equality before the law" clause has continued to find favour, even in our Supreme Court as recently as 1973.

More modern definitions of "equality before the law" have been provided by United Kingdom authorities, but these are still more restrictive than the "egalitarian" interpretation which has been given to the "equal protection of the law" clause in the American Fourteenth Amendment. Thus, Marshall suggests that the doctrine implies "equality of state and individual before the law". Although Marshall acknowledges that since the state imposes its will upon the individual, and since state servants are given specific powers, the state and citizen cannot really be equals, nevertheless, he suggests that it is the duty of the courts to hold an equal balance between citizens and officials. Sir Ivor Jennings, who is one of the leading modern critics of Dicey, expands the concept thus:

> It assumes that among equals the laws should be equal and should be equally administered, that like should be treated alike. The right to sue and be sued, to prosecute and be prosecuted, for the same kind of action should be the same for all citizens of full age and understanding, and without distinction of race, religion, wealth, social status or political influence.

Nevertheless, it will be noted that even this view of "equality before the law" basically restricts it to a procedural concept relating only to the even-handed operation of the legal system in its application and enforcement of the law.

In the twentieth century, particularly after World War II, both national and international Bills of Rights have included "equality" clauses. Essentially three formulations have been adopted. In addition to those of the American "equal protection" clause and the British "equality before the law" clause, a general non-discrimination provision has been introduced. Thus, the European Convention on

Human Rights, which has been ratified by the United Kingdom and over twenty other West European countries, provides that "[t]he enjoyment of the rights and freedoms set forth in this Convention should be secured without discrimination on any grounds such as . . .". Some, such as the Basic Law of the Federal Republic of Germany, provide that "[all] persons shall be equal before the law", that "men and women shall have equal rights" and that "no one may be prejudiced or favoured because of his sex, his parentage, his race, his language, his homeland and origin, his faith or religious or political opinions". Still others, such as the Indian Constitution, combine all three. Thus, article 15(1) provides that "[t]he State shall not discriminate against any citizen on grounds only of religion, race, caste, sex, place of birth or any of them", while article 14 provides that "the State shall not deny to any person equality before the law or the equal protection of the laws". Similarly, the International Covenant on Civil and Political Rights, which was ratified by Canada in 1976 pursuant to a unanimous agreement of all the provinces and the federal government, utilizes all three formulations. Thus, paragraph 1 of article 2 provides:

> 1. Each State Party to the present Covenant undertakes to respect and to ensure to all individuals within its territory and subject to its jurisdiction the rights recognized in the present Covenant, without distinction of any kind, such as race, colour, sex, language, religion, political or other opinion, national or social origin, property, birth or other status.

Similarly, article 25 provides:

> Every citizen shall have the right and the opportunity, without any of the distinctions mentioned in article 2 and without unreasonable restrictions:

to take part in the conduct of public affairs, to vote and be elected, an to have access, on general terms of equality, to public service in his country. In addition, article 14(1) provides that:

> All persons shall be equal before the courts and tribunals.

Furthermore, article 3 makes a special provision for the equal rights of men and women, while article 26 combines a non-discrimination provision along with the clauses on "equality before the law" and "equal protection of the law":

> All persons are equal before the law and are entitled without any discrimination to the equal protection of the law. In this respect, the law shall prohibit any discrimination and guarantee to all persons equal and effective protection against discrimination on any ground such as race, colour, sex, language, religion, political or other opinion, national or social origin, property, birth or other status.

## II. *From Section 1 of the Canadian Bill of Rights to Section 15 of the Charter*

Section 1 of the *Canadian Bill of Rights* includes both a non-discrimination clause and one on "equality before the law". The non-discrimination clause appears in the opening paragraph of section 1 and applies to all the rights and freedoms enumerated, namely, the fundamental freedoms in subsections (c) to (f), the "due process" clause in subsection (a), and the equality clause in subsection (b), which reads "the right of the individual to equality before the law and the protection of the law". Rather than going into a long discussion of the relationship of the non-discrimination clause in the opening paragraph to the "equality before the law" clause in subsection (b), one could refer to the following summation of Laskin J. in *Curr v. The Queen* [[1972] S.C.R. 889 at 896]:

> In considering the reach of s. 1(a) . . .
>
> I would observe . . . that I do not read it as making the existence of any of the forms of prohibited discrimination a *sine qua non* of its operation. Rather, the prohibited discrimination is an additional lever to which federal legislation must respond. Putting the matter another way, federal legislation which does not offend s. 1 in respect of any of the prohibited kinds of discrimination may nonetheless be offensive to s. 1 if it is violative of what is specified in any of the clauses (a) to (f) of s. 1. It is, *a fortiori*, offensive if there is discrimination by reason of race so as to deny equality before the law. That is what this Court decided in *Regina v. Drybones* and I need say no more on this point.

The main focus of the Supreme Court was on the "equality before the law" clause. Since all of the leading cases have been extensively discussed previously, it is not proposed to do so here but rather to summarize briefly.

The only case in which the Supreme Court held that a federal provision contravened the "equality before the law" clause and was therefore inoperative, was *Regina v. Drybones* [,[1970] S.C.R. 282]. In this case Mr. Justice Ritchie, on behalf of the majority of the Supreme Court, held that the provision in the Indian Act which made it an offence for Indians to be intoxicated off a reserve contravened the "equality before the law" clause, and gave that clause the following meaning:

> . . . I think that s. 1(b) means at least that no individual or group of individuals is to be treated more harshly than another under that law, and I am therefore of the opinion that an individual is denied equality before the law if it is made an offence punishable at law, on account of his race, for him to do something which his fellow Canadians are free to do without having committed any offence or having been made subject to any penalty.

However, in the *Lavell* case Mr. Justice Ritchie, held that section 12(1)(b) of the *Indian Act* [R.S.C. 1970, c. I-6, as amended] which provides that an Indian woman who married someone who is not an Indian would thereby lose her band membership, whereas an Indian man not only did not lose his band membership, but gave it to his spouse, did not contravene the "equality before the law" clause. In doing so he made two assertions which have had a clear effect upon the formulation of section 15 of the *Charter*. The first was that he rejected any "egalitarian concept exemplified by the Fourteenth Amendment of the *U.S. Constitution* as interpreted by the courts of that country". Rather, and this was his second assertion, he purported to apply the concept of "equality before the law" as it would have been understood at the time the *Bill of Rights* was enacted, and adopted Dicey's definition of "equal subjection of all classes to the ordinary law of the land administered by the ordinary courts".

Therefore, to the extent that he, as well as Fauteux C.J.C. in *Smythe v. The Queen* [[1971] S.C.R. 680] rejected any possible references to the American "egalitarian" conception, section 15 now includes the "equal protection of the law" clause. To the extent that he adopted the Dicey definition and suggested that *Lavell* could be distinguished from *Drybones* on the basis that in the former case no "inequality of treatment between Indian men and women flows as a necessary result of the application of section 12(1)(b) of the Indian Act", or, in other words, to the extent that he implied there was a distinction between clauses like "equality *before* the law" and "unequal treatment *under* the law", section 15 now includes a reference to equality "*under* the law".

In order to understand the motivation behind the addition of the fourth equality clause, namely "equal *benefit* of the law", it is necessary to recall the *Bliss* case. Stella Bliss was a pregnant woman who had worked long enough to have qualified for ordinary unemployment benefits, that is eight weeks, but not the ten weeks necessary to qualify for maternity benefits. However, she could not claim ordinary benefits because it was assumed that during the maternity period women are not capable of and available for work. She, therefore, challenged section 46, the relevant provision in the *Unemployment Insurance Act, 1971* [S.C. 1970-71-72, c. 48] on the ground that it contravened the "equality before the law" clause in the *Canadian Bill of Rights*. In the Federal Court of Appeal Pratte J. held that this was not discrimination because of sex, but rather a distinction between pregnant women and all other unemployed persons, male or female. When the case reached the Supreme Court of Canada, Ritchie J. gave the unanimous decision upholding the judgment of Pratte J. and, in addition, suggested that there was no contravention of "equality before the law" because section 46 did not involve denial of equality of treatment in the administration and enforcement of the law before the ordinary courts of the land:

> ... There is a wide difference between legislation which treats one section of the population more harshly than all others by reason of race as in the case of *R. v. Drybones*, [1970] S.C.R. 282, and legislation providing additional benefits to one class of women, specifying the conditions which entitle a claimant to such benefits and defining a period during which no benefits are available. The one case involves the imposition of a penalty on a racial group to which other citizens are not subjected; the other involves a definition of the qualifications required for entitlement of benefits. ... [*Bliss v. A.G. Can.* (1978), 92 D.L.R. (3d) 417.]

Since this assertion implied a distinction between "equality before the law" or "equal *protection* of the law", on the one hand, and "equal *benefit* of the law", on the other, this presumed gap, too, has now been covered in section 15 of the Canadian *Charter*.

This very brief survey of how majority decisions on the Supreme Court of Canada limited the "equality before the law" clause in the *Canadian Bill of Rights*, and how these limitations led directly to the incorporation of four equality clauses in section 15(1), also explains, partly, why various women's groups lobbied so hard, both before and after the November, 1981 Accord, for the inclusion of section 28. Although one might have expected that the equality clauses, particularly since section 15(1) lists "sex" as one of the forbidden grounds of discrimination, must require equality between men and women, there was sufficient suspicion amongst women, based upon the Supreme Court judgments referred to above, to press for an "equal rights amendment" in the *Charter*. Another motivation for the action of women in asking for a section 28 will be explained in the succeeding discussion of what might be acceptable distinctions despite an equality provision.

Apart from not providing a more "egalitarian" definition for the "equality before the law" clause, another major limitation on this clause arose from assertions, by majorities on the Supreme Court of Canada, with respect to acceptable distinctions. Without going into a detailed discussion, it might be recalled that in *Regina v. Burnshine* [[1975] 1 S.C.R. 693], the Supreme Court was concerned with the provision in the federal *Prisons and Reformatories Act* [R.S.C. 1970, c. P-21] by which courts in Ontario and British Columbia may sentence anyone apparently under the age of twenty-two, who is convicted of an offence punishable by imprisonment for three months or more, to a fixed term of not less than three months and an indefinite period thereafter of not more than two years less one day, to be served in a special correctional institution, rather than a common jail. Burnshine was sentenced to this maximum, even though the offence for which he had been charged had a maximum punishment of six months. Although the minority judgment, given by Laskin J. would not have found the provision inoperative, but would rather have so "construed and applied" it that the maximum term of detention could not have exceeded that provided under the *Criminal Code*, the majority decision, given by Martland J., held that the provision challenged did not contravene the "equality before the law" clause. The main reason given for coming to this conclusion was that since the object of the law was to reform young offenders by incarceration in an institution other than a jail, "it would be necessary for the respondent, at least, to satisfy this Court that, . . . Parliament was not seeking to achieve a valid federal objective". This "valid federal objective" test was picked up and affirmed again by the Supreme Court of Canada in *Prata v. Minister of Manpower and Immigration* [[1976] 1 S.C.R. 376]. The case concerned provisions in the *Immigration Appeal Board Act* [R.S.C. 1970, c. I-3], providing for a discretion to permit certain deportable persons to remain in Canada on compassionate grounds, unless they are thought to be a threat to national security. In giving the unanimous judgment of the Supreme Court of Canada holding that this discretion did not constitute an infringement of the "equality before the law" clause, Martland J. stated:

> . . . This Court has held that s. 1(b) of the *Canadian Bill of Rights* does not require that all federal statutes must apply to all individuals in the same manner. Legislation dealing with a particular class of people is valid if it is enacted for the purpose of achieving a valid federal objective (*R. v. Burnshine*).

This test was applied again in the *Bliss* case as one of the reasons given for deciding that there was no contravention of the "equality before the law" clause.

In the most recent Supreme Court decision on the topic, *MacKay v. The Queen* [[1980] 2 S.C.R. 370] the issue was whether the provision in the *National Defence Act* [R.S.C. 1970, c. N-4 [am. S.C. 1972, c. 13, s. 73]] providing for prosecution and trial before a military tribunal of an offence under the *Narcotic Control Act* [R.S.C. 1970, c. N-1] offended, *inter alia*, section 1(b) of the *Canadian Bill of Rights*. In giving the majority decision to the effect that there was no such contravention, Ritchie J. referred to the cases discussed above and added very little other than to assert that the National Defence Act was enacted by Parliament "constitutionally competent to do so and exercising its powers in accordance with the tenets of responsible government" and that the Act dealt with a particular class of individuals and, "as it is enacted for the purpose of achieving a valid federal objective, the provisions of s. 1(b) of the *Bill of Rights* do not require that its provisions contain the same requirements as all other federal legislation".

Although McIntyre J. agreed with Ritchie J. in the result, he suggested that the "valid federal objective" test had to mean more than just the issue of whether there was valid legislative competence, because even apart from the *Bill of Rights* an enactment could not be supported constitutionally unless it was within legislative jurisdiction. He suggested that the word "valid" required an analysis beyond the issue of legislative competence, namely, the determination of whether the *Bill of Rights* is also affected:

> ... Our task then is to determine whether in pursuit of an admittedly constitutional federal objective Parliament has, contrary to the provisions of the *Canadian Bill of Rights*, created for those subject to military law a condition of inequality before the law.

Further, he suggested, in distinguishing between valid distinctions and those that contravene the clause,

> ... [t]he question which must be resolved in each case is whether such inequality as may be created by legislation affecting a special class — here the military — is arbitrary, capricious or unnecessary, or whether it is rationally based and acceptable as a necessary variation from the general principle of universal application of law to meet special conditions and to attain a necessary and desirable social objective.

The new test he suggested would require an inquiry into

> ... whether any inequality has been created ... rationally in the sense that it is not arbitrary or capricious and not based upon any ulterior motive or motives offensive to the provisions of the *Canadian Bill of Rights*, and whether it is a necessary departure from the general principle of universal application of the law for the attainment of some necessary and desirable social objective. ...

Although there can be no question but that the making of distinctions between individuals or classes of individuals is an indispensable ingredient of most legislation, and even that the application of an equal law to unequals will not only perpetuate inequality, but even exaggerate it, one must still question whether the test of a "valid legislative objective", or even the more appropriate gauge of "necessary and desirable social objective", is sufficient for all purposes in applying section 15(1). In fact, it may be questioned whether "valid legislative objective" is a test at all. How can one argue successfully that a piece of legislation enacted by a majority does not have a valid legislative objective? Surely, at least, one must accept the argument of McIntyre J. that legislative competence is merely the first step. Legislation valid from the point of view of legislative jurisdiction must still be subjected to the equality test. His suggestion that the test is whether the law "is arbitrary, capricious or unnecessary" or whether instead "it is rationally based and acceptable as a necessary variation from the general principle of universal application of law to meet special conditions and to attain a necessary and desirable social objective", is surely more appropriate. Nevertheless, it is suggested that even this test, which might have been acceptable under section 1(b) of the *Canadian Bill of Rights*, is not sufficient for section 15(1) of the new *Charter*. Even though section 1 of the *Charter* does provide for "reasonable limitations", which clearly contemplates the acceptability of certain legislative distinctions, it would be useful to consider the kinds of tests which the United States Supreme Court developed under the Fourteenth Amendment.

In the United States the equal protection clause does not automatically rule out all legislative classifications. It has not, for instance, been applied to invalidate graduated tax laws, nor special legislation for the protection of infants or mental defectives. Not long after *Brown v. Board of Education* the equal protection clause was described in the following terms:

> What the clause appears to require today is that any classification of "persons" shall be reasonably relevant to the recognized purposes of good government; and furthermore, that there shall be *no* distinction made on the sole basis of race or alienage as to certain rights.

Although this definition would appear to have continuing validity, during the past two decades the United States Supreme Court seems to have developed and applied three levels or intensities of scrutiny: strict, intermediate and minimal. In order to understand the distinction between these three levels, it is useful to start with the first, to then contrast it with the third, and finally to try to identify the second.

The "strict scrutiny" test is applied with respect to what have been termed "inherently suspect" classifications, that is those based on race, religion and nationality, particularly if the classifications are enacted for the purpose of denying the fundamental rights and liberties set out in the Constitution. When faced with an "inherently suspect" classification, the court has applied "close judicial scrutiny" to require proof that the classification was for "an overriding state interest" which could not be accomplished in any less prejudicial manner. The strictness of the scrutiny can be seen in the fact that, if one sets aside the special situation concerned with acceptance of segregation until 1954, the only case of racial discrimination which has passed this test is *Korematsu v. United States* [323 U.S. 214 (1944)], which was a decision dealing with wartime powers applied to exclude Japanese Americans from the west coast.

"Minimal scrutiny" would appear to apply where the classification involves neither an "inherently suspect" group, nor a fundamental constitutional right. These are classifications made essentially for economic or social reasons, and in this instance the court uses a "rational relationship" test. The onus is upon the one who challenges the classification to prove that the legislature did not have a legitimate purpose in mind and that the classification chosen did not have a reasonable rational relationship to the object of the legislation.

It might be noted at this point that the "valid legislative objective" or the "necessary and desirable social objective" tests of the Supreme Court of Canada, developed under the Canadian "equality before the law" clause, would appear to be equivalent to the "minimal scrutiny" test.

Obviously, the test known as "intermediate scrutiny" comes somewhere between "strict" and "minimal" scrutiny. This test has come to be applied with respect to gender- and legitimacy-based classifications. What is important from the point of view of understanding the campaign for the enactment of the Equal Rights Amendment in the United States, as well as the inclusion of section 28 in the Canadian *Charter*, is that "sex" was never included in the "inherently suspect" category along with race, religion and nationality. Whether this was because the courts were male-dominated, or because some of the earlier challenges under the Fourteenth Amendment were with respect to statutes which clearly were enacted for the purpose of protecting women from certain arduous or dangerous occupations, is not clear. In any case, by the mid-1970s the United States Supreme Court had evolved what has come to be called "intermediate scrutiny". The test used is that of "an important governmental objective" which is "substantially related to achievement of those objectives".

Applying this American experience to the Canadian situation one could suggest the following. The inclusion in section 15(1) of four equality clauses must have been intended to cover all possible interactions between citizens and the law, not just for protection, but for benefit as well. Since section 15(1) now lists a number of grounds upon which these clauses are to be interpreted and applied, without discrimination, and since section 28 guarantees the rights and freedoms in the *Charter* equally to male and female persons "notwithstanding anything in this *Charter*", the listed grounds must now be considered "inherently suspect" and subject to "strict judicial scrutiny". Perhaps, in the light of section 1 of the *Charter*, and in light of the fact that some of the listed grounds, such as age and mental or physical disability, are clearly subject to *bona fide* qualifications or requirements, a less stringent test might be applied to these grounds, similar to that of "intermediate scrutiny" in the United States. Finally, with respect to distinctions made on grounds not listed in section 15(1), particularly with respect to legislation having an economic or social purpose, one should expect the courts to defer to legislative opinion on these issues. As in the United States, or under either of the two tests suggested by Justices Ritchie and McIntyre, the legislation would withstand challenge unless the one who challenges it can show that there is no rational relationship between the means and ends chosen and valid legislative activity.

As mentioned earlier, it will not be until after April, 1985 that our courts will come to deal with the meaning and application of section 15(1). In the meantime, however, it should not be forgotten that the "equality before the law" clause in section 1(b) of the *Canadian Bill of Rights* continues to operate. In addition, of course, section 28 is not subject to the three-year delay and operates now "notwithstanding anything in this *Charter*". Therefore, there should be some hope that the earlier decisions concerning contraventions of the "equality before the law" clause, because of sex discrimination, could now be reconsidered in the light of section 28 of the constitutionally entrenched *Charter of Rights and Freedoms*.

## III. *Application of Sections 15 and 28 of the Charter*

In the first place it should be noted that although, by section 52(1) of the *Constitution Act, 1982*, the *Charter* is given primacy over all other laws in Canada, including the *Canadian Bill of Rights*, the three provincial bills of rights of Alberta, Quebec and Saskatchewan, and the anti-discrimination laws of all eleven jurisdictions, none of these has been repealed by section 53(1) of the *Constitution Act, 1982*. In addition, by section 26 of the *Charter*, the guarantees of *Charter* rights and freedoms "shall not be construed as denying the existence of any other rights or freedoms that exist in Canada". Therefore, all the anti-discrimination laws in the country continue to operate except in the very unlikely event that they are found to be inconsistent with the *Charter*. Which, then, is to apply to discrimination within this context — the various anti-discrimination laws or the *Charter*? It will be argued here that discrimination by legislative action will be determined under the *Charter*, discrimination by private action will continue to be dealt with under the anti-discrimination laws, and that discrimination by executive or government action may be challenged under either.

By section 32(1), the *Charter* is specifically made applicable only *to* the Parliament and government of Canada and *to* the legislatures and governments of the provinces "*in respect of* all matters within the authority" of the respective legislative body. It has to be noted that the words "in respect of" were specifically substituted for the words "and to" in the earlier draft of the *Charter*. Therefore, although legislative and executive actions are covered by the *Charter*, the *Charter* is not *per se* applicable to private action.

Second, section 15 refers to equality before and under the *law*, as well as equal protection and benefit of the *law*. Therefore, although an anti-discrimination law would *itself* have to conform to section 15, it, and not section 15, would be directly applicable to discriminatory actions by private persons.

Third, although the United States Supreme Court has extended the "state action" protection of the Fourteenth Amendment to such private activities as privately-owned parking garages on municipally-managed parks, private restaurants on publicly-owned facilities, and restrictive covenants, because these could only be enforced through court action, the reason for the extension must be considered. At the time of such extension there were anti-discrimination laws in only some thirty-five states and very little at the federal level. When, in 1964, Congress enacted the *Civil Rights Act* to apply to the federal sphere, to override any state Civil Rights Acts which were deficient, and to apply to those states which did not have their own, resort to the Fourteenth Amendment became less crucial. Now, private discrimination cases are pursued under the various Civil Rights Acts, and the Fourteenth Amendment is resorted to only for cases involving "state action". In our own case every jurisdiction in Canada has an anti-discrimination statute and so the same extension of "state action" to private activities is unnecessary.

Finally, every anti-discrimination statute in Canada is explicitly made applicable to the Crown. Therefore, executive or governmental discrimination can be challenged either under those statutes or under the *Charter*. However, since a challenge under the *Charter* involves the challenger assuming the cost of the action, unless special provision is made otherwise, whereas under the anti-discrimination laws the various Human Rights Commissions of the various jurisdictions assume the cost of pursuing a complaint of discrimination, it is unlikely that a complainant would resort to a constitutional action in the courts, rather than the complaint process under the anti-discrimination laws, unless such complainant disagrees with the evaluation of his complaint by the Commission. In that event, however, his or her chances of success in the courts under the *Charter* cannot be assumed to be very high.

## IV. *Section 15(2) of the Charter*

Subsection (2) of section 15 is entitled "affirmative action programs" and provides:

> Subsection (1) does not preclude any law, program or activity that has as its object the amelioration of conditions of disadvantaged individuals or groups including those that are disadvantaged because of . . . [the grounds listed in subs. 1].

It would appear that this provision was added to the *Charter* out of excessive caution. In line with the argument suggested earlier, that equal laws can result in inequality if applied to persons in unequal circumstances, it is suggested that "any law, program or activity that has as its object the amelioration of conditions of disadvantaged individuals or groups" cannot be a contravention of subsection (1) of section 15, even without subsection (2) saying so. It would appear that subsection (2) was included partly because of the fear that courts which gave such a limited definition to the "equality before the law" clause, under section 1(b) of the *Canadian Bill of Rights*, might also be inclined to find affirmative action to be discriminatory. The second reason appears to be a mistaken apprehension of the meaning of the *Bakke* case in the United States.

Bakke was a white male who challenged the special admissions scheme of the Medical School of the University of California at Davis, under which sixteen of the one hundred admissions positions were reserved for "economically and/or educationally disadvantaged" members of minority groups defined as blacks, Chicanos, Asians and American Indians. Bakke was able to show that his "bench mark score", although below that of the regular entering class, was higher than that of the sixteen entrants in the special group. Bakke challenged the special admission programme as being contrary to the Fourteenth Amendment, the California Constitution, and section 601 of Title VI of the *Civil Rights Act of 1964*, which provides:

No person in the United States shall, on the ground of race, colour or national origin, be excluded from participation in, be denied the benefits of, or be subjected to discrimination under any programs or activity receiving federal financial assistance.

The United States Supreme Court held, five to four, that the Davis programme was invalid. Nevertheless, a number of points concerning that decision must be noted: (1) Four of the five judges who upheld Bakke's contention based their decisions explicitly and only upon the strict terms of section 601 of the *Civil Rights Act: not* on the equal protection clause of the Fourteenth Amendment. Only Mr. Justice Powell, who joined the majority, based his decision upon the equal protection clause, while the other four members held that the scheme was in accordance with that clause. (2) The four judges who held that the scheme was in accordance with the equal protection clause, were joined by Mr. Justice Powell in holding that race *could* be a factor in admissions decisions and also that racial classifications could be used to eliminate or ameliorate "the disabling effects of identified, specific instances of discrimination", even "at the expense of other innocent individuals", where there have been "judicial, legislative, or administrative findings of constitutional or statutory violations", as part of remedies "for the vindication of constitutional [and statutory] entitlement".

Furthermore, the *Bakke* case was followed exactly one year and one day later by the Supreme Court decision in *United Steel Workers of America v. Weber* [99 S. Ct. 2721 (1979)]. This case concerned a challenge to an affirmative action programme undertaken by Kaiser Aluminium Corporation, pursuant to a collective bargaining agreement with the Union. In this case the equal protection clause was not even relied upon, but rather Title VII of the *Civil Rights Act, 1964*, which is similar to Title VI, dealt with in the *Bakke* case, except that it applies to employment. By a five to two decision the Supreme Court upheld the validity of the affirmative action program. The majority group held that private, voluntary, race-conscious affirmative action plans were valid for the purpose of overcoming manifest racial imbalances or traditional patterns of segregation.

In applying the *Bakke* and *Weber* cases to the Canadian situation a number of points should be noted:

(1) Neither case was decided upon the equal protection clause of the Fourteenth Amendment. Only one of the nine judges in the *Bakke* case found such contravention. Both cases were based upon the explicit wording of the *Civil Rights Act of 1964*. There is no exact Canadian equivalent of the relevant statutory provisions. In fact, the anti-discrimination statutes of all provinces, except Newfoundland and Quebec, as well as the Federal Act, make explicit provision for the adoption of "special" programmes or measures, that is affirmative action programmes, and each of these makes explicit provision that these are *not* to be considered to be in contravention of the anti-discrimination statutes concerned.

(2) The *Bakke* case concerned only a "strict" quota for admission to professional schools, while the *Weber* case concerned voluntarily-adopted special recruitment plans. Neither dealt with the broad spectrum of measures that can be taken in pursuance of an "affirmative action program", such as: special efforts to publicize these programmes; special recruitment measures; special training programmes; a reconsideration of the basis of assessment of "merit", both with respect to initial employment and subsequent promotion; special employment programmes in hinterland areas, taking account of hunting and fishing seasons, or arranging employment obligations by whole communities rather than by individuals; and, of course, the changing of patterns of recruitment and promotion which have resulted in exclusions of disadvantaged minorities and women.

One might add that the undertaking of affirmative action programs, in the context of a requirement to prohibit discrimination, is provided for under the International Convention on the Elimination of all Forms of Racial Discrimination, which has been ratified with the agreement of the federal and all provincial governments. Paragraph 4 of article 1 of that Convention provides:

> 4. Special measures taken for the sole purpose of securing adequate advancement of certain racial or ethnic groups or individuals requiring such protection as may be necessary in order to ensure such groups or individuals equal enjoyment or exercise of human rights and fundamental freedoms shall not be deemed racial discrimination, provided, however, that such measures do not, as a consequence, lead to the maintenance of separate rights for different racial groups and that they shall not be continued after the objectives for which they were taken have been achieved.

Finally, it might be pointed out that although section 28 applies "notwithstanding anything in this Charter", this should not invalidate "affirmative action programs" in favour of women pursuant to section 15(2). Section 28 has to be seen in the light of its purpose, as outlined earlier, to overcome the limitations that had been placed by the courts upon the "equality before the law" clause in section 1(b) of the *Canadian Bill of Rights*, as well as in the light of the fact that under section 33 of the *Charter* a "non obstante clause" could be used to exempt a law which discriminates against women from the ambit of the *Charter*. Therefore, the purpose of section 28 is clear. In addition, subsection (2) of section 15 is not a substantive provision, but rather an explanation of the substantive provision, which is subsection (1). Subsection (2) does not in itself provide for a right, but is merely an amplification of what the right in subsection (1) includes. Therefore, section 28 applies to subsection (1) and not to subsection (2).

## V. *The Effect of Section 27 on the Interpretation of the Charter*

### A. *The Distinction Between Individual Rights and Group Rights.*

There are at least two fundamental distinctions which must be emphasized for the sake of clarity. The first is that an assertion of an individual right emphasizes the proposition that everyone is to be treated the same *regardless* of his or her membership in a particular identifiable group. The assertion of group rights, on the other hand, bases itself upon a claim of an individual or a group of individuals *because of* membership in an identifiable group. This distinction should not be obscured by the fact that certain individual rights are either of no consequence unless enjoyed in community with others, or are asserted on behalf of individuals who happen to be members of identifiable minority groups. Thus, although it is true that the fundamental freedoms of expression, religion, assembly, and association are intended to be exercised by several individuals in common or for the purpose of communication, the intention is that each of these freedoms is to be enjoyed equally by everyone. If one asserts the right to worship as one pleases within the law, this is asserted regardless of whether the person happens to be a Christian, a Jew, a Muslim or a Hindu. However, to the extent that certain rights of religion vary because of special protection for certain religious groups, such a right is no longer an individual right, but a group right. Conversely, although ordinarily one has in mind members of groups identifiable because of race, colour, or religion in asserting a right of equal access, this right is not set out specifically for separate identifiable groups, but for everyone regardless of the fact that that person happens to be a member of an identifiable group.

Certain rights, such as language rights, seem to lie in a borderland. When examined more closely, however, the distinction referred to above becomes clear. A guarantee of freedom of expression, for example, assures one the right to communicate, regardless of which language is used as the medium of communication. It does not, however, give any assurance that the communication will be understood, nor that the reply, if there be any, will be in a language which the initiator of the communication will understand. To put this in a different way, anyone who would like to use a particular language meaningfully is not helped by guarantees of free speech: what is needed is others who can understand and respond in the language of the initiator.

This leads to the second distinction between group rights and individual rights. The guarantee of an individual right like free expression essentially requires the non-interference of the state. A language right on the other hand, requires positive governmental action. It may be that the government is required to have civil servants who can comprehend the language of the citizen and reply in that language, or is required to expend funds to provide instruction in the language to promote cultural activities which protect and promote the guaranteed language. The important thing is that a language guarantee singles out certain groups from others. In a homogeneous country there is no need for constitutional protection for the language which is spoken by the people. For that mater, in a federal multilingual country, where the provincial boundaries coincide with language groups, there is also no need for constitutional guarantees or special government protection. Language rights need constitutional guarantees only in those places where there are minorities who want to safeguard a language other than that spoken by the majority of the country or the province, or where the majority language is threatened by the minority which is a majority in the rest of the country.

In discussing group rights, the matter of intent becomes extremely important. Enforcement of the fundamental freedoms is achieved mainly by invalidation of legislation which abridges or abrogates these freedoms. Similarly, guarantees of fundamental protection for the citizen in the administration of criminal justice, for instance, the right to counsel, could be made enforceable if provision is made for the invalidation of the criminal proceedings in the course of which certain rights were violated. However, how does one enforce the economic, social and cultural rights which require the state to provide something? For example, article 25 of the Universal Declaration of Human Rights proclaims:

> Everyone has the right to a standard of living adequate for the health and well-being of himself and of his family, including food, clothing, housing and medical care and necessary social services, and the right to security in the event of unemployment, sickness, disability, widowhood, old age, or other lack of livelihood in circumstances beyond his control.

How are these rights to be enforced? Clearly, if legislation were enacted which would deny any of these rights or deprive a person of them, such legislation may be invalidated. However, the provision of these rights requires a whole series of activities on the part of legislatures and governments, as well as private individuals and corporations, which it would be very difficult to enforce in a court of law. These are the types of rights that can be proclaimed as an aim or goal of the state concerned. However, the enforcement is achieved mainly through the ballot box, and not a court of law.

On the other hand, constitutions have frequently set out the aims and principles of the particular state concerned, for instance, the "Directive Principles of State Policy" of the Indian and Irish Constitutions. Although not directly and specifically enforceable in courts, they do affect court interpretations of statutes and, what is more important, form an important basis of programmes of political action.

In this line, the Special Joint Committee of the Senate and the House of Commons on the Constitution of Canada (the Molgat-MacGuigan Committee), which reported early in 1972, rejected "the theory that Canada was divided into two cultures", pointed out that there is no "single English-speaking nation" in Canada, and therefore asserted:

> In the face of this cultural plurality there can be no official Canadian culture or cultures.

The Committee recommended that a new Canadian Constitution should have a preamble "which would proclaim the basic objectives of Canadian federal democracy". Two of the six "objectives" suggested were:

> 1. To develop Canada as a bilingual and multicultural country in which all its citizens, male and female, young and old, native peoples and Métis, and all groups from every ethnic origin feel equally at home;

2. To present Canada as a pluralistic mosaic, a free and open society which challenges the talents of her people.

Even before the *Report* was submitted the federal government, in the fall of 1971, officially proclaimed a "policy of multiculturalism" to be at least partly implemented by provision of funds to support the activities of ethno-cultural groups. This had been preceded by the enactment of the *Official Languages Act* [R.S.C. 1970, c. O-2] and the establishment of an Official Languages Commissioner as an "ombudsman" to promote and protect the use, within the federal sphere of jurisdiction, of the two official languages.

The next proposals at the federal level were to be found in the proposed *Constitutional Amendment Act* of mid-summer, 1978 — Bill C-60. Part of the proposed new *Charter of Rights and Freedoms* included rights with respect to the two official languages, while the "aims" provision, in section 4, included a recognition of the pluralism of Canada:

[one of] the stated aims of the Canadian federation shall be:
> (ii) to ensure throughout Canada equal respect for the many origins, creeds and cultures . . . that help shape its society, and for those Canadians who are a part of each of them. . . .

The *Charter* as submitted in October, 1980, however, contained no equivalent provision. Following representations from various ethno-cultural groups, and the Canadian Consultative Council on Multiculturalism, section 27 was introduced.

## B. *The Possible Effect of Section 27.*

The first thing that can be noted about section 27 is that it is impossible to visualize what a court could grand pursuant to that section alone — it is a purely declaratory or interpretive provision. It has to be seen as being similar to a preamble, or an "aims" provision, which are not legally binding in the narrow sense. Nevertheless, it should be noted that in our constitutional history the preamble to the *British North America Act, 1867*, has proved very important. Although there is no reference to the most fundamental characteristics of our constitution, like responsible government, the existence of political parties, the position of the Prime Minister and his cabinet, or the role of the Leader of the Opposition, all of these elements are acknowledged as deriving from a clause in the preamble to the British North America Act, which refers to the Constitution as being "similar in Principle to that of the United Kingdom". Also it should not be forgotten that this same preamble was resorted to as one of the reasons given by several Supreme Court Justices for declaring the *Alberta Press Bill* invalid, and subsequently in restraining the Quebec Government of Maurice Duplessis in his battle with the Jehovah's Witnesses and Communists. Thus, the importance of a preamble, or an "aims" clause, cannot be minimized.

Furthermore, it is quite clear that all of the provisions of the *Charter* have to be interpreted in the light of section 27. Nevertheless, for reasons mentioned earlier, this may not greatly affect the interpretation of the fundamental freedoms, because these in themselves provide protection for the use of one's language, for the practice of one's religion, and for one's right to assemble and associate with others, whether for cultural reasons, or for political or economic ones. So, too, section 27 is not needed with respect to the application of the democratic rights in sections 3, 4 and 5, or the legal rights in sections 7 to 14 inclusive. Whatever the reason for denial, whether for discriminatory ones or otherwise, the infraction should be challengeable. With respect to the language rights in sections 16 to 23 inclusive, section 27 would seem to have application only to section 22, which provides:

> Nothing in sections 16 to 20 abrogates or derogates from any legal or customary right or privilege acquired or enjoyed either before or after the coming into force of this Charter with respect to any language that is not English or French.

Although it would be difficult to see how any language other than those of the native peoples might claim any "customary right or privilege acquired or enjoyed ... before" the coming into force of the *Charter*, one could envisage section 27 as an encouragement to provinces to recognize some linguistic education rights at least "wherever in the province the number of children of citizens ... is sufficient to warrant the provision to them out of public funds of minority language instruction". It must be stated, however, that the use of section 27 to these ends is more likely to have political success, than success in the courts.

The most important provision in respect to which section 27 could have effect is section 15. For the most part, of course, subsection 15(1) does not require the aid of section 27 to provide protection because of one's race, national or ethnic origin, or religion. However, it is possible to envisage that with respect to one of the equality clauses, that is "equal benefit of the law", a claim could be made for equal benefits, particularly concerning grants for cultural activities. Individuals who belong to ethno-cultural groups which do not receive grants equivalent to those received by the ethno-cultural groups that have sometimes been referred to as "the two founding peoples", might be able to invalidate the giving of disproportionate grants to such more fortunate groups. Although it is impossible to envisage a court being prepared to order a government as to whether such money should be spent, or how much should be expended in total, nevertheless, if grants are made pursuant to laws which do not meet the test of "equal benefit" with respect to race, national or ethnic origin, or religion, then invalidity might be sought. Similarly, the granting of licences to such culture-providing institutions as those in the broadcasting field, could be tested under section 27. The reflection of Canada's "multicultural" heritage in such broadcasting institutions as the Canadian Broadcasting Corporation might now be reviewable.

Furthermore, although subsection 15(2) does not provide for a right to compel the adoption of an "affirmative action program", to the extent that affirmative action programmes are adopted, it may be possible to use section 27 as an argument that all under-represented ethno-cultural groups should be considered. Again, this would appear to be a basis for persuasion of legislatures and governments, rather than courts.

For reasons mentioned earlier, it does not appear that a constitutional provision can go further than this with respect to protection of minority groups who make up Canada's "multicultural heritage".

## Note

Mr. Justice Tarnopolsky presented a paper subsequent to the above article at the Comparative Constitutional Law Conference on Limits on Fundamental Rights held at McGill University, Montreal on May 23-4, 1985 (as yet unpublished) suggesting that section 15(1) might *not* cover all differentiations, leaving the test of validity to section 1, but rather only covers "real" limitations:

> Perhaps it will be necessary to consider a different basis for considering some distinctions, because of the very nature of equality rights, particularly when considered in the light of the Aristotelian principle of equality of treatment requiring equals to be treated equally and unequals unequally. In other words, is there a difference between limitations as such, to be dealt with in the light of both sections 15 and 1, and distinctions made for purposes of the Aristotelian notion of equality?
>
> Amongst distinctions which can be described as real limitations are those based on age. A law may stipulate a mandatory retirement age, or a minimum qualifying age for such activities as driving, drinking, voting or consenting to marriage or entering into contracts. These, it would appear, are real limitations, the justification of which would, presumably, have to be made pursuant to section 1.
>
> Similar to age limitations are the various *bona fide* occupational qualifications (b.f.o.qs.) that would have to be proved according to the Supreme Court decision in the *Borough of Etobicoke Firefighters* case, *i.e.*, that the b.f.o.q. is genuinely imposed (subjective test) and really necessary (objective test). Obvious b.f.o.qs. are such matters as sight for a pilot, hearing for a telephone operator, fingers for a typist. Somewhat less precise are such requirements as certain educational or training standards or skills in order to enter into certain occupations or even certain educational institutions. Apart from issues involving "reasonable accommodation" costs and safety, a b.f.o.q. is a real limitation that would have to be dealt with under section 1.
>
> Without attempting an exhaustive list, other examples of real limitations are those based on sex, with respect to such matters as strip searches, or with respect to combat in the armed forces, or such restrictions on liberty of movement or certain civil rights, with respect to inmates in jails or in certain hospital facilities. Again, the limitations imposed would be subject to tests under section 1.
>
> What, however, will be the approach of the courts to distinctions to achieve equal treatment for unequals? Is a progressive income tax a limitation on equality rights or does it constitute equality under the law? Would such government programs as legal aid or educational bursaries, which apply means tests, be dealt with by the courts as limitations or as attempts to achieve equal protection or equal benefit of the law? Is affirmative action (constitutionally protected by section 15(2) of the Charter), otherwise a limitation on those who do not qualify, or is it directed towards achieving equality under the law, or equal protection or equal benefit of the law?
>
> . . . .

The most important difficulty with this view is that it places the onus upon the applicant in section 15(1) rather than upon the government pursuant to section 1 to justify differentiations. In the taxation and bursary examples, the government is the party in possession of the facts and is the one most capable of demonstrating the validity of a limitation. A private applicant will not usually be in a position to do so, and he will accordingly fail at an initial stage even in cases where the government could not have met the section 1 onus had it been forced to carry the burden.

## THE EQUAL PROTECTION OF THE LAWS

Joseph Tussman and Jacobus tenBroek. (1949), 37 Calif. Law Rev. 341
(footnotes omitted).

. . . .

The injunction that no state "shall deny to any person within its jurisdiction the equal protection of the laws" might appear at first glance to be simply a demand for administrative fairness, the historically familiar assertion that all men must stand equal before the law, that justice must be blind to wealth or color, to rank or privilege. But early in its career, the equal protection clause received a formulation which strongly suggested that it was to be more than a demand for fair or equal enforcement of laws; it was to express the demand that the law itself be "equal." In *Yick Wo v. Hopkins* [118 U.S. 356 (1886)] Mr. Justice Matthews said that "The equal protection of the laws is a pledge of the protection of equal laws." This has been frequently cited with approval and has never been challenged by the Court. It is a statement that makes it abundantly clear that the quality of legislation as well as the quality of administration comes within the purview of the clause.

The subsequent career of the equal protection clause as a standard for the criticism of legislation has moved along several lines. First, it has operated as a limitation upon permissible legislative classification. This is its most familiar role. Second, it is used to oppose "discriminatory" legislation. And third, it shares with due process the task of imposing "substantive" limits upon the exercise of the police power.

## 1. EQUAL PROTECTION AND CLASSIFICATION

### a. *The Problem*

. . . .

The contrast here is between "general" legislation which applies without qualification to "all persons" and "special" legislation which applies to a limited class of persons. It is clear that the demand for equal protection cannot be a demand that laws apply universally to all persons. The legislature, if it is to act at all, must impose special burdens upon or grant special benefits to special groups or classes of individuals.

We thus arrive at the point at which the demand for equality confronts the right to classify. For it is the classification which determines the range of persons affected by the special burden or benefit of a law which does not apply to "all persons." "It is of the essence of classification," said Mr. Justice Brewer in 1898, "that upon the class are cast . . . burdens different from those resting upon the general public. . . . Indeed, the very idea of classification is that of inequality. . . . [*Atchison, Topeka & S.F.R.R. v. Matthews*, 174 U.S. 96, 106 (1899)].

Here, then, is a paradox: The equal protection of the laws is a "pledge of the protection of equal laws." But laws may classify. And "the very idea of classification is that of inequality." In tackling this paradox the Court has neither abandoned the demand for equality nor denied the legislative right to classify. It has taken a middle course. It has resolved the contradictory demands of legislative specialization and constitutional generality by a doctrine of reasonable classification.

The essence of that doctrine can be stated with deceptive simplicity. The Constitution does not require that things different in fact be treated in law as though they were the same. But it does require, in its concern for equality, that those who are similarly situated be similarly treated. The measure of the reasonableness of a classification is the degree of its success in treating similarly those similarly situated. The difficulties concealed in this proposition will be analyzed in the following section.

b. *Reasonable Classification*

We begin with an elementary proposition: To define a class is simply to designate a quality or characteristic or trait or relation, or any combination of these, the possession of which, by an individual, determines his membership in or inclusion within the class. A legislature defines a class, or "classifies," when it enacts a law applying to "all aliens ineligible for citizenship," or "all persons convicted of three felonies," or "all citizens between the ages of 19 and 25" or "foreign corporations doing business within the state."

This sense of "classify" (i.e., "to define a class") must be distinguished from the sense in which "to classify" refers to the act of determining whether an individual is a member of a particular class, that is, whether the individual possesses the traits which define the class. Our concern in this essay is with "legislative classification," the first of these senses, since it is the defining of the class to which the law applies which constitutes the distinctly legislative classificatory activity to which the Court refers in conceding that the power to classify belongs to the legislature.

It is also elementary that membership in a class is determined by the possession of the traits which define that class. Individual $X$ is a member of class $A$ if, and only if, $X$ possesses the traits which define class $A$. Whatever the defining characteristics of a class may be, every member of that class will possess those characteristics.

Turning now to the reasonableness of legislative classifications, the cue is to be taken from our earlier reference to the requirement that those similarly situated be similarly treated. A reasonable classification is one which includes all who are similarly situated and none who are not. The question is, however, what does that ambiguous and crucial phrase "similarly situated" mean? And in answering this question we must first dispose of two errors into which the Court has sometimes fallen.

First, "similarly situated" cannot mean simply "similar in the possession of the classifying trait." All members of any class are similarly situated in this respect and consequently, any classification whatsoever would be reasonable by this test. Yet it is instructive to listen to Mr. Justice Harlan in *Powell v. Pennsylvania*, [127 U.S. 678 (1888)]: "The objection that the statute is repugnant to the clause of the Fourteenth Amendment forbidding the denial by the State to any person within its jurisdiction of the equal protection of the laws, is untenable. The Statute places under the same restrictions, and subjects to like penalties and burdens, all who manufacture, or sell, or offer for sale, or keep in possession to sell, the articles embraced by its prohibitions; thus recognizing and preserving the principle of equality among those engaged in the same business."

What is striking about this statement is the easy dismissal of the equal protection issue on the grounds that the law applies equally to all to whom it applies. The law imposes a limitation on the class of "makers ... of margarine." The requirement of equality is held to be satisfied simply because it applies to all makers of margarine. By the same token a law applying to red-haired makers of margarine would satisfy the requirements of equality.

The second error in the interpretation of the meaning of similarly situated arises out of the notion that some classes are unnatural or artificial. That is, a classification is sometimes held to be unreasonable if it includes individuals who do not belong to the same "natural" class. We call this an error without pausing to fight the ancient controversy about the natural status of classes. All legislative classifications are artificial in the sense that they are artifacts, no matter what the defining traits may be. And they are all real enough for the purposes of law, whether they be the class of American citizens of Japanese ancestry, or the class of makers of margarine, or the class of stockyards receiving more than one hundred head of cattle per day, or the class of feeble-minded confined to institutions.

The issue is not whether, in defining a class, the legislature has carved the universe at a natural joint. If we want to know if such classifications are reasonable, it is fruitless to consider whether or not they correspond to some "natural" grouping or separate those who naturally belong together.

But if we avoid these two errors, where are we to look for the test of similarity of situation which determines the reasonableness of a classification? The inescapable answer is that we must look beyond the classification to the purpose of the law. A reasonable classification is one which includes all persons who are similarly situated with respect to the purpose of the law.

The purpose of a law may be either the elimination of a public "mischief" or the achievement of some positive public good. To simplify the discussion we shall refer to the purpose of a law in terms of the elimination of mischief, since the same argument holds in either case. We shall speak of the defining character or characteristics of the legislative classification as the trait. We can thus speak of the relation of the classification to the purpose of the law as the relation of the Trait to the Mischief.

A problem arises at all because the classification in a law usually does not have as its defining Trait the possession of or involvement with the Mischief at which the law aims. For example, let us suppose that a legislature proposes to combat hereditary criminality — an admitted mischief — and that the sterilization of transmitters of hereditary criminality is a permissible means to that end. Now if the legislature were to pass a law declaring that for the purpose of eliminating hereditary criminality, all individuals who are tainted with inheritable criminal tendencies are to be sterilized, and if it provided for proper administrative identification of transmitters of hereditary criminality, our problem would largely disappear. The class, being defined directly in terms of the Mischief, automatically includes all who are similarly situated with respect to the purpose of the law.

This procedure requires, however, delegation of considerable discretion to administrators to determine which individuals to sterilize. Legislators, reluctant to confer such discretion, tend to classify by Traits which limit the range of administrative freedom. Suppose then, that they pass a law providing for the sterilization of all persons convicted of three felonies. The "reasonableness" of this classification depends upon the relation between the class of three-time felons and the class of hereditary criminals.

In other words, we are really dealing with the relation of two classes to each other. The first class consists of all individuals possessing the defining Trait; the second class consists of all individuals possessing, or rather, tainted by, the Mischief at which the law aims. The former is the legislative classification; the latter is the class of those similarly situated with respect to the purpose of the law. We shall refer to these two classes as $T$ and $M$ respectively.

Now, since the reasonableness of any class $T$ depends entirely upon its relation to a class $M$, it is obvious that it is impossible to pass judgment on the reasonableness of a classification without taking into consideration, or identifying, the purpose of the law. That the Court has erred seriously in attempting to do this will be shown subsequently.

There are five possible relationships between the class defined by the Trait and the class defined by the Mischief. These relationships can be indicated by the following diagrams:

(1)    : All $T$'s are $M$'s and all $M$'s are $T$'s

(2)    : No $T$'s are $M$'s

(3)    : All $T$'s are $M$'s but some $M$'s are not $T$'s

(4)    : All $M$'s are $T$'s but some $T$'s are not $M$'s

(5)    : Some $T$'s are $M$'s; some $T$'s are not $M$'s; and some $M$'s are not $T$'s

One of these five relationships holds in fact in any case of legislative classification, and we will consider each from the point of view of its "reasonableness."

The first two situations represent respectively the ideal limits of reasonableness and unreasonableness. In the first case, the classification in the law coincides completely with the class of those similarly situated with respect to the purpose of the law. It is perfectly reasonable. In the second case, no member of the class defined in the law is tainted with the mischief at which the law aims. The classification is, therefore, perfectly unreasonable. These two situations need not detain us.

Classification of the third type may be called "under-inclusive." All who are included in the class are tainted with the mischief, but there are others also tainted whom the classification does not include. Since the classification does not include all who are similarly situated with respect to the purpose of the law, there is a prima facie violation of the equal protection requirement of reasonable classification.

But the Court has recognized the very real difficulties under which legislatures operate — difficulties arising out of both the nature of the legislative process and of the society which legislation attempts perennially to reshape — and it has refused to strike down indiscriminately all legislation embodying the classificatory inequality here under consideration.

In justifying this refusal, the Court has defended under-inclusive classifications on such grounds as: the legislature may attack a general problem in a piecemeal fashion; "some play must be allowed for the joints of the machine" [*Missouri K. & T. Ry. v. May*, 194 U.S. 267, 270 (1904)]; "a statute aimed at what is deemed an evil, and hitting it presumably where experience shows it to be most felt, is not to be upset. . . ." [*Keokee Consol. Coke Co. v. Taylor*, 234 U.S. 224, 227 (1914)]; "the law does all that is needed when it does all that it can . . ." [*Buck v. Bell*, 274 U.S. 200, 208 (1927)]; and — perhaps with some impatience — the equal protection clause is not "a pedagogic requirement of the impracticable."

These generalities, while expressive of judicial tolerance, are not, however, very helpful. They do not constitute a clear statement of the circumstances and conditions which justify such tolerance — which justify a departure from the strict requirements of the principle of equality. Mr. Justice Holmes, in urging tolerance of under-inclusive classifications, stated that such legislation should not be disturbed by the Court unless it can clearly see that there is no fair reason for the law which would not require with equal force its extension to those whom it leaves untouched. But what is a "fair reason" for over-riding the demand for equal treatment?

Forewarned about the dangers of pedagogic impracticability, and fully aware that we cannot subject legislatures to the demands of an impossible perfectionism, we suggest that there are two general sorts of practical considerations to which weight must be given in determining when and how far departures from ideal standards of classification are justified. The first sort raises administrative, the second, political questions.

The legislature cannot very well be required to impose upon administrative agencies tasks which cannot be carried out or which must be carried out on a large scale at a single stroke. While it may be desirable to sterilize all feeble-minded persons, administrative difficulties might justify limiting the law to the sterilization of the institutionalized feeble-minded. The bird in hand may sometimes be plucked before snares are set for those in the bush.

The "piecemeal" approach to a general problem, permitted by under-inclusive classifications, appears justified when it is considered that legislative dealing with such problems is usually an experimental matter. It is impossible to tell how successful a particular approach may be, what dislocations might occur, what evasions might develop, what new evils might be generated in the attempt to treat the old. Administrative expedients must be forged and tested. Legislators, recognizing these factors, may wish to proceed cautiously, and courts must allow them to do so.

This is not to say that any plea of administrative inconvenience or impossibility should receive automatic deference. Nor that the legislative right to "experiment" is very wide. The Magna Carta for legislative curiosity is not to be found even in the Holmesian dictum that "all life is an experiment." But, abuses apart, these factors have weight in justifying under-inclusive classifications.

The political considerations are more difficult to deal with, and at the same time more significant in their implications. The legislature, to be sure, "has done all that is needed when it has done all that it can." But when has it done that? It is one thing to say "this is all we can do within the limits of administrative possibilities." It is quite another thing to say, "this is all we can do within the limits set by certain political considerations, such as the necessity of winning re-election or appeasing powerful pressure groups." Probable retribution at the polls in a coming election unless farmers, for example, are given special classificatory treatment in a law, may set limits to what a legislature thinks it can do — and still be re-elected. But does a legislature have a "right to re-election" to which a court must defer? Does the resentment of the farm vote, or the labor vote, constitute a "fair reason" for failing to extend operation of a law to these groups if they are otherwise tainted with the mischief at which the law aims? Can the legislature successfully plead pressure?

The answer to these questions raises fundamental issues about the theory of legislation and the state. If we accept the pressure group theory, a law is properly the resultant of pressures exerted by competing interests. If so, does it not follow that the stronger groups will succeed in winning legislation of a favorable or "unequal" character? The demand for equal laws becomes meaningless in this context. The legislature, on this view, is simply the focal point of competing forces — a social barometer faithfully registering pressures. Can the Court demand of a barometer that it ignore pressure?

It would appear that the requirement that laws be equal rests upon a theory of legislation quite distinct from that of pressure groups — a theory which puts forward some conception of a "general good" as the "legitimate public purpose" at which legislation must aim, and according to which the triumph of private or group pressure marks the corruption of the legislative process.

The development and evaluation of these alternative theories is an enterprise that falls outside the scope of this essay. We would suggest, however, that the pledge of the protection of equal laws is intelligible only within the framework of the second of these alternatives, and that the pressure theory of legislation and the equal protection requirement are incompatible. Accordingly, if this is true, we must conclude that legislative submission to political pressure does not constitute a fair reason for failure to extend the operation of a law to those similarly situated whom it leaves untouched.

Yet it is impossible altogether to ignore the pressure situation in which legislatures operate. Everything that emerges from the legislative forum is tainted by its journey through the lobby. And the demand for perfection must inevitably compromise with the hard facts of political life. What is at stake here is the extent to which compromise is necessary or desirable. It is not the purpose of this analysis to suggest that the mechanical application of convenient formulae can be substituted for the complex and creative act of judgment. We must rely, as at so many other points, upon judicial statesmanship.

It is probably true, however, that nowhere more than in the area of equal protection does tolerance towards deviation from great principle go by the name of statesmanship. Appreciation of difficulties and sympathetic tolerance are needed. But judicial statesmen are also concerned to strengthen and guard the integrity of the legislative process. This may well require the testing of legislation by higher standards than legislatures sometimes adopt for themselves. With respect to under-inclusive classifications this means that the Court, while giving weight to pleas of administrative difficulties, must stand guard against an overconcern for mere "convenience"; and, while recognizing the facts of pressure politics, must place a barrier in the path of over-eager acquiescence.

A final word about under-inclusive classification. It is possible to avoid the charge of under-inclusiveness by the simple device of giving a narrower formulation of the purpose of the law. But while it may be possible to evade the unreasonable classification charge by this device, it is not possible to escape the equal protection requirement. For that requirement is not limited to reasonable classification. It has other aspects, some of which, as we shall see, are brought into play precisely by the narrow formulation of purpose. Consequently, an attempt to get around the equal protection clause by this evasion of its classificatory requirements will prove futile.

The fourth type of classification imposes a burden upon a wider range of individuals than are included in the class of those tainted with the mischief at which the law aims. It can thus be called "over-inclusive." Herod, ordering the death of all male children born on a particular day because one of them would some day bring about his downfall, employed such a classification. It is exemplified by the quarantine and the dragnet. The wartime treatment of American citizens of Japanese ancestry is a striking recent instance of the imposition of burdens upon a large class of individuals because some of them were believed to be disloyal.

The prima facie case against such departures from the ideal standards of reasonable classification is stronger than the case against under-inclusiveness. For in the latter case, all who are included in the class are at least tainted by the mischief at which the law aims; while over-inclusive classifications reach out to the innocent bystander, the hapless victim of circumstance or association.

It should be noted that such classifications fly squarely in the face of our traditional antipathy to assertions of mass guilt and guilt by association. Guilt, we believe, is individual, and to act otherwise is to deprive the individual of due process of law. But while the courts have preferred to deal with this situation in due process terms, the reasonable classification requirement of the equal protection clause is also violated.

But in spite of the flagrant injustice of over-inclusive classifications, there are circumstances in which legislation of this character has been, and perhaps must be, sustained. The circumstances are those of emergency, which must be grave and imminent if the impositions are harsh and onerous — as in the case of the wartime evacuations of Japanese-Americans — or less grave but still "emergency" if the impositions are relatively mild — as in the case of a police road block. The problem for the court is simply whether there exists or existed a genuine emergency situation calling for emergency measures and whether there was "good faith" in the attempt to deal with it.

The nature of this justification for sustaining over-inclusive classification suggests a further consideration. A genuine emergency will usually involve the exercise of emergency power by some non-legislative agency. The legislative process is not particularly designed for dealing with emergencies. We would expect to find, therefore, very few cases of legislative classification which can successfully plead emergency justification, and it may well be held that the initial presumption, in the case of legislation, should run against the emergency plea.

The final situation to be considered is one in which the previously discussed factors of under-inclusiveness and over-inclusiveness are both present. While it may seem paradoxical to assert that a classification can be at once over-inclusive and under-inclusive, many classifications do, in fact, fall into this category, that is, they can be challenged separately on both grounds.

For example, in the *Hirabayashi* case [*Hirabayashi v. United States*, 320 U.S. 81 (1943)] the classification of "American citizens of Japanese ancestry" for the purpose of meeting the dangers of sabotage can be challenged both on the grounds that it is under-inclusive, since others — American citizens of German or Italian ancestry — are equally under the strain of divided loyalties, and that it is over-inclusive, since it is not supposed that all American citizens of Japanese ancestry are disloyal. The sustaining of this classification, therefore, requires both the finding of sufficient emergency to justify the imposition of a burden upon a larger class than is believed tainted with the Mischief and the establishment of "fair reasons" for failure to extend the operation of the law to a wider class of potential saboteurs.

No problems that have not already been discussed, however, arise in connection with classifications of this type.

Thus far we have spoken of reasonable classification in its bearing upon legislative activity. But it is obvious that the analysis extends to administrative action also. This is true not only because there is delegation of legislative power to non-legislative agencies, but because in the execution of legislatively determined policy there is a considerable range of classificatory discretion remaining in administrative hands. The exercise of that discretion can be judged reasonable or unreasonable by the same criteria as are relevant to the judgment of legislative activity. The reasonable classification requirement applies, in fact, to any classificatory activity involving "state action." Some interesting possibilities are suggested by the discernible tendency to broaden the meaning of "state action."

. . . .

[For a discussion of the usefulness and limitations of American law under the equality guarantee in the Fourteenth Amendment on Canadian law under section 15 of the *Charter*, see Finkelstein, "Section 15, Section 1, and the Relevance of the U.S. Experience" (1985), Advocates Quarterly, *supra.*]

# SECTIONS 1 AND 15 OF THE CANADIAN CHARTER OF RIGHTS AND FREEDOMS AND THE RELEVANCE OF THE U.S. EXPERIENCE

Neil Finkelstein (1985), 6 Advocates Quarterly 188 (footnotes omitted).

## 1. Introduction

Whereas other provisions of the *Canadian Charter of Rights and Freedoms* guarantee particular rights or freedoms, such as freedom of expression or religion or the right to be free of unreasonable searches or seizures, section 15(1) guarantees the right to be treated equally regardless of the substance of law. This gives rise to an immediate interpretive difficulty. All laws make classifications and differentiate between groups. Accordingly, there must be some way to distinguish between prohibited and non-prohibited differentiations. Section 15(1) does not provide the whole answer. The provision reads as follows:

> 15(1) Every individual is equal before and under the law and has the right to the equal protection and equal benefit of the law without discrimination and, in particular, without discrimination based on race, national or ethnic origin, colour, religion, sex, age or mental or physical disability.

The opening lines of section 15(1) are thus textually unlimited, guaranteeing to every individual the right to both the equal protection and benefit of the law without discrimination. There are no restrictions on this language. The enumerated list of prohibited grounds of discrimination is set out only for greater particularity. Other classifications, such as those based upon family status, would clearly be covered even though they are not specifically listed. Even within the enumerated list, not all categories are equally protected *inter se*. For example, it is likely that old age classifications will be more closely scrutinized than those based upon youth. The key is provided by section 1 of the Charter, which reads as follows:

> 1. The *Canadian Charter of Rights and Freedoms* guarantees the rights and freedoms set out in it subject only to such reasonable limits prescribed by law as can be demonstrably justified in a free and democratic society.

A legal classification will therefore be valid pursuant to section 1 provided that, in context, it is reasonable, prescribed by law, and demonstrably justified by reference to what is done in other free and democratic societies.

The legal prescription element of section 1 will not usually create a problem. If there is no legal authority for a classification, the case can be dealt with on administrative law or division of powers principles without reference to the Charter. The critical Charter question in the context of section 1 will therefore usually come down to what is "reasonable" and "demonstrably justified" in the circumstances.

Generally speaking, the courts may interfere in an equality case at one of two stages: (1) the purpose stage, to declare a particular legislative purpose or means invalid, and (2) the nexus stage, to declare that the nexus between the means (*i.e.*, the classification) and the end (*i.e.*, the legislative purpose) is not close enough. At the first stage, the courts must examine the legislative purpose or means by reference to the values embodied in the Charter. If it is illegitimate, the law may be struck down without further analysis. Thus a law which provided for the automatic compulsory sterilization of retarded people would be invalid. In my view, even if it could be proved that mentally retarded people are more likely to have retarded offspring than "normal" people, the state interest in reducing the incidence of retardation does not outweigh the right of people to procreate and propagate their line. As shall be discussed later, access to the future through one's children is a basic human right, an essential attribute of the human dignity which a constitutional equality guarantee is meant to protect.

Once the courts have determined that the purpose of a law or the means used to achieve that purpose is legitimate, they will have to proceed to the next stage of deciding whether the link between the means and the end is close enough. Some classifications, such as those specifically enumerated in section 15 of the Charter, will attract more careful judicial scrutiny because of their nature and context. Others, such as those involving purely economic regulation, will likely be only minimally scrutinized as long as there is a rational relationship between the law and its objective.

The most obvious and accessible source of guidance at the present time is American law. The United States has had over 100 years of experience with a constitutional equality guarantee, so its jurisprudence has had time to mature. While American law will be useful, we must be wary of transporting it *in toto* into the Charter. There are clear differences between our respective constitutional guarantees which make a wholesale transplantation inappropriate.

## 2. Textual Differences between the Canadian and American Equality Guarantees

The Fourteenth Amendment to the *Constitution of the United States of America* reads as follows:

> 1. All persons born or naturalized in the United States, and subject to the jurisdiction thereof, are citizens of the United States and of the State wherein they reside. *No State shall make or enforce any law which shall* abridge the privileges or immunities of citizens of the United States; nor shall

any State deprive any person of life, liberty or property, without due process of law; nor *deny to any person within its jurisdiction the equal protection of the laws.* (Emphasis added.)

The Fourteenth Amendment acts only upon the American states. However, an equal protection element has been implied into the due process component of the Fifth Amendment, a provision which acts upon Congress.

There are significant textual differences between the equality provisions in the U.S. Constitution and sections 1 and 15 of the Charter of Rights. First, there is no specific mention of equal benefits in the Fourteenth Amendment as there is in section 15. Thus in *Dandridge v. Williams* [397 U.S. 471 (1970)] a Maryland Department of Welfare regulation provided for welfare increases up to the fifth child in a family but none beyond that, for a maximum of $250 per family. A family with six children therefore received proportionately less than one with fewer children. The U.S. Supreme Court upheld the regulation on the basis that there is no fundamental right to welfare. In Canada, one could argue that such a regulation is a denial of equal benefits calculated on a per child basis and therefore contrary to section 15 of the Charter.

Second, there is no explicit mention of affirmative action in the Fourteenth Amendment. The American courts have therefore had to fashion principles independently of the text of the Constitution. While the U.S. Supreme Court has accepted affirmative action in principle, it has imposed a relatively strict standard of review. An affirmative action program must bear a "substantial", as opposed to a merely rational, relationship to a legitimate state objective before it will be upheld. Thus in *University of California Regents v. Bakke* [438 U.S. 265 (1978)], the result of a complicated set of decisions was that five members of the U.S. Supreme Court differed among themselves about the validity of a quota system but agreed in principle that the goal of obtaining a racially mixed student population in a state medical school was constitutionally legitimate. Powell J., the swing vote, held that race could be one factor among many to be considered by the admissions officers. However a flat quota system based exclusively upon race was impermissible.

. . . .

In Canada, the provincial legislatures and Parliament had more leeway in the manner in which they chose to implement affirmative action programs even prior to section 15(2) of the Charter. In *Re Athabasca Tribal Council and Amoco Canada Petoleum Co. Ltd.* [[1981] 1 S.C.R. 699] a pre-Charter case decided pursuant to the Alberta *Individual Rights Protection Act*, Ritchie J., speaking for four members of the Supreme Court of Canada in *obiter*, said that any law which was rationally related to "advancing the lot of Indians so that they may be in a competitive position to obtain employment" would be valid. A similar rational relationship standard is postulated by section 15(2) of the Charter, which would validate "any law, program or activity that has as its object the amelioration of conditions of disadvantaged individuals or groups".

Third, the Fourteenth Amendment does not give the courts any guidance about what kinds of classifications should be most closely scrutinized. The provision is textually absolute. This may be contrasted with section 15(1) of the Charter which, while prohibiting all discrimination, at least sets out a list of categories for greater particularity. Canadian courts are put on notice that they should make a careful inquiry into the reasons and purpose behind any law which makes differentiations based upon any of the listed classifications.

Finally, and related to the third difference above, the Fifth and Fourteenth Amendments do not contain any criteria for distinguishing between valid and invalid differentiations. By contrast, section 1 of the *Charter* contains a code of limitations on the rights and freedoms set out in the Charter. In the equality context, legislative or administrative classifications which infringe section 15(1) are invalid unless they are reasonable, prescribed by law, and demonstrably justified in a free and democratic society.

There are, thus, substantial textual differences between the respective Canadian and American equality guarantees. These differences must be considered when applying American law to a Canadian problem.

### 3. Equal Protection Analysis in the United States

Three basic themes underlie the equal protection guarantees in the U.S. Constitution. The first is the basic dignity and worth of the individual. This implies a denial of any governmental power to engage in invidious discrimination between groups, or to imply that any particular group is inferior. The second theme is that of access to a fair distributive share of basic goods and to the future. Equal protection analysis has been applied to protect a limited number of matters which are deemed basic to securing such access. Pursuant to the second theme, American courts have protected the right to travel, to marry, to vote and to litigate. Finally, the equality guarantee has been used as an internal political check. Thus in *Skinner v. Oklahoma* [316 U.S. 535 (1942)], the Oklahoma Legislature could not provide for compulsory sterilization of some criminals but not others. It is clear from Mr. Justice Douglas' reasoning in *Skinner* that the Legislature could not have enacted such a law to govern criminals generally, in effect imposing sterilization as a punishment for conviction. The equal protection clause was an internal political check to protect a group from severe and unwarranted disadvantage.

Professor Tribe has focused the equal protection idea and the above themes by dividing equal protection analysis into two components: (1) treatment as an equal, and (2) equality of treatment. The right to treatment as an equal, deriving from the theme of basic dignity, requires that every individual be treated with equal regard as a person by the government. Not every political judgment which results in disadvantage to an individual is a denial of treatment as an equal. Rather, such treatment means that the government may not make political judgments which appear to be based upon stigmatizing biases or prejudice.

The right to equal treatment, deriving from the second and third themes above, is triggered with respect to only a limited number of interests. Equal treatment thus does not mean that everyone must be treated equally in all cases. On the contrary, the political process is allowed to distinguish unequally between groups as long as the process itself is equal. Distinctions are permissible in order to promote desirable public policies. However where a fundamental right is implicated or a "suspect classification" such as race or ethnic origin is used, a strict standard of review is imposed.

The U.S. Supreme Court has fashioned three standards of judicial review, or "levels of scrutiny", in its equal protection analysis. The first is "minimum rationality" and simply requires that there be a rational relationship between the legislative means used and the objective sought to be accomplished. Most economic legislation is subjected to only this minimal standard. The Supreme Court pays great deference to the legislatures' assumptions about causes and possible solutions to problems where minimum rationality is applied. It will not review the panoply of possible alternatives to see if a better means of accomplishing the objective could be found, nor will it require the legislatures to support their assumptions with hard evidence. Legislatures have great leeway in developing rules and programs where this minimum level of scrutiny is used.

The extent the courts will go to uphold legislation is illustrated by two cases. In *Railway Express Agency v. New York* [336 U.S. 106 (1949)], a municipal traffic law banned advertisements on the sides of vehicles unless they were connected with the vehicle owner's business. In effect, the law prohibited paid advertising. Mr. Justice Douglas, speaking for the majority of the U.S. Supreme Court, held, without demanding evidence, that the city may have decided that those who advertised their own wares were less likely to cause traffic hazards. In *United States Railroad Retirement Bd. v. Fritz* [449 U.S. 116 (1980)], the U.S. Supreme Court went even farther to uphold the statute in question. Before 1974, people who worked for both railroad and non-railroad employers were eligible for both railroad and social security retirement benefits. People who worked for only one type of employer could get only a single set of retirement benefits. Congress tried to remedy this anomaly by providing, *inter alia*, that only those who had worked for railroad and non-railroad employers *and* who were working for a railroad at the time the statute came into force were eligible for the double benefit. All others could receive only a single set of benefits. Thus a person who worked for the railroad first and the non-railroad employer second, and was thus not employed by a railroad when the statute came into force, was excluded from the double benefit. The person working for the railroad at the latter time could collect both sets of benefits even though the only difference between the two people was the order in which they worked for their respective railroad and non-railroad employers. Notwithstanding this strange result, the Supreme Court held that there was a "plausible" relationship between railroad retirement benefits and a current connection with railroading. *Railway Express Agency* and *Railroad Retirement Board* illustrate that it is a rare law indeed which cannot pass the minimum rationality test.

At the other end of the spectrum, the American courts will apply "strict scrutiny" where a fundamental right is implicated or a suspect classification is used. There is an almost *per se* rule of unconstitutionality where strict scrutiny is applied. The law must be neither over-inclusive nor under-inclusive; that is, it must catch all of the people who are the cause of the perceived problem but none who are not. In other words, there must be a unique, totally symmetrical relationship between the legislative means used and the end. Very few laws survive this level of scrutiny.

The difficulty with the American equal protection analysis until recently is that the only real issue before the courts in any particular case was which of these two levels of scrutiny to adopt. Once the court found the right pigeonhole, the constitutional result followed almost automatically. If a fundamental right was implicated or a suspect classification such as race was used, the law was struck down. If the law did not attract strict scrutiny, the other extreme of minimum rationality was applied and the law stood. Theoretically, there was no middle ground, although the courts sometimes stretched principle to accommodate hard cases.

The consequence of this two-tier approach was that the U.S. Supreme Court would often refuse to interfere with the legislative process in economic or social matters even where necessities of modern life were at stake. Thus, in *San Antonio Independent School District v. Rodriguez* [411 U.S. 1 (1973)], the Texas public school system was funded on a district by district basis out of local property taxes. Poorer districts thus received less money for education than wealthy ones. Rather than analyzing the scheme on its own merits, the U.S. Supreme Court applied the traditional minimum rationality/strict scrutiny dichotomy to uphold the scheme. The poor were not a suspect class, and education has never been held to be a fundamental right. In the absence of evidence that a minimum standard of education was not being provided, the scheme was upheld. The Supreme Court has taken the same minimum review approach with respect to other basic necessities such as welfare and decent housing.

In recent years the U.S. Supreme Court has added a third level of scrutiny called "intermediate scrutiny". As stated by Professor Gold:

> This standard is triggered when laws impinge upon interests deemed important, though not fundamental, or when the law employs a basis of classification deemed sensitive, though not suspect.

Where the intermediate standard of review is invoked, the Supreme Court requires that the law bear a "substantial relationship" to an "important governmental objective". This standard was first explicitly adopted by the U.S. Supreme Court in 1976 in *Craig v. Boren* [429 U.S. 190 (1976)]. In that case, an Oklahoma statute prohibited the sale of 3.2% beer to males under 21 and females under 18, purportedly to combat road accidents due to drunkenness. A perusal of the Oklahoma statutes indicated that the state considered 3.2% beer to be non-intoxicating. The statistics indicated that 0.18% of women and 2% of men between the ages of 18 and 20 were arrested for drunk driving. This would have been enough to support the law under the minimum rationality standard. However the Supreme Court held that it was an "unduly tenuous fit" in the gender discrimination context. Restated, a 2% incidence of male drunkenness, even though 10 times that of females in the same age group, was insufficient to support a gender-based system.

Beyond the minimum rationality level of judicial review, the courts require the government to support its policy choices and the means used to achieve them by substantial factual data. The courts are not willing to accept legislative assumptions, be they of a statistical, psychological or sociological nature, where intermediate or strict scrutiny is applied.

### 4. Usefulness of American Jurisprudence on Equal Protection in the Canadian Context

American jurisprudence on equal protection will be useful in analyzing sections 1 and 15 of the Charter for a number of reasons.

First, our systems are predicated on very similar constitutional values. Both are founded upon the value of democratic government. Matters which further this value such as free speech, the right to vote and, notwithstanding *Rodriguez*, the right to a decent education, will find protection in the equality guarantee. Also, both

Canadian and American society are founded upon notions of the value of the individual and the minimization of state intrusion into private affairs. This manifests itself most obviously in the United States, which has had a constitutional *Bill of Rights* for close to two hundred years, but it also has deep roots in Canadian political culture. The value of the individual is now constitutionally protected by the Charter, and perceived threats to it will undoubtedly attract judicial scrutiny pursuant to section 15.

Second, American jurisprudence is a lesson that not all classifications should be treated the same way for constitutional purposes. Some classifications, for reasons rooted in history or other experience, must attract a more intense inspection than others. Where a classification creates invidious or stigmatizing discrimination or seems irrelevant to the legislation's stated purpose, as race or sex often are, it should be closely scrutinized. American law also teaches that a law which appears neutral on its face may in fact create invidious discrimination when one examines the evidence more closely. One must look at the law's history, effect and mode of administration to see whether such is the case.

Third, American cases may be persuasive of a classification's reasonableness, or the lack thereof. This is particularly so where the courts have reviewed the facts extensively and indicated clearly the evidentiary basis of their decisions.

Finally, American cases will be useful as evidence of what is done in another free and democratic society.

Notwithstanding the above, American cases cannot be adopted in Canada without careful analysis. I have already reviewed the textual differences between our respective constitutional guarantees so I shall not repeat the analysis here. In addition, the American two-tiered approach may create distortions. Before 1976, cases which were not subjected to strict scrutiny were automatically left to the minimum rationality standard. That is not appropriate in Canada. Section 1 of the Charter requires the courts to assess each case in light of the evidence and to decide whether a law is reasonable in the circumstances.

To take two examples, let us consider education and age. As to education, *Rodriguez* indicates that great judicial deference is paid in the United States to legislative decisions about public school funding methods. The courts will not interfere with a choice of system which distributes educational financing unequally between rich and poor districts. In Canada, the result would likely be different. Canadian courts are not bound by the two-tier system of review that was in force in the United States at the time of *Rodriguez*. On the contrary, section 1 of the Charter sets the standard of review. Given the importance of education in modern society, I believe that Canadian courts would demand a high standard of proof from the state before allowing public education to be distributed in substantially different qualities to rich and poor groups. I have no doubt that, if such a situation were to arise in Canada, Canadian courts would have to go beyond minimum rationality to determine whether the implementation of such a financing system was reasonable pursuant to section 1 of the Charter. *Prima facie* it is not, and the government would have to lead strong evidence of its reasons for the differentiation.

The two-tier approach has produced a similar distortion with respect to the age classification. In *Massachusetts Bd. of Retirement v. Murgia* [427 U.S. 307 (1976)], a state statute provided a mandatory retirement age of 50 for state uniformed policemen. The U.S. Supreme Court admitted that the state could have chosen "to determine fitness more precisely through individualized testing after age 50". However the court held that people over age 50 were not a discrete and insular group historically subjected to invidious discrimination, and therefore minimum rationality was enough. Because it was not irrational to assume that policemen over 50 were less fit than those below 50 as a general rule, the law survived.

A stricter standard was applied to age in Canada even prior to the Charter. In *Ontario Human Rights Com'n et al. v. Borough of Etobicoke* [[1982] 1 S.C.R. 202], the Supreme Court of Canada considered the validity of a mandatory retirement age for firefighters in the context of the Ontario *Human Rights Code*. Mr. Justice McIntyre held that "impressionistic" evidence that firefighting is not "a young man's game" is not sufficient where prohibited grounds of discrimination are used. Hard statistical data or other scientific evidence must be led where possible before such classifications are upheld. The courts will not defer to legislative assumptions about age.

## 5. Conclusion

American law will be very useful as a guide to interpreting the equality guarantee in the Charter provided that the differences between them are understood and appreciated. No doubt Canadian courts will adopt the minimum rationality standard with respect to most economic regulation. Similarly, classifications which are suspect in the United States will come under heavy scrutiny here. The major area for caution will be with respect to matters which are important but do not implicate fundamental rights or involve suspect classifications. American cases on these subjects decided before the introduction of the intermediate scrutiny standard of review in 1976 in *Craig v. Boren*, or cases decided subsequently but based upon older cases, must be viewed with qualification. The standard of review imposed by section 1 of the Charter in such matters is considerably higher than minimum rationality.

# 23

# Cultural Guarantees:
# Education and Language

## 1. Education: Section 93 and the Charter

### ROMAN CATHOLIC SEPARATE SCHOOL TRUSTEES FOR TINY v. THE KING

In the Privy Council. [1928] A.C. 363.

Viscount Haldane, Lord Buckmaster, Lord Shaw, Lord Wrenbury and
Lord Blanesburgh. June 12, 1928.

Appeal by special leave from a judgment of the Supreme Court of Canada,
[1927] S.C.R. 637, affirming on equal division a judgment of the Ontario Appellate
Division, 60 O.L.R. 15, which affirmed a judgment of Rose J., 59 O.L.R. 96,
dismissing a petition of right by appellants.

VISCOUNT HALDANE: Their Lordships are fully aware that this appeal is
among the most important that have come before them from Canada in recent
years. It relates to the interpretation of the Constitution of Canada in regard to the
separate schools of a large part of her Roman Catholic population, and to the
character of the rights conferred on them by the legislative settlement made at the
time of Confederation under the *British North America Act*. So far as concerns the
question brought before the Judicial Committee of the Privy Council, it will be
found to be a question of pure law, turning on the interpretation and application of
words in that Act. . . .
    These proceedings took the form of a petition of right presented by the
appellants to the Supreme Court of Ontario. The petition claimed that certain Acts
of the legislature of that Province, and certain regulations purporting and to have
been passed under these Acts, prejudicially affected the rights conferred by the
*British North America Act* on the appellants and were *ultra vires*. The appellants
asked for a declaration that the Acts of the legislature, which had sought to alter the
basis of distribution of legislative grants which existed at the date of Confederation,
were *ultra vires* so far as concerned separate schools, and for judgment for a sum
equal to the difference between the amount paid to the trustees of the Roman
Catholic School for school section No. 2 in the Township of Tiny, out of the legislative grant of the Province for 1922, and the amount that would have come to it if
effect had been given to the *Separate School Act*, 1863, which was in force at Confederation, and created (it is claimed) a right which the legislature of the Province
had no power after Confederation to affect prejudicially. The appellants also

claimed that they had the right to establish and conduct in their own schools courses of study and grades of education such as were being conducted in continuation schools, collegiate institutes and high schools, and that all regulations purporting to affect that right were invalid. They asked for a further declaration that the supporters of Roman Catholic separate schools were exempt from the rates imposed for the support of the former kind of schools, unless established or conducted by boards of trustees of Roman Catholic separate schools.

All of these claims were traversed by the Attorney-General of Ontario on behalf of the Government of Ontario.

The question which has to be decided is one of far-reaching magnitude. To understand its scope it is necessary to have in mind the history of education in Canada, including that of s. 93 of the *British North America Act*, 1867. That section embodies a compromise. The language proposed by the conferences of delegates from the various parts of Canada, which passed resolutions at Quebec on October 10, 1864, was not adopted, so far as the final arrangement was concerned, in the form in which the resolutions were passed: see Cartwright's Cases on the B.N.A. Act, vol. ii, Quebec resolution No. 43. Resolution 43 proposed to give power to the local legislatures to make laws as to education, saving the rights and privileges which the Protestant and Catholic minority in both Canadas might possess as to their denominational schools at the time when the Union came into operation. In the *British North America Act*, as passed by the Imperial Parliament, the substance of this resolution is not included in s. 92, but is embodied in a separate section, 93. The separate section enacts that in and for each Province the legislature may exclusively make laws in relation to education, subject and according to certain provisions. These provisions were: (sub-s. 1) that nothing in such law should prejudicially affect any right or privilege with respect to denominational schools which any class of person had by law in the Province at the Union; (sub-s. 2) all the powers, privileges and duties at the Union, conferred and imposed in Upper Canada on the separate schools and school trustees of the Queen's Roman Catholic subjects are extended to the dissentient schools of the Queen's Protestant and Roman Catholic subjects in Quebec (on this sub-section no question arises in the present appeal); and by sub-s. 3, as follows: "Where in any Province a system of separate or dissentient schools exists by law at the Union or is thereafter established by the legislature of the Province, an appeal shall lie to the Governor-General in Council from any Act or decision of any Provincial authority affecting any right or privilege of the Protestant or Roman Catholic minority of the Queen's subjects in relation to education." The fourth sub-section enacts that if a Provincial law which seems to the Governor-General in Council requisite to give effect to his decision is not made or the decision is not executed, then the Parliament of Canada may make the necessary remedial law.

It will be observed that sub-s. 3 goes further than sub-s. 1 in material respects. In the first place, it applies not merely to what exists at the time of Confederation, but also to separate or dissentient schools established afterwards by Provincial legislatures. In the second place, the word "prejudicially", in sub-s. 1, is dropped out from before the expression "affecting", in subs.-3. In the third place, the right or privilege is not confined to one in respect of denominational schools, but is given in respect of education. Their Lordships think that these changes in language are significant. They show that the protection given by sub-s. 1 was deemed, if taken by itself, to be insufficient. It was not considered to be enough protection for the denominational schools to apply to them a restriction which only rendered *ultra vires* of the Provinces a law which took away what was an existing legal right or privilege at the time of Confederation in respect of denominational schools. Sub-s. 3 contemplates that within the powers of the Provincial legislature Acts might be passed which did affect rights and privileges of religious minorities in relation to education, and gives a different kind of remedy, which appears, as has already been pointed out, to have been devised subsequently to the Quebec resolutions of 1864, and before the bill of 1867 was agreed on. Whenever an Act or decision of a Provincial authority affecting any right or privilege of the minority, Protestant or Roman Catholic, in relation to education is challenged, an appeal is to lie to the Governor-General in Council, as distinguished from the Courts of law. No doubt if what is challenged is challenged on the ground of its being *ultra vires*, the right of appeal to a Court of law remains for both parties unimpaired. But there is a further right not based on the principle of *ultra vires*. That this is so is shown by the extension of the power to challenge to any system of separate or dissentient schools established by law after Confederation and which accordingly could not be confined to rights or privileges at the time of Confederation. The omission of the word "prejudicially" in sub-s. 3 tends to bear out the view that something wider than a mere question of legality was intended, and the language of sub-s. 4 enabling the Dominion Parliament to legislate remedially for giving effect, "so far only as the circumstances of each case require", to the decision of the Governor-General in Council, points to a similar interpretation. What is to be dealt with is a right or privilege in relation to education.

Their Lordships are of opinion that where the head of the executive in council in Canada is satisfied that injustice has been done by taking away a right or privilege which is other than a legal one from the Protestant or Roman Catholic minority in relation to education, he may interfere. The step is one from mere legality to administrative propriety, a totally different matter. But it may be that those who had to find a new constitution for Canada when the *British North America Act* was passed in 1867, came to the conclusion that a very difficult situation could be met in no other way than by transferring the question from the region of legality to that of administrative fairness.

There is no question before their Lordships in this case concerning any appeal to the Governor-General in Council, and they abstain from saying anything as to the principles on which, if invoked, he may think fit to proceed. But the view that the rights of the appellants are not necessarily confined to rights under sub-s. 1 has an important bearing on the construction of that sub-section, inasmuch as it no longer takes away all remedy in cases to which the principle of *ultra vires* does not apply. It may even be that the power conferred on the Governor-General in Council enables him to take into account the considerations arising out of what had been done in the course of *de facto* administration, which James L.J. excluded in delivering the judgment of the Judicial Committee in 1874, in *Maher v. Town of Portland*, reported in Wheeler's Confederation Law of Canada, and quoted by the late Lord Chancellor in delivering his recent judgment of the Committee in *Hirsch v. Protestant School Commissioners of Montreal*, [1928] A.C. 200 on February 2 last. The question is one of administrative policy, and it is not before their Lordships. They desire, however, to observe that the view now expressed as to the relations of sub-ss. 1 and 3 of s. 93 is substantially the same as that taken in *Brophy v. Attorney-General of Manitoba*, [1895] A.C. 221. In that case the question arose under the *Constitution Act of Manitoba*, 1870, a Dominion Act under which, as subsequently confirmed by Imperial statute, Manitoba became one of the Provinces of the Dominion of Canada. The Act contains in s. 22 provisions which for present purposes are identical with those of sub-ss. 1, 3 and 4 of s. 93 of the *British North America Act*. It is true that in the second and corresponding sub-section of the *Manitoba Act* the appeal is expressly stated to lie against any Act or decision of the legislature of the Province as well as of any Provincial authority, thus in words saying more than in sub-s. 3 of s. 93 of the Act of 1867. But Lord Herschell in *Brophy's* case expressed his dissent from the argument that the insertion of the additional words in the Manitoba Act showed that in the Act of 1867 it could not have been intended to comprehend the legislatures under the words "any Provincial authority". Their Lordships agree with his view, and they are of opinion that the legislatures are so comprehended. The point may prove to be one of great importance if there is hereafter an appeal to the Governor-General in Council. In *Brophy's* case the Roman Catholic minority in Manitoba appealed to the Governor-General in Council under sub-s. 2 of s. 22 of their Constitutional Act on the ground that rights and privileges of theirs in relation to education had been affected by two statutes of the legislature of Manitoba passed in 1890, which set up a general system of non-sectarian education. The schools of the Roman Catholic minority were deprived of their previously existing proportionate share of the money contributed for school purposes out of the taxes, while for the new non-sectarian schools they were both taxed and assessed for rates. It had been held, in *City of Winnipeg v. Barrett*, [1892] A.C. 445, that the statutes of 1890 did not affect any right or privilege with respect to their schools which the Roman Catholics of Manitoba had by law or practice in their Province at the Union in 1870. The only right or privilege which they then possessed was to establish and maintain for the use of members of their own Church such schools, at their own expense, as they pleased. In *Barrett's* case this was the only question before the Judicial Committee, and it was held that the Acts of 1890 were not *ultra vires*.

But in *Brophy's* case the question was the wholly different one, whether the rights and privileges of Roman Catholics in relation to education had not been so affected by the Acts of 1890 as to enable an appeal to the Governor-General in Council in a quasi administrative capacity. It was held that there was such affection, in fact although not in law, inasmuch as Roman Catholics were to be taxed and rated for the upkeep of schools which were obnoxious to their religious opinion in regard to education. It was no point of illegality. What was decided was that the Governor-General in Council had power to entertain such an appeal under sub-s. 2 of s. 22 of the Constitutional Act, corresponding, as their Lordships have already stated, to sub-s. 3 of s. 93 of the *British North America Act*, 1867.

Their Lordships have dwelt on what was decided in *Brophy's* case in reference to the scope of the appeal against the affection of rights or privileges within the meaning of sub-s. 3 of s. 93 of the *British North America Act*, with a view to bringing out the limitation which has to be placed on the expressions used in sub-s. 1. The rights and privileges there referred to must be such as are given by law, and the redress which may be given in respect of prejudice to them, caused by laws made by the Provincial legislatures which, in other respects, have the exclusive power of legislation in relation to education, is a redress based on the principles of *ultra vires*. Such redress can therefore, for the reasons given in *Brophy's* case, be sought from the Courts of law alone. The other remedy which sub-ss. 3 and 4 afford not only supplements the former but affords cogent reasons why sub-s. 1 should be construed as being confined strictly to questions of *ultra vires*. Were the Acts and regulations complained of in the petition of right assailable under this principle? In order to answer this question it is necessary to understand clearly what was their nature, and to understand this it is essential to see what has been the development of the system of education in Upper Canada.

Before 1867 there were in Canada schools of three principal classes — common schools, grammar schools and separate schools. Since Confederation there have come into existence continuation schools, collegiate institutes and high schools, which have developed out of the three kinds of school last mentioned. The claim of the appellants is that, in 1867, Roman Catholics in Upper Canada enjoyed by law the right to establish denominational schools, to be conducted by boards of trustees chosen by themselves; that, as regards selection of text-books and courses of study, the control of these belonged to the boards of trustees who could sanction in their schools courses of study co-extensive in scope with those, since Confederation, pursued in high schools, collegiate institutes and continuation schools. The case made was that the trustees could do this in the separate schools, inasmuch as these, although common schools, were not under the old order of things, restricted in their scope as regards education of pupils up to twenty-one years of age. It is argued for the appellants that under s. 93, sub-s. 1, the Roman Catholics of Ontario continued to enjoy these autonomous rights, coupled with a consequential right of exemption from taxation for the purposes of the high schools, collegiate institutes and continuation schools, which, it is said, are mere forms of what fall within the scope of existing separate schools, and are, therefore, of a kind for which the Roman Catholics were exempt from taxation.

Their Lordships may say at once that if such a right was really conferred on the boards of separate schools, the right and the title to grants dependent on it were not interrupted by the Act of 1867. . . .

Section 93 was, . . . obviously meant to apply to the future as well as to the past, and to the new Province of Ontario.

This consideration leads up to the crucial point in this appeal. Did the trustees of the separate Roman Catholic schools secure at Confederation a right to maintain, free from control or regulation by the legislature of Ontario, as respects the scope of instruction, denominational schools which could embrace the subjects formerly taught in the separate schools on their higher sides, and afterwards taught in the undenominational high schools, collegiate institutes and continuation schools, as developed after Confederation, or analogous subjects taught in the Roman Catholic separate schools before Confederation, and to exemption from taxation for the support of such undenominational educative organizations? And did the trustees secure a title to receive a share of every grant by the legislature for common school purposes, construed as extending to the maintenance of education of the type given in post-Confederation secondary schools, as well as in those that were merely elementary, based on the number of pupils attending the separate schools, and independent of the subjects taught, or the text-books used, every separate school being entitled to its share, calculated according to a statutory rate, however advanced, however rudimentary, the education and books might be? If these questions are answered in the affirmative then it was *ultra vires* of Ontario to take away the right either to regulate the schools in a manner inconsistent with this freedom, or to diminish the grants or to tax for the support of the undenominational schools, by legislation, or administratively, so far as control was concerned, by State regulation.

The question is a very serious one. Before Confederation the common schools and with them the separate schools were left free, by statute (see *Upper Canada Common Schools Act*, 1859, s. 16), to educate pupils up to the age of twenty-one, and some of them were in the habit of giving to the older pupils advanced teaching such as would fit them to enter the University. But Roman Catholics find a great difficulty in sending their sons and daughters to the higher schools which have now been established for the purposes of this advanced teaching. As the Chief Justice of Canada has said, undenominational education is based on the idea that the separation of secular from religious education may be advantageous. But Roman Catholics, at least, hold that religious instruction and influence should always accompany secular training.

What, then, were the rights of the supporters of the separate schools at the time of Confederation? To answer this, and the question of *ultra vires* which arises out of it, it is necessary to look at the history of the development of education in Canada. [His Lordship here reviewed certain statutes dealing with education in Upper Canada and, after 1840, in the province of Canada.] . . .

In 1859 a Consolidating Act was passed by what had become the Legislative Council and Assembly for the now United Province of Canada. This Act related to common schools. It did not make any important changes in the law, but aimed, for most part, at bringing together the existing statutory provisions relating to common schools. Many of the provisions of this Act were embodied by reference in the Act respecting separate schools passed in the same years as stated below. The office of Chief Superintendent of Education was reconstituted. He was to be under the direction of the Governor. The duty of the Chief Superintendent under the *General Consolidating Act* now cited was among other things, under s. 106, to apportion in each year "all monies granted or provided by the legislature for the support of common schools in Upper Canada, and not otherwise appropriated by law, to the several counties, townships, cities, &c.," according to ratio of population.

There was also to be a Council of Public Instruction of nine persons, appointed by the Governor. Among other things it was to make regulations for the organization, government and discipline of common schools, for the classification of schools and teachers, and for school libraries, and to examine, and at its discretion to recommend or disapprove of text-books for the use of schools or school libraries. By s. 120 the Governor could authorize the expenditure, in Upper Canada, out of the share of the legislative school grant and the additional moneys granted in aid of common and grammar schools "and not otherwise expressly appropriated by law" of certain sums for purposes which were not connected with the separate schools. By s. 121, the whole of the remainder of the grants mentioned in s. 120 and not exclusively appropriated in its sub-sections, were to be expended in aid of the common schools according to the provisions of the Act. There was a conscience section (129) in the Act.

In the same year (1859) the *Separate Schools Act*, already referred to, was passed. The main provisions of the *Common Schools Act* of 1859 were thereby made applicable to the separate schools, but the new Act was designed in ss. 18 to 36 to make clear what was the position in particular of Roman Catholic separate schools. The existing provisions of these were repeated with variations, and it was enacted that the trustees of each separate school should perform the same duties and be subject to the same penalties as trustees of common schools. By s. 33 every separate school was again to be entitled to a proportionate share in the annual grant for common schools. The trustees were to report the names and attendance of the children attending these schools to the Chief Superintendent, who was thereupon to determine what they were entitled to receive out of the legislative grant.

It is now necessary to refer to the final *Separate Schools Act*, passed in 1863, which substituted a new set of provisions in the Act of 1859, in place of ss. 18 to 36, which were by this Act repealed. Amongst those new provisions was s. 20, a re-enactment with additions of the old s. 33 of the Act of 1859; and a section which their Lordships set out later in their judgment.

The appellants contend that the words in s. 106 of the *Common Schools Act* of 1859 "not otherwise appropriated by law" includes the share of the apportioned fund to which they are entitled under s. 20 of the Act of 1863, and shows that they are not excluded from sharing in all the moneys appropriated outside those "granted or provided by the legislature for the support of common schools." But their Lordships think that this is erroneous and that the learned judges were right who thought that the separate schools are only entitled to share in the moneys "granted by the legislature for the support of common schools not otherwise appropriated by law", and also by the Act of 1863 in all other public grants made for common school purposes. The appropriations form in short a first debit item against the money grant. After that, after the appropriations have been made and the debit item satisfied, comes the second stage — namely, that of apportionment; and it is in this apportionment that the separate schools have their share. The apportionment mentioned in s. 106, sub-s. 2, is not that of the total fund, but only of that fund after the trustees of the separate schools had received their share. This their Lordships regard as the true meaning of the Act.

This statute of 1863 is an important one. Its declared purpose was to restore to Roman Catholics in Upper Canada certain rights in respect of separate schools, and to bring the law respecting separate schools more into harmony with the law respecting common schools. It was in force at Confederation, and it has been spoken of as the charter of the denominational schools. The chief points in it were that separate school sections, whether in the same or in adjoining municipalities (not only, as in the earlier Act, the schools in one ward of a city or town), might be joined in a separate school union section. The teachers of separate schools were to be subject to the same examinations, and to receive certificates of qualification in the same way as common school teachers generally. Supporters of separate schools were to be exempt from payment of municipal rates for common schools and libraries, while they continued to be supporters of separate schools, and not merely for the current year, as under the old legislation. The Roman Catholic separate schools were to be subject to such inspection as might be directed by the Chief Superintendent of Education, and were to be subject also to such regulations as might be imposed from time to time by the Council of Public Instruction for Upper Canada. All judges, members of the legislature, heads of local municipal bodies, the Chief Superintendent and the local superintendent of common schools, and clergymen of the Roman Church, were to be visitors of these separate schools.

Section 20 is a section to which much of the argument at their Lordships' bar was directed. It is in these terms: "Every separate school shall be entitled to a share in the fund annually granted by the legislature of this Province for the support of common schools, and shall be entitled also to a share in all other public grants, investments and allotments for common school purposes now made or hereafter to be made by the Province or the municipal authorities, according to the average number of pupils attending such school during the twelve next preceding months, or during the number of months which may elapse from the establishment of a new separate school, as compared with the whole average number of pupils attending school in the same city, town, village or township."

By s. 21, local assessments for common school purposes were excluded from the money to which the separate schools were to be entitled. By s. 26 the Roman Catholic separate schools were to be subject to such inspection as might be directed from time to time by the Chief Superintendent and were to be "subject also to such regulations as might be imposed from time to time by the Council of Public Institution for Upper Canada."

The question which arise on this Act are, first of all, whether, having regard to the provisions quoted, laws have been enacted by the Province which prejudicially affect any legal right or privilege with respect to denominational schools which the Roman Catholic community (a class of persons) had obtained under these statutes at the Union. The second question is whether under these statutes the Roman Catholic schools had become entitled at the Union to grants which were fixed and could not be taken away or interfered with by the authorities of the Province. It has been to render the nature of these questions clear that their Lordships have considered it necessary to examine at some length the history and character of the legislation before Confederation.

The petition of right claims that the suppliants have a legal title to establish and conduct courses of study, with grades of education, such as are now conducted in what are designated as continuation schools, collegiate institutes, and high schools, and that any statutes and regulations purporting to limit or prejudicially affect this title are *ultra vires*. The petition further claims that the class of persons represented by the petitioners are exempt from payment of rates imposed for the support of these organizations when not established by trustees of Roman Catholic separate schools. Consequently on their claim the petitioners ask that the trustees of the Roman Catholic separate schools for section 2, Township of Tiny, may have paid to them certain moneys to which it is said that they would have been entitled on the footing that the general claim as to validity is properly established.

The appellants say that the old common schools were allowed to give such education as was found suitable to pupils up to twenty-one, who were thereby prepared for the University, and that the separate schools enjoyed the right thus permitted, and possessed it at Confederation. For this purpose the classes in the schools were in point of fact "graded". The Courts of Ontario have held in the present case that while this grading was *de facto* permitted it was always subject to the regulations by which the State authorities might from time to time alter and define the work in the common (including the separate) schools. Subject to this supervision, "grading" might take place either in the classes of a single school, or by distributing the teaching where there was a group of schools, as in urban municipalities. It is said for the appellants that the only rival of the common and separate schools as they were up to and after Confederation, was the grammar school, which was not under the common school Acts, but was always organized under separate statutes. The appellants further argued that an Act passed after Confederation in Ontario in 1871 for the improvement of the common and grammar schools really transformed both the common and grammar schools. They were re-arranged in two divisions, in one of which free education was to be given up to the age of twelve, such division to be called a "public school". The other division was to be a "high school", and to give higher instruction with the aid of the old grammar school grant, and of contributions from local revenues by the municipal authorities. The Boards of Grammar school trustees were to take over these high schools, and to administer them under regulation.

The appellants contend that the common school was at the Union entitled to provide for the public, other than separate school supporters, education of every kind which in the judgment of its trustees it was desirable to give and that some of the urban common schools were then known as high schools, in which the teaching extended as far as that in the grammar schools, and was substantially that prescribed for the new high schools after the Act of 1871. The new public and high schools were, it was argued, just divisions of pre-Confederation common schools, with compulsory taxation for the new high schools. From such taxation, it is said, the Roman Catholic separate school supporters must be exempt, and they cannot be affected by the combination brought about by the Act of 1871.

Of the post-Confederation continuation schools, which were established by statutes of 1896 and 1908, it is said that these began by being only continuation classes in public schools in municipalities in which no high school had been established, but were by the Act of 1908 made into continuation schools supported by grants and rates. In any view, as they cannot be given the form of separate schools, Roman Catholics should be free from taxation for them. Of collegiate institutes, it is said that they are only certain high schools to which a special name has been given.

The petition also claims that certain sections in various statutes which infringe the principles thus contended for are *ultra vires*.

The Provincial Legislature is supreme in matters of education, excepting so far as s. 93 of the *British North America Act* restricts its authority. Sub-s. 1 preserves as they stood any rights and the privileges given in relation to denominational schools by law in 1867. The question, therefore, is whether the Province could then as the law stood so control the courses of study and the general range and quality of the text-books used, as to enable the educational authorities of the Province to prescribe the graduation of the separate school and the stages in which instruction should be given in it. Examination of the statutes and of the history of the subject have satisfied their Lordships that, while a settlement was come to in 1863 with both

Roman Catholics and Protestants, a settlement which in so far as it remained unaltered at Confederation, must be strictly maintained, the Province showed in the wording of the successive earlier statutes the intention to preserve for the rest the power to mould the educational system in the interests of the public at large, as distinguished from any section of it, however important. . . .

The examination of the series of statutes relating to education from 1807 onwards has led their Lordships to the view that the Province did provide for the regulation, in the full sense, of its common or public schools. . . .

It is this principle and purpose which appear to their Lordships to be dominant through the statutes, and the language used . . . has brought this Committee to the conclusion that the power of regulation must be interpreted in a wider sense than that given to it in the judgment of the Chief Justice of Canada. They are not at one with him in thinking that separate school trustees could give secondary education in their schools otherwise than by the permission, express or implied, of the Council of Public Instruction. The separate school was only a special form of common school, and the Council could in the case of each determine the courses to be pursued and the extent of the education to be imparted. A full power of regulation, such as the purpose of the statutes quoted renders appropriate, is what suggests itself, and this is the natural outcome of a scheme which never appears to have really varied. Such expressions as "organization", "government", "discipline" and "classification", do, in their Lordships' interpretation of them, imply a real control of the separate schools. The duty of the Judicial Committee is simply to interpret the words used. It may be that even if the contention of the appellants as to the scope of sub-s. 1 is shut out, there will remain to them a remedy of a wholly different kind in the shape of an appeal under sub-s. 3 to the Governor-General in Council in an administrative capacity. That question does not arise in this appeal and is in no way prejudiced by the conclusion to which their Lordships have come.

What has been said on the subject of *ultra vires* in regard to regulation also applies to the title to fixed grants. The appellants rely on s. 20 of the *Separate Schools Act* of 1863. . . . It declares every separate school to be entitled to a share in the fund annually granted by the legislature for the support of common schools, and also to a share in all other public grants, investments and allotments for common school purposes, according to a defined proportion. It is argued that their share of these grants is being withheld from the appellants and from the Roman Catholic separate schools generally. But the question really turns on whether the authorities of the Province had power to make apportionments and payments out of the funds granted before the balance was arrived at which should be available for common school purposes. In their Lordships' opinion it is clear that there was such power. Section 106 of the *Common Schools Act* of 1859 defined as the duty of the Chief Superintendent to apportion the moneys granted or provided by the legislature "and not otherwise appropriated by law" in a manner analogous to that subsequently provided by s. 20 of the Act of 1863. Section 120 of the 1859 Act enabled the Governor to make a number of appropriations out of the sums granted, and s. 121 provides that the whole of the remainder of the grants mentioned and not exclusively appropriated in the earlier sub-sections are to be expended in aid of the common schools according to the provisions of the Act.

In their Lordships' view, in the face of the provisions referred to, it is impossible to contend successfully that it was *ultra vires* after Confederation to make new appropriations out of the grants which would diminish what would otherwise have come to the appellants. Whether the case is looked at from the point of view of regulation, or whether it is regarded from that of discretion in power of appropriation, the result is the same. It is indeed true that power to regulate merely does not imply a power to abolish. But the controversy with which this Board has to deal on the present occasion is a long way from abolition. It may be that the new laws will hamper the freedom of the Roman Catholics in their denominational schools. They may conceivably be or have been subjected to injustice of a kind that they can submit to the Governor-General in Council, and through him to the Parliament of Canada. But they are still left with separate schools, which are none the less actual because the liberty of giving secondary and higher education in them may be abridged by regulation. Such an abridgement may be in the usual course when a national system of education has attained a certain stage in its development, and it would be difficult to forego this power if the grading which may be essential is also to be possible. Their Lordships do not think grading is in itself inconsistent with such rights to separation of schools as was reserved at Confederation. . . .

*Appeal dismissed.*

[See also *Ottawa Separate School Trustees v. Mackell*, [1917] A.C. 62 (P.C.). As to the position of Protestant separate schools in Quebec and the extent to which Quebec legislation could give Jews status in the Protestant school system, see *Hirsch v. Protestant School Com'rs of Montreal*, [1928] A.C. 200 (P.C.). As to the compellability of German Lutherans in Alberta to send their children to public schools, see *R. v. Ulmer*, [1923] 1 D.L.R. 304 (Alta. C.A.). As to the application of section 93 of the *B.N.A. Act* in Saskatchewan, see *McCarthy v. Regina and Regina Public School Trustees*, [1917] 1 W.W.R. 1105 (Sask. C.A.), aff'd [1918] A.C. 911 (P.C.).

In *Reference re Adoption Act*, [1938] S.C.R. 398 at 402, Duff C.J. speaking for the Court said:

It is well not to forget . . . that by section 93 (subject to provisions having for their purpose the protection of religious minorities) education is committed exclusively to the responsibility of the [provincial] legislatures; and that, as regards that subject, the powers of the legislatures are not affected by the clause at the end of section 91. We should perhaps also recall that section 93 (as is well known) embodies one of the cardinal terms of the Confederation arrangement. Education, I may add, is, as I conceive it, employed in this section in its most comprehensive sense.

See, in support, Quebec Resolution 43(6).

Note that by the terms of union with Newfoundland a different provision is substituted for section 93 and declared to be applicable in its stead: see section 17 of the Terms of Union, appended as a schedule to 1949 (Can. 1st sess.), c. 1 and the *British North America Act* (No. 1) 1949 (Imp.), c. 22.

The "education" power is discussed in detail in Lefroy, *Canada's Federal System*, chap. 26 and Clement, *The Canadian Constitution* (3rd ed.), chap. 38. In speaking of the application of section 93 of the *Constitution Act, 1867* to British Columbia, New Brunswick, Nova Scotia and Prince Edward Island, Clement says (at p. 782):

Only in the event of the future establishment of a system of separate or dissentient schools by any of these provinces can their full autonomy in relation to educational matters be interfered with by the parliament of Canada. In none of these provinces could the claim to a 'right or privilege' [with respect to denominational schools which any class of persons have by law in the province at the union — s. 93(1)] existing at the time of the Union be more strongly supported than in New Brunswick; and, as to that province, it has been held by the Privy Council [in *Maher v. Town of Port-*

*land* (1874), 2 Cart. 486n, approving *Ex parte Renaud* (1873), 14 N.B.R. 273 (C.A.); more fully reported in Wheeler's Confederation Law of Canada, p. 362]that no such right or privilege existed there.

See also Lefroy, Annotation, 24 D.L.R. 490; Scott, "The Privy Council and Minority Rights" (1930), 37 Queen's Quarterly 668. For a historical study of separate schools in the various provinces see Sissons, *Church and State in Canadian Education* (1959).

Provincial legislative authority in relation to education is not incompatible with federal activity in the field by way of grants in aid or institutional contributions. *Cf.* Report of the Royal Commission on National Development in the Arts, Letters and Sciences, 1951, pp. 7-8:

> There is no general prohibition in Canadian law against any group, governmental or voluntary, contributing to the education of the individual in its broadest sense. Thus, the activities of the Federal Government and of other bodies in broadcasting, films, museums, libraries, research institutions and similar fields are not in conflict with any existing law. . . . If the Federal Government is to renounce its right to associate itself with other social groups, public and private, in the general education of Canadian citizens, it denies its intellectual and moral purposes, the complete conception of the common good is lost and Canada, as such, becomes a materialistic society. . . . We are convinced that our activities have in no way invaded the rights of the provinces but may rather have been helpful in suggesting means of co-operation.

For a wider view of federal power in relation to higher education, see Corry, "Higher Education in Dominion-Provincial Relations" (1966), 8 University Affairs. No. 2 at 3.

Is religious conviction a tenable ground for refusal to obey provincial compulsory school attendance legislation in the absence of any exemption given on that ground by the legislation? See *Perepolkin v. Superintendent of Child Welfare* (1957), 23 W.W.R. 592 (B.C.S.C.); *Cf. Donald v. Hamilton Board of Education,* [1945] O.R. 518 (C.A.).

Is it open to parents to send their children to a public school and yet claim exemption on religious grounds from certain religious instruction and acts of devotion prescribed as part of the curriculum of the school? See *Chabot v. School Commissioners of Lamorandiere,* [1957] Que. Q.B. 707; and see Scott, *Note* (1958), 36 Can. Bar Rev. 248; *Note* (1958), 4 McGill L.J. 268.]

# LEGAL AND CONSTITUTIONAL ASPECTS OF PUBLIC FUNDING FOR PRIVATE SCHOOLS IN ONTARIO

Neil Finkelstein, Appendix D to Shapiro (Commissioner), Report of the Commission on Private Schools in Ontario (1985) (footnotes omitted)

## Introduction

On June 12, 1984, Premier Davis of Ontario announced in the Legislature that public funding for the Roman Catholic separate school system would be extended past the current Grade 10 level to the end of high school. The fact that Roman Catholic separate schools are publicly financed raised serious constitutional issues about whether the state is obligated to fund private schools in light of certain provisions of the *Canadian Charter of Rights and Freedoms.* With the promulgation of the *Charter* and the coming into force of the equality guarantee in section 15 thereof on April 17, 1985, we must ask i) whether there is now a constitutional right to establish private schools in the first place; ii) if there is, the extent to which the state may regulate them; and iii) what funding obligations, if any, the state has with respect to private schools.

Before dealing with these questions, I shall review both the laws across Canada with respect to funding private schools, with particular emphasis on Ontario, and the scope of provincial legislative jurisdiction over education prior to the *Charter*.

. . . .

## (2) *Pre-Charter Constitutional Position With Respect to Jurisdiction Over Education*

Section 93 of the *Constitution Act, 1867*, the only pre-*Charter* constitutional provision specifically dealing with education, reads as follows:

> 93.  In and for each Province the Legislature may exclusively make Laws in relation to Education, subject and according to the following Provisions:—
> (1) Nothing in any such Law shall prejudicially affect any Right or Privilege with respect to Denominational Schools, which any Class of Persons have by Law in the Province at the Union;
> (2) All the Powers, Privileges, and Duties at the Union by Law conferred and imposed in Upper Canada on the Separate Schools and School Trustees of the Queen's Roman Catholic Subjects shall be and the same are hereby extended to the Dissentient Schools of the Queen's Protestant and Roman Catholic Subjects in Quebec.
> (3) Where in any Province a System of Separate or Dissentient Schools exists by Law at the Union or is thereafter established by the Legislature of the Province, an Appeal shall lie to the Governor General in Council from any Act or Decision of any Provincial Authority affecting any Right or Privilege of the Protestant or Roman Catholic Minority of the Queen's Subjects in relation to Education.
> (4) In case any such Provincial Law as from Time to Time seems to the Governor General in Council requisite for the due Execution of the Provisions of this Section is not made, or in case any Decision of the Governor General in Council on any Appeal under this Section is not duly executed by the proper Provincial Authority in that Behalf, then and in every such Case require, the Parliament of Canada may make remedial Laws for the due Execution of the Provisions of this Section and of any Decision of the Governor General in Council under this section.

Pursuant to section 93, education is a provincial matter subject to the exceptions with respect to minority Roman Catholic or Protestant denominational schools. The promulgation of the *Constitution Act, 1982* has not changed this allocation of legislative jurisdiction, although the *Charter* limits its ambit where guaranteed rights are involved.

Not surprisingly, the litigation with respect to section 93 has been largely concerned with the exceptions concerning denominational schools. The conditions of applicability of these exceptions are well summarized by Chouinard J. in *A.G. Que. v. Lavigne*, [[1984] 2 S.C.R. 575 at 582]:

> In order to claim the protection of [s. 93], the following conditions must of necessity be met:
> (a) there must be a right or privilege affecting a denominational school;
> (b) enjoyed by a particular class of persons;
> (c) by law;
> (d) in effect at the time of the Union;
> (e) and which is prejudicially affected.

Because only rights and privileges protected "by law at the Union" are constitutionally guaranteed, the core of rights protected in each province varies according to the different laws in force at Confederation. "Laws" in this context means statute law, not *de facto* or customary obligations existing at Confederation. It should be noted that the scope of these rights does not vary with developments in society, but rather is frozen in time. In addition, only those rights which are determined by reference to religious belief are guaranteed by section 93. Even as regards those, the Legislature may regulate them as long as the regulation does not "prejudicially affect" their denominational character. For example, a wholesale usurpation of management, even when done for the purpose of enforcing a non-denominational regulation, has been held to "prejudicially affect" separate school rights guaranteed by section 93.

Section 93 draws a demarcation line between legislation which "prejudicially affects" denominational schools, and is therefore *ultra vires*, and legislation which merely "affects" it. The distinction is sometimes difficult to apply in practice. A pair of Ontario cases considering the dismissal of separate school teachers who married outside the Roman Catholic Church illustrates the difficulty of deciding whether a legislative dealing with this issue "affects" or "prejudicially affects" denominational rights in section 93.

In *Re Essex County Roman Catholic Separate School Board and Porter*, [(1978), 21 O.R. (2d) 255 (C.A.)], a provincial board of reference set aside certain separate school teachers' dismissals for marrying outside the faith. The Ontario Court of Appeal held that the right in separate school trustees to dismiss for denominational cause was a right or privilege protected by statute at Confederation. The provincial Legislature, lacking jurisdiction itself, could not give jurisdiction to a board of reference to set aside the dismissals.

On the other hand, in *Essex County Roman Catholic Separate School Board v. Tremblay-Webster* [(1984), 45 O.R. (2d) 83 (C.A.)], provincial legislation permitted collective bargaining. One of the terms in a separate school collective agreement prohibited the discharge of teachers without just cause, in this case for marrying outside the faith. The school board argued on the basis of *Porter* that the Legislature could not empower the parties to negotiate out of protected rights any more than it could empower a board of reference to impose a ruling. The Court of Appeal held that while the statute "affected" protected rights, it did not do so prejudicially because entry into the collective agreement was voluntary. The discharged teacher could therefore use the grievance procedure.

I have difficulty with the Court of Appeal's reconciliation of *Porter* and *Tremblay-Webster*. The "class of persons" protected by section 93 are individual families, not school trustees. The only real difference between *Porter* and *Tremblay-Webster* is that in *Porter* the Legislature restricted the denominational rights. In *Tremblay-Webster* it was done by the trustees who voluntarily entered into the collective agreement. However the parents of children attending these denominational schools may well not have voted for the particular trustees in office and yet, even as dissenters, their section 93 rights are curtailed. In my view, the distinction between the two cases should be reconsidered.

*Roman Catholic Separate School Trustees for Tiny v. The King* [[1928] A.C. 363 (P.C.)] is the *locus classicus* of the law on separate schools in Ontario at Confederation. The statutes in force in Ontario in 1867 were the *Common Schools Act, 1859* [22 Vict., c. 64] and *An Act to Restore to Roman Catholics in Upper Canada Certain Rights in Respect to Separate Schools* [1863, 26 Vict., c. 5] (the *Scott Act*). The separate school trustees in *Tiny* claimed, *inter alia*, the right to establish grades of education and curricula as were established in continuation schools, collegiate institutes and high schools, and the right to exemptions for their supporters in respect of rates for post-elementary schools not regulated by the trustees.

Viscount Haldane, speaking for the Privy Council, reviewed the development of the common and separate school systems in Ontario up to Confederation. Before 1867 there were three principal classes of schools: common schools, grammar schools, and separate schools. The common and separate schools were permitted to educate students up to the age of twenty-one but did not in fact do so. Continuation schools, collegiate institutions and high schools as such only developed after Confederation. The pre-Confederation statutory law showed that the Legislature wanted to bring the common and separate schools under the same regulatory umbrella. The *Scott Act* in 1863 provided that separate school teachers were subject to the same examinations and qualifications as common school teachers, and the separate schools were subject to inspections by the Chief Superintendent of Education and to detailed regulation by the Council of Public Instruction for Upper Canada. Also, the Chief Superintendent and the Council for Public Instruction exercised great discretion over the grades of instruction in separate schools, the stages at which instruction should be given and the funding allocations.

Viscount Haldane held that, given the discretion exercised by the Council at Confederation over grading and levels of instruction, there was no constitutionally guaranteed right in separate school trustees to offer secondary level education. He said [at p. 387 A.C.]:

> [Their Lordships] are not at one with [the Chief Justice of Canada] in thinking that separate school trustees could give secondary education in their schools otherwise than by permission, express or implied, of the Council of Public Instruction. The separate school was only a special form of common school, and the Council could in the case of each determine the courses to be pursued and the extent of the education to be imparted.

The importance of *Tiny* cannot be overstated for the purposes of this paper. It establishes the core area of the section 93(1) constitutional guarantee to Roman Catholic separate schools with regard to public funding. It follows from the Privy Council's holding that, since separate school trustees could offer elementary but not secondary level education as a matter of right, there was no concomitant state obligation to fund separate schools beyond the elementary school level. Accordingly, government funding at the current junior high school level and the contemplated high school level is a matter of government policy rather than constitutional right.

---

3) *What effect if any, has the promulgation of the Canadian Charter of Rights and Freedoms had with respect to state obligations vis à vis private schools?*

I shall now address the issues of i) whether there is a constitutional right to establish private schools; ii) if there is, the extent to which they may be regulated by the state; and iii) whether the state has any funding obligations to these schools.

i) *Constitutional right to establish private schools*

Any constitutional right to establish private parochial or non-parochial schools will be found in sections 2 or 7 of the *Charter*. These provisions read in relevant part as follows:

s. 2. Everyone has the following fundamental freedoms:
(a) freedom of conscience and religion; . . .

s. 7. Everyone has the right to life, liberty and security of the person and the right not to be deprived thereof except in accordance with the principles of fundamental justice.

Section 7 is wider than section 2 because, if the right to establish private schools is comprehended within its "liberty" guarantee, it encompasses both parochial and non-parochial schools. It is unclear at this stage whether section 7 contains a substantive guarantee of life, liberty and security of the person or whether it is limited to procedural safeguards. The question is currently before the Supreme Court of Canada in *Reference re Section 94(2) of the Motor Vehicle Act (B.C.)*, (S.C.C., Dec. 17, 1985), a case which is on appeal from the British Columbia Court of Appeal [[1983] 3 W.W.R. 756]. In *Reference re Section 94(2)*, the impugned statutory provision created an absolute liability offence of driving while one's licence was suspended, punishable by an automatic minimum seven day jail term. The British Columbia Court of Appeal struck down the provision, holding that "fundamental justice" in section 7 requires the courts to examine the substantive content of legislation.

If the British Columbia Court of Appeal is correct, as I believe it is, [since this paper was written, the Supreme Court of Canada has delivered its judgment in *Reference re s. 94(2) of the Motor Vehicle Act (B.C.), supra*, at Chapter 20, affirming the British Columbia Court of Appeal.] the next question is whether the liberty clause in section 7 guarantees the right to establish private schools. Modern human rights documents often contain provisions guaranteeing to parents the right to ensure the religious and moral education of their children. These documents are based on the value in a democratic society of protecting pluralism in thought and belief, coupled with the recognition that the family is the natural place for the inculcation of these matters. In Canada, this right is recognized by provincial statutes which provide for either alternate instruction or the right to withdraw the child from religious instruction to which the parent objects.

In *Donald v. Hamilton Board of Education* [[1945] O.R. 518 (C.A.)], a pre-*Charter* case, a Jehovah's Witness refused on religious grounds to allow his children to salute the flag and sing the national anthem in school. The children were expelled, and he sought an order for *mandamus* to have them readmitted. The education statute in force at the time contained a religious exemption. For most people, saluting the flag and singing the national anthem are displays of patriotism without religious significance. However, the Court of Appeal took a wide view of religion, accepting the complainant's contention of religious faith at face value, and granted sufficient latitude to his divergent beliefs. Gillanders J.A. quoted with approval the following passage from *New York v. Sandstrom* [279 N.Y. 523 at 535 (1939)]:

There are many acts which are not acts of worship and which for most men have no religious significance and are entirely unrelated to the practice of any religious principle or tenet but which may involve a violation of an obligation which other men may think is imposed on them by divine command or religious authority.

In *Chabot v. Commissaires d'Ecoles de Lamorandière* [(1957), 12 D.L.R. (2d) 796 (Que. C.A.)] another pre-*Charter* case and the leading Canadian decision to date on the right of parents to educate their children, Jehovah's Witness children refused to participate in religious exercises at a Catholic public school and were accordingly expelled. The Quebec Court of Appeal granted an order for *mandamus* that the children be readmitted on the basis that, as a matter of statutory interpretation of the relevant legislation, the school could not make participation in Catholic religious courses a condition of attendance. *Chabot* is particularly noteworthy for some of its *obiter* comments about a "natural law" right of parents to control the religious instruction of their children. Pratte J. stated [at 802 D.L.R.]:

It appears useful to recall that the right to give one's children the religious education of one's choice, like freedom of conscience, is anterior to positive law.

As support for this proposition he cited *Re Meades* [(1871), I.R. 5 Esq. 98 at 103] where it is stated:

The authority of a father to guide and govern the education of his child is a very sacred thing, bestowed by the Almighty, and to be sustained to the uttermost by human law. It is not to be abrogated or abridged, without the most coercive reason.

Undoubtedly, the strongest statement on natural law was made by Casey J. [at 807 D.L.R.]:

On this point there can be no doubt for if these rights find their source in positive law they can be taken away. But if, as they do, they find their existence in the very nature of man, then they cannot be taken away and they must prevail should they conflict with the provisions of positive law. Consequently, if the regulations under which, rightly or wrongly, this school is being operated make it mandatory that non-Catholic pupils submit to the religious instructions and practices enacted by the Catholic Committee, then these regulations are *ultra vires* the Committee, and invalid.

Taschereau J., in translation, stated [at 834 D.L.R.]:

It would also be contrary to natural law as well as to the most elementary principles of our democratic institutions that a father could not exercise the right or fulfil his obligation to instruct his children without renouncing his religious faith.

Owen J. stated [at 840 D.L.R.]:

Freedom of worship includes the right of a parent to have his children follow the religious training of the parent's choice and also the right of not being forced to have his children subjected to religious training of another faith.

I do not cite the above passages for the proposition that "natural law" overrides positive law in Canada. The generally accepted view is quite the contrary. However, in my view the statements in *Chabot* go to define the constitutional values which underlie the liberty clause in section 7 and the freedom of religion guarantee in section 2 of the *Charter of Rights*.

American jurisprudence based upon the liberty clause in the Fourteenth Amendment is also instructive. In *Pierce v. Society of Sisters of the Holy Name* [268 U.S. 510 (1925)], Oregon enacted a compulsory public school attendance law. It was challenged by a parochial school and a military academy as an interference with parental liberty to direct their children's education. Justice McReynolds, speaking for the U.S. Supreme Court, stated [at 534-5 U.S.]:

We think it entirely plain that the act of 1922 unreasonably interferes with the liberty of parents and guardians to direct the upbringing and education of children under their control. As often heretofore pointed out, rights guaranteed by the Constitution may not be abridged by legislation which has no reasonable relation to some purpose within the competency of the State. The fundamental theory of liberty upon which all governments in this Union repose excludes any general power of this State to standardize its children by forcing them to accept instruction from public teachers only . . .

The significance of having a military academy as one of the party plaintiffs cannot be overstated. If a parochial school was the sole plaintiff, *Pierce* could be explained as a religion case. Given the presence of the military academy, it establishes that there is a constitutional right to educate one's children outside the public school system, provided the education is consistent with legitimate state interests.

Another source of law which is likely to be persuasive is international law. Numerous international conventions recognize a liberty interest in parents to direct their children's education and, by implication, a concomitant right to establish private schools. While international treaties have no direct application in Canada until implemented by competent legislation, they are evidence of what is done in other free and democratic societies. International law has been considered in both pre-*Charter* and *Charter* cases, and is thereby useful at least indirectly on questions of Canadian law.

In my view, given the consistency among the Canadian, American and international law on the point, the liberty interest in section 7 of the *Charter* comprehends the rights of parents to educate their children and establish private schools.

If I am wrong, perhaps because the Supreme Court of Canada will hold that section 7 is purely procedural, we must consider whether there is a constitutional right pursuant to section 2 of the *Charter*, which is unquestionably substantive in nature, to establish at least parochial schools. I believe that there is. In addition to the above sources, which apply equally to the freedom of religion guarantee in section 2 as to the liberty clause in section 7, the American case of *Wisconsin v. Yoder* [406 U.S. 205 (1971)] indicates that particular deference is given to a parent's right to educate his child in religious matters. In *Yoder*, Amish parents withdrew their children from school after Grade 8 and were convicted of violating Wisconsin's compulsory school attendance laws. They argued that they should be exempted from the law's application because separation from worldly influences and a life-style connected with the land were central tenets of their religious faith. The Court agreed and exempted them. It held that the state had a legitimate interest in universal education, but that interest had to be balanced against fundamental rights such as religion.

### ii) *The extent to which the state may regulate private or parochial schools*

The constitutional right of parents to establish private schools does not denude the state of the right to regulate such schools. The state has a legitimate, and indeed compelling, interest in the universal education of its citizens. I would suggest that this interest is twofold. First, a democracy such as ours operates best where there is an educated citizenry which is capable of making informed choices. This rationale gains nourishment in Canada from Chief Justice Duff's famous passage in the *Alberta Press Case* [*Ref. re Alta. Statutes*, [1938] S.C.R. 106 at 133]:

. . . The [Constitution Act, 1867] contemplates a Parliament working under the influence of public opinion and public discussion. There can be no controversy that such institutions derive their efficacy from free public discussion of affairs, from criticism and answer and counter-criticism, from attack upon policy and administration and defence and counter-attack; from the freest and fullest analysis and examination from every point of view of political proposals . . .

. . . It is axiomatic that the practice of this right of free public discussion of public affairs, notwithstanding its incidental mischiefs, is the breath of life for parliamentary institutions.

It follows that, if Canadian democracy is founded upon free public discussion and dissemination of ideas, the corollary is that the citizenry should be educated and informed, capable of understanding the issues of the day. Similarly if such discussion is the "breath of life of parliamentary institutions", those institutions, in this case the Legislature of Ontario, have a legitimate interest and indeed a high duty to provide universal education provided that adequate allowances are made for parents to make alternative choices. The state's second legitimate interest in universal education is to prepare its children to function as adults without being an excessive burden on the state.

In furtherance of these objectives, the state may inspect and supervise schools, enact compulsory attendance laws provided sufficient religious exemptions are granted, require teachers to be of good moral character, require that essential studies are properly taught and ensure that its health and safety rules are followed. The restriction is that the regulation must be flexible enough to accommodate alternative beliefs and values.

Two American cases illustrate the balancing which must be done to ensure that full rein is given to the expression of alternative family values. In *Meyer v. Nebraska* [262 U.S. 390 (1923)], a Nebraska law forbade the teaching of modern languages other than English in any school in the state. A parochial school instructor was convicted of teaching German. In support of the law, the state argued that it had a legitimate interest in promoting "civic development by inhibiting training and education of the immature in foreign tongues and ideals before they could learn English and acquire American ideals". The Supreme Court accepted the legitimacy of the goal in the abstract, but held that the law went too far in light of the countervailing individual interests involved.

On the other hand, in *Prince v. Massachusetts* [321 U.S. 158 (1944)] a state child labour law prohibited children under twelve from distributing literature on the street. A Jehovah's Witness challenged the law as violative of his free exercise of religion. The U.S. Supreme Court upheld the law as consistent with a compelling state interest. The Court said [at pp. 166-7 U.S.]:

Neither rights of religion or parenthood are beyond limitation. Acting to guard the general interest in youth's well being, the state as *parens patriae* may restrict the parent's control by requiring school attendance, regulating or prohibiting the child's labour and in many other ways. Its authority is not nullified merely because the parent grounds his claim to control the child's course of conduct on religion or conscience. Thus, he cannot claim freedom from compulsory vaccination for the child more than for himself on religious grounds. The right to practise religion freely does not include liberty to expose the community or the child to communicable disease or the latter to ill health or death. . . . The catalogue need not be lengthened. It is sufficient to show what indeed appellant hardly disputes, that the state has a wide range of power for limiting parental freedom and authority in things affecting the child's welfare; and that this includes, to some extent, matters of conscience and religious conviction.

Thus freedom of choice does not include the right to jeopardize the health and safety of the child or the community.

In the international arena, the European Court of Human Rights has considered the degree to which states may regulate schools. Essentially, the state is entitled to pursue its legitimate interests, such as the protection of health and safety and ensuring that parental choices will not leave children unable to take care of themselves as adults. However, as held in *Kjeldsen* [1976 E.C.H.R. 502], the state cannot pursue an "aim of indoctrination". This indoctrination test was affirmed by the Court in *Forty Mothers v. Sweden* [1977 E.C.H.R. 214].

The basic law in other jurisdictions, and I believe in Canada as well pursuant to sections 2 and 7 of the *Charter*, is that the state may regulate the operation of private schools. However, its power does not extend to permit the standardization of children.

### iii) *Whether the state must fund private schools*

As a preliminary matter, it is useful to ask whether there is a constitutionally guaranteed right to at least a government financed public, as opposed to a private, education in Canada. In my view, such a right is found in the liberty clause of section 7 of the *Charter*. It may also exist in section 36, which provides, *inter alia*, that Parliament and the provincial Legislatures are committed to "providing essential public services of reasonable quality to all Canadians". In today's socio-economic and technological environment, I would argue that education is an "essential public service" contemplated by section 36. Regard may also be had to international law, which clearly recognizes a right to a public education.

The more difficult question is whether there is also a constitutionally guaranteed right to public funding for private schools.

In my opinion, neither section 2 nor section 7 of the *Charter* standing alone, unconnected with the equality guarantee in section 15, comprehends a free-standing right to public funding for private schools. As we shall see shortly, there is no such right in other jurisdictions either. Furthermore, section 36 of the *Charter* refers to a commitment to provide "essential *public* services". With respect to the freedom of religion guarantee in section 2 of the *Charter*, the question of the extent of the state's positive obligations, if any, is more difficult than with the liberty clause in section 7. Clearly the state must abstain from impeding or infringing upon a person's free exercise of religion. Furthermore, under the *Charter* the state may as a matter of policy give support to religion, albeit within narrow limits. The preamble to the *Charter* specifically provides that "Canada is founded upon principles that recognize the supremacy of God . . .". Section 27 provides that the *Charter* should be interpreted consistently with "the preservation and enhancement of the multicultural heritage of Canadians". Section 29 of the *Charter* preserves the denominational and separate school rights guaranteed by section 93 of the *Constitution Act, 1867.*

There is thus ample support for the proposition that the state is not prohibited from providing support to religion *as a policy matter*. However there is nothing in section 2 which *obligates* the state to provide such funding, and in my view no such obligation can be implied into section 2.

The same is not true of the equality guarantee in section 15(1) of the *Charter* which reads as follows:

15. (1) Every individual is equal before and under the law and has the right to the equal protection and equal benefit of the law without discrimination and, in particular, without discrimination based on race, national or ethnic origin, colour, religion, sex, age or mental or physical disability.

Section 1 of the *Charter* is also relevant:

1. The Canadian Charter of Rights and Freedoms guarantees the rights and freedoms set out in it subject only to such reasonable limits prescribed by law as can be demonstrably justified in a free and democratic society.

Several points about section 15(1) should be noted. First, while it contains a specific enumeration of prohibited grounds of discrimination, this list is not exhaustive. On the contrary, section 15(1) is a blanket anti-discrimination provision and sets out the list only for greater particularity.

Second, the provision extends to every individual "the right to the equal protection and equal benefit of the law". This distinguishes section 15 of the *Charter* from the equality guarantee in section 1(b) of the statutory federal *Bill of Rights* [S.C. 1960, c. 44]. In *R. v. Drybones* [[1970] S.C.R. 282], the leading case under the *Bill of Rights*, section 94 of the *Indian Act* [R.S.C. 1952, c. 149] made it an offence for an Indian to be intoxicated off a reserve either in public or in private. The *Northwest Territories Liquor Ordinance* [R.O.N.W.T. 1956, c. 60], a law of general application, prohibited any person from being intoxicated in a public place. Thus an Indian could be guilty of an offence off a reserve in places (i.e. private places) where another citizen would not be. In declaring the law inoperative, Ritchie J., speaking for a majority of the Supreme Court of Canada, said [at p. 297 S.C.R.]:

... without attempting any exhaustive definition of 'equality before the law' I think that section 1(b) means at least that *no individual or group of individuals is to be treated more harshly* than another under that law. . . . (emphasis added)

Section 15(1) of the *Charter* is not predicated upon a harshness test. On the contrary, it specifically provides that the equality guarantee can be triggered where the state favours one group of people over another by giving it additional benefits.

State funding of Roman Catholic separate schools but not private schools is therefore *prima facie* discriminatory within the meaning of section 15, because the former receive a benefit not shared by the latter. This is so regardless of the form which the public financing takes. If the government decides to finance the separate schools out of general revenues, the discrimination is obvious because no other groups receive similar funding. Alternatively where, as now, the schools are financed in whole or in part out of rates paid by separate school supporters who receive an exemption from public school taxes, it is equally discriminatory because non-Roman Catholics who wish to educate their children outside the public school system are not accorded a similar exemption. They must pay both public school taxes and private school tuition. The next issue is whether the discrimination is saved by the limitation provision in section 1 of the *Charter*.

Pursuant to section 1, a limitation on a *Charter* right is valid provided that, in context, it is i) reasonable, ii) prescribed by law, and iii) demonstrably justified in a free and democratic society. The burden of proof is on the party seeking to uphold the differentiation. The operation of section 1 has been described by the Ontario Court of Appeal in *Re Southam Inc. and The Queen (No. 1)* [(1983), 41 O.R. (2d) 113 at 124]:

> ... Section 2 states that everyone has the named fundamental freedoms. Section 1 guarantees those rights and, although the rights are not absolute or unrestricted, makes it clear that if there is a limit imposed on these fundamental rights by law, the limits must be reasonable and demonstrably justified in a free and democratic society. The wording imposes a positive obligation on those seeking to uphold the limit or limits to establish to the satisfaction of the court by evidence, by the terms and purpose of the limiting law, its economic, social and political background, and, if felt helpful, by references to comparable legislation of other acknowledged free and democratic societies, that such limit or limits are reasonable and demonstrably justified in a free and democratic society ...

and [at p. 129 O.R.]:

> In determining the reasonableness of the limit in each particular case, the court must examine objectively its argued rational basis in light of what the court understands to be reasonable in a free and democratic society. Further, there is, it appears to me, a significant burden on the proponent of the limit or limits to demonstrate their justification to the satisfaction of the court ...

In my opinion, it is reasonable within the meaning of section 1 for the reasons which follow to exclude non-parochial private schools from public funding. However it is *not* reasonable to finance Roman Catholic separate schools but not other parochial schools.

As to parochial schools, it is clear that a benefit is being given to Roman Catholics which is being denied to other religious denominations. The differentiation is particularly objectionable with respect to junior high school and high school financing. Pursuant to the Privy Council's holding in *Roman Catholic Separate School Trustees for Tiny v. The King* [[1928] A.C. 363], the government is not required to finance secondary level separate school education. It is therefore doing so as a matter of policy rather than constitutional obligation. In my view, this discrimination cannot be saved by section 1 of the *Charter*. If the equality guarantee stands for anything, it stands for the proposition that the government cannot, as a matter of state policy and being under no obligation to do so, favour one group over another strictly on the basis of religion. The government must either terminate the funding of Roman Catholic separate secondary schools or, in the alternative, extend it to other parochial schools.

The issue is more difficult with regard to separate schools at the elementary school level. The primary argument in favour of the continued differentiation between Roman Catholic and other parochial elementary schools is that section 93(1) of the *Constitution Act, 1867* requires that the former be funded. This guarantee was carried forward by section 29 of the *Charter* and, it can be argued, the distinction was thereby preserved even within the *Charter's* framework.

In my view, this argument is misconceived. Section 93 explains why the state must fund Roman Catholic separate elementary schools. It does not explain why it is reasonable not to give other denominational schools the same benefits, particularly since such extended funding would not, in the words of section 29 of the *Charter*, "abrogate or derogate from" separate school rights. It would not affect those rights one way or another. Clearly section 93 does not *restrict* the application of the *Charter*. On the contrary, the two should be interpreted in such a way as to avoid conflict whenever possible. Section 15 of the *Charter* and section 93 can be made compatible by extending equal financing to other parochial schools.

In *Reference re Education Act* [(1984), 47 O.R. (2d) 1], the Ontario Court of Appeal had to decide whether full implementation of the minority language rights in section 23 of the *Charter* would unconstitutionally interfere with the separate school system. The Court said both sections 23 and 93 could apply, stating [at p. 50 O.R.]:

> As we view the Charter, it grants supporters of denominational schools a right in addition to those granted them in 1867 by s. 93. They are now entitled, by virtue of s. 23, to have their children receive denominational education in either the minority or majority language. If, because of s. 93, s. 23 were treated as inapplicable to denominational schools, an anomalous and, indeed, patently unacceptable result would follow. French-speaking members of the Roman Catholic Community would then be required to forego their denominational education rights protected by s. 93 in order to avail themselves of the new minority language educational rights conferred on them by s. 23 of the Charter. We see no conflict between the two provisions compelling that result. In our opinion, s. 23 and s. 93 are compatible and capable of living and operating in harmony with one another.

Admittedly the Court of Appeal's decision in *Reference re Education Act* was made easier by *Ottawa Sep. S. Trustees v. Mackell* [[1917] A.C. 62 (P.C.)] which held that language was not a matter of denominational concern. However, the case is still good authority for the proposition that *Charter* rights will be given full flower where possible as long as they are not inconsistent with section 93.

Whatever the situation in 1867, the Roman Catholic minority in Ontario needs less protection today than other religious minorities. Their roots are longer and better established, and they are numerically superior. If the purpose of the equality guarantee is to guard against majoritarian abuse, weaker minorities should be able to claim at least as much support as Roman Catholics. Section 93 was intended to prevent discrimination, not foster it. It would be very odd indeed if section 93 could be used as the fulcrum to justify religion-based discriminatory funding under the *Charter*. The better view is that section 93 and section 15 of the *Charter* should be read together to oblige the state to fund all denominational schools equally. Additional support for this view can be found in section 27 of the *Charter* which requires the *Charter* to be interpreted consistently with the multicultural heritage of Canadians.

It may be that some religious groups are so small in particular areas that a separate, publicly financed school would be prohibitively expensive. In such cases, it would undoubtedly be reasonable within the meaning of section 1 to impose a restriction on funding limiting it to situations "where numbers warrant" similar to that in section 23 with respect to minority language rights.

In my view, the situation regarding section 1 of the *Charter* is different for non-parochial schools. The government's rationale for excluding private schools from state funding is a concern for maintaining a strong and viable public school system. I believe that a court would find that this rationale is reasonable within the meaning of section 1 provided that the government can prove that funding non-parochial private schools would endanger the public school system.

The counter-argument is that this rationale applies equally to parochial schools, and it is thereby unreasonable to differentiate between parochial and non-parochial schools. A parent should, in view of the freedom of religion and conscience guarantee in section 2 of the *Charter*, be equally free of economic constraint to send his children to non-parochial private schools as to parochial ones. Also, one could argue that freedom from discrimination on religious grounds in section 15 of the *Charter* means not only that the state may not favour one religion over another, but that religion is not a legitimate policy consideration at all under the *Charter*. The government is thus not entitled to differentiate between parochial and non-parochial schools.

The answer to these arguments is that, as set out in the excerpt from the *McBurney* case which has been previously quoted, our public law cannot be said to be entirely neutral with respect to the advancement of religion. The legal and constitutional recognition of God in preambles to both the federal *Bill of Rights* and the *Charter* imports a policy which leans in favour of the profession of religion. Section 2 of the *Charter* guarantees freedom of religion, and language preventing a state establishment of religion similar to that in the First Amendment to the *U.S. Constitution* is notably absent. Finally other provisions, such as sections 27 and 29 of the *Charter* and section 93 of the *Constitution Act, 1867*, militate against a notion of state neutrality. That is not to say that Canada may have an established religion or state theological line. I do not believe that it can. But it is entitled to recognize and advance religion in certain types of situations.

It is therefore my opinion that, while the Ontario Legislature is obliged to extend equal treatment to different religions, it is entitled to differentiate between religious and non-religious schools. If I am wrong in this for the reasons set out above, my comments with respect to the government's obligation to finance parochial schools apply equally to non-parochial schools.

As to the legal prescription element in section 1, it is clear that the government's financing of public and Roman Catholic separate schools to the exclusion of private schools is prescribed by law. Section 10(3) of the Ontario *Education Act* permits the Minister of Education, with the approval of Cabinet, to make regulations for the distribution of public funds for education. The section permits but does not require the financing of private schools. The Minister therefore has jurisdiction as a matter of statutory law to adopt the educational financing system currently in force.

The final element in section 1 is whether Ontario's refusal to finance private non-parochial schools can be justified by reference to what is done in a free and democratic society. The evidence in Canada is inconclusive because the degree of private school financing varies by province from heavy funding in Quebec to none at all in Ontario. In other jurisdictions, the decision about which schools to finance is one of government policy rather than constitutional obligation. The European Court of Human Rights' decision in the *Belgium Linguistics Case* is a good example. Article 2 of the *First Protocol to the European Convention on Human Rights* states:

> No person shall be denied the right to education. In the exercise of any functions which it assumes in relation to education and to teaching, the State shall respect the right of parents to ensure such education and teaching in conformity with their own religious and philosophical convictions.

Article 14 of the Convention states:

> The enjoyment of the rights and freedoms set forth in this Convention shall be secured without discrimination on any grounds such as sex, race, colour, language, religion, political or other opinion, national or social origin, association with the national minority, property, birth or other status.

In Belgium, the state subsidizes virtually all private schools. The Belgian Constitution provides that the use of either of the two official languages, French and Flemish, is optional. The Flemish parts of the country passed regulations limiting the use of French on penalty of loss of state funding. French parents argued on the basis of Articles 2 and 14 that once a state undertakes to provide or subsidize a particular type of education, it must do so without discrimination. The European Court rejected the argument in these terms:

> The negative formulation indicates . . . that the Contracting Parties do not recognize such a right to education as would require them to establish at their own expense, or to subsidize, education of any particular type or of any particular level. . . . There neither was, nor is now, therefore, any question of requiring each State to establish [a general and official educational] system, but merely of guaranteeing to persons subject to the jurisdiction of the Contracting Parties the right, in principle, to avail themselves of the means of instruction existing at a given time.

The European Human Rights Commission in *Forty Mothers v. Sweden*, above, took the same position:

> Article 2 of the Protocol does not go as far as to oblige the High Contracting Parties to subsidize any private education or teaching.

These cases indicate that state subsidization of private schools under the European Convention is a matter of government policy rather than constitutional imperative.

The same is true in the United States, except that the Establishment Clause in the First Amendment prohibits state funding of parochial schools. Otherwise, state governments have discretion to decide as a matter of policy which schools should be publicly funded and how much those schools should receive.

In *San Antonio Independent School District v. Rodriguez* [411 U.S. 1 (1973)], it was argued before the U.S. Supreme Court that the Equal Protection Clause in the Fourteenth Amendment guaranteed equal funding at least as among public schools. In *Rodriguez*, the Texas public school system was financed through local property taxes, with the result that the funds available in any particular district depended upon the size of its tax base. Public schools in poorer areas accordingly received less financing than those in wealthy neighbourhoods. Powell J., speaking for the Court, held that education was not a fundamental right. Accordingly there only had to be a "rational" relationship between the funding system and the way education was provided. The Court found that such a rational relationship existed as long as the system could "provide each child with an opportunity to acquire the basic minimal skills necessary for the enjoyment of the rights of speech and of full participation in the political process". The Court found that the challenged funding system met this test.

In *Norwood v. Harrison* [413 U.S. 455 (1973)], the U.S. Supreme Court struck down a textbook lending program which included private schools with racially discriminatory policies in its ambit. Supporters of these schools argued that students in attendance would be denied the equal protection of the law if their schools were denied access to the program. In the course of his reasons, Chief Justice Burger, speaking for the Court, responded to this argument by saying that the Equal Protection Clause did not guarantee private schools the right to receive public funding:

> It has never been held that if private schools are not given some share of public funds allocated for education that such schools are isolated into a classification violative of the Equal Protection Clause. It is one thing to say that a State may not prohibit the maintenance of private schools and quite another to say that such schools must, as a matter of equal protection, receive state aid.

To summarize the American position with respect to funding non-denominational education, the state has an obligation to provide a minimum level of public education to its residents once it has commenced providing education in the first place. However once it has achieved that minimum, its distribution of funds for public or private schools is, within the limits of the Establishment Clause, a matter of government policy rather than constitutional right.

The result of this survey of other Canadian provinces, the law in international jurisdictions and in the United States is that public funding of non-parochial private schools is largely a matter of public policy. Unequal financing, at least within limits, does not implicate the respective constitutional instruments. My conclusion is therefore that Ontario's refusal to fund non-parochial private schools is reasonable, assuming the government can lead adequate evidence to show that its rationale of public school protection is sound, prescribed by law and demonstrably justified in a free and democratic society. Thus, in my opinion, its policy of differentiation, excluding that with respect to parochial schools, is constitutional.

*Conclusion*

In my opinion, the coming into force of the equality guarantee in section 15(1) of the *Charter of Rights* on April 17, 1985 will, due to the current legal and constitutional context of education in Ontario, require a radical alteration of the government's financing arrangements for schools in the province. My major conclusions may be summarized as follows:

1) Section 93(1) of the *Constitution Act, 1867*, as interpreted by *Roman Catholic Separate School Trustees for Tiny v. The King*, above, guarantees the right of Roman Catholic separate school trustees to offer elementary level education, together with a right to public financing thereof;

2) Pursuant to *Tiny*, separate school trustees do not have a constitutional right to provide post-elementary school education. Accordingly, the government's current financing of separate school junior high school is being done as a matter of policy rather than constitutional obligation;

3) The financing of Roman Catholic separate schools to the exclusion of private schools generally is a *prima facie* violation of section 15(1) of the *Canadian Charter of Rights and Freedoms*, which [came] into force on April 17, 1985. The issue is whether the differentiation is saved by section 1 of the *Charter*;

4) In my view, the constitutional implications of the funding of Roman Catholic separate schools is different for parochial and non-parochial schools:

a) *as to parochial schools*

The funding of Roman Catholic separate schools but not other parochial schools is based exclusively on religion, a specifically enumerated head of discrimination in section 15(1) of the *Charter*, and cannot be saved by section 1 as being reasonable in the circumstances:

(i) The government's financing of separate school junior high schools and its proposal to finance separate school high schools but not other parochial schools is strictly a matter of policy rather than constitutional obligation. In my view, the government is not constitutionally entitled to make such a differentiation in the absence of compelling reasons which are not present in this case. The government's remedy is therefore to either terminate funding for post-elementary separate school education or extend it to other parochial schools equally;

ii) The government's financing of separate school elementary schools is constitutionally required by section 93(1) of the *Constitution Act, 1867*, and this requirement is carried forward by section 29 of the *Charter*. This only explains why Roman Catholic schools must be funded, but it does not explain why it is reasonable within the meaning of section 1 of the *Charter* to exclude other parochial schools from equal funding. Section 93 of the *Constitution Act, 1867* and section 15 of the *Charter* may be made compatible by financing all parochial schools equally, and in my view this must be done. It is unreasonable to use section 93, a provision designed to protect the Roman Catholic minority in Ontario from majoritarian abuse, as the constitutional privot to support discrimination against other religious minorities.

### b) *as to non-parochial private schools*

The law in other jurisdictions is that the government may support private schools but is not required to do so. Subject to the qualifications expressed in this paper that it might be impermissible to differentiate between parochial and non-parochial schools, I believe that the government will not be required by the *Charter* to finance non-parochial schools. The differentiation is predicated on a concern for the maintenance of a strong and viable public school system. Assuming the government can show that funding non-parochial private schools would pose a danger to the system, the government may withhold such financing.

### Appendix A — Section 93, Province by Province

Perhaps the most remarkable feature of section 93 rights and privileges is that they are not uniform across Canada. This is due to their "frozen in time" character and the fact that the various versions of section 93 which are implemented as other provinces joined the Union are not identical. As a result, it is necessary to analyze section 93 rights and privileges province by province.

### New Brunswick and Nova Scotia

There were no special laws with regard to separate schools in these two provinces at Confederation. When the New Brunswick legislature passed *The Common Schools Act, 1871*, which compelled all residents to support a system of common schools, there was strong opposition. Two cases resulted, *Maher v. The Town of Portland* [(1874), Wheeler's Confederation Law of Canada, 338], and *Ex Parte Renaud* [(1874), 2 Cart. 445 (S.C.C.)]. These cases established the principle that section 93 rights must be legal rights guaranteed by statute. The fact that prior to Confederation various denominational schools received public funds did not amount to a right to tax supported denominational schools. It was also found that there was no right to an exemption from assessment for the common schools. As a consequence, the only right in relation to separate schools in these two provinces is the common law rights which existed at Confederation to establish separate schools.

*Manitoba*

The controversy over separate schools in Manitoba in the 1890s was very divisive for Canada. The relevant provision is section 22 of the *Manitoba Act* [33 Vict., c. 3 (Can.)] which reads as follows:

> 22. In and for the Province, the said Legislature may exclusively make Laws in relation to Education, subject and according to the following provisions:—
>
> (1) Nothing in any such Law shall prejudicially affect any right or privilege with respect to Denominational Schools which any class of persons have by Law or practice in the Province at the Union:
>
> (2) An appeal shall lie to the Governor General in Council from any Act or decision of the Legislature of the Province, or of any Provincial Authority, affecting any right or privilege, of the Protestant or Roman Catholic minority of the Queen's subjects in relation to Education:
>
> (3) In case any such Provincial Law, as from time to time seems to the Governor General in Council requisite for the due execution of the provisions of this section, is not made, or in case any decision of the Governor General in Council on any appeal under this section is not duly executed by the proper Provincial Authority in that behalf, then, in every such case, and as far only as the circumstances of each case require, the Parliament of Canada may make remedial Laws for the due execution of the provisions of this section, and of any decision of the Governor General in Council under this section.

Section 22 thus differs from section 93 in that it protects rights and privileges existing in law and practice. These words were added quite deliberately since in 1870 no denominational rights existed in law. As a result, Riel's delegates to Ottawa in 1870 were insistent on the words "in practice" because otherwise no separate school rights would exist. In 1870, Manitoba was divided fairly equally between Protestants and Catholics. By 1890, the Protestants were a clear majority. The *Public Schools Act* of 1890 ended public funding for separate schools and compelled all rate payers to support the public school system. This began what may be compendiously called the Manitoba School Question. A Catholic rate payer went to court in *Barrett v. Winnipeg* [[1892] A.C. 445 (P.C.), reversing (1892) 19 S.C.R. 374]. The separate school supporters were successful before the Supreme Court of Canada, where Chief Justice Ritchie stated [at 385 S.C.R.]:

> While it is quite clear that at the time of the passing of this Act [Manitoba Act] there were no denominational or other schools established and recognized by law, it is equally clear that there were at that time in actual operation or practice a system of denominational schools in Manitoba well established and the *de facto* rights and privileges of which were enjoyed by a large class of persons.

and [at 388 S.C.R.]:

> But it is said that the Catholics as a class are not prejudicially affected by this Act. Does it not prejudicially, that is to say injuriously, disadvantageously, which is the meaning of the word "prejudicially" affect them when they are taxed to support schools of the benefit of which, by their religious belief and the rules and principles of their church, they cannot conscientiously avail themselves, and at the same time by compelling them to find means to support schools to which they can conscientiously send their children, or in the event of their not being able to find sufficient means to do both to be compelled to allow their children to go without either religious or secular instruction?

The Privy Council reversed Lord MacNaghten, in considering the effect of the addition of the word "practice", stated [at 452-3 A.C.]:

These words were no doubt introduced to meet the special case of a country which had not yet enjoyed the security of laws properly so called. It is not perhaps very easy to define precisely the meaning of such an expression as "having a right or privilege by practice". But the object of the enactment is tolerably clear. Evidently the word "practice" is not to be construed as equivalent to "custom having the force of law". Their Lordships are convinced that it must have been the intention of the legislature to preserve every legal right or privilege, and every benefit or advantage in the nature of a right or privilege, with respect to denominational schools, which any class of persons practically enjoyed at the time of the Union.

and [at 454 A.C.]:

[Roman Catholics] would have had by law the right to establish schools at their own expense, to maintain their schools by school fees or voluntary contributions, and to conduct them in accordance with their own religious tenets. Every other religious body, which was engaged in a similar work at the time of the Union would have had precisely the same right with respect to their denominational schools. Possibly this right, if it had been defined or recognized by positive enactment, might have had attached to it as a necessary or appropriate incident the right of exemption from any contribution under any circumstances to schools of a different denomination.

Thus, because the separate school supporters did not have a positive right to a rate exemption when Manitoba entered the Union, their loss thereof did not "prejudicially affect" any guaranteed right or privilege.

*Barrett* was not the end of the matter. Section 22(2), like section 93(3), contains a provision for appeals to the federal Cabinet, which then has the power to direct the province to remedy the situation. If the province fails to do so, Parliament can enact remedial legislation pursuant to section 22(3). The separate school supporters in Manitoba appealed to the federal Cabinet. The appeal was challenged on the ground that the legislation did not "affect" any right or privilege protected by law or practice, and therefore the Cabinet did not have jurisdiction pursuant to section 22(3) to deal with the matter. The Supreme Court of Canada, perhaps chastened by the Privy Council's reversal of *Barrett*, held against the separate school supporters in *Brophy v. A.G. Manitoba* [(1893), 22 S.C.R. 577].

On appeal to the Privy Council [[1895] A.C. 202] the Supreme Court of Canada's decision was again reversed. The Privy Council stated [at p. 227 A.C.]:

Before these [Acts] passed into law there existed denominational schools, of which the control and management were in the hands of Roman Catholics, who could select the books to be used and determine the character of the religious teaching. These schools received their proportionate share of the money contributed for school purposes out of the general taxation of the province, and the money raised for these purposes by local assessment was, so far as it fell upon Catholics, applied only towards the support of Catholic schools. What is the position of the Roman Catholic minority under the Acts of 1890? Schools of their own denomination, conducted according to their views, will receive no aid from the State. They must depend entirely for their support upon the contributions of the Roman Catholic community, while the taxes out of which State aid is granted to the schools provided for by this statute fall alike on Catholics and Protestants. Moreover, while the Catholic inhabitants remain liable to local assessment for school purposes, the proceeds of that assessment are no longer destined to any extent for the support of Catholic schools, but afford the means of maintaining schools which they regard as no more suitable for the education of Catholic children than if they were distinctly Protestant in their character.
In view of this comparison it does not seem possible to say that the rights and privileges of the Roman Catholic minority in relation to education which existed prior to 1890 have not been affected.

The Manitoba School Question was resolved, however unsatisfactorily, by an agreement between Prime Minister Laurier and Premier Greenway of Manitoba in 1896. The remedial part of section 22 was not used. The agreement provided for religious instruction in public schools during the last half-hour of each day and, where numbers warranted, Catholic parents might petition the school trustees to employ a Roman Catholic teacher.

Catholics, of course, were not the only group adversely affected by the new education policy of 1890. There was and is a large community of Mennonites from Russia in Manitoba, which had been encouraged to immigrate to Canada by the federal government. A federal Order-in-Council passed on August 13, 1873 stated in part:

> That the Mennonites will have the fullest privilege of exercising their religious principles, and educating their children in schools, as provided by law, without any kind of molestation or restriction whatever.

In *R. v. Hildebrand* [[1919] 3 W.W.R. 286], the Manitoba Court of Appeal held that the federal Order-in-Council was *ultra vires*, and accordingly was no defence for Mennonite parents convicted of violating compulsory public school atendance laws. Education was a provincial matter, and accordingly the federal Order-in-Council was of no effect so far as education was concerned.

## British Columbia

When British Columbia joined Confederation in 1871, there were no special laws protecting denominational schools. As a consequence, section 93 rights are very limited. As stated by McIntyre J., speaking for the Supreme Court of Canada in *Caldwell v. Stuart* [[1984] 2 S.C.R. 603 at 629]:

> The rights of denominational schools in British Columbia were very limited at the time of Confederation. It has been said that they were limited to the right to exist (see Audrey S. Brent, "The Right to Religious Education and the Constitutional Status of Denominational Schools" (1974-5), 40 Sask. Law Review 239)

It should be noted that British Columbia, quite independent of any section 93 rights, allows for public funding for private schools under the *School Support (Independent) Act* [R.S.B.C. 1977, c. 378], provided that certain conditions are met, as previously discussed in the main body of this paper.

## Prince Edward Island

When Prince Edward Island joined Confederation in 1873, there were no special laws in regard to denominational schools. While in practice denominational schools were publicly supported, there was no law which gave this right. There have been no major disputes with regard to section 93 rights in Prince Edward Island.

## Saskatchewan and Alberta

When Saskatchewan and Alberta joined Confederation as provinces in 1905, section 17 of both the *Alberta Act* [4-5 Edw. VII, c. 3] and the *Saskatchewan Act* [4-5 Edw. VII, c. 42], in identical form, provided for separate school rights as follows:

17. Section 93 of the *British North America Act, 1867*, shall apply to the said province, with the substitution for paragraph (1) of the said section 93, of the following paragraph:—

(1) Nothing in any such law shall prejudicially affect any right or privilege with respect to separate schools which any class of persons have at the date of the passing of this Act, under the terms of chapters 29 and 30 of the Ordinances of the Northwest Territories, passed in the year 1901, or with respect to religious instruction in any public or separate school as provided for in the said ordinances.

(2) In the appropriation by the Legislature or distribution by the Government of the province of any moneys for the support of schools organized and carried on in accordance with the said chapter 29, or any Act passed in amendment thereof, or in substitution therefor, there shall be no discrimination against schools of any class described in the said chapter 29.

(3) Where the expression "by law" is employed in paragraph (3) of the said section 93, it shall be held to mean the law as set out in the said chapters 29 and 30; and where the expression "at the Union" is employed in the said paragraph (3), it shall be held to mean the date at which this Act comes into force.

Section 17 is wider than section 93 in that it extends constitutional protection to religious instruction in all schools. Section 17(2) also explicitly provides that there be no discrimination in the appropriation and distribution of public funds for separate school education. The validity of Parliament's variation of section 93 by section 17 was upheld by the Supreme Court of Canada in *Reference re Section 17 of the Alberta Act* [[1927] S.C.R. 364].

In *Regina Public School v. Grattan Separate School* [(1914), 50 S.C.R. 589], a Saskatchewan statute which altered the allocation of taxes paid by corporations and thereby increased the separate schools' share of taxes was held valid.

In *McCarthy v. The City of Regina* [[1917] 1 W.W.R. 1105 (Sask. C.A.)], it was held that all rate payers of a separate school district who are of the religious faith of the minority establishing the district should be assessed as separate school supporters whether they voted for the establishment of the district or not.

In *McCarthy v. The City of Regina and Board of Trustees of the Public School Board* [[1917] 1 W.W.R. 1088 (Sask. C.A.)], it was held that a person who is not of the religious faith of a minority which has established a separate school cannot escape the obligation of being assessed for the support of the public school.

In *Bintner v. Regina Public School Board District No. 4* [(1965), 55 D.L.R. 646 (Sask. C.A.). Leave to appeal to S.C.C. refused Feb. 8, 1966] the unusual holding was made that members of a minority which has established a separate school district may have a separate school, but this gives them no right to enroll their children in the public school. It was argued, among other things, that this amounted to discrimination on the basis of religion and so was contrary to the Saskatchewan Bill of Rights. Culliton C.J.S. stated [at p. 653 D.L.R.]:

> Under the laws of this Province, a minority group within a public school district has a right to establish a separate school. That group may be "Protestant" or "Roman Catholic". In the Regina public school district the minority which established the separate school district was, and is Roman Catholic. It thus follows that the Public School Board, in limiting its obligations to educating children of the faith of the public school community, do, in fact, refuse to enroll children of the Roman Catholic faith. Such, however, is the inevitable result of the policy but not the purpose thereof.

In Alberta, section 17 was first considered in *R. v. Ulmer* [[1923] 1 W.W.R. 1 (Alta. C.A.)], where a German Lutheran parent was convicted of a violation of *The*

*School Attendance Act* in that his child attended a German Lutheran Protestant School which had not been granted a certificate which exempted its students from attendance at a public school. The school inspector who had the authority to issue certificates had refused to do so on the ground that the instruction in the school was unsatisfactory, without giving further reasons. The Court of Appeal upheld the parents' conviction.

In *Schmidt v. Calgary Board of Education and Alberta Human Rights Commission* [[1976] 6 W.W.R. 717], the Alberta Court of Appeal considered whether the practice in Alberta of charging a fee to parents of students who are enrolled in a school other than that of the parent's religion was discriminatory and in violation of *The Individual's Rights Protection Act*, S.A. 1972, c. 2. The Court upheld the practice. The Court found that there is a statutory right for the establishment of separate school systems based upon a minority religion in Alberta. Further, a person's faith determines which school system his children must attend. Taxes can only be paid to the school system which embraces the tax payer's faith. There was found to be no discrimination in charging a fee if such a parent wishes to send his children to the other school system.

In *Calgary Board of Education v. A.G. Alberta and Board of Trustees of Calgary Roman Catholic Separate School District No. 1* [[1980] 1 W.W.R. 347. Aff'd. [1981] 4 W.W.R. 187 (Alta. C.A.)], a new system of apportioning corporate taxes between public and separate schools was challenged as being in conflict with section 17 rights. This case presented the interesting question of whether section 17 protected the majority, as well as the minority in a school district. The Alberta Court of Appeal held that section 17 gives constitutional protection to the rights of certain minorities with respect to separate schools but does not protect the majority.

## Newfoundland

When Newfoundland joined Confederation in 1949, Term 17 of the *Terms of Union of Newfoundland with Canada* [Constitution Act, 1949 (12-13 Geo. VI, c. 22)] was substituted for section 93. Term 17 is, without question, the widest statutory provision in relation to denominational schools in any province in Canada. Section 17 states:

> 17. In lieu of section 93 of the British North America Act, 1867, the following term shall apply in respect of the Province of Newfoundland:
>
> > In and for the Province of Newfoundland the Legislature shall have exclusive authority to make laws in relation to education, but the Legislature will not have authority to make laws prejudicially affecting any right or privilege with respect to denominational schools, common (amalgamated) schools, or denominational colleges, that any class or classes of persons have by law in Newfoundland at the date of Union, and out of public funds of the Province of Newfoundland, provided for education,
> > > (a) all such schools shall receive their share of such funds in accordance with scales determined on a non-discriminatory basis from time to time by the Legislature for all schools then being conducted under authority of the Legislature; and
> > > (b) all such colleges shall receive their share of any grant from time to time voted for all colleges then being conducted under authority of the Legislature, such grant being distributed on a non-discriminatory basis.

The Newfoundland school system is largely denominational in character. There is no "public" education as such.

*Quebec*

In *Hirsch v. Protestant Board of School Commissioners of Montreal* [[1928] A.C. 200], the Privy Council considered the effect of section 93 on the Quebec school system. The controversy arose over the education of Jewish children primarily in Montreal. In 1903, the province passed an Act which stated that Jewish children should, for school purposes, be treated in the same manner as Protestants. The Privy Council held that this Act was *ultra vires* the province to the extent that it would enable Jewish people to be appointed to the Protestant Board of School Commissioners, as this would prejudicially affect the rights or privileges of denominational school supporters. However the Privy Council held that Jewish children had the right to attend Protestant schools in Montreal and could be admitted as a matter of grace to schools in the rural municipalities. The Privy Council also held that section 93 did not prevent the establishment of schools as a matter of government policy for persons who were neither Protestant nor Catholic.

In *Perron v. Syndics d'Ecole de Rouyn* [[1956] 1 D.L.R. (2d) 414 (Que. C.A.)] a parent who was a Jehovah's Witness successfully sought mandamus against trustees of a dissident school who had refused to let his children attend the school. The parent was a former Catholic and was still on the assessment rolls for the Catholic Public School. Among other things, the school board objected to a Jehovah's Witness being characterized as a Protestant. Bissonnette J. stated [at 417 D.L.R.]:

> In conclusion, to be considered a Protestant it is sufficient to be a Christian and to repudiate the authority of the Pope.

Since Jehovah's Witnesses were Protestants and Protestants were a class of persons with protected rights pursuant to section 93, the Court found that the children of the Jehovah's Witness parent had the right to attend the dissident Protestant school.

In *A.G. Quebec v. Lavigne* [[1984] 2 S.C.R. 575], the Supreme Court of Canada had to deal with a Quebec statute which established a new system of school financing based primarily upon government grants rather than specifically earmarked taxation. The statute, an amendment to the provincial *Education Act*, applied to all public schools in Quebec, whether denominational or not, and provided that 1) the Minister of Education must make rules regarding allowable expenses which are eligible to be covered by grants; 2) school commissioners and trustees must levy taxes to cover non-eligible expenses; 3) the tax assessment was subject to a ceiling; and 4) any taxation in excess of the ceiling had to be approved by referendum of the electors.

The court struck down the statute. After reviewing the education statute in force at Confederation, the Court concluded that the right of Roman Catholics and Protestants in 1867 to direct and control their denominational schools was recognized by law. As to financing, the law recognized a right to receive funds on a proportionate basis from the electors within their municipality. By omitting to state that the grants must be distributed on a proportionate basis, and by making the boards submit to a referendum in respect of certain expenses which could include electors from outside the school district, the statute under consideration in *Lavigne* prejudicially affected rights guaranteed by section 93(1). It was accordingly *ultra vires* the Legislature.

*Ontario*

The important cases in Ontario relating to section 93 rights have already been referred to elsewhere in this paper.

## 2. Constitutional Guarantees Respecting Language

### ATTORNEY-GENERAL OF QUEBEC v. QUEBEC ASSOCIATION OF PROTESTANT SCHOOL BOARDS

In the Supreme Court of Canada. 10 D.L.R. (4th) 321.

Ritchie, Dickson, Beetz, Estey, McIntyre, Lamer and Wilson JJ. July 26, 1984.

Appeal from a judgment of the Quebec Court of Appeal, 1 D.L.R. (4th) 573, 7 C.R.R. 139, affirming a judgment of Deschênes C.J.S.C., 140 D.L.R. (3d) 33, [1982] Que. S.C. 673, 3 C.R.R. 114, declaring that the restrictions on access to English-language education contained in s. 72 *et seq.* of the *Charter of the French Language* (Que.) and the regulations thereunder, to the extent that they are inconsistent with s. 23(1)(*b*), (2) and (3) of the *Canadian Charter of Rights and Freedoms*, are of no force and effect.

BY THE COURT:—

#### I INTRODUCTION

The question is whether the provisions regarding instruction in English contained in chap. VIII of the *Charter of the French Language*, R.S.Q. 1977, c. C-11, and in the regulations adopted thereunder, are inconsistent with the *Canadian Charter of Rights and Freedoms* and of no force or effect to the extent of the inconsistency.

The applicable legislative and constitutional provisions must first be considered.

Chapter VIII of the *Charter of the French Language* ("Bill 101"), which came into effect on August 26, 1977, is entitled "The Language of Instruction". At the time the proceedings were initiated, it consisted of 17 sections, 72 to 88 inclusive. However, ss. 72 and 73 are at the heart of the matter, and only they need be cited:

> 72. Instruction in the kindergarten classes and in the elementary and secondary schools shall be in French, except where this chapter allows otherwise.
>
> This rule obtains in school bodies within the meaning of the Schedule and also applies to subsidized instruction provided by institutions declared to be of public interest or recognized for purposes of grants in virtue of the Act respecting private education (chapter E-9).
>
> 73. In derogation of section 72, the following children, at the request of their father and mother, may receive their instruction in English:
>
> > (*a*) a child whose father or mother received his or her elementary instruction in English, in Québec;
> >
> > (*b*) a child whose father or mother domiciled in Quebec on 26 August 1977, received his or her elementary instruction in English outside Québec;

> (c) a child who, in his last year of school in Québec before 26 August 1977, was lawfully receiving his instruction in English, in a public kindergarten class or in an elementary or secondary school;
> (d) the younger brothers and sisters of a child described in paragraph c.

The applicable constitutional provisions are ss. 1, 23 and 32(1) of the *Canadian Charter of Rights and Freedoms* ("the Charter"), and ss. 52(1) and (2) and 59(1) and (2) of the *Constitution Act, 1982*, of which the Charter is part. These provisions read as follows:

> 1. The *Canadian Charter of Rights and Freedoms* guarantees the rights and freedoms set out in it subject only to such reasonable limits prescribed by law as can be demonstrably justified in a free and democratic society.

Section 23 of the Charter is entitled "Minority Language Educational Rights". It provides:

> 23(1) Citizens of Canada
> (a) whose first language learned and still understood is that of the English or French linguistic minority population of the province in which they reside, or
> (b) who have received their primary school instruction in Canada in English or French and reside in a province where the language in which they received that instruction is the language of the English or French linguistic minority population of the province,
> have the right to have their children receive primary and secondary school instruction in that language in that province.
>
> (2) Citizens of Canada of whom any child has received or is receiving primary or secondary school instruction in English or French in Canada, have the right to have all their children receive primary and secondary school instruction in the same language.
>
> (3) The right of citizens of Canada under subsections (1) and (2) to have their children receive primary and secondary school instruction in the language of the English or French linguistic minority population of a province
> (a) applies wherever in the province the number of children of citizens who have such a right is sufficient to warrant the provision to them out of public funds of minority language instruction; and
> (b) includes, where the number of those children so warrants, the right to have them receive that instruction in minority language educational facilities provided out of public funds.

Section 32(1) of the Charter states:

> 32(1) This Charter applies
> (a) to the Parliament and government of Canada in respect of all matters within the authority of Parliament including all matters relating to the Yukon Territory and Northwest Territories; and
> (b) to the legislature and government of each province in respect of all matters within the authority of the legislature of each province.

However, s. 23(1)(a) of the Charter, cited above, is not in force in Quebec, pursuant to s. 59(1) and (2) of the *Constitution Act, 1982*:

> 59(1) Paragraph 23(1)(a) shall come into force in respect of Quebec on a day to be fixed by proclamation issued by the Queen or the Governor General under the Great Seal of Canada.
>
> (2) A proclamation under subsection (1) shall be issued only where authorized by the legislative assembly or government of Quebec.

Finally, s. 52(1) and (2)(a) of the *Constitution Act, 1982* provides:

> 52(1) The Constitution of Canada is the supreme law of Canada, and any law that is inconsistent with the provision of the Constitution is, to the extent of the inconsistency, of no force or effect.

> (2) The Constitution of Canada includes
> (a) the *Canada Act 1982*, including this Act;

It follows from these provisions that, if ss. 72 and 73 of Bill 101 are inconsistent with s. 23 of the Charter, they are of no force or effect to the extent of the inconsistency as a consequence of s. 52(1) and (2)(a) of the *Constitution Act, 1982*, unless they are legitimized by s. 1 of the Charter to the extent, of course, that s. 1 applies to the rights conferred by s. 23.

. . . .

At the request of respondents Quebec Association of Protestant School Boards, the Protestant School Board of Greater Montreal and Lakeshore School Board, the lamented Laskin C.J.C. stated the following constitutional questions:

> (1) Are the provisions regarding access to English language education contained in Chapter VIII of la *Charte de la langue française* (R.S.Q. 1977, c. C-11) and the regulations thereunder, inconsistent with the *Canadian Charter of Rights and Freedoms* and to the extent of the inconsistency, are they of no force or effect?
>
> (2) Are school boards operating English language primary or secondary schools obliged to admit to English language schooling therein children who qualify pursuant to sections 23(1)(b) and 23(2) of the *Canadian Charter of Rights and Freedoms* whether or not they qualify under la *Charte de la langue française* and have complied with its requirements?
>
> (3) Do school boards have the right to receive grants from public funds for the education of such children on the same basis as applies in respect of children who qualify for English language education under la *Charte de la langue française*?

The Attorney-General of New Brunswick was given leave to intervene and supported the position taken by respondents.

Counsel for the Island of Montreal School Council, the mis-en-cause on the first motion, informed the court that it did not intend to prepare a submission or participate in the hearing.

### III Inconsistency Between ss. 72 and 73 of Bill 101 and s. 23 of the Charter

It is not disputed that ss. 72 and 73 of Bill 101 and s. 23 of the Charter are inconsistent. Nevertheless, it is useful to indicate exactly the nature and extent of this inconsistency. The trial judge made a comparative study of the applicable legislative and constitutional provisions, and described this inconsistency in language the accuracy of which, at least in general terms, does not appear to have been disputed. He said the following, at pp. 46-8 D.L.R., pp. 681-2 Que. S.C., of his judgment:

> Section 72 of Bill 101 enunciates the principle unambiguously: "Instruction . . . shall be in French, except where this chapter allows otherwise."
>
> Section 73 provides the only exceptions which are of interest in this case. "In derogation of section 72": the words at the beginning of s. 73 clearly indicate that it is an exception. Applying traditional canons of construction, s. 73 should receive a restrictive interpretation: only those who fall within the four categories enumerated in s. 73 are to be admitted to English schools.
>
> We are familiar with these categories since the court has already quoted the section.
>
> In the first category, the right follows from father or mother to son or daughter on condition that the mother or father received his or her primary education in English in Quebec.
>
> In the three other categories, still subject to the "Quebec condition", the right will gradually fade away to lapse toward the end of the century: all children falling within these three categories should have completed their secondary schooling by then, and only in the case of a genetic accident will the period be extended.

But under s. 73 the children of immigrants, even English-speaking immigrants from other parts of Canada or from foreign countries, are not to be admitted into English schools in Quebec.

Section 73 sets out what has come to be known, in constitutional jargon in these last few years, as the "Quebec clause".

Undoubtedly, the Minister, Mr. Laurin, had this clause in mind when he spoke, last May 5th, of the "authentically English-speaking minority of Quebec" (R-1).

Without doubt, it was this clause which was contemplated by the White Paper of March, 1977, setting out "La politique québecoise de la langue française" when it described English schooling as "an exceptional system for the present minority in Quebec" (p. 46).

On the other hand, s. 23 of the Charter, in s-ss. 1(*b*) and (2) — the only ones, along with s-s. (3) which are in force in Quebec — allows access to English schools to children whose parents, being citizens of Canada resident in Quebec, have received primary instruction in English in Canada or those children of citizens of Canada having a brother or a sister who has received or is receiving primary or secondary instruction in English in Canada.

Subsection (3) of the same section makes this right subject to the condition of "a sufficient number" of children, etc., but this condition presents no problem in Quebec.

In the same constitutional jargon, s. 23 of the Charter sets out the "Canada clause" in the general sense.

How should these two clauses be compared?

Paragraphs (*a*) and (*b*) of s. 73 of Bill 101 are included in s. 23(1)(*b*) of the Charter, if the condition of citizenship is fulfilled; if not, Bill 101 is more permissive than the Charter.

Paragraphs (*c*) and (*d*) of s. 73 are included within s. 23(2) of the Charter, on the same condition; if not, again it would be necessary to consider Bill 101 as broader than the Charter.

In short, for those who are citizens of Canada, all cases contemplated by s. 73 of Bill 101 are equally covered by the Charter; for non-naturalized aliens Bill 101 is more generous.

Up to this point the applicants cannot complain of any contradiction. But, what of the inverse situation?

Section 23 of the Charter only applies to citizens of Canada: one must keep this premise constantly in mind.

Section 23(1)(*b*) opens English schooling in Quebec to children whose parents have received their primary instruction in English anywhere in Canada.

This general eligibility is prohibited in Quebec by the combined effect of ss. 72 and 73 of Bill 101.

Section 23(2) of the Charter opens English schooling in Quebec to children of citizens of Canada who have a brother or sister who has received or is receiving primary or secondary instruction in English anywhere in Canada.

This general eligibility is, again, denied by the effect of the same provisions of Bill 101.

The conclusion, then, is inevitable: Bill 101 and the Charter are incompatible.

## IV  ARGUMENTS RAISED BY APPELLANT AND THE FIRST CONSTITUTIONAL QUESTION

The arguments raised by appellant may be summarized in three propositions:

(1) s. 1 of the Charter, which guarantees the rights and freedoms contained in that document, applies to all the rights so guaranteed, including that conferred by s. 23;

(2) s. 1 of the Charter does not distinguish between the limit and denial of a right, and makes the reasonable and justifiable nature of the limit the true test of its constitutionality;

(3) the provisions of chap. VIII of Bill 101 place upon the right secured by s. 23 of the Charter reasonable limits that can be justified in a free and democratic society.

The first proposition was approved by the Court of Appeal and the Superior Court. We are disposed to take this proposition as established, but for the sake of discussion only and without deciding the point.

The second and third propositions, like the first, were supported by a thorough memorandum and argument in which, *inter alia*, s. 1 of the Charter, the requirements which it imposes, the presumption of constitutionality and the question of the burden of proof were analysed in light of judicial interpretation of similar clauses in other constitutional charters by the Judicial Committee of the Privy Council for the Commonwealth nations and by the Supreme Court of India, as well as in light of American precedents and decisions of the courts on the *Canadian Bill of Rights*. Counsel for the appellant further argued that not only have respondent applicants not succeeded in establishing that the provisions relating to access to English schooling in Quebec are unreasonable, but also that the latter are reasonable within the meaning of s. 1 of the Charter, in view of factors such as demographic patterns, the physical mobility (migration) and linguistic mobility ("assimilation") of individuals and the regional distribution of interprovincial migrants. It was further argued that other free and democratic societies such as Switzerland and Belgium, which have socio-linguistic situations comparable to that in Quebec, have adopted stricter linguistic measures than Bill 101, and these measures have been held to be reasonable and justified by the Swiss and European courts. Finally, it was argued that the collective right of the Anglophone minority in Quebec to cultural survival is not threatened by Bill 101, which establishes a system providing access to English schooling which is not unreasonable.

We do not think it necessary to go into these arguments, for none of them answers the reasons of Beauregard J.A. of the Court of Appeal in the part of his opinion cited above.

[. . . it is quite apparent, and this seems to me to destroy appellant's argument, that s. 23 was adopted specifically and deliberately to limit the effects of Chapter VIII or other similar statutes, and that accordingly it is pointless to ask which provision limits which.

This is especially true as s. 23 was worded so precisely and guarantees such a specific right, to such a limited number of individuals, that it is hard to see how such an absolute limitation as that in Chapter VIII, however legitimate, could be regarded as other than a prohibited invasion of this right.]

These reasons, with which we agree in substance, are fatal to appellant's position, and in our opinion are conclusive.

Section 23 of the Charter is not, like other provisions in that constitutional document, of the kind generally found in such charters and declarations of fundamental rights. It is not a codification of essential pre-existing and more or less universal rights that are being confirmed and perhaps clarified, extended or amended, and which, most importantly, are being given a new primacy and inviolability by their entrenchment in the supreme law of the land. The special provisions of s. 23 of the Charter make it a unique set of constitutional provisions, quite peculiar to Canada.

This set of constitutional provisions was not enacted by the framers in a vacuum. When it was adopted, the framers knew, and clearly had in mind, the regimes governing the Anglophone and Francophone linguistic minorities in various provinces in Canada so far as the language of instruction was concerned. They also had in mind the history of these regimes, both earlier ones such as Reg. 17, which for a time limited instruction in French in the separate schools of Ontario — *Ottawa Separate Schools Trustees v. Mackell*, [1917] A.C. 62 (P.C.) — as well as more recent ones such as Bill 101 and the legislation which preceded it in Quebec. Rightly or wrongly — and it is not for the courts to decide — the framers of the Constitution manifestly regarded as inadequate some — and perhaps all — of the regimes in force at the time the Charter was enacted, and their intention was to remedy the perceived defects of these regimes by uniform corrective measures, namely, those contained in s. 23 of the Charter, which were at the same time given the status of a constitutional guarantee. The framers of the Constitution unquestionably intended by s. 23 to establish a general regime for the language of instruction, not a special regime for Quebec; but in view of the period when the Charter was enacted, and especially in light of the wording of s. 23 of the Charter as compared with that of ss. 72 and 73 of Bill 101, it is apparent that the combined effect of the latter two sections seemed to the framers like an archetype of the regimes needing reform, or which at least had to be affected, and the remedy prescribed for all of Canada by s. 23 of the Charter was in large part a response to these sections.

Until 1969, the laws of Quebec appear to have been silent on the language of instruction, but in fact the system operated so as to leave almost complete freedom to everyone at all educational levels. Following the conflict that occurred in 1968 at the Saint-Léonard school board, where an attempt had been made to impose instruction in French on children of Italian immigrants — see Joseph Eliot Magnet, "Minority-Language Educational Rights", 4 Supreme Court L. Rev. 195 (1982), at p. 202 — the Quebec legislator adopted the *Act to promote the French Language in Québec*, 1969 (Que.), c. 9, also known as Bill 63. Despite its title, this Act embodied in legislation the freedom of choice regarding language of instruction which had existed up to then. However, the Quebec legislator indicated a concern with immigration in s. 3 [enacting s. 3(*e*) to the *Immigration Department Act*, 1968 (Que.), c. 68], where it directed the Minister of Immigration to

> (*e*) in co-operation with the Minister of Education, take the measures necessary so that the persons who settle in Québec may acquire the knowledge of the French language upon arrival or even before they leave their country of origin, and may have their children instructed in educational institutions where courses are given in the French language.

This Act was replaced in 1974 by the *Official Language Act*, 1974 (Que.), c. 6, also known as Bill 22. Title 1 of this Act stated in its single section [s. 1] that French is the official language of Quebec. Chapter V of Title III is entitled "The Language of Instruction". Sections 40 and 41 gave French a certain degree of priority. The first paragraph of s. 40 provided that the language of instruction shall be French in the schools governed by the school boards, the regional school boards and the corporations of trustees, and the second paragraph stated that school boards, regional school boards and corporations of trustees "shall continue" to provide instruction in English. The third paragraph provided for control over increasing or reducing instruction in English by the Minister of Education, who was not to give his authorization "unless he considers that the number of pupils whose mother tongue is English and who are under the jurisdiction of such body warrants it". Section 41 provided that pupils must have a sufficient knowledge of the language of instruction to receive their instruction in that language, which had the practical effect of closing off French schooling to the majority of Anglophone pupils and English schooling to the majority of Francophone pupils. Section 41 also provided that pupils who do not have a sufficient knowledge of any of the languages of instruction must receive their instruction in French, a provision which, though it did not say so expressly, was directed at immigrants, unless they were French- or English-speaking.

These provisions of the *Official Language Act* were found to be *intra vires* by Deschênes C.J.S.C. in *Protestant School Board of Greater Montreal v. Minister of Education of Quebec; A.-G. Can., Third Party*, [1976] Que. S.C. 430. The Court of Appeal of Quebec dismissed an appeal on the ground that the *Official Language Act* had been replaced by Bill 101: 83 D.L.R. (3d) at p. 679, see note.

Thus, at the time the Charter was adopted, there had for some years been legislation in Quebec which, apart from the Act adopted in 1969, tended to give preferred treatment to French as the language of instruction, and correspondingly to lessen the benefits hitherto given to English, in fact if not in law. The culmination of this legislation was Bill 101.

Although the fate reserved to the English language as a language of instruction had generally been more advantageous in Quebec than the fate reserved to the French language in the other provinces, Quebec seems nevertheless to have been the only province where there was then this tendency to limit the benefits conferred on the language of the minority. In the other provinces at the time, either the earlier situation had remained unchanged, at least so far as legislation was concerned, as in Newfoundland and British Columbia which have no legislation on the language of instruction, or else relatively recent statutes had been adopted improving the situation of the linguistic minority, as in New Brunswick, Nova Scotia and Prince Edward Island: see Alfred Monnin, then a puisne judge of the Manitoba Court of Appeal, "L'égalité juridique des langues et l'enseignment: les écoles françaises hors-Québec", Les Cahiers de Droit, vol. 24, No. 1, March, 1983, p. 157.

It is therefore not surprising that Bill 101 was very much in the minds of the framers of the Constitution when they enacted s. 23 of the Charter, which guarantees "minority language educational rights". This is confirmed when the wording of the section is compared with that of ss. 72 and 73 of Bill 101, and with other provincial statutes on the language of instruction.

To begin with, the fact that Quebec is the only province in Canada in which, by virtue of s. 59(1) and (2) of the *Constitution Act, 1982*, s. 23(1)(a) of the Charter is not yet in force and cannot be brought into force without the consent of Quebec, indicates clearly that the framers of the Constitution had Quebec specially in mind when they enacted s. 23 of the Charter. It may be possible to suggest a reason for this exception: so far as Quebec is concerned, s. 23(1)(a) applies to Canadian citizens whose first language is English but who did not receive their primary school instruction in that language in Canada, that is, in practice, largely immigrants whose first language is English and who have become Canadian citizens. It is therefore plausible to think that this particular provision of the Charter was suspended for Quebec in part so as to calm the concerns regarding immigration, that, long before Bill 101 was adopted, were expressed in Quebec because of the minority status of French in North America.

It is above all when we compare s. 23(1)(b) and (2) of the Charter with s. 73 of Bill 101 that it becomes most apparent that the latter is the type of regime on which the framers of the Constitution modelled s. 23. Both in the Charter and in Bill 101, the criteria that must be considered in deciding the right to instruction in the minority language are the place where the parents received their instruction in the minority language. Both in the Charter and in Bill 101, that place is where the parents received their primary school instruction. Both in the Charter and in Bill 101, satisfying this criterion gives a right to primary and secondary school instruction in the minority language, and Bill 101 adds the right to education at the kindergarten level. Both in the Charter and in Bill 101, the criteria also include the language of instruction of a child's brothers and sisters, though Bill 101 refers to the younger brothers and sisters of children included in a category which is temporary by nature — a limit not found in the Charter.

Now, of all the provincial statutes relating to the language of instruction that were in force at the time the Charter was adopted, only Bill 101 imposes criteria as specific and unique as those we have just indicated: see the statutes listed by Monnin, *op. cit., supra.*

It is true that certain provincial statutes, such as the *Act to Amend the School Act* of Prince Edward Island, S.P.E.I. 1980, c. 48, s. 9, and the *Act to Amend Chapter 81 of the Revised Statutes, 1967, the Education Act* of Nova Scotia, S.N.S. 1981, c. 20, s. 2, contain a definition of the mother tongue similar to that found in s. 23(1)(*a*) of the Charter, or, that others, like the Nova Scotia statute just mentioned, refer to the concept of "a sufficient number of children" found in s. 23(3)(*a*) and (*b*) of the Charter, but equally found in s. 79 of Bill 101, which provides that a school body not already giving instruction in English may not introduce it without authorization from the Minister of Education, who shall grant it if, in his opinion, it is warranted by the number of pupils who come within the jurisdiction of the school body and who are eligible for instruction in English under s. 73.

However, once again, to our knowledge no other provincial statute that was in force at the time the Charter was adopted and which dealt with the language of instruction has criteria as specific as those in s. 73 of Bill 101. These criteria are not only specific, but are also unique as a whole; it may be wondered whether the framers of the Constitution would have drafted s. 23 of the Charter as they did if they had not had in view the model which s. 23 was indeed in large measure meant to override. In their memorandum, the individual respondents, after referring to the Quebec statutes on the language of instruction, add, and in substance, properly so:

Indeed, Sec. 23 was modelled on those laws, except that it provided somewhat broader rights. No other Canadian legislation bases children's education on their parents' in a geographic area.

By incorporating into the structure of s. 23 of the Charter the unique set of criteria in s. 73 of Bill 101, the framers of the Constitution identified the type of regime they wished to correct and on which they would base the remedy prescribed. The framers' objective appears simple, and may readily be inferred from the concrete method used by them: to adopt a general rule guaranteeing the Francophone and Anglophone minorities in Canada an important part of the rights which the Anglophone minority in Quebec had enjoyed with respect to the language of instruction before Bill 101 was adopted.

If, as is apparent, chap. VIII of Bill 101 is the prototype of regime which the framers of the Constitution wished to remedy by adopting s. 23 of the Charter, the limits which this regime imposes on rights involving the language of instruction, so far as they are inconsistent with s. 23 of the Charter, cannot possibly have been regarded by the framers of the Constitution as coming within "such reasonable limits prescribed by law as can be demonstrably justified in a free and democratic society". Accordingly, the limits imposed by chap. VIII of Bill 101 are not legitimate limits within the meaning of s. 1 of the Charter to the extent that the latter applies to s. 23.

In his submission, appellant wrote that the reasoning of Beauregard J.A. amounts to saying that s. 1 of the Charter does not apply to s. 23. With respect, we do not think this observation is correct. We think that Beauregard J.A. in fact says the opposite, when he writes (translation [p. 576 D.L.R.]): "It is true that, strictly speaking, the right guaranteed by s. 23 can be the subject of a limitation under s. 1. ... It is true that even if Chapter VIII denies the s. 23 right absolutely, there is nothing *a priori* to prevent s. 1 validating Chapter VIII."

Beauregard J.A. then wrote the passage cited at the beginning of these reasons. We interpret this passage to mean that the limits imposed by chap. VIII of Bill 101 cannot be regarded as legitimate limits within the meaning of s. 1 of the Charter, since they are precisely the type of limit struck down by s. 23. However, Beauregard J.A. adds that it "is hard to see how a limit as absolute as that in Chapter VIII, whatever its legitimacy, could be regarded otherwise than as a prohibited invasion of this right".

Accordingly, in his opinion, limits less absolute than those in chap. VIII of Bill 101 could be legitimized by s. 1 of the Charter.

It does not appear necessary to decide this last point, since the only limits we have to consider are those in chap. VIII of Bill 101. In addition, we repeat that we have only assumed for the sake of discussion, without deciding the point, the truth of the proposition that s. 1 of the Charter applies to s. 23.

The reasons of Beauregard J.A., like those developed above, are based on a teleological interpretation of s. 23 of the Charter, that is to say, on a method of interpretation which looks to the purpose sought by the framers in drafting this section. Such an interpretation is possible because Bill 101 was adopted prior to the Charter; but it should be noted that, even without this argument, the result would be the same.

Let us assume that chap. VIII of Bill 101 had been enacted after the Charter, or that a province other than Quebec were now to adopt an Act drafted like chap. VIII of Bill 101, but designed to limit the right to instruction in French. Could it be said that s. 1 of the Charter is capable of legitimizing such legislation, to the extent that s. 1 applies to s. 23?

We do not think so.

Whatever their scope, the limits which s. 1 of the Charter allows to be placed on the rights and freedoms set out in it cannot be equated with exceptions such as those authorized by s. 33(1) and (2) of the Charter, which in any event do not authorize any exception to s. 23:

> 33(1) Parliament or the legislature of a province may expressly declare in an Act of Parliament or of the legislature, as the case may be, that the Act or a provision thereof shall operate notwithstanding a provision included in section 2 or sections 7 to 15 of this Charter.
>
> (2) An Act or a provision of an Act in respect of which a declaration made under this section is in effect shall have such operation as it would have but for the provision of this Charter referred to in the declaration.

Nor can those limits be tantamount to amendments to the Constitution of Canada, the procedure for which is prescribed in s. 38 *et seq.* of the *Constitution Act, 1982.*

Now, the real effect of s. 73 of Bill 101 is to make an exception to s. 23(1)(*b*) and (2) of the Charter in Quebec; yet those subsections are not provisions to which exceptions can be made under s. 33(1) and (2) of the Charter. In addition, s. 73 of Bill 101 directly alters the effect of s. 23 of the Charter for Quebec, without following the procedure laid down for amending the Constitution.

The rights stated in s. 23 of the Charter are guaranteed to very specific classes of persons. This specific classification lies at the very heart of the provision, since it is the means chosen by the framers to identify those entitled to the rights they intended to guarantee. In our opinion, a legislature cannot by an ordinary statute validly set aside the means so chosen by the framers and affect this classification. Still less can it remake the classification and redefine the classes.

The following arguments made by the Attorney-General of New Brunswick in his submission seem to us to be conclusive:

> Section 59 modifies the classes of parents entitled to have their children instructed in English by suspending the operation of paragraph 23(1)(a) in Quebec. By implication, the other classes of beneficiaries entitled to enjoy section 23 rights cannot be redefined by ordinary legislative enactment.
>
> The detailed definition of classes of parents is at the heart of Section 23. Any effort to redefine the classes of parents entitled to educational rights effectively represents an attempt to amend the Constitution without resort to the amending formula and is accordingly not comprehended by section 1.

The Attorney-General of Canada expresses the same idea in his memorandum, where he writes, after referring to s. 1 of the Charter (translation):

> . . . it does not allow the categories of individuals who enjoy the right conferred by s. 23 to be altered by imposing different rules which run directly counter to those expressly stated in that section. The exception clause provided for in s. 33 does not cover s. 23, and the *Canadian Charter of Rights and Freedoms* can only be amended in accordance with the terms of the procedure for amending the Constitution contained in Part V of the *Constitution Act, 1982.*

As the Attorney-General of Canada notes in his memorandum, s. 73 of Bill 101 constitutes exactly the kind of redefinition of the classes of persons protected by s. 23 of the Charter which is prohibited and invalid if undertaken by any means other than a constitutional amendment (translation):

> Section 73 of the *Charter of the French language* does not limit the right conferred by s. 23: rather, it constitutes a permanent alteration of the classes of citizens who are entitled to the protection afforded by that section. By laying down conditions of access which run directly counter to those expressly stated in s. 23, and which by their very nature have the effect of permanently depriving an entire class of individuals of the right conferred by s. 23, s. 73 alters the very content of that right . . .

It goes without saying that in adopting s. 73 of Bill 101 the Quebec Legislature did not intend, and could not have intended, to create an exception to s. 23 of the Charter or to amend it, since that section did not then exist; but its intent is not relevant. What matters is the effective nature and scope of s. 73 in light of the provisions of the Charter, whenever the section was enacted. If, because of the Charter, s. 73 could not be validly adopted today, it is clearly rendered of no force or effect by the Charter and this for the same reason, namely the direct conflict between s. 73 of Bill 101 and s. 23 of the Charter. The provisions of s. 73 of Bill 101 collide directly with those of s. 23 of the Charter, and are not limits which can be legitimized by s. 1 of the Charter. Such limits cannot be exceptions to the rights and freedoms guaranteed by the Charter nor amount to amendments of the Charter. An Act of Parliament or of a legislature which, for example, purported to impose the beliefs of a State religion would be in direct conflict with s. 2(a) of the Charter, which guarantees freedom of conscience and religion, and would have to be ruled of no force or effect without the necessity of even considering whether such legislation could be legitimized by s. 1. The same applies to chap. VIII of Bill 101 in respect of s. 23 of the Charter.

This other method of interpretation, based on the true nature and effects of chap. VIII of Bill 101 in light of the *Charter* provisions, takes an opposite route to that based on the purpose of the framers, but leads to the same result: chap. VIII is of no force or effect.

For these reasons, we would answer "yes" to the first constitutional question stated by Chief Justice Laskin.

### V  THE OTHER TWO CONSTITUTIONAL QUESTIONS

Respondents and the interveners argued that these two questions should be answered in the affirmative, whereas appellant argued that the court should give no answer to them.

It will be recalled that in the judgment which he rendered on the first motion for a declaratory judgment, Deschênes C.J.S.C. answered in the affirmative the two questions cited above, which were practically identical to the two constitutional questions stated by Chief Justice Laskin. These questions were put to Deschênes C.J.S.C. by the respondent who were parties to the first motion. However, it is important to note the basis on which Deschênes C.J.S.C. answered in the affirmative. He explained his reasoning at p. 709 Que. S.C., of his judgment as follows:

> At the hearing, counsel for Quebec agreed that, if the petitioners' application were to be allowed, then the laws in force would impose the obligations claimed in the first question on the school boards and would give them the right claimed in the second question of the petition.

Appellant argued that he had reasserted his position in the Court of Appeal, which did not discuss these questions; but, as it dismissed the appeal, it left standing the affirmative answers given by Deschênes C.J.S.C. as well as the basis on which those answers were given.

Appellant explained in his memorandum why, in his opinion, this court should not answer the last two constitutional questions. After noting the basis on which Deschênes C.J.S.C. answered in the affirmative the two questions put to him by respondent applicants in the first motion for a declaratory judgment, he went on (translation):

> 11. The Attorney General of Quebec repeats that if this Court answers the first constitutional question in the affirmative, the *laws in effect* in Quebec impose the obligation claimed in the second question and gives [sic] them the right claimed in the third question. Accordingly, the facts of the case at bar cannot be a basis for such questions, since there is no issue respecting the points raised.
> 12. To the extent that, by means of these questions which correspond to some of the conclusions of the motions for a declaratory judgment, this Court is being urged to rule on the meaning of s. 23 of the *Canadian Charter* as it applies to respondent school boards, the Attorney General of Quebec submits that there is no basis for this Court to do so in the case at bar.

. . . . .

The Attorney General of Quebec respectfully submits that:

(1) it is not necessary in order to dispose of the appeal at bar to decide whether s. 23 of the Canadian Charter gives *school boards* the right claimed in the third question and imposes on them the obligation claimed in the second question, and that therefore, this Court should not rule on the point (*Citizens Insurance Co. of Canada v. Parsons*, (1881-82) 7 App. Cas. 96, at 109; *John Deere Plow Co. Ltd. v. Wharton*, [1915] A.C. 330, at 339);

(2) in any case the case is not ripe [for consideration], since the obligations and rights claimed depend on the application of s. 23(3) of the Canadian Charter, and that no argument or evidence was submitted to the trial court on the basis of which it could decide whether the conditions imposed by s. 23(3)(*a*) and (*b*) had been met.

The Quebec Association of Protestant School Boards, the Protestant School Board of Greater Montreal and the Lakeshore School Board answered appellant in their memorandum as follows:

12. Appellant, at paragraphs 8 to 15 of his Factum, contends that Questions 2 and 3 ought not to be answered on the basis that the rights and obligations which they seek to confirm are secured under existing Quebec law if the answer to Question 1 is in the affirmative.

13. At issue in this case however are the rights and obligations which flow from the Canadian Charter and it was to these rights and obligations, not those under Quebec law for the time being, that the Motion for Declaratory Judgment was addressed.

Finally, in their memorandum the individual respondents took the following position:

Before beginning their argument, Respondents observe that, while they agree with Appellant that the first of the three questions drafted following the obtaining of leave to appeal is the most important but they submit that all three should be answered in order that no further dispute arise from the application of Section 23 in Quebec.

We believe that appellant is right on this point. It is possible that the questions put in the first motion for a declaratory judgment can be interpreted as covering the rights and obligations resulting from the Charter rather than the rights and obligations resulting from the laws in effect in Quebec. However, this is not the basis on which the trial judge answered, and it can be assumed that, if he answered as he did on the basis of an admission by the Attorney-General of Quebec as to the effect of the laws in force in Quebec, and not as if he had to answer constitutional questions, it was because the parties did not provide him with the means of answering on any other basis, in the evidence presented to him or the arguments which were made.

We consider that this court should not answer these constitutional questions, on which we do not know the opinions of either the Court of Appeal or the trial judge. We are not even sure we could given an enlightened answer, if we wished to. We think it is significant in this respect that, even though respondents and the interveners argued that we should answer these two questions in the affirmative, they did not discuss either in their memoranda or orally any reasons of fact or law as to why the court should answer in the affirmative.

The parties will have to content themselves with the two answers given by the trial judge on the basis used by him. His judgment has, on this basis, the force of *res judicata*.

## VI CONCLUSIONS

The first constitutional question is answered in the affirmative.

The other two constitutional questions are left unanswered.

The appeal is dismissed with costs. However, there will be no order as to costs for or against the Attorney-General of Canada and the intervener.

*Appeal dismissed.*

# REFERENCE RE LANGUAGE RIGHTS UNDER SECTION 23 OF THE MANITOBA ACT, 1870, AND SECTION 133 OF THE CONSTITUTION ACT, 1867

In the Supreme Court of Canada. [1985] 4 W.W.R. 385.

Dickson C.J.C., Beetz, Estey, McIntyre, Lamer, Wilson and LeDain JJ.
June 13, 1985.

PER CURIAM:—

I

THE REFERENCE

This Reference combines legal and constitutional questions of the utmost subtlety and complexity with political questions of great sensitivity. The proceedings were initiated by *Order in Council*, P.C. 1984-1136, dated 5th April 1984, pursuant to s. 55 of the *Supreme Court Act*, R.S.C. 1970, c. S-19. The *Order in Council* reads:

WHEREAS the Minister of Justice reports:

1. That it is important to resolve as expeditiously as possible legal issues relating to certain language rights under section 23 of the *Manitoba Act, 1870* and section 133 of the *Constitution Act, 1867*.

2. That in order that such legal issues be addressed without delay, it is considered necessary that the opinion of the Supreme Court of Canada be obtained in relation to the following questions, namely:

*Question #1*

Are the requirements of section 133 of the *Constitution Act, 1867* and of section 23 of the *Manitoba Act, 1870* respecting the use of both the English and French languages in
(a) the Records and Journals of the Houses of the Parliament of Canada and of the Legislatures of Quebec and Manitoba, and
(b) the Acts of the Parliament of Canada and of the Legislatures of Quebec and Manitoba mandatory?

*Question #2*

Are those statutes and regulations of the Province of Manitoba that were not printed and published in both the English and French languages invalid by reason of section 23 of the *Manitoba Act, 1870?*

*Question #3*

If the answer to question 2 is affirmative, do those enactments that were not printed and published in English and French have any legal force and effect, and if so, to what extent and under what conditions?

*Question #4*

Are any of the provisions of *An Act Respecting the Operation of section 23 of the Manitoba Act in Regard to Statutes*, enacted by S.M. 1980, Ch. 3, inconsistent with the provisions of section 23 of the *Manitoba Act, 1870*, and if so are such provisions, to the extent of such inconsistency, invalid and of no legal force and effect?

THEREFORE, HIS EXCELLENCY THE GOVERNOR GENERAL IN COUNCIL, on the recommendation of the Minister of Justice, pursuant to section 55 of the *Supreme Court Act*, is pleased hereby to refer the questions immediately above set forth to the Supreme Court of Canada for hearing and consideration.

## Section 23 of the *Manitoba Act, 1870*, provides:

23. Either the English or the French language may be used by any person in the debates of the Houses of the Legislature, and both those languages shall be used in the respective Records and Journals of those Houses; and either of those languages may be used by any person, or in any Pleading or Process, in or issuing from any Court of Canada established under the *British North America Act* [*Constitution Act*], *1867*, or in or from all or any of the Courts of the Province. The Acts of the Legislature shall be printed and published in both those languages.

The provisions of *s. 133 of the Constitution Act, 1867*, are virtually identical to those of s. 23 of the *Manitoba Act, 1870*.

. . . .

## II

MANITOBA'S LANGUAGE LEGISLATION

Section 23 of the *Manitoba Act, 1870*, was the culmination of many years of co-existence and struggle between the English, the French, and the Metis in Red River Colony, the predecessor to the present day province of Manitoba. Though the region was originally claimed by the English Hudson's Bay Company in 1670 under its Royal Charter, for much of its pre-confederation history, Red River Colony was inhabited by anglophones and francophones in roughly equal proportions. On 19th November 1869 the Hudson's Bay Company issued a deed of surrender to transfer the North-West Territories, which included the Red River Colony, to Canada. The transfer of title took effect on 15th July 1870.

Between 19th November 1869 and 15th July 1870, the provisional government of Red River Colony attempted to unite the various segments of the Red River Colony and drew up a "Bill of Rights" to be used in negotiations with Canada. A Convention of Delegates was elected in January 1870 to prepare the terms upon which Red River Colony would join the Confederation. The convention was made up of equal numbers of anglophones and francophones elected from the various French and English parishes.

The final version of the Bill of Rights which was used by the convention delegates in their negotiations with Ottawa contained these provisions:

That the English and French languages be common in the Legislature, and in the courts, and that all public documents, as well as all Acts of the Legislature, be published in both languages. That the judge of the Superior Court speak the English and French languages.

These clauses were re-drafted by the Crown lawyers in Ottawa and included in a Bill to be introduced in Parliament. The Bill passed through Parliament with no opposition from either side of the House, resulting in s. 23 of the *Manitoba Act, 1870*. In 1871 this Act was entrenched in the *British North America Act, 1871* (renamed *Constitution Act, 1871*, in the *Constitution Act, 1982*, s. 53). The *Manitoba Act, 1870*, is now entrenched in the Constitution of Canada by virtue of s. 52(2)(*b*) of the *Constitution Act, 1982*.

In 1890 the *Official Language Act*, 1890 (Man.), c. 14, (hereafter "the *Official Language Act*") was enacted by the Manitoba legislature. This *Act* provides:

> 1) Any statute or law to the contrary notwithstanding, the English language only shall be used in the records and journals of the House of Assembly for the Province of Manitoba, and in any pleadings or process in or issuing from any court in the Province of Manitoba. The Acts of the Legislature of the Province of Manitoba need only be printed and published in the English language.
>
> 2) This Act shall only apply so far as this Legislature has jurisdiction so to enact, and shall come into force on the day it is assented to.

Upon enactment of the *Official Language Act, 1890*, the province of Manitoba ceased publication of the French version of legislative records, journals and Acts.

### III

### LEGAL CHALLENGES TO MANITOBA'S LANGUAGE LEGISLATION

The *Official Language Act, 1890*, was challenged before the Manitoba courts soon after it was enacted. It was ruled *ultra vires* in 1892 by Judge Prud'homme of the County Court of St. Boniface, who stated: "Je suis donc d'opinion que le c. 14, 53 Vict. est *ultra vires* de la législature du Manitoba et que la clause 23, de l'Acte de Manitoba, ne peut pas être changée et encore moins abrogée par la législature de cette province": *Pellant v. Hebert*, first published in "Le Manitoba" (a French language newspaper), 9th March 1892, reported in (1981), 12 R.G.D. 242. This ruling was not followed by the legislature or the government of Manitoba. The 1890 *Act* remained in successive revisions of the Statutes of Manitoba; the government did not resume bilingual publication of legislative records, journals or Acts.

In 1909, the 1890 *Act* was again challenged in Manitoba courts and again ruled unconstitutional: *Bertrand v. Dussault*, 30th January 1909, Prud'homme Co. Ct. J., County Court of St. Boniface (unreported), reproduced in *Forest v. Registrar of Man. Ct. of Appeal*, [1977] 5 W.W.R. 347 at 361 (Man. C.A.). According to Monnin J.A. in *Forest*, at [p. 361]: "This latter decision, not reported, appears to have been unknown or ignored."

In 1976 a third attack was mounted against the 1890 *Act* and the *Act* was ruled unconstitutional: *R. v. Forest*, [1977] 1 W.W.R. 363 (Man. Co. Ct.). Nonetheless, the 1890 *Act* remained on the Manitoba statute books; bilingual enactment, printing and publication of Acts of the Manitoba legislature was not resumed.

In 1979 the constitutionality of the 1890 Act was tested before this court. On 13th December 1979, in *A. G. Man. v. Forest*, [1979] 2 S.C.R. 1032, this court, in unanimous reasons, held that the provisions of Manitoba's *Official Language Act* were in conflict with s. 23 of the *Manitoba Act, 1870*, and unconstitutional.

On 9th July 1980, after the decision of this court in *Forest*, the legislature of Manitoba enacted *An Act Respecting the Operation of section 23 of the Manitoba Act in Regard to Statutes*, S.M. 1980, c. 3 (also C.C.S.M., c. S207). The validity of this Act is the subject of Q. 4 of this Reference.

In the 4th session (1980) and the 5th session (1980-1981) of the 31st legislature of Manitoba, the vast majority of the Acts of the legislature of Manitoba were enacted, printed and published in English only.

Since the first session of the 32nd legislature of Manitoba (1982), the Acts of the legislature of Manitoba have been enacted, printed and published in both English and French. However, those Acts that only amend Acts that were enacted, printed and published in English only and private Acts have in most instances been enacted in English only.

In *Bilodeau v. A.G. Man.*, [1981] 5 W.W.R. 393, the Manitoba Court of Appeal held that Manitoba's *Highway Traffic Act*, C.C.S.M. 1970, c. H60, and *Summary Convictions Act*, C.C.S.M. 1970, c. S230, although enacted in English only, were valid. This decision is under appeal to this court. (Judgment in *Bilodeau v. A.G. Man.* will be delivered at the time of delivery of judgment in *MacDonald v. Montreal* [[1982] C.S. 998 [Que.], leave to appeal to S.C.C. granted 50 N.R. 160].)

On 4th July 1983 the Attorney General of Manitoba introduced into the Legislative Assembly of Manitoba a resolution to initiate a constitutional amendment under s. 43 of the *Constitution Act, 1982.* The purpose of the resolution was to amend the language provisions of the *Manitoba Act, 1870.* The 2nd session of the 32nd legislature was prorogued on 27th February 1984, without the resolution having been adopted.

It might also be mentioned that on 13th December 1979, in *A.G. Que. v. Blaikie; A.G. Que. v. Laurier*, [1979] 2 S.C.R. 1016 ("*Blaikie No. 1*"), this court held that the provisions of Quebec's *Charter of the French Language* (Bill 101), enacted in 1977, were in conflict with s. 133 of the *Constitution Act, 1867.* The *Charter* purported to provide for the introduction of Bills in the legislature in French only, and for the enactment of statutes in French only. The day after the decision of this court in *Blaikie No. 1*, the legislature of Quebec re-enacted in both languages all those Quebec statutes that had been enacted in French only: see *An Act respecting a judgment rendered in the Supreme Court of Canada on 13 December 1979 on the language of the legislature and the courts in Québec*, S.Q. 1979, c. 61.

The implication of this court's holdings in *Blaikie No. 1*, and *Forest*, both supra, was that provincial legislation passed in accordance with the *ultra vires* statutes, i.e., enacted in one language only, was itself in derogation of the constitutionally entrenched language provisions of the *Constitution Act, 1867*, and the *Manitoba Act, 1870*, and therefore invalid. In *Soc. Asbestos Ltée v. Soc. Nat. de l'Amiante*, [1979] C.A. 342, the Quebec Court of Appeal held, in a judgment also rendered 13th December 1979, that this was indeed the consequence of unilingual enactment and struck down two statutes that had not been enacted in English.

In *A.G. Que. v. Blaikie; A.G. Que. v. Laurier*, [1981] 1 S.C.R. 312 ("*Blaikie No. 2*"), this court elaborated its earlier decision in *Blaikie No. 1* by holding that regulations adopted by or subject to the approval of the government of Quebec and Rules of Court were subject to the requirements of s. 113. However, regulations adopted by subordinate bodies, outside the government of Quebec, and not subject to the approval of the government of Quebec, as well as municipal by-laws and school board by-laws, were not subject to the requirements of s. 133.

The Manitoba Court of Appeal, in *Bilodeau*, supra, was faced with a similar challenge to unilingually enacted legislation. That court held that the unilingual legislation of the Manitoba legislature was not invalid. The majority (*per* Freedman

C.J.M.) held that the requirement for bilingual enactment was *directory* rather than *mandatory* and that therefore the consequence of disobedience was not invalidity. Monnin J.A. thought that s. 23 was mandatory but would have applied the doctrine of state necessity (of which more anon) to prevent invalidity.

IV

QUESTION 1

*The Mandatory Nature of s. 133 of the Constitution Act, 1867, and s. 23 of the Manitoba Act, 1870*

Question 1 of this Reference asks whether the requirements of s. 133 of the *Constitution Act, 1867*, and s. 23 of the *Manitoba Act, 1870*, respecting the use of both English and French in the records, journals and Acts of the Parliament of Canada and of the legislatures of Quebec and Manitoba, are "mandatory".

The Attorney General of Manitoba responds to this question in his written argument with the plain assertion that:

> Since the decisions of this Court in *Attorney General of Quebec v. Blaikie*, [1979] 2 S.C.R. 1016 and *Attorney General of Manitoba v. Forest*, [1979] 2 S.C.R. 1032 it is beyond dispute that statutes of the Parliament of Canada, of the National Assembly of Quebec and of the Legislature of Manitoba are required to be enacted in both the English and the French languages. The requirement is imperative, rather than permissive, in the sense that the legislative bodies have no option in the matter.

And later:

> Obviously it was intended that the requirement of enactment in both languages be observed. The relevant question is: What is the consequence of non-observance?

The consequence of non-observance will be addressed when QQ. 2 and 3 are under consideration.

For present purposes, it seems clear that the bilingual record-keeping and the printing and publication requirements of s. 23 of the *Manitoba Act, 1870*, and s. 133 of the *Constitution Act, 1867*, are mandatory in the sense that they were meant to be obeyed.

Section 23 of the *Manitoba Act, 1870*, provides that both English and French "*shall* be used in the ... Records and Journals" of the Manitoba legislature. It further provides that "[t]he Acts of the Legislature *shall* be printed and published in both those languages." Section 133 of the *Constitution Act, 1867*, is strikingly similar. It provides that both English and French "*shall* be used in the respective Records and Journals" of Parliament and the Legislature of Quebec. It also provides that "[t]he Acts of the Parliament of Canada and of the legislature of Quebec *shall* be printed and published in both those Languages."

As used in its normal grammatical sense, the word "shall" is presumptively imperative: see *Odgers' Construction of Deeds and Statutes*, 5th ed. (1967), at p. 377; *Interpretation Act*, S.C. 1867, c. 1, s. 6(3); *Interpretation Act*, R.S.C. 1970, c. I-23, s. 28 ("'shall' is to be construed as imperative"). It is therefore incumbent upon this court to conclude that Parliament, when it used the word "shall" in s. 23 of the *Manitoba Act, 1870*, and s. 133 of the *Constitution Act, 1867*, intended that those sections be construed as mandatory or imperative, in the sense that they must be obeyed, unless such an interpretation of the word "shall" would be utterly inconsistent with the context in which it has been used and would render the sections irrational or meaningless: see, e.g., *Re Pub. Fin. Corp. and Edwards Garage Ltd.* (1957), 22 W.W.R. 312 at 317 (Alta. S.C.).

There is nothing in the history or the language of s. 23 of the *Manitoba Act, 1870*, or s. 133 of the *Constitution Act, 1867*, to indicate that "shall" was not used in its normal imperative sense. On the contrary, the evidence points ineluctably to the conclusion that the word "shall" was deliberately and carefully chosen by Parliament for the express purpose of making the bilingual record-keeping and printing and publication requirements of those sections obligatory. In particular, Parliament's use of the presumptively imperative word "shall" twice in s. 23 of the *Manitoba Act, 1870*, and twice in s. 133 of the *Constitution Act, 1867*, contrasts starkly with its use of the presumptively permissive word "may" twice in the same sections. Section 23 provides that either English or French "*may* be used" by anyone in the debates of the Manitoba legislature and that either language "*may* be used" by anyone in the Manitoba courts. Similarly, s. 133 provides that either English or French "*may* be used" by anyone in the debates of Parliament and the legislature of Quebec, and in the courts of Canada and Quebec.

The French versions of both sections leave no doubt that the choice of these contrasting terms was deliberate. In the French version of s. 23, "shall" appears as "sera obligatoire" and "seront", while "may" appears as "sera facultatif" and "pourra être ... à faculté". Similarly, in the French version of s. 133, "shall" is expressed as "sera obligatoire" at one point, and as "devront être" at another, while "may" is expressed as "sera facultatif" in the first clause in which it appears and as "pourra être ... à faculté" in the second.

In *Blaikie v. A.G. Que.*, [1978] C.S. 37 (Que. S.C.), Deschênes C.J.S.C. had this to say about the may/shall dichotomy in s. 133 of the *Constitution Act, 1867*:

> The Imperial Parliament has passed s. 133 with, from all evidence, extreme care and even the most mildly attentive observer cannot help but be struck by the alternation of the means of expression that are found in considering the use of the two languages: first part, 'Either ... may'; second part, 'Both ... shall'; third part, 'Either ... may'; fourth part, 'Shall ... both'.
>
> The Court is totally incapable of finding in the second part of s. 133 justification for the alternates or the sequence of the languages that the Attorney General of Quebec suggests can be read there: *this is not one or the other language as a choice, but the two at the same time which must be used in the records and journals of the Legislature.* (Any emphasis throughout this judgment is added.)

See also *Jones v. A.G. N.B.*, [1975] 2 S.C.R. 182 at 192-93.

. . . .

There is no authority in Canada for applying the mandatory/directory doctrine to constitutional provisions. It is our belief that the doctrine should not be applied when the constitutionality of legislation is in issue....

In answer to Q. 1, s. 23 of the *Manitoba Act, 1870*, and s. 133 of the *Constitution Act, 1867*, are mandatory.

V

## QUESTIONS 2 AND 3

Question 2 asks whether the unilingual statutes and regulations of Manitoba are invalid. Question 3 asks about the force and effect of these statutes and regulations if they are found to be invalid. . . .

### B) *The Consequences of the Manitoba Legislature's Failure to Enact, Print and Publish in Both Languages*

Section 23 of the *Manitoba Act, 1870*, entrenches a mandatory requirement to enact, print, and publish all Acts of the legislature in both official languages: see *Blaikie No. 1.* It establishes a constitutional duty on the Manitoba legislature with respect to the manner and form of enactment of its legislation. This duty protects the substantive rights of all Manitobans to equal access to the law in either the French or the English language.

Section 23 of the *Manitoba Act, 1870*, is a specific manifestation of the general right of Franco-Manitobans to use their own language. The importance of language rights is grounded in the essential role that language plays in human existence, development and dignity. It is through language that we are able to form concepts; to structure and order the world around us. Language bridges the gap between isolation and community, allowing humans to delineate the rights and duties they hold in respect of one another, and thus to live in society.

The constitutional entrenchment of a duty on the Manitoba legislature to enact, print and publish in both French and English in s. 23 of the *Manitoba Act, 1870*, confers upon the judiciary the responsibility of protecting the correlative language rights of all Manitobans including the Franco-Manitoban minority. The judiciary is the institution charged with the duty of ensuring that the government complies with the Constitution. We must protect those whose constitutional rights have been violated, whomever they may be, and whatever the reasons for the violation.

The constitution of a country is a statement of the will of the people to be governed in accordance with certain principles held as fundamental and certain prescriptions restrictive of the powers of the legislature and government. It is, as s. 52 of the *Constitution Act, 1982*, declares, the "supreme law" of the nation, unalterable by the normal legislative process, and unsuffering of laws inconsistent with it. The duty of the judiciary is to interpret and apply the laws of Canada and each of the provinces, and it is thus our duty to ensure that the constitutional law prevails.

As this court said in *Amax Potash Ltd. v. Sask.*, [1977] 2 S.C.R. 576 at 590:

> A state, it is said, is sovereign and it is not for the Courts to pass upon the policy or wisdom of legislative will. As a broad statement of principle that is undoubtedly correct, but the general principle must yield to the requisites of the constitution in a federal state. By it the bounds of sovereignty are defined and supremacy circumscribed. The Courts will not question the wisdom of enactments which, by the terms of the Canadian Constitution are within the competence of the Legislatures, *but it is the high duty of this Court to insure that the legislatures do not transgress the limits of their constitutional mandate and engage in the illegal exercise of power.*

See also *Re Resolution to Amend the Constitution*, [1981] 1 S.C.R. 753 at 841, 848, 877.

Since 17th April 1982, the mandate of the judiciary to protect the Constitution has been embodied in s. 52 of the *Constitution Act, 1982*. This section reads:

> 52(1) The Constitution of Canada is the supreme law of Canada, and any law that is inconsistent with the provisions of the Constitution is, to the extent of the inconsistency, of no force or effect.

Prior to enactment of the *Constitution Act, 1982*, the governing provision was, pursuant to the *Statute of Westminster, 1931*, s. 2 of the *Colonial Laws Validity Act, 1865* (U.K.) (28 & 29 Vict., c. 63), which provides:

> 2. Any Colonial Law which is or shall be in any respect repugnant to the Provisions of any Act of Parliament extending to the Colony to which such Law may relate, or repugnant to any Order or Regulation made under Authority of such Act of Parliament, or having in the Colony the Force and Effect of such Act, shall be read subject to such Act, Order, or Regulation, and shall, to the Extent of such Repugnancy, but not otherwise, be and remain *absolutely void and inoperative*.

The constitutional jurisprudence, developed under the *Colonial Laws Validity Act, 1865*, was based on the invalidity doctrine. If Parliament or a provincial legislature was ultra vires its constitutionally allocated powers in enacting a certain Act, then the repugnancy of that Act with the provisions of the *British North America Act, 1867*, would mean that the Act was "absolutely void and inoperative".

Section 52 of the *Constitution Act, 1982*, does not alter the principles which have provided the foundation for judicial review over the years. In a case where constitutional manner and form requirements have not been complied with, the consequence of such non-compliance continues to be invalidity. The words "of no force or effect" mean that a law thus inconsistent with the Constitution has no force or effect because it is invalid.

Canadian courts have been unanimous in finding that failure to respect mandatory requirements to enact, print and publish statutes and regulations in both official languages leads to inconsistency and thus invalidity: see, *Soc. Asbestos Ltée v. Soc. Nat. de l'Amiante*, supra; *P.G. Qué. v. Collier*, [1983] C.S. 366 (Que.); *P.G. Qué. v. Brunet*, J.E. 83-510, reversed on other grounds, J.E. 84-62 (Que. S.C.). These cases accord with the general principle that failure to comply with constitutional provisions dealing with the manner and form of the enactment of legislation will result in inconsistency and thus invalidity: see *Bribery Commr. v. Ranasinghe*, supra.

In the present case the unilingual enactments of the Manitoba legislature are inconsistent with s. 23 of the *Manitoba Act, 1870*, since the constitutionally required manner and form for their enactment has not been followed. Thus they are invalid and of no force or effect.

C) *The Rule of Law*

1. *The Principle*

The difficulty with the fact that the unilingual Acts of the legislature of Manitoba must be declared invalid and of no force or effect is that, without going further, a legal vacuum will be created with consequent legal chaos in the province of Manitoba. The Manitoba legislature has, since 1890, enacted nearly all of its laws in English only. Thus, to find that the unilingual laws of Manitoba are invalid and of no force or effect would mean that only laws enacted in both French and English *before 1890* would continue to be valid, and would still be in force even if the law had purportedly been repealed or amended by a post-1890 unilingual statute; matters that were not regulated by laws enacted before 1890 would now be unregulated by law, unless a pre-confederation law or the common law provided a rule.

The situation of the various institutions of provincial government would be as follows: the courts, administrative tribunals, public officials, municipal corporations, school boards, professional governing bodies, and all other bodies created by law, to the extent that they derive their existence from or purport to exercise powers conferred by Manitoba laws enacted since 1890 in English only, would be acting without legal authority.

Questions as to the validity of the present composition of the Manitoba legislature might also be raised. Under the *Manitoba Act, 1870*, the Legislative Assembly was to be composed of 24 members (s. 14), and voters were to be male and over 21 (s. 17). By laws enacted after 1890 in English only, the size of the Legislative Assembly was increased to 57 members, and all persons, both women and men, over 18 were granted the right to vote: see *Act to Amend the Manitoba Election Act*, S.M. 1916, c. 36; *Act to Amend the Election Act*, S.M. 1969 (2nd Sess.), c. 7; the *Legislative Assembly Act*, C.C.S.M., c. L110, s. 4(1). If these laws are invalid and of no force or effect, the present composition of the Manitoba legislature might be invalid. The invalidity of the post-1890 laws would not touch the existence of the legislature or its powers since these are matters of federal constitutional law: *Constitution Act, 1867*, ss. 92, 92A, 93, 95; *Manitoba Act, 1870*, s. 2.

Finally, all legal rights, obligations and other effects which have purportedly arisen under all Acts of the Manitoba legislature since 1890 would be open to challenge to the extent that their validity and enforceability depend upon a regime of unconstitutional unilingual laws.

In the present case, declaring the Acts of the legislature of Manitoba invalid and of no force or effect would, without more, undermine the principle of the rule of law. The rule of law, a fundamental principle of our Constitution, must mean at least two things. First, that the law is supreme over officials of the government as well as private individuals, and thereby preclusive of the influence of arbitrary power. Indeed, it is because of the supremacy of law over the government, as established in s. 23 of the *Manitoba Act, 1870*, and s. 52 of the *Constitution Act, 1982*, that this court must find the unconstitutional laws of Manitoba to be invalid and of no force and effect.

Second, the rule of law requires the creation and maintenance of an actual order of positive laws which preserves and embodies the more general principle of normative order. Law and order are indispensable elements of civilized life. "The Rule of Law in this sense implies ... simply the existence of public order." (I. Jennings, *The Law and the Constitution*, 5th ed. (1959), at p. 43.) As John Locke once said, "A government without laws is, I suppose, a mystery in politics, inconceivable to human capacity and inconsistent with human society" (quoted by Lord Wilberforce in *Carl Zeiss-Stiftung v. Rayner & Keeler Ltd.; Rayner & Keeler Ltd. v. Courts*, [1967] 1 A.C. 853 (H.L.)). According to Wade and Phillips, *Constitutional and Administrative Law*, 9th ed. (1977), at p. 89:

> ... the rule of law expresses a preference for law and order within a community rather than anarchy, warfare and constant strife. In this sense, the rule of law is a philosophical view of society which in the Western tradition is linked with basic democratic notions.

It is this second aspect of the rule of law that is of concern in the present situation. The conclusion that the Acts of the legislature of Manitoba are invalid and of no force or effect means that the positive legal order which has purportedly regulated the affairs of the citizens of Manitoba since 1890 will be destroyed and the rights, obligations and other effects arising under these laws will be invalid and unenforceable. As for the future, since it is reasonable to assume that it will be impossible for the legislature of Manitoba to rectify *instantaneously* the constitutional defect, the Acts of Manitoba legislature will be invalid and of no force or effect until they are translated, re-enacted, printed and published in both languages.

Such results would certainly offend the rule of law. As we stated in the *Patriation Ref.*, supra, at pp. 805-806:

> The 'rule of law' is a highly textured expression ... conveying, for example, *a sense of orderliness, of subjection to known legal rules* and of executive accountability to legal authority.

Dr. Raz has said: "'The rule of law' means literally what it says: the rule of the law ... It has two aspects: (1) that people should be ruled by the law and obey it, and (2) that the law should be such that people will be able to be guided by it": *The Authority of Law* (1979), at pp. 212-13. The rule of law simply cannot be fulfilled in a province that has no positive law.

The constitutional status of the rule of law is beyond question. The preamble to the *Constitution Act, 1982*, states:

> Whereas Canada is founded upon principles that recognize the supremacy of God and the *rule of law*: ...

This is explicit recognition that "the rule of law [is] a fundamental postulate of our constitutional structure": per Rand J. in *Roncarelli v. Duplessis*, [1959] S.C.R. 121 at 142. The rule of law has always been understood as the very basis of the English Constitution characterising the political institutions of England from the time of the Norman Conquest: A.V. Dicey, *The Law of the Constitution*, 10th ed. (1959), at p. 183. It becomes a postulate of our own Constitutional order by way of the preamble to the *Constitution Act, 1982*, and its implicit inclusion in the preamble to the *Constitution Act, 1867*, by virtue of the words "with a Constitution similar in Principle to that of the United Kingdom".

Additional to the inclusion of the rule of law in the preambles of the *Constitution Acts* of 1867 and 1982, the principle is clearly implicit in the very nature of a constitution. The Constitution, as the supreme law, must be understood as a purposive ordering of social relations providing a basis upon which an actual order of positive laws can be brought into existence. The founders of this nation must have intended, as one of the basic principles of nation building, that Canada be a society of legal order and normative structure: one governed by rule of law. While this is not set out in a specific provision, the principle of the rule of law is clearly a principle of our Constitution.

This court cannot take a narrow and literal approach to constitutional interpretation. The jurisprudence of the court evidences a willingness to supplement textual analysis with historical, contextual and purposive interpretation in order to ascertain the intent of the makers of our Constitution.

The court has in the past inferred constitutional principles from the preambles to the Constitution Acts and the general object and purpose of the Constitution. In the *Patriation Ref.*, supra, the court found the federal principle to be inherent in the Constitution in this way. At pp. 905-906 the court said:

> The reason for the rule is the federal principle. Canada is a federal union. The preamble of the B.N.A. Act states that
>
> > . . . the Provinces of Canada, Nova Scotia, and New Brunswick have expressed their Desire to be federally united . . .
>
> The federal character of the Canadian Constitution was recognized in innumerable judicial pronouncements. We will quote only one, that of Lord Watson in *Liquidators of the Maritime Bank of Canada v. Receiver-General of New Brunswick, supra*, at pp. 441-42:
>
> > The object of the Act was neither to weld the provinces into one, nor to subordinate provincial governments to a central authority, but to create a federal government in which they should all be represented, entrusted with the exclusive administration of affairs in which they had a common interest, each province retaining its independence and autonomy.
>
> The federal principle cannot be reconciled with a state of affairs where the modification of provincial legislative powers could be obtained by the unilateral action of the federal authorities. It would indeed offend the federal principle that 'a radical change to . . . [the] constitution [be] taken at the request of a bare majority of the members of the Canadian House of Commons and Senate' (Report of Dominion Provincial Conference, 1931, at p. 3).

Martland and Ritchie JJ. in their dissent stated (at p. 841):

> However, on occasions, this Court has had to consider issues for which the *B.N.A. Act* offered no answer. In each case, this Court has denied the assertion of any power which would offend against the basic principles of the Constitution.

They went on to discuss a number of the more important decisions rendered by this court and concluded with the following (at pp. 844-45):

> It may be noted that the above instances of judicially developed legal principles and doctrines share several characteristics. *First, none is to be found in express provisions of the British North America Acts or other constitutional enactments. Second,* all have been perceived to represent constitutional requirements that are derived from the federal character of Canada's Constitution. *Third, they have been accorded full legal force in the sense of being employed to strike down legislative enactments. Fourth,* each was judicially developed in response to a particular legislative initiative in respect of which it might have been observed, as it was by Dickson J. in the *Amax (supra)* case at p. 591, that: 'There are no Canadian constitutional law precedents addressed directly to the present issue . . .'.

In other words, in the process of Constitutional adjudication, the court may have regard to unwritten postulates which form the very foundation of the Constitution of Canada. In the case of the *Patriation Ref.* this unwritten postulate was the principle of federalism. In the present case it is the principle of rule of law.

### 2) *Application of the Principle of the Rule of Law*

It is clear from the above that: (i) the law as stated in s. 23 of the *Manitoba Act, 1870*, and s. 52 of the *Constitution Act, 1982*, requires that the unilingual Acts of the Manitoba legislature be declared to be invalid and of no force or effect, and (ii) without more, such a result would violate the rule of law. The task the court faces is to recognize the unconstitutionality of Manitoba's unilingual laws and the legislature's duty to comply with the "supreme law" of this country, while avoiding a legal vacuum in Manitoba and ensuring the continuity of the rule of law.

A number of the parties and interveners have suggested that the court declare the unilingual Acts of the Manitoba legislature to be invalid and of no force or effect and leave it at that, relying on the legislatures to work out a constitutional amendment. This approach because it would rely on a future and uncertain event, would be inappropriate. A declaration that the laws of Manitoba are invalid and of no legal force or effect would deprive Manitoba of its legal order and cause a transgression of the rule of law. For the court to allow such a situation to arise and fail to resolve it would be an abdication of its responsibility as protector and preserver of the Constitution.

Other solutions suggested by the parties and interveners are equally unsatisfactory. Counsel for the Attorney General of Manitoba argues that the linguistic rights guaranteed by s. 23 of the *Manitoba Act, 1870*, can be protected by the Lieutenant Governor of the province, who can either withhold royal assent to a unilingual bill or reserve the bill for the signification of the Governor General's pleasure: *Constitution Act, 1867*, ss. 55, 57, 90; see also *Manitoba Act, 1870*, s. 2. Though this legal power continues to exist, it has not been exercised in recent years: see *Ref. re Power of Disallowance and Power of Reservation*, [1938] S.C.R. 71.

The fundamental difficulty with the Attorney General of Manitoba's suggestion is that it would make the executive branch of the federal government, rather than the courts, the guarantor of constitutionally entrenched language rights. It should be noted that a decision of a provincial Lieutenant Governor as to whether to withhold assent or reserve a bill is not reviewable by the courts: *Ref. re Disallowance and Reservation*, at p. 95. The overall effect of implementing the suggestion of the Attorney General of Manitoba would be to insulate the legislature's failure to comply with s. 23 of the *Manitoba Act, 1870*, from judicial review. Such a result would be entirely inconsistent with the judiciary's duty to uphold the Constitution.

Similar considerations would apply to the six Manitoba citizen interveners' contention that the federal power of disallowance in the *Constitution Act, 1867*, could be used as an alternative to judicial invalidation. This is not an appropriate alternative solution because it asks the court to abdicate its responsibility to enforce the dictates of the Constitution.

The only appropriate resolution to this Reference is for the court to fulfil its duty under s. 52 of the *Constitution Act, 1982*, and declare all the unilingual Acts of the legislature of Manitoba to be invalid and of no force and effect and then to take such steps as will ensure the rule of law in the province of Manitoba.

There is no question that it would be impossible for all the Acts of the Manitoba legislature to be translated, re-enacted, printed and published overnight. There will necessarily be a period of time during which it would not be possible for the Manitoba legislature to comply with its constitutional duty under s. 23 of the *Manitoba Act, 1870*.

. . . .

The only appropriate solution for preserving the rights, obligations and other effects which have arisen under invalid Acts of the legislature of Manitoba and which are not saved by the de facto or other doctrines is to declare that, in order to uphold the rule of law, these rights, obligations and other effects have, and will continue to have, the same force and effect they would have had if they had arisen under valid enactments, for that period of time during which it would be impossible for Manitoba to comply with its constitutional duty under s. 23 of the *Manitoba Act, 1870*. . . .

## VI

### THE DURATION OF THE TEMPORARY PERIOD

The difficult question, then, is what is the duration of the minimum period necessary for translation, re-enactment, printing and publishing of the unilingual Acts of the Manitoba legislature?

It was argued by the Attorney General of Canada and by the Fédération Des Francophones Hors Québec that this court fix some arbitrary period such as a year or two years during which the Manitoba legislature could re-enact its unilingual legislation in both languages.

This solution would not be satisfactory. We do not know how many of the Acts of the legislature have already been translated. We know nothing as to the availability of translators or their daily output. We thus have no factual basis for determining a period during which compliance with s. 23 of the *Manitoba Act, 1870*, would not be possible.

As presently equipped the court is incapable of determining the period of time during which it would not be possible for the Manitoba legislature to comply with its constitutional duty. The court will, however, at the request of either the Attorney General of Canada, or the Attorney General of Manitoba, made within 120 days of the date of this judgment, make such a determination. The Attorney General of Canada was granted carriage of this Reference and the Attorney General of Manitoba represents the province whose laws are in issue in this case. Following such a request, a special hearing will be set and submissions will be accepted from the Attorney General of Canada and the Attorney General of Manitoba and the other interveners.

The period of temporary validity will not apply to any unilingual Acts of the legislature enacted after the date of judgment. From the date of judgment, laws which are not enacted, printed, and published in both languages will be invalid and of no force and effect *ab initio*.

. . . .

## VIII

### CONCLUSIONS

i) Section 133 of the *Constitution Act, 1867*, and s. 23 of the *Manitoba Act, 1870*, are mandatory;

ii) All Acts of the Manitoba legislature that were not printed and published in both the English and French languages are, and always have been, invalid and of no force and effect;

iii) The Acts of the Manitoba legislature which would currently be in force were it not for their constitutional defect (i.e. current Acts) are deemed to have temporary validity and force and effect from the date of this judgment to the expiry of the minimum period required for translation, re-enactment, printing and publishing;

iv) Rights, obligations and any other effects which have arisen under current Acts, and purportedly repealed or spent Acts, of the legislature of Manitoba, which are not saved by the *de facto* doctrine or doctrines such as *res judicata* and mistake of law, are deemed temporarily to have been, and to continue to be, valid, and of force and effect until the expiry of the minimum period required for translation, re-enactment, printing and publishing;

v) The court will, at the request of either the Attorney General of Canada or the Attorney General of Manitoba, made within 120 days of the date of this judgment, establish the minimum period necessary for translation, re-enactment, printing and publishing of (1) unilingual Acts of the legislature of Manitoba which would be currently in force were it not for their constitutional defect, and (2) the unilingual repealed and spent Acts of the legislature of Manitoba. Following such a request, a special hearing will be set and submissions will be accepted from the Attorney General of Canada and the Attorney General of Manitoba and the other interveners.

vi) *An Act Respecting the Operation of section 23 of the Manitoba Act in Regard to Statutes*, S.M. 1980, c. 3, is invalid and of no force and effect in its entirety if it was not enacted, printed, and published in both official languages. In any event, ss. 1-5 are invalid and of no force and effect.

## IX

ANSWER TO THE QUESTIONS

*Question 1*

Are the requirements of section 133 of the *Constitution Act, 1867* and of section 23 of the *Manitoba Act, 1870* respecting the use of both the English and French languages in

(a) the Records and Journals of the Houses of the Parliament of Canada and of the Legislatures of Quebec and Manitoba, and
(b) the Acts of the Parliament of Canada and of the Legislatures of Quebec and Manitoba

mandatory

*Answer:*

Yes.

*Question 2*

Are those statutes and regulations of the Province of Manitoba that were not printed and published in both the English and French languages invalid by reason of section 23 of the *Manitoba Act, 1870?*

*Answer:*

Yes, but, for the reasons given by the court, the invalid current Acts of the legislature will be deemed temporarily valid for the minimum period necessary for their translation, re-enactment, printing and publication.

*Question 3*

If the answer to question 2 is affirmative, do those enactments that were not printed and published in English and French have any legal force and effect, and if so, to what extent and under what conditions?"

*Answer:*

The Acts of the legislature that were not enacted, printed and published in English and French have no legal force and effect because they are invalid, but, for the reasons given by the court, the current Acts of the legislature will be deemed to have temporary force and effect for the minimum period necessary for their translation, re-enactment, printing and publication.

*Question 4*

Are any of the provisions of *An Act Respecting the Operation of section 23 of the Manitoba Act in Regard to Statutes*, enacted by S.M. 1980, Ch. 3, inconsistent with the provisions of section 23 of the *Manitoba Act, 1870*, and if so are such provisions, to the extent of such inconsistency, invalid and of no legal force and effect?

*Answer:*

If the *Act* was not enacted, printed and published in both official languages, then it is invalid and of no force and effect in its entirety.

If the *Act* was enacted, printed and published in both official languages, then ss. 1-5 are invalid and of no force and effect.

*Judgment accordingly.*

### Note on Language Rights

In *Reference re Education Act of Ontario and Minority Language Education Rights* (1984), 47 O.R. (2d) 1 (C.A.), certain provisions of the *Education Act*, R.S.O. 1980, c. 129 required school boards to establish French language elementary and secondary schools or classes where French-speaking pupils elected instruction in French, and could be assembled in classes of 25 at the elementary level and 20 at the secondary level. Where these minimum class sizes could not be met, the boards had discretion about whether to establish French schools. The Ontario Court of Appeal held that the legislation conflicted with section 23 of the *Charter* in four respects.

*First*, the Court of Appeal held that section 23 protects the rights of parents, not children. The reference in the legislation to French-speaking pupils was therefore too restrictive. *Second*, the discretion given to school boards as to when to provide French language instruction and facilities was too broad. Section 23(3) makes it mandatory to provide such instruction and facilities whenever numbers warrant. *Third*, albeit related to the aforesaid deficiency, the imposition of a requirement of French language instruction only where groups of 20 or 25 pupils could be assembled was arbitrary. Section 23 requires that the "where numbers warrant" test be done on a locality by locality basis, and there was no evidence that the selection of an arbitrary figure of 20 or 25 to be applied across the province without any qualifications was justified. *Fourth*, the *Education Act* delegated the responsibility of deciding when to establish French schools to the various school boards, with the consequence that decisions would be made on the basis of need within the geographical jurisdiction of each individual board. The Court held that section 23 transcends school district boundaries. It applies whenever numbers warrant, and includes those situations where pockets of people cross school district boundaries. Thus, for example, it applies where two groups on either side of the district line would meet the "where numbers warrant" test if considered together, even though neither group considered separately would qualify.

On the general interpretation of section 23, the Court of Appeal held that section 23(3)(b), which deals with the provision of "educational facilities", is wider than section 23(3)(a) which merely deals with language of instruction. As well, the "facilities" in section 23(3)(b) must be separate from the majority language facilities where numbers warrant and, in light of the provisions of section 27 regarding the preservation of the multicultural heritage of Canadians, the educational environment must be that of the linguistic minority. Furthermore, the quality of the education provided must be equal to that given to the majority.

An interesting argument was made in *Reference re Education Act* that the legislation conflicted with the denominational rights of separate schools contrary to section 93 of the *Constitution Act, 1867* and section 29 of the *Charter*. The Court of Appeal held that there was no such conflict. Its holding was made easier by the Privy Council's decision in *Ottawa Separate School Trustees v. Mackell*, [1917] A.C. 62 that language is not a matter of denominational concern (see also *Protestant School Board of Greater Montreal v. Min. of Education of Quebec* (1976), 83 D.L.R. (3d) 645 (Que. S.C.)). However, the Court went on to say that one should interpret the provisions of the *Charter* in such a way as to make them compatible where possible. This has obvious implications for the relationship between section 93 of the *Constitution Act, 1867* and section 29 of the *Charter* on one hand and section 15(1) on the other with respect to the issue of the financing of private schools: see Finkelstein, "Legal and Constitutional Aspects of Public Funding for Private Schools", *supra*, in this chapter.

It should be noted that section 23 has been held to guarantee the right of the linguistic minority to education in the minority language but not that of the majority: see *Societe des Acadiens du Nouveau-Brunswick Inc. v. Minority Language School Board No. 50* (1983), 48 N.B.R. (2d) 361 (N.B.Q.B.).

Apart from section 23 of the *Charter of Rights* dealing with minority language education rights, sections 16-22 of the *Charter* provide the following with respect to language:

16.(1) English and French are the official languages of Canada and have equality of status and equal rights and privileges as to their use in all institutions of the Parliament and government of Canada.

(2) English and French are the official languages of New Brunswick and have equality of status and equal rights and privileges as to their use in all institutions of the legislature and government of New Brunswick.

(3) Nothing in this Charter limits the authority of Parliament or a legislature to advance the equality of status or use of English and French.

17.(1) Everyone has the right to use English or French in any debates and other proceedings of Parliament.

(2) Everyone has the right to use English or French in any debates and other proceedings of the legislature of New Brunswick.

18.(1) The statutes, records and journals of Parliament shall be printed and published in English and French and both language versions are equally authoritative.

(2) The statutes, records and journals of the legislature of New Brunswick shall be printed and published in English and French and both language versions are equally authoritative.

19.(1) Either English or French may be used by any person in, or in any pleading in or process issuing from, any court established by Parliament.

(2) Either English or French may be used by any person in, or in any pleading in or process issuing from, any court of New Brunswick.

20.(1) Any member of the public in Canada has the right to communicate with, and to receive available services from, any head or central office of an institution of the Parliament or government of Canada in English or French, and has the same right with respect to any other office of any such institution where

(a) there is a significant demand for communications with and services from that office in such language; or
(b) due to the nature of the office, it is reasonable that communications with and services from that office be available in both English and French.

(2) Any member of the public in New Brunswick has the right to communicate with, and to receive available services from, any office of an institution of the legislature or government of New Brunswick in English or French.

21. Nothing in sections 16 to 20 abrogates or derogates from any right, privilege or obligation with respect to the English and French language, or either of them, that exists or is continued by virtue of any other provision of the Constitution of Canada.

22. Nothing in sections 16 to 20 abrogates or derogates from any legal or customary right or privilege acquired or enjoyed either before or after the coming into force of this Charter with respect to any language that is not English or French.

In addition, section 133 of the *Constitution Act, 1867*, which is preserved by s. 21 of the Charter, reads as follows:

133. Either the English or the French Language may be used by any Person in the Debates of the Houses of the Parliament of Canada and of the Houses of the Legislature of Quebec; and both those Languages shall be used in the respective Records and Journals of those Houses; and either of those Languages may be used by any Person or in any Pleading or Process in or issuing from any Court of Canada established under this Act, and in or from all or any of the Courts of Quebec.

The Acts of the Parliament of Canada and of the Legislature of Quebec shall be printed and published in both those Languages.

The Manitoba equivalent of section 133 is contained in section 23 of the *Manitoba Act, 1870* and is in substantially the same form. It should be noted that section 23 of the *Manitoba Act, 1870* has been held to give a constitutional right to speak either English or French in Court, but not the right to be heard by a bilingual judge: see *Robin v. College de St-Boniface* (1984), 15 D.L.R. (4th) 198 (Man. C.A.).

*A.G. Que. v. Blaikie (No. 1)*, [1979] 2 S.C.R. 1016, and *A.G. Que. v. Blaikie (No. 2)*, [1981] 1 S.C.R. 312 and the *Manitoba Language Reference, supra*, are the leading cases on the scope of section 133 of the *Constitution Act, 1867*. These are particularly important with respect to Quebec because it will be noted that only Canada and New Brunswick, and not Quebec, are referred to in the "Official Languages" sections in sections 16-22 of the *Charter*.

In *Blaikie (No. 1)*, the plaintiffs, members of the Bar of Quebec, sought a declaration that certain provisions of Chapter III of Title I of the *Charter of the*

*French Language*, S.Q. 1977, c. 5, sections 7-13, making French the language of the Courts and the Legislature and making French the only official language with respect to statutes and regulations, were *ultra vires* the Quebec Legislature as being inconsistent with section 133.

Counsel for Quebec argued that the Legislature could unilaterally amend or modify the provisions of section 133, insofar as they relate to the Legislature and courts of Quebec, pursuant to its power in section 92(1) to amend the provincial Constitution. The Court rejected this argument, saying at 1025 S.C.R.:

> It does not seem necessary to come to a determination whether s. 128 is part of the Constitution of the Province and amendable as such under s. 92(1), so as to lend support to the appellant's contention of the amendability by unilateral action of s. 133. The reasons for this transcend even the widest operation of s. 92(1) and are cogently set out in the judgment of Deschênes C.J., followed by the Quebec Court of Appeal. He found that s. 133 is not part of the Constitution of the Province within s. 92(1) but is rather part of the Constitution of Canada and of Quebec in an indivisible sense, giving official status to French and English in the Parliament and in the Courts of Canada as well as in the Legislature and Courts of Quebec. Concerning the qualification in s. 91(1) of the *British North America Act* (enacted by 1949 (U.K.), c. 81) to the power of Parliament to amend the "Constitution of Canada", except (*inter alia*), "as regards the use of the English or French language" it is difficult to see how this amendment enacted in the terms requested by Parliament, can be of any help in interpreting a statute expressly passed for the purpose of giving effect to a political arrangement, made more than eighty years earlier, which did not contemplate such federal power.
>
> There is, moreover, another consideration noticed in the Courts below which should also be brought into account. In *Jones v. Attorney-General of New Brunswick*, [1975] 2 S.C.R. 182, which concerned the validity of the federal *Official Languages Act*, the Court had this to say about s. 133 (at pp. 192-3):
>
>> ... Certainly, what s. 133 itself gives may not be diminished by the Parliament of Canada, but if its provisions are respected there is nothing in it or in any other parts of the *British North America Act* (reserving for later consideration s. 91(1)) that precludes the conferring of additional rights or privileges or the imposing of additional obligations respecting the use of English and French, if done in relation to matters within the competence of the enacting Legislature.
>>
>> The words of s. 133 themselves point to its limited concern with language rights; and it is, in my view, correctly described as giving a constitutionally based right to any person to use English or French in legislative debates in the federal and Quebec Houses and in any pleading or process in or issuing from any federally established Court or any Court of Quebec, and as imposing an obligation of the use of English and French in the records and journals of the federal and Quebec legislative Houses and in the printing and publication of federal and Quebec legislation. There is no warrant for reading this provision, so limited to the federal and Quebec legislative chambers and their legislation, and to federal and Quebec Courts, as being in effect a final and legislatively unalterable determination for Canada, for Quebec and for all other Provinces, of the limits of the privileged or obligatory use of English and French in public proceedings, in public institutions and in public communications. On its face, s. 133 provides special protection in the use of English and French; there is no other provision of the *British North America Act* referable to the Parliament of Canada (apart from s. 91(1)) which deals with language as a legislative matter or otherwise. I am unable to appreciate the submission that to extend by legislation the privileged or required public use of English and French would be violative of s. 133 when there has been no interference with the special protection which it prescribed ...

What the *Jones* case decided was that Parliament could enlarge the protection afforded to the use of French and English in agencies and institutions and programmes falling within federal legislative authority. There was no suggestion that it could unilaterally contract the guarantees or requirements of s. 133. Yet it is contraction not enlargement that is the object and subject of

Chapter III, Title I of the *Charter of the French language*. But s. 133 is an entrenched provision, not only forbidding modification by unilateral action of Parliament or of the Quebec Legislature but also providing a guarantee to members of Parliament or of the Quebec Legislature and to litigants in the Courts of Canada or of Quebec that they are entitled to use either French or English in parliamentary or legislative assembly debates or in pleading (including oral argument) in the Courts of Canada or of Quebec.

Subject to consideration of the range of protection given by s. 133 in the use of either French or English, there does not appear any need to expand any further on the main issue in this case. On matters of detail and of history, we are content to adopt the reasons of Deschênes C.J. as fortified by the Quebec Court of Appeal.

Dealing now with the question whether "regulations" issued under the authority of acts of the Legislature of Quebec are "Acts" within the purview of s. 133, it is apparent that it would truncate the requirement of s. 133 if account were not taken of the growth of delegated legislation. This is a case where the greater must include the lesser. Section 9 of the impugned provisions, in giving official status only to the French text of regulations as well as of statutes and s. 10 in providing for the subordinate position of an English version of bills, statutes and regulations appear to put all these instruments on an equal footing with respect to language and, consequently, towards s. 133.

There is, however, a more compelling answer not only to the question of the language of delegated legislation but also to the question of the language of Court pleading, Court processes, oral argument before the Courts and Court judgments, and it is to be found in s. 7 of Chapter III of Title I of the *Charter of the French language*. The generality of s. 7, "French is the language of the legislature and the courts in Quebec" sweeps in the particulars spelled out in the succeeding ss. 8 to 13. It encompasses in its few and direct words what the succeeding sections say by way of detail. Indeed, as already pointed out, Chapter III of Title I, and especially s. 7 thereof, is a particular projection of Title I, Chapter I of the *Charter of the French language*, saying that "French is the official language of Quebec". Although as a matter of construction, the particular in a statute may modify or limit the general, nothing in ss. 8 to 13 indicates any modification or limitation of s. 7. If anything, there is an extension of the term "Courts" as it appears in s. 7 to include "bodies discharging judicial or quasi-judicial functions": see ss. 11 and 12. In s. 13, the reference is to "judgments . . . by courts and by bodies discharging judicial or quasi-judicial functions" in making only the French text of such judgments official. Again, this appears to envisage an enlarged appreciation of the meaning of "Courts of Quebec", as that term appears in s. 133.

Even if this not be the view of the Quebec Legislature in enacting ss. 11, 12 and 13 above-mentioned, the reference in s. 133 to "any of the Courts of Quebec" ought to be considered broadly as including not only so-called s. 96 Courts but also Courts established by the Province and administered by provincially-appointed Judges. It is not a long distance from this latter class of tribunal to those which exercise judicial power, although they are not courts in the traditional sense. If they are statutory agencies which are adjudicative, applying legal principles to the assertion of claims under their constituent legislation, rather than settling issues on grounds of expediency or administrative policy, they are judicial bodies, however some of their procedures may differ not only from those of Courts but also from those of other adjudicative bodies. In the rudimentary state of administrative law in 1867, it is not surprising that there was no reference to non-curial adjudicative agencies. Today, they play a significant role in the control of a wide range of individual and corporate activities, subjecting them to various norms of conduct which are at the same time limitations on the jurisdiction of the agencies and on the legal position of those caught by them. The guarantee given for the use of French or English in Court proceedings should not be liable to curtailment by provincial substitution of adjudicative agencies for Courts to such extent as is compatible with s. 96 of the *British North America Act*.

. . . .

It follows that the guarantee in s. 133 of the use of either French or English "by any person or in any pleading or process in or issuing from . . . all or any of the Courts of Quebec" applies to both ordinary Courts and other adjudicative tribunals. Hence, not only is the option to use either language given to any person involved in proceedings before the Courts of Quebec or its other adjudicative tribunals (and this covers both written and oral submissions) but documents emanating from such bodies or issued in their name or under their authority may be in either language, and this option extends to the issuing and publication of judgments or other orders.

In *Walsh v. Montreal*, [1980] C.S. 1054 (Que. S.C.), the appellant argued on the basis of section 133 that, because both his traffic ticket and Municipal Court summons were in French only, his conviction for breach of a municipal traffic by-law should be quashed. Hugessen A.C.J., citing the last sentence quoted above from *Blaikie (No. 1)*, dismissed the appeal.

The Supreme Court of Canada comments in *Blaikie (No. 1)* that regulations issued under the authority of statutes are "Acts" within the meaning of section 133 gave rise to the question of the extent to which delegated legislation was reached by section 133. A rehearing was ordered on the question of whether section 133 applies to regulations or orders of municipalities, school boards and other statutory bodies. A list was provided to the Supreme Court which indicated that there were over 2,000 provincial law-making agencies in Quebec alone, ranging from the provincial Government at one end to municipal councils and school boards at the other.

The Court in *A.G. Quebec v. Blaikie (No. 2)*, [1981] 1 S.C.R. 312, held that enactments of a legislative nature issued by the Government or one or more of its Ministers fell within the ambit of section 133, saying at 319 S.C.R.:

> The provincial executive power is vested in the Queen (*Liquidators of the Maritime Bank of Canada v. Receiver General of New Brunswick* [1892] A.C. 437) represented by the Lieutenant-Governor (*B.N.A. Act*, s. 58) whose office is beyond the competence of the Legislature to modify (*B.N.A. Act* s. 92(1)).
>
> The Lieutenant-Governor is part and parcel of the Legislature (*B.N.A. Act*, s. 71; *Legislature Act*, R.S.Q. 1977, c. L-1, s. 1). He appoints members of the Executive Council and ministers (*B.N.A. Act*, s. 63; *Executive Power Act*, R.S.Q. 1977, c. E-18, ss. 3 to 5) and these, according to constitutional principles of a customary nature referred to in the preamble of the *B.N.A. Act* as well as in some statutory provisions (*Executive Power Act*, R.S.Q. 1977, c. E-18, ss. 3 to 5, 7, 11(1); *Legislature Act*, R.S.Q. 1977, c. L-1, s. 56(1)), must be or become members of the Legislature and are expected, individually and collectively, to enjoy the confidence of its elected branch. There is thus a considerable degree of integration between the Legislature and the Government.
>
> The Government of the province is not a body of the Legislature's own creation. It has a constitutional status and is not subordinate to the Legislature in the same sense as other provincial legislative agencies established by the Legislature. Indeed, it is the Government which, through its majority, does in practice control the operations of the elected branch of the Legislature on a day to day basis, allocates time, gives priority to its own measures and in most cases decides whether or not the legislative power is to be delegated and, if so, whether it is to hold it itself or to have it entrusted to some other body.
>
> Legislative powers so delegated by the Legislature to a constitutional body which is part of itself must be viewed as an extension of the legislative power of the Legislature and the enactments of the Government under such delegation must clearly be considered as the enactments of the Legislature for the purposes of s. 133 of the *B.N.A. Act*.
>
> It is true that the above-mentioned conventions of the Constitution were well-established in 1867 and the delegation of legislative powers to the Executive was not then unknown. But such delegation was used sparingly and almost by way of exception. The exception has now become the rule in some matters to the point where a large and important part of the laws in force in the Province consists of regulations made by the Executive. The requirements of s. 133 of the *B.N.A. Act* would be truncated, as was said by this Court at p. 1027 of its reasons, should this section be construed so as not to govern such regulations.
>
> Regulations enacted by the Government to alter regulations made by a subordinate body must also be included in this class. This was not conceded by the Attorney General of Quebec. But there is no valid reason for distinguishing such regulations from ordinary Government regulations. (There would appear to be very few regulations of this type under statutes now in force in Quebec.)

As to other regulations of the civil administration, excluding municipal bodies and school boards, the Court said at 328 S.C.R.:

In order to determine the proper test, one must keep two sets of considerations in mind.

First, the proliferation of these other regulations was at least as unforeseeable as that of Government regulations which, unlike municipal and school board by-laws could not have been originally intended to escape the operation of s. 133 of the *B.N.A. Act.*

Second, while the ordinary meaning of the words "Acts . . . of the Legislature" in s. 133 must be departed from to prevent the requirements of the section from being frustrated, it cannot be stretched beyond what is necessary to accomplish this purpose.

Inadequate as they may be, the two tests suggested by counsel for the Attorney General of Quebec, the Attorney General of Canada and the Attorney General of Manitoba nevertheless point in the right direction in that they both emphasize some connexion between the Legislature and delegated legislation, apart from the delegation itself. This connexion is the decisive factor in so far as the subjection of Government regulations to s. 133 of the *B.N.A. Act* is concerned. There is no reason to select a different element with respect to other regulations. It is because in our constitutional system the enactments of the Government should be assimilated with the enactments of the Legislature that they are governed by s. 133. Other regulations must in our opinion be viewed in the same light when they can also properly be said to be the enactments of the Government.

This happens whenever these other regulations are made subject to the approval of the Government.

The particular form of words used in this respect by various statutes matters little. Whether it be provided that some regulations "shall have no force and effect until approved and sanctioned by the Lieutenant-Governor in Council" or "shall not be carried into execution until approved by the Lieutenant-Governor in Council" or "shall not have force and effect until confirmed by the Lieutenant-Governor in Council", they can be assimilated with the enactments of the Government and therefore of the Legislature as long as positive action of the Government is required to breathe life into them. Without such approval or confirmation, they are a nullity (*North Coast Air Services Ltd. v. Canadian Transport Commission*, [1968] S.C.R. 940) or at least inoperative. The Government does legislate in approving them in the same way as one house legislates in a bicameral legislature when it passes a bill already passed by the other house, or the Lieutenant-Governor when he assents to a bill passed by the house of the now unicameral Legislature.

Regulations which are subject to disallowance by the Government are different. They have an independent life of their own. Their disallowance is a contingency. And even when they are disallowed, they probably are fully effective for the period preceding their disallowance. (See, by analogy, the effect of disallowance on provincial legislation under a similarly worded enactment: *Wilson v. Esquimalt and Nanaimo Ry. Co.*, [1922] 1 A.C. 202).

Under the statutes now in force in Quebec, regulations which are subject to the approval of the Government and therefore to s. 133 of the *B.N.A. Act* seem to be almost as numerous as those of the Government itself.

Similarly, section 133 was held to apply to rules of practice enacted by courts and quasi-judicial tribunals.

Only the by-laws of municipalities and their emanations and school boards were exempt, and these were exempt for essentially historical reasons.

Pre-Confederation statutes provided that municipal by-laws were to be published in only one language (see "An Act to incorporate the Town of Joliette", S.Q. 1863, 27 Vict., c. 23, s. 43) or in French or English "unless the use of either of the said languages be dispensed with" (see "An Act respecting Municipalities and Roads in Lower Canada", C.S.L.C. 1861, c. 24, s. 10(2)). The Supreme Court found that language was a sensitive issue even in 1867 and the Fathers of Confederation would have specifically mentioned language in section 133 in relation to municipalities and school boards if they had intended to cover it. As the Court said at 324 S.C.R.: "It is a purposeful silence to which effect must be given . . ."

It should be noted that section 133 is a bare minimum. It does not limit the ability of either Parliament or the Quebec Legislature from expanding on the linguistic rights contained therein: see *Jones v. A. G. Can.*, [1975] 2 S.C.R. 182 (see the passages previously quoted from *Blaikie (No. 1), supra*, dealing with *Jones*).

For additional literature on language rights, see Magnet, "The Charter's Official Languages Provisions: The Implications of Entrenched Bilingualism" (1982), 4 Sup. Ct. L.R. 163; Magnet, "Minority Language Education Rights" (1982), 4 Sup. Ct. L.R. 195; Tremblay, "The Language Rights", in *The Canadian Charter of Rights and Freedoms: Commentary* (1982), Tarnopolsky and Beaudoin, (eds.).

# 24

# General

## 1. Enforcement — Section 24

### (a) The Threshold Issues: Retrospectivity and Notice

*Note on Retrospectivity and Notice*

(i) *Retrospectivity*

The question of the retrospectivity of section 24 is inextricably bound up with the retrospectivity, or lack thereof, of the right or freedom at issue in the particular case. The general rule of statutory interpretation is that, in the absence of an explicit or implicit statutory direction to the contrary, substantive provisions are prospective only. Procedural rules are retrospective. As set out by Lord Blackburn in *Gardner v. Lucas* (1878), 3 App. Cas. 582 at 603:

> Alterations in the form of procedure are always retrospective, unless there is some good reason or other, why they should not be.

See also *Re Joseph Suche & Co. Ltd.* (1875), 1 Ch. D. 48 at 50; *Re Athlumney*, [1898] 2 Q.B. 547 at 551-2. For a general discussion of the proposition that statutes respecting procedural matters as opposed to substantive matters or vested rights are retrospective, see *Craies on Statute Law* (6th ed.), 1863 at p. 400 *et seq* and *Maxwell on Interpretation of Statutes* (12th ed., 1969) at p. 222 *et seq.*

The right in section 10(b) of the *Charter* to be informed of the right to retain and instruct counsel has been held to be a new substantive right rather than a procedural one. Accordingly it does not operate retrospectively: see *R. v. Lee* (1982), 142 D.L.R. (3d) 574 (Sask. C.A.); *Re Potma and The Queen* (1982), 67 C.C.C. (2d) 19 (Ont. H.C.) (an appeal from the decision of Eberle J. was dismissed by the Ontario Court of Appeal at (1983), 2 C.C.C. (3d) 383 without consideration of the retrospectivity issue); *R. v. Longtin* (1983), 147 D.L.R. (3d) 604 at 608 (Ont. C.A.). Similarly, the right to be free of unreasonable searches or seizures has been held to be a new substantive right, and thus prospective only: see *R. v. Longtin, supra*. See also *R. v. Calgary Rent-a-Fridge Ltd.* (1982), 8 W.C.B. 507 (Alta. Q.B.). However, see *R. v. Davidson* (1982), 40 N.B.R. (2d) 702 (Q.B.) holding that the *Charter* applies to evidence tendered at trial even where it consists of things seized prior to the proclamation of the *Charter*. Along the same lines as *Davidson, quaere* whether the Ontario Court of Appeal's *obiter* in *Re Chapman and The Queen* (1984), 9 D.L.R. (4th) 244 respecting the possible application of section 24(2) of the *Charter* to items seized prior to proclamation, or at least having the question open, is inconsistent with *Longtin.*

On the other hand, section 24(1) may be applied retrospectively to enforce a *Charter* guarantee which is itself retrospective: see *R. v. Antoine* (1983), 41 O.R. (2d) 607 (C.A.), holding that section 24(1) may apply to the right pursuant to section 11(b) to be tried within a reasonable time even where the proceeding was commenced before the proclamation of the *Charter*.

There is an argument to be made that even substantive *Charter* guarantees are retrospective insofar as criminal matters are concerned. That possibility is clearly adverted to by Morden J.A. for the Ontario Court of Appeal in *Re McDonald and the Queen* (1985), 51 O.R. (2d) 745. While a retrospective application of section 15 of the *Charter* was arguably not necessary on the facts of the case, Morden J.A. said at p. 763:

> Further, to the extent that the Charter does involve retroactive or retrospective application. . . . then I would give effect to the consideration that it is the Charter and not an ordinary statute that is sought to be applied and its purposes are beneficial.

It must be remembered that the policy underlying the rule against retrospectivity is that it is unfair to litigants to alter their rights in midstream. This rationale does not apply to criminal prosecutions, as the Crown is not an ordinary litigant in this context. In the American case of *Calder v. Bull*, 3 U.S. (3 Dall.) 386 at 391 (1798), Chase J. discussed the effect of a "benevolent" law in the context of the constitutional prohibition against *ex post facto* laws, saying:

> But I do not consider any law *ex post facto* within the prohibition, that nullifies the rigour of the criminal law, but only those that create or aggravate the crime, or increase the punishment or change the rules of evidence for the purpose of conviction . . .

*Quaere* whether this rationale would support the *Re Chapman supra, obiter* respecting section 24(2) referred to earlier in this Note. For further discussion, see Black "Charter of Rights — Application to Pre-enactment Events", U.B.C.L. Rev., Charter ed. 59 (1982).

### (ii) *Notice to the Attorneys General*

Notice should be given to the federal and (home) provincial attorneys general pursuant to the constitutional questions provisions in the various provincial *Judicature Acts* where the validity of federal or provincial enactments are called into question on *Charter* grounds: see *Re Koumoudouros and Metro. Toronto* (1982), 136 D.L.R. (3d) 373 (Ont. H.C.); *Butler v. York University* (1983), 44 O.R. (2d) 259 (Div. Ct.); *Re Broddy and Director of Vital Statistics* (1982), 142 D.L.R. (3d) 151 (Alta. C.A.). It does not, of course, have to be given where administrative acts as opposed to the validity of legislative or regulatory enactments are called into question.

### (b)  Court of Competent Jurisdiction

### (i) *Availability of prerogative writs*

# RE ANSON AND THE QUEEN

In the British Columbia Court of Appeal. 4 C.C.C. (3d) 119.

Craig, Macdonald and MacFarlane JJ.A. February 18, 1983.

Appeal by the accused from a judgment of Toy J., [1983] 2 W.W.R. 654, dismissing his application for prohibition.

The judgment of the Court was delivered by

MacFarlane J.A.: — The question raised by this appeal is whether a Supreme Court Judge properly exercised his discretion in refusing to make an order prohibiting a county court judge from proceeding with the trial of the appellant under the provisions of s. 8 of the *Narcotic Control Act*, R.S.C. 1970, c. N-1.

The appellant had been charged under s. 4(2) of the *Narcotic Control Act* that he possessed narcotics for the purpose of trafficking. He had pleaded not guilty, and then, before any evidence was adduced, he challenged the constitutionality of s. 8, contending that part of s. 8 was inconsistent with ss. 7, 11(*c*) and (*d*) of the *Canadian Charter of Rights and Freedoms*, being Part I of the *Constitution Act, 1982*, and therefore it was of no force and effect by reason of s. 52 of the *Constitution Act, 1982*. Wetmore Co. Ct. J. held that the application of s. 8 was not inconsistent with the Charter.

Section 4(2) and (3) of the *Narcotic Control Act* reads:

> 4(2) No person shall have in his possession any narcotic for the purpose of trafficking.
>
> (3) Every person who violates subsection (1) or (2) is guilty of an indictable offence and is liable to imprisonment for life.

Section 8 of the *Narcotic Control Act* reads:

> 8. In any prosecution for a violation of subsection 4(2), if the accused does not plead guilty, the trial shall proceed as if it were a prosecution for an offence under section 3, and after the close of the case for the prosecution and after the accused has had an opportunity to make full answer and defence, the court shall make a finding as to whether or not the accused was in possession of the narcotic contrary to section 3; if the court finds that the accused was not in possession of the narcotic contrary to section 3, he shall be acquitted but *if the court finds that the accused was in possession of the narcotic contrary to section 3, he shall be given an opportunity of establishing that he was not in possession of the narcotic for the purpose of trafficking, and thereafter the prosecutor shall be given an opportunity of adducing evidence to establish that the accused was in possession of the narcotic for the purpose of trafficking; if the accused establishes that he was not in possession of the narcotic for the purpose of trafficking, he shall be acquitted of the offence as charged but he shall be convicted of an offence under section 3 and sentenced accordingly; and if* the accused fails to establish that he was not in possession *of the narcotic for the purpose of trafficking, he shall be convicted of the offence as charged and sentenced accordingly.*

(The italicizing identifies the impugned law.)

Section 52(1) of the *Constitution Act, 1982* reads:

> 52(1) The Constitution of Canada is the supreme law of Canada, and any law that is inconsistent with the provisions of the Constitution is, to the extent of the inconsistency, of no force or effect.

The appellant limited his argument before us to ss. 7 and 11(*d*) of the Charter which read:

7. Everyone has the right to life, liberty and security of the person and the right not to be deprived thereof except in accordance with the principles of fundamental justice.

. . . . .

11. Any person charged with an offence has the right

. . . . .

(*d*) to be presumed innocent until proven guilty according to law in a fair and public hearing by an independent and impartial tribunal;

Toy J. had to consider whether an order in the nature of *certiorari, mandamus* or prohibition should be granted. Counsel for the appellant now concedes that *certiorari* and *mandamus* would not lie. That was the conclusion reached by Toy J. Counsel asks only for an order in the nature of prohibition.

The reasons of Toy J. for exercising his discretion against granting prohibition may be summarized in this way. The ruling which the trial judge made was within his jurisdiction to make. It involved the legal question whether part of s. 8 was of no force and effect by reason of being inconsistent with the Charter. The trial judge did not lose his jurisdiction if he erred in deciding that question of law. An appeal from such error, if it exists, is to the Court of Appeal and not by way of an application for prerogative relief. The fundamental rights of the accused were not being infringed. There are cases where prerogative relief may be granted on constitutional grounds: see *Re Rutherford and The Queen* (1981), 63 C.C.C. (2d) 97, where Berger J. granted prohibition in a case where two counts in a multi-count indictment were found to be nullities. This was not such a case. The court has a discretion to refuse prohibition even where there may be an anticipated infringement of Charter rights. In exercising that discretion the court may have regard to a number of factors. Toy J. decided that relief ought not to be granted because the question was premature and was more appropriate for appellate consideration. He stated that the applicant had a right of appeal and that the jurisdiction to grant prerogative relief should not be used as an alternative to the appeal process. He did not think it was appropriate for him to sit in appeal from a decision on a question of law which the trial judge had jurisdiction to decide.

The purpose of the prerogative writ is to keep an inferior tribunal within its jurisdiction. For the most part, the use of the writ has been discretionary. In earlier days, when there was no right of appeal, or a limited right of appeal, the discretion was exercised more freely than now is the case. Canadian law now recognizes that a denial of natural justice goes to jurisdiction: see *Forsythe v. The Queen*, [1980] 2 S.C.R. 268 at 272. An exception to the jurisdictional basis for interference has developed in cases where the statute under which the court is exercising its jurisdiction is *ultra vires*: see *Re Thodas*, 10 C.R.N.S. 290 (B.C.C.A.), and *Re Rutherford* (1981), 63 C.C.C. (2d) 97 (B.C.S.C.). The tendency in recent years has been to limit the use of the prerogative writ rather than extend it.

Toy J. cited *R. v. Roe* (unreported, C.A. No. 423/68, November 7, 1968), in which this court held that prohibition is not a writ of right, but one to be granted after a proper exercise of judicial discretion and *only* in a *substantially clear case of want of jurisdiction*. Toy J. did not find this to be such a case.

. . . .

Toy J. concluded that in this case it would be more appropriate to consider the questions raised after there had been a trial on the merits, when it would be apparent whether or not the rights of the accused had been infringed, and whether the question was academic or not.

. . . .

Policy considerations have played an important part in deciding not to extend the use of the prerogative writ, and to resist the temptation to premature review, especially when other remedies, such as an appeal, will be available. McDermid J.A., in *Re Gilberg and The Queen*, [1975] 2 W.W.R. 171 (Alta. C.A.), expressed such views:

> I shall turn first to a consideration of the public interest. In my opinion the concept of a trial Judge losing jurisdiction by an error in his procedure should be restricted. Unless this is done the conduct of a trial might be under continuous review by successive applications for prohibition resulting in intolerable delays. The preferable manner to correct errors by a trial Judge is on an appeal and not by way of writs of prohibition. Accordingly, when "it is difficult to draw a sharp line between lack or excess of jurisdiction which gives the right and the improper exercise of jurisdiction which gives no right", I would in cases of doubt resolve the matter in favour of appeal rather than prohibition.

In *Re R. and Jones (Nos. 1 and 2)* (1974), 16 C.C.C. (2d) 338 at 348 (Ont. C.A.), Schroeder J.A. said:

> These principles have been adopted and applied consistently in our Courts, and for the best of reasons. If a disappointed litigant were at liberty to obtain an order of *mandamus* or prohibition whenever he was dissatisfied with an order or ruling made by a Court in the course of a trial, this would constitute a disastrous interference with the orderly administration of justice and the wheels of justice would soon grind to a halt. Moreover, the burden of expense which such a course of procedure would impose upon the State is not to be left out of consideration.

When errors in relation to evidentiary questions have been the subject of application for review, prerogative relief has been refused: see *Patterson v. The Queen*, [1970] S.C.R. 409; *R. v. Norgren*, [1976] 3 W.W.R. 196 (B.C.C.A.); *R. v. Kopan* (1975), 3 B.C.L.R. 102 (C.A.); *Re R. and Collos*, [1977] 5 W.W.R. 284 (B.C.C.A.); *Re Skogman and The Queen*, [1982] 3 W.W.R. 367 (B.C.C.A.); *Re Depagie and The Queen*, [1976] 6 W.W.R. 1 (Alta. C.A.); *Re R. and Commisso (No. 2)* (1977), 35 C.C.C. (2d) 237 (B.C.S.C.); *Re Madden and The Queen* (1977), 35 C.C.C. (2d) 381 (Ont. H.C.). In all those cases it was held that the alleged errors were made within jurisdiction.

In *Re Kendall and The Queen*, [1983] 2 W.W.R. 70 (Alta. C.A.) Prowse J.A. (McGillivray C.J.A. and Kerans J.A. concurring) dismissed an application for prohibition, saying:

> The submissions made by the applicants were that the requirements of s. 235 of the *Criminal Code* violated the following rights of an individual secured under the *Constitution Act, 1982*:
>
> (i) the right not to be compelled to be a witness in proceedings against himself;
> (ii) the right to a fair hearing, which was denied because the applicant was not supplied with a sample of his breath, and
> (iii) the right to be presumed innocent until proven guilty
>
> and that as a consequence s. 235 is inoperative or in the alternative, *ultra vires* the Parliament of Canada.
>
> On the dismissal in provincial court of the applications the trials were not proceeded with as the applications were made to this court for an order prohibiting the continuance of the charges against the applicants on the grounds set out above.

That prohibition is a discretionary remedy in cases such as this is not in issue. The problem is in what circumstance the discretion should be exercised to grant that remedy.

Whatever older authorities may have said, one of the circumstances in which a court now generally will decline to grant that remedy is set out in the following statement of Beetz J. in delivering the majority judgment in the Supreme Court of Canada in *Re Harelkin and University of Regina*, [1979] 2 S.C.R. 561:

> I have reached the conclusion that the appellant's right of appeal to the senate committee provided him with an adequate alternative remedy. In addition, *this remedy was in my opinion a more convenient remedy* for appellant as well as for the university in terms of costs and expeditiousness.

(Italics for emphasis.)

In the present case the provincial court judges had jurisdiction to hear the respective application prior to the plea or at the end of the case. Where there are no special circumstances, such as an allegation that the expense of a lengthy trial would be avoided or where there is an allegation of a continuing infringement of his rights, we are of the view that the court in exercising its jurisdiction should decline to grant the remedy sought and permit the trial to proceed.

Prowse J.A. concluded by saying: "If, following trials, the issues raised are not academic the applicants will have the *normal* and usual remedy of appeal."

In *Re Potma and The Queen*, Robins J.A. (speaking for Brooke, Martin, Zuber and Blair JJ.A.) concluded his judgment with these words [31 C.R. (3d) 231]:

> I would, however, add that it is manifestly undesirable that trials be interrupted to test allegedly wrong evidentiary rulings: see, *Re Kendall and The Queen*, [[1983] 2 W.W.R. 70], and that cases in which such rulings can amount to jurisdictional error are few and far between.

Whether an alleged error is jurisdictional or legal is, in many cases, difficult to ascertain.

In his work *The Prerogative Writs in Canadian Criminal Law and Procedure* (1976), G. Létourneau concludes that the concept of jurisdiction is a tool which is at bottom a question of policy and not logic. At pp. 341-2 he writes.

> Like jurisdiction, natural justice includes violations of procedural safeguards which are prejudicial to an accused. The difficulty is to identify which of those violations are serious enough to amount to either an excess of jurisdiction or to a violation of the rules of natural justice. There is no doubt that the concept of jurisdiction could be given a much narrower meaning and be put on a more logical and consistent basis. However, the fact is that the "question is at bottom one of policy, not of logic". Jurisdiction is a tool to achieve a judicial review where it is deemed expedient that there be an immediate review rather than one at a later stage. For instance, on considerations of time and expense, it appeared expedient to the courts that an accused should have, if he wishes to exercise it, an immediate right to challenge before the superior courts the unconstitutionality of a criminal law. Then the issue was made jurisdictional in order that a writ of prohibition could issue to bring the matter before the superior courts.

Prerogative relief may be granted to prevent jurisdictional error, but the mere fact that error may be jurisdictional in nature does not mean that prerogative relief must be granted. If that were so then there would be no discretion to refuse prerogative relief once jurisdictional error had been established. The writ has always been discretionary, and so it should remain.

An examination of the cases indicates that policy considerations lie at the root of the matter. A balance must be struck in many cases between the intolerable delay and possible fragmentation of a trial which would "constitute a disastrous interference with the orderly administration of justice" — see *Re. R. and Jones (Nos. 1 and*

*2)* [(1974), 16 C.C.C. (2d) 338 (C.A.)] and the "subjection to illegal proceedings which involve delays, costs, damaging publicity, fatigue, anguish and which, after having created perhaps a lasting feeling of pique, must be quashed [on appeal] and started anew" (Létourneau, The Prerogative Writs in Canadian Criminal Law and Procedure (1976) at p. 123).

No one test can be formulated to balance those considerations. It is of the essence of discretion that it must be exercised on a case-by-case basis.

In this case, Toy J. considered the question whether a breach of natural justice or a breach of the fundamental principles of justice would occur if he did not grant prohibition. He concluded, in effect, that the accused could have a fair trial.

Lamer J. in *Korponey v. A.-G. Can.* (1982), 26 C.R. (3d) 343 (S.C.C.), discussed the operation of s. 8 of the *Narcotic Control Act*:

> Under s. 8, the rights of an accused are fourfold:
>
> (1) a trial conducted during the first phase as if the charge were one under s. 3;
> (2) a full answer and defence to the issue of possession *before* being put in actual jeopardy of conviction of an offence under s. 4(2);
> (3) a finding on possession *before* deciding on a defence and revealing its nature as regards the purpose of that possession in the event that finding be affirmative;
> (4) an opportunity of presenting that defence.

Another dimension may be added in the light of what was said in *R. v. Rankin*, [1971] 5 W.W.R. 188 (Y.T.C.A.), in which it was held that if the Crown adduces evidence on the issue of purpose that the accused is entitled to call rebuttal evidence.

Turning to the question of natural justice, there is no suggestion in this case of the tribunal not acting fairly, in good faith, without bias and in a judicial temper. The accused knows the charge which he faces. He will know when the first stage is completed precisely what narcotics he has been found to have possessed. He will know the case he has to meet and he will have the last word in meeting it. It is a case where the accused has within his own knowledge the means of establishing that his purpose was not to traffic. It is also to be remembered that he is not compelled to testify in order to establish that proposition. It may be established by calling or relying on other evidence, or by cross-examination. The court may be persuaded by argument based on the evidence that the purpose was not to traffic.

The crucial legal question, rather than the jurisdictional one, is whether the closing words of s. 8 shift the ultimate burden of proof to the accused, thereby offending the Charter which will tolerate only reasonable limits upon the rights to be protected. Toy J. recognized that if such were the case the accused should not be convicted of the full offence, and that such conviction, if it occurred, would be set aside on appeal. But should a judge exercising his discretion on an application for prerogative relief sit in appeal on that question of law? Toy J. said "no". Section 24(1) of the Charter reads:

> 24(1) Anyone whose rights or freedoms, as guaranteed by this Charter, have been infringed or denied may apply to a court of competent jurisdiction to obtain such remedy as the court considers appropriate and just in the circumstances.

In the context of this case where the accused submits that part of the procedure under s. 8 of the *Narcotic Control Act* is of no force and effect, as a matter of constitutional law, the court to which he is to address that complaint is the trial court. If the question of law is decided against him then it, like other questions of law, may be dealt with on appeal. There may be cases where the question is such that immediate review is required. If an immediate remedy is needed then the court reviewing the question may make such order as it considers appropriate and just in the circumstances. For instance, if a statute provided that a person be tried for a particular offence without a jury, and if that person fell within the provisions of s. 11(f) of the Charter then it would be essential to determine the question before the proceedings commenced. Otherwise a whole trial might be conducted by a court which did not have any jurisdiction at all. But such cases will be rare. If it were otherwise then every time it was contended that a legislative provision was inconsistent with the Charter the trial would stop while an application was made for prerogative relief, while an appeal was taken to the Court of Appeal and while a further appeal might be taken to the Supreme Court of Canada. It is possible that several such points could arise during the course of one trial, and intolerable delays might result. It is to be remembered that the Charter also provides that any person charged with an offence has the right to be tried within a reasonable time. He has a right to have his trial started and concluded without unreasonable delay.

Toy J. had to consider whether the constitutional exception to the jurisdictional rule was a ground for granting relief. The usual question raised by a plea that legislation is unconstitutional is whether there is any offence in law for the court to try. The basis for granting prerogative relief in such an event appears to be that the trial court ought not to be permitted to try a charge which has no legal existence. That is not the case here. The charge under s. 4(2) is valid. Furthermore, it includes a charge under s. 3(1) of the *Narcotic Control Act*, namely, possession of a narcotic. There is a valid offence to be tried. The constitutional question does not relate to the included offence of possession and the accused may be found guilty of that offence without reliance at all upon the "reverse onus" provisions of s. 8. They do not apply to the first stage of the trial. The accused may be acquitted on the charge of possession and if that occurs the matter ends. He may be found guilty of possession and if so he is not entitled to escape punishment because a procedure, unrelated to the lesser offence, may be found to be unconstitutional. If he is found to have been in possession then he may, despite the "reverse onus" clause, be acquitted. The whole question of infringement of rights may then become academic. So far as delays, costs, damaging publicity, fatigue and anguish are concerned he would have no complaint about the effect of the "reverse onus" procedure because that machinery would not have been applied to him had he not been found guilty of possession. It is not the case of a man who is completely innocent of any crime being subjected to an entire trial when he ought not to have been tried at all. He can only be convicted of the full offence if he has first of all, in effect, been convicted of possession. If he is convicted of the full offence then he may appeal and have that conviction set aside. I do not understand that such an appeal would affect the finding of possession and his guilt on that lesser offence. It is understandable, therefore, that the trial judge would conclude that immediate review was not called for in the circumstances of this case. The point of law was raised prematurely. It is better that such objections be made and dealt with when the issue arises. Unless the accused is found to have been in possession the issue will not arise. It is still open to Wetmore Co. Ct. J., if the question arises, to reconsider and to order that the trial be proceeded with in a different way. Toy J. had reference to that possibility in considering whether to exercise his discretion for or against granting relief. I think it was open to Toy J. to weigh the interests of the administration of justice against the interests of the accused in such circumstances and to find that the balance lay in favour of refusing to intervene. On that point it was contended on behalf of the appellant that prohibition should have been granted to prevent an unconstitutional trial, appeals and new trials. But if every case is to be interrupted each time a constitutional point arises while prerogative relief is sought, while appeals are taken to this court and to the Supreme Court of Canada then the administration of justice would be chaotic, the cost of accused persons would be oppressive and the cost to the public unjustified — particularly when many such points would prove to have been academic.

Counsel submitted that we ought to treat this as a special case because there is a need for early clarification of this issue at the appellate level. Such clarification will come reasonably quickly in the ordinary course. Already the Ontario Court of Appeal in *R. v. Oakes* (1983), 40 O.R. (2d) 660, and the Prince Edward Island Supreme Court, *in banco*, in *R. v. Carroll* (February 4, 1983) [unreported] have, for different reasons, struck down the "reverse onus" provisions of s. 8. (Neither case involved the question of prerogative relief.) Those cases will provide strong persuasive authority for trial judges in this province, who may choose to resolve any doubts they have on the issue in favour of the accused until the matter is finally settled by a higher court. In most situations the Crown can establish its case in the ordinary way, and without reliance on the "reverse onus" provisions of the Act. It has been a great temptation to jump into the forefront of the resolution of this legal question but I think it is of greater importance to make it clear at the outset of questions arising under the *Constitution Act, 1982* (and there will be many of them based on s. 52) that each level of the judiciary should be free to perform its proper function, and that counsel should not be encouraged to seek solutions to legal questions prematurely at the supervisory or appellate level. I repeat, however, that there will be cases where it may be appropriate to grant prerogative relief. Such cases should be few and far between, but it is best to leave the decision in those cases to the fair and proper exercise of the discretion of the judge charged with the responsibility for deciding whether immediate review and intervention is justified in the particular case.

Mr. Justice Toy has exercised his discretion in this case on a number of apparently sound grounds. I am not persuaded that there was any error in his doing so and I would dismiss the appeal.

*Appeal dismissed.*

## Note

The example postulated by MacFarlane J.A. in *Re Anson and The Queen supra* of the right to be tried within a reasonable time pursuant to section 11(b) of the *Charter* arose in *Re Krakowski and The Queen* (1983), 4 C.C.C. (3d) 188 (Ont. C.A.). In *Krakowski*, the Ontario Court of Appeal purported to follow *Anson*, citing MacFarlane J.A.'s language that "counsel should not be encouraged to seek solutions to legal questions prematurely at the supervisory or appellate level", however it does not appear to have considered the possibility left open by *Anson* that a section 11(b) case might be an appropriate case for an exception to be made. There is a difference in principle between *Anson* and *Krakowski* which does not appear to have been appreciated by the Ontario Court of Appeal. In *Anson*, the proceeding clearly was not void *ab initio*. There was at least the stub of a case apart from the possible constitutional invalidity of part of the statute, in that a proper case of possession was to be tried. In *Krakowski*, where an infringement of section 11(b) was alleged, different considerations may be said to arise. It is clear that compliance with certain kinds of constitutional guarantees are conditions precedent to the validity of the trial process itself. Infringement of these guarantees vitiates the trial process *ab initio*. The right to trial by jury in section 11(f) and the right to trial within a reasonable time pursuant to section 11(b) are illustrations of this kind of right. Where these are at issue, there are good grounds for saying that a person should not be put through the anxieties and tribulations of a trial when the entire proceeding may well be void. A remedy analogous to the civil remedy of objection by way of demurrer should be available. Evidence of the constitutional violation, but not the merits of the charge, will, of course, have to be taken by the lowest court of competent jurisdiction. Thus where an infringement of section 11(b) is alleged, the trial judge would have to hear evidence as to the four relevant factors which must be considered in assessing whether the accused has been deprived of his right to a speedy trial; namely, the length of the delay, the reasons therefor, the accused's assertion of his right, and the prejudice to him: see *R. v. Antoine* (1983), 41 O.R. (2d) 607 (C.A.); *R. v. Thompson* (1983), 3 D.L.R. (4th) 642 (B.C.C.A.); *R. v. Donald* (1983), 5 D.L.R. (4th) 382 (B.C.C.A.), and he would have to balance the conduct of the accused and the prosecution: see *Re R. and Beason* (1983), 43 O.R. (2d) 65 (C.A.). However, once this evidence is taken and the trial judge makes a determination, the accused should be entitled to apply for a prerogative writ before the trial on the merits is commenced.

It appears from a comparison of *Anson* and *Krakowski* that there is a wider availability of prerogative writs in British Columbia than Ontario. In my view, the British Columbia position is to be preferred.

In any event, it is clear that the appropriate forum for relief is, in the absence of special circumstances, the lowest level of court which has jurisdiction, independently of the *Charter*. As stated by Howland C.J.O. in *Krakowski, supra* at pp. 191-2:

> The right of an accused to be tried within a reasonable time is a right which was granted by the Charter. We agree with Trainor J. that the provincial court, as the court which had jurisdiction to hear the charges independently of the Charter, was a court of competent jurisdiction within s. 24(1) of the Charter. There is no merit in the contention that the provisional court has lost jurisdiction by fixing a date for trial, or that it was no longer an impartial tribunal which could grant a fair hearing.
>
> It is not necessary for the purposes of this appeal to decide whether the Supreme Court was also a court of competent jurisdiction based on its inherent jurisdiction as a court of general jurisdiction. Assuming, without deciding, that it had such jurisdiction in addition to its power to grant prerogative relief, it had a discretion to refuse to exercise such jurisdiction where the provincial court in turn had jurisdiction, and the right could be enforced in that court. If the Supreme Court has inherent jurisdiction, it should only be assumed where a Supreme Court Judge in the exercise of his discretion considered that the special circumstances of a particular case merit it. This is the same approach which should be taken by the Supreme Court in deciding whether to grant prerogative relief. Counsel should be discouraged from seeking to enforce rights under the Charter, such as the right to a trial within a reasonable time, prematurely in the Supreme Court.
>
> . . . . .
>
> In most instances it is preferable where the charges are to be tried in the provincial court that the provincial court decide whether the accused has been denied the right to a trial within a reason-

able time as guaranteed by the Charter. The provincial court is in the position to hear viva voce evidence and is familiar with any problems so far as its case-load is concerned. The Supreme Court, on the other hand, might be faced with the difficulty of trying to deal with the matter on the basis of conflicting affidavits. Furthermore, there would be resulting delay if cross-examination of the deponents was required. It is much more satisfactory for the matter to be dealt with at a supervisory or appellate level on the basis of the entire record in the provincial court where all of the relevant issues have been considered in one forum, rather than having been litigated piecemeal.

To the same effect, see *Re United States and Smith* (1984), 44 O.R. (2d) 705 (C.A.), holding that a court should refuse to review the decision of a judge at an extradition hearing on questions of the admissibility of evidence before a committal order is issued. Review by way of *habeas corpus* for infringement of *Charter* rights is available, afterwards if the fugitive is ultimately committed for extradition.

It should be noted that it is not a rule of law that a prerogative writ may not issue where an appeal lies. Rather, the "rule" regulates the exercise of judicial discretion. Thus a prerogative writ may issue notwithstanding the existence of a right of appeal: see *Re R. and Beason* (1983), 43 O.R. (2d) 65 (C.A.).

(ii) *Appeals*

## CAN. NEWSPAPERS CO. v. A.G. CAN.; R. v. D.D.

In the Ontario Court of Appeal. 49 O.R. (2d) 557.

Howland C.J.O., Lacourcière and Goodman JJ.A. October 16 and 17, 1984.

The judgment of the Court was delivered by

HOWLAND C.J.O.: — This is an application by the Attorney-General for Ontario to quash two alternative appeals from the order of The Honourable Mr. Justice Osborne, one in a criminal proceeding and the other in a civil proceeding. The criminal proceeding was the trial of an accused, D.D., on a charge of sexual assault. The civil proceeding was an application by originating notice before Osborne J., a judge of the Supreme Court of Ontario, to declare s. 442(3) of the *Criminal Code* unconstitutional. Osborne J. did not grant leave to intervene in the criminal proceeding and dismissed the application by the appellant for a declaration that s. 442(3) of the *Criminal Code* is of no force and effect as it is inconsistent with the provisions of the *Canadian Charter of Rights and Freedoms* (the Charter). This Court reserved its decision on the applications to quash, and proceeded to hear the appeals. The following important issues are raised:

1. Can the appellant either in criminal or in civil proceedings challenge the validity of an order made by the trial judge banning publication of the identity of the complainant where the accused is charged with sexual assault?
2. Is s. 442(3) of the *Code* of no force and effect because it contravenes the freedom of the press or the right to a public hearing under the Charter?

. . . .

[The Court's discussion of the second issue is reproduced at Chapter 17, *supra*.]

*Issues*

Three issues were raised before this Court on the hearing of the application to quash and of the appeals:

(1) Did the appellant have any right to appeal to this Court from the order of Osborne J. in so far as it was an order in the criminal proceeding?
(2) (a) In making his order on an application by way of originating notice in the civil proceeding, was Osborne J. a court of competent jurisdiction pursuant to s. 24 of the Charter?
    (b) Is there a right of appeal to this Court from such an order?
(3) Is s. 442(3) of the *Code* of no force and effect on the ground that it is inconsistent with ss. 2(*b*) and 11(*d*) of the Charter?

. . . .

[His Lordship's discussion of issue #3 is reproduced at Chapter 17, *supra.*]

*Right of appeal in the criminal proceeding*

The notice of appeal in the criminal proceeding was on the grounds that the appellant should have been allowed to intervene in the criminal proceeding and that Osborne J. erred in concluding that s. 442(3) was not unconstitutional.

Before turning to the question whether there was any right to appeal to this Court from the order of Osborne J. in so far as it was made in the criminal proceeding, it is important to consider the status of the appellant in the criminal proceeding. The case before the Court is the trial of the accused in respect of a charge that he committed sexual assault. The conduct of that trial from the beginning to the end is the responsibility of the trial judge. It is of great importance to the accused that his trial should not be delayed or disrupted by lengthy collateral proceedings and resultant appeals, to his prejudice. The making of an order by the trial judge under s. 442(3) is a matter incidental to the trial which may be of great importance to the complainant and of concern to the media. On the other hand the appellant is not given any right to intervene in any proceeding under s. 442(3) and such intervention is a matter lying within the discretion of the trial judge.

In *R. v. Thomson Newspapers Ltd.* (unreported, released December 8, 1983 [summarized 11 W.C.B. 436]) motions were made to Anderson J. by way of originating notice by the Canadian Broadcasting Corporation and by Canadian Newspapers Limited during the course of the trial of charges under the *Combines Investigation Act* [R.S.C. 1970, c. C-23] requesting access to the exhibits entered into evidence for filming or other purposes. Alternatively, the right of intervention for those purposes was sought. Anderson J. in dismissing the motions expressed the view that an application by originating notice was not appropriate in the circumstances nor was a right of intervention. He did not consider that freedom of the press or any constitutional issue had been raised. He left open the question whether leave to intervene would be appropriate if a constitutional issue were raised on different facts.

Although I am inclined to think that the trial judge was correct in not granting the appellant the right to intervene, it is not necessary to express a final opinion on this point. We are only concerned with whether there is a right of appeal to this Court from his refusal to grant permission to intervene.

Any right of appeal from an order of Osborne J. in a criminal proceeding in respect of an indictable offence must be found either in the *Criminal Code* or in other legislation of the Parliament of Canada: *R. v. Forget* (1982), 35 O.R. (2d) 238 (C.A.). Under ss. 602 and 603 of the *Code* there is no right of appeal in respect of indictable offences except in the event of an acquittal or a conviction. This was recently confirmed in the decision of this Court in *R. v. Morgentaler* (1984), 48 O.R. (2d) 519 (C.A.). There is no inherent jurisdiction to entertain an appeal in criminal cases: *Welch v. The King*, [1950] S.C.R. 412.

The next question which arises is whether any relief can be obtained pursuant to s. 24(1) of the Charter and s. 52(1) of the *Constitution Act, 1982* where the constitutional validity of legislation is involved. These sections are as follows:

> 24(1) Anyone whose rights or freedoms, as guaranteed by this Charter, have been infringed or denied may apply to a court of competent jurisdiction to obtain such remedy as the court considers appropriate and just in the circumstances.     . . . .

> 52(1) The Constitution of Canada is the supreme law of Canada, and any law that is inconsistent with the provisions of the Constitution is, to the extent of the inconsistency, of no force or effect.

This matter was fully considered by this Court in *R. v. Morgentaler, supra*. In that case the Court had to consider whether there was a right of appeal from an order of the trial judge [47 O.R. (2d) 353] dismissing a motion to quash the indictment or stay the proceedings on the ground that the provisions of the *Code* which the accused was alleged to have infringed were inconsistent with the provisions of the Charter. It was conceded that the accused would have a right of appeal in the event that they were convicted. This Court concluded that s. 24(1) of the Charter merely vested additional powers in courts which had already been found to be competent independently of the Charter; it did not create courts of competent jurisdiction.

As Brooke J.A. stated in delivering the judgment of this Court at [pp. 525-7 O.R.]:

> The meaning to be ascribed to the phrase "court of competent jurisdiction" in s. 24(1) of the Charter has been the subject of consideration in a number of cases. The weight of authority is that s. 24(1) does not create courts of competent jurisdiction, but merely vests additional powers in courts which are already found to be competent independently of the Charter. We agree with Mr. Doherty that a court is competent if it has jurisdiction, conferred by statute, over the person and the subject-matter in question and, in addition, has authority to make the order sought. The Court presided over by Associate Chief Justice Parker was the court of competent jurisdiction to which the accused could apply under s. 24(1). It has declared that the rights and freedoms guaranteed to the accused by the Charter have not been infringed or denied by charging them under the section of the *Criminal Code* upon which the count in the indictment was founded. Section 24(1) does not purport to create a right of appeal or bestow appellate powers on this or any other court. Rather it authorizes those courts which have statutory appellate jurisdiction independent of the Charter to exercise the remedial power in s. 24(1) in appropriate cases when disposing of appeals properly brought before the court.     . . . . .

This was also the view of the Alberta Court of Appeal in *R. v. Crate* (1983), 7 C.C.C. (3d) 127, 1 D.L.R. (4th) 149, 27 Alta. L.R. (2d) 214.     . . . . .

In two recent judgments delivered by Lacourcière J.A., this Court has expressed agreement with the judgment in *Crate*: see *R. v. Langevin* (1984), 45 O.R. (2d) 705; *R. v. Petrovic* (1984), 47 O.R. (2d) 97. The same conclusion has been reached in other cases: see *Re Ritter and The Queen*, [1984] 2 W.W.R. 623, a judgment of the British Columbia Court of Appeal. This is an important case as many of the judgments and texts which deal with the question are considered. See also: *R. v. Toker and McKinney* (1984), 13 C.C.C. (3d) 472 (Alta. C.A.).

Brooke J.A. then went on to consider s. 52(1) of the *Constitution Act, 1982.* He came to the conclusion that s. 52(1) did not create a right of appeal to this Court and give the Court jurisdiction to hear an appeal from an interlocutory motion where a constitutional issue is raised. He did not consider that the Manitoba Court of Appeal had reached a contrary conclusion in *Re Bird and Peebles and The Queen* (1984), 12 C.C.C. (3d) 523, 27 Man. R. (2d) 241, 9 C.R.R. 69. It might be that the Manitoba Court of Appeal was concerned that it should not foreclose the *Constitution Act, 1982* as a possible basis for jurisdiction if there were circumstances where there was no lower court to which to apply for a remedy if rights and freedoms guaranteed by the Charter were refused or denied. He pointed out that there were strong policy reasons against interrupting the trial process with appeals to the Court of Appeal. Furthermore, there was a right of appeal to this Court in the event that the accused was convicted and any constitutional issue could be raised at that time.

Accordingly, I am of the opinion that there is no right of appeal to this Court from the order of Osborne J. in the criminal proceeding either under the *Criminal Code*, or under s. 24(1) of the Charter, or s. 52(1) of the *Constitution Act, 1982*. I would grant the application to quash the appeal in the criminal proceeding and quash the appeal.

## Right of appeal in civil proceeding

It is necessary to turn now to consider the civil proceeding by way of originating notice. While it is important that the right of the accused to be tried for the criminal offence with which he is charged should not be disrupted by collateral proceedings with resultant delays necessitated by appeals, it is also of importance that those who are given rights by the Charter which may conflict with provisions of the *Criminal Code* should have the opportunity to have these rights determined by the courts.

It was contended by counsel for the Attorney-General for Ontario that the proper procedure for the determination of the validity of the Charter rights which the appellant considered were in conflict with s. 442(3) of the *Code* was in an action commenced by writ of summons for declaratory relief.

Counsel for the appellant contended that the appellant was entitled to have its rights determined by originating notice of motion under Rule 11 of the Rules of Practice which provides in part:

11(1) Where by any statute an application may be made to a court or a judge thereof and where such application may be made without the institution of an action, the application may be made by originating notice of motion.

She submitted that the statutory basis for such an application is s. 24(1) of the Charter. The Charter comprises part of the *Constitution Act, 1982*. It was her contention that while s. 24(1) forms part of the Constitution, it also forms part of a statute, and could be the basis for an application by originating notice under Rule

11. As I have already pointed out, before remedies under s. 24(1) can be exercised it must be concluded that the Supreme Court of Ontario was a court of competent jurisdiction apart from the Charter.

Section 18, para. 2 of the *Judicature Act*, R.S.O. 1980, c. 223, provides that:

> 18. In every civil cause or matter, law and equity shall be administered according to the following rules:
>
> . . . .
>
> 2. No action or proceeding is open to objection on the ground that a merely declaratory judgment or order is sought thereby and the court may make binding declarations of right, whether or not any consequential relief is or could be claimed.

It has been held that the Supreme Court of Ontario has jurisdiction to grant declaratory relief on an originating application where it is authorized to do so by the rules rather than in an action or proceeding: *Re Oil, Chemical & Atomic Workers Int'l Union, Local 9-14 and Polymer Corp. Ltd.*, [1966] 1 O.R. 774 at 783-4 (H.C.). It would therefore seem to be clear that the Supreme Court of Ontario was a court of competent jurisdiction to grant declaratory relief under s. 24(1) of the Charter.

The rules do not create new jurisdiction, but provide a mode by which the jurisdiction conferred by s. 18, para. 2 of the *Judicature Act* can be exercised: *Re Toronto General Trusts Corp. and McConkey* (1917), 41 O.L.R. 314 at 315 (H.C.). The question remains whether the broad powers which are given by s. 24(1) of the Charter to anyone whose rights or freedoms under the Charter are infringed or denied to obtain such remedy as the court considers appropriate and just in the circumstances can be treated as statutory authorization for a summary application by way of originating notice within Rule 11.

The wording of s. 24(1) is very broad and the courts have been left to formulate the rules whereby the appropriate remedies can be granted. On the other hand there is considerable substance in the contention that Rule 11 contemplates a statute which specifically authorizes a summary application and specifies the manner in which it is to be made. It is not necessary for the purpose of this appeal to decide whether the application by originating notice was properly brought under Rule 11. Even if Osborne J. erred in proceeding under Rule 11, the order made by him is not thereby rendered void. Under Rule 186 non-compliance with the rules does not render any act or proceeding void, but it may be set aside, either wholly or in part, as irregular, or may be amended, or otherwise dealt with as seems just.

In *R. v. Bales, Ex parte Meaford General Hospital*, [1971] 2 O.R. 305 (H.C.), relief was sought by way of an order for prohibition on application by way of originating notice against the order of the Minister of Labour appointing a conciliation officer. Osler J. concluded that the proper relief was by way of declaratory judgment. He decided that even though the preferable course would have been for the person aggrieved to have brought an action for a declaration, he should not be deprived of relief because he had proceeded by way of originating notice. At p. 315 O.R., he stated:

> It is highly desirable that in proceedings dealing with the operation of collective agreements the most expeditious method of determining the rights of parties should be adopted, all of such agreements being, as they are, of relatively short duration and, in my opinion, the present applicant should not be prevented from obtaining the relief which I have found to be proper merely because

he adopted the more expeditious procedures of an originating notice of motion in preference to issuing a writ of summons.

It is important that persons who allege that their rights under the Charter have been infringed should have an opportunity of having their legal position determined expeditiously. The appellant should not be prevented from obtaining the declaratory relief to which it was entitled because it proceeded by originating notice rather than by commencing an action.

It should be noted that other issues respecting the Charter have been determined in proceedings instituted by originating notice: *Re Skapinker* (1982), 38 O.R. (2d) 116 (H.C.); reversed 40 O.R. (2d) 481 (C.A.); reversed [1984] 1 S.C.R. 357; *Germany v. Rauca* (1982), 38 O.R. (2d) 705 (H.C.); affirmed 41 O.R. (2d) 225 (C.A.); *Reference re Constitutional Validity of s. 12 of Juvenile Delinquents Act* (1982), 38 O.R. (2d) 748 (H.C.), [affirmed (*sub nom. Re Southam Inc. and The Queen (No. 1)*) (1983), 41 O.R. (2d) 113. *Re Southam Inc. and the Queen (No. 1) supra* is particularly in point because the issue before the Court was whether s. 12(1) of the *Juvenile Delinquents Act*, R.S.C. 1970, c. J-3, which in effect required that the trial of all juveniles shall be held *in camera*, was unconstitutional because it was in conflict with the right of freedom of the press under s. 2(*b*) of the Charter. The matter originally came before Smith J. in motions court for an order in the nature of *mandamus* compelling the provincial court judge to permit representatives of the media to be present at the proceedings in the provincial court (family division) pursuant to the *Juvenile Delinquents Act*. While initially in its appellant's statement the Crown argued that the respondent, Southam Inc., did not have the status to bring the application and that the Supreme Court of Ontario was not a court of competent jurisdiction within s. 24(1) of the Charter, this contention was not pressed during argument. The Crown agreed that the application was properly brought before Smith J. It was also agreed that the Crown had a right of appeal under s. 28 of the *Judicature Act*, R.S.O. 1980, c. 223.

Osborne J. was faced with a very considerable dilemma. He was commencing an important criminal trial in which the prime consideration was that the accused receive a fair and expeditious trial. As the trial judge he had a discretion not only to refuse to grant the appellant the right to intervene in the criminal proceeding, but to decline to hear the application by originating notice under Rule 11. He took a course of action which was in keeping with the spirit of the Charter and gave the appellant an opportunity to have its rights determined promptly in the civil proceeding.

In my opinion the validity of the order of Osborne J. in the civil proceeding should be upheld. His order was a final order and accordingly an appeal lies to this Court under s. 28(1)(*a*) of the *Judicature Act*. The application to quash the appeal in the civil proceeding should accordingly be dismissed.

It is not necessary for the purposes of this appeal to consider the appropriate procedure to be followed in future cases under the [Ontario] Rules of Civil Procedure which came into force on January 1, 1985. It would seem desirable that such applications for declaratory relief should be made in separate civil proceedings at as early a date as possible.

. . . .

Appeal in criminal case quashed; appeal in civil proceeding allowed.

(iii)  *General*

### Note on Court of Competent Jurisdiction

The view expressed by the three justices out of six in *Singh v. Min. of Employment and Immigration*, [1985] 1 S.C.R. 177, who based their decision on the *Charter* was that a "court of competent jurisdiction" for the purposes of section 24(1) is one which gains such jurisdiction, inherent or otherwise, from sources external to the *Charter* itself. Restated, section 24(1) does not operate to extend the jurisdiction of otherwise limited courts or tribunals.

The following is a non-exhaustive list for illustrative purposes of bodies which have or have not been held to be courts of competent jurisdiction:

1) The Federal Court, Trial Division has jurisdiction to grant an injunction to prevent the deportation of an alien where the deportation would violate his *Charter* rights: see *Re Gittens and The Queen*, [1983] F.C. 152 (T.D.). In fact, provincial superior courts have been held not to have jurisdiction to hear *Charter* questions where the matter is otherwise within the exclusive jurisdiction of the Federal Court: see *Gandam v. Minister of Employment*, [1982] 6 W.W.R. 378 (Sask. Q.B.); see also *Jackson v. Minister of Finance* (1982), 21 Sask. R. 221 (Q.B.). *Quaere* whether *Gandam* is inconsistent with *A. G. Can. v. Law Society of British Columbia; Jabour v. Law Society of British Columbia*, [1982] 2 S.C.R. 307, which held that, although the Federal Court is empowered to administer the "laws of Canada", it does not have jurisdiction to determine the constitutional validity of those laws. It is submitted that the better view is that *Jabour* is based up protection of federalism notions, and a declaration of unconstitutionality based upon the *Charter* does not implicate the federal-provincial balance of power.

2) A provincial court judge has no power apart from that conferred by statute to review the decision of another provincial court judge (e.g. with respect to the section 11(e) guarantee of reasonable bail); *Re R. and Brooks* (1982), 38 O.R. (2d) 545 (Ont. H.C.).

3) The Federal Court, Trial Division has no jurisdiction pursuant to section 24(1) of the *Charter* to grant a stay of execution, or interlocutory injunctive relief with respect to orders of the Canada Labour Relations Board. The Federal Court of Appeal is the appropriate forum for review pursuant to section 122 of the *Canada Labour Code*, R.S.C. 1970, c. L-1 and section 28 of the *Federal Court Act*: see *Re Vergis and Canada Labour Relations Board* (1982), 142 D.L.R. (3d) 747 (Fed T.D.).

4) The Immigration Appeal Board is, within the limits of its statutory jurisdiction, a court of competent jurisdiction pursuant to section 24(1). Sections 59(1) and 72(1) of the *Immigration Act, 1976*, S.C. 1976-77, c. 52 give the Board jurisdiction to hear and determine all questions of law arising with respect to the making of a removal order and, as well, to deal with the issues and constitutionality of a Ministerial certificate issued pursuant to section 83 of the Act: see *Law v. Solicitor-General of Canada* (1984), 11 D.L.R. (4th) 608 at 613 (Fed. C.A.).

5) In the absence of an express statutory right of appeal in the applicable legislation (in this case the *Extradition Act*, R.S.C. 1970, c. E-21), the provincial superior court, as a court of inherent jurisdiction and no other forum being available, has jurisdiction to review the decision of an extradition judge banning the publication of

the proceedings at the fugitive's bail application: see *Re Global Communications and A.G. Can.* (1983), 44 O.R. (2d) 609 (Ont. C.A.).

6) The Court of Appeal, as a statutory court whose jurisdiction in criminal matters is established by sections 601 and 602 of the *Criminal Code*, is not a court of competent jurisdiction to decide questions of the constitutionality of *Code* provisions (in this case regarding the right to trial by jury pursuant to section 11(f) of the *Charter*) where the application comes before the court by way of pre-trial motion rather than appeal from conviction: see *R. v. Crate* (1983), 7 C.C.C. (3d) 127 (Alta. C.A.). This view that section 24(1) does not bestow appellate jurisdiction or create new rights of appeal has been concurred in *R. v. Langevin* (1984), 45 O.R. (2d) 705 (C.A.); *R. v. Petrovic* (1984), 47 O.R. (2d) 97 (C.A.); *R. v. Ritter*, [1984] 2 W.W.R. 623 (B.C.C.A.); *R. v. Morgentaler* (1984), 48 O.R. (2d) 519 (C.A.); *Canadian Newspapers Company Limited v. A.G. Can.* (1985), 49 O.R. (2d) 557 (C.A.): see extract, *supra*. See also in *Re Laurendeau and The Queen* (1983), 4 D.L.R. (4th) 702 (Que. C.A.) that the Court of Appeal has no jurisdiction to grant a remedy in the nature of a declaration that the accused has the right to trial by jury for contempt *ex facie* pursuant to section 11(f) of the *Charter*.

7) The provincial court is a statutory court without jurisdiction to stay summary conviction proceedings and, accordingly, the provincial superior court as a court of inherent jurisdiction is the appropriate forum: see *R. v. Century Helicopters Inc.* (1983), 51 A.R. 395 (Q.B.). Similarly, a provincial court judge has no jurisdiction to quash or stay a charge of an indictable offence prior to the accused's being put to his election: see *Re R. and Henyu* (1984), 8 D.L.R. (4th) 596 (B.C.S.C.).

8) As there is no provision in the *National Defence Act*, R.S.C. 1970, c. N-4 for the release of a convicted serviceman on bail pending an appeal to the Court Martial Appeal Court, and as the common law jurisdiction to grant *habeas corpus* exists only prior to conviction pending trial, section 11(e) of the *Charter* is the only relief available for a convicted serviceman pending appeal. The provincial superior court is accordingly a court of competent jurisdiction pursuant to section 24(1) for the enforcement of this right: see *Re Hinds and The Queen* (1983), 147 D.L.R. (3d) 730 (B.C.S.C.).

## (c)  Remedies and Standards of Review

### Note on Remedies and Standards of Review

Section 24(1) of the *Charter* empowers a court of competent jurisdiction to grant "such remedy as the court considers appropriate and just in the circumstances". It therefore has jurisdiction to fashion new remedies as the need arises. However, the courts have been reluctant to date to go beyond the traditional legal and equitable remedies such as damages, prerogative writs, declarations, injunctions and the like, or to undertake the supervision of large institutions or programs as is routinely done in the United States. Thus, the courts will not use section 24(1) to amend legislation or, in effect, legislate to grant a "remedy". In *R. v. Varga* (1985), 44 C.R. (3d) 377 (C.A.) the accused argued that section 563 of the *Criminal Code*, which granted 48 stand-asides to the Crown in a jury selection and none to the accused, was violative of section 7 of the *Charter*. The trial judge agreed but, rather than strike down the section, he reduced the Crown's stand-asides from 48 to 12 and gave the accused 12 stand-asides, even though there was no statutory authority for doing so in the *Criminal Code*. Mackinnon A.C.J.O. held that section 24 of the *Charter* does not empower the courts to fashion such a remedy. He said at p. 383:

> I do not believe that s. 24(1) was intended to grant to a court the power to amend legislation or introduce new legislation at its discretion and, in effect, re-write the section. That is still, surely, Parliament's function.

Similarly, the courts have been loath to take over the administration of large systems. Thus in *Re Maltby and A. G. Sask.* (1984), 10 D.L.R. (4th) 745 (Sask. C.A.) the Saskatchewan Court of Appeal refused to hear an appeal on the merits on mootness grounds. One of the factors considered was that the applicants were seeking a sweeping condemnation of the entire system of correctional practices used for remand inmates. It is likely that, at least until Canadian courts have achieved more familiarity with their new functions under the *Charter*, they will be as reluctant to take over large systems now as they were in pre-*Charter* days. Laskin C.J.C.'s remarks in *Morgentaler v. The Queen*, [1976] 1 S.C.R. 616 at 634-5 about the absence of "judicially manageable standards" in the statutory *Bill of Rights* context are instructive:

> Finally, in the catalogue of submissions under the *Canadian Bill of Rights* is point (5) which, understandably, shows concern for the effect of place or area of residence (where remote from hospitals or where there is a dearth of qualified physicians) and the economic status on the availability and accessibility of the services under s. 251(4) and (5) of the *Criminal Code*, through which an abortion may be sought without risk of criminality. The contention that there is here a denial of equality before the law and the protection of the law necessarily assesses s. 251(4) and (5) according to whether it gives its advantages to all sections of the Canadian community, enabling them to avail themselves of it in whatever part of Canada they may be and regardless of their economic status. Assessment on this basis would make the operation of s. 251(4) and (5) depend on there being a certain distribution of physicians throughout the country and on the availability of hospitals in all areas. It would mean too that the Court would have to come to some conclusion on what distribution would satisfy equality before the law, and that the Court would have to decide how large or small an area must be within which an acceptable distribution of physicians and hospitals must be found. This is a reach for equality by judicially unmanageable standards, and is posited on the theory that the Court should either give directions for the achievement of relative equality of access to therapeutic abortion committees and approved hospitals to overcome an alleged legislative shortcoming, or should strike down not only s-ss. (4) and (5) of s. 251 (which would leave an unqualified prohibition of abortion) but the whole section as being inseverable.
>
> I do not regard s. 1(b) of the *Canadian Bill of Rights* as charging the Courts with supervising the administrative efficiency of legislation or with evaluating the regional or national organization of its administration, in the absence of any touchstone in the legislation itself which would indicate a violation of s. 1(b) including the specified prohibitions of discrimination by reason of race, national origin, colour, religion or sex . . .

The cases to date suggest that the question of remedies and the notion of "court of competent jurisdiction" interact, and that the latter expression requires that the court have independent jurisdiction apart from the *Charter* over the person, the proceeding and the remedy sought. If so, one cannot go to a court of limited jurisdiction for a new remedy even if it is otherwise the appropriate forum. One would have to apply to a court of inherent jurisdiction, and show that the remedies which the court of limited jurisdiction is empowered to grant are insufficient.

For an excellent enumerated summary of cases decided and remedies granted, see *The Canadian Charter of Rights Annotated*, Laskin, Greenspan, Dunlop, Rosenberg, Dambrot (eds.), section 24.

For discussion of section 24, see Fairley, "Enforcing the Charter: Some Thoughts on an Appropriate and Just Standard for Judicial Review" (1982), 4 Sup. Ct. L.R. 217; Gibson, "Enforcement of the Canadian Charter of Rights and Freedoms", *Canadian Charter of Rights and Freedoms: Commentary* (1982, Tarnopolsky and Beaudoin, eds.), Ch. 16; Hogg, *Constitutional Law of Canada* (2d ed. 1985), p. 694; Pilkington, "Damages as a Remedy for Charter Infringement" (1984), 62 Can. Bar Rev. 517.

# 2. Exclusion of Evidence

## R. v. THERENS

In the Supreme Court of Canada. [1985] 1 S.C.R. 613.

Dickson C.J.C., Ritchie, Beetz, Estey, McIntyre, Chouinard, Lamer, Wilson, LeDain JJ. May 23, 1985.

[Ritchie J. did not take part in the judgment.]

DICKSON C.J.C. (dissenting in part): — I agree with LeDain J., for the reasons he has given in his judgment, that the respondent was "detained" within the meaning of s. 10 of the Charter of Rights and Freedoms, Constitution Act, 1982, Pt. I, and that his rights under subs. (*b*) were violated. I also agree with LeDain J. that s. 235(1) [of the Criminal Code, R.S.C. 1970, c. C-34] does not create a limit, prescribed by law, under s. 1 of the Charter, on a detained person's right to be informed of the right to retain and instruct counsel. Section 235(1) does not expressly or by necessary implication compel the police to deny a detained person's right to be informed of his s. 10(*b*) rights.

I agree with Lamer J., for the reasons he has given, that the breathalyzer evidence tendered in this case was obtained in a manner which infringed and denied the respondent's rights under s. 10(*b*) and that it has been established that, having regard to all the circumstances, the admission of this evidence in the proceedings would bring the administration of justice into disrepute. Accordingly, the certificate of analysis prepared pursuant to s. 237 of the Criminal Code should be excluded under s. 24(2) of the Charter.

Since this evidence may properly be excluded by the operation of s. 24(2) of the Charter, I do not wish to be taken as expressing any view on the availability of the exclusion of evidence as an appropriate and just remedy under s. 24(1) of the Charter.

I would accordingly dismiss this appeal.

The judgment of Beetz, Estey, Chouinard and Wilson JJ. was delivered by

ESTEY J.:

I have had the benefit of reading the judgment of my colleague LeDain J. in this appeal and, while I am in agreement, as shall be seen below, with much of what has been there written, I am in respectful disagreement as to the disposition. I would dismiss the appeal [from 33 C.R. (3d) 204, affirming 16 M.V.R. 285] for these reasons.

I am in agreement that the respondent-defendant was "detained" within the meaning of s. 10 of the Charter of Rights and Freedoms when the police officers administered the breathalyzer test under s. 235 of the Criminal Code. That section of the Criminal Code clearly anticipates a delay in some circumstances for the administration of this test. This is in contrast to s. 234.1(1) of the Code. In the former section the Code provides that the peace officer may "by demand made . . . forthwith or as soon as practicable" require such person to provide samples "then or as soon thereafter as is practicable". Section 234.1(1) requires that the person driving the motor vehicle "provide forthwith such a sample of his breath".

Section 10(*b*) of the Charter of Rights provides:

10. Everyone has the right on arrest or detention . . .

(*b*) to retain and instruct counsel without delay and to be informed of that right . . .

Neither of the two rights assured in s. 10(*b*) of the Charter was honoured by the police authority. The peace officers did not accord to the respondent the right "without delay" to retain and instruct counsel, nor did they inform the respondent of that right. There is nothing in this record to suggest that the officers would have been unable to afford the respondent a reasonable time to contact his counsel.

The provisions of s. 235 cannot constitute a cause for failure to assure these rights. As noted above, action under s. 235 by the respondent need only be taken "as soon as practicable". We are not here faced with a proceeding under s. 234.1 which may raise different issues. Neither are we here, on this record, required to determine the more difficult question of what the peace officer may do pursuant to s. 235 of the Code after s. 10(*b*) of the Charter has been accommodated. Furthermore, because s. 24(2) of the Charter, as we shall see, operates to exclude the evidence thereby obtained, s. 24(1) of the Charter need not be invoked.

I am therefore in respectful agreement with my colleague that the rights of the respondent under s. 10(*b*) have been violated.

Because Parliament has not purported to place a limitation on the right of the respondent under s. 10(*b*) of the Charter, in s. 235(1), the court is not here concerned with s. 1 of the Charter. That section subjects all Charter rights, including s. 10, "only to such reasonable limits prescribed by law . . ." Here Parliament has not purported to prescribe any such limit and hence s. 1 of the Charter does not come into play. The limit on the respondent's right to consult counsel was imposed by the conduct of the police officers and not by Parliament.

This brings one to the core issue in this appeal, namely, the admissibility of the evidence as to the alcohol content in the respondent's blood as determined by the test taken under s. 235(1) of the Code. The admissibility of this evidence in my view, and again I am in respectful agreement with my colleague LeDain J., falls to be determined by s. 24(2) of the Charter and not by reason of subs. (1) of that section, as was the view of the Court of Appeal below. Subsection (2) alone in the Charter of

Rights empowers a court to exclude evidence where "that evidence was obtained in a manner that infringed or denied any rights or freedoms guaranteed by this Charter . . ." Subsection (2) goes on to direct, in mandatory terms:

> . . . the evidence *shall* be excluded if it is established that, having regard to all the circumstances, the admission of it in the proceedings would bring the *administration of justice into disrepute*. [The italics are mine.]

Here the police authority has flagrantly violated a Charter right without any statutory authority for so doing. Such an overt violation as occurred here must, in my view, result in the rejection of the evidence thereby obtained. We are here dealing only with direct evidence or evidence thereby obtained directly and I leave to another day any consideration of evidence thereby indirectly obtained. To do otherwise than reject this evidence on the facts and circumstances in this appeal would be to invite police officers to disregard Charter rights of the citizen and to do so with an assurance of impunity. If s. 10(*b*) of the Charter of Rights can be offended without any statutory authority for the police conduct here in question and without the loss of admissibility of evidence obtained by such a breach then s. 10(*b*) would be stripped of any meaning and would have no place in the catalogue of "legal rights" found in the Charter.

The violation by the police authority of a fundamental Charter right, which transpired here, will render this evidence inadmissible. Admitting this evidence under these circumstances would clearly "bring the administration of justice into disrepute". I am strongly of the view that it would be most improvident for this court to expatiate, in these early days of life with the Charter of Rights, upon the meaning of the expression "administration of justice" and particularly its outer limits. There will no doubt be, over the years to come, a gradual build-up in delineation and definition of the words used in the Charter in s. 24(2).

For these reasons, I would therefore dismiss this appeal.

McINTYRE J. (dissenting): — I am in full agreement with the reasons for judgment of LeDain J. I would add that to exclude the questioned evidence in this case solely on a finding that a Charter right was breached in obtaining it would be to disregard the provisions of s. 24(2) of the Canadian Charter of Rights and Freedoms. In my view, this section must have its effect. The exclusion of such evidence is not automatic. It must be excluded only where it is established that its admission, having regard to all the circumstances, would bring the administration of justice into disrepute. In my view, that is not established here. The exclusion of the evidence in the circumstances of this case would itself go far to bring the administration of justice into disrepute.

LAMER J. (dissenting in part): — The issues that require determination in this case are the following: was the respondent "detained", within the meaning of s. 10(*b*) of the Charter; was there a violation of his rights under s. 10(*b*); if so, is the violation in this case a reasonable limit prescribed by law; if not, what is the proper remedy and disposition of this case?

I have had the advantage of reading the judgments of my colleagues Estey and LeDain JJ.

I agree with my brother LeDain for the reasons set out in his judgment that the respondent was detained. I also agree with LeDain J. that there was here a violation of the respondent's rights under s. 10(*b*). Clearly he was not, as a detainee, in any way informed of his right to retain and instruct counsel without delay. As set out in the reasons of Estey J., the violation of the respondent's rights is not the result of the operation of law but of the police action and there is no need, in my view, to consider in this case whether under s. 1 of the Charter the "breathalyzer scheme" set up through ss. 235(1) and 237 of the Criminal Code is a reasonable limit to one's rights under the Charter. That issue will certainly arise in some other case given the content which I think must be given to s. 10(*b*).

At first blush, there would appear not to be any need to expand upon the content of s. 10(*b*) given that the facts of this case indicate a clear violation of the section, whatever be that content. However, in order to meet the requirements for exclusion of evidence under s. 24(2) there must not only exist a violation of a Charter right, but there must also be, as was said by LeDain J., "some connection or relationship between the infringement or denial of the right or freedom in question and the obtaining of the evidence the exclusion of which is sought by the application".

With respect, however, I cannot subscribe to the proposition later advanced by LeDain J. that this requirement is met by the simple fact that the infringement or denial of the right has preceded the obtaining of the evidence. Indeed, if there is no relationship other than a temporal one, the evidence was not "*obtained* in a manner that infringed" the Charter.

Thus, when one addresses the consequences that should flow under s. 24 as a result of the violation in this case, one has to go back and give some content to s. 10(*b*) if one is to consider whether, under s. 24(2), the "breathalyzer evidence" was obtained in a manner that infringed or denied that right. Indeed, if a literal construction is given to s. 10(*b*), there is then no nexus whatsoever between the requirement of the taking of breath samples on the one hand and, on the other hand, informing the detainee of his rights and not preventing him from exercising them.

I do not want to be taken here as giving an exhaustive definition of the s. 10(*b*) rights and will limit my comments in that respect to what is strictly required for the disposition of this case. In my view, s. 10(*b*) requires at least that the authorities inform the detainee of his rights, not prevent him in any way from exercising them and, where a detainee is required to provide evidence which may be incriminating and refusal to comply is punishable as a criminal offence, as is the case under s. 235 of the Code, s. 10(*b*) also imposes a duty not to call upon the detainee to provide that evidence without first informing him of his s. 10(*b*) rights and providing him with a reasonable opportunity and time to retain and instruct counsel. Failure to abide by that duty will lead to the obtainment of evidence in a manner which infringes or denies the detainee's s. 10(*b*) rights. Short of that, s. 10(*b*) would be a near empty right, as remedies could seldom affect the admissibility of evidence obtained through the accused.

Whether s. 10(*b*) extends any further, so as to encompass, for example, the principle of *Miranda v. Airzona*, 384 U.S. 436, 16 L. Ed. 2d 694, 86 S. Ct. 1602 (1966), and apply to matters such as interrogation and police line-ups, need not be decided in this case and I shall refrain from so doing.

Whether s. 235(1) of the Code in general, and its two-hour limitation in particular, are in conflict with s. 10(*b*), especially that aspect of being given a reasonable time to speak to counsel, does not arise in this case and I would choose not to address that question for the following reason. Were we to find that s. 235(1) does impose a limit on the amount of time the peace officer can give a detainee to exercise his rights under s. 10(*b*) before requiring a breath sample, we would in my view be faced with a very incomplete file when called upon to determine whether the limitation is one that is reasonable under the test set out in s. 1 of the Charter. I think that question, if to be addressed, will be more properly considered in a case where there will have been adduced evidence in support of the demonstration the authorities have the burden to make under s. 1. As an example, why is there a two-hour limit? Is it for scientific reasons related to reliability? I suspect so but do not find any evidence in the record.

In this case, the test was required by the peace officer and then given to the detainee prior to his being informed of his right to counsel. By so doing, the police officer violated the accused's rights under s. 10(*b*) and obtained the "breathalyzer evidence" in a manner which infringed and denied those rights.

I would decide the disposition of this case as does Estey J., and for the reasons he sets out in his judgment. Indeed, I am of the view that admitting the breathalyzer evidence in this case would bring the administration of justice into disrepute. Having so concluded, I need not express any views as regards the exclusion of evidence under s. 24(1).

I would therefore dismiss the appeal.

LeDain J. (dissenting): — This appeal [from (1983), 5 C.C.C. (3d) 409, affirming 70 C.C.C. (2d) 468] raises the following questions on which there have been differing opinions in provincial Courts of Appeal:

1. Does a person upon whom a demand is made pursuant to s. 235(1) of the Criminal Code to accompany a police officer to a police station and to submit to a breathalyzer test have the right to counsel guaranteed by s. 10 of the Canadian Charter of Rights and Freedoms?

2. If there has been an infringement or denial of the right to counsel, can the evidence obtained by the breathalyzer test be excluded pursuant to s. 24(1) of the Charter on the ground that its exclusion is considered by the court to be appropriate and just in the circumstances or may it be excluded pursuant only to s. 24(2) on the ground that it was obtained in a manner that infringed or denied the right to counsel and that, having regard to all the circumstances, its admission would bring the administration of justice into disrepute?

3. If the evidence was obtained in a manner that infringed or denied the right to counsel, and its exclusion is to be governed exclusively by the test in s. 24(2) of the Charter, what is the meaning and application to be given to that test in the circumstances of the present case?

Section 235(1) of the Criminal Code and ss. 10 and 24 of the Charter are as follows:

> 235.(1) Where a peace officer on reasonable and probable grounds believes that a person is committing, or at any time within the preceding two hours has committed, an offence under section 234 or 236, he may, by demand made to that person forthwith or as soon as practicable, require him to provide then or as soon thereafter as is practicable such samples of his breath as in the opinion of a qualified technician referred to in subsection 237(6) are necessary to enable a proper analysis to

be made in order to determine the proportion, if any, of alcohol in his blood, and to accompany the peace officer for the purpose of enabling such samples to be taken.

10. Everyone has the right on arrest or detention

(*a*) to be informed promptly of the reasons therefor;

(*b*) to retain and instruct counsel without delay and to be informed of that right; and

(*c*) to have the validity of the detention determined by way of *habeas corpus* and to be released if the detention is not lawful . . .

24.(1) Anyone whose rights or freedoms, as guaranteed by this Charter, have been infringed or denied may apply to a court of competent jurisdiction to obtain such remedy as the court considers appropriate and just in the circumstances.

(2) Where, in proceedings under subsection (1), a court concludes that evidence was obtained in a manner that infringed or denied any rights or freedoms guaranteed by this Charter, the evidence shall be excluded if it is established that, having regard to all the circumstances, the admission of it in the proceedings would bring the administration of justice into disrepute.

I

The appeal is by leave of this court from the judgment of the Saskatchewan Court of Appeal on 15th April 1983 dismissing an appeal by way of stated case from a judgment of Muir Prov. J. of the Provincial Court of Saskatchewan on 30th July 1982, which dismissed a charge that the respondent.

. . . on or about the 25th day of April A.D. 1982 at the City of Moose Jaw, in the Province of Saskatchewan, did unlawfully drive a motor vehicle while having consumed alcohol in such quantity that the proportion thereof in this blood exceeds 80 milligrams of alcohol in 100 millilitres of blood, contrary to Section 236(1) of the Criminal Code.

The facts found by Muir Prov. J. at the trial of the respondent are set out in the stated case as follows:

(a) On April 24th, 1982, at approximately 10:30 P.M., the accused was operating a motor vehicle in a street in the City of Moose Jaw at which time he lost control of the vehicle and it collided with a tree at the side of the street.

(b) Very shortly thereafter, Constable Measner of the Moose Jaw City Police Department arrived at the scene and conducted an investigation. Constable Measner, having reasonable and probable grounds for doing so, made a demand on the accused under the provisions of Section 235(1) of the Criminal Code requiring the accused to accompany him for the purpose of obtaining samples of the accused's breath for analysis. The accused accompanied the officer and supplied samples of his breath in compliance with the demand.

(c) The accused was at no time informed of any rights to retain and instruct counsel.

(d) The accused was co-operative throughout the investigation and was at no time placed under arrest.

In the reasons which he delivered on behalf of the majority for the Saskatchewan Court of Appeal Tallis J.A. said at p. 420 [C.C.C.]:

It is common ground between counsel that after a demand was made under s. 235(1) of the *Criminal Code*, the respondent accompanied the officer in a patrol car to the City Police Station in Moose Jaw, where the breathalyzer tests were subsequently conducted.

There was no evidence that the accused, of his own knowledge, was aware of his right to retain and instruct counsel.

At the trial of the respondent the Crown sought to tender in evidence the certificate of analysis prepared, pursuant to s. 237 of the Criminal Code, by the technician who conducted the breathalyzer test. Counsel for the respondent objected to the admission of the certificate and applied, pursuant to s. 24 of the Charter, for its exclusion on the ground that the respondent had been denied the right, guaranteed by s. 10 of the Charter, to be informed, upon arrest or detention, of his right to retain and instruct counsel without delay. The trial judge allowed the application, ordered the exclusion of the certificate, and for lack of other evidence of the respondent's blood-alcohol level dismissed the charge. He held that the respondent had been "detained" within the meaning of s. 10 of the Charter and that the court was empowered by s. 24(1) thereof to exclude the certificate if it considered such exclusion to be appropriate and just in the circumstances, and that it was not confined to the test laid down in s. 24(2) — that the admission of the evidence would bring the administration of justice into disrepute.

The questions put to the Court of Appeal in the stated case were as follows:

> (1) Did the court err in law in holding that the accused person, Paul Mathew Therens, had been detained within the meaning of Section 10 of the Canadian Charter of Rights and Freedoms?
>
> (2) Did the court err in law in holding that it had a power to exclude evidence under sub-section (1) of Section 24 of the Canadian Charter of Rights and Freedoms whether or not admitting the evidence in question would bring the administration of justice into disrepute?
>
> (3) Did the court err in law in holding that it was just and appropriate in the circumstances of this case to exclude from evidence the Certificate of Analyses tendered by the prosecution?

At the hearing of the appeal the third question was abandoned by counsel for the Crown on the ground that it did not involve a question of law alone. A majority of the Saskatchewan Court of Appeal answered the first two questions in the negative and dismissed the appeal. Tallis J.A., with whom Bayda C.J.S. and Hall and Cameron JJ.A. concurred, held that the restraint of the respondent's liberty effected by the demand pursuant to s. 235(1) of the Criminal Code amounted to a detention within the meaning of s. 10 of the Charter and that accordingly there had been an infringement or a denial of the respondent's right to be informed of his right to retain and instruct counsel without delay, and, further, that the certificate of analysis could be excluded from the evidence pursuant to s. 24(1) of the Charter, notwithstanding the terms of s. 24(2), which refer expressly to the exclusion of evidence obtained in a manner that infringes or denies any right or freedom guaranteed by the Charter. Bayda C.J.S. wrote a separate concurring opinion with reference to the power to exclude evidence under s. 24(2). Brownridge J.A., dissenting, held that there had not been a detention within the meaning of s. 10 of the Charter, but that in any event the exclusion of evidence as a remedy under s. 24 was governed exclusively by the terms of subs. (2) thereof.

[His Lordship's discussion of section 10 of the Charter is omitted. Having found a *prima facie* breach of section 10, His Lordship proceeded with a section 1 analysis.]

For these reasons I am of the opinion that the s. 235(1) demand to accompany the police officer to a police station and to submit to a breathalyzer test resulted in the detention of the respondent within the meaning of s. 10 of the Charter.

The respondent was accordingly entitled at the time of his detention to be informed of his right to retain and instruct counsel without delay, and there was an infringement or denial of this right, unless it can be shown that the right to retain and instruct counsel (and consequently the right to be informed of such right) does not exist in the context of a s. 235(1) demand by reason of a limit which meets the requirements of s. 1 of the Charter:

> 1. *The Canadian Charter of Rights and Freedoms* guarantees the rights and freedoms set out in it subject only to such reasonable limits prescribed by law as can be demonstrably justified in a free and democratic society.

Section 1 requires that the limit be prescribed by law, that it be reasonable, and that it be demonstrably justified in a free and democratic society. The requirement that the limit be prescribed by law is chiefly concerned with the distinction between a limit imposed by law and one that is arbitrary. The limit will be prescribed by law within the meaning of s. 1 if it is expressly provided for by statute or regulation, or results by necessary implication from the terms of a statute or regulation or from its operating requirements. The limit may also result from the application of a common law rule. Section 235(1) and the related breathalyzer provisions of the Criminal Code do not expressly purport to limit the right to counsel. Such a limit, if it exists, must result by implication from their terms or operating requirements. For example, the Saskatchewan Court of Appeal in *R. v. Talbourdet* [(1984) 39 C.R. (3d) 210] found that such a limit resulted from the requirement under s. 234.1(1) of the Criminal Code that a sample of breath be provided "forthwith" into a roadside screening device. The court held that this requirement precluded contact with counsel prior to compliance with a s. 234.1(1) demand. In the case of a s. 235(1) demand, the implications from the terms and operating requirements are somewhat different. A s. 235(1) demand must be made "forthwith or as soon as practicable" and the person upon whom the demand is made is required to provide a sample of breath "then or as soon thereafter as is practicable". Such samples can be used in evidence as proof of an offence under s. 234 or s. 236 of the Criminal Code only if (s. 237(1)(*c*)(ii)):

> (ii) each sample was taken as soon as practicable after the time when the offence was alleged to have been committed and in any event not later than two hours after that time, with an interval of at least fifteen minutes between the times when the samples were taken.

This two-hour operating requirement does not, as in the case of the "forthwith" requirement of a s. 234.1(1) demand, preclude any contact at all with counsel prior to the breathalyzer test. The right, at the time of the detention effected by a s. 235(1) demand, to be informed of the right to retain and instruct counsel without delay is not, therefore, subject to a limit prescribed by law within the meaning of s. 1 of the Charter. Whether the two-hour operating requirement of s. 237(1) imposes a justified limit on the nature or extent of the access to counsel that may be afforded in particular circumstances is something that need not be considered in this case.

### III

It is necessary now to consider whether the evidence provided by the breathalyzer test should have been excluded, pursuant to s. 24 of the Charter, because of this infringement or denial of the right to counsel. For convenience I set out s. 24 again as follows:

> 24. (1) Anyone whose rights or freedoms, as guaranteed by this Charter, have been infringed or denied may apply to a court of competent jurisdiction to obtain such remedy as the court considers appropriate and just in the circumstances.

EXCLUSION OF EVIDENCE 1385

(2) Where, in proceedings under subsection (1), a court concludes that evidence was obtained in a manner that infringed or denied any rights or freedoms guaranteed by this Charter, the evidence shall be excluded if it is established that, having regard to all the circumstances, the admission of it in the proceedings would bring the administration of justice into disrepute.

As indicated earlier in these reasons, the first issue under s. 24 is whether, as was held by the majority of the Saskatchewan Court of Appeal, evidence may be excluded pursuant to s. 24(1) on the ground that it is appropriate and just in the circumstances to do so, or whether it may be excluded pursuant only to s. 24(2) on the ground that, having regard to all the circumstances, the admission of it in the proceedings would bring the administration of justice into disrepute. Tallis J.A., with whom Hall and Cameron JJ.A. concurred, said that the view which would limit the exclusion of evidence to the terms of s. 24(2) would in many cases leave an individual whose rights or freedoms had been infringed or denied without any suitable or effective remedy. In his separate concurring reasons on this issue, Bayda C.J.S. said that had Parliament intended that s. 24(2) should be the exclusive basis for the exclusion of evidence because of an infringement or denial of a right or freedom guaranteed by the Charter it would have used the word "only" after the word "excluded" in the subsection. Although it was not necessary for him to express an opinion on this issue, in view of his conclusion on the question of detention, Brownridge J.A. briefly indicated that in his opinion evidence could be excluded under s. 24 of the Charter only if its admission would bring the administration of justice into disrepute. He said [at p. 393]:

It appears anomalous to me that the very power which is so circumscribed in s. 24(2) should be available to a court under s. 24(1) without any such restriction.

The trial judge and the majority of the Court of Appeal held that, while s. 24(2) imposed a *duty* to exclude evidence if its admission would bring the administration of justice into disrepute, s. 24(1) conferred a *discretion* to exclude it if such exclusion appeared to the court to be appropriate and just in the circumstances. It would appear that this distinction between duty and discretion was the principal rationale for the majority view that the framers of the Charter intended to provide two different bases for the exclusion of evidence where there has been an infringement or a denial of a guaranteed right or freedom.

I do not find it necessary to consider whether we should look, as was suggested by counsel for the appellant, at the legislative history of s. 24 as an aid to the determination of this issue. I am satisfied from the words of s. 24 that s. 24(2) was intended to be the sole basis for the exclusion of evidence because of an infringement or a denial of a right or freedom guaranteed by the Charter. It is clear, in my opinion, that in making explicit provision for the remedy of exclusion of evidence in s. 24(2), following the general terms of s. 24(1), the framers of the Charter intended that this particular remedy should be governed entirely by the terms of s. 24(2). It is not reasonabe to ascribe to the framers of the Charter an intention that the courts should address two tests or standards on an application for the exclusion of evidence — first, whether the admission of the evidence would bring the administration of justice into disrepute and, if not, secondly, whether its exclusion would nevertheless be appropriate and just in the circumstances. The inevitable result of this alternative test or remedy would be that s. 24(2) would become a dead letter.

The framers of the Charter could not have intended that the explicit and deliberately adopted limitation in s. 24(2) on the power to exclude evidence because of an infringement or a denial of a guaranteed right or freeom should be undermined or circumvented in such a manner. The opening words of s. 24(2) "Where, in proceedings under subsection (1)" simply refer, in my view, to an application for relief under s. 24(1). They reinforce the conclusion that the test set out in s. 24(2) is to be the exhaustive one for the remedy of exclusion of evidence. I conclude, therefore, that the Saskatchewan Court of Appeal erred in law in affirming the exclusion of the evidence provided by the breathalyzer test on the ground that it was appropriate and just in the circumstances, within the meaning of s. 24(1) of the Charter.

IV

It is necessary, then, to consider the meaning of the test or standard prescribed by s. 24(2) and its application to the facts as established by the record in this case. There are two requirements for the exclusion of evidence pursuant to s. 24(2): (a) that the evidence has been obtained in a manner that infringed or denied a right or freedom guaranteed by the Charter; and (b) that, having regard to all the circumstances, the admission of the evidence would bring the administration of justice into disrepute. The first requirement suggests that there must be some connection or relationship between the infringement or denial of the right or freedom in question and the obtaining of the evidence the exclusion of which is sought by the application. Some courts have held, or appear to have assumed, that the relationship must be one of causation, similar to the "but for" causation requirement of tort law: see Fleming, The Law of Torts, 6th ed. (1983), p. 171. This was essentially the view applied by Gushue J.A. on behalf of the Newfoundland Court of Appeal in *R. v. Trask* [(1983), 6 C.C.C. (3d) 132] where he said at 137:

> The evidence was not obtained in contravention of the Charter. It was properly obtained in accordance with the provisions of the *Criminal Code*. There is no evidence that the accused had any reasonable excuse to refuse to provide samples of his breath. If he had been informed of his right to retain and instruct counsel and had indeed consulted counsel, counsel would have undoubtedly advised him of his obligation to provide the samples demanded.

In my opinion, the words "obtained in a manner that infringed or denied any rights or freedoms guaranteed by this Charter", particularly when they are read with the French version, "obtenus dans des conditions qui portent atteinte aux droits ou libertés garantis par la présente charte", do not connote or require a relationship of causation. It is sufficent if the infringement or denial of the right or freedom has preceded, or occurred in the course of, the obtaining of the evidence. It is not necessary to establish that the evidence would not have been obtained but for the violation of the Charter. Such a view gives adequate recognition to the intrinsic harm that is caused by a violation of a Charter right or freedom, apart from its bearing on the obtaining of evidence. I recognize, however, that in the case of derivative evidence, which is not what is in issue here, some consideration may have to be given in particular cases to the question of relative remoteness.

In the result, I am of the opinion that the evidence represented by the certificate of analysis in this case was obtained in a manner that infringed or denied the respondent's right to be informed of his right to retain and instruct counsel without delay and thus meets the first requirement under s. 24(2).

The meaning and application of the words in s. 24(2) "if it is established that, having regard to all the circumstances; the admission of it in the proceedings would bring the administration of justice into disrepute" have been the subject of considerable judicial and academic commentary, which has looked for guidance not only to the words of s. 24(2) but to a variety of sources, including the common law respecting the exclusion of illegally obtained evidence in Canada, England and other jurisdictions of the Commonwealth, experience with the American "absolute" exclusionary rule, various recommendations for change in the law prior to the Charter, the judgments of Estey J. and Lamer J. in *Rothman v. R.*, [1981] 1 S.C.R. 640 and the legislative history of s. 24(2).

On the whole, Courts of Appeal have adopted, in some cases with certain reservations, what has come to be known as the "community shock" test suggested by Lamer J. in *Rothman*: see *R. v. Collins*, [1983] 5 W.W.R. 43 (B.C.C.A.); *R. v. Cohen* (1983), 33 C.R. (3d) 151 (B.C.C.A.); *R. v. Stevens* (1983), 35 C.R. (3d) 1 (N.S.C.A.); *R. v. Chapin* (1983), 43 O.R. (2d) 458, (C.A.); *R. v. Manninen* (1983), 43 O.R. (2d) 731 (C.A.); and *R. v. Simmons* (1984), 45 O.R. (2d) 609 (C.A.).

The issue in *Rothman* was the admissibility of a statement made by the accused while he was in his cell, and after he had indicated to the police that he did not wish to make a statement, to a police officer posing as a truck driver detained for a traffic violation. The majority of this court held that the statement by the accused was voluntary and therefore admissible. Lamer J., while agreeing in the result, held that a statement, although elicited under circumstances which would not render it inadmissible, should nevertheless be excluded if its use in the proceedings would, as a result of what was said or done by any person in authority in eliciting the statement, bring the administration of justice into disrepute. He held that what would bring the administration of justice into disrepute would be police conduct that shocked the community.

Estey J., dissenting, with whom Laskin C.J.C. concurred, held that the statement should be ruled inadmissible because it was given in circumstances which would bring the administration of justice into disrepute. The test of what would bring the administration of justice into disrepute, in his view, was what would be prejudicial to the public interest in the integrity of the judicial process.

The test suggested by Estey J. has been perceived as a less restrictive one than that suggested by Lamer J., partly, it would seem, because it led to a different conclusion, on the facts of the case, as to whether the police conduct would bring the administration of justice into disrepute.

In *Cohen*, supra, Anderson J.A., dissenting, said that he favoured the test suggested by Estey J. Several academic commentaries have expressed or implied agreement with this view.

In *Manninen, Chapin*, and *Simmons*, all supra, the Ontario Court of Appeal, while acknowledging that what would shock the community would clearly bring the administration of justice into disrepute, indicated that it did not think the application of the words in s. 24(2) should be limited to this test. In *Simmons*, Howland C.J.O. said at 634:

> If the evidence is obtained in such a manner as to shock the Canadian community as a whole, it would no doubt be inadmissible as bringing the administration of justice into disrepute. There may, however, be instances where the administration of justice is brought into disrepute within s. 24(2) without necessarily shocking the Canadian community as a whole. In my opinion, it is pref-

erable to consider every case on its merits as to whether it satisfies the requirements of s. 24(2) of the Charter and not to substitute a "community shock" or any other test for the plain words of the statute.

I agree, with respect, that we should not substitute for the words of s. 24(2) another expression of the standard, drawn from a different jurisprudential context. The values which must be balanced in making the determination required by s. 24(2) have been placed in a new relationship of relative importance by the constitutional status given to guaranteed rights and freedoms by the Charter. The central concern of s. 24(2) would appear to be the maintenance of respect for and confidence in the administration of justice, as that may be affected by the violation of constitutional rights and freedoms. There is clearly, of course, by implication, the other value which must be taken into consideration in the application of s. 24(2) — that is, the availability of otherwise admissible evidence for the ascertainment of truth in the judicial process, particularly in the administration of the criminal law. The issue under s. 24(2) is the circumstances in which that value must yield to the protection and enforcement of constitutional rights and freedoms by what may be in a particular case the only remedy.

The factors or circumstances to be taken into consideration in determining whether the admission of evidence would bring the administration of justice into disrepute have also been the subject of considerable commentary by courts and scholars. It would not be wise to attempt an exhaustive identification of the relevant factors in this case. However, certain of them have, in my opinion, been properly affirmed in the cases as being of particular relevance and weight, expecially in the context of the right under s. 8 of the Charter to be secure against unreasonable search and seizure. In this context the two principal considerations in the balancing which must be undertaken are the relative seriousness of the constitutional violation and the relative seriousness of the criminal charge. The relative seriousness of the constitutional violation has been assessed in the light of whether it was committed in good faith, or was inadvertent or of a merely technical nature, or whether it was deliberate, wilful or flagrant. Another relevant consideration is whether the action which constituted the constitutional violation was motivated by urgency or necessity to prevent the loss or destruction of the evidence.

The application of these factors to a denial of the right to counsel involves, in my view, a different balance because of the importance of that right in the administration of criminal justice. In my opinion, the right to counsel is of such fundamental importance that its denial in a criminal law context must prima facie discredit the administration of justice. That effect is not diminished but, if anything, increased by the relative seriousness of the possible criminal law liability. In view, however, of the judgment of this court in *Chromiak*, the police officer in this case was in my opinion entitled to assume in good faith that the respondent did not have a right to counsel on a demand under s. 235(1) of the Criminal Code. Because of this good faith reliance, I am unable to conclude, having regard to all the circumstances, as required by s. 24(2) of the Charter, that the admission of the evidence of the breathalyzer test in this particular case would bring the administration of justice into disrepute: see Tarnopolsky J.A. in *Simmons*, supra, at 645. The evidence cannot, therefore, be excluded.

As this conclusion indicates, I am also of the opinion that the question whether evidence must be excluded because, having regard to all the circumstances, its admission would bring the administration of justice into disrepute is a question of law which may be determined by a court without evidence of the actual or likely effect of such admission on public opinion. Obviously the application of the relevant factors or considerations will turn in some cases on matters of fact which must be established by evidence, but the meaning and application of the standard in s. 24(2) is, like other questions of admissibility of evidence, a question of law. A court is the best judge of what would bring the administration of justice into disrepute. There is no reliable evidentiary basis for determining what the actual effect on public opinion would be of the admission of evidence in the circumstances of a particular case. The suggestion of opinion polls (see D. Gibson, "Determining Disrepute: Opinion Polls and the Canadian Charter of Rights and Freedoms" (1983), 61 Can. Bar Rev. 377) encounters, in my opinion, two fatal objections. The first is the requirement which Professor Gibson refers to as "specificity". How could "all the circumstances" of a case and the necessary balancing exercise be conveyed in an opinion poll or survey? The second objection is the cost of requiring such evidence, which, since it would have to be borne by the person whose constitutional right or freedom had been violated, would surely be a further factor reducing availability of the remedy provided by s. 24(2). The exlcusion of evidence under s. 24(2) does not, as has been suggested by some, involve the exercise of a discretion. Section 24(2) involves the application of a broad test or standard, which necessarily gives a court some latitude, but that is not, strictly speaking, a discretion. A discretion exists where there is a choice to do one thing or another, not merely because what is involved is the application of a flexible standard. Under the terms of s. 24(2), where a judge concludes that the admission of evidence would bring the administration of justice into disrepute, he or she has a duty, not a discretion, to exclude the evidence. This distinction is of some importance, of course, with reference to the scope and review of a determination under s. 24(2).

I would accordingly allow the appeal, set aside the judgments of the Saskatchewan Court of Appeal and Muir Prov. J., and order a new trial.

# 3. Application and Supremacy — Sections 32 and 52

## (a) General

### Note on the Application of the Charter

Pursuant to section 32(1) of the *Charter*, the *Charter* applies to Parliament, the provincial legislatures and the federal and provincial governments. While section 32 does not specifically say so, in my view the presence of section 32 clearly implies that the *Charter* does not apply directly to private activity: *Bhindi v. B.C. Projectionists Local 348 of Int'l Alliance of Picture Machine Operators* (1985), 63 B.C.L.R. 352 (S.C.); *Re Peg Win Real Estate Ltd. and Winnipeg Real Estate Board* (1985), 19 D.L.R. (4th) 438 (Man. Q.B.); *Chyz v. Appraisal Institute of Canada* (1984), 36 Sask.

R. 266 (Q.B.); *Re Wark and Green* (1984), 15 D.L.R. (4th) 577 at 579 (N.B.Q.B.). Sections 1 and 32(1) of the *Charter* provide as follows:

> 1. The *Canadian Charter of Rights and Freedoms* guarantees the rights and freedoms set out in it subject only to such reasonable limits prescribed by law as can be demonstrably justified in a free and democratic society.

> 32.(1) This Charter applies

>> (a) to the Parliament and government of Canada in respect of all matters within the authority of Parliament including all matters relating to the Yukon Territory and Northwest Territories; and

>> (b) to the legislature and government of each province in respect of all matters within the authority of the legislature of each province.

Section 1 thus commences with the proposition that the *Charter* guarantees the rights set out therein. However, it does not say against whom those rights may be asserted. Section 32(1) goes on to say that the *Charter* applies to the Parliament and government of Canada and the provincial legislatures and governments. Because section 32(1) does not contain the word "only" or some other words of exclusivity, there is arguably an ambiguity as to whether section 32(1) is an exclusive code of the *Charter*'s application or whether it may apply beyond the boundaries of section 32(1) to private activity generally. The better view is that the *Charter* applies only to legislation and government but not to private activity.

This position is supported by *Chyz v. Appraisal Institute of Canada, supra*, where the applicant, a real estate appraiser and accredited member of the respondent Institute was the subject of disciplinary action. The Institute was established as a non-share corporation pursuant to the provincial *Companies Act* essentially to promote and advance the profession. The Court found that the Institute was a voluntary, private organization and, while membership was important to any person practising as an appraiser in Canada, lack of membership would not preclude a person from carrying on an appraisal practice in the province. Further, Wright J. held at 273

> The authority exercised by the committee as a creation of the institute is not statutory. Certiorari and prohibition, generally speaking, will not lie against a private body which derives its jurisdiction from the consent of its members banded together in a voluntary association. The institute is such an association.

In response to the applicant's argument that his rights under section 7 of the *Charter* which provides that "everyone" is entitled to life, liberty and security of the person, were infringed, Wright J. considered whether the *Charter* could apply in light of section 32(1). Wright J. said

> Views vary as to how far the language of s. 32 of the *Charter* ought to be extended. I note on one side the vigorous arguments of Professor Dale Gibson that the *Charter* should apply equally to the public and private sectors of Canadian life and apply as much to those engaged in private activities as employers, entrepreneurs or parents as those who exercise governmental responsibilities: *The Charter of Rights and the "Private Sector"* (1982) 12 Man. Law Journal 213. Others, such as Professor Hogg, author of *The Canada Act* annotated and Professor Swinton, a contributor to *The Canadian Charter of Rights and Freedoms* — commentary, (1982) are not so convinced. A bench mark may be found in this debate, I have concluded, by considering again the criterion applied earlier to determine what administrative functions fall within and without the area of judicial review. If a body exercises statutory power — that is authority expressly granted by a legislative

body — it may be brought within the scope of the *Charter* as it represents a kind of governmental power. Conversely, if the body scrutinized is a private and voluntary association or corporation created pursuant to a general or public law of the legislature, it cannot and should not be categorized as governmental in nature even if its activities affect important interests of its members. There are provincial laws to regulate such private entities and the general equitable powers of the courts are available also. As vital a balm as the *Charter* may be for the cure of society's ills and injustices it is not, with the greatest respect to the views of those otherwise minded, a panacea. Creative and liberal application of the *Charter* is to be encouraged but interpreters must remember that the words of s. 32 are inherently restrictive, and that apparently by design.

Accordingly Wright J. held that the *Charter* did not apply to the Institute as a private body. See also *Bhindi, supra; Re Peg Win Real Estate Ltd., supra.*

In *Re McCutcheon and Toronto* (1983), 41 O.R. (2d) 652 (H.C.) Linden J. had to consider whether municipal by-laws were subject to the *Charter*. His reasoning appears to assume that the *Charter* applies only to government, and that the relevant issue is simply whether a municipal by-law comes within that term. His reasoning in full on the point is set out at 662-3 as follows:

> Second, s. 32(1) contemplates municipal by-laws being subject to the Charter. Counsel for the respondents point out there is no express mention of municipal governments and their by-laws in s. 32 which provides that the Charter applies to the Parliament and Government of Canada and the Legislature and government of each province. Absent a specific reference to municipal governments in s. 32(1), it is contended, that the Charter does not apply to them and, hence, it cannot render inoperative their by-laws, notwithstanding any inconsistency between a by-law and constitutionally guaranteed right or freedom.
>
> This cannot be the case, for it would permit circumvention of the Charter through delegation to any body that is not classified as part of the Government of Canada or of a province. This is contrary to the tenor of s. 32(1), which provides that subordinates (the Governments of Canada and of each province) cannot do that which their principals (Parliament and the Legislatures) cannot do. It must be that more junior subordinates, like municipalities, are to be similarly bound by the Charter.
>
> The American experience is of help here. The *Bill of Rights* in the United States is, on its face, addressed exclusively to the federal and state governments. Private activity offensive to the Bill's guarantees of liberty and equality can be enjoined, however, where "state" (i.e., governmental) action or inaction can be characterized as tacit affirmation of the private action. Most particularly, delegation of government authority will permit a conclusion of "state action", as in *Evans et al. v. Newton*, 382 U.S. 296 at 299 (1966), where the U.S. Supreme Court declared:
>
> > [W]hen private individuals or groups are endowed by the State with powers or functions governmental in nature, they become agencies or instrumentalities of the State and subject to its constitutional limitations.
>
> It follows that municipal governments in the U.S. are bound by the *Bill of Rights*. Thus, in *Buchanan v. Warley*, 245 U.S. 60 at 81 (1917), the U.S. Supreme Court used constitutional principles to strike down a municipal ordinance which denied members of one race the right to occupy a house on a block inhabited primarily by persons of another race. Speaking for the court, Mr. Justice Day stated:
>
> > It is urged that this proposed segregation will promote the public peace by preventing race conflicts. Desirable as this is, and important as is the preservation of the public peace, this aim cannot be accomplished by laws *or ordinances* which deny rights created or protected by the federal constitution. (Emphasis added.)
>
> In the U.S. the concept of "state action" is subtle and elusive. The U.S. Supreme Court itself has knowledge that formulating "an infallible test" is "an impossible task": *Reitman v. Mulkey*, 387 U.S. 369 at 378 (1967). There are many cases grappling with the issue and the scholars have not yet resolved it definitively: see Tribe, *American Constitutional Law* (1978), at p. 1155.

The Charter of Rights and Freedoms is meant to curtail *absolute* parliamentary and legislative supremacy in Canada. As such, the Charter addresses itself expressly to the two levels of government whose primary legislative organs have been held in the past to be sovereign within their respective spheres. Municipalities, though a distinct level of government for some purposes, have no constitutional status; they are merely "creatures of the legislature", with no existence independent of the Legislature or government of the province. Hence, just as the provincial Legislatures and governments are bound by the Charter, so too are municipalities, whose by-laws and other actions must be considered, for the purposes of s. 32(1), as actions of the provincial government which gave them birth. Thus, these by-laws must comply with the Charter by virtue of both s. 52 and s. 32.

It is useful as well in this connection to quote the views of Professor Hogg in *Canada Act, 1982 Annotated* (1982) at pp. 76-7:

Private activity is not covered by the Charter. Such actions as an employer restricting an employee's freedom of speech or assembly, a parent restricting mobility of a child, or a landlord discriminating on the basis of race in his selection of tenants, cannot be breaches of the Charter, because in no case is there any action by the Parliament or government of Canada or by the Legislature or government of a province. (Accord, Testimony of Mr. F.J.E. Jordan, Senior Counsel, Public Law, federal Department of Justice, in *Minutes of Proceedings and Evidence of the Special Joint Committee of the Senate and of the House of Commons on the Constitution of Canada*, First Session of Thirty-second Parliament, 1980-81, p. 49:47 (January 30, 1981).) In cases where private activity results in a restriction of a civil liberty there may be a remedy for the aggrieved person under a human rights code (but cf. *Bd. of Governors of Seneca College v. Bhadauria* (1981) 124 D.L.R. (3d) 193), under labour law or family law, tort or contract or property, or under some other branch of the law governing relations between private individuals or organizations; but there will be no breach of the Charter. The exclusion of private activity is not only clear from s. 32, it is the result one would expect: one would expect a constitution to empower and regulate the institutions of government, not the relationships between private individuals or organizations. Indeed, the application of the Charter to private activity would create a vast new body of constitutionally-based tort law, because the Charter's enforcement provision (s. 24) would authorize lawsuits for redress of private infringements of the civil liberties specified in the Charter. That would be a strange new branch of constitutional law. (In the United States the Bill of Rights has been held inapplicable to private action; "state action" must be present before the bill of rights can be invoked: Tribe, *American Constitutional Law* (1978), ch 18).

There is perhaps a faint argument that the Charter applies to the actions of all Canadian corporations, whether publicly or privately owned, and even if they are engaged only in commercial activity. The argument would start from the premise that the existence and powers of a modern corporation depend upon the statute which authorized its incorporation. In that sense, it could be argued, all modern corporations act under statutory authority and should be held to be bound by the Charter. But the better view is that a corporation, once it has been brought into existence and empowered (admittedly under statutory authority), is thereafter exercising the same proprietary and contractual powers as are available to any private person. In the context of distribution-of-powers limitations, it is reasonably clear that a corporation is not confined to activities which are within the legislative authority of the incorporating jurisdiction (Hogg, *Constitutional Law of Canada* (1977), 347-353). It is therefore probable that corporations are not subject to the restrictions of the Charter either. This conclusion is reinforced by the consideration, advanced in the previous paragraph, that in the absence of very clear language a constitution should not be interpreted as regulating the relationships between private individuals or organizations.

Professor Hogg repeats this view in expanded form in Hogg, *Constitutional Law of Canada* (2d ed., 1985) at pp. 670-8.

The above is reinforced by the fact that section 32(1) falls under the heading "Application of Charter", which points to the conclusion that sections 32 and 33 provide the exclusive code of the *Charter*'s application. The Supreme Court of Canada has already relied heavily on the "Mobility" heading in the *Charter* in *Law*

*Society of Upper Canada v. Skapinker* (1984), 9 D.L.R. (4th) 161 at 176-7 (S.C.C.) to interpret the mobility rights guarantee in section 6 of the *Charter* restrictively.

Professor Swinton is not as definite in her views as *Chyz, Bhindi,* or Hogg, but rather perceives a wider scope for the argument that parts of the *Charter* may apply to private activity. Nevertheless she agrees on balance both on policy and interpretational grounds in her article in Tarnopolsky and Beaudoin (eds.), *Canadian Charter of Rights and Freedoms: Commentary* (1982), ch. 3 at page 44-9, that the presence of s. 32(1) tilts the matter in favour of an interpretation that the *Charter of Rights* was designed to bind only governments. She states at page 44:

> That is the nature of a constitutional document: to establish the scope of governmental authority and to set out the term of the relationship between the citizen and the state and those between the organs of government. The purpose of a Charter of Rights is to regulate the relationship of an individual with the government by invalidating laws and governmental activity which infringe the rights guaranteed by the document, while relationships between individuals are left to the regulation of human rights codes, other statutes, and common law remedies, such as libel and slander laws.

This view is reinforced by the wording of section 32(1) which provides that the *Charter of Rights* applies "to the Parliament and government of Canada *in respect* of all matters within the authority of Parliament" (emphasis added). The earlier version debated in the House of Commons in April, 1981 referred to "the Parliament and government of Canada *and to all matters within* the authority of Parliament" (emphasis added). The change of "and to all matters" to "in respect of all matters" supports the view that a more restrictive interpretation was intended by the drafters of the document which was ultimately promulgated.

It should be noted, however, that, in the European Economic Community (E.E.C.), certain provisions in the Treaty of Rome have been applied directly to private activity. In *Defrenne v. SABENA*, [1976] 2 C.M.L.R. 98 (E.C.J.), Article 119 provides that:

> Each member-State shall during the first stage ensure and subsequently maintain the application of the principle that men and women should receive equal pay for equal work.

In the claim by an employee against her employer for equal pay for equal work, the European Court of Justice held at p. 124:

> The fact that certain provisions of the Treaty are formally addressed to the member-State does not prevent rights from being conferred at the same time on any individual who has an interest in the performance of the duties thus laid down.

For the endorsement of this principle in other equal pay cases, see *Macarthys v. Smith*, [1980] 2 C.M.L.R. 205 (E.C.J.) aff'd [1981] Q.B. 180 (Eng. C.A.); *Worringham and Humphreys v. Lloyds Bank*, [1981] 2 C.M.L.R. I (E.C.J.). A similar conclusion has been reached with respect to articles of the Treaty which require member-States to secure freedom of movement (Art. 48(1)), and to abolish discrimination based upon nationality in both employment (Art. 48(2)) and the establishment of non-citizens (Art. 52): see *Costa v. Ente Nazionale per l'Energia Elettrica (ENEL)*, [1964] C.M.L.R. 425 at 458 (E.C.J.).

It is questionable whether these cases are transferrable to the Canadian context. The provisions of the Treaty in question imposed an obligation on the member-State to take positive steps to secure the individual interests involved and to eliminate trade barriers. In the Canadian context, one would have to argue that the *Charter* imposes a positive burden on Parliament and the legislatures to scrutinize all of the common law and, where it violates a *Charter* provision, to legislate a remedy. Apart from section 23 of the *Charter* with regard to the establishment of minority language education facilities, the *Charter* does not contain language similar to the Treaty of Rome imposing positive obligations. Swinton says in her article at page 47 of *Canadian Charter of Rights and Freedoms: Commentary, supra*:

> The Charter of Rights contemplates no such positive obligations on governmental bodies to eliminate private discrimination or to enact protective legislation to ensure the continued existence of fundamental freedoms from private encroachment, except with regard to the establishment of minority language education facilities pursuant to s. 23. It might be suggested that the guarantee of "equal benefit" of the laws in s. 15(1) imposes such a positive obligation on governments, but the argument is tenuous. The reference to equal benefit of the laws is more appropriately invoked when a litigant claims that a statute provides benefits for one group and not another. The section does not impose an obligation of redistribution on governments, nor does it contemplate positive action. Because the Charter's purpose is to restrain government action, not to generate legislative action, the rationale invoked by the European Court of Justice for direct application of the Treaty — protection from reluctant legislatures — does not exist.

Notwithstanding the above, the view that the Charter applies exclusively to government activity has been rejected in two Alberta decisions. In *R. v. Lerke* (1984), 13 C.C.C. (3d) 515 (Alta. Q.B.), a tavern supervisor searched an accused's jacket and found a bag of marijuana. The trial judge excluded the evidence on the basis that it was obtained by way of an unreasonable search or seizure contrary to section 8 of the *Charter* and its admission would bring the administration of justice into disrepute. Rowbotham J. rejected the analogy of American cases on the basis that the wording in the *U.S. Constitution* is specifically limited to state action. By contrast, section 32(1) deals with Parliament, legislatures and governments but does not specifically exclude private activity. Rowbotham J. said at 518:

> It is obvious that, if the draftsman involved had intended to restrict the application of the Charter to matters between Government and citizen and not to matters between citizen and citizen this could have been achieved by the simple addition to the word 'only' in the first line so that it would have read 'This Charter *only* applies . . .'

Rowbotham J. relies for much of his reasoning upon a short comment by Professor Gibson, "The Charter of Rights and the Private Sector" (1982) 12 Man. L.J. 213. It should be noted that even Gibson admits that certain guarantees are specifically limited in their terms to government. By way of example, he notes in his article at p. 217 that the equality guarantee in s. 15(1) of the *Charter* is expressly limited to "laws" and that s. 11 is restricted to those "charged with an offence". He therefore concludes with respect to these guarantees that:

> Control of discrimination in the private sector therefore remains in the hands that dealt with the problem prior to the enactment of the *Charter*: federal and provincial human rights Commissions, provincial bills of rights, and so on. Legal rights under section 11 would similarly seem to be restricted by the words 'person charged with an offence' to those who have run afoul of the law and are prosecuted by governmental authorities.

The other Alberta case which would apply the *Charter* to private activity is *Re Edmonton Journal and A. G. Alta.* (1983), 4 C.C.C. (3d) 59 (Alta. Q.B.), where Dea J. said at 63:

On the issue of the applicability of American cases, a review of the two constitutions will disclose that the one (American) addresses itself to the question of whether a Congressional Act abridges the stated right whereas the other (Canadian) guarantees a particular right or freedom. Put simply the American Constitution protects the rights of citizens against government interference whereas the Canadian Constitution protects the rights of citizens against any interference, be it government or private. Because of that difference in concept the contest in Canada may be as in the United States, *i.e.* between government and citizen or it may be quite different, *i.e.*, between citizen and citizen. That difference makes the description, extent and quality of the guaranteed freedoms in Canada rather more significant, I think, than the same process in the United States. This is so because as the guaranteed freedoms are defined under the Charter, the freedoms so guaranteed not only limit government action which infringes or denies but also private action which has the same effect.

The major difficulty with Dea J.'s remarks in the *Edmonton Journal* case is that he looked at the freedom of expression guarantee in section 2(b) of the *Charter* in isolation, without any reference whatsoever to the possible limiting effect of section 32(1) of the *Charter*.

For a thoughtful piece advocating a wider application of the *Charter*, see Slattery, "Comment", (1985), 63 Can. Bar Rev. 148.

The most obvious source of international assistance in determining the extent of the *Charter*'s application is by analogy to the *U.S. Constitution*. As quoted earlier, Linden J. stated in *Re McCutcheon and Toronto, supra* that American cases are useful in Canada to determine the scope of the *Charter*'s application.

The *U.S. Constitution* clearly only applies to "state action" where, for example, the First Amendment provides that "Congress shall make no law ..." and the Fourteenth Amendment provides that "no State shall ... deny to any person within its jurisdiction the equal protection of the laws". Accordingly, the *U.S. Constitution* does not apply to transactions where there is insufficient government involvement: *Jackson v. Metropolitan Edison Co.* 419 U.S. 345 (1947); *Moose Lodge No. 107 v. Irvis*, 407 U.S. 163 (1972).

In *Jackson v. Metropolitan Edison*, the U.S. Supreme Court held that the due process clause in the Fourteenth Amendment did not govern Metropolitan Edison's dealings with its customers. This was so notwithstanding that the utility was heavily regulated in all aspects of its business and performed an important public function. In *Moose Lodge No. 107 v. Irvis*, the U.S. Supreme Court refused to apply the Fourteenth Amendment to a private club's policy of racial discrimination notwithstanding that the state had extended the privilege of a liquor licence to the club.

On the other hand, the U.S. Supreme Court has applied the *Constitution* even to private bodies where there was a high degree of government involvement in the enterprise, or where the enterprise itself had the trappings of government. Thus in *Burton v. Wilmington Parking Authority* 365 U.S. 715 (1961), the Fourteenth Amendment was held to prevent a private restaurateur from refusing to serve blacks where the restaurant was located in a building owned and operated by an agency of the State of Delaware and the premises were leased from that agency. Similarly, the U.S. Supreme Court held in *Marsh v. Alabama* 326 U.S. 501 (1946) that a state cannot impose criminal punishment on a person who undertakes to distribute religious literature on the premises of a company-owned town contrary to the wishes of the town's management. In *Marsh*, except for the private ownership, the town had all the characteristics of any other American town. It is interesting to note that the U.S. Supreme Court has refused to extend this "public function" test to shopping centre premises. While the initial jurisprudence in this regard was ambiguous, it is now settled that shopping centre owners are not engaged in "state action": see *Hudgens v. National Labour Relations Board* 424 U.S. 507 (1976); *Lloyd Corp. v. Tanner* 407 U.S. 551 (1972); *C.F. Amalgamated Food Employees' Union v. Logan Valley Plaza Inc.* 391 U.S. 308 (1968) (explained in *Hudgens* to have been overruled by *Lloyd Corp. v. Tanner*).

The most difficult state action case in the United States, and one which has the potential to obliterate the distinction between public and private activity, is *Shelley v. Kraemer* 334 U.S. 1 (1948). In that case, racially restrictive covenants were entered into among property owners to exclude, *inter alia*, blacks. In spite of these covenants a number of black people purchased houses from white owners. The beneficiaries of the covenants sued to enjoin the purchasers from taking possession of their property. The U.S. Supreme Court held that the equal protection guarantee in the Fourteenth Amendment was applicable and accordingly dismissed the suit. The Court held that, in having the state judicial machinery brought to bear to gain a remedy, there was sufficient state action to implicate the *Constitution*.

The difficulty with *Shelley v. Kraemer* is that all disputes among private litigants are ultimately enforceable in courts. One possible explanation of the case is that its principle may be applied only where the *Constitution* is used as a shield to prevent the state's judicial machinery from directly imposing a remedy upon the individual which is contrary to the *Constitution*. It may not be used as a sword to found a direct cause of action. This would explain the result in *New York Times v. Sullivan*, 376 U.S. 254 (1964), where a defendant was able to raise the First Amendment as a shield to bar a court from imposing damages for libel where the state common law standards did not meet the First Amendment test, and at the same time provide a point of reconciliation for cases like *Jackson v. Metropolitan Edison* and *Moose Lodge No. 107* where the U.S. Supreme Court refused to apply the *Constitution* to what it found to be private activity.

It is legitimate to ask whether the American authorities are applicable in Canada, given the somewhat different wording of our respective constitutional instruments. As previously discussed, Linden J. used American law in *Re McCutcheon* to interpret section 32. The Supreme Court of Canada cases decided to date indicate that American jurisprudence must be viewed with care, but is nonetheless highly persuasive. Thus in the recent *Lord's Day Act* case, *R. v. Big M Drug Mart Ltd.*, [1985] 1 S.C.R. 295 (S.C.C.) Dickson J. (as he then was) referred extensively to American jurisprudence and commentators in striking down the federal law. Similarly, in *Lawson v. Hunter*, [1984] 6 W.W.R. 577 (S.C.C.) Dickson J. (as he then was) used jurisprudence under the Fourth Amendment to interpret the guarantee against unreasonable search or seizure in section 8 of the *Charter*, notwithstanding that the Fourth Amendment is worded in a substantially different way.

In summary, in my view the inclusion of section 32(1), which in its wording is limited to government, together with the analogy to the American cases, is persuasive that the *Charter* does not apply directly to private activity.

It may, of course, apply indirectly by rendering invalid statutes or other laws which themselves regulate the relations of private persons *inter se*.

While the principle that the *Charter* applies to government but not private activity is easy to state, it is difficult to apply in practice. Naturally, it clearly applies to Parliament, the Legislatures, and their direct emanations in the form of government departments and agencies, and independent bodies such as provincial Bar Associations exercising statutory jurisdiction: see *Malartic Hygrade Gold Mines v. The Queen in Right of Quebec* (1982), 142 D.L.R. (3d) 512 (Que. S.C.); *Black v. Law Society of Alberta* (1983), 144 D.L.R. (3d) 439 (Alta. Q.B.), rev'd on other grounds 8 D.L.R. (4th) 346 (Alta. C.A.). Similarly, it applies to the activities and enactments of municipal governments and agencies: *Re McCutcheon and Toronto* (1983), 41 O.R. (2d) 652 (Ont. H.C.), and *at least* to those sorts of bodies exercising delegated state authority which the Supreme Court of Canada held in *A. G. Que. v. Blaikie (No. 2)*, [1981] S.C.R. 312 to fall within the ambit of s. 133 of the *Constitution Act, 1867*. Of course, as indicated by *McCutcheon, supra* in its holding that section 32 reaches down to municipalities, *Blaikie (No. 2)* is not an exhaustive definition for the purposes of section 32(1) of the *Charter*.

A number of sources may be useful in determining the reach of section 32. For example, cases holding that a given institution is entitled to crown immunity are strong authority for saying that the institution in question is part of "government" for *Charter* purposes and subject to its proscriptions. In addition, American cases and authorities on the state action doctrine will also be useful in their assessment and weighing of the various indicia of state involvement: see, for example, *Burton v. Wilmington Parking Authority, infra; Jackson v. Metropolitan Edison Co., infra; Moose Lodge No. 107 v. Irvis*, 407 U.S. 163 (1972). The American "public function" cases may be of some help as well, although they are in sufficient disarray that their usefulness is limited: *Marsh v. Alabama*, 326 U.S. 501 (1946); *Amalgamated Food Employees Local 590 v. Logan Valley Plaza*, 391 U.S. 308 (1968); *Lloyd Corp. v. Tanner*, 407 U.S. 551 (1972); *Hudgens v. NLRB*, 424 U.S. 507 (1976). On the state action doctrine generally, see Tribe, *American Constitutional Law* (1978), Ch. 18.

While pre-*Charter* cases and those from other jurisdictions will be useful, Canadian courts will have to devise new tests which are appropriate to the *Charter* context. Section 32 clearly casts a wide net, going beyond *Blaikie (No. 2)* and the Crown immunity cases. The courts must give "government" a definition which is sufficient to prevent government from directly or indirectly, and by commission or omission, proscribing *Charter* rights. The tests should include:

(1) the method by which the institution is created: for example, a body which is established by statute is at least *prima facie* a state organism. One should not overstate the importance of this indicator, because even purely private corporations derive their existence from the various *Corporations Acts*. The distinction between public and private activity would be obliterated if the mere fact of statutory creation was controlling;

(2) whether the organization performs functions that are public and governmental in nature. The degree to which the body performs a public function in the public interest is an important indicator of government action: *Marsh v. Alabama*, 326 U.S. 501 (1946); *Evans v. Newton*, 382 U.S. 296 (1966). The provincial Bar Associations are a good example: *Malartic, supra; Black, supra*. Crown corporations such as the Post Office or the Atomic Energy Commission are good illustrations as well. There is a presumption that Crown corporations are established in the public interest. This is so even where the function of the corporation may in one aspect be commercial. For example, Air Canada is a commercial airline, but at the same time is an integral part of the overall system of aeronautics regulation in Canada. The

CBC sells advertising air time, but its most important function is the preservation of Canadian culture. *Quaere*, whether the government can operate free of the strictures of the *Charter* when it intervenes in the economy in the same way as a private person or investor, be it through the medium of the Crown corporation or otherwise;

(3) extent of the intermingling of private and public actors for the performance of their functions: *Burton v. Wilmington Parking Authority*, 365 U.S. 715 (1961); *Buckton v. Nat'l Collegiate Athletic Assoc*, 366 F. Supp. 1152 (D. Mass. 1973); *Evans v. Newton, supra; cf. Jackson v. Metropolitan Edison Co.*, 419 U.S. 345 (1974).

(4) degree of state financing and control: it is arguable, for example, that Canadian universities are governed by the *Charter* notwithstanding that the government exercises very little control over staffing, curricula, tenure or day to day operations. Most if not all Canadian universities are established by statute to provide higher education, a quintessential public function, and receive the vast preponderance of their financing through government grants and subsidies. Thus, as with the state universities in the United States (see *University of California Regents v. Bakke*, 438 U.S. 265 (1978)), Canadian universities should be part of "government" for the purposes of section 32 of the *Charter*. See also *Cooper v. Aaron*, 358 U.S. 1 at 19 (1958).

(5) involvement of the body or person as part of an over-arching statutory or regulatory scheme.

## (b) Judicial Review of Cabinet Decisions, Justiciability and The Political Questions Doctrine

# OPERATION DISMANTLE v. R.

In the Supreme Court of Canada. [1985] 1 S.C.R. 441.

Dickson C.J.C., Ritchie, Estey, McIntyre, Chouinard, Lamer and Wilson JJ.
May 9, 1985.

[Ritchie J. did not take part in the judgment]

The judgment of Dickson C.J.C. and Estey, McIntyre, Chouinard and Lamer JJ. was delivered by

DICKSON C.J.C.:

This case arises out of the appellants' challenge under s. 7 of the *Canadian Charter of Rights and Freedoms* to the decision of the Federal Cabinet to permit the testing of the cruise missile by the United States of America in Canadian territory. The issue that must be addressed is whether the appellants' statement of claim should be struck out, before trial, as disclosing no reasonable cause of action. In their statement of claim, the appellants seek: (i) a declaration that the decision to permit the testing of the cruise missile is unconstitutional; (ii) injunctive relief to prohibit the testing; and (iii) damages. Cattanach J. of the Federal Court, Trial Division, refused the respondents' motion to strike. The Federal Court of Appeal unanimously allowed the respondents' appeal, struck out the statement of claim and dismissed the appellants' action.

The facts and procedural history of this case are fully set out and discussed in the reasons for judgment of Madame Justice Wilson. I agree with Madame Justice Wilson that the appellants' statement of claim should be struck out and this appeal dismissed. I have reached this conclusion, however, on the basis of reasons which differ somewhat from those of Madame Justice Wilson.

In my opinion, if the appellants are to be entitled to proceed to trial, their statement of claim must disclose facts, which, if taken as true, would show that the action of the Canadian Government could cause an infringement of their rights under s. 7 of the *Charter*. I have concluded that the causal link between the actions of the Canadian Government, and the alleged violation of appellants' rights under the *Charter* is simply too uncertain, speculative and hypothetical to sustain a cause of action. Thus, although decisions of the Federal Cabinet are reviewable by the Courts under the *Charter*, and the government bears a general duty to act in accordance with the *Charter*'s dictates, no duty is imposed on the Canadian Government by s. 7 of the *Charter* to refrain from permitting the testing of the cruise missile.

. . . .

### (b) *The Allegations of the Statement of Claim*

The principal allegation of the statement of claim [which is set out in relevant part in the judgment of Wilson J. *infra*] is that the testing of the cruise missile in Canada poses a threat to the lives and security of Canadians by increasing the risk of nuclear conflict, and thus violates the right to life, liberty and security of the person guaranteed by s. 7 of the *Charter*.

As a preliminary matter, it should be noted that the exact nature of the deprivation of life and security of the person that the appellants rely upon as the legal foundation for the violation of s. 7 they allege is not clear. There seem to be two possibilities. The violation could be the result of actual deprivation of life and security of the person that would occur in the event of a nuclear attack on Canada, or it could be the result of general insecurity experienced by all people in Canada as a result of living under the increased threat of nuclear war.

The first possibility is apparent on a literal reading of the statement of claim. The second possibility, however, appears to be more consistent with the appellants' submission at p. 31 of their factum, that:

> at the minimum, the above allegations show [in paragraph 7 of the statement of claim] that there is a 'threat' to the life and security of the appellants which 'threat', depending upon the construction of the concept 'infringe' or 'deny' in section 7 [sic], could arguably constitute an infringement of the person. The amendment to the Statement of Claim, rejected by the Court of Appeal, would have made the infringement or denial more explicit when it states: 'The very testing of the cruise missile per se in Canada endangers the *Charter of Rights and Freedoms* Section 7: (sic) Rights.'

I believe that we are obliged to read the statement of claim as generously as possible and to accommodate any inadequacies in the form of the allegations which are merely the result of drafting deficiencies.

Thus, I am prepared to accept that the appellants intended both of these possible deprivations as a basis for the violation of s. 7. It is apparent, however, that the violation of s. 7 alleged turns upon an actual increase in the risk of nuclear war, resulting from the Federal Cabinet's decision to permit the testing of the cruise missile. Thus, to succeed at trial, the appellants would have to demonstrate, inter alia, that the testing of the cruise missile would cause an increase in the risk of nuclear war. It is precisely this link between the Cabinet decision to permit the testing of the cruise and the increased risk of nuclear war which, in my opinion, they cannot establish. It will not be necessary therefore to address the issue of whether the deprivations of life and security of the person advanced by the appellants could constitute violations of s. 7.

As I have noted, both interpretations of the nature of the infringement of the appellants' rights are founded on the premise that *if* the Canadian Government allows the United States Government to test the cruise missile system in Canada, *then* there will be an increased risk of nuclear war. Such a claim can only be based on the assumption that the net result of all the various foreign powers' reactions to the testing of the cruise missile in Canada will be an increased risk of nuclear war.

The statement of claim speaks of weapons control agreements being "practically unenforceable", Canada being "more likely to be the target of a nuclear attack", "increasing the likelihood of either a pre-emptive strike or an accidental firing, or both", and "escalation of the nuclear arms race". All of these eventualities, culminating in the increased risk of nuclear war, are alleged to flow from the Canadian Government's single act of allowing the United States to test the cruise missile in Canada.

Since the foreign policy decisions of independent and sovereign nations are not capable of prediction, on the basis of evidence, to any degree of certainty approaching probability, the nature of such reactions can only be a matter of speculation; the causal link between the decision of the Canadian Government to permit the testing of the cruise and the results that the appellant alleges could never be proven.

An analysis of the specific allegations of the statement of claim reveals that they are all contingent upon the possible reactions of the nuclear powers to the testing of the cruise missile in Canada. The gist of paras. (a) and (b) of the statement of claim is that verification of the cruise missile system is impossible because the missile cannot be detected by surveillance satellites, and that, therefore, arms control agreements will be unenforceable. This is based on two major assumptions as to how foreign powers will react to the development of the cruise missile: first, that they will not develop new types of surveillance satellites or new methods of verification, and second, that foreign powers will not establish new modes of co-operation for dealing with the problem of enforcement. With respect to the latter of these points, it is just as plausible that lack of verification would have the effect of enhancing enforceability than of undermining it, since an inability on the part of the nuclear powers to verify systems like the cruise could precipitate a system of enforcement based on co-operation rather than surveillance.

As for para. (c), even if it were the case that the testing of the air-launched cruise missile would result in an increased American military presence and interest in Canada, to say that this would make Canada more likely to be the target of a nuclear attack is to assume certain reactions of hostile foreign powers to such an increased American presence. It also makes an assumption about the degree to which Canada is already a possible target of nuclear attack. Given the impossibility of determining how an independent sovereign nation might react, it can only be a matter of hypothesis whether an increased American presence would make Canada more vulnerable to nuclear attack. It would not be possible to prove it one way or the other.

Paragraph (d) assumes that foreign states will not develop their technology in such a way as to meet the requirements of effective detection of the cruise and that there will therefore be an increased likelihood of pre-emptive strike or an accidental firing, or both. Again, this assumption concerns how foreign powers are likely to act in response to the development of the cruise. It would be just as plausible to argue that foreign states would improve their technology with respect to detection of missiles, thereby decreasing the likelihood of accidental firing or pre-emptive strike.

Finally, para. (e) asserts that the development of the cruise will lead to an escalation of the nuclear arms race. This again involves speculation based on assumptions as to how foreign powers will react. One could equally argue that the cruise would be the precipitating factor in compelling the nuclear powers to negotiate agreements that would lead to a de-escalation of the nuclear arms race.

One final assumption, common to all the paragraphs except (c), is that the result of testing of the cruise missile in Canada will be its development by the United States. In all of these paragraphs, the alleged harm flows from the production and eventual deployment of the cruise missile. The effect that the testing will have on the development and deployment of the cruise can only be a matter of speculation. It is possible that as a result of the tests, the Americans would decide *not* to develop and deploy the cruise since the very reason for the testing is to establish whether the missile is a viable weapons system. Similarly, it is possible that the Americans would develop the cruise missile even if testing were not permitted by the Canadians.

In the final analysis, exactly what the Americans will decide to do about development and deployment of the cruise missile, whether tested in Canada or not, is a decision that they, as an independent and sovereign nation, will make for themselves. Even with the assistance of qualified experts, a Court could only speculate on how the American Government may make this decision, and how important a factor the results of the testing of the cruise in Canada will be in that decision.

What can be concluded from this analysis of the statement of claim is that all of its allegations, including the ultimate assertion of an increased likelihood of nuclear war, are premised on assumptions and hypotheses about how independent and sovereign nations, operating in an international arena of radical uncertainty, and continually changing circumstances, will react to the Canadian Government's decision to permit the testing of the cruise missile.

The point of this review is not to quarrel with the allegations made by the appellants about the results of cruise missile testing. They are, of course, entitled to their opinion and belief. Rather, I wish to highlight that they are raising matters that, in my opinion, lie in the realm of conjecture, rather than fact. In brief, it is simply not possible for a Court, even with the best available evidence, to do more than speculate upon the likelihood of the Federal Cabinet's decision to test the cruise missile resulting in an increased threat of nuclear war.

. . . .

II. *The Cabinet's Decision to Permit the Testing of the Cruise Missile and the Application of the Charter of Rights and Freedoms*

(a) *Application of the Charter to Cabinet Decisions*

I agree with Madame Justice Wilson that Cabinet decisions fall under s. 32(1)(a) of the *Charter* and are therefore reviewable in the Courts and subject to judicial scrutiny for compatability with the Constitution. I have no doubt that the executive branch of the Canadian Government is duty bound to act in accordance with the dictates of the *Charter*. Specifically, the Cabinet has a duty to act in a manner consistent with the right to life, liberty and security of the person and the right not to be deprived thereof except in accordance with the principles of fundamental justice.

(b) *The Absence of a Duty on the Government to Refrain from Allowing Testing*

I do not believe the action impugned in the present case can be characterized as contrary to the duties of the executive under the *Charter*. Section 7 of the *Charter* cannot reasonably be read as imposing a duty on the government to refrain from those acts which *might* lead to consequences that deprive or threaten to deprive individuals of their life and security of the person. A duty of the Federal Cabinet cannot arise on the basis of speculation and hypothesis about possible effects of government action. Such a duty only arises, in my view, where it can be said that a deprivation of life and security of the person could be proven to result from the impugned government act.

The principles governing remedial action by the Courts of the basis of allegations of future harm are illustrative of the more general principle that there is no legal duty to refrain from actions which do not prejudice the legal rights of others. A person, whether the government or a private individual, cannot be held liable under the law for an action unless that action causes the deprivation, or threat of deprivation, of legal rights. And an action cannot be said to cause such deprivation where it is not provable that the deprivation will occur as a result of the challenged action. I am not suggesting that remedial action by the Courts will be inappropriate where future harm is alleged. The point is that remedial action will not be justified where the link between the action and the future harm alleged is not capable of proof.

The reluctance of Courts to provide remedies where the causal link between an action and the future harm alleged to flow from it cannot be proven is exemplified by the principles with respect to declaratory relief. According to Fager, *The Declaratory Judgment Action* (1971), at p. 5:

> The remedy [of declaratory relief] is not generally available where the controversy is not presently existing but merely possible or remote; the action is not maintainable to settle disputes which are contingent upon the happening of some future event which may never take place.

> Conjectural or speculative issues, or feigned disputes or one-sided contentions are not the proper subjects for delcaratory relief.

Similarly, Sarna has said, "The court does not deal with unripe claims, nor does it entertain proceedings with the sole purpose of remedying only possible conflicts." (*The Law of Declaratory Judgments* (1978), at p. 179.)

None of this is to deny the preventative role of the declaratory judgment. As Madame Justice Wilson points out in her judgment, Borchard, *Declaratory Judgments* (2nd ed., 1941), at p. 27 states that,

> no 'injury' or 'wrong' need have been actually committed or threatened in order to enable the plaintiff to invoke the judicial process; he need merely show that some legal interest or right of his has been placed in jeopardy or grave uncertainty.

Nonetheless, the preventative function of the declaratory judgment must be based on more than mere hypothetical consequences; there must be a cognizable threat to a legal interest before the Courts will entertain the use of its process as a preventive measure. As this Court stated in *Solosky v. R.*, [1980] 1 S.C.R. 821, a declaration could issue to affect future rights, but not where the dispute in issue was merely speculative. In *Solosky* supra, one of the questions was whether an order by a director of a prison to censor correspondence between the appellant inmate and his solicitor could be declared unlawful. The dispute had already arisen as a result of the existence of the censorship order and the declaration sought was a direct and present challenge to this order. This Court found that the fact that the relief sought would relate to letters not yet written, and thereby affect future rights, was not in itself a bar to the granting of a declaration. The Court made it clear, however, (at p. 832)

> that a declaration will not normally be granted when the dispute is over and has become academic, *or where the dispute has yet to arise and may not arise.* (emphasis added)

A similar concern with the problems inherent in basing relief on the prediction of future events is found in the principles relating to injunctive relief. Professor Sharpe, *Injunctions and Specific Performance* (1983), clearly articulates the difficulties in issuing an injunction where the alleged harm is prospective at pp. 30-31:

> All injunctions are future looking in the sense that they are intended to prevent or avoid harm rather than compensate for an injury already suffered. . . . Where the harm to the plaintiff has yet to occur the problems of prediction are encountered. Here, the plaintiff sues quia timet — because he fears — and the judgment as to the propriety of injunctive relief must be made without the advantage of actual evidence as to the nature of harm inflicted on the plaintiff. The court is asked to predict that harm will occur in the future and that the harm is of a type that ought to be prevented by injunction.

The general principle with respect to such injunctions appears to be that "there must be a high degree of probability that the harm will in fact occur." (Sharpe, *supra*, at p. 31). In *Redland Bricks Ltd. v. Morris*, [1970] A.C. 652 at 665, per Lord Upjohn, the House of Lords laid down four general propositions concerning the circumstance in which mandatory injunctive relief could be granted on the basis of prospective harm. The first of these stated:

> A mandatory injunction can only be granted where the plaintiff shows a very strong probability upon the facts that grave damage will accrue to him in the future . . . It is a jurisdiction to be exercised sparingly and with caution but in the proper case unhesitantly.

It is clearly illustrated by the rules governing declaratory and injunctive relief that the Courts will not take remedial action where the occurrence of future harm is not probable. This unwillingness to act in the absence of probable future harm demonstrates the Courts' reluctance to grant relief where it cannot be shown that the impugned action will cause a violation of rights.

In the present case, the speculative nature of the allegation that the decision to test the cruise missile will lead to an increased threat of nuclear war makes it manifest that no duty is imposed on the Canadian Government to refrain from permitting the testing. The government's action simply could not be proven to cause the alleged violation of s. 7 of the *Charter* and, thus, no duty can arise.

### III. *Justiciability*

The approach which I have taken is not based on the concept of justiciability. I agree in substance with Madame Justice Wilson's discussion of justiciability and her conclusion that the doctrine is founded upon a concern with the appropriate role of the Courts as the forum for the resolution of different types of disputes. I have no doubt that disputes of a political or foreign policy nature may be properly cognizable by the Courts. My concerns in the present case focus on the impossibility of the Court finding, on the basis of evidence, the connection, alleged by the appellants, between the duty of the government to act in accordance with the *Charter of Rights and Freedoms* and the violation of their rights under s. 7. As stated above, I do not believe the alleged violation — namely, the increased threat of nuclear war — could ever be sufficiently linked as a factual matter to the acknowledged duty of the government to respect s. 7 of the *Charter*.

### IV. *Section 52 of the Constitution Act, 1982 and Section 1 of the Charter*

I would like to note that nothing in these reasons should be taken as the adoption of the view that the reference to "laws" in s. 52 of the *Charter* is confined to statutes, regulations and the common law. It may well be that if the supremacy of the Constitution expressed in s. 52 is to be meaningful, then all acts taken pursuant to powers granted by law will fall within s. 52. Equally, it is not necessary for the resolution of this case to express any opinion on the application of s. 1 of the *Charter* or the appropriate principles for its interpretation.

### V. *Conclusion*

I would accordingly dismiss the appeal with costs.

WILSON J. (concurring in result only):

This litigation was sparked by the decision of the Canadian Government to permit the United States to test the cruise missile in Canada. It raises issues of great difficulty and considerable importance to all of us.

### 1. *The facts*

The appellants are a group of organizations and unions claiming to have a collective membership of more than 1.5 million Canadians. They allege that a decision made by the Canadian Government on July 15, 1983, to allow the United States to test cruise missiles within Canada violates their constitutional rights as guaranteed by the *Canadian Charter of Rights and Freedoms*. More specifically, quoting from their statement of claim:

7. The Plaintiffs state and the fact is that the testing of the cruise missile in Canada is a violation of the collective rights of the Plaintiffs and their members and all Canadians, specifically their right to security of the person and life in that:

(a) the size and eventual dispersion of the air-launched cruise missile is such that the missile cannot be detected by surveillance satellites, thus making verification of the extent of this nuclear weapons system impossible;

(b) with the impossibility of verification, the future of nuclear weapons' control and limitation agreements is completely undermined as any such agreements become practically unenforceable;

(c) the testing of the air-launched cruise missiles would result in an increased American military presence and interest in Canada which would result in making Canada more likely to be the target of a nuclear attack;

(d) as the cruise missile cannot be detected until approximately eight minutes before it reaches its target, a 'Launch on Warning' system would be necessary in order to respond to the cruise missile thereby eliminating effective human discretion and increasing the likelihood of either a pre-emptive strike or an accidental firing, or both;

(e) the cruise missile is a military weapon, the development of which will have the effect of a needless and dangerous escalation of the nuclear arms race, thus endangering the security and lives of all people.

The plaintiffs, in addition to declaratory relief, seek consequential relief in the nature of an injunction and damages. The defendants, by a motion pursuant to R. 419(1) of the Federal Court Rules moved to strike out the plaintiff's statement of claim and to dismiss it as disclosing no reasonable cause of action. Cattanach J. dismissed the defendants' motion to strike on the grounds that the *Charter* applied to the Government of Canada, including executive acts of the Cabinet, and that the statement of claim contained "the germ of a cause of action" and raised a "justiciable issue". The Federal Court of Appeal unanimously allowed the defendants' appeal.

3. *The issues*

The issues to be addressed on the appeal to this Court may be conveniently summarized as follows:

(1) Is a decision made by the Government of Canada in relation to a matter of national defence and foreign affairs unreviewable on any of the following grounds:
   (a) it is an exercise of the royal prerogative;
   (b) it is, because of the nature of the factual questions involved, inherently non-justiciable;
   (c) it involves a "political question" of a kind that a Court should not decide?
(2) Under what circumstances can a statement of claim seeking declaratory relief concerning the constitutionality of a law or governmental decision be struck out as disclosing no cause of action?
(3) Do the facts as alleged in the statement of claim, which must be taken as proven, constitute a violation of s. 7 of the *Canadian Charter of Rights and Freedoms*? and

(4) Do the plaintiffs have a right to amend the statement of claim before the filing of a statement of defence?

### (1) *Is the Government's decision reviewable?*

### (a) *The royal prerogative*

The respondents submit that at common law the authority to make international agreements (such as the one made with the United States to permit the testing) is a matter which falls within the prerogative power of the Crown and that both at common law and by s. 15 of the *Constitution Act*, 1867 the same is true of decisions relating to national defence. They further submit that since by s. 32(1)(a) the *Charter* applies "to the Parliament and Government of Canada in respect of all matters within the authority of Parliament", the *Charter*'s application must, so far as the government is concerned, be restricted to the exercise of powers which derive directly from statute. It cannot, therefore, apply to an exercise of the royal prerogative which is a source of power existing independently of Parliament; otherwise, it is argued, the limiting phrase "within the authority of Parliament" would be deprived of any effect. The answer to this argument seems to me to be that those words of limitation, like the corresponding words "within the authority of the legislature of each province" in s. 32(1)(b), are merely a reference to the division of powers in ss. 91 and 92 of the *Constitution Act*, 1867. They describe the subject matters in relation to which the Parliament of Canada may legislate or the Government of Canada may take executive action. As LeDain J. points out, the royal prerogative is "within the authority of Parliament" in the sense that Parliament is competent to legislate with respect to matters falling within its scope. Since there is no reason in principle to distinguish between Cabinet decisions made pursuant to statutory authority and those made in the exercise of the royal prerogative, and since the former clearly fall within the ambit of the *Charter*, I conclude that the latter do so also.

### (b) *Non-justiciability*

LeDain and Ryan JJ. in the Federal Court of Appeal were of the opinion that the issues involved in this case are inherently non-justiciable, either because the question whether testing the cruise missile increases the risk of nuclear war is not susceptible of proof and hence is not triable (per Ryan J.) or because answering that question involves factors which are either inaccessible to a Court or are of a nature which a Court is incapable of evaluating (per LeDain J.). To the extent that this objection to the appellants' case rests on the inherent evidentiary difficulties which would obviously confront any attempt to prove the appellant's allegations of fact, I do not think it can be sustained. It might well be that, if the issue were allowed to go to trial, the appellants would lose simply by reason of their not having been able to establish the factual basis of their claim but that does not seem to me to be a reason for striking the case out at this preliminary stage. It is trite law that on a motion to strike out a statement of claim the plaintiff's allegations of fact are to be taken as having been proved. Accordingly, it is arguable that by dealing with the case as they have done LeDain and Ryan JJ. have, in effect, made a presumption against the appellants which they are not entitled, on a preliminary motion of this kind, to make.

I am not convinced, however, that LeDain and Ryan JJ. were restricting the concept of non-justiciability to difficulties of evidence and proof. Both rely on Lord Radcliffe's judgment in *Chandler v. D.P.P.*, [1962] 3 All E.R. 142 (H.L.), and especially on the following passage at p. 151:

> The disposition and equipment of the forces and the facilities afforded to allied forces for defence purposes constitute a given fact and it cannot be a matter of proof or finding that the decisions of policy on which they rest are or are not in the country's best interests. I may add that I can think of . few issues which present themselves in less triable form. It would be ingenuous to suppose that the kind of evidence that the appellants wanted to call could make more than a small contribution to its final solution. The facts which they wished to establish might well be admitted: even so, throughout history men have had to run great risk for themselves and others in the hope of attaining objectives which they prize for all. *The more one looks at it, the plainer it becomes, I think, that the question whether it is in the true interests of this country to acquire, retain or house nuclear armaments depends on an infinity of considerations, military and diplomatic, technical, psychological and moral, and of decisions, tentative or final, which are themselves part assessments of fact and part expectations and hopes.* I do not think that there is anything amiss with a legal ruling that does not make this issue a matter for judge or jury. (Emphasis added)

In my opinion, this passage makes clear that in Lord Radcliffe's view these kinds of issues are to be treated as non-justiciable not simply because of evidentiary difficulties but because they involve moral and political considerations which it is not within the province of the Courts to assess. LeDain J. maintains that the difficulty is one of judicial competence rather than anything resembling the American "political questions" doctrine. However, in response to that contention it can be pointed out that, however unsuited Courts may be for the task, they are called upon all the time to decide questions of principle and policy. As Melville Weston points out in "Political Questions" (1925), 38 Harv. L. Rev. 296 at 299:

> The word 'justiciable' . . . is legitimately capable of denoting almost any question. That is to say, the questions are few which are intrinsically incapable of submission to a tribunal having an established procedure, with an orderly presentation of such evidence as is available, for the purpose of an adjudication from which practical consequences in human conduct are to follow. For example, when nations decline to submit to arbitration or to the compulsory jurisdiction of a proposed international tribunal those questions of honour or interest which they call 'non-justiciable', they are really avoiding that broad sense of the word, but what they mean is a little less clear. Probably they mean only that they will not, or deem they ought not, endure the presentation of evidence on such questions, nor bind their conduct to conform to the proposed adjudications. So far as 'non-justiciable' is for them more than an epithet, it expresses a sense of a lack of fitness, and not of any inherent impossibility, of submitting these questions to judicial or quasi-judicial determination.

In the 1950's and early 1960's there was considerable debate in Britain over the question whether restrictive trade practices legislation gave rise to questions which were subject to judicial determination: see Marshall, "Justiciability" in *Guest Oxford Essays in Jurisprudence* (1961); Summers, "Justiciability" (1963), 26 M.L.R. 530; Stevens, "Justiciability: The Restrictive Practices Court Re-Examined", [1964] Public Law 221. I think it is fairly clear that the British restrictive trade practices legislation did not involve the Courts in the resolution of issues more imponderable than those facing American Courts administering the *Sherman Act*. Indeed, there is significantly less "policy" content in the decisions of the Courts in those cases than there is in the decisions of administrative tribunals such as the Canadian Transport Commission or the C.R.T.C. The real issue there, and perhaps also in the case at Bar, is not the *ability* of judicial tribunals to make a decision on the questions presented, but the *appropriateness* of the use of the judicial techniques for such purposes.

I cannot accept the proposition that difficulties of evidence or proof absolve the Court from making a certain kind of decision if it can be established on other grounds that it has a duty to do so. I think we should focus our attention on whether the Courts *should* or *must* rather than on whether they *can* deal with such matters. We should put difficulties of evidence and proof aside and consider whether as a constitutional matter it is appropriate or obligatory for the Courts to decide the issue before us. I will return to this question later.

### (c)  *The Political Questions Doctrine*

It is a well established principle of American constitutional law that there are certain kinds of "political questions" that a Court ought to refuse to decide. In *Baker v. Carr*, 369 U.S. 186 (1962) at pp. 210-11 Brennan J. discussed the nature of the doctrine in the following terms:

> We have said that 'In determining whether a question falls within [the political question] category, the appropriateness under our system of government of attributing finality to the action of the political departments and also the lack of satisfactory criteria for a judicial determination are dominant considerations.' *Coleman v. Miller*, 307 U.S. 433, 454-455. The nonjusticiability of a political question is primarily a function of the separation of powers. Much confusion results from the capacity of the 'political question' label to obscure the need for case-by-case inquiry. Deciding whether a matter has in any measure been committed by the Constitution to another branch of government, or whether the action of that branch exceeds whatever authority has been committed, is itself a delicate exercise in constitutional interpretation, and is a responsibility of this Court as ultimate interpreter of a Constitution.

> It is apparent that several formulations which vary slightly according to the settings in which the questions arise may describe a political question, although each has one or more elements which identify it as essentially a function of the separation of powers. Prominent on the surface of any case held to involve a political question is found a textually demonstrable constitutional commitment of the issue to a coordinate political department; or a lack of judicially discoverable and manageable standards for resolving it; or the impossibility of deciding without an initial policy determination of a kind clearly for nonjudicial discretion; or the impossibility of a court's undertaking independent resolution without expressing lack of the respect due coordinate branches of government; or an unusual need for unquestioning adherence to a political decision already made; or the potentiality of embarrassment from multifarious pronouncements by various departments on one question.

While one or two of the categories of political question referred to by Brennan J. raise the issue of judicial or institutional competence already referred to, the underlying theme is the separation of powers in the sense of the proper role of the Courts vis-à-vis the other branches of government. In this regard it is perhaps noteworthy that a distinction is drawn in the American case law between matters internal to the United States on the one hand and foreign affairs on the other. In the area of foreign affairs the Courts are especially deferential to the executive branch of government: see e.g. *Atlee v. Laird*, 347 F. Supp. 689 (1972) (U.S. Dist. Ct.) at pp. 701 ff.

While Brennan J.'s statement, in my view, accurately sums up the reasoning American Courts have used in deciding that specific cases did not present questions which were judicially cognizable, I do not think it is particularly helpful in determining when American Courts will find that those factors come into play. In cases from *Marbury v. Madison*, 5 U.S. (1 Cranch) 137 (1803) to *United States v. Nixon*, 418 U.S. 683 (1974) the Court has not allowed the "respect due coordinate branches of government" to prevent it from rendering decisions highly embarrassing to those holding executive or legislative office. In *Baker v. Carr* itself, supra, Frankfurter J., in dissent, expressed concern that the judiciary could not find manageable standards for the problems presented by the reapportionment of political districts. Indeed, some would say that the enforcement of the desegregation decision in *Brown v. Bd. of Educ.*, 347 U.S. 483 (1954) gave rise to similar problems of judicial unmanageability. Yet American Courts have ventured into these areas undeterred.

Academic commentators have expended considerable effort trying to identify when the political questions doctrine should apply. Although there are many theories (perhaps best summarized by Professor Scharpf in his article "Judicial Review and the Political Question: A Functional Analysis" (1966), 75 Yale L.J. 517), I think it is fair to say that they break down along two broad lines. The first, championed by scholars such as Weston ("Political Questions", (1925), 38 Harv. L.R. 296) and Wechsler (*Principles, Politics and Fundamental Law* (1961); Wechsler, Book Review (1966), 75 Yale L.J. 672) define political questions principally in terms of the separation of powers as set out in the Constitution and turn to the Constitution itself for the answer to the question when the Courts should stay their hand. The second school, represented by Finkelstein ("Judicial Self-Limitation", (1924), 37 Harv. L.R. 338) and Bickel (*The Least Dangerous Branch* (1962), especially c. 4, "The Passive Virtues"), roots the political questions doctrine in what seems to me to be a rather vague concept of judicial "prudence" whereby the Courts enter into a calculation concerning the political wisdom of intervention in sensitive areas. More recently, commentators such as Tigar ("Judicial Power, the 'Political Question Doctrine' and Foreign Relations" (1970), 17 U.C.L.A. L.R. 1135) and Henkin ("Is there a 'Political Question' Doctrine?" (1976), 85 Yale L.J. 597) have doubted the need for a political questions doctrine at all, arguing that all the cases which were correctly decided can be accounted for in terms of orthodox separation of powers doctrine.

Professor Tigar in his article suggests that the political questions doctrine is not really a doctrine at all but simply "a group of quite different legal rules and principles, each resting in part upon deference to the political branches of government" (p. 1163). He sees Justice Brennan's formulation of the doctrine in *Baker v. Carr*, supra, as an "unsatisfactory effort to rationalize a collection of disparate precedent" (p. 1163).

In the House of Lords in *Chandler*, supra, Lord Devlin expressed a similar reluctance to retreat from traditional techniques in the interpretation of the phrase "purpose prejudicial to the safety or interests of the State . . ." in the *Official Secrets Act*, 1911 (U.K., 1 & 2 Geo. 5), c. 28. His colleagues, in particular Lord Radcliffe and Lord Reid, seem to have been of the view that in matters of defence the Crown's opinion as to what was prejudicial to the safety or interests of the State was conclusive upon the Courts. Lord Devlin agreed with the result reached by his colleagues on the facts before him, and with the observation of Lord Parker on the Court of Criminal Appeal ([1962] 2 All E.R. 314 at p. 319) that "the manner of exercise of . . . (the Crown's) prerogative powers (over the disposition and armament of the military) cannot be enquired into by the Courts, whether in a civil or a criminal case . . ." ([1962] 3 All E.R. at p. 157) but went on to make three observations in clarification of his position.

Lord Devlin's first observation was that the principle that the *substance* of discretionary decisions is not reviewable in the Courts is one basic to administrative law and is not confined to matters of defence or the exercise of the prerogative. The second point was even though review on the merits of a discretionary decision was excluded, that did not mean that judicial review was excluded entirely. The third comment was that the nature and effect of the principle of judicial review is "(to limit) the issue which the court has to determine . . ." ([1962] 3 All E.R. at p. 158).

Lord Devlin then proceeded to apply these propositions to the case before him and asked what it was that the jury was required to determine. In his view "the fact to be proved is the existence of a purpose prejudicial to the state — not a purpose which 'appears to the Crown' to be prejudicial to the state" ([1962] 3 All E.R. at p. 158). He accordingly went on to conclude at p. 159:

> Consequently, the Crown's opinion as to what is or is not prejudicial in this case is just as inadmissible as the appellant's. The Crowns' evidence about what its interests are is an entirely different matter. They can be proved by an officer of the Crown wherever it may be necessary to do so. In a case like the present, it may be presumed that it is contrary to the interests of the Crown to have one of its airfields immobilised just as it may be presumed that it is contrary to the interests of an industrialist to have his factory immobilised. The thing speaks for itself as the Attorney-General submitted. But the presumption is not irrebuttable. Men can exaggerate the extent of their interests and so can the Crown. The servants of the Crown, like other men animated by the highest motives, are capable of formulating a policy ad hoc so as to prevent the citizen from doing something that the Crown does no want him to do. *It is the duty of the courts to be as alert now as they have always been to prevent abuse of the prerogative.* But in the present case there is nothing at all to suggest that the Crown's interest in the proper operation of its airfields is not what it may naturally be presumed to be or that it was exaggerating the perils of interference with their effectivenness." (Emphasis added)

It seems to me that the point being made by Lord Devlin, as well as by Tigar and Henkin in their writings, is that the Courts should not be too eager to relinquish their judicial review function simply because they are called upon to exercise it in relation to weighty matters of state. Equally, however, it is important to realize that judicial review is not the same thing as substitution of the Court's opinion on the merits for the opinion of the person or body to whom a discretionary decision-making power has been committed. The first step is to determine who as a constitutional matter has the decision-making power; the second is to determine the scope (if any) of judicial review of the exercise of that power.

It might be timely at this point to remind ourselves of the question the Court is being asked to decide. It is, of course, true that the federal Legislature has exclusive legislative jurisdiction in relation to defence under s. 91(7) of the *Constitution Act*, 1867 and that the federal executive has the powers conferred upon it in ss. 9-15 of that Act. Accordingly, if the Court were simply being asked to express its opinion on the wisdom of the Executive's exercise of its defence powers in this case, the Court would have to decline. It cannot substitute its opinion for that of the Executive to whom the decision-making power is given by the Constitution. Because the *effect* of the appellants' action is to challenge the wisdom of the government's defence policy, it is tempting to say that the Court should in the same way refuse to involve itself. However, I think this would be to miss the point, to fail to focus on the question which is before us. The question before us is not whether the government's defence policy is sound but whether or not it violates the appellants' rights under s. 7 of the *Charter of Rights and Freedoms*. This is a totally different question. I do not think there can be any doubt that this is a question for the Courts. Indeed, s. 24(1) of the *Charter*, also part of the Constitution, makes it clear that the adjudication of that question is the responsibility of "a court of competent jurisdiction". While the Court is entitled to grant such remedy as it "considers appropriate and just in the circumstances", I do not think it is open to it to relinquish its jurisdiction either on the basis that the issue is inherently non-justiciable or that it raises a so-called "political question": see Martin H. Redish, "Abstention, Separation of Powers, and the Limits of the Judicial Function" (1984), 94 Yale L.J. 71.

I would conclude, therefore, that if we are to look at the Constitution for the answer to the question whether it is appropriate for the Courts to "second guess" the executive on matters of defence, we would conclude that it is not appropriate. However, if what we are being asked to do is to decide whether any particular act of the executive violates the rights of the citizens, then it is not only appropriate that we answer the question; it is our obligation under the Charter to do so.

One or two hypothetical situations will, I believe, illustrate the point. Let us take the case of a person who is being conscripted for service during wartime and has been ordered into battle overseas, all of this pursuant to appropriate legislative and executive authorization. He wishes to challenge his being conscripted and sent overseas as an infringement of his rights under s. 7. It is apparent that his liberty has been constrained and, if he is sent into battle, his security of the person and, indeed, his life are put in jeopardy. It seems to me that it would afford the conscriptee a somewhat illusory protection if the validity of his challenge is to be determined by the Executive. On the other hand, it does not follow from these facts that the individual's rights under the Charter have been violated. Even if an individual's rights to life and liberty under s. 7 are interpreted at their broadest, it is clear from s. 1 that they are subject to "such reasonable limits prescribed by law as can be demonstrably justified in a free and democratic society". If the Court were of the opinion that conscription during wartime was a "reasonable limit" within the meaning of s. 1, a conscriptee's challenge on the facts as presented would necessarily fail.

By way of contrast, one can envisage a situation in which the government decided to force a particular group to participate in experimental testing of a deadly nerve gas. Although the government might argue that such experiments were an important part of our defence effort, I find it hard to believe that they would survive judicial review under the Charter. Equally we could imagine a situation during wartime in which the army began to seize people for military service without appropriate enabling legislation having been passed by Parliament. Such "press gang" tactics would, one might expect, be subject to judicial review even if the Executive thought they were justified for the prosecution of the war.

Returning then to the present case, it seems to me that the Legislature has assigned to the Courts as a constitutional responsibility the task of determining whether or not a decision to permit the testing of cruise missiles violates the appellants' rights under the *Charter*. The preceding illustrations indicate why the Legislature has done so. It is therefore, in my view, not only appropriate that we decide the matter; it is our constitutional obligation to do so.

[Her Ladyship's discussion of declaratory relief is omitted.]

(3) *Could the facts as alleged constitute a violation of s. 7 of the Charter?*

Section 7 of the *Charter of Rights and Freedoms* provides as follows:

> 7. Everyone has the right to life, liberty and security of the person and the right not to be deprived thereof except in accordance with the principles of fundamental justice.

Whether or not the facts that are alleged in the appellants' statement of claim could constitute a violation of s. 7 is, of course, the question that lies at the heart of this case. If they could not, then the appellants' statement of claim discloses no reasonable cause of action and the appeal must be dismissed. The appellants submit that on its proper construction s. 7 gives rise to two separate and presumably independent rights, namely the right to life, liberty and security of the person, and the right not to be deprived of such life, liberty and security of the person except in accordance with the principles of fundamental justice. In their submission, therefore, a violation of the principles of fundamental justice would only have to be alleged in relation to a claim based on a violation of the second right. As Marceau J. points out in his reasons, the French text of s. 7 does not seem to admit of this two-rights interpretation since only one right is specifically mentioned. Moreover, as the respondents point out, the appellants' suggestion does not accord with the interpretation that the Courts have placed on the similarly structured provison in s. 1(a) of the *Canadian Bill of Rights*: see e.g. *R. v. Miller*, [1977] 2 S.C.R. 680 *per* Ritchie J.

The appellants' submission, however, touches upon a number of important issues regarding the proper interpretation of s. 7. Even if the section gives rise to a single unequivocal right not to be deprived of life, liberty or security of the person except in accordance with the principles of fundamental justice, there nonetheless remains the question whether fundamental justice is entirely procedural in nature or whether it has a substantive aspect as well. This, in turn, leads to the related question whether there might not be certain deprivations of life, liberty or personal security which could not be justified no matter what procedure was employed to effect them. These are among the most important and difficult questions of interpretation arising under the *Charter* but I do not think it is necessary to deal with them in this case. It can, in my opinion, be disposed of without reaching these issues.

In my view, even an independent, substantive right to life, liberty and security of the person cannot be absolute. For example, the right to liberty, which I take to be the right to pursue one's goals free of governmental constraint, must accommodate the corresponding rights of others. The concept of "right" as used in the *Charter* postulates the inter-relation of individuals in society all of whom have the same right. The aphorism that "A hermit has no need of rights" makes the point. The concept of "right" also premises the existence of someone or some group against whom the right may be asserted. As Mortimer J. Adler expressed it in *Six Great Ideas* (1981), at p. 144:

> Living in organized societies under effective government and enforceable laws, as they must in order to survive and prosper, human beings neither have autonomy nor are they entitled to unlimited liberty of action. Autonomy is incompatible with organized society. Unlimited liberty is destructive of it.

The concept of "right" used in the *Charter* must also, I believe, recognize and take account of the political reality of the modern state. Action by the state or, conversely, inaction by the state will frequently have the effect of decreasing or increasing the risk to the lives or security of its citizens. It may be argued, for example, that the failure of the government to limit significantly the speed of traffic on the highways threatens our right to life and security in that it increases the risk of highway accidents. Such conduct, however, would not, in my view, fall within the scope of the right protected by s. 7 of the *Charter*.

In the same way, the concept of "right" as used in the *Charter* must take account of the fact that the self-contained political community which comprises the state is faced with at least the possibility, if not the reality, of external threats to both its collective well-being and to the individual well-being of its citizens. In order to protect the community against such threats it may well be necessary for the state to take steps which incidentally increase the risk to the lives or personal security of some or all of the state's citizens. Such steps, it seems to me, cannot have been contemplated by the draftsman of the Charter as giving rise to violations of s. 7. As John Rawls states in *A Theory of Justice* (1971), at p. 213:

> The government's right to maintain public order and security is . . . a right which the government must have if it is to carry out its duty of impartially supporting the conditions necessary for everyone's pursuit of his interests and living up to his obligations as he understands them.

The rights under the *Charter* not being absolute, their content or scope must be discerned quite apart from any limitation sought to be imposed upon them by the government under s. 1. As was pointed out by the Ontario Court of Appeal in *Re Fed. Republic of Germany and Rauca* (1983), 41 O.R. (2d) 225 at 244,

> The *Charter* was not enacted in a vacuum and the rights set out therein must be interpreted rationally having regard to existing law.

There is no liberty without law and there is no law without some restriction of liberty: see Dworkin, *Taking Rights Seriously* (1977) p. 267. This paradox caused Roscoe Pound to conclude:

> There is no more ambiguous word in legal and juristic literature than the word right. In its most general sense it means a reasonable expectation involved in civilized life. (See *Jurisprudence*, (1959) Vol. IV, p. 56.)

It is not necessary to accept the restrictive interpretation advanced by Pratte J., which would limit s. 7 to protection against arbitrary arrest or detention, in order to agree that the central concern of the section is direct impingement by government upon the life, liberty and personal security of individual citizens. At the very least, it seems to me, there must be a strong presumption that governmental action which concerns the relations of the state with other states, and which is therefore not directed at any member of the immediate political community, was never intended to be caught by s. 7 even although such action may have the incidental effect of increasing the risk of death or injury that individuals generally have to face.

I agree with LeDain J. that the essence of the appellants' case is the claim that permitting the cruise missile to be tested in Canada will increase the risk of nuclear war. But even accepting this allegation of fact as true, which as I have already said I think we must do on a motion to strike, it is my opinion for the reasons given above that this state of affairs could not constitute a breach of s. 7. Moreover, I do not see how one can distinguish in a principled way between this particular risk and any other danger to which the government's action vis-à-vis other states might incidentally subject its citizens. A declaration of war, for example, almost certainly increases the risk to most citizens of death or injury. Acceptance of the appellants' submissions, it seems to me, would mean that any such declaration would also have to be regarded as a violation of s. 7. I cannot think that that could be a proper interpretation of the *Charter*.

This is not to say that every governmental action that is purportedly taken in furtherance of national defence would be beyond the reach of s. 7. If, for example, testing the cruise missile posed a direct threat to some specific segment of the populace — as, for example, if it were being tested with live warheads — I think that might well raise different considerations. A Court might find that that constituted a violation of s. 7 and it might then be up to the government to try to establish that testing the cruise with live warheads was justified under s. 1 of the *Charter*. Section 1, in my opinion, is the uniquely Canadian mechanism through which the Courts are to determine the justiciability of particular issues that come before it. It embodies through its reference to a free and democratic society the essential features of our constitution including the separation of powers, responsible government and the rule of law. It obviates the need for a "political questions" doctrine and permits the Court to deal with what might be termed "prudential" considerations in a principled way without renouncing its constitutional and mandated responsibility for judicial review. It is not, however, called into operation here since the facts alleged in the statement of claim, even if they could be shown to be true, could not in my opinion constitute a violation of s. 7.

. . . .

## Conclusions

In summary, it seems to me that the issues raised on the appeal are to be disposed of as follows:

(1) The government's decision to permit testing of the cruise missile in Canada cannot escape judicial review on any of the grounds advanced;

(2) The statement of claim may be struck out if the facts as alleged do not disclose a reasonable cause of action which in this case could be either

  (a) a cause of action under s. 24(1) of the *Charter*; or

  (b) a cause of action for declaratory relief at common law on the principle of *Dyson v. A.G.*, [1911] 1 K.B. 410 (C.A.); or

  (c) a cause of action under s. 52(1) of the *Charter* for a declaration of unconstitutionality.

(3) Taking the facts alleged as proven, they could not constitute a violation of s. 7 of the *Charter* so as to give rise to a cause of action under s. 24(1);

(4) The appellants could not establish their status to sue at common law for declaratory relief for the same reason that they could not establish a cause of action under s. 24(1); and

(5) The appellants could not establish a cause of action for declaratory relief under s. 52(1) since the facts as alleged could not constitute a violation of s. 7 and therefore no inconsistency with the provisions of the Constitution could be established.

I would accordingly dismiss the appeal with costs.

# Addendum

## R. v. OAKES

In the Supreme Court of Canada.

Dickson C.J.C. and Estey, McIntyre, Chouinard, Lamer, Wilson and LeDain JJ. February 28, 1986.

The judgment of Dickson, C.J.C., and Chouinard, Lamer, Wilson and LeDain JJ. was delivered by

DICKSON J.:

This appeal concerns the constitutionality of section 8 of the *Narcotic Control Act*, R.S.C. 1970, c. N-1. The section provides, in brief, that if the Court finds the accused in possession of a narcotic, he is presumed to be in possession for the purpose of trafficking. Unless the accused can establish the contrary, he must be convicted of trafficking. The Ontario Court of Appeal held that this provision constitutes a "reverse onus" clause and is unconstitutional because it violates one of the core values of our criminal justice system, the presumption of innocence, now entrenched in section 11(d) of the *Canadian Charter of Rights and Freedoms*. The Crown has appealed.

### I

*STATUTORY AND CONSTITUTIONAL PROVISIONS*

Before reviewing the factual context, I will set out the relevant legislative and constitutional provisions:

*Narcotic Control Act*, R.S.C. 1970, c. N-1

s.3(1) Except as authorized by this Act or the regulations, *no person shall have a narcotic in his possession.*
　　(2) *Every person who violates subsection (1) is guilty of an indictable offence and is liable*

　　　　(a) upon summary conviction for a first offence, to a fine of one thousand dollars or to imprisonment for six months or to both fine and imprisonment, and for a subsequent offence, to a fine of two thousand dollars or to imprisonment for one year or to both fine and imprisonment; or
　　　　(b) *upon conviction on indictment, to imprisonment for seven years.*

s.4(1) No person shall traffic in a narcotic or any substance represented or held out by him to be a narcotic.
　　(2) *No person shall have in his possession a narcotic for the purpose of trafficking.*
　　(3) *Every person who violates subsection (1) or (2) is guilty of an indictable offence and is liable to imprisonment for life.*

s.8 *In any prosecution for a violation of subsection 4(2)*, if the accused does not plead guilty, *the trial shall proceed as if it were a prosecution for an offence under section 3*, and after the close of the case for the prosecution and after the accused has had an opportunity to make full answer and defence, *the court shall make a finding as to whether or not the accused was in possession of the narcotic contrary to section 3*; if the court finds that the accused was not in possession of the narcotic contrary to section 3, he shall be acquitted but *if the court finds that the accused was in possession of the narcotic contrary to section 3, he shall be given an opportunity of establishing that he was not in possession of the narcotic for the purpose of trafficking*, and thereafter the prosecutor shall be given an opportunity of adducing evidence to establish that the accused was in possession of the narcotic for the purpose of trafficking; *if the accused establishes that he was not in possession of the narcotic for the purpose of trafficking, he shall be acquitted of the offence* as charged but he shall be convicted of an offence under section 3 and sentenced accordingly; and *if the accused fails to establish that he was not in possession of the narcotic for the purpose of trafficking, he shall be convicted of the offence as charged and sentenced accordingly.*

(Emphasis added)

## Canadian Charter of Rights and Freedoms:

s.11 Any person charged with an offence has the right

. . .

(d) to be presumed innocent until proven guilty according to law in a fair and public hearing by an independent and impartial tribunal.

s.1 The *Canadian Charter of Rights and Freedoms* guarantees the rights and freedoms set out in it subject only to such reasonable limits prescribed by law as can be demonstrably justified in a free and democratic society.

II

## FACTS

The respondent, David Edwin Oakes, was charged with unlawful possession of a narcotic for the purpose of trafficking, contrary to section 4(2) of the *Narcotic Control Act.* He elected trial by magistrate without a jury. At trial, the Crown adduced evidence to establish that Mr. Oakes was found in possession of eight one gram vials of *cannabis* resin in the form of hashish oil. Upon a further search conducted at the police station, $619.45 was located. Mr. Oakes told the police that he had bought ten vials of hashish oil for $150 for his own use, and that the $619.45 was from a workers' compensation cheque. He elected not to call evidence as to possession of the narcotic. Pursuant to the procedural provisions of section 8 of the *Narcotic Control Act*, the trial judge proceeded to make a finding that it was beyond a reasonable doubt that Mr. Oakes was in possession of the narcotic.

Following this finding, Mr. Oakes brought a motion to challenge the constitutional validity of section 8 of the *Narcotic Control Act*, which he maintained imposes a burden on an accused to prove that he or she was not in possession for the purpose of trafficking. He argued that section 8 violates the presumption of innocence contained in s. 11(d) of the *Charter.*

. . . .

IV

## THE ISSUES

The constitutional question in this appeal is stated as follows:

Is section 8 of the *Narcotic Control Act* inconsistent with section 11(d) of the *Canadian Charter of Rights and Freedoms* and thus of no force and effect?

Two specific questions are raised by this general question: (1) does section 8 of the *Narcotic Control Act* violate section 11(d) of the *Charter*; and, (2) if it does, is section 8 a reasonable limit prescribed by law as can be demonstrably justified in a free and democratic society for the purpose of section 1 of the *Charter*? If the answer to (1) is affirmative and the answer to (2) negative, then the constitutional question must be answered in the affirmative.

V

## Does Section 8 of the Narcotic Control Act violate Section 11(d) of the Charter?

### (a) *The Meaning of Section 8*

Before examining the presumption of innocence contained in section 11(d) of the *Charter*, it is necessary to clarify the meaning of section 8 of the *Narcotic Control Act*. The procedural steps contemplated by section 8 were clearly outlined by Branca J.A. in *R. v. Babcock and Auld*, [1967] 2 C.C.C. 235 (B.C.C.A.) at 247:

(A) the accused is charged with possession of a forbidden drug for the purpose of trafficking;

(B) the trial of the accused on this charge then proceeds as if it was a prosecution against the accused on a simple charge of possession of the forbidden drug; . . .

(C) when the Crown has adduced its evidence on the basis that the charge was a prosecution for simple possession, the accused is then given the statutory right or opportunity of making a full answer and defence to the charge of simple possession; . . .

(D) when this has been done the Court must make a finding as to whether the accused was in possession of narcotics contrary to s. 3 of the new Act; (Unlawful possession of a forbidden narcotic drug);

(E) Assuming that the Court so finds, it is then that an onus is placed upon the accused in the sense that an opportunity must be given to the accused of establishing that he was not in possession of a narcotic for the purpose of trafficking;

(F) when the accused has been given this opportunity the prosecutor may then establish that the possession of the accused was for the purpose of trafficking; . . .

(G) it is then that the Court must find whether or not the accused has discharged the onus placed upon him under and by the said section;

(H) if the Court so finds, the accused must be acquitted of the offence as charged, namely, possession for the purpose of trafficking, but in that event the accused must be convicted of the simple charge of unlawful possession of a forbidden narcotic;

(I) if the accused does not so establish he must then be convicted of the full offence as charged.

### Mr. Justice Branca then added at 247-48:

It is quite clear to me that under s. 8 of the new Act the trial must be divided into two phases. In the first phase the sole issue to be determined is whether or not the accused is guilty of simple possession of a narcotic. This issue is to be determined upon evidence relevant only to the issue of possession. In the second phase the question to be resolved is whether or not the possession charged is for the purpose of trafficking.

Against the backdrop of these procedural steps, we must consider the nature of the statutory presumption contained in section 8 and the type of burden it places on an accused. The relevant portions of section 8 read:

> s. 8 . . . if the court finds that the accused was in possession of the narcotic . . . he shall be given an opportunity of establishing that he was not in possession of the narcotic for the purpose of trafficking . . .
>
> if the accused fails to establish that he was not in possession of the narcotic for the purpose of trafficking, he shall be convicted of the offence as charged. . . .

In determining the meaning of these words, it is helpful to consider in a general sense the nature of presumptions. Presumptions can be classified into two general categories: presumptions *without* basic facts and presumptions *with* basic facts. A presumption without a basic fact is simply a conclusion which is to be drawn until the contrary is proved. A presumption with a basic fact entails a conclusion to be drawn upon proof of the basic fact (see *Cross On Evidence* 5th ed., pp. 122-23).

Basic fact presumptions can be further categorized into permissive and mandatory presumptions. A permissive presumption leaves it optional as to whether the inference of the presumed fact is drawn following proof of the basic fact. A mandatory presumption requires that the inference be made.

Presumptions may also be either rebuttable or irrebuttable. If a presumption is rebuttable, there are three potential ways the presumed fact can be rebutted. First, the accused may be required merely to raise a reasonable doubt as to its existence. Secondly, the accused may have an evidentiary burden to adduce sufficient evidence to bring into question the truth of the presumed fact. Thirdly, the accused may have a legal or persuasive burden to prove on a balance of probabilities the non-existence of the presumed fact.

Finally, presumptions are often referred to as either presumptions of law or presumptions of fact. The latter entail "frequently recurring examples of circumstantial evidence" (*Cross On Evidence, supra*, p. 124) while the former involve actual legal rules.

To return to section 8 of the *Narcotic Control Act*, it is my view that, upon a finding beyond a reasonable doubt of possession of a narcotic, the accused has the legal burden of proving on a balance of probabilities that he or she was not in possession of the narcotic for the purpose of trafficking. Once the basic fact of possession is proven, a mandatory presumption of law arises against the accused that he or she had the intention to traffic. Moreover, the accused will be found guilty of the offence of trafficking unless he or she can rebut this presumption on a balance of probabilities. This interpretation of section 8 is supported by the courts in a number of jurisdictions: *R. v. Carroll* (1983), 147 D.L.R. (3d) 92 (P.E.I. S.C. *in banco*), affirmed 32 C.R. (3d) 235 (P.E.I. C.A.); *R. v. Cook* (1983), 4 C.C.C. (3d) 419 (N.S.C.A.); *R. v. O'Day* (1983), 5 C.C.C. (3d) 227 (N.B.C.A.); *R. v. Landry* (1983), 7 C.C.C. (3d) 555 (Que. C.A.); *R. v. Stanger* (1983), 7 C.C.C. (3d) 337 (Alta. C.A.).

In some decisions it has been held that section 8 of the *Narcotic Control Act* is constitutional because it places only an evidentiary burden rather than a legal burden on the accused. The ultimate legal burden to prove guilt beyond a reasonable doubt remains with the Crown and the presumption of innocence is not offended. (*R. v. Therrien* (1982), 67 C.C.C. (2d) 31 (Ont. G.S.P.); *R. v. Fraser* (1982), 138 D.L.R. (3d) 488 (Sask. Q.B.); *R. v. Kupczyniski*, (June 23, 1982, unreported, Ont. Co. Ct.)).

This same approach was relied on in *R. v. Sharpe* (1961), 131 C.C.C. 75 (Ont. C.A.), a *Canadian Bill of Rights* decision on the presumption of innocence. In that case, a provision in the *Opium and Narcotic Drug Act*, R.S.C. 1952, c. 201, similar to section 8 of the *Narcotic Control Act*, was interpreted as shifting merely the secondary burden of adducing evidence onto the accused. The primary onus remained with the Crown. In *R. v. Silk*, [1970] 3 C.C.C. (2d) 1 (B.C.C.A.), the British Columbia Court of Appeal held that s. 2(f) of the *Canadian Bill of Rights* had not been infringed because section 33 (now section 35) of the *Food and Drugs Act*, R.S.C. 1970, c. F-27, required only that an accused raise a reasonable doubt that the purpose of his or her possession was trafficking. This decision, however, was not followed in *R. v. Appleby*, [1972] S.C.R. 303, nor in *R. v. Erdman* (1971), 24 C.R.N.S. 216 (B.C.C.A.).

Those decisions which have held that only the secondary or evidentiary burden shifts are not persuasive with respect to the *Narcotic Control Act*. As Ritchie J. found in *R. v. Appleby, supra*, (though addressing a different statutory provision) the phrase "to establish" is the equivalent of "to prove". The legislature, by using the word "establish" in section 8 of the *Narcotic Control Act*, intended to impose a legal burden on the accused. This is most apparent in the words "if the accused fails to establish that he was not in possession of the narcotic for the purpose of trafficking, he shall be convicted of the offence as charged".

In the *Appleby* case, Ritchie J. also held that the accused is required to disprove the presumed fact according to the civil standard of proof, on a balance of probabilities. He rejected the criminal standard of beyond a reasonable doubt, relying, *inter alia*, upon the following passage from the House of Lords' decision in *Public Prosecutor v. Yuvaraj*, [1970] A.C. 913 at 921 (P.C.):

> Generally speaking, no onus lies upon a defendant in criminal proceedings to prove or disprove any fact: it is sufficient for his acquittal if any of the facts which, if they existed, would constitute the offence with which he is charged are "not proved". But exceptionally, as in the present case, an enactment creating an offence expressly provides that if other facts are proved, a particular fact, the existence of which is a necessary factual ingredient of the offence, shall be presumed or deemed to exist "unless the contrary is proved". In such a case the consequence of finding that that particular fact is "disproved" will be an acquittal, whereas the absence of such a finding will have the consequence of a conviction. Where this is the consequence of a fact's being "disproved" there can be no grounds in public policy for requiring that exceptional degree of certainty as excludes all reasonable doubt that that fact does not exist. In their Lordships' opinion the general rule applies in such a case and it is sufficient if the court considers that upon the evidence before it it is more likely than not that the fact does not exist. The test is the same as that applied in civil proceedings: the balance of probabilities.

I conclude that section 8 of the *Narcotic Control Act* contains a reverse onus provision imposing a legal burden on an accused to prove on a balance of probabilities that he or she was not in possession of a narcotic for the purpose of trafficking. It is therefore necessary to determine whether section 8 of the *Narcotic Control Act* offends the right to be "presumed innocent until proven guilty" as guaranteed by section 11(d) of the *Charter*.

(b) *The Presumption of Innocence and Section 11(d) of the Charter*

Section 11(d) of the *Charter* constitutionally entrenches the presumption of innocence as part of the supreme law of Canada. For ease of reference, I set out this provision again:

> s.11 Any person charged with an offence has the right
>
>     . . .
>
> > (d) to be presumed innocent until proven guilty according to law in a fair and public hearing by an independent and impartial tribunal.

To interpret the meaning of section 11(d), it is important to adopt a purposive approach. As this Court stated in *R. v. Big M Drug Mart Ltd.*, [1985] 1 S.C.R. 295 at 344:

> The meaning of a right or freedom guaranteed by the *Charter* was to be ascertained by an analysis of the *purpose* of such a guarantee; it was to be understood, in other words, in the light of the interests it was meant to protect.
>
> In my view this analysis is to be undertaken, and the purpose of the right or freedom in question is to be sought by reference to the character and the larger objects of the *Charter* itself, to the language chosen to articulate the specific right or freedom, to the historical origins of the concepts enshrined, and where applicable to the meaning and purpose of the other specific rights and freedoms . . .

To identify the underlying purpose of the *Charter* right in question, therefore, it is important to begin by understanding the cardinal values it embodies.

The presumption of innocence is a hallowed principle lying at the very heart of criminal law. Although protected expressly in section 11(d) of the *Charter*, the presumption of innocence is referable and integral to the general protection of life, liberty and security of the person contained in section 7 of the *Charter* (see *Reference re s. 94(2) of the Motor Vehicle Act*, December 17, 1985, unreported, per Lamer J.). The presumption of innocence protects the fundamental liberty and human dignity of any and every person accused by the State of criminal conduct. An individual charged with a criminal offence faces grave social and personal consequences, including potential loss of physical liberty, subjection to social stigma and ostracism from the community, as well as other social, psychological and economic harms. In light of the gravity of these consequences, the presumption of innocence is crucial. It ensures that until the State proves an accused's guilt beyond all reasonable doubt, he or she is innocent. This is essential in a society committed to fairness and social justice. The presumption of innocence confirms our faith in humankind; it reflects our belief that individuals are decent and law-abiding members of the community until proven otherwise.

The presumption of innocence has enjoyed longstanding recognition at common law. In the leading case, *Woolmington v. Director of Public Prosecutions*, [1935] A.C. 462 (H.L.), Viscount Sankey wrote at 481-482:

> Throughout the web of the English Criminal Law one golden thread is always to be seen, that it is the duty of the prosecution to prove the prisoner's guilt subject to what I have already said as to the defence of insanity and subject also to any statutory exception. If, at the end of and on the whole of the case, there is a reasonable doubt, created by the evidence given by either the prosecution or the prisoner, as to whether the prisoner killed the deceased with a malicious intention, the prosecution has not made out the case and the prisoner is entitled to an acquittal. No matter what the charge or

> where the trial, the principle that the prosecution must prove the guilt of the prisoner is part of the common law of England and no attempt to whittle it down can be entertained.

Subsequent Canadian cases have cited the *Woolmington* principle with approval (see, for example, *Manchuk v. The King*, [1938] S.C.R. 341 at 349; *R. v. City of Sault Ste. Marie*, [1978] 2 S.C.R. 1299 at 1316).

Further evidence of the widespread acceptance of the principle of the presumption of innocence is its inclusion in the major international human rights documents. Article 11(1) of the *Universal Declaration of Human Rights*, adopted December 10, 1948 by the General Assembly of the United Nations, provides:

> Art. 11(1) Everyone charged with a penal offence has the right to be presumed innocent until proved guilty according to law in a public trial at which he has had all the guarantees necessary for his defence.

In the *International Covenant on Civil and Political Rights*, 1966, art. 14(2) states:

> Art. 14(2) Everyone charged with a criminal offence shall have the right to be presumed innocent until proved guilty according to law.

Canada acceded to this Covenant, and the Optional Protocol which sets up machinery for implementing the Covenant, on May 19, 1976. Both came into effect on August 19, 1976.

In light of the above, the right to be presumed innocent until proven guilty requires that section 11(d) have, at a minimum, the following content. First, an individual must be proven guilty beyond a reasonable doubt. Second, it is the State which must bear the burden of proof. As Mr. Justice Lamer stated in *Dubois v. The Queen*, [1986] 1 W.W.R. 193 at 213 (S.C.C.):

> Section 11(d) imposes upon the Crown the burden of proving the accused's guilt beyond a reasonable doubt as well as that of making out the case against the accused before he or she need respond, either by testifying or calling other evidence.

Third, criminal prosecutions must be carried out in accordance with lawful procedures and fairness. The latter part of s. 11(d), which requires the proof of guilt "according to law in a fair and public hearing by an independent and impartial tribunal", underlines the importance of this procedural requirement.

. . . .

[His Lordship's discussion of the authorities on reverse onus provisions and the presumption of innocence is omitted.]

### (d) Conclusion Regarding Section 11(d) of the Charter and Section 8 of the Narcotic Control Act

This review of the authorities lays the groundwork for formulating some general conclusions regarding reverse onus provisions and the presumption of innocence in section 11(d). We can then proceed to apply these principles to the particulars of section 8 of the *Narcotic Control Act*.

In general one must, I think, conclude that a provision which requires an accused to disprove on a balance of probabilities the existence of a presumed fact, which is an important element of the offence in question, violates the presumption of innocence in s. 11(d). If an accused bears the burden of disproving on a balance of probabilities an essential element of an offence, it would be possible for a conviction to occur despite the existence of a reasonable doubt. This would arise if the accused adduced sufficient evidence to raise a reasonable doubt as to his or her innocence but did not convince the jury on a balance of probabilities that the presumed fact was untrue.

The fact that the standard is only the civil one does not render a reverse onus clause constitutional. As Sir Rupert Cross commented in the *Rede Lectures*, "The Golden Thread of the English Criminal Law: The Burden of Proof", delivered in 1976 at the University of Toronto, pp. 11-13:

> It is sometimes said that exceptions to the Woolmington rule are acceptable because, whenever the burden of proof on any issue in a criminal case is borne by the accused, he only has to satisfy the jury on the balance of probabilities, whereas on issues on which the Crown bears the burden of proof the jury must be satisfied beyond a reasonable doubt. ... The fact that the standard is lower when the accused bears the burden of proof than it is when the burden of proof is borne by the prosecution is no answer to my objection to the existence of exceptions to the Woolmington rule as it does not alter the fact that a jury or bench of magistrates may have to convict the accused although they are far from sure of his guilt.

As we have seen, the potential for a rational connection between the basic fact and the presumed fact to justify a reverse onus provision has been elaborated in some of the cases discussed above and is now known as the "rational connection test". In the context of section 11(d), however, the following question arises: if we apply the rational connection test to the consideration of whether section 11(d) has been violated, are we adequately protecting the constitutional principle of the presumption of innocence? As Professors MacKay and Cromwell point out in their article "Oakes: A Bold Initiative" (1983), 32 C.R. (3d) 221 at 233:

> The rational connection test approves a provision that forces the trier to infer a fact that may be simply rationally connected to the proved fact. Why does it follow that such a provision does not offend the constitutional right to be proved guilty beyond a reasonable doubt?

A basic fact may rationally tend to prove a presumed fact, but not prove its existence beyond a reasonable doubt. An accused person could thereby be convicted despite the presence of a reasonable doubt. This would violate the presumption of innocence.

I should add that this questioning of the constitutionality of the "rational connection test" as a guide to interpreting section 11(d) does not minimize its importance. The appropriate stage for invoking the rational connection test, however, is under section 1 of the *Charter*. This consideration did not arise under the *Canadian Bill of Rights* because of the absence of an equivalent to section 1. At the Court of Appeal level in the present case, Martin J.A. sought to combine the analysis of s. 11(d) and s. 1 to overcome the limitations of the *Canadian Bill of Rights* jurisprudence. To my mind, it is highly desirable to keep section 1 and section 11(d) analytically distinct. Separating the analysis into two components is consistent with the approach this Court has taken to the *Charter* to date (see *R. v. Big M Drug Mart Ltd., supra*; *Hunter v. Southam Inc.*, [1984] 2 S.C.R. 145; *Law Society of Upper Canada v. Skapinker*, [1984] 1 S.C.R. 357).

To return to section 8 of the *Narcotic Control Act*, I am in no doubt whatsoever that it violates section 11(d) of the *Charter* by requiring the accused to prove on a balance of probabilities that he was not in possession of the narcotic for the purpose of trafficking. Mr. Oakes is compelled by section 8 to prove he is *not* guilty of the offence of trafficking. He is thus denied his right to be presumed innocent and subjected to the potential penalty of life imprisonment unless he can rebut the presumption. This is radically and fundamentally inconsistent with the societal values of human dignity and liberty which we espouse, and is directly contrary to the presumption of innocence enshrined in section 11(d). Let us turn now to section 1 of the *Charter*.

## VI

*Is Section 8 of the Narcotic Control Act a Reasonable and Demonstrably Justified Limit Pursuant to s. 1 of the Charter?*

The Crown submits that even if section 8 of the *Narcotic Control Act* violates section 11(d) of the *Charter*, it can still be upheld as a reasonable limit under section 1 which, as has been mentioned, provides:

> s.1 The *Canadian Charter of Rights and Freedoms* guarantees the rights and freedoms set out in it subject only to such reasonable limits prescribed by law as can be demonstrably justified in a free and democratic society.

The question whether the limit is "prescribed by law" is not contentious in the present case since section 8 of the *Narcotic Control Act* is a duly enacted legislative provision. It is, however, necessary to determine if the limit on Mr. Oakes' right, as guaranteed by section 11(d) of the *Charter*, is "reasonable" and "demonstrably justified in a free and democratic society" for the purpose of section 1 of the *Charter*, and thereby saved from inconsistency with the Constitution.

It is important to observe at the outset that section 1 has two functions: first, it constitutionally guarantees the rights and freedoms set out in the provisions which follow; and, second, it states explicitly the exclusive justificatory criteria (outside of section 33 of the *Constitution Act, 1982*) against which limitations on those rights and freedoms must be measured. Accordingly, any section 1 inquiry must be premised on an understanding that the impugned limit violates constitutional rights and freedoms — rights and freedoms which are part of the supreme law of Canada. As Madame Justice Wilson stated in *Singh v. Min. of Employment and Immigration*, [1985] 1 S.C.R. 177 ". . . it is important to remember that the courts are conducting this inquiry in light of a commitment to uphold the rights and freedoms set out in the other sections of the *Charter*."

A second contextual element of interpretation of section 1 is provided by the words "free and democratic society". Inclusion of these words as the final standard of justification for limits on rights and freedoms refers the Court to the very purpose for which the *Charter* was originally entrenched in the Constitution: Canadian society is to be free and democratic. The Court must be guided by the values and principles essential to a free and democratic society which I believe embody, to name but a few, respect for the inherent dignity of the human person, commitment to social justice and equality, accommodation of a wide variety of beliefs, respect for cultural and group identity, and faith in social and political institutions which enhance the participation of individuals and groups in society. The underlying values and principles of a free and democratic society are the genesis of the rights and freedoms guaranteed by the *Charter* and the ultimate standard against which a limit on a right or freedom must be shown, despite its effect, to be reasonable and demonstrably justified.

The rights and freedoms guaranteed by the *Charter* are not, however, absolute. It may become necessary to limit rights and freedoms in circumstances where their exercise would be inimical to the realization of collective goals of fundamental importance. For this reason, section 1 provides criteria of justification for limits on the rights and freedoms guaranteed by the *Charter*. These criteria impose a stringent standard of justification, especially when understood in terms of the two contextual considerations discussed above, namely, the violation of a constitutionally guaranteed right or freedom and the fundamental principles of a free and democratic society.

The onus of proving that a limit on a right or freedom guaranteed by the *Charter* is reasonable and demonstrably justified in a free and democratic society rests upon the party seeking to uphold the limitation. It is clear from the text of section 1 that limits on the rights and freedoms enumerated in the *Charter* are exceptions to their general guarantee. The presumption is that the rights and freedoms are guaranteed unless the party invoking section 1 can bring itself within the exceptional criteria which justify their being limited. This is further substantiated by the use of the word "demonstrably" which clearly indicates that the onus of justification is on the party seeking to limit: *Hunter v. Southam Inc., supra.*

The standard of proof under section 1 is the civil standard, namely, proof by a preponderance of probability. The alternative criminal standard, proof beyond a reasonable doubt, would, in my view, be unduly onerous on the party seeking to limit. Concepts such as "reasonableness", "justifiability" and "free and democratic society" are simply not amenable to such a standard. Nevertheless, the preponderance of probability test must be applied rigorously. Indeed, the phrase "demonstrably justified" in section 1 of the *Charter* supports this conclusion. Within the broad category of the civil standard, there exist different degrees of probability depending on the nature of the case: see Sopinka and Lederman, *The Law of Evidence in Civil Cases* (Toronto: 1974), p. 385. As Lord Denning explained in *Bater v. Bater*, [1950] 2 All E.R. 458 (C.A.) at 459:

> The case may be proved by a preponderance of probability, but there may be degrees of probability within that standard. The degree depends on the subject-matter. A civil court, when considering a charge of fraud, will naturally require a higher degree of probability than that which it would require if considering whether negligence were established. It does not adopt so high a standard as a criminal court, even when considering a charge of a criminal nature, but still it does require a degree of probability which is commensurate with the occasion.

This passage was cited with approval in *Hanes v. Wawanesa Mutual Insurance Co.*, [1963] S.C.R. 154 at 161. A similar approach was put forward by Cartwright J. in *Smith v. Smith & Smedman*, [1952] 2 S.C.R. 312 at 331-32:

> I wish, however, to emphasize that in every civil action before the tribunal can safely find the affirmative of an issue of fact required to be proved it must be satisfied, and that whether or not it will be so satisfied must depend on the totality of the circumstances on which its judgment is formed including the gravity of the consequences.

Having regard to the fact that section 1 is being invoked for the purpose of justifying a violation of the constitutional rights and freedoms the *Charter* was designed to protect, a very high degree of probability will be, in the words of Lord Denning, "commensurate with the occasion". Where evidence is required in order to prove the constituent elements of a section 1 inquiry, and this will generally be the case, it should be cogent and persuasive and make clear to the Court the consequences of imposing or not imposing the limit. See *Law Society of Upper Canada v. Skapinker, supra*, at 384; *Singh v. Ministry of Employment and Immigration, supra*, at 217. A court will also need to know what alternative measures for implementing the objective were available to the legislators when they made their decisions. I should add, however, that there may be cases where certain elements of the section 1 analysis are obvious or self-evident.

To establish that a limit is reasonable and demonstrably justified in a free and democratic society, two central criteria must be satisfied. First, the objective, which the measures responsible for a limit on a *Charter* right or freedom are designed to serve, must be "of sufficient importance to warrant overriding a constitutionally protected right or freedom": *R. v. Big M Drug Mart Ltd., supra*, at 352. The standard must be high in order to ensure that objectives which are trivial or discordant with the principles integral to a free and democratic society do not gain section 1 protection. It is necessary, at a minimum, that an objective relate to concerns which are pressing and substantial in a free and democratic society before it can be characterized as sufficiently important.

Second, once a sufficiently significant objective is recognized, then the party invoking section 1 must show that the means chosen are reasonable and demonstrably justified. This involves "a form of proportionality test": *R. v. Big M Drug Mart Ltd., supra*, at 352. Although the nature of the proportionality test will vary depending on the circumstances, in each case courts will be required to balance the interests of society with those of individuals and groups. There are, in my view, three important components of a proportionality test. First, the measures adopted must be carefully designed to achieve the objective in question. They must not be arbitrary, unfair or based on irrational considerations. In short, they must be rationally connected to the objective. Second, the means, even if rationally connected to the objective in this first sense, should impair "as little as possible" the right or freedom in question: *R. v. Big M Drug Mart Ltd., supra*, at 352. Third, there must be a proportionality between the *effects* of the measures which are responsible for limiting the *Charter* right or freedom, and the objective which has been identified as of "sufficient importance".

With respect to the third component, it is clear that the general effect of any measure impugned under section 1 will be the infringement of a right or freedom guaranteed by the *Charter*; this is the reason why resort to section 1 is necessary. The inquiry into effects must, however, go further. A wide range of rights and freedoms are guaranteed by the *Charter*, and an almost infinite number of factual situations may arise in respect of these. Some limits on rights and freedoms protected by the *Charter* will be more serious than others in terms of the nature of the right or freedom violated, the extent of the violation, and the degree to which the measures which impose the limit trench upon the integral principles of a free and democratic society. Even if an objective is of sufficient importance, and the first two elements of the proportionality test are satisfied, it is still possible that, because of the severity of the deleterious effects of a measure on individuals or groups, the measure will not be justified by the purposes it is intended to serve. The more severe the deleterious effects of a measure, the more important the objective must be if the measure is to be reasonable and demonstrably justified in a free and democratic society.

Having outlined the general principles of a section 1 inquiry, we must apply them to section 8 of the *Narcotic Control Act*. Is the reverse onus provision in section 8 a reasonable limit on the right to be presumed innocent until proven guilty beyond a reasonable doubt as can be demonstrably justified in a free and democratic society?

The starting point for formulating a response to this question is, as stated above, the nature of Parliament's interest or objective which accounts for the passage of section 8 of the *Narcotic Control Act*. According to the Crown, section 8 of the *Narcotic Control Act* is aimed at curbing drug trafficking by facilitating the conviction of drug traffickers. In my opinion, Parliament's concern with decreasing drug trafficking can be characterized as substantial and pressing. The problem of drug trafficking has been increasing since the 1950's at which time there was already considerable concern. (See *Report of the Special Committee on Traffic in Narcotic Drugs*, Appendix to Debates of the Senate, Canada, Session 1955, pp. 690-700; see also *Final Report, Commission of Inquiry into the Non-Medical Use of Drugs* (Ottawa, 1973)). Throughout this period, numerous measures were adopted by free and democratic societies, at both the international and national levels.

At the international level, on June 23, 1953, the *Protocol for Limiting and Regulating the Cultivation of the Poppy Plant, the Production of, International and Wholesale Trade in, and Use of Opium*, to which Canada is a signatory, was adopted by the United Nations Opium Conference held in New York. The *Single Convention on Narcotic Drugs, 1961*, was acceded to in New York on March 30, 1961. This treaty was signed by Canada on March 30, 1961. It entered into force on December 13, 1964. As stated in the Preamble, "addiction to narcotic drugs constitutes a serious evil for the individual and is fraught with social and economic danger to mankind, . . . ."

At the national level, statutory provisions have been enacted by numerous countries which, *inter alia*, attempt to deter drug trafficking by imposing criminal sanctions (see, for example, *Misuse of Drugs Act*, 1975, No. 116 (New Zealand); *Misuse of Drugs Act*, 1971, c. 38 (United Kingdom)).

The objective of protecting our society from the grave ills associated with drug trafficking, is, in my view, one of sufficient importance to warrant overriding a constitutionally protected right or freedom in certain cases. Moreover, the degree of seriousness of drug trafficking makes its acknowledgement as a sufficiently important objective for the purposes of section 1, to a large extent, self-evident. The first criterion of a section 1 inquiry, therefore, has been satisfied by the Crown.

The next stage of inquiry is a consideration of the means chosen by Parliament to achieve its objective. The means must be reasonable and demonstrably justified in a free and democratic society. As outlined above, this proportionality test should begin with a consideration of the rationality of the provision: is the reverse onus clause in section 8 rationally related to the objective of curbing drug trafficking? At a minimum, this requires that section 8 be internally rational; there must be a rational connection between the basic fact of possession and the presumed fact of possession for the purpose of trafficking. Otherwise, the reverse onus clause could give rise to unjustified and erroneous convictions for drug trafficking of persons guilty only of possession of narcotics.

In my view, section 8 does not survive this rational connection test. As Martin J.A. of the Ontario Court of Appeal concluded, possession of a small or negligible quantity of narcotics does not support the inference of trafficking. In other words, it would be irrational to infer that a person had an intent to traffic on the basis of his or her possession of a very small quantity of narcotics. The presumption required under section 8 of the *Narcotic Control Act* is overinclusive and could lead to results in certain cases which would defy both rationality and fairness. In light of the seriousness of the offence in question, which carries with it the possibility of imprisonment for life, I am further convinced that the first component of the proportionality test has not been satisfied by the Crown.

Having concluded that section 8 does not satisfy this first component of proportionality, it is unnecessary to consider the other two components.

## CONCLUSION

The Ontario Court of Appeal was correct in holding that section 8 of the *Narcotic Control Act* violates the *Canadian Charter of Rights and Freedoms* and is therefore of no force or effect. Section 8 imposes a limit on the right guaranteed by section 11(d) of the *Charter* which is not reasonable and is not demonstrably justified in a free and democratic society for the purpose of section 1. Accordingly, the constitutional question is answered as follows:

*Question*:

> Is section 8 of the *Narcotic Control Act* inconsistent with section 11(d) of the *Canadian Charter of Rights and Freedoms* and thus of no force and effect?

*Answer*: Yes

I would, therefore, dismiss the appeal.

[The concurring judgment of Estey J., McIntyre J. concurring, is omitted.]

# APPENDICES

# APPENDIX I

## Constitution Act, 1867

U.K., 30 & 31 Victoria, c. 3.

(Consolidated with amendments)

An Act for the Union of Canada, Nova Scotia, and New Brunswick, and the Government thereof; and for Purposes connected therewith.

*(29th March, 1867.)*

WHEREAS the Provinces of Canada, Nova Scotia and New Brunswick have expressed their Desire to be federally united into One Dominion under the Crown of the United Kingdom of Great Britain and Ireland, with a Constitution similar in Principle to that of the United Kingdom:

And whereas such a Union would conduce to the Welfare of the Provinces and promote the Interests of the British Empire:

And whereas on the Establishment of the Union by Authority of Parliament it is expedient, not only that the Constitution of the Legislative Authority in the Dominion be provided for, but also that the Nature of the Executive Government therein be declared:

And whereas it is expedient that Provision be made for the eventual Admission into the Union of other Parts of British North America: (1)

### I. – PRELIMINARY.

**1.** This Act may be cited as the *Constitution Act, 1867.*(2)   Short title.

---

(1) The enacting clause was repealed by the *Statute Law Revision Act, 1893*, 56-57 Vict., c. 14 (U.K.). It read as follows:

> Be it therefore enacted and declared by the Queen's Most Excellent Majesty, by and with the Advice and Consent of the Lords Spiritual and Temporal, and Commons, in this present Parliament assembled, and by the Authority of the same, as follows:

(2) As enacted by the *Constitution Act, 1982*, which came into force on April 17, 1982. The section, as originally enacted, read as follows:

> **1.** This Act may be cited as The British North America Act, 1867.

**2.** Repealed.(3)

## II. – Union.

Declaration of Union.

**3.** It shall be lawful for the Queen, by and with the Advice of Her Majesty's Most Honourable Privy Council, to declare by Proclamation that, on and after a Day therein appointed, not being more than Six Months after the passing of this Act, the Provinces of Canada, Nova Scotia, and New Brunswick shall form and be One Dominion under the Name of Canada; and on and after that Day those Three Provinces shall form and be One Dominion under that Name accordingly. (4)

Construction of subsequent Provisions of Act.

**4.** Unless it is otherwise expressed or implied, the Name Canada shall be taken to mean Canada as constituted under this Act.(5)

Four Provinces.

**5.** Canada shall be divided into Four Provinces, named Ontario, Quebec, Nova Scotia, and New Brunswick.(6)

---

(3) Section 2, repealed by the *Statute Law Revision Act, 1893,* 56-57 Vict., c. 14 (U.K.), read as follows:

> **2.** The Provisions of this Act referring to Her Majesty the Queen extend also to the Heirs and Successors of Her Majesty, Kings and Queens of the United Kingdom of Great Britain and Ireland.

(4) The first day of July, 1867, was fixed by proclamation dated May 22, 1867.

(5) Partially repealed by the *Statute Law Revision Act, 1893,* 56-57 Vict., c. 14 (U.K.). As originally enacted the section read as follows:

> **4.** The subsequent Provisions of this Act, shall, unless it is otherwise expressed or implied, commence and have effect on and after the Union, that is to say, on and after the Day appointed for the Union taking effect in the Queen's Proclamation; and in the same Provisions, unless it is otherwise expressed or implied, the Name Canada shall be taken to mean Canada as constituted under this Act.

(6) Canada now consists of ten provinces (Ontario, Quebec, Nova Scotia, New Brunswick, Manitoba, British Columbia, Prince Edward Island, Alberta, Saskatchewan and Newfoundland) and two territories (the Yukon Territory and the Northwest Territories).

The first territories added to the Union were Rupert's Land and the North-Western Territory, (subsequently designated the Northwest Territories), which were admitted pursuant to section 146 of the *Constitution Act, 1867* and the *Rupert's Land Act,* 1868, 31-32 Vict., c. 105 (U.K.), by the *Rupert's Land and North-Western Territory Order* of June 23, 1870, effective July 15, 1870. Prior to the admission of those territories the Parliament of Canada enacted *An Act for the temporary Government of Rupert's Land and the North-Western Territory when united with Canada* (32-33 Vict., c. 3), and the *Manitoba Act, 1870,* (33 Vict., c. 3), which provided for the formation of the –Province of Manitoba.

British Columbia was admitted into the Union pursuant to section 146 of the *Constitution Act, 1867,* by the *British Columbia Terms of Union,* being Order in Council of May 16, 1871, effective July 20, 1871.

Provinces of
Ontario and
Quebec.

**6.** The Parts of the Province of Canada (as it exists at the passing of this Act) which formerly constituted respectively the Provinces of Upper Canada and Lower Canada shall be deemed to be severed, and shall form Two separate Provinces. The Part which formerly constituted the Province of Upper Canada shall constitute the Province of Ontario; and the Part which formerly constituted the Province of Lower Canada shall constitute the Province of Quebec.

Provinces of Nova
Scotia and New
Brunswick.

**7.** The Provinces of Nova Scotia and New Brunswick shall have the same Limits as at the passing of this Act.

Decennial Census.

**8.** In the general Census of the Population of Canada which is hereby required to be taken in the Year One thousand eight hundred and seventy-one, and in every Tenth Year thereafter, the respective Populations of the Four Provinces shall be distinguished.

### III. – EXECUTIVE POWER.

Declaration of
Executive Power
in the Queen.

**9.** The Executive Government and Authority of and over Canada is hereby declared to continue and be vested in the Queen.

Application of
Provisions
referring to
Governor General.

**10.** The Provisions of this Act referring to the Governor General extend and apply to the Governor General for the Time being of Canada, or other the Chief Executive Officer or Admin-

---

Prince Edward Island was admitted pursuant to section 146 of the *Constitution Act, 1867,* by the *Prince Edward Island Terms of Union,* being Order in Council of June 26, 1873, effective July 1, 1873.

On June 29, 1871, the United Kingdom Parliament enacted the *Constitution Act, 1871* (34-35 Vict., c. 28) authorizing the creation of additional provinces out of territories not included in any province. Pursuant to this statute, the Parliament of Canada enacted the *Alberta Act* (July 20, 1905, 4-5 Edw. VII, c. 3) and the *Saskatchewan Act,* (July 20, 1905, 4-5 Edw. VII, c. 42), providing for the creation of the provinces of Alberta and Saskatchewan, respectively. Both these Acts came into force on Sept. 1, 1905.

Meanwhile, all remaining British possessions and territories in North America and the islands adjacent thereto, except the colony of Newfoundland and its dependencies, were admitted into the Canadian Confederation by the *Adjacent Territories Order,* dated July 31, 1880.

The Parliament of Canada added portions of the Northwest Territories to the adjoining provinces in 1912 by *The Ontario Boundaries Extension Act,* 1912, 2 Geo. V, c. 40, *The Quebec Boundaries Extension Act,* 1912, 2 Geo. V, c. 45 and *The Manitoba Boundaries Extension Act,* 1912, 2 Geo. V, c. 32, and further additions were made to Manitoba by *The Manitoba Boundaries Extension Act,* 1930, 20-21 Geo. V., c. 28.

The Yukon Territory was created out of the Northwest Territories in 1898 by *The Yukon Territory Act,* 61 Vict., c. 6, (Canada).

Newfoundland was added on March 31, 1949, by the *Newfoundland Act* (U.K.), 12-13 Geo. VI, c. 22, which ratified the Terms of Union between Canada and Newfoundland.

istrator for the Time being carrying on the Government of Canada on behalf and in the Name of the Queen, by whatever Title he is designated.

**Constitution of Privy Council for Canada.**

**11.** There shall be a Council to aid and advise in the Government of Canada, to be styled the Queen's Privy Council for Canada; and the Persons who are to be Members of that Council shall be from Time to Time chosen and summoned by the Governor General and sworn in as Privy Councillors, and Members thereof may be from Time to Time removed by the Governor General.

**All Powers under Acts to be exercised by Governor General with Advice of Privy Council, or alone.**

**12.** All Powers, Authorities, and Functions which under any Act of the Parliament of Great Britain, or of the Parliament of the United Kingdom of Great Britain and Ireland, or of the Legislature of Upper Canada, Lower Canada, Canada, Nova Scotia, or New Brunswick, are at the Union vested in or exerciseable by the respective Governors or Lieutenant Governors of those Provinces, with the Advice, or with the Advice and Consent, of the respective Executive Councils thereof, or in conjunction with those Councils, or with any Number of Members thereof, or by those Governors or Lieutenant Governors individually, shall, as far as the same continue in existence and capable of being exercised after the Union in relation to the Government of Canada, be vested in and exerciseable by the Governor General, with the Advice or with the Advice and Consent of or in conjunction with the Queen's Privy Council for Canada, or any Member thereof, or by the Governor General individually, as the Case requires, subject nevertheless (except with respect to such as exist under Acts of the Parliament of Great Britain or of the Parliament of the United Kingdom of Great Britain and Ireland) to be abolished or altered by the Parliament of Canada.(7)

**Application of Provisions referring to Governor General in Council.**

**13.** The Provisions of this Act referring to the Governor General in Council shall be construed as referring to the Governor General acting by and with the Advice of the Queen's Privy Council for Canada.

**Power to Her Majesty to authorize Governor General to appoint Deputies.**

**14.** It shall be lawful for the Queen, if Her Majesty thinks fit, to authorize the Governor General from Time to Time to appoint any Person or any Persons jointly or severally to be his Deputy or Deputies within any Part or Parts of Canada, and in that Capacity to exercise during the Pleasure of the Governor General such of the Powers, Authorities, and Functions of the

(7) See the notes to section 129, *infra.*

Governor General as the Governor General deems it necessary or expedient to assign to him or them, subject to any Limitations or Directions expressed or given by the Queen; but the Appointment of such a Deputy or Deputies shall not affect the Exercise by the Governor General himself of any Power, Authority or Function.

**15.** The Command-in-Chief of the Land and Naval Militia, and of all Naval and Military Forces, of and in Canada, is hereby declared to continue and be vested in the Queen.

Command of armed Forces to continue to be vested in the Queen.

**16.** Until the Queen otherwise directs, the Seat of Government of Canada shall be Ottawa.

Seat of Government of Canada.

## IV. – LEGISLATIVE POWER

**17.** There shall be One Parliament for Canada, consisting of the Queen, an Upper House styled the Senate, and the House of Commons.

Constitution of Parliament of Canada.

**18.** The privileges, immunities, and powers to be held, enjoyed, and exercised by the Senate and by the House of Commons, and by the Members thereof respectively, shall be such as are from time to time defined by Act of the Parliament of Canada, but so that any Act of the Parliament of Canada defining such privileges, immunities, and powers shall not confer any privileges, immunities, or powers exceeding those at the passing of such Act held, enjoyed, and exercised by the Commons House of Parliament of the United Kingdom of Great Britain and Ireland, and by the Members thereof.(8)

Privileges, etc. of Houses.

**19.** The Parliament of Canada shall be called together not later than Six Months after the Union.(9)

First Session of the Parliament of Canada.

---

(8) Repealed and re-enacted by the *Parliament of Canada Act, 1875*, 38-39 Vict., c. 38 (U.K.). The original section read as follows:

> **18.** The Privileges, Immunities, and Powers to be held, enjoyed, and exercised by the Senate and by the House of Commons and by the Members thereof respectively shall be such as are from Time to Time defined by Act of the Parliament of Canada, but so that the same shall never exceed those at the passing of this Act held, enjoyed, and exercised by the Commons House of Parliament of the United Kingdom of Great Britain and Ireland and by the Members thereof.

(9) Spent. The first session of the first Parliament began on November 6, 1867.

**20.** Repealed.(10)

### The Senate.

Number of
Senators.

**21.** The Senate shall, subject to the Provisions of this Act, consist of One Hundred and four Members, who shall be styled Senators.(11)

Representation of
Provinces in
Senate.

**22.** In relation to the Constitution of the Senate Canada shall be deemed to consist of Four Divisions:–

1. Ontario;
2. Quebec;
3. The Maritime Provinces, Nova Scotia and New Brunswick, and Prince Edward Island;
4. The Western Provinces of Manitoba, British Columbia, Saskatchewan, and Alberta;

which Four Divisions shall (subject to the Provisions of this Act) be equally represented in the Senate as follows: Ontario by twenty-four senators; Quebec by twenty-four senators; the Maritime Provinces and Prince Edward Island by twenty-four senators, ten thereof representing Nova Scotia, ten thereof representing New Brunswick, and four thereof representing Prince Edward Island; the Western Provinces by twenty-four senators, six thereof representing Manitoba, six thereof representing British Columbia, six thereof representing Saskatchewan, and six thereof representing Alberta; Newfoundland shall be entitled to

---

(10) Section 20, repealed by the Schedule to the *Constitution Act, 1982*, read as follows:

**20.** There shall be a Session of the Parliament of Canada once at least in every Year, so that Twelve Months shall not intervene between the last Sitting of the Parliament in one Session and its first Sitting in the next Session.

Section 20 has been replaced by section 5 of the *Constitution Act, 1982*, which provides that there shall be a sitting of Parliament at least once every twelve months.

(11) As amended by the *Constitution Act, 1915*, 5-6 Geo. V, c. 45 (U.K.) and modified by the *Newfoundland Act*, 12-13 Geo. VI, c. 22 (U.K.), and the *Constitution Act (No. 2), 1975*, S.C. 1974-75-76, c. 53.

The original section read as follows:

**21.** The Senate shall, subject to the Provisions of this Act, consist of Seventy-two Members, who shall be styled Senators.

The *Manitoba Act, 1870*, added two for Manitoba; the *British Columbia Terms of Union* added three; upon admission of Prince Edward Island four more were provided by section 147 of the *Constitution Act, 1867*; the *Alberta Act* and the *Saskatchewan Act* each added four. The Senate was reconstituted at 96 by the *Constitution Act, 1915*. Six more Senators were added upon union with Newfoundland, and one Senator each was added for the Yukon Territory and the Northwest Territories by the *Constitution Act (No. 2), 1975*.

be represented in the Senate by six members; the Yukon Territory and the Northwest Territories shall be entitled to be represented in the Senate by one member each.

In the Case of Quebec each of the Twenty-four Senators representing that Province shall be appointed for One of the Twenty-four Electoral Divisions of Lower Canada specified in Schedule A. to Chapter One of the Consolidated statutes of Canada.(12)

**23.** The Qualification of a Senator shall be as follows:

Qualifications of Senator.

(1)  He shall be of the full age of Thirty Years:

(2)  He shall be either a natural-born Subject of the Queen, or a Subject of the Queen naturalized by an Act of the Parliament of Great Britain, or of the Parliament of the United Kingdom of Great Britain and Ireland, or of the Legislature of One of the Provinces of Upper Canada, Lower Canada, Canada, Nova Scotia, or New Brunswick, before the Union, or of the Parliament of Canada, after the Union:

(3)  He shall be legally or equitably seised as of Freehold for his own Use and Benefit of Lands or Tenements held in Free and Common Socage, or seised or possessed for his own Use and Benefit of Lands or Tenements held in Franc-alleu or in Roture, within the Province for which he is appointed, of the Value of Four thousand Dollars, over and above all Rents, Dues, Debts, Charges, Mortgages, and Incumbrances due or payable out of or charged on or affecting the same:

---

(12) As amended by the *Constitution Act, 1915*, the *Newfoundland Act*, 12-13 Geo. VI, c. 22 (U.K.), and the *Constitution Act (No. 2), 1975*, S.C. 1974-75-76, c. 53. The original section read as follows:

> **22.** In relation to the Constitution of the Senate, Canada shall be deemed to consist of Three Divisions:
>
> 1. Ontario;
>
> 2. Quebec;
>
> 3. The Maritime Provinces, Nova Scotia and New Brunswick; which Three Divisions shall (subject to the Provisions of this Act) be equally represented in the Senate as follows: Ontario by Twenty-four Senators; Quebec by Twenty-four Senators; and the Maritime Provinces by Twenty-four Senators, Twelve thereof representing Nova Scotia, and Twelve thereof representing New Brunswick.
>
> In the case of Quebec each of the Twenty-four Senators representing that province shall be appointed for One of the Twenty-four Electoral Divisions of Lower Canada specified in Schedule A. to Chapter One of the Consolidated Statutes of Canada.

(4)  His Real and Personal Property shall be together worth Four thousand Dollars over and above his Debts and Liabilities:

(5)  He shall be resident in the Province for which he is appointed:

(6)  In the case of Quebec he shall have his Real Property Qualification in the Electoral Division for which he is appointed, or shall be resident in that Division.(13)

**Summons of Senator.**

**24.** The Governor General shall from Time to Time, in the Queen's Name, by Instrument under the Great Seal of Canada, summon qualified Persons to the Senate; and, subject to the Provisions of this Act, every Person so summoned shall become and be a Member of the Senate and a Senator.

**25.** Repealed.(14)

**Addition of Senators in certain cases.**

**26.** If at any Time on the Recommendation of the Governor General the Queen thinks fit to direct that Four or Eight Members be added to the Senate, the Governor General may by Summons to Four or Eight qualified Persons (as the Case may be), representing equally the Four Divisions of Canada, add to the Senate accordingly.(15)

**Reduction of Senate to normal Number.**

**27.** In case of such Addition being at any Time made, the Governor General shall not summon any Person to the Senate, except upon a further like Direction by the Queen on the like Recommendation, to represent one of the Four Divisions until

---

(13) Section 2 of the *Constitution Act (No. 2), 1975,* S.C. 1974-75-76, c. 53 provided that for the purposes of that Act (which added one Senator each for the Yukon Territory and the Northwest Territories) the term "Province" in section 23 of the *Constitution Act, 1867,* has the same meaning as is assigned to the term "province" by section 28 of the *Interpretation Act,* R.S.C. 1970, c. I-23, which provides that the term "province" means "a province of Canada, and includes the Yukon Territory and the Northwest Territories."

(14) Repealed by the *Statute Law Revision Act, 1893,* 56-57 Vict., 14 (U.K.). The section read as follows:

> **25.** Such Persons shall be first summoned to the Senate as the Queen by Warrant under Her Majesty's Royal Sign Manual thinks fit to approve, and their Names shall be inserted in the Queen's Proclamation of Union.

(15) As amended by the *Constitution Act, 1915,* 5-6 Geo. V, c. 45 (U.K.). The original section read as follows:

> **26.** If at any Time on the Recommendation of the Governor General the Queen thinks fit to direct that Three or Six Members be added to the Senate, the Governor General may by Summons to Three or Six qualified Persons (as the Case may be), representing equally the Three Divisions of Canada, add to the Senate accordingly.

such Division is represented by Twenty-four Senators and no more.(16)

**28.** The Number of Senators shall not at any Time exceed One Hundred and twelve.(17)

Maximum Number of Senators.

**29.** (1) Subject to subsection (2), a Senator shall, subject to the provisions of this Act, hold his place in the Senate for life.

Tenure of Place in Senate.

(2) A Senator who is summoned to the Senate after the coming into force of this subsection shall, subject to this Act, hold his place in the Senate until he attains the age of seventy-five years.(18)

Retirement upon attaining age of seventy-five years.

[Sections 30 to 36 are omitted.]

## The House of Commons.

**37.** The House of Commons shall, subject to the Provisions of this Act, consist of two hundred and eighty-two members of whom ninety-five shall be elected for Ontario, seventy-five for Quebec, eleven for Nova Scotia, ten for New Brunswick, fourteen for Manitoba, twenty-eight for British Columbia, four for Prince Edward Island, twenty-one for Alberta, fourteen for Saskatchewan, seven for Newfoundland, one for the Yukon Territory and two for the Northwest Territories.(20)

Constitution of House of Commons in Canada.

---

(16) As amended by the *Constitution Act, 1915*, 5-6 Geo. V, c. 45 (U.K.). The original section read as follows:

> **27.** In case of such Addition being at any Time made the Governor General shall not summon any Person to the Senate except on a further like Direction by the Queen on the like Recommendation, until each of the Three Divisions of Canada is represented by Twenty-four Senators and no more.

(17) As amended by the *Constitution Act, 1915*, 5-6 Geo. V, c. 45 (U.K.). and the *Constitution Act (No. 2), 1975*, S.C. 1974-75-76, c. 53. The original section read as follows:

> **28.** The Number of Senators shall not at any Time exceed Seventy-eight.

(18) As enacted by the *Constitution Act, 1965*, Statutes of Canada, 1965, c. 4 which came into force on the 1st of June 1965. The original section read as follows:

> **29.** A Senator shall, subject to the Provisions of this Act, hold his Place in the Senate for Life.

(20) The figures given here result from the application of section 51, as enacted by the *Constitution Act, 1974*, S.C. 1974-75-76, c. 13, amended by the *Constitution Act (No. 1), 1975*, S.C. 1974-75-76, c. 28 and readjusted pursuant to the *Electoral Boundaries Readjustment Act*, R.S.C. 1970, c. E-2. The original section (which was altered from time to time as the result of the addition of new provinces and changes in population) read as follows:

> **37.** The House of Commons shall, subject to the Provisions of this Act, consist of one hundred and eighty-one members, of whom Eighty-two shall be elected for Ontario, Sixty-five for Quebec, Nineteen for Nova Scotia, and Fifteen for New Brunswick.

Summoning of
House of
Commons.

**38.** The Governor General shall from Time to Time, in the Queen's Name, by Instrument under the Great Seal of Canada, summon and call together the House of Commons.

[Sections 39 to 49 are omitted.]

Duration of House
of Commons.

**50.** Every House of Commons shall continue for Five Years from the Day of the Return of the Writs for choosing the House (subject to be sooner dissolved by the Governor General), and no longer.(26)

[Section 51 is omitted.]

Constitution of
House of
Commons.

**51A.** Notwithstanding anything in this Act a province shall always be entitled to a number of members in the House of Commons not less than the number of senators representing such province.(29)

Increase of
Number of House
of Commons.

**52.** The Number of Members of the House of Commons may be from Time to Time increased by the Parliament of Canada, provided the proportionate Representation of the Provinces prescribed by this Act is not thereby disturbed.

*Money Votes; Royal Assent.*

Appropriation and
Tax Bills.

**53.** Bills for appropriating any Part of the Public Revenue, or for imposing any Tax or Impost, shall originate in the House of Commons.

Recommendation
of Money Votes.

**54.** It shall not be lawful for the House of Commons to adopt or pass any Vote, Resolution, Address, or Bill for the Appropriation of any Part of the Public Revenue, or of any Tax or Impost, to any Purpose that has not been first recommended to that House by Message of the Governor General in the Session in which such Vote, Resolution, Address, or Bill is proposed.

Royal Assent to
Bills, etc.

**55.** Where a Bill passed by the Houses of the Parliament is presented to the Governor General for the Queen's Assent, he shall declare, according to his Discretion, but subject to the Provisions of this Act and to Her Majesty's Instructions, either that he assents thereto in the Queen's Name, or that he with-

---

(26)  The term of the twelfth Parliament was extended by the *British North America Act, 1916,* 6-7 Geo. V, c. 19 (U.K.), which Act was repealed by the *Statute Law Revision Act, 1927,* 17-18 Geo. V, c. 42 (U.K.). See also subsection 4(1) of the *Constitution Act, 1982,* which provides that no House of Commons shall continue for longer than five years from the date fixed for the return of the writs at a general election of its members, and subsection 4(2) thereof, which provides for continuation of the House of Commons in special circumstances.

(29)  As enacted by the *Constitution Act, 1915,* 5-6 Geo. V, c. 45 (U.K.).

holds the Queen's Assent, or that he reserves the Bill for the Signification of the Queen's Pleasure.

**56.** Where the Governor General assents to a Bill in the Queen's-Name, he shall by the first convenient Opportunity send an authentic Copy of the Act to one of Her Majesty's Principal Secretaries of State, and if the Queen in Council within Two Years after Receipt thereof by the Secretary of State thinks fit to disallow the Act, such Disallowance (with a Certificate of the Secretary of State of the Day on which the Act was received by him) being signified by the Governor General, by Speech or Message to each of the Houses of the Parliament or by Proclamation, shall annul the Act from and after the Day of such Signification.

*Disallowance by Order in Council of Act assented to by Governor General.*

**57.** A Bill reserved for the Signification of the Queen's Pleasure shall not have any Force unless and until, within Two Years from the Day on which it was presented to the Governor General for the Queen's Assent, the Governor General signifies, by Speech or Message to each of the Houses of the Parliament or by Proclamation, that it has received the Assent of the Queen in Council.

*Signification of Queen's Pleasure on Bill reserved.*

An Entry of every such Speech, Message, or Proclamation shall be made in the Journal of each House, and a Duplicate thereof duly attested shall be delivered to the proper Officer to be kept among the Records of Canada.

## V. – PROVINCIAL CONSTITUTIONS.

### Executive Power.

**58.** For each Province there shall be an Officer, styled the Lieutenant Governor, appointed by the Governor General in Council by Instrument under the Great Seal of Canada.

*Appointment of Lieutenant Governors of Provinces.*

**59.** A Lieutenant Governor shall hold Office during the Pleasure of the Governor General; but any Lieutenant Governor appointed after the Commencement of the First Session of the Parliament of Canada shall not be removeable within Five Years from his Appointment, except for Cause assigned, which shall be communicated to him in Writing within One Month after the Order for his Removal is made, and shall be communicated by Message to the Senate and to the House of Commons within One Week thereafter if the Parliament is then sitting, and if not then within One Week after the Commencement of the next Session of the Parliament.

*Tenure of Office of Lieutenant Governor.*

**Salaries of Lieutenant Governors.**

**60.** The Salaries of the Lieutenant Governors shall be fixed and provided by the Parliament of Canada.(30)

**Oaths, etc., of Lieutenant Governor.**

**61.** Every Lieutenant Governor shall, before assuming the Duties of his Office, make and subscribe before the Governor General or some Person authorized by him Oaths of Allegiance and Office similar to those taken by the Governor General.

**Application of provisions referring to Lieutenant Governor.**

**62.** The Provisions of this Act referring to the Lieutenant Governor extend and apply to the Lieutenant Governor for the Time being of each Province, or other the Chief Executive Officer or Administrator for the Time being carrying on the Government of the Province, by whatever Title he is designated.

**Appointment of Executive Officers for Ontario and Quebec.**

**63.** The Executive Council of Ontario and of Quebec shall be composed of such Persons as the Lieutenant Governor from Time to Time thinks fit, and in the first instance of the following Officers, namely, – the Attorney General, the Secretary and Registrar of the Province, the Treasurer of the Province, the Commissioner of Crown Lands, and the Commissioner of Agriculture and Public Works, with in Quebec, the Speaker of the Legislative Council and the Solicitor General.(31)

**Executive Government of Nova Scotia and New Brunswick.**

**64.** The Constitution of the Executive Authority in each of the Provinces of Nova Scotia and New Brunswick shall, subject to the Provisions of this Act, continue as it exists at the Union until altered under the Authority of this Act.(32)

**Powers to be exercised by Lieutenant Governor of Ontario or Quebec with Advice, or alone.**

**65.** All Powers, Authorities, and Functions which under any Act of the Parliament of Great Britain, or of the Parliament of the United Kingdom of Great Britain and Ireland, or of the Legislature of Upper Canada, Lower Canada, or Canada, were or are before or at the Union vested in or exerciseable by the respective Governors or Lieutenant Governors of those Provinces, with the Advice or with the Advice and Consent of the respective Executive Councils thereof, or in conjunction with those Councils, or with any Number of Members thereof, or by those Governors or Lieutenant Governors individually,

---

(30) Provided for by the *Salaries Act*, R.S.C. 1970, c. S-2.

(31) Now provided for in Ontario by the *Executive Council Act*, R.S.O. 1980, c. 147, and in Quebec by the *Executive Power Act*, R.S.Q. 1977, c. E-18.

(32) A similar provision was included in each of the instruments admitting British Columbia, Prince Edward Island, and Newfoundland. The Executive Authorities for Manitoba, Alberta and Saskatchewan were established by the statutes creating those provinces. See the notes to section 5, *supra*.

shall, as far as the same are capable of being exercised after the Union in relation to the Government of Ontario and Quebec respectively, be vested in and shall or may be exercised by the Lieutenant Governor of Ontario and Quebec respectively, with the Advice or with the Advice and consent of or in conjunction with the respective Executive Councils, or any Members thereof, or by the Lieutenant Governor individually, as the Case requires, subject nevertheless (except with respect to such as exist under Acts of the Parliament of Great Britain, or of the Parliament of the United Kingdom of Great Britain and Ireland,) to be abolished or altered by the respective Legislatures of Ontario and Quebec.(33)

**66.** The Provisions of this Act referring to the Lieutenant Governor in Council shall be construed as referring to the Lieutenant Governor of the Province acting by and with the Advice of the Executive Council thereof.

*Application of Provisions referring to Lieutenant Governor in Council.*

**67.** The Governor General in Council may from Time to Time appoint an Administrator to execute the office and Functions of Lieutenant Governor during his Absence, Illness, or other Inability.

*Administration in Absence, etc., of Lieutenant Governor.*

**68.** Unless and until the Executive Government of any Province otherwise directs with respect to that Province, the Seats of Government of the Provinces shall be as follows, namely, – of Ontario, the City of Toronto; of Quebec, the City of Quebec; of Nova Scotia, the City of Halifax; and of New Brunswick, the City of Fredericton.

*Seats of Provincial Governments.*

*Legislative Power.*

### 1.–ONTARIO.

**69.** There shall be a Legislature for Ontario consisting of the Lieutenant Governor and of One House, styled the Legislative Assembly of Ontario.

*Legislature for Ontario.*

[Section 70 is omitted.]

### 2.–QUEBEC.

**71.** There shall be a Legislature for Quebec consisting of the Lieutenant Governor and of Two Houses, styled the Legis-

*Legislature for Quebec.*

---

(33) See the notes to section 129, *infra.*

lative Council of Quebec and the Legislative Assembly of Quebec.(35)

[Sections 72 to 85 are omitted.]

Yearly Session of
Legislature.

**86.** There shall be a Session of the Legislature of Ontario and of that of Quebec once at least in every Year, so that Twelve Months shall not intervene between the last Sitting of the Legislature in each Province in one Session and its first Sitting in the next Session.

[Section 87 is omitted.]

### 4.–NOVA SCOTIA AND NEW BRUNSWICK.

Constitutions of
Legislatures of
Nova Scotia and
New Brunswick.

**88.** The Constitution of the Legislature of each of the Provinces of Nova Scotia and New Brunswick shall, subject to the Provisions of this Act, continue as it exists at the Union until altered under the Authority of this Act.(42)

**89.** Repealed.(43)

---

(35) The Act respecting the Legislative Council of Quebec, S.Q. 1968, c. 9, provided that the Legislature for Quebec shall consist of the Lieutenant Governor and the National Assembly of Quebec, and repealed the provisions of the *Legislature Act*, R.S.Q. 1964, c. 6, relating to the Legislative Council of Quebec. Sections 72 to 79 following are therefore completely spent.

(42) Partially repealed by the *Statute Law Revision Act, 1893*, 56-57 Vict., c. 14 (U.K.), which deleted the following concluding words of the original enactment:

> and the House of Assembly of New Brunswick existing at the passing of this Act shall, unless sooner dissolved, continue for the Period for which it was elected.

A similar provision was included in each of the instruments admitting British Columbia, Prince Edward Island and Newfoundland. The Legislatures of Manitoba, Alberta and Saskatchewan were established by the statutes creating those provinces. See the footnotes to section 5, *supra*.

See also sections 3 to 5 of the *Constitution Act, 1982,* which prescribe democratic rights applicable to all provinces, and subitem 2(2) of the Schedule to that Act, which sets out the repeal of section 20 of the *Manitoba Act, 1870*. Section 20 of the *Manitoba Act, 1870,* has been replaced by section 5 of the *Constitution Act, 1982.*

Section 20 reads as follows:

> **20.** There shall be a Session of the Legislature once at least in every year, so that twelve months shall not intervene between the last sitting of the Legislature in one Session and its first sitting in the next Session.

(43) Repealed by the *Statute Law Revision Act, 1893,* 56-57 Vict., c. 14 (U.K.). The section read as follows: .

> 5. – Ontario, Quebec, and Nova Scotia.

> **89.** Each of the Lieutenant Governors of Ontario, Quebec and Nova Scotia shall cause Writs to be issued for the First Election of Members of the Legislative Assembly thereof in such Form and by such Person as he thinks

## 6.–THE FOUR PROVINCES.

**90.** The following Provisions of this Act respecting the Parliament of Canada, namely, – the Provisions relating to Appropriation and Tax Bills, the Recommendation of Money Votes, the Assent to Bills, the Disallowance of Acts, and the Signification of Pleasure on Bills reserved, – shall extend and apply to the Legislatures of the several Provinces as if those Provisions were here re-enacted and made applicable in Terms to the respective Provinces and the Legislatures thereof, with the Substitution of the Lieutenant Governor of the Province for the Governor General, of the Governor General for the Queen and for a Secretary of State, of One Year for Two Years, and of the Province for Canada.

Application to Legislatures of Provisions respecting Money Votes, etc.

## VI. – DISTRIBUTION OF LEGISLATIVE POWERS.

### *Powers of the Parliament.*

**91.** It shall be lawful for the Queen, by and with the Advice and Consent of the Senate and House of Commons, to make Laws for the Peace, Order, and good Government of Canada, in relation to all Matters not coming within the Classes of Subjects by this Act assigned exclusively to the Legislatures of the Provinces; and for greater Certainty, but not so as to restrict the Generality of the foregoing Terms of this Section, it is hereby declared that (notwithstanding anything in this Act) the exclusive Legislative Authority of the Parliament of Canada extends to all Matters coming within the Classes of Subjects next hereinafter enumerated; that is to say, –

Legislative Authority of Parliament of Canada.

1.  Repealed. (44)

---

fit, and at such Time and addressed to such Returning Officer as the Governor General directs, and so that the First Election of Member of Assembly for any Electoral District or any Subdivision thereof shall be held at the same Time and at the same Places as the Election for a Member to serve in the House of Commons of Canada for the Electoral District.

(44) Class 1 was added by the *British North America (No. 2) Act, 1949*, 13 Geo. VI, c. 8 (U.K.). That Act and class 1 were repealed by the *Constitution Act, 1982*. The matters referred to in class 1 are provided for in subsection 4(2) and Part V of the *Constitution Act, 1982*. As enacted, class 1 read as follows:

1.  The amendment from time to time of the Constitution of Canada, except as regards matters coming within the classes of subjects by this Act assigned exclusively to the Legislatures of the provinces, or as regards rights or privileges by this or any other Constitutional Act granted or secured to the Legislature or the Government of a province, or to any class of persons with respect to schools or as regards the use of the English or the French language or as regards the requirements that there shall be a session of the Parliament

1A. The Public Debt and Property.(45)
 2. The Regulation of Trade and Commerce.
2A. Unemployment insurance.(46)
 3. The raising of Money by any Mode or System of Taxation.
 4. The borrowing of Money on the Public Credit.
 5. Postal Service.
 6. The Census and Statistics.
 7. Militia, Military and Naval Service, and Defence.
 8. The fixing of and providing for the Salaries and Allowances of Civil and other Officers of the Government of Canada.
 9. Beacons, Buoys, Lighthouses, and Sable Island.
10. Navigation and Shipping.
11. Quarantine and the Establishment and Maintenance of Marine Hospitals.
12. Sea Coast and Inland Fisheries.
13. Ferries between a Province and any British or Foreign Country or between Two Provinces.
14. Currency and Coinage.
15. Banking, Incorporation of Banks, and the Issue of Paper Money.
16. Savings Banks.
17. Weights and Measures.
18. Bills of Exchange and Promissory Notes.
19. Interest.
20. Legal Tender.
21. Bankruptcy and Insolvency.
22. Patents of Invention and Discovery.
23. Copyrights.
24. Indians, and Lands reserved for the Indians.
25. Naturalization and Aliens.
26. Marriage and Divorce.
27. The Criminal Law, except the Constitution of Courts of Criminal Jurisdiction, but including the Procedure in Criminal Matters.

---

of Canada at least once each year, and that no House of Commons shall continue for more than five years from the day of the return of the Writs for choosing the House: provided, however, that a House of Commons may in time of real or apprehended war, invasion or insurrection be continued by the Parliament of Canada if such continuation is not opposed by the votes of more than one-third of the members of such House.

(45) Re-numbered by the *British North America (No. 2) Act, 1949.*

(46) Added by the *Constitution Act, 1940,* 3-4 Geo. VI, c. 36 (U.K.).

28. The Establishment, Maintenance, and Management of Penitentiaries.

29. Such Classes of Subjects as are expressly excepted in the Enumeration of the Classes of Subjects by this Act assigned exclusively to the Legislatures of the Provinces.

And any Matter coming within any of the Classes of Subjects enumerated in this Section shall not be deemed to come within the Class of Matters of a local or private Nature comprised in the Enumeration of the Classes of Subjects by this Act assigned exclusively to the Legislatures of the Provinces.(47)

---

(47) Legislative authority has been conferred on Parliament by other Acts as follows:

**1.** The *Constitution Act, 1871*, 34-35 Vict., c. 28 (U.K.).

**2.** The Parliament of Canada, may from time to time establish new Provinces in any territories forming for the time being part of the Dominion of Canada, but not included in any Province thereof, and may, at the time of such establishment, make provision for the constitution and administration of any such Province, and for the passing of laws for the peace, order, and good government of such Province, and for its representation in the said Parliament.

**3.** The Parliament of Canada may from time to time, with the consent of the Legislature of any province of the said Dominion, increase, diminish, or otherwise alter the limits of such Province, upon such terms and conditions as may be agreed to by the said Legislature, and may, with the like consent, make provision respecting the effect and operation of any such increase or diminution or alteration of territory in relation to any Province affected thereby.

**4.** The Parliament of Canada may from time to time make provision for the administration, peace, order, and good government of any territory not for the time being included in any Province.

**5.** The following Acts passed by the said Parliament of Canada, and intituled respectively, – "An Act for the temporary government of Rupert's Land and the North Western Territory when united with Canada"; and "An Act to amend and continue the Act thirty-two and thirty-three Victoria, chapter three, and to establish and provide for the government of "the Province of Manitoba", shall be and be deemed to have been valid and effectual for all purposes whatsoever from the date at which they respectively received the assent, in the Queen's name, of the Governor General of the said Dominion of Canada.

**6.** Except as provided by the third section of this Act, it shall not be competent for the Parliament of Canada to alter the provisions of the last-mentioned Act of the said Parliament in so far as it relates to the Province of Manitoba, or of any other Act hereafter establishing new Provinces in the said Dominion, subject always to the right of the Legislature of the Province of Manitoba to alter from time to time the provisions of any law respecting the qualification of electors and members of the Legislative Assembly, and to make laws respecting elections in the said Province.

*Exclusive Powers of Provincial Legislatures.*

Subjects of
exclusive
Provincial
Legislation.

**92.** In each Province the Legislature may exclusively make Laws in relation to Matters coming within the Classes of Subject next hereinafter enumerated; that is to say, –

1. Repealed.(48)
2. Direct Taxation within the Province in order to the raising of a Revenue for Provincial Purposes.
3. The borrowing of Money on the sole Credit of the Province.
4. The Establishment and Tenure of Provincial Offices and the Appointment and Payment of Provincial Officers.
5. The Management and Sale of the Public Lands belonging to the Province and of the Timber and Wood thereon.
6. The Establishment, Maintenance, and Management of Public and Reformatory Prisons in and for the Province.
7. The Establishment, Maintenance, and Management of Hospitals, Asylums, Charities, and Eleemosynary Institutions in and for the Province, other than Marine Hospitals.

---

The *Rupert's Land Act 1868,* 31-32 Vict., c. 105 (U.K.) (repealed by the *Statute Law Revision Act, 1893,* 56-57 Vict., c. 14 (U.K.)) had previously conferred similar authority in relation to Rupert's Land and the North Western Territory upon admission of those areas.

2. The *Constitution Act, 1886,* 49-50 Vict., c. 35 (U.K.).

> **1.** The Parliament of Canada may from time to time make provision for the representation in the Senate and House of Commons of Canada, or in either of them, of any territories which for the time being form part of the Dominion of Canada, but are not included in any province thereof.

3. The *Statute of Westminster, 1931,* 22 Geo. V, c. 4 (U.K.).

> **3.** It is hereby declared and enacted that the Parliament of a Dominion has full power to make laws having extra-territorial operation.

4. Section 44 of the *Constitution Act, 1982,* authorizes Parliament to amend the Constitution of Canada in relation to the executive government of Canada or the Senate and House of Commons. Sections 38, 41, 42, and 43 of that Act authorize the Senate and House of Commons to give their approval to certain other constitutional amendments by resolution.

(48) Class 1 was repealed by the *Constitution Act, 1982.* As enacted, it read as follows:

> **1.** The Amendment from Time to Time, notwithstanding anything in this Act, of the Constitution of the province, except as regards the Office of Lieutenant Governor.

Section 45 of the *Constitution Act, 1982,* now authorizes legislatures to make laws amending the constitution of the province. Sections 38, 41, 42, and 43 of that Act authorize legislative assemblies to give their approval by resolution to certain other amendments to the Constitution of Canada.

8. Municipal Institutions in the Province.
9. Shop, Saloon, Tavern, Auctioneer, and other Licences in order to the raising of a Revenue for Provincial, Local, or Municipal Purposes.
10. Local Works and Undertakings other than such as are of the following Classes: –

    (*a*) Lines of Steam or other Ships, Railways, Canals, Telegraphs, and other Works and Undertakings connecting the Province with any other or others of the Provinces, or extending beyond the Limits of the Province;

    (*b*) Lines of Steam Ships between the Province and any British or Foreign Country;

    (*c*) Such Works as, although wholly situate within the Province, are before or after their Execution declared by the Parliament of Canada to be for the general Advantage of Canada or for the Advantage of Two or more of the Provinces.

11. The Incorporation of Companies with Provincial Objects.
12. The Solemnization of Marriage in the Province.
13. Property and Civil Rights in the Province.
14. The Administration of Justice in the Province, including the Constitution, Maintenance, and Organization of Provincial Courts, both of Civil and of Criminal Jurisdiction, and including Procedure in Civil Matters in those Courts.
15. The Imposition of Punishment by Fine, Penalty, or Imprisonment for enforcing any Law of the Province made in relation to any matter coming within any of the Classes of Subjects enumerated in this Section.
16. Generally all Matters of a merely local or private Nature in the Province.

*Non-Renewable Natural Resources, Forestry Resources and Electrical Energy.*

**92A.** (1) In each province, the legislature may exclusively make laws in relation to

   (*a*) exploration for non-renewable natural resources in the province;

   (*b*) development, conservation and management of non-renewable natural resources and forestry resources in the province, including laws in relation to the rate of primary production therefrom; and

   (*c*) development, conservation and management of

Laws respecting non-renewable natural resources, forestry resources and electrical energy.

sites and facilities in the province for the generation and production of electrical energy.

Export from provinces of resources.

(2) In each province, the legislature may make laws in relation to the export from the province to another part of Canada of the primary production from non-renewable natural resources and forestry resources in the province and the production from facilities in the province for the generation of electrical energy, but such laws may not authorize or provide for discrimination in prices or in supplies exported to another part of Canada.

Authority of Parliament.

(3) Nothing in subsection (2) derogates from the authority of Parliament to enact laws in relation to the matters referred to in that subsection and, where such a law of Parliament and a law of a province conflict, the law of Parliament prevails to the extent of the conflict.

Taxation of resources.

(4) In each province, the legislature may make laws in relation to the raising of money by any mode or system of taxation in respect of
  (a) non-renewable natural resources and forestry resources in the province and the primary production therefrom, and
  (b) sites and facilities in the province for the generation of electrical energy and the production therefrom,
whether or not such production is exported in whole or in part from the province, but such laws may not authorize or provide for taxation that differentiates between production exported to another part of Canada and production not exported from the province.

"Primary production".

(5) The expression "primary production" has the meaning assigned by the Sixth Schedule.

Existing powers or rights.

(6) Nothing in subsections (1) to (5) derogates from any powers or rights that a legislature or government of a province had immediately before the coming into force of this section.(49)

*Education.*

**93.** In and for each Province the Legislature may exclusively make Laws in relation to Education, subject and according to the following Provisions: –

---

(49) Added by the *Constitution Act, 1982.*

(1)   Nothing in any such Law shall prejudicially affect any Right or Privilege with respect to Denominational Schools which any Class of Persons have by Law in the Province at the Union:

(2)   All the Powers, Privileges, and Duties at the Union by Law conferred and imposed in Upper Canada on the Separate Schools and School Trustees of the Queen's Roman Catholic Subjects shall be and the same are hereby extended to the Dissentient Schools of the Queen's Protestant and Roman Catholic Subjects in Quebec:

(3)   Where in any Province a System of Separate or Dissentient Schools exists by Law at the Union or is thereafter established by the Legislature of the Province, an Appeal shall lie to the Governor General in Council from any Act or Decision of any Provincial Authority affecting any Right or Privilege of the Protestant or Roman Catholic Minority of the Queen's Subjects in relation to Education:

(4)   In case any such Provincial Law as from Time to Time seems to the Governor General in Council requisite for the due Execution of the Provisions of this Section is not made, or in case any Decision of the Governor General in Council on any Appeal under this Section is not duly executed by the proper Provincial Authority in that Behalf, then and in every such Case, and as far only as the Circumstances of each Case require, the Parliament of Canada may make remedial Laws for the due Execution of the Provisions of this Section and of any Decision of the Governor General in Council under this Section.(50)

---

(50) Altered for Manitoba by section 22 of the *Manitoba Act, 1870*, 33 Vict., c. 3 (Canada), (confirmed by the *Constitution Act, 1871*), which reads as follows:

> **22.** In and for the Province, the said Legislature may exclusively make Laws in relation to Education, subject and according to the following provisions: –

> (1) Nothing in any such Law shall prejudicially affect any right or privilege with respect to Denominational Schools which any class of persons have by Law or practice in the Province at the Union:

> (2) An appeal shall lie to the Governor General in Council from any Act or decision of the Legislature of the Province, or of any Provincial Authority, affecting any right or privilege, of the Protestant or Roman Catholic minority of the Queen's subjects in relation to Education:

> (3) In case any such Provincial Law, as from time to time seems to the Governor General in Council requisite for the due execution of the

provisions of this section, is not made, or in case any decision of the Governor General in Council on any appeal under this section is not duly executed by the proper Provincial Authority in that behalf, then, and in every such case, and as far only as the circumstances of each case require, the Parliament of Canada may make remedial Laws for the due execution of the provisions of this section, and of any decision of the Governor General in Council under this section.

Altered for Alberta by section 17 of the *Alberta Act*, 4-5 Edw. VII, c. 3, 1905 (Canada), which reads as follows:

17. Section 93 of the *Constitution Act, 1867*, shall apply to the said province, with the substitution for paragraph (1) of the said section 93 of the following paragraph: –

(1) Nothing in any such law shall prejudicially affect any right or privilege with respect to separate schools which any class of persons have at the date of the passing of this Act, under the terms of chapters 29 and 30 of the Ordinances of the Northwest Territories, passed in the year 1901, or with respect to religious instruction in any public or separate school as provided for in the said ordinances.

2. In the appropriation by the Legislature or distribution by the Government of the province of any moneys for the support of schools organized and carried on in accordance with the said chapter 29 or any Act passed in amendment thereof, or in substitution therefor, there shall be no discrimination against schools of any class described in the said chapter 29.

3. Where the expression "by law" is employed in paragraph 3 of the said section 93, it shall be held to mean the law as set out in the said chapters 29 and 30, and where the expression "at the Union" is employed, in the said paragraph 3, it shall be held to mean the date at which this Act comes into force.

Altered for Saskatchewan by section 17 of the *Saskatchewan Act*, 4-5 Edw. VII, c. 42, 1905 (Canada), which reads as follows:

17. Section 93 of the *Constitution Act, 1867*, shall apply to the said province, with the substitution for paragraph (1) of the said section 93, of the following paragraph: –

(1) Nothing in any such law shall prejudicially affect any right or privilege with respect to separate schools which any class of persons have at the date of the passing of this Act, under the terms of chapters 29 and 30 of the Ordinances of the Northwest Territories, passed in the year 1901, or with respect to religious instruction in any public or separate school as provided for in the said ordinances.

2. In the appropriation by the Legislature or distribution by the Government of the province of any moneys for the support of schools organized and carried on in accordance with the said chapter 29, or any Act passed in amendment thereof or in substitution therefor, there shall be no discrimination against schools of any class described in the said chapter 29.

3. Where the expression "by law" is employed in paragraph (3) of the said section 93, it shall be held to mean the law as set out in the said chapters 29 and 30; and where the expression "at the Union" is employed in the said paragraph (3), it shall be held to mean the date at which this Act comes into force.

## Uniformity of Laws in Ontario, Nova Scotia and New Brunswick.

**94.** Notwithstanding anything in this Act, the Parliament of Canada may make Provision for the Uniformity of all or any of the Laws relative to Property and Civil Rights in Ontario, Nova Scotia, and New Brunswick, and of the Procedure of all or any of the Courts in Those Three Provinces, and from and after the passing of any Act in that Behalf the Power of the Parliament of Canada to make Laws in relation to any Matter comprised in any such Act shall, notwithstanding anything in this Act, be unrestricted; but any Act of the Parliament of Canada making Provision for such Uniformity shall not have effect in any Province unless and until it is adopted and enacted as Law by the Legislature thereof.

*Legislation for Uniformity of Laws in Three Provinces.*

## Old Age Pensions.

**94A.** The Parliament of Canada may make laws in relation to old age pensions and supplementary benefits, including survivors, and disability benefits irrespective of age, but no such law shall affect the operation of any law present or future of a provincial legislature in relation to any such matter.(51)

*Legislation respecting old age pensions and supplementary benefits.*

Altered by Term 17 of the Terms of Union of Newfoundland with Canada (confirmed by the *Newfoundland Act,* 12-13 Geo. VI, c. 22 (U.K.)), which reads as follows:

> **17.** In lieu of section ninety-three of the *Constitution Act, 1867,* the following term shall apply in respect of the Province of Newfoundland:
>
> In and for the Province of Newfoundland the Legislature shall have exclusive authority to make laws in relation to education, but the Legislature will not have authority to make laws prejudicially affecting any right or privilege with respect to denominational schools, common (amalgamated) schools, or denominational colleges, that any class or classes of persons have by law in Newfoundland at the date of Union, and out of public funds of the Province of Newfoundland, provided for education,
>
> (*a*) all such schools shall receive their share of such funds in accordance with scales determined on a non-discriminatory basis from time to time by the Legislature for all schools then being conducted under authority of the Legislature; and
>
> (*b*) all such colleges shall receive their share of any grant from time to time voted for all colleges then being conducted under authority of the Legislature, such grant being distributed on a non-discriminatory basis.

See also sections 23, 29, and 59 of the *Constitution Act, 1982.* Section 23 provides for new minority language educational rights and section 59 permits a delay in respect of the coming into force in Quebec of one aspect of those rights. Section 29 provides that nothing in the *Canadian Charter of Rights and Freedoms* abrogates or derogates from any rights or privileges guaranteed by or under the Constitution of Canada in respect of denominational, separate or dissentient schools.

(51) Added by the *Constitution Act, 1964,* 12-13 Eliz. II, c. 73 (U.K.). As originally enacted by the *British North America Act, 1951,* 14-15 Geo. VI, c. 32 (U.K.), which was repealed by the *Constitution Act, 1982,* section 94A read as follows:

*Agriculture and Immigration.*

Concurrent Powers
of Legislation
respecting
Agriculture, etc.

**95.** In each Province the Legislature may make Laws in relation to Agriculture in the Province, and to Immigration into the Province; and it is hereby declared that the Parliament of Canada may from Time to Time make Laws in relation to Agriculture in all or any of the Provinces, and to Immigration into all or any of the Provinces; and any Law of the Legislature of a Province relative to Agriculture or to Immigration shall have effect in and for the Province as long and as far only as it is not repugnant to any Act of the Parliament of Canada.

## VII. – JUDICATURE.

Appointment of
Judges.

**96.** The Governor General shall appoint the Judges of the Superior, District, and County Courts in each Province, except those of the Courts of Probate in Nova Scotia and New Brunswick.

Selection of Judges
in Ontario, etc.

**97.** Until the laws relative to Property and Civil Rights in Ontario, Nova Scotia, and New Brunswick, and the Procedure of the Courts in those Provinces, are made uniform, the Judges of the Courts of those Provinces appointed by the Governor General shall be selected from the respective Bars of those Provinces.

Selection of Judges
in Quebec.

**98.** The Judges of the Courts of Quebec shall be selected from the Bar of that Province.

Tenure of office of
Judges.

**99.** (1) Subject to subsection two of this section, the Judges of the Superior Courts shall hold office during good behaviour, but shall be removable by the Governor General on Address of the Senate and House of Commons.

Termination at age
75.

(2) A Judge of a Superior Court, whether appointed before or after the coming into force of this section, shall cease to hold office upon attaining the age of seventy-five years, or upon the coming into force of this section if at that time he has already attained that age.(52)

---

**94A.** It is hereby declared that the Parliament of Canada may from time to time make laws in relation to old age pensions in Canada, but no law made by the Parliament of Canada in relation to old age pensions shall affect the operation of any law present or future of a Provincial Legislature in relation to old age pensions.

(52) Repealed and re-enacted by the *Constitution Act, 1960,* 9 Eliz. II, c. 2 (U.K.), which came into force on the 1st day of March, 1961. The original section read as follows:

**99.** The Judges of the Superior Courts shall hold Office during good Behaviour, but shall be removable by the Governor General on Address of the Senate and House of Commons.

**100.** The Salaries, Allowances, and Pensions of the Judges of the Superior, District, and County Courts (except the Courts of Probate in Nova Scotia and New Brunswick), and of the Admiralty Courts in Cases where the Judges thereof are for the Time being paid by Salary, shall be fixed and provided by the Parliament of Canada.(53)

*Salaries etc., of Judges.*

**101.** The Parliament of Canada may, notwithstanding anything in this Act, from Time to Time provide for the Constitution, Maintenance, and Organization of a General Court of Appeal for Canada, and for the Establishment of any additional Courts for the better Administration of the Laws of Canada.(54)

*General Court of Appeal, etc.*

VIII. – REVENUES; DEBTS; ASSETS; TAXATION.

[Sections 102 to 104 are omitted.]

**105.** Unless altered by the Parliament of Canada, the Salary of the Governor General shall be Ten thousand Pounds Sterling Money of the United Kingdom of Great Britain and Ireland, payable out of the Consolidated Revenue Fund of Canada, and the same shall form the Third Charge thereon.(55)

*Salary of Governor General.*

[Sections 106 and 107 are omitted.]

**108.** The Public Works and Property of each Province, enumerated in the Third Schedule to this Act, shall be the Property of Canada.

*Transfer of Property in Schedule.*

**109.** All Lands, Mines, Minerals, and Royalties belonging to the several Provinces of Canada, Nova Scotia, and New Brunswick at the Union, and all Sums then due or payable for such Lands, Mines, Minerals, or Royalties, shall belong to the several Provinces of Ontario, Quebec, Nova Scotia, and New Brunswick in which the same are situate or arise, subject to any Trusts existing in respect thereof, and to any Interest other than that of the Province in the same.(56)

*Property in Lands. Mines, etc.*

[Sections 110 to 116 are omitted.]

**117.** The several Provinces shall retain all their respective Public Property not otherwise disposed of in this Act, subject to the Right of Canada to assume any Lands or Public Property required for Fortifications or for the Defence of the Country.

*Provincial Public Property.*

---

(53) Now provided for in the *Judges Act*, R.S.C. 1970, c. J-1.

(54) See the *Supreme Court Act*, R.S.C. 1970, c. S-19, and the *Federal Court Act*, R.S.C. 1970, (2nd Supp.) c. 10.

(56) The three prairie provinces were placed in the same position as the original provinces by the *Constitution Act, 1930*, 21 Geo. V, c. 26 (U.K.).

[Sections 118 to 120 are omitted.]

Canadian
Manufactures, etc.

**121.** All Articles of the Growth, Produce, or Manufacture of any one of the Provinces shall, from and after the Union, be admitted free into each of the other Provinces.

Continuance of
Customs and
Excise Laws.

**122.** The Customs and Excise Laws of each Province shall, subject to the Provisions of this Act, continue in force until altered by the Parliament of Canada.(60)

[Sections 123 and 124 are omitted.]

Exemption of
Public Lands, etc.

**125.** No Lands or Property belonging to Canada or any Province shall be liable to Taxation.

[Section 126 is omitted.]

## IX. – MISCELLANEOUS PROVISIONS.

### General.

[Sections 127 and 128 are omitted.]

Continuance of
existing Laws,
Courts, Officers,
etc.

**129.** Except as otherwise provided by this Act, all Laws in force in Canada, Nova Scotia, or New Brunswick at the Union, and all Courts of Civil and Criminal Jurisdiction, and all legal Commissions, Powers, and Authorities, and all Officers, Judicial, Administrative, and Ministerial, existing therein at the Union, shall continue in Ontario, Quebec, Nova Scotia, and New Brunswick respectively, as if the Union had not been made; subject nevertheless (except with respect to such as are enacted by or exist under Acts of the Parliament of Great Britain or of the Parliament of the United Kingdom of Great Britain and Ireland), to be repealed, abolished, or altered by the Parliament of Canada, or by the Legislature of the respective Province, according to the Authority of the Parliament or of that Legislature under this Act.(64)

[Sections 130 and 131 are omitted.]

Treaty
Obligations.

**132.** The Parliament and Government of Canada shall have all Powers necessary or proper for performing the Obligations of Canada or of any Province thereof, as Part of the British

---

(60) Spent. Now covered by the *Customs Act,* R.S.C. 1970, c. C-40, the *Customs Tariff,* R.S.C. 1970, c. C-41, the *Excise Act,* R.S.C. 1970, c. E-12 and the *Excise Tax Act,* R.S.C. 1970, c. E-13.

(64) The restriction against altering or repealing laws enacted by or existing under statutes of the United Kingdom was removed by the *Statute of Westminster, 1931,* 22 Geo. V, c. 4 (U.K.) except in respect of certain constitutional documents. Comprehensive procedures for amending enactments forming part of the Constitution of Canada were provided by Part V of the *Constitution Act, 1982,* (U.K.) 1982, c. 11.

Empire, towards Foreign Countries, arising under Treaties between the Empire and such Foreign Countries.

**133.** Either the English or the French Language may be used by any Person in the Debates of the Houses of the Parliament of Canada and of the Houses of the Legislature of Quebec; and both those Languages shall be used in the respective Records and Journals of those Houses; and either of those Languages may be used by any Person or in any Pleading or Process in or issuing from any Court of Canada established under this Act, and in or from all or any of the Courts of Quebec.

The Acts of the Parliament of Canada and of the Legislature of Quebec shall be printed and published in both those Languages.(66)

[Sections 134 to 145 are omitted.]

## XI. – ADMISSION OF OTHER COLONIES.

**146.** It shall be lawful for the Queen, by and with the Advice of Her Majesty's Most Honourable Privy Council, on Addresses from the Houses of the Parliament of Canada, and from the Houses of the respective Legislatures of the Colonies or Provinces of Newfoundland, Prince Edward Island, and British Columbia, to admit those Colonies or Provinces, or any of them, into the Union, and on Address from the Houses of the Parliament of Canada to admit Rupert's Land and the Northwestern Territory, or either of them, into the Union, on such Terms and Conditions in each Case as are in the Addresses expressed and as the Queen thinks fit to approve, subject to the Provisions of this Act; and the Provisions of any Order in

*Power to admit Newfoundland etc., into the Union*

---

(66) A similar provision was enacted for Manitoba by Section 23 of the *Manitoba Act, 1870,* 33 Vict., c. 3 (Canada), (confirmed by the *Constitution Act, 1871)*. Section 23 read as follows:

> **23.** Either the English or the French language may be used by any person in the debates of the Houses of the Legislature, and both those languages shall be used in the respective Records and Journals of those Houses; and either of those languages may be used by any person, or in any Pleading or Process, in or issuing from any Court of Canada established under the British North America Act, 1867, or in or from all or any of the Courts of the Province. The Acts of the Legislature shall be printed and published in both those languages.

Sections 17 to 19 of the *Constitution Act, 1982,* restate the language rights set out in section 133 in respect of Parliament and the courts established under the *Constitution Act, 1867,* and also guarantees those rights in respect of the legislature of New Brunswick and the courts of that province.

Section 16 and sections 20, 21 and 23 of the *Constitution Act, 1982,* recognize additional language rights in respect of the English and French languages. Section 22 preserves language rights and privileges of languages other than English and French.

Council in that Behalf shall have effect as if they had been enacted by the Parliament of the United Kingdom of Great Britain and Ireland.(75)

[Section 147 is omitted.]

## SCHEDULES

[The first and second schedules are omitted.]

## THE THIRD SCHEDULE.

---

*Provincial Public Works and Property to be the Property of Canada.*

1. Canals, with Lands and Water Power connected therewith.
2. Public Harbours.
3. Lighthouses and Piers, and Sable Island.
4. Steamboats, Dredges, and public Vessels.
5. Rivers and Lake Improvements.
6. Railways and Railway Stocks, Mortgages, and other Debts due by Railway Companies.
7. Military Roads.
8. Custom Houses, Post Offices, and all other Public Buildings, except such as the Government of Canada appropriate for the Use of the Provincial Legislature and Governments.
9. Property transferred by the Imperial Government, and known as Ordinance Property.
10. Armouries, Drill Sheds, Military Clothing, and Munitions of War, and Lands set apart for general Public Purposes.

[The fourth and fifth schedules are omitted.]

## THE SIXTH SCHEDULE. (78)

---

*Primary Production from Non-Renewable Natural Resources and Forestry Resources.*

1. For the purposes of section 92A of this Act,
   (*a*) production from a non-renewable natural resource is primary production therefrom if

---

(75) All territories mentioned in this section are now part of Canada. See the notes to section 5, *supra.*

(78) As enacted by the *Constitution Act, 1982.*

·(i) it is in the form in which it exists upon its recovery or severance from its natural state, or

(ii) it is a product resulting from processing or refining the resource, and is not a manufactured product or a product resulting from refining crude oil, refining upgraded heavy crude oil, refining gases or liquids derived from coal or refining a synthetic equivalent or crude oil; and

(b) production from a forestry resource is primary production therefrom if it consists of sawlogs, poles, lumber, wood chips, sawdust or any other primary wood product, or wood pulp, and is not a product manufactured from wood.

# APPENDIX II

## Canada Act 1982

U.K., 1982, c. 11

An Act to give effect to a request by the Senate and House of Commons of Canada

Whereas Canada has requested and consented to the enactment of an Act of the Parliament of the United Kingdom to give effect to the provisions hereinafter set forth and the Senate and the House of Commons of Canada in Parliament assembled have submitted an address to Her Majesty requesting that Her Majesty may graciously be pleased to cause a Bill to be laid before the Parliament of the United Kingdom for that purpose.

Be it therefore enacted by the Queen's Most Excellent Majesty, by and with the advice and consent of the Lords Spiritual and Temporal, and Commons, in this present Parliament assembled, and by the authority of the same as follows:

*Constitution Act. 1982* enacted

**1.** The *Constitution Act, 1982* set out in Schedule B to this Act is hereby enacted for and shall have the force of law in Canada and shall come into force as provided in that Act.

Loi donnant suite à une demande du Sénat et de la Chambre des communes du Canada

Sa Très Excellente Majesté la Reine, considérant: qu'à la demande et avec le consentement du Canada, le Parlement du Royaume-Uni est invité à adopter une loi visant à donner effet aux dispositions énoncées ci-après et que le Sénat et la Chambre des communes du Canada réunis en Parlement ont présenté une adresse demandant à Sa Très Gracieuse Majesté de bien vouloir faire déposer devant le Parlement du Royaume-Uni un projet de loi à cette fin,

sur l'avis et du consentement des Lords spirituels et temporels et des Communes réunis en Parlement, et par l'autorité de celui-ci, édicte :

**1.** La *Loi constitutionnelle de 1982*, énoncée à l'annexe B, est édictée pour le Canada et y a force de loi. Elle entre en vigueur conformément à ses dispositions.

Adoption de la *Loi constitutionnelle de 1982*

Termination of power to legislate for Canada

**2.** No Act of the Parliament of the United Kingdom passed after the *Constitution Act, 1982* comes into force shall extend to Canada as part of its law.

**2.** Les lois adoptées par le Parlement du Royaume-Uni après l'entrée en vigueur de la *Loi constitutionnelle de 1982* ne font pas partie du droit du Canada.

Cessation du pouvoir de légiférer pour le Canada

French version

**3.** So far as it is not contained in Schedule B, the French version of this Act is set out in Schedule A to this Act and has the same authority in Canada as the English version thereof.

**3.** La partie de la version française de la présente loi qui figure à l'annexe A a force de loi au Canada au même titre que la version anglaise correspondante.

Version française

Short title

**4.** This Act may be cited as the *Canada Act 1982*.

**4.** Titre abrégé de la présente loi: *Loi de 1982 sur le Canada*.

Titre abrégé

# APPENDIX III

## Constitution Act, 1982

### Schedule B to Canada Act 1982 (U.K.)

PART I

PART I

CANADIAN CHARTER OF RIGHTS AND FREEDOMS

Whereas Canada is founded upon principles that recognize the supremacy of God and the rule of law:

*Guarantee of Rights and Freedoms*

Rights and freedoms in Canada

**1.** The *Canadian Charter of Rights and Freedoms* guarantees the rights and freedoms set out in it subject only to such reasonable limits prescribed by law as can be demonstrably justified in a free and democratic society.

*Fundamental Freedoms*

Fundamental freedoms

**2.** Everyone has the following fundamental freedoms:
(*a*) freedom of conscience and religion;
(*b*) freedom of thought, belief, opinion and expression, including freedom of the press and other media of communication;
(*c*) freedom of peaceful assembly; and
(*d*) freedom of association.

PARTIE I

CHARTE CANADIENNE DES DROITS ET LIBERTÉS

Attendu que le Canada est fondé sur des principes qui reconnaissent la suprématie de Dieu et la primauté du droit:

*Garantie des droits et libertés*

Droits et libertés au Canada

**1.** La Charte canadienne des droits et libertés garantit les droits et libertés qui y sont énoncés. Ils ne peuvent être restreints que par une règle de droit, dans des limites qui soient raisonnables et dont la justification puisse se démontrer dans le cadre d'une société libre et démocratique.

*Libertés fondamentales*

Libertés fondamentales

**2.** Chacun a les libertés fondamentales suivantes:
*a*) liberté de conscience et de religion;
*b*) liberté de pensée, de croyance, d'opinion et d'expression, y compris la liberté de la presse et des autres moyens de communication;
*c*) liberté de réunion pacifique;
*d*) liberté d'association.

## Democratic Rights

*Democratic rights of citizens*

**3.** Every citizen of Canada has the right to vote in an election of members of the House of Commons or of a legislative assembly and to be qualified for membership therein.

*Maximum duration of legislative bodies*

**4.** (1) No House of Commons and no legislative assembly shall continue for longer than five years from the date fixed for the return of the writs at a general election of its members.

*Continuation in special circumstances*

(2) In time of real or apprehended war, invasion or insurrection, a House of Commons may be continued by Parliament and a legislative assembly may be continued by the legislature beyond five years if such continuation is not opposed by the votes of more than one-third of the members of the House of Commons or the legislative assembly, as the case may be.

*Annual sitting of legislative bodies*

**5.** There shall be a sitting of Parliament and of each legislature at least once every twelve months.

## Mobility Rights

*Mobility of citizens*

**6.** (1) Every citizen of Canada has the right to enter, remain in and leave Canada.

*Rights to move and gain livelihood*

(2) Every citizen of Canada and every person who has the status of a perma-

## Droits démocratiques

*Droits démocratiques des citoyens*

**3.** Tout citoyen canadien a le droit de vote et est éligible aux élections législatives fédérales ou provinciales.

*Mandat maximal des assemblées*

**4.** (1) Le mandat maximal de la Chambre des communes et des assemblées législatives est de cinq ans à compter de la date fixée pour le retour des brefs relatifs aux élections générales correspondantes.

*Prolongations spéciales*

(2) Le mandat de la Chambre des communes ou celui d'une assemblée législative peut être prolongé respectivement par le Parlement ou par la législature en question au-delà de cinq ans en cas de guerre, d'invasion ou d'insurrection, réelles ou appréhendées, pourvu que cette prolongation ne fasse pas l'objet d'une opposition exprimée par les voix de plus du tiers des députés de la Chambre des communes ou de l'assemblée législative.

*Séance annuelle*

**5.** Le Parlement et les législatures tiennent une séance au moins une fois tous les douze mois.

## Liberté de circulation et d'établissement

*Liberté de circulation*

**6.** (1) Tout citoyen canadien a le droit de demeurer au Canada, d'y entrer ou d'en sortir.

*Liberté d'établissement*

(2) Tout citoyen canadien et toute personne ayant le statut de résident

nent resident of Canada has the right

(*a*) to move to and take up residence in any province; and

(*b*) to pursue the gaining of a livelihood in any province.

permanent au Canada ont le droit:

*a*) de se déplacer dans tout le pays et d'établir leur résidence dans toute province;

*b*) de gagner leur vie dans toute province.

Limitation

(3) The rights specified in subsection (2) are subject to

(*a*) any laws or practices of general application in force in a province other than those that discriminate among persons primarily on the basis of province of present or previous residence; and

(*b*) any laws providing for reasonable residency requirements as a qualification for the receipt of publicly provided social services.

(3) Les droits mentionnés au paragraphe (2) sont subordonnés:

*a*) aux lois et usages d'application générale en vigueur dans une province donnée, s'ils n'établissent entre les personnes aucune distinction fondée principalement sur la province de résidence antérieure ou actuelle;

*b*) aux lois prévoyant de justes conditions de résidence en vue de l'obtention des services sociaux publics.

Restriction

Affirmative action programs

(4) Subsections (2) and (3) do not preclude any law, program or activity that has as its object the amelioration in a province of conditions of individuals in that province who are socially or economically disadvantaged if the rate of employment in that province is below the rate of employment in Canada.

(4) Les paragraphes (2) et (3) n'ont pas pour objet d'interdire les lois, programmes ou activités destinés à améliorer, dans une province, la situation d'individus défavorisés socialement ou économiquement, si le taux d'emploi dans la province est inférieur à la moyenne nationale.

Programmes de promotion sociale

## Legal Rights

## Garanties juridiques

Life, liberty and security of person

7. Everyone has the right to life, liberty and security of the person and the right not to be deprived thereof except in accordance with the principles of fundamental justice.

7. Chacun a droit à la vie, à la liberté et à la sécurité de sa personne; il ne peut être porté atteinte à ce droit qu'en conformité avec les principes de justice fondamentale.

Vie, liberté et sécurité

Search or seizure

**8.** Everyone has the right to be secure against unreasonable search or seizure.

**8.** Chacun a droit à la protection contre les fouilles, les perquisitions ou les saisies abusives.

Detention or imprisonment

**9.** Everyone has the right not to be arbitrarily detained or imprisoned.

**9.** Chacun a droit à la protection contre la détention ou l'emprisonnement arbitraires.

Arrest or detention

**10.** Everyone has the right on arrest or detention
(*a*) to be informed promptly of the reasons therefor;
(*b*) to retain and instruct counsel without delay and to be informed of that right; and
(*c*) to have the validity of the detention determined by way of *habeas corpus* and to be released if the detention is not lawful.

**10.** Chacun a le droit, en cas d'arrestation ou de détention:
*a*) d'être informé dans les plus brefs délais des motifs de son arrestation ou de sa détention;
*b*) d'avoir recours sans délai à l'assistance d'un avocat et d'être informé de ce droit;
*c*) de faire contrôler, par *habeas corpus*, la légalité de sa détention et d'obtenir, le cas échéant, sa libération.

Proceedings in criminal and penal matters

**11.** Any person charged with an offence has the right
(*a*) to be informed without unreasonable delay of the specific offence;
(*b*) to be tried within a reasonable time;
(*c*) not to be compelled to be a witness in proceedings against that person in respect of the offence;
(*d*) to be presumed innocent until proven guilty according to law in a fair and public hearing by an independent and impartial tribunal;
(*e*) not to be denied reasonable bail without just cause;
(*f*) except in the case of an offence under military

**11.** Tout inculpé a le droit:
*a*) d'être informé sans délai anormal de l'infraction précise qu'on lui reproche;
*b*) d'être jugé dans un délai raisonnable;
*c*) de ne pas être contraint de témoigner contre lui-même dans toute poursuite intentée contre lui pour l'infraction qu'on lui reproche;
*d*) d'être présumé innocent tant qu'il n'est pas déclaré coupable, conformément à la loi, par un tribunal indépendant et impartial à l'issue d'un procès public et équitable;
*e*) de ne pas être privé sans juste cause d'une

law tried before a military tribunal, to the benefit of trial by jury where the maximum punishment for the offence is imprisonment for five years or a more severe punishment;

(g) not to be found guilty on account of any act or omission unless, at the time of the act or omission, it constituted an offence under Canadian or international law or was criminal according to the general principles of law recognized by the community of nations;

(h) if finally acquitted of the offence, not to be tried for it again and, if finally found guilty and punished for the offence, not to be tried or punished for it again; and

(i) if found guilty of the offence and if the punishment for the offence has been varied between the time of commission and the time of sentencing, to the benefit of the lesser punishment.

mise en liberté assortie d'un cautionnement raisonnable;

f) sauf s'il s'agit d'une infraction relevant de la justice militaire, de bénéficier d'un procès avec jury lorsque la peine maximale prévue pour l'infraction dont il est accusé est un emprisonnement de cinq ans ou une peine plus grave;

g) de ne pas être déclaré coupable en raison d'une action ou d'une omission qui, au moment où elle est survenue, ne constituait pas une infraction d'après le droit interne du Canada ou le droit international et n'avait pas de caractère criminel d'après les principes généraux de droit reconnus par l'ensemble des nations;

h) d'une part de ne pas être jugé de nouveau pour une infraction dont il a été définitivement acquitté, d'autre part de ne pas être jugé ni puni de nouveau pour une infraction dont il a été définitivement déclaré coupable et puni;

i) de bénéficier de la peine la moins sévère, lorsque la peine qui sanctionne l'infraction dont il est déclaré coupable est modifiée entre le moment de la perpétration de l'infraction et celui de la sentence.

Treatment or punishment

**12.** Everyone has the right not to be subjected to any cruel and unusual treatment or punishment.

**12.** Chacun a droit à la protection contre tous traitements ou peines cruels et inusités.

Cruauté

Self-crimination

**13.** A witness who testifies in any proceedings has the right not to have any incriminating evidence so given used to incriminate that witness in any other proceedings, except in a prosecution for perjury or for the giving of contradictory evidence.

**13.** Chacun a droit à ce qu'aucun témoignage incriminant qu'il donne ne soit utilisé pour l'incriminer dans d'autres procédures, sauf lors de poursuites pour parjure ou pour témoignages contradictoires.

Témoignage incriminant

Interpreter

**14.** A party or witness in any proceedings who does not understand or speak the language in which the proceedings are conducted or who is deaf has the right to the assistance of an interpreter.

**14.** La partie ou le témoin qui ne peuvent suivre les procédures, soit parce qu'ils ne comprennent pas ou ne parlent pas la langue employée, soit parce qu'ils sont atteints de surdité, ont droit à l'assistance d'un interprète.

Interprète

### Equality Rights

### Droits à légalité

Equality before and under law and equal protection and benefit of law

**15.** (1) Every individual is equal before and under the law and has the right to the equal protection and equal benefit of the law without discrimination and, in particular, without discrimination based on race, national or ethnic origin, colour, religion, sex, age or mental or physical disability.

**15.** (1) La loi ne fait acception de personne et s'applique également à tous, et tous ont droit à la même protection et au même bénéfice de la loi, indépendamment de toute discrimination, notamment des discriminations fondées sur la race, l'origine nationale ou ethnique, la couleur, la religion, le sexe, l'âge ou les déficiences mentales ou physiques.

Égalité devant la loi, égalité de bénéfice et protection égale de la loi

Affirmative action programs

(2) Subsection (1) does not preclude any law, program or activity that has as its object the amelioration of conditions of disadvantaged individuals or groups including those that are disadvantaged because of race, national or ethnic origin, colour, religion, sex, age or mental or physical disability.

(2) Le paragraphe (1) n'a pas pour effet d'interdire les lois, programmes ou activités destinés à améliorer la situation d'individus ou de groupes défavorisés, notamment du fait de leur race, de leur origine nationale ou ethnique, de leur couleur, de leur religion, de leur sexe, de leur âge ou de leurs déficiences mentales ou physiques.

Programmes de promotion sociale.

## Official Languages of Canada

## Langues officielles du Canada

**Official languages of Canada**

**16.** (1) English and French are the official languages of Canada and have equality of status and equal rights and privileges as to their use in all institutions of the Parliament and government of Canada.

**16.** (1) Le français et l'anglais sont les langues officielles du Canada; ils ont un statut et des droits et privilèges égaux quant à leur usage dans les institutions du Parlement et du gouvernement du Canada.

**Langues officielles du Canada**

**Official languages of New Brunswick**

(2) English and French are the official languages of New Brunswick and have equality of status and equal rights and privileges as to their use in all institutions of the legislature and government of New Brunswick.

(2) Le français et l'anglais sont les langues officielles du Nouveau-Brunswick; ils ont un statut et des droits et privilèges égaux quant à leur usage dans les institutions de la Législature et du gouvernement du Nouveau-Brunswick.

**Langues officielles du Nouveau-Brunswick**

**Advancement of status and use**

(3) Nothing in this Charter limits the authority of Parliament or a legislature to advance the equality of status or use of English and French.

(3) La présente charte ne limite pas le pouvoir du Parlement et des législatures de favoriser la progression vers l'égalité de statut ou d'usage du français et de l'anglais.

**Progression vers l'égalité**

**Proceedings of Parliament**

**17.** (1) Everyone has the right to use English or French in any debates and other proceedings of Parliament.

**17.** (1) Chacun a le droit d'employer le français ou l'anglais dans les débats et travaux du Parlement.

**Travaux du Parlement**

**Proceedings of New Brunswick legislature**

(2) Everyone has the right to use English or French in any debates and other proceedings of the legislature of New Brunswick.

(2) Chacun a le droit d'employer le français ou l'anglais dans les débats et travaux de la Législature du Nouveau-Brunswick.

**Travaux de la Législature du Nouveau-Brunswick**

**Parliamentary statutes and records**

**18.** (1) The statutes, records and journals of Parliament shall be printed and published in English and French and both language versions are equally authoritative.

**18.** (1) Les lois, les archives, les comptes rendus et les procès-verbaux du Parlement sont imprimés et publiés en français et en anglais, les deux versions des lois ayant également force de loi et celles des autres documents ayant même valeur.

**Documents parlementaires**

New Brunswick statutes and records

(2) The statutes, records and journals of the legislature of New Brunswick shall be printed and published in English and French and both language versions are equally authoritative.

(2) Les lois, les archives, les comptes rendus et les procès-verbaux de la Législature du Nouveau-Brunswick sont imprimés et publiés en français et en anglais, les deux versions des lois ayant également force de loi et celles des autres documents ayant même valeur.

Documents de la Législature du Nouveau-Brunswick

Proceedings in courts established by Parliament

**19.** (1) Either English or French may be used by any person in, or in any pleading in or process issuing from, any court established by Parliament.

**19.** (1) Chacun a le droit d'employer le français ou l'anglais dans toutes les affaires dont sont saisis les tribunaux établis par le Parlement et dans tous les actes de procédure qui en découlent.

Procédures devant les tribunaux établis par le Parlement

Proceedings in New Brunswick courts

(2) Either English or French may be used by any person in, or in any pleading in or process issuing from, any court of New Brunswick.

(2) Chacun a le droit d'employer le français ou l'anglais dans toutes les affaires dont sont saisis les tribunaux du Nouveau-Brunswick et dans tous les actes de procédure qui en découlent.

Procédures devant les tribunaux du Nouveau-Brunswick

Communications by public with federal institutions

**20.** (1) Any member of the public in Canada has the right to communicate with, and to receive available services from, any head or central office of an institution of the Parliament or government of Canada in English or French, and has the same right with respect to any other office of any such institution where
  (a) there is a significant demand for communications with and services from that office in such language; or
  (b) due to the nature of the office, it is reasonable that communications with and services from

**20.** (1) Le public a, au Canada, droit à l'emploi du français ou de l'anglais pour communiquer avec le siège ou l'administration centrale des institutions du Parlement ou du gouvernement du Canada ou pour en recevoir les services; il a le même droit à l'égard de tout autre bureau de ces institutions là où, selon le cas:
  a) l'emploi du français ou de l'anglais fait l'objet d'une demande importante;
  b) l'emploi du français et de l'anglais se justifie par la vocation du bureau.

Communications entre les administrés et les institutions fédérales that office be available in both English and French.

**Communications by public with New Brunswick institutions**

(2) Any member of the public in New Brunswick has the right to communicate with, and to receive available services from, any office of an institution of the legislature or government of New Brunswick in English or French.

(2) Le public a, au Nouveau-Brunswick, droit à l'emploi du français ou de l'anglais pour communiquer avec tout bureau des institutions de la législature ou du gouvernement ou pour en recevoir les services.

**Communications entre les administrés et les institutions du Nouveau-Brunswick**

**Continuation of existing constitutional provisions**

**21.** Nothing in sections 16 to 20 abrogates or derogates from any right, privilege or obligation with respect to the English and French languages, or either of them, that exists or is continued by virtue of any other provision of the Constitution of Canada.

**21.** Les articles 16 à 20 n'ont pas pour effet, en ce qui a trait à la langue française ou anglaise ou à ces deux langues, de porter atteinte aux droits, privilèges ou obligations qui existent ou sont maintenus aux termes d'une autre disposition de la Constitution du Canada.

**Maintien en vigueur de certaines dispositions**

**Rights and privileges preserved**

**22.** Nothing in sections 16 to 20 abrogates or derogates from any legal or customary right or privilege acquired or enjoyed either before or after the coming into force of this Charter with respect to any language that is not English or French.

**22.** Les articles 16 à 20 n'ont pas pour effet de porter atteinte aux droits et privilèges, antérieurs ou postérieurs à l'entrée en vigueur de la présente charte et découlant de la loi ou de la coutume, des langues autres que le français ou l'anglais.

**Droits preserves**

### Minority Language Educational Rights

### Droits à l'instruction dans la langue de la minorité

**Language of instruction**

**23.** (1) Citizens of Canada
(*a*) whose first language learned and still understood is that of the English or French linguistic minority population of the province in which they reside, or
(*b*) who have received their primary school instruction in Canada in English or French and re-

**23.** (1) Les citoyens canadiens:
*a*) dont la première langue apprise et encore comprise est celle de la minorité francophone ou anglophone de la province où ils résident,
*b*) qui ont reçu leur instruction, au niveau primaire, en français ou en anglais au Canada et qui résident dans une pro-

**Langue d'instruction**

side in a province where the language in which they received that instruction is the language of the English or French linguistic minority population of the province, have the right to have their children receive primary and secondary school instruction in that language in that province.

vince où la langue dans laquelle ils ont reçu cette instruction est celle de la minorité francophone ou anglophone de la province, ont, dans l'un ou l'autre cas, le droit d'y faire instruire leurs enfants, aux niveaux primaire et secondaire, dans cette langue.

Continuity of language instruction

(2) Citizens of Canada of whom any child has received or is receiving primary or secondary school instruction in English or French in Canada, have the right to have all their children receive primary and secondary school instruction in the same language.

(2) Les citoyens canadiens dont un enfant a reçu ou reçoit son instruction, au niveau primaire ou secondaire, en français ou en anglais au Canada ont le droit de faire instruire tous leurs enfants, aux niveaux primaire et secondaire, dans la langue de cette instruction.

Continuité d'emploi de la langue d'instruction

Application where numbers warrant

(3) The right of citizens of Canada under subsections (1) and (2) to have their children receive primary and secondary school instruction in the language of the English or French linguistic minority population of a province
(a) applies wherever in the province the number of children of citizens who have such a right is sufficient to warrant the provision to them out of public funds of minority language instruction; and
(b) includes, where the number of those children so warrants, the right to have them receive that instruction in minority language educational facilities provided out of public funds.

(3) Le droit reconnu aux citoyens canadiens par les paragraphes (1) et (2) de faire instruire leurs enfants, aux niveaux primaire et secondaire, dans la langue de la minorité francophone ou anglophone d'une province:
a) s'exerce partout dans la province où le nombre des enfants des citoyens qui ont ce droit est suffisant pour justifier à leur endroit la prestation, sur les fonds publics, de l'instruction dans la langue de la minorité;
b) comprend, lorsque le nombre de ces enfants le justifie, le droit de les faire instruire dans des établissements d'enseignement de la minorité linguistique financés sur les fonds publics.

Justification par le nombre

## Enforcement

**Enforcement of guaranteed rights and freedoms**

**24.** (1) Anyone whose rights or freedoms, as guaranteed by this Charter, have been infringed or denied may apply to a court of competent jurisdiction to obtain such remedy as the court considers appropriate and just in the circumstances.

**Exclusion of evidence bringing administration of justice into disrepute**

(2) Where, in proceedings under subsection (1), a court concludes that evidence was obtained in a manner that infringed or denied any rights or freedoms guaranteed by this Charter, the evidence shall be excluded if it is established that, having regard to all the circumstances, the admission of it in the proceedings would bring the administration of justice into disrepute.

## General

**Aboriginal rights and freedoms not affected by Charter**

**25.** The guarantee in this Charter of certain rights and freedoms shall not be construed so as to abrogate or derogate from any aboriginal, treaty or other rights or freedoms that pertain to the aboriginal peoples of Canada including
(*a*) any rights or freedoms that have been recognized by the Royal Proclamation of October 7, 1763; and
(*b*) any rights or freedoms that now exist by way of land claims agreements or may be so acquired.(1)

## Recours

**24.** (1) Toute personne, victime de violation ou de négation des droits ou libertés qui lui sont garantis par la présente charte, peut s'adresser à un tribunal compétent pour obtenir la réparation que le tribunal estime convenable et juste eu égard aux circonstances.

**Recours en cas d'atteinte aux droits et libertés**

(2) Lorsque, dans une instance visée au paragraphe (1), le tribunal a conclu que des éléments de preuve ont été obtenus dans des conditions qui portent atteinte aux droits ou libertés garantis par la présente charte, ces éléments de preuve sont écartés s'il est établi, eu égard aux circonstances, que leur utilisation est susceptible de déconsidérer l'administration de la justice.

**Irrecevabilité d'éléments de preuve qui risqueraient de déconsidérer l'administration de la justice**

## Dispositions générales

**25.** Le fait que la présente charte garantit certains droits et libertés ne porte pas atteinte aux droits ou libertés – ancestraux, issus de traités ou autres – des peuples autochtones du Canada, notamment:
*a*) aux droits ou libertés reconnus par la Proclamation royale du 7 octobre 1763;
*b*) aux droits ou libertés existants issus d'accords sur des revendications territoriales ou ceux susceptibles d'être ainsi acquis.(1)

**Maintien des droits et libertés des autochtones**

---

(1)  Paragraph 25(b) was repealed and the present paragraph 25(b) was substituted by the Constitution Amendment Proclamation, 1983.

Other rights and freedoms not affected by Charter

**26.** The guarantee in this Charter of certain rights and freedoms shall not be construed as denying the existence of any other rights or freedoms that exist in Canada.

**26.** Le fait que la présente charte garantit certains droits et libertés ne constitue pas une négation des autres droits ou libertés qui existent au Canada.

Maintien des autres droits et libertés

Multicultural heritage

**27.** This Charter shall be interpreted in a manner consistent with the preservation and enhancement of the multicultural heritage of Canadians.

**27.** Toute interprétation de la présente charte doit concorder avec l'objectif de promouvoir le maintien et la valorisation du patrimoine multiculturel des Canadiens.

Maintien du patrimoine culturel

Rights guaranteed equally to both sexes

**28.** Notwithstanding anything in this Charter, the rights and freedoms referred to in it are guaranteed equally to male and female persons.

**28.** Indépendamment des autres dispositions de la présente charte, les droits et libertés qui y sont mentionnés sont garantis également aux personnes des deux sexes.

Égalité de garantie des droits pour les deux sexes

Rights respecting certain schools preserved

**29.** Nothing in this Charter abrogates or derogates from any rights or privileges guaranteed by or under the Constitution of Canada in respect of denominational, separate or dissentient schools.

**29.** Les dispositions de la présente charte ne portent pas atteinte aux droits ou privilèges garantis en vertu de la Constitution du Canada concernant les écoles séparées et autres écoles confessionnelles.

Maintien des droits relatifs à certaines écoles

Application to territories and territorial authorities

**30.** A reference in this Charter to a province or to the legislative assembly or legislature of a province shall be deemed to include a reference to the Yukon Territory and the Northwest Territories, or to the appropriate legislative authority thereof, as the case may be.

**30.** Dans la présente charte, les dispositions qui visent les provinces, leur législature ou leur assemblée législative visent également le territoire du Yukon, les territoires du Nord-Ouest ou leurs autorités législatives compétentes.

Application aux territoires

Legislative powers not extended

**31.** Nothing in this Charter extends the legislative powers of any body or authority.

**31.** La présente charte n'élargit pas les compétences législatives de quelque organisme ou autorité que ce soit.

Non-élargissement des compétences législatives

## Application of Charter

## Application de la charte

Application of
Charter

**32.** (1) This Charter applies
(*a*) to the Parliament and government of Canada in respect of all matters within the authority of Parliament including all matters relating to the Yukon Territory and Northwest Territories; and
(*b*) to the legislature and government of each province in respect of all matters within the authority of the legislature of each province.

Application de la
charte

**32.** (1) La présente charte s'applique :
*a*) au Parlement et au gouvernement du Canada, pour tous les domaines relevant du Parlement, y compris ceux qui concernent le territoire du Yukon et les territoires du Nord-Ouest;
*b*) à la législature et au gouvernement de chaque province, pour tous les domaines relevant de cette législature.

Exception

(2) Notwithstanding subsection (1), section 15 shall not have effect until three years after this section comes into force.

Restriction

(2) Par dérogation au paragraphe (1), l'article 15 n'a d'effet que trois ans après l'entrée en vigueur du présent article.

Exception where express declaration

**33.** (1) Parliament or the legislature of a province may expressly declare in an Act of Parliament or of the legislature, as the case may be, that the Act or a provision thereof shall operate notwithstanding a provision included in section 2 or sections 7 to 15 of this Charter.

Dérogation par déclaration expresse

**33.** (1) Le Parlement ou la législature d'une province peut adopter une loi où il est expressément déclaré que celle-ci ou une de ses dispositions a effet indépendamment d'une disposition donnée de l'article 2 ou des articles 7 à 15 de la présente charte.

Operation of exception

(2) An Act or a provision of an Act in respect of which a declaration made under this section is in effect shall have such operation as it would have but for the provision of this Charter referred to in the declaration.

Effet de la dérogation

(2) La loi ou la disposition qui fait l'objet d'une déclaration conforme au présent article et en vigueur a l'effet qu'elle aurait sauf la disposition en cause de la charte.

Five year limitation

(3) A declaration made under subsection (1) shall cease to have effect five years after it comes into

Durée de validité

(3) La déclaration visée au paragraphe (1) cesse d'avoir effet à la date qui y est précisée ou, au plus tard,

force or on such earlier date as may be specified in the declaration.

cinq ans après son entrée en vigueur.

Re-enactment

**(4)** Parliament or the legislature of a province may re-enact a declaration made under subsection (1).

**(4)** Le Parlement ou une législature peut adopter de nouveau une déclaration visée au paragraphe (1).

Nouvelle adoption

Five year limitation

**(5)** Subsection (3) applies in respect of a re-enactment made under subsection (4).

**(5)** Le paragraphe (3) s'applique à toute déclaration adoptée sous le régime du paragraphe (4).

Durée de validité

## Citation

## Titre

Citation

**34.** This Part may be cited as the *Canadian Charter of Rights and Freedoms.*

**34.** Titre de la présente partie: *Charte canadienne des droits et libertés.*

Titre

## PART II

## PARTIE II

### RIGHTS OF THE ABORIGINAL PEOPLES OF CANADA

### DROITS DES PEUPLES AUTOCHTONES DU CANADA

Recognition of existing aboriginal and treaty rights

**35. (1)** The existing aboriginal and treaty rights of the aboriginal peoples of Canada are hereby recognized and affirmed.

**35. (1)** Les droits existants – ancestraux ou issus de traités – des peuples autochtones du Canada sont reconnus et confirmés.

Confirmation des droits existants des peuples autochtones

Definition of "aboriginal peoples of Canada"

**(2)** In this Act, "aboriginal peoples of Canada" includes the Indian, Inuit and Métis peoples of Canada.

**(2)** Dans la présente loi, «peuples autochtones du Canada» s'entend notamment des Indiens, des Inuit et des Métis du Canada.

Définition de «peuples autochtones du Canada»

Land claims agreements

**(3)** For greater certainty, in subsection (1) "treaty rights" includes rights that now exist by way of land claims agreements or may be so acquired.

**(3)** Il est entendu que sont compris parmi les droits issus de traités, dont il est fait mention au paragraphe (1), les droits existants issus d'accords sur des revendications territoriales ou ceux susceptibles d'être ainsi acquis.

Accords sur des revendications territoriales

Aboriginal and treaty rights are guaranteed equally to both sexes

**(4)** Notwithstanding any other provision of this Act, the aboriginal and treaty rights referred to in subsection (1) are guaranteed

**(4)** Indépendamment de toute autre disposition de la présente loi, les droits – ancestraux ou issus de traités – visés au paragraphe (1)

Égalité de garantie des droits pour les deux sexes

equally to male and female persons. (2)

sont garantis également aux personnes des deux sexes. (2)

Commitment to participation in constitutional conference

**35.1** The government of Canada and the provincial governments are committed to the principle that, before any amendment is made to Class 24 of section 91 of the "*Constitution Act, 1867*", to section 25 of this Act or to this Part,

(*a*) a constitutional conference that includes in its agenda an item relating to the proposed amendment, composed of the Prime Minister of Canada and the first ministers of the provinces, will be convened by the Prime Minister of Canada; and

(*b*) the Prime Minister of Canada will invite representatives of the aboriginal peoples of Canada to participate in the discussions on that item.(3)

**35.1** Les gouvernements fédéral et provinciaux sont liés par l'engagement de principe selon lequel le premier ministre du Canada, avant toute modification de la catégorie 24 de l'article 92 de la «*Loi constitutionnelle de 1867*», de l'article 25 de la présente loi ou de la présente partie:

*a*) convoquera une conférence constitutionnelle réunissant les premiers ministres provinciaux et lui-même et comportant à son ordre du jour la question du projet de modification;

*b*) invitera les représentants des peuples autochtones du Canada à participer aux travaux relatifs à cette question.(3)

Engagement relatif à la participation à une conférence constitutionnelle

## PART III

### EQUALIZATION AND REGIONAL DISPARITIES

## PARTIE III

### PEREQUATION ET INEGALITES REGIONALES

Commitment to promote equal opportunities

**36.** (1) Without altering the legislative authority of Parliament or of the provincial legislatures, or the rights of any of them with respect to the exercise of their legislative authority, Parliament and the legislatures, together with the government of Canada and the provincial governments, are committed to

**36.** (1) Sous réserve des compétences législatives du Parlement et des législatures et de leur droit de les exercer, le Parlement et les législatures, ainsi que les gouvernements fédéral et provinciaux, s'engagent à :

*a*) promouvoir l'égalité des chances de tous les Canadiens dans la recherche de leur bien-être;

Engagements relatifs à l'égalité des chances

---

(2) Subsections (3) and (4) of s. 35 were added by the Constitution Amendment Proclamation, 1983.

(3) Section 35.1 was added by the Constitution Amendment Proclamation, 1983.

(*a*) promoting equal opportunities for the well-being of Canadians;

(*b*) furthering economic development to reduce disparity in opportunities; and

(*c*) providing essential public services of reasonable quality to all Canadians.

*Commitment respecting public services*

(2) Parliament and the government of Canada are committed to the principle of making equalization payments to ensure that provincial governments have sufficient revenues to provide reasonably comparable levels of public services at reasonably comparable levels of taxation.

*b*) favoriser le développement économique pour réduire l'inégalité des chances;

*c*) fournir à tous les Canadiens, à un niveau de qualité acceptable, les services publics essentiels.

(2) Le Parlement et le gouvernement du Canada prennent l'engagement de principe de faire des paiements de péréquation propres à donner aux gouvernements provinciaux des revenus suffisants pour les mettre en mesure d'assurer les services publics à un niveau de qualité et de fiscalité sensiblement comparables.

*Engagement relatif aux services publics*

## PART IV

### CONSTITUTIONAL CONFERENCE

*Constitutional conference*

**37.** (1) A constitutional conference composed of the Prime Minister of Canada and the first ministers of the provinces shall be convened by the Prime Minister of Canada within one year after this Part comes into force.

*Participation of aboriginal peoples.*

(2) The conference convened under subsection (1) shall have included in its agenda an item respecting constitutional matters that directly affect the aboriginal peoples of Canada, including the identification and definition of the rights of those peoples to be included in the Constitution

## PARTIE IV

### CONFERENCE CONSTITUTIONNELLE

**37.** (1) Dans l'année suivant l'entrée en vigueur de la présente partie, le premier ministre du Canada convoque une conférence constitutionnelle réunissant les premiers ministres provinciaux et lui-même.

*Conférence constitutionnelle*

(2) Sont placées à l'ordre du jour de la conférence visée au paragraphe (1) les questions constitutionnelles qui intéressent directement les peuples autochtones du Canada, notamment la détermination et la définition des droits de ces peuples à inscrire dans la Constitution du Canada. Le

*Participation des peuples autochtones*

of Canada, and the Prime Minister of Canada shall invite representatives of those peoples to participate in the discussions on that item.

premier ministre du Canada invite leurs représentants à participer aux travaux relatifs à ces questions.

**Participation of territories**

(3) The Prime Minister of Canada shall invite elected representatives of the governments of the Yukon Territory and the Northwest Territories to participate in the discussions on any item on the agenda of the conference convened under subsection (1) that, in the opinion of the Prime Minister, directly affects the Yukon Territory and the Northwest Territories.

**(3)** Le premier ministre du Canada invite des représentants élus des gouvernements du territoire du Yukon et des territoires du Nord-Ouest à participer aux travaux relatifs à toute question placée à l'ordre du jour de la conférence visée au paragraphe (1) et qui, selon lui, intéresse directement le territoire du Yukon et les territoires du Nord-Ouest.

**Participation des territoires**

PART IV.1

PARTIE IV.1

CONSTITUTIONAL CONFERENCES

CONFERENCES CONSTITUTIONNELLES

**Constitutional conferences**

**37.1** (1) In addition to the conference convened in March 1983, at least two constitutional conferences composed of the Prime Minister of Canada and the first ministers of the provinces shall be convened by the Prime Minister of Canada, the first within three years after April 17, 1982 and the second within five years after that date.

**37.1** (1) En sus de la conférence convoquée en mars 1983, le premier ministre du Canada convoque au moins deux conférences constitutionnelles réunissant les premiers ministres provinciaux et lui-même la première dans les trois ans et la seconde dans les cinq ans suivant le 17 avril 1982.

**Conférences constitutionnelles**

**Participation of aboriginal peoples**

(2) Each conference convened under subsection (1) shall have included in its agenda constitutional matters that directly affect the aboriginal peoples of Canada, and the Prime Minister of Canada shall invite

(2) Sont placées à l'ordre du jour de chacune des conférences visées au paragraphe (1) les questions constitutionnelles qui intéressent directement les peuples autochtones du Canada. Le premier ministre

**Participation des peuples autochtones**

(4) Part IV.1, consisting of s. 37.1, was added by the Constitution Amendment Proclamation, 1983.

representatives of those peoples to participate in the discussions on those matters.

du Canada invite leurs représentants à participer aux travaux relatifs à ces questions.

Participation of territories

(3) The Prime Minister of Canada shall invite elected representatives of the governments of the Yukon Territory and the Northwest Territories to participate in the discussions on any item on the agenda of a conference convened under subsection (1) that, in the opinion of the Prime Minister, directly affects the Yukon Territory and the Northwest Territories.

(3) Le premier ministre du Canada invite des représentants élus des gouvernements du territoire du Yukon et des territoires du Nord-Ouest ,à participer aux travaux relatifs à toute question placée à l'ordre du jour des conférences visées au paragraphe (1) et qui, selon lui, intéresse directement le territoire du Yukon et les territoires du Nord-Ouest.

Participation des territoires

Subsection 35(1) not affected

(4) Nothing in this section shall be construed so as to derogate from subsection 35(1).(4)

(4) Le présent article n'a pas pour effet de déroger au paragraphe 35(1).

Non-dérogation au paragraphe 35(1)

PART V

PROCEDURE FOR
AMENDING
CONSTITUTION
OF CANADA

PARTIE V

PROCEDURE
DE MODIFICATION
DE LA CONSTITUTION
DU CANADA

General procedure for amending Constitution of Canada

**38.** (1) An amendment to the Constitution of Canada may be made by proclamation issued by the Governor General under the Great Seal of Canada where so authorized by
(a) resolutions of the Senate and House of Commons; and
(b) resolutions of the legislative assemblies of at least two-thirds of the provinces that have, in the aggregate, according to the then latest general census, at least fifty per cent of the population of all the provinces.

**38.** (1) La Constitution du Canada peut être modifiée par proclamation du gouverneur général sous le grand sceau du Canada, autorisée à la fois:
a) par des résolutions du Sénat et de la Chambre des communes;
b) par des résolutions des assemblées législatives d'au moins deux tiers des provinces dont la population confondue représente, selon le recensement général le plus récent à l'époque, au moins cinquante pour cent de la population de toutes les provinces.

Procédure normale de modification

Majority of members

(2) An amendment made under subsection (1) that derogates from the legislative powers, the proprietary rights or any other rights or privileges of the legislature or government of a province shall require a resolution supported by a majority of the members of each of the Senate, the House of Commons and the legislative assemblies required under subsection (1).

(2) Une modification faite conformément au paragraphe (1) mais dérogatoire à la compétence législative, aux droits de propriété ou à tous autres droits ou privilèges d'une législature ou d'un gouvernement provincial exige une résolution adoptée à la majorité des sénateurs, des députés fédéraux et des députés de chacune des assemblées législatives du nombre requis de provinces.

Majorité simple

Expression of dissent

(3) An amendment referred to in subsection (2) shall not have effect in a province the legislative assembly of which has expressed its dissent thereto by resolution supported by a majority of its members prior to the issue of the proclamation to which the amendment relates unless that legislative assembly, subsequently, by resolution supported by a majority of its members, revokes its dissent and authorizes the amendment.

(3) La modification visée au paragraphe (2) est sans effet dans une province dont l'assemblée législative a, avant la prise de la proclamation, exprimé son désaccord par une résolution adoptée à la majorité des députés, sauf si cette assemblée, par résolution également adoptée à la majorité, revient sur son désaccord et autorise la modification.

Désaccord

Revocation of dissent

(4) A resolution of dissent made for the purposes of subsection (3) may be revoked at any time before or after the issue of the proclamation to which it relates.

(4) La résolution de désaccord visée au paragraphe (3) peut être révoquée à tout moment, indépendamment de la date de la proclamation à laquelle elle se rapporte.

Levée du désaccord

Restriction on proclamation.

**39.** (1) A proclamation shall not be issued under subsection 38(1) before the expiration of one year from the adoption of the resolution initiating the amendment procedure thereunder, unless the legislative

**39.** (1) La proclamation visée au paragraphe 38(1) ne peut être prise dans l'année suivant l'adoption de la résolution à l'origine de la procédure de modification que si l'assemblée législative de chaque province

Restriction

assembly of each province has previously adopted a resolution of assent or dissent.

a préalablement adopté une résolution d'agrément ou de désaccord.

Idem

(2) A proclamation shall not be issued under subsection 38(1) after the expiration of three years from the adoption of the resolution initiating the amendment procedure thereunder.

(2) La proclamation visée au paragraphe 38(1) ne peut être prise que dans les trois ans suivant l'adoption de la résolution à l'origine de la procédure de modification.

Idem

Compensation

**40.** Where an amendment is made under subsection 38(1) that transfers provincial legislative powers relating to education or other cultural matters from provincial legislatures to Parliament, Canada shall provide reasonable compensation to any province to which the amendment does not apply.

**40.** Le Canada fournit une juste compensation aux provinces auxquelles ne s'applique pas une modification faite conformément au paragraphe 38(1) et relative, en matière d'éducation ou dans d'autres domaines culturels, à un transfert de compétences législatives provinciales au Parlement.

Compensation

Amendment by unanimous consent

**41.** An amendment to the Constitution of Canada in relation to the following matters may be made by proclamation issued by the Governor General under the Great Seal of Canada only where authorized by resolutions of the Senate and House of Commons and of the legislative assembly of each province:
(*a*) the office of the Queen, the Governor General and the Lieutenant Governor of a province;
(*b*) the right of a province to a number of members in the House of Commons not less than the number of Senators by which the province is entitled to be represented

**41.** Toute modification de la Constitution du Canada portant sur les questions suivantes se fait par proclamation du gouverneur général sous le grand sceau du Canada, autorisée par des résolutions du Sénat, de la Chambre des communes et de l'assemblée législative de chaque province:
*a*) la charge de Reine, celle de gouverneur général et celle de lieutenant-gouverneur;
*b*) le droit d'une province d'avoir à la Chambre des communes un nombre de députés au moins égal à celui des sénateurs par lesquels elle est habilitée à être représentée lors de l'entrée en

Consentement unanime

at the time this Part comes into force;

(c) subject to section 43, the use of the English or the French language;

(d) the composition of the Supreme Court of Canada; and

(e) an amendment to this Part.

vigueur de la présente partie;

c) sous réserve de l'article 43, l'usage du français ou de l'anglais;

d) la composition de la Cour suprême du Canada;

e) la modification de la présente partie.

**Amendment by general procedure**

**42.** (1) An amendment to the Constitution of Canada in relation to the following matters may be made only in accordance with subsection 38(1):

(a) the principle of proportionate representation of the provinces in the House of Commons prescribed by the Constitution of Canada;

(b) the powers of the Senate and the method of selecting Senators;

(c) the number of members by which a province is entitled to be represented in the Senate and the residence qualifications of Senators;

(d) subject to paragraph 41(d), the Supreme Court of Canada;

(e) the extension of existing provinces into the territories; and

(f) notwithstanding any other law or practice, the establishment of new provinces.

**42.** (1) Toute modification de la Constitution du Canada portant sur les questions suivantes se fait conformément au paragraphe 38(1):

a) le principe de la représentation proportionnelle des provinces à la Chambre des communes prévu par la Constitution du Canada;

b) les pouvoirs du Sénat et le mode de sélection des sénateurs;

c) le nombre des sénateurs par lesquels une province est habilitée à être représentée et les conditions de résidence qu'ils doivent remplir;

d) sous réserve de l'alinéa 41d), la Cour suprême du Canada;

e) le rattachement aux provinces existantes de tout ou partie des territoires;

f) par dérogation à toute autre loi ou usage, la création de provinces.

**Procédure normale de modification**

**Exception**

(2) Subsections 38(2) to (4) do not apply in respect of amendments in relation to matters referred to in subsection (1).

(2) Les paragraphes 38(2) à (4) ne s'appliquent pas aux questions mentionnées au paragraphe (1).

**Exception**

**Amendment of provisions relating to some but not all provinces**

**43.** An amendment to the Constitution of Canada in relation to any provision

**43.** Les dispositions de la Constitution du Canada applicables à certaines pro-

**Modification à l'égard de certaines provinces**

that applies to one or more, but not all, provinces, including

(a) any alteration to boundaries between provinces, and

(b) any amendment to any provision that relates to the use of the English or the French language within a province, may be made by proclamation issued by the Governor General under the Great Seal of Canada only where so authorized by resolutions of the Senate and House of Commons and of the legislative assembly of each province to which the amendment applies.

vinces seulement ne peuvent être modifiées que par proclamation du gouverneur général sous le grand sceau du Canada, autorisée par des résolutions de Sénat, de la Chambre des communes et de l'assemblée législative de chaque province concernée. Le présent article s'applique notamment:

a) aux changements du tracé des frontières interprovinciales;

b) aux modifications des dispositions relatives à l'usage du français ou de l'anglais dans une province.

**Amendments by Parliament**

**44.** Subject to sections 41 and 42, Parliament may exclusively make laws amending the Constitution of Canada in relation to the executive government of Canada or the Senate and House of Commons.

**44.** Sous réserve des articles 41 et 42, le Parlement a compétence exclusive pour modifier les dispositions de la Constitution du Canada relatives au pouvoir exécutif fédéral, au Sénat ou à la Chambre des communes.

**Modification par le Parlement**

**Amendments by provincial legislatures**

**45.** Subject to section 41, the legislature of each province may exclusively make laws amending the constitution of the province.

**45.** Sous réserve de l'article 41, une législature a compétence exclusive pour modifier la constitution de sa province.

**Modification par les législatures**

**Initiation of amendment procedures**

**46.** (1) The procedures for amendment under sections 38, 41, 42 and 43 may be initiated either by the Senate or the House of Commons or by the legislative assembly of a province.

**46.** (1) L'initiative des procédures de modification visées aux articles 38, 41, 42 et 43 appartient au Sénat, à la Chambre des communes ou à une assemblée législative.

**Initiative des procédures**

**Revocation of authorization**

(2) A resolution of assent made for the purposes of this Part may be revoked at any time before the issue

(2) Une résolution d'agrément adoptée dans le cadre de la présente partie peut être révoquée à tout

**Possibilité de révocation**

of a proclamation authorized by it.

moment avant la date de la proclamation qu'elle autorise.

Amendments without Senate resolution

**47.** (1) An amendment to the Constitution of Canada made by proclamation under section 38, 41, 42 or 43 may be made without a resolution of the Senate authorizing the issue of the proclamation if, within one hundred and eighty days after the adoption by the House of Commons of a resolution authorizing its issue, the Senate has not adopted such a resolution and if, at any time after the expiration of that period, the House of Commons again adopts the resolution.

**47.** (1) Dans les cas visés à l'article 38, 41, 42 ou 43, il peut être passé outre au défaut d'autorisation du Sénat si celui-ci n'a pas adopté de résolution dans un délai de cent quatre-vingts jours suivant l'adoption de celle de la Chambre des communes et si cette dernière, après l'expiration du délai, adopte une nouvelle résolution dans le même sens.

Modification sans résolution du Sénat

Computation of period

(2) Any period when Parliament is prorogued or dissolved shall not be counted in computing the one hundred and eighty day period referred to in subsection (1).

(2) Dans la computation du délai visé au paragraphe (1), ne sont pas comptées les périodes pendant lesquelles le Parlement est prorogé ou dissous.

Computation du délai

Advice to issue proclamation

**48.** The Queen's Privy Council for Canada shall advise the Governor General to issue a proclamation under this Part forthwith on the adoption of the resolutions required for an amendment made by proclamation under this Part.

**48.** Le Conseil privé de la Reine pour le Canada demande au gouverneur général de prendre, conformément à la présente partie, une proclamation dès l'adoption des résolutions prévues par cette partie pour une modification par proclamation.

Demande de proclamation

Constitutional conference

**49.** A constitutional conference composed of the Prime Minister of Canada and the first ministers of the provinces shall be convened by the Prime Minister of Canada within fifteen years after this Part comes into force to review the provisions of this Part.

**49.** Dans le quinze ans suivant l'entrée en vigueur de la présente partie, le premier ministre du Canada convoque une conférence constitutionnelle réunissant les premiers ministres provinciaux et lui-même, en vue du réexamen des dispositions de cette partie.

Conférence constitutionnelle

PART VI

AMENDMENT TO THE
CONSTITUTION ACT, 1867

PARTIE VI

MODIFICATION DE LA LOI
CONSTITUTIONNELLE DE
1867

[Sections 50 and 51 are omitted. They added a new s. 92A and a new Sixth Schedule to the Constitution Act, 1867. The new provisions have been reproduced as part of the Constitution Act, 1867.]

PART VII

GENERAL

PARTIE VII

DISPOSITIONS GENERALES

Primacy of Constitution of Canada

**52.** (1) The Constitution of Canada is the supreme law of Canada, and any law that is inconsistent with the provisions of the Constitution is, to the extent of the inconsistency, of no force or effect.

**52.** (1) La Constitution du Canada est la loi suprême du Canada; elle rend inopérantes les dispositions incompatibles de toute autre règle de droit.

Primauté de la Constitution du Canada

Constitution of Canada

(2) The Constitution of Canada includes
(a) the *Canada Act 1982*, including this Act;
(b) the Acts and orders referred to in the schedule; and
(c) any amendment to any Act or order referred to in paragraph (a) or (b).

(2) La Constitution du Canada comprend :
a) la *Loi de 1982 sur le Canada*, y compris la présente loi;
b) les textes législatifs et les décrets figurant à l'annexe;
c) les modifications des textes législatifs et des décrets mentionnés aux alinéas a) ou b).

Constitution du Canada

Amendments to Constitution of Canada

(3) Amendments to the Constitution of Canada shall be made only in accordance with the authority contained in the Constitution of Canada.

(3) La Constitution du Canada ne peut être modifée que conformément aux pouvoirs conférés par elle.

Modification

Repeals and new names

**53.** (1) The enactments referred to in Column I of the schedule are hereby repealed or amended to the extent indicated in Column II thereof and, unless repealed, shall continue as law in Canada under the names set out in Column III thereof.

**53.** (1) Les textes législatifs et les décrets énumérés à la colonne I de l'annexe sont abrogés ou modifiés dans la mesure indiquée à la colonne II. Sauf abrogation, ils restent en vigueur en tant que lois du Canada sous les titres mentionnés à la colonne III.

Abrogation et nouveaux titres

Consequential amendments

(2) Every enactment, except the *Canada Act 1982*, that refers to an enactment referred to in the schedule by the name in Column I thereof is hereby amended by substituting for that name the corresponding name in Column III thereof, and any British North America Act not referred to in the schedule may be cited as the *Constitution Act* followed by the year and number, if any, of its enactment.

(2) Tout texte législatif ou réglementaire, sauf la *Loi de 1982 sur le Canada,* qui fait mention d'un texte législatif ou décret figurant à l'annexe par le titre indiqué à la colonne I est modifié par substitution à ce titre du titre correspondant mentionné à la colonne III; tout Acte de l'Amérique du Nord britannique non mentionné à l'annexe peut être cité sous le titre de *Loi constitutionnelle* suivi de l'indication de l'année de son adoption et éventuellement de son numéro.

Modifications corrélatives

Repeal and consequential amendments

**54.** Part IV is repealed on the day that is one year after this Part comes into force and this section may be repealed and this Act renumbered, consequentially upon the repeal of Part IV and this section, by proclamation issued by the Governor General under the Great Seal of Canada.

**54.** La partie IV est abrogée un an après l'entrée en vigueur de la présente partie et le gouverneur général peut, par proclamation sous le grand sceau du Canada, abroger le présent article et apporter en conséquence de cette double abrogation les aménagements qui s'imposent à la présente loi.

Abrogation et modifications qui en découlent

Repeal of Part IV.1 and this section

**54.1** Part IV.1 and this section are repealed on April 18, 1987.(5)

**54.1** La Partie IV.1 et le présent article sont abrogés le 18 avril 1987.

Abrogation de la Partie IV.1 et du présent article

French version of Constitution of Canada

**55.** A French version of the portions of the Constitution of Canada referred to in the schedule shall be prepared by the Minister of Justice of Canada as expeditiously as possible and, when any portion thereof sufficient to warrant action being taken has been so prepared, it shall be put forward for enactment by proclamation issued by the Governor General under

**55.** Le ministre de la Justice du Canada est chargé de rédiger, dans les meilleurs délais, la version française des parties de la Constitution du Canada qui figurent à l'annexe; toute partie suffisamment importante est, dès qu'elle est prête, déposée pour adoption par proclamation du gouverneur général sous le grand sceau du Canada, conformément à la procé-

Version française de certains textes constitutionnels

(5) Section 54.1 was added by the Constitution Amendment Proclamation, 1983.

the Great Seal of Canada pursuant to the procedure then applicable to an amendment of the same provisions of the Constitution of Canada.

dure applicable à l'époque à la modification des dispositions constitutionnelles qu'elle contient.

**English and French versions of certain constitutional texts**

**56.** Where any portion of the Constitution of Canada has been or is enacted in English and French or where a French version of any portion of the Constitution is enacted pursuant to section 55, the English and French versions of that portion of the Constitution are equally authoritative.

**56.** Les versions française et anglaise des parties de la Constitution du Canada adoptées dans ces deux langues ont également force de loi. En outre, ont également force de loi, dès l'adoption, dans le cadre de l'article 55, d'une partie de la version française de la Constitution, cette partie et la version anglaise correspondante.

**Versions française et anglaise de certains textes constitutionnels**

**English and French versions of this Act**

**57.** The English and French versions of this Act are equally authoritative.

**57.** Les versions française et anglaise de la présente loi ont également force de loi.

**Versions française et anglaise de la présente loi**

**Commencement**

**58.** Subject to section 59, this Act shall come into force on a day to be fixed by proclamation issued by the Queen or the Governor General under the Great Seal of Canada.

**58.** Sous réserve de l'article 59, la présente loi entre en vigueur à la date fixée par proclamation de la Reine ou du gouverneur général sous le grand sceau du Canada.

**Entrée en vigueur**

**Commencement of paragraph 23(1)(a) in respect of Quebec**

**59.** (1) Paragraph 23(1)(*a*) shall come into force in respect of Quebec on a day to be fixed by proclamation issued by the Queen or the Governor General under the Great Seal of Canada.

**59.** (1) L'alinéa 23(1)*a*) entre en vigueur pour le Québec à la date fixée par proclamation de la Reine ou du gouverneur général sous le grand sceau du Canada.

**Entrée en vigueur de l'alinéa 23(1)*a*) pour le Québec**

**Authorization of Quebec**

(2) A proclamation under subsection (1) shall be issued only where authorized by the legislative assembly or government of Quebec.

(2) La proclamation visée au paragraphe (1) ne peut être prise qu'après autorisation de l'assemblée législative ou du gouvernement du Québec.

**Autorisation du Québec**

**Repeal of this section**

(3) This section may be repealed on the day paragraph 23(1)(*a*) comes into force in respect of Quebec

(3) Le présent article peut être abrogé à la date d'entrée en vigueur de l'alinéa 23(1)*a*) pour le Qué-

**Abrogation du présent article**

and this Act amended and renumbered, consequentially upon the repeal of this section, by proclamation issued by the Queen or the Governor General under the Great Seal of Canada.

bec, et la présente loi faire l'object, dès cette abrogation, des modifications et changements de numérotation qui en découlent, par proclamation de la Reine ou du gouverneur général sous le grand sceau du Canada.

Short title and citations

**60.** This Act may be cited as the *Constitution Act, 1982,* and the Constitution Acts 1867 to 1975 (No. 2) and this Act may be cited together as the *Constitution Acts, 1867 to 1982.*

**60.** Titre abrégé de la présente loi : *Loi constitutionnelle de 1982;* titre commun des lois constitutionnelles de 1867 à 1975 (n° 2) et de la présente loi : *Lois constitutionnelles de 1867 à 1982.*

Titres

References

**61.** A reference to the *"Constitution Acts, 1867 to 1982"* shall be deemed to include a reference to the *"Constitution Amendment Proclamation, 1983".*(6)

**61.** Toute mention des *«Lois constitutionnelles de 1867 à 1982»* est réputée constituer également une mention de la *«Proclamation de 1983 modifiant la Constitution».*

Mentions

## SCHEDULE

### to the

### Constitution Act, 1982

### Modernization of the Constitution

| Item | Column I<br>Act Affected | Column II<br>Amendment | Column III<br>New Name |
|---|---|---|---|
| 1. | British North America Act, 1867, 30-31 Vict., c. 3 (U.K.) | (1) Section 1 is repealed and the following substituted therefor:<br>"1. This Act may be cited as the *Constitution Act, 1867.*"<br>(2) Section 20 is repealed.<br>(3) Class 1 of section 91 is repealed.<br>(4) Class 1 of section 92 is repealed. | Constitution Act, 1867 |

(6) Section 61 was added by the Constitution Amendment Proclamation, 1983.

# SCHEDULE

## to the
## Constitution Act, 1982 – *Continued*

| Item | Column I<br>Act Affected | Column II<br>Amendment | Column III<br>New Name |
|------|--------------------------|------------------------|------------------------|
| 2. | An Act to amend and continue the Act 32-33 Victoria chapter 3; and to establish and provide for the Government of the Province of Manitoba, 1870, 33 Vict., c. 3 (Can.) | (1) The long title is repealed and the. following substituted therefor:<br>"*Manitoba Act, 1870.*"<br>(2) Section 20 is repealed. | Manitoba Act, 1870 |
| 3. | Order of Her Majesty in Council admitting Rupert's Land and the North-Western Territory into the union, dated the 23rd day of June, 1870 | | Rupert's Land and North-Western Territory Order |
| 4. | Order of Her Majesty in Council admitting British Columbia into the Union, dated the 16th day of May, 1871 | | British Columbia Terms of Union |
| 5. | British North America Act, 1871, 34-35 Vict., c. 28 (U.K.) | Section 1 is repealed and the following substituted therefor:<br>"1. This Act may be cited as the *Constitution Act, 1871.*" | Constitution Act, 1871 |
| 6. | Order of Her Majesty in Council admitting Prince Edward Island into the Union, dated the 26th day of June, 1873 | | Prince Edward Island Terms of Union |
| 7. | Parliament of Canada Act, 1875, 38-39 Vict., c. 38 (U.K.) | | Parliament of Canada Act, 1875 |
| 8. | Order of Her Majesty in Council admitting all | | Adjacent Territories Order |

## SCHEDULE

### to the
### Constitution Act, 1982 – *Continued*

| Item | Column I<br>Act Affected | Column II<br>Amendment | Column III<br>New Name |
|---|---|---|---|
|  | British possessions and Territories in North America and islands adjacent thereto into the Union, dated the 31st day of July, 1880 | | |
| 9. | British North America Act, 1886, 49-50 Vict., c. 35 (U.K.) | Section 3 is repealed and the following substituted therefor:<br>"3. This Act may be cited as the *Constitution Act, 1886.*" | Constitution Act, 1886 |
| 10. | Canada (Ontario Boundary) Act, 1889, 52-53 Vict., c. 28 (U.K.) | | Canada (Ontario Boundary) Act, 1889 |
| 11. | Canadian Speaker (Appointment of Deputy) Act, 1895, 2nd Sess., 59 Vict., c. 3 (U.K.) | The Act is repealed. | |
| 12. | The Alberta Act, 1905, 4-5 Edw. VII, c. 3 (Can.) | | Alberta Act |
| 13. | The Saskatchewan Act, 1905, 4-5 Edw. VII, c. 42 (Can.) | | Saskatchewan Act |
| 14. | British North America Act, 1907, 7 Edw. VII, c. 11 (U.K.) | Section 2 is repealed and the following substituted therefor:<br>"2. This Act may be cited as the *Constitution Act, 1907.*" | Constitution Act, 1907 |
| 15. | British North America Act, 1915, 5-6 Geo. V, c. 45 (U.K.) | Section 3 is repealed and the following substituted therefor:<br>"3. This Act may be cited as the *Constitution Act, 1915.*" | Constitution Act, 1915 |

# SCHEDULE

## to the
## Constitution Act, 1982 – *Continued*

| Item | Column I<br>Act Affected | Column II<br>Amendment | Column III<br>New Name |
|---|---|---|---|
| 16. | British North America Act, 1930, 20-21 Geo. V, c. 26 (U.K.) | Section 3 is repealed and the following substituted therefor:<br>"3. This Act may be cited as the *Constitution Act, 1930*." | Constitution Act, 1930 |
| 17. | Statute of Westminster, 1931, 22 Geo. V, c. 4 (U.K.) | In so far as they apply to Canada,<br>(*a*) section 4 is repealed; and<br>(*b*) subsection 7(1) is repealed. | Statute of Westminster, 1931 |
| 18. | British North America Act, 1940, 3-4 Geo. VI, c. 36 (U.K.) | Section 2 is repealed and the following substituted therefor:<br>"2. This Act may be cited as the *Constitution Act, 1940*." | Constitution Act, 1940 |
| 19. | British North America Act, 1943, 6-7 Geo. VI, c. 30 (U.K.) | The Act is repealed. | |
| 20. | British North America Act, 1946, 9-10 Geo. VI, c. 63 (U.K.) | The Act is repealed. | |
| 21. | British North America Act, 1949, 12-13 Geo. VI, c. 22 (U.K.) | Section 3 is repealed and the following substituted therefor:<br>"3. This Act may be cited as the *Newfoundland Act*." | Newfoundland Act |
| 22. | British North America (No. 2) Act, 1949, 13 Geo. VI, c. 81 (U.K.) | The Act is repealed. | |
| 23. | British North America Act, 1951, 14-15 Geo. VI, c. 32 (U.K.) | The Act is repealed. | |

# SCHEDULE

## to the
## Constitution Act, 1982 – *Continued*

| Item | Column I<br>Act Affected | Column II<br>Amendment | Column III<br>New Name |
|---|---|---|---|
| 24. | British North America Act, 1952, 1 Eliz. II, c. 15 (Can.) | The Act is repealed. | |
| 25. | British North America Act, 1960, 9 Eliz. II, c. 2 (U.K.) | Section 2 is repealed and the following substituted therefor:<br>"2. This Act may be cited as the *Constitution Act, 1960*." | Constitution Act, 1960 |
| 26. | British North America Act, 1964, 12-13 Eliz. II, c. 73 (U.K.) | Section 2 is repealed and the following substituted therefor:<br>"2. This Act may be cited as the *Constitution Act, 1964*." | Constitution Act, 1964 |
| 27. | British North America Act, 1965, 14 Eliz. II, c. 4, Part I (Can.) | Section 2 is repealed and the following substituted therefor:<br>"2. This Part may be cited as the *Constitution Act, 1965*." | Constitution Act, 1965 |
| 28. | British North America Act, 1974, 23 Eliz. II, c. 13, Part I (Can.) | Section 3, as amended by 25-26 Eliz. II, c. 28, s. 38(1) (Can.), is repealed and the following substituted therefor:<br>"3. This Part may be cited as the *Constitution Act, 1974*." | Constitution Act, 1974 |
| 29. | British North America Act, 1975, 23-24 Eliz. II, c. 28, Part I (Can.) | Section 3, as amended by 25-26 Eliz. II, c. 28, s. 31 (Can.), is repealed and the following substituted therefor:<br>"3. This Part may be cited as the *Constitution Act (No. 1), 1975*." | Constitution Act (No. 1), 1975 |

# SCHEDULE

## to the
## Constitution Act, 1982 – *Concluded*

| Item | Column I<br>Act Affected | Column II<br>Amendment | Column III<br>New Name |
|------|--------------------------|------------------------|------------------------|
| 30. | British North America Act (No. 2), 1975, 23-24 Eliz. II, c. 53 (Can.) | Section 3 is repealed and the following substituted therefor:<br>"3. This Act may be cited as the *Constitution Act (No. 2), 1975.*" | Constitution Act (No. 2), 1975 |

# APPENDIX IV

## Canadian Bill of Rights

### S.C. 1960, c. 44

The Parliament of Canada, affirming that the Canadian Nation is founded upon principles that acknowledge the supremacy of God, the dignity and worth of the human person and the position of the family in a society of free men and free institutions;

Affirming also that men and institutions remain free only when freedom is founded upon respect for moral and spiritual values and the rule of law;

And being desirous of enshrining these principles and the human rights and fundamental freedoms derived from them, in a Bill of Rights which shall reflect the respect of Parliament for its constitutional authority and which shall ensure the protection of these rights and freedoms in Canada:

THEREFORE Her Majesty, by and with the advice and consent of the Senate and House of Commons of Canada, enacts as follows:

### PART I

#### BILL OF RIGHTS

1. It is hereby recognized and declared that in Canada there have existed and shall continue to exist without discrimination by reason of race, national origin, colour, religion or sex, the following human rights and fundamental freedoms, namely,

    (a) the right of the individual to life, liberty, security of the person and enjoyment of property, and the right not to be deprived thereof except by due process of law;

    (b) the right of the individual to equality before the law and the protection of the law;

    (c) freedom of religion;

    (d) freedom of speech;

    (e) freedom of assembly and association; and

    (f) freedom of the press.

2. Every law of Canada shall, unless it is expressly declared by an Act of the Parliament of Canada that it shall operate notwithstanding the Canadian Bill of Rights, be so construed and applied as not to abrogate, abridge or infringe or to authorize the abrogation, abridgment or infringement of any of the rights or freedoms herein recognized and declared, and in particular, no law of Canada shall be construed or applied so as to

    (a) authorize or effect the arbitrary detention, imprisonment or exile of any person;

(b)   impose or authorize the imposition of cruel and unusual treatment or punishment;

(c)   deprive a person who has been arrested or detained
   (i) of the right to be informed promptly of the reason for his arrest or detention,
   (ii) of the right to retain and instruct counsel without delay, or
   (iii) of the remedy by way of *habeas corpus* for the determination of the validity of his detention and for his release if the detention is not lawful;

(d)   authorize a court, tribunal, commission, board or other authority to compel a person to give evidence if he is denied counsel, protection against self crimination or other constitutional safeguards;

(e)   deprive a person of the right to a fair hearing in accordance with the principles of fundamental justice for the determination of his rights and obligations;

(f)   deprive a person charged with a criminal offence of the right to be presumed innocent until proved guilty according to law in a fair and public hearing by an independent and impartial tribunal, or of the right to reasonable bail without just cause; or

(g)   deprive a person of the right to the assistance of an interpreter in any proceedings in which he is involved or in which he is a party or a witness, before a court, commission, board or other tribunal, if he does not understand or speak the language in which such proceedings are conducted.

3.   The Minister of Justice shall, in accordance with such regulations as may be prescribed by the Governor in Council, examine every proposed regulation submitted in draft form to the Clerk of the Privy Council pursuant to the *Regulations Act* and every Bill introduced in or presented to the House of Commons, in order to ascertain whether any of the provisions thereof are inconsistent with the purposes and provisions of this Part and he shall report any such inconsistency to the House of Commons at the first convenient opportunity.

4.   The provisions of this Part shall be known as the *Canadian Bill of Rights.*

## PART II

5.   (1) Nothing in Part I shall be construed to abrogate or abridge any human right or fundamental freedom not enumerated therein that may have existed in Canada at the commencement of this Act.

(2) The expression "law of Canada" in Part I means an Act of the Parliament of Canada enacted before or after the coming into force of this Act, any order, rule or regulation thereunder, and any law in force in Canada or in any part of Canada at the commencement of this Act that is subject to be repealed, abolished or altered by the Parliament of Canada.

(3) The provisions of Part I shall be construed as extending only to matters coming within the legislative authority of the Parliament of Canada.

6. Section 6 of the *War Measures Act* is repealed and the following substituted therefor:

"6.    (1) Sections 3, 4, and 5 shall come into force only upon the issue of a proclamation of the Governor in Council declaring that war, invasion or insurrection, real or apprehended, exists.

(2) A proclamation declaring that war, invasion or insurrection, real or apprehended, exists shall be laid before Parliament forthwith after its issue, or, if Parliament is then not sitting, within the first fifteen days next thereafter that Parliament is sitting.

(3) Where a proclamation has been laid before Parliament pursuant to subsection (2), a notice of motion in either House signed by ten members thereof and made in accordance with the rules of that House within ten days of the day the proclamation was laid before Parliament, praying that the proclamation be revoked, shall be debated in that House at the first convenient opportunity within the four sitting days next after the day the motion in that House was made.

(4) If both Houses of Parliament resolve that the proclamation be revoked, it shall cease to have effect, and sections 3, 4 and 5 shall cease to be in force until those sections are again brought into force by a further proclamation but without prejudice to the previous operation of those sections or anything duly done or suffered thereunder or any offence committed or any penalty or forfeiture or punishment incurred.

(5) Any act or thing done or authorized or any order or regulation made under the authority of this Act, shall be deemed not to be an abrogation, abridgement or infringement of any right or freedom recognized by the *Canadian Bill of Rights*."

# APPENDIX V

## American Bill of Rights

### AMENDMENTS TO THE CONSTITUTION OF THE UNITED STATES

First Ten Amendments passed by Congress September 25, 1789.
Ratified by three-fourths of the States December 15, 1791.

### ARTICLE I

Congress shall make no law respecting an establishment of religion, or prohibiting the free exercise thereof; or abridging the freedom of speech, or of the press; or the right of the people peaceably to assemble, and to petition the government for a redress of grievances.

### ARTICLE II

A well regulated militia, being necessary to the security of a free State, the right of the people to keep and bear arms, shall not be infringed.

### ARTICLE III

No soldier shall, in time of peace be quartered in any house, without the consent of the owner, nor in time of war, but in a manner to be prescribed by law.

### ARTICLE IV

The right of the people to be secure in their persons, houses, papers, and effects, against unreasonable searches and seizures, shall not be violated, and no warrants shall issue, but upon probable cause, supported by oath or affirmation, and particularly describing the place to be searched, and the persons or things to be seized.

### ARTICLE V

No person shall be held to answer for a capital, or otherwise infamous crime, unless on a presentment or indictment of a grand jury, except in cases arising in the land or naval forces, or in the militia, when in actual service in time of war or public danger; nor shall any person be subject for the same offense to be twice put in jeopardy of life or limb; nor shall be compelled in any criminal case to be a witness against himself, nor be deprived of life, liberty, or property, without due process of law; nor shall private property be taken for public use without just compensation.

### ARTICLE VI

In all criminal prosecutions, the accused shall enjoy the right to a speedy and public trial, by an impartial jury of the State and district wherein the crime shall have been committed, which district shall have been previously ascertained by law, and to be informed of the nature and cause of the accusation; to be confronted with the witnesses against him; to have compulsory process for obtaining witnesses in his favor, and to have the assistance of counsel for his defense.

## ARTICLE VII

In suits at common law, where the value in controversy shall exceed twenty dollars, the right of trial by jury shall be preserved, and no fact tried by a jury shall be otherwise reexamined in any court of the United States, than according to the rules of the common law.

## ARTICLE VIII

Excessive bail shall not be required, nor excessive fines imposed, nor cruel and unusual punishments inflicted.

## ARTICLE IX

The enumeration in the Constitution of certain rights shall not be construed to deny or disparage others retained by the people.

## ARTICLE X

The powers not delegated to the United States by the Constitution, nor prohibited by it to the States, are reserved to the States respectively, or to the people.

## ARTICLE XIII

Passed by Congress January 31, 1865. Ratified December 6, 1865.

SECTION 1. Neither slavery nor involuntary servitude, except as punishment for crime whereof the party shall have been duly convicted, shall exist within the United States, or any place subject to their jurisdiction.

SECTION 2. Congress shall have power to enforce this article by appropriate legislation.

## ARTICLE XIV

Passed by Congress June 13, 1866. Ratified July 9, 1868.

SECTION 1. All persons born or naturalized in the United States, and subject to the jurisdiction thereof, are citizens of the United States and of the State wherein they reside. No State shall make or enforce any law which shall abridge the privileges or immunities of citizens of the United States; nor shall any State deprive any person of life, liberty, or property, without due process of law; nor deny to any person within its jurisdiction the equal protection of the laws. . . .

SECTION 5. The Congress shall have power to enforce, by appropriate legislation, the provisions of this article.

## ARTICLE XV

Passed by Congress February 26, 1869. Ratified February 3, 1870.

SECTION 1.   The right of citizens of the United States to vote shall not be denied or abridged by the United States or by any State on account of race, color, or previous condition of servitude.

SECTION 2.   The Congress shall have power to enforce this article by appropriate legislation.

## ARTICLE XIX

Passed by Congress June 4, 1919. Ratified August 18, 1920.

The right of citizens of the United States to vote shall not be denied or abridged by the United States or by any State on account of sex.

The Congress shall have power by appropriate legislation to enforce the provisions of this article.

## ARTICLE XXIV

Passed by Congress August 27, 1962. Ratified January 23, 1964.

SECTION 1.   The right of citizens of the United States to vote in any primary or other election for President or Vice President, for electors for President or Vice President, or for Senator or Representative in Congress, shall not be denied or abridged by the United States or any State by reason of failure to pay any poll tax or other tax.

SECTION 2.   The Congress shall have the power to enforce this article by appropriate legislation.

## ARTICLE XXVI

Passed by Congress March 23, 1971. Ratified June 30, 1971.

SECTION 1.   The right of citizens of the United States, who are eighteen years of age or older, to vote shall not be denied or abridged by the United States or any State on account of age.

SECTION 2.   The Congress shall have the power to enforce this article by appropriate legislation.